# FINANCIAL INSTITUTIONS AND MARKETS

# FINANCIAL INSTITUTIONS AND MARKETS

## Second Edition

Murray E. Polakoff

University of Maryland


Thomas A. Durkin

Board of Governors of the Federal Reserve System

and Pennsylvania State University


## and Others

HOUGHTON MIFFLIN COMPANY   Boston

Dallas   Geneva, Illinois · Hopewell, New Jersey

Palo Alto   London

Printed in the U.S.A.

Library of Congress Catalog Card Number: 80-82758

ISBN: 0-395-29191-7

# CONTENTS

# PREFACE

The decade since publication of the first edition of *Financial Institutions and Markets* in 1970 has witnessed developments and changes even more rapid and remarkable than could have been contemplated at that time. Financial markets and institutions have grown enormously over the decade and have become more integrated and competitive, domestically and worldwide. Furthermore, growth and integration have taken place in an environment characterized by inflation, stagflation, a slowdown in productivity and real growth, rapid and substantial swings in interest rates, and frequent changes in governmental economic policies. Nevertheless, despite these developments, a primary goal that prompted preparation of the first edition is as appropriate today as it was when the first edition was published—if not more so. This concerned the need for broadening the traditional field known as "money and banking" to include nonmonetary financial assets and nonbank financial intermediaries. The reasoning behind this goal, which seems well supported by events of the intervening decade, was effectively summarized by Houghton Mifflin Company's then General Editor of Finance in his introduction to the 1970 edition:

"Money" has traditionally been defined as currency (including coins) in circulation plus commercial bank demand deposits after deductions of interbank deposits, cash items in process of collection, U.S. government demand deposits, and Federal Reserve float. This is still the accepted definition, but in the past few decades controversies have developed over just what else should be called "money." Witness, for example, the debate as to whether the money supply should include foreign individual, corporate, and commercial bank deposits held in U.S. commercial banks and the demand deposits of foreign central banks and international organizations with the Federal Reserve. Note, too, the contention of Milton Friedman that the money stock should include time deposits of commercial banks. And, finally, we may call attention to the August 1969 federal revision in the money supply data resulting from the growth of Eurodollars.

But whatever the changes involved in the definition of "money," there has been a still more important development in the last two decades. This is the growth of "near-monies" and "not-so-near monies." The liabilities of certain financial institutions and of the government cannot satisfy the definition of "money," since they are not universally accepted means of payment; that is, one cannot buy a cup of coffee with a Treasury bill. In order to include these liabilities, we add to the definition of money in the narrow sense the time deposits in commercial banks and in savings banks and arrive at a figure called cash assets. We may then add to cash assets, the share capital of savings and loan associations and U.S. government securities and the resulting figure is the Federal Reserve concept of liquid assets. If we then add the net cash values of life insurance, we will have a still broader concept of liquid assets.

All of these things involving less liquidity than "money" can be called "near-monies." However, it is not terribly important where we draw the line between "monies" and "near-monies." The significant point is that we recognize that levels of income, prices, and employment are influenced by the operations of our entire financial system, a financial system producing both "monies" and "near-monies" wherever the line of separation is drawn. It is this recognition that has given rise to some of the most profound changes in monetary theory since World War II and these changes in theory have, in turn, significantly affected monetary policy. The precise impact of substitutes for money on the nation's economic aggregates is a matter of controversy, but that there is an impact, no one doubts.

If we are to expand the study of money to include near-monies, then we must also broaden the concept of "banking" to include the institutions which bring into existence the substitutes for money. These include savings banks, savings and loan associations, insurance companies, and government agencies, among others. The study of money and banking is thus fast approaching a status where it is indistinguishable from a study of the financial system as a whole. In such a system, the commercial and central banking sector of the financial structure retains its predominance, but we must also include other sectors, namely, the nonbank financial sector as well as the households, business firms, government units, and rest-of-the-world sectors. This total system approach constitutes in essence a flow of funds analysis and necessarily involves consideration of the principal financial intermediaries, many of whose liabilities constitute our supply of money substitutes.

To employ a systems approach encompassing all financial assets and financial intermediaries there was the need for a text not only analytical in nature but one sufficiently comprehensive so as to do justice, even by 1970, to the already huge, complex, and rapidly growing field known as macrofinance. This is even more true today. However, the expertise necessary for producing such a comprehensive text above the introductory level is usually beyond the capabilities of one or two people. Consequently, there were twenty-eight contributors to the first edition and there are thirty-one contributors to the second, each a specialist in a particular area. Each author in both editions has faced the challenge of developing required material so as to bring it into conformity with the overall design of the book, but the task has still remained for the editors to incorporate the various chapters into a unified whole. As a result, no drafts of individual chapters (including those of the editors) have escaped the discipline of constant and continuous rewriting and revision. The total effort by all involved in producing such a book is great. To quote from the preface to the first edition: "Ideally, the book which has emerged should appear to the student as one written by a single author with respect to level of analysis, substantive content, internal consistency, and stylistic uniformity."

Part I of the new edition presents an overview and introduction to the structure of the book—concentrating on the saving-investment process, the rationale for financial markets, the role of financial intermediaries, and the framework of the flow of funds. Part II expands on this introductory section by examining the sources of funds to financial markets with chapters on each of the major intermediaries. In Part III the demand for funds is studied with multiple chapters on the consumer sector, the business sector, and the public and foreign sectors. Supply of and demand for funds are brought together in Part IV. This section examines the money and capital markets and the important interactions of financial markets with the rest of the macroeconomy; understanding these interactions is important for comprehending causes of fluctuations in financial market prices, that is, changes in interest rates. These changes are then analyzed in considerable depth in various chapters in Part V. Part VI builds upon the discussion and analysis of the determinants of interest rates by looking at methods of forecasting. Econometric models are studied as well as more traditional forecasting methods. The final section, Part VII, examines public policy with respect to financial markets and institutions, including a review of macroeconomic policy and the role of government regulation.

All parts of the text can be covered in a one-year course. However, if the course is one semester in duration, it is recommended that Chapters 1 and 2 in Part I and Chapters 4–6 in Part II be covered along with all the chapters comprising Parts IV, V, and VII. Other chapters can be read in conjunction with those covered in the classroom.

The format for the second edition is basically similar to that of the first edition, revolving as it does around flow of funds analysis as the central organizing device and conceptual framework. Also, as in the earlier edition, the new one is designed primarily for college upperclassmen and beginning graduate students in a school of business or in liberal arts, students with some background in elementary economics who are or will be taking courses or even specializing in the field of financial institutions and markets or money and banking.

Most of the chapters in this edition have been completely rewritten with the remaining few sufficiently altered and updated so as to reflect the many changes which have occurred in the decade of the

1970s. In addition, the current edition has two chapters devoted to money and banking (exclusive of its structure and regulation) as compared to only one in the older edition. Also, Part V has brought together all chapters dealing with interest rate determination, including two new chapters on liquidity preference and portfolio theory, the latter in an attempt to generalize many of the other, more partial approaches to the subject by explicitly taking into account the necessary trade-offs between the yields on various financial assets and their respective risk differentials. Further, and more than in the earlier work, the text attempts to bridge the still existing gap between macro- and microfinance. Thus, in addition to coverage of the relation of financial intermediaries to the total financial system, various chapters in the book—especially the ones concerning specific intermediaries—address some of the problems associated with internal management of these institutions. The current edition has also developed an extensive series of subheadings for each chapter in the Table of Contents, something which was missing in the older edition. Finally, and unlike the first edition, this edition is accompanied by an Instructor's Manual in the form of suggested answers to the questions posed at the end of each chapter.

In addition to the contributors, acknowledgments and thanks are due to a host of individuals both known and unknown who helped in some way to bring the manuscript to press. Among those known and gladly acknowledged are Professor Theodor Kohers of Mississippi State University and Professor Harold C. Krogh of the University of Kansas, who made important and timely contributions by reading and critiquing the manuscript; Mr. Gregory Elliehausen and Ms. Mary Pat McNulty, graduate students who updated certain tables as new data appeared; Mrs. Sharon Johnson, the Administrative Aide of one of the editors, who kept ingoing and outgoing drafts of individual chapters in some semblance of order as well as keeping an eagle eye on the obtaining of copyright permissions; and Mrs. Ethel Thom, who typed and retyped many of the chapters. Credit is gratefully given to the late Professor Herman Krooss of New York University for much of the historical material found in the earlier and present editions, as well as to Dr. Albert M. Wojnilower of First Boston Corporation for graciously allowing the co-authors of the chapter on portfolio analysis of interest rates the right to use some of the institutional material to be found in the first edition of the book. One of the co-authors of Chapter 7 also wishes to thank Richard D. Irwin, Inc., the publisher of his text on life insurance, for permission to adapt parts of it for this edition of the book. Likewise, the author of Chapter 27 wishes to express his appreciation to Professor William Silber of New York University for some of the ideas in this chapter and to Barbara Muller for her many helpful suggestions.

Finally, it is customary in most books to express thanks and appreciation to one's spouses, children, or friends for their love, interest, support, inspiration, and what have you, which helped lead to a culmination, hopefully successful, of their endeavors in the form of publication. Since the co-editors view themselves as traditionalists, at least in this context, conventional utterances and protestations seem appealing and appropriate, and so this edition is dedicated to their respective wives, Sheila D. Polakoff and Carolyn I. Durkin.

Murray E. Polakoff
Thomas A. Durkin

# NOTES ON CONTRIBUTORS

**Murray E. Polakoff** is Provost of the Division of Behavioral and Social Sciences, the University of Maryland at College Park, and Professor of Finance and Economics. Previously he was Dean and Leading Professor of Finance in the School of Management at the State University of New York at Binghamton and Professor of Economics and Finance and Vice Dean, Graduate School of Business Administration, New York University. He has also taught at the University of Texas at Austin and at the University of Rochester where he served as Chairman of the Department of Economics and Finance. He has been a Visiting Professor of Economics at the University of California at Los Angeles and, under the auspices of the U.S. Agency for International Development, has lectured in Brazil on money and capital markets and economic development. Dr. Polakoff has been a contributor to several books in the fields of banking, finance, and economic development and is the author of numerous articles in professional journals, including the *Journal of Finance*, the *Journal of Financial and Quantitative Analysis*, the *Antitrust Bulletin, Economic Development and Cultural Change*, the *Indian Economic Journal, Revista Internazionale di Scienze Economiche e Commerciali*, and the *Industrial and Labor Relations Review*. He has served on the Board of Directors of an industrial conglomerate, the Board of Trustees of a hospital, and on the Advisory Committee of a bank. He has testified before several Congressional committees on housing and mortgage finance as well as on the mutual fund industry.

**Thomas A. Durkin** is an economist in the Division of Research and Statistics of the Board of Governors of the Federal Reserve System and Associate Professor of Finance at the Pennsylvania State University. His research on aspects of consumer credit markets has been published in various professional journals in economics and business as well as in the Technical Studies of the National Commission on Consumer Finance and in other monograph series. Formerly, he served as Visiting Professor at the Federal Reserve Board and as consultant to the Board's Division of Research and Statistics and Division of Consumer Affairs.

**Victor L. Andrews** is Mills Bee Lane Professor of Banking and Finance and Chairman, Department of Finance, Georgia State University. Previous faculty affiliations have been with Harvard University and M.I.T. Dr. Andrews is coauthor, with Pearson Hunt, of *Financial Management: Cases and Readings,* and wrote one of the Commission on Money and Credit monographs, "Noninsured Corporate and State and Local Government Retirement Funds in the Retirement Structure," published in *Private Capital Markets*. He is also the author of various journal articles. He was the founding editor of *Financial Management*, serving in the years 1971–1976, was President of the Financial Management Association for 1978–1979, and serves it now as a trustee.

**H. Robert Bartell, Jr.** is Chairman of PMI Mortgage Insurance Co. and formerly President of the Federal Home Loan Bank of Chicago. He has served as Commissioner of Banks and Trust Companies for the State of Illinois, economist for the United States League of Savings Associations, and a member of the research staff of the National Bureau of Economic Research. His academic career included professorships at Washington University, Northwestern University, and the University of California at Los Angeles. He has authored a number of articles and studies on pension funds, mortgage markets, the savings and loan business, and regulation of financial institutions. He was a founding member and president of the Society of Financial Examiners and holds the designation of Certified Financial Examiner.

**H. Prescott Beighley** is Managing Associate, Beighley and Associates, and Consulting Economist to the Federal Home Loan Bank of Chicago. He was formerly Vice President of that institution as well as Associate Professor of Finance in the Kellog Graduate School of Management at Northwestern University and a research associate at its Banking Research Center. He has also served as a financial economist for the Federal Deposit Insurance Corporation. He has authored numerous articles in the areas of banking and finance, and has served as a consultant to banks, bank supervisory agencies, and trade organizations.

**Robert L. Bennett** received his Ph.D. from the University of Texas and is Associate Professor of Economics at the University of Maryland. He was a postdoctoral fellow at the University of Wisconsin in 1963 and a Ford Foundation Faculty Research Fellow in 1966. He is author of *The Financial Sector and Economic Development* and numerous articles in professional journals. Currently he is developing a dynamic microanalytic simulation model of the U.S. economy.

**George A. Bishop** is Director of Economic Research, American Council of Life Insurance. Previously, he was Director of Federal Affairs Research at the Tax Foundation and, before that, an economist at the Federal Reserve Bank of Boston. He is the author of *Capital Formation Through Life Insurance: The Response of Life Insurance Investments to Changes in Monetary Policy 1965–1970,* and various articles in professional journals.

**Martin R. Blyn** is Dean of the School of Management and Professor of Business Administration and Economics at California State University, Dominguez Hills. Formerly, Dr. Blyn was on the faculty of New York University and, previous to that, was an economist with the Federal Reserve Bank of Cleveland. He has published several articles and books in the fields of money and banking and U.S. economic history, including *A History of Financial Intermediaries,* co-authored with Herman E. Krooss.

**Robert O. Edmister** is Associate Professor of Finance, College of Business and Management, University of Maryland. Previously he taught at the Krannert Graduate School of Industrial Administration, Purdue University. He has been a research consultant with the Federal Deposit Insurance Corporation, has testified before state banking commission hearings, and has taught commercial bank management at banking schools. He has published articles in the *Journal of Finance* and the *Journal of Financial and Quantitative Analysis.*

**Peter C. Eisemann** is Associate Professor of Finance, Georgia State University. He teaches courses primarily on the management of financial institutions. His articles have appeared in such publications as the *Journal of Banking and Finance, Journal of Bank Research, Financial Analysts' Journal,* and *Bankers Magazine.*

**Holger L. Engberg** is Associate Professor of Finance and International Business, Graduate School of Business Administration, New York University. Previously, he taught at Columbia University and at several African universities, most recently at the University of Ghana in West Africa. He is the author of several monographs and articles, including studies on the emerging financial markets in Africa. He has been a contributor to professional journals such as the *Journal of Finance,* the *Journal of Economic History,* and the *Journal of Modern African Studies.*

**Paul C. Grier** is Associate Professor of Finance, School of Management, State University of New York at Binghamton. He previously taught at Baruch College and served as an economist for the New York Stock Exchange. Dr. Grier has contributed to several books and has published numerous articles on economics and finance in such journals as the *Journal of Business, Financial Management,* and *Health Services Research.*

**John H. Hand** is Associate Professor of Finance at Auburn University, specializing in money and financial institutions. He has authored or co-authored three books and more than a dozen journal articles in finance and economics, and has served as a consultant for governments and businesses.

**John A. Haslem** is Professor and Chairman of Finance, College of Business and Management, University of Maryland. A graduate of Duke University and the University of North Carolina, Dr. Haslem's research articles have appeared in the *Journal of Finance; Journal of Financial and Quantitative Analysis; Journal of Money, Credit and Banking; Journal of Business; Journal of Accountancy,* and other journals. His early research focused on commercial bank profitability, while his more recent empirical studies have analyzed the behavior of individual investors. Dr. Haslem is a corporate director and has been a consultant to the Director of Supersonic Transport Development, National Aeronautics and Space Administration, and the U.S. Department of Justice.

**Robert G. Hawkins** is Professor of Economics and Vice Dean, Graduate School of Business Administration, New York University. He also serves as Executive Secretary-Treasurer of the American Finance Association. He has contributed to several professional journals, including the *Journal of Finance; Journal of Money, Credit and Banking;* and *Journal of International Business Studies;* and has been a member of the board of editors of the *Journal of Finance* and *Journal of International Business Studies.* His testimony on international financial issues has been presented to several Congressional committees, and he is editor of the annual series on *Research in International Business and Finance.*

**George H. Hempel** is Professor of Finance at the School of Business, Southern Methodist University, where he teaches courses in commercial bank management, money and capital markets, and financial management. He is currently chairman of its Finance Subject Area. He received his Ph.D. from the University of Michigan. He previously taught at Washington University, Austin College, and the University of Michigan. He has served as a consultant to and has been on the board of directors of several banks. He also is an Instructor at the Stonier Graduate School of Banking, the ABA National School of Bank Investments, the School of Banking of the South, the New Mexico School of Banking, and several AIB senior management seminars. Dr. Hempel is the author of many books and monographs as well as numerous articles in professional journals. Some of his more recent books and monographs are *Postwar Quality of State and*

*Local Debt, Management Policies for Commercial Banks, Financial Institutions: Notes and Cases, Determining and Meeting a Bank's Capital Needs*, and *Financial Management of Financial Institutions*.

**W. Michael Keenan** is an Associate Professor of Finance at the Graduate School of Business, New York University, where he teaches corporation finance, investments, and a seminar in mergers and acquisitions. He received his Ph.D. from Carnegie Mellon University. His research in recent years has focused on evolving trends in the securities industry. Publications include a monograph, *Profile of the New York Based Securities Industry*, published by the Center for the Study of Financial Institutions at New York University, and the chapter "The Scope of the Deregulation in the Securities Industry" in *The Deregulation of the Banking and Securities Industry*, by L. Goldberg and L. White.

**Richard Kolodny** is Associate Professor of Finance, College of Business and Management, University of Maryland. Prior to his present appointment, he was Associate Professor and Chairman of the Masters in Business Administration Program at the State University of New York at Binghamton. Dr. Kolodny's publications include numerous articles in professional journals such as the *Journal of Finance, Review of Economics and Statistics,* the *Bell Journal of Economics,* and the *Journal of Financial and Quantitative Analysis*.

**Richard M. Levich** is Associate Professor of Finance and International Business, Graduate School of Business Administration, New York University, and is also a Research Associate with the National Bureau of Economic Research. He previously taught at the University of Chicago and was a Visiting Scholar at the Federal Reserve Board. His research on international financial markets has appeared in several scholarly publications, including the *Journal of Political Economy*. He is the author of *The International Money Market: An Assessment of Forecasting Techniques and Market Efficiency,* and the co-editor, with Clas G. Wihlborg, of *Exchange Risk and Exposure: Current Developments in International Financial Management*.

**Michael E. Levy** received his Ph.D. from Columbia University and taught there from 1956 to 1959. He also served at the United Nations as an Economic Affairs Officer and Economic Consultant. He joined The Conference Board in 1959 as Senior Economist; he became Manager of its Fiscal and Monetary Department in 1965 and Director of Economic Policy Research in 1970. Over the years he has served repeatedly as an economic consultant to the U.S. Office of Management and Budget, the General Accounting Office, and several prominent corporations. He has taught frequently at New York University and the New School for Social Research. A member of the Interna-

tional Institute of Public Finance and a former Director of the American Finance Association (1976–1978), Dr. Levy is the author of numerous monographs, including *Income Tax Exemptions*; *Fiscal Policy, Cycles and Growth*; *Cycles in Government Securities*; and *Revenue Sharing with the States*. Since 1967, he has been the editor and senior author of *The Federal Budget: Its Impact on the Economy,* a review of U.S. fiscal policy published annually until 1976, and three times a year thereafter.

**William E. Mitchell** is Associate Professor of Economics and Chairman, Department of Economics, University of Missouri–St. Louis. His primary research concentrates on integrating public choice theory into the study of state and local government financial and political institutions. This research has appeared in a monograph as well as in professional journals such as the *Public Finance Quarterly* and the *National Tax Journal,* and as chapters in several books. He also is co-author or co-editor of several textbooks in public finance and macroeconomics. In addition, Dr. Mitchell has been a consultant to city governments, private corporations, and individuals on various aspects of financial planning.

**Roger F. Murray** is S. Sloan Colt Professor Emeritus of Banking and Finance, Graduate School of Business, Columbia University. His career in finance has included executive positions at Bankers Trust Company and the College Retirement Equities Fund. He is a director of three mutual funds and serves as a public member of the Board of Governors of the Investment Company Institute. He has served on the Advisory Committee of Pension Benefit Guaranty Corporation and as a public director of the Chicago Board Options Exchange. His writings have been largely in the field of investment management and the management of financial institutions. He is a past president of the American Finance Association.

**Lawrence S. Ritter** Professor of Finance and former Chairman of the Department of Finance, Graduate School of Business Administration, New York University, previously taught at Michigan State University and at Yale University. He has been an economist for the Federal Reserve Bank of New York, a staff economist for the Commission on Money and Credit, a member of the Advisory Committee on Commercial Bank Supervision to the Superintendent of Banks of the State of New York, and a consultant to the United States Treasury, The Federal Deposit Insurance Corporation, and the Board of Governors of the Federal Reserve System. Dr. Ritter also has served as editor of the *Journal of Finance* and is a past President of the American Finance Association.

**Thomas R. Robinson** is Senior Economist of the American Council of Life Insurance in Washington, D.C. His primary responsibility is the analysis of changing conditions in financial markets. Dr. Robinson received his Ph.D. in economics from The George Washington University in Washington, D.C., where he currently serves as Associate Professorial Lecturer in economics. Dr. Robinson was an economist for the Bureau of Economic Analysis of the U.S. Department of Commerce from 1971 until joining the ACLI in 1973.

**Sally S. Ronk** is a financial economist at the U.S. Treasury Department and has also served as Vice President and Chief Economist at Drexel Burnham & Co., Inc., and as Vice President and Economist at Bankers Trust Company. Dr. Ronk has worked extensively in the field of financial analysis through the flows of funds technique, having pioneered some of the developments in this area in the late 1940s and early 1950s, and is the author of several articles in professional and business journals based on this approach. Currently serving on the board of directors of the National Economists' Club, she has been on the boards of several professional associations and has served as President of the Metropolitan Economic Association and Chairman of the Downtown Economists Luncheon Group. Also, she has been elected a fellow both of the National Association of Business Economists and of the American Statistical Association.

**Arnold W. Sametz** received his Ph.D. in economics from Princeton University and taught there from 1948 to 1957. Since then, he has been at the Graduate School of Business Administration of New York University as Professor of Economics and Finance, Editor of the Institute of Finance *Bulletin,* and Director of the Salomon Brothers Center for the Study of Financial Institutions. His current research centers on long-term financial forecasting with particular emphasis on the business sector and, within that sector, on corporate securities. He is also engaged in studies of the National (automated) Securities Market System and in analyzing the costs and impact of foreign direct investment in the United States. Dr. Sametz has published extensively in academic journals. He is also the author of several monographs and texts in the fields of economics and finance, both domestic and international. Among his recent publications are a monograph entitled "A Modest Proposal for a National Market System and Its Governance" (with E. Bloch), *Monographs in Finance and Economics,* and a book entitled *Prospects for Capital Formation and Capital Markets: Financial Requirements Over the Next Decade.*

**Richard T. Selden** is Carter Glass Professor of Economics and former Chairman in the James Wilson Department of Economics at the University of Virginia. Previously he taught at the University of Massachusetts, Vanderbilt University, Columbia University, and Cornell University. In addition, he has served as a member of the research staff at the National Bureau of Economic Research and

as staff economist at Citibank. Currently he serves as a director and economic consultant at First Virginia Banks, Inc., a multibank holding company which operates throughout the state of Virginia. Dr. Selden is the author of several monographs, including *Trends and Cycles in the Commercial Paper Market* and, with George R. Morrison, *Time Deposit Growth and the Employment of Bank Funds.* He also has published many articles on monetary and financial topics in professional journals and has testified before several committees of the Congress.

**Bernard Shull** Professor of Economics, Hunter College of the City University of New York, was formerly Associate Adviser, Director for Research Projects for the Reappraisal of the Federal Reserve Discount Mechanism, and Chief of the Banking Markets Section, Board of Governors of the Federal Reserve System; Senior Economist and Associate Editor of the *National Banking Review* in the Office of the Comptroller of the Currency; and Economist at the Federal Reserve Bank of Philadelphia. In recent years he has been a consultant to a number of federal agencies, including the Federal Reserve Board, the Federal Deposit Insurance Corporation, the Justice Department, and the President's Commission on Financial Structure and Regulation. He is the author of a number of articles and monographs published in scholarly journals and by governmental agencies.

**Seymour Smidt** is Nicholas H. Noyes Professor of Economics and Finance in the Graduate School of Business and Public Administration, Cornell University. He teaches in the areas of corporate finance, capital markets, finance theory, and the economics of securities markets, and has written many articles and several books on these and related subjects, including *The Capital Budgeting Decision,* co-authored with Harold Bierman, Jr. During 1969–1970 he was Associate Director of the S.E.C.'s Institutional Investors Study.

**Paul Wachtel** is Associate Professor of Economics at the Graduate School of Business Administration, New York University. He has also been a Research Associate at the National Bureau of Economic Research and a visiting economist at the Federal Reserve Bank of New York. He has published articles on saving behavior and inflation in the *American Economic Review, Brookings Papers on Economic Activity,* the *Journal of Monetary Economics,* and other journals. He is also the Proceedings Editor of the *Journal of Finance,* and co-editor of and contributor to *Understanding Capital Markets: The Financial Environment and the Flow of Funds in the Next Decade.* Recently completed research includes "Age Structure and Personal Saving Behavior," and "Inflation and the Saving Behavior of Households: A Survey," both for the American Council of Life Insurance Study on Capital Formation.

**Albert M. Wojnilower** is a Managing Director and Economist of The First Boston Corporation, and has served also as Adjunct Professor of Finance at New York University. Previous positions held by him include Chief of Financial Statistics Division, and Chief of Domestic Research Division, Federal Reserve Bank of New York, as well as Associate Economist at First National City Bank of New York. Dr. Wojnilower has written many articles in the field of finance as well as a monograph entitled *The Quality of Bank Loans*. One of his most recent publications is a chapter entitled "The Central Role of Credit Crunches in Recent Financial History" in *Brookings Papers on Economic Activity*.

# FINANCIAL INSTITUTIONS AND MARKETS

# Introduction

# 1

# Institutionalization of Saving and Financial Markets

For most people, finance is what they see in the financial pages of a newspaper. It is arcane and remarkably detailed. It is a jumble of debentures, margins, bill rates, stock prices, machine tool orders, stockholders' meetings—a bewildering variety of special terms and special events. Even if people are familiar with the terms, they often find it difficult to see the connections between the events.

This book is aimed at making visible those connections and making clear the significant economic forces that lie behind the daily flow of financial activities.

A major objective of this introductory chapter is to provide an overview of the many financial institutions and markets that are analyzed in greater detail in subsequent chapters of this book. This chapter utilizes a broad conceptual framework so that much of what follows will be seen as a cohesive and interrelated whole. Among other things, it will be shown, not only that financial factors are related to one another in certain ways, but that they are also interrelated with such "real" factors as saving and investment. For example, it will be found that, in a market economy, the process of capital formation—that is, saving and investment—is intimately associated with such financial factors as lending and borrowing, the creation of financial assets, the role of financial intermediaries, and the functioning of money and capital markets.[1] In order

[1]At this point acknowledgment must be made to John Gurley and the late Edward Shaw of Stanford University for their many contributions in developing a conceptual framework within which it might be possible to understand the interrelationship of real and financial factors and the importance of financial intermediation. Some of these contributions can be found in the following: J. G. Gurley, "Financial Institutions in the Saving-Investment Process," *Conference on Savings and Residential Financing,* Proceedings of the U.S. Savings and Loan League, 1959; J. G. Gurley and E. S. Shaw, "Financial Aspects of Economic Development," *American Economic Review* (September 1955); Gurley and Shaw, "Financial Intermediaries and the Saving-Investment Process," *Journal of Finance* (May 1956); Gurley and Shaw, "The Growth of Debt and Money in the United States, 1800–1950: A Suggested Interpretation," *Review of Economic Statistics* (August 1957); Gurley and Shaw, "Intermediaries and Monetary Theory: Reply," *American Economic Review* (March 1958); Gurley, "Liquidity and Financial Institutions in the Postwar Period," Study Paper No. 14, Joint Economic Committee, *Employment, Growth and Price Levels,* U.S. Congress, January 25, 1960; Gurley,

to comprehend and appreciate these interrelationships fully, it will be helpful to begin with a brief review of the importance of the saving-investment process.

## Role of the Saving-Investment Process

The process of capital formation plays a major role in all economies, including our own. This is readily understandable when one remembers that many current economic objectives—such as price stability, high levels of income and employment, and high rates of economic growth—are closely bound up with the relationship of savings to investment.[2] Since, in a modern market economy, this relationship is highly complex, it might prove helpful to look first at the saving-investment process in its most simple and pristine form. For the economist, this invariably involves a highly imaginary illustration taken from the pages of Daniel Defoe, featuring Robinson Crusoe and his friend Friday.

Crusoe and Friday have fallen on evil days to the extent that, in order to survive, a minimal daily catch of fish is indispensable. However, being human, they would like to *increase* their daily catch of fish in order to attain a *higher* level of living. Hence, it becomes desirable to take some time off from fishing to produce a capital good, such as a fishing net, which will increase their productivity. The problem, however, is that they must continue to eat while they are constructing the net. This, in turn, implies that they must produce a surplus of fish (a consumer good) to sustain them in the interim. In building up an excess supply of fish they are, in effect, consuming less than the full amount

of their real income or output—that is, they are *saving*. This act of abstaining from the consumption of all of their current catch of fish enables them, in turn, to devote their time to the construction of the fishing net—an act of *investment*. The real effect of saving, therefore, is to *release* productive resources from the current production of consumer goods. Investment, on the other hand, is the *use* of such freed resources to produce capital goods.[3]

While the basic nature of the saving-investment process is no different in a modern market economy, the relationship is far more complex, since those who refrain from consuming all of their income—that is, who save—are rarely the same persons or groups as those desiring to invest. Unlike Robinson Crusoe's economy, where *ex ante* (or planned) saving was always equal to *ex ante* (or desired) investment, it is only by the sheerest of coincidences that one can expect planned saving and investment to be equal in a modern market economy.

As is well known, even to those students who have had only one basic course in economics, the importance of this observation lies in the fact that while *ex post* (or actual) saving and *ex post* investment must always be equal as a matter of definition,[4] *ex ante* (or desired) saving and investment

[3]Strictly speaking, the Crusoe-Friday saving-investment example is not quite accurate if one interprets the catching of, say, ten fish, the eating of eight, and the saving of two *already* as an act of investment—in inventories. Given this interpretation when Crusoe and Friday do take a day off to build the net, eating the two fish, they in fact are disinvesting two fish in inventories and investing $x$ in a net. Whatever the terminology employed, the essence of the saving-investment relationship lies in the act of forgoing the immediate consumption of some part of all currently produced consumer goods, thereby freeing productive resources so that time can be spent in the production of capital goods.

[4]Thus, in very simple terms, we know that

$$C + S = Y$$
$$C + I = Y$$
$$Y - C = S$$
$$Y - C = I$$
$$\therefore S = I$$

where

$C$ = aggregate consumption expenditures
$S$ = aggregate saving
$I$ = aggregate investment
$Y$ = national income, or the value of output at factor cost of all final goods and services

"The Influence on Prices of Changes in the Effective Supply of Money," Joint Economic Committee, *Employment, Growth and Price Levels*, U.S. Congress, May 25, 1959; and Gurley and Shaw, *Money in a Theory of Finance*, The Brookings Institution, Washington, D.C., 1960.

[2]In economics the term *investment* is usually understood to mean real investment, the purchase of capital goods—plant and equipment and homes, for example. While the acquisition of financial assets—stocks or bonds—is also referred to in the financial literature as *investment*, it really denotes the various financial claims in which *savings* are held. Throughout this book, the context in which the term *investment* is employed should make clear whether the reference is to financial or real investment.

are brought into equality only by fluctuations in the level of national income and the rate of interest. This is analogous to the demand for, and supply of, any particular commodity, such as prunes, for example. Thus, *ex post,* the supply of and demand for prunes are always equal. In other words, the amount of prunes purchased must always equal the quantity of prunes sold. In *ex ante* terms, however, the amounts demanded and amounts supplied are brought into equilibrium only by changes in the prices of prunes so that, at their equilibrium price, the market is cleared. The equilibrating mechanism in this instance is the price of prunes rather than the level of national income and the interest rate, as in the saving-investment process.

Let us return now to our saving-investment example. When intended saving is greater than intended investment, national income or gross national product (GNP) will fall. Conversely, when desired investment is greater than desired saving, national income or GNP will increase. Whether this decrease or increase in national income and gross national product will, at the same time, be associated with changes in the general price level depends, in the first instance, upon the flexibility of the pricing structure and, secondly, on the relationship of the employment of productive resources to productive capacity. For example, if the prices of goods and services respond readily to the demand for them, and if, in the short run, the economy is fully utilizing all of its resources, including labor, then increases in aggregate demand will be reflected rather promptly in increases in the price level. Regardless of price movements, however, short-run fluctuations in income will be closely related to employment rates, and they will tend to rise and fall together.

Nor does the relationship of saving to investment end with fluctuations in income, employment, and prices. Over a period of time, the fraction of income devoted to saving and investment, as well as the efficiency with which such saving is allocated among alternative investment opportunities, helps determine a country's rate of economic growth. Thus, the greater the amounts of aggregate saving and investment at each level of national income, other things being equal, the more rapidly will output increase in the future. This is because investment in new plant and equipment helps increase productivity. Furthermore, the more efficient the allocation of saving (the more such savings flow into capital projects with the highest rates of return, or net productivities), the higher the rate of economic growth and the greater the contribution of the saving-investment process to economic well-being.

So far we have emphasized the importance of saving and investment in terms of their effects on such major economic goals as full employment levels of income, price stability, and high growth rates. In so doing, however, we have said nothing about the fundamental problems of just what kind of institutional mechanism is necessary to bring together savers and investors in order to achieve these objectives. The transfer process by which saving becomes *available* for investment involves a highly complex financial system. In a modern market economy, real and financial variables must interact in complex ways if the capital formation process is to take place, or if it is to take place at its fullest potential. The following section considers such interaction and the emergence of financial or credit markets.

## Relationship of Saving and Investment to Lending and Borrowing

In order to show the relationship of saving and investment to lending and borrowing let us, for the moment, make the improbable assumption that any saving performed by nonfinancial economic units—such as households, business firms, and government—out of current income is, in turn, *always* accompanied by an equal amount of *desired internal* investment by them, as in our Robinson Crusoe example. Under these conditions, all saving would be absorbed in the production of planned new capital goods by each of these economic units. Consequently, there would be no surplus or excess saving available to be loaned out for investment by others. In effect, each economic unit would be fully self-financed, a balanced-budget unit, with its saving always equal to its desired internal investment.

Picture now a more realistic situation where, instead of all economic units being balanced-budget units, some of them are in a position where their saving out of income is *greater* than their desired or planned internal investment. We can refer to these units as *surplus units* or *ultimate lenders.* Others are in a position where their saving is *less* than their desired internal investment. We can call these units *deficit units* or *ultimate borrowers.*

What options might be available to these unbalanced budget units in this setting?

To the extent that saving is greater than desired investment, surplus units would have the alternatives open to them of repaying some of their outstanding liabilities or adding to their stock of financial assets. If they choose the latter, they might add to their money holdings or they might make loans and acquire nonmonetary financial assets, such as corporate and municipal bonds or U.S. government securities. Such lending can be thought of as supplying loanable funds—credit—or, equivalently, as demanding financial assets.

Similarly, to the extent that there are economic units whose savings are less than their planned investment, such deficit units could finance the difference either by decreasing their stock of financial assets (decreasing their money holdings or their holdings of other financial assets) or by borrowing.[5] Such borrowing in turn, can be thought of as demanding loanable funds or, conversely, of borrowers supplying securities or claims against themselves to acquire loanable funds. The primary source of credit and debt, therefore, arises from the difference between internally generated saving and planned investment on the part of ultimate lenders and ultimate borrowers in the economy.[6]

## Institutionalization of Saving and Financial Markets

Given the emergence of potential lending and borrowing, some financial link or conduit is necessary if excess saving is actually to be transferred to deficit units. A major rationale for the existence of credit or financial markets, in fact, lies precisely in this imbalance between planned saving and investment *within* economic units and, consequently, the desire and need by them for external financing. As we have seen, if all units in the economy were always content to be balanced-budget units, lending and borrowing would never take place and credit markets would never emerge.

Given the existence of financial markets,[7] surplus and deficit units can be brought together either directly through external financing or indirectly through intermediation. *Direct* financing involves the use of marketing techniques in which primary securities (or the liabilities of ultimate borrowers) in such forms as U.S. bonds, corporate securities, and mortgages are distributed among surplus units (or ultimate lenders) anxious to acquire these financial assets. Examples of distributive techniques in our early history include the widespread role of lotteries in financing public and private investment projects as well as the employment of face-to-face loans by local lenders and borrowers. Current distributive techniques include the use of brokerage facilities and investment banking services.

*Indirect* financing, on the other hand, involves the existence of financial intermediaries that place themselves between ultimate lenders and ultimate borrowers by purchasing the primary securities of the latter and issuing *claims against themselves*—indirect securities—for the portfolios of ultimate lenders.[8] Thus, savings and loan associations issue claims against themselves in the form of savings shares that are, in turn, "purchased" by the public with some of their excess saving. Most of the proceeds are then employed by these associations to finance the building and purchase of new and existing homes by households, the latter issuing IOUs against themselves in the form of mortgages, which

---

[5] For a more detailed analysis, see Chapter 2. The term *securities* includes any and all kinds of financial assets: bonds, stocks, mortgages, all kinds of loans, and so on. While equities, strictly speaking, are not liabilities, they do help supply loanable funds in the same manner that debt instruments do.

[6] It should be remembered, however, that apart from major wars and depressions, the larger share of investment in the United States since 1900 has been financed internally rather than by borrowing. At the same time, the aggregative trend of internal financing may have slightly declined over the first half of this century. See, in this connection, Simon Kuznets, *Capital in the American Economy: Its Formation and Financing,* Princeton University Press, Princeton, N.J., 1961, pp. 268–271.

[7] The two major components of such markets may be termed the money and capital markets. The distinction between the two lies in the fact that, in the former, money is exchanged for other financial assets having a maturity of one year or less while, in the latter, the exchange involves claims with a maturity greater than one year. This is simply a matter of definition and, as such, is similar to the convention adopted for classifying consumer goods and investment goods.

[8] In terms of balance sheets, the major distinction between nonfinancial and financial institutions lies on the asset side of their respective ledgers. While the bulk of assets of nonfinancial corporations is in the form of real assets, such as plant and equipment and inventories of goods, most of the assets of financial corporations take the form of paper claims.

## Figure 1-1  The Market for Loanable Funds

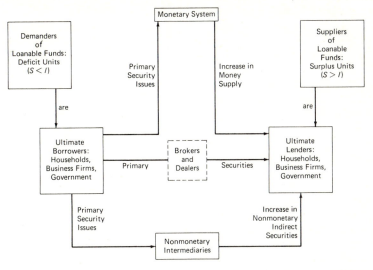

Source: Adapted from the chart presented by John G. Gurley in *Liquidity and Financial Institutions in the Postwar Period,* Study Paper No. 14; materials prepared for the Joint Economic Committee's *Study of Employment, Growth, and Price Levels,* U.S. Congress, January 25, 1960.

are taken by the S&Ls. In addition to savings and loan associations, there are many other financial intermediaries performing similar functions. These include, among others, commercial banks; mutual savings banks; credit unions; life, fire and casualty insurance companies; public and private pension funds; and investment companies.[9] The process whereby primary and indirect securities are distributed through the money and capital markets is shown in Figure 1-1.

Figure 1-1 illustrates that, during any year, nonfinancial economic units that are ultimate borrowers (demanders of loanable funds, in other words) may acquire funds: (1) by selling their primary security issues, or IOUs, directly to other nonfinancial economic units that are ultimate lenders—that is, surplus units that are suppliers of loanable funds; (2) by selling their primary securities indirectly to them through the monetary system, in which case ultimate lenders accumulate indirect securities in the form of money rather than primary

securities; and (3) by selling their primary securities indirectly to ultimate lenders through nonmonetary intermediaries. In this instance, ultimate lenders receive nonmonetary indirect securities such as life insurance policies and time deposits at mutual savings banks.[10]

### The Price of Loanable Funds

On certain social occasions, such as Christmas and certain other holidays, presents are exchanged without the parties involved necessarily expecting a strictly *quid pro quo* based on equivalent market values. The transfer of real and financial assets under ordinary circumstances, however, takes place at prices that reflect the exchange of equivalents. Furthermore, just as the supply of, and demand for, various commodities (such as copper) and factor inputs (such as labor) are cleared at their respective equilibrium prices in real markets, so there is an equilibrium price that clears the market

[9]Some of the forms that such indirect securities take, in addition to saving shares, are demand deposits, credit union shares, life insurance policies, retirement policies, and mutual fund shares.

[10]For a further and more detailed discussion and analysis of the role of financial intermediaries and how, under certain circumstances, they can actually *augment* the supply of loanable funds, see Chapter 22.

for financial assets at any given moment of time. In other words, there is an equilibrium price that equates the supply of loanable funds with the demand for these funds. This equilibrium price is called the rate of interest, the amount per dollar per annum that the lender (or supplier of loanable funds) receives for parting with those funds for a specified time period and which the borrower (or demander of loanable funds) must pay to acquire them. Chapter 22 devotes considerable time to a discussion and analysis of the various determinants of loanable funds and "the" rate of interest. Suffice it at this point to show that the supply of loanable funds, or what is the same thing, the demand for securities, and the demand for loanable funds, or the supply of securities, can be depicted graphically as shown in Figure 1-2.

In Figure 1-2(a), the supply of loanable funds schedule ($S_{lf}$) is positively sloped, indicating that lenders are prepared to increase the amount of loanable funds they supply as the rate of interest rises. Similarly, the demand for loanable funds schedule ($D_{lf}$) is negatively sloped, indicating that borrowers will demand larger amounts of loanable funds as the interest rate declines. Given the position and slope of the two schedules, the loanable funds market will be cleared at an equilibrium rate of interest of $i_e$ with the amount of loanable funds offered and accepted equal to $OA$.

Figure 1-2(b) is the alter ego of Figure 1-2(a), with the volume of securities substituting for loanable funds and with the average price per security depicted on the vertical axis in place of the rate of

### Figure 1-2(a)  The Supply and Demand for Loanable Funds, and Interest Rate Determination

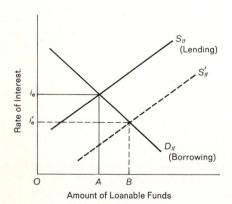

Amount of Loanable Funds

### Figure 1-2(b)  The Supply and Demand for Securities, and Price Determination

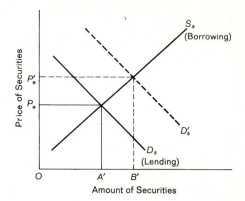

Amount of Securities

interest.[11] The demand schedule for securities ($D_s$) is negatively sloped, indicating that the lower the price of securities, the greater the amount of them that lenders will be prepared to demand. Similarly, the supply schedule of securities ($S_s$) is positively sloped, indicating that borrowers are prepared to increase the amounts of securities that they offer as their price rises. Given the positions and slopes of the two schedules, the market will be cleared at the equilibrium price ($P_e$), with the amount of securities exchanged equal to $OA'$. Of course, $OA$ in Figure 1-2(a) and $OA'$ in Figure 1-2(b) must be equal to each other—assuming that the units of measurement on the horizontal axes are the same in both instances.

Suppose that there is a shift to the right in the supply of loanable funds curve in Figure 1-2(a) such

[11] To analyze interest rate determination in terms of the supply and demand for loanable funds, or security prices in terms of the demand and supply of securities, amounts to one and the same thing. To say that when security prices fall interest rates rise, is really to say the same thing twice. It is no accident that when security prices fall, interest rates rise. The rate of interest ($i$) is *defined* as $d/p$, where $d$ equals the annual dollar income return yielded by a security and $p$ stands for its price. If the dollar income return is contractually fixed, as is usually the case with debt instruments, the effective rate of interest and the price of the security *must* move inversely. If, for example, a perpetual bond carrying a $100 income, contractually fixed, sells for $1,000, the rate of interest would be 10 percent. If the same bond rose in price to $2,000, the effective rate of interest would drop to 5 percent. If you bought that bond for only $500, on the other hand, you would receive an effective yield of 20 percent.

that, at each rate of interest, the amount of loanable funds supplied is greater than previously. This is tantamount to saying that the demand for securities schedule in Figure 1-2(b) also shifts to the right to the same degree, so that at each price the amount of securities demanded is greater than previously. The result of an increase in the demand for securities, with the supply of securities remaining constant, is an increase in its equilibrium price from $P_e$ to $P'_e$ in Figure 1-2(b). The counterpart of this price increase in Figure 1-2(a) is a corresponding decrease in the effective yield on such securities. Furthermore, as a result of the rightward shifts in the schedules in Figures 1-2(a) and 1-2(b), the volume of loanable funds traded in the market will increase from $OA$ to $OB$, while the volume of newly issued securities exchanged will increase from $OA'$ to $OB'$. Since the volume of loanable funds exchanged is nothing more nor less than the volume of securities traded, it must follow that, after the shift, $OB$ is equal to $OB'$.

## The Growth of Financial Intermediation

Apart from the prices at which financial assets are exchanged, surplus units, or ultimate lenders, and deficit units, or ultimate borrowers, are brought together, as noted earlier, either through the use of distributive or intermediative techniques. For approximately the past six decades, at least (that is, from 1920 to 1978), intermediation has played a constantly expanding role in capturing a greater share of household saving. The magnitude of the shift from direct market acquisition of primary securities to mediation of saving flows over the last six decades can be illustrated by the fact that during the 1920s direct purchases of primary securities averaged somewhat over half of the net increase in household financial assets; by the mid-1950s this share had fallen to below 20 percent,[12] and it averaged only some 10 percent for the period 1961–1978.[13] The remainder flowed through financial intermediaries.

What can possibly account for this dramatic rise in the importance of financial intermediaries in attracting a constantly higher proportion of personal savings since the turn of the century? For one thing, the steady rise in real per capita income, in which most groups in the economy have participated, has led to the emergence of many small savers. These savers, traditionally, have shown a high preference for liquidity and safety of principal as represented by the liabilities of such deposit-type financial institutions as commercial banks (especially their time and saving deposits), mutual savings banks, savings and loan associations, and credit unions. Two facts have tended to favor these institutions: the liabilities issued by these intermediaries to acquire net saving are, in practice if not by law, payable on demand and they are redeemable at a fixed face value as compared to fluctuations in the prices of negotiable primary securities.

Furthermore, the difficulty, at times, of the small saver in gaining access to markets where primary securities are bought and sold and the relatively high costs of effecting small transactions, combined with the large denominations in which they usually take place, has resulted again in a preference by the public for those financial intermediaries featuring claims against themselves that emphasize the attributes of liquidity and safety.[14] In recent decades, the latter features have been enhanced in the eyes of the holders of excess saving by the evolution and development of governmental insurance and guarantee programs respecting the liabilities of such institutions. The growth of claims against deposit-type intermediaries in the postwar period may be seen in Table 1-1. Except for the relatively slow growth of the money supply, the growth of such liabilities of depository institutions has, in most instances, either kept pace with or far outdistanced the growth of gross national product.

Given the constraints imposed by a relatively modest income, small savers, as well as other groups in the economy, have also sought the protection of the insurance principle in making provision for members of their families given the possibility of premature death. The pooling of risks inherent in the insurance principle has given them the opportunity to make such provisions at a minimal cost to themselves and their families as compared with any attempt on their parts at self-insur-

[12]Daniel H. Brill, "The Role of Financial Intermediaries in U.S. Capital Markets," *Federal Reserve Bulletin* (January 1967), 19.
[13]Board of Governors of the Federal Reserve System, *Flow of Funds Accounts,* Washington, D.C., August 1979.

[14]Brill, "The Role of Financial Intermediaries," 19.

**Table 1-1   Assets of Nonfinancial Sectors in Form of Claims on Selected Financial Intermediaries, 1939–1978 (in billions of dollars)**

| End of Year | Money Supply | Time Deposits Commercial Banks | Time Deposits Savings Banks | Savings and Loan Shares | Credit Union Shares | Life Insurance Reserves[a] | Private and Public Pension Reserves[b] | Mutual Fund Net Assets | Gross National Product |
|---|---|---|---|---|---|---|---|---|---|
| 1939 | $ 36.2 | $ 15.3 | $ 10.5 | $ 4.1 | $ 0.2 | $ 25.8 | $ 3.0[c] | $ 0.4[d] | $ 91.1 |
| 1945 | 102.4 | 30.1 | 15.4 | 7.4 | 0.4 | 38.7 | 5.4 | 1.3 | 213.6 |
| 1950 | 116.2 | 36.7 | 20.0 | 14.0 | 0.8 | 55.0 | 11.7 | 2.5 | 284.6 |
| 1955 | 135.2 | 50.2 | 28.1 | 32.1 | 2.4 | 75.4 | 26.8 | 7.8 | 397.5 |
| 1960 | 141.2 | 72.7 | 36.3 | 62.1 | 5.0 | 98.5 | 52.8 | 17.0 | 562.6 |
| 1965 | 167.2 | 146.9 | 52.4 | 110.3 | 9.4 | 127.6 | 91.6 | 35.2 | 681.2 |
| 1970 | 219.6 | 229.2 | 71.6 | 146.4 | 15.5 | 167.8 | 157.3 | 47.6 | 982.4 |
| 1975 | 295.4 | 462.6 | 109.9 | 285.7 | 33.0 | 237.1 | 249.9 | 42.2[e] | 1,528.8 |
| 1977 | 338.7 | 556.4 | 134.0 | 386.8 | 46.8 | 281.0 | 312.0 | 45.0[e] | 1,889.5 |
| 1978 | 361.2 | 612.1 | 142.7 | 431.0 | 53.0 | 318.5 | 350.7 | 45.0[e] | 2,235.2 |
| | | | | *Percent Growth* | | | | | |
| 1945– 1978 | 252.7 | 1933.6 | 826.6 | 5724.3 | 13,150.0 | 723.0 | 6,394.4 | 3,361.5 | 946.4 |

[a]Also includes individual and group annuities.

[b]Reserves of private noninsured pension funds and state and local pension reserves. Does not include Old Age and Survivors Disability Insurance.

[c]Figure is for 1940 rather than 1939.

[d]Figure is for 1941 rather than 1939.

[e]Excludes money market funds.

Sources: Data for commercial banks, mutual savings banks, savings and loan associations, credit unions, and gross national product are from Board of Governors of the Federal Reserve System. *Federal Reserve Bulletin*, various issues; *Flow of Funds Accounts*, December 1976, August 1979; and *Flow of Funds Accounts, Assets and Liabilities Outstanding, 1968–1978*. Those for life insurance companies are from the American Council of Life Insurance, *Life Insurance Fact Book, 1979*. Those for private and public pension reserves are from the U.S. Securities and Exchange Commission, *Statistical Bulletin*, May 1969, November 1976, May 1978, and August 1979. Data on mutual fund net assets are from the Investment Company Institute, *Mutual Fund Fact Book*, 1979.

ance. The fact that life insurance reserves have grown at only a slightly lower rate than GNP in the postwar period (see Table 1-1) attests to the importance of the insurance principle in attracting saving.

The last few decades have also witnessed higher living standards and aspirations, advances in medicine leading to greater longevity, a larger number of senior citizens sixty-five years of age and over as a percentage of our total population, earlier retirements, a more sophisticated understanding of the erosion of future purchasing power through secular price inflation, and fundamental changes in our economic philosophy and social structure. These changes, in turn, have led to increasing preoccupation with problems associated with old age. The result has been the emergence and proliferation, in recent decades, of such new and dynamic intermediaries as public and private pension funds and open-ended investment companies—mutual funds. In the same way that contractual saving flows to life insurance companies represent, in the eyes of

the saver, a hedge against premature death, so does saving flowing into pension funds represent a hedge against living too long, for life expectancy has risen at the same time that the average job retirement age has fallen.

Moreover, the demands of our highly complex industrial and urban society, as compared with a rural and agricultural economy, have fostered the steady increase of population mobility at the same time that they have downgraded the institution of the extended family with its philosophy of familial aid for its older members. The result of all these changes has been the need, greater than ever before, for the individuals to provide financial sustenance for themselves and their families during their advanced years. This need is reflected, as seen in Table 1-1, in the very rapid growth of private noninsured and public pension funds during the postwar period.

At the same time as these changes have been taking place, it has become of vital importance that lower- and middle-income households, as well as some of those with higher incomes, have the opportunity during their productive years to build a source of invested capital, the income of which could be used to supplement federal Old Age and Survivors Disability Insurance as well as state, local, and private pension benefits. Except for the very affluent, however, and/or those with enough leisure time and interest to follow closely current market developments, the great mass of financial investors do not have sufficient accumulated saving to provide adequately for common-stock diversification.[15] Such financial intermediaries as mutual funds, with their built-in advantages of diversification, selection, and professional management help meet these risk needs and, therefore, are an important vehicle for financial investment by individuals.[16]

## Portfolio Management by Financial Institutions

Earlier in this chapter, we had occasion to discuss the supply of, and demand for, loanable funds and the equilibrium rate of interest that clears the financial markets. At the same time, as we have just seen, financial intermediation has played an ever expanding role in attracting excess saving and in utilizing such saving to acquire primary securities. Its growing importance in transferring loanable funds, therefore, is obvious. However, it is difficult to discuss the *aggregate supply* of loanable funds, or the *aggregate demand* for financial assets by different types of financial intermediaries, without at the same time becoming involved in an analysis of the *composition* of each of their portfolios. Consequently, it may be useful, at this time, to review briefly some of the general principles of asset management that help to explain the *allocation* of loan-

able funds by different financial intermediaries, especially as these matters will come up in later sections of this book. It will become obvious even from this brief introduction to the subject that a realistic explanation also demands institutional knowledge of the laws and regulations regarding the asset choices of intermediaries and of the operating constraints underlying such choices.

To highlight the problem of portfolio choice, let us begin by assuming a world of complete certainty—that is, a world with perfect knowledge of the future so that there are, in effect, no financial risks involved in the selection of securities. In such a world, asset management by financial intermediaries—as well as by others—would consist simply of so selecting various claims as to maximize total net revenue. In other words, profitability would be the dominant consideration.

In the real world, however, where there is uncertainty about future events, financial institutions not only must take account of current and anticipated yields on financial assets but must also consider how safe such returns are. In other words, in a world filled with uncertainty, decision making for the financial firm is infinitely more complex than in a world with perfect foresight since it involves taking into explicit consideration such financial characteristics as various kinds of risk, in addition to net yields.

The notion of risk of financial assets is multidimensional. One kind of risk, called *liquidity risk,* refers to the possibility that price concessions will have to be made if an asset is sold prior to maturity.[17] *Credit risk* refers to the possibility of default on income and principal by the borrower. *Money* or *market risk,* on the other hand, refers to variability of income and fluctuations in the market price of a security. A fourth kind of risk, *purchasing power risk,* refers to changes in rates of return induced by fluctuations in the cost of living.[18]

---

[15]It is interesting to note that, apart from their acquisition of mutual fund shares, individuals have been net sellers of preferred and common stock for many years. See U.S. Securities and Exchange Commission, *Statistical Bulletin,* various issues.

[16]The recent phenomena of inflationary expectations and of double-digit inflation with their adverse impacts on common stock prices have severely affected the rate of growth of those mutual funds whose assets are held in the form of equities (see Table 1-1). In fact, for some years now, redemptions by investors in such funds have exceeded the sales of mutual fund shares. On the other hand, there has been a phenomenal growth of money market funds in the years 1978 to 1980. Investment Company Institute, *Mutual Fund Fact Book,* 1980.

[17]Liquidity may be defined in terms of the speed of conversion of an asset into money with the certainty of little or no capital loss. Thus, the most liquid of all liquid assets, and the yardstick against which they all can be measured on a liquidity scale, is money. Money has no liquidity risk.

[18]Thus, while money has no liquidity or market risk and little credit risk, financial assets held in this or other forms are subject to persistent erosion in their purchasing power when the general level of prices increases, assuming there is no proportional increase in the prices of such assets.

These risks are present, in varying degrees, in most of the financial assets held by intermediaries.

The difficulty is that return (or yields) and risk are positively correlated; consequently, the problem of portfolio management becomes one of some trade-off between higher yields with the associated degree of greater risk, and lower yields, with a corresponding reduction in the degree of risk. The degree to which risk can be taken relative to yields earned depends, in the first instance, on the nature of any particular intermediary's liability structure and the ability of its management to predict with a fair degree of certainty its cash inflows and outflows. In a general sense, such decision variables are significantly different for such broad categories as deposit-type and insurance-type intermediaries. Thus, in the case of such depository institutions as commercial banks, mutual savings banks, and savings and loan associations, their liabilities, in the form of demand and time deposits and shares, are relatively liquid as compared to the obligations incurred by life insurance companies and pension funds. The latter can predict, with less error than these depository institutions, both their cash inflows arising out of contractual obligations and their cash outflows primarily in the form of death and retirement benefits. To meet such benefit payments they need not sell securities. The large excess of their cash receipts over their benefit payments give them cash reserves so that they can make their needed cash payments. Both saving inflows into, and outflows from, depository intermediaries are voluntary and noncontractual in nature and, consequently, more volatile. As a result, it is not surprising to discover that the proportion of liquid assets held in the form of cash, U.S. government and agency securities, and open-market paper, is higher, on the average, for deposit-type institutions than for their contractual brethren,[19] nor that the average maturity of earning assets is higher for life insurance companies and pension funds than, for

example, commercial banks.[20] Since yields and risk are highly correlated and since, typically, the degree of money risk is greater for financial assets of longer than shorter maturity, it follows that the *expected* average yield will be higher on primary securities held by insurance-oriented intermediaries than on claims held by depository institutions.

*Within* each broad class of financial intermediary, one also can discern differences in portfolio composition and asset management that can be explained, in some measure, by the general principles mentioned. Thus, the fact that the average turnover rate on demand and time deposits held by commercial banks is considerably higher than those on savings deposits and shares held by savings banks and savings and loan associations helps account, in part, for the fact that the former hold a much higher fraction of their assets in liquid form than do the latter,[21] and that a much larger fraction of the earning assets of commercial banks are short term and intermediate in nature. On the other hand, given the fixed nature of their contractual obligations and the great differences in the degree of market risk between equities and fixed-income securities, life insurance companies hold only a small fraction of their total assets in the form of common stocks compared to the significant percentage held in this form by private noninsured pension funds.[22]

While the general principles of asset management help to explain many of the differences in the portfolio composition of different financial institutions, a more complete explanation presupposes familiarity, as well, with differing legal and tax provisions as they apply to the various classes of intermediaries. Thus, savings and loan associations, both by

[19]At the end of 1978, 5.3 percent of the total financial assets of life insurance companies were held in these liquid forms; the corresponding figure for private noninsured pension funds was 12.1 percent. Compare these percentages with those for savings and loan associations, mutual savings banks, and commercial banks for the same year, namely, 7.6 percent, 12.8 percent, and 18.2 percent respectively. Calculations are from data in the Board of Governors of the Federal Reserve System, *Flow of Funds Accounts, Assets and Liabilities Outstanding 1968–1978.*

[20]Since life insurance companies, pension funds, and commercial banks are, in effect, multi-product financial firms such a comparison is relevant. On the other hand, due to federal and state regulatory restrictions as to the types of earning assets they may acquire, mutual savings banks and savings and loan associations are primarily specialized mortgage lenders. Consequently, no relevant comparison based on the general principles of asset management alluded to above can be made between them and life insurance companies and pension funds with regard to allocation of earning assets.

[21]See footnote 19.

[22]At the end of 1978, life insurance companies held only 9.4 percent of their total assets in equities compared with 54.3 percent held in that form by noninsured pension funds. *Flow of Funds Accounts, Assets and Liabilities, 1968–1978.*

law and tradition, are predominantly mortgage lenders. While mutual savings banks are authorized to acquire a somewhat broader variety of financial assets, they, too, tend in practice to specialize in mortgage lending.[23] While part of this represents a traditional response on the part of savings bankers, a good part lies in the fact that security acquisitions by them are often circumscribed by state regulations limiting them to approved lists of securities as well as their responsibility under the "prudent man" rule.[24]

The huge acquisitions of municipal securities by commercial banks since the mid-1950s, as compared with the net disposal of such securities by state and local pension funds over the same period, cannot be fully understood unless one is aware that commercial banks have to pay the normal corporate profits tax as compared with the tax-free status of public pension funds. While the pretax yields on municipals were still *relatively* low over much of this period, their after-tax yields, in many instances, were greater than those on taxable securities of similar maturity, such as government bonds. Therefore, given the tax status of commercial banks, the reasons for their large acquisitions of such securities during this period become understandable, as does the net decrease of municipals in the portfolios of state and local pension funds. While many similar illustrations could be given, suffice it to say that portfolio management by financial intermediaries is a highly complex subject in which general principles of asset management must be supplemented with specific institutional knowledge before one is in a position fully to understand how such intermediaries allocate their loanable funds among various sectors of the money and capital markets.

## Financial Intermediation and Economic Growth

Until now, we have devoted ourselves to an analysis of the role of saving and investment with respect to their impacts on such economic objectives as price stability, high levels of income and employment, and a high rate of economic growth. We have also observed the manner in which saving and investment are transformed into lending and borrowing by surplus and deficit units, the financial mechanisms for transferring excess saving in the form of the money and capital markets, the price at which loanable funds are exchanged in these markets, the reasons for the growth of financial intermediation and, finally, the general principles and institutional factors that these intermediaries must take into account in making their asset choices. With all this in mind, we can now explore in greater depth the relationship of financial assets and financial intermediation to those problems associated with economic growth.

To understand the impact of financial assets on economic growth, let us attempt to visualize an economy without any claims, including money. In such an economy, each economic unit, in effect, would *have* to be a balanced-budget unit, inasmuch as it would be forced to invest in real goods that part of its current income which it did not consume. In this claimless economy, no economic unit could invest more than its saving, even if it desired to do so, because there would be no way to finance such excess expenditures through borrowing. Conversely, no unit could invest less than its actual saving, even if it wished to do so, since no financial assets, including money, would be available in which to put its excess saving.[25] Therefore, each economic unit would be forced to end up in a balanced-budget position, with its saving equal to its internal investment.[26]

---

[23]Even within the area of mortgage loans, however, there are interesting differences. For example, at the end of 1978, 80.0 percent of all mortgage loans by savings and loan associations were held in the form of one- to- four-family mortgages compared with 65.9 percent for mutual savings banks. National Association of Mutual Savings Banks, *1979 National Fact Book of Mutual Savings Banks.*

[24]This rule states, in effect, that the security acquisitions by those serving in a fiduciary capacity must be of such high quality as would induce their purchase by a conservative investor were that investor employing his or her own funds.

[25]This also assumes, of course, no nonfinancial borrowing and lending among economic units—that is, borrowing and lending of real goods. In all probability, however, even where such nonfinancial borrowing and lending existed, it would be relatively insignificant in an economy devoid of financial claims.

[26]Unfortunately, the distribution of income and saving is rarely, if ever, matched by the distribution of productive ability and initiative. As a result, some groups desire to specialize in saving while others prefer to concentrate on investing.

The fact that for some of the potential deficit units desired investment would be *greater* than the amounts that could actually be invested would imply lower growth rates than would have been attained had such units been able to borrow additional funds for investment purposes through the creation of claims against themselves. Likewise, for other units, desired saving would be less than actual saving, thereby leading to a condition of economic disequilibrium and to the adjustment of actual to desired saving through the process of spending more out of current income for consumer goods. In this manner, actual saving would decline and a new equilibrium between desired saving and actual saving levels would be established. The end result of an economy with no financial assets, therefore, would be *lower* levels of saving and investment at each level of income than for one with such claims and, hence, a *lower* rate of economic growth.[27]

We have already noted that the bulk of saving by ultimate lenders finds its way into financial intermediaries in exchange for their liabilities. It is fairly obvious, therefore, that their growth and proliferation, to the extent that they result in a greater and more varied assortment of attractive claims than would be possible in their absence, encourage higher levels of saving and investment at each level of income. This is the first way that financial intermediaries encourage economic growth.

A second way intermediation encourages growth is by allocating funds to productive users. In the introductory section of this chapter, the observation was made that the rate of economic growth is dependent not only upon the proportion of income saved and invested but also upon "the efficiency with which such saving is allocated among alternative investment opportunities." Still another way of saying the same thing is that the rate of economic growth not only depends on that portion of income devoted to new capital expenditures, or investment, but also on the net productivity of such increments to the capital stock. In a competitive market economy, the payment of interest reflects the fact that capital funds are limited in amount and this, when combined with the demand for such funds among different sectors of the economy,

helps determine the level of interest rates. Presumably, the payment of interest will ensure that saving will flow only into those capital projects where the net return, after due allowance for risk, is equal to or greater than the relevant interest rate. Thus, given a fixed amount of saving, the latter will be allocated among those available investment projects offering the highest rates of return and, therefore, having the highest net productivities. This means that, given the fraction of income devoted to investment, the more efficient the allocation of saving the higher will be the rate of economic growth.

In a world without financial assets, or lending and borrowing, there would inevitably be an inefficient allocation of real resources. In such a world some economic units would be faced with a situation in which some of their desired investments, based on anticipated rates of return, exceeded their actual saving. Other economic units would find that their actual saving exceeded the amounts they desired to invest given the expected rates of return on many of these projects. In the absence of lending and borrowing, no financial mechanism would exist whereby investment projects were allocated among the various economic units in a manner different from the distribution of saving among them. Consequently, a successful *execution* of investment projects based on a rational *ranking* of investment opportunities could not be accomplished for society as a whole, and allocational efficiency would suffer. The result would be lower growth rates and standards of living.[28]

The emergence of financial assets, brought about through lending and borrowing by surplus and deficit units through financial markets, helps change this state of affairs by redistributing saving from investment projects with relatively low net productivities to those with higher expected rates of return. *How far* such a process can go, however, in enlarging the area of market efficiency depends, among other things, upon the *extent* of asset choices facing lenders and borrowers, their asset *preferences,* and the *costs* involved in transferring excess saving. Let us see the *why* and *how* of each, in terms of both direct and indirect finance.

The use and development of distributive techniques leads to a more efficient resource allocation

---

[27]Gurley, "Financial Institutions in the Saving-Investment Process," 12.

[28]Ibid.

as local loans, with the passage of time, are supplemented by a vast network of national brokerage and dealer facilities. These facilities include organized stock exchanges and over-the-counter securities trading in equities, corporate, municipal, and federal government debt, as well as investment banking services, all of which perform the basic function of marketing primary securities throughout the country. The emergence of these institutions, which specialize in bringing lenders and borrowers together via an effective communications network, leads to lower transaction costs (those costs incurred in the search for potential lenders and borrowers) or, what amounts to the same thing, they result in more economic and financial information per dollar spent in this manner. This, in turn, leads to a broadening of the area of market choice for surplus units, since ultimate lenders are now better informed about the many types and characteristics of debt and equity instruments available for purchase. Ultimate borrowers, on the other hand, are enabled to issue primary securities whose terms more fully reflect their borrowing needs, given a vastly broader range of potential lenders from whom to borrow. In sum, widening the area of market choice can only enhance the utilities of potential lenders while, at the same time, lowering the disutilities of potential borrowers.

Even distributive techniques, however, suffer from certain inherent limitations, the most important of which is the fact that though claims may be distributed more efficiently, lenders must still end up with primary securities. To the extent that such claims are not that highly regarded by some potential lenders, borrowers may be forced to pay higher rates of interest as well as altering still other terms of the debt contract so as to induce their purchase. Consequently, not only the cost but also the disutility of borrowing will be increased, thereby hampering an efficient allocation of resources. For example, some lenders, as typical risk averters,[29] prefer short-term financial assets with a high degree of liquidity to long-term claims that involve the

distinct possibility of capital losses. On the other hand, some borrowers prefer to issue long-term debt in line with the use of such funds in the acquisition of fixed real assets. To the extent that surplus saving is redistributed at all, it will be at a market rate of interest reflecting the additional risk premiums to lenders, as well as changes in the other terms of credit. As has just been noted, this not only increases the cost but also the disutility of such borrowing for deficit units.

The development of financial intermediation changes much of this by extending the financial choices of lenders and borrowers. By their very nature, financial intermediaries are middlemen who place themselves between the ultimate lenders and borrowers, offering the former additional choices, in terms of claims against themselves, which such lenders may desire to accumulate while, at the same time, acquiring the IOUs of borrowers at terms more congenial to the latter. In this manner, intermediaries increase still further the marginal utility of surplus units while, at the same time, lowering the marginal disutility of deficit units. Claims that are more attractive to surplus units include liquid claims, such as time deposits and savings shares, which deposit-type institutions offer to the public, and the issuance of such indirect securities as life insurance policies, retirement contracts, and mutual fund shares by insurance-type and investment-oriented intermediaries. On the borrowing side, financial intermediation may decrease the disutility of borrowing by such techniques as direct placement of corporate bonds with life insurance companies. With direct placements the terms of the debt contract are specifically tailored to meet the particular needs of the borrowing firm.[30]

---

[29]It is commonly assumed that most people, in terms of utility or satisfaction, weigh the prospects of capital losses more heavily than they do the possibility of equivalent capital gains. Hence, given the equal probability of an event, most people are unwilling to participate unless they receive some premium in the form of favorable odds as to the likely outcome of that event. In this sense, a

majority of people are risk averters rather than risk takers. For an application of this principle to the relationship of various rates of interest to one another, see Chapters 23 and 24.

[30]The past quarter century has seen further widening of the choices open to ultimate lenders and borrowers. Thus, the pressures of increased competition among financial intermediaries has resulted in a proliferation of new indirect securities (financial innovations) designed to meet the needs and wants of the public. For example, commercial banks have pioneered in the development of negotiable time certificates of deposit to attract short-term funds held by business firms and governmental units. Similarly, they have developed their equivalent for house-

At the same time that intermediaries have been widening the alternatives available both to lenders and borrowers, they have further lowered transaction costs by making the market for loanable funds less imperfect through the additional gathering, dissemination, and use of information. Because they are large organizations capable of attracting and pooling huge amounts of small saving, they are in a position, via professional management, to provide for asset diversification by the holders of their liabilities and, therefore, for insurance against default and money risks. In this manner, they are further able to take advantage of large-scale economies in making saving both more available, and less costly, to capital-intensive borrowers—that is, to borrowers requiring large amounts of capital funds. Such improvements in the organization and structure of financial markets accelerate the economy's growth by expediting the flow of funds from savers to investors.

While intermediation, in general, has led to a more efficient allocation of resources, it must be noted that the process of indirect finance has involved some economic costs. One such cost lies in the degree of spread between the rate paid by financial institutions to surplus units and the rates paid to those intermediaries by deficit units. The narrower the differential, the greater the operational efficiency of financial intermediation. In the short run, public regulation, which has sometimes been less than diligent in fostering competitive behavior, combined with varying degrees of monopolistic competition and oligopoly within and among various types of intermediaries, has prevented the spread from being as narrow as it might have been in the absence of such rigidities.[31] Over the course of many decades, however, there appears to be

little doubt that increasing competition among intermediaries has systematically narrowed spreads by raising rates of return to ultimate lenders while at the same time lowering costs to ultimate borrowers.[32]

Increasingly, competition has been breaking down overspecialization and the "unique" services previously claimed by different types of intermediaries so that, in the process, intermediative costs have declined. Thus, the last few decades have witnessed commercial banks offering consumer credit earlier reserved for personal and sales financial companies, or competing with factoring companies in purchasing the accounts receivable of business firms; mutual savings banks competing with life insurance companies by offering their depositors insurance policies; life insurance companies, in turn, expanding their area of operations to include health and accident benefits, insured pension plans, mutual funds, and so on. The future should witness further declines in specialization as financial intermediaries, spurred on by competitive pressures and by less restrictive government regulation, become increasingly anxious to enlarge their markets. In sum, the net result of this pro-

---

holds in the form of consumer savings certificates or notes. Likewise, life insurance companies now issue benefit contracts in the form of variable annuities. These permit beneficiaries to share in the advantages of potential price appreciation of common stocks as well as continuing to guarantee fixed-income benefits.

[31] Still other sources of intermediative inefficiency are differences in unit costs at each scale of operation among individual financial firms in the same industry that cannot be satisfactorily accounted for by differences in product mix, location, factor prices, or growth rates, as well as a tendency, at times, to evaluate improperly risk in attracting saving and acquiring primary securities, a situation

most prevalent where economic efficiency has been sacrificed by individual institutions to the dictates of less than optimal growth rates.

For an analysis of the impact of oligopoly on profit spreads and the performance of the savings and loan industry, see Edward S. Shaw, *Savings and the Loan Market Structure and Market Performance: A Study of California State-Licensed Savings and Loan Associations,* California Savings and Loan Commission, Los Angeles, 1962. While recent studies of market structure and performance among commercial banks are too numerous to cite, note might be taken of the classic study in this field, namely, David P. Alhadeff's *Monopoly and Competition in Banking,* University of California Press, Berkeley, 1954. For a similar analysis applied to listed common stocks traded off the organized stock exchanges, see Murray E. Polakoff and Arnold W. Sametz, "The Third Market—The Nature of Competition in the Market for Listed Securities Traded Off-Board," *The Antitrust Bulletin* (January–April 1966). For a detailed discussion of these and other areas of market imperfection, see Chapters 31 and 32, as well as the references listed in those chapters.

[32] Thus, for example, the spread between borrowing and lending rates for depository intermediaries has narrowed, through the passage of time, within a range of approximately 1 to 1½ percent. See Brill, "The Role of Financial Intermediaries," 29.

**Table 1-2  Increases and Decreases in Outstanding Debt and GNP, 1919–1976 (in billions of dollars)**

| Debtor | 1919–1929 | 1929–1941 | 1941–1945 | 1945–1957 | 1957–1967[a] | 1967–1976 | Total 1919–1976 |
|---|---|---|---|---|---|---|---|
| Nonfarm households and noncorporate | $21.1 | $ (4.7) | $ (2.2) | $129.7 | $251.1 | $ 557.2 | $ 977.1 |
| Corporate | 42.9 | (17.5) | 3.1 | 185.1 | 243.7 | 861.1 | 1259.4 |
| State and local governments | 9.8 | 3.0 | (3.6) | 38.7 | 63.4 | 123.5 | 228.4 |
| Federal government | (8.4) | 47.2 | 213.4 | (2.3)[b] | 63.6 | 229.4 | 491.8 |
| Total | $65.4 | $ 28.0 | $210.7 | $351.2 | $621.8 | $1771.2 | $2956.7 |
| GNP | $24.2 | $ (3.4) | $112.3 | $229.1 | $344.0 | $ 903.8 | $1610.0 |

[a] Figures from 1957 are not strictly comparable with earlier data.

[b] The reduction in the federal debt between 1945 and 1957 resulted from the large cash balances built up by the end of the war that were subsequently used to reduce the government debt outstanding.

Sources: U.S. Bureau of the Census, Department of Commerce, *Historical Statistics of the United States: Colonial Times to 1957; Economic Report of the President,* January 1977; and Marshall A. Robinson, "Debt and the American Economy," 5.

gressive overlapping of functions and purposes can only be a continuing downtrend in the economic costs of financial intermediation.

## Economic Growth and Debt

It should be fairly obvious by now that there exists a very close relationship between economic growth and the growth of debt. After all, debt, or the issuance of claims, is the principal financial link putting the excess saving of surplus units at the disposal of ultimate borrowers for productive and other uses. Without access to such borrowing, deficit units desiring to invest more than their saving would not be able to do so, and economic growth would suffer. Yet one still hears statements such as the following campaign statement by an elder statesmen who announced with rage and shock, "the debts of the American people today are higher than ever before in our history!"[33] While having the political advantage of being almost always true, the statement also suggests a moral abhorrence to debt that is part of our Puritan ethic. At the same time, economic growth is looked upon everywhere with approbation and respect. What seems to be lacking is the realization that economic growth (desirable) and the growth of debt (undesirable) are not independent entities but are closely related to

one another. If the economy is to grow rapidly, a significant increase in its liabilities and a rapid accumulation of financial assets must occur.[34]

Debt does not always grow at the same rate in all sectors, however. It can be shown that, over time, different sectors of the economy have alternately taken the lead in increasing their debt relative to other sectors, but in most instances rapid debt increases have been accompanied by corresponding changes in GNP regardless of the source of the debt. Thus, as Table 1-2 indicates, during World War II the vast increase in aggregate debt resulted almost exclusively from the borrowing activities of the federal government. This was made necessary by the huge increases in federal expenditures brought about by the war. Not so surprisingly, then, GNP also increased substantially in those five years. Similarly, the huge increases in GNP since World War II have been accompanied by correspondingly large increases in the aggregate debt, the largest share of which has been the very rapid increase in debt of the private sector. In fact, the tremendous postwar increases in GNP are, to a large extent, a tribute to the spending habits of households and business firms. On the other hand, during the decade of the Great Depression in the 1930s, when GNP actually declined from its pre-

[33] Quoted in Marshall A. Robinson, "Debt and the American Economy," *The Brookings Institution,* Reprint No. 31, June 1959, 1. This paper was first published in the *Proceedings,* Fifty-first Annual Conference on Taxation, The National Tax Association, 1958.

[34] If one wished to feel better regarding the growth of debt, one might recall that the existence of credit and debt are merely two sides of the same coin. Thus, for every dollar of debt issued by a borrower, there must be an equivalent dollar of credit held by a lender. In this connection, see Chapter 2.

vious peak in 1929, total net debt increased relatively little, and such increases as did occur were primarily due to increases in the debt of the federal government as it attempted to revive the economy through deficit financing. Conversely, there were actual *decreases* in individual and corporate debt outstanding as these sectors curtailed their spending, in the process liquidating some of their debt during this decade of economic stagnation.

In conclusion, it should be borne in mind that, while no attempt has been made throughout this discussion to attribute causal primacy either to debt or to economic growth in terms of each other, it seems indisputably clear that both are highly interrelated. Furthermore, when the economy is broken down into its primary sectors, interesting differences have emerged in terms of each sector's role in both the growth and debt process at different times in our economic history.

## Conclusion

At the beginning of this chapter, we mentioned Robinson Crusoe and the delightful simplicity of capital formation in an economy where savers and investors were one and the same people, and where there were no financial assets or institutions to complicate life. The fact that in a modern market economy, savers and investors are usually different individuals or groups implies the need for a whole complex of financial institutions and markets to transfer excess saving efficiently and promptly from surplus to deficit units. While Crusoe may well have heaved a sigh of relief at being spared the ordeal of living in such a complex society, it does seem to have certain advantages of its own, not the least of which is its ability to produce more than the minimal quota of fish constituting his basic diet.

## Questions

1. Define what is meant by saving and investment and explain how the saving-investment process helps determine such economic objectives as: (a) full employment level of income; (b) price stability; and (c) high rates of economic growth.
2. What is the relationship between saving and investment, on the one hand, and lending and borrowing, on the other?

3. What is the difference, if any, between a financial institution and a financial intermediary?
4. Discuss and analyze the implications of the following statements:
   a. "Complete self-financing by all units in the economy is incompatible with the existence of financial markets."
   b. "The growth of financial intermediation is an historical accident and is unnecessary for the proper functioning of credit markets."
   c. "The existence of claims on wealth is synonymous with the existence of financial markets."
5. Discuss the notion that the supply of loanable funds is really the same as the demand for securities while the demand for loanable funds is synonymous with the supply of securities.
6. Over the course of the last six decades, financial intermediation has played a constantly expanding role in capturing an ever-increasing share of household saving. How would you account for this trend?
7. How would you explain the differences in portfolio composition between the assets of commercial banks and life insurance companies? Between the assets of commercial banks and S&Ls?
8. What is the relationship, if any, between financial intermediation and economic growth?
9. Why are economic growth and debt indissolubly bound together?
10. Why is the process of capital formation much more complex in modern times than in the world of Robinson Crusoe?

## Selected Bibliography

Alhadeff, David P. *Monopoly and Competition in Banking.* University of California Press, Berkeley, 1954.

Board of Governors of the Federal Reserve System. *Flow of Funds Accounts.* Washington, D.C., August 1979.

Brill, Daniel H. "The Role of Financial Intermediaries in U.S. Capital Markets." *Federal Reserve Bulletin* (January 1967).

Gurley, John G. "Financial Institutions in the Saving-Investment Process." *Conference on Savings and Residential Financing,* Proceedings of the U.S. Savings and Loan League, 1959.

———. *"Liquidity and Financial Institutions in the Postwar Period."* Study Paper No. 14, Joint Economic Committee, *Employment, Growth and Price Levels,* U.S. Congress, May 25, 1959.

Gurley, John G., and Edward Shaw, "Financial Aspects of Economic Development." *American Economic Review* (September 1955).

———. "Financial Intermediaries and the Saving-Investment Process." *Journal of Finance* (May 1956).

———. "The Growth of Debt and Money in the United States, 1800–1950: A Suggested Interpretation." *Review of Economic Statistics* (August 1957).

———. "Intermediaries and Monetary Theory: Reply." *American Economic Review* (March 1958).

———. *Money in a Theory of Finance.* The Brookings Institution, Washington, D.C., 1960.

Kuznets, Simon. *Capital in the American Economy: Its Formation and Financing.* Princeton University Press, Princeton, N.J., 1961.

Light, J. O., and William L. White. *The Financial System.* Irwin, Homewood, Ill., 1979.

Polakoff, Murray E., and Arnold W. Sametz. "The Third Market—The Nature of Competition in the Market for Listed Securities Traded Off-Board." *The Antitrust Bulletin* (January–April 1966).

Robinson, Marshall A. *Debt and the American Economy.* The Brookings Institution, Washington, D.C., Reprint No. 31, June 1959.

Shaw, Edward S. *Saving and the Loan Market Structure and Market Performance: A Study of California State-Licensed Savings and Loan Associations.* California Savings and Loan Commission, Los Angeles, 1962.

# 2

# The Flow of Funds Accounts: A Framework for Financial Analysis

The preceding chapter developed a broad conceptual framework within which much of what follows in subsequent chapters will fall into place quite naturally instead of remaining a jumble of unrelated facts. This chapter is closely related to the preceding one inasmuch as it presents the empirical counterpart of that chapter's conceptual framework, a counterpart known as the Flow of Funds Accounts.

## What Are the Flow of Funds Accounts?

This chapter is about a form of accounting known as the Flow of Funds Accounts. We will be concerned mainly with developing the logical structure of these accounts, rather than with analyzing the implications of any particular set of numbers over any particular time span. That is done elsewhere in the book, most particularly in Chapter 25.

Throughout most of its history, accounting has been concerned primarily with record keeping in individual business firms. About a generation or two ago, however, economists started applying accounting principles and techniques to the whole economy: record keeping for the whole society. Out of such "social accounting" has come the National Income Accounts of the Department of Commerce, which by now are well known. More recently, the Board of Governors of the Federal Reserve System developed a companion set of bookkeeping entries on the financial side, the Flow of Funds Accounts.

Flow of funds accounting is used to analyze borrowing and lending in financial markets. It traces financial transactions by recording the payments that each economic sector makes to other sectors and the receipts that it receives from them. It also traces how financial flows interact with and influence "real" savings and investment. To appreciate all these implications, however, we will first have to learn what flow of funds accounting is all about. Very briefly, it is a system of social accounting in which (1) the economy is divided into a number of sectors; and (2) a "sources and uses of funds statement" is constructed for each sector. When the sources and uses of funds statements for each sector are integrated with each other, we obtain (3) a flow of funds matrix for the economy as a whole. This matrix shows the real and financial interrelations that are taking place within the economy. The rest of this chapter explains how this is done.

## Dividing the Economy into Sectors

In geometry, the word *sector* refers to the area bounded by two radii and the included arc of a circle. It is a subdivision or a section of the circle. In the same sense, a sector in economics refers to a subdivision of the economy, in particular to a group of decision-making units within the economy that are considered more or less homogeneous.

In the National Income Accounts, for example, the economy is usually divided into three main sectors: consumers, business firms, and government. In the Flow of Funds Accounts, on the other hand, financial institutions are separated from other business firms and grouped together in a sector of their own. The number of sectors into which the economy is divided is not especially important, provided the sectoring is done on some consistent basis. There should be more than one sector, of course, in order to be able to trace transactions between sectors. The maximum practical number of sectors will depend on such factors as the relative homogeneity of groups of decision-making units within the economy, the availability of raw data and, perhaps most important, ease of handling. Too many sectors make it difficult to analyze interrelations among them. Thus, although we are well aware that all consumers are not really homogeneous, we still group them all together, and the same goes for commercial banks, nonfinancial business firms, and the like. In any event, whatever the number of sectors, it is important that they be exhaustive—in other words, taken all together they should encompass the whole economy.

One objective, as mentioned, is to construct a model sector "sources and uses of funds statement." This is a hybrid accounting statement that combines the balance sheet and the income statement into one. It is the fundamental basis of the Flow of Funds Accounts, and the explanation of its derivation will occupy us through most of this chapter.

## Constructing a Sectoral Sources and Uses of Funds Statement

A sectoral sources and uses of funds statement is nothing more than a statement of the changes in a sector's balance sheet from one point in time to another in terms of which transactions caused inflows of funds and which transactions caused outflows. Although many changes can take place in a sector's balance sheet over time, these can be classified into only two groups in describing the sectoral sources and uses of funds statement. The first group includes changes resulting from income-statement transactions—transactions involving flows of current income receipts, current expenditures, and current savings. The second group includes pure balance-sheet changes: asset exchanges and transactions that involve issuance of liabilities to purchase other assets. Both of these groups will now be considered in more detail, first by looking at the structure of sectoral income statements and balance sheets and then by examining how the flow of funds is a method of accounting for the changes.

## A Generalized Sector Income Statement

Taking first things first, a simplified income statement, general enough to apply to any sector, would look something like the following:

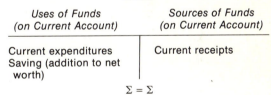

*(1) A Generalized Income Statement for a Single Sector*

| Uses of Funds (on Current Account) | Sources of Funds (on Current Account) |
|---|---|
| Current expenditures Saving (addition to net worth) | Current receipts |
| $\Sigma = \Sigma$ | |

An income statement like the one shown merely lists a sector's current receipts during a period of time as a source (inflow) of funds, and its current expenditures as a use (outflow) of funds. Current receipts differ depending on which sector is involved; they consist mainly of wages and salaries for the household sector, sales receipts for the business sector, and tax revenues for the government. Similarly, the composition of current expenditures also differs, depending on which sector we are looking at.

In all cases, however, one sector's payments become another sector's receipts. For example, tax payments, a major use of funds for households and business firms, become tax receipts, a major source of funds for the government. As we shall see, it is this mutual interaction that gives the eventual flow of funds matrix its interlocking nature.

Saving, on the left-hand side, is defined as any excess of a sector's current receipts over and above its current spending. For households, saving means disposable income minus consumer spending. When it involves the government sector, it is usually called a budget surplus; when applied to the business sector, it is frequently labeled either retained earnings or addition to net worth. In any case, since it is defined as the difference between current receipts and current expenditures, it is the balancing entry on an income statement. Thus, summation equality signs are at the bottom of income statement (1).

### A Generalized Sector Balance Sheet

Let us leave income statements for a moment and examine the structure of balance sheets. Income statements show current receipts and expenditures over a period of time (say during the year 1980), whereas a balance sheet shows not receipts and expenditures but assets and liabilities, and not over a period of time but at an instant in time (say on December 31, 1980). A simplified balance sheet, general enough to apply to any sector, would look something like the following:

(2) *A Generalized Balance Sheet for a Single Sector*

| Assets | Liabilities & Net Worth |
|---|---|
| Financial assets | Liabilities |
|   a. Money | |
|   b. Other | |
| Real assets | Net worth |
| $\Sigma = \Sigma$ | |

Like income statements, the principal difference between the balance sheets of different sectors is in the characteristic items that appear under each heading—consumer durable goods, such as automobiles and furniture, are typical real assets for consumers, inventories and capital equipment are typical real assets for business firms, and so on. Also, like income statements, balance sheets must balance, in this case because the net worth entry is defined as the difference between total assets and total liabilities. Thus, our simplified balance sheet also contains summation equality signs.

On the balance sheet in our example, assets are divided into two broad categories, real and financial. A *real* asset, like a car or a calculator, appears on only one balance sheet, that of its owner. However, a *financial* asset, like money or bonds, always appears on two balance sheets: that of whoever owns it (as an asset), and that of whoever owes it (as a liability). This is because every financial asset is a claim by someone against someone else—an IOU of some sort—like a government bond (an asset to whoever owns it, a liability of the government) or a bank deposit (again an asset to the owner, a liability of the bank).[1]

While only *financial* assets appear on two different balance sheets, *all* liabilities do, because all liabilities *by definition* represent debts owed to others. Thus, any time a liability is listed on anyone's balance sheet, a corresponding financial asset must appear on some other balance sheet.

If we examine the wealth (or net worth) of society as a whole, this correspondence between financial assets and liabilities has interesting consequences. It is well known that the net worth (or wealth) of any one entity is equal to its total assets minus its total liabilities. Using familiar examples, the net worth of any family or business firm is equal to its real assets plus its financial assets minus its liabilities. For society as a whole, however, every time a financial asset is entered for any firm or family, a corresponding liability has to be rung up on the balance sheet of some other firm or family.

Imagine a single lengthy balance sheet for the entire economy. It would be possible, theoretically, to construct such a balance sheet for society as a

---

[1]A complication arises in this connection with respect to corporate equities (corporate stocks), because they are financial assets to whoever holds them but are not, legally, liabilities of the issuing corporation. For most purposes, the simplest way to handle this is to assume that corporate stocks and bonds are roughly the same thing, despite their legal differences, and treat them as liabilities of the corporation.

A related problem, which also remains unresolved, is that both bonds and stocks are traded on organized markets and change in price, so they may be valued differently by the holder and the issuing corporation. For example, a $100 bond issued by a corporation may rise in price to $120; to the holder it is now a $120 financial asset, but to the corporation it is still a $100 liability. The difference is saving to the sector holding the bond, although strictly speaking there is no funds inflow to the bondholder unless the bond is sold.

whole by entering all the assets and liabilities of every firm, every family, and every governmental unit on one huge balance sheet. However, every time a financial asset was entered for someone, sooner or later it would also be necessary to enter a liability of equal amount for someone else. Thus, after all the records had been entered, in figuring the net worth of society liabilities and financial assets would be equal and would cancel each other out. For all of society taken as a whole, only real assets and net worth would be left.

In sum, the wealth of any one unit within society is equal to its real assets plus its financial assets less its liabilities, *but the wealth of society as a whole must be equal to just its real assets.* The difference between a single unit and society as a whole arises because for any one unit or sector its financial assets need not equal its own liabilities, but for society as a whole total financial assets must equal total liabilities.

This conclusion—that the net worth, or wealth, of society as a whole equals only its real assets—always pleases conservatives, because it implies that printing money cannot in and of itself make a country richer. After all, money is a financial asset and, therefore, appears on two balance sheets, as an asset of the holder but as a liability of the issuer. Most of our money is in the form of demand deposits, for example, and these are liabilities of commercial banks. The part of our money in the form of coin or currency is a liability of either the U.S. Treasury or the Federal Reserve, depending on which agency issued it. Thus, merely printing money can hardly make a nation richer, no matter how much it prints. Liabilities go up as much as assets. To become richer—to increase its net worth—a country must increase its output of real assets, its production of real goods and services. As conservatives are fond of pointing out, if we want to become wealthier we must work harder and produce more. Printing money will not do it.

However, the same logic implies that one of the favorite incantations of conservatives is equally false, namely, the belief that increasing the national debt makes a country poorer. Government bonds—the total outstanding being the national debt—are liabilities of the government but are financial assets to whoever owns them. As long as the national debt is held within the country, someone's financial assets go up as much as the government's liabili-

ties. A government bond is, after all, an asset for whoever buys it. The very term *national debt* is a half-truth. If it is a domestically held debt, it could just as well be called the national credit. As with all liabilities, it is both a debt (to the borrower) and a credit (to the lender). To become poorer—to reduce its net worth—a country must reduce its holdings of real assets, curtail its production of real goods and services. Increasing the national debt, no matter how high it goes, will not in itself make a country poorer. The equality between financial assets and liabilities for society as a whole turns out to be a two-edged sword.

## The Sources and Uses Statement: Saving and Investment

As noted, funds flows occur because of income-statement transactions such as saving, and because of alterations of balance sheets due either to changes in asset preferences or to financial transactions such as lending and borrowing. Let us see how these changes can be integrated starting with the income-statement concept of saving.

Going back to our simplified balance sheet (2), let us take the bottom pair of entries, real assets and net worth—ignoring financial assets and liabilities for the time being—and see how we can convert those stock figures, snapped at a moment in time, into flows covering a period of time. The change ($\Delta$) between two dates could be displayed like this:

*(3) A Partial Sector Sources and Uses of Funds Statement, on Capital Account*

| Uses of Funds (on Capital Account) | Sources of Funds (on Capital Account) |
| --- | --- |
| $\Delta$ Real assets (investment) | $\Delta$ Net worth (saving) |

$$\Sigma \neq \Sigma$$

Since (3) is derived from only part of the balance sheet, it need not balance, so there are no summation equality signs at the bottom. Notice also that the column headings are different from (2): "Assets" and "Liabilities and Net Worth" have been replaced by "Uses of Funds" and "Sources of Funds," the same as in income statement (1). Now, however, they refer to uses and sources of funds on capital rather than current account—that is, to long-term rather than short-term uses and sources.

On the uses side, the change in real assets refers only to capital expenditures, as contrasted with an income statement's current expenditures. Capital expenditures involve the purchase of *real* assets with an expected useful life of a year or more; the term is synonymous with real investment spending (or simply investment spending).[2] Such capital expenditures are not included in an income statement; in accordance with conventional accounting practice, income statements are confined to current expenditures—the purchase of assets with an expected useful life of less than a year.

A distinction has to be made between *investment spending* as economists use the word (it always refers to the purchase of *real* assets with a useful life of a year or more, such items as houses or machine tools), and the use of the word in general conversation, where it often refers to the purchase of *financial* assets, like stocks or bonds. In this chapter, when we say simply *investment,* we always have reference to buying real assets; if we want to refer to the purchase of financial assets, we will always say, explicitly, *financial investment.*

On the sources of funds side, the change in a sector's net worth during the period is exactly the same thing as saving on its income statement covering that time interval. This deserves a word of explanation, since it is not immediately obvious (even though the fact that saving is frequently labeled "addition to net worth" should provide a clue that they are one and the same). On a balance sheet, net worth is defined as a sector's total assets minus its total liabilities. A change in net worth must therefore equal any change in total assets less any change in total liabilities. On an income statement, in contrast, saving refers to an excess of current receipts over current expenditures. But any excess of current receipts over current expenditures (flows) must imply a resulting build-up of total assets or a reduction of liabilities, or some combination of the two. Conclusion: Saving on a sector's income statement must become an equivalent change in the net worth on its balance sheet.

[2]Real investment can be recorded on either a net or gross basis, depending on whether or not depreciation is deducted from original value.

Put somewhat differently, as a "use" of funds on current account (on the income statement), saving means *not* spending. It means retention or accumulation. As such, it represents an addition to one's wealth or net worth and becomes available as a source of funds for capital account.[3]

Since statement (3) is derived from only part of the balance sheet, and thus does not have to balance, it follows that an individual unit or sector may invest (that is, buy capital goods) just equal to its current saving. Or, it may save more than it invests or invest more than it saves. These possibilities give rise to some important concepts. As was indicated in the previous chapter, if a unit or sector invests an amount equal to its current saving it is called a balanced-budget sector. If it saves more than it invests, it is called a surplus sector; if it saves less than it invests, it is called a deficit sector.[4]

How could a sector invest more than it saves? One way is simply to borrow enough to finance its deficit, which brings us to the other pair of balance-sheet entries—liabilities and financial assets.

## The Sources and Uses Statement: Borrowing, Lending, and Hoarding

The remaining causes of a sector's funds flows involve purely balance-sheet transactions. One cause—changes in asset preference—is obvious and requires almost no explanation. Occasionally a sector will reduce its holdings of one type of asset (a source of funds) and will use the funds thus generated to purchase other assets. Quantitatively, however, changes like this are not very important in the flow of funds tables since holdings of all forms of assets tend to grow over time and only rarely does a net reduction in a category become a net source of funds. The other major class of balance-sheet transaction—lending and borrow-

[3]As with investment, saving can be measured on a net or gross basis. It should be noted that even if depreciation is deducted, so that saving is measured on a net basis, depreciation would still be a source of funds for capital account since it represents a noncash "expense" rather than an actual current outlay of funds.

[4]Alternatively, a surplus sector is one that spends (on consumption plus real investment) *less* than its current income; a deficit sector is one that spends *more* than its current income.

ing—is much more important in the funds-flow matrix.

## Converting Balance Sheet Stocks to Flows: Borrowing, Lending, and Hoarding

So far we have largely ignored the possibility of changes in liabilities and financial assets, the remaining entries on (2), our generalized sector balance sheet. Such changes between two balance sheet dates would look like this:

*(4) A Partial Sector Sources and Uses of Funds Statement, on Capital Account*

| Uses of Funds (Financial, on Capital Account) | Sources of Funds (Financial, on Capital Account) |
|---|---|
| Δ Financial assets other than money (lending) Δ Money (hoarding) | Δ Liabilities (borrowing) |

$$\Sigma \neq \Sigma$$

Since (4), like (3), is derived from only partial balance sheets, it need not balance and thus contains no summation equality signs. But where (3) dealt with nonfinancial or real sources and uses of funds, (4) is concerned with *financial* transactions: with *borrowing* (an increase in outstanding liabilities) as a source of funds, and with *lending* (an increase in holdings of financial assets other than money) and *hoarding* (increased money holdings) as uses of funds.

Strictly speaking, we should separate short-term financial transactions from long-term transactions, in the same way that we distinguished between short- and long-term spending on real assets. However, in flow of funds accounting such distinctions are rarely made with respect to financial transactions and all borrowing and lending, regardless of duration, is typically considered as on capital account.

The three possibilities in (4)—borrowing, lending, and hoarding—do not exhaust all the potential financial sources or uses of funds open to a sector. For instance, another possible financial source of funds was already mentioned: selling off some holdings of financial assets. Still another source of

funds is *dis*hoarding. And an additional possible use of funds would be repayment of debts. These alternatives do not appear on (4) because only *net* changes are considered there, and it is implicitly assumed that they are all positive. Potential negative changes would add the three just mentioned. By convention, if the net change in any entry turns out to be negative over a period, it is kept on the side where it presently appears in (4) but preceded by a minus sign. If the net change in financial assets for a sector turns out to be minus, for example, as when a person liquidates some of his government bonds to raise cash, it would be recorded on the uses side but be preceded by a minus sign and be referred to as a negative use of funds. A negative use, however, is actually a source of funds.

## A Complete Sector Sources and Uses of Funds Statement

If we now string together everything we have done so far, we will have before us a complete sector sources and uses of funds statement.

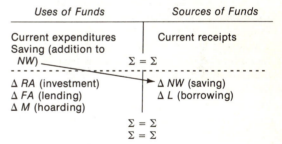

*(5) = (1) + (3) + (4)  A Complete Sector Sources and Uses of Funds Statement*

| Uses of Funds | Sources of Funds |
|---|---|
| Current expenditures Saving (addition to NW) | Current receipts |
| | $\Sigma = \Sigma$ |
| Δ RA (investment) Δ FA (lending) Δ M (hoarding) | Δ NW (saving) Δ L (borrowing) |
| | $\Sigma = \Sigma$ |
| | $\Sigma = \Sigma$ |

Above the dashed line is the income statement, below the dashed line the changes in the balance sheet. Since the income statement must balance, as must the aggregate changes in the balance sheet, the summation of all the sources must equal the summation of all the uses of funds, and therefore we have summation equality signs all over the place.

We are now able to define more precisely what we mean by a sector's sources and uses of funds. *Sources* of funds consist of *current receipts,* any *increase in a liability item* (borrowing), or any *de-*

crease in any asset item (selling off assets, dishoarding).

Uses of funds consist of current expenditures; any increase in an asset item—increased holdings of real assets (investment), of financial assets (lending), or of money (hoarding); or any decrease in a liability item (debt repayment).

We could simplify (5) by eliminating current receipts from sources and current expenditures from uses, taking only the difference between them—saving—as a source of funds (if positive, or as a use if negative). That is what we have, in effect, if we look only below the dashed line. (This is, in fact, the way the Flow of Funds Accounts are currently published by the Federal Reserve.)

The requirement that everything below the dashed line must balance means that each sector's investing + lending + hoarding must equal its saving + borrowing. As we know, however, a sector might save more than it invests (a surplus sector) or invest more than it saves (a deficit sector). If there is a discrepancy between its saving and its investing, this necessarily implies a corresponding differential between its financial sources and uses of funds. To be more specific: A surplus sector, with saving greater than investment, must dispose of its surplus by lending, repaying debts, or hoarding (building up its cash holdings) in an amount equal to its surplus. And a deficit sector, with investment in excess of its saving, has to finance its deficit by borrowing, selling off financial assets, or dishoarding (running down its cash holdings) in an amount equal to its deficit.[5]

These conclusions flow from the fact that below the dashed line, as well as above it, the sum of all a sector's uses of funds must equal the sum of all its sources. Putting the same thing rather formally:

For any one sector:

$$\text{Investment} + \text{Lending} + \text{Hoarding} =$$
$$\text{Saving} + \text{Borrowing}$$

[5] A deficit sector might also finance its deficit by issuing new money. Until very recently, however, only two sectors were legally able to exercise that unique option—commercial banks (by creating demand deposits) and the federal government (by creating dollar bills). If they did so, it would be entered on their statement(s) as an increase in their liabilities (borrowing), because while money is an asset to whoever owns it, it is a liability to whoever issues it.

So if:

$$\text{Saving} > \text{Investment, then Lending} +$$
$$\text{Hoarding} > \text{Borrowing}$$

And if:

$$\text{Investment} > \text{Saving, then Borrowing} >$$
$$\text{Lending} + \text{Hoarding}$$

## The Flow of Funds Matrix for the Whole Economy

Early in this chapter we said that flow of funds accounting records payments between and among sectors via sector sources and uses of funds statements. Since one sector's payments become another sector's receipts, when we put all these individual sector statements together we get a flow of funds matrix for the economy as a whole, an interlocking grid that reveals financial interrelationships among all the sectors. When the flow of funds matrix was first published by the Federal Reserve in 1955, it contained the complete statements for each sector in the form of statement (5). Since 1959, however, it has consisted of only partial sector sources and uses statements, namely that part of (5) below the dashed line. Current receipts and current expenditures are not shown explicitly in the presently published format, but they are implicitly there in that the difference between them—saving (or dissaving)—is included.

Assuming a total of three sectors and omitting some detail, we can present the flow of funds matrix as presently published in Matrix (6).

This matrix does nothing more than place the sector sources and uses statements side by side, each in the form of that part of (5) below the dashed line. The resulting matrix forms an interlocking self-contained system, showing the balanced sources and uses of funds for each sector, interrelations among the sectors, and the aggregate totals of saving, investment, borrowing, lending, and hoarding for the economy as a whole.

For each individual sector, as we know, its investment + lending + hoarding must equal its saving + borrowing. Since that is true for each individual sector, it is also true in summation for all the sectors taken together, that is, for the economy as a whole.

### (6)  Flow of Funds Matrix for the Whole Economy

| | Sector A | | Sector B | | Sector C | | All Sectors | |
|---|---|---|---|---|---|---|---|---|
| | Uses | Sources | Uses | Sources | Uses | Sources | Uses | Sources |
| Saving (Δ NW) | | s | | s | | s | | S |
| Investment (Δ RA) | i | | i | | i | | I | |
| Borrowing (Δ L) | | b | | b | | b | | B |
| Lending (Δ FA) | l | | l | | l | | L | |
| Hoarding (Δ M) | h | | h | | h | | H | |
| | $\Sigma = \Sigma$ | | $\Sigma = \Sigma$ | | $\Sigma = \Sigma$ | | $\Sigma = \Sigma$ | |

Note: The small letters within the matrix represent the data for sector saving ($s$), investment ($i$), borrowing ($b$), lending ($l$), and hoarding ($h$), and are placed in the appropriate space where such data would be entered. The large letters similarly represent the aggregate sum totals for the whole economy. Thus $s+s+s=S$, $i+i+i=I$, and so on.

In addition, something else is true for the economy as a whole that need not be true for any one sector taken by itself: saving must equal investment. For the whole economy:

$$\text{Investment} + \text{Lending} + \text{Hoarding} =$$
$$\text{Saving} + \text{Borrowing}$$

But since one sector's financial asset is another sector's liability:

$$\text{Lending} + \text{Hoarding} = \text{Borrowing}$$

Therefore:

$$\text{Investment} = \text{Saving}$$

The conclusion that saving must equal investment applies only to the entire economy taken in the aggregate, not to any single sector taken by itself. As we have seen, any single sector may save more than it invests or invest more than it saves. But since saving must equal investment for the economy as a whole, it follows that for each sector that saves more than it invests there must, somewhere, be other sectors that invest correspondingly more than they save.[6]

In coming chapters we shall have frequent oc-

[6]This is true not only because the economywide total of saving must equal investment, but also because a surplus sector must dispose of its surplus either by lending, repaying debts, or hoarding an amount equal to its surplus. This implies the existence of deficit sectors to borrow, reduce their financial assets, or dishoard.

Similarly, deficit sectors, which invest more than they save, necessarily imply the existence of surplus sectors. A deficit sector must finance its deficit by borrowing, selling off financial assets, or dishoarding. This implies the presence of surplus sectors to do the lending, buying of the securities, or hoarding.

casion to use this framework in analyzing financial institutions and markets and the interdependencies among them. The economic function of financial markets, after all, is to provide channels through which the excess funds of surplus units (whose saving exceeds their investment) can be transferred to potential deficit units (who want to invest more than they are saving). The flow of funds matrix enables us to trace these transactions and see how various spending flows are financed.

### Financial Markets and GNP

The economic function of financial markets, as we have said, is to provide channels through which the excess funds of surplus units can be transferred to potential deficit units. Those who can visualize and exploit potentially profitable investment opportunities are not always the same ones who are generating sufficient current saving to finance themselves. Financial markets are the conduits that link surplus and deficit units together, providing the means whereby, directly or indirectly, one can finance the other.

Without such markets, surplus units would be unable to do anything with their surpluses except hoard them, and deficit units would be unable to finance any spending over and above their current income except insofar as they were fortunate enough to have previously hoarded that which they could now draw on.[7] Financial markets give sur-

[7]We here assume that there is available one financial asset, money, as compared to the assumption in the previous chapter that *no* financial assets exist while tracing the implications of the latter for economic growth. See Chapter 1.

plus units additional options besides that of hoarding surpluses; they can, if they wish, *buy securities* with the money. That is, they can lend their funds (by buying securities that represent the liabilities of others) or repay debts (by buying back securities that represent their own liabilities).

Similarly, deficit sectors can finance their deficits through financial markets even though they may not have a previously accumulated hoard of cash to draw upon: they can sell securities to raise the funds they need. That is, they can borrow the money (by selling securities representing their own liabilities) or dispose of some financial assets they had previously acquired (sell off securities representing the liabilities of others).

The existence of highly developed, widely accessible, and smoothly functioning financial markets is thus of crucial importance in transmitting saved funds into the hands of those desiring to make investment expenditures. If the transmission mechanism is underdeveloped, inaccessible, or imperfect, the flow of funds from surplus units to deficit units will be impeded and GNP will fall below its potential.

While it is true, as we have seen, that for the whole economy saving must equal investment, *ex post,* this equality may take place at low or high magnitudes of saving and investment, implying consequent low or high magnitudes of GNP, production, and employment. The equality between realized (or *ex post*) saving and investment does not mean that all planned (or *ex ante*) saving must inevitably flow into or be matched by an equal volume of investment spending.

Assume, for example, that a significant portion of otherwise feasible investment plans is not undertaken because of lack of financing, due to the failure of financial markets to channel funds effectively from surplus units able to lend to potential deficit units anxious to borrow. The end result of such a curtailment of investment spending is likely to be a lower level of GNP, which will then generate a reduced volume of saving. Realized (or *ex post*) saving and investment will be equal, after all is said and done, but at levels below their potential and at a level of GNP lower than that which could have been reached had financial markets operated more effectively.

The distinction should be emphasized between planned (or *ex ante*) transactions and realized (or *ex post*) transactions. Since one sector's financial asset is another sector's liability, it follows that for the whole economy, *ex post,* lending and hoarding must equal borrowing and dishoarding. But this does not mean that the *planned* lending and hoarding of the surplus sectors need equal the *planned* borrowing and dishoarding of the deficit sectors.

Surplus sectors may be planning, at the start of a period, to lend very little. Deficit sectors may simultaneously be planning to borrow a great deal. Obviously, such plans are mutually inconsistent. Such a situation is likely to result in an increase in interest rates and, in light of the now higher interest rates, revisions in plans by both lenders and borrowers. If investment plans are then revised, as borrowers find themselves unable to borrow as much as they had expected at the old level of interest rates, GNP will fall. With saving and investment decisions partially dependent on GNP, the surplus or deficit position of various sectors is likely to change and lead to further revisions in borrowing and lending plans, with the consequent ramifications upon interest rates and GNP.

*Ex post,* actual lending and hoarding for the whole economy will turn out to be equal to borrowing and dishoarding. They must. The same is true of saving and investment. But the dynamics of this adjustment process, through which initial *ex ante* inequalities at the start of a period are eventually resolved into *ex post* equalities, and the magnitudes at which those equalities will finally be realized—with their implications for interest rates and GNP—is quite another story, as will be seen in Chapter 22.

## A Postscript

Some final comments should be made about the differences between the Federal Reserve's Flow of Funds Accounts and the Department of Commerce's National Income Accounts. Three differences are of special interest.

First, the National Income Accounts confine themselves exclusively to nonfinancial transactions. They contain no data on borrowing, lending, or hoarding. Second, the National Income Accounts treat all real investment (with the exception of housing) as a business activity; neither consumers nor governments can invest. In the Flow of Funds Accounts, however, consumer purchases of durable goods are treated as real investments. This removes the purchase of consumer durables from the category of current (or consumer) expenditures and greatly increases the volume of recorded household (and national) saving. Finally, the sectoring is more detailed in the Flow of Funds Accounts than it is in the National Income Accounts; this makes integration and reconciliation of the two a rather complicated affair. In principle, one should be able to move easily from one set of accounts to the other, but in practice the sectoring and the treatment of various transactions are so different as to make it awkward to do so.

## Appendix: The Flow of Funds Matrix, 1978

In the body of this chapter, the explanation of the construction of the Flow of Funds Accounts culminated in Matrix (6), the Flow of Funds Matrix for the Whole Economy. That matrix assumed a total of only three sectors, and for purposes of clarity omitted a considerable amount of detail. Table 2-1 is the actual flow of funds matrix for the year 1978 as presented by the Board of Governors of the Federal Reserve System. *Ex ante* it appears to bear little resemblance to Matrix (6); *ex post* it turns out to be the same thing, merely more elaborate. The best way to see this is to relate the accompanying table to Matrix (6), column by column and line by line.

First the columns. Instead of only three sectors, the actual matrix contains four major sectors: the private domestic nonfinancial sector, the rest of the world, the U.S. government, and the financial sector. These, in turn, are subdivided into a number of subsectors, making nine in all. The names of each are self-explanatory, except perhaps for "Sponsored Agency and Mtg. Pools," which is short for federally sponsored credit agencies and mortgage pools, and the "Monetary Authority," which consists of the Federal Reserve plus the U.S. Treasury's monetary accounts. For some unexplained reason, the "State and Local Governments" subsector is included in the *private* part of the economy. Some other incidental observations: the "Household" sector includes nonprofit organizations within it; "Private Nonbank Finance" includes savings and loan associations, mutual savings banks, insurance companies, pension funds, mutual funds, and credit unions.

The last two columns are new. Neither appeared in Matrix (6). The "Discrepancy" column results from the fact that deficiencies and inconsistencies often exist in the raw statistical data. Things often do not add up as logic tells us they should. Borrowers report liabilities of *x* dollars, while lenders report they are owed *y* dollars. Errors in data collection, omissions, differences in coverage or classification all give rise to inconsistencies in the data. The "Discrepancy" column is the statistician's way of reconciling such problems so that the accounts balance.

We know, for example, that for "All Sectors," the financial uses of funds (line 12) should equal the financial sources (line 13). Thus the differences between them (line 11) should be zero. However, financial uses of funds for All Sectors are $843.4 billion, and financial sources are $843.6 billion. They are *not* equal. So in the "Discrepancy" column a $0.2 billion "use" is posted; *now* they balance. By convention, all discrepancies are entered on the uses side of the accounts, making them positive or negative as appropriate to create the equality that logic tells us should exist.

The last column, "National Saving and Investment," is merely a measure of *domestic* saving and investment. It consists of data for saving and investment for all sectors, plus any discrepancies in those accounts, minus the "Rest of the World" sector. Included here is any increase in net financial claims on foreigners.

Turning now to the lines (or rows), there are two main differences between the table and Matrix (6): first, a slight rearrangement of the entries (including differences in terminology); and second, the presentation of considerably greater detail.

The first line of the table, "Gross Saving," corresponds to "Saving" on the first line of Matrix (6). The table also gives an estimate of depreciation (capital consumption, line 2) and thus data for "Net Saving" (line 3) as well. Line 5 corresponds to the entry "Investment" on our model matrix. Lines 6–10 are a breakdown by type of investment. Line 12 corresponds to "Lending" on Matrix (6) and line 13 to "Borrowing." Line 16 is roughly equivalent to what we have called "Hoarding."

## Table 2-1 Summary of Flow of Funds Accounts for the Year 1978 (in billions of dollars)

| Transaction Category | Households U | Households S | Business U | Business S | State and Local Governments U | State and Local Governments S | Total U | Total S | Rest of the World U | Rest of the World S | U.S. Government U | U.S. Government S |
|---|---|---|---|---|---|---|---|---|---|---|---|---|
| 1 Gross saving | .... | 338.3 | .... | 195.6 | .... | 7.6 | .... | 541.5 | .... | 23.5 | .... | (34.9) |
| 2 Capital consumption | .... | 181.0 | .... | 172.7 | .... | .... | .... | 353.7 | .... | .... | .... | .... |
| 3 Net savings (1 − 2) | .... | 157.3 | .... | 22.9 | .... | 7.6 | .... | 187.7 | .... | 23.5 | .... | (34.9) |
| 4 Gross investment (5 + 11) | 380.1 | .... | 174.1 | .... | .5 | .... | 554.8 | .... | 12.7 | .... | (36.6) | .... |
| 5 Private capital expenditures | 298.2 | .... | 249.9 | .... | .... | .... | 548.1 | .... | (2.0) | .... | .... | .... |
| 6 Consumer durables | 200.3 | .... | .... | .... | .... | .... | 200.3 | .... | .... | .... | .... | .... |
| 7 Residential construction | 92.0 | .... | 16.3 | .... | .... | .... | 108.3 | .... | .... | .... | .... | .... |
| 8 Plant and equipment | 5.9 | .... | 209.3 | .... | .... | .... | 215.2 | .... | .... | .... | .... | .... |
| 9 Inventory change | .... | .... | 22.3 | .... | .... | .... | 22.3 | .... | .... | .... | .... | .... |
| 10 Mineral rights | .... | .... | 2.0 | .... | .... | .... | 2.0 | .... | .... | .... | (2.0) | .... |
| 11 Net financial investment (12 − 13) | 81.9 | .... | (75.7) | .... | .5 | .... | 6.7 | .... | 12.7 | .... | (34.7) | .... |
| 12 Financial uses | 248.3 | .... | 84.6 | .... | 25.1 | .... | 358.0 | .... | 55.7 | .... | 28.9 | .... |
| 13 Financial sources | .... | 166.4 | .... | 160.4 | .... | 24.6 | .... | 351.4 | .... | 43.0 | .... | 63.5 |
| 14 Gold and official foreign exchange | .... | .... | .... | .... | .... | .... | .... | .... | 1.2 | .2 | (2.6) | .... |
| 15 Treasury currency | .... | .... | .... | .... | .... | .... | .... | .... | .... | .... | .... | .5 |
| 16 Demand deposits and currency | 18.2 | .... | 5.4 | .... | (1.1) | .... | 22.5 | .... | (.2) | .... | 4.0 | .... |
| 17 Private domestic | 18.2 | .... | 5.4 | .... | (1.1) | .... | 22.5 | .... | .... | .... | .... | .... |
| 18 Foreign | .... | .... | .... | .... | .... | .... | .... | .... | (.2) | .... | .... | .... |
| 19 U.S. government | .... | .... | .... | .... | .... | .... | .... | .... | .... | .... | 4.0 | .... |
| 20 Time and savings accounts | 105.2 | .... | 2.0 | .... | 8.1 | .... | 115.2 | .... | 1.1 | .... | .1 | .... |
| 21 At commercial banks | 44.1 | .... | 2.0 | .... | 8.1 | .... | 54.1 | .... | 1.1 | .... | .1 | .... |
| 22 At savings institutions | 61.1 | .... | .... | .... | .... | .... | 61.1 | .... | .... | .... | .... | .... |
| 23 Fed funds and security RPs | .... | .... | 5.5 | .... | 2.0 | .... | 7.5 | .... | .... | .... | .... | .... |
| 24 Money market fund shares | 6.9 | .... | .... | .... | .... | .... | 6.9 | .... | .... | .... | .... | .... |
| 25 Life insurance reserves | 12.0 | .... | .... | .... | .... | .... | 12.0 | .... | .... | .... | .... | .3 |
| 26 Pension fund reserves | 65.8 | .... | .... | .... | .... | .... | 65.8 | .... | .... | .... | .... | 6.9 |
| 27 Net interbank claims | .... | .... | .... | .... | .... | .... | .... | .... | 5.4 | .... | .... | .... |
| 28 Corporate equities | 6.2 | .... | .... | 2.6 | .... | .... | (6.2) | 2.6 | 2.4 | (.5) | .... | .... |
| 29 Credit market instruments | 58.0 | 162.6 | (1.2) | 125.6 | 14.6 | 23.6 | 71.4 | 311.8 | 37.7 | 32.8 | 20.4 | 53.7 |
| 30 U.S. Treasury securities | 17.3 | .... | (7.1) | .... | 9.8 | .... | 20.0 | .... | 28.2 | .... | .... | 55.1 |
| 31 Federal agency securities | 9.7 | .... | .7 | .... | 2.8 | .... | 13.3 | .... | .... | .... | 7.7 | (1.3) |
| 32 State and local govt. securities | 3.3 | .... | .2 | 3.2 | 1.0 | 25.1 | 4.5 | 28.3 | .... | .... | .... | .... |
| 33 Corporate and foreign bonds | 1.4 | .... | .... | 20.1 | .... | .... | (1.4) | 20.1 | 1.6 | 4.0 | .... | .... |
| 34 Mortgages | 14.5 | 104.8 | .... | 43.3 | 1.0 | .... | 15.5 | 148.2 | .... | .... | (.4) | (.1) |
| 35 Consumer credit | .... | 50.6 | 3.2 | .... | .... | .... | 3.2 | 50.6 | .... | .... | .... | .... |
| 36 Bank loans n.e.c. | .... | 3.4 | .... | 33.9 | .... | .... | .... | 37.3 | .... | 18.3 | .... | .... |
| 37 Open-market paper | 14.6 | .... | 1.7 | 5.2 | .... | .... | 16.3 | 5.2 | 7.9 | 6.6 | .... | .... |
| 38 Other loans | .... | 3.8 | .... | 19.9 | .... | (1.6) | .... | 22.2 | .... | 3.9 | 13.0 | .... |
| 39 Security credit | 1.4 | 1.4 | .... | .... | .... | .... | 1.4 | 1.4 | 0 | 0 | .... | .... |
| 40 Trade credit | .... | 1.4 | 54.9 | 45.5 | .... | 1.0 | 54.9 | 47.9 | 3.4 | (.3) | 2.7 | 2.4 |
| 41 Taxes payable | .... | .... | .... | 3.4 | 1.6 | .... | 1.6 | 3.4 | .... | .... | 3.5 | .... |
| 42 Equity in noncorporate business | (20.8) | .... | .... | (20.8) | .... | .... | (20.8) | (20.8) | .... | .... | .... | .... |
| 43 Miscellaneous | 7.6 | 1.1 | 18.1 | 4.0 | .... | .... | 25.7 | 5.0 | 4.7 | 10.8 | .7 | (.3) |
| 44 Sector discrepancies (1−4) | (41.8) | .... | 21.4 | .... | 7.0 | .... | (13.3) | .... | 10.8 | .... | 1.7 | .... |

Source: Board of Governors of the Federal Reserve System.

## Table 2-1   (cont.)

| | | Financial Sectors | | | | | | | | | | | |
|---|---|---|---|---|---|---|---|---|---|---|---|---|---|
| Total | | Sponsored Agency and Mtg. Pools | | Monetary Authority | | Commercial Banking | | Private Nonbank Finance | | All Sectors | | Discrepancy | National Saving and Investment |
| L | S | U | S | U | S | U | S | U | S | U | S | U | |
| .... | 18.4 | .... | 1.0 | .... | .7 | .... | 3.4 | .... | 13.3 | .... | 548.5 | .......... | 524.9 |
| .... | 6.0 | .... | .... | .... | .... | .... | 2.7 | .... | 3.3 | .... | 359.7 | .......... | 359.7 |
| .... | 12.4 | .... | 1.0 | .... | .7 | .... | .7 | .... | 10.0 | .... | 188.7 | .......... | 165.2 |
| 20.7 | .... | .5 | .... | .7 | .... | 9.6 | .... | 9.8 | .... | 551.6 | .... | (3.1) | 539.0 |
| 5.6 | .... | .... | .... | .... | .... | 4.2 | .... | 1.4 | .... | 551.8 | .... | (3.3) | 551.8 |
| .... | .... | .... | .... | .... | .... | .... | .... | .... | .... | 200.3 | .... | .......... | 200.3 |
| (.3) | .... | .... | .... | .... | .... | .... | .... | (.3) | .... | 108.0 | .... | .......... | 108.0 |
| 5.9 | .... | .... | .... | .... | .... | 4.2 | .... | 1.7 | .... | 221.1 | .... | .......... | 221.1 |
| .... | .... | '.... | .... | .... | .... | .... | .... | .... | .... | 22.3 | .... | .......... | 22.3 |
| .... | .... | .... | .... | .... | .... | .... | .... | .... | .... | .... | .... | .......... | .......... |
| 15.0 | .... | .5 | .... | .7 | .... | 5.4 | .... | 8.4 | .... | (.2) | .... | .2 | (12.7) |
| 400.8 | .... | 46.7 | .... | 13.3 | .... | 141.2 | .... | 199.6 | .... | 843.4 | .... | .2 | 43.0 |
| .... | 385.7 | .... | 46.2 | .... | 12.6 | .... | 135.8 | .... | 191.2 | .... | 843.6 | .......... | 55.7 |
| 1.6 | .... | .... | .... | 1.6 | .... | .... | .... | .... | .... | .2 | .2 | .......... | .......... |
| .6 | .... | .... | .... | .6 | .... | .... | .... | .... | .... | .6 | .5 | .......... | .......... |
| 2.6 | 28.2 | .... | .... | .... | 6.3 | .3 | 22.0 | 2.3 | .... | 28.9 | 28.2 | (.7) | .......... |
| 2.6 | 24.8 | .... | .... | .... | 9.3 | .3 | 15.5 | 2.3 | .... | 25.1 | 24.8 | (.3) | .......... |
| .... | (.2) | .... | .... | .... | .1 | .... | .3 | .... | .... | (.2) | (.2) | .......... | .......... |
| .... | 3.7 | .... | .... | .... | (3.1) | .... | 6.8 | .... | .... | 4.0 | 3.7 | (.3) | .......... |
| 7.8 | 124.2 | .... | .... | .... | .... | .... | 65.0 | 7.8 | 59.2 | 124.2 | 124.2 | .......... | .......... |
| 9.7 | 65.0 | .... | .... | .... | .... | .... | 65.0 | 9.7 | .... | 65.0 | 65.0 | .......... | .......... |
| (2.0) | 59.2 | .... | .... | .... | .... | .... | .... | (2.0) | 59.2 | 59.2 | 59.2 | .......... | .......... |
| 4.0 | 20.9 | 1.4 | .... | .... | .... | .... | 18.8 | 2.6 | 2.1 | 11.5 | 20.9 | 9.4 | .......... |
| .... | 6.9 | .... | .... | .... | .... | .... | .... | .... | 6.9 | 6.9 | 6.9 | .......... | .......... |
| .... | 11.7 | .... | .... | .... | .... | .... | .... | .... | 11.7 | 12.0 | 12.0 | .......... | .......... |
| .... | 58.9 | .... | .... | .... | .... | .... | .... | .... | 58.9 | 65.8 | 65.8 | .......... | .......... |
| 9.5 | 15.6 | .... | .... | 3.6 | 5.9 | 5.9 | 9.7 | .... | .... | 14.9 | 15.6 | .7 | .......... |
| 7.6 | 1.7 | .... | .... | .... | .... | .... | 1.1 | 7.5 | .5 | 3.7 | 3.7 | .......... | .......... |
| 348.4 | 79.8 | 44.6 | 41.4 | 7.0 | .... | 128.7 | 6.9 | 168.1 | 31.5 | 478.0 | 478.0 | .......... | .......... |
| 6.9 | .... | .5 | .... | 7.7 | .... | (6.5) | .... | 5.2 | .... | 55.1 | 55.1 | .......... | .......... |
| 19.1 | 41.4 | .1 | 41.4 | (.4) | .... | 7.0 | .... | 12.3 | .... | 40.1 | 40.1 | .......... | .......... |
| 23.8 | .... | .... | .... | .... | .... | 9.6 | .... | 14.2 | .... | 28.3 | 28.3 | .......... | .......... |
| 31.3 | 7.5 | .... | .... | .... | .... | .3 | .2 | 31.6 | 7.3 | 31.6 | 31.6 | .......... | .......... |
| 133.9 | .9 | 30.6 | .... | .... | .... | 35.0 | .... | 68.3 | .9 | 149.0 | 149.0 | .......... | .......... |
| 47.3 | .... | .... | .... | .... | .... | 26.9 | .... | 20.4 | .... | 50.6 | 50.6 | .......... | .......... |
| 58.4 | 2.8 | .... | .... | 0 | .... | 58.4 | .... | .... | 2.8 | 58.4 | 58.4 | .......... | .......... |
| 2.2 | 14.6 | (1.2) | .... | (.4) | .... | (1.3) | 6.7 | 5.1 | 7.9 | 26.4 | 26.4 | .......... | .......... |
| 25.5 | 12.5 | 14.6 | 0 | .... | .... | .... | .... | 10.9 | 12.5 | 38.6 | 38.6 | .......... | .......... |
| (1.1) | (1.0) | .... | .... | .... | .... | (2.9) | .... | 1.8 | (1.0) | .4 | .4 | .......... | .......... |
| 1.3 | .... | .... | .... | .... | .... | .... | .... | 1.3 | .... | 62.3 | 50.0 | (12.3) | .......... |
| .... | 1.7 | .... | .... | .... | .... | .... | .3 | .... | 1.4 | 5.2 | 5.2 | .......... | .......... |
| .... | .... | .... | .... | .... | .... | .... | .... | .... | .... | (20.8) | (20.8) | .......... | .......... |
| 18.5 | 37.1 | .6 | 4.8 | .5 | .5 | 9.1 | 11.9 | 8.2 | 19.9 | 49.6 | 52.6 | 3.0 | .......... |
| (2.3) | .... | .5 | .... | 0 | .... | (6.3) | .... | 3.5 | .... | (3.1) | .... | (3.1) | (14.1) |

Thus, if we were to list the rows in the table that correspond to the entries in Matrix (6)—Saving, Investment, Borrowing, Lending, and Hoarding—they would be, in the same order, lines 1, 5, 13, 12 minus 16, and 16.[1]

Line 11, called "Net Financial Investment," refers to a sector's lending plus hoarding minus its borrowing, as we have been using these terms. And line 4, called "Gross Investment," refers to a sector's real investment plus lending plus hoarding minus its borrowing.

To determine whether a particular sector is a surplus or deficit sector, we should compare the entry for that sector on line 1 with the entry on line 5. (Or, if we deducted depreciation from both saving and investment, we would compare the entry on line 3 with line 5 minus line 2.) Thus, we see that during 1978 households were a surplus sector by $40.1 billion, business a deficit sector by $54.3 billion.

The remainder of the table, from line 14 down, breaks down in detail the various forms of borrowing and lending by type of liability (or asset) involved. For example, line 35 indicates that consumers borrowed $50.6 billion in the form of consumer credit during 1978. Who did the lending?

---

[1]If a money-*issuing* sector were involved, this would become 1, 5, 13 minus 16, 12, and 16. Money creation is a financial source of funds to those who issue it. See footnote 5 in the main body of the chapter.

Line 35 shows that $26.9 billion was from commercial banks, $20.4 billion from nonbank financial institutions, and $3.2 billion from nonfinancial business firms.

## Questions

1. Explain why a balance sheet must balance.
2. Does an income statement "balance" also?
3. Distinguish between a *financial* asset and a *real* asset.
4. Why do we refer to changes in money holdings as "hoarding"?
5. If there were no money, and therefore no financial markets, could an individual invest more than he or she saved? Or save more than he or she invested?
6. If an internally held national debt does not make a nation poorer, does it therefore make no difference at all whether the debt is high or low?
7. For an individual sector, is prior saving necessary to make investment expenditures? For the economy as a whole?
8. For the economy as a whole, *ex post,* can saving exceed investment? Can investment exceed saving? Explain.
9. For an individual sector, must total sources of funds equal total uses of funds? For the economy as a whole?

## Selected Bibliography

Bain, A. D. "Flow of Funds Analysis." *Economic Journal* (December 1973).

Board of Governors of the Federal Reserve System. *Introduction to Flow of Funds.* Washington, D.C., 1975.

# 3

# The Evolution of the U.S. Money and Capital Markets and Financial Intermediaries

Chapter 1 analyzed, among other things, the reasons for the emergence of financial intermediaries and markets in this country. This chapter is intended to supplement those general statements as well as to provide a background for subsequent chapters by showing the historical origins and evolution of those intermediaries and financial markets from colonial times until the mid-1970s. In other words, this chapter is expressly designed to add the flesh, or substance, of historical description to the anatomy of financial analysis.

None of the capital markets and the financial intermediaries analyzed in the succeeding chapters of this text existed in the colonial period. Some of them are of quite recent origin. Once capital markets and financial intermediaries did appear, however, they grew very rapidly. Indeed, financial intermediaries grew faster than the population and much faster than the economy in general. It is estimated that throughout the course of American history, the assets of financial institutions (in constant prices per capita) grew at a rate of 2½–3 percent a year, half again as high as the rise in total production per capita.[1]

As late as 1800, when America had passed the halfway mark in its present history, the total assets of the few existing commercial banks and insurance companies probably amounted to less than $10 per capita, or about $50 million in the aggregate. How far we have come since then. The assets of the financial intermediaries discussed in this chapter are presently equal to about $10,000 for every man, woman, and child in the population.

Each of the various institutions in the money and capital markets first appeared at a different time. Each came into existence as a need for its services developed. Some grew rapidly from the moment they began operations, while others gathered momentum much more slowly. But all of them had their ups and downs. They rose or faltered in response to the external environment and because of the ingenuity, imagination, and aggressiveness of their managers or, in the language of the economic historian, of the entrepreneurs who made the decisions that guided them. In the process of growth, these entrepreneurs had to overcome a series of

[1]Raymond W. Goldsmith, *Financial Intermediaries in the American Economy Since 1900,* Princeton University Press, Princeton, N.J., 1958, p. 3.

obstacles and, what is much more important, they had to take advantage of every encouraging factor in the economic, social, and political milieu.

Deeply embedded in the American culture is an antagonism toward the pillars of finance—the stock exchange, investment banking, and commercial banking—everything, in other words, that has been denounced under the generic term *Wall Street*. Yet, at the same time, the culture has always lauded thrift, admired money making, and praised saving; and this latter set of values has encouraged the rise of financial intermediaries. Their growth has been further aided and abetted by changes in how Americans made their living, where they lived, how they managed their businesses, how they spent their income, and how their governments regulated the money and capital markets. This chapter describes how and why the various financial institutions grew by overcoming their obstacles and by profiting from their advantages.[2]

Before embarking on this story, it will be helpful to present a rough timetable showing when the various institutions were born and when they attained their peak rates of growth. The first investment bank began in Philadelphia in 1764. The first commercial bank, the Bank of North America, opened in the same city in 1781. The first investment company, the Massachusetts Hospital Life Insurance Company, was founded in 1818 in Boston. The Philadelphia Saving Fund Society (1816) is usually designated as the first savings bank.[3] Insurance companies are as old as the country itself, but mutual life insurance companies first began operations in the 1840s. Savings and loan associations, or building and loan associations as they were originally called, go all the way back to 1831. Credit unions, funded pension systems, and the

[2]The specialized literature on the history of financial institutions is not very plentiful. It includes G. W. Edwards, *The Evolution of Finance Capitalism,* Longmans, Green & Co., New York, 1938; Herman E. Krooss and Martin R. Blyn, *A History of Financial Intermediaries,* Random House, New York, 1971; Margaret G. Myers, *The New York Money Market,* Columbia University Press, New York, 1931; and Fritz Redlich, *The Molding of American Banking,* Hafner Publishing Company, New York, 1946–1951.

[3]Lest Boston and New York object, let it be said that the Provident Institution for Savings in the Town of Boston and the Bank of Savings in the City of New York also have a claim to the honor.

now discontinued postal savings system are all products of the twentieth century.

Mutual savings banks have, from their inception, grown slowly, gradually, and almost uninterruptedly. Life insurance companies have experienced a similar growth, but at a higher rate. Commercial banks and general insurance companies, on the other hand, have grown at a very rapid rate but not as steadily. They, along with the population in general, have suffered severely from the effects of the catastrophic depressions that sporadically engulfed the economy. Building and loan associations occupied a small niche in the financial world until the 1920s at which time they, along with investment companies, enjoyed a phenomenal growth.

Let us look at the evolution of financial institutions in another way: from the standpoint of the changing needs and demands of their users—households, business firms, and the government. Viewed in this way, the history of capital markets can be divided into four rather loosely dated periods. In the first period, the years before 1850, individuals did not rely very heavily on intermediaries. When, as ultimate lenders, they did acquire indirect securities, these were primarily in the form of deposits. As ultimate borrowers, they had little need for credit except for the purchase of real property. As for business units, they were small scale and agriculturally oriented and most of their funds could best be supplied directly by ultimate lenders in the form of intermediate- or long-term credit. Governments borrowed only occasionally, but when they did, they resorted directly to the securities market. Indeed, in this period the shortage, or inadequacy, of a circulating medium (money) was perhaps the major financial constraint on the economy.

During the second period, the last half of the nineteenth century, the federal government was engaged in paying off the huge debt incurred to finance the Civil War and, because the government employed a regressive tax system, it was to some small extent redistributing income from lower-income to higher-income households. The latter, therefore, were able to save more, but in general their relations with financial institutions were much the same as they had been earlier in the century. The end of this second period, that is, the late 1880s and the 1890s, saw a great expansion of direct financing via the securities markets to meet the emerging needs of heavy industry.

In the third era, the 1920s, a great change occurred in both the sources and uses of loanable funds. Households began to purchase more consumer durable goods, and consumer credit began to be important. Business firms relied less on the short-term money markets where they had formerly obtained most of their external funds, and more on the capital markets, the equity portion of which became extremely important. Once again, the federal government paid off a major fraction of its debt, but this retirement was more than matched by a rise in state and local debt.

Further developments have occurred in the period since World War II. The federal, state, and local governments are now major factors in the capital and money markets inasmuch as all three have increased their debt almost continuously since the 1930s. Business firms, much more sophisticated in the management of their money, rely less and less on the traditional sources of borrowing, such as bank loans. Households, on the other hand, have increased their stake in the mortgage market and in consumer credit. At the same time, pensions have become a major outlet for business and household saving and a major source of long-term capital funds.

## The Growth of Financial Institutions Before 1850

As we have already noted, modern capital markets as we know them today did not exist in the colonial period, when there was neither a need nor a desire for them. In today's complicated financial structure, savers who supply capital funds are rarely the same people who demand capital funds for investment spending. In the undeveloped economy of early America, by contrast, investors were very often their own savers. Most people worked for themselves as farmers, shopkeepers, artisans, and small manufacturers. They expanded their enterprise by plowing back some of their earnings or by investing their own labor, but they borrowed relatively little from those who had surplus saving. Farmers needed external funds to buy land, tools, and seed, but they built their own barns and fences, cleared their land, and increased their herds without recourse to intermediaries. Small business owners used part of their profits to buy more machinery or to expand their plants.

This is not to say, however, that there were no financial institutions of any sort or that there was no demand for the services of intermediaries. There were land banks, which issued paper money against mortgages on land, but these enterprises did not discount notes or accept demand deposits. They were, therefore, not commercial banks by today's definition. They were "batches of paper money." Ideally, they were designed to give land liquid value, which the owner could use to finance capital investment. Often, however, the loans went to finance unproductive consumer spending and ended disastrously. The fact that most land banks were government, not private, enterprises shows that the community, especially the mercantile interests, felt a strong need for such institutions. The same fact also suggests that land banking schemes were not particularly profitable business ventures. Though the history of these early experiments makes interesting reading, suffice it to note that most met with quick and unhappy ends.

But if this was the case, if these institutions left so much to be desired, why didn't some ambitious entrepreneur start a modern bank? Many merchants in the big cities thought about doing so, but the difficulties were too great. The primitive nature of an economy that was 90 percent agricultural, where most transactions were handled on a barter rather than on a money basis, did not offer a tempting environment for banking. Nor did the widespread hostility toward banking as a privileged monopoly make entry into the field any easier. In fact, as we shall see, the first commercial bank was actually created by means of subterfuge. Perhaps, too, the land banks were not as unsuccessful as they might have seemed from the vantage point of later banking theory; whatever their defects, they did at least provide a supplementary means of payment at a time when specie was hard to come by and was leaving the colonies almost as fast as it entered. The shortage of money was especially hard on the merchant and middle classes. John Coleman, a Boston merchant, in 1720 bared the plight of that city in a letter to a friend in this manner:

The Medium of Exchange, the only thing which gives life to Business, Employs the Poor, Feeds the Hungry, and Cloaths the Naked, is so Exhausted; that in a little time we shall not have wherewithal to Buy our Daily Bread, much less to pay our Debts or Taxes. How happy are you in the Countrey, who have your Milk and Honey of your own, while we depend on the ready Penny from day to day; and there are so few Bills Circulating (for Silver there is not a Penny passing) that People are distressed to a very great degree, to get Bills to procure the Necessaries of Life; and that not the Poor only, but good substantial House-keepers, who have good real Estates in the Place, such as we call the middling sort, who it must be acknowledged bear the greatest part of the Burthen; and by these Taxes support, both the Government, Ministry, and the Poor.

This unhappy merchant goes on to tell his seemingly happy country friend:

Now People work for half, & some for two thirds Goods, and so have a little Money coming in, but what will they do when it comes to working for all Goods, Is it possible for Men to Truck for a Pound of Butter, a Pound of Candles, or a Loaf of Bread, or many other things a Family is Daily in need of? No. It is impossible.[4]

Another reason for the slow development of American banking lay in the fact that the creation of credit was dominated by English suppliers of capital funds. We must remember that until well into the nineteenth century, foreign trade was immensely important, and that trade with England was most important of all. Almost every American importer carried an account with an English merchant or banker who advanced credit to the importer on what would now be considered scandalous terms. Thus, English capitalists would make intermediate-term loans on which interest would not begin for nine months and, with such arrangements, they had close to a monopoly on the largest volume of credit in the American capital market.

The American merchant who obtained this credit offered it, in turn, to his customers and, in essence, carried on a banking business as a sideline to merchandising. Thus, the dry-goods merchant who imported from Britain on the basis of British credit sold on credit to a jobber who, in turn, sold on credit to the retailer. Typical were the dealings of Thomas Hancock, a leading Boston merchant, whose ordinary terms of sale required payment at the end of six months or a year, charging interest at 6 percent on overdue balances. A similar link existed between the Southern plantation owner and British bankers. The plantation owner borrowed from a factor in New Orleans or Charleston who was financed by a big city merchant who was, in turn, financed by a member of the London money market.

Eventually, some merchants found themselves spending so much of their time acting as intermediaries between American retailers and British exporters, or bankers, that they gave up their merchandising businesses and became full-fledged bankers. These merchants entered the money market as private bankers, that is, they did not operate under a charter granted by a state or the federal government. Because the economy was very small, these merchants-turned-bankers conducted a very diversified business. They were something more than commercial bankers and something less than investment bankers. They dealt in long-term credit and foreign exchange. They bought bills of exchange and occasionally securities, although the latter were scarce during these early years.[5] In 1764 Thomas A. Biddle and Company of Philadelphia formed a banking house, which has the distinction of being the first bank, but not the first commercial bank, in the United States. Somewhat later, Alexander Brown, who had emigrated from Ireland to Baltimore to sell linens, left his dry-goods business and, together with his sons, embarked on a long banking career. Still later, some merchants and general store proprietors who had been advancing credit to their wholesale and retail customers in domestic trade made the same transition from selling goods to selling credit. The list is long and would include, among others, Astor and Sons; Corcoran and Riggs; Kuhn, Loeb & Co.; Goldman, Sachs & Co.; and Lehman Brothers.

Despite the proliferation of American banking houses, England remained in a position of primary importance. London continued to finance the small volume of securities issued in the United States. The American market was so important in England

---

[4]Stuart Bruchey, *The Colonial Merchant,* Harcourt, Brace & World, New York, 1966, pp. 83–85.

[5]A bill of exchange is a written order issued by the drawer calling on a second party (the drawee) to pay a certain sum of money on a certain date in the future to a named party (the payee).

that a group of houses, known as the Anglo-American merchant bankers, devoted most of their time to exporting capital to America. They permitted American importers to draw drafts against them and they underwrote the securities of the federal government, state and city governments, and such private enterprises as the Bank of the United States. The three Ws—the firms headed by Timothy Wiggin, George Wildes, and Thomas Wilson, all of which failed—were very aggressive in pursuit of American trade. Eventually, the House of Rothschild discovered America. But by far the most important merchant banker in the American market was the House of Baring Brothers.

Except in time of severe depression, losses on the extensive credit arrangements in effect were not excessive if the few examples that remain from business history have any validity. At first, the English practice of granting "long-term" credit—from six to nine months—prevailed, and the market was localized because merchants were forced to rely on their own limited knowledge or on the recommendation of other merchants. But, by midcentury, the credit system had greatly improved. The invention of credit agencies, such as Lewis Tappan's Mercantile Agency (later R. G. Dun & Company) founded in 1841 and Bradstreet's Commercial Agency (1849), provided merchants with a means of checking on borrowers, thus making it possible for them to extend credit over wider areas. At the same time, improvements in transportation and communication speeded the marketing of goods. The two things—wider knowledge and better communication—led to a rapid reduction in terms, and, by the 1850s, mercantile credit ran from thirty to sixty days.

In the early years, private bankers did very little investment banking, that is, underwriting of securities. To be sure, Nicholas Biddle, a most brilliant financial innovator, and a few houses, such as the North American Trust Company, the Morris Canal and Banking Company, and J. L. and S. Josephs (agents for the Rothschilds), handled some government and other securities. But all of these failed in the depression that began in 1837. With recovery, a new group of investment bankers, including Prime, Ward, and King; August Belmont; E. W. Clark & Co.; and Drexel & Co., appeared. Nevertheless, American investment banking remained a small and precarious business until long after the

Civil War for the simple reason that the raw materials for a thriving securities business did not exist. As late as the 1850s the U.S. Treasury estimated that outstanding securities totaled only about $1.5 billion, although there was some dealing in securities on organized exchanges. The first transactions in securities began to take place in 1792, primarily to deal in the "stock" of the newly formed federal government, which had just funded its Revolutionary War debt. In 1800 Philadelphia opened a formal exchange. Then, in 1817, New York formed the New York Stock and Exchange Board and quickly became the center of securities trading. One of the reasons for New York's dominance was that it had already surpassed Philadelphia in the export and import business. But, much more important, its entrepreneurs had the imagination and vision to create a call-money market (that is, a market where loans payable on demand are made to finance security transactions). This call-money market elicited a supply of short-term loanable funds and contributed to the liquidity and efficiency of the equities market.

Government, bank, and insurance stocks monopolized the early trading on the New York Stock Exchange. Railroad securities did not exist until the 1830s, although by 1850 dealings in rails exceeded all other trading. The first industrial shares (New York Gas Light and Schuylkill Coal) appeared in the early 1830s, but, at midcentury, only a dozen industrials were listed. In Boston, on the other hand, the stocks of textile firms and copper mining companies totaled somewhat more than a dozen.

On all exchanges, the volume of trading was very light. Before the speculative boom of the 1830s, brokers considered a 100-share day as fair; in the years that ended with the panic of 1837, 1,000-share days were not unusual, and, on one day in the 1850s, trading rose to the then astronomical height of 71,000 shares.[6] Most would-be borrowers and potential leaders could not use the new market mechanisms that have just been described. Most firms were not large enough or sufficiently well known to go to the stock exchanges, and their business did not fit into the Anglo-American financial network. For these people, impromptu arrangements and personal contacts were satisfactory

[6]Myers, *The New York Money Market.*

mechanisms so long as business relations could be conducted in the face-to-face manner that prevailed in a small-town atmosphere. In the early years of the nineteenth century, and probably much later as well, more funds were transferred through informal and direct arrangements than through financial intermediation. It was an almost unbroken custom for sellers of real estate to offer to keep a mortgage on the houses or land they offered for sale. Individuals who saved more than they invested internally tried to find their opposites in the coffee houses or "on change" or by advertising in the daily newspapers. A typical example was an advertisement in the *New York Evening Post* in March 1802, which offered "TO LOAN 1600 dollars on real security in this city." In this case, apparently, the demand for capital must have been very low, or the lender's liquidity preference must have been very high, for the same advertisement ran all through the month of April. While this suggests that direct finance was moderately successful, it also ought to suggest that the absence of financial intermediaries worked against more rapid economic growth.

Of all the direct methods for raising funds, lotteries were the most interesting and probably the most widely used in the colonial period and the early part of the nineteenth century.[7] Individuals occasionally resorted to them as a means of paying off debts but, much more frequently, they were conducted by manufacturing companies, turnpike companies, governments, schools and colleges, and charitable institutions. Since lotteries seemed so painless, governments used them in lieu of taxes to raise capital to construct internal improvements, such as bridges, canals, and public buildings. One of the most ambitious, albeit least successful, lotteries was organized by Samuel Blodgett in order "to improve the City of Washington." The first prize in this enterprise was "one superb hotel with baths, outhouses, etc."[8]

Organizations and institutions that depended on gifts and endowments were the most prolific lottery entrepreneurs. All religious groups, except the Quakers and other plain sects of Pennsylvania, sold tickets and distributed prizes in order to build and furnish churches and hospitals. Private elementary and secondary schools raised money through lotteries, and so did every early college, including Harvard, Yale, Columbia, Princeton, and Pennsylvania.

In the colonial period, lotteries were authorized by law and were organized and conducted just as they are today by volunteers, that is, unpaid managers. With rare exceptions, they followed a well-accepted format. From the proceeds of the ticket sale, the organizers took 10 to 15 percent and distributed the rest as prizes. Almost everyone, including George Washington, played the lotteries, but two examples will give a more precise indication of their size and importance. In a 1765 Pennsylvania lottery, 13,350 tickets were sold at 30 shillings each. The manager's share was over £3,000. In the lottery that was held in 1762 to raise money to rebuild Faneuil Hall, 6,000 tickets were sold and 1,486 prizes totaling over $10,000 were distributed.

Although they always ran into some opposition, lotteries became increasingly popular, and by 1800 they had all the characteristics of a big business. By then their management had been taken over by professionals: note brokers, lottery contractors, and proprietors of exchange offices. These entrepreneurs underwrote the lottery by buying all the tickets at a discount. In a way, therefore, they were predecessors of the syndicate underwriters, who appeared somewhat later in the securities markets.[9]

By 1815 every town of 1,000 people had one or more lottery offices. Every daily paper carried five or six advertisements urging the reader to grasp the opportunity to get rich fast. In the late 1820s there were 60 contractors in Philadelphia and 160 in New York. Total business in four states was conservatively estimated at around $5 million. In the midst of the economic boom of the early 1830s, when lotteries were probably at the peak of their popularity, there were in Philadelphia alone over 200 lottery offices, employing an average of two people plus a few part-time salespeople. It was estimated that revenues of $30,000 a week were received by

[7] The best book on lotteries is John S. Ezell, *Fortune's Merry Wheel*, Harvard University Press, Cambridge, Mass., 1960.

[8] This same Samuel Blodgett later achieved some recognition by posterity for his pioneer estimates of the national wealth of the United States.

[9] The first syndicate was composed of John Jacob Astor, David Parish, and Stephen Girard, who bought most of the $16 million war loan floated by the U.S. Treasury in 1813.

these offices, and $53 million was paid out in prizes in one year.

Many of the successful lottery contractors later became private or commercial bankers and established a lineage that can be traced to businesses operating today. The history of S. and M. Allen & Company is a good illustration. In August 1808 Solomon Allen, a printer from Albany, New York, began selling lottery tickets. He was so successful that in 1812 he abandoned everything else and gave his entire attention to the "lottery, exchange, and broking business." In 1815, he and his brother opened Allen's Truly Lucky Office in New York City, and by the 1820s they had offices in ten different cities as well as contracts with outlets in other cities. However, anticipating a rise in public hostility and realizing that the best years of public lotteries were over, they sold fewer and fewer tickets and increasingly turned to banking and brokerage. Some of their employees also took heed of the shifting tides. E. W. Clark, a relative of the Allens, founded an exchange business that later became Jay Cooke & Co., which was, in turn, the lineal antecedent of the house of Smith, Barney, Harris, Upham & Co. John Thompson, however, best illustrated the connection between lotteries and commercial banking. He began as a seller of lottery tickets and later founded both the First National Bank and the Chase National Bank of New York City.

The lottery was a maze of paradoxes. It appealed, of course, to the speculative and gambling spirit that is ubiquitous among human beings. But it also ran counter to the prevalent American culture with its emphasis on Calvinism. Social reformers argued that the lottery had immensely harmful effects on the lower-income classes and that it encouraged dishonesty as well as a flight from the realities of hard work. Merchants added their weight to the opposition by insisting that lottery tickets diverted large sums of money from trade and commerce. Despite their inherent appeal, lotteries could not withstand rising public hostility. Legislature after legislature outlawed them and, by the decade that Van Wyck Brooks once called "the God-intoxicated forties," the lottery had faded into relative unimportance.

Organized capital markets and formal financial intermediaries were clearly superior to the personal arrangements that were still in wide use in the early 1800s. Financial intermediaries could attract more saving, which meant that they could be more diversified. Since they had the advantages that go with specialization, they were ostensibly more skillful in bringing together savers and investors than individual operators could be. The impromptu arrangements we have just discussed were, therefore, used with less and less frequency as time passed. Although they have never completely disappeared, many of their functions were taken over by commercial banks, which first appeared in the late eighteenth century, and by savings banks, which were born just before 1820.

Because their operations were badly understood, commercial banks were regarded suspiciously and had great difficulty in getting started. Indeed, most of the first commercial banks entered the financial community through the back door. The first truly commercial bank, the Bank of North America, would probably not have opened in 1781 if the public had understood its real objective. Robert Morris, the bank's founder, appealed for a charter, not on the ground that a bank was needed, but because the Continental Congress needed a fiscal agent "to furnish a supply for the armies of the United States." Still later, the Manhattan Company was formed ostensibly to provide a water supply for New York City.

The opening of commercial banks called forth from strong boxes, old stockings, and cookie jars a horde of hidden savings. Equity issues by the big city banks were subscribed to freely, and in a very short time the commercial bank became by far the most important type of financial institution. The statistics on early commercial banking are poor, but as Table 3-1 indicates, it seems safe to say that the number of commercial banks increased more than twenty-five times and their capital seven times in the first fifty years of the nineteenth century.

How rapidly commercial banking grew can be demonstrated by events in the four largest cities: New York, Phiiladelphia, Baltimore, and Boston. In 1790, each city had one bank. Their combined capitalization was $2.5 million. By 1810, there were nineteen banks (excluding the Bank of the United States) with a total capital of $25 million. In another ten years, or, by 1820, the number of commercial banks had increased 50 percent and their capitalization was not quite $40 million. And by 1850 the four cities had eighty-five banks with an aggregate

**Table 3-1  Commercial and Savings Banks, 1800–1850 (in millions of dollars)**

| Year | Number of Commercial Banks | Estimated Bank Capital | Estimated Deposit & Note Circulation | Savings Bank Deposits |
|------|------|------|------|------|
| 1800 | 29 | $ 30 | $ 20 | $— |
| 1820 | 307 | 135 | 90 | 1 |
| 1830 | 329 | 150 | 120 | 7 |
| 1840 | 901 | 350 | 215 | 14 |
| 1850 | 824 | 200 | 325 | 43 |

Sources: *Historical Statistics of the United States; Annual Report of the Comptroller of the Currency*, 1876; A. Piatt Andrew, *Statistics for the United States, 1887–1909*, Government Printing Office, Washington, D.C., 1910; David Kinley, *The Independent Treasury of the U.S., and Its Relation to the Banks of the Country*, Government Printing Office, Washington, D.C., 1910.

net worth of close to $70 million. The number of banks in the big cities was growing at a much slower rate than in the country as a whole, but their net worth was rising at about the same rate.[10] In theory at least, the functions of a commercial bank were well understood. The petition of the Massachusetts bank argued that its creation would save borrowers "from the griping usurer," would provide a means for safekeeping one's liquid wealth, and would increase the "medium of trade" (that is, the money supply). Whether nineteenth-century commercial banks fulfilled these functions in a satisfactory way is still the subject of some debate, but it is true that they quickly became the most versatile of all financial institutions. They held deposits for safekeeping and deposits against which checks could be written. They made short-term loans to manufacturers, merchants, and small shopkeepers. More frequently, they made loans against real estate mortgages and so-called accommodation loans, that is, intermediate or long-term loans to finance fixed capital investment or even consumer purchases. They also bought government bonds, thereby supplying much of the funds needed to finance wars and the construction of public works and internal improvements.

But, broad as their activities were, commercial banks could not make all the loans that were asked of them. This was especially true in the big cities where the banks tried, often unsuccessfully, to follow what is known as the *real bills doctrine*. This doctrine, once part of the decalogue of orthodox banking but now in relative disrepute, taught that commercial banks should restrict their assets to short-term, self-liquidating commercial loans. In other words, banks should confine themselves to working capital loans that would be repaid in a short time. In the very early years, the city banks sincerely tried to follow this rule by taking nothing but short-term, nonrenewable loans. They almost immediately found this to be totally impracticable and began to make longer-term loans, sometimes for as long as two years. Country banks, from the start, did a substantial business in accommodation paper. This was quite natural given the need for long-term agricultural capital in their communities. As business and commerce expanded and transportation improved, the city banks were gradually able to reduce their accommodation loans, so that such loans were almost nonexistent by 1850. However, at country banks, lending on real property maintained its dominance.

To the extent that commercial banks succeeded in following the real bills doctrine, they avoided acquiring mortgages and long-term securities and loans. As a by-product of this policy, they discouraged time deposits, especially small accounts.[11] But an efficient capital market structure cannot afford to ignore small savings. To fill this gap, mutual savings banks appeared in the boom years after the War of 1812.

Savings banks originally were regarded as benevolent institutions, or charities, and had as their objective "to ameliorate the condition of the poorer classes" or "to aid and assist the poor and middling classes of society in putting their money out to advantage." Some savings banks hewed closely to this line. The Savings Bank of Baltimore, for ex-

[10] Herman E. Krooss, "Financial Institutions," in *The Growth of the Seaport Cities*, ed. David T. Gilchrist, Eleutherian Mills-Hagley Foundation, Wilmington, Del., 1967.

[11] In its first few years the Massachusetts Bank *charged* depositors. It was not until 1804 that a commercial bank (the Farmers' Bank, Annapolis, Maryland) paid interest on deposits.

ample, would not allow a depositor to deposit over $10 in any one week, but other savings banks, exhibiting more entrepreneurial ingenuity, defined the "poor and middling classes" much more liberally. The New York Bank of Savings, for example, often accepted funds of as much as $1,000 or $2,000. It is true that institutions made most of the large deposits, but deposits quickly grew to over $1.5 million distributed among 30,000 depositors whose occupations ranged from domestic, porter, and carter to physician, attorney, and merchant. The funds deposited were loaned out on mortgages, used to purchase bank stocks and, most important of all, employed to help finance the construction of the Erie Canal.[12]

The early nineteenth century produced three additional financial intermediaries: the building and loan association, the investment company, and the mutual life insurance company. The Oxford Provident Building Association was founded in Philadelphia in 1831 as a cooperative engaged in financing the building and purchasing of homes. This early association bore little resemblance to its present-day counterpart, the savings and loan association. Its members subscribed to shares of stock on which they made regular payments until the full purchase price was paid. Then the assets were divided among the members.

Although it has often been called the first trust company, the Massachusetts Hospital Life Insurance Company was really an investment company. It was created in 1818 to achieve two main objectives: to provide a corporate trustee to supervise the large estates of New England capitalists, and to provide an income for the Massachusetts General Hospital. The estates that were deposited with the trustees were invested as a common fund, not as a series of segregated funds—the usual practice in a trust company. The MHLIC was immensely successful and was well worth the fee of 0.5 percent charged against the principal. By 1830, it was the leading financial institution in New England. Thereafter, although it continued to grow, it declined from its leading position. Nevertheless, in 1850 it had $7.5 million in assets. Of this, $4.1

million was in mortgages and $2.9 million in "notes."[13]

Willard Phillips, of the Boston merchant family, formed the first modern mutual insurance company, the New England Mutual Life Insurance Company, in 1835, although it did not begin operations until 1842. As late as 1840, life insurance was clearly a sideline of trust companies, some of which wrote life insurance on a renewable term basis. In 1841 only some 1,200 policies were written and only $4 million was in force. In that same year, total premiums were a little over $250,000. Two developments propelled the industry forward. The first was the inauguration of mutual companies that catered to all members of society; the other was the creation of the agency system and the beginning of modern selling. This latter innovation was started by the Connecticut Mutual Life Insurance Company in 1846. It was not, however, until 1853 that the first sales manager or general agent appeared in the person of Henry W. Hyde of the Mutual of New York.

By the middle of the nineteenth century, most of the specialized financial markets and institutions with which we are concerned had been created to accommodate the needs of specialized entrepreneurs and to serve different classes of savers. Four of these—the securities markets, commercial banks, savings banks, and insurance companies—had already attained considerable importance. Households that had more savings than they cared to self-invest could find a convenient outlet in the securities market and in the commercial and savings banks. The securities market, centered in the stock exchange and handled by domestic and foreign private bankers, met the long-term credit requirements of government and some of the needs of business. Commercial banks satisfied the short-term needs of trade and commerce through commercial paper[14] and foreign exchange, and savings banks pooled and transferred small savings into the mortgage and securities markets.

---

[12]*First Annual Report of the Bank for Savings in the City of New York,* New York, 1820; Peter Lester Payne and Lance E. Davis, *The Savings Bank of Baltimore, 1816–1866,* Johns Hopkins University Press, Baltimore, Md., 1954.

[13]Gerald T. White, *History of the Massachusetts Hospital Life Insurance Company,* Harvard University Press, Cambridge, Mass., 1955.

[14]Like so many terms in economics, the meaning of *commercial paper* has changed over the years. Originally, it meant any instrument, except a bond, that was used as a basis for a business loan. It included bills of exchange, trade acceptances, and promissory notes. In the broad

The other intermediaries still had their popularity ahead of them. To be sure, trust companies were already supervising the large estates of financiers and manufacturers, and toward the end of the period, building and loan associations and mutual life insurance companies joined the venerable general insurance companies in lending on real estate and in making long-term loans to those businesses requiring large amounts of fixed capital. The era of pension funds was, of course, far in the future.

## Financial Institutions in the Late 1800s

During the second half of the nineteenth century, the American economy was developing very rapidly. These were the years when the westward movement reached its height, when the Census Bureau, in 1890, announced that there was no longer any frontier line. These were also the years when the United States became an urban country. The number of people living in cities first surpassed those living on farms in 1890. It was an age of more than ordinary technological progress, the age of the railroad, of steel, and toward the end of the period, of electricity and the first faint hints of the internal combustion engine. In 1850, there were only 9,000 miles of railroad, and steel production totaled only a few thousand pounds; by 1900, the rail network covered about 200,000 miles and steel production, at 10 million tons, was greater than that of Great Britain and Germany combined. Encouraged by the expansion of the market area and under the pressure of technological change and the prodding of their own entrepreneurs, large-scale industrial firms, so-called big business, began to appear with greater frequency. All of these impressive accomplishments and sweeping changes were reflected in a significant rise in national income and the dollar volume of saving. Real per capita income probably doubled between 1850 and 1900, a considerably higher rate of growth than seems to have been experienced in the first half of the century. Since

the *rate* of saving remained relatively constant, this meant that the dollar volume of saving also doubled.

The vigorous and salubrious developments that were taking place in the economic and business world had profound ramifications for the capital markets and the growth of financial intermediaries. As in the earlier years, part of the capital needs of the economy were self-financed, but, much more frequently than in the past, external financing was resorted to either through the direct sale of primary securities in the capital markets or through financial intermediation.

For the financial system, five developments in the fifty or sixty years after 1850 were especially significant. First of all, the assets of financial intermediaries grew at a much faster rate than they did in the first half of the century. Second, most of the increased saving that fed the intermediaries flowed through commercial banks, savings banks, and life insurance companies. Third, the investment banker emerged as an independent and vital force in the capital market. Fourth, during the final years of the period, industrial securities became increasingly important in the equities market. Finally, and closely related to the others, the latter half of the nineteenth century witnessed the integration of local and regional financial markets along national lines. Let us examine each of these developments in more detail.

The total assets of all financial intermediaries grew from about $650 million in 1850 to about $20 billion in 1900. Per capita assets (deflated for price changes) multiplied some six-and-a-half times from a mere $25 in 1850 to approximately $165 in 1900, a rate of increase probably 25 percent higher than in the years before 1850. Clearly the most important reason for the better-than-previous performance of the intermediaries was the high rate of growth in national income and saving. But, even if national income had not grown more rapidly, commercial banks as well as other intermediaries might still have fared better than the general economy, for savers were continuously investing less of their own savings directly and channeling more saving through intermediaries. With the passage of time, the number of self-employed persons declined relative to the population as a whole. Conversely, there were more city dwellers and employees. This trend toward urbanization and industrialization re-

_____
sense, it still means any short-term business obligation. We say, for example, that the Federal Reserve banks rediscount commercial paper, but technically commercial paper today means unendorsed, short-term promissory notes issued by large, creditworthy borrowers and sold in the open market.

sulted in an ever-widening cleavage between the functions of saving and investing. The farmers and the self-employed both saved and invested internally, while city dwellers and employees rarely invested their own savings but entrusted them to intermediaries instead.

The separation of the functions of saving and investment represented a windfall for the banking system. By 1900 there were at least eleven times as many commercial banks with at least twenty times as many assets as in 1850. Savings banks enjoyed even greater success. Their deposits climbed some fiftyfold.[15] Most of this increase occurred between 1850 and 1870. The growth rate of savings banks declined with the settlement of the trans-Mississippi West, for these institutions, although plentiful in the East, failed to gain a foothold in the West. Westerners who wished to deposit their savings in a bank opened interest-bearing time deposit accounts in commercial banks. By 1900, time deposits made up 20 percent of total commercial bank deposits and were equal to about 40 percent of savings bank deposits. Such time deposits would have been even greater except for the fact that the big-city bankers would not accept them.[16]

Life insurance companies and trust companies were carried along with the tide, although much of the success of the former has to be attributed to significantly more aggressive handling of the marketing function.[17] The rise in national income and the increase in the number of people depending on someone else for their jobs and their livelihood further encouraged the growth of life insurance. In the last half of the century, life insurance company assets grew about one hundredfold, or at twice the rate of assets of savings banks.

The trust company (an institution formed to manage as a segregated fund the assets of individuals or estates), although almost unknown in the early years, had achieved considerable influence by the end of the century. If we exclude the Massachusetts Hospital Life Insurance Company, the first trust company was the Farmers Loan and Trust Company founded in 1823. In 1850, there were only a handful of such trust companies, and by 1875 only 35, but there were 200 by 1890, and 500 by 1900.[18]

Until the early 1850s, trust companies were mostly involved in personal asset administration, especially estate administration. Later on, as securities markets broadened, their activities expanded to include trusteeship under bond indentures. In addition, they became registrars and agents for stock transfer and dividend payments. The rise of the trust companies in the latter part of the nineteenth century was due to several advantages they possessed over the commercial banks. They could hold a greater variety of earning assets, including mortgages and various public and private securities; their deposits were more stable; they held lower cash reserves; and they paid interest on deposits. Because they were less closely regulated than commercial banks, trust companies were able to participate more actively in the rapidly expanding securities markets.

The rise of the trust company was a symptom of a striking transformation in the capital market in the late nineteenth century. The period has often been portrayed as the heyday of investment banking, and some economic historians have labeled it the era of finance capitalism. This is not altogether inaccurate. In the early part of the century, American investment banking, powerful though it may have seemed, was really a subsidiary of the older international banking houses of Europe. But, as national income and the volume of domestic saving

[15] The statistics on the growth of most financial intermediaries are from Goldsmith, *Financial Intermediaries in the American Economy Since 1900*; on commercial and savings banks and insurance companies from Board of Governors of the Federal Reserve System, *All-Bank Statistics,* Washington, D.C., 1959; and U.S. Department of Commerce, *Historical Statistics of the United States,* Washington, D.C., 1960.

[16] Consider, for example, the testimony of Frank A. Vanderlip, President of the National City Bank of New York, at the hearings on the Federal Reserve Act in 1913: "Taking up the savings bank feature, I have paid no attention to that, because in any event it probably would not interest the large city banks."

[17] Douglass North, "Capital Accumulation in Life Insurance Between the Civil War and the Investigation of 1905," in *Men in Business,* ed. William Miller, Harper & Row Publishers, New York, 1952.

[18] George E. Barnett, *State Banks and Trust Companies,* Government Printing Office, Washington, D.C., 1911. The uncertainty of the data is illustrated by the difference between this estimate and one made by the Comptroller of the Currency. The latter estimated the number of trust companies at 285 in 1900. See *Annual Report of the Comptroller of the Currency,* 1915.

rapidly increased in the late nineteenth century, American investment bankers quickly freed themselves from dependence on the European houses and emerged as preeminent role players in the capital markets. Indeed, at the outset of the last quarter of the 1800s, such houses as J. P. Morgan & Co. and Kuhn, Loeb & Co. were beginning to play a part in financing the investment needs of the rest of the world as well as in reorganizing the capital markets of the United States.

The securities market—the stage on which the investment banker played his role—underwent a very marked change in the late nineteenth century. Before the 1880s, the volume of business on the New York Stock Exchange was very small. Up to that time, the largest number of shares sold on any single day was 700,000, a record set in 1879. It was not until December 1886 that brokers enjoyed a 1,000,000-share day.[19] Most trading was in railroad stocks, for railroads were, of course, large concerns with heavy capital requirements and, consequently, their shares were widely held. There were, for example, 2,500 shareholders in the New York Central even before the Civil War. A number of medium-sized companies in textile manufacturing were listed on the Boston Exchange, but in the late 1800s only one large manufacturing firm—the Pullman Palace Car Company—was traded on the New York Exchange. Most companies were small, and even the large ones, such as Carnegie Steel, McCormick Reaper, Standard Oil, and Singer Sewing Machine, were closely owned, that is, their shares were not publicly traded.[20]

Toward the end of the century, all this was beginning to change. Large-scale enterprises were becoming increasingly common in manufacturing as a result of internal growth and because of the merger wave that began in the 1890s. As they became more common, large industrial firms began to offer their shares for public purchase. Going public was not only a natural way of life for large business, but it had very decided advantages for the various groups with a stake in business enterprises: the owners, the managers, the financiers, and the public. For the owner, the sale of equity shares provided an opportunity both to liquidate capital tied up in the business and to diversify his investments. It also meant an enhancement of wealth, for by experience the financial community had arrived at a rule of thumb that said that a family-owned company was worth three times earnings, but a publicly owned company—due to the greater liquidity of its shares—was worth ten times earnings. It was also true that public ownership could limit the owner's decision-making power, but this was regarded as an advantage by the nonowner managers who were appearing with greater frequency in the large firms. To them, one-man control was an obstacle to progress and a barrier to growth. Their view was shared by the bankers who were beginning to participate more frequently in industrial enterprises and who were more at home in the stock exchanges than in the factories. The last group—the investing public—also welcomed public ownership, for it could now put its excess saving into securities as well as into real estate loans, savings banks, and commercial bank time deposits.

These changes helped to create the atmosphere and lay the groundwork on which enterprising promoters, such as John R. Dos Passos, Charles R. Flint, and the Moore Brothers, and investment bankers, like J. Pierpont Morgan, financed the huge aggregations of capital that made the development of big business possible. Between 1898 and 1902 such industrial giants as American Can, International Harvester, United States Steel, and United Fruit appeared on the Exchange. By 1903 the stocks of 136 large industrial companies were listed. In 1901 over 3 million shares were sold in one day, a record which would stand until 1916. Long before then, stock trading had become so active that Lord Bryce, the perceptive English observer of the American scene, commented on its ubiquity. But it must be said that Bryce's sample was limited, for as a critic once wrote, he "looked at America over a champagne glass." Nevertheless, it is estimated that in 1900 there were some 1 million stockholders out of an adult population of 42 million.[21]

Until the late 1800s, in fact almost up to the turn of the century, financial markets were of a local or regional nature. Despite the supposed propensity of economic man to arbitrage between markets

[19]New York Stock Exchange, *Fact Book*, 1975.
[20]Thomas Navin and Marian V. Sears, "The Rise of a Market for Industrial Securities, 1887–1902," *Business History Review*, 29 (1955).
[21]Edwin B. Cox, *Trends in the Distribution of Stock Ownership*, University of Pennsylvania Press, Philadelphia, 1963.

(that is, to equalize net rates of return in different markets), substantial interest rate differentials, both on short- and long-term securities, persisted among the different regions of the country. Differences in risk and in transportation costs explain part of regional variation in rates. Yet even after adjusting for these factors the pronounced regional differences remained. In the 1890s, bank loan rates on short-term commercial loans ranged from less than 5 percent in New England and the eastern states to more than 7 percent in the South to nearly 9 percent in the western and Pacific states. Due, in large measure, to the activities of commercial paper houses, these differentials were for the most part eliminated by the beginning of World War I. Somewhat the same story carries over to the capital markets, where the spread of mortgage and life insurance companies brought large reductions in regional mortgage-rate differentials between 1870 and 1890.[22]

## Financial Institutions in the 1920s

Until the 1920s, financial institutions competed against one another only in the broad sense that they were outlets for the saving of those who did not consume and invest all of their income. Each financial intermediary—even the commercial banks—was highly specialized, performing distinctive functions that rarely overlapped. Thus, commercial banks in the big cities were not interested in time deposits or in long-term loans. Savings banks did not make short-term loans. Building and loan associations did not accept funds for deposit. Life insurance companies insured lives and granted annuities, but they did not describe themselves in any way as savings institutions. Investment bankers monopolized the flotation of new securities. To be sure, country banks welcomed time deposits and made some long-term loans, and private bankers accepted some accounts that might otherwise have gone to commercial banks, but there was no aggressive competition. The business of financial intermediation was, as Bagehot had said about banking in Victorian days, "a watchful, but not laborious trade."

Circumstances were somewhat altered in the 1920s. Financial intermediaries became more diversified and competition among them increased. World War I had something to do with this, for it affected financial institutions as it did everything else. During the war, businesspeople and the general public became much more familiar with the securities markets as the federal government increased its debt by over $25 billion and offered to the public the widely publicized liberty loans. The public also gained a broader acquaintance with insurance through the federal government's ambitious program for insuring each member of the armed forces.

Trends in business organization and finance had even more to do with the reshaping of financial institutions. The continued growth of large-scale enterprise and the increasing importance of the professional manager in the 1920s brought a greater sophistication into business behavior. The professional managers relied much more on internal financing and the capital markets than on the money markets. That is to say, they made more use of retained earnings and the sale of long-term securities to raise capital and depended less on short-term borrowing from the banks. In addition, the professional managers exercised closer control over their cash and working capital than had been the previous custom. The more far-sighted managers were already subjecting their cash to inventory controls in the same way that their predecessors had handled raw materials and, thus, they were less dependent on the commercial banks.[23]

The spreading familiarity with some of the more complicated financial instruments was an unexpected boon to the life insurance industry. Government military insurance, which the private companies had initially regarded with dismay, turned out in the long run to be highly advantageous. Just as Social Security later kindled an interest in building a retirement fund, military insurance made the

---

[22]Lance E. Davis, "The Investment Market, 1879–1914: The Evolution of a National Market," *Journal of Economic History,* 25 (1965).

[23]One of the ablest of the career executives, Alfred P. Sloan, Jr., tells what happened in General Motors in 1922: "We began calculating a month ahead what our cash would be each day of the month. . . . Against this projected curve we compared each day the corporation's actual cash balances. . . . By reducing our cash balances in banks, this system enabled us to invest the excess cash, principally in short-term government securities." *My Years with General Motors,* Doubleday & Company, New York, 1963, p. 123.

public more familiar with insurance in general and, thereby, led to greater sales. The private companies, reacting to what they thought was certain disaster, had tried desperately to save themselves by creating new policies that stressed saving over protection. As a result, life insurance assets, instead of declining, rose sharply from less than $2 billion in 1900 to almost $20 billion in 1929. In the process, life insurance became the largest private absorber of financial saving. In 1900 the public paid $325 million in premiums. By 1929 this had risen to $3.3 billion.[24]

The securities markets gained even more from the spreading familiarity with the intricacies of finance and twentieth-century trends in business management. Activity on the stock exchange accelerated rapidly as businesses turned to the sales of securities for more of their capital funds and the public consumed whatever bonds and stocks were offered. New security issues totaled less than $3 billion in 1919; they were about $10 billion in 1929. The number of shareholders climbed in the same proportion—from 3 million to 10 million.[25] The number of firms engaged in selling securities increased almost as rapidly as the number of securities sold, creating a new type of competition in the capital market and a fundamental change in investment banking leadership. Investment companies, practically unknown in 1900, had assets of $3 billion by 1929. The number of businesses engaged in selling securities increased from 485 in 1920 to 665 in 1929, while the number of branch offices expanded from 203 to 1,237. With one office

for every 64,000 people, almost every county seat had its brokerage office, complete with stock ticker and stock board. Activity on the New York Stock Exchange grew at the same furious pace. In 1900 the exchange handled over 100 million shares of stock, equal to a turnover of 172 percent of all listed shares. During the 1920s, volume averaged about 475 million shares, and in 1929 business soared to a phenomenal 1.1 billion shares, a turnover rate of 119 percent of all listed stock.[26] Not until the early 1960s did the number of shares traded exceed the volume of 1929.

The trend away from bank borrowing, which was highlighted by the prosperity of the securities business and investment banking, was, of course, a disaster for the commercial banks. And their relative deterioration was further aggravated by the continued drift to the city and the wider use of the automobile, which rendered superfluous many rural banks. In the midst of the general prosperity of the era, the rate of bank suspensions increased rapidly, averaging over 600 a year and reducing the number of commercial banks from almost 30,000 in 1919 to fewer than 24,000 in 1929. The assets of commercial banks, as may be seen in Tables 3-2 and 3-3, grew by only 5 percent in the 1920s, and their market share of all financial assets held by private financial institutions declined from over 50 percent in 1922 to some 43 percent in 1929 (see Table 3-4).

The performance of commercial banks would have been far worse had not some innovators taken action to change the basic nature of the industry. As they watched their best depositors taking their

**Table 3-2   Financial Assets of Selected Financial Intermediaries for Selected Years, 1900–1939 (in billions of dollars)**

| Years | Commercial Banks | Mutual Savings Banks | Savings & Loan Assns. | Life Ins. Co's. | Other Ins. Co's. | Private Noninsured Pension Funds | Investment Companies | Other[a] |
|---|---|---|---|---|---|---|---|---|
| 1900 | $10.0 | $ 2.4 | $0.5 | $ 1.7 | $0.5 | — | — | $ 3.8 |
| 1912 | 21.8 | 4.0 | 1.0 | 4.4 | 1.2 | — | — | 8.4 |
| 1922 | 47.5 | 6.6 | 2.8 | 8.7 | 2.8 | $0.1 | $0.1 | 22.6 |
| 1929 | 66.2 | 9.9 | 7.4 | 17.5 | 5.5 | 0.5 | 3.0 | 43.4 |
| 1933 | 46.1 | 10.8 | 6.2 | 20.9 | 4.5 | 0.7 | 1.3 | 29.3 |
| 1939 | 66.3 | 11.9 | 5.4 | 29.2 | 6.0 | 1.0 | 1.6 | 40.6 |

[a]"Other" includes finance companies, personal trust departments, mortgage companies, securities brokers and dealers, credit unions.

Source: Raymond W. Goldsmith, *Financial Intermediaries in the American Economy Since 1900*, Princeton University Press, Princeton, N.J., 1958.

[24]*Historical Statistics of the United States.*
[25]Cox, *Trends in the Distribution of Stock Ownership.*

[26]Edwards, *The Evolution of Finance Capitalism*; New York Stock Exchange, *Fact Book, 1965.*

**Table 3-3  Growth Rates of Selected Financial Intermediaries, 1900–1939**

| Years | Commercial Banks | Mutual Savings Banks | Savings & Loan Assns. | Life Ins. Co's. | Other Ins. Co's. | Private Noninsured Pension Funds | Investment Companies | Other[a] |
|---|---|---|---|---|---|---|---|---|
| 1900–1912 | 6.7% | 4.4% | 5.9% | 8.2% | 7.6% | — | — | 6.8% |
| 1912–1922 | 9.2 | 5.1 | 10.9 | 7.1 | 8.8 | — | — | 10.4 |
| 1922–1929 | 4.9 | 6.0 | 14.9 | 10.5 | 10.1 | 0.1% | 62.6% | 9.8 |
| 1929–1933 | −8.7 | 2.2 | −4.3 | 4.5 | −4.9 | 0.5 | −18.9 | −9.4 |
| 1933–1939 | 6.2 | 1.6 | −2.3 | 5.7 | 5.9 | 0.7 | 3.5 | 5.6 |

[a]"Other" includes finance companies, personal trust departments, mortgage companies, securities brokers and dealers, credit unions.

Source: Same as Table 3-2.

**Table 3-4  Assets of Selected Private Financial Intermediaries as a Percentage of Assets of All Private Financial Institutions, 1900–1939**

| Years | Commercial Banks | Mutual Savings Banks | Savings & Loan Assns. | Life Ins. Co's. | Other Ins. Co's. | Private Noninsured Pension Funds | Investment Companies | Other[a] |
|---|---|---|---|---|---|---|---|---|
| 1900 | 52.9% | 12.7% | 2.6% | 9.0% | 2.6% | — | — | 20.1% |
| 1912 | 53.4 | 9.8 | 2.5 | 10.8 | 2.9 | — | — | 20.6 |
| 1922 | 52.1 | 7.2 | 3.1 | 9.5 | 3.1 | .1% | .1% | 24.8 |
| 1929 | 43.2 | 6.5 | 4.8 | 11.4 | 3.6 | .3 | 2.0 | 28.3 |
| 1933 | 38.5 | 9.0 | 5.2 | 17.4 | 3.8 | .6 | 1.1 | 24.5 |
| 1939 | 40.9 | 7.3 | 3.3 | 18.0 | 3.7 | .6 | 1.0 | 25.1 |

[a]"Other" includes finance companies, personal trust departments, mortgage companies, securities brokers and dealers, credit unions.

Source: Same as Table 3-2.

business elsewhere, the more aggressive and far-sighted commercial bankers in the big cities realized that if they were to maintain their relative position, they would have to revolutionize both the asset and the liability sides of their balance sheets. They entered the retail business by welcoming time deposits and seeking small accounts. In 1920, time deposits totaled a little over $10 billion, or one-third of all deposits. By the end of 1928, they had doubled and were equal to 45 percent of all deposits.[27] It would not be long, it seemed, before time deposits would exceed demand deposits.

On the asset side, the banks gradually jettisoned the real bills doctrine with its emphasis on short-term, self-liquidating, commercial paper. They persuaded Congress to include in the McFadden Branch Banking Act of 1927 provisions that permitted national banks to purchase investment securities and that also enlarged their power to make real estate loans. The banks were quick to take advantage of their powers. During the 1920s, the dollar volume of commercial loans remained relatively constant, but security loans increased 120 percent; real estate loans, 175 percent; and security acquisitions, 65 percent.

Meanwhile, the largest commercial banks were seeking to retain their corporate connections as well as to participate in the Great Bull Market of the late 1920s by invading the investment banking field. Although commercial banks were active in investment banking long before the 1920s, it was not until then that they began to assume all the functions of that business—including the origination of new security issues, formation of, and participation in, underwriting syndicates, and the retail distribution of securities through networks of branch offices. The vehicle for accomplishing this was the security affiliate. The first such affiliates were set up by the First National Bank of New York in 1908 and by the National City Bank of New York in 1911. They remained isolated cases until World War I; however, the movement gained momentum in the early and middle twenties. In 1928, in response to the bull market, the idea of separate investment banking affiliates took on the

[27]Board of Governors of the Federal Reserve System, *All-Bank Statistics.*

proportions of a craze. By 1929 nearly all the largest commercial banks had acquired one or more investment banking houses.

Yet what happened in commercial banking, important as it was, did not constitute a revolution. First of all, it is easy to exaggerate the importance of the real bills doctrine in restraining long-term loans in earlier times. Except for city banks, the theory was probably ignored more often than it was observed. This is not to imply that the real bills doctrine was without force. It certainly influenced the regulation of commercial banks by various government agencies as well as the attitudes of bankers. Nevertheless, it never dominated banking practice in America as it did in England. Secondly, although the business of commercial banking was quite different in the twenties from what it had been earlier, the new ways of thinking, underlying the changes that had taken place, still did not permeate the whole industry. This remained to be accomplished in the post–World War II era.

## Financial Institutions During the Depression

Both the volume and the rate of saving fell sharply during the depression that crippled the country in the years 1930–1933. Indeed, in 1932, net capital formation was negative, as depreciation and obsolescence allowances exceeded investment. In the general flight to liquidity that accompanied an almost total loss of confidence in the economy, savings banks with their emphasis on safety of principal increased their assets slightly. Life insurance companies managed to do somewhat better, while the government-owned and operated postal savings system fared still better, achieving some importance in the financial community for the first and only time in its career. As can be seen from Tables 3-2 and 3-3, all other financial intermediaries watched the volume of their business drop sharply as safety and liquidity came to be uppermost in the minds of frightened Americans.

In the shift toward greater risk aversion by the public, the securities markets and investment banking were the major casualties, and they did not fully recover for two decades. Corporate security issues did not surpass the 1929 figure until 1955 when the gross national product was more than three times as large. The number of stockholders shrank from

about 10 million in 1929 to about 5 million in 1950 and did not exceed the 1929 figure until the late 1950s. The volume of transactions also fell far short of the heady pace set in the 1920s. It was not until 1961 that the New York Stock Exchange again witnessed the billion-share year it had experienced in 1929. Even then, the turnover rate was only 15 percent of all listed shares.

There were a number of reasons why investment banking declined as a supplier of loanable funds for business. As has already been noted, when the market collapsed, emphasis on security temporarily replaced the sky's-the-limit psychology of the 1920s. In desperate pursuit of liquidity, asset holders rushed out of the stock market into the savings banks and the postal savings system and, eventually, into currency and gold. Later in the thirties, government legislation and fiscal policy also contributed to the decline in the importance of investment banking. The government, largely as a result of popular sentiment, passed legislation that separated commercial from investment banking, prohibited pools and wash sales, restricted margin trading, required publicity for new security issues of over $300,000, regulated stock exchange operations, and required competitive bidding for certain types of new security issues. Those who did not believe in government intervention charged that fiscal policy, by placing constantly greater emphasis on progressive taxation, reduced the number of persons who could afford to buy large blocks of securities. At the same time, it seemed to some observers foolish to buy risk securities in the face of high tax rates. The return of prosperity was to render many of these issues of academic importance only.

Commercial banking was also badly hurt by the depression, partly because of a decline in the demand for short-term funds and partly because the public feared for the safety of its demand and time deposits. Commercial bank assets in 1933 were below what they had been in 1922, and in 1939 they were only slightly higher than they had been in 1929 (see Table 3-2). The demand for loanable funds declined much faster than the supply, and banks were hard pressed to find outlets for their excess reserves. Having no other recourse, they purchased government bonds in large quantities at the same time that the supply of the latter increased as a consequence of deficit financing by the federal government. By 1939 holdings of government bonds exceeded total loans in the portfolios of commercial banks. Thus, to a marked degree commercial banks during the thirties became warehouses of government bonds, rather than suppliers of short- and intermediate-term business credit.

## Financial Institutions Since World War II

The objective of this chapter has been to recount the history of the growth of the United States money and capital markets and financial intermediaries. It is not essential that the story be brought up to the present in any great detail. What has been happening over the last few decades will be developed at many other points in this book. All that is intended here is to make a few broad statements about the postwar period.

A comparison of the postwar era with that of the twenties brings to the fore several similarities and differences between the two periods that emphasize both the continuity of history and the amount of change that has occurred. One of the most striking differences between the two periods lies in the area of political economy. In the 1920s, the federal government was a relatively passive and unimportant factor in the economy, and the public apparently liked it that way. In the present era the federal government plays a highly influential and, indeed, expanding role in economic life, and today's public apparently likes it that way or at least accepts it as a seemingly necessary consequence of modern life.[28] What this has meant to financial institutions is illustrated by the increased importance of government in capital formation and in the composition of total debt. In the years around the turn of the century, government units of all types were responsible for about 10 percent of gross domestic capital formation; business units accounted for about 70 percent; and household investment (that is, residential housing) constituted the remaining 20 percent. In the decade following World War II, by contrast, the government's share of gross capital formation swelled to over 20 percent, while the

business and household shares declined to 65 percent and 15 percent respectively.[29] Similar changes occurred in the composition of debt. In 1929 business firms owed 65 percent of net public and private debt; individuals were obligated for another 20 percent; and government borrowing made up the remaining 15 percent. By the mid-1970s, business debt had declined to 50 percent of the total; household debt had increased to 25 percent; and the debt of the various governmental units had expanded sharply to account for the remaining 25 percent.

Business firms, governments, and households have also altered their savings behavior and their use of financial intermediaries since the twenties. Over much of the past century, gross savings remained at somewhat over 20 percent of GNP. However, data for the postwar period suggest that the rate of capital formation has declined. (The decline in *net* capital formation has been much more pronounced and of longer duration.) But much depends on the particular definition of capital formation and saving being used. The inclusion of consumer durables as well as government in the definition, for example, results in the ratio remaining relatively stable. The relationship of personal savings to disposable income likewise did not change very much from the earlier period. It was 5 percent of disposable income in 1929; from 1947 to 1979 it ranged from lows of 4.6 percent in 1979 and 4.7 percent in 1963 to highs of 7.8 percent in 1973 and 1975.[30]

In contrast to the general comparability in overall savings ratios, very substantial changes have occurred in the *forms* of saving over the past fifty years. Most significant has been the continued growth of indirect finance—that is, the transference of saving into investment through financial intermediation—and further erosion in the shares of direct investment. The contribution of financial intermediaries to external financing rose from less than 50 percent in the years 1901–1912 and 1923–1929 to more than two-thirds in the immediate postwar years. By the late 1960s, financial intermediaries were supplying 85 percent of the funds raised in the credit markets compared to about 75 percent

---

[28]Nevertheless, the traditional American objection to "big" government continues to find expression in the repeated clamor for less government spending, balanced budgets, and more control at the local level, as well as in the frequent defeat of state and local bond issues.

[29]Simon S. Kuznets, *Capital in the American Economy*, Princeton University Press, Princeton, N.J., 1961, p. 178.

[30]Board of Governors of the Federal Reserve System, *Flow of Funds Accounts*, 1979.

in the 1950s. And, by the late 1970s, nearly 90 percent of all funds raised in the money and capital markets was acquired through financial intermediaries.[31]

On the whole, financial intermediaries expanded rapidly in the years since World War II, with total assets growing ninefold, clearly outstripping the growth of GNP. However, the growth of financial intermediation did not affect all intermediaries alike, as can be seen in Table 3-5. Some, such as credit unions, savings and loans associations, and pension funds, grew exceptionally rapidly. Others, however, like mutual savings banks and life insurance companies, encountered problems in keeping pace. And still others (investment companies and banks, for example) found that growth did not occur at a steady rate, but rather had its ups and downs.

The most striking development to take place in the recent history of financial institutions has been the increase in diversification and competition. This development was first discernible in the 1920s, but the trend accelerated in the 1950s and 1960s, and in the 1970s it reached a point unmatched in our history. Diversification and competition have, perhaps, been most visible on the liability side of the balance sheet—in the battle for savings by deposit-type institutions. They have also, however, extended to the asset, or lending, side.

During the first decade and a half of the postwar period, demand and time deposits of commercial banks lagged behind the growth of mutual savings bank time deposits and of savings and loan shares, particularly the latter. Beginning in 1933, commercial banks were not allowed to pay interest on demand deposits, and, with interest rates on money substitutes rising throughout the postwar period, individuals and businesses naturally sought to economize on their demand-deposit balances. Furthermore, the maximum rate permitted on bank time and savings deposits was considerably below the then unregulated rates paid by savings banks. The savings bank rate was, in turn, somewhat lower than the rates paid by the S&Ls. Rates were unregulated for these institutions until 1966 because the monetary authorities and legislators deliberately wished to encourage the flow of deposits into them. Even after 1966, mutual savings banks and S&Ls were permitted to pay higher rates than commercial banks. The commercial banks faced an added disadvantage in that the so-called thrift institutions also received more favorable tax treatment.

Commercial banks were slow to react. Until the mid-fifties, they still preferred to concentrate on attracting low-cost demand deposits and on making commercial loans. Indeed, during most of the fifties, even in the face of strong competition, many commercial banks were paying lower rates on their time and savings deposits than the legal ceilings permitted.

By the late 1950s, however, commercial banks were making concerted efforts to recapture their preeminence as financial institutions. They offered more services. They began to advertise on a relatively large scale, stressing the advantages of one-stop banking. On the asset side, the banks reacted to the decline in business borrowing by competing effectively for consumer loans, mortgages, and in other ways that had been considered inappropriate at the beginning of the century.[32] More dramatic changes, however, appeared on the liability side of the balance sheet. To attract time deposits, the banks lobbied successfully for a liberalization of deposit rate ceilings. In 1957 maximum interest rates on commercial bank time deposits were raised for the first time since 1936, and they have been raised on various occasions since then. (They are now scheduled to be phased out by 1986.) Aided by the permissive stance of the regulatory author-

[31] This does not imply that the share of funds flowing through intermediaries has been stable in the short run. It has in fact varied in response to credit market conditions. Thus, high interest rates in 1969 and 1973 led to sharp declines in the share of funds passing through financial institutions, as individuals sought the higher yields of primary securities. Whereas household net acquisitions of the liabilities of financial institutions accounted for nearly half of the sector's gross saving (which includes capital consumption) in 1968, the proportion dropped to just over one-fourth in 1969; similarly, the share declined from three-fifths in 1972 to 45 percent in 1973. Historically, disintermediation has resulted, in part, from a widening of the gap between unregulated interest rates on certain primary securities and the regulated, or otherwise less flexible, rates paid on secondary securities—a widening that has occurred particularly during periods of tight money.

[32] In the 1950s and early sixties, businesses raised most of their funds internally. Bank loans accounted for only about 15 percent of the funds raised externally.

**Table 3-5 Total Assets of Selected Financial Intermediaries at Year-End, 1945–1978[a] (in billions of dollars)**

|  | 1945 | 1950 | 1955 | 1960 | 1965 | 1970 | 1975 | 1978[b] |
|---|---|---|---|---|---|---|---|---|
| Commercial banks | $160.3 | $168.9 | $210.7 | $257.6 | $377.3 | $ 576.2 | $ 964.9 | $1,284.0 |
| Savings and loan associations | 8.7 | 16.9 | 37.7 | 71.5 | 129.6 | 176.2 | 338.2 | 523.6 |
| Life insurance companies | 44.8 | 64.0 | 90.4 | 119.6 | 158.9 | 207.3 | 289.3 | 389.0 |
| Mutual savings banks | 17.0 | 22.4 | 31.3 | 40.6 | 58.2 | 79.0 | 121.1 | 158.2 |
| Finance companies | 4.3 | 9.3 | 18.3 | 26.9 | 44.8 | 64.0 | 97.7 | 143.4 |
| Investment companies | 1.3 | 3.3 | 7.8 | 17.0 | 35.2 | 47.6 | 42.2 | 45.2 |
| Credit unions | 0.4 | 1.0 | 2.7 | 5.7 | 10.6 | 18.0 | 38.0 | 62.6 |
| Private pension funds | 2.8 | 6.7 | 18.3 | 38.2 | 73.6 | 110.6 | 148.9 | 205.1 |
| State and local pension funds | 2.6 | 4.9 | 10.8 | 19.6 | 33.2 | 60.3 | 104.7 | 146.5 |
| Total | $242.2 | $297.4 | $428.0 | $596.7 | $921.4 | $1,339.2 | $2,145.0 | $2,957.6 |

[a]Discrepancies appear to exist between these data and those in Table 1-1 because the latter refer only to financial assets, whereas the former encompass not only financial but *real* assets as well.
[b]Preliminary.

Source: U.S. League of Savings Associations, *Savings and Loan Fact Book,* 1979.

ities, commercial banks successfully innovated new deposit-type claims or renewed claims that had been long dormant. The most important of these, of course, has been the negotiable certificate of deposit (CD), which grew from almost nothing in 1960 to about $100 billion at the end of 1978. Consumer CDs grew rapidly as a result of a similar attempt to segment the market for financial savings—a game the other deposit-type intermediaries were quick to play. As a consequence of these and other actions (including the development of Federal Funds and the Eurodollar markets), commercial banks, whose rate of growth had for many years been lower than that of other financial institutions, were again holding their own with their deposit-type competitors (see Table 3-6).

During the 1950s savings and loan institutions experienced very rapid growth for a number of reasons, including tax and interest rate advantages over their commercial bank competitors, and because many of them, especially those with the fastest rates of growth, were favorably located in the capital-scarce Far West. In addition, they benefited enormously from their specialization in the growing field of mortgage financing, and many were managed by aggressive entrepreneurs who advertised all over the country for the savings of households.

In the 1960s, however, their growth slowed (though only in relative terms), partly in response to much more aggressive competition from the

commercial banks and partly because their intense specialization in home mortgages left them vulnerable to violent and sudden increases in interest rates and to periodic contractions in construction activity, such as occurred in the latter part of the decade. By then, savings and loans were trying to persuade government authorities to liberalize regulations so that they might diversify by entering the market for consumer loans. At the same time, they and other deposit-type intermediaries were trying to lessen the distinction between checking accounts and savings accounts. In this latter effort, the savings and loans have had some success and are likely to be even more successful in the years ahead. At present a number of savings and loans will transfer interest-bearing savings funds, on demand, to a customer's checking account (at a commercial bank), thus allowing the customer to maintain little or no noninterest-paying demand balances. Potentially more significant are the electronic funds transfer systems (EFTS), which permit consumers to pay for purchases by having funds instantly transferred from a customer's account to the store's account. Similarly, using point-of-sales terminals, customers can deposit funds with a retailer for transference to a savings institution. The extent to which the potential benefits of EFTS accrue to the thrift institutions depends, in part, on the ability of commercial banks to pay interest on demand deposits. As of year-end 1979, interest-bearing de-

**Table 3-6 Percentage Distribution of Assets of Selected Financial Intermediaries at Year-End, 1945–1978**

| | 1945 | 1950 | 1955 | 1960 | 1965 | 1970 | 1975 | 1978[a] |
|---|---|---|---|---|---|---|---|---|
| Commercial banks | 66.2% | 56.8% | 49.2% | 43.2% | 40.9% | 43.1% | 44.7% | 43.4% |
| Savings and loan associations | 3.6 | 5.7 | 8.8 | 12.0 | 14.1 | 13.2 | 15.8 | 17.8 |
| Life insurance companies | 18.5 | 21.5 | 21.1 | 20.0 | 17.2 | 15.5 | 13.5 | 13.2 |
| Mutual savings banks | 7.0 | 7.5 | 7.3 | 6.8 | 6.3 | 5.9 | 5.6 | 5.4 |
| Finance companies | 1.8 | 3.1 | 4.3 | 4.5 | 4.9 | 4.7 | 4.3 | 4.8 |
| Investment companies | 0.5 | 1.1 | 1.8 | 2.8 | 3.8 | 3.6 | 2.0 | 1.5 |
| Credit unions | 0.2 | 0.3 | 0.6 | 1.0 | 1.2 | 1.3 | 1.8 | 2.1 |
| Private pension funds | 1.2 | 2.3 | 4.3 | 6.4 | 8.0 | 8.3 | 7.3 | 6.9 |
| State and local pension funds | 1.1 | 1.6 | 2.5 | 3.3 | 3.6 | 4.4 | 5.0 | 5.0 |
| Total | 100.0% | 100.0% | 100.0% | 100.0% | 100.0% | 100.0% | 100.0% | 100.0% |

[a]Preliminary.

Source: Table 3-5.

mand deposits were not allowed (except for NOW accounts in New York, New Jersey, and the New England states), but major changes appear likely in the early 1980s.[33]

Mutual savings banks have continued to grow during the postwar period as they have always grown—except for the 1930s—slowly and steadily. Indeed, their growth has been the slowest of all deposit-type intermediaries. In the postwar world mutuals had an advantage over commercial banks because mutuals paid higher interest rates on savings deposits, but they were also frequently accused of being stodgy, stuffy, and stultified. During the 1950s, however, this stereotype began to change. The more enterprising managers of savings banks began to advertise aggressively for deposits. They also invaded territory hitherto considered the exclusive province of commercial banks. Indeed, in New England, where the savings banks are most strongly entrenched, they have been offering what are in fact interest-paying checking accounts in the form of negotiable orders of withdrawal (NOW accounts). Also, they extend passbook loans against deposits as well as mortgage loans against the increased equity in residential housing. Both of these activities have allowed the mutual savings banks to

[33]Such changes came sooner than expected with the passage of the Financial Institutions Deregulation and Monetary Control Act of 1980, signed by the president on March 31, 1980. References to some of these changes will be found in later chapters of the book.

compete against finance companies, credit unions, and commercial banks in the consumer loan field.

With credit unions entering the mortgage loan business, S&Ls and mutual savings banks attempting to move further into the consumer loan business, all of them trying to give their liabilities demand deposit-like attributes, and commercial banks competing aggressively in the savings and consumer loan markets, the lines of demarcation that previously separated the deposit-type intermediaries are rapidly blurring. It is likely that in the years ahead quite a few special distinctions will be obliterated and all depository institutions will be put on roughly similar footing with respect to many assets they can acquire and the types of liabilities they can issue.

Turning to other intermediaries, open-end investment companies (better known as mutual funds) continued to grow in the 1920s, as Americans found them to be a convenient and seemingly less risky way of participating in the stock market upsurge that characterized much of the postwar period. From the Great Depression until the mid-1960s, prices of common stock showed a fairly steady upswing, rising about sixfold. Declines were brief, though sometimes sharp. The shift to a somewhat higher rate of inflation by the 1960s and the early concern of people to protect themselves against purchasing-power risk encouraged the buying of common stock, directly as well as through mutual funds and pension plans. The conventional wisdom was that common stock was a good hedge against inflation, since stock prices were bound to rise along with other prices. To small investors, mutual funds seemed a particularly attractive way to enter the market, as they offered relatively low transaction costs and the presumed benefits of diversification and professional management.

But these illusions were shattered, as they were in the thirties, by the failure of the market to maintain its upward thrust. Stock prices fluctuated after 1966 and were lower in early 1980 than they had been fourteen years earlier as one shock after another (including undreamed of rates of inflation, greater government regulation, and political and social turmoil) acted to depress the equities market. To the disappointment of shareholders, the recent advent of double-digit inflation meant not a rise in stock prices but a fall in real profits. Contrary to the view that stock prices would rise in line with other prices, investors found that stock prices exhibited a greater correlation with corporate profits (after allowing for inflationary effects). Furthermore, the notion that fund managements could pick winners was not generally supported by the results. Studies found that one could have done at least as well by buying the stocks underlying the major stock price average (the Dow-Jones, for example) as by buying mutual funds. Consequently, from the late 1960s on, investment companies found their assets shrinking as a result of market losses and net redemptions by a disappointed public. By the beginning of the 1980s one of the few bright spots on the investment company scene was the spectacular growth in the numbers and assets of funds specializing in money market securities, a growth brought on by the very high yields of the money market instruments in their portfolios, and reflecting, in part, the double-digit inflation and rapidly accelerating inflationary expectations of the second half of the 1970s.

Another type of financial intermediary, operating much like investment companies, that experienced a brief moment of glory and an equally abrupt fall was the real estate investment trust (REIT). Starting in the mid-sixties, REITs were formed, often by commercial banks, to make real estate investments. Starting from virtually nothing in 1967, their assets increased to $20 billion in 1973, as investors sought to participate in the lucrative construction market and to benefit from various tax advantages.

Their decline followed a severe weakening of the market that left many REITs unable to cover fixed interest charges.

The position of life insurance in contractual savings was rapidly taken over in the 1950s and 1960s by noninsured pension plans and investment companies. Indeed, life insurance companies grew more slowly than any other major financial institution in the postwar period. The accumulation of saving through the purchase of life insurance was simply not seen as an effective means of keeping up with inflation. By contrast, pension plans experienced rapid growth as a means of meeting the retirement needs of an increasingly affluent society. Private noninsured pension funds, which invested heavily in common stock, exhibited the fastest growth.[34] The life insurance companies responded to competitive pressures by issuing policies (term insurance, for example) that did not have a heavy savings component. The major force stimulating the growth of life insurance company reserves was the rising number of insured pension plans.

## Conclusion

Thus, all financial intermediaries in the post–World War II period mirrored the vast changes that had taken place in the country's economic, social, and legal environment. They were more aggressive in pursuing their entrepreneurial functions. They had adjusted to the expanded role of government in the economy and to the increased sophistication of businesses and consumers. They had, in short, adapted to the market and, in the process, the whole system had become increasingly complex and more competitive. But perhaps the essence of this transformation lay in the increased importance of the household in the operations of most financial intermediaries. Commercial banks, savings banks, savings and loan associations, life insurance companies, credit unions, investment companies, and pension funds, among others, competed for the savings of individuals, and many financial intermediaries vied with each other to lend to them.

[34]Recently the growth of private pension plans has slowed down due to the failure of stock prices to show sustained appreciation.

## Questions

1. What factors accounted for the slow development of financial institutions in the colonial period?
2. In what ways did the development of securities markets and the rise of investment banking contribute to the formation of big business and the rise of the professional managements that came to run these enterprises?
3. To what extent does it appear that financial innovation took place in response to economic development? To what extent did financial innovation occur independently of economic development and, therefore, provide a spur to growth?
4. What has been the effect of inflation on the various types of financial intermediaries over the most recent decade? How would continued inflation affect the flow of savings into primary and secondary securities?
5. Among all the varieties of financial institutions, commercial banks are, and have long been, the most diversified and versatile in their operations. What has this meant in terms of the success of commercial banking? Does this suggest that in the future the American financial system will consist of specialized or of multifunctional institutions?
6. What factors have periodically resulted in disintermediation?
7. What factors contributed to the growth of indirect finance in the second half of the nineteenth century?
8. What possible effects will financial innovation have on how we define the money supply?
9. Compare the commercial banking innovations of the 1920s with those of the late 1950s and 1960s.
10. Compare the role of the consumer as lender and borrower in the late 1800s and in the years after World War II.

## Selected Bibliography

Carosso, Vincent P. *Investment Banking in America: A History.* Harvard University Press, Cambridge, Mass., 1970.

Davis, Lance E. "The Investment Market, 1870–1914." *Journal of Economic History*, 25, No. 2 (1965).

Edwards, G. W. *The Evolution of Finance Capitalism.* Longmans, Green & Co., New York, 1938.

Goldsmith, Raymond W. *Financial Institutions.* Random House, New York, 1968.

———. *Financial Intermediaries in the American Economy Since 1900.* Princeton University Press, Princeton, N.J., 1958.

Greef, Albert. *The Commercial Paper House in the United States.* Harvard University Press, Cambridge, Mass., 1938.

Keller, Morton. *The Life Insurance Enterprise, 1885–1910.* Harvard University Press, Cambridge, Mass., 1963.

Krooss, Herman E., and Martin R. Blyn. *A History of Financial Intermediaries.* Random House, New York, 1971.

Kuznets, Simon S. *Capital in the American Economy.* Princeton University Press, Princeton, N.J., 1961.

Mitchell, Wesley C. "The Role of Money in Economic History." *Journal of Economic History,* 4, Tasks (1944).

Myers, Margaret G. *The New York Money Market.* Columbia University Press, New York, 1931.

Navin, T. R., and Marian V. Sears. "The Rise of a Market for Industrial Securities." *Business History Review,* 29, No. 2 (1955).

Redlich, Fritz. *The Molding of American Banking.* Hafner Publishing Company, New York, 1946–1961, 2 vols.

Stalson, J. Owen. *Marketing Life Insurance.* Harvard University Press, Cambridge, Mass., 1942.

# II

# The Supply of Loanable Funds

# 4

# Commercial Banking as a Business

If you were to ask a banker to define the business of banking, you would probably be told something like this: "Banking is a business in which money is borrowed from the public in the form of deposits and used to make loans and purchase securities. The banks' 'product' is money, and banks try to sell it at a price in excess of its cost and the costs of doing business, thereby making a profit." While this response would be correct and probably reflects the view held by many bankers, banking plays a more important role in economic activity than this view alone suggests.

In their role as the nation's largest financial intermediaries, commercial banks perform a number of important interrelated functions. First, on the liability side, commercial banks are the primary source of the most important ingredient of the U.S. money supply—demand deposits.[1] Second, banks provide these monetary liabilities through creation of credit in the form of loans and investments.[2] In this way banks provide liquidity to the nation's economy. Banks are the largest suppliers of short-term loanable funds to business and consumers, and they supply over one-half of the external funds needed by state and local governments. In addition, they are large purchasers of securities of the U.S. government and its agencies. Third, banks are the custodians of their communities' money and the managers of most monetary transfers. For those customers who seldom borrow, the depository and savings-accumulation functions of banks may be

---

[1]Other depository institutions have gained permission to create liabilities similar to demand deposits—for example, share drafts and NOW accounts. The implications of this for commercial banks and the economy are discussed in Chapters 6 and 28.

[2]Bank creation of deposit liabilities is heavily influenced by the policy decisions of the Federal Reserve. Their policy actions interact with the profit-seeking activities of banks to determine the supply of loanable (and investable) funds to the banking system. While banks "create" money through their lending (credit creation) activities, the Federal Reserve's open-market operations as well as its reserve and discount policies affect the extent to which the banking system has funds available to pursue its activities. Consequently, by controlling the cost and availability of bank loanable funds, the Federal Reserve has a major impact on the quantity and price of the banks' primary "products"—money and liquidity. For further discussion of the interaction of the Federal Reserve and the banking system in determining the nation's money supply, see Chapters 5 and 28.

**Table 4-1 Services Provided by a Sample Commercial Bank**

| *Personal Banking Services* | *Commercial Banking Services* |
| --- | --- |
| Deposit Services | Deposit Services |
|   Personal Checking Accounts |   Commercial Checking Accounts |
|   Statement Savings Accounts |   Commercial Night Depsitory |
|   Regular Savings Accounts |   Lock Box Service |
|   Christmas Clubs | Loan Services |
|   Automatic Investment Service |   Commercial Loans |
| Loan Services |   Leasing |
|   Instalment Loans |   Construction Loans |
|   *Tuition Helper* Loans |   Retail Instalment Financing for Dealers |
|   *Check Command* |   Floor Planning |
|   *Visa* |   *Visa* for Merchants |
| Trust Services | Trust Services |
|   Executor under Will |   Pension and Profit Sharing Plans |
|   Trustee under Will |   Self-Employed Retirement Plans |
|   Living Trusts |   Trustee of Charitable Trusts and Foundations |
|   Investment Management Accounts |   Corporate Trust Services |
|   Custodianship Accounts | International Banking Services |
| Other Services |   Foreign Exchange |
|   *24 Hour Teller* |   Travelers Letters of Credit |
|   Safe Deposit Boxes |   Commercial Letters of Credit |
|   Travelers Checks |   Foreign Collection |
|   Travel Service |   Letters of Introduction |
| |   Foreign Loans |
| |   Foreign Trade Information |
| |   Foreign Market Conditions |
| |   Foreign Credit Data |
| | Other Services |
| |   *Pay Command* |
| |   *Freight Command* |
| |   Interline Services |
| |   Computer Output Microfilm |

the most important, but most customers also use the convenience of transferring funds to third parties by writing checks. Most transfers of any size or over any distance are made through the banking system. Fourth, most banks provide important fiduciary services, such as safekeeping of customers assets and trust department services. Finally, banks provide various miscellaneous services, from foreign exchange to travelers checks. The services provided by a regional bank are listed in Table 4-1 and are illustrative of the variety of banking services which a commercial bank often offers.

This chapter analyzes the important managerial problems that banks must face as they perform their functions as financial intermediaries. As Chapter 1 points out in regard to all intermediaries, these problems involve questions that relate to the structure of their liabilities and the risk and return of their assets. The next section addresses these questions in a general way, using portfolio theory to develop a theoretical framework. Following this discussion, we examine some practical approaches to the activities of day-to-day bank management. Finally, the chapter presents a consolidated balance sheet and income statement for commercial banks and relates them to general institutional and regulatory constraints.

## Basic Risk-Return Trade-offs in Banking

### Measuring Returns (Costs) and Risks on Individual Assets or Liabilities

Typically, most commercial bank assets are loans, securities of the U.S. government and its agencies, and state and local government securities. Bank liabilities consist primarily of demand deposits, various types of time and savings deposits, and borrowings. These assets and liabilities generally require payment of fixed-dollar amounts at maturity, although most can be sold prior to maturity, and some, particularly demand deposits, are payable at the option of the holder.

The yield on a financial instrument of any maturity is the rate of discount (internal rate of return) that equates the discounted value of interest and principal flows to the investor with the current market price of the security. If the interest payments are assumed to occur at the end of the period, then the yield on a debt instrument can be determined by solving the following equation for $r$,

$$M = \frac{C}{1 + r} + \frac{C_2}{(1 + r)^2} + \frac{C_3}{(1 + r)^3}$$
$$+ \cdots + \frac{C_n + B_n}{(1 + r)^n} \quad (4\text{-}1)$$

where $M$ is the current market price of the instrument, $C$ is the amount of interest payments to the investor in period $i$, $B_n$ is the principal payment at maturity, and $r$ is the rate of discount or yield.[3] The rate of discount ($r$) is easily found in bond-yield tables or by using special calculators.

There are several potential weaknesses in this method for measuring the return on debt securities, although it is widely used. First, there may be differences in income tax rates applied to interest (for example, interest payments on state and local government debts are exempt from federal income taxes) or to differences between purchase price and sale or maturity price. Second, if there is any risk of default on interest or principal payments, the rate of discount will be the maximum return and not the expected return. Third, there is an implicit assumption that as cash flows are received they can be reinvested at the rate of discount. Finally, the return calculated from Equation (4-1) is a yield to maturity and may differ from the holding-period yield if the debt security is sold prior to maturity.[4]

Recognizing these weaknesses, bank managers generally use the calculated interest rate of return as a convenient representation of yield.

Just as measuring returns is somewhat complex, so too is measuring risk. Actually, as Chapter 1 mentions, there are four potential sources of risk for debt securities:

1. There is the risk that the investor will be forced to sell a particular security that does not have broad marketability prior to maturity. The price concessions necessary to sell the security may decrease the security's return appreciably. This risk is sometimes called liquidity risk.

2. A second source of risk comes from changes in the general level of interest rates. Changes in the market value of outstanding securities are inversely related to changes in interest rates. For most bonds, the magnitude of such changes will increase with the maturity of the debt instrument. This rate of increase declines as the maturity of the security increases.[5] These changes in security prices, known as *market risk* or *interest rate risk*, are, of course, of greater concern to institutions whose portfolios are continually revalued and/or offered for sale than to institutions that usually hold debt securities to maturity.

3. A third risk is the possibility of the borrower's default on interest and/or principal payments. The possibility of nonpayment, often labeled the *credit risk* or *default risk*, is a relevant consideration for most debt securities. Obligations of the federal government do not have this risk.

4. Finally, there is a *purchasing-power risk* associated with all debt instruments. If dollars received as interest or principal payments will purchase less than the dollars used to purchase the debt instruments, the investor suffers a loss of purchasing power. The investor attempts to overcome this risk by requiring a higher return and/or by having dollar liabilities that are paid in lower-purchasing-power dollars. To the extent that interest rate and price-level changes are positively correlated, it is difficult to separate interest rate and purchasing-power risk. That is, nominal (market)

[3] For more detailed calculations of returns on debt securities—for example, when interest is paid more than once a year—see George H. Hempel, *Investment Management in a Commercial Bank,* Bankers Publishing Company, Boston, 1979.

[4] These potential weaknesses are discussed in greater detail in Sidney Homer and Martin L. Leibowitz, *Inside*

*the Yield Book,* Prentice-Hall, Englewood Cliffs, N.J., 1972.

[5] See Jess Yawitz, George H. Hempel, and William Marshall, "Average Maturity as a Risk Proxy in Investment Decisions," *Journal of Finance* (May 1975), 325–333, for a discussion of the relationship between maturity and price changes on debt instruments.

interest rates normally adjust to changes in the expected rate of inflation.[6]

The costs associated with the liabilities of commercial banks are the opposite of their returns. Instead of receiving inflows, the bank must make agreed-upon payments. Thus, in this case, the rate of discount in Equation (4-1) represents the cost of the liability to the institution throughout the liability's life.

Two primary types of risks are associated with liabilities. First, there is the possibility of inability to repay the debt at maturity. This risk is especially important to banks because they hold such a large proportion of short-term liabilities—including liabilities that are payable on demand. For this reason, most banks hold substantial portions of their assets in liquid form in order to be able to meet deposit outflows. When a bank is unable to meet some of its liabilities at maturity, either from cash inflows or by selling assets, it is usually also on the verge of failure. For this reason, risk of nonpayment is often referred to as solvency risk because it is usually equivalent to the risk of bank failure.[7] The second type of liability risk concerns the relation between the cost of the liability during its life and the cost of refinancing it at maturity. If, for example, the bank might have borrowed at a significantly lower cost some time during the life of the liability, it has suffered an opportunity cost. The reverse is true if rates increase after issuance of the liability. At maturity the bank will be forced to borrow again at the higher prevailing rate of interest.

[6]The formula for converting nominal rates of return ($R_n$) to real rates ($R_r$) is

$$R_r = \frac{1 + R_n}{1 + \dot{q}} - 1$$

where $\dot{q}$ denotes the actual rate of change in the general price level over the holding period. This equation is commonly expressed as

$$R_r \approx R_n - \dot{q}$$

which is a simpler approximation of $R_r$. The relation between expected inflation and interest rates is discussed further in Chapter 22.

[7]Solvency risk is sometimes referred to as liquidity risk because it arises from the inability of the bank to generate sufficient liquidity to meet its obligations on time. Solvency (liquidity) risk on the liability side is closely related to asset-side liquidity risk, which we mentioned earlier.

## Using Portfolio Theory to Analyze Returns and Risks

In a world of certainty, the asset and liability decisions in banking degenerate into simply obtaining the maximum return on assets and paying the minimum cost for liabilities. Without risk, the quantification of available risk-return combinations and the identification of optimal portfolios poses no problem. However, as we have seen, banking involves a number of kinds of risks on the asset side: liquidity risk, market risk, default risk, and purchasing power risk, among others. In addition, there are liability risks as well. Portfolio theory is a theoretical framework for joint analysis of the impact of risk and return on the selection of optimal combinations of assets and liabilities. Because of the impact of risk and return on financial institutions like commercial banks, we now turn to examination of some important conclusions that derive from portfolio analysis.[8]

The assumption of investor risk-aversion serves as the cornerstone for much of portfolio analysis. Risk aversion refers to the notion that, other things (such as returns or rewards) being equal, investors prefer less risk to more risk. This undoubtedly reflects the views of most investors.[9]

From the assumption that investors are averse to risk, we are able to develop a portfolio model that reflects the trade-off between expected return (or, where liabilities are concerned, the cost) and risk. Both the asset- and liability-acquisition decisions involve a two-step process. On the asset side, the manager must first ascertain the set of portfolios offering the highest possible return for each level of risk. Then the manager must choose the most desirable from among those portfolios. Similarly, proper liability management requires the manager first to generate those combinations requiring the least cost commitment for the level of risk and then to choose the wealth-maximizing solution. The complete portfolio decision takes proper account of the trade-off between net return (return minus

[8]For a further elaboration and analysis of portfolio theory, see Chapter 24.

[9]While any number of individual utility functions are consistent with risk aversion, they share the common quality of being concave with respect to wealth. That is, while wealth and utility are positively related, a given increase in wealth has a smaller effect on utility, the greater the initial level of wealth.

cost) and overall risk, where risk encompasses the uncertainty associated with both sides of the balance sheet.

The potential benefits from portfolio analysis can be demonstrated quite well intuitively by examining the risk-return behavior of a portfolio composed of two assets or two liabilities. The key feature is the relationship between the benefits of risk pooling that accompany diversification and the correlation between returns. Let us now examine this relationship using the example of a portfolio of two assets.[10]

*Risk-pooling* occurs in a portfolio of assets or liabilities whenever the overall risk of the portfolio is less than the weighted average of the risk from each of the individual components. If the rates of return on the two assets in question (or the cost of the two liabilities) are negatively correlated (inversely related) over time, risk-pooling benefits will be considerable when the assets or liabilities are combined in a portfolio. As an illustration, consider a portfolio composed of equity positions in a procyclical steel mill and in a countercyclical residential construction company. In an expanding economy with high interest rates, the return from the steel mill will be above average, thereby compensating for the below-average return from the construction firm. The situation is reversed in a sluggish economy. In this case, the above-average return from the construction firm would compensate for the below-average return from the steel mill. In effect, diversifying, or holding assets with negatively correlated returns, over time, results in reduced variability or riskiness in the two-asset portfolio compared to either one-asset portfolio. This benefit would not be present if returns on the assets were positively correlated. Where returns are positively correlated, variations in return would generally be in the same direction over the business cycle, and risk-pooling benefits would be restricted.

A portfolio is deemed *efficient* if, for a given expected return, it has the lowest possible exposure to risk; or for a given risk level it has the highest expected return. The first problem, then, is to determine the set of portfolios that satisfy this criterion. Two models have been developed to select efficient portfolios of risky assets: the Markowitz

model and the Sharpe model.[11] While the portfolios selected by the two models are similar, the data and computational requirements vary considerably.

The Markowitz model was the first model to be developed for obtaining efficient portfolios of risky assets. The locus (set) of all such portfolios comprises what is referred to as the efficient frontier. The Markowitz procedure uses quadratic programming to determine this efficient frontier.

Sharpe developed a portfolio-selection model that considerably reduces both the computational and data requirements of the Markowitz model. In spite of this simplification, the Sharpe model has performed well in comparative tests on identical sets of data. The Sharpe model is based on the premise that security price changes can be attributed to two phenomena: (1) factors related to general business conditions in the economy, and (2) factors affecting either one firm or only a small number of firms. Price changes resulting from general economic activity give rise to *systematic risk*. Such price movements are assumed to be perfectly correlated among all assets. On the other hand, price changes that result from factors specific to the firm are uncorrelated (independent) among all assets. Such *nonsystematic risk* commands no premium in the capital markets since it can be eliminated by diversification.

In a version of the Sharpe model known as the Sharpe-Lintner-Mossin Capital Asset Pricing Model (CAPM),[12] an asset's return is related to a single index of economic activity. Candidates for this index include: national income, the Dow-Jones Index, and a composite of all stock returns. While the CAPM has been shown to provide a reasonable explanation for the structure of historical rates of return in the equity market,[13] its application to practical decisions of commercial banks has been

[10]The example is developed more fully with the use of mathematics in one of the appendices to this chapter.

[11]A computational procedure for determining the efficient set of portfolios was first reported by Harry Markowitz in "Portfolio Selection," *Journal of Finance* (March 1952), 77–91. Sharpe's model is described in William F. Sharpe, *Portfolio Theory and Capital Markets,* McGraw-Hill Book Company, New York, 1970.

[12]For an evaluation of the CAPM, see Michael C. Jensen, "Capital Markets: Theory and Evidence," *Bell Journal* (Autumn 1972), 357–398.

[13]As an example, see E. Fama and J. MacBeth, "Risk, Return, and Equilibrium: Empirical Tests," *Journal of Political Economy* (May–June 1973), 607–635; and M. Miller and M. Scholes, "Rates of Return in Relation to

limited. This lack of application can be explained in part by the difficulty of obtaining the required return data for assets and liabilities that are not traded in efficient capital markets. Furthermore, most commercial banks operate in an environment that places on their activities constraints not found in the assumptions of the CAPM. Such constraints may take the form of legal limits on asset and liability composition as well as a general cash-flow constraint. For these reasons, one hesitates to suggest that optimal management policies require commercial banks simply to apply the Sharpe model appropriately in order to maximize valuation.

Recognizing the limitations of the model, however, it is still possible to think in general terms of the commercial bank as a portfolio of assets, liabilities, and capital, to which portfolio principles apply. The important conclusions are that diversification can reduce or eliminate unsystematic risk and that the remaining (systematic) risk will be directly correlated with return. The result for financial institutions like banks is that trade-offs between risk and return must be evaluated by the institution's managers in conjunction with any regulatory constraints.

## Developing a Model to Manage Risk-Return Trade-offs

### The Wealth-Maximization Criterion

Now that we have examined some principles of portfolio choice in a general way, we need to develop a model for managing risk-return trade-offs in banking. The first step is to establish an objective for bank management. As with other businesses, the primary goal for bank managers that is consistent with optimal allocation of resources in a market economy is maximization of the owners' wealth. Wealth maximization denotes maximizing the benefits (whether cash payments or increases in the value of holdings) to the residual contributors of funds—the common stockholders. Contributors with prior claims are paid contractually promised sums; however, shareholders gain from higher actual or potential residual cash benefits. The max-

imization of these benefits is consistent with the efficient allocation of scarce financial resources.[14]

Now we can state the wealth-maximization criterion in an objective manner. Wealth maximization is the maximization of the discounted net cash benefits to shareholders. This condition can be expressed algebraically as:

$$W = \frac{B_1}{(1 + r)^1} + \frac{B_2}{(1 + r)^2} + \frac{B_3}{(1 + r)^3}$$
$$+ \cdots + \frac{B_n}{(1 + r)^n} \quad (4\text{-}2)$$

where $W$ is the wealth position of the firm's shareholders, $B$ denotes the net cash benefits to the shareholders in periods 1, 2, 3, . . . and $n$; and $r$ is the appropriate rate of discount which reflects both the timing and the risk associated with the net cash receipts.[15]

The key variables comprising $B$ and $r$ are shown in the following equations:

$$B = R - (C + O + T) \quad (4\text{-}3)$$
$$r = i + p \quad (4\text{-}4)$$

In Equation (4-3), $R$ denotes the gross receipts from the commercial bank's assets ($A$), $C$ represents the costs of its financial liabilities ($L$), $O$ is the overhead costs associated with $R$ and $C$, and $T$ is the taxes the bank must pay. Depreciation and other noncash costs are generally a relatively small percentage of $O$, so net cash benefits and net income are reasonably similar for most financial institutions. In Equation (4-4), $i$ is an estimated riskless interest rate that reflects the time value of money, and $p$ is the appropriate risk premium associated with the assets ($A$) and liabilities ($L$) of the institution. Substituting Equations (4-3) and (4-4) into Equation (4-2), we obtain:

[14]While not wishing to deemphasize the social responsibilities of firms, the quantification of social costs and benefits does require one to employ the opinions of individuals rather than relying on market forces for the efficient allocation of resources. By providing needed financial services in a wealth-maximizing manner, a commercial bank generally performs a needed economic function and tends to carry out its social and other obligations over a span of time, provided these obligations are brought to bear on management's decisions.

[15]The model is more fully developed in George H. Hempel and Jess Yawitz, *Financial Management of Financial Institutions*, Prentice-Hall, Englewood Cliffs, N.J., 1977.

Risk: A Re-Examination of Some Recent Findings,'' in *Studies in the Theory of Capital Markets*, ed. M. Jensen, Frederick A. Praeger, New York, 1972, pp. 47–78.

$$W = \frac{R_1 - (C_1 + O_1 + T_1)}{1 + (i + p)} + \frac{R_2 - (C_2 + O_2 + T_2)}{[1 + (i + p)]^2}$$

$$+ \cdots + \frac{R_n - (C_n + O_n + T_n)}{[1 + (i + p)]^n} \quad (4\text{-}5)$$

The interdependent nature of these variables should be evident. $R$ represents the flow of benefits from the stock of asset $A$, and $C$ represents the flow of negative benefits (costs) from the stock of liabilities $L$, which the bank uses to obtain funds. $O$, which has both fixed and variable components, will depend at least partially on the nature of the asset and liability positions, and $T$ can be taken to be a variable cost that is a function of $R - (C + O)$. While the riskless rate $(i)$ is beyond the control of the bank, it will tend to be strongly correlated with both $R$ and $C$. Finally, $p$ is a function of the interaction of the systematic risks associated with the diversified portfolios of assets and liabilities. Conceptually, it is useful to think of the required return $(i + p)$ as determined by the market's perception of the riskiness of the bank's asset, liability, and capital composition.

Equation (4-5) illustrates an important consideration for management, namely that in order to make prudent management decisions, the manager of a bank must consider the combined effect of *all* variables relevant for wealth maximization. For example, if management considers purchasing liabilities at 8 percent and investing the proceeds in assets earning 10 percent, it must also take account of changes in $O$, $T$, and $p$ from the transaction. It may well be that, in spite of the positive spread between $R$ and $C$, the total effect, including increases in overhead, taxes, or risks, may actually reduce the wealth of the bank's owners.

Using a numerical example for a hypothetical bank shows the necessity of taking all variables into account. For simplicity, assume constant average returns and constant costs over the perpetual life of the bank.[16] Equations (4-2) and (4-5) can then be restated as follows:

$$W = \frac{B}{r} \quad (4\text{-}2a)$$

[16]With constant returns and costs a series of

$$\frac{B_1}{(1 + r)^1} + \frac{B_2}{(1 + r)^2} + \frac{B_3}{(1 + r)^3} + \frac{B_4}{(1 + r)^4}$$

$$+ \cdots + \frac{B_n}{(1 + r)^n} = \frac{B}{r}$$

$$W = \frac{R = (C + O + T)}{(i + p)} \quad (4\text{-}5a)$$

Assume that the hypothetical bank, Second National Bank, has $200 million in assets allocated among: required reserves $(A_0)$, which are determined by the Federal Reserve and earn a zero return;[17] short-term securities $(A_1)$, which offer a relatively low risk and a low return; longer-term securities $(A_2)$, which have higher returns and risks than $A_1$; and loans $(A_3)$, which offer the highest return and highest risk of all the bank's assets. These assets are financed by $184 million in deposits and other liabilities (composed of lower-cost, high risk $D_1$ and higher-cost, low-risk $D_2$) and $16 million in capital. The returns and costs on these assets and liabilities, the assumed overhead and income tax rate, and the capitalization rates applied to various risky income streams appear in Table 4-2. Given the available alternatives, the question is what are the optimal asset and liability allocation decisions of Second National Bank.

Six possible situations are presented in Table 4-3. In the first case, it is assumed that Second National Bank obtained $104 million of $D_1$ and $80 million of $D_2$ and had $16 million of capital. Second National Bank had $19.0 million in $A_0$ ($18.7 million were required revenues and $.3 million were held in correspondent balances with other banks). The bank lent $121 million $(A_3)$ and chose to invest $40 million in short-term securities $(A_1)$ and $20 million in longer-term securities $(A_2)$. These asset, liability, and capital decisions produced net benefits, after overhead and taxes, of $2,262,000. When benefits are capitalized at a 14 percent rate, the wealth of the bank's owners is $16.2 million. The capitalization rate reflects the combined risk of the bank's portfolios of assets and liabilities.

In Cases 2 and 3, it is assumed that the bank's funds sources (deposits, other liabilities, and other capital) are as in Case 1, while the bank has chosen to emphasize higher earnings in Case 2 and lower risk in Case 3, in its asset allocation decisions. In

[17]A bill in Congress, which would have allowed some payment of interest on reserves, came close to passage in 1978 and may pass in the future. As long as the return on required reserves is less than the return on earning assets, such as securities or loans, no fundamental changes are needed in the analysis that follows, although some minor changes in the calculations would be necessary.

## Table 4-2  Assumptions About Second National Bank

Balance-Sheet Totals
Assets        $200,000,000

Deposits and other liabilities        $184,000,000
Capital                                  16,000,000

Available asset returns
$A_1$ (short-term securities) = 8%
$A_2$ (long-term securities) = 9%
$A_3$ (loans) = 11%

Costs of acquiring funds, overhead, and taxes
$D_1$ (low-cost deposits) = 6%
$D_2$ (higher-cost deposits) = 8%
$O$ (overhead per period) = $1,900,000
$t$ (income tax rate)
$T = t[R - (C + O)]$

Reserve requirements ($A_0$ earns 0%)
$A_0$ (for $D_1$) = 14%
$A_0$ (for $D_2$) = 5%

Capitalization rates
$i$ (riskless rate) = 10%
$P_1$ (low-risk premium) = 2%
$P_2$ (medium-risk premium) = 4%
$P_3$ (high-risk premium) = 6%

Case 2, Second National Bank had a lower proportion in short-term securities ($A_1$), and a higher proportion in loans ($A_2$). The results, as expected, are a higher net after-tax benefit of $2,622,000 and a higher capitalization rate, assumed to be 16 percent. The total effect is a slight improvement in the owners' wealth position to nearly $16.4 million. In Case 3, it is assumed that Second National's desire for lower risk resulted in an increase in its holdings of short-term securities ($A_1$) and a decrease in loans ($A_3$). The lower level of net benefits, $1,902,000, capitalized at the appropriately lower risk rate of 12 percent implies an owners' wealth position of approximately $15.9 million.

The mixture of deposits, other liabilities, and capital are allowed to vary in Cases 4, 5, and 6. In Case 4 it is assumed that Second National Bank obtained $80 million in $D_1$ and $104 million in $D_2$ and that its capital remained at $16 million. Under the assumptions presented in Table 4-2, these sources constitute a higher-cost, lower-risk liability structure than the sources for Cases 1, 2, and 3. After meeting its required reserves of $16 million, the bank chose an aggressive asset structure of $141 million in loans, $23 million in short-term securities, and $20 million in long-term securities in Case 4. The bank's owners have a wealth position

## Table 4-3  Alternative Decisions by Second National Bank (in thousands of dollars)

|  | Case 1 | Case 2 | Case 3 | Case 4 | Case 5 | Case 6 |
|---|---|---|---|---|---|---|
| **Balance sheet** | | | | | | |
| $A_0$ | $ 19,000 | $ 19,000 | $ 19,000 | $ 16,000 | $ 19,000 | $ 19,000 |
| $A_1$ | 40,000 | 20,000 | 60,000 | 23,000 | 20,000 | 60,000 |
| $A_2$ | 20,000 | 20,000 | 20,000 | 20,000 | 20,000 | 20,000 |
| $A_3$ | 121,000 | 141,000 | 101,000 | 141,000 | 143,000 | 101,000 |
| $D_1$ | $104,000 | $104,000 | $104,000 | $ 80,000 | $104,000 | $104,000 |
| $D_2$ | 80,000 | 80,000 | 80,000 | 140,000 | 80,000 | 82,000 |
| $E$ | 16,000 | 16,000 | 16,000 | 16,000 | 18,000 | 14,000 |
| **Returns and costs** | | | | | | |
| $R$ | $ 18,310 | $ 18,910 | $ 17,710 | $ 19,150 | $ 18,910 | $ 17,710 |
| $C$ | 12,640 | 12,640 | 12,640 | 13,120 | 12,640 | 12,800 |
| $O$ | 1,900 | 1,900 | 1,900 | 1,900 | 1,900 | 1,900 |
| $I$ | 1,508 | 1,748 | 1,268 | 1,652 | 1,748 | 1,204 |
| $B$ | 2,262 | 2,622 | 1,902 | 2,478 | 2,628 | 1,806 |
| **Capitalization rates and wealth** | | | | | | |
| $i$ | 10% | 10% | 10% | 10% | 10% | 10% |
| $p$ | 4% | 6% | 2% | 4% | 6% | 2% |
| $i + p$ | 14% | 16% | 12% | 14% | 16% | 12% |
| $W$ | $ 16,157 | $ 16,388 | $ 15,850 | $ 17,700 | $ 16,425 | $ 15,050 |
| $W - E$ | $    157 | $    388 | $   (150) | $  1,700 | $    425 | $  1,050 |

of $17.7 million, assuming that the net benefits of $2,478,000 are capitalized at a 14 percent (medium-risk) rate.

Cases 5 and 6 illustrate an additional dimension of Second National Bank's management trade-offs. In Case 5, it is assumed that Second National chose to seek high returns on assets aggressively (as in Case 2) but that its regulatory authorities forced the bank to raise $2 million of additional capital. If the additional $2 million were then loaned out and the bank's other assets and liabilities were the same as in Case 2, the bank's net benefits would be $2,628,000 and its capitalized value would be $16,425,000. In Case 6, it is assumed that Second National chose the low-risk, lower-return approach (like Case 3), but because of this lower risk, the regulatory authorities required the bank to have only $14 million of capital rather than $16 million. Assuming the bank had $2 million more in $D_2$ and its other assets and liabilities were the same as in Case 3, the bank's net benefits would be $1,806,000 and its capitalized value would be $15.1 million on a capital investment of $14 million.

While we could present many other situations for even the relatively simple asset and liability decisions facing the Second National Bank (for example, other risk-return possibilities and combinations of assets and liabilities could be considered; overhead or taxes could be varied with side effects on asset and liability combinations; a different capital position could affect both net benefits and risks, and so on), three basic points seem evident. First, changes in any one variable will typically affect nearly all other variables. Second, since risk affects the capitalization rate, one must consider the interactive effect on risk of decisions regarding the portfolio of assets, liabilities, and capital. Finally, while the effect on the net wealth of the common shareholders is the primary consideration in bank-management decisions, further elaboration of the specific decision-making criteria is needed in order for bank management to decide on its objective.

The overall decision-making criterion should be to maximize the net wealth of the owners, which is the wealth of the owners less their investment in the bank ($E$). Thus, among the cases considered in Table 4-3, Case 4 would be the optimal choice. Case 6 is preferable to Case 5 if the regulatory authorities have varying capital requirements. A possible exception to this criterion would be the

situation in which the owners' investments were markedly different. For example, would $W$ of $14.5 million and $E$ of $14 million be preferable to $W$ of $20.6 million and $E$ of $20 million? In unusual situations where this disparity exists, the ratio of $W$ to $C$ is the appropriate decision criterion. (In the situation described above, 1.04 of the first example would be preferable to 1.03 for the second example.) When the assumption of similar size is relaxed, nearly all decisions relating to management policies causing changes in asset, liability, and capital should employ maximization of net wealth of the owners ($W - E$) as the ultimate objective.

### Management Decision Making

Although, as we have seen, the criterion for every decision should be its effect on the shareholders' net wealth, practical decision making requires emphasis on selected variables for day-to-day management actions. Commercial banks can group the key variables affecting their wealth-maximization objective into four interrelated categories: spread management, control of overhead, liquidity management, and capital management.

*Spread management* focuses on the difference or spread between the return on assets ($R$) and the cost of liabilities ($C$) over time. Although a high positive spread is generally desirable, two limitations need to be stressed. First, spread management should seek a high positive spread *over time*. A bank using short-term liabilities as a source of funds may not want to buy long-term assets, even if they provide a highly favorable spread, because of the possible adverse movements in the spread over time. Similarly, a bank may purchase long-term assets rather than higher-yield, short-term assets because of the possibility that the latter may yield a low or negative spread later in the life of the liability. Recent efforts to maintain the spread over time has involved the increased use by banks of variable-return assets (such as floating-rate loans) and variable-cost liabilities. Second, spread management cannot ignore the effect of $R$ and $C$ on overhead ($O$) and risk ($p$). For example, additional overhead and risk may negate the appreciably higher gross spread when banks make consumer instalment loans.

Table 4-4 illustrates the first point, using rates and cost data for each of the two types of assets

## Table 4-4 Rate and Cost Data for Second National Bank

Available asset returns
$A_1$ = 7%; a callable business loan at prime plus ½%
$A_2$ = 9%; a five-year instalment credit loan

Costs of acquiring funds
$D_1$ = 6%; a time-deposit account at approximately ½% under prime.
$D_2$ = 8%; a five-year maturity certificate of deposit

and liabilities available to Second National Bank. If the bank pursues a policy of maximizing current spread, the asset and liability choices are obvious—obtain funds from time deposits at 6 percent and allocate these funds to five-year instalment loans. The gross operating spread from the bank's portfolio would be a healthy 3 percent. Unfortunately, such a policy of borrowing short to lend long, in an environment with an upward-sloping yield curve,[18] almost insures that the spread will deteriorate in the future. To demonstrate this point, assume that, after two years of anticipation of higher rates, rates rise appreciably in the money market. Specifically, the rates on the financial instruments listed in Table 4-4 have increased by a full 3 percentage points. Since the bank originally elected to borrow at the short-term rate, it must now pay 9 percent on time deposits to remain competitive with alternative financial instruments (Treasury bills, savings accounts, and the like) and, thereby, avoid a runoff in its deposit base. The return on the asset portfolio that seemed to be quite profitable two years earlier is now equal to the cost of obtaining funds, that is, the gross spread is now zero. The lesson to be learned from this example is obvious. By "locking-in" the 9 percent rate on assets two years earlier, Second National Bank created a situation in which its spread is highly sensitive to changes in the interest rate. The strategy of maximizing the current spread had serious implications for the future profitability of the bank.

As an alternative, suppose Second National had elected to finance the 9 percent instalment loans by issuing 7 percent CDs[19] with the same maturity. Regardless of the movements in rates over the five-year period, the bank has guaranteed itself a stable 2 percent spread since it will not be forced to pay a higher rate on its liabilities.

Second National could have also pursued a policy of financing short-term assets with short-term liabilities and been fairly certain of the stability of its spread over time. Such a policy would have generated a 2 percent spread with the original array of rates—8 percent and 6 percent. After two years, the 3 percent increase in all rates would have again resulted in a 2 percent spread.

*Control of overhead costs* is a second major area for consideration in bank management. Many statements on control of overhead costs by some security analysts are probably oversimplifications. They include remarks like, "Whenever I see excavation work start on a new building by a bank, I sell their stock short." Nevertheless, two of the major causes of financial stress for a bank are large fixed-overhead costs in periods of stress and the high overhead costs that might accompany apparently high-profit opportunities. A bank can meet the first problem by examining the impact of any increase in overhead costs on net cash flows at varying levels of activity, not just for the most optimistic projections. To meet the second problem, rational spread-management decisions cannot and must not ignore the effect on overhead costs.

*Liquidity management* involves the structuring of the interactive portfolios of assets ($A$) and liabilities ($L$) so that funds are available to meet the cash flow demands of both existing and potential deposit and loan customers. Liquidity management should be applied so as to maximize the spread ($R - C$) at a risk level the commercial bank is willing to accept. At an elementary level, liquidity management may emphasize matching the maturity structure of an institution's assets and liabilities.[20] Liquidity management is, however, usually more complex. Factors such as expected fund inflows, access to purchased liabilities, credit risks on assets, and purchasing-power risks must be consid-

---

[18] A yield curve has yield to maturity on the vertical axis and maturity on this security on the horizontal axis. An upward-sloping yield curve would indicate higher yields on long-term securities than on short-term securities. Chapter 23 describes yield curves in detail.

[19] Certificates of deposits (CDs) are time deposits with specified maturity dates. Withdrawal earlier than the date specified lowers the rate of interest paid on the CD.

[20] The term *matching maturity structure* is used to denote a matching of the time profile of cash flows on assets and liabilities.

ered. For example, a commercial bank that expects its annual cash inflows to exceed matured liabilities over the next several years may structure its portfolio so that the maturities of its assets exceed the maturities of its liabilities in order to attain a higher spread without placing excessive pressure on its liquidity position. Some commercial banks can legitimately use liability management (the purchase of funds rather than the liquidation of assets to meet liquidity needs) if they can purchase the acquired funds at a positive spread in periods of credit ease and tightness. Firms with lower liquidity pressures may take somewhat greater credit risks in their asset portfolios because they will not be under pressure to sell these assets.

*Capital management* is the final major category of bank-management decisions. A bank's capital position is based on the residual from assets minus liabilities. If capital is too high, the return per dollar of capital may be low and shareholders may not receive sufficient benefits (dividends, appreciation on common stock, higher interest on savings shares, lower insurance costs, and the like). If capital is too low, higher risk may offset the higher return per dollar of capital. Growth of assets and liabilities may also be constrained by the lack of capital to support that growth.

These categories of bank-management decisions are often brought together in mathematical programming models, which are mathematical formulations for analyzing problems that can be expressed as goals with constraints. Though more elaborate techniques are justified in modeling particular tasks performed by bank management, the relatively simple linear programming seems sufficiently powerful for representing the overall management of a bank and is attractive in its computational ease.[21]

## Managing the Interest-Sensitivity Gap as a Technique for Wealth Maximization

Another technique for maximizing the bank owner's wealth is managing the interest-sensitivity gap between assets and liabilities. While this technique is only part of a complete wealth-maximization model, it emphasizes the dynamic changes that may occur in interest rates. Increasingly, banks have sought to hedge and improve interest margins by acting on their expectations regarding credit cycle and interest rates. Evidence of this behavior during periods of rising market interest rates includes the increase in the percentage of bank loans made with interest rates indexed to the prime rate[22] as well as the lengthening of maturities on CD liabilities sold.

Interest margins ought to benefit from such behavior. Gross interest revenues should rise automatically as loan yield rates are indexed with rises in the prime rate. On the other hand, gross interest expense should tend to stabilize at relatively low levels as cost rates remain fixed on long-maturity CDs contracted in the early stages of the rise in market rates.[23] In an environment of rising market rates, therefore, a bank's interest margin might benefit in proportion to its position in market-rate-sensitive assets (such as floating-rate loans) and its position in market-rate-insensitive sources of funds. Conversely, in an environment of falling rates, interest margins will deteriorate in proportion to such positions. Recent analyses set forth the concept of a *funds gap* or "*net* position in market rate assets," defined as the difference between rate-sensitive-assets and rate-sensitive-sources of funds. This difference represents the amount of rate-sensitive-assets financed by rate-*in*sensitive-sources of funds. In theory, this amount should be increased when market rates are expected to rise and reduced when rates are expected to fall. Recent empirical analyses find that banks' behavior is consistent with this theory.[24] The funds-gap concept is illustrated in Table 4-5, where an individual

[21] For further discussion of linear programming models in banking, see Kalman J. Cohen and Stephen E. Gibson, eds., *Management Science in Banking,* Warren, Gorham & Lamont, Boston, 1978.

[22] The prime rate is the short-term interest rate that banks charge their best customers. It is usually set by large, money-market banks, which look at competitive rates on short-maturity financial instruments. For further discussion, see Murray E. Polakoff and Morris Budin, *The Prime Rate,* Association of Reserve City Bankers, Chicago, 1973.

[23] This assumes that buyers of such CDs form conservative expectations for future rates; that is, *ex post,* rates so contracted prove to be less than the average of subsequent, realized short-term rates.

[24] For a more complete discussion plus simulated and actual examples of "gap" management, see Donald Simonson, Ronald Olson, Stanley Reber, and George H. Hempel, "Bank Interest Rate Fluctuations and the Credit

**Table 4-5  Illustration of the Funds Gap Concept**

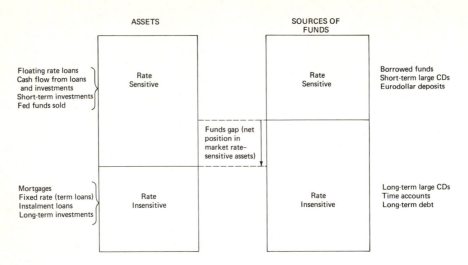

bank's assets and sources of funds are classified according to rate sensitivity.

## Consolidated Balance Sheet of All Insured Commercial Banks

So far we have discussed the general principles and techniques that can be used in attracting and allocating various sources and uses of bank funds in order to attain the objective of maximizing stockholders' wealth in a world replete with uncertainty and risk. We shall now discuss the specific types of assets and liabilities held by the banking system and their relative importance in banks' portfolios. The data on which the discussion is based are to be found in Table 4-6, which is a consolidated balance sheet of all insured commercial banks as of September 30, 1978. In analyzing the balance sheet as well as the income statement that follows, we must keep in mind that, in addition to risk, institutional factors arising from the liquidity requirements of demand-deposit banking and from various federal and state regulations act as side constraints on portfolio allocations and wealth maximization. As already indicated, our purpose here is to ex-

amine these impacts in some detail by carefully reviewing banks' sources and uses of funds.

The major institutional constraint for banks arises from the role of commercial banks as the primary source of highly liquid deposits. Checking deposits are payable on customer demand, and much of time and savings deposits are effectively payable on demand as well. This institutional characteristic of commercial banking permeates and constrains all major asset decisions by management. It means, for example, that management decisions must reflect anticipated and unanticipated deposit withdrawals as well as profitability considerations.

Traditionally, banks have ensured their ability to meet liquidity needs by holding adequate quantities of specific types of liquid assets, an approach known as *asset allocation*. This approach dominated bank-management practice for many years, until at least the mid-1960s, and it is still influential today, especially in smaller banks. It suggests that bank funds comprise a "pool" from which asset allocations are made based on, first, liquidity needs and requirements and, second, profitability objectives. The priorities for uses of funds from the pool are (1) liquidity-reserve assets, (2) loans, and (3) investments for income.

Liquidity reserves consist of primary reserves (nonearning cash assets held to satisfy legal re-

————
Cycle,'' working paper at Southern Methodist University, Dallas, 1979.

**Table 4-6  Commercial Bank Assets and Liabilities, All Insured Commercial Banks, 1978 (in millions of dollars)**

| | Sept. 30, 1978 | Percentage of Total |
|---|---|---|
| **Assets** | | |
| Cash and bank balances | $ 158.3 | 13.2% |
| Currency and coin | 12.1 | 1.0 |
| Reserves with Federal Reserve banks | 28.0 | 2.3 |
| Deposits at other banks | 49.0 | 4.1 |
| Cash items in process of collection | 69.2 | 5.8 |
| Securities | 262.3 | 21.9 |
| U.S. Treasury | 95.1 | 7.9 |
| U.S. government agencies | 40.1 | 3.3 |
| State and local | 121.3 | 10.1 |
| Other securities | 5.8 | 0.5 |
| Loans | 692.8 | 57.8 |
| Federal Funds sold and securities purchased under resale agreements | 41.3 | 3.4 |
| Other loans, net | 651.5 | 54.4 |
| Other assets | 85.1 | 7.1 |
| Total assets | $1,198.5 | 100.0% |
| **Liabilities and capital** | | |
| Deposit liabilities | $ 960.9 | 80.2% |
| Demand deposits | 369.0 | 30.8 |
| Savings deposits | 223.3 | 18.6 |
| Time deposits | 368.6 | 30.8 |
| Nondeposit liabilities | 146.3 | 12.2 |
| Federal Funds purchased and securities sold under repurchase agreements | 92.0 | 7.7 |
| Other liabilities | 54.3 | 4.5 |
| Capital accounts | 91.3 | 7.6 |
| Subordinated notes and debentures | 5.8 | 0.5 |
| Preferred stock | 0.1 | 0.01 |
| Common stock and surplus | 50.2 | 4.2 |
| Undivided profits | 33.5 | 2.8 |
| Other reserves | 1.7 | 0.1 |
| Total liabilities and capital | $1,198.5 | 100.0% |

Source: Adapted from *Federal Reserve Bulletin* (November 1979).

quirements) and secondary reserves (highly liquid earning assets held to meet anticipated or unanticipated deposit withdrawals and loan requests). Because these needs often are not immediate, these funds can be invested in earning assets with the following characteristics: (1) short maturity (to minimize interest rate or market risk); (2) highest credit quality (to minimize default or credit risk); (3) high degree of marketability (to minimize liquidity risk). Securities that meet these characteristics include open-market commercial paper, bankers' acceptances, short-term (or near-term) U.S. government securities, and selected municipal securities. Each of these kinds of securities, which are described more fully later in this chapter and in Chapter 20, offers a compromise between risk and yield.

Beginning in the early 1960s the emphasis on asset sources of liquidity has been supplemented by the development of *liability management*. Using this concept, banks utilize the liability side of the balance sheet to obtain supplemental liquidity. The basic idea underlying liability management is the purchase of funds (liabilities) in the money market to meet loan demand and other liquidity needs. The sources of funds include (1) sale of negotiable CDs, (2) borrowings in the Federal Funds market, (3) Eurodollar borrowings, and (4) sale of commercial paper by bank holding companies and their nonbank affiliates.

A second major constraint in banking is the relatively small capital position of commercial banks. A relatively small capital ratio is necessitated by the need to earn an adequate return on stockholder equity with a narrow spread between asset returns and liability costs. With a small capital base, a small loss on assets from credit risk, defalcation, or theft has a magnified impact on capital. If capital is 8 percent of total assets, a 1 percent loss in assets results in a 12 percent loss in capital. In this sense, capital protects depositors by providing ultimate protection against insolvency. In a broader sense, however, the primary role of capital is to provide the confidence that the bank can remain viable while repaying any losses from future earnings. Because of their relatively small capital ratios, bank asset portfolios must maintain relatively low levels of liquidity, market, and credit risk.

In addition to these fundamental constraints, banks have also long been subjected to a variety of state and federal laws and regulations. In recent years, four forms of controls have tended to exert the strongest impact on bank management.[25] These controls may be summarized as follows:

1. Certain proportions of "transaction" accounts (including demand deposits), nonpersonal time deposits, and selected other liabilities cannot be invested in earning assets but must be held in the form of reserves. Within statutory limits, the Federal Reserve determines the reserve ratio percentage required for the various deposit forms and permits member banks to hold these reserves in vault cash or on deposit in their district's Federal Reserve bank. Following implementation of the Monetary Control Act of 1980, nonmember banks and other institutions required to hold reserves (that is, any institutions offering either transaction accounts or nonpersonal time deposits) can hold their reserves either at their district's Federal Reserve Bank (or other federal regulatory agency) or at a member bank in pass-through form. The original purpose of these required reserves was to ensure a maximum level of bank liquidity. Now, the reserve ratio requirement helps the Federal Reserve to control the money supply.[26]

2. The capital position of a bank is closely supervised by bank regulatory authorities. Future expansion of banking assets and deposits can be severely constrained by regulators' demands to raise more capital following a period in which asset and deposit growth exceeded the growth in capital from retained earnings. Many economists believe that this capital constraint may severely limit banking growth in the coming decade.[27]

3. Both regulatory authorities and bank management carefully monitor a bank's liquidity position, that is, its ability to satisfy the need for funds to meet loan demands or deposit withdrawals. Such liquidity needs have traditionally been met by unpledged short-term securities and cash. In recent years, regulatory authorities have recognized that the purchase of liabilities is another liquidity source for many larger banks. Nevertheless, most banks' decisions regarding the allocation of assets are affected by management and regulatory desires to maintain adequate liquidity.

4. The Federal Reserve has in the past employed Regulation Q to restrict the interest rates banks are able to pay for some categories of deposits. In periods of generally high interest rates, this constraint has restricted the banks' ability to compete with other financial institutions and with some primary security instruments. As long as Regulation Q remains in effect, banks must take its impact into account before reaching financial management decisions.

The major asset, liability, and capital items of all commercial banks are shown in Table 4-6. These balance sheet items reflect the interaction of managerial decisions in a world of uncertainty, as well as reflecting decisions which are limited by institutional and regulatory constraints. The relative overall impact of these constraints (in contrast to the behavior of unfettered bank management) might be summarized as follows: (1) a higher proportion of liquid assets; (2) a more conservative asset portfolio; (3) a shorter asset-maturity structure; (4) a lower overall interest cost of deposit liabilities; (5) a larger capital ratio; and (6) a slower asset growth (limited by capital adequacy constraint).

Table 4-6 shows that in 1978 over 80 percent of bank sources of funds (liabilities and capital) were in the form of *deposits*. These funds include the deposits of individuals, nonprofit organizations, corporations and other business organizations, foreign and domestic governmental units and official institutions, and foreign and domestic commercial banks and other financial intermediaries. Of these total deposits, approximately 40 percent were demand deposits and 60 percent were time and savings deposits.

*Demand deposits* are depositor checking-account balances. These balances are payable upon demand—that is, the funds in the account may be withdrawn in cash or transferred by draft (typically, check) to other parties without prior notice to the bank holding the deposits. Approximtely 75 percent of total demand-deposit balances are owned by individuals, partnerships, and corporations. In our market economy, these deposits, of course, play a major role as money, thereby facilitating exchange through the efficient transfer of financial resources.

[25] For a detailed discussion of banking structure and regulation, see Chapter 31.

[26] Reserve ratios and the money supply are discussed further in the following chapter.

[27] See George H. Hempel, *Bank Capital: Determining and Meeting Your Bank's Capital Needs,* Bankers Publishing Co., Boston, 1977, for a discussion of the bank capital issue.

*Savings deposits,* often known as regular savings accounts, are interest-bearing accounts that represented approximately 40 percent of total time and savings deposits in 1978. (Savings deposits are often classified as a type of time deposit.) Savings deposits have no specified maturity, but depositors can be required to give written notice of intent to withdraw funds. In practice, however, savings deposits are payable on demand by presentation of a savings passbook or other acceptable evidence of ownership (account number, for example). Over 90 percent of savings deposit balances are owned by individuals and nonprofit organizations, especially the former. Significant amounts are also owned by corporations and other business organizations and by the U.S. government. According to federal legislation enacted in 1980, interest rate ceilings on deposits are to be phased out over six years. In the past, the Federal Reserve, through its Regulation Q, set the maximum interest rate that member banks could pay on savings deposits, and the Federal Deposit Insurance Corporation set the maximum rates for insured, nonmember banks.[28]

Time deposits are generally classified as either time certificates of deposit or time deposits, open account. *Time certificates of deposit* (CDs) specify on their face (certificate) the amount of deposit. The deposit is payable to bearer or to the order of the depositor on a specific date no less than thirty days after deposit, date of the instrument, or required written notice of withdrawal. *Time deposits, open account,* are similar to CDs except that they are "open" to additional deposits and are frequently automatically renewed at maturity unless either party gives the required written notice of termination. Time deposits, open account, also include special purpose accounts, such as Christmas club and vacation-club accounts.

CDs are either nonnegotiable or negotiable. *Nonnegotiable CDs* are often advertised by such names as consumer savings certificates to reflect their "retail" orientation. These retail certificates are designed to attract deposits of from $1,000 (typical minimum) to $100,000 from individual savers who are sensitive to interest rate differentials. Most savings certificates have maturities ranging from one to three years, but longer maturities are generally available and they are frequently renewable. One important class of certificate, the *money market certificate,* has a maturity of six months and a minimum deposit size of $10,000. Being nonnegotiable, savings certificates cannot be sold prior to maturity, but they can be withdrawn prior to maturity if the required notice is given and the holder is willing to incur the interest penalty. Savings certificates pay higher interest rates than regular savings deposits. Of course, market rates may be lower than the legal maximum rates, but this has not been the case for many years.

*Negotiable CDs* are designed to attract large deposits from "wholesale" investors in money market securities. These investors include large individual savers, businesses, foreign and domestic governmental units, and foreign and domestic banks and other financial intermediaries. However, corporations are by far the largest purchasers of these CDs.

*Nondeposit liabilities* were approximately 12 percent of total liabilities and capital in 1978. They include: Federal Funds purchased and securities sold under repurchase agreements, and "Other" liabilities. Other liabilities refer to, among other things, mortgages on bank property, bankers' acceptances outstanding, Eurodollar borrowings, and borrowings from the Federal Reserve.

*Federal Funds* as bank liabilities refers to the borrowing of balances of member banks in their reserve accounts at Federal Reserve banks or borrowing from other sources of immediately available funds.[29] The lending institution acquires an asset (*Federal Funds sold*—a use of funds) and the borrowing bank acquires a liability (*Federal Funds purchased*—a source of funds). The instructions and entries are subsequently reversed at maturity, typically the next day.

*Bank sales of securities under repurchase agreements* have traditionally been used as a means of meeting temporary shortfalls in required reserves. Under this arrangement, a borrowing bank "sells" securities to a dealer with a simultaneous agreement to "repurchase" them (repay the loan) at a

---

[28]Interest rate ceilings on all types of deposits can be found in current issues of the *Federal Reserve Bulletin.*

[29]Federal Funds, along with other money market instruments, including bankers' acceptances and Eurodollars, are discussed in more detail in Chapter 20. See also C. M. Lucas, M. T. Jones, and T. B. Thurston, "Federal Funds and Repurchase Agreements," *Quarterly Review,* Federal Reserve Bank of New York (Summer 1977).

predetermined price and maturity, usually the next business day.[30]

*Bank (bankers') acceptances outstanding* include unmatured 30–180 day drafts "accepted" for future payment by the bank. A bank acceptance is, therefore, a time draft drawn on and accepted by a bank. Most commonly, acceptances arise out of commercial transactions involving the import and export of goods.

*Eurodollars* are dollar deposits held in foreign banks and dollars purchased by foreign banks for lending and investing. The market in Eurodollars is created by foreign banks and foreign branches of U.S. banks that accept dollar deposits and make dollar loans. Eurodollar borrowings by domestic banks became significant in the mid-1960s when Regulation Q ceilings prevented banks from offering competitive interest rates on domestic negotiable CDs.

*Bank borrowings from the Federal Reserve* arise from temporary deficits in reserves needed to meet legal reserve requirements. Borrowing by member banks has traditionally been considered a privilege rather than a right of Federal Reserve membership. Under the Monetary Control Act of 1980, all institutions required to hold reserves are eligible to borrow from the Federal Reserve. Regulation A states that this type of credit is appropriate on a short-term basis to enable banks and other depository institutions to adjust their assets to meet unanticipated deposit withdrawals and requests for credit. Borrowings from the Federal Reserve are traditionally called discounts and advances—thus the name "discount window" to describe the Federal Reserve's bank-credit facility.[31]

As indicated in Table 4-6, bank *capital* (total capital accounts, including subordinated notes and debentures) represented 7.6 percent of total liabilities and capital in 1978. Contrasted to nonfinancial firms, bank capital is relatively small, which explains in large part banks' traditional conservatism toward assuming risk in their loans and investments.

Qualified issues of *subordinated notes and debentures* (capital notes) are included as capital account items although they constitute debt rather than equity financing. Capital notes are long-term debt with specified maturities ranging from seven years (to qualify for inclusion as a capital account item) to typically twenty to twenty-five years. Most issues of capital notes require periodic sinking-fund payments to reduce the principal amount. Call provisions may also be used to facilitate retirement of the issues prior to maturity. The justification for including capital notes is that such notes are subordinated with respect to payment of interest and principal to depositor and other creditor claims. Thus, capital notes are equivalent to equity from the standpoint of creditors but remain debt from the standpoint of preferred and common stockholders. Compared to the issuance of preferred or common stock, capital notes offer several advantages: interest payments are tax deductible (dividends are not); issuance costs are generally lower; there is leverage to bank earnings, to the extent that the returns earned with the funds exceed their cost; and there is less immediate earnings dilution. Disadvantages include fixed interest and repayment schedules, uncertainty about conditions when refinancing is required, and less than enthusiastic acceptance by some regulatory authorities.[32]

The issuance of capital notes in noncrisis situations is a relatively recent phenomenon although they were originally used for emergency financing during the depression of the 1930s. In 1961 the Comptroller of the Currency ruled that national banks could issue subordinated notes and debentures, and since that ruling, other federal and most state regulatory agencies have permitted their issuance under various conditions. The appropriate role of capital notes as part of the broader issue of capital adequacy is still an unsettled issue, however.

*Preferred stock* is a minor source of bank capital. In general, capital notes have been a more desirable source of financing because of lower cost and the fact that interest expenses are tax deductible while preferred dividends are not. While preferred stock can offer more leverage and less dilution than comparable amounts of common stock, banks have made relatively little use of this source of funds.

---

[30] For a discussion of recent developments in repurchase agreements, see Lucas, et al., "Federal Funds and Repurchase Agreements."

[31] For a further discussion of member-bank borrowing from the Federal Reserve, see Chapters 5 and 28.

[32] For a thorough discussion of the advantages of using subordinated debt as bank capital, see George H. Hempel, *Bank Capital: Determining and Meeting Your Bank's Capital Needs.*

*Common stock, surplus, undivided profits,* and *other reserves* represent the equity base of the bank. As such, the common stockholders hold a residual claim on their bank's assets. "Other reserves" represent earmarked portions of capital for such items as contingencies and dividends payable. In Table 4-6, valuation reserves for loan losses have been netted against loans.

The asset side of the statement of condition for all commercial banks (Table 4-6) indicates the uses to which funds have been placed. *Cash and bank balances* in 1978 represented approximately 13 percent of total assets. This asset category includes currency and coin, cash items in process of collection, deposits at other banks, and reserve (deposit) balances at the Federal Reserve.

*Currency and coin* represent only a very small percentage of total assets. These funds are the banks' "till and vault" cash needed for daily operations.

*Cash items in process of collection* are contingent assets indicating out-of-town checks and other items not yet available as deposits with other banks or the Federal Reserve. Banks attempt to minimize these items because they represent nonearning assets.

*Deposits at other banks* ("due from banks") are the largest of the cash and bank-balance items. These balances arise out of the correspondent banking system, which evolved before the Federal Reserve System was established in 1913. Prior to that time, national banks kept their reserves in cash or as deposits with banks in so-called reserve cities. While this system of reserve management for banks changed with the passage of the Federal Reserve Act, the correspondent system has retained its importance. Correspondent banks are banks that seek and accept deposits from other banks in return for services provided. The banks receiving the services are often called respondent banks. They usually compensate the correspondent banks for the services provided by keeping deposits at those banks. These funds, like any other deposits, are loaned and invested for a profit by the correspondents.

The services provided by correspondent banks are many and varied. The major ones include: check clearing and collections; loan participations (by both correspondents and respondents); asset-management services, including reports on economic conditions, securities portfolio review and analysis, Federal Funds transactions, and lines of credit; international banking services; credit information; specialized lending programs; interpretation of banking laws and regulations; and data processing. While there is growing impetus for banks to charge explicitly for their services rather than negotiate deposit balances from respondents, most banks, especially the smaller ones using the services, probably favor the current system.[33]

*Loan participations* are an important aspect of the correspondent-respondent bank relationship. Correspondents often assist respondent banks by participating in loans originated by respondents or by purchasing loans outright. In this way, respondents are able to make loans in excess of their own legal lending limits (10 percent of capital, surplus, and capital notes for national banks) and generate funds to meet new credit requests if they are loaned up. Correspondents prefer participations in high-quality short-term or seasonal loans with competitive interest rates originated by long-time respondents with quality management and large and profitable correspondent balances. Most participations involve loans originated by respondents, but many are originated by correspondents. Small banks with low loan demand frequently request participations in loans originated by correspondent banks as a means of earning higher than money-market yields. Most participations involve business loans, but real estate and farm loans are also used.

*Reserve balances at the Federal Reserve* represent the required reserves—and any excess—of banks. As already mentioned, member banks must keep specified percentages of deposits in the form of vault cash and/or deposits with the Federal Reserve. However, only to the extent that these reserves exceed legal requirements do they provide funds for bank and customer contingency needs (in the usual sense of the word *reserves*).

Securities in 1978 represented approximately 22 percent of bank assets (Table 4-6). Bank holdings of *U.S. Treasury securities* were nearly 8 percent of total assets and second only to holdings of tax-exempt securities of states and their political sub-

---

[33] For a thorough discussion of correspondent banking and services, see the three-part article by Robert E. Knight, "Correspondent Banking," Federal Reserve Bank of Kansas City *Monthly Review* (November 1970), 3–14; (December 1970), 12–24; and (December 1971), 3–17.

divisions. Holdings of U.S. Treasury obligations fall into three maturity categories: short-term holdings (maturity within one year) of bills, certificates of indebtedness, notes, and bonds; intermediate-term holdings (one to five years) of notes and bonds; and long-term holdings (over five years) of notes and bonds. Over one-half of bank holdings of U.S. Treasury obligations are intermediate term, and approximately one-third are short-term securities.

Bank holdings of *U.S. government agency obligations* are relatively small. These securities include bonds, notes, and debentures issued by agencies and corporations of the U.S. government that are not direct obligations of the U.S. Treasury. Among the many agencies issuing these obligations are the Federal National Mortgage Association, the Federal Home Loan Bank System, and the Federal Land Banks. These holdings include the mortgage-backed securities and securities secured by pooled mortgages of the Government National Mortgage Association.[34]

Holdings of *state and local obligations* in 1978 were slightly over 10 percent of total bank assets. These so-called municipals are the obligations of state and local governments, agencies, districts, and authorities. Municipals are classified as general obligation bonds, revenue bonds, assessment bonds, and "hybrid" bonds. General obligation bonds ("full faith and credit bonds") are backed by the full taxing power of the issuing governmental unit. Because of this, general obligation bonds represent the largest category of bank holdings of municipal bonds. Revenue bonds are backed by the revenue generated by the issuing district, agency, or authority (for example, toll roads). Assessment bonds are backed by the proceeds of assessments for public improvements (for example, sewer assessments). These bonds are generally of lower credit quality than the other types of municipal bonds and are less frequently found in bank portfolios. Hybrid bonds are combinations of other bond types. For example, the full faith and credit of an issuing government could be added to a revenue bond.[35]

*"Other securities"* is a residual category and represented less than 1 percent of total assets in 1978. It includes other bank holdings of trusts, notes, and debentures; required member-bank holdings of Federal Reserve stock; stock required as collateral for defaulted loans; foreign stock held for investment; and trading-account securities held for resale as underwriters or dealers.

Lending is the basic business of commercial banking. Loans include direct extensions of credit and loan assets purchased from other lenders. Therefore, the fact that loans are approximately 58 percent of total assets in Table 4-6 seems reasonable. Federal Funds sold and securities purchased under resale agreements in 1978 were less than 5 percent of total assets. These uses of funds represent the reverse side of the Federal Funds and securities repurchase-agreement transactions discussed previously as sources of funds. Federal Funds sold represent the temporary "sale" (loan) of immediately available funds, and the securities purchased under resale agreements represent the temporary "purchase" of short-term U.S. government securities or other money-market instruments.

The category of *"other loans"* sounds residual in nature but, in fact, represents the heart of the commercial bank loan function. Based on the general purpose or type of borrower, these loans include: real estate loans, including loans for construction and land development, mortgage loans on farm land and residential and other property (residential mortgages involve "conventional" loans as well as FHA-insured and VA-guaranteed loans); loans to financial institutions, including real estate investment trusts (REITs) and mortgage companies, domestic and foreign banks, and other depository and financial institutions; loans to security brokers and dealers; loans to "carry" or purchase securities; loans to farmers (other than real estate); commercial and industrial ("business") loans; loans to individuals;[36] and all other loans.[37] The major loan categories are business loans (35 percent of total loans), real estate loans (29 percent of total

---

[34]U.S. government agencies and their securities are discussed further in Chapter 11.

[35]For greater detail on state and local bonds, see "Understanding State and Local Bonds," in *Investment Management in a Commercial Bank,* ed. George H. Hempel, Bankers Publishing Co., Boston, 1979.

[36]Loans to individuals include instalment loans—automobile and mobile home loans, residential repair and modernization loans, and credit card and other revolving credit loans—and single-payment loans to individuals.

[37]All other loans are those not otherwise classified, such as loans to nonprofit organizations and to foreign central banks.

loans), and loans to individuals (22 percent of total loans).

Loans made with the cooperation of other banks and financial institutions are called *participation loans*. Loan participations purchased from other banks are included as loans and classified according to the type of loan—business loans, for example. These participations represent a pro rata share in a pool of loans and carry similar maturity and interest rate terms as the underlying loans. The bank selling participations deletes them from its loan assets. In those cases where the participation certificate bears maturity and interest rate terms different from those of the underlying loans, the purchasing bank carries the participation as a loan but the selling bank keeps the participation on its books as a loan asset, which is offset by a liability ("Other liabilities" in Table 4-6).

Bank purchases of commercial paper, mortgages, bankers' acceptances, and the like, under resale agreements or carrying another bank's endorsement or guarantee are included as loans to the other party (bank, broker, dealer, or other financial institution) to the agreement.

The residual category of "*Other assets*" was approximately 7 percent of total assets in 1978. These assets include direct lease-financing arrangements, bank premises and related assets, and investments in unconsolidated subsidiaries and associated companies.

## Income Statement for All Commercial Banks

Table 4-7 provides a summary report of income and dividends (an income statement) for all insured commercial banks for the year 1978. Like the balance sheet items, these income-statement items reflect the interaction of managerial decisions operating in a world of uncertainty, as well as a world which is limited by institutional and regulatory constraints.

As shown in Table 4-7, interest and fees on loans is the major source of operating income, representing more than 65 percent of the total in 1978. If interest on Federal Funds sold and securities sold under repurchase agreements and interest from other banks is included, the total reaches 76 percent. The importance of loan revenue reflects, of course, the fact that lending is the primary business of commercial banks. Income on securities

**Table 4-7  Consolidated Report of Income, All Insured Commercial Banks, 1978 (in millions of dollars)**

|  |  | Percentage of Total Operating Income |
|---|---:|---:|
| Total operating income | $113.2 | 100.0% |
| Interest and fees on loans | 75.9 | 67.1 |
| Other interest | 10.3 | 9.0 |
| Income on securities | 16.4 | 14.5 |
| Trust department | 2.1 | 1.9 |
| Service charges on deposits | 2.0 | 1.8 |
| Other charges and fees | 3.8 | 3.4 |
| Other operating income | 2.5 | 2.2 |
| Total operating expenses | 98.1 | 86.7 |
| Salaries, wages, and benefits | 18.7 | 16.5 |
| Interest on deposits | 50.0 | 44.2 |
| Other interest expense | 9.1 | 8.0 |
| Net occupancy expense (furniture, equipment, etc.) | 5.6 | 5.0 |
| Provision for loan losses | 3.5 | 3.1 |
| Other operating expenses | 11.2 | 9.9 |
| Income before taxes and securities, gains and losses | 15.1 | 13.3 |
| Income taxes | 4.2 | 3.7 |
| Net securities gains or losses after taxes | (.2) | (0.2) |
| Other charges or credits after taxes | .0 | — |
| Net income | $ 10.7 | 9.5% |
| Cash dividends declared | $ 3.7 | 3.3% |

Source: Adapted from *Federal Reserve Bulletin* (September 1979).

was nearly 15 percent of total revenue in 1978 and was the second most important source of gross income. Income from securities is provided by U.S. Treasury securities, U.S. government agency and corporate securities, municipal securities, and all other securities. The importance of the income from municipals is emphasized by their tax-exempt status. All other revenue sources were less than 15 percent of total operating income in 1978.

Total operating expenses in that year were approximately 87 percent of total operating income. The major expense items as percentages of total operating income were salaries and related costs (16.5 percent), interest on deposits (44 percent), other interest expenses (8 percent), and all other expenses (nearly 20 percent). Other interest expenses included Federal Funds purchased and securities sold under repurchase agreements and interest on capital notes, debentures, and other borrowings. Thus, the costs of labor and funds were the major expense items for commercial banks. The spread between revenues and expenses was a before-tax profit of 13 percent of total operating income in 1978, which was reduced to nearly 10 percent after taxes and security gains and losses. Dividends totaled nearly 40 percent of this after-tax net income figure.

Statistical analyses of the differential preferences of bank management in earning after-tax profits on total capital lead to several important conclusions.[38] It appears that, in general, successful management performance is determined more by the relative use made of funds rather than the types of funds acquired. An important exception is the lower proportion of capital for high-profitability banks. High-performance management earns higher gross returns on loans and taxable securities and brings a higher net return through to net income. This requires close attention to the gains and losses on loans and securities.

## Conclusion

Commercial banks are financial intermediaries whose liabilities include one of the most important ingredients of the U.S. money supply—demand deposits. The importance of banks' intermediation and money functions has affected both their structure and the ways in which they are regulated. Any discussion analyzing risks and returns on individual financial assets and liabilities and on the portfolios of these assets and liabilities—those things that commercial banks typically manage—must be tempered by the institutional and regulatory environment in which banks operate. Nevertheless, it is clear that, by using a wealth-maximization criterion, modern financial management techniques such as portfolio theory, linear programming, and gap management can be helpful in bank management. A detailed analysis of the balance sheet and income statement of all commercial banks provides important insights into the ways banks manage their assets and liabilities subject to institutional and regulatory constraints in an environment characterized by uncertainty.

## Appendix 4-1: Mathematics for Illustrative Two-Asset Portfolio

The mathematics required for computing the risk and return for a two-asset portfolio is quite simple. For assets $A$ and $B$, let $(\chi_a, \chi_b)$, $(E_a, E_b)$, and $(\sigma_a, \sigma_b)$ denote the proportions of each asset in the portfolio, the expected rates of return, and the standard deviation on return, respectively. The portfolio's expected return is computed by

$$E_p = \chi_a E_a + \chi_b E_b \qquad (4\text{-}6)$$

We obtain $E_p$ by weighing each asset's return by its proportion in the portfolio. The standard deviation of the portfolio's return is given by

$$\sigma_p = \sqrt{\chi_a^2 \sigma_a^2 + \chi_b^2 \sigma_b^2 + 2\chi_a\chi_b \text{COV}_{ab}} \qquad (4\text{-}7)$$

where the covariance between $A$ and $B$'s returns is computed as

$$\text{COV}_{ab} = \sigma_a \sigma_b \rho_{ab} \qquad (4\text{-}8)$$

$\rho_{ab}$ being the simple correlation coefficient.

Earlier, we indicated the importance of the correlation between assets' returns in determining the risk-pooling benefits available from diversification. Here we demonstrate the quantitative significance of this relationship. Let us assume the two assets in question have the following expected returns and risks:

$$E_a = 8\% \qquad \sigma_a = 4\%$$
$$E_b = 12\% \qquad \sigma_b = 6\%$$

The importance of the correlation coefficient in determining the portfolio's risk is evidenced in Table 4-8. We compute $\sigma_p$ for values of $\rho_{ab}$ from $-1$ to $+1$ by 0.2 intervals for portfolios composed of proportions of asset $A$ from 0 to 0.1 intervals. The expected return for every portfolio on a given row in Table 4-8 is identical (column 2). Therefore, the

[38]John A. Haslem, "A Statistical Analysis of the Relative Profitability of Commercial Banks," *Journal of Finance* (March 1968), 167–176; John A. Haslem, "A Statistical Estimation of Commercial Bank Profitability," *Journal of Business* (January 1969), 22–35; and John A. Haslem and William A. Longbrake, "A Discriminant Analysis of Commerical Bank Profitability," *Quarterly Review of Economics and Business* (Autumn 1971), 39–46.

**Table 4-8  Deviation in Return for a Two-Asset Portfolio for Various Values of $\rho_{ab}$**

| % of Portfolio in Asset A | % Return | Correlation Coefficient ($\rho_{ab}$) | | | | | | | | | | |
|---|---|---|---|---|---|---|---|---|---|---|---|---|
| | | −1 | −0.8 | −0.6 | −0.4 | −0.2 | 0 | 0.2 | 0.4 | 0.6 | 0.8 | 1.0 |
| 0 | 12.0 | 6.0 | 6.00 | 6.00 | 6.00 | 6.00 | 6.00 | 6.00 | 6.00 | 6.00 | 6.00 | 6.0 |
| 10 | 11.6 | 5.0 | 5.09 | 5.17 | 5.25 | 5.33 | 5.41 | 5.49 | 5.57 | 5.65 | 5.73 | 5.8 |
| 20 | 11.2 | 4.0 | 4.19 | 4.37 | 4.54 | 4.71 | 4.87 | 5.02 | 5.17 | 5.32 | 5.46 | 5.6 |
| 30 | 10.8 | 3.0 | 3.32 | 3.61 | 3.88 | 4.13 | 4.37 | 4.59 | 4.81 | 5.01 | 5.21 | 5.4 |
| 40 | 10.4 | 2.0 | 2.51 | 2.93 | 3.30 | 3.64 | 3.94 | 4.22 | 4.49 | 4.74 | 4.97 | 5.2 |
| 50 | 10.0 | 1.0 | 1.84 | 2.41 | 2.86 | 3.26 | 3.61 | 3.92 | 4.22 | 4.49 | 4.75 | 5.0 |
| 60 | 9.6 | 0 | 1.52 | 2.15 | 2.63 | 3.04 | 3.39 | 3.72 | 4.02 | 4.29 | 4.55 | 4.8 |
| 70 | 9.2 | 1.0 | 1.74 | 2.24 | 2.65 | 3.01 | 3.33 | 3.62 | 3.89 | 4.14 | 4.38 | 4.6 |
| 80 | 8.8 | 2.0 | 3.35 | 2.66 | 2.93 | 3.18 | 3.42 | 3.64 | 3.84 | 4.04 | 4.22 | 4.4 |
| 90 | 8.4 | 3.0 | 3.11 | 3.28 | 3.40 | 3.53 | 3.65 | 3.77 | 3.88 | 3.99 | 4.10 | 4.2 |
| 100 | 8.0 | 4.0 | 4.00 | 4.00 | 4.00 | 4.00 | 4.00 | 4.00 | 4.00 | 4.00 | 4.00 | 4.0 |

risk-pooling benefits from diversification can be measured by the difference between standard deviation of the portfolio with $\rho_{ab} = +1$ and that of the portfolio in question.

For an $n$-asset or $n$-liability portfolio, the computation of risk and return is more difficult. Return is obtained by

$$E_p = \sum_{i=1}^{n} \chi_i E_i \qquad (4\text{-}9)$$

while risk is computed as

$$\sigma_p = \sqrt{\Sigma \chi_i^2 \sigma_i^2 + \Sigma\Sigma_{i \neq j} \chi_i \chi_j \overline{COV}_{ij}} \qquad (4\text{-}10)$$

From Equation (4-10), we are aware of the importance of covariability in determining the contribution of a given asset to the risk of the portfolio.

It is necessary to have information on $E$ and $\sigma$ for each asset and the COV between each pair of assets. For a sample of $n$ assets, the data requirements for the Markowitz model include $n$ return and $n$ standard deviation measures and $n^2 - n/2$ covariances.

Before presenting the computational procedures of the Markowitz model, we digress briefly to consider the methods available for obtaining the required data on each asset's risk and return. The simplest and most commonly used method for obtaining the data required for any portfolio-selection model is historical return observations. While this method generally yields satisfactory results, it has two major shortcomings. First, one may be forced to employ risk-return observations that, for some assets, are contrary to the hypothesis that investors are risk averse. That is, assets having a positive

risk sometimes achieve a negative return over a given sample period. Using this return figure as an estimate for the next period's expected return is wholly unsatisfactory since a rational investor would never hold such an asset. The second drawback of employing only historical return data is that one is unable to incorporate specific forecasts of future returns into the asset-selection process.

The objective function of the Markowitz model is the minimization of the portfolio's variance ($\sigma_p^2$) for a given expected return. From Equation (4-10) we express $\sigma_p^2$ as

$$\sigma_p^2 = \Sigma \chi_i^2 \sigma_i^2 + \Sigma\Sigma_{i \neq j} \chi_i \chi_j COV_{ij} \qquad (4\text{-}11)$$

Two constraints are required:

$$C_1: \Sigma\chi_i = 1$$
$$C_2: \chi_i \geq 0 \text{ for all } i$$

The first constraint simply assures us that the proportions of the portfolio in each asset equal a total of one. The second constraint limits the portfolio to nonnegative holdings of any asset, that is, no short sales.

Observe that both of the above constraints are linear in the $\chi_i$s. For this reason conventional techniques of linear programming are incapable of generating the efficient frontier. Rather, one must employ quadratic programming to obtain the minimum value of $\sigma_p^2$ for each possible value of $E_p$.

In one version of the Sharpe model, an asset's return is related to a single index of economic activity. Candidates for this index include gross national product, the Dow-Jones Index, and a composite of all stock returns. The following regression equation is employed to obtain estimates of each asset's risk and return.

$$R_{it} = \alpha_i + \beta_i R_{mt} + \epsilon_{it} \qquad (4\text{-}12)$$

In Equation (4-12), $R_{it}$ denotes $i$'s return in period $t$, $R_{mt}$ denotes the index value, $\epsilon_{it}$ denotes the random error term, and $\alpha_i$ and $\beta_i$ are coefficients obtained from the regression. The size of the $\beta$ coefficient measures the degree of co-movement between the index and the asset's return. Since the index serves as a proxy for economic activity, $\beta$ can be interpreted as a measure of the procyclical response of the asset's return. While the Sharpe model in general allows for both positive and negative values for $\beta$, the evidence suggests that the majority of equity returns move in unison with economic activity ($+\beta$s).

The data requirements for generating an efficient frontier with the Sharpe single-index model represent a significant simplification over the Markowitz model. The Sharpe model requires estimates for each asset's $\alpha$ and $\beta$ coefficients and a forecast for the value of the index in the next period (perhaps simply $\overline{X}_m$). The computational time required for the Sharpe calculation has been estimated to be as little as 2 percent of that required for the Markowitz analysis when 2,000 assets are available. From Equation (4-13) we obtain an expression for the expected return on assets $i$,

$$E(R_i) = \alpha_i + \beta_i \overline{R}_m \qquad (4\text{-}13)$$

where $\overline{R}_m$ is the average value of the index over the period. Note that this form, $E(R_i)$, is solely a function of historical return behavior.

## Appendix 4-2: Applying Linear Programming as a Technique for Wealth Maximization

In recent years, a great deal of effort has been devoted to the construction of mathematical models to facilitate commercial bank management. Most have taken the form of mathematical programming models. In banking the goal is to maximize some measure of performance while satisfying both internal and external constraints on behavior, such as liquidity and capital adequacy. Though more elaborate techniques are justified in modeling particular tasks performed by management, the relatively simple linear programming format seems sufficiently powerful for representing the overall management of the bank and is attractive in its computational ease. A description of the general characteristics of one linear programming model of a commercial bank follows.

The objective of this linear programming model is to maximize shareholder wealth. This objective will be accomplished by maximizing the market value of the bank's common equity. The value of the bank's equity is determined by the residual value of assets over liabilities. Thus, the objective function (that is, the mathematical representation of the goal) becomes

$$
\begin{aligned}
\text{MAX } V_B = {} & \\
& V_C X_C + V_G X_G + V_M X_M + V_L X_L + V_F X_F \\
& - V_{DD} D_{DD} - V_{TD} X_{TD} - V_{CN} X_{CN} - V_{PS} X_{PS} \\
& - 0.0\, B_e \qquad (4\text{-}14)
\end{aligned}
$$

where $V_i$ is the market value of dollars expended for corresponding assets, or received in exchange for the respective liabilities; $X_i$ represents dollars invested in the $i$th asset or obtained through the $i$th liability; and $B_e$ is the book value of the bank's common equity. The book value is set equal to zero to simplify constraints in the model. The subscript $C$ stands for cash and due from banks, $G$ for government securities, $M$ for municipal securities, $L$ for loans, $F$ for fixed assets, $DD$ for demand deposits, $TD$ for time deposits, $CN$ for capital notes, and $PS$ for preferred stock.

Once the objective function has been specified, linear constraints can be constructed so as to model various regulations and behaviors that typify the banking environment. One such constraint on bank activities is the reserve requirement for demand and time deposits. Any progressive nature of the reserve requirement on demand deposits can be incorporated into the model by breaking demand deposits into categories. Upper bounds are placed on these categories to get the model to evaluate this constraint at various levels of demand deposits. Thus, reserve requirement constraints may be modeled as

$$
\begin{aligned}
0 \le X_C - 0.08 X_{DD_1} - {}&.105 X_{DD_2} - .125 X_{DD_3} \\
& - .135 X_{DD_4} - 0.18 X_{DD_5} - 0.06 X_{TD}
\end{aligned}
$$

$$X_{DD_1} \le 2,\ X_{DD_2} \le 8,\ X_{DD_3} \le 90,\ X_{DD_4} \le 300 \qquad (4\text{-}15)$$

Another constraint upon banks is the capital-adequacy constraint which requires banks to have a sufficient level of capital given the risk and liquidity embodied in its asset structure and the volatility of bank deposits. To accomplish this within the model, weights can be assigned to assets in a way that reflects liquidity and to deposits so as to reflect the risk of withdrawal (volatility). As an example the illiquidity of assets might be represented by $A$.

$$A = 0.01X_G + 0.5X_M + 0.10X_L \qquad (4\text{-}16)$$

and the volatility of deposits and Federal Funds is denoted by $D$.

$$D = 0.47X_{DD} + 0.36X_{TD} + 1.0X_F \qquad (4\text{-}17)$$

The computation of the capital requirement depends on the types of assets (denoted by $R_i$) held against liabilities in $D$. The types hypothesized in this model are as follows:

$$R_1 = X_C + 0.8X_G \qquad (4\text{-}17\text{a})$$
$$R_2 = R_1 + 0.18X_G \qquad (4\text{-}17\text{b})$$
$$R_3 = R_2 + 0.20X_M \qquad (4\text{-}17\text{c})$$

To develop the actual capital adequacy constraint, the following assumptions are made:

1. For every dollar that $D$ exceeds $R_i$, 0.065 dollars of capital are needed.
2. For every dollar that $D$ exceeds $R_2$, 0.040 dollars of capital are needed.
3. For every dollar that $D$ exceeds $R_3$, 0.095 dollars of capital are necessary.

Taking all of the above assumptions into account, the capital adequacy constraint becomes

$$B_e + X_{CN} + X_{PS} \geq A + 0.065(D - R_1)$$
$$+ 0.04\,(D - R_2) + 0.095(D - R_3) \qquad (4\text{-}18)$$

Other aspects of the banking environment could also be included in the model as well. For example, there might be a requirement that deposits of state and local political subdivisions be matched dollar for dollar by securities. Historically these deposits have been about 4 percent of total demand deposits, and about 12 percent of total time deposits. Hence, this constraint is written as follows:

$$X_G + X_M \geq 0.04X_{DD} + 0.12X_{TD} \qquad (4\text{-}19)$$

Another example of a constraint would be to incorporate the fact that the use of capital notes to raise capital is limited in the banking industry. This constraint on bank behavior could be depicted in linear fashion as

$$X_{CN} \leq 0.22B_e \quad \text{or} \quad X_{CN} \leq 0.25(X_{PS} + B_e) \qquad (4\text{-}20)$$

Two other constraints must be added. One is the balance-sheet identity constraint:

$$B_e + X_{PS} + X_{CN} + X_F + X_{TD} + X_{DD}$$
$$- X_L - X_M - X_G - X_C = 0 \quad (4\text{-}21)$$

Another is the nonnegativity constraint:

$$X_i \geq 0 \qquad \text{for all } i \qquad (4\text{-}22)$$

Any number of linear constraints can be added to better reflect the bank's environment. Only a few were included here to indicate how the bank's environment can be depicted in a linear programming model that maximizes the wealth of the stockholders as its objective function.

## Questions

1. If banks are private, profit-seeking businesses, why are they so heavily regulated? List the functions performed by banks in your answer.
2. List and discuss four potential sources of risk for debt securities held as assets by banks.
3. Discuss two types of risks associated with bank liabilities.
4. Contrast bank asset and liability decision making under certainty and uncertainty.
5. A bank's risk position is largely determined by the interrelationship between its assets, liabilities, and owner equity. What are the particular aspects of each that determine its contribution?
6. Discuss the types of regulatory controls that exert the strongest impact on bank management.
7. Describe the effect of a downward-sloping yield curve (that is, short-term rates exceed long-term rates) on the decisions of a bank trying to maximize the net wealth position of its owners.
8. Referring to specific account items on bank balance sheets and income statements, discuss why each item selected might be significantly larger or smaller if banks were unregulated. Discuss one item for each of the types of regulatory control in Question 5
9. Describe the major types of loans that commercial banks make. What factors determine the types of loans made by an individual commercial bank?
10. Discuss the income and expense items that seem to have the most positive effects on bank earnings. How do these items affect the bank's risk position?

## Selected Bibliography

American Bankers Association. *The Commercial Banking Industry*. Prentice-Hall, Englewood Cliffs, N.J., 1962.

Cohen, Kalman J. and Stephen F. Gibson, eds. *Management Science in Banking*. Warren, Gorham & Lamont, Boston, 1978.

Crosse, Howard, and George H. Hempel. *Management Policies for Commercial Banks,* 3rd ed. Prentice-Hall, Englewood Cliffs, N.J. 1979.

Hempel, George H. *Bank Capital: Determining and Meeting Your Bank's Capital Needs*. Bankers Publishing Company, Boston, 1977.

———. *Investment Management in a Commercial Bank*. Bankers Publishing Company, Boston, 1979.

———. and Jess B. Yawitz. *Financial Management of Financial Institutions*. Prentice-Hall, Englewood Cliffs, N.J., 1977.

Jessup, Paul F., ed. *Innovations in Bank Management: Selected Readings*. Holt, Rinehart and Winston, New York, 1969.

Mason, John M. *Financial Management of Commercial Banks*. Warren, Gorham & Lamont, Boston, 1979.

Reed, Edward W., Richard V. Cotter, Edward K. Gill, and Richard K. Smith. *Commercial Banking*. Prentice-Hall, Englewood Cliffs, N.J., 1976.

Robinson, Roland I. *Management of Bank Funds,* 2nd ed. McGraw-Hill Book Company, New York, 1962.

Sharpe, William. *Portfolio Theory and Capital Markets*. McGraw-Hill Book Company, New York, 1970.

For professional publications specializing in bank management topics, see *ABA Banking Journal, Bankers Magazine, Bankers Monthly, Journal of Bank Research, Journal of Commercial Bank Lending, Magazine of Bank Administration,* and the periodicals of the Federal Reserve banks.

# 5

# The Supply of Money and Bank Credit

Few things, if any, have attracted as much attention in the history of mankind as money. Money, it is alleged, can motivate individuals to satisfy the needs of others while, at the same time, satisfying their own needs. Money, it is argued, can also provoke evil; the quest for money has sometimes been called the "root of all evil." Money is controversial in other ways as well. American political leaders have often argued there is not enough of it; others have contended that the problem is there is too much of it.[1] Government policy with respect to its creation has, on occasion, been simultaneously praised and condemned as both inflationary and deflationary. In the 1970s, even the types and sources of money became controversial. Daily newspapers and nightly newscasts speak of M1-A, M1-B, M2, Eurodollars, petrodollars, offshore currencies, and even paper gold. The interrelationships among all these concepts are often difficult to comprehend.

The purpose of this chapter is to discuss the most important characteristics of money, to analyze how it is created and by whom, and to examine the limits of its expansion and contraction. In the course of this chapter, it will be seen that both commercial banks and the Federal Reserve System are important participants in the monetary process. In a later chapter we will be able to analyze how monetary policy affects such economic objectives as full employment, price stability, economic growth, and equilibrium in our balance of payments.

## Money Defined

Defining money is not easy. Many things have served as money in the history of the world—among them precious metals, grains, cattle, checking accounts at banks, salt, cigarettes, and certain green pieces of paper with pictures of George Washington and other famous people on them. It might be asked what all these things have in common that makes them money while other commod-

[1] Although this dispute has a modern ring to it, students of American economic history know that the controversy over the optimal quantity of money and monetary growth has been central to American economic debate for a century and a half. For a thorough discussion, see Milton Friedman and Anna Schwartz's monumental work, *A Monetary History of the United States, 1867–1960,* Princeton University Press, Princeton, New Jersey, 1963.

ities are not money. In itself, this list of things is not very helpful in revealing the essential characteristic of money—the "moneyness" of money—since none of these forms of money is universal. Cattle and grains, for example, have served as money only in certain tribal societies, cigarettes only in prisoner and refugee camps, and green paper picturing George Washington only in the United States. Even precious metals like gold and silver, which have served as money throughout much of the world's history, do not circulate widely as money in the 1980s. What, then, is the essence of money, the factor that causes something to be categorized as *money*? Put differently, how can we define money in a way that includes all the essential elements and eliminates the nonessential ones?

Perhaps the most comprehensive definition of money is that money is anything which is generally acceptable in the uses to which money is ordinarily put. The word *anything* quickly suggests that money can take any of the forms mentioned earlier as well as a myriad of others so long as most people in a society are willing to accept them as money. However, for this definition of money to be meaningful, an obvious query must be answered: what are the "purposes to which money is ordinarily put"? In a modern economy, such as the United States in the 1980s, one can identify at least four such uses or functions of money: (1) a store of value, (2) a medium of exchange, (3) a unit of account, and (4) a standard of deferred payment.

First of all, money is an asset that can be held. As an asset, money performs an economic function—namely, it serves as a store of value. This means simply that money, like other assets, is a way the public can hold its wealth. It represents purchasing power in someone's hands and, while it is held, it serves as a store of wealth for the holder. Of course, this is not a function unique to money. All assets, including cattle, real estate, and corporate bonds serve as stores of value. However, these assets are not so liquid as to be immediately convertible into goods, services, or other financial assets—the distinguishing characteristic of money as a medium of exchange.

Money is a special asset because it is the most liquid of all assets. As was mentioned in Chapter 1, liquidity refers to the speed of conversion of an asset with certainty of little or no capital loss. Money is instantly convertible with no risk of cap-

ital loss. Anyone who has ever visited a retail store or taken a short shopping trip knows that money is readily convertible into goods and services. Other assets, including extremely valuable ones, are much less liquid. Hundreds of thousands of merchants, it seems, are willing to accept money for purchases, but relatively few accept real estate or cattle. Money can also be exchanged easily for other assets, including both financial and real assets. In contrast, assets that are not money are not as easily exchanged. U.S. Treasury bills, for example, cannot generally be used to purchase corporate stocks without an intermediate exchange of those bills for money. Likewise, corporate stocks cannot easily be exchanged for desired goods and services. Thus, it appears that a key characteristic of money is its liquidity, its readiness and ability to be spent.

This liquidity or exchangeability of money contributes to its second economic function. Besides being a store of value along with other assets, money uniquely serves as a medium of exchange. The medium of exchange in an economy is the factor or asset which facilitates exchanges and avoids the necessity of barter.[2] Thus, in modern economies like twentieth-century America, for example, there is relatively little barter because a convenient asset is available (money) that facilitates exchange. Values and prices are expressed in money, and most exchanges are made for money. It is the easy exchangeability of money and its role as the medium of exchange that, ultimately, makes money valuable. Things that are sometimes used as money (for example, gold or cattle) may have inherent values because of other uses. As we have seen, however, value does not make an asset money. An asset is money only when it also is a medium of exchange, and some kinds of money have value *only* because they can be exchanged. Green pieces of paper picturing George Washington are valuable only because of their exchangeability, and the same is true of deposits in checking ac-

---

[2] For money to serve as a medium of exchange there must exist a market or exchange economy. While the absence of the latter is difficult to imagine for participants in a modern economy, there have been societies where the allocation of goods does not come about through market exchange. In the Egypt of the pharaohs, for example, goods that were produced were sent to a central location and reallocated.

counts. Of course, both these forms of money retain their value only as long as they are readily acceptable to others.[3]

Besides serving as a store of value and a medium of exchange, money has two additional economic functions—it serves as a unit of account or common denominator and also as a standard of deferred payment. The unit of account is the unit in which values and prices are expressed. In the United States, for example, values and prices are expressed in monetary units (dollars and cents) rather than in terms of some nonmonetary measure, such as feet or inches. The standard of deferred payment refers to the tendency in modern credit economies to denote debts in monetary units rather than in terms of some other commodity. While these functions of money seem almost obvious today, they are important in a modern economy.

Having defined money and briefly discussed its functions, we can certainly see that currency, coins, and demand deposits owned by the public fall within the purview of money. The question is whether this list is all-inclusive or whether other assets should also be counted. What about NOW accounts at commercial and savings banks and S&Ls; share drafts at credit unions; and the automatic transfer of savings deposits into demand deposit accounts at commercial banks? Both NOW accounts and share drafts are subject to transfer by check to third parties and are readily acceptable in exchange for goods and services. A decade ago these financial assets were nonexistent; today they are increasingly being recognized as additional forms of money along with currency and demand deposits. How does one go about classifying another recent entry into the monetary sweepstakes, namely, money market funds which, beyond a certain minimum amount, are subject to transfer by check? Will they not in time become another new form of money? And how does one go about describing other financial assets, such as time and savings deposits at commercial banks, deposits at nonbank intermediaries, and even short-term securities, such as Treasury bills or corporate commercial paper, all of which are highly liquid and, if not recognized as money, are certainly very close substitutes for money? All of these near-money substitutes have, like money, an impact on the level of economic activity.

The Federal Reserve System, the central bank in the American economy and the agency charged with the conduct of monetary policy, has attempted to respond to this dilemma by proposing a series of formal definitions of money and liquidity—a series that has changed as the forms of money and its close substitutes have changed. No one definition of money and liquidity is regarded as sufficient; instead, a variety of measures are monitored and studied.

The first part of Table 5-1 provides a list of definitions of money and liquidity used by the Federal Reserve System during the 1970s. Table 5-1 also contains a list of new definitions adopted by the Federal Reserve in January 1980 to account for financial, regulatory, and market changes in the types of assets that might be used as money.[4] M-1 in the first part of the table is, of course, the traditional form of money in the American economy—currency and coin plus demand deposits (checking accounts) at commercial banks. In contrast, the new definition of M-1 actually involves two alternative measures. M1-A consists of the traditional components of M-1, but it subtracts deposits of foreign commercial banks and official agencies (such as central banks). M1-B adds some new kinds of accounts widely used by consumers for transaction purposes. These include negotiable order of withdrawal (NOW) accounts at commercial banks and savings institutions, demand deposits at savings institutions, share draft accounts at credit unions, and savings accounts that will be transferred automatically into a checking account by the financial institution in response to a checking overdraft (automatic transfer or ATS accounts). Each of these accounts has elements of traditional savings accounts (such as payment of interest on all but the demand deposits at savings institutions), but each is also readily available for spending.

The remaining definitions of money (both old and new) include additional assets that are highly liquid and moneylike, but which, as we have seen, are

---

[3]These forms of money might become less acceptable if their supply increased more rapidly than the demand for them and their value, therefore, declined in terms of goods and services and other financial assets. Both this condition (known as inflation) and the demand for money are discussed in more detail in Chapters 21, 22, and 28.

[4]See Thomas D. Simpson, "The Redefined Monetary Aggregates," *Federal Reserve Bulletin* (January 1980).

**Table 5-1  Traditional and New Monetary Definitions (in billions of dollars, not seasonally adjusted)**

| *Traditional Definitions, Prior to January 1980* | | *Definitions,[a] since January 1980* | |
|---|---|---|---|
| *Aggregate and Components* | *Amount, as of November 1979* | *Aggregate and Components* | *Amount, as of November 1979* |
| M-1 | $ 106.6 | M1-A | $ 372.2 |
| Currency | | Currency | 106.6 |
| PLUS: Demand deposits at | | Demand deposits[b] | 265.6 |
|     commercial banks | 265.6 | M1-B | 387.9 |
|       Total | 372.2 | M1-A | 372.2 |
| M-2 | | Other checkable deposits[c] | 15.7 |
|   M-1 | 372.2 | M-2 | 1,510.0 |
| PLUS: Savings balances at | | M-1B | 387.9 |
|     commercial banks | 209.6 | Overnight RPs issued by | |
|     Time deposits at | |   commercial banks | 20.3 |
|     commercial banks | 445.7 | Overnight Eurodollar deposits | |
| LESS: Negotiable CDs at large | |   held by U.S. nonbank residents | |
|     banks | 95.9 |   at Caribbean branches of U.S. | |
|       Total | 940.5 |   banks | 3.2 |
| M-3 | | Money market mutual fund | |
|   M-2 | 940.5 |   shares | 40.4 |
| PLUS: Savings and time | | Savings deposits at all | |
|     deposits at thrift | |   depositary institutions | 420.0 |
|     institutions | 664.1 | Small time deposits at all | |
|       Total | 1604.6 |   depositary institutions[d] | 640.8 |
| | | M-2 consolidation component[e] | (2.7) |
| M-4 | | M-3 | 1,759.1 |
|   M-2 | 940.5 | M-2 | 1,510.0 |
| PLUS: Negotiable CDs at large | | Large time deposits at all | |
|     banks | 95.9 |   depositary institutions[f] | 219.5 |
|       Total | 1036.4 | Term RPs issued by commercial | |
| | |   banks | 21.5 |
| M-5 | | Term RPs issued by savings and | |
|   M-3 | 1604.6 |   loan associations | 8.2 |
| PLUS: Negotiable CDs at large | | L | 2,123.8 |
|     banks | 95.9 |   M-3 | 1,759.1 |
|       Total | 1700.5 | Other Eurodollar deposits of | |
| | |   U.S. residents other than | |
| | |   banks | 34.5 |
| | | Bankers acceptances | 27.6 |
| | | Commercial paper | 97.1 |
| | | Savings bonds | 80.0 |
| | | Liquid Treasury obligations | 125.4 |

[a]Components of M-2, M-3, and L measures generally exclude amounts held by domestic depositary institutions, foreign commercial banks and official institutions, the U.S. government (including the Federal Reserve), and money market mutual funds. Exceptions are bankers acceptances and commercial paper for which data sources permit the removal only of amounts held by money market mutual funds and, in the case of bankers acceptances, amounts held by accepting banks, the Federal Reserve, and the Federal Home Loan Bank System.

[b]Net of demand deposits due to foreign commercial banks and official institutions.

[c]Includes NOW, ATS, and credit union share draft balances and demand deposits at thrift institutions.

[d]Time deposits issued in denominations of less than $100,000.

[e]In order to avoid double counting of some deposits in M-2, those demand deposits owned by thrift institutions (a component of M1-B), which are estimated to be used for servicing their savings, and small time deposit liabilities in M-2, are removed.

[f]Time deposits issued in denominations of $100,000 or more.

Source: *Federal Reserve Bulletin* (January 1980).

nevertheless not perfect substitutes for M-1. Typically, these assets must be transferred into money before spending, even though transfer may be relatively easy. The traditional definition of M-2 includes M-1 and adds savings and time deposits at commercial banks, with the exception of negotiable certificates of deposit. M-3 is broader still; it encompasses both M-2 and similar time and savings deposits at nonbank institutions. M-4 and M-5 are the same as M-2 and M-3 with the addition of negotiable certificates of deposit at large banks. The new 1980 measures are designed to replace the traditional M-1–M-5 aggregates in a way that responds to market changes. Policymakers and economists in the future undoubtedly will have to study a variety of new monetary measures as they attempt to understand better the impact of monetary forces on the economy.

## Structure and Functions of the Federal Reserve System

Before proceeding to a discussion of the sources and creation of money and credit, it seems worthwhile to review briefly the structure and functions of the Federal Reserve System. The Federal Reserve System is, of course, the nation's central bank, the institution charged with planning and implementing the country's monetary policies. Designed in a uniquely American fashion as a "decentralized" central bank, the Federal Reserve System has a number of independent but interrelated components that interact to carry out the System's monetary and other functions.[5]

The Federal Reserve System was established by the Federal Reserve Act of 1913 to consist of twelve regional Federal Reserve banks and a Board of Governors with headquarters in the nation's capital. Unlike central banks in other developed countries, the System has a decentralized character as a result of an early compromise between those favoring establishment of a central bank and those fearful of centralized economic and financial power.[6] The Act established district banks primarily because Congress intended to create autonomous institutions that were limited in financial power but responsive to the needs of each geographic region of the country. Each of the twelve banks is a federally chartered corporation, privately owned by its member commercial banks but charged with public responsibilities. Of the nine individuals comprising the Board of Directors of each Reserve bank, six are elected by the member banks in that district and three are appointed by the Board of Governors in Washington. Each bank's Board of Directors is responsible for the policy and operation of its district bank subject to overall coordination and approval by the Board of Governors.

The regional banks participate in the monetary policy and other functions of the System in a number of important ways. One way is through the holding, by the regional Reserve banks, of banks' required reserves. According to federal and state banking laws and regulations, all banks must keep a specified proportion of their deposit liabilities in the form of reserve requirements. Historically, for banks that were not members of the Federal Reserve System (typically, these were smaller banks chartered by their home states), reserves could be held in whatever forms were permitted by state law.[7] However, if the bank was a member of the Federal Reserve System, reserves could be kept only in the form of currency in the bank's vault or as deposit balances in its regional Reserve bank. This dichotomy was altered in 1980 by the Mone-

---

[5] Fuller accounts of the origins, history, and structure of the Federal Reserve System may be found in many textbooks in the field of money and banking. For the System's own view, see Board of Governors of the Federal Reserve System, *The Federal Reserve: Purposes and Functions*, Washington, D.C., 1974; for an interesting account of the System's early years through a biography of one of its formative influences, see Lester V. Chandler, *Benjamin Strong, Central Banker*, The Brookings Institution, Washington, D.C., 1967.

[6] These twin concerns of the need for a strong monetary authority and fear of centralized economic power have been central to the American political economy since the presidency of George Washington. For a discussion of the historical aspects, see Bray Hammond, *Banks and Politics in America from the Revolution to the Civil War*, Princeton University Press, Princeton, N.J., 1957; and Friedman and Schwartz, *A Monetary History*.

[7] See R. Alton Gilbert and Jean M. Lovatis, "Bank Reserve Requirements and their Enforcement: A Comparison Across States," Federal Reserve Bank of St. Louis *Review* (March 1978); and R. Alton Gilbert, "Effectiveness of State Reserve Requirements," Federal Reserve Bank of St. Louis *Review* (September 1978).

tary Control Act, which required all financial institutions offering "transaction accounts" (demand deposit–like accounts) or nonpersonal time deposits to hold reserves like member banks. Originally, the idea of requiring banks to hold reserves was associated with the desire to ensure adequate liquidity in banks to protect depositors. More recently, required reserves have become an important fulcrum of monetary policy since they limit the individual bank's and the banking system's ability to expand money and credit. (This will be discussed further in the next section of this chapter.)

Member banks' deposit balances at their Reserve banks also are important in the monetary payments mechanism. The great majority of monetary transfers in this country are made by checks drawn on commercial banks. Many of these transfers are processed ("cleared") by the Federal Reserve banks through debiting the reserve account of the paying bank and crediting the account of the receiving bank. Although not all payments are processed through Federal Reserve banks (some are cleared directly by commercial banks), the Federal Reserve banks clear millions of checks each day.

A second function of the Reserve banks is to make loans (called discounts or advances) to institutions that are subject to reserve requirements on their transaction accounts; this is done for short periods of time either to accommodate seasonal demands or to help with short-term liquidity needs. Although discount policy and discount rates are elements of monetary policy and must be centrally coordinated, discount rates are actually established by the individual Reserve banks (subject to approval by the Board of Governors) and the loans are actually made by the regional banks. Since discounting is an instrument of monetary policy, it will be discussed more fully in Chapter 28.

The district Federal Reserve banks also provide a variety of other services for member banks, the federal government, and the public. For one thing, they maintain a continuous program of bank examinations whereby they supervise directly the safety, soundness, and banking law compliance of member banks that are not national banks.[8] The

regional banks and their branches also serve as fiscal agents for the U.S. Treasury, providing checking accounts and processing U.S. government bonds. In addition, they provide for monetary transfers, not only through the check-clearing process, but also through currency distribution and automated (computerized) clearing houses for electronic funds transfers. Finally, the regional Reserve banks aid in economic analysis through their research departments, statistical preparation and assembly, and dissemination of information on economic and financial topics. The decentralized nature of the central bank even produces, on occasion, divergent viewpoints on economic policy matters that challenge the conventional wisdom. The soul searching and questioning that result undoubtedly help the central bank keep its thinking fresh and up to date.

Member banks comprise a second important segment of the Federal Reserve System, although they are not actually part of the central bank itself. Member banks include all national banks (banks chartered by the federal government under the National Banking Act must be members of the System) and state-chartered banks that choose to be members. In the past, advantages of membership included access to the check-clearing and monetary-transfer facilities of the System as well as eligibility for discounts and advances. Disadvantages consisted primarily of the necessity for holding required reserves in the form of noninterest-earning deposit accounts at Federal Reserve banks or in vault cash that also provided no interest return. As interest rates rose through most of the 1970s, the nonearning nature of these required reserves caused Federal Reserve membership to become increasingly unattractive, especially to smaller banks, and many members resigned their System membership. Declining System membership caused the Federal Reserve to argue that its control over monetary conditions was being slowly eroded, and a variety of reform proposals circulated in the latter part of the decade. In general, the reform proposals

---

[8]The Federal Reserve System directly examines only banks that are state chartered and are members of the System (about 1,000 banks). National banks are examined by the Office of the Comptroller of the Currency, and state-chartered insured banks that are not members of the Federal Reserve System are examined by the Federal Deposit Insurance Corporation (FDIC). State-chartered banks are also examined by state authorities. Supervisory responsibilities of the various banking agencies are discussed further in Chapter 31.

took either of two forms: making membership mandatory or making it more attractive by paying interest on reserves held at the Federal Reserve banks. Neither of the choices was especially attractive to Congress since mandatory membership might be burdensome to small institutions, and paying interest on reserves would require spending federal revenues. Fortunately, the option of doing nothing was also unattractive since Congress realized that control over monetary conditions could be affected. Congress finally resolved this problem in March 1980 by specifying, in the Monetary Control Act, uniform reserve requirements for all institutions offering either checking-type accounts or nonpersonal time deposits, while phasing in the requirements for non–Federal Reserve members over eight years. This legislation sharply reduced the advantages of nonmembership.

At the center of the Federal Reserve System is the Board of Governors. The Board operates as a quasi-independent agency of the federal government with seven governors, each appointed by the President and confirmed by the Senate for fourteen-year, nonrenewable terms.[9] One term expires every two years (at the end of January of the even-numbered years), so, if there are no resignations, the President will have the opportunity to appoint only two Board members during each term of office.[10] The reason for the long, staggered terms is to insulate the central bank, as much as possible, from the pressures of government and politics. Nevertheless, because the governors are appointed by the President and confirmed by the Senate, and because Congress can change banking law, including the Federal Reserve Act, at any time, the Federal Reserve is not totally independent of the checks and balances inherent in American government.

The Federal Reserve Board is, of course, highly involved in the System's monetary policy, but actual policy decisions are made by a somewhat larger group, again illustrating the decentralized nature of the American central bank. Monetary policy decisions are made by the Federal Open Market Committee (FOMC) which is composed of the seven Board governors plus five Reserve bank presidents. The president of the Federal Reserve Bank of New York is a permanent voting member of the Committee, and the other presidents serve on a rotating basis.[11] All the Reserve bank presidents participate in the formulation of monetary policy. Furthermore, all attend and can speak at FOMC meetings, although only five can vote at any one time. Meetings are held regularly, approximately every four weeks, at the Board's headquarters in Washington. Telephone conferences are held between meetings if changing economic conditions warrant immediate attention. Decisions made at the meetings usually involve giving to the System guidelines for purchases and sales of government securities in the financial markets. As will be discussed in a later section of this chapter and in Chapter 28, the System's purchases and sales of these securities affect the volume of money and credit in the financial system, and these open-market operations are the chief instrument of monetary policy. Actual market activities are carried out for the System by the Federal Reserve Bank of New York.

Besides assigning the Board of Governors a central role in the formulation of monetary policy, Congress has also given the Board a number of other financial and regulatory functions. One responsibility, examination and supervision of state-chartered member banks, has already been mentioned. In addition, under the Bank Holding Company Act, the Board must evaluate whether purchases of banks by holding companies meet the "convenience and needs" of the public and whether the acquisitions have any adverse competitive implications before the acquisition can be finalized. Also, the Board must determine whether any *nonbank* acquisitions by bank holding companies (such as purchases of finance companies or mortgage banking firms) are "closely related to banking" as required by the Act, and whether there will be net public benefits from the consolidation. Net public benefits might come about if gains in

---

[9]Board members appointed to serve the remaining years of an unexpired term created by a resignation can be reappointed by the President to their own fourteen-year term. Thus, William McChesney Martin, who was Chairman of the Board from 1951 to 1970, served five years of an unexpired term and was reappointed by President Eisenhower to his own fourteen-year term.

[10]In recent years, resignations have caused the turn-over to be considerably higher.

[11]The presidents of the Chicago and Cleveland banks alternate, and the others serve once every three years.

efficiency, capital, or managerial capabilities might result from a merger and if these are not out-weighed by anticompetitive or monopolistic tend-encies. In deciding such questions, the Board is aided by economic and legal researchers at the Board headquarters in Washington and in the re-gional Reserve banks.[12] In recent years, the Board has also been tapped by Congress to write the rules and guidelines for enforcing a variety of pieces of legislation affecting consumer financial services. Probably best known among these laws are the Truth-in-Lending Act, the Fair Credit Billing Act, the Equal Credit Opportunity Act, and the Elec-tronic Funds Transfer Act. Each of these Acts specifies that the Board must work out the details of administering the Act (write the implementing rules) and then mount, usually in conjunction with other federal regulatory agencies, the necessary enforcement efforts. In recent years, it seems, these and other regulatory matters initiated by Con-gress have consumed increasing amounts of time on the part of the Board staff, over and beyond the efforts devoted to traditional aspects of monetary policy.

## The Process of Money and Credit Creation

### Commercial Banks and the Supply of Money and Credit

Even some careful readers of the financial press might report, if asked, that the Federal Reserve supplies the American economy with money. Ac-tually, this statement by itself may be misleading, since the Federal Reserve directly creates only a small portion of the money supply. Most money is created by banks and some of the rest is created by the U.S. Treasury. Consequently, while it may be correct to say that the Federal Reserve influ-ences or even controls money creation, a clear picture requires a fuller description of how banks, the public, the Treasury, and the Federal Reserve interact in the process of supplying money. The purpose of this section of the chapter is to examine the monetary process more closely.

For a moment let us recall the definition of money introduced earlier in this chapter. Money, we said, is an asset that is readily acceptable in exchange for goods and services or other financial assets. We also mentioned that, in the United States, the main component of the supply of money is bank demand deposits that can be readily spent. These include traditional checking deposits as well as the newer forms of deposits such as NOW ac-counts and share drafts. This suggests that even a simple answer to the question of where money comes from must involve an understanding of how banks create demand deposits. (In much of the discussion that follows the term *banks* can be viewed as also applying to those nonbank deposi-tory intermediaries that offer monetary "transac-tion accounts," as permitted by the Monetary Con-trol Act mentioned previously.)

Banks create demand deposits in only three ways. Of these, the first way has no impact on the supply of money because for every dollar of de-mand deposits created by a bank, simultaneously another dollar of money is extinguished. In con-trast, the other two ways do have impacts on the supply of money; and one of these, the purchase of assets and the extension of credit by banks, is quantitatively the most important cause of mone-tary changes.

The first case is the obvious one: a bank estab-lishes or increases a demand-deposit account when someone brings money to the bank in exchange for the deposit. Examples are familiar and they con-stitute a very large category of bank transactions, but no creation of money is involved. There is no money creation because the inflow consists of al-ready-existing money—either checks drawn on ex-isting accounts or currency.[13] In the former case, new demand deposits may be created in Bank A, but Banks B and C lose demand deposits when the checks are cleared. The result is no new money. The same is true if the deposit is made in the form of currency. Again, a deposit is established or in-creased, and this account is money if it is a demand deposit, but now the *bank* has the currency, and currency in vaults is generally not counted as

---

[12]These and other issues of financial structure are con-sidered further in Chapter 31.

[13]It is possible, of course, that a deposit of money (currency, coin, or check) might be made into a savings account, in which case the supply of money might actually *decrease*.

money since it is not in the hands of the public. Again, the net effect is no increase in the money supply, just a change of form. Consequently, ordinary acts of depositing funds in banks do not result in any change in the available supply of money.

The second way banks add to demand-deposit accounts is by shifting funds from deposit accounts that are not demand-deposit accounts into deposit accounts that are. A familiar example is the case of an account holder with a savings account who requests the bank to move the funds into a checking account. In this situation, the supply of money increases because now the asset can be spent immediately. However, the overall impact of transactions like this on the total supply of money is minor because, although shifting funds into demand-deposit accounts increases the supply of money, the reverse shift, which also is common, decreases the supply of money. While the net effect may lead to monetary increases or decreases on a given day or over a short period, they are not a major cause of monetary changes over time.

Acquiring financial assets is the third and major way in which banks augment demand deposits. Whenever a bank acquires a financial asset (for example, by buying a security or making a loan) the bank pays for the asset by increasing its own demand-deposit liabilities or by issuing a check that can be deposited in another bank. If a check is issued and it is deposited in another bank, the latter creates in exchange for it an additional demand-deposit liability against itself. In either case, the total supply of money has increased since no one else's money has decreased as a result of the transaction.

To provide a framework for showing a variety of such transactions as well as others, we can employ the T-accounts concept introduced in Chapter 2. A T-account is simply a bookkeeping device where asset changes are shown to the left of the vertical member of a "T," and changes in liabilities are shown on the right. It is particularly useful for illustrating money creation because it also shows the relationship between deposit creation and loanable funds.[14]

[14]Loanable funds in the macroeconomy are discussed in Chapter 22.

Transaction 1 in Figure 5-1 illustrates the typical case of monetary and credit expansion by the banking system. The First National Bank makes a loan (acquires an asset), paying for it by opening and crediting an account for a customer. The amount of demand deposits and loans at the bank increases and, since deposits and loans do not decrease anywhere else as a result of the transaction, the supply of money and credit increases. This is the typical case of money and credit creation by a bank.

Now, if banks are responsible for money creation, what, if anything, will limit their ability to expand demand deposits at will? The answer is that individual banks are limited by the amount of their reserves over requirements—in other words, by their excess reserves.[15] Only by having excess reserves can individual banks augment the supply of loanable funds or credit by acquiring IOUs, in the process creating additional liabilities against themselves in the form of demand deposits.[16]

Now, households and firms normally do not borrow for the purpose of leaving the new deposits idle. Instead, they typically borrow (and pay interest on the loans) for the purpose of spending the funds, and this means, as we shall shortly see, that an individual bank can expect to lose its excess reserves after a loan is made. This is illustrated by transaction 2 in Figure 5-1. After a loan for $100 has been made by First National, the borrower spends the money by writing a check for that amount to a merchant (as he does so, the demand-deposit liability of First National Bank for $100 is extinguished). If the merchant deposits the check drawn on First National in a different bank, say the Second National Bank (there are some 14,500 banks in the United States), then Second National

[15]As was pointed out earlier, institutions offering "transaction accounts" are required to hold a portion of these liabilities in the form of required reserves. For example, if reserve requirements are 12 percent, this would mean that for every additional dollar of demand deposits, banks must hold an additional 12 cents in required reserve balances. On the other hand, excess reserves constitute reserves in excess of requirements. Thus, excess reserves = total reserves − required reserves.

[16]Thus banks do not create credit and demand deposits out of thin air as many unfamiliar with the process of deposit creation seem to think. Like individuals and business firms, banks must have free cash or excess reserves available to acquire other assets.

**Figure 5-1 Illustration of Monetary Expansion and Contraction**

*Trans-action*

1)

*Customer*

| | | | |
|---|---|---|---|
| Deposit | +100 | Debt | +100 |

*First National Bank*

| | | | |
|---|---|---|---|
| Loan | +100 | Deposit | +100 |

2)

*Customer*

| | | | |
|---|---|---|---|
| Deposit | −100 | | |
| Goods | +100 | | |

*First National Bank*

| | | | |
|---|---|---|---|
| Reserves | −100 | Deposits of customer | −100 |

*Merchant*

| | | | |
|---|---|---|---|
| Goods | −100 | | |
| Deposit | +100 | | |

*Second National Bank*

| | | | |
|---|---|---|---|
| Reserves | +100 | Deposit of merchant | +100 |
| Loan | +100 | Deposit of borrower | +100 |
| Reserves | −100 | Deposit of borrower | −100 |

*Federal Reserve*

| | | | |
|---|---|---|---|
| | | Reserve of First NB | −100 |
| | | Reserve of Second NB | +100 |

3)

*Federal Reserve*

| | | | |
|---|---|---|---|
| Securities | +100 | Reserve of First NB | +100 |

*Dealer*

| | | | |
|---|---|---|---|
| Securities | −100 | | |
| Deposit | +100 | | |

*First National Bank*

| | | | |
|---|---|---|---|
| Reserves | +100 | Deposits | +100 |
| (Required | +10) | | |
| (Excess | +90) | | |

4)

*Borrowers*

| | | | |
|---|---|---|---|
| Deposits | +90 | Debt | +90 |

*First National Bank*

| | | | |
|---|---|---|---|
| Loans | +90 | Deposits | +90 |

5)

*Federal Reserve*

| | | | |
|---|---|---|---|
| Securities | −10 | Reserve of First NB | −10 |

*Dealer*

| | | | |
|---|---|---|---|
| Securities | +10 | | |
| Deposit | −10 | | |

*First National Bank*

| | | | |
|---|---|---|---|
| Reserves | −10 | Deposits | −10 |
| (Required | −1) | | |
| (Excess | −9) | | |

6)

*Federal Reserve*

| | | | |
|---|---|---|---|
| | | Reserve of First NB | +9 |
| | | Reserve of Second NB | −9 |

*Dealer*

| | | | |
|---|---|---|---|
| Bonds | +9 | | |
| Deposit | −9 | | |

*First National Bank*

| | | | |
|---|---|---|---|
| Bonds | −9 | | |
| Reserves | +9 | | |

*Second National Bank*

| | | | |
|---|---|---|---|
| Reserves | −9 | Deposits | −9 |
| (Required | −0.9) | | |
| (Excess | −8.1) | | |

will increase its demand-deposit liabilities to the merchant by $100 (equal to the amount of the check) and send the latter to its Federal Reserve bank for clearing and collection. The Federal Reserve bank, in turn, will credit (increase) Second National's reserve balances with it by $100 and debit (decrease) First National's account by an equivalent amount. The result is an increase in demand-deposit liabilities and reserves for Second National of $100 and a decrease in both for First National of $100.[17]

Transaction 2 in Figure 5-1 also illustrates the consequences that would ensue should banks extend credit and create additional demand deposits beyond their excess reserves. Suppose, for example, that First National had no excess reserves when it made the loan in question. Now, having made the loan anyway and having lost reserves to Second National when the check cleared, First National finds itself in a required-reserve deficit position amounting to $100. Similarly, if Second National were to make a loan greater than its recently acquired excess reserves (assuming a 10 percent reserve requirement against the $100 demand-deposit liability to the merchant, its required reserves would be an additional $10 and its excess reserves would amount to $100 − $10, or $90), it would shortly lose not only its excess reserves ($90) to some other bank, but it would also lose the reserves required against the still-existing demand deposit of the merchant, thereby putting Second National in a required reserve deficit position ($10). Simply put, avoidance of deficits in their required reserves is what, ultimately, limits banks in their lending and the resultant creation of demand deposits.[18] And since the Federal Reserve System controls the total amount of reserves in the System at any point in time, the central bank can influence and control monetary expansion, even if it does not actually create money itself.

In sum, commercial banks in the United States and not the central bank are responsible for the bulk of money creation in the form of demand deposits. When commercial banks purchase anything—securities and the IOUs of borrowers are the most familiar examples, but the same principles apply to purchases of buildings, stationery and supplies, and labor services—money is created. The bank simply purchases something that is not money by exchanging something that *is* money. As has been stated several times, however, banks are limited in their ability to create demand deposits by their reserve requirements. In this way, the central bank influences the money supply, since it can control (or at least strongly influence) both total and required reserves.

### The Federal Reserve and Bank Reserves

The Federal Reserve affects the supply of bank reserves in much the same way as banks affect the supply of money. Whenever Federal Reserve banks purchase anything or extend credit (the usual examples are the purchase of U.S. government securities and borrowing by member banks), they pay for the purchase or loan either by creating a deposit on their books or by issuing a check. In either case, new bank reserves are created—in the first case directly and, in the second case, when the check is deposited in a commercial bank which then demands payment from the Federal Reserve bank. In both cases new reserves are created which banks can then use to create money.[19] These changes are illustrated in more detail by transaction 3 in Figure 5-1. (Although the examples involve banks, the principles apply equally to nonbank depository intermediaries that provide monetary liabilities and must adhere to reserve requirements.)

In transaction 3, suppose that, for policy reasons, the Federal Reserve has decided that an increase in the supply of money is appropriate. Knowing that an increase in bank reserves is

---

[17]Some checks are cleared directly by commercial banks that hold accounts for other banks, and the Federal Reserve is accordingly bypassed. Nevertheless, the result is the same: one bank gains reserves and another loses them.

[18]As will be discussed further both in this chapter and in Chapter 28, banks with reserve deficits may be able to borrow from other banks with reserve surpluses. However, not all banks can be in deficit simultaneously. Thus, the possibility of borrowing reserves does not contradict the contention that individual banks' lending is limited by their reserve requirements.

[19]If a check is issued, some money is also created, which is how the Federal Reserve directly creates money. The Federal Reserve's impact on money creation goes far beyond this small amount of money created directly, however, as will be seen.

needed, the System purchases $100 million of government securities from a government securities dealer and issues a check in payment. The dealer firm then deposits the check in the First National Bank and First National sends the check to its Federal Reserve bank for clearing. When the check arrives, the Federal Reserve bank increases the reserve account of First National on its own books. The net changes are shown in transaction 3, leaving out the intermediate steps involving movement of the Federal Reserve's check.[20]

This transaction has a number of important results. In the first place, the dealer has fewer securities in inventory but has a greater deposit balance at First National Bank. Other things equal, this could encourage dealers to replenish inventories, which would tend to raise security prices. In addition, First National has more demand deposits and so the supply of money has increased. Even more important to the bank, however, its total reserves and excess reserves have also risen, and this allows it to make more loans. Suppose that First National had no excess reserves before the Federal Reserve entered the market and that required reserves on demand deposits are 10 percent. First National's deposits have increased $100 million but its required reserves have increased only $10 million (10 percent of $100 million). This leaves First National with new excess reserves of $90 million, which enables it to make $90 million of new loans. Now suppose that potential borrowers desire a full $90 million of new loans and First National accommodates their demand by crediting their accounts with $90 million of new money (transaction 4 in Figure 5-1). At this stage the total amount of new money in the economy is $190 million—$90 million *more than* the Federal Reserve's initial injection of reserves into the banking system!

The process does not stop here, though. Since borrowers do not borrow $90 million to keep in the bank while paying interest on the borrowed funds, we can assume that checks are written to various merchants and suppliers and these checks are eventually deposited in the Second National Bank. As a result, Second National now has $90 million in

new reserves, only $9 million of which are required reserves for the $90 million of new deposits. This means that Second National, like First National earlier, now has new lending capacity. If it lends the full amount of its new excess reserves ($81 million), the total amount of new money in the economy would now be $271 million ($190 million + $81 million). But still the process does not stop. If borrowers pay out the new money and eventually the $81 million is deposited in the Third National Bank, then Third National has new reserves and new lending capacity. The process of lending and creating money, reserve transfer, and further lending and creating money will continue, theoretically, until all of the original new excess reserves created by the Federal Reserve are employed as required reserves. The amount of new money that will be created in the process can be calculated from a simple equation. If new reserves are given by $NR$, new demand deposits by $\Delta DD$, and the required reserve ratio by $rr\%$, then

$$NR = rr\% \cdot \Delta DD \qquad (5\text{-}1)$$

or, rearranging

$$\Delta DD = \frac{1}{rr\%} \cdot NR \qquad (5\text{-}2)$$

In other words, total new demand deposits (new money) created as a result of the Federal Reserve's action theoretically can reach (that is, if there are no leakages and the lending process continues) a total far greater than the amount of the new excess reserves: the new reserves times the reciprocal of the required reserve ratio. In the example, total new deposits could reach $1 billion ($1/.1 \cdot $100 million = $1 billion).

This example, and Equations (5-1) and (5-2), illustrate the principle known as the *multiple expansion of money*. Briefly stated, when the Federal Reserve increases bank reserves by some amount, the increase in money and credit is not limited to that amount; money and loanable funds can increase by a *multiple* of the increase in reserves.[21] The recip-

---

[20] To be sure that the student fully understands all the changes involved, the transaction should be reproduced on scratch paper, but adding the intermediate steps of the movements of the Federal Reserve's check from the Federal Reserve to the dealer, to First National Bank, and back again to the Federal Reserve.

[21] This applies to the banking system as a whole; it does not apply to individual banks comprising the system because, as we have seen, the individual bank will shortly lose its excess reserves after making a loan to another bank, whereas the system does not have this leakage (loss of excess reserves) to contend with. Consequently, for the latter, a multiple expansion of demand deposits is possible.

rocal of the required reserve ratio ($1/.1 = 10$ in the example) is called the *reserve multiplier*. It is the ratio of the potential increase in money to the increase in bank reserves. This multiple expansion of money shows the power of Federal Reserve policy initiatives. For every $1 of reserves injected, the impact on the money supply and loanable funds can be many times that $1.

If, in contrast to the expansionary case, the Federal Reserve should desire a contraction in the supply of money, exactly the opposite policy can be followed. Instead of buying government securities, which would lead to an increase in bank reserves, the Federal Reserve can sell securities. Transaction 5 in Figure 5-1 illustrates the contractionary case. First, assume that the Federal Reserve sells $10 million of U.S. government securities from its portfolio. The government securities dealer pays for the securities with a check drawn against its account at First National Bank. Next, the Federal Reserve clears the check by decreasing the reserve account of First National by $10 million. Now, if First National did not have sufficient excess reserves, it finds itself in a required-reserve deficit position. Suppose, for example, that First National had no excess reserves before the Federal Reserve sold the securities to the dealer. Now the bank finds that its deposits have declined by $10 million, freeing $1 million of required reserves; its total reserves, however, have declined by $10 million. This means that First National has a required-reserve deficit of $9 million.

If First National believes its reserve deficit is temporary, it could do a number of things to offset the deficit, including borrowing reserves from other banks or from its Federal Reserve bank. Eventually, however, if the deficit is not temporary and permanent reserves do not materialize from another source, First National would be forced to acquire additional reserves by liquidating assets. Suppose that First National decides to raise $9 million by selling securities from its portfolio to a dealer. The dealer firm, of course, must pay for the securities by writing a check on its bank, say, Second National Bank. First National would then send the check drawn on Second National to the Federal Reserve for clearing. The Reserve bank would increase the reserve account of First National by the amount of the check and reduce the reserves of Second National. These changes are shown in transaction 6 in Figure 5-1.

Transaction 6 in Figure 5-1 shows that the sale of securities by First National Bank did not eliminate the required-reserve deficiency, it merely passed most of it on to Second National Bank. Now Second National must respond and, if it cannot find sufficient reserves either, it must also reduce assets. In this way the impact of a Federal Reserve sale of securities can pass through the entire banking system. This case shows, however, that whenever the Federal Reserve sells anything, the result is a contraction in bank reserves and a multiple contraction in the supply of money and credit. As in the expansion case, the theoretical limit to the monetary contraction—as the required-reserve deficit is passed to Third National, Fourth National, and so on—is equal to the amount of the initial contraction in reserves times the reciprocal of the required-reserve ratio. The contractionary case is simply the mirror image of the expansionary case.[22]

The transactions reviewed in Figure 5-1 show the interaction between the Federal Reserve and the banking system in the process of money and credit creation. The important points are that whenever the Federal Reserve System purchases securities and extends credit, the supply of bank reserves increases, and whenever the banking system does the same, the supply of demand deposits and money increases. Furthermore, Federal Reserve policy concerning bank reserves has a powerful impact on the supply of deposits and money because of the potential for multiple expansion. This is the reason why bank reserves are occasionally referred to as *high-powered money*.[23]

## Other Influences on Bank Reserves

Actually, the Federal Reserve does not have complete control over bank reserves. Policy actions with respect to the purchase and sale of govern-

---

[22]In both of these cases it is assumed that the banks are fully loaned up, that is, they do not hold excess reserves beyond requirements. As will be discussed later in this chapter, if banks hold excess reserves the potential reserve multiplier and "money multiplier" (defined later) are reduced.

[23]The term *high-powered money* is also often applied to the total of all liabilities in the economy that could *potentially* serve as bank reserves. In this sense the term refers to the sum of bank reserves and currency and coin in the hands of the public. This is also known as the *monetary base*.

ment securities constitute one important group of factors affecting bank reserves, but there is also another, more diverse, group known as the *operating factors*. In the long run, changes caused by the operating factors are overshadowed by policy-induced changes but, in a short period, such as a week or month, the operating factors can be highly important in influencing bank reserves. As a result, for many years much of the Federal Reserve System's day-to-day activities in financial markets involved policy actions designed primarily to offset the impact of various operating factors that might have undesirable consequences. Although, more recently, the System has chosen to devote less attention to offsetting the operating factors, they are still important and merit examination if weekly changes in monetary statistics are to be understood fully.[24]

Probably the most important operating factors affecting bank reserves are currency movements and changes in U.S. Treasury checking-account balances at Federal Reserve banks. Currency movements can occur whenever the public desires a change in the amount of its pocket currency and currency is either withdrawn or deposited in banks. Substantial withdrawals might occur, for example, before a holiday weekend or during vacation periods or the year-end retail shopping period. Currency withdrawals or "drains" may cause severe operating problems for banks, though, since currency in vaults is considered part of banks' required reserves. The problem is that currency withdrawals that cause required-reserve deficits force the banking system to contract loans, investments, and money in the same way as Federal Reserve policy actions.

Transaction 1 in Figure 5-2 illustrates a currency drain. Suppose depositors at First National Bank, noting the onset of the "summer sales" season, decide to carry $100,000 more cash in their wallets and purses. Furthermore, they decide to acquire the additional currency by writing checks against

their deposits at First National Bank. The supply of money remains the same, since one form of money is simply exchanged for another, but First National loses deposits in this process. More importantly from the bank's standpoint, it also loses reserves. The decline in deposits means that *required* reserves are reduced somewhat, but total reserves decline even more. In the example, deposits decline by $100,000 and required reserves by $10,000, but total reserves decline by the full amount of the cash drain—$100,000. The $90,000 decline in additional reserves would put First National in a required-reserve deficit position unless it held excess reserves. And, as pointed out earlier, required-reserve deficits can produce a multiple contraction of deposits and money.

Typically, the Federal Reserve has attempted to limit the impact of cash drains on the banking system by offsetting the drains with policy actions. These actions might take the form of System purchases of U.S. government securities from dealers before long weekends or during certain seasons of the year. In this way, cash needs of the public can be accommodated without causing an undesired contraction of bank lending and money. When the cash is redeposited by merchants and other recipients following the weekend or shopping season, Federal Reserve sales of securities could be undertaken to avoid buildup of reserves in the banking system. In any case, the key point is that the Federal Reserve can offset the cash drain, if it wishes to, by ordinary purchases and sales of securities. If a forecast suggests that a cash drain is likely to cause only temporary tightness in the banking system, the Federal Reserve will very often undertake both sides of the purchase-sale transaction at the same time, but with a delayed effective date of the resale.[25]

Changes in U.S. Treasury checking-account balances at Federal Reserve banks are another class of transactions which affect bank reserves but

[24]In October 1979, Federal Reserve Chairman, Paul Volcker, announced new System procedures which would involve less attention to day-to-day fluctuations in the operating factors. However, the new policies did not alter the short-run importance of the operating factors or long-standing System programs to make gradual improvements in the payments mechanism that lessen the influence of these factors.

[25]A transaction of this kind is known as a System repurchase agreement or *Repo*. The reverse transaction—where a sale of securities that reduces reserves is matched a few days later by a prearranged purchase—is called a matched sale-purchase or a *Reverse Repo*. Private institutions may enter into repos and reverse repos with one another for a variety of investment purposes, but when the Federal Reserve enters into transactions of this kind, it does so solely for purposes associated with monetary policy.

# Figure 5-2  Illustration of the Impact of Operating Factors on Bank Reserves

**Transaction**

**1)**

*Depositor*

| | |
|---|---|
| Deposit | −100 |
| Cash | +100 |

*First National Bank*

| | | Deposits | −100 |
|---|---|---|---|
| Cash | −100 | | |
| (Required | −10) | | |
| (Excess | −90) | | |

**2)**

*Public*

| | |
|---|---|
| Treasury bond | +100 |
| Deposits | −100 |

*Treasury*

| Check | +100 | Debt | +100 |
|---|---|---|---|

**3)**

*First National Bank*

| | | Deposits | −100 |
|---|---|---|---|
| Reserves | −100 | | |
| (Required | −10) | | |
| (Excess | −90) | | |

*Treasury*

| | |
|---|---|
| Check | −100 |
| Deposit at Fed | +100 |

*Federal Reserve*

| | Deposit of Treasury | +100 |
|---|---|---|
| | Reserve of First NB | −100 |

**4)**

*First National Bank*

| Cash items in process of collection | +500 | Deposits | +500 |
|---|---|---|---|

*Federal Reserve*

| Cash items in process of collection | +500 | Deferred availability items | +500 |
|---|---|---|---|

**5)**

*First National Bank*

| | | |
|---|---|---|
| Cash items in process of collection | −500 | |
| Reserves | +500 | |
| (Required | +50) | |
| (Excess | +450) | |

*Federal Reserve*

| | Deferred availability items | −500 |
|---|---|---|
| | Reserve of First NB | +500 |

**6)**

*Federal Reserve*

| Cash items in process of collection | −500 | Reserve of Second NB | −500 |
|---|---|---|---|

*Second National Bank*

| | | Deposits | −500 |
|---|---|---|---|
| Reserves | −500 | | |
| (Required | −50) | | |
| (Excess | −450) | | |

**7)**

*First National Bank*

| Reserves | +10 | Debt to Federal Reserve | +10 |
|---|---|---|---|

*Federal Reserve*

| Loan to First NB | +10 | Reserve of First NB | +10 |
|---|---|---|---|

which, traditionally, the Federal Reserve has tried to forecast and offset. Whenever payments are made by the public to the Treasury, whether for tax payments, bond sales, or other reasons, the supply of money is immediately reduced, because Treasury deposits are not considered as part of the money supply. Payment to the Treasury is illustrated by transaction 2 in Figure 5-2. In the example, the public buys $100 million of new government bonds issued by the Treasury and pays for them by check, in the process extinguishing $100 million of its demand deposits. More important to the banking system, however, is the question of what the Treasury does with the check. If it deposits its new funds back again into the commercial banking system, the Treasury does not affect bank reserves. On the other hand, if the Treasury uses the funds to add to its checking account with the Federal Reserve System, bank reserves will be reduced when the check clears (transaction 3 in Figure 5-2). Unless the reduction in bank reserves is offset by the Federal Reserve or the banking system is holding excess reserves, a multiple contraction of bank credit and money could follow.

Over time, the Treasury has used a number of methods of allocating its deposits among banks to minimize disruptions to bank reserves. Nevertheless, since the Treasury has consistently made all of its payments from its Federal Reserve account, this means that some disruptions are inevitable as deposits are shifted from commercial banks to deposits at Federal Reserve banks and back again to the banking system as revenues are spent by the Treasury and eventually find their way back into banks. A large portion of Federal Reserve day-to-day open market purchases and sales, often through the repo or reverse repo method, are undertaken to offset fluctuations in the Treasury's checking account balances. On occasion, these fluctuations can be quite large, and they have a distinct seasonal pattern associated with patterns of tax collections, borrowing, and federal spending.

Changes in Federal Reserve *float* are another important short-run operating factor affecting bank reserves. Float arises in the process of check clearing whenever a bank acquiring new reserves receives credit for the increase before the bank losing them has its reserve account deducted. This can occur because the Federal Reserve System has rules governing the timing of crediting and debiting

reserve accounts as part of the check-clearing process and, depending on the circumstances, these events may not take place simultaneously. Full explanation requires a closer look at details of the check-clearing process.

Suppose a merchant customer of the First National Bank (which is in the New York Federal Reserve district) receives in payment for some goods a check for $500 drawn against a bank in California. On its books First National increases the deposits of the merchant, but it does not immediately increase the entry for its reserves with the Federal Reserve because reserves are not available that quickly under Federal Reserve rules. Instead, First National sends the check to its Federal Reserve bank for clearing and increases an account titled "cash items in process of collection."[26] When the Federal Reserve receives the check, it does not immediately credit or debit reserve accounts either since, at this stage, the California bank does not know yet that the check has been written and that it will lose reserves. Instead, adequate time for notice is allowed. On its books the Federal Reserve Bank of New York increases both an account entitled "cash items in the process of collection" and an offsetting liability account called "deferred availability items" and sends the check to the Federal Reserve Bank of San Francisco. The events up to this point are shown in transaction 4 in Figure 5-2.

Under Federal Reserve rules, reserves will be credited automatically to First National after a certain length of time that varies according to distance, but with a maximum of two days. Consequently, after a short while, the Federal Reserve will automatically reduce its deferred availability items and credit First National's reserve account as shown in transaction 5 in Figure 5-2. Float arises because the offsetting deduction of reserves from the account of the California bank does not take place until the check is presented to the bank by the Federal Reserve Bank of San Francisco, and the timing of this event depends, among other things, on the vagaries of the transportation system. If, for example, snow somewhere in the country tempo-

[26]This account is important to banks because it may be deducted from deposits in calculating required reserves. Thus, in the example, First National's deposits have increased, but it does not yet have to include these deposits in calculating its required reserves.

rarily grounds some airplanes and check presentations slow down, float could build up rapidly. Other causes of float include strikes, computer failures, and checks written on banks in inconvenient locations.

In essence, Federal Reserve float is credit extended by the Reserve banks in the process of check clearing. Banks receiving reserves can obtain them before they are deducted from other banks, and this amounts to an extension of credit by the central bank. Technically, Federal Reserve float is the difference on the Federal Reserve books between cash items in the process of collection and deferred availability items. This may be seen by combining the entries for the Federal Reserve System from transactions 4 and 5 in Figure 5-2. Deferred availability items cancel, and now cash items in process of collection exceed deferred availability items by $500 ($500 − $0 = $500). This is precisely the amount of new reserves in the System as a result of the float. Of course, the net addition to reserves is temporary and will be reversed when the check in question is finally presented to the California bank. The final presentation of the check and cancellation of the float are illustrated by transaction 6 in Figure 5-2. In the interim, however, the Federal Reserve System may undertake offsetting policy actions if it desires to keep bank reserves steady. On occasion, float may be quite disruptive and, for this reason, the Federal Reserve System has, over time, made many changes in the payments system to improve its efficiency.

A final operating factor to be mentioned is Federal Reserve lending or *discounting*. Actually, discounting is not the same as the other operating factors mentioned because it is also an instrument of Federal Reserve monetary policy, which will be discussed further in Chapter 28. However, it is included here among operating factors as well because discounting, like other operating factors, causes fluctuations in bank reserves that are not initiated by the System's policy actions. Rather, discounting is initiated by commercial banks that find themselves short of reserves. Under the guidelines articulated in Federal Reserve Regulation A, banks may borrow from their district Reserve bank, and this increases the total amount of bank reserves. This is illustrated by transaction 7 in Figure 5-2. If the First National Bank borrows $10 million from its Reserve bank, the System responds

by increasing First National's reserve account, and total bank reserves increase by $10 million. The Federal Reserve, of course, may offset this action by sales of U.S. government securities from its own portfolio, if it desires to do so.

In sum, the commercial banking system creates most of the money in the American economy, but it is strongly influenced by the activities of the Federal Reserve System. Although banks can create money by making loans and purchasing assets, their creation of money is ultimately limited by the extent of their reserves, and the volume of reserves is, in large part, the province of the nation's central bank. The Federal Reserve System's control over bank reserves is not absolute, but the System can anticipate and offset the other major influences. Because of this fact, while it is not correct that the central bank is directly responsible for money creation, it is true that the central bank must be willing before monetary expansion can proceed. These ideas are summarized more formally in the remaining portion of this chapter.

### The Bank Reserve Equation and the Money Multiplier

All of the potential influences on bank reserves can be summarized in a single accounting statement known as the bank reserve equation. The *bank reserve equation* is derived from the balance sheet of the Federal Reserve System, with modification to account for U.S. Treasury actions affecting bank reserves. In its simplest form, the equation is merely the expression that potential sources of bank reserves minus their potential uses equals bank reserves. The main elements of the equation are listed in more detail in Table 5-2.[27] Information about each of the components is compiled weekly by the Federal Reserve System, and averages for the seven days ending each Thursday are released by the System each Friday afternoon. Complete listings or summaries of the equation's parts are usually carried in financial newspapers each Saturday. Table 5-3 contains detailed information about the reserve bank equation for the week ending February 8, 1980.

[27]Fuller detail and description of all the components of the bank reserve equation may be found in Federal Reserve Bank of New York, *Glossary: Weekly Federal Reserve Statements.*

## Table 5-2  The Bank Reserve Equation

---

I. Potential Sources of Bank Reserves
  1) Federal Reserve Bank Credit
    a) Open-market account
    b) Discounts and advances
    c) Federal Reserve float
  2) Gold stock and Special Drawing Rights
  3) Treasury currency outstanding

II. (Minus) Potential Uses of Bank Reserves
  4) Currency in circulation (outside the Treasury, Federal Reserve Banks, and commercial banks)
  5) Deposits of the United States Treasury in Federal Reserve Banks
  6) Treasury cash holdings
  7) Nonbank deposits at Federal Reserve Banks
  8) Foreign deposits in Federal Reserve Banks
  9) Other Federal Reserve liabilities and capital (net)

III. (Equals) Bank Reserves

---

The most important source of bank reserves is Federal Reserve Credit, which consists of all credit generated by the Reserve banks. This includes the System's main policy instrument—its purchases of government securities (the open-market account)—as well as some elements of Reserve bank credit that are not completely under the System's control. These include discounts and advances (Reserve bank lending to banks) and Federal Reserve float arising from the check-clearing process. Like other operating factors, these may be important over short time periods, but they can be offset by policy actions if the central bank desires.

The remaining items in the bank reserve equation are the other operating factors that are outside the central bank's control. In general, their impact on bank reserves is not very great, either because they tend to change relatively slowly (being balanced by concurrent changes in other operating factors) or because they are offset by policy actions undertaken by the Reserve System. On occasion, however, one or more operating factors may be influential in affecting reserves because the policymakers decide *not* to offset them. This might happen, for example, if operating factors were supplying reserves in a week during which the System wanted reserves to increase. In this case, additional System policy actions might become unnecessary, and the operating factors might serve as the policy action for that week.

The gold stock consists of so-called monetary gold purchased by the Treasury in the past and held today by the Treasury in its vaults. In the past the Treasury purchased most of the gold mined in this country and also acquired gold as a result of transactions with foreign governments and central banks. Purchases of gold affected bank reserves because, in effect, the Treasury paid for the purchases by check which, when deposited, increased bank reserves. The Treasury would replenish its checking account by issuing gold certificates to the Federal Reserve System. The result of this (somewhat complex) transaction was an increase in the monetary gold stock and the supply of bank reserves with no change in Treasury checking-account balances at the Federal Reserve. While transactions of this kind were once fairly important influences on bank reserves, they are much less common or important today. Changes in holdings of foreign currencies and Special Drawing Rights (SDRs or "paper gold") also result from international transactions, and they affect bank reserves in exactly the same way as changes in the gold stock. In recent years foreign currencies and SDRs have replaced gold for international payments.

The remaining factor listed in Table 5-2 as increasing bank reserves is Treasury currency outstanding. Treasury currency consists primarily of coins, although a few miscellaneous kinds of currency are also included. When new coins are minted, they are transferred to the Federal Reserve System for distribution, and the Federal Reserve credits the Treasury's account on its books. As expenditures are made from the Treasury's checking account, the supply of bank reserves increases. As a result, the amount of Treasury currency is a factor potentially increasing bank reserves.

Table 5-2 also lists the factors that must be subtracted from potential sources of bank reserves to calculate the amount of reserves at any point in time. Two of these, currency in circulation and Treasury deposits at Federal Reserve banks, have already been mentioned as factors affecting bank reserves. Whenever deposits are withdrawn by the public in the form of currency, bank reserves are reduced by the amount of the withdrawal. Likewise, whenever Treasury deposits at Federal Reserve banks increase as bank deposits are paid to the Treasury, bank reserves are reduced. The opposite is true whenever the public's currency hold-

## Table 5-3 Federal Reserve: Factors Affecting Bank Reserves and Condition Statement of F.R. Banks (in millions of dollars)

| Member Bank Reserves, Reserve Bank Credit, and Related Items | Averages of Daily Figures | | | Wednesday Feb. 6, 1980* |
|---|---|---|---|---|
| | Week Ended Feb. 6, 1980* | Change from Week Ended | | |
| | | Jan. 30, 1980 | Feb. 7, 1979 | |
| Reserve Bank credit: | | | | |
| U.S. government securities | | | | |
| Bought outright—System account | 115,570[a] | −74 | +10,693 | 111,849[b] |
| Held under repurchase agreements | — | −684 | −671 | — |
| Federal agency obligations | | | | |
| Bought outright | 8,216 | — | +729 | 8,216 |
| Held under repurchase agreements | — | −241 | −91 | — |
| Acceptances | | | | |
| Bought outright | — | — | — | — |
| Held under repurchase agreements | — | −143 | −170 | — |
| Loans | | | | |
| Total member bank borrowing | 759 | −1,062 | −58 | 343 |
| Includes seasonal borrowing of: | 73 | −14 | −29 | 43 |
| Other borrowing | — | — | — | — |
| Float | 5,074 | +1,487 | −901 | 5,910 |
| Other F.R. assets | 5,366 | −43 | −213 | 5,365 |
| Total Reserve Bank credit | 134,984 | −762 | +9,316 | 131,683 |
| Gold stock | 11,172 | — | −406 | 11,172 |
| Special Drawing Rights certif. acct. | 2,968 | +167 | +1,668 | 2,968 |
| Treasury currency outstanding | 13,017 | +19 | +1,106 | 13,035 |
| | 162,142 | −576 | +11,685 | 158,858 |
| Currency in circulation† | 121,078 | +78 | +10,514 | 121,656 |
| Treasury cash holdings† | 458 | +5 | +169 | 450 |
| Treasury deposits with F.R. banks | 2,976 | −63 | −691 | 3,733 |
| Foreign deposits with F.R. banks | 322 | +9 | +35 | 362 |
| Other deposits with F.R. banks | 367 | +54 | −444 | 275 |
| Other F.R. liabilities and capital | 5,073 | −284 | +920 | 4,573 |
| | 130,274 | −201 | +10,505 | 131,049 |
| Reserves | | | | |
| With F.R. banks[c] | 31,868 | −374 | +1,180 | 27,809 |
| Currency and coin | 11,831 | −420 | +1,147 | 11,831 |
| Total reserves held[d] | 43,914 | −751 | +2,397 | 39,855 |
| Required reserves | 43,358 | −1,028 | +2,120 | 43,358 |
| Excess reserves[d] | 556 | +277 | +277 | −3,503 |

Note: A net of $146 million of surplus reserves were eligible to be carried forward from the week ended January 30 into the week ending February 6.

On February 6, 1980, marketable U.S. government securities held in custody by the Federal Reserve banks for foreign official and international accounts were $80,707 million, a decrease of $92 million for the week.

[a]Net of $3,011 million, daily average, matched sale-purchase transactions outstanding during the latest statement week, of which $2,083 million was with foreign official and international accounts. Includes securities loaned—fully secured by U.S. government securities.

[b]Net of $6,733 million matched sale-purchase transactions outstanding at the end of the latest statement week, of which $1,949 million was with foreign official and international accounts. Includes $158 million securities loaned—fully secured by U.S. government securities.

[c]Includes reserves of member banks, Edge Act Corporations, and U.S. agencies and branches of foreign banks.

[d]Adjusted to include $215 million waivers of penalties for reserve deficiencies in accordance with Board policy effective November 19, 1975.

*Estimated (Richmond District).

†Estimated (Treasury's figures).

Source: Board of Governors of the Federal Reserve System.

ings decrease or Treasury deposits at Federal Reserve banks decline. In both of these cases bank reserves increase.[28]

Treasury cash holdings affect bank reserves in exactly the same way that the public's cash holdings affect reserves. Similarly, changes in foreign deposits at Federal Reserve banks affect bank reserves in the same way as changes in Treasury deposits. In particular, whenever Treasury cash holdings or foreign deposits increase, they do so at the expense of bank reserves. In reverse, whenever either of these quantities decrease, the result is an increase in bank reserves. The final potential use of bank reserves consists of other deposits at Federal Reserve banks and Federal Reserve capital net of other Federal Reserve assets (line 9 of Table 5-2). All of these changes and their impacts on bank reserves are summarized in Table 5-3 for the week ending February 8, 1980.

The elements of the bank reserve equation may be rearranged slightly to produce a concept that is even more useful for monetary analysis than bank reserves alone. Equation (5-3) is in the bank reserve equation from Table 5-2.

(FRC + other sources)
$$- \text{(CUR + other uses)} = \text{BR} \qquad (5\text{-}3)$$

where FRC = Federal Reserve Credit
CUR = currency in the hands of the public
BR = bank reserves

If the terms are rearranged slightly by moving the public's holdings of currency from the left side to the right side, a new monetary concept is introduced, one known as the monetary base.

(FRC + other sources) − (other uses)
$$= \text{BR} + \text{CUR} \qquad (5\text{-}4)$$

The *monetary base* is defined as bank reserves plus currency in the hands of the public. Functionally, the monetary base is important because it is the sum of current high-powered money (bank reserves) and potential high-powered money in the form of the public's currency holdings. Both of these have the potential of supporting a multiple expansion of money through the banking system.

[28]All the components of the bank reserve equation are discussed in considerably more detail in the Federal Reserve Bank of New York's *Glossary*.

However, the monetary base concept is somewhat more useful for monetary analysis than the bank reserve component alone because it separates, to a greater degree than the bank reserve equation, the items under the central bank's control from the elements not under its control. By removing the influence of changes in consumers' cash balances from the left-hand side of the equation, the monetary base equation highlights the critical role played by changes in Federal Reserve credit.

Thus, even though the central bank may not be able to create money, or even be able to influence its creation with a high level of precision, it can exercise rather substantial control by influencing the monetary base.

The *relationship* between the supply of money and the monetary base is known as the money multiplier. The multiplier is the amount by which each dollar of monetary base is multiplied to equal the total money supply. This definition is illustrated by Equations (5-5) and (5-6). If $M$ is the supply of money, $B$ the monetary base, and $m$ the money multiplier, then

$$M = m \cdot B \qquad (5\text{-}5)$$

or

$$m = M/B \qquad (5\text{-}6)$$

The question which immediately comes to mind is the size of the money multiplier, the actual relationship between $M$ and $B$.

In an economy with no cash, no bank deposits that are not demand deposits (that is, no bank deposits that do not qualify as money), and no banks that hold excess reserves, the money multiplier takes on a particularly simple form. In such an economy the monetary base is the same as bank reserves and the supply of money is the same as bank demand deposits. Since banks hold no excess reserves, the money multiplier is the same as the theoretical reserve multiplier discussed in the preceding section of this chapter. Returning to that example, if the Federal Reserve should desire to expand the supply of money, it might undertake an open-market operation to increase bank reserves (increase the monetary base). Now banks armed with new reserves could make new loans, expanding demand deposits (money) in the process. Theoretically, assuming no leakages, demand-deposit (monetary) expansion could continue until all the new reserves (new monetary base) were employed as required reserves. As was illustrated earlier by Equations (5-1) and (5-2), the theoretical limit of new deposits (new money) in this case would be an amount equal to the reciprocal of the required reserve ratio ($rr\%$) times the increase in bank reserves (the increase in the monetary base). In sum, for this simple economy with no currency and no other leakages in the monetary expansion process in the form of time deposits or excess reserve holdings, the money multiplier would be equal to the reciprocal of the required reserve ratio.

$$m = \frac{1}{rr\%} \qquad (5\text{-}7)$$

Obviously the economy is much more complex than this simple example and, not surprisingly, the monetary expansion process and the money multiplier are more complex as well. Leakages occur in the deposit expansion process that cause actual monetary expansion to be considerably less than the theoretical maximum. Prominent among the possible leakages are changes in the public's demand for currency, the exchange of new demand deposits into time or savings (nonmonetary) form, and the holding of excess reserves by banks. These leakages will limit the potential expansion of demand deposits and the size of the money multiplier.

The impact of these potential limitations on deposit expansion may be seen by comparing the money multiplier derived when currency holding is possible with the multiplier for the economy with no currency. The latter multiplier is, of course, $1/rr\%$, which was derived in Equations (5-2) and (5-7). Assume now that the public desires to hold some of its money in the form of currency and that the amount it desires to hold is related to its demand-deposit holdings. For simplicity, assume that this amount is some fraction ($c$) of its demand deposits $DD$. Now, employing the same symbols as used earlier. Equation (5-2) may be rewritten.

$$\Delta DD = \frac{1}{rr\%} \cdot NR \qquad (5\text{-}2)$$

$$= \frac{1}{rr\%} \Delta(B - CUR) \qquad (5\text{-}8)$$

$$= \frac{1}{rr\%} \Delta(B - cDD) \qquad (5\text{-}9)$$

where $\Delta DD$ = the change in demand deposits
$NR$ = new bank reserves
$B$ = the monetary base
$CUR$ = currency in the hands of the public.

Algebraic manipulation of Equation (5-9) shows that if the public desires to hold more currency when demand deposits increase, then the money multiplier is reduced when compared to the case with no currency. The common sense explanation is that, for a given increase in the monetary base, a smaller expansion of deposits will result because some of the new monetary base will be siphoned into currency holdings. The latter, of course, do not support a multiple expansion of deposits, and so monetary expansion is limited. More formally, beginning with Equation (5-9), multiplying both sides by $rr\%$, and shifting currency holding to the left-hand side,

$$(rr\% \cdot \Delta DD + c\Delta DD = \Delta B \qquad (5\text{-}10)$$

and solving for $\Delta DD$,

$$\Delta DD (rr\% + c) = \Delta B \qquad (5\text{-}11)$$

$$\Delta DD = \left(\frac{1}{rr\% + c}\right) \Delta B \qquad (5\text{-}12)$$

Now, since new money is the sum of new demand deposits plus new currency, it is necessary to calculate new currency holdings:

$$\Delta CUR = c\Delta DD = c \left(\frac{1}{rr\% + c}\right) \Delta B \qquad (5\text{-}13)$$

With this information, it is possible to calculate the money multiplier for the economy with currency holdings:

$$\Delta M = \Delta DD + \Delta CUR = \frac{1}{rr\% + c} \Delta B$$

$$+ \frac{c}{rr\% + c} \Delta B \qquad (5\text{-}14)$$

$$= \frac{1 + c}{rr\% + c} \Delta B \qquad (5\text{-}15)$$

A simple example can demonstrate that the money multiplier of Equation (5-15) is smaller than the multiplier of Equation (5-2). If the required reserve ratio ($rr\%$) is .1, then the multiplier in the no-currency case is 10. Suppose, however, that the public desires a currency ratio ($c$) of .3 in relation to demand deposits. This makes the multiplier in the currency case [Equation (5-15)] equal to only [(1 + .3) ÷ (.1 + .3) = 3.25]. Clearly, in this example, the money multiplier in the economy with currency will be much smaller than in the economy without currency.

Similarly, if the public should desire to hold some time and savings deposits and banks are required to hold reserves against these deposits, the money multiplier will be reduced. Again, the common sense explanation is that if part of the monetary base is used for purposes other than as required reserves against demand deposits, less is available for expansion of these deposits. The result, simply stated, is a reduction in the money multiplier. If, for example, the public desires to hold $n$ dollars of time and savings deposits for every dollar of demand deposits and, furthermore, reserves of $t\%$ are required on time and savings deposits, then another term $nt\% \cdot \Delta DD$ must be added to the uses of the monetary base in Equation (5-10).

$$rr\% \cdot \Delta DD + c\Delta DD + nt\% \cdot \Delta DD = \Delta B \quad (5\text{-}16)$$

Solving in exactly the same manner as in Equations (5-10) through (5-15) produces the analogous result.

$$\Delta M = \frac{1 + c}{rr\% + c + nt\%} \Delta B \quad (5\text{-}17)$$

Again, as long as $n$ and $t\%$ are both positive, the multiplier in Equation (5-17) is smaller than the multiplier in Equation (5-15) [or Equation (5-2)]. For example, if the public desires to hold $2 of time and savings deposits for every dollar of demand deposits ($n = 2$) and reserve requirements on time and savings deposits are 5 percent ($t\% = .05$), the money multiplier in Equation (5-17) is (1 + .3) ÷ (.1 + .3 + .1) = 2.6.

As can be seen, allocation of parts of the monetary base for purposes other than as required reserves for demand deposits limits the size of the monetary multiplier. One other leakage from the multiple expansion process arises from banks' holding at times some fraction of their excess reserves idle instead of fully employing them through making loans and investments. If there is an excess of reserves held idle in the banking system as a whole, the money multiplier is reduced further.[29]

In sum, the size of the money multiplier is dependent on a range of factors. If all the parameters of these factors were known, it would be possible to specify the changes in the money supply assuming complete knowledge of changes in the monetary base. Unfortunately, some of the parameters [like $c$ and $n$ in Equation (5-17)] may not be constant in either the long or short run. Some of them may be functions of other variables, such as rates of interest and levels of income, and the functional forms may be quite complex. Nevertheless, as shown in Figure 5-3, the money multiplier in the American economy is fairly constant over periods of intermediate length, such as a few months or a year.[30] This suggests that, because of their impact on the monetary base, policy actions by the Federal Reserve during a year will have somewhat predictable impacts on the supply of money.

## Conclusion

In conclusion, money, the most liquid of all assets, serves a number of important economic functions. Besides being a store of value like other assets, money is also a medium of exchange, a unit of account, and a standard for deferred payments. Although many commodities have served as money throughout the course of history, these features describe the essence of money, the "moneyness" of money. In the American economy, currency, coins, and demand deposits have long served as money; but in recent years new kinds of assets, such as consumers' NOW accounts, have also exhibited moneylike features. As a result, the Federal Reserve System, as the nation's central bank, monitors more than one monetary measure as it carries out its responsibilities in the monetary area.

Although the Federal Reserve has a variety of regulatory and financial duties, conducting monetary policy is its central function. The Fed does not directly create much of the supply of money, but it exercises strong influence over bank reserves, and this gives it substantial control over the money supply process. Still, it is the commercial banking system that creates most of the money in the American economy, employing available reserves in the creation of bank credit. Thus, one of

---

[29] Algebraically, there is another term in the denominator of Equation (5-17).

[30] The validity of this statement depends to some extent, however, on the method of calculation employed. In this connection, see Chapter 28, footnotes 21 and 23.

**Figure 5-3  The Money Multiplier**

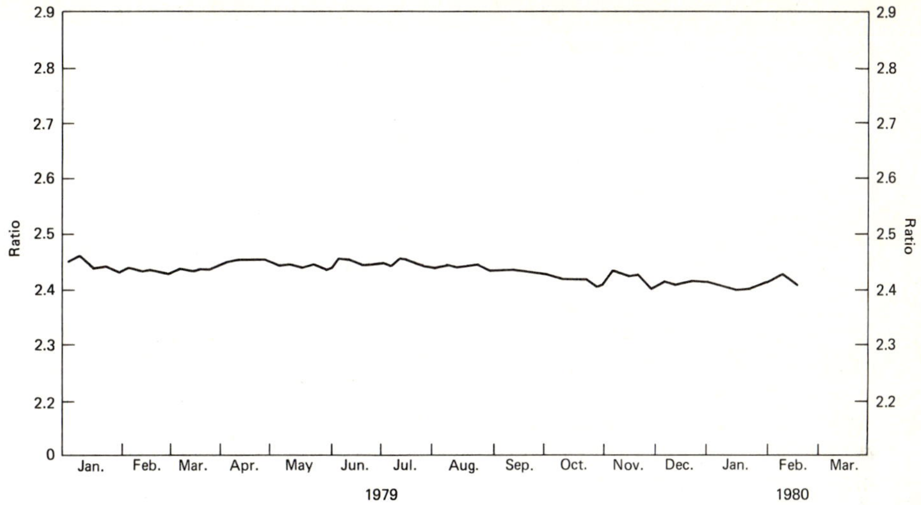

Source: Federal Reserve Bank of St. Louis.

the most important problems that the Federal Reserve has in conducting monetary policy is that it does not have complete control over bank reserves. This complication, and the longer-run problem of the relationship between monetary variables and the macroeconomy, are a central concern of Chapter 28.

## Questions

1. Compare the traditional definitions of money used by the Federal Reserve System with the new definitions adopted in 1980. Explain why more than one definition is employed.

2. Outline the structure of the Federal Reserve System and the roles of each of its important parts.

3. Explain what is meant by the term *multiple expansion of money*. Explain the major limitations of this process.

4. Can an individual bank, in contrast to the banking system, engage in a multiple expansion of money? Explain why or why not.

5. Occasionally the view is expressed that banks create money "out of the air" or "with the stroke of a pen." Is this view correct? Explain why or why not.

6. Show the effects of each of the following transactions on the balance sheet of (1) the First National Bank,

(2) all banks, and (3) the Federal Reserve System:

a. First National sells $50 million of Treasury bills to a Federal Reserve bank and lends $75,000 to a corporation, crediting its demand deposit account for that amount.

b. First National sells $10 million of Treasury bills to a government securities dealer who pays by check drawn against Second National.

c. First National borrows $50 million from the Federal Reserve. Half of the loan is added to its reserve account at the Federal Reserve and the other half is taken in the form of Federal Reserve notes (currency), which are liabilities of the Federal Reserve System. The new notes are immediately paid out to depositors who write checks for cash.

7. Describe the effect of each of the transactions in Question 6 on (a) the supply of money, (b) the amount of bank reserves, and (c) the monetary base.

8. Explain the major components of the bank reserve equation. Using the Federal Reserve statement for a recent week, explain the major causes of changes in member bank reserves.

9. What are the *operating factors* with respect to Federal Reserve policy affecting bank reserves? Explain their importance for Federal Reserve policy making.

10. What is the *money multiplier*? What are its major components? Explain how the money multiplier might cause some complications for monetary policy.

## Selected Bibliography

Board of Governors of the Federal Reserve System. *The Federal Reserve: Purposes and Functions*. Washington, D.C., 1974.

Chandler, Lester V. *Benjamin Strong, Central Banker*. The Brookings Institution, Washington, D.C., 1967.

Federal Reserve Bank of Chicago. *Modern Money Mechanics*. Chicago, 1975.

Federal Reserve Bank of New York. *Glossary: Weekly Federal Reserve Statements*. New York, 1975.

Friedman, Milton, and Anna J. Schwartz. *A Monetary History of the United States, 1867–1960*. Princeton University Press, Princeton, N.J.

Hammond, Bray. *Banks and Politics in America from the Revolution to the Civil War*. Princeton University Press, Princeton, N.J., 1957.

Havrilesky, Thomas M., and John T. Boorman, *Monetary Macroeconomics*. AHM Publishing Company, Arlington Heights, Ill., 1978.

Simpson, Thomas D. "The Redefined Monetary Aggregates." *Federal Reserve Bulletin* (January 1980).

Wrightsman, Dwayne. *An Introduction to Monetary Theory and Policy*. The Free Press, New York, 1976.

# 6

# Deposit-Type Intermediaries: Bank and Nonbank

There are four types of depository intermediaries in the United States: commercial banks, savings and loan associations, mutual savings banks, and credit unions. Each of these major categories can be subdivided in various ways, such as whether or not the institution is federally chartered or federally insured. The distinguishing characteristic of deposit-type intermediaries is the form of their major liabilities—their deposits. Although there are significant differences among the types of deposits that are issued by these institutions, they have the following characteristics in common: they announce conditions for the "sale" of the deposit and fully supply the quantity demanded by the depositor under those conditions;[1] they agree to "repay" in the future the nominal sum of money deposited; they provide financial assets that can be purchased in small amounts; and the federal government has made insurance available for a portion of their deposits.

At the end of 1978, commercial banks held 62 percent of the financial assets of all depository intermediaries, down from 80 percent at the end of 1948.[2] Savings and loan associations were next in relative importance with 27 percent of the sector's financial assets—an increase from 8 percent at the end of 1948. Mutual savings banks accounted for 8 percent of the financial assets of depository institutions at the end of 1978—down from 12 percent at the end of 1948—while credit unions increased from 0.4 percent to 3 percent their share of the financial assets of depository intermediaries be-

[1]An exception to this completely elastic supply of deposits is the large-denomination certificate of deposit (CD), which has been available since 1961.

[2]The intent of this chapter is to describe and analyze the behavior of depository intermediaries in the period since World War II. The year 1948, rather than 1946, was chosen as the initial year of the analysis because of the importance of the disequilibria in financial markets in 1946, the end of World War II. The wartime combination of price controls, production controls, and increased incomes left the public with substantial excess supplies of liquid assets by 1946. During the following two years prices were bid up considerably while production of consumer goods also increased dramatically. This combination of circumstances had important consequences for financial intermediaries. For example, between 1946 and 1948 the ratio of depository intermediary financial assets to gross national product declined from 0.78 to 0.67 and the ratio of depository intermediary liabilities of households to disposable personal income declined from 0.74 to 0.63.

tween 1948 and 1978. A later section of this chapter analyzes some of the major reasons for the changes in the relative importance of these types of intermediaries. First, however, the types of institutions will be described briefly.

## Types of Depository Institutions

The characteristic that traditionally has distinguished a commercial bank from other deposit-type intermediaries is that it issues demand deposits payable to the owner or to third parties at the demand of the owner.[3] From the early 1930s until recently, this type of liability had the advantage from the point of view of the bank of requiring no explicit interest payment to its owners, since federal law specifically forbade payment of interest on demand deposits. It had the disadvantage of requiring unconditional payment on demand by the owner, thus introducing a substantial element of uncertainty concerning the quantity and timing of demands for payment.

Currently, the nature of deposit transactions is changing dramatically from the use of checks to the use of electronic funds transfers (EFTs). The EFT is an electronic order (usually generated by magnetic computer tape or plastic card) that requests a bank to transfer funds. The transfer may be to pay another person whose bank is also notified of the transaction electronically, or it may simply be a transfer in the depositor's account. Today EFTs are largely used in connection with large payrolls or regular payments, such as those associated with social security. Increased use of this type of transaction may reduce the banking system's burden of paperwork and, perhaps, will have consequences as far-reaching as the shift from bank notes to deposits as the main bank liability, a shift which occurred largely during the nineteenth century.[4]

At the end of 1978, there were 14,712 commercial banking firms in the United States. Generally, a commercial bank is limited to establishing banking

offices only in its home state, and many states either entirely prohibit or severely restrict the ability of a bank to open branch offices. Federally chartered banks are required to observe the state limitations on branching.

In 1978, of the 14,712 commercial banks in existence, 4,616 had national charters issued by the federal government, whereas state banking commissions had chartered 10,096 state banks. All national banks must become members of the Federal Reserve System—and observe the rules of membership. Also, at the end of 1978, 949 state banks were members of the Federal Reserve System. All of these member banks—and all but 322 other banks in 1978—subscribe to the Federal Deposit Insurance Corporation's insurance of deposits up to the current limit of $100,000. Detailed regulation and inspection are provided for national banks by the U.S. Comptroller of the Currency, for state member banks by the Board of Governors of the Federal Reserve System (hereafter, Federal Reserve Board), and for insured nonmember banks by the Federal Deposit Insurance Corporation (FDIC). By their regulations, these agencies impose accounting practices, such as the conditions under which certain assets will be written off as bad debts and the method of evaluating bonds, as well as offer suggestions and requirements of general banking practices, such as those associated with overdraft privileges.[5]

The asset portfolios of commercial banks generally are more diversified with respect to both maturities and types of financial instruments than are the portfolios of other types of depository intermediaries. Their holdings of short-term obligations include Treasury bills as well as short-term loans to businesses and consumers. Intermediate-maturity assets include federal, state, and local government securities; term loans to businesses; and consumer instalment loans. Longer-term assets include mortgages as well as private and government bonds. Banks are generally prohibited from holding stock except in carefully controlled circumstances. Because they have this great flexibility in their choice of instruments, commercial banks are in a better position than the other depository intermediaries to adjust their portfolios in response to

---

[3] The lines of distinction between commercial banks and the other deposit-type intermediaries are being blurred significantly by the relatively new share drafts of credit unions and NOW (Negotiable Order of Withdrawal) deposits of the other depository intermediaries.

[4] For a discussion of EFTs, see Federal Reserve Bank of Boston, *The Economics of a National Electronic Funds Transfer System*, Boston, 1974.

[5] For a more complete description of commercial banks and their regulation, see Chapter 31.

changes in the relative attractiveness of various financial assets.

Commercial banks are also less specialized in their liabilities than are the other depository intermediaries. In addition to demand deposits, commercial banks may issue a variety of liabilities ranging from savings accounts to long-term bonds and stocks. Most of them have substantial liabilities in the form of demand deposits, savings deposits (which pay interest and could require up to thirty days notice before withdrawal), and time certificates of deposit (which pay interest and have specific maturity dates). In addition many commercial banks, particularly larger, money-market banks, issue large ($100,000 and above) negotiable certificates of deposit (CDs) and various types of notes, bonds, and stocks. Borrowing in foreign markets, such as the Eurodollar market, is also a possibility for many of the larger banks. Thus, commercial banks have greater latitude than the other depository intermediaries in managing their liabilities.

The distinctive features of savings and loan associations (S&Ls) is that they issue passbook savings shares to "depositors" as well as a variety of savings certificates and use the funds almost exclusively to purchase residential mortgages. Originally the savings and loan associations developed as mutual organizations in which the deposits were legally "shares" evidencing owner as distinct from creditor status. The management of these mutual associations is largely self-perpetuating as a result of proxies obtained by the management from new shareholders. Today more than one-eighth of the savings and loan associations are stock corporations.[6]

Of the 4,723 savings and loan associations at the end of 1978, 4,053 had national charters, and the remainder had state charters. Federally chartered associations are required to belong to the Federal Home Loan Bank System; three-fourths of the state-chartered associations had also opted for

membership by the end of 1978. At that time member associations accounted for approximately 98 percent of all S&L assets. Regulation of member S&Ls is primarily through the Federal Home Loan Bank Board, which exercises, among other powers, the following: (a) setting the reserves required of members as a percentage (between 4 percent and 10 percent) of savings deposits—these reserves may be in the form of cash, government securities, or commercial bank time deposits; and (b) providing advances with maturities as long as ten years in amounts up to 50 percent of the member's savings accounts. Formerly, the FHLBB also set maximum rates that member S&Ls could pay on deposits, but federal legislation in 1980 provided for a phase-out of all ceilings by 1986. This legislation also specified new, higher levels of reserves for "transaction accounts," which include NOW accounts and similar accounts from which payments may be made to third parties. The Federal Savings and Loan Insurance Corporation (FSLIC), a government institution, insures up to $100,000 per deposit for all federal S&Ls as well as insuring nearly all the state-chartered associations that are members of the Federal Home Loan Bank System.

Historically, savings and loan associations (originally known as building and loan associations) issued only share deposits and invested almost exclusively in mortgages on the family residences of their shareholders. These practices to a significant extent were gradually written into the laws and regulations governing S&Ls. In more recent times, the regulatory trend has been toward relaxing the restrictions placed on the form of S&L assets and liabilities. All associations are now permitted to lend to nondepositors, and most may purchase mortgages on property outside the immediate locality of the association. Most associations in recent years also have been permitted to make consumer loans on the security of their savings deposits. As part of the omnibus federal financial reform legislation enacted in early 1980, federally chartered S&Ls received authority to invest up to 20 percent of assets in consumer loans, commercial paper, and corporate debt securities.

In recent years, S&Ls have also been permitted greater latitude in the form of their liabilities. The mutual associations still do not issue open-market securities, but the stock associations may issue stocks and bonds, and a significant number of

---

[6]A source of current information on savings and loan associations is the annual *Savings and Loan Fact Book*, U.S. League of Savings Associations, Chicago. A good short description of the activities of S&Ls is found in George H. Hempel and Jess B. Yawitz, *Financial Management of Financial Institutions*, Prentice-Hall, Englewood Cliffs, N.J., 1977. A more definitive treatment is found in Federal Home Loan Bank Board, *Study of the Savings and Loan Industry*, Washington, D.C., 1969.

S&Ls have been permitted to convert from the mutual to the stock form of organization. Federally insured S&Ls can issue NOW accounts nationwide beginning in January 1981 in addition to the usual passbook savings accounts, and fixed-maturity certificates of deposit have increased dramatically as a source of funds in the last few years.

Mutual savings banks are a third type of depository intermediary in the United States.[7] As of early 1980 all mutual savings banks were state chartered although in 1980 a few applied for federal charters under enabling legislation passed in 1978. All exhibit the mutual form of ownership, in which the depositors ostensibly (but management proxy-holders actually) elect the governing body. Unlike most savings and loan deposits, which legally are *shares* (but give the owner a claim senior to creditors in the event of bankruptcy, although permitting the remote possibility of the institution's refusing to return the deposit on demand), the deposits of mutual savings banks give creditor status to the owner. The shareholder-depositor distinction is of little practical significance, however, in view of the insurance of shares by the FSLIC and the insurance of deposits by the FDIC (or state insurance in the cases of Connecticut and Massachusetts).

Although there are mutual savings banks in seventeen states, approximately three-fourths of the 465 institutions were located in Connecticut, Massachusetts, and New York in 1980, and only some 5 percent of the total were found outside the northeastern section of the country. Virtually all mutual savings banks are required by their state regulatory authorities either to have state deposit insurance (Connecticut and Massachusetts) or deposit insurance with the Federal Deposit Insurance Corporation. The Federal Home Loan Bank System allows membership by mutual savings banks and some 13 percent have opted for it—in all probability to become eligible for the advances mentioned ear-

lier. The Federal Reserve Board sets maximum interest rates payable on the mutual savings bank deposits—generally at the level permitted by the Federal Home Loan Bank Board for savings and loan associations. As mentioned previously, all deposit rate ceilings are to be phased out by 1986.

Although the liabilities of mutual savings banks are quite similar to those of savings and loan associations, the mutual savings banks have a more diversified portfolio of assets. Whereas, in the past, S&Ls have been specifically prohibited from holding corporate stocks and bonds, corporate bonds have long formed a substantial part of mutual savings bank assets. Mutual savings banks' mortgage holdings contain relatively large quantities of mortgages on property other than one- to four-family residences. This reflects the fact that mutual savings banks are located primarily in the Northeast—a part of the country heavily populated by apartment dwellers. Finally, mutual savings banks have operated under fewer restrictions than savings and loan associations with respect to the location of mortgages acquired.

Credit unions are the fourth type of depository intermediary in the United States. The distinguishing characteristic of credit unions is the requirement that the depositors and borrowers have some "common bond," such as their place of employment, occupation, or residence. This legal requirement has severely restricted the growth of credit unions until recently, and it is one reason why their financial assets at the end of 1978 were only 3.0 percent of the assets of all deposit-type intermediaries.[8] The deposits of credit unions are analogous to the passbook accounts of the mutual savings and loan associations in that legally they are shares, evidencing owner rather than creditor status, but *de facto* they are deposits that are paid on demand. However, the depositors of credit unions are far more likely than the depositors of the other mutual

---

[7] Current information on mutual savings banks is available in the annual *National Fact Book of Mutual Savings Banks* published by the National Association of Mutual Savings Banks. A short description of their history and activities is found in Donald P. Jacobs et al., *Financial Institutions,* Richard D. Irwin, Homewood, Ill., 1972, Chap. 11; and Hempel and Yawitz, *Financial Management of Financial Institutions,* Chap. 6. A more thorough treatment is found in National Association of Mutual Savings Banks, *Mutual Savings Banks,* Prentice-Hall, Englewood Cliffs, N.J., 1962.

[8] For further discussion of the regulation of credit unions, see Chapter 31. Current information on them is available from the Credit Union National Association, Madison, Wisconsin. More detailed treatment of their activities can be found in Mark J. Flannery, *An Economic Evaluation of Credit Unions in the United States,* Federal Reserve Bank of Boston, Boston, 1974; and U.S. Bureau of Federal Credit Unions, *Regular Reserves of Federal Credit Unions,* Washington, D.C., 1968. See also Hempel and Yawitz, *Financial Management of Financial Institutions.*

depository institutions to exercise some significant voice in the control of the institution's activities.

Approximately 23,000 credit unions were in existence in 1978, of which three-fifths were federally chartered and the remainder had state charters. All of the federally chartered credit unions have their deposits insured up to $100,000 by the National Credit Union Share Insurance Fund and are regulated by the National Credit Union Administration. Some 3,500 of the state-chartered credit unions have opted for membership in NCUA and for deposit insurance with it.

While the liabilities of credit unions are similar to those of the other depository intermediaries, credit unions are far more restricted in their asset holdings. Traditionally, credit has been limited almost solely to consumer loans (such as automobile loans), although loans have also been extended to other credit unions and some government securities or deposits in other institutions have been held for liquidity purposes. In recent years, legislative changes have permitted some credit unions to make mortgage and home improvement loans. The requirement that they lend only to members is the major factor explaining the relatively small size of most credit unions, and relaxation of restrictions on the type of lending and, in some states, on the nature of the common bond are major explanations for their rapid growth in the 1970s.

## The Growth of Depository Intermediaries Since World War II

From 1948 through 1978, total financial assets of depository intermediaries as a group grew from $173.6 billion to $1,965.9 billion—an average annual compound growth rate of 8.4 percent. During the same period, gross national product grew at a rate of only 7.2 percent. Likewise, in the twenty-two years between the end of 1956 and the end of 1978, the total financial assets of depository intermediaries grew at an annual rate of 9.4 percent while GNP grew by only 7.6 percent annually. In sharp contrast, however, during the earlier period 1948–1956, financial assets of these intermediaries grew by 5.9 percent per year while GNP grew by 6.2 percent. What were the reasons for this relative turnaround in performance by the depository intermediaries?

Deposit-type financial institutions are no exception to the rule that a firm's growth depends in the long run on its ability to sell its liabilities and equities to the public or to retain its own earnings.[9] For a nonfinancial corporation, the major determinant of its ability to sell liabilities or increase equity is the profitability of operating its plant and equipment. Anything that increases the net return from operating the plant and equipment will enhance the firm's position in the interfirm competition for funds. The financial firm differs from the nonfinancial primarily in the relative composition of its assets—the financial firm's earning assets are almost exclusively financial assets, such as loans and securities of various types. But the financial firm's growth is still determined basically by the profitability of its earning assets, which, together with regulatory constraints, determines the explicit and implicit return that it can offer to depositors and others who provide funds. Hence, its profitability determines the growth of liabilities and capital. Later in this chapter the assets of deposit-type intermediaries are discussed. Our attention in this section is on their liabilities and capital as the long-run sources of their funds.

In competing for savers' funds, the depository intermediaries have some advantages and some disadvantages as compared with nonfinancial firms, governmental units, and other intermediaries. Depository intermediaries offer liabilities in small denominations with exceptionally low risk, thereby appealing to a group of savers whose loanable funds are not readily available to many segments of the capital market. Some deposit liabilities, such as bank demand deposits or NOW accounts, serve both as a means of payment and store of value, joint attributes denied the liabilities of other borrowers. The major disadvantages suffered by depository intermediaries in their competition for funds are those imposed by government regulation, primarily in the interest of protecting depositors. Federal and state governments specify in detail the legal characteristics of the liabilities and equities that depository intermediaries may issue. In addition to specifying the type of financial instruments, in many cases the maximum return is specified by

[9]See, for example, Robin Marris, *The Economic Theory of "Managerial" Capitalism,* The Free Press, New York, 1964.

**Table 6-1   Selected Assets and Liabilities of Households (end-of-year percentages of total non-equity financial assets)**

|  | *1948* | *1956* | *1966* | *1978* |
|---|---|---|---|---|
| **FINANCIAL ASSETS** | | | | |
| Demand deposits and currency | 19% | 15% | 10% | 9% |
| Commercial bank time deposits | 11 | 10 | 15 | 19 |
| Other time deposits | 10 | 15 | 20 | 24 |
| U.S. govt. securities | 23 | 16 | 10 | 7 |
| Other govt. securities | 3 | 5 | 5 | 3 |
| Corporate bonds | 3 | 2 | 1 | 2 |
| Other nonequity financial assets | 31 | 37 | 39 | 36 |
| Total excluding equities | 100 | 100 | 100 | 100 |
| Equities | 34 | 68 | 65 | 30 |
| **LIABILITIES** | | | | |
| Home mortgages | 11% | 21% | 26% | 28% |
| Instalment consumer credit | 3 | 7 | 9 | 11 |
| Other consumer and securities credit | 2 | 4 | 3 | 3 |
| Other liabilities | 2 | 4 | 5 | 5 |
| Total liabilities | 18 | 36 | 43 | 47 |

Source: Board of Governors of the Federal Reserve System, *Flow of Funds Accounts.*

law or regulation, as in the case of the Federal Reserve Board's specification of maximum rates payable on bank time deposits.

Some idea of the success of depository intermediaries in competing for the savings of households and firms can be gained by looking at the composition of their portfolios in Tables 6-1 and 6-2, respectively. Currency and deposit liabilities of depository intermediaries amounted to 52 percent of total financial assets—excluding equities[10]—in the portfolios of households and nonprofit institutions by the end of 1978. This percentage had risen gradually from 40 percent at the end of 1948 and 1956. For nonfinancial businesses, on the other hand, the percentage of total financial assets accounted for by deposits and currency had declined from 39 percent at year-end 1948 to 14 percent at the end of 1978.

In the case of households, the increase in the relative importance of deposits and currency was matched by a decline in the relative importance of government securities (both federal and local) from

26 percent of total financial assets (excluding equities) at the end of 1948 to 10 percent at the end of 1978. This largely reflects the federal government's failure to keep the yields on savings bonds competitive with alternative uses of savers' funds. Private bonds were 3 percent of household nonequity financial assets in 1948 and 2 percent in 1978; the remainder (31 percent in 1948 and 36 percent in 1978) was accounted for largely by insurance reserves and retirement funds. Thus, even with substantial government regulation of their liabilities, the depository intermediaries as a group have improved their position in the competition for household funds during the last thirty years.

The nonfinancial firms' reduction in deposits and currency from 39 percent to 14 percent of financial assets over the 1948–1978 period was part of a general reduction in the importance of their liquid assets relative to other financial assets. Their holdings of government securities, for example, declined during this period from 12 percent to 1 percent of their total financial assets, while their holdings of other financial assets—primarily accounts receivable and direct foreign investments—increased substantially in relative importance. From the viewpoint of the financial institutions involved, the decline in the relative importance of their liabilities in the portfolios of nonfinancial businesses was far less salient than the increase in the

[10]It is difficult to compare household holdings of equities with their holdings of other financial assets, since the latter are valued at maturity values while equities are valued at market prices that have varied markedly over the last twenty years. At the end of 1948 equities were 34 percent of other financial assets; they rose to 68 percent in 1956 and declined to 30 percent by the end of 1978.

**Table 6-2   Selected Assets and Liabilities of Nonfinancial Firms (end-of-year percentages of total nonequity financial assets)**

|  | 1948 | 1956 | 1966 | 1978 |
|---|---|---|---|---|
| **FINANCIAL ASSETS** | | | | |
| Demand deposits and currency | 38% | 27% | 17% | 10% |
| Time deposits | 1 | 1 | 3 | 4 |
| U.S. government securities | 12 | 10 | 4 | 1 |
| Corporate bonds | 1 | 1 | 1 | 1 |
| Other financial assets | 48 | 61 | 75 | 84 |
| Total financial assets | 100 | 100 | 100 | 100 |
| **LIABILITIES** | | | | |
| Bank loans | 19% | 21% | 28% | 31% |
| Mortgages | 23 | 25 | 37 | 48 |
| Corporate bonds | 30 | 33 | 35 | 39 |
| Other liabilities | 45 | 51 | 55 | 63 |
| Total liabilities | 117 | 130 | 155 | 181 |

Source: Board of Governors of the Federal Reserve System, *Flow of Funds Accounts*.

relative importance of their liabilities in the portfolios of households, since households' deposits and currency were $1,279 billion and nonfinancial business' deposits and currency were only $111 billion at the end of 1978.

### Growth of Deposits Relative to Other Financial Assets

To explain the reasons for the behavior we have just described, consider the following decision framework. Assume that depository intermediaries make available only one type of liability—deposits—which carry no explicit return. Savers can hold either these deposits, or they can hold other financial assets on which the annual return is positive, say, 10 percent. Assume that deposits and other financial assets are relatively good substitutes for each other for some purposes; for other purposes, assume that they are not close substitutes. For instance, both deposits and other financial assets are forms in which savings can be held, but deposits have the special advantage of serving as a means of payment, whereas life insurance policies (one of the other financial assets) have the special advantage of providing protection for the insured's beneficiaries.

If none of these special advantages or disadvantages attended the ownership of the different financial assets, then a saver would wish to own only the one financial asset that paid the highest return (or, alternatively, the one that cost the least). In

the presence of these special characteristics, however, the typical saver will probably divide his or her portfolio between deposits and other financial assets, considering the returns and costs of the assets together with the other attributes of each in making a decision as to how to allocate the portfolio.[11]

Figure 6-1 illustrates the decision-making process for an individual. The horizontal axis measures deposits delivered one year in the future; the vertical axis measures other financial assets, also delivered one year in the future. Thus, any point in the plane represents a specific combination of deposits and other financial assets. Point *A,* for example, represents a portfolio of *OX* deposits and *OY* other financial assets, both measured in units of their value after one year. To calculate their cost or present value at the time that the decision is made (today) in terms of portfolio allocation, one would divide their value one year in the future by the annual rate of return on the asset plus 1. For

[11]Both the explicit and implicit costs of the assets would be considered. An example of explicit costs would be brokers' fees for purchasing bonds, while implicit costs might include riskiness of the assets. In this chapter it is not necessary to consider risk explicitly because it can be assumed that deposits are risk-free and that the riskiness of other assets is both known and constant. Riskiness will affect substitutability of assets and, consequently, the slopes of the indifference curves used in this chapter, but it does not alter the analysis or conclusions. For further consideration of investment in risky assets, see Chapter 24.

**Figure 6-1  Portfolio Allocation Between Deposits and Other Financial Assets**

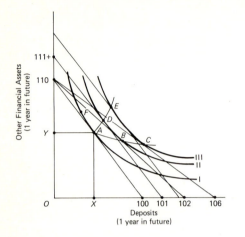

example, if other financial assets have an annual return of 10 percent, then the present value or cost of $110 would be $110/1.10 = $100. The cost of the portfolio represented by point A would be $OX/1.00 + OY/1.10$ if deposits have a zero return and other financial assets yield 10 percent annually. An individual wishing to allocate $100 among other financial assets and deposits can purchase $110 of other financial assets ($100 × 1.10) if their explicit return is 10 percent annually and the entire $100 is allocated to other financial assets; the depositor can purchase only $100 of deposits if their explicit return is zero and the entire portfolio is allocated to deposits. A straight line (called a budget or price line) connecting point $110 on the y-axis and point $100 on the x-axis will include all possible combinations of these two assets that can be purchased today for $100 if the return is 10 percent for other financial assets and zero for deposits (negative quantities of an asset are not permitted). The slope of the budget or price line is −$110 ÷ $100 and measures the quantity of other financial assets that the purchaser must forgo in order to add one unit of deposits to the portfolio. Any line that is parallel to line $110–$100 will have the same slope (and, hence, will represent the same relative prices of deposits and other financial assets) but will involve the current expenditure of a budget other than $100.

At the time an individual is making the allocation decision for his or her portfolio, he or she knows both the relative prices of the two assets (the slope of the budget line) and the amount of the budget that is to be allocated (the level of the budget line). The only question remaining is what specific combination of assets to choose from among those lying on that specific budget line. Our individual allocating $100 and facing relative prices of $110–$100 will want to choose the combination of deposits and other financial assets that has, from his or her viewpoint, the best group of attributes and can be purchased for $100. The individual's preferences, represented by indifference curves (such as curves I, II, and III in Figure 6-1), are the final necessary ingredient of the portfolio-allocation decision. An *indifference curve* is the locus of all combinations of deposits and other financial assets that the individual considers to be equally rewarding after all attributes of the assets have been considered. Curve I in Figure 6-1 is just such a curve. The indifference curves are drawn to reflect the assumptions that an individual: (a) prefers more to less of each asset (and, hence, would be indifferent to a loss of some of one asset only if equally compensated by receipt of some of the other); and (b) requires ever-larger compensation of one asset per unit loss of the other as the stock of the latter declines (the curves are convex to the origin). The individual, when comparing point A on indifference curve I in Figure 6-1 with another combination, such as F—which includes a larger quantity of other financial assets but fewer deposits—believes that the loss of the deposits (which may entail having to postpone some purchase due to a cash shortage) is just matched by the value of the gain in other financial assets (which may, for example, provide more insurance coverage for family members). And, as one goes farther along curve I from A past F, an increasing quantity of other financial assets per dollar's worth of deposits is required to maintain this indifference between the combinations.

The assumption that an individual prefers more of each asset to less implies that the individual would prefer to be on an indifference curve as far from the origin as possible in Figure 6-1. For the individual with a budget of $100 to spend on the two assets, facing relative prices of $110–$100, the best combination of deposits and other financial assets is represented by point A, which is a point of tangency between budget line $110–$100 and indifference curve I. Curve I is the highest level of satisfaction obtainable within the $100 budget constraint. At such a point of tangency between a budget line and an indifference curve, the ratio of the prices of the two assets (the slope of the budget line) is just equal to the marginal rate of indifference substitution between the assets in the preferences of the individual (the slope of the indifference curve), indicating that the individual thinks the price is right for keeping that combination of assets. For any other point on the budget line, the slope of the indifference curve passing through that point will be either greater or less than that of the budget line, indicating that the individual thinks the price is right for changing the combination of assets until an equilibrium is reached at point A.

Suppose now that the return on deposits is increased (the cost of deposits reduced), while the return on other financial assets is unchanged. In this case, the individual would probably decide to hold more deposits. This response is depicted in Figure 6-1 with budget lines rotating counterclockwise around $110 on the vertical axis. If the deposit return rises to 2 percent, the appropriate budget line for a budget of $100 becomes $110–$102, and that for a return of 10 percent on deposits is $110–$110. These new budget lines become tangent to indifference curves II and III at points B and C, respectively. When points A, B, and C are connected, the resulting curve indicates the portfolio allocation of the individual that results from various relative prices of the assets. By drawing budget lines that are parallel to $110–$100, but just tangent to indifference curves II and III at points D and E, respectively, we can follow the responses of the individual to increased budgets in the face of the original relative prices of the assets. In this case, the individual purchases more of *each* of the assets.

Let us now relate this individual portfolio-allocation process to the growth of depository intermediaries since World War II. By making several simplifying assumptions (the most unrealistic of which is that individuals have the same preferences), it is possible to multiply the values on the vertical and horizontal axes in Figure 6-1 by the number of individual decision makers to arrive at the aggregate behavior for the United States. By further assuming that tastes or preferences did not change between 1948 and 1978, one can ignore the fact that Figure 6-1 has no time dimension. During

the period between 1948 and 1978, personal disposable income increased dramatically, and each year part of that income was saved. The stock of all financial assets owned by individuals at a particular time is determined by all of their past saving and the effect of capital gains, losses, and bequests. The budget constraint for the aggregate household sector at the end of 1948 was $293 billion for allocation between deposits and other financial assets (excluding equities); by the end of 1978, this figure had risen to $2,595 billion, as a result primarily of the additional saving that occurred between the two dates. Thus, households accumulated quite large additional quantities of both deposits and other financial assets: deposits increased from $118 to $1,279 billion and other financial assets rose from $175 to $1,316 billion.

If there had been no changes in the relative prices of deposits and other financial assets between 1948 and 1978, it seems that due to "income effects" of the relaxed budget constraint, portfolios would have followed an expansion path like the sequence A, D, E in Figure 6-1. But the share of deposits in the total portfolio increased from 40 percent in 1948 to 49 percent in 1978, and it is reasonable to attribute a significant portion of the shift to increased returns (reduced prices) of deposits relative to other financial assets. There are several reasons for this conclusion. First, the proportion of deposits accounted for by nonearning demand deposits declined from 46 percent in 1948 to 17 percent of total deposits in 1978, thus increasing the proportion of deposits on which explicit interest was received. Second, a larger and larger fraction of time deposits in recent years has been in the form of longer-term certificates of deposit (CDs), which have returns that are quite competitive with open-market securities. Third, since 1957, commercial banks have been permitted to pay rates on their time deposits that are significantly higher relative to open-market securities' rates than was the case in the early postwar period.

Like households, nonfinancial firms have dramatically increased their holdings of both deposits and other financial assets since 1948. Their portfolio of financial assets rose from $104 billion at the end of 1948 to $815 billion by the end of 1978. However, for the nonfinancial firms, deposits declined significantly in importance relative to other financial assets from a 1948 figure of 39 percent to

14 percent by the end of 1978. Two major factors explain this difference in the behavior of firms and households. First, firms were prohibited from owning deposit liabilities of nonbank intermediaries and, until recently, were also prohibited from owning the savings account liabilities of banks. Thus nonfinancial firms were little affected until recently by the higher rates permitted on time deposits. Second, financial assets to some extent perform a different function in the portfolios of the two groups. Households are more likely to view financial assets as a repository of savings, whereas firms are more likely to view them as a producer good that is a necessary part of the process of producing income. Thus, a firm holds deposits largely for transaction purposes and holds other financial assets, such as trade and consumer credit, largely to facilitate sales. As the yields on other financial assets have risen since 1948 relative to demand deposits, firms have experienced added incentives both to economize on their holdings of cash and to obtain the higher rates paid by the trade and consumer credit advanced.

## The Growth of Time Deposits Relative to Demand Deposits

The major types of deposit liabilities—demand and time deposits—behaved quite differently in the portfolios of savers during the post-1948 period. Demand deposits, while increasing absolutely, declined consistently in relative importance in the portfolios of both households and nonfinancial firms. For households, demand deposits and currency were 19 percent of nonequity financial assets at the end of 1948, but were only 9 percent by the end of 1978. For firms, the decline was even greater during the same period, falling from 38 percent to 10 percent of all financial assets. Time deposits, on the other hand, increased from 22 percent to 43 percent in the portfolios of households, and from 1 percent to 4 percent in the portfolios of nonfinancial firms. Let us now consider the reasons for this remarkable development.

Figure 6-2 adapts the decision-making framework discussed earlier with respect to deposits and other financial assets to the decisions allocating the deposit portion of the portfolio between demand deposits and time deposits. The vertical axis shows demand deposits and the horizontal axis shows

**Figure 6-2  Portfolio Allocation Between Demand Deposits and Time Deposits**

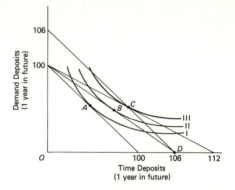

time deposits, both delivered one year in the future. For an investment of $100 now, one can receive only $100 of demand deposits. An investment of the $100 in time deposits would result a year hence in $100 if the yield on them were also zero, $106 if the yield were 6 percent, and $112 if the yield were 12 percent. Indifference curves I, II, and III represent successively higher levels of satisfaction from a portfolio and are drawn to take into account all differences between demand and time deposits other than differences in returns (costs).

During the 1948–1978 period, households and nonfinancial firms moved in sequences like A, B, C as the yields on time deposits rose relative to the zero yield on demand deposits. For the bulk of time deposits, the yield was below 2½ percent in 1948. By the end of 1978, it was over 6 percent, and longer-term CDs paid more. This significant change in the relative prices of these two assets accounts for a portion of the shift from demand to time deposits in the portfolios of individuals and businesses.

Another factor accounting for the shift from demand to time deposits is the advent of financial innovations that have made savings and time deposits better substitutes for demand deposits. Traditionally, with demand (but not with time and savings) deposits, banks could be ordered by holders of these deposits to pay a third party through the writing of checks drawn on the bank. This distinction has been altered dramatically in the last few years by NOW accounts and share drafts, both of which are expected to become vastly more important as a means of payment in the future. Also important in the last two decades has been the increase in the number of branch offices, which makes it less expensive in terms of time and of money to convert a time deposit into a demand deposit.[12] The major difference currently between demand deposits, on the one hand, and savings and time deposits, on the other, is the speed of conversion into money, a possibility which prevents their becoming perfect substitutes for demand deposits. However, such innovations as NOW accounts, share drafts, and telephone transfers in terms of Figure 6-2 have made the slopes of the indifference curves more nearly approach the limiting case of perfect substitutes in which the curve is a straight line, such as $106–$106 with a slope of $-1$. If time and savings deposits and demand deposits were perfect substitutes—that is, if the only difference between them was the fact that time and savings deposits paid interest—then the individual or firm would spend $100 now for a demand deposit only if it would buy the same value one year in the future as spending $100 for a time or savings deposit would. Thus, where the one type of deposit is a perfect substitute for the other, portfolios will be allocated entirely to time and savings deposits, at points such as $D$ for a 6 percent yield on time and savings deposits, so long as the rate of interest on them is positive. As time and savings deposits approach this case of perfect substitution—and they have become close substitutes during the last twenty years—there would be a substitution of such deposits for demand deposits even if the yield on time deposits were constant over time.[13]

These two factors—the increasing interest yield on time and savings deposits relative to demand deposits, and the increasing substitutability of such deposits for demand deposits—are the major factors explaining the declining importance of demand deposits relative to time and savings deposits in the portfolios of individuals and businesses in the United States in the post-1948 period. Since com-

mercial banks are the only issuers of demand deposits, they have felt the full impact of the decline in the public's relative preference for demand deposits. One should note, however, that despite the decline of demand deposits relative to time and savings deposits, the growth rate of demand deposits in an average year for the past decade has been 7 percent.

## Changes in the Relative Size of the Various Depository Intermediaries

Thus far we have analyzed the dramatic post-1948 increase in the size of the entire depository intermediary sector and the dramatic decline in the importance of demand deposits relative to savings and time deposits. Now let us turn to an explanation of the important changes in the relative size of particular types of depository intermediaries. Table 6-3 is a summary of the relevant statistics, using total financial assets as the basis for comparison. For all of these intermediaries, the basic determinant of their asset size is their ability to "sell" deposits. Public policy plays a role so important with respect to these liabilities that it may well be the primary explanation for changes that are not accounted for in the preceding discussion. Commercial banks have felt the full force of the declining market for demand deposits relative to savings and time deposits, but these banks also issue the latter and would have experienced no change in relative size if their savings and time deposit liabilities had increased to the same extent that their demand deposit liabilities decreased. This did not happen, however. In 1948 commercial banks were liable for 52 percent of depository intermediary savings and time deposits; such liability had declined to only 40 percent by the end of 1956, after which it rose gradually to 45 percent by the end of 1978. Thus, the nonbank depository intermediaries grew dramatically relative to banks between 1948 and 1956 because both demand deposits and commercial banks' savings and time deposits were declining proportions of the public's portfolio. Since 1956, commercial banks' savings and time deposits have held their own relative to nonbank savings and time deposits, while demand deposits have continued to decline in relative importance.

The effect of changing the yield on commercial banks' savings and time deposits relative to those of

---

[12]Some banks even provide a telephone transfer service, and, beginning November 1, 1978, regulatory changes permit banks to provide automatic transfers to cover overdrafts.

[13]Commercial banks could prevent time deposits from becoming perfect substitutes for demand deposits by requiring compensating balances in the form of demand deposits as a condition for making loans.

**Table 6-3  Relative Size of Financial Assets of Depository Intermediaries (percentages)**

|  | 1948 | 1956 | 1966 | 1978 |
|---|---|---|---|---|
| Commercial banks | 80.3% | 70.9% | 63.7% | 62.3% |
| Savings and loan associations | 7.5 | 15.6 | 23.4 | 26.6 |
| Mutual savings banks | 11.8 | 12.2 | 10.8 | 8.1 |
| Credit unions | .4 | 1.3 | 2.1 | 3.0 |
| Total depository intermediaries | 100.0 | 100.0 | 100.0 | 100.0 |

Source: Board of Governors of the Federal Reserve System, *Flow of Funds Accounts.*

savings institutions can be analyzed in terms of Figure 6-3. Let commercial banks' savings and time deposits one year in the future be measured on the vertical axis and thrift institutions' savings and time deposits one year in the future be measured on the horizontal axis. Again identify the amount of each asset that a current expenditure of $100 will purchase. If thrift institutions' savings and time deposits return 2½ percent per year, an expenditure of $100 now will purchase $102.50 one year hence. If commercial banks' savings and time deposits also pay 2½ percent, one can also purchase $102.50 for the expenditure of $100. Raising the yield on savings institutions' time and savings deposits will shift the typical individual from a point, such as *A*, to a point, such as *B*, with an increase in holdings of savings and time deposits at thrift institutions at the expense of commercial banks' savings and time deposits.

Since, in all probability, there is greater substitutability between savings and time deposits issued by different institutions than between savings and time deposits and demand deposits, the indifference curves are more likely to approach the shape of perfect substitutes in Figure 6-3 than in Figure 6-2.[14] Thus, the response in terms of substitution of these assets is likely to be greater for a given percentage point change in the interest rates in Figure 6-3 than in Figure 6-2.

Let us now analyze, in terms of Figure 6-3, the effects of some major changes in public policy since 1948 on the relative importance of commercial banks and thrift institutions. From the beginning of Federal Reserve power to set maximum rates pay-

able on commercial bank savings and time deposits until 1957, the maximum permitted rate was 2½ percent. Other depository institutions during that period and until 1966 were not constrained directly by public policy in the rates they could pay on their savings and time deposits. Beginning in 1957 the Federal Reserve Board raised the rate that commercial banks could pay, and generally kept it only slightly below the rate that the savings institutions were paying. In 1966 the Federal Reserve Board, Federal Deposit Insurance Corporation, and Federal Home Loan Bank Board began to set jointly the maximum rates that could be paid by all of the institutions (except credit unions); since then the commercial bank rate has generally been a uniform ¼ percent below the savings institution rates.[15]

The situation in 1948 was approximately that indicated in Figure 6-3 by point *A*. Both banks and other depository institutions were paying 2½ percent or less on savings and time deposits. The public's ratio of commercial banks' savings and time deposits to savings institutions' time deposits was the slope of a ray through the origin, *OA*, approximately 1.08. Between 1948 and the end of 1956, movement to a point such as *B* occurred as savings institutions gradually raised their rates to 4½ percent, while banks were restricted to offering a maximum of 2½ percent. The resulting ratio, the slope of the line *OB*, was 0.67. With the new, more comparable treatment of commercial banks beginning in 1957, movement was toward points such as *C* and *D*—with the ratio of commercial banks' to savings institutions' savings and time deposits 0.74 at the end of 1966 and 0.83 at the end of 1978.

Although the behavior of interest rates during the period 1957–1978 has improved the position of

[14]A survey of much of the recent literature on the subject of elasticity of substitution among financial assets is presented in Edgar L. Feige and D. K. Pearce, "The Substitutability of Money and Near-Monies: A Survey of the Time-Series Evidence," *Journal of Economic Literature* (June 1977).

[15]A relatively complete chronology of statutory and regulatory matters of importance to savings institutions, together with relevant statistics, can be found in the current *Savings and Loan Fact Book.*

**Figure 6-3  Portfolio Allocation Between Time Deposits at Commercial Banks and Time Deposits at Savings Institutions**

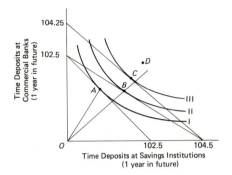

commercial banks relative to other deposit intermediaries in terms of the sale of savings and time deposits, other factors have worked in the opposite direction. After initial experimentation with NOW accounts for mutual savings banks in Massachusetts and New Hampshire in the early 1970s, nearly all New England depository institutions now offer these liabilities, and these powers were extended to S&Ls and mutual savings banks nationwide, as well as to banks, beginning in 1981. Furthermore, in 1977, federal credit unions were authorized to issue share drafts. More recently, credit unions have been permitted to use electronic funds transfers and to issue credit cards, such as VISA.[16] In 1980, federally chartered S&Ls received authority to issue credit cards. All of these innovations have reduced the advantage of the full-service bank as a place to do business. As some of the differences other than interest rates have disappeared, the time and savings deposits of the various institutions have become more nearly perfect substitutes. This trend will probably continue, as interest rate ceilings on deposits are phased out during the period 1980–1986.

In sum, demand factors such as prices, incomes, and preferences have important influences on the relative growth rates of the various intermediaries and on the variety of liabilities they provide. How-

ever, as was observed in Chapter 4, other factors, such as risk, return, and regulation also influence intermediaries' products, especially their asset choices. Because there remain significant differences in the types of loans available from the various depository intermediaries, in addition to differences in their liabilities, we now examine the asset side in more detail.

### Depository Intermediaries as Suppliers of Loanable Funds

At the end of 1978, households in the United States had liabilities of $361 billion in the form of consumer and securities debt; depository intermediaries held two-thirds of such debt.[17] Also, households at the end of 1978 had $738 billion of home mortgages outstanding, of which three-fourths were held by depository intermediaries. These and other liabilities of households came to $1,208 billion, of which depository intermediaries owned at least 66 percent. Nonfinancial firms had $393 billion of mortgages outstanding at the end of 1978, of which one-half was held by depository intermediaries. Of the $1,480 billion total liabilities of nonfinancial firms at the end of 1978, depository intermediaries owned at least 39 percent. At the end of 1978 the federal government (including federal agencies) had securities outstanding of $825 billion, with deposit-type intermediaries owning 24 percent. These statistics indicate the overwhelming importance of depository intermediaries in these major markets for loanable funds. A relatively small (from the viewpoint of the financial sector) shift in the preferences of deposit intermediaries for financial assets may cause severe consequences for particular classes of ultimate borrowers. Thus, from the viewpoint of the entire economy, it is important to identify the factors that determine the aggregate quantity of funds supplied by the deposit intermediaries and the allocation of those funds among specific financial assets.

Chapter 4 discussed the general decision-making framework for an individual financial intermediary. Although Chapter 4 concentrated on the commercial bank, there are some general characteristics of the process common to all depository intermedi-

---

[16]See, for instance, the testimony of the chairman of the Federal Reserve Board in *Federal Reserve Bulletin* (July 1977), 636–643; and *Washington Post* (October 14, 1977), p. B3.

[17]These data are from Board of Governors of the Federal Reserve System, *Flow of Funds Accounts*.

aries.[18] First, they have some goal or goals, which the decision makers attempt to attain. Much of economic analysis assumes that this goal is to maximize the wealth of the owners. Second, due to the nature of their sources of funds, uncertainty and risk are particularly important constraints on the behavior of depository intermediaries. Because these intermediaries are uncertain as to the timing and size of changes in their deposits, they must carefully consider this uncertainty in allocating their portfolios. For this reason, these institutions tend to hold relatively liquid, lower-return assets where at all possible.[19] Although there exists a wealth of legal and regulatory restraints on the purchase of risky assets by depository intermediaries, it is important to understand that, even in the absence of such restraints, the nature of their sources of funds would dictate prudence. Third, to the extent they can do so within their regulatory confines, depository intermediaries attempt to diversify their asset portfolios in order to reduce unsystematic risk. Attempts by intermediaries to diversify both their assets and liabilities have led to financial innovations and to pressures for regulatory changes.[20]

Let us now consider how the four types of depository intermediaries have in actual practice allocated their funds in the post-1948 period.

## The Decision-Making Process for Commercial Banks

Detailed treatment of the decision-making process for commercial banks is found in Chapter 4. In addition, important aspects of commercial bank regulation are treated in Chapter 31. For these reasons, only balance-sheet data and the briefest of descriptions appear here, and only so that the reader can compare the data for commercial banks

with those for the other depository intermediaries discussed in this chapter. Table 6-4 shows a consolidated balance sheet for all commercial banks broken down by percentage distribution of selected assets and liabilities for the years 1948, 1956, 1966, and 1978. One can see from Table 6-4 that banks obtain most of their funds from savings and time deposits; most of the rest from demand deposits; and some funds from longer-term sources, such as bonds and common stocks. Twenty years ago demand deposits were considerably more important as a source of funds than were savings and time deposits. In using their funds, commercial banks have shifted away from U.S. government securities toward loans to consumers and businesses as well as toward investments in state and local government securities. At the present time, a smaller fraction of the funds available to commercial banks is tied up in nonearning reserves than was formerly the case. It will be seen that, compared with the other depository intermediaries, commercial banks have greater variety both in their assets and their liabilities.

Although commercial banks have a greater variety of sources of funds than the other intermediaries, the average turnover rate on their demand and time deposits is considerably higher than that on savings deposits and shares held by the savings banks and S&Ls and helps account, in part, for banks' holding a higher fraction of their assets in liquid form than do savings banks or S&Ls. Also, a larger proportion of banks' earning assets are short term and intermediate in nature.

## The Decision-Making Process for Savings and Loan Associations

Data for savings and loan associations for the postwar period are shown in Table 6-5. Compared with commercial banks, savings and loan associations are extremely specialized in their assets and liabilities. Savings shares or deposits accounted for 82 percent of their liabilities and capital at the end of 1978. Among their assets on the same date, mortgages accounted for 83 percent of total financial assets. Savings shares are sold to all who wish to purchase them under the conditions announced by the association, and the owner of a share can in practice sell it back to the association on demand for the initial purchase price, although legally some

[18]Further treatment of the decision-making process for financial institutions generally and its application to the individual depository institution is found in Hempel and Yawitz, *Financial Management of Financial Institutions.*

[19]Regulatory constraints, especially severe in the case of S&Ls and savings banks, dictate a higher percentage of mortgage holdings and acquisitions than would exist if such regulations were liberalized.

[20]The extraordinary extent and implications of financial innovations are to be found in William L. Silber, *Financial Innovation,* Lexington Books, Lexington, Mass., 1975.

**Table 6-4  Selected Assets and Liabilities of All Commercial Banks (percentages)**

|  | 1948 | 1956 | 1966 | 1978 |
|---|---|---|---|---|
| FINANCIAL ASSETS | | | | |
| Demand deposits and currency | 16.3% | 11.8% | 7.3% | 7.7% |
| Money market instruments not elsewhere classified | .3 | .5 | 1.0 | 1.1 |
| U.S. government securities | 46.7 | 31.7 | 17.3 | 11.3 |
| State and local securities | 4.1 | 6.7 | 11.3 | 10.1 |
| Corporate bonds | 1.6 | .7 | .3 | .6 |
| Home mortgages | 5.3 | 8.3 | 9.0 | 10.4 |
| Other mortgages | 2.5 | 3.3 | 5.9 | 7.1 |
| Business loans | 16.9 | 25.0 | 31.9 | 28.1 |
| Consumer credit | 5.1 | 10.0 | 13.2 | 15.3 |
| Misc. financial assets | 1.0 | 1.6 | 2.7 | 8.3 |
| Total financial assets | 100.0 | 100.0 | 100.0 | 100.0 |
| LIABILITIES AND CAPITAL | | | | |
| Gross demand deposits | 64.2% | 60.0% | 41.6% | 28.1% |
| Time deposits (excl. large CDs) | 26.0 | 27.0 | 39.6 | 42.4 |
| Large negotiable CDs | .0 | .0 | 4.3 | 8.2 |
| Federal Funds and repurchases | .0 | .0 | .3 | 1.9 |
| Borrowing from foreign banks | .0 | .0 | .0 | 1.4 |
| Miscellaneous liabilities | 3.0 | 5.5 | 7.3 | 12.7 |
| Total liabilities | 93.2 | 92.6 | 93.2 | 94.7 |
| Equity in financial assets | 6.8 | 7.4 | 6.8 | 5.3 |
| Total liabilities and equity | 100.0 | 100.0 | 100.0 | 100.0 |

Source: Board of Governors of the Federal Reserve System, *Flow of Funds Accounts.*

substantial delay could be enforced. At the present time, more than half of the share and deposit accounts are certificates of deposit, which provide specific maturity dates and, hence, reduce the uncertainty to associations concerning the timing of withdrawals. The mortgages are primarily on one- to four-family residences and usually are amortized with level monthly payments of principal and interest over a fifteen- to thirty-year period. Traditionally, the interest rate is set when the mortgage is issued and remains unchanged over its life. In recent years in California, however, there has been experimentation with variable-rate mortgages, and in 1979 the Federal Home Loan Bank Board authorized federally chartered S&Ls nationwide to offer mortgages on which rates will vary with the cost of money.

The extreme specialization of the savings and loan associations is not a voluntary matter; it has been forced on them by law and by federal and state regulation (see Chapter 31). Thus, the major short-run problem of a savings and loan association is to predict, prepare for, and manage the cash flows resulting from its mortgage holdings and deposits. Amortizations of existing mortgages result

in predictable inflows of funds. Withdrawals of funds by existing depositors result in an outflow of funds that, in the short run, is at the discretion of the depositor and is somewhat uncertain, though not so uncertain as withdrawals of demand deposits from commercial banks.[21] Inflows of funds result from sales of new deposits and this flow is relatively unpredictable and uncontrolled in the short run. The sum of the inflow of interest and amortizations and new deposits less withdrawals of old deposits is the basic source of funds for purchases of new mortgages. However, the association is not free to purchase any amount of new mortgages that it would like at a particular time, due to the behavior of the new mortgage market. The association at any particular time will have to honor commitments to purchase new mortgages that were made several months earlier, often before the construction of the homes was started. Thus, at any given time, the cash outflow from actual purchases of new mort-

[21]Since bank demand deposits are used primarily for transactions, their rate of turnover is greater and, hence, they are subject to greater short-run variations than other deposits, which have been used primarily as repositories of savings.

**Table 6-5  Selected Assets and Liabilities of Savings and Loan Associations (percentages)**

| | *1948* | *1956* | *1966* | *1978* |
|---|---|---|---|---|
| FINANCIAL ASSETS | | | | |
| Demand deposits and currency | 4.1% | 3.3% | 1.7% | .3% |
| Time deposits or shares | .0 | .0 | .1 | .9 |
| Money market instruments not elsewhere classified | .0 | .0 | .0 | 2.2 |
| U.S. government securities | 11.2 | 6.9 | 6.4 | 6.9 |
| State and local securities | .0 | .0 | .0 | .2 |
| Home mortgages | 75.5 | 79.3 | 72.7 | 68.0 |
| Other mortgages | 3.6 | 4.0 | 12.7 | 14.6 |
| Consumer credit | .9 | 1.3 | 1.0 | 2.3 |
| Misc. financial assets | 4.8 | 5.1 | 5.3 | 4.4 |
| Total financial assets | 100.0 | 100.0 | 100.0 | 100.0 |
| LIABILITIES AND CAPITAL | | | | |
| Savings shares or deposits | 84.2% | 86.6% | 85.1% | 82.3% |
| Mortgages loans in process | 1.8 | 2.1 | .9 | 2.1 |
| Bank loans | .7 | .3 | .4 | .6 |
| Fed. Home Loan Bank advances | 3.9 | 2.9 | 5.2 | 6.2 |
| Miscellaneous liabilities | 2.0 | 1.3 | 1.6 | 1.8 |
| Total liabilities | 92.6 | 93.1 | 93.2 | 94.5 |
| Equity in financial assets | 7.4 | 6.9 | 6.8 | 5.5 |
| Total liabilities and equity | 100.0 | 100.0 | 100.0 | 100.0 |

Source: Board of Governors of the Federal Reserve System, *Flow of Funds Accounts.*

gages is almost as predetermined as is the inflow from interest and amortizations of old mortgage holdings. The short-run problem is to obtain funds from some source to finance any excess of new mortgage purchases and share withdrawals over old mortgage amortizations and interest payments and new share sales; or in the opposite case, to use any net inflow of funds to reduce liabilities or increase assets.

The associations can turn to their reserve accounts to meet some cash outflows to the extent that reserves exceed legal requirements. Excess reserves are held in the form of demand deposits, time deposits, and U.S. government securities, all of which can be sold on short notice with little, if any, risk of capital loss due to changed conditions in the money market. The associations' holdings of these assets accounted for 8.1 percent of total financial assets at the end of 1978. (They also held relatively small quantities of other money-market instruments and state and local government securities, which together accounted for 2.4 percent of their total financial assets.)

The association that experiences a short-run cash outflow could also look to the possibility of issuing liabilities to meet the cash deficiency. Relatively small quantities of commercial bank loans to sav-

ings and loan associations accounted for approximately 1 percent of association financial liabilities at the end of 1978. Much more important than bank loans are advances from the Federal Home Loan banks. These advances, which are secured by mortgage collateral, accounted for approximately 6 percent of savings and loan total liabilities at the end of 1978. These advances are much more important to the S&Ls than are the discounts and advances of the Federal Reserve System to borrowing banks. This reflects the greater enforced specialization of the associations, which prevents them from issuing so varied a list of liabilities and from holding so varied a set of financial assets as banks. Thus, a relatively small percentage decline in share liabilities or increase in mortgages (each of which accounts for approximately 85 percent of total financial assets) would exhaust an association's ability to sell other financial assets or issue other liabilities to meet a cash drain. The Federal Home Loan banks make advances to alleviate these short-run problems—thus providing an extremely important service for the associations in the short-run management of their funds.

The longer-run problems of the savings and loan associations involve growth in their shares outstanding and their capital stock or reserve accounts to provide the possibility of growth in their mortgage portfolio. Commercial banks can increase the size of commercial bank liabilities (somewhere in the system) *simultaneously* with increasing their loan and investment activities; and regulation by the monetary authorities of the rate of growth of these commercial bank liabilities is largely through managing the quantity of reserves available to and required of those banks. No similar process exists for savings and loan associations. They must sell liabilities or capital or other assets to someone *before* they can make payment for the assets they purchase. The associations can change the conditions of their offers of shares in an attempt to regulate the inflow of funds from share sales in the longer run, but, in the past, this power has been restricted by the ceiling on interest rates imposed by the Federal Home Loan Bank Board. Most businesses could attempt to increase the level of their activity by lowering their prices, but the savings and loan associations have been prevented from doing at their discretion what for them is comparable to lowering their prices—raising the dividend rates paid on shares. This fact of life for the associations was particularly troublesome when rates rose for financial assets that are substitutes for S&L shares in the portfolios of savers. For instance, as the yields on short-term government securities rose in the past, shareholders were likely to convert shares into government securities since yields on shares remained constant. Protecting savings institutions (and the home mortgage market) from difficulties of this kind is, of course, a major reason for financial reforms in 1980 phasing out interest rate ceilings on deposits.[22]

On three recent occasions—in 1966, 1969, and 1973–1974—the savings and loan industry and, indeed, the entire depository intermediary sector, was faced with the problem of disintermediation.[23] Here is the sequence of events in these "credit crunches": (1) the Federal Reserve pursued a tight-money policy that significantly raised long- and short-term interest rates; (2) depository institutions either would not or could not raise deposit rates as rapidly as open-market rates were rising; (3) depositors withdrew deposits and used the proceeds to purchase open-market securities; (4) some intermediaries were forced to dispose of assets or issue other liabilities to meet deposit withdrawals; and (5) interest rates other than those on deposits rose even higher as a result of (4), thereby moving the sequence back to (2) for a new round. Some of the effects of these credit crunches are seen in Table 6-6. It is apparent that the major factor explaining the decline in mortgage acquisitions for 1966, 1969, and 1974 was the decline in net deposits for those years. The problem was so acute in the third quarter of each of those years that the quantity of S&Ls' outstanding legal liabilities actually declined even as interest rates on new mortgages rose to historically high levels.

Past inability of the S&Ls to offer higher deposit rates as a result of regulation, however, is only a partial explanation of their behavior during credit crunches. A somewhat more fundamental explanation is the profit squeeze that occurs as deposit rates rise on virtually all deposits, while the association's income rises only on the relatively small fraction of the asset portfolio that is replaced with higher-yield mortgages.[24] Thus, even if there were no deposit-rate ceilings, the phenomenon of disintermediation might well accompany periods of tight money and high interest rates, although perhaps in a less virulent form than was observed in 1966, 1969, and 1974. Experience in 1980 following partial removal of deposit rate ceilings is probably illus-

[22]Commercial banks also are prevented from lowering their prices, but the effect on them is not as great as for savings and loan associations. Conversion of an S&L deposit into a Treasury bill results in a loss of funds for the S&L industry. Conversion of a commercial bank time deposit into a Treasury bill results in no loss to the banking system, but only in the conversion of a time deposit into a demand deposit opened by the person selling the Treasury bill.

[23]For an additional discussion of disintermediation, see Henry Kaufman, "Financial Crises: Market Impact, Consequences, and Adaptability," in *Financial Crises,* eds. Edward I. Altman and Arnold W. Sametz, John Wiley & Sons, New York, 1977; also, Allan Sinai, "Credit Crunches—An Analysis of the Postwar Experience," in *Parameters and Policies in the U.S. Economy,* ed. Otto Eckstein, North-Holland Publishing Co., Amsterdam, 1976.

[24]The effective lifetime of the average home mortgage is approximately seven years prior to the sale and refinancing of a used home. Consequently, on average, only 15 percent of the mortgage portfolio of the typical association turns over during the course of a year, enabling the funds so freed to take advantage of higher mortgage yields during periods of high and rising interest rates.

**Table 6-6 Savings and Loan Associations: Selected Sources and Uses of Funds, 1965–1978 (in billions of dollars or percentages)**

| | Sources | | Use | FHA New |
|---|---|---|---|---|
| | Net Change in Savings Deposits | Interest & Amortization of Mortgage Portfolio[a] | Acquisitions of New Mortgages | Mortgage Yields |
| 1965 | $ 8.5 | $17.5 | $ 26.7 | 5.5% |
| 1966 | 3.6 | 14.3 | 18.2 | 6.3 |
| 1967 | 10.6 | 14.6 | 22.3 | 6.6 |
| 1968 | 7.5 | 15.0 | 24.4 | 7.1 |
| 1969 | 4.1 | 14.5 | 24.3 | 8.2 |
| 1970 | 11.0 | 14.8 | 25.2 | 9.1 |
| 1971 | 28.0 | 23.0 | 47.2 | 7.8 |
| 1972 | 32.7 | 30.1 | 62.3 | 7.5 |
| 1973 | 20.2 | 30.1 | 56.8 | 8.1 |
| 1974 | 16.1 | 27.4 | 45.0 | 9.5 |
| 1975 | 42.8 | 34.2 | 63.8 | 9.2 |
| 1976 | 50.6 | 46.8 | 91.8 | 8.8 |
| 1977 | 51.0 | 63.5 | 122.2 | 8.7 |
| 1978 | 44.9 | 68.9 | 121.5 | 9.7 |

[a]Includes use of mortgages as collateral for loans.

Source: U.S. League of Savings Associations, *Savings and Loan Fact Book; Federal Reserve Bulletin.*

trative of the kinds of problems that may develop in the future.[25]

The closest substitutes for S&L shares and CDs are savings accounts and time deposits at commercial banks. Since 1966 the maximum S&L rates have been maintained approximately ¼ percent above comparable commercial bank rates.[26] This difference is permitted in an attempt to offset the greater convenience of commercial bank liabilities, which is supposed to result from the wider range of services available to a customer at com-

mercial banks. Although this maintaining of a fixed differential appears to give equality of regulatory treatment to commercial banks and savings and loan associations, in fact the results of deposit-rate ceilings are much more restrictive on the operations of savings and loan associations. This results from the somewhat greater latitude available to commercial banks in issuing alternative liabilities to obtain funds and the substantial short-term assets that they can allow to mature without replacing them—thus avoiding capital losses in obtaining funds for lending to their major customers. But, as we have seen, the savings and loan associations' portfolios are almost entirely in mortgages. These obligations are longer-term than the bulk of earning assets held by commercial banks and, until recently, had quite poorly developed secondary markets. Thus, a moderate change in the current yield on mortgages would result in substantial changes in the opposite direction in the market prices of outstanding mortgages. Whereas a commercial bank, in adjusting to an outflow of deposits, could reallocate a substantial portion of its portfolio of assets without incurring capital losses, the savings and loan association finds almost all of its assets either nonmarketable or subject to substantial fluctuations in market value. The goal of insulating S&Ls from difficulties of this kind is a major reason why the Financial Institutions Deregulation and

[25]On June 1, 1978, S&Ls, along with mutual savings and commercial banks, were given the authority to issue six-month savings certificates of $10,000 minimum denominations with rates fixed at slightly higher yields than the weekly auction rates on comparable-maturity Treasury bills. (This yield differential has since been rescinded.) The result was greater ability on the part of thrift institutions to retain and even attract funds during a period of high and rising money market rates. How long such disintermediation can be thwarted in the face of rising costs and dwindling profit margins for S&Ls, however, is not at all clear. A credit crunch was averted in the spring of 1980 when interest rates tumbled in a very short period. Nevertheless, the impact on profitability of many S&Ls was severe, and mortgage credit growth slowed sharply in the first half of 1980. For further discussion of conditions in 1980 see Charles A. Luckett, "Recent Financial Behavior of Households," *Federal Reserve Bulletin* (June 1980).

[26]See various issues of the *Federal Reserve Bulletin* for specific rates.

Monetary Control Act of 1980 that ordered the phasing out of deposit rate ceilings over six years also allowed federally chartered S&Ls to hold 20 percent of their assets in shorter-term consumer loans and commercial paper and (marketable) corporate securities.

A thorough discussion of the mortgage market—and the wealth of government and quasi-governmental agencies that participate in it—appears in Chapters 11 and 13; suffice it to note here that the Government National Mortgage Association, the Federal National Mortgage Association, and the Federal Home Loan Mortgage Corporation provide secondary markets in mortgages and commitments to purchase mortgages. The availability of secondary markets, plus advances from the Federal Home Loan Bank Board, further reduce the liquidity problem for S&Ls caused by cyclical swings in monetary and credit policy.

### The Decision-Making Process for Mutual Savings Banks

The decision-making process for mutual savings banks is similar to that for savings and loan associations because of the similarities in their liabilities. They have to be prepared to repay depositors on short notice, even though in an emergency the repayment could be delayed legally. This means that mutual savings banks must be able to issue other liabilities on short notice or sell assets in the event of net withdrawals of deposits. Those few mutual savings banks that are members of the Federal Reserve System can obtain advances of funds from the Federal Reserve bank in their district; members of the Federal Home Loan Bank System can borrow from their Federal Home Loan banks to obtain funds on short notice. All of the mutual savings banks can draw down their cash accounts or sell the limited quantities of their short-term securities to meet short-run demands for funds or withdrawals without incurring substantial risk of capital losses. The longer-run uses of funds of these mutual savings banks are in the higher-return assets: mortgages, corporate bonds, and longer-term government securities. Table 6-7 provides data on the balance sheet for these institutions.

Mutual savings banks are somewhat more circumscribed than S&Ls in their liabilities—with approximately 90 percent of their assets financed by savings shares or deposit liabilities. The difference is mainly due to the lesser importance of Federal Home Loan Bank advances in the case of the mutual savings banks. For the last two decades, the fraction of total assets matched by these deposits has remained almost constant. Miscellaneous lia-

**Table 6-7   Selected Assets and Liabilities of Mutual Savings Banks (percentages)**

|  | 1948 | 1956 | 1966 | 1978 |
|---|---|---|---|---|
| FINANCIAL ASSETS |  |  |  |  |
| Demand deposits and currency | 3.2% | 2.3% | 1.3% | 1.0% |
| Time deposits or shares | 1.1 | .5 | .3 | 1.4 |
| Money market instruments not elsewhere classified | .3 | .4 | .7 | 2.1 |
| U.S. government securities | 56.4 | 24.2 | 9.4 | 11.6 |
| State and local securities | .3 | 2.0 | .4 | 2.1 |
| Corporate bonds | 9.1 | 7.9 | 5.2 | 13.6 |
| Home mortgages | 13.8 | 41.6 | 57.9 | 39.3 |
| Other mortgages | 14.5 | 17.0 | 19.0 | 20.8 |
| Consumer credit | .2 | .4 | 1.0 | 2.4 |
| Misc. financial assets | .2 | .4 | 1.0 | 2.5 |
| Total financial assets | 100.0 | 100.0 | 100.0 | 100.0 |
| LIABILITIES AND CAPITAL |  |  |  |  |
| Savings shares or deposits | 89.8 | 89.2 | 89.4 | 90.1 |
| Miscellaneous liabilities | .4 | 1.1 | 1.8 | 2.9 |
| Total liabilities | 90.2 | 90.3 | 91.2 | 93.0 |
| Equity in financial assets | 9.8 | 9.7 | 8.8 | 6.7 |
| Total liabilities and equity | 100.0 | 100.0 | 100.0 | 100.0 |

Source: Board of Governors of the Federal Reserve System, *Flow of Funds Accounts.*

bilities have gradually increased from approximately 1 percent to 3 percent of financial assets in the last twenty years. Total liabilities have increased somewhat more, from 90 percent to 93 percent of financial assets, reflecting the decline in the importance of equity in various financial assets.

Approximately 60 percent of mutual savings bank assets are in mortgages. These are divided between home mortgages and "others," with approximately two-thirds in home mortgages. "Other" mortgages are divided approximately evenly between mortgages on rental residential units and on other commercial property, such as office buildings. The increase in the relative importance of other mortgages is largely due to diversification of bank portfolios. Over the last twenty years, other mortgages increased gradually in relative importance from approximately 15 percent to 21 percent of total financial assets. Home mortgages rose rather dramatically in relative importance from 42 percent to 58 percent of financial assets between 1956 and 1966, after which they declined to 39 percent by 1978. Next in importance are corporate bonds, which have risen during the last two decades from 8 percent to 14 percent of total financial assets. United States government securities in 1978 accounted for 12 percent of financial assets—down from 24 percent in 1956 and up from 7 percent at the end of 1971. The behavior of government securities is almost a mirror image of the behavior of home mortgages—probably indicating that government securities are used as temporary investments when residential mortgages are not available or have unattractive yields.

Relatively small fractions of mutual savings bank portfolios are devoted to state and local government securities and consumer credit—in both cases no more than approximately 2 percent. The relatively small holdings of state and local government securities result directly from the tax-exempt status of mutual savings banks. While state and local government securities show no particular trend in relative importance, consumer credit has risen consistently over the last twenty years. Mutual savings banks hold demand deposits, time deposits, and other money-market instruments as reserves. These, in the aggregate, have changed little in relative importance during the last twenty years, but their composition has altered from a predominance of demand deposits and currency to a predominance of money-market instruments.

### The Decision-Making Process for Credit Unions

Although they are still quite small relative to the other deposit-type intermediaries, credit unions have doubled in size in the last twenty years, and relaxation in 1977 of many federal legal restraints on their growth may result in still more advances in the next few years.

Table 6-8 shows that some 91 percent of the assets of credit unions at the end of 1978 was financed through the issuance of savings shares; 9

**Table 6-8  Selected Assets and Liabilities of Credit Unions (percentages)**

|  | 1948 | 1956 | 1966 | 1978 |
|---|---|---|---|---|
| FINANCIAL ASSETS |  |  |  |  |
| Demand deposits and currency | 12.5% | 7.3% | 4.8% | 2.3% |
| Time deposits or shares | 17.2 | 24.6 | 17.3 | 3.8 |
| U.S. government securities | 11.6 | 4.3 | 3.9 | 8.4 |
| Home mortgages | 7.1 | 6.6 | 5.3 | 5.7 |
| Consumer credit | 51.6 | 57.4 | 68.8 | 78.9 |
| Total financial assets | 100.0 | 100.0 | 100.0 | 100.0 |
| LIABILITIES AND CAPITAL |  |  |  |  |
| Savings shares or deposits | 93.2 | 83.0 | 83.9 | 91.1 |
| Total liabilities | 93.2 | 83.0 | 83.9 | 91.1 |
| Equity in financial assets | 6.8 | 17.0 | 16.1 | 8.9 |
| Total liabilities and equity | 100.0 | 100.0 | 100.0 | 100.0 |

Source: Board of Governors of the Federal Reserve System, *Flow of Funds Accounts.*

percent was financed by various types of liability and reserve accounts. This high degree of specialization in share accounts increased somewhat in the last decade from 84 percent of liabilities in 1966. More than four-fifths of the financial assets of credit unions were loans to their depositors at the end of 1978—with approximately 79 percent of financial assets in the form of consumer credit (typically automobile loans) and 6 percent in home mortgages. Consumer credit rose from 57 percent of financial assets at the end of 1956, while mortgage lending declined slightly from 7 percent.

Funds which are available to the credit unions but which they cannot or will not lend to depositors are held primarily as demand deposits, time deposits, or United States government securities. For the last decade these assets have accounted for between 15 percent and 25 percent of their total assets—down from 35 percent at the end of 1956. Within these reserve accounts, credit unions have gradually switched from time deposits or shares into government securities. This shift has been substantial: time deposits or shares were 25 percent of total financial assets at the end of 1956; they were only 4 percent at the end of 1978. Government securities rose from 4 percent in 1956 to 8 percent in 1978. Demand deposits declined during the last two decades from approximately 7 percent to 2 percent of all credit unions' financial assets.

The remarkably high degree of liquidity observed for credit unions is a result of the requirement that they lend only to their members or to other credit unions. Thus, the credit union may find itself unable to find sufficient borrowers among its members to utilize the available funds fully. In such cases, credit unions purchase government securities, lend to other credit unions, or leave money idle in the form of bank deposits. As restrictions on the type of permissible loans made by credit unions have been relaxed in recent years, they have utilized their funds more fully in loans to their members. As a result, lending between credit unions has declined.

## Conclusion

This chapter has presented the broad outline of the post-1948 history of depository intermediaries. Their growth in the aggregate and by individual types has been spectacular. The growth of demand deposit liabilities has been much slower than the growth of time deposits. Prior to 1957 the growth of commercial bank deposits proceeded at a much slower pace than that of the other depository intermediaries. Commercial banks declined in relative importance, while savings and loan associations increased dramatically in size. Since 1957, commercial banks have roughly maintained their market share of savings relative to the other thrift institutions. In the portfolios of all of these intermediaries, government securities have declined significantly in importance relative to customer-related financial assets, such as loans and mortgages. Innovations in new types of liabilities have developed, such as those represented by negotiable CDs and NOW accounts.

All of these developments have been influenced heavily by public policies. Public restrictions on the types of assets that savings and loan associations could purchase forced extreme specialization on them. Credit unions and mutual savings banks were permitted somewhat more variety in their assets, and commercial banks were granted the greatest degree of discretion of any of the depository institutions. Commercial banks have been permitted to issue demand deposits and, in the early post-1948 period, the rates they could pay on their time deposits liabilities were set at relatively low levels. Finally, the maximum rates that all of these institutions, with the exception of credit unions, can pay on their deposits has been made more uniform since 1966, and ceilings on deposit rates at all depository institutions are scheduled to be phased out by 1986.

These obvious and important connections between public policies and long-run growth and profitability of different types of depository intermediaries have given rise to repeated proposals for change in the regulatory structure. Nearly all of the proposals that have been given serious consideration in recent years have been in the direction of removing restrictions on various types of assets and liabilities. Many of these proposals were enacted in the federal financial reform legislation signed by President Carter in March 1980.

There is also interaction between the behavior of depository intermediaries and countercyclical monetary policy. As the Federal Reserve pursues a tight-money policy to counteract inflation, it drives up interest rates on open market securities. This, in turn, affects households' and nonfinancial firms' allocations of funds between deposits and other financial assets. With the degree of specialization required in thrift institution assets, the allocation of funds to markets, such as those for home mortgages, can be greatly affected. The relative growth of the various intermediaries can also be affected. The initial impact and subsequent effects of monetary policy on the financial system are discussed further in Chapter 28.

## Questions

1. Describe the size of the various types of depository intermediaries relative to the entire sector. Explain the reasons behind any differences in size.
2. Explain the forces acting to change the relative importance of demand deposits and time deposits in individual portfolios in the last three decades.
3. Discuss the impact on profits of the averge maturity of an intermediary's portfolio during a business cycle.
4. List major changes in the last three decades of government policy with respect to maximum interest rates on time deposits. Discuss the effects of these changes on individual portfolios.
5. What explains the growth of depository intermediaries relative to gross national product in recent decades?
6. Discuss relative asset specialization among depository intermediaries. How do you explain this asset specialization?
7. Discuss relative liabilities specialization among depository intermediaries. How do you explain this liabilities specialization?
8. Describe two recent financial innovations important to depository intermediaries and discuss the likely impact of each on the intermediaries and their customers.
9. Are depository intermediaries becoming more or less similar in their portfolios and services? Explain.
10. What explains the dramatic decline in liquid assets of nonfinancial businesses in recent decades?

## Selected Bibliography

Altman, Edward I., and Arnold W. Sametz, eds. *Financial Crises*. John Wiley & Sons, New York, 1977.

Board of Governors of the Federal Reserve System. *Federal Reserve Bulletin*. Washington, D.C.

Eckstein, Otto, ed. *Parameters and Policies in the U.S. Economy*. North-Holland Publishing Co., Amsterdam, 1976.

*Economic Report of the President*. Government Printing Office, Washington, D.C., 1980.

Federal Home Loan Bank Board. *Study of the Savings and Loan Industry*. Washington, D.C., 1969.

Feige, Edgar L., and D. K. Pearce. "The Substitutability of Money and Near-Monies: A Survey of the Time-Series Evidence." *Journal of Economic Literature* (June 1977).

Flannery, Mark J. *An Economic Evaluation of Credit Unions in the United States*. Federal Reserve Bank of Boston, Boston, 1974.

Hempel, George H., and Jess B. Yawitz. *Financial Management of Financial Institutions*. Prentice-Hall, Englewood Cliffs, N.J., 1977.

Jacobs, Donald P., et al. *Financial Institutions*. Richard D. Irwin, Homewood, Ill., 1972.

Kaufman, Henry. "Financial Crises: Market Impact, Consequences, and Adaptability," in *Financial Crises*, Edward I. Altman and Arnold W. Sametz, eds. John Wiley & Sons, New York, 1977.

Marris, Robin. *The Economic Theory of "Managerial" Capitalism*. The Free Press, New York, 1964.

National Association of Mutual Savings Banks. *Mutual Savings Banks*. Prentice-Hall, Englewood Cliffs, N.J., 1962.

Silber, William L. *Financial Innovation*. Lexington Books, Lexington, Mass., 1975.

Sinai, Allan. "Credit Crunches—An Analysis of the Postwar Experience," in *Parameters and Policies in the U.S. Economy*, ed. Otto Eckstein. North-Holland Publishing Co., Amsterdam, 1976.

U.S. Bureau of Federal Credit Unions. *Regular Reserves of Federal Credit Unions*. Washington, D.C., 1968.

U.S. League of Savings Associations. *Savings and Loan Fact Book*. Chicago, 1980.

# 7

# Insurance-Type Intermediaries: Insurance Companies

## Life Insurance Companies

Life insurance companies provide over 80 percent of all families in the United States with financial protection in case of the death of a member, and they also offer many other forms of insurance, including health, accident, and disability insurance. In addition, life insurance companies provide pension plans for over half of the employed labor force covered by private pension plans.[1] In varying degrees, these forms of insurance protection involve the accumulation of funds, which are an important part of the public's financial assets and also a source of capital funds to business and government. The treatment here of life insurance companies is organized into four main sections: (1) an examination of life insurance companies as financial intermediaries—firms that offer the public, as a part of insurance contracts, an outlet for its savings and that provide a means of channeling the accumulated funds to borrowers and investors; (2) an examination of the long-term growth of life insurance assets; (3) an analysis of the activity of life insurance companies in major sectors of the capital market and long-term shifts in their asset holdings; and (4) an analysis of the responsiveness of life insurance investments to cyclical changes in credit conditions.

The role of property and casualty insurance companies is treated in the concluding section of this chapter.

## Life Insurance Companies as Financial Intermediaries

### Life Insurance as a Vehicle for Saving

*Forms of Saving*   Beyond the general choice between spending or not spending income for current consumption, individuals also have choices among ways of accumulating funds for future use. Saving, defined as disposable income not spent for current consumption, includes outlays for additions to financial assets and for reductions in financial liabilities. While there are problems in defining these terms (as well as in obtaining appropriate data), the

---

[1]Nearly half of the employed labor force is covered by private pension plans. Because of problems of duplication and the definition of "coverage," precise figures cannot be given.

general concepts and orders of magnitude may be illustrated by the Federal Reserve Board's Flow of Funds Accounts for saving by individuals. As shown in Table 7-1, individuals' saving in selected recent years was allocated to increases in demand deposits, savings deposits, holdings of government and corporate securities, insurance and pension reserves, and miscellaneous financial assets. Increases in holdings of durable real goods (tangible assets) are also reflected in Table 7-1, although definition and measurement problems are especially severe in this area.[2] Offsetting the increases in assets are increases in debt: mortgage debt, consumer credit, and other debt of individuals—including life insurance policy loans—which must be subtracted from assets in order to measure the amount of saving.

Financial assets may be grouped into two broad categories: (1) those that involve current discretionary decisions that are made frequently; and (2) those that involve long-term decisions to purchase regularly certain amounts of assets with little leeway for change once the commitment has been made, or where a change in the decision may involve significant costs. Examples of the first category include additions to demand deposits and savings accounts. The second category, frequently called *contractual saving,* includes additions to life insurance and pension fund reserves.

Such additions to life insurance reserves, a by-product of the purchase of financial protection against premature death, characteristically involve a long-term commitment. Individual life insurance policies with cash values are typically purchased as part of an overall financial plan and fitted into the family budget as continuing payments, much like payments on a mortgage. Similarly, the use of pension plans, motivated by a need for financial protection in old age, entails a commitment to set aside specific amounts at regular intervals. Typically, becoming a participant in a pension plan is part of the decision to take a job, and the contributions are made by the employer and/or the em-

ployee as long as the employee continues on that job.[3]

Since life insurance is a unique financial instrument—no other contract offers its guarantees—the opportunity to substitute other instruments in its place is strictly limited. Some observers believe there is evidence of a degree of substitution between life insurance and other forms of saving in response to differences in their relative rates of return.[4] However, since the interest factor in life insurance cash values is obscure and can as a rule only be estimated, any comparison between the so-called investment return on life insurance and the yield on other financial instruments is usually more a matter of conjecture rather than simple arithmetic. The same would hold true for an annuity because it typically guarantees an income for the life of the annuitant, who may far outlive the return generated by the annuity viewed strictly as an investment. Thus, it would be difficult for an individual to replace an annuity by accumulating other assets for the same purpose, since these could be eroded by time where an annuity could not. Some scholars have raised the possibility that there may be a high degree of substitutability between potential social security benefits and private pension plans, but these results require further testing, especially in light of recent legislation on both private pension plans and social security.[5]

*Types of Insurance Contracts* The role of saving through life insurance may be seen more clearly by contrasting the two basic types of life insurance, namely, term insurance and whole life insurance.

---

[2]Purchases of durable goods other than housing are classified as current consumption expenditures in the National Income and Product Accounts and are, therefore, deducted, along with other current consumption, from disposable personal income in deriving personal saving for purposes of these accounts.

[3]For a study of the determinants of contractual saving, see William C. Reher, ''A Multivariate Analysis of Contractual Saving,'' *Review of Economics and Statistics* (February 1966), 61–68. Unfortunately, Reher examined total life insurance premiums, rather than a measure of the saving element involved. His findings emphasize the primary importance of the size of family income in the purchase of individual life insurance.

[4]For a study of the degree of substitutability between life insurance and other financial assets, see Robert S. Headen and J. Findley Lee, ''Life Insurance Demand and Household Portfolio Behavior,'' *Journal of Risk and Insurance* (December 1974), 685–698.

[5]See Alicia H. Munnell, ''The Interaction of Social Security and Private Pensions,'' prepared for the American Enterprise Institute for Public Policy Research Conference on Social Security Financing, October 27–28, 1977.

**Table 7-1  Analysis of Individuals' Saving[a] (in billions of dollars)**

|  | 1970 | 1974 | 1977 | 1978 |
|---|---|---|---|---|
| Individuals' saving (equals increase in financial assets plus net investment in tangible assets less net increase in debt) | $76.5 | $126.2 | $166.9 | $191.3 |
| Increase in financial assets | 78.9 | 142.4 | 241.7 | 275.3 |
| Demand deposits and currency | 8.9 | 7.1 | 22.7 | 18.3 |
| Savings accounts | 43.6 | 55.9 | 109.2 | 105.2 |
| Money market fund shares | 0 | 2.3 | .2 | 6.9 |
| Securities[b] | (3.0) | 32.3 | 18.5 | 37.3 |
| Private life insurance reserves | 5.4 | 6.6 | 11.4 | 11.7 |
| Private insured pension reserves | 3.2 | 6.4 | 13.9 | 19.5 |
| Private noninsured pension reserves | 6.9 | 10.7 | 17.7 | 19.6 |
| Govt. insurance and pension reserves | 8.9 | 12.6 | 22.4 | 27.1 |
| Miscellaneous financial assets | 5.4 | 8.5 | 25.7 | 29.7 |
| Net investment in tangible assets[c] | 31.9 | 51.8 | 99.0 | 116.6 |
| Net increase in debt | 34.3 | 68.0 | 173.8 | 200.6 |
| Mortgage debt on nonfarm homes | 14.1 | 35.4 | 93.2 | 103.8 |
| Policy loans | 2.3 | 2.7 | 1.7 | 2.6 |
| Other[d] | 17.9 | 29.9 | 78.9 | 94.2 |

[a]Combined statement for households, farm, and nonfarm noncorporate business.
[b]Includes U.S. government, state and local, corporate, and foreign bonds.
[c]Includes investment in homes and consumer durables.
[d]Includes noncorporate business mortgage debt, consumer credit, security credit, and other credit.

Source: Board of Governors of the Federal Reserve System, *Flow of Funds Accounts*.

*Term insurance* provides temporary protection for a specified period, which may be one year, five years, or ten or more years. If the term insurance is renewed at the end of the period, the premium increases to reflect the higher risk of mortality as the policyholder's age increases. Since term insurance premiums are calculated to meet expected benefit payments over short periods of time, only a very limited accumulation of assets and reserves is needed.[6]

[6]As a simplified example, assume that a life company has a large number of policyholders each with a $1,000 one-year term policy. The company can estimate the benefits to be paid each year by multiplying the expected number of deaths (number of policyholders at each age times the mortality rate for that age) by $1,000. Similarly, apart from administrative and other business costs, the company can calculate the premium for policyholders at each age by multiplying the mortality rate at that age by $1,000. In this type of insurance, the pooling of risks is essentially a pay-as-you-go operation: the premiums for each age group are calculated to meet the expected death benefits for that age group and, hence, there is little need for accumulation of reserves except to provide a margin

The *whole life policy,* an important innovation dating from the eighteenth century, involves a level (that is, constant) annual premium for a given amount of life insurance paid over the full span of a policyholder's life. The level premium is larger than the term premium for an equal amount of life insurance in the early years of a policyholder's life and less in the later years, when higher mortality risks are reflected in higher premiums for term insurance.[7] The level premium is calculated to take account of the interest that can be earned on the

for annual fluctuations in claims. The main disadvantage of this type of insurance is the rise in the premium as the mortality rate increases with age.

[7]The whole life plan may be written so that premiums are payable up to a specific age or for a fixed number of years. If the premium is actually payable for the lifetime, the policy is referred to as a *straight life policy.* Beyond this, there is the *endowment policy,* a special type of life insurance contract under which the cash value equals the face value after a stated number of years. This contract is designed to assure the payment of a given amount of savings at the end of the stated period.

excess of the level premium over the term premium in the early years of a policyholder's life. Because contractual inflows in the early years are less than outflows, the level-premium plan involves a larger accumulation of reserves by life insurance companies than term insurance.

The whole life policy also provides stated cash values, which the policyholder will receive if he or she terminates the policy—that is, the policy guarantees that the holder will in effect receive back some of the savings in the policy if he or she should decide to give it up. These cash values are also the basis on which the policyholder may obtain a policy loan at a guaranteed rate of interest specified in the contract. For these reasons, the cash values are often referred to as the savings element in whole life insurance. Surveys of buyers show, however, that life insurance is bought primarily for protection, rather than for these cash value savings.[8]

Despite problems of legal and theoretical interpretation, the level-premium, whole life plan was a very important innovation for financial markets because, with this plan, life insurers became major financial intermediaries. The premiums on new policies produce a pool of funds for investment, and the interest earned on those funds had to at least equal the amount assumed in the calculation of the premium. Later in this chapter the size and uses of this pool are reviewed.

The typical individual annuity contract is essentially similar to the whole life contract, except that instead of a fixed death benefit, the life insurance company promises to pay a specified monthly or annual amount to the annuitant for life, with the payments usually beginning at age 65. The individual has various options in the method of paying for such contracts. Either an annual amount ("consideration") may be paid on an instalment basis over a period of years, or the individual may make a single payment at 65 (or other age) in exchange for an immediate annuity—under which benefit payments are made for life beginning in the year in which the annuity is purchased. Employers and other purchasers of group annuities have similar options. The annuity contract necessarily involves a substantial accumulation of assets by the life insurer and savings by the purchaser because the annuity benefit is designed as a combination of both interest and a return of capital.

Life insurance and annuities are distinct products or types of insurance contracts from the standpoint of the buyer. From the standpoint of the life insurer, however, the assets held by the company are pooled to meet liabilities under both life insurance contracts and annuity contracts.[9] As a consequence, part of every payment for life insurance contracts and for annuities (including insured pension plans[10]) goes into a single pool of assets held by the life insurance company. Saving through life insurance companies, as one type of financial intermediary, thus encompasses accumulations of assets both for whole life insurance contracts and for their close cousins, annuity contracts. We now turn to the other side of the intermediary process, the role of life insurers as investors in the capital markets.

### Life Insurance Companies as Lenders and Investors

*Sources of Investment Funds*  The net flow of new money for investment by life insurance companies arises from two main sources: (1) the excess of premiums over benefit payments, expenses, sales commissions, and taxes that results largely from level-premium policies; and (2) net investment income, which consists of the earnings on invested assets held less investment expenses and related taxes. The net flow of new money for investment rose from $12 billion in 1971 to an estimated $29

---

[8]For a recent discussion of the nature of the savings element, see Robert I. Mehr, "The Concept of the Level-Premium Whole Life Insurance Policy—Reexamined," *Journal of Risk and Insurance* (September 1975), 502–507; see also, *The Nature of Whole Life Contract,* Institute of Life Insurance, 1974. (The Institute of Life Insurance has been merged into the American Council of Life Insurance).

[9]The exceptions to this statement are variable annuities, variable life insurance, and other contracts under which the benefits paid are related to earnings on a separate pool of assets (or "separate account"). Under these contracts, the buyer accepts the risk of fluctuations in the earnings on such assets.

[10]*Insured pension plans* include all plans administered by life insurance companies. The group contracts offered by insurers, however, may differ little in the guarantees involved from pension plans not administered by life insurance companies. For descriptions of various types of plans, see *Pension Facts,* published annually by the American Council of Life Insurance.

billion in 1977, a period of unusually rapid increase. A rough allocation of the sources of this flow, under a reasonable set of assumptions on the use of investment income, indicates that approximately half of net investable funds comes from insurance operations and half from investment operations.[11]

In addition to the net flow of new funds for investment, life companies must make decisions on the reinvestment of a large return flow from past investments. The total flow of investment funds includes return flows from maturities and scheduled principal repayments on bonds and mortgages, prepayments of mortgage loans when the related properties are sold, calling in of securities, and proceeds of the sale of securities in the public markets as well as sales of other assets. In 1977 the total gross flow of investment funds amounted to an estimated $53 billion, compared to a net flow of $29 billion. Return flows from existing investments do not necessarily go back into the type of investment that produced the flow, since pressure to maximize earnings involves a continual reconsideration of risks and returns on all types of alternative investments.

*Characteristics of Investment Policies* The investment decisions of life insurance companies are concerned primarily with the allocation of current gross flows of investment funds to various portfolio assets. In many companies, finance committees provide guidelines for overall allocations of funds to bonds, mortgages, and other assets; within these broad classes, decisions are made to satisfy preference regarding risk and return. Legal limitations and the desire to maintain good customer relations and to retain expertise in various sectors of the capital market also affect broad allocations, but companies may considerably modify these allocations in a given period depending on interest rate differentials and the demand for funds in the form of mortgage loan applications and available corporate securities. The major elements in investment decisions are elaborated in the following discussion.[12]

(1) EMPHASIS ON LONG-TERM INVESTMENTS Life insurance companies make payments to policyholders and beneficiaries on the occurrence of reasonably predictable events: the number of policyholders who will die at different ages, and the number of annuitants who will live to various ages. As premium payments flow into life companies, it is appropriate for the companies to invest a large portion of these payments in longer-term securities, which will serve to provide funds for liabilities that stretch out over many years. At the end of 1978, corporate bonds and mortgages accounted for 67 percent of total assets of U.S. life insurance companies. Corporate stocks, real estate, policy loans, and government securities with a maturity of over one year accounted for a further 27 percent of assets. (See Table 7-5 for details on asset holdings.)

The liquidity needs of life companies are relatively small compared with those of other financial institutions. At the end of 1978, securities with a maturity of one year or less amounted to only about 2 percent of total assets of U.S. life companies. Life insurance companies require cash, bank deposits, and short-term securities for their ordinary daily and monthly transactions. In addition, there are fluctuations in claims for benefits, in policy loans, and in disbursements under investment commitments that may require temporary borrowing as well as sales of assets. Life company holdings of short-term securities are relatively small in their balance sheets, but because of the turnover, the volume of transactions in a year is sizable. In general, the predictability of cash flow minimizes liquidity needs. Forecasting cash flow is a well-developed function in most companies, which reduces the need for short-term security holdings.

(2) RISK AND RETURN Life insurance companies generally put a high priority on investment quality, partly because of their responsibilities as fiduciaries and partly because of state regulations. Bond investments are generally in the better grades of bonds—Baa or higher for publicly issued bonds, and similar qualities for bonds that are not sold through the public-issue market. Mortgage loans

---

[11]See George A. Bishop, *Capital Formation Through Life Insurance Companies,* Richard D. Irwin, Homewood, Ill., 1976, pp. 84–85.

[12]For detailed studies, see Lawrence D. Jones, *Investment Policies of Life Insurance Companies,* Graduate School of Business Administration, Harvard University, Boston, 1968; *Investment Activities of Life Insurance*

*Companies,* ed. J. David Cummins, Huebner Foundation Lectures. Wharton School, University of Pennsylvania, Richard D. Irwin, Homewood, Ill., 1977; and John D. Stowe, "Life Insurance Company Portfolio Behavior," *Journal of Risk and Insurance* (September 1978), 431–448.

are secured by real property that can be sold in the event of default, and in some cases, they are also secured by the general financial position and earnings of the borrower.

Although life insurance companies, as major fiduciaries, must be concerned with the safety of principal, competition within the industry is strong and the incentive to provide dividends to policyholders and stockholders makes the maximization of investment return a major objective of investment policy. The higher the investment return, the lower net premiums can be. Since World War II, the long-term upward trend in investment returns has contributed to a substantial reduction in premium outlays per $1,000 of life insurance coverage.

(3) STATE REGULATION   State laws governing the establishment and operation of life insurance companies are designed in part to require diversification of assets and limitation of investment risks.[13] Although investment requirements vary from state to state, these laws typically limit the proportions of total assets that can be invested in common stocks, real estate, and certain other assets. For example, most states limit holdings of common stocks to 10 percent of the general assets of a company; a similar limitation applies to preferred stocks. Some states place an overall limit on the proportion of mortgages to total assets. State laws also limit the percentage of a life company's assets that may be invested in the obligations or equities of one issuer. In general, life companies operate well within the portfolio-allocation limits fixed by law.

There are also legal constraints on the quality of investments. A maximum loan-to-value ratio is typically provided for mortgages, and the location of the property is generally limited to the United States and Canada. Companies selling bonds to life companies usually must meet earnings tests—in other words, earnings must exceed fixed charges in recent years by a stipulated multiple, or net earn-ings must bear some minimum ratio to fixed charges. Similar standards apply to preferred stocks. Standards for common stocks typically state that the stock must be listed on a public securities exchange or be regularly traded with public quotations for over-the-counter stocks. In these ways, regulatory influences are important in the investment environment of life insurance companies, setting various limits within which companies make more specific decisions on the makeup of their portfolios.

(4) FORWARD COMMITMENTS   The long-term nature of most of their liabilities and the normally steady inflow of funds for investment enabled life companies to develop the forward investment commitment earlier than did other institutional investors. A *forward investment commitment* is an agreement on the part of the company to lend or invest a specific amount of money, usually at a stated interest rate for a specified period, with agreed dates for disbursement of funds some months or years after the forward commitment is made. The lender is legally obligated to provide the funds on the terms stated in the commitment, and the borrower also has an obligation to meet the terms of the agreement, although the commitment may be cancelled by the borrower at the cost only of any commitment fee paid. The forward commitment has long been used for most life company acquisitions of mortgages and corporate bonds.[14]

The forward-commitment process limits the possibilities of following a cyclical investment policy, timing investments to take maximum advantage of short-term changes in interest rates. For most life companies, however, the more important objective

---

[13] For a detailed description of investment limitations, see *Comparative Regulations of Financial Institutions*, Subcommittee on Domestic Finance, Committee on Banking and Currency, U.S. House of Representatives, November 22, 1963, pp. 277–342. Although not up to date, this compilation of laws still provides a good description of the types of limitations imposed by states. For an evaluation of the significance of the state regulations for investment decisions, see Mendes Hershman, "The Impact of Life Insurance Company Investment Regulations," in *Investment Activities of Life Insurance Companies*, ed. J. David Cummins, pp. 309–336.

[14] Interest rates agreed to in these commitments involve some view on the part of both borrowers and lenders of the future course of interest rates, although there has been relatively little research on the role of expectations in the forward-commitment process. Recently, however, Michel Fleuriet found a significant relationship between the volume of forward commitments and the forward interest rate implicit in the yield curve ("Public and Private Offerings of Public Debt: Changes in the Yield Spread," *The Bulletin*, Graduate School of Business Administration of New York University [1975] p. 1). More recently, John Lintner developed a model of the impact of interest rate expectations on forward commitments in his paper, "Interest Rate Expectations and Optimal Forward Commitments for Institutional Investors," *Explorations in Economic Research*, National Bureau of Economic Research (Fall 1976).

is to find permanent outlets for the large volume of funds flowing in for investment. The forward-commitment process also helps to maintain good relations with mortgage bankers, investment bankers, and corporate borrowers.

(5) EFFECTS OF TAXATION  Life insurers are taxed under the Life Insurance Company Income Tax Act of 1959. Under this act, life companies are taxed at regular corporation income tax rates on all sources of income under a four-stage formula for calculation of the tax base.[15] The major parts of the tax base are taxable investment income and underwriting income. Taxable investment income is determined by taking certain deductions from total investment income, primarily the interest needed to meet reserve and other contractual liabilities. The latter portion, known as the policyholders' share, is calculated by a special five-year averaging formula that has, in effect, raised effective tax rates on life companies as the rate of investment income rose, particularly in recent years.

Since the total policyholders' share is already a deduction, tax-exempt income has only a partial effect on the tax liabilities of life companies and they usually have had little incentive to buy tax-exempt bonds. In the 1970s, however, life companies purchased somewhat more of these bonds as tax rates on life companies rose.

The 85 percent dividend exclusion applies to life companies' holdings of common and preferred stocks, although again the same allocation applies as between the company's share and the policyholder's share, and the advantage for a life insurance company is not as great as for a typical corporation.

The regular corporation capital gains tax rate applies to capital gains of life companies. Some insurers have found bonds and mortgages selling at a discount in secondary markets to be an attractive investment for tax reasons. Similarly, direct investment in real estate may be attractive because one can expect the return to be largely in the form of capital gains.

On the whole, tax considerations do not have a substantial impact on most life company investment decisions.

*Combining Investment Objectives*  Different companies combine investment objectives in different ways, both as a matter of choice as to the degree of risk that is acceptable and as a reflection of the types of products the company is selling. Some companies may accept a considerable degree of risk in order to achieve a higher rate of return on their portfolios; other companies prefer to be very conservative in their investment policies. In a sample of thirty larger companies in 1977, the average ratio of net investment income to invested assets ranged from 6.07 percent to 8.39 percent, around an average of 7.05 percent for the sample. Higher portfolio rates tend to be associated with relatively large holdings of privately issued bonds, which generally carry higher rates because of their illiquidity.

In a study of 100 life insurance companies, Rennie found that life companies classified by different product mixes showed small though discernible differences in portfolio mixes.[16] Life insurance companies with a high proportion of health insurance tend to have relatively high proportions of government bonds and preferred and common stocks in their portfolios—reflecting their greater needs for liquidity and the short-term nature of liabilities under health insurance. Companies with a high proportion of group term insurance tend to have a higher than average proportion of government bonds and a lower proportion of mortgages in their portfolios. Companies with a high proportion of annuities have a higher than average proportion of mortgage loans and corporate bonds.

The shifting of asset holdings over time in relation to changes in interest rate differentials is discussed in a separate section of this chapter.

## Growth of Life Insurance Saving and Assets

This section examines the major influences on the growth of life insurance, life insurance companies, assets, and saving through life insurance over the past twenty-five years. A few of the major determinants of growth can be summarized easily. For example, the demand for life insurance, as well as for pensions and annuities, is closely related to the size of family income and reflects the need for

[15] For an explanation, see William B. Harman, Jr., "Taxation of Companies," in *Life and Health Insurance Handbook,* eds. David W. Gregg and Vane B. Lucas, 3rd ed. Richard D. Irwin, Homewood, Ill., 1973.

[16] Robert A. Rennie, "Investment Strategy for the Life Insurance Company," in *Investment Activities of Life Insurance Companies,* ed. J. David Cummins, pp. 20–24.

protection as well as the ability to buy. Another variable is price, although this measure is very difficult to define for a composite "product" involving saving and protection elements that are not separable except by rather arbitrary allocations. A third influence is the growth of competing forms of financial assets, which are, in varying degrees, alternatives to life insurance products. Even the growth of social security, which is not, strictly speaking, a financial asset, may have important effects on the demand for life insurance.[17]

## Growth of Life Insurance Pensions and Annuities

As the slope of the lines in Figure 7-1 shows, total life insurance in force (face amounts) has grown more rapidly over the past twenty-five years than total disposable personal income (DPI) and total financial assets of individuals. The most rapid growth was in group life insurance, which is largely in the form of one-year term insurance involving little accumulation of reserves. In contrast to most other kinds of life insurance, group life insurance is essentially an "indexed" product. Sales and renewals are made to employers on the basis of ratios of insurance to current wages and salaries. Thus, part of the growth of group insurance can be attributed to higher wages and salaries, although part is also due to expanded coverage.[18] However, since 1960, individual life insurance in force has also grown approximately in proportion to DPI. Since the proportion of population covered has been reasonably stable, the growth in demand for individual insurance as incomes increase has apparently offset any adverse effects of inflation on the fixed dollar amounts of outstanding insurance sold in earlier years. Thus, the ratio of total insurance in force (a stock variable) to DPI (a flow variable) has

grown despite the fact that the denominator is more affected by inflation than the numerator.

Substantial declines in the cost of life insurance coverage are reflected in the ratios of insurance premiums to insurance in force and to DPI.[19] Declines in the ratio of premiums per $1,000 of face value result from rising investment returns, improved mortality, a decline in the average age of buyers, and a shift from permanent insurance toward term insurance. About the same degree of individual insurance coverage (insurance in force in relation to income) has been possible with a decline in the ratio of life insurance premiums to DPI. Much of this decline can be attributed to higher investment earnings available to life insurance companies in recent years. As shown in Table 7-2, the ratio of ordinary (individually purchased) life insurance premiums to DPI has shown a considerable decline, from 2.48 percent in 1960 to 1.81 percent in 1978. In the case of group insurance, there has been an even sharper decline in the ratio of premiums to group life insurance in force, even though the amount in force has been rising in relation to personal income.[20]

The ratio of annuity considerations (that is, payments by individuals for individual annuities and by employers for group annuities under insured pension plans) to DPI has been rising significantly in recent years, largely as a result of increases in pension coverage. Indeed, payments to all private pension plans have been rising in relation to DPI, indicating a growing demand for retirement security in general.[21]

In the past decade, payments into insured pension plans have been increasing more rapidly than payments into other private plans. This shift reflects a number of changes in the position of life

---

[17]Research on the demand for life insurance has been relatively limited. For a recent analysis and review of research, see Headen and Lee, "Life Insurance Demand." For an analysis of the demand for pension saving, see Norman B. True with Barbara A. Fields, *The Future of Private Pension Plans*, American Enterprise Institute for Public Policy Research, Washington, D.C., 1976.

[18]Under group insurance, all members of a group are covered under one contract and the essential condition for coverage is membership in the group. Term insurance is typical, and the employer usually pays the premiums for employees.

[19]As an example of the decline in costs, the average annual premium per $1,000 of new purchases of individual straight life insurance for adult males declined 25 percent from 1949 to 1976 based on data from the Life Insurance Marketing and Research Association.

[20]The ratio of group premiums to group life insurance in force declined by about one-third from 1960 to 1978. Various factors, including the average age and size of groups covered, affect this ratio, but the chief influence appears to be a real decline in price.

[21]See *Security Expenditures in the United States, An Analysis of 1960–76 Spending for Life, Health, and Retirement Coverage and a Forecast Through 1990*, Research Report 1978-2, Life Insurance Marketing and Research Association, Hartford, Conn., 1978.

**Figure 7-1 Life Insurance in Force in Relation to Disposable Personal Income and Total Financial Assets of Individuals, 1950-1977**

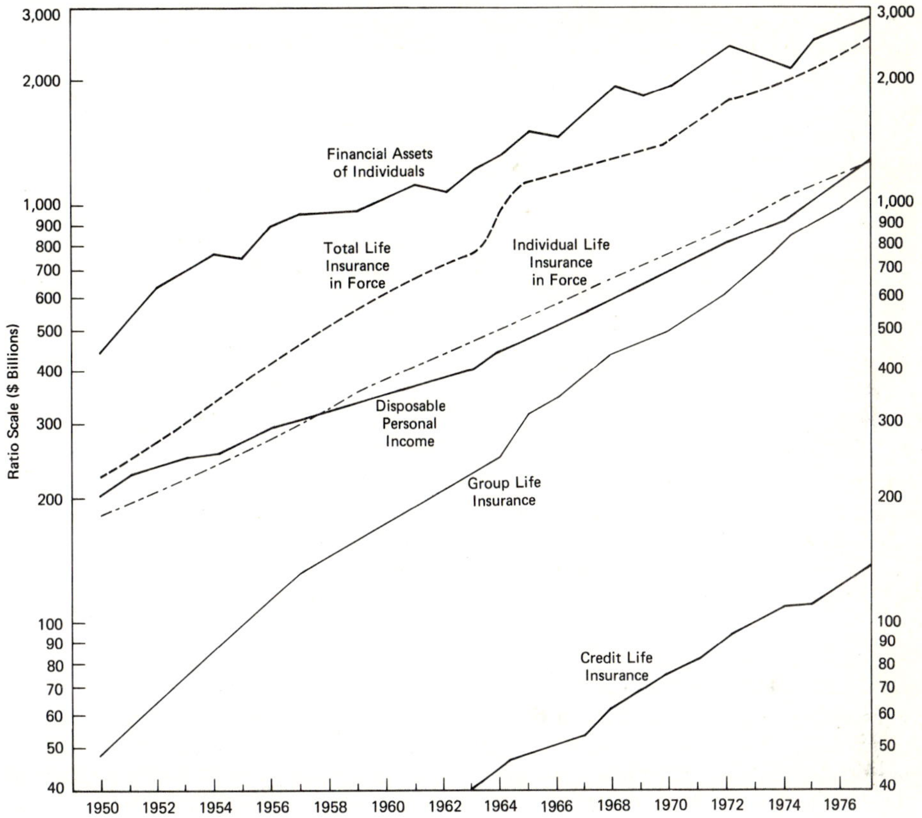

Sources: American Council of Life Insurance; Federal Reserve Board; and U.S. Department of Commerce.

insurance companies competing for pension business, including new types of pension contracts better adapted to the needs of different groups of customers. The Life Insurance Company Tax Act of 1959 provided for the gradual elimination of federal income taxation on the investment earnings credited to qualified pension plan reserves, thereby giving life companies tax treatment parallel to noninsured pension plans (that is, private plans not administered by life insurance companies). In the early 1960s, most states began to permit life companies to invest pension funds through *separate accounts,* which are not subject to the overall investment limitations on types of assets held in the general accounts; in particular, life companies could invest in common stocks up to 100 percent

of assets held in separate accounts. Life companies were also permitted to use an interest rate related to earnings on new investments in crediting investment returns to group annuities rather than using the average investment return on the total portfolio.

With such changes in the regulatory environment, life companies have been able to compete more effectively with bank-administered and other pension funds. Moreover, the poor performance of the stock market in recent years, combined with historically high levels of interest rates, has meant greater interest in life companies' offerings of pension plans based on fixed-income securities. The Employee Retirement Income Security Act of 1974 gave additional impetus to life companies, as recognized fiduciaries, in gaining pension-fund busi-

**Table 7-2  Ratio of Life Insurance Premiums and Annuity Considerations to Disposable Personal Income (percentages)**

| Year | Life Insurance Premiums | | | Annuity Considerations[c] | Total Life Premiums and Annuity Considerations |
|---|---|---|---|---|---|
| | Ordinary Life[a] | Other[b] | Total Life Insurance | | |
| 1950 | 2.18% | 0.86% | 3.04% | 0.46% | 3.50% |
| 1955 | 2.28 | 0.97 | 3.26 | 0.47 | 3.73 |
| 1960 | 2.48 | 0.96 | 3.43 | 0.38 | 3.82 |
| 1965 | 2.48 | 0.92 | 3.41 | 0.48 | 3.88 |
| 1966 | 2.46 | 0.90 | 3.36 | 0.47 | 3.84 |
| 1967 | 2.43 | 0.89 | 3.32 | 0.49 | 3.81 |
| 1968 | 2.39 | 0.90 | 3.29 | 0.51 | 3.80 |
| 1969 | 2.35 | 0.90 | 3.25 | 0.60 | 3.85 |
| 1970 | 2.28 | 0.88 | 3.16 | 0.54 | 3.70 |
| 1971 | 2.23 | 0.86 | 3.09 | 0.66 | 3.75 |
| 1972 | 2.21 | 0.87 | 3.08 | 0.69 | 3.77 |
| 1973 | 2.08 | 0.84 | 2.92 | 0.75 | 3.68 |
| 1974 | 2.01 | 0.81 | 2.82 | 0.79 | 3.61 |
| 1975 | 1.94 | 0.76 | 2.71 | 0.94 | 3.65 |
| 1976 | 1.90 | 0.75 | 2.64 | 1.18 | 3.82 |
| 1977 | 1.85 | 0.74 | 2.58 | 1.14 | 3.72 |
| 1978 | 1.81 | 0.71 | 2.52 | 1.13 | 3.65 |

Note: Credit life premiums were included in the "Ordinary Life" category prior to 1973. Beginning with 1973, credit life insurance premiums on loans of ten years or less duration are excluded. In some cases, the sum of "Total Life Insurance" and "Annuity Considerations" may not add to "Total" owing to rounding.
[a]Includes term insurance purchased directly by individuals.
[b]Includes group, industrial, and, except as noted, credit life insurance premiums.
[c]Includes payments by individuals for individual annuities and payments by employers for group annuities under pension plans administered by life insurers.

Source: American Council of Life Insurance, *1979 Life Insurance Fact Book*.

ness by mandating standards for investments and funding of liabilities. This act also provided, for the first time, tax advantages for individual retirement accounts for employees not covered by pension plans on their jobs and liberalized the provisions on Keogh plans for the self-employed.

Since 1960 the number of workers covered by pension plans administered by life insurance companies has grown by about 7 percent annually, while the rate of growth of the larger number covered by other private pension plans has grown by less than 3 percent annually (see Table 7-3). From 1970 to 1978, reserves of pension plans administered by life insurers grew at an annual rate of 13.6 percent per year, while assets of other private pension plans grew at an average rate of almost 10 percent per year.

On balance, the growth of life insurance and insured pension plans has, for a variety of reasons, been impressive during the 1970s, especially in view of the rapid inflation of recent years that could

be expected to have an adverse effect on insurers selling products involving long-term liabilities fixed in current dollar terms. However, with the numerous influences at work, it is difficult to isolate the effects of one variable, such as inflation.[22]

### Growth of Life Insurance Company Assets

As shown by Figure 7-2, life insurance companies long ranked next to commercial banks in holdings of financial assets. In 1972, after an extended period of rapid growth, the financial assets of saving and loan associations surpassed those of life companies. The average annual growth rate of life insurers' assets rose from a post–World War II low of 5.5 percent in the period 1965–1970 to a 10 per-

[22]See J. Robert Ferrari, "Impact of Inflation on the Life Insurance Industry and Its Investment Policies," in *Investment Activities of Life Insurance Companies,* ed. J. David Cummins, pp. 249–267.

**Table 7-3 Workers Covered and Reserves or Assets of Private Pension Plans in the United States**

| Year or Period | Administered by Life Insurance Companies | | Other Private Plans | |
| | Persons (thousands) | Reserves (millions) | Persons (thousands) | Assets (millions) |
|---|---|---|---|---|
| 1950 | 2,755 | $ 5,600 | 7,500 | $ 6,500 |
| 1960 | 5,475 | 18,850 | 17,540 | 33,100 |
| 1970 | 10,580 | 41,175 | 25,520 | 97,000 |
| 1975 | 15,190 | 71,700 | 30,300 | 145,200 |
| 1976 | 16,965 | 88,400 | N.A.[a] | 160,400 |
| 1978 | 21,615 | 119,110 | N.A.[a] | 202,240 |
| | *Annual compound rate of increase* | | | |
| 1950–60 | 7.1% | 12.9% | 8.5% | 17.7% |
| 1960–70 | 6.9 | 8.1 | 3.0 | 11.4 |
| 1970–78 | 7.7 | 13.6 | 2.8[b] | 9.7 |

Note: It is impossible to obtain a total for the number of persons covered by pension plans because of differences in definitions of *coverage* and duplications of coverage. The data also represent various dates during the year, since the plans' fiscal years are not necessarily the same.
[a]Not available on a consistent basis.
[b]1970–1975.

Source: American Council of Life Insurance, *Pension Facts 1978–79*.

cent rate in the years 1975–1978. Inflation, of course, tended to increase the growth rate of all financial assets in the 1970s.

Important influences on the rate of growth of assets are the changing makeup of life insurance products or sales and the rate of growth of net investment income. As noted in the preceding section, group life insurance in force has been growing much faster than individual life insurance, and group life insurance involves less accumulation of reserves and assets than individual life insurance.[23] This shift in the type of life insurance coverage has tended to slow the growth of assets. In the 1970s, however, a major contribution to faster growth of life company assets was the expansion of life companies' pension business. From 1970 to 1978, payments into insured pension plans tripled (approximately), while benefits paid increased more than 100 percent.[24] It is difficult to measure precisely

the contributions of pension plan business to the growth of life companies' assets because, as noted earlier, the assets backing group annuities (with the exception of variable annuities) are not distinguishable among the total assets held by life insurance companies. However, since the reserves for group annuities and various types of life insurance are calculated separately, the growth of reserves, as explained in the following section, gives a broad indication of the contribution of different products, or lines of business, to the growth of assets. The rising rate of return on invested assets has also contributed substantially to asset growth.

### Growth of Life Insurance and Other Policy Reserves

Policy reserves constitute the major part of the liabilities of life insurance companies. The total is not a sum of specific amounts owed by the life company to individual policyholders, but an amount calculated by the life company as an estimate of its total liabilities to groups of policyholders.[25] The calculation is designed to answer the

[23]The makeup of individual insurance has also shifted toward relatively more term insurance and less whole life and endowment contracts, so that premium receipts from individual life insurance add less to assets than they did in previous years. (See *Life Insurance Fact Book* for data on the mix of individual life insurance sales.)

[24]For further details, see *Pension Facts,* published annually by the American Council of Life Insurance, Washington, D.C.

[25]For a detailed discussion, see William H. Schmidt, "Reserves," in *Life and Health Insurance Handbook,* eds. Davis W. Gregg and Vane B. Lucas, Richard D. Irwin, Homewood, Ill., 1973, Chap. 12.

**Figure 7-2  Total Financial Assets of Major Types of Financial Institutions, 1950–1977**

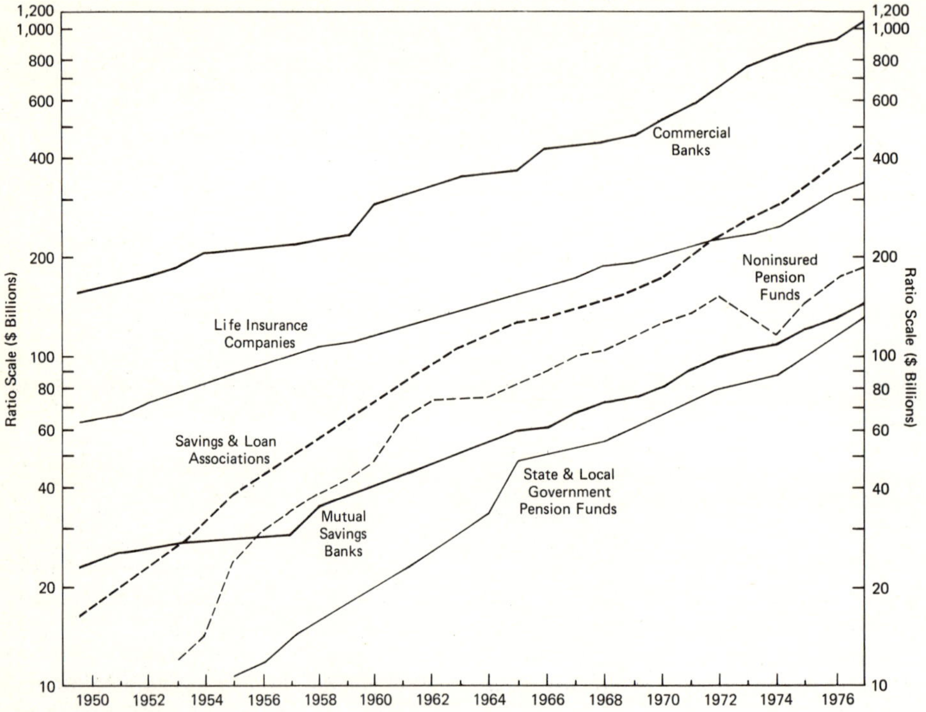

Note: Life insurance company assets include assets attributable to pension funds.

Source: Board of Governors of the Federal Reserve System.

question: Taking into account expected premiums, what should the company hold in order to meet policy obligations as they come due? At the beginning of any year, reserves equal the discounted value of future benefits (based on appropriate mortality statistics for the policies outstanding) less the discounted value of future premium receipts. The essential elements in the calculation are mortality statistics and the interest rate used for calculating present values. Under state laws, conservative assumptions both on mortality and interest rates are used in calculating minimum reserves. For example, an interest rate of 4½ percent is used for individual life insurance reserves, with the result that reserves are substantially larger than an assumption of a higher interest rate would provide. The reserves, thus, are liabilities calculated on somewhat arbitrary assumptions, not totals of amounts in

each separate policy contract. (By contrast, assets are the sum of specific securities, loans, real estate, and so forth, which can be valued at cost, market price, or estimated market price.)

Since reserves result from a calculation based on selected assumptions, changes in the amounts of policy reserves are a poor statistical measure of saving through life insurance, a purpose for which they are widely used. Year-to-year changes in such liabilities have only a loose relationship to the actual flow of funds to life companies and the growth of their assets.[26] Over long periods, however, the growth of reserves provides a rough indication of the sources of growth in assets.

[26] For a measure of saving through life insurance based on the asset side of the accounts, see Bishop, *Capital Formation Through Life Insurance,* especially Chap.

Table 7-4 shows the growth of reserves by line of product. The rate of growth of individual life insurance reserves has been somewhat less than the rate of growth in total assets, while the rate of growth of policy reserves for group life insurance, health insurance, and group annuities in the last five years has been more than double the rate of growth for individual life insurance reserves. In absolute terms, however, reserves for group life and health insurance are small because these products are essentially term insurance written for short periods of time. Over the last decade, the growth in group annuity reserves has been large in both absolute and relative terms. From 1970 to 1978, group annuity reserves grew by almost $65 billion, slightly more than the $56 billion growth in individual life insurance reserves. For the period 1970–1978, the average annual rate of growth of group annuity reserves was almost 14 percent compared with 7.1 percent for total assets.

## Investment Activity in Major Sectors of the Capital Market and Shifts in Asset Holdings

This section examines the activity of life insurance companies as investors of long-term capital funds. Life companies specialize in the private markets for bonds and mortgages—that is, the markets where securities and loans are placed directly with lenders who generally expect to hold them until maturity—in contrast with the markets for publicly issued and widely traded securities.

Although they typically hold securities for long periods, life companies contribute to the efficiency of the capital markets because their current investable funds are quickly shifted from one type of asset to another as interest rates and spreads change. Funds flow quickly to uses with the greatest needs—as measured by market rates of return. Life companies' assets are among the most diversified of major financial institutions, and although the mix of holdings changes slowly from year to year, the mix of new investment commitments and acquisitions can change substantially even from

month to month with changes in the demands for funds. Strong competition among life insurers and other lenders in private markets for bonds and mortgages generally ensures quick availability of funds with small rate differentials for different types of borrowers. Rate differentials among major sectors of the credit markets in which life companies are important have been relatively smaller in recent years than in the early 1960s (see Figure 7-3).

### Corporate Bond Markets

Life insurance companies have long been the major institutional investor in corporate bonds. At the end of 1978, life companies held about one-third of outstanding corporate bonds (including notes and debentures with a maturity of more than one year).

For a long period in the 1950s and early 1960s, life companies increased their corporate bond holdings less rapidly than their mortgage holdings (see Figure 7-4). In that period, mortgage contract rates generally were higher than yields on corporate bonds (Figure 7-3). By the 1970s, in contrast, corporate bond holdings rose in importance, increasing from 34.2 percent of total life company assets at the end of 1970 to 38.4 percent at the end of 1978 (see Table 7-5). In this period, yields on corporate bonds were generally higher in relation to yields on mortgages, and demands for mortgage funds lagged with successive recessions in 1970 and 1974–1975. As a result, the share of corporate bonds in total assets increased while the mortgage share decreased.

*The Private Placement Market* Privately placed bonds (also referred to as direct placements) are sold directly, or with the aid of an investment banker, by the borrower to the lender. Several lenders may participate in a given loan, and the terms of privately placed bonds are tailored to the special needs of the borrowers. Publicly issued bonds, on the other hand, must be registered with the Securities and Exchange Commission (SEC). They are then sold through underwriters, who typically form groups or syndicates to handle the sale of bonds to large numbers of investors on uniform terms under a standard contract. The Securities Act of 1933 exempted private placements from registration requirements because institutional lenders

---

5. Such a statistical measure is broader in scope than saving as measured by changes in policy reserves, because it includes assets reflecting all liabilities, including surplus and capital funds.

Table 7-4   Assets, Policy Reserves, and Other Obligations of U.S. Life Insurance Companies (in millions of dollars)

| End of Year | Total Assets of Life Insurance Companies | Policy Reserves | | | | | | | | Other Obligations and Unassigned Surplus[c] |
|---|---|---|---|---|---|---|---|---|---|---|
| | | Total | Life Insurance | | | | Health Insurance | Group Annuities | Other[b] | |
| | | | Total[a] | Individual | | Group[a] | | | | |
| | | | | Ordinary | Industrial | | | | | |
| 1950 | $ 64,020 | $ 54,946 | N.A. | N.A. | N.A. | N.A. | N.A. | N.A. | N.A. | $ 9,074 |
| 1960 | 119,576 | 98,473 | $ 70,791 | $ 58,897 | $10,627 | $1,267 | $ 865 | $14,952 | $11,865 | 21,103 |
| 1970 | 207,254 | 167,779 | 115,442 | 100,076 | 12,273 | 3,093 | 3,474 | 34,009 | 14,854 | 39,475 |
| 1977 | 351,722 | 287,932 | 167,281 | 147,414 | 12,624 | 6,415 | 8,329 | 84,285 | 28,037 | 63,790 |
| 1978 | 389,924 | 318,483 | 177,743 | 156,862 | 12,627 | 7,219 | 9,596 | 98,673 | 32,471 | 71,441 |
| As a percentage of total assets: | | | | | | | | | | |
| 1950 | 100.0 | 85.8 | N.A. | N.A. | N.A. | N.A. | N.A. | N.A. | N.A. | 14.2 |
| 1960 | 100.0 | 82.4 | 59.2 | 49.3 | 8.9 | 1.1 | 0.7 | 12.5 | 9.9 | 17.6 |
| 1970 | 100.0 | 81.0 | 55.7 | 48.3 | 5.9 | 1.5 | 1.7 | 16.4 | 7.2 | 19.0 |
| 1977 | 100.0 | 81.9 | 47.6 | 41.9 | 3.6 | 2.1 | 2.4 | 24.0 | 7.9 | 18.1 |
| 1978 | 100.0 | 81.7 | 45.6 | 40.2 | 3.2 | 1.9 | 2.5 | 25.3 | 8.3 | 18.3 |
| Compound Annual Rate of Increase | | | | | | | | | | |
| 1950–60 | 6.4% | 6.0% | N.A. | N.A. | N.A. | N.A. | N.A. | N.A. | N.A. | 8.8% |
| 1960–70 | 5.7 | 5.5 | 5.0% | 5.4% | 1.5% | 9.3% | 14.9% | 8.5% | 2.2% | 6.5 |
| 1970–78 | 7.1 | 7.4 | 5.0 | 5.9 | 0.4 | 12.9 | 13.3 | 13.8 | 9.3 | 7.7 |

N.A. = Not Available

[a]Includes reserves for credit life insurance.

[b]Includes reserves for individual annuities and supplementary contracts with and without life contingencies.

[c]Includes policy dividend accumulations and funds set aside for such dividends, securities valuation reserves, special surplus funds, unassigned surplus, capital of stock companies, and other items.

Source: American Council of Life Insurance.

**Figure 7-3  Selected Bond Yields and Contract Rate on Income-Property Mortgages (Quarterly Averages, 1960–1978)**

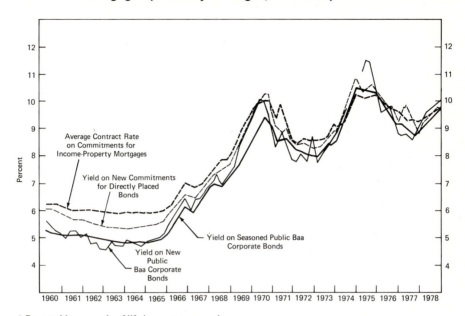

a Reported by a sample of life insurance companies.
b During 1974–75, no yields were recorded for 14 months of a 17-month period by Moody's on new public Baa corporate bond issues.

Sources: American Council of Life Insurance and Moody's Investor Service, Inc.

presumably had adequate capacity to investigate new issues and, therefore, had no need for protective regulation.[27]

Life companies are in a good position to engage in the private placement market because their needs for liquidity are small and their liabilities are suited to long-term loans. Other financial institutions typically have much larger proportions of short-term liabilities and are less able to make long-term, illiquid loans.

The privately placed bond has important advantages to the borrower. First, issuing costs in relation to the size of the offering are lower for private placements than for publicly issued bonds. Second,

new firms, or firms that are not well known, have limited access to the public market because they lack a historical earnings record or a high credit rating. The private placement market provides them with a source of funds.[28] Third, the borrower can negotiate loan terms to suit his or her particular needs for repayment schedules, maturity, renegotiation privileges, and so on. Fourth, a private placement can be arranged quickly, often within a day or two. Public issues have a waiting period of at least twenty days from the time an issue is registered with the SEC, thereby exposing the borrower to the risks of market changes that could result in withdrawal of an issue. To the lender, the privately placed bond typically offers a higher return to the investor than a publicly issued bond,

[27]For a detailed analysis, see Eli Shapiro and Charles R. Wolf, *The Role of Private Placements in Corporate Finance,* Harvard Graduate School of Business Administration, Boston, 1972. See also Charles R. Wolf, "The Demand for Funds in the Public and Private Corporate Bond Markets," *The Review of Economics and Statistics* (February 1974), 23–29.

[28]Most states have a "leeway" clause in investment laws relating to life insurance companies. This clause allows them to hold a small percentage of assets in securities of small or new firms that otherwise would not be of "investment quality."

**Figure 7-4   U.S. Life Insurance Company Assets by Major Type, 1948–1977**

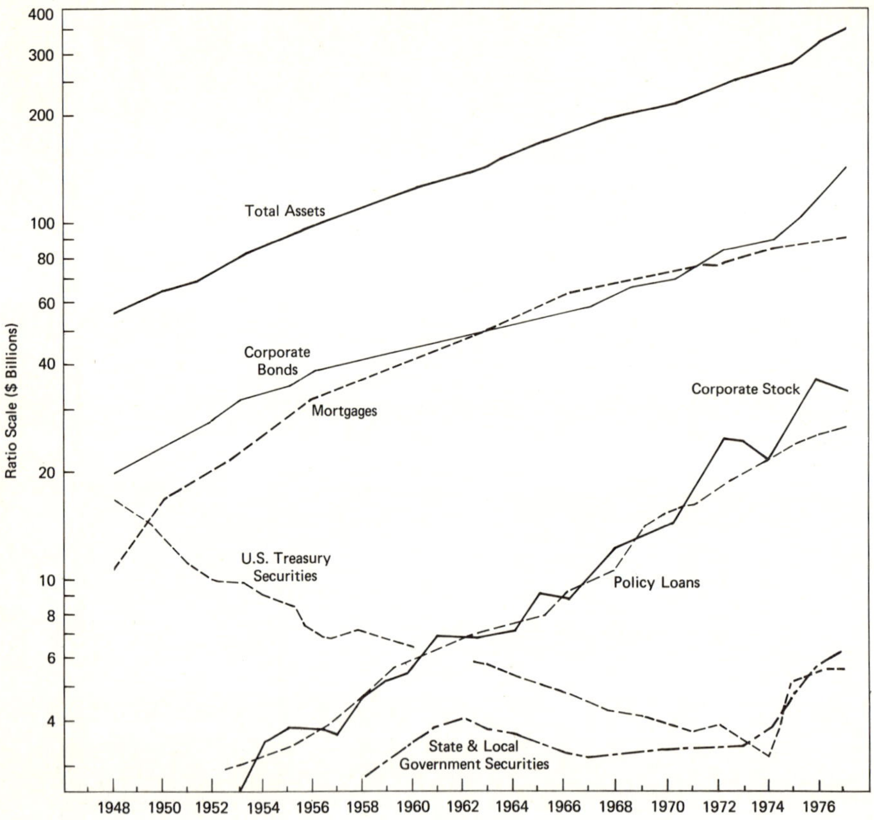

Source: American Council of Life Insurance.

but it lacks the liquidity of the publicly issued bond. There is a small resale market in private placements, but it is unlikely to become important because of high transaction costs and legal restrictions.

The supply of investment funds of life companies is an important element in the total volume of new issues of privately placed bonds. When life company investment funds are plentiful, as in the years 1975–1976, the rate differential between publicly issued bonds and private placements tends to narrow, and many firms shift their borrowing from the public to private markets. At these times, the private placement market becomes more important in relation to the public-issues market. When the investment funds of life companies are limited, as

they were in the late 1960s, the private placement market declines in relative importance to the public-issue market.

*The Public Bond Market*   As market conditions and interest rate differentials change, some part of the investment funds of life companies may shift from the private placement market to the public-issues market. In recent years, the rate spread between private and public issues has not been large, and because of the impact of successive periods of tight money conditions on their investable funds, some life companies have a greater need for liquidity, which can be met in part by publicly issued bonds. To small and medium-sized life companies with limited facilities for making private place-

**Table 7-5  Assets of U.S. Life Insurance Companies (in billions of dollars)**

| | 1950 Amount | 1950 Percent | 1960 Amount | 1960 Percent | 1970 Amount | 1970 Percent | 1977 Amount | 1977 Percent | 1978 Amount | 1978 Percent |
|---|---|---|---|---|---|---|---|---|---|---|
| Corporate bonds, notes, and debentures | $23.2 | 36.3 | $ 46.7 | 39.1 | $ 73.1 | 35.3 | $137.9 | 39.2 | $156.0 | 40.0 |
| Short-term: 1 year or less | a | | a | | 2.1 | 1.0 | 4.9 | 1.4 | 6.3 | 1.6 |
| Other: over 1 year | 23.2 | 36.3 | 46.7 | 39.1 | 71.0 | 34.3 | 133.0 | 37.8 | 149.7 | 38.4 |
| Corporate stocks | 2.1 | 3.3 | 5.0 | 4.2 | 15.4 | 7.4 | 33.8 | 9.6 | 35.5 | 9.1 |
| Preferred | 1.5 | 2.3 | 1.8 | 1.5 | 3.5 | 1.7 | 9.7 | 2.8 | 10.5 | 2.7 |
| Common | 0.6 | 1.0 | 3.2 | 2.7 | 11.9 | 5.7 | 24.1 | 6.8 | 25.0 | 6.4 |
| Mortgages, total | 16.1 | 25.2 | 41.8 | 35.0 | 74.4 | 35.9 | 96.8 | 27.5 | 105.8 | 27.2 |
| Land and construction | 0.2 | 0.3 | 0.7 | 0.6 | 2.0 | 1.0 | 3.9 | 1.1 | 4.0 | 1.0 |
| Residential | 11.0 | 17.2 | 28.2 | 23.6 | 41.3 | 19.9 | 31.9 | 9.1 | 32.2 | 8.3 |
| Nonresidential and farm | 4.9 | 7.7 | 12.9 | 10.8 | 31.1 | 15.0 | 61.0 | 17.3 | 69.6 | 17.9 |
| Government securities | 16.2 | 25.2 | 11.8 | 9.9 | 11.1 | 5.3 | 23.6 | 6.7 | 26.6 | 6.8 |
| Short-term: 1 year or less | a | | a | | 0.3 | 0.1 | 0.7 | 0.2 | 0.7 | 0.2 |
| Other: over 1 year | a | | a | | 10.8 | 5.2 | 22.9 | 6.5 | 25.9 | 6.6 |
| U.S. government | 13.5 | 21.0 | 6.5 | 5.5 | 4.3 | 2.1 | 8.6 | 2.5 | 10.8 | 2.8 |
| U.S. state and local | 1.2 | 1.8 | 3.6 | 3.0 | 3.3 | 1.6 | 6.1 | 1.7 | 6.4 | 1.6 |
| Foreign government and international | 1.5 | 2.4 | 1.7 | 1.4 | 3.2 | 1.5 | 8.2 | 2.3 | 8.7 | 2.2 |
| Real estate | 1.4 | 2.2 | 3.8 | 3.1 | 6.3 | 3.0 | 11.1 | 3.2 | 11.8 | 3.0 |
| Policy loans | 2.4 | 3.8 | 5.2 | 4.3 | 16.1 | 7.8 | 27.6 | 7.8 | 30.1 | 7.7 |
| Other[b] | 2.6 | 4.0 | 5.3 | 4.4 | 10.9 | 5.3 | 20.9 | 6.0 | 24.1 | 6.2 |
| Total | $64.0 | 100.0 | $119.6 | 100.0 | $207.3 | 100.0 | $351.7 | 100.0 | $389.9 | 100.0 |

Note: Separate account assets in 1970 and 1977, included in the data, totaled $5.1 and $16.9 billion, including common stocks amounting to $4.0 and $10.9, for these years, respectively. Amounts for separate accounts in 1950 and 1960 were not significant.

[a] Breakdown of securities of date of maturity is not available. Short-term securities in 1950 and 1960 are combined with the over one-year categories.

[b] Two major components accounting for over two-thirds of "Other" are due and deferred premiums and due and accrued interest. Another item is cash holdings. Other assets include electronic data processing equipment and oil, mineral, and timber rights.

Source: American Council of Life Insurance, *Life Insurance Fact Book 1979.*

ments, public bond issues may provide a more convenient and appropriate outlet for their investment funds.

### Mortgage Markets

The same features that make life insurance companies important in the privately placed bond market also explain their significance in the mortgage market, especially the commercial mortgage market: a long-term investment horizon and the ability to negotiate individual loans. For a time in the early 1950s, life companies were the largest institutional holders of mortgage debt of all kinds.

In the 1950s, life companies were major participants in the one- to four-family mortgage market. At that time, yields on home mortgages generally exceeded those on commercial mortgages. For example, in 1955 the average contract rate on conventional home mortgage commitments by life companies was 4.87 percent, while interest rates on commercial mortgage commitments by life companies averaged 4.66 percent. Both categories of mortgage rates exceeded the average yield on directly placed corporate bonds.

In the early 1960s, the structure of mortgage yields shifted, and rates on commercial mortgages rose above those on home mortgages. As a result, life companies began to invest more funds in commercial mortgages. By the late 1960s, U.S. life companies as a whole reduced their holdings of one- to four-family mortgages, and since that time, they have concentrated on the income-property mortgage market. Life companies have been active in the development of retail complexes, large office buildings, industrial properties, hotels and motels, recreational centers, and institutional properties. Commercial construction fell to a low level in the 1974–1975 recession, however, and mortgage acquisitions of life companies were relatively small as a result. Mortgage acquisitions picked up again with construction activity following the recession.

### Stock Markets

Before 1951, life companies in the United States were not important investors in common stocks. In 1951, for the first time in more than forty years, New York State (where many of the largest life companies have their headquarters) permitted life

companies to invest in common stocks—up to a limit of 3 percent of their assets or one-third of their surplus, whichever was less. This limit was raised in 1969 to 10 percent of assets or 100 percent of surplus, whichever was less. A number of other states have similar limitations on common-stock holdings. In terms of life company accounting, preferred stocks are more like bonds in that they are valued at cost instead of market and they are less exposed to capital losses when stock prices decline. Hence, many life companies are more willing to invest in preferred stocks than in common stocks.

Common-stock holdings of life companies have been small not only because of legal restrictions but also because of the view held by some companies that common stocks were not an appropriate investment against fixed-dollar liabilities. Since common stocks (unlike preferred stocks) are valued at market prices, a substantial drop in stock prices could result in a large unrealized capital loss and have a heavy impact on surplus, thereby endangering the technical solvency of the life company. Many life companies, however, have viewed common stocks as a useful form of diversification and as a means of increasing the total return on investments in the long run. Moreover, the growth of pension fund business and the sale of variable annuities gave a strong impetus to common stock acquisitions—at least until recent years of poor common-stock performance.

Common-stock holdings grew from $650 million at the end of 1950 to $25 billion at the end of 1978. In recent years, life companies have been the third largest institutional investor in common stocks—after noninsured private pension funds and open-end investment companies. In terms of the net annual flow of funds into the stock market, life companies' net acquisitions have generally ranged from $2 to $3 billion, or about one-fourth of the net purchases of all institutional buyers. In 1974–1975, however, net acquisitions of common stocks by life companies fell below $2 billion. They were still below that level in 1978.

### Other Assets

Holdings of U.S. government securities by life insurance companies fell almost without interruption from 1950 to 1974. The decline was reversed in the 1975–1978 period, however, as yield differentials between U.S. government and high-grade corporate bonds narrowed. Net investments in federal agency issues, which typically carry higher yields than Treasuries, reached a record volume in 1978.

Holdings of U.S. state and local government securities, after a bulge in the early 1960s and a subsequent decline, have been growing since 1967. At the end of 1978 these securities accounted for 1.6 percent of total assets. Rising effective tax rates on life companies will probably mean a continued increase in holdings of tax-exempt issues.

At the end of 1978, life insurance companies directly owned real estate valued at $11.8 billion, or 3.0 percent of total assets. The real estate share of total assets has gradually increased over the past decade. Some life companies are important participants in joint ventures—in which they supply most of the capital while other participants supply development and management services. Real estate subsidiaries are also used for real estate investment, often as a part of a holding company complex.

Policy loans of life companies continue to increase and have recently represented almost 8 percent of total assets. As explained in the following section, market rates of interest for more than a decade, especially at the peaks in periods of tight money, have exceeded the rates at which policy loans are available to policyholders. When the differential widens between market rates and policy-loan rates, the increase in policy loans accelerates, diverting investment funds from the life companies' normal long-term investments in bonds and mortgages.

## Cyclical Responses of Life Insurance Investment Flows

In the 1950s and early 1960s, the flow of investment funds through life insurance companies was fairly stable. In the second half of the 1960s and early 1970s, the flow became less stable, largely a result of successive periods of unusually tight credit conditions and rising interest rates.

The main interest-sensitive and cyclically responsive elements in the flow of investable funds to life companies are the following: net changes in policy loans; mortgage prepayments; and calls of securities. These flows contrast with the relatively stable flows from amortization of mortgages,

scheduled bond maturities, and the annual net increase in assets, which derives from net investment income and the excess of premiums over benefit payments, expenses, and taxes.[29]

The net increase in policy loans was a primary source of instability in the flow of investable funds in the last half of the 1960s. Because the maximum policy-loan rate on a large proportion of outstanding policies was fixed at 5 percent at that time, a rise in market rates of interest well above this level provided an incentive for policyholders, not only to obtain policy loans rather than borrow elsewhere, but also to use proceeds of policy loans to invest directly in market instruments that provided a higher yield. The net increase in policy loans again reached a high level in 1973 and early 1974, when interest rates soared to a double-digit level, but in that period, life companies were more prepared than they had been earlier for this type of diversion of funds. They were able to hold more liquid assets and more accurately forecast cash flow. In 1975 and 1976, the net increase in policy loans was down to a more normal volume.[30]

Prepayments of mortgages in full usually accompany a high level of housing activity as owners sell existing homes, pay off old mortgages, and take out new mortgages on new homes. Turnover of ownership of commercial properties also contributes to an increase in mortgage prepayments. Since housing construction and sales vary substantially with business activity and credit conditions, the inflow of funds from mortgage prepayments to life companies rises and falls with business activity.

Calls of securities—in effect prepayments of bonds and retirements of preferred stocks—tend to increase when interest rates fall and to decrease when interest rates rise, thus providing more funds for reinvestment by life companies when money and credit conditions are easy. Corporations try to refund debt when interest rates fall, although they may call securities for other reasons as well.

The fluctuations in the flow of investment funds for market investment (that is, cash flow) are shown

[29] For a detailed discussion of these flows, see George A. Bishop, *The Response of Life Insurance Investments to Changes in Monetary Policy 1965–70,* Life Insurance Association of America, 1971.
[30] Maximum interest rates on policy loans in many states have been raised in recent years to 8 percent for new policies.

as a quarterly moving average in Figure 7-5. Also plotted is a quarterly moving average of new forward investment commitments. To relate these series to monetary conditions, the approximate dates of substantial changes in the Federal Reserve policy actions and periods of ease or tightness in credit markets are shown.

The relatively steady growth of investment funds in the first half of the 1960s contrasts with the large fluctuations in investment funds during the second half of the decade, which was marked by episodes of tight money conditions in 1966 and 1969. A period of ease in monetary policy and declining interest rates beginning in late 1970 and continuing through 1972 brought a rapid rise in the investment funds of life companies. The rise continued until monetary policy again shifted to restraint and interest rates rose sharply in 1973. Tight money and credit conditions continued through the first half of 1974, and the investment funds of life companies again fell sharply in this period. A shift once more to easy money and credit conditions in 1975 and 1976 again led to a rapid rise in life insurance investment funds.

This record over the past decade shows that the investment funds available to life companies and their forward investment commitments are quite sensitive to changes in Federal Reserve policy and credit conditions. Tight credit serves to restrict the supply of funds in the capital market; easy credit increases it. There is, moreover, little lag in the change in investment funds and in commitments following a substantial change in money and credit conditions. Hence, life insurance investment operations serve to reinforce the effects of changes in monetary policy.[31] The impact on capital markets is generally felt most strongly in the market for privately placed corporate debt, where life insurance companies are major participants.

## Conclusion

Life insurance companies, a major type of financial intermediary, offer the public products involving both insurance protection and a means of saving.

[31] For an econometric analysis, including a simulation of the effects of higher interest rates, see James E. Pesando, "The Interest Sensitivity of the Flow of Funds Through Life Insurance Companies," *Journal of Finance* (September 1974), 1105–1121.

At the same time, life companies are important participants in the capital markets providing equity capital and other loanable funds for a wide range of borrowers.

In the 1970s, life insurance companies' assets increased above the long-term historic rate of about 7 percent a year since 1900. This recent growth reflected higher rates of investment earnings and accelerated growth in certain products, particularly pension plans, group life insurance, and other employee benefits. Over the past twenty-five years, various legal and regulatory obstacles to life company participation in pension business have been removed. Individual life insurance in force has continued to grow in line with total disposable income, although the ratio of premiums paid for individual life insurance to disposable personal income has declined.

The long-term nature of much of life insurers' liabilities allows them to hold the bulk of their assets in long-term maturities. Moreover, the large and relatively predictable flow of investable funds of life insurers means that it is rarely necessary to sell assets to obtain funds for unexpected policy claims or for policy loans. Thus, with limited needs for liquidity, only a small proportion of assets is in securities with maturities of one year or less.

Short-term influences on the growth of life insurance assets have become more significant with the substantial rise in the level of interest rates in the past decade. The gross and net investments of life insurance companies show a material response to changes in money and credit conditions, partly because the growth of policy loans is sensitive to interest rate fluctuations. Cyclical changes in life insurance investments are such as to reinforce the objectives of monetary policy—that is, new forward commitments and purchases of investments increase rapidly in periods of easy money but decline in periods of tight money and credit conditions.

Life companies are most important in the capital markets for corporate bonds and for mortgages on commercial properties. Life companies are the major lenders in the market for privately placed securities, where bonds are sold directly by the borrower to one or a few lenders and there is little secondary trading in such bonds once they are issued. Life companies also participate in the public bond markets, where bonds are publicly issued to

**Figure 7-5   Total Cash Flow for Market Investment and Total New Commitments Estimated for All U.S. Life Insurance Companies (Quarterly Moving Averages, 1959–1977)**

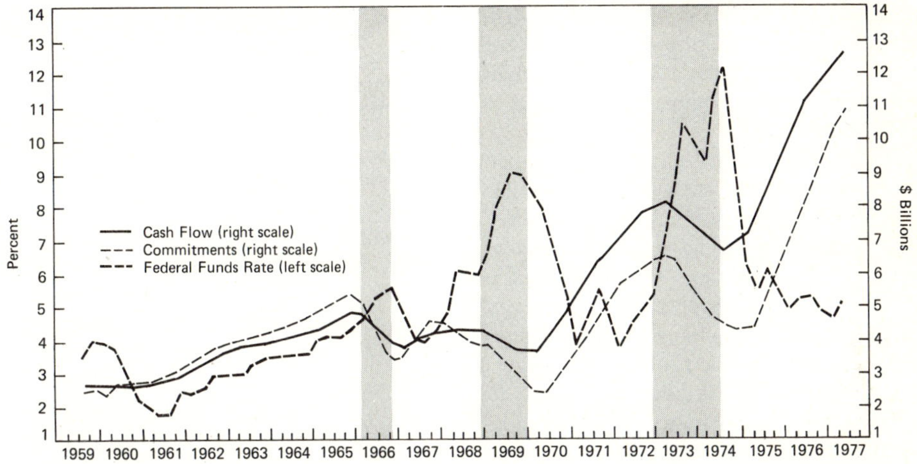

Note: Shaded areas are periods of tight money and credit conditions. These periods were selected on the basis of policy attitudes contained in directives of the Federal Open Market Committee together with significant changes in money market rates.

Sources: American Council of Life Insurance and Federal Reserve Board.

a large number of investors and widely traded after issue, but they participate on a comparatively limited scale.

In the mortgage markets, life companies once were very active lenders on single-family homes. In recent years, however, in response to shifts in interest rates, they have been active mainly in making loans on income-producing properties.

Life companies are a significant source of equity capital as well as of debt financing to business borrowers. Their net purchases of common stocks usually represent a substantial proportion of the net issues of common stock, though common stocks remain a small proportion of life companies' total assets.

Through policy loans, life companies also lend substantial amounts to households. The essential role of life companies, however, is to serve as intermediaries that attract a substantial part of the public's financial savings through insurance products and then invest these funds largely in long-term bonds and mortgages. In this role, life insurance companies in the 1970s improved their rate of growth despite high rates of inflation and the fact

that they deal largely in long-term fixed dollar liabilities.

**Property and Casualty Insurance Companies**

Property and casualty insurance companies comprise more than 2,500 companies that sell property and casualty insurance and related lines, including inland marine coverages and surety and fidelity bonds.[32] This group of insurance companies had accumulated assets of more than $150 billion as of year-end 1978, making them roughly comparable in size to mutual savings banks and finance companies. In terms of asset growth, they have enjoyed much faster expansion in the postwar period than life companies. In fact, their financial assets have increased even more rapidly than financial assets in the economy as a whole.

[32]*Surety bonds* are agreements to provide monetary compensation if specified acts are not performed within a stated period of time. *Fidelity bonds* protect employers against losses caused by dishonest or fraudulent acts of employees.

Sales of various lines of insurance resulted in more than $80 billion in premium income in 1978. As Table 7-6 shows, about 40 percent of all premiums written are for automobile collision and liability insurance, but multiple peril, fire, and workers' compensation lines also provide a sizable proportion of premium income. Slightly over half of all premiums arise from commercial or business coverages.

In the past, property and casualty insurance companies tended to concentrate on particular types of coverage, but today many companies are multiple-line companies, selling several classes of property and casualty insurance.[33] In recent years, some property and casualty companies have even begun to sell life insurance, and many also sell large amounts of accident and health insurance. Diversification in this industry has been prompted, in part, by the highly volatile nature of the underwriting performance in various lines; because cycles in underwriting experience are usually not coincidental, these diversification efforts should smooth out income.

It is useful to draw a distinction between property insurance and casualty insurance coverages because of the importance of the characteristics of the liabilities to which they give rise. Property insurance provides coverage against loss to property from fire and other hazards, with indemnification of damage losses up to the limits set in the policy. The loss experience on these policies is highly variable. Casualty insurance covers losses deriving from personal injuries and from damage to the property of others. In comparison with property

**Table 7-6  Premiums Written by Property and Casualty Insurance Companies, 1978 (in billions of dollars)**

|  | Amount | *Percentage of All Premiums* |
|---|---|---|
| Commercial total | $47.4 | 58% |
| Workers' compensation | 11.3 | 14 |
| Commercial auto | 6.7 | 8 |
| General liability | 7.7 | 9 |
| Commercial multiple peril | 6.3 | 8 |
| Others | 15.4 | 19 |
| Individual total | $34.3 | 42% |
| Auto | 26.5 | 32 |
| Homeowners multiple peril | 7.8 | 10 |
| All premiums written | $81.7 | 100% |

Source: *Best's Aggregates and Averages, Property-Liability,* 1979.

insurance, loss experience on casualty lines is generally more stable.

In a discussion of the property and casualty group, it is also useful to distinguish between mutual and stock companies.[34] Numerically, the mutuals predominate, but stock companies are larger in terms of assets and premium volume, a situation which is the opposite of the life insurance industry. Stock companies differ in certain important respects from mutual companies, as we shall see.

Despite the fact that there are more than 2,500 property and casualty insurance companies, the top 10 companies in terms of premiums write about 40 percent of the business. This high degree of concentration apparently has not precluded extensive price and nonprice competition, however.[35] State

[33]Legal tradition in the United States established a threefold classification system (called the mono-line system) for insurance companies and companies specialized in one of these lines. The categories were broken down as follows: (1) life and health insurance; (2) casualty and surety insurance; and (3) fire and marine insurance. Since 1955 all states have enacted permissive legislation for multiple-line companies, although the distinction between life and property-casualty insurance has been retained. Some life companies, however, now sell property-casualty insurance and vice versa. The operations, nevertheless, remain distinct, with direct ownership or control exercised through a common financial group. For greater detail on the evolution of the general regulatory history of the insurance industry, see S. S. Huebner, Kenneth Black, Jr., and Robert S. Cline, *Property and Liability Insurance,* 2nd ed., Prentice-Hall, Englewood Cliffs, N.J., 1976.

[34]Two other minor classes of property and casualty companies exist: reciprocal exchanges and American Lloyd's. A reciprocal exchange combines persons into a group to insure each other at cost. Subscribers receive protection for a certain amount of risk and they, in turn, underwrite coverage for the membership. Lloyd's-type companies are patterned after the famous Lloyd's of London and consist of associations of individuals, each of which agrees to accept a portion of the risk in a given contract.

[35]Measurement of the degree of competition in the property and casualty insurance industry is extremely complex and highly controversial. For a discussion of some of the issues involved, see Paul L. Joskow, "Cartels, Competition, and Regulation in the Property-Liability Insurance Industry," *The Bell Journal of Economics and Management Science* (Autumn 1973), 375–427. Using

insurance departments, the regulators of the property and casualty industry, set the upper and lower limits of the range of premium rates for various lines.[36] This procedure leaves considerable room for competition on premium rates, particularly in periods when the industry enjoys favorable underwriting and investment results. Such a period of keen competition occurred in the early 1970s. In that period, personal automobile premiums actually declined by about 3 percent, even though medical and repair costs rose by 20 percent. There are limits to the degree of price competition, however, and nonprice competition can be, and often is, important in this industry.

## Financial Intermediation Function

The most significant characteristic of a financial intermediary is that it provides a mechanism for the transfer of funds from surplus to deficit economic units. The fact that a financial institution has a significant amount of assets is taken as evidence that holders of the liabilities of those institutions have a surplus of funds in excess of current needs. Property and casualty insurance companies do not usually think of themselves as possessing these critical features. Instead, they view their primary purpose as the sale of specialized current services. In order to evaluate this industry argument, let us spend a few moments contrasting insurance contracts in the property and casualty lines with those in life insurance.

For life insurance companies, the incidence of risk is generally lower in the earlier years than in the later years of a contract period. For these companies, level-premium plans imply that premium payments exceed the actual cost of insurance protection in the early years of a contract. The excess, then, can be invested in financial assets until later in the contract period when the costs of protection exceed the premium payments. Clearly, to the extent the company can continue to sell new level-

premium policies, this procedure implies a substantial build-up in assets.

For property and casualty companies, the incidence of occurrence of insured risk is evenly distributed throughout the contract period, and this factor results in a shorter average lapse of time between receipts of premium income and claim payments than for life insurance companies.[37] Indeed, much of the yearly inflows of property and casualty insurance companies is returned in the same year to policyholders suffering an insured loss. So, despite the fact that premiums received by property and casualty companies are only moderately below yearly premiums of life companies, asset accumulation of the property and casualty companies is considerably less.

Nevertheless, while strictly speaking it may be true that purchasers of property and casualty insurance are not undertaking an act of saving, the point remains that property and casualty insurance companies do accumulate surplus and reserve funds from an excess of inflows from all sources above underwriting outflows.[38] This net cash flow, as suggested earlier, is small compared with life companies and, consequently, property and casualty insurers are a relatively minor force in capital markets. However, while they do not supply sizable amounts of funds to the money and capital markets in the aggregate each year, they are significant participants in one important segment of these markets, the market for state and local government securities. Moreover, a substantial part of the net income of property and casualty insurers

---

[37]Indeed, in consideration of the specialized features of the business, the National Income and Product Accounts treat premium income less claims paid as personal consumption expenditures for services. This classification in the National Income and Product Accounts differs from the classification of life companies, where the build-up in reserves is treated as a form of personal saving. Whether this treatment is appropriate for all life insurance reserves is a matter of some debate but, nevertheless, the treatment persists.

[38]In the nature of the property and casualty insurance company contract there are several reasons for surplus and reserve funds to accumulate. One of the more important may be attributed to the payment of premiums in advance of coverage mixed with staggered timing of the takedowns of coverage by individual policyholders. Also, larger reserves are accumulated for certain lines than for others, and to the extent those lines grow more rapidly, reserve accumulation is larger.

---

more sophisticated methods than employed in the text, Professor Joskow concludes that the property and casualty insurance industry is not highly concentrated. Overall, his evidence strongly suggests that the industry exhibits essentially competitive characteristics.

[36]It is worth noting, however, that some twenty-two states now have "file and use" provisions in their insurance rating laws.

derives from their investments. In fact, in many years, net investment income exceeds underwriting gains or serves to offset underwriting losses.[39] For these reasons, it is analytically useful to treat property and casualty insurance companies as financial intermediaries.

### Reserves, Net Worth, and Income

In the last section we demonstrated that property and casualty insurance companies accumulate surplus and reserve funds by generating an excess of inflows from all sources above underwriting outflows. This section describes more fully the process by which this accumulation occurs and introduces the reader to certain concepts pertinent to an understanding of how the inflows to property and casualty insurance companies are handled in their accounting.

In the property and casualty industry, the majority of all liabilities are reserves against losses or reserves for premiums collected but not yet earned. The net worth of these companies is commonly identified with the policyholders' surplus, but this discussion shows that actual net worth needs to be defined somewhat more broadly than policyholders' surplus alone. As background, data on reserves and policyholders' surplus for selected years from 1950 to 1978 are shown in Table 7-7.

When property and casualty insurers sell policies, they generate gross premium income, which is largely allocated between loss reserves and unearned premium reserves.[40] Additions to loss reserves are based on (1) estimates of liabilities on which claimants have filed but which have not yet been paid; and (2) claims expected from losses but

for which policyholders have not yet filed. The companies compute loss reserves on the basis of past experience, but property and casualty insurers cannot predict the actual claims with the same degree of accuracy that life insurers can estimate their claims. Moreover, they cannot know the total amount of liability to a claimant with certainty; the actual repair or other costs depend on current factors which might not be captured in estimates based upon past experience.[41] Hence, the actual loss experience may differ from estimates, and loss reserves may not reflect actual needs.

The unearned premium reserve arises from the fact that premium income is collected (or the company acquires the right to collect) in advance of the actual provision of protection, which can only be provided as time elapses during the contract period. The full premium is not earned until the policy itself has expired. The unearned portion of a premium is held as a reserve to cover the costs of protection throughout the contract's life, and if the policy is canceled before the term is complete, the amount of unearned premium reserve is returned to the policyholder.

In general, analysts believe the formula specifying the additions to unearned premium reserves to be in excess of actual need, in that expenses are incurred at the time of issue of the policy and the risks being insured could be reinsured for less than the prepaid premiums. Particularly when analysts assess the performance of stock companies, they argue that the companies should classify a portion of this reserve as net worth.[42]

---

[39]Property and casualty insurance premium rates are determined without regard to investment income, in sharp contrast to life companies where such income is critical in setting premium levels. There has been considerable interest recently in revising this procedure to incorporate profits from investment operations into rate making in the property and casualty area.

[40]In the Federal Reserve's Flow of Funds Accounts, the allocation of premium income to these two reserve accounts is referred to as "policy payables." It is also worth noting that the Flow of Funds Accounts refer to property and casualty insurance as "Other Insurance Companies" on the theory that all nonlegal reserve life companies are in this sector. In practice, however, only property and casualty insurers make up the "Other Insurance Companies" sector in the Flow of Funds Ac-

counts. In order to derive data on the asset and liability side, the Flow of Funds Accounts combines data on stock and mutual companies, reciprocals, and American Lloyd's from *Best's Aggregate and Averages.* In the case of mutuals, there are minor adjustments of the Best's data to arrive at the total.

[41]For example, few would have predicted the sharp increases in automobile repair costs over the last few years. The Insurance Information Institute estimates that the total costs of replacing a set of frequently damaged parts (front bumper, grille, hood, and front fender) on one type of popular automobile rose by about 90 percent between 1971 and 1977, with the cost of parts increasing more rapidly than labor costs.

[42]Reserves are computed on the basis of instructions by the insurance commissioners in the various states. Financial analysts may judge these calculated reserves as leading to an unrealistic picture of net worth and, hence,

**Table 7-7   Reserves and Net Worth of Property and Casualty Insurance Companies, Selected Years (in billions of dollars)**

|  | 1950 | 1960 | 1965 | 1970 | 1975 | 1978 |
|---|---|---|---|---|---|---|
| Loss reserves | $ 2.8 | $ 7.5 | $11.0 | $19.6 | $37.9 | $ 65.7 |
| Stock companies | 2.1 | 5.4 | 7.9 | 14.0 | 29.3 | 51.3 |
| Mutual companies | 0.7 | 2.1 | 3.1 | 5.6 | 8.6 | 14.4 |
| Unpaid premium reserves | 4.2 | 8.2 | 10.1 | 14.7 | 20.5 | 29.4 |
| Stock companies | 3.7 | 6.6 | 8.0 | 11.4 | 16.1 | 22.5 |
| Mutual companies | 0.6 | 1.6 | 2.1 | 3.3 | 4.4 | 6.9 |
| Policyholders' surplus | 5.2 | 11.6 | 16.8 | 18.0 | 24.2 | 43.1 |
| Stock companies | 4.2 | 9.5 | 13.7 | 14.0 | 18.5 | 32.5 |
| Mutual companies | 1.0 | 2.1 | 3.1 | 4.0 | 5.7 | 10.6 |
| Total reserves and net worth | 12.2 | 27.3 | 37.9 | 52.3 | 82.6 | 138.2 |
| Stock companies | 10.0 | 21.5 | 29.6 | 39.4 | 63.9 | 106.3 |
| Mutual companies | 2.3 | 5.8 | 8.3 | 12.9 | 18.7 | 31.9 |
| Total liabilities and net worth | $13.4 | $30.1 | $41.8 | $58.6 | $94.0 | $160.1 |

Source: *Best's Aggregates and Averages, Property-Liability,* 1979.

The net worth of a property and casualty insurance company is equivalent to policyholders' surplus. This is largely the capital and surplus accounts of stock companies or the net surplus account of mutuals. Important additions of policyholders' surplus come from underwriting profits or from investment gains. These last concepts bear some further brief elaboration.

Net *underwriting* profits are the direct outcome of insurance operations over a specified period of time, without taking investment operations into account. They are determined by deducting from gross premiums written increases in unearned premium reserves, losses, and underwriting expenses, such as acquisition costs and agents' commissions.[43]

Figure 7-6 highlights for the property and casualty insurance industry the wide variability of underwriting profits from year to year, particularly in recent years when underwriting gains and losses have been the largest in the history of the industry. Also interesting is the greater number of years of

losses than of profits. This has necessarily increased the importance of investment performance in the overall operations of property and casualty insurers.

It should be added that the erratic behavior of underwriting income goes a long way toward explaining observed short-term fluctuations in annual capital market flows. It also suggests why there is

sider the data for all stock companies for 1977 as an example.

*Underwriting Account Summary*
*(in billions of dollars)*

| | |
|---|---|
| Net premiums written | $51.165 |
| Increase in unearned premium reserve | 2.433 |
| Net premiums earned | 48.732 |
| Losses and adjustment expenses incurred | 34.180 |
| Expenses incurred | 13.748 |
| Net underwriting profit | .804 |

Source: *Best's Aggregates and Averages, Property-Liability,* 1978.

Underwriting results in the industry are often measured in terms of the so-called combined ratio. This ratio is the sum of the ratio of expenses (before federal income taxes) to premiums written and the ratio of losses to premiums written. Again using 1977, the combined ratio for stock companies was 96.0, as the sum of a loss ratio of 70.7 and an expense ratio of 25.3. The combined ratio implies an underwriting profit for the year of 4.0 percent, roughly. A ratio of 102 percent, by contrast, would indicate a loss of approximately 2.0 percent.

choose to make certain adjustments in reported figures to obtain estimates of net worth. The procedure used by analysts is described in a number of places but, for a simplified treatment, see Herbert E. Dougall, *Investments,* 9th ed., Prentice-Hall, Englewood Cliffs, N.J., 1973, Chap. 30.

[43] The underwriting account of property and casualty insurance companies is part of their income statement. To show the derivation of net underwriting profits, con-

**Figure 7-6  Underwriting Profit or Loss Experience of Stock Property-Casualty Company[a]**

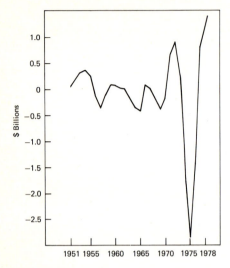

<sup>a</sup> Before federal income taxes.

Source: A.M. Best Data Center, *Best's Aggregates and Averages, Property-Liability, 1979.*

decline, investment losses can be quite large and can occasionally threaten the solvency of some companies. However, investment profits generally have been positive and have served to maintain the income of property and casualty insurers at higher levels than the underwriting account alone would indicate (see Figure 7-7). This fact has led to some interest in modifying industry calculations of profits to include both investment and underwriting income rather than, as is now the case, considering only underwriting income. Such a change would permit investment results to be utilized in arriving at reasonable premium rates.

### Determinants of Asset Mix

In general, property and casualty insurance companies, like other financial institutions, seek to maximize their return on invested assets consistent with an acceptable level of risk as determined by the nature of their business and the regulatory environment in which they operate.[45] Unlike life in-

a need to invest relatively more in assets providing tax-exempt income in some years than in others. When underwriting income is high, property and casualty insurers invest more heavily in state and local government securities and corporate stocks than in years when underwriting income is negative or less favorable. The following section presents a more detailed analysis of the determinants of asset mix.

*Investment* results appear in the investment income account and are measured by "Net investment gain." The net investment gain includes investment income, net profits on the sale of investments, and unrealized capital gains or losses.[44] With large portfolios of common stocks, property and casualty insurers are particularly sensitive to capital gains and losses. Not only are these included in net investment gain, but they also enter into calculations of surplus. Surplus is designed in part to provide a cushion against declines in asset values, but in periods of substantial stock market

[44]In a similar manner to the underwriting account, the investment account is part of the income account. For

1977, stock companies had the following experience:

*Investment Account Summary*
*(in billions of dollars)*

| | |
|---|---|
| Investment income | $4.906 |
| Investment expenses | .259 |
| Net investment income | 4.647 |
| Net profit on sale of investments | .332 |
| Net investment profit | 4.979 |
| Unrealized capital gains or losses | (.260) |
| Net investment gain | 4.720 |

Source: *Best's Aggregates and Averages, Property-Liability, 1978.*

The annual statements of property and casualty companies show a net yield on investments. The data are not entirely comparable (in the treatment of realized capital gains and losses), but the net yield for these companies is generally lower than for life companies. This reflects lower gross before-tax yields on certain major components of the portfolios of property and casualty companies, namely, tax-exempts and corporate stocks (where dividend yields are the relevant measure).

[45]Scholarly analytic studies of the optimal asset mix of property and casualty insurance companies have been quite limited. However, the recent work by Professors Kahane and Nye has been an important first step in remedying this shortcoming in the literature. In particular, Kahane and Nye have sought to develop an efficiency frontier linking asset mix directly with the liability struc-

**Figure 7-7  Combined Underwriting and Investment Gain Experience of Stock Property-Casualty Companies[a]**

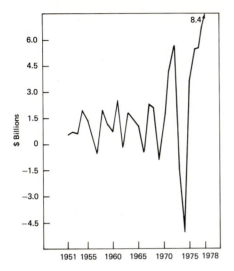

[a] Includes investment income.

Source: A.M. Best Data Center, *Best's Aggregates and Averages, Property-Liability, 1979.*

*Safety of Principal*  The need to meet policyholders' claims in timely fashion dictates considerable emphasis on the safety of principal. Statutory regulations are also quite strict on this aspect of investment policy, permitting only high-grade assets in the portfolios of property and casualty insurers. There are no restrictions on the purchase of federal government securities, but for purchases of either public utility or state and local government obligations, the issuing body cannot ever have been in default of either principal or interest for many years. Even stricter requirements are applicable to the obligations of industrial corporations where, among the requirements, a debt-paying history of both principal and interest must be established. Similar requirements exist for corporate equities.

*Investment Return*  Any financial institution attempts to maximize its effective yield consistent with an acceptable level of risk, and property and casualty insurers are no exception to this general rule. The more effectively they meet this objective, the less will be the total premium outlays for policyholders or the greater the rate of return on surplus or net worth. Stock companies are often more aggressive in their investment policy than mutual companies inasmuch as they are prepared to accept somewhat greater risk in order to increase the profitability of their investments.

Another reason insurers attempt to maximize return is to obtain as high a degree of inflation protection as possible. The costs of repair and replacement of property as well as of personal liability claims have risen rapidly in recent years, and this has encouraged many companies to seek ways to protect the real value of their assets. Many companies have felt that one way of meeting this objective was to concentrate more assets in common stocks in an effort to obtain the advantages of price appreciation. Such a policy has not always been successful, however. In the poor stock market environment of 1973–1974, for example, property and casualty insurers encountered the same problem as other large investors in equities in those years, with many of the gains from appreciation in earlier periods being sizably reduced.

*Diversification*  Property and casualty insurers seek to diversify their asset holdings in an effort to reduce the risks inherent in any portfolio of assets where the return is uncertain. The management

surance companies, property and casualty insurance companies typically purchase their assets in the secondary market since they require a high degree of marketability to assure their ability to meet liabilities as they arise. This factor is particularly important because, as mentioned earlier, these companies are unable to estimate future claims with a high degree of accuracy. In the preceding section, the discussion focused on the reserves and net worth side of the balance sheets of property and casualty insurers. This section discusses the factors that influence the distribution or allocation of funds among alternative investment outlets. Many of these are directly related to regulatory requirements for the industry, which is one of the most closely regulated in the United States.

ture of these companies and to test their model by using data on nineteen insurance lines and two types of assets for the period 1956–1971. See Yehuda Kahane and David Nye, "A Portfolio Approach to the Property-Liability Insurance Industry," *The Journal of Risk and Insurance* (December 1975), 579–598.

policy of property and casualty insurers gives strong support to the principle of diversification and, in most cases, adopts more conservative standards than the regulatory authorities require.

The regulatory requirements on diversification of assets are quite extensive, giving due regard to investment concentration by geographic regions, by industry, and by investment media. State insurance statutes are both restrictive and prescriptive. They restrict the amounts that may be invested with any one borrower by limiting those funds to a stated percentage of assets (typically 5 to 10 per cent). Percentage limitations for various broad classes of issuers are also set and are more stringent for the riskier potential acquisitions. Investments to meet capital requirements are carefully prescribed. In the case of New York State, for example, at least 60 percent of minimum capital requirements must be in federal government obligations (or in those guaranteed by it) or obligations of New York State and its political subdivisions (with some relaxation for out-of-state insurers).

*Federal Taxation* Stock companies, and mutuals since 1962, are taxed at the full corporate income tax rate. However, mutual companies do receive some permanent and temporary deferrals of portions of their underwriting gains.[46] Tax-exempt obligations of state and local governments, therefore, are favored over corporate debt by the need for tax relief in years when investment and underwriting experiences are good. Corporate stocks also enjoy considerable favor for tax reasons because of the provision for the exclusion of 85 percent of intercorporate dividend payments from taxation. In addition, long-term capital gains are taxed at lower rates.

*Liquidity and Marketability*[47] Property and casualty underwriters sell policies that cover the in-

[46] For a general discussion of the federal tax law as well as state and local tax laws pertaining to property and casualty insurers, see John D. Long and Davis W. Gregg, eds., *Property and Liability Insurance Handbook*, Richard D. Irwin, Homewood, Ill., 1965, Chap. 66.

[47] The views on liquidity and marketability expressed in this section of the chapter have been questioned recently in an article on asset-liability management in the property and casualty area. The relevant finding of the authors is that investment policy need not become relatively more conservative as risk increases in the insurance portfolio. See Kahane and Nye, "A Portfolio Approach," 594–596.

sured for a relatively shorter time period than life insurers. Companies writing property and casualty insurance, therefore, often place substantial stress on liquidity. The need for instruments that can be converted into cash quickly also requires that no serious loss of value should be incurred. Hence, property and casualty companies prefer bonds and stocks with high investment quality and ready markets. However, the maintenance of adequate liquidity and marketability for property and casualty companies has been particularly burdensome for investment officers in recent years. In the 1970s inflation accelerated, raising the amount of individual claims but, at the same time, it was also a critical factor in the move to higher interest rates. As interest rates rose to new highs, the market value of fixed-income assets was reduced. Moreover, common stock losses were often significant, particularly during the dark days of underwriting losses for some companies when they were forced into distress selling of common stocks.

### Trends in Portfolio Structure

Table 7-8 shows combined assets outstanding, by type, for all classes of property and casualty insurance companies for selected years in the period since World War II. This section discusses the changes in portfolio structure in this industry and compares them with trends in the life insurance industry.

The first feature to be observed in Table 7-8 is the relatively large place fixed-income obligations occupied in the portfolios of property and casualty insurers over the entire period. Indeed, the proportion of total assets accounted for by U.S. government securities, state and local government bonds, and corporate bonds was stable at about 50 percent over much of the two decades of 1950–1970. Since 1970, however, the proportion of assets held in fixed-income obligations has grown to over 65 percent. This extraordinary change in the structure of this industry's portfolio has accompanied a move to sharply higher interest rates on these obligations in U.S. financial markets. The 1970s, however, were generally a period of weak stock market performance, and depressed and fluctuating equity values weakened the interest of property and casualty insurers in common stocks. This development, naturally, lowered the percentage of assets accounted for by common stocks and favored a

**Table 7-8 Year-End Assets of Large Property and Casualty Insurance Companies, Amounts and Percentages, Selected Years**

| | 1950 | | 1960 | | 1965 | | 1970 | | 1978 | |
|---|---|---|---|---|---|---|---|---|---|---|
| | Billions of Dollars | Percent | Billions of Dollars | Percent | Billions of Dollars | Percent | Billions of Dollars | Percent | Billions of Dollars | Percent |
| U.S. gov't. securities | $ 5.5 | 41.0% | $ 6.0 | 19.9% | $ 6.5 | 15.6% | $ 5.4 | 9.2% | $ 15.1 | 10.1% |
| State and local bonds | 1.1 | 8.2 | 8.2 | 27.2 | 10.2 | 24.4 | 16.8 | 28.7 | 62.4 | 41.8 |
| Corporate bonds | 0.6 | 4.5 | 1.7 | 5.6 | 2.6 | 6.2 | 8.6 | 14.7 | 20.3 | 13.6 |
| Preferred stocks | 0.7 | 5.2 | 0.8 | 2.7 | 1.1 | 2.6 | 1.6 | 2.8 | 4.5 | 3.2 |
| Common stocks | 2.8 | 20.9 | 8.6 | 28.6 | 14.1 | 33.7 | 16.1 | 27.5 | 20.9 | 14.0 |
| Mortgages | 0.1 | 0.1 | 0.1 | a | 0.1 | a | 0.2 | a | 0.4 | 0.3 |
| Other assets[b] | 2.6 | 19.4 | 4.7 | 15.6 | 7.2 | 17.2 | 9.9 | 16.9 | 25.5 | 17.0 |
| Total Assets | 13.4 | 100.0 | 30.1 | 100.0 | 41.8 | 100.0 | 58.6 | 100.0 | 149.1 | 100.0 |

Note: Because of rounding, components may not add to totals shown.

[a]Less than 0.1 percent.

[b]Primarily cash and premium balances.

Source: *Best's Aggregates and Averages, Property-Liability* for selected years.

growing proportion of fixed-income obligations enjoying high and climbing yields.

The shift into fixed-income obligations was not without its problems, however. These obligations are carried on balance sheets at amortized cost, but if these assets are needed to meet claims in any year, they must be sold at market values. And market values were, of course, declining over much of this period. Fortunately, the return flow from investments was substantial enough to keep investment income growing and provide some cushion to poor underwriting performance in some years.

Within the fixed-income category, corporate and state and local government bonds have increased their relative importance, while the holdings of U.S. government securities have declined dramatically. In 1950, U.S. government securities accounted for over 40 percent of all assets, but by the 1970s, this proportion had fallen to around 10 percent. The rapid growth in the industry in the postwar years meant that the gains in premiums could often pay claims and expenses, thereby reducing the need for the high degree of liquidity of the 1940s and early 1950s. Moreover, the growth in the availability of other investment alternatives contributed to the decline. Still, U.S. government securities continue to be a major source of liquidity to property and casualty underwriters, and their relative importance in the portfolio structure of these companies has diminished less than it has for life insurance companies.

The dramatic growth in holdings of state and local securities from under 10 percent of assets in 1950 to more than 40 percent in 1978 reflects the increasing concern of many property and casualty companies with obtaining tax-exempt income, particularly after the recovery from the record underwriting losses of 1975. In fact, their large acquisitions of state and local government securities have made them the third largest holder of these securities, behind commercial banks and individuals. Property and casualty insurers, therefore, are a major force in the support of the tax-exempt market.

Property and casualty insurers hold considerably more state and local debt than do life insurance companies. This is traceable to differences in the tax treatment of the two industries. Life companies do not pay taxes on that portion of net investment income necessary to meet policy reserve requirements. Property and casualty companies, by contrast, are taxed on the full amount of their net investment income without exemption; hence, the tax savings can be appreciable.

Corporate bonds have more than tripled in relative importance in the portfolios of property and casualty insurers in the last quarter century but still account for only a little over one-eighth of all assets, a much smaller proportion than for life insurance companies. The reason for the lesser importance of corporate bonds in the portfolios of property and casualty companies than of life companies is largely attributable to the types of marginal tax rate considerations just discussed. In some recent years, however, large underwriting losses served to make corporate bonds relatively more attractive. When these underwriting losses were offset against net investment income, the need for tax-exempt income for the industry was reduced. In such situations, the tax position is less significant, and the higher yields on corporate debt than on tax-exempts becomes a more important factor influencing investment behavior.

The holdings of equities have varied between one-quarter and one-third of all assets of property and casualty insurers in much of the postwar period, a much larger percentage of assets than for life companies. The nature of the claim liabilities of property and casualty insurers is markedly different from life insurers, who sell fixed-dollar claims and ordinarily wish to invest in fixed-income obligations. Rising claims for property and casualty insurers can be offset only partly by adjustments in premium rates. Therefore, the need for potential capital appreciation through the acquisition of equities is critical. An additional incentive for holding corporate equities is the tax consideration provided by the intercorporate dividend credit and the lower tax on capital gains than on other types of income.

The importance of common stocks in the combined portfolio is particularly evident in the valuation of total industry assets. Property and casualty insurance companies carry stock holdings at market value. Hence, fluctuations in market values are an important part of observed changes in assets. In recent years, the extreme fluctuations in stock market prices have made this investment medium relatively less attractive. Because they need reasonably stable or rising market values for assets to assure the availability of funds to meet claims commitments in a timely fashion, property and casualty insurers returned only cautiously to the equities market after the stock market losses of 1973–1974.

## Conclusion

Property and casualty insurers essentially provide protection against losses to policyholders and, as part of their operations, do accumulate financial assets and significantly contribute to the support of at least one important component of financial markets.

The sale of property and casualty insurance gives rise to certain liabilities, most of which are reserves for losses and unearned premiums. The policyholders' surplus (or net worth) of these companies is a useful cushion against losses in asset values and helps to insure timely payment of claims.

The asset mix of property and casualty insurers depends on both the legal requirements and the demands of the business. In general, these companies have exhibited a decided preference for investments that provide at least some tax-exempt income. They also value liquidity quite highly to insure that they can meet claims as they arise. Consistent with these and other objectives, the companies seek to maximize their yields on market investments.

## Questions

1. What are the special characteristics of saving through life insurance and pension plans?
2. Distinguish whole life insurance from term insurance and explain the significance for the intermediary role of life insurance companies.
3. In what ways is an annuity contract similar to a whole life insurance contract?
4. What are the main sources of the gross flow of investment funds to life insurance companies?
5. What are the main influences on the portfolio mix of assets held by life insurance companies?
6. What major shifts have occurred in the liabilities of life insurance companies since World War II?
7. How have shifts on the liability or product side affected the growth of assets?
8. How is the flow of investable funds through life companies affected by changes in money and credit conditions?

9. What special role do life insurance companies play in the corporate bond market?
10. In terms of the growth of financial assets, how have life insurance companies fared since World War II?
11. What reasons could be suggested for the recent trend in the insurance industry toward diversification into a broader range of insurance lines?
12. What specific characteristics of financial intermediaries do property and casualty companies possess?
13. Why would property and casualty insurers ever show a greater preference—among fixed-income securities—for corporate bonds over debt of state and local governments, considering their tax treatment?
14. What problems do common stocks pose for portfolio management in the insurance industry? Do they possess offsetting advantages?

## Selected Bibliography

American Council of Life Insurance. *Economic and Investment Report* (annual).
———. *Life Insurance Fact Book* (annual).
———. *Pension Facts* (annual).
Bishop, George A. *Capital Formation Through Life Insurance.* Richard D. Irwin, Homewood, Ill., 1976.
Commission on Money and Credit. *Life Insurance Companies as Financial Institutions.* Prentice-Hall, Englewood Cliffs, N.J., 1962.
———. *Property and Casualty Insurance Companies: Their Role as Financial Intermediaries.* Prentice-Hall, Englewood Cliffs, N.J., 1962.
Cummins, J. David. *An Econometric Model of the Life Insurance Sector of the U.S. Economy.* D.C. Heath and Company, Lexington, Mass., 1975.
Cummins, J. David, ed. *Investment Activities of Life Insurance Companies.* Richard D. Irwin, Homewood, Ill., 1977.
Dougall, Herbert E. *Investments,* 9th ed. Prentice-Hall, Englewood Cliffs, N.J., 1973, Chap. 30.
Fleuriet, Michel. "Public and Private Offerings of Public Debt: Changes in the Yield Spread." *The Bulletin,* Graduate School of Business Administration of New York University, 1 (1975).
Gregg, Davis W., and Vane B. Lucas, eds. *Life and Health Insurance Handbook.* Richard D. Irwin, Homewood, Ill., 1973.
Headen, Robert S., and J. Findley Lee. "Life Insurance Demand and Household Portfolio Behavior." *The Journal of Risk and Insurance* (December 1974).
Huebner, S. S., Kenneth Black, Jr., and Robert S. Cline. *Property and Liability Insurance.* 2nd ed. Prentice-Hall, Englewood Cliffs, N.J., 1976.
Insurance Information Institute. *Insurance Facts* (annual).

Jones, Lawrence D. *Investment Policies of Life Insurance Companies*. Graduate School of Business Administration, Harvard University, Boston, 1968.

Joskow, Paul L. "Cartels, Competition and Regulation in the Property-Liability Insurance Industry." *The Bell Journal of Economics and Management Science* (Autumn 1973).

Kahane, Yehuda, and David Nye. "A Portfolio Approach to the Property-Liability Insurance Industry." *The Journal of Risk and Insurance* (December 1975).

Levine, Sumner N., ed. *Financial Analysis Handbook II: Analysis by Industry*. Dow Jones-Irwin, Homewood, Ill., 1975, Chap. 17.

Long, John D., and Davis W. Gregg, eds. *Property and Liability Insurance Handbook*. Richard D. Irwin, Homewood, Ill., 1965.

Shapiro, Eli, and Charles R. Wolf. *The Role of Private Placements in Corporate Finance*. Graduate School of Business Administration, Harvard University, Boston, 1972.

# 8

# Insurance-Type Intermediaries: Pension Funds

Virtually everywhere in the Western world, the enormous change that has occurred in the age structure of populations in the twentieth century has prompted the growth of social devices providing income transfers to retired persons. The prevailing legal framework and relative maturity of each nation's financial system has conditioned the form assumed by each transfer system.

It is sometimes said that the United States evolved a dual retirement system—overlapping systems of income assurances to retired persons. We have both the Old Age, Survivors and Disability Insurance System (OASDI) of the federal government (known as "social security") and the diverse and vast retirement systems operated by private and governmental employers, unions, fraternal associations, and others. Because OASDI and some federally supervised retirement systems, such as Railroad Retirement, do not rely on asset accumulation, these funds are only nominally linked to the capital market. On the other hand, public and private employee pension systems rely on calculated accumulation of funds invested largely free of federal government constraints. Thus, this chapter focuses on private pension plans, private profit-sharing plans with deferred payment schemes, and the pension funds operated by state and local governments for their employees.[1]

The reason for limiting the scope of the chapter in this manner becomes fairly obvious when one looks at the numbers of persons covered by and the assets of the various types of governmental and private funds. In book value terms,[2] assets of the OASDI fund totaled $35.9 billion in 1977. At that date the Civil Service pension fund was $52.6 billion, and the Railroad Retirement fund held $2.6 billion of assets. State and local government employee funds, one of the two principal types of funds that are of interest here, totaled $130.8 billion at the same date. Of the private funds, noninsured private employee funds[3] accounted for an esti-

---

[1]A thoughtful overview of the social security system and its many problems is provided in Alicia H. Munnell, "Social Security," *New England Economic Review* (July-August 1977), 16–43.

[2]*Book value* means cost at acquisition in the case of most funds.

[3]Noninsured private employee funds generally include deferred profit-sharing funds and pension funds of cor-

mated $181.5 billion and insured pension reserves were $98.1 billion.[4] In 1975, private noninsured pension plans covered more than 30 million employees; state and local government retirement plans covered 11.2 million employees.

In short, despite the overwhelming differences in coverage, in 1977 private plans held assets more than seven times as large, and state and local funds something less than four times the assets of the OASDI fund.

This chapter will attempt to explain the role of private and state and local pension funds in the saving-investment process. Portfolio practices will be examined in light of the operational constraints imposed on these funds and the changing conditions in capital markets. We will find that pension funds have been a potent influence on the shape of financial markets, and, furthermore, that the nature of the influence has changed dramatically over the last few decades.

The passage of the Employee Retirement Income Security Act (ERISA) in 1974 ensured that pension funds will continue to change. This law has already exerted significant influence on the management of pension funds, and its numerous provisions will surely affect them greatly in the future. Virtually every aspect of pension management has been or will be touched by the act. Because of its pervasive influence, references to ERISA are frequent.

## Pension Funds in the Saving-Investment Process

Pension saving can be viewed as a part of the economy's saving-investment process on several distinct planes. On one level of abstraction, retirement saving and equilibrium levels of investment can be linked to the economy's capital stock, the rate of real output, and demographic factors.[5] This set of

---

porations, unions, multiemployer groups, and nonprofit organizations.

[4]Insured pension funds are those issued by life insurance companies. Noninsured pension funds, the subject of this chapter, are placed with a trustee—typically a bank or trust company.

[5]The discussion in this section has profited greatly from the work of John O. Blackburn, "The Macroeconomics of Pension Funds," in Joint Economic Committee, *Old Age Income Assurance, Part V, Financial Aspects of Pension Plans*, 90th Cong., 1st Sess., 1967. For a rigorous treatment, the reader should consult this reference.

associations is of profound long-run economic significance and is of the utmost importance. A second vantage point contrasts pension saving with rival forms of saving. On this level, the effect of retirement saving on the fraction of income saved is relevant. A third view looks at the pension fund as a type of financial intermediary through which saving flows materialize as loanable funds.

## The Real Investment Effects of Pension Saving

An unfunded plan does not accumulate assets; instead, benefits are paid from current income sources. These plans are frequently called pay-as-you-go plans. Although social security has a fund, its size in relation to current and prospective benefit payments is so small that social security is usually categorized as an unfunded plan. A funded plan makes provisions for future outflows by setting aside assets. The amount of assets depends on the actuarial method used. The importance of the funding distinction will become clear as the discussion unfolds; however, it should be obvious at this point that only funded pension plans are of interest as financial intermediaries.

The tie between real investment and pension saving is most easily visualized if, for expositional convenience, the assumption is made that *all* saving in an economy is for retirement. Under this assumption, there is a one-for-one parallel between reasoning with respect to a single pension fund and the entire economy.

If all saving is for retirement, the economy's capital stock must be a synonym for the pension fund. The latter is the cumulant of net fund inflows; by the same token, the economywide capital stock is simply the cumulated sum of net saving. The parallel will hold one step further: the rate of return on a pension fund is a direct analogue of real rate of return on, or productivity of, the capital stock. And this is all we need to establish a crucial point.

For any fund, it is easy to see that, given a certain working life and life expectancy of covered members, which determine the length of time benefits are paid, the rate of return on the fund governs the level of benefits. The higher the rate of earnings, the greater the capability to pay benefits, and vice versa. An alternative interpretation is possible too: if the level of benefits is fixed, rate of return must vary as either or both working life and life expectancy vary.

To an economist, the parallel generalization of this last point to the level of the economy as a whole is of paramount significance. At a level of complete generality, the real rate of return or productivity of the economy's capital stock[6] must vary as either or both working life and life expectancy vary to keep income transfers to retired persons constant at a given level. Further, if life expectancy increases or working life decreases, return on capital must rise to maintain income payments to retirees. Of course, the opposite must also hold true.

The implications of these findings for the problem of macroeconomic stability are apparent. In a dynamic economy in which demographic features (working life and life expectancy, for example) are in flux, flexibility of the real return on capital is crucially important to the maintenance of stability. If the rate of output or returns relative to the capital stock is rigid, macroeconomic equilibrium is threatened when demographic characteristics are in transition.

Some observers believe that the seeming inability of the United States economy to absorb private saving at full employment rates prior to its Vietnamese engagement in the 1960s may be linked to a sudden increase of the fraction of income saved traceable to accumulation via pension funds. Whether this hypothesis is correct or not, the existence of a mechanical link between pension saving and the productivity of capital makes it clear that flexibility of the latter will become increasingly important to the achievement of smooth economic adjustments as pension saving bulks larger in total saving.

## Pension Saving Within Total Personal Saving

Although individuals save for a variety of reasons, retirement is undoubtedly an important one. The time pattern of saving can be described using the life-cycle hypothesis of consumption-saving.[7] This hypothesis states that individuals save to smooth out their lifetime consumption. In early productive years workers save; after retirement they dissave. This changing pattern of saving over their lifetimes allows them to even out consumption over time.

Our concern is with the saving method used to fund this retirement need. Broadly speaking, there are two alternatives—nondiscretionary and discretionary. One can further segregate the nondiscretionary alternative into public and private outlets. Of particular interest is whether saving through nondiscretionary media *per se* affects the total amount of saving and, within total saving, how important nondiscretionary saving is when compared with discretionary saving.

The public form of nondiscretionary saving, social security, is not "saving" in accounting terms. Social security taxes reduce disposable income; there is normally no planned increase in assets of OASDI. But, when it is recognized that the social security system is based on a scheme of contingently guaranteed intergenerational transfers of funds, it becomes apparent why many individuals may informally or even formally consider social security as a saving vehicle. If this forced form of purchasing retirement income is treated as a close substitute for other forms of saving, its increasing importance might reduce the relative importance of other saving.

Empirical evidence supports the presumption of a substitute relationship.[8] Because social security is a type of forced saving, individuals decrease their private saving, both nondiscretionary and discretionary. However, social security has also had an impact in the opposite direction. The limitation on the amount of income that may be earned while

[7]See Albert Ando and Franco Modigliani, "The Life Cycle Hypothesis of Saving: Aggregate Implications and Tests," *American Economic Review* (March 1963), 55–89.

[8]The substitute position is strongly argued by Martin Feldstein in "The Social Security Fund and National Capital Accumulation," *Funding Pensions: Issues and Implications for Financial Markets,* Federal Reserve Bank of Boston, Conference Series No. 16, 1976; and by Alicia H. Munnell in *The Effect of Social Security on Personal Savings,* Ballinger Publishing Company, Cambridge, Mass., 1974. An example of the opposing viewpoint is Joseph A. Pechman, "Discussion," *Funding Pensions: Issues and Implications for Financial Markets,* Federal Reserve Bank of Boston, Conference Series No. 16, 1976, pp. 65–68.

[6]*Rate of return* is earnings or output relative to capital stock per unit of time. The reader may have encountered the inverse of this notion in economic literature, namely, the capital/output ratio. Where a reference is found here to return on capital or productivity of capital, it is perfectly permissible, if less handy, to read the reciprocal of the capital/output ratio.

receiving social security payments forces workers largely to drop out of the labor market once they start collecting. To compensate for this increased dissaving in retirement years, individuals must save more in early years. Furthermore, the social security retirement age of 65 has probably induced some workers to retire at 65 rather than later, causing additional compensatory increases in earlier saving. While the two changes in retirement experience have counteracted some of the effect of substitutability, the overall effect of social security on other saving appears to be modestly negative.

The other form of nondiscretionary saving is saving through private pension funds. Once again we would expect the tremendous growth in pension assets to have caused discretionary private saving to grow much less. Again, empirical evidence supports the substitute relationship.[9] Workers with larger expected retirement benefits save less than those without large benefits. During two recent decades, when pension assets grew rapidly, private pension saving as a percentage of personal saving rose from about 20 percent in 1950 to 30 percent in 1970.[10]

The increase in popularity of pensions as a form of retirement saving may be the result of cost advantages. Pension plans that meet IRS requirements (known as *qualified plans*) have a number of tax advantages: within limitations, employers can deduct the pension cost as an expense; workers defer payment of tax on the employer contribution until benefits are received; and earnings of pension funds are tax exempt. There are also efficiencies of the group administration of annuities and opportunities to gain access to higher-earning investments in pension plans.

The evidence indicates that nondiscretionary and discretionary forms of saving are substitutes. They

are not perfect substitutes, however, and their relationship is quite complex. The existence of pension plans has affected the work experience of individuals, and this has further effects on the need for saving. The environment is also changing: confidence in the social security system is declining; less reliance is placed on the guarantee of intergenerational transfers of funds. One can only conjecture as to the effect of this loss of confidence on other forms of saving. Finally, the future growth of pension plans *vis-à-vis* other savings forms may be affected by the recent liberalization of laws relating to pension plans set up by individuals. Because some of the advantages of pensions discussed earlier have been bestowed on individuals, this may lessen the attractiveness of some group pension plans.

### Pension Funds as Intermediaries and Flows of Loanable Funds

A third perspective from which to visualize pension saving looks at the funds as financial intermediaries linking funds-surplus and funds-deficit units in the economy through the financial markets. This conception of pension funds puts them in their most familiar terms.

Prolonged debate among financial economists over the last few years has resulted, if nothing else, in focusing on the issue of whether or not financial intermediaries possess the capability of augmenting the supply of loanable funds through their own actions. Some may consider the issue still moot, but when one considers the characteristics of flows through pension funds there is little doubt that, while some intermediaries may function this way, pension funds do not. Rather, one must conclude that pension funds act as rather passive conduits of a flow of loanable funds determined elsewhere. Put in the terms of theory, pension funds as intermediaries do not affect the position of the supply schedule of loanable funds.

Loanable funds may emanate from three sources: (1) saving out of current income by surplus units; (2) dishoarding, or acceleration of the turnover rate, or velocity, of the money stock; and (3) net additions to the money stock. Clearly, pension funds are not associated with the last of these. Pension funds have no mechanism for creating money within any of the received definitions. It is

[9] For evidence of the substitute relationship, see Alicia H. Munnell, "Private Pensions and Saving: New Evidence," *Journal of Political Economy* (October 1976), 1013–1032. Earlier studies hypothesizing a positive effect are Philip Cagan, *The Effect of Pension Plans on Aggregate Saving: Evidence From a Sample Survey,* National Bureau of Economic Research Occasional Paper No. 95, Columbia University Press, New York, 1965; and George Katona, *Private Pensions and Individual Saving,* Monograph No. 40. Survey Research Center, Institute for Social Research, The University of Michigan, Ann Arbor, 1965.

[10] Private-pension saving excludes saving through public retirement systems. Personal saving includes retirement saving plus saving for all other purposes.

equally clear that pension fund accumulation does fall within the first category, net saving out of current income. However, this saving flow is quasi-contractual and deeply embedded in terms of employment; it will not easily vary outside narrow limits. Hence, the funds cannot increase or decrease this flow through their actions alone. A legitimate question, though, relates to the second source: can pension funds succeed in increasing the supply of loanable funds by reducing the demand for money or, conversely, by accelerating the turnover of the money stock? If acceleration of velocity is to be effected by pension funds, it must perforce take the form of an intensified rate of exchange of claims on the funds for money inflows or outflows per unit of time. However, acquisition of claims on pension funds takes place only as contributions are made on account of covered service. Furthermore, benefits are paid only on stated conditions. Hence, acquisition and discharge of claims is nondiscretionary. No apparent means exists, therefore, for pension funds to affect fund inflows through manipulation of claims as deposit intermediaries do. Thus, we can dismiss the last possible connection between pension funds and shifts in the supply schedule of loanable funds. Rather, pension funds are truly middlemen in transferring net saving out of current income to ultimate borrowers.

## The Foundations of Portfolio Policy

The touchstone of a pension fund's portfolio policy is the long period of sustained growth that it may usually anticipate with confidence. Other influences are material but of lesser importance.

### Actuarial Foundations and the Time Horizon of Net Growth

An understanding of some basic actuarial concepts and paralleling terminology is fundamental to the examination of portfolio policy. Pension plans are of two major types: defined-benefit and defined-contribution. A *defined-benefit plan* promises a periodic fixed payment to workers after retirement. The amount of the payment is determined by a schedule usually relating years of service and income to benefits. The sponsor of the plan (a corporation, for example) bases its contributions to the fund on actuarial assumptions. In other words, the benefit is treated as given and the contributions are variable. With a *defined-contribution plan* the annual pension contribution is fixed by the pension plan and the benefit is variable. The investment experience of the fund determines the actual level of benefits.

Notions of actuarial solvency or actuarial soundness as they are applied to pension funds relate the present value of future benefits payments, the present value of future contributions to the fund, and the value of assets on hand. *Actuarial solvency* requires that assets presently held plus the present value of future contributions must equal the present value of anticipated benefits. For defined-benefit plans, actuaries make assumptions about mortality, employee turnover, retirement age, salary scales, discount factors, and other inputs—depending on the nature of the particular plan—to arrive at the present value of benefits. An infinite number of contribution patterns over the life of the plan will yield the required-contribution present value. However, actuaries have devised a limited number of actuarial cost methods that are actually used to calculate annual contributions. In each case the annual contribution is separated into the portion relating to the present value of benefits earned during the year (the normal cost) and to the present value of benefits earned in prior years (the past service cost). This latter category arises for two reasons: first, when pension plans are initiated, coverage is usually extended to workers for years of service prior to the initiation date. Second, each time the pension plan is modified to increase the level of benefits, the portion of the increase relating to years of service prior to the date of change must then be funded. Typically, the annual pension contribution includes all normal cost plus a portion of the past service cost. The latter is normally amortized over a number of years.

Despite the variety of plans and funding methods, a simplified, abstract picture of the growth of a fund has expository usefulness. To begin the analysis of prolonged growth, assume the existence of a fund associated with a pension plan that "promises" to retired persons a level of benefits determined principally, let us say, by years of service and level of wages. Imagine, now, an employee who enters the coverage of the plan at, say, twenty-five years of age. If the employee does not change employers and retires at age sixty-five, credited service of forty years will result. Therefore, the "liability" of the fund with respect to our hypothetical employee will be to make payments after forty years, depending in amount and nature upon the kind of benefit promised. At the point of retirement, that portion of the fund attributable to our employee should equal the present value of the stream of future payments expected. Over the forty working years, contributions to the fund together with their earnings must cumulate to equal the discounted value of this stream of payments. Since earnings and demographic characteristics are not precisely foreseeable, required contributions must be estimated actuarially.

Net growth of the fund as a whole takes place so long as contributions on behalf of covered and currently employed workers exceed the payments made to retirees. Crudely, a pension fund would peak in size when the number of retired persons receiving benefits bulked large enough relative to active covered employees so that inflows of contributions on their account exactly met benefit payments. As benefits paid exceeded contributions, assets would, perforce, be liquidated to finance the net difference.

A startling implication of all this is that the period of prospective net growth of a new fund is at least a generation in length. Several influences may act separately or together to delay, possibly indefinitely, the date when net growth stops. Foremost, and often the most powerful among the possibilities, is continued expansion of the covered active work force. If expansion in the number of covered employees is great enough, expansion alone can lead to growth in current contributions more than sufficient to defray current benefit payments. Liberalization of promised benefit payments to currently active employees can lead to the same result. Higher anticipated benefit levels lead to greater current contributions. Without offsetting developments, the margin of current contributions over current benefit payments will increase.

The same model of net accumulation does not apply without qualification to retirement funds using defined-contribution–variable-benefit schemes or to profit-sharing plans. The inflow of contributions to the former type will vary directly with the number of covered employees and not on the basis of actuarial estimates. Net growth will occur, as in the case of fixed-benefit plans, so long as contri-

butions on behalf of active employees exceed disbursements to retired workers. Net growth of deferred-benefit profit-sharing plans will be the net result of the vagaries of employer profits and fund earnings.

## Predictability of Fund Outflows

With the exception of minor operating costs and the withdrawal of employee contributions when an employee leaves a plan, the only cash outflow from a fund is for benefit payments. Save for exceptions that prove the rule, withdrawals (payments) from a fund are not discretionary; they occur only under stated or determinable conditions. In short, employees cannot draw at will upon the fund; there are no demand liabilities. With respect to benefits to retired employees, uncertainties are few and minor. New retirements are the only occasion for starting new benefit payments, and retirements are known in advance from age schedules, especially as employee turnover is slight in upper age brackets. Mortality, before and after retirement, is predictable from experience within narrow limits. Thus, in the absence of demand obligations, actuarially predictable forces and semicontractual benefit schedules lead to cash outflows foreseeable within narrow limits.

It is difficult to exaggerate the force of the foregoing for pension-fund portfolio policy. An expectation of long-term, sustained, net asset growth implies that cash outflows for benefit payments will be "financed" by current cash inflows. In short, the principal of the fund need not be invaded to meet benefit payments. Without the hazard of forced liquidation, a pension fund can hold long-term debt and common stocks and expect to wait out changes in their market price. Thus, bonds and stocks are a common item in pension-fund portfolios. The commonness of fixed liabilities accounts for the early dominance of bonds in pension-fund portfolios and for their continued prominence.[11]

---

[11]Note that the immediate operational key to the lack of liquidity needs is the positive fund inflows. With a change in demographics, this fund inflow could change to an outflow. An interesting speculation is the effect on net flows of currently changing birthrates and composition of the populace. Liquidity may become a more important issue in the future.

## Accounting Latitude

At one time freedom from constrictive accounting was another important element in the ability to hold variable-valued securities. Valuation of assets was discretionary, but most funds carried assets at cost, not reflecting market-price variations. Parties at interest tended to subordinate effects of fluctuations in market value of assets (together with their accounting reflection) when making portfolio decisions.

The environment of accounting for pension assets, however, has altered appreciably in recent years. The accounting profession has presumably taken a position with respect to reporting to the parties at interest, namely the trustees, the sponsor, and the plan participants. Although generally accepted accounting principles permit a variety of valuation methods, there seems to be a growing commitment to disclosure of market-value information along with cost.[12] In fact, ERISA requires that market-value data be provided to plan participants. Considering the volatility of asset values this may have the effect of reducing the freedom to hold variable-valued assets. This is especially true as declining asset prices would force actuaries to require larger pension payments to maintain fund solvency.

At this writing, the ultimate extent of the influence that will be exerted on management of pension assets by extended reporting and valuation of assets at market is unpredictable.

## Tax Exemption

Investment income of both corporate and state and local government funds is exempt from federal income taxation. Thus, the tax-exempt status of state and local government bonds is meaningless to pension funds. The same implication applies to the tax treatment of profit realized from interest payments on bonds or dividends versus capital gain (or loss!) in the case of stocks.

If tax exemption of income to the investor has no real meaning, yields from state and local gov-

ernment bonds are inferior. Thus, their appearance in the assets of pension funds is anomalous.

Meaninglessness of the preferential tax treatment of capital gains implies that pension funds find neither virtue nor harm in trading for profit versus receipt of income in dividends or interest. The decision to trade versus buy-and-hold, therefore, rests entirely on other grounds.

## Alternative Uses of Fund Earnings

Earnings on fund assets can be used to increase benefits or to reduce the contributions required by a given level of benefits. An oft-quoted statistic is that, for funds having "typical" experience otherwise, an increment of one percentage point in rate of return on the portfolio can decrease contributions by approximately 20 percent or raise benefits by approximately one-fourth.

Leverage exerted by fund earnings interacts with the benefit pattern in motivating the parties at interest. If a plan promises fixed benefit levels, the employer can trade off, in essence, fund earnings for contributions or barter the elbow room given by enlarged earnings for higher benefit levels. This goes far toward explaining the determined drive over the last few years, particularly among corporate employers, for aggressiveness in fund investments, specifically the drive, until recently, toward common-stock usage.

The apparent motivations of the different parties are responsible, in part, for the division of responsibilities in fund portfolio policy.

## Legal Constraints

*Private Pension Plans*   Legal requirements of private pension plans are proscriptive rather than prescriptive. Until 1974 the major federal legislation affecting private plans was the Internal Revenue Code and the Welfare and Pension Plans Disclosure Act of 1958. Both of these were rather weak in their demands. In 1974 Congress passed the Employee Retirement Income Security Act (ERISA). Unlike its predecessors, this law imposes stringent requirements on private pension plans. A number of state statutes require disclosure but, in general, they are weak.

In point of fact, a corporate trustor can impose any circumscription on a trustee. Nominally, there-

---

[12] For an excellent treatment of the accounting and operating procedures for pension plans, see Felix Pomeranz, Gordon P. Ramsey, and Richard M. Steinberg, *Pensions: An Accounting and Management Guide*, The Ronald Press Company, New York, 1976.

fore, the latitude of trust statutes matters only in discretionary trusts. In the fishbowl existence of trustees, however, the touchstone of the law must surely play a role in any portfolio policy that they advocate.

Circumstances converged to force upon trust officers the virtues of common stock after World War II. Rapid price-level increases eroded the real value of fixed-price securities as well as the income they generated. Fears of postwar economic collapse gave way with recovery from the 1949 recession, and the stock market recovered from its depressed level of early postwar years. Investment officers of many different stripes argued persistently that institutional investments should incorporate increased proportions of common stock. In 1950, perseverance by the New York State Bankers Association secured liberalization of New York's statutes to an intermediate position between the mandatory legal list and full freedom of the prudent man rule. This rule states, in effect, that the security acquisitions by those serving in a fiduciary capacity must be of such high quality as to induce their purchase by a conservative investor using personal funds. After the liberalization of the statutes, discretionary investments were then permitted to the extent of 35 percent of a trust. The strong swing of corporate pension trust investments to common stock went into motion shortly afterward.

The prudent man rule subsequently became applicable to pension trusts in most states. A few problems prevented this from becoming a fully workable governing system. First, because there was no federal statute imposing the prudent man rule, not all private pensions were subject to the constraint. Second, the prudent man rule had been developed primarily through personal trust court decisions, and its applicability to pension management was in doubt. Third, the prudent man rule could be avoided by adding an exculpatory clause in the trust agreement. ERISA sought to overcome these problems by declaring that ERISA superseded all state laws. A prudent man concept was applied to all private pension trusts and exculpatory clauses were forbidden.[13] Much confu-

sion remains about the actual application of this rule, and we will have more to say about it later on.

*State and Local Government Plans*  Statutory circumscription of the state and local government-administered funds is, by contrast, confining. Federal law, including ERISA, does not apply to public pension plans. Although extension of ERISA to these plans has been proposed, there is little likelihood of this occurrence. There is, however, the possibility of individual states passing laws with some of ERISA's provisions. State law usually establishes a class of investments legal for the funds. Sometimes the law states directly what the permissible investments are; in some cases, the law states that investments legal for financial institutions, such as savings banks, in that state are legal for public employee pension funds, possibly with an exclusion, such as mortgages. In a few instances, investments legal for public funds of the state are the investments legal for public employee pension funds.

Laying aside the precise character of state statutes, there is little question but that they tend toward the illiberal. Thus, in 1970, funds administered by eight states did not hold any corporate equities. Many states liberalized their laws, but the potential of diverse investment for public funds is still less than for private funds.

No-default, no-arrearages imperatives are common. Such tests may or may not be stated in conjunction with requirements that bonds held must lie in the top two or three grades as established by two out of the three widely recognized rating agencies. Some states add industry limitations. Quality tests for state and local government bonds usually include a minimum-population stipulation for the issuing jurisdiction and a maximum relationship between outstanding indebtedness of the issuer and assessed or market property values. Sometimes only full faith and credit bonds are permitted.

For most funds, preferred stock must stand a test of earnings coverage. Also, when permitted, common stock often must meet quality tests, some of dubious value. Sustained cash dividend records and the requirement that a subject corporation must earn a certain percentage of par or stated value would fall among the latter. The common specification that stock must be listed on a public exchange is more understandable.

[13] For a broader treatment of the prudent man rule and ERISA, see Robert C. Pozen, "The Prudent Person Rule and ERISA: A Legal Perspective," *Financial Analysts Journal* (March-April 1977), 30–35.

## The Influence of Administrative Structure and the Division of Interest

Administrative considerations and the characteristics of the quasi-legal and legal framework that embraces the parties at interest influence profoundly the investment policy of a given fund. Table 8-1 indicates that banks and trust companies manage roughly two-thirds of private noninsured pension fund assets, while only about 15 percent of private noninsured funds are self-managed. Although similar statistics are not available for state and local government pension funds, the proportion of self-management among them is much higher.

*Externally Administered Private Funds* Institutional trusteeship and its broad alternative, self-administration, exert characteristic influences on portfolio theory. External trusteeship adds to the potpourri of governing forces, the elaborate structure of formal trust agreements, the characteristics of institutional investing, and the evolving mores of the fiduciary world.

Trust officers live under a system where rewards for success are rather fixed, but penalties for failure are severe. This is true in purely monetary terms where fees and salaries tend strongly to a slowly

**Table 8-1 Management of Private Noninsured Pension Funds Market Value (in billions of dollars)**

| Managed by | 1972 | 1973 | 1974 | 1975 |
|---|---|---|---|---|
| Banks and trust companies | $104.6 | $ 87.8 | $ 73.4 | $ 93.5 |
| Self-managed[a] | 23.7 | 20.6 | 17.2 | 21.8 |
| Broker-dealers | 2.2 | 1.9 | 1.7 | 2.6 |
| Other investment advisors | 23.9 | 21.9 | 19.4 | 27.7 |
| Total | 154.4 | 132.2 | 111.7 | 145.6 |
| *Percentages* | | | | |
| Banks and trust companies | 67.7 | 66.4 | 65.7 | 64.2 |
| Self-managed | 15.3 | 15.6 | 15.4 | 15.0 |
| Broker-dealers | 1.4 | 1.4 | 1.5 | 1.8 |
| Other investment advisors | 15.5 | 16.6 | 17.4 | 19.0 |
| Total | 100.0 | 100.0 | 100.0 | 100.0 |

[a]Those plans that are self-managed by banks, trust companies, broker-dealers, and other investment advisors are not included in this item, but instead are included under their respective category.

Source: Securities and Exchange Commission, *Statistical Bulletin* (November 1976).

moving modest norm, but penalties can be loss of an account and possibly a career. Penalties at the extreme could be a surcharge by a court for negligence. Clearly, in a transparent world where invidious comparisons are forever being drawn, where rewards are modest and penalties severe, departures and innovations will come slowly. The nominally fixed-payment promise of most corporate pension trusts neatly provides a rationale that converges with the sustained, painful, legal and environmental constraints on the trustee to produce bond-dominated portfolios.

A formidable, yet practical, consideration is the problem of flexibility faced by the bank trust departments. In the case of most large banks, a small staff must handle huge amounts of trust funds, including personal and other trusts as well as pension funds. With limited personnel, investing and investment policy must be formulated in broad terms admitting of comparatively little discrimination at the level of individual accounts. Buying and selling typically takes place in large lots, and there is not always time for negotiation of private transactions, particularly small ones. Thus, maneuvering takes place in coarse terms.

The instability that comes from overwhelming dominance of a given predisposition led to swift, widespread change of pension-fund portfolio policy among externally trusteed funds after the early 1950s. Watchful waiting for the first move led to uniformity and slow change, but a decisive switch of new fund inflows toward common stock by a few prestigious trust departments produced a veritable parade of followers.

A deed of trust can delegate all, some, or none of the investing authority for a pension fund. That is, a trust department can serve merely as custodian, as custodian and investor, as custodian and part of a joint authority over investment, or, in rarer instances, as investment adviser only.

We lack the necessary data to be certain of the mix of relationships currently prevailing among externally trusteed funds. Even if these statistics were available, though, it is certainly not obvious that the truth would be evident from them. The rise of pension costs, the realization among employers of the power of portfolio earnings, the drama of the securities markets in the 1950s and 1960s, and the departures in portfolio policy they evoked produced a determined drive by many corporate managers for improved portfolio earnings. Various devices were used to motivate the external trustees in this regard. A common device calls for distributing a given fund among several managers and keeping track of comparative earnings. Sometimes comparative earnings data are supplied to the managers concerned for the obvious purpose. In some instances, these data serve as the basis for an explicit incentive system, such as funneling new contributions to the higher-earning funds or making disbursements from the funds having lesser performance. In sum, for many companies, resignation and credulity in dealing with institutional trustees were replaced by aggressiveness and close scrutiny. Thus, irrespective of the formal arrangement of trust instruments, standards of investing performance applied to the external trustee are far more exacting now than in earlier years of pension-fund history.

In sum, externally administered private pension funds evolved from simple security devices constructed to finance fixed, known liabilities to the current view of them as assets subject to aggressive use by employers to minimize the cost of an unknown level of future commitments. One authority was moved to the following statement in this regard:

> The problem of investment management, then, is not to earn any particular rate but to earn the best possible rate which investment opportunities permit. . . . The fund is not analogous to life insurance assets or to a personal trust or to an investment company or to any other financial institution. It is *sui generis*. There is simply no other type of trust fund like it.[14]

*Self-Administered Private Funds* A number of major corporations eschewed the encumbrances of institutional trusteeship for the supposed advantages of self-administration. In their investing activities, these externally trusteed funds are, of course, simply the tangible manifestation of the employer's will. Virtually all prerogatives rest with the employer where trusteeship and administration are performed by officers of the corporation or by a board appointed by the corporation.

In the case of large funds directly administered by the employer, full-time professional managers and staffs are the investing alter egos of corporate management. A good number of billion-dollar funds and more funds of several hundreds of millions of dollars fall into this category. More than any other single illustration, they are an expression of the drive by management to employ pension-plan assets aggressively as a resource operating indirectly to defray retirement costs. The success of aggressive leaders in portfolio management exerted an influence over other funds of the same administrative form as well as over the externally trusteed funds. As a generality to which there are some notable exceptions, the larger employer-administered funds moved more swiftly and perhaps farther than others in the direction of maximizing earnings. They did this for the most part by enlarging the proportions of common stock and, sometimes, by including higher-risk equities in the portfolio. One well-known fund led the way in the purchase of equity-sweetened privately placed debt issues.

*State and Local Government-Administered Funds* Several features of the administration of state and local government funds influence their investment policy. As a rough generality, the level of the administering authority affects the portfolio through the sophistication it brings to investment.

To understand the relevance of the multitude of political levels of administration, one must appreciate their great diversity. Without exaggeration, there are instances of authorities involved in fund administration from very nearly the lowest local level through the highest state offices. Within a given state, it is not unusual to find a large fund of, say, the public school teachers invested by a body at the state level. Similarly, state employees may be covered by a fund administered at the same level, but city and/or county employees may be covered under funds administered by their elected local officials. Roughly, higher levels of government bring larger, more capable staffs, more effort, and more sophistication to the problem of using the fund assets to maximum earnings advantage than do lower levels of administering authority. In any given comparision, however, size disparities of the fund reverse this relationship for the simple reason that economies of scale make it possible to maintain investing staffs for large, but not for small, funds. City-administered funds may well be as large as state-administered funds—at least in the case of major metropolitan areas within a given state—and,

[14]Joint Economic Committee, *Old Age Income Assurance: Part V, Financial Aspects of Pension Plans,* 90th Cong., 1st Sess., p. 83.

of course, it is certainly true that city funds of major metropolitan areas are larger than the funds administered by many smaller states. Thus, level of authority and sophistication of fund management are related, but only loosely.

The interests of employees and government are protected and implemented formally by representation of administering boards of trustees. Informally, though, control of investments and investment policy within legally defined limits falls mostly into the hands of the financial officer of the administering government. Typically, state and local government retirement funds are administered by boards of trustees (often called the retirement board) comprised invariably of governmental representatives and frequently include employee representatives. The former are either members appointed by the executive officer of the administering government or are members *ex officio,* such as the state insurance commissioner, the commissioner of banking, the state treasurer or controller, the superintendent of education, and so forth. Local officials serve in this capacity at the lower levels. It seems to be uniformly true, though, that the financial officer is a member of the trustees whether by appointment or *ex officio.* Employee representation may be appointive or elected. State law might provide, for instance, that several members of the retirement board may be appointed from the membership of the retirement system, sometimes on a rotating basis.

In formal terms, a system of administration such as this is replicated at each level of government that administers a retirement fund, but an important qualification must be added. The stock of trained personnel thins out badly at the lower end of the scale of governments and there may, in effect, be no financial officer to serve on the board of trustees. The town accountant or auditor will be employed instead, and although he may know more about the investment problem than other members of the board, his perspective is usually not great.

The most important implication of this power structure is the extent of discretion left by default in the hands of the financial officer representing the administering government. That officer is charged formally with the task of representing the interests of the government, particularly its budgetary pressures. Equally important, that officer must report to the administrative hierarchy about his or her representation of its interests as well as be a trustee

for the employees covered by the retirement system. In short, he wears more than one hat. In addition, it is very often the case that other trustees are wholly untutored in financial affairs and knowingly abdicate their responsibility for investment policy and investment selection to the financial officer.

Some large funds employ an investment officer to winnow out securities being offered and to make investments or investment recommendations. When these functions devolve on an untrained person, as is often the case with local governments, the problem is sometimes solved by completely avoiding policy formation and investment selection by taking a path of least resistance—for example, exclusive investment in government securities.

### The History of Asset Holdings and Gross Fund Flows

Portfolio policy determines the channels taken by savings flows through financial intermediaries to the capital markets and, thence, to the economy's real investment process. Hence, it is important to analyze the asset composition and the nature of growth for private and public employee pension funds.

### Asset Holdings and Private Noninsured Funds

Statistics relating to the years before the 1950s are meager. Data are sufficient, however, to indicate that private noninsured funds were not quantitatively imposing.

It appears that assets of private employee funds failed to reach the billion-dollar mark until the late 1930s—in 1938, according to one estimate.[15] This much is certain: annual increases in assets ran only in the tens of millions of dollars through the 1930s. However, net asset increases rose sharply during World War II, and by the latter part of the 1940s, they were well up into the hundreds of millions of dollars annually. By 1950, total estimated assets were $5.2 billion. In that year net growth was $900 million, and the era of proliferating plans and mushrooming assets was at hand.

[15]Raymond W. Goldsmith, *A Study of Saving in the United States*, Princeton University Press, Princeton, N.J., 1955, Vol. I, Table 4-15.

Portfolio breakdowns for these earlier years are, if anything, shakier than figures on asset totals. Despite this, it may be said that private funds before the 1950s were confined overwhelmingly to investment in U.S. government securities and corporate bonds. Corporate stock played only a minor role.

We must rely on statistics of the Securities and Exchange Commission for information on the portfolio history of private funds after 1950. While these data allow us to paint a fairly complete picture of the nature of pension investment, we must be careful not to impute an unrealistic degree of accuracy to the figures.

Table 8-2 shows that, at book value, the assets of private funds rose by $144.1 billion in the thirteen years ending with 1978. A growth rate of roughly 10 percent carried the total at that date to $202.2 billion.[16]

One invariant feature of assets—perhaps the only one—was full financial investment. The dollar amount of cash held drifted upward but, in the face of strong asset growth, generally stayed below 2 percent. This policy of minimal liquidity reflects the underlying structural features of fund management mentioned earlier.

Broad shifts in portfolio policy are evident in Table 8-2. Corporate and other bonds decreased in proportion to the total portfolio throughout most of the period from 39.1 percent to 26.6 percent, and preferred stock, unimportant in 1965, continued to decline further to less than 1 percent of assets in 1978. U.S. government securities, which declined from about 30 percent of assets in the early 1950s to 5.2 percent in 1965, continued to slide until 1975 when there was an increase. By 1978, U.S. government securities totaled 9.7 percent of assets. The other major category of fixed-income investment—mortgages—showed a steady decline throughout the period and is now proportionately insignificant.

Common stocks continued the portfolio rise begun in the 1950s. By 1978, equities, at book value, amounted to 49.7 percent of all assets. It is interesting to note, however, that the peak level was

[16]In terms of market value, assets increased from $66.2 billion in 1966 to $201.5 billion in 1978, for a slightly larger growth rate. The difference in value is primarily related to the common-stock portfolio. The market value of stock holdings totaled $106.7 billion in 1978.

63.7 percent in 1973. During 1974 there was actual disinvestment in common stocks and, in 1975, 1977, and 1978, net new investment was modest. This moderation of the change in equity holdings coincided with an increased investment in U.S. government securities. The reasons for this are threefold. First, stock prices began a sharp decline in 1974. Second, interest rates at the time were very high, especially on short-term securities such as U.S. Treasury bills. These two factors together changed the relative attractiveness of equities and U.S. government securities for many investors, including pension funds. A third possible reason for the shift was the passage of ERISA in 1974.

### Gross Fund Flows of Private Noninsured Funds

Consideration of gross flows of funds through private noninsured pension funds highlights their activities in capital markets and permits analysis of their role as major financial intermediaries.

The data in Table 8-3, which relate only to the private noninsured funds flow, lay bare the sources of spectacular growth. In 1965 the net inflow was $6.4 billion, and by 1975 the comparable figure was $13.9 billion. Behind this, of course, lay the increasing annual gross inflows to the funds. Both sources and uses of funds are revealed in detail in Table 8-3. The table also shows the changes over time caused by growing maturity of these intermediaries.

Increasing maturation of pension funds normally brings with it two notable developments. One sign of maturity is the rising importance of investment income among inflows. In the decade prior to 1965 the percentage of gross inflows attributable to investment income doubled from about 12 to 24 percent, and there has been little change since then. The cause of this stabilization is the liberalization of benefit levels in existing pension plans. In recent years much attention has been placed on the pension portion of total wages. As promised benefits are increased, past service costs rise and so must contributions. The increase in contributions has caused the investment-income portion of funds flows to remain constant on a percentage basis. Relative contributions of employer and employee have been changing toward a larger share for employers. Finally, while unrealized capital gains and

Table 8-2　Assets of Private Noninsured Pension and Deferred Profit-Sharing Funds,[a] 1965–1978[b] (in billions of dollars)

| | 1965 | 1966 | 1967 | 1968 | 1969 | 1970 | 1971 | 1972 | 1973 | 1974 | 1975 | 1976 | 1977 | 1978 |
|---|---|---|---|---|---|---|---|---|---|---|---|---|---|---|
| Cash and deposits | $ .9 | $ .9 | $ 1.3 | $ 1.6 | $ 1.6 | $ 1.8 | $ 1.6 | $ 1.9 | $ 2.3 | $ 4.3 | $ 3.0 | $ 2.2 | $ 3.7 | $ 8.1 |
| U.S. government securities | 3.1 | 2.6 | 2.3 | 2.8 | 2.8 | 3.0 | 2.7 | 3.7 | 4.4 | 5.5 | 10.8 | 14.7 | 20.1 | 19.7 |
| Corporate and other bonds | 22.7 | 24.5 | 26.4 | 27.0 | 27.6 | 29.7 | 29.0 | 28.2 | 30.3 | 35.0 | 37.8 | 39.0 | 45.6 | 53.8 |
| Preferred stock | .8 | .8 | 1.0 | 1.3 | 1.8 | 1.7 | 1.8 | 1.5 | 1.3 | 1.1 | 1.2 | 1.3 | 1.2 | 1.3 |
| Common stock | 24.5 | 28.3 | 34.9 | 41.7 | 47.9 | 51.7 | 62.8 | 74.6 | 80.6 | 79.3 | 83.7 | 93.4 | 97.0 | 100.4 |
| Mortgages | 3.3 | 3.8 | 4.1 | 4.1 | 4.2 | 4.2 | 3.7 | 2.7 | 2.4 | 2.4 | 2.4 | 2.4 | 2.5 | 2.8 |
| Other assets | 2.8 | 3.2 | 4.2 | 4.6 | 4.7 | 4.9 | 4.8 | 5.0 | 5.2 | 6.1 | 6.4 | 7.5 | 11.4 | 16.1 |
| Total assets[c] | $58.1 | $64.0 | $74.2 | $83.1 | $90.6 | $97.0 | $106.4 | $117.6 | $126.5 | $133.7 | $145.3 | $160.5 | $181.5 | $202.2 |
| *Percentages* | | | | | | | | | | | | | | |
| Cash and deposits | 1.5 | 1.4 | 1.8 | 1.9 | 1.9 | 1.9 | 1.5 | 1.6 | 1.8 | 3.2 | 2.1 | 1.4 | 2.0 | 4.0 |
| U.S. government securities | 5.3 | 4.1 | 3.1 | 3.4 | 3.1 | 3.1 | 2.5 | 3.1 | 3.5 | 4.1 | 7.4 | 9.2 | 11.1 | 9.7 |
| Corporate and other bonds | 39.1 | 38.3 | 35.6 | 32.5 | 30.5 | 30.6 | 27.3 | 24.0 | 24.0 | 26.2 | 26.0 | 24.3 | 25.1 | 26.6 |
| Preferred stock | 1.4 | 1.3 | 1.3 | 1.6 | 2.0 | 1.8 | 1.7 | 1.3 | 1.0 | .8 | .8 | .8 | .7 | .6 |
| Common stock | 42.2 | 44.2 | 47.0 | 50.2 | 52.9 | 53.3 | 59.0 | 63.4 | 63.7 | 59.3 | 57.6 | 58.2 | 53.4 | 49.7 |
| Mortgages | 5.7 | 5.9 | 5.5 | 4.9 | 4.6 | 4.3 | 3.5 | 2.3 | 1.9 | 1.8 | 1.7 | 1.5 | 1.4 | 1.4 |
| Other assets | 4.8 | 5.0 | 5.7 | 5.5 | 5.2 | 5.1 | 4.5 | 4.3 | 4.1 | 4.6 | 4.4 | 4.7 | 6.3 | 8.0 |
| Total assets[c] | 100.0 | 100.0 | 100.0 | 100.0 | 100.0 | 100.0 | 100.0 | 100.0 | 100.0 | 100.0 | 100.0 | 100.0 | 100.0 | 100.0 |

[a]Book value
[b]Includes deferred profit-sharing funds and pension funds of corporations, unions, multiemployer groups, and nonprofit organizations.
[c]Figures may not add to totals because of rounding.

Source: Securities and Exchange Commission, various issues of *Statistical Bulletin*.

**Table 8-3  Flow of Funds Through Private Noninsured Pension Funds, 1965–1975 (in billions of dollars)**

| | Inflows | | | | | | Outflows | | | |
|---|---|---|---|---|---|---|---|---|---|---|
| | Contributions | | Investment Income | Capital Gain | Other Income | Total Gross Inflow | Benefit Payments | Expenses | Total Outflow | Net Inflow of Funds |
| Years | Employer | Employee | | | | | | | | |
| 1975 | $19.828 | $1.604 | $6.703 | $(1.659) | $.107 | $26.583 | $12.334 | $.263 | $12.597 | $13.986 |
| 1974 | 16.971 | 1.460 | 5.982 | (3.477) | .127 | 21.063 | 10.740 | .290 | 11.030 | 10.033 |
| 1973 | 14.370 | 1.270 | 4.840 | (.920) | .110 | 19.670 | 9.310 | .230 | 9.540 | 10.130 |
| 1972 | 12.740 | 1.200 | 4.300 | 1.720 | .100 | 20.070 | 8.300 | .200 | 8.490 | 11.580 |
| 1971 | 11.320 | 1.120 | 4.100 | .900 | .100 | 17.540 | 7.080 | .180 | 7.260 | 10.280 |
| 1970 | 9.720 | 1.070 | 3.870 | (1.590) | .130 | 13.200 | 6.030 | .150 | 6.180 | 7.020 |
| 1969 | 8.490 | 1.010 | 3.550 | .990 | .110 | 14.150 | 5.290 | .140 | 5.430 | 8.720 |
| 1968 | 7.700 | .890 | 3.190 | 1.260 | .100 | 13.150 | 4.500 | .120 | 4.620 | 8.530 |
| 1967 | 7.040 | .790 | 2.940 | 1.000 | .060 | 11.820 | 3.880 | .120 | 3.990 | 7.830 |
| 1966 | 6.360 | .710 | 2.670 | .520 | .070 | 10.330 | 3.380 | .110 | 3.480 | 6.840 |
| 1965 | 5.600 | .670 | 2.390 | .570 | .050 | 9.280 | 2.800 | .090 | 2.880 | 6.400 |

*Percentages (of total gross inflows)*

| | | | | | | | | | | |
|---|---|---|---|---|---|---|---|---|---|---|
| 1975 | 74.6 | 6.0 | 25.2 | (6.2) | .4 | 100.0 | 46.4 | 1.0 | 47.4 | 52.6 |
| 1974 | 80.6 | 6.9 | 28.4 | (16.5) | .6 | 100.0 | 51.0 | 1.4 | 52.4 | 47.6 |
| 1973 | 73.1 | 6.5 | 24.6 | (4.7) | .1 | 100.0 | 47.3 | 1.2 | 48.5 | 51.5 |
| 1972 | 63.5 | 6.0 | 21.4 | 8.6 | .5 | 100.0 | 41.4 | 1.0 | 42.3 | 57.7 |
| 1971 | 64.5 | 6.4 | 23.4 | 5.1 | .6 | 100.0 | 40.4 | 1.0 | 41.4 | 58.6 |
| 1970 | 73.6 | 8.1 | 29.3 | (12.0) | 1.0 | 100.0 | 45.7 | 1.1 | 46.8 | 53.2 |
| 1969 | 60.0 | 7.1 | 25.1 | 7.0 | .8 | 100.0 | 37.4 | 1.0 | 38.4 | 61.6 |
| 1968 | 58.6 | 6.8 | 24.3 | 9.6 | .8 | 100.0 | 34.2 | .9 | 35.1 | 64.9 |
| 1967 | 59.6 | 6.7 | 24.9 | 8.5 | .5 | 100.0 | 32.8 | 1.0 | 33.8 | 66.2 |
| 1966 | 61.6 | 6.9 | 25.8 | 5.0 | .7 | 100.0 | 32.7 | 1.1 | 33.7 | 66.2 |
| 1965 | 60.3 | 7.2 | 25.8 | 6.1 | .5 | 100.0 | 30.2 | 1.0 | 31.0 | 69.0 |

Source: Securities and Exchange Commission, various issues of *Statistical Bulletin*.

losses are not included in investment income in Table 8-3, they are part of total investment return. As the stock market became depressed in recent years, private pensions suffered considerable capital losses on their portfolios. Table 8-3 reflects only realized losses.

A second sign of maturation is that benefits paid by private pension funds have reached levels high enough to absorb significant proportions of gross inflows. This is visible either directly, in the percentage of benefits paid relative to gross funds inflows or, indirectly, in the steady downward drift of the relationship of net to gross inflows. Benefit payments now absorb almost half of all cash flowing into these funds.

In a macrofinancial context, the points of greater importance are the continuous growth of net annual fund inflows and the minor yearly variations in growth rate. This net annual flow is virtually a synonym for one important component of the economy's saving. Moreover, with negligible changes in cash held by the funds, it is a synonym for the annual net money flows to the securities markets through the pension-plan conduit.

## Asset Holdings of State and Local Government Funds

Employee funds administered by state and local government, like private funds, were also marked by slow growth until the 1950s. During the early years, these funds invested almost completely in U.S. government and state and local government bonds.

Portfolio practices took a dramatic turn in the late 1950s. Many of the changes are evident from Tables 8-4 and 8-5. These tables should be examined together because of the dissimilarities among subaggregates.

Total assets grew from $31.8 billion to $142.6 billion over the period 1965–1978. The annual growth rate of 12 percent slightly overshadowed the growth rate of private funds over the same period.

As with private funds, cash held was proportionately insignificant over the period. This holds more strongly for state-administered than for local funds, but, as a generality, is true at both levels. In 1965, U.S. government securities were an important part

**Table 8-4  Assets of All State and Local Government-Administered Employees Retirement Funds, 1965–1978 (in billions of dollars)**

| | 1965 | 1966 | 1967 | 1968 | 1969 | 1970 | 1971 | 1972 | 1973 | 1974 | 1975 | 1976 | 1977 | 1978 |
|---|---|---|---|---|---|---|---|---|---|---|---|---|---|---|
| Cash | $ .3 | $ .3 | $ .4 | $ .5 | $ .5 | $ .5 | $ .6 | $ .8 | $ 1.1 | $ 1.5 | $ 2.0 | $ 1.4 | $ 1.7 | $ 2.4 |
| U.S. government securities | 7.4 | 7.0 | 6.7 | 6.1 | 5.8 | 5.2 | 4.5 | 3.7 | 3.5 | 5.3 | 6.6 | 9.2 | 12.2 | 18.4 |
| State and local government bonds | 2.7 | 2.5 | 2.4 | 2.4 | 2.4 | 2.2 | 2.0 | 2.4 | 1.5 | 1.4 | .7 | 3.1 | 3.6 | 3.7 |
| Nongovernmental securities | 21.4 | 25.3 | 29.7 | 34.7 | 40.2 | 47.1 | 54.5 | 61.8 | 72.3 | 79.2 | 88.7 | 97.7 | 106.0 | 118.0 |
| Corporate bonds | 15.1 | 17.7 | 20.3 | 23.3 | 26.7 | 30.1 | 34.7 | 37.9 | 43.3 | 47.4 | 53.6 | 57.4 | 56.8 | 63.9 |
| Corporate stocks | 1.4 | 1.8 | 2.4 | 3.3 | 4.9 | 6.9 | 9.5 | 12.6 | 17.1 | 19.6 | 21.8 | 24.6 | 28.0 | 31.3 |
| Mortgages | 3.4 | 4.1 | 4.8 | 5.3 | 5.5 | 6.6 | 6.9 | 7.0 | 6.8 | 6.6 | 7.3 | 7.9 | 10.9 | 10.5 |
| Other | 1.4 | 1.8 | 2.2 | 2.8 | 3.1 | 3.5 | 3.5 | 4.3 | 5.1 | 5.7 | 6.0 | 7.8 | 10.3 | 12.3 |
| Total assets[a] | $31.8 | $35.3 | $39.3 | $43.7 | $48.9 | $55.0 | $61.6 | $68.7 | $78.4 | $87.4 | $98.0 | $111.4 | $123.5 | $142.6 |
| *Percentages* | | | | | | | | | | | | | | |
| Cash | .9 | .8 | 1.1 | 1.1 | 1.0 | .9 | 1.0 | 1.2 | 1.4 | 1.7 | 2.0 | 1.3 | 1.1 | 1.7 |
| U.S. government securities | 23.3 | 19.8 | 16.9 | 14.0 | 11.9 | 9.5 | 7.3 | 5.4 | 4.5 | 6.1 | 6.7 | 8.3 | 9.9 | 12.9 |
| State and local government bonds | 8.5 | 7.1 | 6.2 | 5.5 | 4.9 | 4.0 | 3.2 | 3.5 | 1.9 | 1.6 | .7 | 2.8 | 2.9 | 2.6 |
| Nongovernmental securities | 67.3 | 71.7 | 75.7 | 79.4 | 82.2 | 85.6 | 88.5 | 90.0 | 92.2 | 90.6 | 90.5 | 87.7 | 85.8 | 82.7 |
| Corporate bonds | 47.5 | 50.1 | 51.7 | 53.3 | 54.6 | 54.7 | 56.3 | 55.2 | 55.1 | 54.2 | 54.7 | 51.5 | 46.0 | 44.8 |
| Corporate stocks | 4.4 | 5.1 | 6.1 | 7.6 | 10.0 | 12.5 | 15.4 | 18.3 | 21.8 | 22.4 | 22.2 | 22.1 | 22.7 | 22.0 |
| Mortgages | 10.7 | 11.6 | 12.2 | 12.1 | 11.2 | 12.0 | 11.2 | 10.2 | 8.7 | 7.6 | 7.4 | 7.1 | 8.8 | 7.4 |
| Other | 4.4 | 5.1 | 5.6 | 6.4 | 6.3 | 6.4 | 5.7 | 6.3 | 6.5 | 6.5 | 6.1 | 7.0 | 8.3 | 8.2 |
| Total assets[a] | 100.0 | 100.0 | 100.0 | 100.0 | 100.0 | 100.0 | 100.0 | 100.0 | 100.0 | 100.0 | 100.0 | 100.0 | 100.0 | 100.0 |

[a] Figures may not add to totals because of rounding.

Source: U.S. Bureau of the Census, various annual issues of *Finances of Employee-Retirement Systems of State and Local Governments*.

**Table 8-5  Assets of State and Local, State, and Locally Administered Retirement Funds[a] 1965, 1977, 1978 (in billions of dollars)**

| | 1965 | | | 1977 | | | 1978 | | |
|---|---|---|---|---|---|---|---|---|---|
| | State and Local | State | Local | State and Local | State | Local | State and Local | State | Local |
| Cash | $ .3 | $ .2 | $ .2 | $ 1.7 | $ .8 | $ .9 | $ 2.4 | $ 1.3 | $ 1.1 |
| U.S. government securities | 7.4 | 5.2 | 2.2 | 12.2 | 9.5 | 2.7 | 18.4 | 14.3 | 4.0 |
| State and local government bonds | 2.7 | .9 | 1.8 | 3.6 | .6 | 3.0 | 3.7 | .3 | 3.4 |
| Nongovernmental securities | 21.4 | 15.8 | 5.5 | 106.0 | 84.0 | 22.0 | 118.0 | 94.0 | 23.7 |
| Corporate bonds | 15.1 | 10.6 | 4.5 | 56.8 | 45.4 | 11.5 | 63.9 | 51.3 | 12.6 |
| Corporate stock | 1.4 | 1.2 | .3 | 28.0 | 21.7 | 6.2 | 31.3 | 24.4 | 6.9 |
| Mortgages | 3.4 | 3.0 | .4 | 10.9 | 10.2 | .6 | 10.5 | 9.8 | 0.7 |
| Other | 1.4 | 1.0 | .4 | 10.3 | 6.7 | 3.6 | 12.3 | 8.9 | 3.5 |
| Total assets[b] | $31.8 | $22.1 | $ 9.7 | $123.5 | $94.9 | $28.5 | $142.6 | $110.4 | $32.2 |
| | | | *Percentages* | | | | | | |
| Cash | .9 | .9 | 2.1 | 1.1 | .8 | 3.2 | 1.7 | 1.2 | 3.4 |
| U.S. government securities | 23.3 | 23.5 | 22.7 | 9.9 | 10.0 | 9.5 | 12.9 | 13.0 | 12.4 |
| State and local government bonds | 8.5 | 4.1 | 18.6 | 2.9 | .6 | 10.5 | 2.6 | 0.3 | 10.6 |
| Nongovernmental securities | 67.3 | 71.5 | 56.7 | 85.8 | 88.5 | 77.2 | 82.7 | 85.1 | 73.6 |
| Corporate bonds | 47.5 | 48.0 | 46.4 | 46.0 | 47.8 | 40.4 | 44.8 | 46.5 | 39.1 |
| Corporate stock | 4.4 | 5.4 | 3.1 | 22.7 | 22.9 | 21.8 | 22.0 | 22.1 | 21.4 |
| Mortgages | 10.7 | 13.6 | 4.1 | 8.8 | 10.7 | 2.1 | 7.4 | 8.9 | 2.2 |
| Other | 4.4 | 4.5 | 4.1 | 8.3 | 7.1 | 12.6 | 8.6 | 8.1 | 10.9 |
| Total Assets[b] | 100.0 | 100.0 | 100.0 | 100.0 | 100.0 | 100.0 | 100.0 | 100.0 | 100.0 |

[a]Local funds include cities and all other local levels of government.
[b]Figures may not add to totals because of rounding.

Source: See Table 8-4.

of portfolios at all levels, accounting for 23.3 percent overall. By 1973 the continuing trend toward the relative reduction in federal securities brought this percentage down to 4.5. In the following five years, the U.S. government proportion rose from its nadir to 12.9 percent. Most likely, this shift has the same cause as a similar shift by private funds, namely, yield differentials changing to favor government securities.

State and local securities, a major holding in the 1950s, amounted to only 8.5 percent of all public fund assets in 1965. This proportion decreased to a low point in 1975 of 0.7 percent. Then, in 1976, there was an increase to 2.8 percent. Interestingly, most of the increase came within the local funds. This increase is puzzling. To a tax-free investor, tax-exempt yields are not competitive with those of taxable securities having an equal risk. One guess is that public pension plans administered by financially troubled authorities increased their investment in these assets in order to supply a market for troubled securities. Table 8-6 provides some

support for this hypothesis. In 1976, New York State-administered funds increased their holdings of state and local government securities by $1.0 billion, equivalent to the net addition of all state plans. At the same time, New York City-administered plans provided $1.4 billion to this market, an amount equal to all city pension fund flows into the state and local security market. Considering both return and risk, the prudence of such a move on the part of these funds must be questioned. By 1978 most of the holdings of tax-exempt securities had been eliminated by the state-administered funds, but tax-exempt holdings of the city-administered funds continue to expand.

In dollar terms, holdings of corporate bonds grew tremendously from $15.1 billion in 1965 to $63.9 billion in 1978 but, on a percentage basis, the growth was moderate. Still, corporate bonds are now the major investment for public funds at 44.8 percent of all assets. State funds are slightly more invested in these securities than those of local governments.

**Table 8-6  New York State–Administered and New York City–Administered Employee Retirement Fund Holdings of State and Local Government Securities (in thousands of dollars)**

|  | 1975 | 1976 | Increase, 1975 to 1976 | 1978 | Increase, 1975 to 1978 |
|---|---|---|---|---|---|
| State administered: |  |  |  |  |  |
| General | $72,237 | $ 756,527 |  | $187,851 |  |
| Teachers | — | 339,000 |  | 28,940 |  |
| Total | $72,237 | $1,095,527 | $1,023,290 | $216,791 | $144,554 |
| City administered: |  |  |  |  |  |
| General | $165,088 | $ 856,541 |  | $1,658,121 |  |
| Policemen | 98,729 | 264,739 |  | 407,839 |  |
| Firemen | 11,711 | 73,521 |  | 94,966 |  |
| School employees | 6,295 | 26,295 |  | 66,035 |  |
| Teachers | 109,994 | 617,264 |  | 1,125,070 |  |
| Total | $391,827 | 1,838,360 | $1,446,533 | $3,352,031 | $2,960,204 |
| Total increase in holdings |  |  | $2,469,823 |  | $3,124,758 |

Source: See Table 8-4.

Mortgages have enjoyed some following in public portfolios. After reaching a maximum of about 12 percent during the late 1960s, growth declined so that mortgages accounted for only 7.4 percent of assets in 1978. Differences between types of public funds are important, with states investing in them to the extent of 8.9 percent in 1978 and local governments only 2.2 percent.

The growth in corporate stock held by public funds was dramatic. Starting with only 4.4 percent of assets comprised of stock in 1965, public funds added $29.9 billion to their portfolios by 1978 to raise the proportion in stock to 22.0 percent. The last few years saw this percentage hold fairly constant as the stock market slumped.

Fragmentary evidence has indicated the existence of variations in portfolio policy between funds of different sizes and between regions of the country. The simple truth, however, is that the raw data are not rich enough and/or the investigatory work is as yet too shallow to enable us to speak with much power or conviction about such issues as the influence of fund size on asset policy.

### Gross Fund Flows of State and Local Government Funds

Table 8-7 provides summary data of the gross funds flows through state and locally administered pension plans. The local category includes cities as well as other forms of local government.

Total gross inflows rose steadily for all three types of public pension funds for the period 1965–1978. Within the positive trend of total inflows some important changes occurred. As with private funds, the employee contributions to public funds declined substantially. This decline was met partially by an increase in employer contributions, in this case contributions of state and local governments. However, the relative size of the governmental contribution is substantially lower than the corresponding employer contribution for private funds. The other major source of funds to public pensions has been investment income. This, too, has been increasing as a percentage of total inflows.

A sign of maturation is the increasing percentage of gross cash inflows absorbed by benefit payments. Local and city plans pay out in benefits a higher portion of total funds received than state plans. However, over the last decade, the difference has narrowed. State-administered plans showed an increase of about 4 percentage points in the portion of inflows paid out in benefits, while the other plans experienced a slight decline of the same statistic. It is unclear, however, how much of this difference is attributable to maturation and how much to low funding rates.

The last major element of fund outflows, withdrawals, was rather volatile between 1965 and 1978.

Overall, public funds enjoyed large increases in gross fund inflows in the last decade. Although outflows also grew, the relatively constant ratio

**Table 8-7  Flow of Funds Through State and Locally Administered Public Employee Retirement Systems, 1965, 1978 (in billions of dollars)**

| Administered by | Year | Inflows | | | | | Outflows | | | |
| --- | --- | --- | --- | --- | --- | --- | --- | --- | --- | --- |
| | | Contributions | | | Investment Income | Total Gross Inflow[a] | Benefit Payments | Withdrawals | Total Outflow[b] | Net Inflow of Funds |
| | | Employee | State Govt. | Local Govt. | | | | | | |
| State | 1978 | $4.619 | $5.704 | $4.263 | $6.868 | $21.455 | $6.821 | $.990 | $7.811 | $13.644 |
| | 1965 | 1.208 | .994 | .582 | .849 | 3.632 | .995 | .243 | 1.238 | 2.394 |
| Local | 1978 | 1.068 | .123 | 3.529 | 1.807 | 6.528 | 2.728 | .234 | 2.963 | 3.565 |
| | 1965 | .418 | .042 | .800 | .368 | 1.628 | .690 | .080 | .770 | .858 |
| | | | | | *Percentages* | | | | | |
| State | 1978 | 21.5 | 26.6 | 19.9 | 32.0 | 100.0 | 31.8 | 4.6 | 36.4 | 63.6 |
| | 1965 | 33.3 | 27.4 | 16.0 | 23.4 | 100.0 | 27.4 | 6.7 | 34.1 | 65.9 |
| Local | 1978 | 16.4 | 1.9 | 54.1 | 27.7 | 100.0 | 41.8 | 3.6 | 45.4 | 54.6 |
| | 1965 | 25.7 | 2.6 | 49.1 | 22.6 | 100.0 | 42.4 | 4.9 | 47.3 | 52.7 |

[a] Figures may not add to totals because of rounding.
[b] Negligible amount of expenses not separately itemized.

Source: See Table 8-4.

of net inflows to gross inflows translated into a large overall growth in public pension assets. This increased their impact on the financial markets.

## Pension Funds in the Securities Markets

Demands on the financial markets trace back, directly and indirectly, to the participation of real investors in the economy's saving-investment process. The most proximate association of pension funds with the saving-investment process is via the financial markets, and so this section traces the recent history of net issues of various financial assets and net purchases by pension funds.

In general, pension funds are not significant suppliers of funds to the market for U.S. government securities or to real estate, either directly or indirectly. Earlier portfolio figures showed private pension funds in 1978 holding $19.7 billion of U.S. government securities and the public employee funds holding $18.4 billion of such securities. Except to indicate their truly minuscule role, it serves little purpose to compare these holdings with the $487.5 billion of marketable government securities outstanding in 1978 and even less purpose to compare yearly net purchases by the funds with growth in the total outstanding.

Likewise, it is not particularly informative, except in a negative way, to trace the net acquisitions of mortgages by pension funds to their aggregate holdings of $13.3 billion in 1978 against a backdrop of more than $1 trillion of mortgages then outstanding. An interesting speculation is whether this small degree of market participation may change with the increased use of mortgage-backed securities.

In point of bald fact, pension funds are noteworthy as suppliers of funds only to the markets for corporate and state and local government bonds and the market for corporate stock. Table 8-8 contains the record of net issues of these securities for 1964 to 1978. Throughout the 1964–1978 period, the corporate world emerged as the principal recipient of pension money supplied to the capital market. Although there has been substantial yearly variation, in dollar amounts the total investment in corporate debt has been upward. To a total increase of $314.8 billion outstanding for the fifteen-year period, private noninsured funds contributed increases in their holdings of $35.7 billion and public funds added $68.2 billion.

The movement into the corporate stock market is even more dramatic. Although there has been a slowdown during the past few years, the investment was huge. Public funds acquired $30.4 billion and private funds $83.1 billion despite the fact that corporations sold only $94.8 billion of new stock during the period. Acquisition by pension funds equaled all of net new issues and more. Indeed, this increase in pension-fund activity in the stock market is a matter of concern to many observers.

Although public pension plans were once large holders of state and local government securities, Table 8-8 clearly indicates a current contrary trend. From 1964 through 1975, the net investment in these securities by public funds was −$2.8 billion. In 1976 the situation reversed, with public funds investing $2.4 billion. However, this departure from the trend was explained by the activity of a few funds rather than the inclinations of the entire group (New York funds in particular).

### Pension Plans and Inflation

The effects of inflation are numerous, and they are often difficult to sort out. Some, such as the effects of inflation on total saving and its composite effects on the various types of saving, while interesting, are clearly beyond our scope. It is doubtful that they are known, and they may or may not be discoverable. However, we can make some direct observations about the effects of inflation on pension-fund operations.

Inflation affects pension plans directly, both through its effects on pension benefits and the return on pension-fund assets. The effect on benefits depends on the nature of the specific plan but, because promised benefits are usually tied to future salaries, inflation is a positive and direct spur to benefits and, thus, costs. Pension costs are further magnified by inflation for plans that provide beneficiaries with cost-of-living increases after retirement. To the extent that the actual returns are positively correlated with inflation, there is a counterbalancing influence. The net effect depends on the nature of cost-of-living increases in benefits and whether or not and, if so, to what degree, returns are positively correlated with inflation.[17,18]

---

[17] For a rigorous treatment of the effects of inflation on pension costs, see Howard E. Winklevoss, *Pension*

**Table 8-8 Net Issues of Corporate Bonds and Stocks and State and Local Government Bonds and Net Acquisitions by Pension Funds, 1964–1978 (in billions of dollars)**

| | 1964 | 1965 | 1966 | 1967 | 1968 | 1969 | 1970 | 1971 | 1972 | 1973 | 1974 | 1975 | 1976 | 1977 | 1978 |
|---|---|---|---|---|---|---|---|---|---|---|---|---|---|---|---|
| *Net issues of* | | | | | | | | | | | | | | | |
| State and local government securities | $6.0 | $7.3 | $5.6 | $7.8 | $9.5 | $9.9 | $11.2 | $17.4 | $14.7 | $14.7 | $16.5 | $16.1 | $15.7 | $23.7 | $28.3 |
| Corporate and foreign bonds | 6.8 | 8.1 | 11.1 | 16.6 | 14.4 | 13.8 | 23.3 | 23.5 | 18.4 | 13.6 | 23.9 | 36.4 | 37.2 | 36.1 | 31.6 |
| Corporate stock[a] | 1.5 | .3 | 1.1 | 2.5 | .6 | 5.2 | 7.7 | 13.7 | 13.8 | 10.4 | 4.8 | 10.8 | 12.9 | 4.9 | 4.7 |
| *Net acquisition of* | | | | | | | | | | | | | | | |
| *State and local government securities by* | | | | | | | | | | | | | | | |
| All state and local employee funds | (.4) | (.4) | (.2) | (.1) | — | — | (.2) | (.2) | .4 | (.9) | (.1) | (.7) | 2.4 | .5 | .1 |
| State-administered funds | (.2) | (.3) | (.1) | (.1) | — | (.1) | — | (.1) | .2 | (.4) | — | (.1) | 1.0 | (.6) | (.3) |
| Locally administered funds | (.2) | (.1) | — | (.1) | — | .1 | (.2) | (.1) | .2 | (.5) | (.1) | (.6) | 1.4 | 1.1 | .4 |
| *Corporate and foreign bonds by* | | | | | | | | | | | | | | | |
| All state and local employee funds | 1.8 | 1.8 | 2.6 | 2.6 | 3.0 | 3.4 | 3.4 | 4.6 | 3.2 | 5.4 | 4.1 | 6.2 | 3.8 | 8.3 | 7.0 |
| State-administered funds | 1.4 | 1.2 | 1.8 | 1.9 | 2.6 | 3.1 | 2.7 | 3.5 | 3.4 | 4.3 | 3.1 | 4.7 | 3.4 | 7.2 | 5.9 |
| Locally administered funds | .4 | .6 | .7 | .8 | .4 | .3 | .8 | .9 | (.1) | .9 | 1.0 | 1.5 | .4 | 1.1 | 1.1 |
| Noninsured corporate funds | 1.4 | 1.2 | 1.7 | 4.0 | .6 | .6 | 2.1 | (.7) | (.8) | 2.1 | 4.7 | 2.8 | 1.2 | 6.5 | 8.2 |
| *Corporate stock by* | | | | | | | | | | | | | | | |
| All state and local employee funds | .2 | .3 | .4 | .6 | .9 | 1.6 | 2.0 | 2.6 | 3.1 | 4.5 | 2.5 | 2.2 | 2.8 | 3.4 | 3.3 |
| State-administered funds | .2 | .3 | .3 | .4 | .7 | 1.1 | 1.4 | 1.9 | 2.2 | 2.9 | 2.6 | 1.7 | 2.6 | 2.7 | 2.7 |
| Locally administered funds | — | .1 | — | .2 | .2 | .5 | .6 | .7 | .9 | 1.6 | (.1) | .4 | .3 | .6 | .7 |
| Noninsured corporate funds | 2.6 | 3.5 | 3.5 | 8.2 | 6.8 | 6.2 | 3.8 | 11.1 | 11.6 | 6.0 | (1.3) | 4.4 | 9.7 | 3.6 | 3.4 |

[a]Excludes shares of open-end investment companies.

Source: Federal Reserve *Flow of Funds Accounts*, 1946–1975; *Flow of Funds Accounts*, August 1978; also, derived from Tables 8-2, 8-4, and U.S. Bureau of Census, various annual issues of *Finances of Employee-Retirement Systems of State and Local Governments* by taking net differences from year to year; Securities and Exchange Commission, *Statistical Bulletin*, various issues.

Properly, investors are interested in the real returns from financial assets. Therefore, as the rate of price rise intensifies, investors will demand higher nominal rates of return as compensation for loss in purchasing power.[19] However, the change in nominal returns will be determined by a variety of complex factors in addition to investor demands. Furthermore, the degree of adjustment may be different for various classes of financial assets.

Although we cannot say how well actual returns will adjust to future inflation, we do have empirical evidence concerning the historical level of real returns for various financial assets. These data provide some insight into the reasonableness of the assumption that the effects of inflation on pension asset returns will be realized.

The major work, and the basis for later work, on the returns of common stock was done by Fisher and Lorie.[20] They found that over the period 1926–1965, the compound rate of return on common stocks was 9.5 percent. Because this substantially exceeded the inflation rate of the period, that figure has since been used as the basis of a claim that common stocks are a hedge against inflation. However, the realized return is quite sensitive to the time period chosen for study.

A more recent study updated the Fisher-Lorie work and, in addition, looked at real returns for other financial assets.[21] For the period 1926–1974,

stocks returned 8.5 percent per year compounded annually and, after adjusting for inflation, 6.1 percent. This overall return, however, disguises variability in year-to-year returns. The average annual return for common stocks deflated for inflation was 8.8 percent, but the range of values was 53.5 to −43.7 percent. Eighteen of the forty-nine annual periods showed negative returns. Extreme variability was also evident in the results for other financial assets. Inflation-adjusted corporate-bond returns had an average annual return of 1.4 percent and a range of 23.5 to −13.9 percent. Eighteen years showed negative returns. Holding periods other than one year showed much less range, but still showed substantial variability between time periods.

The implications for pension-fund portfolio management are that we cannot assume that the favorable effects of inflation will always cancel out the negative effects, and common stocks are not always preferable to other financial assets—corporate bonds, for one. The trend toward pension-fund investment in corporate equities in the 1960s and early 1970s and the subsequent emphasis on bonds in the last few years may well indicate recognition of this last fact. Unfortunately, the evidence on inflation and security returns is so limited that little more can be said about the effects of inflation on the investment selections of pension funds. Additional questions relating to the real incidence of inflation on pension sponsors and beneficiaries must await research.

## Pension Funds and Investment Theory

During the 1960s and 1970s investment theory made dramatic advances. This section attempts to state theory's challenge to the management of pension funds.

### Investment Theory

The proposition that financial markets are efficient rests in part on the presumption (or argument) that information is quickly and inexpensively disseminated through financial markets.[22] The result, it is

---

*Mathematics with Numerical Illustrations,* Richard D. Irwin, Homewoood, Ill., 1977.

[18]For a theoretical discussion and empirical test of market efficiency, inflation, and interest rates, see Eugene F. Fama, *Foundations of Finance,* Basic Books, New York, 1976, Chap. 6. For applications to common stocks, see Papers and Proceedings of the American Finance Association, *Journal of Finance* (May 1976), 447–487.

[19]This relationship is known as the Fisher Effect. See Irving Fisher, *The Theory of Interest,* Macmillan, New York, 1930.

[20]Lawrence Fisher and James Lorie, "Rates of Return on Investments in Common Stock," *Journal of Business* (January 1964), 1–21; and Fisher and Lorie, "Rates of Return on Investments in Common Stock: The Year-by-Year Record, 1926–1965," *Journal of Business* (July 1968), 291–316.

[21]Roger G. Ibbotson and Rex A. Sinquefield, "Stocks, Bonds, Bills and Inflation: Year-By-Year Historical Returns (1926–1974)," *Journal of Business* (January 1976), 11–47. See also Alexander Robichek, Richard Cohn, and John Pringle, "Returns on Alternative Investment Media and Implications for Portfolio Construction," *Journal of Business* (July 1972), 427–443.

[22]See Fama, *Foundations of Finance,* Chap. 5, for a formal specification of the theory and review of much of the empirical evidence.

said, is that security prices at any time fully reflect all available information and, thus, current prices are the best estimates of value. The implications of this for investment managers are twofold. First, most research efforts will be valueless or even wasted because it is unlikely that the research will uncover new information of economic value. Second, because all investment managers have available the same information, they should not attempt individually to outguess the market consensus by actively trading securities.

Risk, defined in terms of variability of returns, must also be explicitly considered in making portfolio choices.[23] Variability in individual security returns can be divided conceptually into diversifiable and nondiversifiable components. All of the diversifiable risk may be eliminated so that the remainder relates to the composite riskiness of all securities in the market. Theory asserts that, regardless of their risk preferences, investors should hold as assets the "market" portfolio composed of a weighted combination of all securities in the market. Variations in individual risk preferences are satisfied in theory by purchasing riskless assets along with the market portfolio (lowering risk) or by borrowing additional money to further invest in the market portfolio (raising risk). In the abstract a distinction between promissory and nonpromissory assets is not required.

Modern investment theory concludes that active portfolio management is not profitable. Because assets are efficiently valued, there can be no expected windfall gain and transaction costs will be incurred by trading. In theory, a pension fund should buy a market portfolio of securities, adjust risk level by added borrowing or by investing in riskless assets, and make infrequent changes in proportionate asset composition.

## Pension Investment Performance

A number of researchers have measured the performance of private pension funds without complimentary results—with only a few exceptions.[24]

After adjusting for risk, funds managed by banks and independent investment advisors underperformed the market. Where funds were able to earn a higher return than the market rate, it was because those funds accepted levels of risk higher than the market portfolio's risk.[25]

Consistent with theoretical predictions, managers trying to manage funds actively ended with below-market returns. For the most part, pension funds would have been better off following efficiently diversified buy-and-hold strategies. This last statement should be qualified because the efficient market theory does not claim that no one can outperform the market, only that consistent outperformance should be rare.

## Applicability of Investment Theory to Pensions

Despite the conclusions of the previous two sections regarding investment theory and pension-fund performance, there may be barriers to their use. One difficulty confronting managers intent on applying the principles of modern investment theory is the question of whether or not these principles are consistent with the prudent man rule. Recall that ERISA imposed the prudent man rule on all pension funds. Because the statute does not define prudence, its interpretation has been left to the courts. To this date, court interpretations of prudence have applied the prudent man rule of personal trusts to pre-ERISA pension trusts.

[23]Ibid.

[24]The major studies claiming that pension funds do not perform well are Edward Malca, *Pension Fund and Other Institutional Investors,* Lexington Books, Lexington, Mass., 1975; Martin J. Schwimmer and Edward Malca, *Pension and Institutional Portfolio Management,* Praeger

Publishers, New York, 1976; and Frank L. Voorheis, "Do Banks Manage Pension Funds Well?" *Financial Analysts Journal* (September-October 1976), 35–40. One study claiming that some pension managers are able to consistently do better than others is Gilbert L. Beebower and Gary L. Bergstrom, "A Performance Analysis of Pension and Profit-Sharing Portfolios: 1966–1975," *Financial Analysts Journal* (May-June 1977), 31–42.

[25]Recent work by Roll questions the methodology used in all performance-evaluation studies, leaving the performance question unsettled. See Richard Roll, "A Critique of the Capital Asset Pricing Theory's Tests," *Journal of Financial Economics* (1977), 129–176; and Richard Roll, "Why the Securities Market Line Cannot Distinguish Superior Assets (or Portfolios) from Inferior Assets (or Portfolios), *ex post* or *ex ante*," Working Paper 4-77, Study Center in Managerial Economics and Finance, Graduate School of Management, UCLA, March 1977.

The importance of the interpretation of the prudent man rule is underscored by the fact that under traditional court interpretations in personal trust cases, the prescriptions of modern investment theory would be unacceptable. Specifically, courts have always placed emphasis on safety of the individual security rather than the portfolio as an entity. Even if the portfolio as a whole earns a reasonable or spectacular return, the trustee may have violated his fiduciary responsibility by investing in one speculative issue that loses money.[26] On the other hand, modern investment theory accepts the portfolio rather than the security as the appropriate focus of attention, and individual securities are important only as they interrelate with the remainder of the portfolio.

Some commentators familiar with the regulatory and legislative background of ERISA have stated that the legislative intent was to have a flexible law.[27] Thus, it is possible that the courts will be more receptive to the prescriptions of investment theory in future interpretations.

Two other problems confront the fund manager trying to implement portfolio theory. First, how can large pension funds invest in a broad range of securities if there are only a limited number of securities that provide liquidity to the fund?[28] For the largest funds there must be a large amount of stock outstanding and subject to trading to provide liquidity. Thus, the largest funds must invest in a subset of the securities population if they are to maintain liquidity. However, as we discussed earlier, liquidity has not been a major factor in pension investment decisions. Furthermore, even if large funds invested only in a small group of stocks, research has shown that most of the gains from diversification can be achieved with a modest number of stocks in the portfolio.[29]

A second major problem in implementing portfolio theory in pension-fund investing is the choice of the proper level of risk assumed. ERISA clearly states that the fiduciary is to make investment decisions for the benefit of the participants in the pension plan. With a defined-benefit plan, however, a rise in the return on the portfolio benefits the sponsor through reducing required contributions, rather than benefiting the participant. If the gain in return was achieved by increasing the level of risk assumed, there is a serious question as to whether or not the law is violated.

One feature of ERISA may actually encourage the use of portfolio theory. In its broadest form, portfolio theory dictates proportional investment in all financial assets, not just equities. A provision of ERISA requires diversification of a fund's investments to minimize the risk of large losses. As we saw earlier, large negative returns are sometimes earned. To the extent that ERISA forces managers to consider financial assets other than equities because of the fear of losses, more efficient diversification might occur. Interestingly, as has already been observed, common stock as a percentage of total fund assets has recently declined for both private and public funds. As long as this provision does not force managers to underinvest in equities, it might favor the implementation of portfolio theory. A related point is that research showing that markets are reasonably efficient was conducted for the most part in our presumably most efficient markets—the New York Stock Exchange and Treasury bills. As pension funds invest in less efficient markets (for example, unlisted equities, mortgages, corporate debt, real estate), there may be greater opportunities to outperform the market.

Investment theory as we have outlined it is far from wholly academic. Currently, many institutional money managers have embraced portfolio theory and its mandates and are actively applying it to the funds under their management. Indexed mutual funds have conspicuously adopted the findings of theory and applied research. However, it is conjectural whether there will ever be an engi-

---

[26] For a discussion of this legal problem and the application of portfolio theory to pension trusts, see John H. Langbein and Richard A. Posner, "Market Funds and Trust Investments Law," *American Bar Foundation Research Journal* (1976), 1–34. Also, Robert C. Pozen, "The Prudent Person Rule and ERISA: A Legal Perspective," *Financial Analysts Journal* (March-April 1977), 30–35.

[27] Gary A. Kesch, "Interpreting the Prudent Man Rule of ERISA," *Financial Analysts Journal* (January-February 1977), 26–32; and Marilyn V. Brown, "Prudence Under ERISA: What the Regulators Say," *Financial Analysts Journal* (January–February 1977), 33–39.

[28] An interesting effect of this problem is discussed in Frank Reilly, "A Three-Tier Stock Market and Corporate Financing," *Financial Management* (Autumn 1975), 7–15.

[29] See Bruce D. Fielitz, "Indirect Versus Direct Diversification," *Financial Management* (Winter 1974), 54–62.

neered fit of portfolio theory to pension-fund management because of the institutional constraints already stated.

## ERISA and the Future of Pension Funds

In addition to the foregoing section's comments, ERISA reduced the amount of time a person must work before he or she is covered by his or her pension plan. It also extended coverage and benefits to the employee and the employee's family. ERISA mandated increased disclosure as well as changes in accounting standards. Another provision of the law is its new vesting requirements. Pension costs are reduced when vesting is long delayed because labor turnover will diminish the need to pay future benefits. ERISA adds tough vesting requirements by allowing three methods for determining vesting with the longest allowable period being fifteen years.

Our discussion of the actuarial foundations of portfolio policy noted the distinction between normal costs and past service costs. A plan is fully funded when contributions plus the fund's assets equal benefits earned. While the normal costs are funded immediately, past service costs are usually amortized over a long period of time and, thus, total funding is not immediate. ERISA sets explicit rules for the allowable amortization periods for different plans. Furthermore, actuarial assumptions must be reevaluated every three years and adjustments resulting from experience gains and losses must be made to the funding rate.

Congress included a provision in ERISA requiring all private plans to pay termination-insurance premiums to a new governmental agency, the Pension Benefit Guaranty Corporation (PBGC). If a plan terminates and is unable to pay all obligations, the PBGC will provide limited pension benefits. This insurance fund will also be used to allow plan sponsors to lay off the risk of claims against them arising from the pension plan. Before ERISA, the sponsor's responsibility for unfunded liabilities was limited to the assets of the pension fund. The new law makes the sponsor liable for up to 30 percent of its net worth. The PBGC requires sponsors to insure against this risk.

An obvious concern to pension plans is the cost of all these provisions. While there will undoubt-

edly be cost increases occasioned for some or many, for most larger plans little will be changed.[30] Many large plans were already following vesting and funding requirements at least as stringent as ERISA's. Disparities, where present, were often not very great. Large cost effects will be centered on the smaller plans. An interesting corollary of this proposition is that ERISA itself should not cause much of an increase in the size of pension-fund assets.

Another important point is that pension costs are just part of total labor costs. To the extent that pension costs do increase, reduction in wages may offset the increase. Indeed, there is evidence that in collective bargaining the firm will determine the total labor cost and then bargain on the distribution between wages and fringe benefits.

A recent survey showed that perhaps as many as 30 percent of private plans have terminated since ERISA.[31] While the exact number is in doubt, it is certain that many smaller plans have ceased to exist. This attrition is not related solely to cost increases. ERISA also reduced the relative advantage of pension saving versus other private saving by liberalizing Keogh plans and introducing Individual Retirement Accounts (IRAs). These new savings avenues allow individuals to gain many of the tax advantages of saving through a regular pension plan. Keogh plans allow self-employed individuals to deduct the lesser of $7,500 or 15 percent of gross income. Both plans allow the deferral of taxes on these annual contributions and related investment incomes until benefits are received in retirement. Although the assets in both of these plans are still small relative to the assets of all private funds, they represent a growing pool of money.

It is still early to make any firm statement about the effects of ERISA on private pension plans. Nonetheless, it appears that the largest impact will be on portfolio policy and on the growth of small funds.

---

[30] For further discussion of this point, see Randall D. Weiss, "Private Pensions: The Impact of ERISA on the Growth of Retirement Plans," *Funding Pensions: Issues and Implications for Financial Markets,* Federal Reserve Bank of Boston Conference Series No. 16, 1976, pp. 137–151.

[31] *Pension and Investments,* August 1, 1977, p. 1.

## Conclusion

In the perspective of the history of financial institutions, the tenure of pension funds, regarded as a sizable entity, has been brief. Statistics given here, though inclusive of pension funds' span of significance, relate to a scant twenty-five years. The relative absence of legal fetters, unique freedom from cash-flow pressures, and rapidly shifting stimuli from the socioeconomic environment of financial markets and institutions, however, have converged to accelerate their portfolio evolution. Thus, in a short time we have witnessed not only adaptive response, but also what may be interpreted as affirmative evidence of the maneuverability of pension funds as a financial intermediary.

A perennial question is whether or not the widespread restrictions imposed legislatively and administratively on financial institutions and aimed usually at claimants' protection, are self-defeating, not only in the cost in terms of reduced portfolio freedom and earnings, but also in the resulting unwieldy, encrusted alignments of institutions and segments of the capital markets. One gains some measure of reassurance from the demonstrated flexibility of the rapidly growing pension funds. The ability to pivot and turn in the direction of attractive earning opportunities is a precious one socially, for it is synonymous with the ability of the financial markets to perform the allocation of funds flows that is at the heart of efficient direction of saving and investment.

## Questions

1. Explain the circumstances that lead to net accumulation of a pension fund. What limits the growth of a given fund?
2. What is the meaning of the phrase *actuarial solvency*? What is its importance to a pension fund?
3. Account for the differences between public and private funds with respect to the composition of cash flows through the funds. What are the principal reasons behind the different net growths of the public and private funds?
4. Explain why the following types of securities occupy proportionately small or insignificant places in the portfolios of pension funds: (1) U.S. Treasury bonds; (2) residential home mortgages; (3) short-term securities of practically all types.
5. Imagine that you are the manager of investments for a self-administered corporate pension fund that prom-

ises stated levels of benefits. (a) Recommend a portfolio policy that will emphasize safety of payments to retirees in the future. (b) Recommend a portfolio policy that will minimize cost to your employer. Be specific in your recommendations about the proportions of the portfolio to be devoted to various classes of securities. Do your recommendations avoid conflicts of interest?
6. Are the variances in the respective portfolio policy of public and private funds justifiable?
7. Are flows of cash to various segments of the capital markets from retirement funds responsive to differentials in yield on the various types of securities? Over short periods? Over long periods? What is the evidence for your answer?
8. What is your best guess about the effect of retirement saving through pension funds on total saving? Does social security influence total saving? Does saving through pension funds merely substitute for other forms of saving or does it augment them? Can you substantiate your guess?
9. Is modern portfolio theory consistent with the sound management of pension-fund assets?
10. Examine and evaluate the barriers to the implementation of modern portfolio theory by pension funds.
11. Recommend a portfolio strategy for a private pension fund that is consistent with the provisions of ERISA. Be specific in your recommendations.
12. What will the likely effects of ERISA be on: (a) pension-plan formation and termination; (b) secrecy of plan operations; and (c) security selection?
13. Can inflation increase net pension costs? Decrease costs? Explain, giving the necessary conditions for your answers.
14. Should limitations be imposed on the present freedom of corporate pension funds in portfolio policy?
15. What changes would you recommend in public policy toward private and public employee pension funds?

## Selected Bibliography

Andrews, Victor L. "Noninsured Corporate and State and Local Government Retirement Funds in the Financial Structure." In *Private Capital Markets,* published by the Commission on Money and Credit. Prentice-Hall, Englewood Cliffs, N.J., 1964.

Barro, Robert T. *The Impact of Social Security on Private Saving: Evidence from the U.S. Time Series.* American Enterprise Institute for Public Policy Research, Washington, D.C., 1978.

*Funding Pensions: Issues and Implications for Financial Markets.* Federal Reserve Bank of Boston, Conference Series No. 16, 1976.

Greenbough, William C., and Francis P. King. *Pension Plans and Public Policy*. Columbia University Press, New York, 1976.

Malca, Edward. *Pension Funds and Other Institutional Investors*. Lexington Books, Lexington, Mass., 1975.

*Old Age Income Assurance: Part V, Financial Aspects of Pension Plans*. Joint Economic Committee, 90th Cong., 1st Sess., 1967.

Pomeranz, Felix, Gordon P. Ramsey, and Richard M. Steinberg. *Pensions: An Accounting and Management Guide*. The Ronald Press Company, New York, 1976.

Schwimmer, Martin J., and Edward Malca. *Pension and Institutional Portfolio Management*. Praeger Publishers, New York, 1976.

Tilove, Robert. *Public Employee Pension Funds*. A Twentieth Century Fund Report, Columbia University Press, New York, 1976.

Trowbridge, C. L., and C. E. Farr. *The Theory and Practice of Pension Funding*. Richard D. Irwin, Homewood, Ill., 1976.

Ture, Norman, and Barbara A. Fields. *The Future of Private Pension Plans*. American Enterprise Institute for Public Policy Research, Washington, D.C., 1976.

Winklevoss, Howard E. *Pension Mathematics with Numerical Illustrations*. Richard D. Irwin, Homewood, Ill., 1977.

# 9

# Investment-Type Intermediaries

As outlined in Chapter 1, the role of financial intermediaries in the economy is to stand between savers and investors and to aid in the allocation of accumulated savings among competing uses of funds. As they perform this function, financial intermediaries provide a variety of services to lenders and borrowers that make the funds transfer mechanism and the saving-investment process more efficient. In this chapter we examine in more detail the specific services provided by a particular class of intermediaries, the investment-oriented intermediaries. In this introductory section, we discuss the motivations of savers who choose to use the services of these intermediaries. The remainder of the chapter is devoted to the factors that determine the growth of these intermediaries, their record and characteristics of performance, and implications for the capital markets.

Financial intermediaries of the investment type function essentially as substitutes for portfolios of primary securities that an individual might otherwise hold for a variety of purposes. Households may choose intermediaries over the direct-investment alternative in order to secure some of the following advantages or services that the financial intermediary can provide:

1. superior diversification as a means of reducing specific or nonmarket risk
2. superior marketability
3. lower portfolio transaction costs
4. access to capital-market sectors not generally open to the saver/investor of modest means
5. selection, continuing supervision, and adjustment of specific portfolio holdings
6. safekeeping, accounting, and tax services
7. economies of scale in all such functions

Most of these features are also offered by deposit- and insurance-type intermediaries, but an investment-type intermediary is distinctive in at least three major respects:

1. It does not create fixed liabilities as an underwriter, guarantor, borrower, or issuer of deposit liabilities.
2. It does not promise any particular rate of return to asset holders, who instead receive whatever the portfolio produces after the deduction of their share of management and administration expenses.

3. It receives compensation from a defined fee which is typically related to the market value of assets, rather than from a spread between the earnings on assets acquired and the return to be paid on liabilities.

The saver or holder of accumulated financial assets exchanges money or primary securities, then, for a participation in a portfolio that the intermediary undertakes to manage in a fiduciary capacity to meet a defined set of investment objectives. As a participant, rather than as a claimant or creditor, the saver shares fully in the gains from successful portfolio management in a favorable capital market environment or in the losses from inferior management in less auspicious markets.

The individual who rationally uses an investment-type intermediary rather than a deposit-type institution has decided to forgo liquidity[1] in the expectation of earning a higher average total return. Unfortunately for the individual, however, higher returns are also associated with greater risk, measured by the variability of returns. The reward for accepting illiquidity and variability of returns has been substantial over a recent fifty-year period in the capital markets of the United States, as can be seen in Table 9-1. Nevertheless, the exposure to losses from business failures and the increased volatility of an *undiversified* portfolio of common stocks makes it desirable, or even essential, for the inexperienced individual of modest means to consider at least the diversification feature of an investment-type intermediary.[2]

Until the past few years, no data were available on individual investors' experience in actively managing their own portfolios. A recent study, however, concludes that a large sample of individuals did about as well, on average, as a large group of equity mutual funds.[3] It should be expected,

[1]Here defined as those characteristics of an asset that make it readily convertible into cash on short notice without risk of material loss.

[2]Portfolio diversification criteria can be found in Lawrence Fisher and James H. Lorie, "Some Studies of Variability of Returns on Investments in Common Stocks," *Journal of Business* (April 1970). See also Chapter 24 of this text.

[3]Gary G. Schlarbaum, Wilbur G. Lewellen, and Ronald C. Lease, "The Common Stock Portfolio Performance of Individual Investors 1964–70," *Journal of Finance* (May 1978). Earlier reports on this research project appeared in the *Journal of Finance* (May 1974) and the *Journal of*

**Table 9-1  Total Annual Returns of Selected Securities, 1926–1976**

| | Geometric Mean of Total Returns | Standard Deviation of Annual Returns |
|---|---|---|
| U. S. Treasury bills | 2.4% | 2.1% |
| Long-term government bonds | 3.4 | 5.8 |
| Long-term corporate bonds | 4.1 | 5.6 |
| Common stocks | 9.2 | 22.4 |

Source: Roger G. Ibbotson and Rex A. Sinquefield, *Stocks, Bonds, Bills, and Inflation: The Past (1926–1976) and the Future (1977–2000),* Financial Analysts Research Foundation, Charlottesville, Va., 1977.

though, that the dispersion of results was substantially greater than for the more widely diversified mutual fund portfolios; but this conclusion has not yet been verified. Of course, the funds with which the comparison was made also provided a range of other valuable services to investors—for example safekeeping of securities, accounting for transactions, providing tax information, and monitoring corporate changes.

Thus, diversification within the higher risk–higher return segments of the capital markets is an important service provided by the investment intermediaries. By reducing the exposure to losses and poor performance, investment-type intermediaries make investing for higher returns less risky for individuals with modest capital or savings flows. This is not their only service, however. As is characteristic of the intermediation process in any of its forms, investing institutions, including the investment intermediaries, gather small savings and expedite their flow into large pools of capital. The economies and efficiencies are presumably shared between the suppliers and the users of funds, which results in some reduction in the cost of capital. Another measure of the possible contribution of intermediaries to capital market efficiency is their ability consistently to facilitate the transfer of risk capital to the most productive employment. It is necessary to measure the performance (realized return allowing for risk) of intermediaries in order to evaluate both saver/investor experience

*Business* (April 1978). The analysis covers some 2,500 individual brokerage accounts for the seven years 1964 through 1970.

and intermediaries' contribution to the capital market as an efficient allocator of investment funds.

## Mutual Funds

As we have pointed out, to the individual whose time, experience, and access to information are limited, investment intermediaries, such as mutual funds, are appealing because they eliminate problems of selecting, trading, and supervising securities. They also provide services, such as safekeeping of securities and accounting for transactions. Moreover, for almost any defined investment objective there is a mutual fund, or combination of funds, that will seek to meet that goal. Terms like *growth, aggressive growth, growth and income,* and *income* apply to various categories of common-stock funds. Many fund management groups also provide convenient transfer privileges among their several funds, which may include municipal bond and money-market funds for those whose objectives change. Recent innovations in the industry have attempted to make this form of investing even more attractive to small savers. For example, the mutual fund *open account,* like a passbook savings account, facilitates systematic saving in small amounts and reinvestment of income to achieve the compounding effect. In many cases, individuals quite logically make their first or second common-stock investment in a mutual fund. Employee savings and profit-sharing plans frequently include such an option. Thus introduced to equity investing, the individual may make subsequent purchases and get direct ownership of stocks and bonds.

### Corporate Structure

Mutual funds are investment companies that issue variable liabilities in the form of shares redeemable on demand at net asset value. Disregarding relatively small current receivable and payable accounts, the investment portfolio at market value and working cash balances constitute the net assets of a typical mutual fund. The fund's net assets also constitute its liabilities; there are no reserve or surplus accounts.

Substantially all mutual funds qualify as regulated investment companies under the provisions of the Internal Revenue Code. This means they are recognized as a conduit through which flow to stockholders all net investment income and capital gains. Thus, both types of return are taxed to the stockholders, not to the fund.

The fund as a corporate entity makes a commitment to stockholders only to supervise management of the assets in accordance with objectives stated in the fund prospectus. A banking institution typically holds the assets, maintains the records of ownership, and redeems shares at net asset value as calculated at least once a day.

Most funds have management contracts with organizations that provide administrative services as well as portfolio management. Expenses charged to the fund, other than management fees, include the cost of auditing and legal services, stock transfers and dividend disbursements, bank custody of the assets, stockholder reports, and local taxes. Because of the high proportion of fixed costs in rendering these services, the expense ratio is extremely sensitive to the size of the fund. For this reason the rise in costs of the 1970s, which was frequently not accompanied by asset growth, has stimulated an active merger movement among funds. However, assets were highly concentrated even before this period.[4]

The organizers of a fund are usually the owners of the company holding the management contract. The management fee, often starting at one-half of 1 percent of the first $100 or $200 million of assets, is typically tapered to reflect the economies of scale inherent in the investment-management function. The management company also acts as the distributor of fund shares in most instances.

Studies of mutual funds do not show any significant relationships between investment performance adjusted for variability and size, management expenses, portfolio turnover, or sales charges.[5] The evidence is fragmentary on the question of

---

[4]On June 30, 1969, the top five fund complexes managed 34.6 percent of mutual fund assets, the top twenty-five managed 75.4 percent, and the top fifty firms 90.0 percent. *Institutional Investor Study Report of the Securities and Exchange Commission,* House Document No. 92-64, 92nd Cong., 1st Sess., March 1971, Chap. 4.

[5]Wharton School of Finance and Commerce, *A Study of Mutual Funds, Prepared for the Securities and Exchange Commission,* House Report No. 2274, 87th Cong., 2nd Sess., August 1962; Securities and Exchange Commission, *Public Policy Implications of Investment Company Growth,* House Report No. 2337, 89th Cong., 2nd Sess., December 1966; and Irwin Friend, Marshall

whether a positive cash flow (excess of sales over redemptions) materially enhances performance; but the experience of fund managers with heavy net redemptions makes clear the difficulties of achieving satisfactory results under those conditions. A steady drain of share repurchases leaves the portfolio manager in a state of uncertainty as to funds available for investment and the relevant time horizon for making new investments. The increased pressure to emphasize near-term results runs counter to strategies based on portfolio-management theory.

Thus, for this reason, the economics of performing investment-management services provide a strong incentive for the manager to try to increase fund size. Since shareholders may also benefit from economies of scale and a tapered management fee, there is an argument for sharing distribution expenses with existing shareholders instead of charging them entirely to new investors in the form of a sales fee (or *load*). At present, *no-load funds* may have a slightly higher management fee because the manager is providing advertising, promotional materials, and other distribution services. As investors have become better informed in recent years about mutual funds, they have bought more shares on the no-load basis.

### Postwar Growth

The Investment Company Act of 1940, which established the present framework of regulation by the Securities and Exchange Commission, restored confidence in this type of financial institution, which had been severely damaged by the Great Depression. At the end of 1940, fewer than 300,000 stockholders in sixty-eight funds held about $450 million worth of shares. From this small base, the next thirty years of growth were phenomenal, as shown in Table 9-2.

In viewing the record of growth for the 1943–1971 period of persistent net sales of shares, it is evident that many influences have been at work. The early postwar years reflect a widespread and successful sales effort to attract new investors

when they turned to common stocks for growth and income as fear of a postwar depression receded. Some diminution of the rate of growth was visible by 1960, however, after assets had reached $20 billion and the number of shareholder accounts approached six million.[6] This represented a significant penetration of the market for the care of existing financial assets in modest accumulations as evidenced by the fact that the *number* of regular accounts (those with no provision for automatic reinvestment of dividends and capital gain distributions) showed no increase for the next decade. Even though there was a surge of speculative interest in the late 1960s, by the early 1960s the traditional equity mutual funds had reached the maturity stage where the primary determinants of growth were steady savings flows and market appreciation, rather than steady sales to new investors.

To encourage and facilitate savings flows, substantially all funds provided dividend reinvestment plans in addition to regular accounts. These savings-type accounts accounted for all of the 44 percent increase in the number of shareholder accounts between 1961 and 1971. A feature designed to encourage accumulations for retirement was the withdrawal plan account, which grew from 32,000 to 280,000 accounts in the same period. Subsequently, Keogh Plans, which fund tax-deferred retirement plans for the self-employed, developed rapidly. By the end of 1977, there were 236,000 plans with 344,000 participants and almost $2 billion in assets. Individual Retirement Accounts, available to employees not covered under a group plan, had $243 million in 67,000 accounts at the end of 1977, the third year of their availability.

A sign of maturity among the traditional equity mutual funds is the instability in the rate of both net sales and redemptions of fund shares (Table 9-2). This instability contrasts sharply with the steadier growth that might be expected in a less mature market. Each period of market decline since 1943 has been followed by a decline in sales, but the declines in sales have tended to become propor-

---

Blume, and Jean Crockett, *Mutual Funds and Other Institutional Investors,* McGraw-Hill Book Company, New York, 1970.

[6]Because of duplications in holdings, the number of individual stockholders is less than the number of shareholder accounts. The Investment Company Institute estimated the number of stockholders at 7.5 million, compared with 8.5 million accounts at the end of 1977.

**Table 9-2  Mutual Fund Growth, 1943–1978 (in millions of dollars)**

| Calendar Years | Sales of Shares | Repurchases of Shares | Net Flow of Funds | | Appreciation or (Depreciation)[b] | | Net Assets at Year End |
|---|---|---|---|---|---|---|---|
| | | | Amount | Percentage[a] | Amount | Percentage[a] | |
| 1943/47 | $1,214.8 | $ 464.3 | $ 750.5 | 154.1 | $ 171.8 | 35.3 | $ 1,409.2 |
| 1948/52 | 2,635.6 | 1,033.1 | 1,602.5 | 113.7 | 919.7 | 65.3 | 3,931.4 |
| 1953/57 | 5,479.6 | 1,919.6 | 3,560.0 | 90.6 | 1,222.7 | 31.1 | 8,714.1 |
| 1958 | 1,619.8 | 511.3 | 1,108.5 | 12.7 | 3,419.8 | 39.3 | 13,242.4 |
| 1959 | 2,280.0 | 785.6 | 1,494.4 | 11.3 | 1,081.2 | 8.2 | 15,818.0 |
| 1960 | 2,097.2 | 841.8 | 1,255.4 | 7.9 | (48.3) | (0.3) | 17,025.7 |
| 1961 | 2,950.9 | 1,160.4 | 1,790.5 | 10.5 | 3,972.6 | 23.3 | 22,788.8 |
| 1962 | 2,699.0 | 1,122.7 | 1,576.4 | 6.9 | (3,094.5) | (13.6) | 21,270.7 |
| 1963 | 2,459.1 | 1,505.3 | 953.8 | 4.5 | 2,989.9 | 24.0 | 25,214.4 |
| 1964 | 3,403.0 | 1,874.1 | 1,528.9 | 6.1 | 2,373.0 | 9.4 | 29,116.3 |
| 1965 | 4,358.1 | 1,962.4 | 2,395.7 | 8.2 | 3,708.2 | 12.7 | 35,220.2 |
| 1966 | 4,671.8 | 2,005.1 | 2,666.8 | 7.6 | (3,057.6) | (8.7) | 34,829.4 |
| 1967 | 4,669.8 | 2,744.2 | 1,925.4 | 5.5 | 7,946.5 | 22.8 | 44,701.3 |
| 1968 | 6,819.8 | 3,838.7 | 2,981.1 | 6.7 | 4,994.8 | 11.2 | 52,677.2 |
| 1969 | 6,718.3 | 3,661.6 | 3,056.6 | 5.8 | (7,443.1) | (14.1) | 48,290.7 |
| 1970 | 4,625.8 | 2,987.6 | 1,638.2 | 3.4 | (2,310.8) | (4.8) | 47,618.1 |
| 1971 | 5,147.2 | 4,750.2 | 347.0 | 0.8 | 7,030.2 | 14.8 | 55,045.3 |
| 1972 | 4,892.5 | 6,562.9 | (1,670.7) | (3.0) | 6,456.0 | 11.7 | 59,830.6 |
| 1973 | 4,359.3 | 5,651.1 | (1,291.8) | (2.2) | (12,020.3) | (20.1) | 46,518.5 |
| 1974 | 3,091.5 | 3,380.9 | (289.5) | (0.6) | (12,167.2) | (26.2) | 34,061.8 |
| 1975 | 3,307.2 | 3,686.3 | (379.1) | (1.1) | 8,496.0 | 24.9 | 42,178.7 |
| 1976 | 4,360.3 | 6,801.2 | (2,440.9) | (5.8) | 7,844.8 | 18.6 | 47,582.6 |
| 1977 | 6,399.7 | 6,026.0 | 373.7 | 0.8 | (2,907.3) | (6.1) | 45,049.0 |
| 1978 | 6,705.3 | 7,232.4 | (527.1) | (1.2) | (596.1) | (1.3) | 44,980.0 |

[a] Amount shown as a percentage of the market value of net assets at the start of the period.
[b] Calculated by subtracting from period's change in net assets, the excess of sales over repurchases of shares. This is not, of course, a measure of performance.

Source: Investment Company Institute, *Mutual Fund Fact Book, 1979* and news releases. Data are for all members of the Institute and exclude money market funds.

tionally larger over time. Conversely, the pace of fund sales has quickened in periods of subsequent price recovery. Operating to moderate these fluctuations in sales is a tendency of individuals to feel less need for professional management when stock prices are in a broad upward movement. A sharp decline in prices, on the other hand, tends to emphasize the value of a diversified portfolio.

The pattern of *redemptions* also discloses some interesting characteristics of investor behavior. In years of market declines like 1949, 1957, 1962, 1966, 1970, and 1974 shareholders feel "locked in" and reluctant to take a loss; but a subsequent recovery may touch off the familiar "even and out" wave of redemptions. The opinion is widely held that high-performance funds were sold in the late 1960s to people who did not recognize the volatility of prospective returns, and they were eager to re-

deem during the 1971–1972 recovery in share prices. The 1975–1978 wave of redemptions, concentrated in equity products, is part of the widespread disillusionment with common stocks.

The stability and continuity of fund flows into mutual funds is obviously a major concern to the capital market, particularly to the market for equity securities. Nevertheless, the revival of growth in equity mutual fund products seems to depend on the future trend of stock prices. The 1973–1978 investor experience with equities disappointed even the reasonable expectations of serious, long-term investors. The broadening of the mutual fund product line (which we discuss in the next section) and the conversion feature offered by fund complexes have combined to improve the economics of the investment company business, but stabilizing the base of the fund complex does not necessarily contribute to stabilization of capital market flows. In fact, these facilities may contribute to instability and the execution of knee-jerk responses to changes in expectations. The tendency of equity funds to hold their maximum cash reserves at market troughs and minimum liquidity at market peaks, furthermore, results in the funds' exaggerating the variations in the pattern of sales and redemptions created by the decisions of shareholders.

There has been a sharp rise in the rate of turnover in mutual fund stock portfolios since the mid-1960s, as shown in Table 9-3. This substantially higher level of turnover in stock portfolios reflects more than simple market turbulence of recent years. As performance lagged, more frequent shifts were made among market sectors and attempts, not very productive, were made at market timing. The shortened time horizon of investors generally was shared by fund managers as they sought to improve disappointing results. Years of large net share redemptions, of course, produced an increment of about 2½ percentage points to the turnover rate if one simply takes account of net sales reflecting share repurchases rather than investment policy.

### New Products

For fund managers attempting to sustain sales, a major strategy is to offer new products that respond to the changing preferences of savers/investors. Table 9-4 shows the breakdown of sales by type of fund, excluding money-market funds, for selected recent years. As can be seen, new products—types of funds that did not exist five years earlier, such as bond funds—made up more than one-third of 1978 sales.

Dramatic shifts in saver/investor preferences are mirrored in Table 9-4. In the late 1960s, the emergence of the aggressive growth style of management conformed to the speculative mood that fueled the hot new-issue market and sharply diminished equity risk premiums. From 1966 through 1973, the period of the so-called two-tier market, growth funds accounted for between 40 and 51 percent of sales each year as investors lengthened their time horizons and emphasized growth relative to current return. However, the traumatic experience of investors in the third quarter of 1974, which witnessed the sharpest market decline since the second quarter of 1932, drastically altered preferences

**Table 9-3  Annual Turnover Rates of Common Stocks in Mutual Fund Portfolios, 1957–1978**

| Period | Mutual Fund Turnover Rate | Period | Mutual Fund Turnover Rate |
|---|---|---|---|
| 1957–1961 | 19.6% | 1970 | 42.2% |
| 1962 | 17.3 | 1971 | 50.6 |
| 1963 | 18.6 | 1972 | 45.0 |
| 1964 | 18.7 | 1973 | 37.4 |
| 1965 | 21.1 | 1974 | 28.9 |
| 1966 | 33.6 | 1975 | 34.5 |
| 1967 | 42.3 | 1976 | 32.3 |
| 1968 | 46.6 | 1977 | 34.0 |
| 1969 | 49.9 | 1978 | 44.5 |

Note: Turnover rates are computed as the total of purchases and sales divided by twice the average of common-stock holdings.

Source: Investment Company Institute, *Mutual Fund Fact Book, 1979.*

away from the long term and toward the immediate realization of current income.

Fund complexes responded with new income and bond funds in the years 1974–1978. In addition to these bond funds sold by traditional mutual fund complexes, municipal bond dealers sold $8,148 million of municipal bond trusts to the public in the seven years 1970–1976. Blocks of bonds were packaged in the form of fixed trusts, with no right of redemption but some resale market. This vehicle provided six of the seven advantages of intermediation cited earlier; only continuing supervision and management of the pool was lacking. Passage of the Tax Reform Act of 1976 in October of that year permitted traditional mutual fund groups to pass through to shareholders the tax-exempt status of the interest earned. During the rest of 1976, $476 million of shares were sold as new funds were rapidly formed, providing the additional features of portfolio management, dividend reinvestment, and the redemption privilege.

The newest entry in the mutual fund field is the option fund, designed to increase the current return of a common-stock portfolio by writing covered call options against it. This development awaited growth of the market for listed options and passage of an amendment of the Internal Revenue Code to treat expired option premiums as investment income. A variation on participation in the listed option market is available through funds that buy call options in combination with liquid assets.

**Table 9-4  Mutual Fund Sales by Investment Objective, 1962, 1969, 1973, 1977, and 1978 (in millions of dollars)**

| Investment Objective | 1962 Amount | 1962 Percentage | 1969 Amount | 1969 Percentage | 1973 Amount | 1973 Percentage | 1977 Amount | 1977 Percentage | 1978 Amount | 1978 Percentage |
|---|---|---|---|---|---|---|---|---|---|---|
| Aggressive growth | $   7.2 | 0.3 | $   887.5 | 13.2 | $   368.1 | 8.4 | $   407.4 | 6.4 | $   480.4 | 7.2 |
| Growth | 990.6 | 36.7 | 2,992.5 | 44.6 | 2,054.1 | 47.2 | 829.1 | 13.0 | 1,015.2 | 15.1 |
| Growth and income | 983.8 | 36.5 | 1,788.5 | 26.6 | 1,212.5 | 27.8 | 1,033.6 | 16.1 | 1,060.6 | 15.8 |
| Balanced | 516.1 | 19.0 | 329.8 | 4.9 | 244.5 | 5.6 | 168.4 | 2.6 | 239.4 | 3.6 |
| Income | 201.3 | 7.5 | 720.0 | 10.7 | 480.1 | 11.0 | 633.0 | 9.9 | 649.7 | 9.7 |
| Bond[a] | N.A. | | N.A. | | N.A. | | 983.0 | 15.4 | 1,306.8 | 19.5 |
| Municipal bond | N.A. | | N.A. | | N.A. | | 2,056.1 | 32.1 | 1,812.8 | 27.0 |
| Option | N.A. | | N.A. | | N.A. | | 289.1 | 4.5 | 140.4 | 2.1 |
| Total | $2,699.0 | 100.0 | $6,718.3 | 100.0 | $4,359.3 | 100.0 | $6,399.7 | 100.0 | $6,705.3 | 100.0 |

N.A. = Not Applicable
[a]Bond funds prior to 1975 are included in the "Income" category.

Source: Investment Company Institute, *Mutual Fund Fact Book, 1979.*

Shareholders are also giving conventional equity funds authority to engage in option transactions as part of their portfolio-management activity.

Fund complexes ordinarily offer to shareholders, for a nominal charge, the privilege of shifting their capital from one fund to another within the complex. Such conversions are not included in the sale/repurchase statistics, but they have become an important service to savers/investors as they choose to adjust their positions. If we include money market funds, conversions in 1977 reached $2.2 billion, compared with $363 million ten years earlier. These arrangements permit shareholders to attempt market-timing virtually without transaction costs to the investor; however, they do not relieve the timer of the formidable problems of making reliable forecasts of market swings.

By far the biggest recent innovation in mutual funds, a by-product of Federal Reserve Regulation Q, which specifies interest ceilings on bank deposits, is the money market fund. The removal of interest rate ceilings on large (over $100,000) bank certificates of deposit prior to the sharp increase in money rates in 1973 and 1974 represented a new opportunity for mutual funds to offer small savers the high short-term yields previously available only to the large holder of liquid assets. Strong growth in 1974 and 1975, renewed in 1977, brought the totals of fifty funds reporting to the Investment Company Institute up to $10.9 billion in assets by year-end 1978. Growth was even more rapid in 1979 and early 1980 as assets reached $75 billion at the end of June 1980. Some funds offer a withdrawal privilege—an account in this type of fund strongly resembles an interest-bearing checking account. Money market funds, like municipal bond funds, offer access to capital market sectors not generally open to the holder of modest amounts of liquid assets. The distribution of holdings of the fifty funds at year-end 1977 and 1978 is found in Table 9-5. Over a recent period, the ten largest money-market funds produced a return, after expenses, close to the discount rate on 90-day U.S. Treasury bills with a portfolio having an average maturity fluctuating around the 90-day mark.

## Performance

It is a truism to state that the average performance of all equity mutual funds will tend to be less than the average for the markets in which they participate by the cost of transactions, administration, and services provided to shareholders. Since large segments of the equity markets are relatively efficient, broadly diversified funds should be expected, on average, to underperform the market as measured by the Standard & Poor's 500 Stock Index by the amount of the expense ratio of close to 1 percent plus brokerage and transaction costs and amortization over the holding period of any sales load. Only funds that accept nonmarket risk by being substantially less than broadly diversified or are successful at market timing can expect to show superior performance across a market cycle. Some funds, perhaps one out of eight or ten, have consistently produced superior total returns, adjusted for volatility,[7] over many years. They have done so by identifying an imperfectly efficient sector of the equity capital markets in which they have analytical selection skills. Having identified such a sector, they make purchases and sales so as to gain from the drift of market prices toward intrinsic values.[8] However, successful market timing has proved to be elusive.

It is not possible to prove that mutual funds have necessarily enhanced the capital market's efficiency in allocating resources to the most productive uses, but they have certainly contributed to the process. Early recognition of fundamental changes in the economics of an industry or in the position of a company is the key to superior stock selection in a zero-sum game played against capable and well-informed asset managers. The prevailing view is likely to be fully reflected in share prices; only the detection of a disparity from the

[7] The conventional measure of volatility used here is the beta coefficient in the equation $R_f = \alpha + \beta R_m$ for describing the relationship at regular intervals between the return from the fund ($R_f$) and the return from the market index ($R_m$). The constant $\alpha$ is the positive or negative contribution of management. The slope of the linear relationship between the observations is the portfolio beta ($\beta$), the measure of volatility relative to the market index.

[8] For extensive treatment of fund performance and questions of market efficiency in this context, see the sources cited in footnote 5; Michael C. Jensen, "Risk, The Pricing of Capital Assets, and the Evaluation of Investment Portfolios," *Journal of Business* (April 1969); and J. Peter Williamson, "Measuring Mutual Fund Performance," *Financial Analysts Journal* (November-December 1972).

**Table 9-5  Assets of Money Market Funds, Year-End 1977 and 1978 (in millions of dollars)**

|  | 1977 | | 1978 | |
|---|---|---|---|---|
|  | Amount | Percentage | Amount | Percentage |
| Certificates of deposit | $1,793.0 | 46.1 | $ 5,293.8 | 48.8 |
| Commercial paper | 941.3 | 24.2 | 2,842.0 | 26.2 |
| Letters of credit | 22.0 | 0.6 | 71.9 | 0.7 |
| Bankers' acceptances | 100.5 | 2.6 | 764.7 | 7.1 |
| U.S. government securities | 882.5 | 22.7 | 1,489.3 | 13.7 |
| Cash reserves | 27.9 | 0.7 | 68.2 | 0.6 |
| Other assets | 120.5 | 3.1 | 327.7 | 3.0 |
|  | $3,887.7 | 100.0 | $10,857.6 | 100.0 |

Source: Investment Company Institute, *Mutual Fund Fact Book, 1979.*

consensus interpretation of widely disseminated information will provide superior returns or avoid losses. Clearly, fund managers are active participants in this endless contest, bringing pressure on prices to measure more promptly and accurately economic values of the industry and the company.

Because of the availability of the extensive data base, investor experience with mutual funds has been endlessly analyzed and different conclusions drawn from different periods. The decade of the 1960s is a good example. The Friend, Blume, and Crockett analysis compared 136 mutual funds with unmanaged portfolios of New York Stock Exchange issues, both equally weighted and weighted by market value. For the January 1960 to March 1964 period, the funds outperformed the equally weighted portfolios but underperformed the value-weighted portfolios, just as in 1973–1976. This period, including the 1962 market break, was one of high aversion to volatility. When the high-performance phase of April 1964 to June 1968 replaced the sober period with speculative fever, the funds outran the value-weighted portfolios but did not match the returns of equally weighted, unmanaged portfolios, just as in 1977.

Typically, fund portfolios are composed of positions that are more nearly equally weighted than value weighted. Thus, their performance relative to a value-weighted index, like the Standard & Poor's 500 or the New York Stock Exchange Composite, will be a function not of flashes of brilliance and stupidity but of changes in the risk-premium differentials between large and small companies. The logical measurement, therefore, is over a complete market cycle—which is, unfortunately, identifiable only in retrospect. The saver/investor will

not find it easy to select the small minority of superior performers because of this uncertainty about the correct measurement period and because past history is not a reliable guide to future results. Nevertheless, the average fund will still provide a useful bundle of financial services and protection from the aberrations of an inadequately diversified portfolio that occur when the art of security selection has been practiced without discipline and experience.

## Closed-End Investment Companies

### The Traditional Group

Any investment company is classified as closed end if it holds a portfolio of assets but does not stand ready to redeem its shares at net asset value. If the shares sell at a discount from net asset value, as has most frequently been the case since the Great Crash, new shares cannot be sold without diluting the equity of existing stockholders. The investment company becomes "closed," therefore, in the sense of not being open to the sale or redemption of shares.[9]

Under the circumstances, it is not surprising that this group of investment companies has shown little growth. The ranks have also been thinned by mergers, including those with open-end funds to eliminate the discount. Of nine large companies listed on the New York Stock Exchange and having $2.2 billion net assets, none was currently selling at a

[9]Internal management is another common characteristic of both the fully diversified and the nondiversified closed-end investment companies.

premium over asset value in 1977. The discount appears to be attributable to potentially taxable unrealized appreciation in portfolio securities, the character of assets, and policies governing the realization and distribution of gains.[10] The fact that the discount tends to widen in rising markets and to narrow in periods of decline makes a closed-end common-stock investment company less variable than its underlying net asset value, which may track the general market closely.

In the early 1970s, especially in 1973, a number of closed-end bond funds were marketed in response to the shift of investor interest away from equity products. These funds were marketed as closed-end funds because the fund managers did not wish to make the shares redeemable when the portfolios were heavily concentrated in long-term bonds. However, the benefits of active management have not been sufficient to prevent the shares from trading at moderate discounts (typically 6 to 9 percent) from net asset values. The permitted use of leverage is designed to bring prices up to or above net asset values, but it has not been widely employed because of its riskiness. Borrowing against long-term bonds is helpful only so long as there is a positive carry—that is, short-term interest rates are below long-term rates. Since short-term rates are inherently more variable, the spread may fluctuate widely and even turn negative in periods of tight money.

In 1967 established investment advisory organizations offered the public a new type of closed-end fund, called a *dual purpose fund,* to provide investors with the opportunity to meet specific portfolio objectives more precisely than was possible by the use of any other type of fund. Offerings by seven firms came to a total of $330 million usually divided equally between two classes of shares: (1) the income shares (which receive the entire net income from investments, including a preferential minimum rate) do not share in asset growth and are to be redeemed twelve to eighteen years from the original offering date at a fixed call price; and (2) the capital shares, which receive no income but stand to benefit from all increases in value. After redemption of the income shares, the fund can be converted to an open-end investment company, which would close the discounts from net asset value of the capital shares which have fluctuated around 20 percent.[11]

This new type of closed-end investment company was stimulated by the euphoric growth expectations of the 1967–1968 market environment and was destined to have limited life in that form as a high-quality hedge fund for the ordinary investor. The prompt appearance of discounts from net asset values on the capital share brought new offerings to a halt. The equity markets of future years will make the final determination of investor experience.

## Real Estate Investment Trusts

Real Estate Investment Trusts (REITs), formed under provisions of the Real Estate Investment Act of 1960, are investment companies that hold most or all of their investments in the form of real estate loans and securities. These trusts showed the most rapid growth in the years immediately after 1970 when the combination of high current return and moderate growth offered by the trusts appeared extremely attractive to individual investors following the sharp stock-market decline of 1970 and the ensuing deterioration in their experience. Consequently, certificates of beneficial interest in Real Estate Investment Trusts and their convertible subordinated debentures found a ready market among the large number of investors who had long sought an entry into the real estate sector of the capital markets on a full-participation basis. Commercial banks provided large credit lines at the senior level. Strong sponsorship by major financial institutions encouraged expectations of good management.

In amending the Internal Revenue Code to give Real Estate Investment Trusts the same conduit tax treatment as registered investment companies, Congress sought to provide the small investor with a sound means of participating in the real estate lending and equity markets and to encourage construction of residential housing. The 1960 legislation provided, therefore, for public ownership of

---

[10] For a discussion of factors contributing to the discount, see Burton G. Malkiel, ''The Valuation of Closed-End Investment Company Shares,'' *Journal of Finance* (June 1977).

[11] For an analysis of the dual-purpose fund concept, see Robert H. Litzenberger and Howard B. Sosin, ''The Theory of Recapitalizations and the Evidence of Dual-Purpose Funds,'' *Journal of Finance* (December 1977).

REITs, full distribution of income to the holders of the certificates of beneficial interest, and restriction of holdings to real estate mortgages, construction loans, and equities. This structure, which permitted no retention of earnings or capital gains, created immense pressure to lend and invest funds as soon as they were raised and made no provision for establishing general reserves for possible future losses.

Apart from long-term improvement in the value of real estate equities, the REITs' principal strategies for achieving growth in returns to investors were (1) borrowing short in the commercial-paper market and from commercial banks for high-rate construction loans or lending long; and (2) also increasing the leverage in the trust's capital structure by the sale of senior and subordinated debentures. The independent organizations, predominantly banks, insurance companies, and mortgage bankers, that sponsored the REITs created management companies to perform under the management contracts with the trusts. Their fees were based on total assets, providing an incentive to increase the use of borrowed funds.

In the early years, 1961 through 1967, some thirty-eight equity REITs were launched with equity capital of about $240 million. Mortgage REITs came to market in tremendous volume in the subsequent years as investors turned away from an erratic and unrewarding common-stock market. At the end of 1969 Securities and Exchange Commission data show all REITs having $2.5 billion of assets and $1.6 billion of equity. By the end of 1972, the corresponding figures were $14 billion and $5.9 billion. At approximately the peak in mid-1974, assets had increased to almost $21 billion but net worth only to $6.6 billion. At this point, mortgage loans accounted for 86 percent of assets, including a major proportion in the form of construction and development loans.[12]

The 1973–1974 doubling of the bank prime lending rate, the severity of the credit crunch, and the emergence of borrowers' defaults as borrowers were hurt by a deteriorating housing market and escalating building costs, all combined to produce a disastrous experience for investors. Despite the

handful of REITs that weathered the period of severe strain, dividends to shareholders declined by 79 percent from the fourth-quarter 1974 peak rate to mid-1977. An index of share prices declined by 75 percent from the 1972 level. A number of trusts have changed to become real estate operating companies so as to carry forward operating losses against future earnings.

The final outcome of the REIT episode will depend on the success of managers in working out compromises and swaps with lenders and the extent of the improvement in real estate markets. Because the lessons taught by the experience are highly visible, regulation of these trusts may be tightened somewhat. On the other hand, the few successful REITs have set a pattern of policies that can carry a trust through difficult periods in the capital markets.

## Bank Common Trust Funds

### Function

Commercial bank personal trust departments have turned to the common trust fund as a means of handling personal trust accounts of modest size more economically and more effectively. By pooling the assets of many small accounts and a portion of the assets of some moderately larger accounts, banks have been able to check the drain on earnings of much unprofitable business. The beneficiaries have been content to have a participation in a large pool of primary securities replace their interests in their own portfolios because of the promise of broader diversification and better investment management. More individuals have undoubtedly made use of personal trust services as a consequence of the availability of this more efficient investment vehicle.

Only assets held under wills or voluntary trust agreements can participate in the variety of funds a bank can create. Advertising of results is prohibited. Most of the assets are trusteed for long periods of time, such as the life of a widow or children of the creator of the trust. Additions and withdrawals are made on quarterly valuation dates.

By having common-stock, fixed-income, and tax-exempt bond funds, as well as balanced common trust funds, banks have been able to meet the particular problems of individual trust accounts with

---

[12]In addition to the Securities and Exchange Commission and the usual financial services, data are compiled by the National Association of Real Estate Investment Trusts and Audit Investment Research.

greater precision than if they all had to participate in a single balanced or diversified fund. As a consequence, there are more than twice as many funds as banks managing them. The bank is compensated on the basis of the fees provided in the trust agreement or in the statutes of the state of jurisdiction.

### Asset Composition

Assets in common trust funds have grown rapidly as more individual accounts participated and specialized funds, such as those for tax-exempt bonds, were started. The annual *Trusts and Estates* survey of 382 common trust funds in 1979 showed total assets of more than $6.6 billion; the distribution of these funds is found in Table 9-6. Diversified common trust funds typically had about two-thirds of their assets in equity securities. Also, assets of the diversified funds reflect a need for current income in many small accounts.

Common trust funds show greater diversity of portfolio holdings than might be expected. The annual tabulations of common stocks made by the magazine *Trusts and Estates* show little tendency for concentration in a limited number of issues. The breadth of choices made by portfolio managers reflects more than mere differences in opinion about blue-chip stocks. The common trust fund

### Table 9-6 Assets of Bank Common Trust Funds in 1978

| Asset | Amount (in millions of dollars) | Percentage of Total |
|---|---|---|
| Cash and savings | $ 176.6 | 2.7 |
| Commercial paper | 409.4 | 6.2 |
| U.S. government and agencies | 715.0 | 10.9 |
| Municipals | 1,142.1 | 17.4 |
| Corporate and foreign bonds | 659.0 | 10.0 |
| Mortgages | 58.0 | 0.9 |
| Preferred stocks | 30.2 | 0.5 |
| Common stocks and convertibles | 3,210.1 | 48.8 |
| Miscellaneous | 174.8 | 2.7 |
| | $6,575.2 | 100.0 |

Note: These statistics are based solely on the responses of 382 selected banks.

Source: Communication Channels, Inc., *Trusts and Estates*, May 1979.

portfolio is something of a showpiece in the solicitation of new business, and management often cites its performance when competing for pension funds and large personal trust accounts.

### Bank-Administered Personal Trusts

### Purposes and Functions

Estate administration and investment management of family assets have become increasingly complex with the development of progressive estate, gift, and income taxation. The duration of management is extended by trusts that skip a generation to save estate taxes and administration expenses. The charitable remainder unitrust concept is an example of an effort to enhance prospects for a life income that will keep pace with inflation. A typical vehicle names a charitable remainder interest and provides a return to the life beneficiary of 5 percent of the market value of the fund determined annually. Without some such arrangement, provisions for the invasion of principal to supplement conventional interest and dividend income are common. Safekeeping, accounting, and tax services are provided along with investment management.

Since wealthy people need an executor-trustee to carry out an estate plan, the only question is whether an individual or a bank should be appointed to serve. Banking institutions can staff the various specialized services and spread the cost over a substantial volume of assets. They also provide permanence, and their capital stands behind their acceptance of accountability. Because of the amount of personal services required, banks cannot handle small estates and trusts profitably, even with common trust funds available. About 53 percent of the assets managed by commercial bank trust departments are employee benefit trusts and agency accounts. Much of the rest consists of personal trusts.

### Asset Composition

The distribution of assets in personal trusts and estates is shown in Table 9-7. The indicated reduction in the common-stock proportion is only in part a consequence of the decline in prices; an increase in the bond position was an investment-policy decision.

**Table 9-7  Distribution of Assets of Bank-Managed Personal Trusts and Estates**

|  | 1972 | 1975 | 1977 |
|---|---|---|---|
| Cash and savings accounts | 2.9% | 3.6% | 4.0% |
| U.S. governments and agencies | 4.0 | 8.7 | 9.0 |
| Municipals | 9.7 | 5.4 | 11.7 |
| Corporate and foreign bonds | 6.7 | 16.5 | 11.4 |
| Preferred stocks | 1.7 | 1.4 | 1.2 |
| Common stocks | 69.9 | 56.7 | 52.9 |
| Real estate mortgages | 1.1 | 1.6 | 1.6 |
| Real estate | 2.7 | 3.9 | 6.3 |
| Miscellaneous | 1.3 | 2.3 | 2.0 |
|  | 100.0 | 100.0 | 100.0 |

Source: Federal Deposit Insurance Corporation, *Trust Assets of Insured Commercial Banks*, 1972, 1975, 1977.

Bank trust departments manage agency accounts for nonprofit organizations as well as for wealthy individuals. As a consequence of the Supreme Court decision in the case of *I.C.I. v. Camp,* banks cannot open pooled agency accounts because of the Glass-Steagall Act's prohibition of their underwriting of corporate securities. Even the operation of dividend reinvestment accounts by banks has been questioned.

## Growth

Personal trust assets of commercial banks probably doubled between 1958 and 1965, but the increase in the market value of common-stock holdings accounts for a substantial fraction of this growth.[13] Since 1965, the growth rate has probably been about 4 percent a year. The spread of estate planning and the use of corporate fiduciaries for trusts designed to minimize taxation contribute to growth in assets under administration. Offsets are the stream of terminations of trusts and the redistribution of assets. In the case of estates, of course,

[13] For a longer view of bank-administered personal trusts, see "Commercial Banks and the Trust Function," *The Commercial Banking Industry,* Prentice-Hall, 1962, Chap. 4 (Monograph prepared for the Commission on Money and Credit by the American Bankers Association). See also Edward S. Herman, *Conflicts of Interest: Commercial Bank Trust Departments,* Twentieth Century Fund, New York, 1975.

gross assets collected are substantially reduced by outright bequests, estate taxes, and administrative expenses. The result is a rather modest rate of growth, apart from appreciation in the value of equity holdings.

## Role in the Capital Market

Bank-administered personal trusts play their most important role in the capital markets as the largest group of institutional holders of common stocks. Banks' personal trust departments are not only the largest institutional owners of stocks, but they are also by far the oldest and probably the most stable holders. Due to the nature of their operations, they are apt to be net suppliers of shares as they sell to meet taxes and other large cash payments.

As executors and trustees, banks administer accumulated wealth, often in the form of controlling interests in businesses. To shift from the position of owner to that of investor may involve marketing closely held securities and diversifying the portfolio of assets to provide regular income. Such duties play a key role in broadening public ownership of business firms. This happens, for example, when trustees sell equities, on balance, and purchase municipal bonds to meet the requirements of individuals who are largely dependent on the income from trusts for current living expenses.

Under the guidance of the long-established prudent man rule, bank trustees deal with the myriad differences of individual circumstances and problems. Except in common trust funds, there need be no uniformity in the application of investment management policies. As a consequence, few identifiable trends can be detected in the distribution of trust portfolios. About the only general trends that can be asserted confidently are the moves to higher proportions in common stocks, the substitution of municipal bonds for corporate and federal government securities, and more emphasis on maintaining the real purchasing power of trust assets instead of merely conserving dollar values. In recent years, greater consciousness of the quality of investment management has been evident, with a resulting increase in the rate of portfolio turnover.

As financial institutions, bank trust departments play no real part in the accumulation of financial assets. Theirs is the function of taking over the management of existing assets and redistributing their ownership—an important financial service in a complicated world of intricate problems in taxation and administration. In addition, they seek to participate effectively in the allocation of capital to its most productive uses. Such activities are most conspicuous in the secondary market for outstanding securities.

## Investment-Type Intermediaries as a Whole

### As Suppliers of Equity Capital

We have seen that investment-type financial intermediaries serve both as savings institutions and as managers of existing wealth. They are important as net institutional suppliers of loanable funds, major suppliers of equity capital, and net demanders of financial assets, as these magnitudes are conventionally measured. They are, however, of even greater importance in total capital-market transactions, which include exchanges of existing securities as well as new issues.

During the decade 1967–1976, net new issues of common stock averaged $6.7 billion a year, but corporate retained earnings averaged $31.3 billion a year. Retained earnings are, in effect, equivalent to a fully subscribed preemptive rights offering to existing stockholders.[14] As holders of about 13 percent of all corporate stocks, investment companies and bank-administered personal trusts can be ranked as major suppliers of equity capital if "purchases" of retained earnings averaging $4 billion per year during that decade are considered.

### As Portfolio Managers

The second major role of these intermediaries is as decision makers in the allocation of wealth among alternative financial investment opportunities. In the secondary market for common stocks in particular, their pace and scale of activities can change market structure and the mechanism designed to accommodate them. Their operations also affect both the level and stability of the cost of equity capital for different risk classes.

The changing pattern of portfolio diversification over a span of time also is important in developing new markets and ventures. Because risks to the participant in an investment-type intermediary are greatly reduced, these institutions can take greater individual risks than would be acceptable to those who have entrusted their capital to such institutions. The net effect is that these intermediaries make available a greater amount of risk capital than would otherwise be the case.

The management of large aggregations of capital for profit provides incentives to employ and train capable individuals in financial analysis. Improvements in information, techniques, and the analytical process contribute to greater rationality in valuation and, therefore, in the process of allocating real resources. The experienced structure of investment management contributes skills as well as funds to the working of the capital market.

Because these analytical skills are applied to investment, current prices fully reflect all that is known or knowable about particular companies. For this reason, superior returns cannot be earned consistently by extensive analysis of this body of knowledge. This is the essence of the efficient market hypothesis.[15] We have stated the semi-strong form of this hypothesis. Acceptance of this position implies that security analysts and portfolio managers perform a socially desirable service in keeping the market efficient but that they need not be highly rewarded for incurring transaction costs in the futile effort to detect market inefficiencies. In the judgment of some law experts, prudence calls for investing in a market or index fund.[16]

There are, however, several opposing views: (1) the rewards to active portfolio management are obscured in the broad averages compiled in most studies; (2) the inefficiency of the analytical and

---

[14]That is to say, apart from certain transaction costs and tax consequences, it makes no difference if a corporation retains earnings or if it pays them out in dividends but then sells new shares to each stockholder in proportion to his or her existing holdings to raise the equivalent of the earnings paid out.

[15]For a brief summary of this hypothesis and its implications, see James H. Lorie and Mary T. Hamilton, *The Stock Market: Theories and Evidence,* Richard D. Irwin, Homewood, Ill., 1973, Chaps. 4 and 5.

[16]John H. Langbein and Richard A. Posner, "Market Funds and Trust-Investment Law," *American Bar Foundation Research Journal,* 1976, No. 1, Part I, and 1977, No. 1, Part II. For an opposing view, see Roger F. Murray, "Investment Risk in Pension Funds; The Pension Benefit Guaranty Corporation View," *Evolving Concepts of Prudence,* Financial Analysts Research Foundation, Charlottesville, Va., 1976.

selective process in probing the future, not the efficiency of the market, explains why superior returns are earned by only a few asset managers; (3) rewards from the selection of equity securities come from making superior forecasts of the future of the economy, the industry, and the company—all of which are inaccurately reflected in share prices (witness the major price changes that occur when that future unfolds)—but *current knowledge* about the company is an unreliable guide to its future (the problem is to anticipate change rather than the repetition of past performance by a firm);[17] and (4) the usefulness of inactive management in the form of an index fund for a low-cost, diversified portfolio does not preclude a role for actively managed accumulations of capital to which specialized analytical techniques are applied on a consistent basis. In addition, some observers believe that the index-fund concept as widely applied is primarily a commitment to a portfolio weighted by market values as compared with a more equally weighted portfolio. There is, however, little or no evidence that the market is especially efficient at making this weighting decision. It is not clear that adjustments for volatility deal adequately with the evaluation of results. Furthermore, new studies are required to take account of how the use of options in portfolio management can change the risk/return characteristics of various portfolio mixes.

The conventional test for the efficient market hypothesis is whether actively managed portfolios can consistently outperform passive ones after taking into account their variability characteristics. A different criterion is the efficiency with which capital markets allocate resources to the most productive (profitable) uses. On this score, the test is more difficult. The experience of observers has been that the market is chronically late in taking account of fundamental changes in the economics of industries and in the effectiveness of business firms. Yet the market does its work across time more effectively than any known alternative system. Investment-type intermediaries are competitively active participants in this process.[18]

## As Market Participants

The increased role of investing institutions as participants in the equity capital market has been the subject of numerous studies and investigations. These studies have posed various questions.

1. What is the significance to the equity capital markets of the increased emphasis on performance, the higher rate of turnover, and the possible concentration of ownership?[19]

2. Have the securities markets adapted to the explosion in institutional volume, with the need to handle block transactions in an auction market structure designed for a large flow of round-lot orders? (In 1952, individuals accounted for 69 percent of the public volume on the New York Stock Exchange and institutions 31 percent. By 1971, individuals' share was only 40 percent, while institutions accounted for almost 60 percent of public volume.)[20]

3. Does the concentration of ownership and control have potentially deleterious effects on the risk-capital allocation process? Does the large investing institution, for example, have to concentrate its funds in corporate giants with a resulting deprivation of smaller, newer, risk-taking enterprises?[21]

The *Institutional Investor Study* showed that imbalances in trading among institutions frequently left 25 percent of a purchase or sale to be supplied or acquired by market makers or other investors. That is to say, a separate market for institutions would not be a promising solution for the problem of short-run price instability.

Contrary to many preconceptions, the study concluded: "The findings indicate that situations in which the trading of an institution may create or accentuate price movements are more or less matched in number and importance by situations in which the trading behavior of an institution *reduces* the magnitude of the price impacts of trading

[17]See John Lintner and Robert Glauber, "Higgledy Piggledy Growth in America," in *Modern Development in Investment Management,* ed. James Lorie and Richard Brealey, Frederick A. Praeger, New York, 1972.

[18]Tests of the efficient market hypothesis are discussed further in Chapter 32.

[19]These are among the central questions addressed by the *Institutional Investor Study.*

[20]New York Stock Exchange, *Public Transaction Study,* 1971. See also six papers comprising "Individuals and the Corporate Equity Market," *Journal of Contemporary Business* (Winter 1974).

[21]Cf. Carol J. Loomis, "How the Terrible Two-Tier Market Came to Wall Street," *Fortune* (July 1973), 82–89, 186–190. For a differing view, see Roger F. Murray, "Institutionalization of the Stock Market: To Be Feared Or Favored?" *Financial Analysts Journal* (March-April 1974).

by others."[22] Although some people believe that institutions play "follow the leader," draw on many of the same investment research sources, and, therefore, tend to think alike and to accentuate the range of individual stock price fluctuations, these impressions were not borne out by this most careful analysis of the Institutional Investor Study team.

The notion that markets really do not work is periodically revived. The so-called two-tier market of 1971–1973 was the most recent revival,[23] and the occasion for it was a recurrence of the 1961 market phenomenon. By the third quarter of 1974, just as in the summer of 1962, increased value disparities between different market sectors once again proved to be transitory. There is reliable evidence that group movements (that is, growth, cyclical, stable market sectors) are significant across time,[24] but it is also clear that the market's discipline eventually brings prices into line with risk-adjusted and realistic expected returns. Competition for investor patronage goads investing institutions into activity designed to bring prices into line with economic values.

## As Participants in the Saving Process

Through the activities of investment-type intermediaries, equities in corporate retained earnings are accumulated for the benefit of households. This is the major role of investment-type intermediaries in the saving process. Nonetheless, investing institutions have also become efficient providers of saving facilities through mutual fund accumulation accounts in the form of Keogh or Individual Retirement Accounts. Of course, the investment companies' money-market funds compete directly with deposit-type institutions' saving and liquid-asset products.

Banks have attempted to remain competitive and have had major success in the development of dividend reinvestment plans. Attempts to offer broadly diversified portfolios to individuals on an agency basis, however, have repeatedly run afoul of the Glass-Steagall Act's prohibition of the underwriting by banks of nongovernmental securities. Furthermore, congressional committees show concern about the concentration of voting securities in financial institutions, possible conflicts between investing functions and commercial lending activity, and the lack of public information about portfolio transactions. Nevertheless, the efforts of banking institutions to penetrate markets for investment services will undoubtedly continue.

These trends illustrate the broad tendency of financial institutions to become increasingly similar in their functions, and one can expect that specialization will continue to diminish among intermediaries of all types.

## Questions

1. Which characteristics of an investment-type intermediary influence the types of assets held and the duration of holding periods?
2. How would you go about making a forecast of mutual fund sales, repurchases, and net increase in assets?
3. How would you change the preceding forecast if banks were permitted to underwrite and distribute mutual fund shares?
4. What is a reasonable span of time for the measurement of mutual fund performance? What are the problems with using shorter periods?
5. What, if any, limitations should be placed on withdrawal privileges from money market funds? Why?
6. Do higher turnover rates in common-stock portfolios contribute to the breadth, liquidity, and continuity of markets or simply to the volatility of share prices?
7. What lessons can be learned from investor experience with Real Estate Investment Trusts?
8. In terms of the structure and functioning of the capital markets, what difference does it make whether individuals accumulate equity investments directly or through investment-type intermediaries?
9. Bank trust departments are large suppliers and demanders of securities. How does the size of these activities affect the structure and efficiency of the capital markets?
10. Distinguish the role of investment-type intermediaries from deposit and insurance types in terms of the capital-allocation function performed.

[22]Vol. 4, Chap. 10, 1465.

[23]See sources in footnote 20.

[24]James L. Farrell, Jr., "Analyzing Covariance of Return to Determine Homogeneous Stock Groupings," *Journal of Business* (April 1974); "Homogeneous Stock Groupings," *Financial Analysts Journal* (May-June 1975); and *The Multi-Index Model and Practical Portfolio Analysis,* Financial Analysts Research Foundation, Charlottesville, Va., 1976.

## Selected Bibliography

Friend, Irwin, Marshall Blume, and Jean Crockett. *Mutual Funds and Other Institutional Investors.* McGraw-Hill Book Company, New York, 1970.

Herman, Edward S. *Conflicts of Interest: Commercial Bank Trust Departments*. Twentieth Century Fund, New York, 1975.

*Institutional Investor Study Report of the Securities and Exchange Commission*. House Document No. 92-64, 92nd Cong., 1st Sess., March 1971.

Investment Company Institute. *Mutual Fund Fact Book*, published annually.

*Report of Special Study of Securities Markets of the Securities and Exchange Commission*. House Document No. 95, 88th Cong., 1st Sess., April-September 1963.

Securities and Exchange Commission. *Public Policy Implications of Investment Company Growth*. House Report No. 2337, 89th Cong., 2nd Sess., December 1966.

Wharton School of Finance and Commerce. *A Study of Mutual Funds, Prepared for the Securities and Exchange Commission*. House Report No. 2274, 87th Cong., 2nd Sess., August 1962.

# 10

# Consumer-Oriented Intermediaries

One of the more interesting developments in U.S. credit markets during the twentieth century has been the rapid growth of consumer credit. Around the turn of the century, household indebtedness other than mortgage debt consisted mainly of charge accounts at retail outlets and outstanding doctors' bills. Instalment credit was used for only a few items, such as pianos, encyclopedias, and sewing machines, and these made up a minuscule portion of total household expenditures. Moreover, financial intermediaries played almost no direct role in the extension of such credit.

Today, with the increased emphasis on consumer durable goods, such as automobiles, boats, and household appliances, the situation is vastly different. Consumer credit has become large from any point of view, even though it is still less than one-third the size of residential mortgage debt. The instalment portion has far outstripped single-payment loans and charge accounts; and financial institutions now provide almost 90 percent of instalment credit.

There is a straightforward explanation for this turnaround: both demand for and supply of consumer credit have increased sharply in recent decades. Instalment credit demand has grown as a result of the rising importance of high-priced consumer durable goods, the most obvious example being the automobile. But growth in demand, by itself, would not have led to the huge increase in volume. There had to be an increase in supply as well, and this required relaxation of state usury laws that applied to consumer credit along with other types of credit.

Consumer credit is inherently costly for two basic reasons. First, the typical transaction is small in size relative to other types of credit. Since many of the costs associated with lending do not vary significantly with loan size, the average cost per dollar loaned (that is, total cost divided by loan size) of a small loan is usually much higher than that of a large loan. Second, like all loans, consumer credit is subject to risk and, in certain respects, these risks are greater than those attached to other forms of credit. For example, most households do not keep accurate and easily verifiable records for lenders to inspect. There is the obvious risk that a borrower's income will fall because of loss of job, sickness, or death. Moreover, it is not always feasible for a household to provide collateral; even when collateral is available, it usually remains in the borrower's custody and is difficult for the lender to locate and seize in the event of default.

For both reasons, it was uneconomic for lenders to provide consumer credit so long as it was subject to the interest rate ceilings imposed by usury laws. Not until these ceilings were lifted—or alternatively, until ways of circumventing them were devised—did consumer credit begin to thrive as a legitimate form of lending.[1]

At the end of 1978, outstanding consumer credit totaled $340.0 billion, of which $275.6 billion was instalment debt.[2] Table 10-1 presents a two-way classification of this $275.6 billion, by lender and by type of credit. It can be seen that three principal types of financial intermediaries—commercial banks, finance companies, and credit unions—provide instalment credit to households, and that the credit takes the form of auto paper, mobile home credit, revolving credit, and "other" (which is chiefly personal loans and credit for purchase of nonautomotive durable goods).[3]

The purpose of this chapter will be (1) to describe briefly each intermediary; (2) to analyze selected features of instalment credit markets; and (3) to examine the responsiveness of instalment lenders to monetary policy. The latter topic is of special interest since consumer instalment lenders have often been considered to be largely impervious to monetary policy or—worse still—to be sources of short-run business fluctuations.

## Description of Major Instalment Lenders

### Commercial Banks

At the end of 1978, commercial banks held consumer instalment credit of $136.2 billion, or 49.4 percent of the total amount outstanding, and were thus by far the most important providers of such credit. Moreover, banks provide additional funds to this market through loans (and loan commitments) to finance companies and retailers. Through holding companies, banks have acquired a substantial number of finance companies in recent years. They are also important noninstalment lenders to consumers. It seems fair to say, therefore, that the commercial banking system is the foundation of consumer credit, as it is in so many other credit markets.

From Table 10-1 it can be seen that banks are important in every branch of consumer credit. In 1978, they held about 59 percent of all automobile paper, 59 percent of mobile home credit, and 42 percent of all other consumer instalment credit. They obtained 59 percent of their auto-paper holdings through purchase from automobile dealers. The remainder, of course, consisted of direct loans to car purchasers. As a concomitant of the purchase of automobile paper, banks have become involved heavily in the extension of "wholesale" credit to dealers for the carrying of inventories.

The category "revolving credit" comprises two relatively new forms of instalment credit: bank check credit and bank credit cards. Under check credit an individual may arrange for a line of credit that enables him to write checks against nonexistent balances—essentially an overdraft system. Within limits, repayment can proceed at the borrower's preferred pace. Bank credit cards offer the same flexibility with regard to repayment. However, cards can be used only for purchases from participating merchants (or for cash advances at participating banks). They do have the important advantage, of course, of being more widely acceptable than a personal check. Retailers as well as banks offer revolving credit plans.

---

[1] For discussions of the history of consumer credit, see John M. Chapman and Robert P. Shay, *Licensed Lending in New York*, Columbia University Press, New York, 1970; and David H. Rogers, *Consumer Banking in New York*, Columbia University Press, New York, 1975.

[2] The best source of data on consumer credit is the *Federal Reserve Bulletin*. Beginning with the January 1976 issue, the *Bulletin* has included data only for the instalment portion of consumer credit. Noninstalment credit, which is discussed further in Chapter 14, represents only about 15 percent of consumer credit.

[3] Unfortunately, classification by type of credit involves ambiguities. For example, a cash loan by a bank for an unspecified purpose, or for a purpose other than the purchase of an automobile or a mobile home, is classified as a "personal loan." On the other hand, if the purpose is to acquire an automobile, this cash loan is included in the auto-paper category, along with instalment sales contracts that banks purchase from automobile dealers. From some points of view, a direct cash loan of this sort is more akin to a personal loan than to indirect auto financing arranged through a dealer, since it involves face-to-face negotiations between the purchaser and the ultimate lender. There are other anomalies as well.

**Table 10-1   Consumer Instalment Credit Outstanding, December 31, 1978 (in millions of dollars)**

| Type of Credit | Commercial Banks | Finance Companies | Credit Unions | Retailers | Others[a] | Total |
|---|---|---|---|---|---|---|
| | | | Holders | | | |
| Automobiles | $ 60,564 | $19,937 | $21,967 | — | — | $102,468 |
| Mobile homes | 9,553 | 3,152 | 489 | — | $ 2,848 | 16,042 |
| Revolving | 24,434 | — | — | $19,377 | 3,240 | 47,051 |
| Other | 41,638 | 31,209 | 23,483 | 5,499 | 8,239 | 110,068 |
| Total | $136,189 | $54,298 | $45,939 | $24,876 | $14,327 | $275,629 |

[a]Credit held by automobile dealers has been included in "Others."

Source: Board of Governors of the Federal Reserve System, *Federal Reserve Bulletin.*

While banks are major providers of consumer instalment credit, this credit is a relatively small portion of total bank earning assets—13.4 percent at the end of 1978. Among the broad loan and investment categories presented each month in the *Federal Reserve Bulletin,* consumer credit ranked well behind commercial and industrial loans, real estate loans, U.S. government securities, and state and local government securities. However, when allowance is made for an estimated $6 to $10 billion of bank loans to finance companies, much of which finds its way into consumer credit, plus an unknown amount of lending to merchants in support of charge account and other retail credit, it is clear that consumer credit directly or indirectly makes up a significant share of total bank credit.

Banks were latecomers as instalment lenders. In 1919 (the earliest date for which reliable data exist), banks held a mere 2.4 percent of all instalment credit, and their share had grown to only 5.7 percent a decade later. An estimated 5,000 banks were engaged in consumer lending in 1940, and this figure had risen to nearly 11,000 by the end of World War II.[4] As of December 31, 1974, fewer than 50 of the 14,200 insured banks reported no holdings of consumer credit.[5]

We have already suggested a major reason why banks were slow in entering the instalment credit business: usury ceilings, in some states as low as 6 percent per annum, made this an unattractive market for banks. In addition, in the early decades

of the century, most banks operated out of single offices, without branches, making it difficult for them to compete effectively. The reluctance of banks to advertise or to stay open beyond the traditional 3 P.M. closing time also hampered their participation in the market for instalment credit.

Banks met the challenge of usury ceilings in a number of ways. In place of simple annual interest, they commonly calculated instalment loan rates on a *discount* or *add-on* basis. The effect was to apply the quoted interest rate to the initial amount borrowed, rather than to the average amount outstanding. In the case of an instalment loan with repayments of uniform size, the latter would be only about one-half of the initial amount borrowed, implying that the simple annual interest counterpart of a 6 percent discount or add-on rate would be close to 12 percent.[6] Another way of achieving the same objective was the use of "hypothecated deposits" in conjunction with a consumer loan. Under this arrangement, which was employed mainly by "industrial" or "Morris-plan banks," the loan was not repaid until final maturity but the borrower agreed to accumulate funds in a deposit according to a prearranged schedule, to permit repayment of the loan.[7] Obviously, the hypothecated-deposit device meant that the borrower did not have use of the full amount borrowed; hence, once again, the effect was a substantial increase in interest costs

[4]American Bankers Association, *The Commercial Banking Industry,* a monograph prepared for the Commission on Money and Credit, Prentice-Hall, Englewood Cliffs, N.J., 1963, p. 164.

[5]"Consumer Lending at Commercial Banks," *Federal Reserve Bulletin* (May 1975), 271.

[6]For a clear discussion of alternative methods of stating instalment finance charges, see Wallace P. Mors, *Consumer Credit Finance Charges: Rate Information and Quotation,* National Bureau of Economic Research, New York, 1965.

[7]Most industrial banks have now been absorbed into the mainstream of commercial banking since most of them have diversified into various other activities.

over the stated amount. Still another method of circumventing usury ceilings was to purchase consumer instalment contracts from retailers. English common law had established long ago that the difference between a cash price and the sum of a series of instalments, known as the "time-price differential," is not interest. Hence it is not subject to the usury laws.[8]

In the aftermath of the Great Depression, banks began in earnest to penetrate instalment credit markets, especially under the impetus of the Federal Housing Administration's home repair and modernization program. Business loan demand was weak then and banks quickly saw the potential profits in lending to consumers, particularly when it could be carried out at convenient branches, under liberalized branching rules. In addition, many states adopted statutes that provided more generous loan rates for bank instalment loans.

The basic federal banking statutes in the U.S. are silent on consumer credit. Nevertheless, the states have gradually brought banks under rate regulation for most types of instalment credit, and today banks are regulated almost as thoroughly as other types of consumer lenders. The federal government also has played a considerably more active role in instalment credit markets during the past decade, especially since enactment of the Consumer Credit Protection Act in 1968. This new regulatory environment, which relates to all instalment lenders, is discussed later in the chapter and in Chapter 14.

### Finance Companies

Next in importance, after commercial banks, are finance companies. They held 20 percent of total instalment credit at the end of 1978, primarily in the form of personal loans and automobile paper. Finance companies are the largest providers of personal instalment loans in the United States.

When one examines the finance company category, one finds a rather heterogeneous collection of intermediaries that seem to have just two features in common: they are regulated closely by the states, and they obtain most loan funds from sources other than deposits. Until recently, a distinction was made between sales finance and consumer finance companies, the former consisting of firms that purchase instalment sales contracts from retailers, the latter of firms that make direct cash loans to households. During the 1960s this distinction became increasingly blurred, both as a result of sales finance company shifts into cash lending, leasing, and business financing and because of consumer finance company entry into retail finance through the acquisition of retail chains. Consequently, the Federal Reserve merged the two types of companies in its statistical reports beginning in September 1970. Even within the sales finance industry there have been sharp differences among companies, some specializing heavily in automobile financing, others engaging exclusively in purchases of other consumer-goods paper. Moreover, since 1919, when General Motors Corporation formed its wholly owned finance subsidiary, General Motors Acceptance Corporation, there has been an important distinction between *independents* and *captives*. Many manufacturers have formed captive finance companies—or finance subsidiaries, as they might better be called—and they now account for the bulk of new-car financing by finance companies.[9]

The first sales finance company was formed in 1904 to acquire instalment contracts from piano dealers.[10] The rise of the automobile in the next few years led to the formation of hundreds of new sales finance companies. By 1922 it was estimated that as many as 1,000 firms were in operation. The legal foundation of instalment sales financing was, as noted earlier, the doctrine that a time-price differential is not subject to the usury laws since it is not interest. Thus, sales finance companies arose spontaneously to meet a market demand, and they did not come under close public supervision until much later.

---

[8]However, the courts have recognized many exceptions to the time-price doctrine. See Mors, *Consumer Credit Finance Charges*, pp. 19–20.

[9]This can be seen rather vividly by examining the annual reports of the huge independent sales finance companies, Commercial Credit Company and C.I.T. Financial Corporation, which (together with General Motors Acceptance Corporation) were the leading financers of new automobiles several decades ago. Auto paper now constitutes only 1 to 2 percent of total consumer receivables of these companies.

[10]See Rolf Nugent, *Consumer Credit and Economic Stability*, Russell Sage Foundation, New York, 1939, pp. 78–79.

Consumer finance companies came into existence at about the same time as sales finance companies, but under entirely different circumstances. For some time there had been discussion of the desirability of permitting "small loan companies" to provide instalment loans, subject to close government regulation, at interest rates sufficiently high to cover costs. The object was to eliminate illegal loan sharks who, quite naturally, were lending money at much higher rates of interest. Under leadership of the Russell Sage Foundation, a Uniform Small Loan Law was drafted in 1916, and one version or another of this law was adopted by a majority of the states during the next few decades. Initially, most of these laws permitted licensed lenders to make cash loans of up to $300, at interest rates as high as 3½ percent per month on the unpaid balance, repayable in monthly instalments within 10 to 20 months. Over the years, however, the laws have been amended to permit much larger loans and longer maturities, but at markedly lower rate ceilings.

Both types of companies have been largely free from federal regulation. In contrast to banks, they have been able to operate across state lines, usually through holding companies. Indeed, the largest finance companies have between 800 and 2,000 loan offices, covering all parts of the United States and extending to other countries as well. As a consequence, there is substantially greater concentration among finance companies than among banks at the national level. In its most recent quinquennial survey of finance companies, dated June 30, 1975, the Federal Reserve presented data for 3,376 firms, of which 190 had gross receivables of $25 million or more; their consumer receivables were equal to 93.8 percent of the industry's total.[11] However, since instalment credit markets are inherently local in nature, the existence of high concentration nationally has little relevance to market performance. In most communities, medium-size and small firms manage to survive in competition with the giants, not to mention the competition among the giants themselves and between finance companies and other lenders.

[11]"Survey of Finance Companies, 1975," *Federal Reserve Bulletin* (March 1976), Appendix Table 1. Results of the 1980 survey should become available around mid-year 1981.

Table 10-2 presents a simplified balance sheet for all finance companies as of the end of 1978. Assets consist mainly of receivables. Cash is a minor asset; finance companies are not subject to legal reserve requirements, and they protect themselves against run-offs of short-term debt by maintaining open lines of credit at banks. In fact, most finance company cash represents compensating balances demanded by line-granting banks. These balance requirements usually are 10 percent of the credit line plus 10 percent of actual borrowings, in the case of the larger companies, or 15 percent of the line regardless of the intensity of its use, in the case of smaller companies. However, they tend to be somewhat higher during periods of monetary restraint than during periods of slack.

Finance companies tend to be highly leveraged, especially the largest firms. As of December 1978, debt was 6.1 times net worth. Throughout the mid-1970s, there was a fairly even balance between short- and long-term debt, with commercial paper far outweighing bank loans. The 1975 Federal Reserve survey indicates that 91 percent of finance company commercial paper had been sold directly by the issuers rather than through paper dealers. Companies with less than $25 million in receivables

**Table 10-2  Assets and Liabilities of Finance Companies, December 31, 1978 (in billions of dollars)**

| ASSETS | |
|---|---:|
| Accounts receivable, gross | |
|   Consumer | $ 52.6 |
|   Business | 63.3 |
|     Total | 116.0 |
| Less reserves for unearned income and losses | (15.6) |
|     Accounts receivable, net | 100.4 |
| Cash | 3.5 |
| Securities | 1.3 |
| Other | 17.3 |
|     Total assets | $122.4 |
| LIABILITIES | |
| Short-term debt | |
|   Bank loans | $ 6.5 |
|   Commercial paper | 34.5 |
|   Other | 8.1 |
|     Total | 49.1 |
| Long-term debt | 56.2 |
| Net worth | 17.2 |
|     Total liabilities and net worth | $122.4 |

Source: *Federal Reserve Bulletin* (November 1979).

sold only negligible amounts of commercial paper, relying heavily on bank loans for their funds.

## Credit Unions

The last major financial institution in the instalment credit market is the credit union. At the end of 1978, credit union holdings of consumer instalment credit were $45.9 billion—85 percent as large as those of finance companies (see Table 10-1). As recently as the end of 1968, credit unions were only 37.5 percent as large as finance companies. Credit union growth has been spectacular throughout the postwar period, and their share of total instalment credit has risen from 4 percent in 1952 to 17 percent in 1978.

Credit unions arrived in the United States about the same time as sales and consumer finance companies, the first one being established in 1909. In contrast to other instalment lenders, however, credit unions are cooperative associations. Members must be linked by some common bond, such as employment, church or labor union membership, or place of residence. Funds are derived almost entirely from members' share accounts, which typically are accumulated in small increments under payroll deduction schemes. They are used largely for instalment cash loans, exclusively to members.

Credit unions may operate under either federal or state charter. At the end of 1978, there were more than 22,000 active unions, slightly over half of which were federal credit unions (see Table 10-3). More than 4,000 of the state-chartered unions were insured by the National Credit Union Share Insurance Fund, which, since 1970, has performed the same function for credit unions as the Federal Deposit Insurance Corporation has for commercial banks. Thus, a sizable majority of all credit unions are subject to federal supervision. Federal credit unions may not offer dividends on shares in excess of 7 percent per year on savings shares (except on certificates of deposit for specified maturities), and loan rates are limited to 15 percent per year, simple interest. Annual reports must be filed with the National Credit Union Administration, which examines federal credit unions each year. State-chartered credit unions generally face similar regulations.

It is obvious from the foregoing facts that credit unions are almost entirely local institutions and that

their average size is small—under $3 million in assets in 1978.[12] Despite their small size, credit unions have come to play an important role in instalment credit markets.

## Other Instalment Lenders

The three financial intermediaries discussed so far—commercial banks, finance companies, and credit unions—held 86 percent of all consumer instalment credit in December 1978. An additional 4 percent was held by two other intermediaries—mutual savings banks and savings and loan associations—leaving just 9 percent in the hands of retailers. The share held by retailers has declined steadily, from 28.9 percent in 1940 to 9.0 percent in 1978.

Except for a small amount of auto paper that is held by automobile dealers, instalment credit held by retailers consists of other consumer-goods paper, much of it being balances in revolving credit accounts at department stores. Mutual savings banks and savings associations provide mainly home improvement and personal loans. Needless to say, these are minute segments of their total earning assets.

## Selected Features of Instalment Credit Markets

### Finance Charges, Maturities, and Other Terms

In contrast to most other types of credit in the United States, data on interest rates and other charges for consumer instalment credit have not been readily available until quite recently. Students of this subject had to rely on bits and pieces of information contained in occasional research reports.[13] Fortunately, the Federal Reserve Board now publishes interest rates each month on selected types of instalment credit at a sample of banks and finance companies. Table 10-4 presents figures for 1972 and 1975–1978.

---

[12]In contrast, the average size of finance companies exceeds $26 million in assets.

[13]See, for example, Robert P. Shay, *New-Automobile Finance Rates, 1924–62,* Occasional Paper 86, National Bureau of Economic Research, New York, 1963.

**Table 10-3  Assets and Liabilities of Credit Unions, as of December 31, 1978 (in billions of dollars)**

|  | Federal | State | Total |
|---|---|---|---|
| **Assets** |  |  |  |
| Loans to members | $28.6 | $23.2 | $51.8 |
| Other assets | 6.1 | 4.7 | 10.8 |
| Total assets | $34.7 | $27.9 | $62.6 |
| **Liabilities and capital** |  |  |  |
| Deposits and shares | $29.3 | $23.7 | $53.0 |
| Other liabilities | 5.4 | 4.2 | 9.6 |
| Total liabilities and capital | $34.7 | $27.9 | $62.6 |
| Number of credit unions | 12,757 | 9,515 | 22,272 |
| Number of members | 22,079,000 | 17,488,000 | 39,567,000 |

Source: *Federal Reserve Bulletin*; National Credit Union Administration, *Credit Union Statistics*.

Several features of instalment credit finance charges are illustrated in Table 10-4. First, rates differ substantially by type of credit and type of lender. It can be seen that charges are lowest for new-auto paper and highest for credit-card balances and personal loans. Moreover, charges appear to be consistently higher at finance companies, on average, than at banks. Evidence from other sources indicates that credit union finance charges are generally lower than those of finance companies. Finally, the movements over time are interesting. Between 1972 and 1978, finance charges followed a path broadly similar to other interest rates (for example, the bank prime rate), first rising during the price explosion of 1973–1974, then falling as the effects of the deep recession of 1973–1975 were felt with a lag of a year or two.[14] Even though these rates do not appear to oscillate widely over time, they do vary with the general state of the economy.

This latter point has important implications. It simply is not true, as is often claimed, that instalment credit finance charges are persistently pushing against legally mandated ceilings. A detailed study by the National Commission on Consumer Finance found that, as of the second quarter of 1971, a very large share of all transactions carried finance rates less than 90 percent as high as ceiling rates.[15] For example, in the case of commercial bank direct new-auto paper with balances of $2,000 and maturities of 24 months, it was found that only in three states—Alaska, Georgia, and the District of Columbia—were all contracts in the sample carrying rates as high as 90 percent of the ceiling rate. Six states had no legally specified maximum rate on such credit. Among the remaining states, the median state response was 2.85 percent, which means that in half of the states only 2.85 percent or less of all contracts had rates within 10 percent of the legal ceiling. In thirteen states, in fact, *no* contracts carried rates as high as 90 percent of the ceiling. The NCCF made similar analyses for other types of contracts at banks and at other lenders. While personal loan rates tended to stay closer to ceilings than did rates on other types of consumer credit, not even in that instance did the NCCF find rates tending to bump against ceilings.

The rate differences across lenders and types of credit that exist at each point in time can be explained plausibly by conventional economic theory. The most important single contributor to these differences is average loan size.[16] As was mentioned earlier, many costs of lending are no greater for a large loan than for a small loan. Occupancy costs, of course, are completely independent of loan size

[14]Rates on bank credit-card plans provide an exception: they fell steadily from 1972 to 1977.

[15]Milton W. Schober and Robert P. Shay, *State and Regional Estimates of the Price and Volume of the Major Types of Consumer Instalment Credit in Mid-1971*, National Commission on Consumer Finance, Technical Studies, Government Printing Office, Washington, D.C., 1973, Vol. 3. The information referred to in the text can be found on pp. 99ff.

[16]For a thorough empirical analysis of instalment lenders' costs, see George J. Benston's recent studies: "Risk on Consumer Finance Company Personal Loans," *Journal of Finance* (May 1977), "Graduated Interest Rate Ceilings and Operating Costs by Size of Small Consumer Cash Loans," *Journal of Finance* (June 1977), and "Rate Ceiling Implications of the Cost Structure of Consumer Finance Companies," *Journal of Finance* (September 1977). Benston's bibliographies provide citations to nearly all other studies on this subject.

**Table 10-4   Terms on Selected Types of Credit**

| Lender and Type of Credit | April 1972 | April 1975 | April 1976 | April 1977 | May 1978 |
|---|---|---|---|---|---|
| Commercial banks: interest rates | | | | | |
| New automobiles (36 months) | 10.00 | 11.44 | 11.08 | 10.82 | 10.84 |
| Mobile homes (84 months) | 10.45 | 11.78 | 11.66 | 11.73 | 12.01 |
| Other consumer goods (24 months) | 12.37 | 13.22 | 12.95 | 12.92 | 13.11 |
| Other personal expenditures (12 months) | 12.58 | 13.55 | 13.16 | 13.41 | 13.56 |
| Credit card plans | 17.22 | 17.17 | 17.04 | 16.91 | 16.97 |
| Prime business loans, short-term | 5.25 | 7.50 | 6.75 | 6.25 | 8.50 |
| Finance companies: interest rates | | | | | |
| New automobiles (all) | 11.87 | 13.07 | 13.13 | 13.14 | 13.11 |
| Used automobiles (all) | 16.40 | 17.58 | 17.58 | 17.67 | 17.68 |
| Mobile homes (all) | 12.57[a] | 13.59[a] | 13.35[b] | 13.65[b] | 13.50 |
| Other consumer goods (all) | 19.75[a] | 20.00[a] | 19.37[b] | 18.85[b] | 18.90 |
| Personal loans (all) | 21.21[a] | 20.86[a] | 20.93[b] | 20.32[b] | 20.29 |
| Finance companies: average maturities (mos.) | | | | | |
| New automobiles (all) | 35.0 | 37.6 | 38.7 | 40.4 | 42.8 |
| Used automobiles (all) | 29.1 | 29.6 | 30.3 | 31.4 | 33.0 |
| Mobile homes (all) | 102.1[a] | 120.2[a] | 122.7[b] | 126.2[b] | 129.1 |
| Other consumer goods (all) | 21.6[a] | 20.6[a] | 22.9[b] | 22.9[b] | 25.4 |
| Personal loans (all) | 32.3[a] | 35.6[a] | 37.4[b] | 44.4[b] | 47.4 |
| Finance companies: average loan-to-value ratio | | | | | |
| New automobiles (all) | .87 | .86 | .86 | .87 | .88 |
| Used automobiles (all) | .99 | .97 | .95 | .96 | .97 |

[a]March data.
[b]May data.

Source: *Federal Reserve Bulletin* (September 1977) and statistical releases.

(at least in the short run), and such costs as advertising, legal fees, computer rentals, record-keeping costs, and many others are not much affected by the size of loans. It is evident, therefore, that the lender's average cost per dollar loaned will fall sharply as loan size increases. Thus, it is not surprising that used-car credit is substantially more expensive than new-car credit; used-car contracts, according to Federal Reserve data,[17] average only about half the size of new-car contracts. The Federal Reserve also reports that finance company personal loans, on average, are only about half as large as balances on used-car paper, while other consumer-goods paper average amounts are only one-third the size of personal loans. Again, this pattern would cause one to predict higher rates for personal loans and other consumer-goods paper, which is just what we see in Table 10-4.

Another relevant factor, of course, is risk. Many personal loans are unsecured, making the risk of

default greater than in the case of automobile, mobile home, and other consumer-goods credit.[18] Similarly, used-car loans made by finance companies have loan-to-value ratios substantially higher than those of new-car loans. Obviously, the lack of substantial owner equity in used cars makes such loans relatively risky.

Other factors—for example, degree of competition and state regulation of rates—contribute somewhat to rate variations, especially across states. However, it appears that loan size and risk play the dominant roles.

Finally, one sees in Table 10-4 a pronounced trend toward longer maturities, especially in new-

[17]See Federal Reserve Statistical Release No. G.26. As of November 1978, the average contract sizes were $5,856 for new cars, $3,335 for used cars.

[18]The relative riskiness of personal loans is reflected in the magnitudes of reserves for losses, expressed as ratios to outstanding instalment receivables, of finance companies that specialize in cash lending compared with companies that make relatively few cash loans. See, for example, the data presented in Robert J. Hampton, "Analysis of 1976 Composite Ratios of Instalment Sales Finance and Consumer Finance (Direct Cash Lending) Companies," *The Journal of Commercial Bank Lending* (August 1977).

car, mobile home, and personal loan paper. This reflects the attempt of borrowers to prevent monthly payments from rising as prices of items financed have escalated in recent years.

## Regulatory Trends

Until fairly recently, consumer instalment credit markets were regulated solely by the states. The only exception occurred during and immediately after World War II, when the Federal Reserve Board exercised controls over downpayments and maturities under its Regulation W. Interestingly, Regulation W applied not just to member banks, nor to all commercial banks, but to all instalment lenders, including retailers. Its aim was to control demand for consumer durables, especially automobiles, by making downpayments sufficiently high and maturities sufficiently short to ration some prospective purchasers out of durable goods markets. Regulation W was in effect on four separate occasions between September 1, 1941, and May 7, 1952; the Federal Reserve's authority to institute such controls lapsed in September 1952. Direct controls were reinstated briefly by the Federal Reserve in 1980 under new authority granted to the President in 1969, but they were removed after only three months. Many other countries, however, continue to use hire-purchase controls (as they are often called, following British terminology).

At the state level, regulation has been curiously schizophrenic. On the one hand, the initial intention of the Uniform Small Loan Law was to increase credit availability by *raising* legally permitted finance charges above the regular usury limits. More recently, the emphasis has been on *reducing* rate ceilings by shifting to graduated rate structures, presumably on the theory that lenders often are in a position to extract monopoly profits. Coupled with the emergence of severe inflation in recent years, this development has seriously limited credit availability in many states. Also, since the early 1930s, most states have added "convenience and advantage" clauses to their laws regulating finance companies. The practical effect of such clauses, which state that a charter is to be granted only if the convenience and advantage of the community will be served, has been to limit competition, thereby possibly contributing to higher finance rates. Since there is no federal chartering of

finance companies, a charter denial by state authorities means exclusion from the market.

The federal government has become heavily involved in consumer credit regulation since passage of the Truth in Lending Act (officially, Title I of the Consumer Credit Protection Act) in 1968. The key aspect of Truth in Lending (TIL) is disclosure: lenders must inform borrowers in writing of all terms relating to instalment credit transactions. This, in itself, was not new since most states had long required lenders to disclose the dollar amount of finance charges, along with other items of information. The novel features of TIL were the intrusion of the federal government into an area that had been thought to be a preserve of the states and the *method* of the required disclosure. Specifically, lenders were required to state finance charges in the form of annual percentage rates (APRs)—that is, simple annual interest rates. Thus, consumer finance companies that had been advertising rates on personal loans of (say) 3 percent per month were obliged to inform borrowers that such a rate is equivalent to an APR of about 36 percent. The objective was twofold: to make consumers more cautious about burdening themselves with debts by dramatizing the costs, and to enable them to shop for credit more intelligently by clarifying the relative costs of alternative sources of credit.

The task of policing lender compliance with TIL was spread among nine federal agencies, the most important being the Federal Reserve Board, the Comptroller of the Currency, the Federal Deposit Insurance Corporation, the National Credit Union Administration, the Federal Home Loan Bank Board, and the Federal Trade Commission. However, Congress placed responsibility for the drafting of detailed rules for implementing TIL with the Federal Reserve Board, which has done so in its Regulation Z. The regulatory task has been complicated enormously not only by the fragmentation of supervision but by adoption of several other pieces of legislation as amendments to the Consumer Credit Protection Act. Achieving an acceptable level of lender understanding and compliance has been a major challenge for the supervisory agencies.[19]

[19]"Complying with Consumer Credit Regulations: A Challenge," *Federal Reserve Bulletin* (September 1977); also, Board of Governors of the Federal Reserve System, "Annual Report to Congress on Truth in Lending for the

**Table 10-5 Concentration Ratios, Instalment Lenders in Virginia, 1971 (percentages)**

| Type of Credit | All Holders | Banks | Finance Companies | Credit Unions | Retail Outlets |
|---|---|---|---|---|---|
| All credit | 18.9 | 30.3 | 36.5 | 11.2 | 54.4 |
| Auto paper | 26.4 | 30.4 | 87.7 | 11.9 | — |
| Mobile home paper | 39.7 | 31.7 | 95.5 | 24.3 | — |
| Total: auto, mobile home, aircraft, boat, & recreational vehicle paper | 25.4 | 30.6 | 78.9 | 11.9 | — |
| Other consumer goods paper | 30.0 | 26.8 | 68.1 | 11.2 | 58.5 |
| Home repair & modernization credit | 19.6 | 23.0 | — | 9.0 | — |
| Personal loans | 17.4 | 26.3 | 29.4 | 10.8 | — |
| Retail revolving credit | 40.4 | 55.5 | — | — | 60.5 |

Note: All concentration ratios reported in the above table are based on dollar amounts outstanding. The Schober and Shay study also presents ratios based on dollar amount of credit extended and on number of contracts outstanding and extended. All ratios relate to shares of credit held by the four largest holders.

Source: Milton W. Schober and Robert P. Shay, *State and Regional Estimates of the Price and Volume of the Major Types of Consumer Instalment Credit in Mid-1971,* National Commission on Consumer Finance, Technical Studies, Volume III, Government Printing Office, Washington, D.C., 1973, pp. 145–167.

While a full assessment of the impact of TIL remains to be made, it is safe to say that neither the hopes of its sponsors nor the fears of lenders have been fully realized. Contrary to the expectations of many finance company leaders, APR disclosure has not triggered a rebellion by customers. Apparently, the level of consumer ignorance prior to TIL was less than many observers believed. Nor has there been any discernible scaling down in credit use, now that the true cost of instalment credit has been revealed. Undoubtedly, the move to uniform rate quotations has eliminated a certain amount of confusion about relative costs and has contributed to sharper competition among lenders. However, whatever gain has been reaped in this respect must be balanced against very substantial costs in added paper work, legal expenses, and other compliance burdens that are now being shouldered by lenders (ultimately, by borrowers), not to mention the large army of supervisors that has

come into existence. The net gain in consumer welfare probably has been modest—perhaps even negative.

### Competition and Market Structure

In a typical community, there are many sources of instalment credit. Hence, lender concentration tends to be low. The most comprehensive investigation of instalment credit market structures to date was conducted by the National Commission on Consumer Finance and is based on 1971 data. The NCCF calculated statewide concentration ratios for each type of instalment credit, both within and across lender groups. There is no simple way of summarizing the findings, but their general flavor can be perceived by considering the results for one fairly typical state, Virginia. The first column in Table 10-5 shows the share of outstanding credit held by the four largest holders, for all instalment credit and seven categories of such credit. Except for mobile home paper and retail revolving credit, it can be seen that concentration in Virginia was quite low, relative to prevailing levels in manufacturing and other nonfinancial sectors of the U.S. economy. Similarly, if we make comparisons across states, we find that the median concentration ratio in automobile loans, to take one example, was a moderate 29.9 percent.

Year 1977," January 3, 1978. The additional legislation referred to in the text includes the following: Fair Credit Billing (1974), Equal Credit Opportunity (1974), Amendments to Truth in Lending (1974), Real Estate Settlement Procedures (1974), Federal Trade Commission Improvement (1975), Home Mortgage Disclosure (1976), Consumer Leasing (1976), Amendments to Equal Credit Opportunity (1976), Electronic Funds Transfer (1978), and Truth in Lending Simplification (1980).

These numbers should not be taken too literally, of course. Within a particular region of any state, concentration levels are bound to be higher than those reported by the NCCF. In addition, there is a considerable degree of specialization within market categories, especially with respect to the type of risk exposure that lenders are willing to accept. Thus, low-risk borrowers tend to gravitate to the banks, leaving higher-risk borrowers as the main customers of finance companies.

## Instalment Credit and Economic Instability

In this final section, we look at consumer-oriented intermediaries from a macroeconomic perspective. This was a lively area of discourse during the 1950s—a period of rapid but unstable growth in instalment credit. There was considerable concern over the possibility that the volatility of instalment credit markets was adding to the overall problem of economic instability. This notion seems to have been the impetus behind the Federal Reserve Board's massive study of consumer credit in 1957.[20] A related concern was the widely held view that instalment credit is unresponsive to monetary policy.[21]

### Business Fluctuations

It must be conceded at once that instalment credit has displayed a considerable degree of volatility in the short run. There are clear undulations in instalment credit growth rates corresponding to business cycles, in addition to substantial month-to-month choppiness. Figure 10-1 reveals that instalment credit growth tends to peak far ahead of general cycle peaks and to reach troughs a few months ahead of cycle troughs. Thus, instalment credit growth can be regarded as a leading indicator of economic activity, even though the Commerce Department does not so classify it.

Many time series, however, display more or less regular cyclical movements. This fact alone provides little basis for concluding that instalment

credit plays a role as either a cause or an amplifier of short-run instability. Indeed, when one compares cycles in instalment credit growth with those of other types of credit, one finds that the swings in instalment credit (expressed in dollars) are typically much smaller than those in mortgage debt and business loans—to name just two examples.[22] The case for implicating instalment credit as a source of instability is far from obvious.[23] Only on rare occasions—as in 1955, when large sales finance subsidiaries promoted a sudden lengthening of standard maturities for auto paper—have there been exogenous shifts in credit supply of a possibly destabilizing nature.

A more reasonable interpretation of instalment credit cycles is that they reflect, rather than cause, cycles in durable goods expenditures. This can be tested in various ways. One method is to run regressions of instalment credit on expenditures for consumer durable goods, introducing leads and lags. When this is done, it turns out that the closest relationship exists when current-quarter instalment credit growth is related to durable goods purchases of the preceding two quarters. When leads were used, rather than lags, incorrect signs resulted. Thus, the regression results are more consistent with the hypothesis that spending drives credit than the other way around.

A second method points even more convincingly toward this interpretation. As we have seen, instalment credit can be analyzed by type. Auto paper and other consumer-goods paper, being closely linked to the acquisition of durable goods, should display strong cycles in their rates of growth, according to this interpretation. Personal loans, on the other hand, are used to finance purchases of services (for example, vacations, schooling, weddings, and funerals) as well as purchases of goods, both durable and nondurable. Since purchases of

[20]*Consumer Instalment Credit,* Government Printing Office, Washington, D.C., 1957, Parts I–IV.

[21]For example, see Marcus Nadler, ''For Standby Consumer Credit Control,'' in *Consumer Instalment Credit,* Part II, Vol. 2 (Conference on Regulation).

[22]The evidence is discussed at some length in Richard T. Selden, ''Monetary Restraint and Instalment Credit,'' in *Consumer Spending and Monetary Policy: The Linkages,* Conference Series No. 5, Federal Reserve Bank of Boston, Boston, 1971.

[23]See Milton Friedman and David Meiselman, ''The Relative Stability of Monetary Velocity and the Investment Multiplier in the United States, 1897–1958,'' in *Stabilization Policies,* Prentice-Hall, Englewood Cliffs, N.J. 1963; and Milton Friedman and Anna J. Schwartz, ''Money and Business Cycles,'' *Review of Economics and Statistics* (February 1963), Part 2.

**Figure 10-1    Instalment Credit Growth Rates, by Lender, 1953–1978**

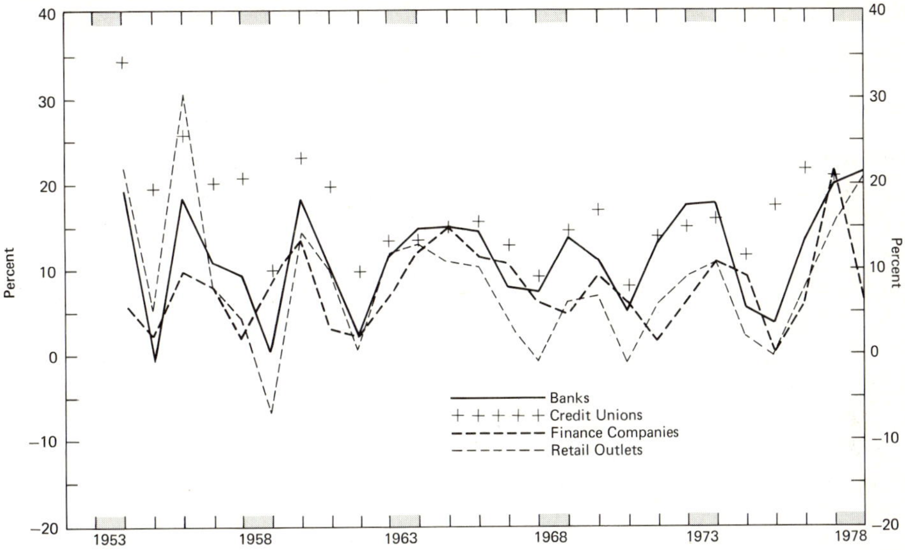

services and nondurables are less cycle-prone than those of durables, one would expect to find that personal-loan growth rates also are much less cyclical than growth rates in auto and other consumer-goods paper. This implication is strongly supported by the facts.

## Monetary Policy

Even though there seems to be scant evidence that instalment credit contributes much (if anything at all) toward the severity of business cycles, some analysts are fearful that the existence of such credit tends to undermine the potency of monetary policy. As was pointed out earlier, instalment credit is supplied by a diverse group of lenders, some of whom would appear to be little affected by a general policy of monetary restraint. Credit unions, for example, obtain funds mainly from their members, often under payroll deduction plans, rather than by borrowing. Finance companies protect themselves against tight money by negotiating massive credit lines at banks during periods of slack. Moreover, since the largest finance companies are subsidiaries of manufacturers, it is not clear that the parents would allow sales objectives to be missed simply on account of a higher cost of funds. As for banks, presumably they always have the option of main-

taining instalment credit volume by shifting funds away from other types of credit.

Once again, however, the evidence suggests that such fears are misplaced.[24] From Figure 10-1, it can be seen that credit unions are subject to the same kinds of cycles in instalment credit growth rates as other lenders. The similarity is especially clear when one allows for the fact that credit unions are relatively more active in personal loans than in more volatile types of paper. And finance companies turn out to be remarkably similar to banks, in terms of cyclical volatility and timing of instalment credit growth. Other (unpublished) evidence indicates that the behavior of the major finance subsidiaries corresponds very closely to that of the large independent finance companies, and that there were no significant differences among large, medium, and small finance companies during the three business cycles between 1953 and 1961. Finally, while it is true that bank-held instalment credit experiences somewhat wider cyclical swings in growth than does the aggregate of all other bank credit, the timing of peaks and troughs is almost identical.[25] This suggests that instalment credit responds to

[24]Much of this evidence is reviewed in Selden, "Monetary Restraint and Instalment Credit."
[25]Ibid., Chart 4.

changes in monetary policy in much the same way as other types of credit. Thus, every piece of available evidence suggests that there has been no tendency of instalment credit to undermine the effectiveness of monetary policy.

Taken by itself, this conclusion certainly is reassuring with respect to the potency of monetary policy. But the implications go far beyond the question of whether or not instalment credit markets can be controlled by the monetary authorities; they suggest that the structure of our economic system is rather different from what it is widely presumed to be. The conventional wisdom in this regard is that monetary policy works mainly through changes in the supply of credit.[26] A restrictive policy, for example, means that growth in bank reserves slows down, causing banks to sell securities (driving down their prices and increasing their yields), to raise loan rates, and to tighten credit standards. Finance companies would feel the effects of tight money when banks raise rates on loans to them and when open-market rates begin to climb. Both groups of instalment credit lenders would pass along the higher costs to borrowers, assuming that rates are not already at ceiling levels. Faced with higher borrowing costs, many would-be consumers would decide to defer purchases. Thus, a tightening of monetary policy is linked, in this conventional view, to a slowing of aggregate demand for goods and services, mainly through a shrinkage in the supply of funds.

Undoubtedly, there is some truth in this conventional picture of the transmission mechanism. However, our evidence strongly suggests the existence of a radically different sort of transmission mechanism, one that affects credit markets from the demand side.[27] According to this demand-oriented view, a tightening of monetary policy implies a slowdown in the rate of monetary growth. Would-be consumers, finding their cash balances less than expected, decide to reduce their rate of acquisition of consumer durable goods. Hence, the demand for

instalment credit falls, as does the rate of growth of instalment credit. Note that this alternative view of the transmission mechanism can easily explain the otherwise paradoxical finding of similarity in timing among lenders that face widely divergent supply conditions for funds. It is also consistent with the fact that finance companies invariably experience declining growth during tight money periods despite the availability of huge open credit lines at banks.

Fortunately, we do not face an either/or choice on this issue. It is quite possible—indeed, highly likely—that monetary policy works through more than one channel. Nevertheless, it would be a serious mistake to focus solely on funds-supply channels when attempting to assess the effectiveness of general monetary controls on a particular sector, such as the market for consumer instalment credit.

## Conclusion

Instalment credit is provided to American consumers by a diverse group of intermediaries. Foremost among them is the commercial banking system. Following a slow start, it has assumed a commanding leadership position. The dominance of banks extends to every subdivision of the instalment credit market. Finance companies (combining the former small loan companies and sales finance companies) are next in importance, followed by credit unions. These (and other) instalment lenders differ widely in balance-sheet structures, regulations to which they are subject, methods of operation, and type of customer. Nevertheless, there is clear evidence of effective competition across lender groups, despite their differences.

Instalment credit markets have experienced much turmoil since the early 1960s. Sales finance companies, faced with sharp competition from banks and credit unions, have tended to move away from automobile financing and into cash lending, making them increasingly indistinguishable from small loan (consumer finance) companies. They also have shifted toward business financing in many instances. Large finance companies of all types have tended to diversify their operations by merging with retailers and manufacturers. In the meantime, bank holding companies have bought up a substantial number of finance companies, enabling them to extend their operations across state lines.

---

[26] For a simple but representative discussion of the conventional view, see Frank de Leeuw and Edward M. Gramlich, "The Channels of Monetary Policy," *Federal Reserve Bulletin* (June 1969).

[27] The transmission mechanism that is sketched in this paragraph is similar to the mechanism articulated by Milton Friedman and his associates. See Friedman and Meiselman, "The Relative Stability," and Friedman and Schwartz, "Money and Business Cycles."

The emergence of rapid inflation in the mid-1960s and the changing regulatory environment of the late 1960s and early 1970s have further complicated these structural changes. Inflation has had two adverse effects on instalment lenders. First, it has pushed up interest rates generally, but rate ceilings imposed by states have been slow to reflect these changes, which implies, in many instances, adverse cost-price trends for lenders. Second, inflation has reduced the real value of limits on loan size, forcing lenders to make a larger share of their loans at low rates, as specified by state laws.

The principal regulatory developments have been at the federal level, with enactment of Truth in Lending in the Consumer Credit Protection Act in 1968. The requirement of rate disclosure by all lenders on the basis of annual percentage rates has proven to be less earthshaking in its effects than the sponsors of Truth in Lending had hoped, or than instalment lenders had feared. But Truth in Lending has turned out to be just the thin edge of the wedge, as Congress has extended its efforts at protection of instalment borrowers in a number of other ways since 1968.

Despite all of the changes, the market for instalment credit was not greatly different in the late 1970s from its condition a decade or two earlier. There continues to be a multiplicity of lenders, competition seems to be reasonably effective, and patterns of credit use appear to be much the same as before. Probably the best hope for significant improvements in the functioning of markets lies in policies designed to promote competition rather than in rate and loan-size ceilings and protective legislation.

## Questions

1. Explain why consumer instalment credit was not important in the U.S. economy prior to the twentieth century.
2. Name the three major financial intermediaries engaged in providing instalment credit to consumers and indicate the particular type of credit emphasized in each case.
3. What is wholesale credit?
4. Banks participate in the market for consumer credit in a number of ways. List as many of these as you can and give some rough indication of their relative importance.
5. Explain the reasons for the wide range of finance charges for instalment credit, both across lenders for a given type of credit and across credit types at given lenders.
6. Discuss the major impacts of the rapid inflation of recent years on instalment credit markets.
7. What sorts of factors might explain the more rapid growth of credit unions than of finance companies as consumer instalment lenders in recent years?
8. The Truth in Lending Act has been in effect for more than a decade. Explain the benefits and costs associated with this legislation.
9. Why are lines of credit at commercial banks important to finance companies even though these firms do not usually obtain a large share of their funds from banks?
10. What was Regulation W? During what periods was it in effect?
11. Describe how finance companies use the commercial paper market. Distinguish between the large "direct" sellers and the smaller firms that sell paper through dealers.
12. What evidence can be marshaled for and against the notion that finance companies and credit unions, which are not regulated directly by the Federal Reserve, tend to offset and weaken monetary policy?

## Selected Bibliography

Benston, George J. "Graduated Interest Rate Ceilings and Operating Costs by Size of Small Consumer Cash Loans." *Journal of Finance* (June 1977).

———. "Rate Ceiling Implications of the Cost Structure of Consumer Finance Companies." *Journal of Finance* (September 1977).

———. "Risk on Consumer Finance Company Personal Cash Loans." *Journal of Finance* (May 1977).

Boczar, Gregory E. "Competition Between Banks and Finance Companies: A Cross Section Study of Personal Loan Debtors." *Journal of Finance* (March 1978).

Chapman, John M., and Robert P. Shay, eds. *The Consumer Finance Industry*. Columbia University Press, New York, 1967.

*Consumer Credit in the United States*. Report of the National Commission on Consumer Finance. Government Printing Office, Washington, D.C., 1972.

Peterson, Richard L. "Factors Affecting the Growth of Bank Credit Card and Check Credit." *Journal of Finance* (May 1977).

———. "The Impact of General Credit Restraint on the Supply of Commercial Bank Consumer Instalment Credit." *Journal of Money, Credit and Banking* (November 1976).

Selden, Richard T. "Monetary Restraint and Instalment Credit." In *Consumer Spending and Monetary Policy: The Linkages*. Conference Series No. 5, Federal Reserve Bank of Boston, Boston, 1971.

# 11

# Government Lending Agencies

The federal government's first major venture into the credit business came in 1916, when it established the Federal Land Bank System. The Federal Intermediate Credit Banks followed in 1923, but it was the Great Depression that made the U.S. government a really major factor in credit markets. During that time, federal lending activities grew enormously both in number and in scope, and this growth has continued in the years since. Today there are more than 150 programs serving mainly housing, agriculture, education, small business, and international trade. By the end of 1978, federal programs had acquired private securities or made loans to the private sector totaling $296 billion, in addition to guaranteeing $210 billion of private loans.[1] This enumeration, moreover, excludes the largest lending agency, the Federal Reserve System, as well as the largest programs for guaranteeing loans, those of the Federal Deposit Insurance Corporation and the Federal Savings and Loan Insurance Corporation. Thus, there can be little doubt about the importance of federal activity in private credit markets.

This chapter examines the major federal credit programs. The first section presents the rationale for establishing and continuing these programs. The next section describes the structure and functions of the federal institutions providing direct credit or guarantees. Quantitative estimates of their size are made in this section. Finally, the last section attempts to assess the impact of these programs on the economy as a whole as well as on the sectors served by the programs.

### Reasons for Federal Credit Activity

Federal credit programs, like federal activities of all types, are usually established to correct inequities and inefficiencies perceived by Congress. These problems can be classified into four types: encouragement of economic growth and alleviation of economic recessions, correction of inefficiencies in private markets, encouragement of activities providing external economies,[2] and redistribution of income.

---

[1] There is some double-counting in these figures. More than 40 percent of guaranteed securities have been acquired by government agencies (see Table 11-3).

[2] An external economy is said to exist if an activity's marginal social benefits exceed marginal social costs even

The Great Depression occasioned a massive increase in federal credit programs. The private financial system was in complete disarray—beset, on the one hand, by depositors attempting to withdraw funds and, on the other, by debtors unable to honor their obligations. The government responded by establishing agencies empowered to provide liquidity to financial institutions and to offer alternative sources of credit to borrowers. Although the Depression is far behind us, economic stabilization remains a primary function of federal credit agencies. It is generally believed that by altering the cost and availability of credit, the agencies can encourage output and employment.

Misallocation of resources even in a full employment context may come about because of market inefficiencies. On occasion a lack of funds may prevent exploitation of investment opportunities that have higher returns given their risk than some opportunities which are receiving funds. This situation can arise from such imperfections as monopolistic elements in the structure of financial markets; ignorance of available investment opportunities; legal or regulatory restrictions on behavior; organizational inertia; and prejudice.

Government activity in the credit markets can eliminate market imperfections. Competition from the government can break down monopolistic barriers: pioneering activity by the government can dispel ignorance and overcome inertia, can change laws and regulations, and can give victims of discrimination the chance to show their true worth. These statements do not prove that a *permanent* role for government is justified. Indeed, when monopolies are broken, ignorance and inertia swept away, and other inefficiencies removed, the presumption in a market economy is that the government program should be terminated. A permanent government-lending program cannot be defended under the efficiency criterion unless it can be shown that elimination of the government's role would lead to a less efficient use of society's resources.

Both policymakers and those who carry out federal credit policy appear to take it for granted that serious inefficiencies exist in some credit markets,

particularly in those serving housing and agriculture. The conventional wisdom is that, in the absence of government help, credit flowing into these sectors will be insufficient to fund all investment opportunities with expected returns (at a given risk level) higher than opportunities being funded in other sectors.

Another major rationale for intervention in private markets is the presence of special social benefits that are not properly rewarded by private markets. Most people consider homeownership, family farms, education, national security, and independent small businesses to possess virtues that transcend monetary rewards won in the marketplace. These areas would probably receive government assistance even if markets were perceived to be economically efficient.

The final *raison d'être* for government programs, redistribution of income, is easily identified as a major goal of many government credit programs. There are numerous special programs to enable the poor to obtain housing, education, or other desirable goods. Veterans of military service, too, receive program benefits as a delayed reward for service to the nation.

Alleviation of recessions, elimination of perceived shortcomings of the market, encouragement of socially desirable activities, and redistribution of income are well-established goals of public credit agencies. While financial experts have no special wisdom about the determination of national goals, it is pertinent to ask whether federal credit programs are an effective means of attaining the goals set by society. We address this issue in the last section of the chapter; our first task is to describe the various federal credit agencies and the programs they administer.

## Functions and Financing of Federal Credit Programs

It is impossible to provide detailed descriptions of all 150 federal credit programs. The programs discussed in this chapter are the largest and most important, but there are many others of considerable significance. All seven federally *sponsored* agencies are discussed here: the Federal National Mortgage Association, the Federal Home Loan Bank System, the Federal Home Loan Mortgage Corporation, the Federal Land Banks, the Federal Intermediate Credit Banks, the Banks for Coop-

---

if marginal private benefits equal marginal private costs. For example, government subsidies for education are supported on the ground that increased education for an individual may benefit society in ways not reflected in rewards to that individual alone.

eratives, and the Student Loan Marketing Association. In addition, eleven federally *owned* agencies, including the Federal Financing Bank, the Government National Mortgage Association, the Agency for International Development, the Small Business Administration, the Export-Import Bank, the Rural Electrification Administration, the Commodity Credit Corporation, the Farmers Home Administration, the Federal Housing Administration, the Low Rent Public Housing program of the Department of Housing and Urban Development (HUD), and the Veterans' Administration are discussed in turn.

### Federally Sponsored Credit Agencies

A federally sponsored agency, in contrast to a federal agency, is characterized by the absence of any federal contribution to its capital. All capital is raised from private sources and the programs must be self-financing. Sponsored agencies acquire funds from earnings and borrowings; they are not recipients of appropriations from the U.S. Treasury. Despite the superficial resemblance of sponsored agencies' financing to that of private businesses, the federal government, nonetheless, plays a substantial role. All of the programs have been established by the government for some public purpose. All are subject to direction and supervision by appropriate government officials and the government appoints some or all members of their boards of directors. Thus, even though the agencies are capitalized like private firms, ownership of the capital does not give private interests the power to elect directors or to set overall policies.

Federally sponsored agencies are accorded important privileges not available to purely private firms. They can require users of their services to buy stock in the agency and can assess their members if the need arises. Even though the programs are nominally self-supporting, they have access to Treasury loans in case of an emergency. The securities they issue to private capital markets have certain favorable characteristics: they are exempt from registration with the SEC; they are issued and redeemed through the Federal Reserve banks; they are eligible collateral for Federal Reserve advances and discounts; they may be held without limit by national banks; and they are legal financial investments for federally supervised institutions. These

characteristics, plus the fact that the securities are issued by authority of various acts of Congress and with the approval of the Secretary of the Treasury, gives the debt of sponsored agencies almost the same standing in the capital markets as direct federal debt. The Treasury does not guarantee the interest or principal of agency debt, but it is obvious that the market believes the Treasury would not allow any defaults. The Treasury's ties to these agencies are too close for it to take a hands-off attitude if problems should arise.

*Federal National Mortgage Association* (FNMA, or "Fannie Mae") The Federal National Mortgage Association, the largest and most significant of the federally sponsored agencies, was created during the Depression to provide liquidity to mortgage-lending institutions. Subsequent legislation has substantially altered its operations. The most recent major change occurred in 1968, when the Housing and Urban Development Act split FNMA into two separate organizations. Federally subsidized functions were given to a new corporation, the Government National Mortgage Association (GNMA, or "Ginnie Mae"), a wholly owned government enterprise in the Department of Housing and Urban Development. Ginnie Mae has become almost as large and important as its older sister, and it will be discussed in the section on government agencies. The remainder of this discussion is confined to FNMA as it has existed since 1968.[3]

The primary purpose of FNMA is to improve the liquidity of the mortgage instrument by providing secondary market facilities. The availability of a secondary outlet for mortgages is especially important for mortgage bankers. These institutions originate mortgage loans, but they do not intend to hold the loans permanently. Instead, the originator sells the mortgage to a bank, savings and loan association, insurance company, or some other institution. The difficulty is that flows of funds into these institutions tend to move together, so that in periods of high interest rates when consumers withdraw funds from these institutions, the loss of funds affects all potential buyers of mortgages. In addition, some of the institutions follow their customers into higher-yield open-market securities. Under these

[3] For a description and analysis of FNMA's activities before its 1968 reorganization, see Federal National Mortgage Association, *Background and History*, 1973.

conditions, mortgage originators are happy to sell their mortgages to FNMA despite the required commitment fee.

The basic procedure under which FNMA purchases mortgages is the weekly free-market auction. A prospective seller specifies the amount and bids the yield he or she is willing to offer. FNMA determines the lowest yield it will accept, and the successful bidders have four months to deliver the mortgages. Delivery is entirely optional with the seller. If a better price can be obtained from the private market, the selling institution can sell in that market instead of to FNMA. Fannie Mae also offers twelve-month standby agreements, which can be converted into the standard four-month contract.

Although FNMA is often said to provide secondary market facilities, its failure to sell mortgages except under rare circumstances makes its program dissimilar to the usual secondary market operation. In a true secondary market, the agent both buys and sells, keeping an inventory only large enough to meet temporary net outflows. FNMA's mortgage holdings of more than $41 billion at the end of 1978 were too large to serve that purpose. By buying far more than it sells, it is actively injecting into the mortgage market funds that have been raised elsewhere.

Like all federally sponsored credit agencies, FNMA raises funds primarily by selling securities competitively in the open market. Most of its securities are long-term debentures (up to 25-years maturity), but it also sells short-term notes. As Table 11-1 shows, Fannie Mae had more than $41 billion of debt outstanding at the end of 1978.

It is likely that FNMA's move to nongovernmental status in 1968 actually increased the aggressiveness of its support of the mortgage markets. While a government agency, it was subject to the politics of federal budgets, deficits, and debt. FNMA purchased huge amounts of mortgages in the credit crunch of 1969–1970, and even more in 1973 and 1974. Of course, it is possible that FNMA might have followed a similar policy even if it had remained completely under government control.

*Federal Home Loan Bank System* (FHLB) Established July 22, 1932, the Federal Home Loan Bank System was the first depression-born federal agency designed to assist residential mortgage fi-

nancing. Like FNMA, its primary function is to provide liquidity to mortgage lenders. Membership in the system is open to three of the four major types of mortgage lending institutions: savings and loan associations, insurance companies, and mutual savings banks.[4] Of nearly 4,300 members, all but 200 are savings and loan associations and the System has become identified as an organization for S&Ls.

The structure of the FHLB System superficially resembles that of the Federal Reserve System: There are twelve regional Federal Home Loan Banks; each bank exercises regulatory and supervisory control of members in its district; the System sets minimum liquidity requirements; member institutions hold deposits in their district bank; and members may borrow from their bank. Despite these similarities, the FHLB System cannot compare in importance to the Federal Reserve. The basic reason is that the Fed is a money-creating authority and the FHLB System is not; the FHLB System must raise funds by borrowing in the private markets. This difference is the cause of another: while the Federal Reserve is responsible for the conduct of monetary policy and will put financial pressure on the banks in pursuit of policy goals, the FHLBS is free to accommodate its members. This helps explain why the Home Loan banks do not discourage long-term borrowing.

The System's most important function, and the one that makes it a financial institution rather than merely a regulatory body, is the lending of funds to member institutions. The amounts involved can be substantial: total loans to members were $27,563 million at the end of 1978. As Table 11-1 indicates, the volume of these loans fluctuates substantially from year to year. These movements occur because, when credit conditions tighten, savings and loan associations find themselves under severe liquidity pressure, caught between deposit withdrawals and continuing disbursements from past loan commitments. At this point the associations call upon the FHLB System and it is inclined to help.[5]

[4]Commercial banks are the fourth major type.

[5]The FHLB System has now adopted a countercyclical housing policy, one that it did not always follow in the past. Prior to 1967 it passively accommodated credit demands when housing demand was strong, supplying credit even when credit from private sources was plentiful. The previous policy and the changeover are described by

**Table 11-1  Federally Sponsored Credit Agencies: Loans to Public and Liabilities (in millions of dollars)**

| | 1969 | 1970 | 1971 | 1972 | 1973 | 1974 | 1975 | 1976 | 1977 | 1978 |
|---|---|---|---|---|---|---|---|---|---|---|
| **Loans and securities held by:** | | | | | | | | | | |
| Federal National Mortgage Association (FNMA) | $10,945 | $15,502 | $17,791 | $19,791 | $23,002 | $28,167 | $29,693 | $30,565 | $31,890 | $ 41,080 |
| Federal Home Loan Bank System (FHLB) [advances] | 9,289 | 10,614 | 7,936 | 7,979 | 15,147 | 21,804 | 17,845 | 15,862 | 20,173 | 32,670 |
| Federal Home Loan Mortgage Corporation (FHLMC) | | | | | | | | | | |
| Direct holdings | | 325 | 968 | 1,789 | 2,604 | 4,586 | 4,987 | 4,269 | 3,267 | 3,064 |
| Mortgage pools | | | 441 | 766 | 757 | 1,598 | 2,671 | 6,610 | 11,892 | |
| Farm Credit System | | | | | | | | | | |
| Federal Land Banks (FLB) | 6,714 | 7,186 | 7,917 | 9,107 | 11,071 | 13,863 | 16,563 | 17,127 | 19,118 | 20,360 |
| Federal Intermediate Credit Banks (FICB) | 4,275 | 4,974 | 5,669 | 6,094 | 7,198 | 8,848 | 9,947 | 10,494 | 11,174 | 11,469 |
| Banks for Cooperatives (BC) | 1,732 | 2,030 | 2,076 | 2,298 | 2,577 | 3,575 | 3,979 | 4,330 | 4,434 | 4,843 |
| Student Loan Marketing Association (SLMA) | | | | | 100 | 180 | 296 | 410 | 515 | 915 |
| Total assets | 32,955 | 40,631 | 42,357 | 47,499 | 62,465 | 81,780 | 84,908 | 85,728 | 97,181 | 126,293 |
| **Borrowings:** | | | | | | | | | | |
| Federal National Mortgage Association (FNMA) | $10,511 | $15,206 | $17,701 | $19,238 | $23,002 | $28,167 | $29,963 | $30,565 | $31,890 | $41,080 |
| Federal Home Loan Bank System (FHLB) | | | | | | | | | | |
| (Private) | 8,423 | 10,189 | 7,139 | 7,096 | 15,362 | 21,883 | 18,900 | 16,811 | 18,345 | 27,563 |
| (Treasury) | | | | | | | 1,247 | 1,534 | | |
| (Member deposits) | 1,041 | 2,332 | 1,789 | 1,548 | 1,745 | 2,484 | 2,700 | 4,024 | 4,286 | 6,243 |
| Federal Home Loan Mortgage Corporation (FHLMC) | | | | | | | | | | |
| Bonds | | 315 | 615 | 1,240 | 1,784 | 1,551 | 1,550 | 1,690 | 1,686 | 2,262 |
| Pool certificates | | | | 441 | 766 | 757 | 1,598 | 2,671 | 6,610 | 11,892 |
| Farm Credit System | | | | | | | | | | |
| Federal Land Banks (FLB) | 6,088 | 6,547 | 7,220 | 8,181 | 10,062 | 12,653 | 15,000 | 17,127 | 19,118 | 20,360 |
| Federal Intermediate Credit Banks (FICB) | 4,132 | 4,857 | 5,531 | 5,828 | 6,932 | 8,589 | 9,254 | 10,494 | 11,174 | 11,469 |
| Banks for Cooperatives (BC) | 1,492 | 1,762 | 1,814 | 1,961 | 2,695 | 3,589 | 3,655 | 4,330 | 4,434 | 4,843 |
| Student Loan Marketing Association (SLMA) (Federal Financing Bank only beginning 1974) | | | | | 200 | 220 | 310 | 410 | 515 | 915 |
| Total debt | 31,687 | 41,208 | 41,809 | 45,533 | 62,548 | 79,893 | 84,636 | 90,384 | 99,644 | 129,412 |

Sources: *Federal Reserve Bulletin; Treasury Bulletin; Federal Home Loan Bank Journal.*

Later, when changed market conditions result in share reintermediation, S&Ls are able to repay their borrowings.

The FHLB System is financed mainly by bonds and notes sold to the public in competitive markets. The loans from the Treasury reported in the years 1974–1976 are a product of emergency legislation designed to help the housing market through the difficult credit crunch of 1974. These funds went directly to the Federal Home Loan Mortgage Corporation to purchase mortgages from savings and loan associations.

*Federal Home Loan Mortgage Corporation* (FHLMC or "Freddie Mac") This "little brother" of Fannie Mae and Ginnie Mae was created on July 24, 1970, by enactment of the Emergency Home Finance Act of 1970. It is sometimes called the FNMA for savings and loan associations. It is permitted by law to serve members of the FLHB System and other authorized institutions whose deposits are insured by a government agency. This obviously excludes mortgage bankers, who are the main customers of Fannie Mae.

Freddie Mac is authorized to purchase conventional mortgages from private lenders. Before its creation in 1970, only FHA- or VA-guaranteed mortgages were eligible for purchase by FNMA and GNMA. This "gap" was no doubt a major reason for establishing another agency whose functions are essentially the same as FNMA and GNMA. However, there are small operational differences between FHLMC and its larger sisters; for example, Freddie Mac will buy participations as well as whole mortgages.

Freddie Mac, like other sponsored agencies, is financed mainly by borrowings from the public. In its effort to encourage a private secondary market in conventional mortgages, it has created some rather novel debt instruments. One is the Mortgage Participation Certificate, which represents an undivided interest in a pool of mortgages held by FHLMC. The certificates are *pass-through securities* in the sense that Freddie Mac collects the payments on the mortgages and passes them

through to the certificate holders. If the mortgages are prepaid, the certificates are retired early. Freddie Mac guarantees payments on the certificates regardless of the fate of the mortgages in its pools.

The Guaranteed Mortgage Certificate, created in 1975, also represents an undivided interest in a mortgage pool. This certificate, which resembles a bond, is designed for the benefit of investors accustomed to bonds and not mortgages. Interest on the certificates is paid every six months and amortization payments are made once a year. They mature in thirty years, but may be redeemed in fifteen at the option of the holder. Certificates are guaranteed by FHLMC. These certificates are so completely divorced from the underlying mortgages that they do not qualify as real estate loans for savings and loan associations.

Freddie Mac is also financed by loans from the FHLB System and the Treasury. The $1,534 million owed by the FHLB to the Treasury at the end of 1976 was passed through to Freddie Mac. In addition, the FHLB System passed through $2,700 million of the $16,811 million it raised from the public. The transactions between the System and Freddie Mac are excluded from the debt portion of Table 11-1 to avoid double-counting.

Freddie Mac has grown rapidly. At the end of 1978, it owned more than $3 billion in mortgages. Its mortgage pools and mortgage-backed securities totaled nearly $11.9 billion.

*Farm Credit System* The Farm Credit System provides credit to farmers, fishermen, rural homeowners, some farm-related businesses, and farmers' cooperatives. The country is divided into twelve Farm Credit districts, each with a Federal Land Bank (FLB), a Federal Intermediate Credit Bank (FICB), and a Bank for Cooperatives (BC).[6] The three groups of banks are separately financed and independently operated.

We have already mentioned that the Federal Land Banks, established in 1916, were the first government venture into the credit business. They are generally given credit for originating the amortized loan and for greatly extending the maturities of farm mortgages. While no one can say for sure whether or not these developments would have

Harry S. Schwartz, "The Role of Government-Sponsored Intermediaries in the Mortgage Market," *Housing and Monetary Policy,* Federal Reserve Bank of Boston, Boston, 1970.

[6]There is a Central Bank for Cooperatives in Denver, which participates in large loans made by the other twelve Banks for Cooperatives.

occurred anyway, the banks certainly accelerated these changes.

The Federal Land Banks do not lend directly to farmers. Instead, they lend to cooperatives which, in turn, lend to farmers. These cooperatives, known as federal land bank associations, are organized by farmers who wish to obtain credit from a land bank. If an association approves a loan, it applies to the land bank for an advance equal to that amount. Farmers who borrow from the land banks must buy stock in their land bank association, which in turn buys stock in the land bank. The land banks are financed primarily by sale of bonds in the private capital market.

Federal Intermediate Credit Banks (FICBs) serve the short- and medium-term credit needs of farmers in much the same way that Federal Land Banks serve their long-term requirements. The FICBs provide credit mainly through cooperative institutions called production credit associations, just as the land banks work through land bank associations. However, the FICBs also lend to, and discount paper for, commercial banks and other private lenders. The loans supported by FICBs are for such purposes as the purchase and raising of livestock, purchase of equipment, improvement of buildings, preparation of crops, living expenses, and refinancing of debt. The banks are financed primarily by ''bonds,'' most of which have maturities of less than one year. All the stock is owned by production credit associations.

Banks for Cooperatives (BCs) serve production and marketing cooperatives formed by farmers. As Table 11-1 shows, they operate by far the smallest of the Farm Credit System programs. BCs offer credit to cooperatives for purchase of capital equipment, preparation of products for sale, and for operating expenses. Most loans are for one year or less, though loans for capital equipment can be for up to twenty years. Like the FICBs, the BCs raise their funds primarily by offering short-term securities in the market. The capital is owned by cooperatives.

The Farm Credit System began issuing discount notes on behalf of the entire System early in 1975. These issues are designed to provide additional flexibility in System financing. There were $3,257 million outstanding at the end of 1978.

*Student Loan Marketing Association* (SLMA, or ''Sallie Mae'') Sallie Mae was created in 1972 to provide liquidity to student loans guaranteed by the Department of Health, Education and Welfare. It is empowered to buy and sell issued student loans, in effect creating a secondary market for banks, institutions of higher learning, and others who provide loans to students.

Since the Federal Financing Bank (FFB) was established in 1974, Sallie Mae has borrowed exclusively from it.[7] No securities are currently in the hands of the public.

### Federal Credit Agencies

There is one obvious difference between federally sponsored credit agencies and federal agencies: the former are privately owned, while the latter are owned by the federal government. Often a program needs government ownership because it is intended to provide a direct subsidy to some group. These subsidies have to be financed by the Treasury, making financial independence for the agency impossible.

Federal credit agencies provide two services: direct loans, and guarantees of private loans. Under a guarantee, the federal agency expends no funds unless default occurs, in which case it pays an agreed amount to the lender. The two services have one important feature in common: the government agency bears the risk of the credit transaction. When the government agency acts as an intermediary and does the actual lending and borrowing, the risk of the debt it issues is not affected by the risk of the loans it makes. For loan guarantees, the risk of the debtor is also irrelevant; in either case, the government has substituted its own credit standing for that of the borrower. This reduction of risk should enable borrowers to obtain approximately the same credit terms from private lenders that they could have obtained from a government agency itself.

There remain two important differences between a direct agency loan and a government loan guarantee. Most guarantee programs do not cover the full face value of the private loan, leaving the private lender exposed to at least some of the risk. The guarantee also requires the lender to undertake effort and expense to foreclose in case of default

[7]As Sallie Mae is the only federally sponsored agency authorized to issue debt guaranteed by the U.S. government, it is the only one that can sell its securities to the FFB. This is discussed in the following section.

and often to wait weeks or months for reimbursement. The effect is to force the private lender to behave like a private lender—that is, to screen out poor risks.

The second difference has to do with the financial statements of the government agency. If the agency is a borrower and lender, both loan and debt appear on its balance sheet. If it merely guarantees private debt, the transaction appears nowhere on its financial statements unless the guarantee is called for payment. In effect, the guarantee is a contingent liability, to be paid only in the event of a specified contingency (namely, default of the loan). This difference could very well affect the behavior of the agency. If there are constraints on agency expenditures, a shift of program emphasis from loans to guarantees frees the agency's resources for additional activity. If, as in the case of FHA guarantees under Section 203 of the National Housing Act, the claims are fully financed by premiums and fees, there are no financial constraints on the program's size.

The first part of Table 11-2 shows direct loans and guarantees outstanding made by each of the major federal credit agencies. At the end of 1978, federal agencies held over $166 billion in loans to the private sector and had guaranteed over $210 billion in private loans. The latter figure exaggerates the importance of loan guarantees, for many of the guaranteed loans have been acquired by federally owned or federally sponsored agencies and, thus, are part of the $166 billion of loans held by federal agencies or the $124 billion held by federally sponsored agencies. In fact, despite the apparently impressive growth of guaranteed loans since 1974, the amount of guaranteed loans remaining in private hands has actually declined since 1973.[8]

The second part of Table 11-2 shows the debt owed by the federal lending agencies. Some agencies have borrowed directly from the public through private capital markets, just as the federally sponsored agencies have done. Others have borrowed from the Treasury or from the Federal Financing Bank, a government agency housed in the Treasury that serves mainly as a conduit for funds from the Treasury to the agencies.[9] A few

agencies have shifted most of their borrowing from the Treasury or from private capital markets to the Federal Financing Bank, but it appears unlikely that all agencies will make the switch.

The agencies' total debt falls far short of their loans outstanding; for example, at the end of 1978, $166 billion in loans were backed up by only $139 billion in debt. There are small amounts of miscellaneous assets and liabilities, but nearly all the discrepancy is due to capital contributed by the federal government. For a few agencies, such as the Export-Import Bank, the capital funds were paid in as if the agencies were private corporations. In most cases, however, the capital accounts represent nothing more than regular congressional appropriations, which have been duly spent. The capital item is a dummy, created to make the balance sheet balance. There is no logical reason why some agencies, such as the Agency for International Development or the Commodity Credit Corporation, are financed in this way, while others, such as the Export-Import Bank or the Veterans' Administration, are financed mainly by loans. To some extent, use of appropriations indicates a desire by Congress to subsidize a service that cannot be self-financing, but some heavily subsidized programs are also financed by borrowing. The remainder of this section describes the agencies, their programs, and their financing.

*Government National Mortgage Association* (GNMA, or "Ginnie Mae") This agency was created in 1968, when the Housing and Urban Development Act split the Federal National Mortgage Association into two parts. FNMA kept the secondary market operations and was converted into a privately financed agency. GNMA was given the subsidized programs and was assigned to the Department of Housing and Urban Development. Currently, GNMA operates three distinct types of programs: the mortgage-backed securities program, the special assistance function, and the management and liquidation function.

Under the mortgage-backed securities program, GNMA encourages private mortgage-financing institutions to originate FHA-insured or VA-guaranteed mortgages and set them aside in pools. The mortgage loans are financed by issuing securities secured by the pools. These securities are fully guaranteed by GNMA (and the full faith and credit of the U.S. government); it will pay the interest

[8]See Table 11-3. The total amount of guaranteed loans held by private lenders was $80,625 million at the end of 1978.

[9]The Federal Financing Bank is described in a later section of this chapter.

**Table 11-2 Loans, Guarantees, and Debt Outstanding of Federal Agencies (in millions of dollars)**

|  | 1974 | | 1975 | |
|---|---|---|---|---|
|  | Loans | Guarantees | Loans | Guarantees |
| Agency for International Development (AID) | $13,840 | $ 376 | $ 13,934 | $ 453 |
| Commodity Credit Corporation (CCC) | 5,135 | | 6,031 | |
| Farmers Home Administration (FmHA) | | | | |
|   Direct | 6,292 | 8,067 | 2,066 | 16,269 |
|   Pools | 11,273 | | 14,283 | |
| FHA Revolving Fund | 1,974 | 84,571 | 2,997 | 85,601 |
| Low Rent Public Housing | 75 | 12,920 | 84 | 13,277 |
| Govt. National Mortgage Assoc. (GNMA) | | | | |
|   Direct | 4,740 | | 7,321 | |
|   Pools | 11,769 | | 18,257 | |
| Veterans' Administration (VA) | 2,973 | 29,108 | 3,027 | 29,700 |
| Small Business Administration (SBA) | 2,952 | 3,619 | 3,149 | 3,890 |
| Export-Import Bank | 8,668 | 3,596 | 9,970 | 3,914 |
| Rural Electrification Administration (REA) | 7,512 | | 8,164 | |
| Other | 16,367 | 13,632 | 18,025 | 15,912 |
| Total | $93,570 | $155,889 | $107,308 | $169,016 |
| Memo: Federal Financing Bank | 4,474 | | 17,154 | |

**Table 11-2 (continued)**

|  | 1974 | | | 1975 | | |
|---|---|---|---|---|---|---|
|  | Debt to Public | Debt to Treasury | Debt to FFB | Debt to Public | Debt to Treasury | Debt to FFB |
| AID | | $ 327 | | | $ 228 | |
| CCC | | 5,481 | | | 2,314 | |
| FmHA:  Direct | $ 492 | 2,570 | | 492 | 1,482 | |
|       Pools | 8,773 | | $2,500 | $ 7,283 | | $ 7,000 |
| FHA Revolving Fund | 440 | 3,082 | | 564 | 4,382 | |
| Low Rent Public Housing | | 60 | | | 0 | |
| GNMA  Direct | 1,216 | 4,476 | | 1,173 | 7,494 | |
|       Pools | 11,769 | | | 18,257 | | |
| VA | 1,223 | 1,730 | | 1,186 | 1,730 | |
| SBA | 444 | | | 444 | | |
| Eximbank | 2,893 | 3,213 | | 2,625 | 183 | 4,595 |
| REA | | 7,207 | | | 7,502 | 566 |
| Other | 2,283 | 6,165 | 359 | 2,146 | 3,910 | 1,343 |
| Total | $29,533 | $34,311 | $2,859 | $34,170 | $29,225 | $13,504 |
| Memo: FFB | 1,471 | 3,050 | | 0 | 17,153 | |

Sources: *Treasury Bulletin; Federal Reserve Bulletin.*

and principal regardless of payments received on the pool mortgages. GNMA has no claim on the mortgage originators for any deficiencies. Mortgage-backed securities are frequently called *pass-throughs* for, as the name implies, they provide for passing monthly payments from the borrower through GNMA to the security holder. If the mortgage is paid off early, payment on the securities is accelerated. The mortgage-backed securities pro-

gram is the largest program run by GNMA; its pools totaled $54,347 million at the end of 1978.[10]

The mortgage-backed securities program offers competition for FNMA's operations. A lender has

[10]This total includes pools formed under the special assistance function, described later in this chapter. This function's commitment to the support of subsidized housing makes GNMA's pools riskier on the average than FNMA's holdings.

**Table 11-2**

| 1976 | | 1977 | | 1978 | |
|---|---|---|---|---|---|
| Loans | Guarantees | Loans | Guarantees | Loans | Guarantees |
| $ 14,277 | $    561 | $ 12,589 | $    611 | $ 13,748 | $    695 |
| 7,754 | | 12,641 | | 15,107 | |
| 1,952 | 19,155 | 2,845 | 22,618 | 3,079 | 29,333 |
| 16,558 | | 18,783 | | 22,394 | |
| 3,348 | 87,623 | 3,259 | 90,241 | 3,446 | 92,017 |
| 102 | 13,877 | 60 | 14,259 | 47 | 14,567 |
| 4,305 | | 3,570 | | 3,429 | |
| 30,572 | | 44,896 | | 54,347 | |
| 2,747 | 31,627 | 2,701 | 34,563 | 2,748 | 36,911 |
| 3,096 | 4,572 | 3,288 | 5,331 | 5,606 | 6,352 |
| 11,226 | 3,010 | 11,431 | 4,016 | 11,608 | 3,793 |
| 8,712 | | 9,310 | | 9,307 | |
| 19,415 | 17,987 | 20,252 | 20,913 | 21,882 | 27,191 |
| $124,064 | $178,412 | $145,625 | $192,552 | $166,748 | $210,859 |
| 28,711 | | 38,580 | | 51,298 | |

| 1976 | | | 1977 | | | 1978 | | |
|---|---|---|---|---|---|---|---|---|
| Debt to Public | Debt to Treasury | Debt to FFB | Debt to Public | Debt to Treasury | Debt to FFB | Debt to Public | Debt to Treasury | Debt to FFB |
| | $    0 | | | | | | | |
| | 3,505 | | $ 6,128 | | | | $11,261 | |
| $   492 | 1,892 | | $   451 | 1,922 | | $   318 | 2,222 | |
| 5,808 | | $10,750 | 2,688 | | $16,095 | | | $23,825 |
| 575 | 4,878 | | 579 | 3,529 | | 601 | 3,969 | |
| | 0 | | | | | | | |
| 1,133 | 5,134 | | 980 | 4,908 | | 806 | 5,248 | |
| 30,572 | | | 44,896 | | | 52,732 | | |
| 1,146 | 1,730 | | 1,105 | 1,730 | | 871 | 1,730 | |
| 444 | | | 342 | | | 311 | | |
| 3,366 | 7 | 5,208 | 2,858 | 3 | 5,834 | 2,141 | | 6,898 |
| | 7,514 | 1,768 | | 7,865 | 2,647 | | 7,865 | 4,604 |
| 2,039 | 4,071 | 4,717 | 1,908 | 4,332 | 6,782 | 1,758 | 4,737 | 6,951 |
| $45,575 | $28,731 | $22,443 | $55,807 | $30,417 | $31,358 | $59,538 | $37,032 | $42,278 |
| 0 | 28,731 | | 0 | 35,418 | | 0 | 48,078 | |

the option of selling a mortgage to a private investor, selling to FNMA, or forming a pool with GNMA backing and selling mortgage-backed securities to the public. An advantage to the GNMA operation is the guarantee by GNMA of the pass-through securities.[11] The pass-through innovation may attract investors who would not otherwise invest in mortgages. If so, the total supply of funds to the mortgage market may be increased, thereby providing benefits to originators as well as promoting a policy objective of the agency. The spectacular growth of GNMA since its formation in 1968 is evidence that this advantage has been acknowledged.

As part of the special assistance function, GNMA encourages and subsidizes categories of mortgages specified by law. Most of the mortgages

[11]FNMA, as a private agency, cannot offer the backing of the U.S. government for any securities.

are on subsidized housing, which has little chance of being self-supporting. An example of programs thus supported is Section 221 (rent subsidy) of the Housing and Urban Development Act. Recently, the special assistance function has been broadened to include providing funds to the market during periods of slack in home-building activity.

In order to reduce Treasury outlays and borrowing, most special assistance programs operate under a system called the Tandem Plan. GNMA enters into commitments to purchase mortgages from the private sector at prices higher than the going market price. It then sells the commitments or the mortgages themselves either to FNMA or, preferably, to private investors at the market price, absorbing the loss as a subsidy. GNMA's outlays are thus limited to the losses incurred, not the much larger gross value of the mortgages.

GNMA has a large portfolio of mortgages that have not been sold to other investors under the Tandem Plan. Most of these were acquired before the invention of the Tandem Plan; a few were acquired under programs that have not yet been operated under the plan. However, GNMA has reduced its holdings through the formation of pools or direct sales. GNMA's portfolio is financed by borrowing from the Treasury.

The third GNMA function, the management and liquidation function, requires GNMA to manage and oversee the liquidation of certain mortgages it acquired in 1968 as the successor to the old FNMA; $189 million remained at the end of 1978. In addition, at that time and shortly after, it was assigned mortgages held by other agencies, notably the Small Business Administration, the Veterans' Administration, and the Farmers Home Administration.[12] These mortgages were formed into pools against which participation certificates were issued. At the end of 1978, there were $4,120 million of these certificates in the hands of the public. As the certificates are the obligation of the agencies that own the pool mortgages, only $806 million are liabilities of GNMA. No certificates have been issued since 1969.

*Agency for International Development* (AID) AID administers the foreign aid program. It must tailor its activities to meet the requirements of U.S. economic and political policy; hence, its credit programs for less developed nations have extremely restrictive conditions.

AID funds must not compete with private investment or with U.S. international agencies. Thus, the agency is a lender of last resort for programs unable to attract private or other unsubsidized funds. The terms are heavily subsidized: maturities are long, interest rates are far below market rates, and renegotiation of terms is relatively easy to obtain. All funds for the program are currently obtained from the Treasury by direct appropriation.

*Small Business Administration* (SBA) The SBA was established to encourage the flow of loanable funds and capital to small businesses. Many people contend that these businesses do not have access to organized national markets and must rely on local financing where costs are higher and availability uncertain. Congress created the SBA in response to complaints that the private money and capital markets do not adequately meet the credit needs of small firms.

SBA loans are made in two main programs. Under its disaster loan program, the SBA provides loans and guarantees of private credit for victims of natural disasters. The business loan program provides direct loans, participations in loans made by private lenders, and guarantees of private credit. To qualify, a firm must show that it cannot obtain money on reasonable terms elsewhere and that it is "small" in the sense that it is independently operated and is not dominant in its field. The rules for defining smallness depend on the precise program and on the industry in which the applicant operates.

Most of the SBA's funds are provided by congressional appropriations to its revolving funds.[13] If loan disbursements exceed cash inflows from interest and amortization payments, the fund can be exhausted. The terms on which credit is granted depend, therefore, on the state of the SBA's finances as well as on the general economic situation.

The SBA also provides capital to small business through its support of small business investment companies (SBICs), which supply loans and capital to small firms. The SBICs are privately incorporated, but they operate under SBA license and su-

---

[12] For a complete list of agencies, see Table FD-7 of the *Treasury Bulletin*.

[13] The SBA sold participation certificates through GNMA until 1969.

pervision. The SBA will supply up to two-thirds of their capital by purchasing their debentures or by guaranteeing debentures sold to the Federal Financing Bank. The debentures may have maturities up to 15 years. The interest rate paid is determined by the Treasury and is based on Treasury borrowing costs. Under certain circumstances, the SBA may also buy preferred stock from the SBICs.

*Export-Import Bank of the United States* (Eximbank)  Established in 1934 as an independent agency of the U.S. government, Eximbank has as its primary purpose the facilitation of U.S. export trade through direct loans and guarantees of private loans. The terms of assistance vary somewhat depending on the maturity of the credits involved. Usually long-term financing (up to 15 years) is supported by a combination of guarantees and direct loans. The borrower is expected to finance 10 percent of the transaction; Eximbank will lend 30 percent to 55 percent; and the remainder of the transaction is financed by a private loan guaranteed by Eximbank.

An inherent conflict in Eximbank's role has led to considerable criticism. On the one hand, the agency is expected to cover its operating expenses and loan losses with earnings, and this encourages strict credit standards. In contrast, it is also charged with encouraging exports and this usually involves easier credit standards. Unfortunately for U.S. exporters and Eximbank, foreign competitors of U.S. exporters often have the advantage of subsidized credit from their own governments. Obviously, it is difficult for Eximbank to meet subsidized competition without itself being subsidized by the U.S. government.

Eximbank was originally established with a $1 billion capital grant from the U.S. Treasury. Its profits have allowed it to increase capital through retained earnings. Its borrowings are also large: at the end of 1978 it owed $2,141 million to the public at large and $6,898 million to the Federal Financing Bank.

*Rural Electrification Administration* (REA)  This agency provides loans to cooperatives, power companies, municipalities, and other qualified power suppliers in eligible rural communities for construction of electric facilities. Financial aid is also available from the REA for telephone facilities.

For many years the heart of the REA program was the 2 percent, 35-year loan. The generous sub-

sidy inherent in these terms was much criticized by the power companies, who have to compete in the marketplace with recipients of these loans. As a result, in 1973 REA's rules were changed to provide 2 percent loans only to sparsely populated or other needy borrowers; others must pay 5 percent.

The degree of subsidization in REA programs forces the agency to rely on the Treasury and the FFB for financing. It can no longer borrow from the Treasury at 2 percent; it pays the average cost of funds paid by the Treasury. The difference between REA's borrowing and lending rates are covered by direct Treasury appropriations. The amounts thus paid are not part of the federal budget because the REA is an off-budget agency.

*Commodity Credit Corporation* (CCC), U.S. Department of Agriculture  The CCC administers the well-known price-support programs for feed grains, wheat, rice, rye, soybeans, honey, cotton, dairy products, peanuts, and tobacco. At harvest time, the farmer applies for a short-term (6 to 10 months) loan and pledges the crop as collateral. The amount loaned is determined by the legal support price. The farmer may market the crop at any time and retire the loan. The unique characteristic of this program is that the loans are nonrecourse: the farmer may retire the loan by forfeiting the crop without having to make good any decrease in the value of the crop below that determined by the support price. Thus, the farmer is given time to market products to best advantage knowing that a minimum value is guaranteed.

One may question whether this program is a loan program or a grant. Its tie with price supports and the optional nature of cash repayments offer reasonable argument for excluding it from this chapter altogether. However, credit *is* given for the length of the marketing period, and the fact that repayment is heavily subsidized does not differentiate it from any other subsidized federal credit program.

Under the Public Law 480 loan program, also known as the Food for Peace program, the CCC provides loans on highly favorable terms to finance the sale of U.S. agricultural commodities to developing nations. It should be noted that the CCC acts only as a financing agency; the sales are made by private agencies.

The heavy subsidies inherent in all CCC programs require exclusive reliance on Treasury financing. Most of the money is provided by direct appropriations, but a significant amount of loans have been made by the Treasury as well.

*Farmers Home Administration* (FmHA or FHDA), U.S. Department of Agriculture   The FmHA provides financial assistance for farms, rural housing, community facilities, and industrial development in rural areas. Of the many programs offered by the agency, two are especially significant.

Farm ownership loans are available to farmers unable to obtain credit on reasonable terms to buy, improve, or enlarge a farm. The direct loans are secured by mortgages on farm real estate, cannot exceed $100,000, must mature in no more than 40 years, and carry an interest rate of 5 percent.

Farm operating loans are also available for farmers unable to obtain private financing. These are secured by chattel mortgages on seed, fertilizer, feed, machinery, or livestock and are intended to provide short- to medium-term production financing. Direct loans are limited to $50,000, mature in 1 to 7 years, and carry an interest rate that is set annually by the FmHA.

The direct loan programs are financed by revolving funds, which are continually replenished by repayments. Outside money is obtained mainly by sale of certificates of beneficial ownership, which provide investors with a share of the payments from pools of loans. These certificates are essentially the same as the pass-through securities sold under the auspices of the housing agencies. In 1975, sale of the certificates to the public was discontinued and the Federal Financing Bank became the sole source of financing. These transactions are treated in Table 11-2 as guarantees by FmHA and as mortgage pools.

*Federal Housing Administration* (FHA)   This agency, a part of the Department of Housing and Urban Development, administers many loan guarantee and direct loan programs. In this section, we identify the FHA with its largest and best-known programs, which provide revolving funds for insuring private mortgage loans. Under Section 203(b) of the National Housing Act, the FHA insures lenders against losses incurred on mortgages secured by one- to four-family housing. In order to qualify for insurance, a number of conditions must be met by the borrower and the loan contract. The most important characteristic of the borrower is that he or she be capable of repaying the loan; this

program is not designed to subsidize marginal borrowers.[14] The home to be purchased may be new or used, but it must meet certain minimum standards with respect to construction and livability. The loan cannot exceed $65,000 if the structure is for a single family, and the normal maximum term is 30 years.

At one time, the interest rate ceiling on FHA-guaranteed mortgages was fixed by law, which meant that use of the program fluctuated markedly. Currently, HUD is authorized to vary the ceiling in accordance with market conditions. Nevertheless, there are still times when the rate is not competitive. At such times, use of FHA-insured loans declines. Since 1972 there has been a strong trend away from FHA insurance; a major reason appears to be the increased availability of private mortgage insurance. The FHA was a major factor in the single-family mortgage market from the end of World War II until 1972; as a result, it still has guarantees in excess of $85 billion in force on non-subsidized housing.

In the last decade or so, FHA has also begun to support *subsidized* housing through insured loans. The most important programs involve *low-rent public housing.* There are many programs under different sections of the Housing and Urban Development Act, but they serve essentially the same purpose: to encourage financing of projects that bring decent housing within the means of low- and moderate-income families.

Direct subsidies are paid out of Treasury appropriations. Other financing needs are met by borrowing from the Treasury. Given the excellent default record of the unsubsidized activities, borrowing has been relatively low. The $601 million in debt to the public in 1978 reported in Table 11-2 is not the product of a deliberate effort to finance part of the loan insurance program by borrowing from the public. In general, when a multifamily project is involved, the FHA has settled default claims by issuing long-term debentures. The $601 million is the amount of these debentures outstanding. They are transferable and are fully guaranteed by the U.S. government.

_____

[14]The programs for unsubsidized housing have always earned in insurance premiums more than they have paid out in claims.

*Veterans' Administration* (VA)  The VA operates a program similar to that run by the FHA under Section 203. It is available to certain categories of veterans regardless of their income. A lending institution has two options under the program. It may accept a guarantee against loss for up to 60 percent of the loan, with a limit of $25,000. Alternatively, the lender may be insured for total losses in a given case with a limit equal to 15 percent of the aggregate of all VA-insured loans made or purchased by that lender.[15] Most lenders favor the former program. Loans cannot exceed the reasonable value of the property and the property must meet minimum standards of construction and livability. No fee is charged for the service, making it impossible for the program to be self-financing despite a good record on defaults.

The VA also offers direct loans to veterans living in areas where guaranteed or insured loans are not available. Loans may be made for up to $25,000 and may be used for improvements and repairs as well as for purchase or construction of a home. As in the insurance program, loans cannot exceed the reasonable value of the property and minimum standards of housing quality must be maintained.

The VA's programs are currently financed by direct Treasury appropriations. Borrowings from the Treasury have been constant at $1,730 million for several years.

*Federal Financing Bank* (FFB)  The Federal Financing Bank was established by an act of Congress on December 29, 1973, and began operations in May 1974. It is wholly owned by the federal government, and the Secretary of the Treasury is the chairman of its board of directors. The Secretary is given statutory authority to supervise and direct the bank's activities.

Congress assigned the FFB three general functions: (1) to assure coordination of federal and federally assisted borrowing programs with the overall economic and fiscal policies of the government; (2) to reduce the costs of federal and federally assisted borrowings from the public; and (3) to assure that such borrowings are financed in a manner that least disrupts private financial markets and institutions. To pursue these ends, the FFB is authorized to

buy and sell any security issued, sold, or guaranteed by a federal agency. The bank itself is an *off-budget* agency, so its disbursements are not part of federal budget totals, nor are they subject to expenditure ceilings.

The FFB may finance its activity either by issuing securities to the public or by borrowing from the U.S. Treasury. Early in its existence, it did issue notes to the public, but the notes carried a higher interest rate than was paid on comparable direct Treasury securities. After that experience, the FFB's board of directors decided to borrow exclusively from the Treasury. It may do so at the Treasury's own borrowing rate. The bank's debt to the Treasury totaled $28,731 million at the end of 1976 and $48,078 million at the end of 1978.

The Treasury's ability to borrow at rates lower than those usually paid on agency debt enables the FFB to make credit available to other agencies at a lower cost than they would pay if they sought funds in the market themselves.[16] As a result, a number of agencies have shifted their financing from the private market to the FFB.

Perhaps the more significant of the bank's powers in the long run is its authority to purchase securities *guaranteed* by a federal agency. When the FFB buys a security issued by a federal agency, it merely substitutes Treasury borrowing for agency borrowing, a change that is not likely to be significant. However, when guaranteed debt instruments are purchased, the FFB is substituting federal credit for private (though federally guaranteed) credit.[17] As yet, the bank has not fully exploited its power to acquire guaranteed debt.

Table 11-2 shows the spectacular growth of the FFB since its formation in mid-1974. At the end of 1978, it held $51,298 million in federal agency securities and guaranteed loans. In order to avoid double-counting, the FFB's loans and debts are reported as a memo item and excluded from the totals reported in Table 11-2. The reason for this treatment is that, at the present time, the FFB

---

[15]Although *loan guarantees* and *loan insurance* technically refer to different programs, the usual practice is to use the terms interchangeably.

[16]It does not follow that *total* government borrowing will cost less, for the Treasury must borrow more to supply funds to the FFB. The extra borrowing will raise the cost of all Treasury borrowing unless the elasticity of demand for Treasury debt is infinite.

[17]We shall later suggest that the difference between federal loans and guarantees is often exaggerated. No one would claim, however, that there is no difference.

serves almost exclusively as a conduit for funds between the Treasury and the other federal agencies. These agencies make loans to the public; hence, it would be improper to count FFB loans to them as an increase in lending by the federal government. The debt of all federal agencies to the FFB is below the bank's loans outstanding. The difference is due to loans to the Student Loan Marketing Association, the Tennessee Valley Authority, and the U.S. Postal Service. SLMA is excluded from Table 11-2 because it is a federally sponsored agency; the others are excluded because they are not lending agencies.

## Economic Significance of Federal Credit Programs

As the program descriptions indicate, federal credit agencies are both numerous and large: collectively they control billions of dollars in financial assets. As yet, however, nothing has been said about their size relative to financial flows in the sectors they serve or in the economy as a whole. Also, nothing has been said about their importance to the economy and, in particular, whether they affect the economy in the ways envisioned by their designers. This section discusses these issues, beginning with the relative size of the agency programs. Following this discussion the importance of the agencies can be evaluated.

### Relative Size of Federal Credit Programs

Table 11-3 compares total credit flows in the economy and in the housing sector with the amounts of credit that the federal government provides through its owned or sponsored agencies.[18] Table 11-3 includes credit provided by direct loans, guaranteed loans, and the formation of loan pools against which guaranteed securities are issued. Thus, before making these comparisons, it is necessary to decide whether the impact of a federal credit program is affected by the form the credit takes. The question, in other words, is whether increases in direct loans, in guarantees, or in loan pools have the same effect on credit flows and economic activity.

---

[18]See Chapter 15 for an assessment of the government's role in financing agriculture.

GNMA, FHLMC, and FmHA encourage private lenders to originate mortgage loans and to form them into pools. The lenders issue securities against these pools; interest and amortization payments by the borrowers provide the funds for interest and principal payments on the securities. The important factor is that the three agencies both service and guarantee the pool securities; this arrangement gives the pools characteristics of both guaranteed loans and direct agency credit. However, their similarity to direct agency debt is more impressive. The basic reason is that the agencies service the pool securities as if they were their own debt. Interest and principal payments are automatically made in the agreed amounts and at the agreed times. The security holder need not take any action to receive payment, even in case of default of all or part of the payments of the pool mortgages. In short, the pool securities are so divorced from the underlying pools—and even more so from the individual mortgages in the pools—that they take on a life of their own. For this reason, they have been added to agency direct borrowing and lending in Table 11-3 to derive a measure of total agency activity.

The proper treatment of loan guarantees is not as easily determined. It is possible to make a case either for treating a dollar of guarantees as equivalent to a dollar of direct loans or for ignoring guarantees altogether. The rationale for adding guarantees to direct loans and pools is that, in both cases, the risk of the loan is passed from the private lender to the federal government. Theoretically, this shift should enable the borrower to obtain essentially the same cost and quantity of credit regardless of how the government assumes the risk of default. However, as the earlier discussion pointed out, there are significant differences between a direct loan and a federal guarantee. First, nearly all guarantee programs leave the private lender exposed to some risk: the guarantee does not cover the full value of the loan, and the lender must expend money and effort to collect from the government in case of default. Second, in a guarantee program, no government funds are expended unless default actually occurs. If defaults are rare, as they are under the VA and FHA programs, the amount of funds expended are small and may even be covered by fees generated by the program. In these cases, the government's assumption of risk has little effect, for there is little risk to be assumed.

**Table 11-3  Credit Supplied by Federal and Federally Sponsored Programs (in billions of dollars)**

| | 1970 | 1971 | 1972 | 1973 | 1974 | 1975 | 1976 | 1977 | 1978 |
|---|---|---|---|---|---|---|---|---|---|
| Total funds raised | $116.4 | $168.9 | $206.1 | $253.7 | $229.0 | $219.5 | $296.8 | $392.5 | $481.7 |
| Supplied by | | | | | | | | | |
| Federal agencies[a] | 3.0 | 7.9 | 7.5 | 5.9 | 16.4 | 15.2 | 19.3 | 22.1 | 22.4 |
| Sponsored agencies | 7.7 | 1.7 | 5.1 | 16.1 | 19.6 | 3.8 | 5.4 | 9.3 | 29.8 |
| Total supplied by government | 10.7 | 9.7 | 12.7 | 22.0 | 36.0 | 19.1 | 24.7 | 31.4 | 52.2 |
| Percentage supplied by government | 9.2% | 5.7% | 6.2% | 8.7% | 15.7% | 8.7% | 8.3% | 8.0% | 10.8% |
| Guarantees made by government or agencies | $ 13.4 | $ 12.7 | $ 13.4 | $ 12.8 | $ 4.2 | $ 13.1 | $ 9.4 | $ 14.2 | $ 18.3 |
| Less government holdings of guaranteed loans[b] | 6.8 | 7.7 | 7.4 | 6.6 | 11.1 | 12.7 | 12.7 | 20.2 | 26.6 |
| Net guarantees | 6.6 | 5.0 | 6.0 | 6.2 | (6.9) | 0.4 | (3.3) | (6.0) | (8.3) |
| Sum of net guarantees and holdings | $ 17.3 | $ 14.7 | $ 18.7 | $ 28.2 | $ 29.1 | $ 19.5 | $ 21.4 | $ 25.4 | $ 43.9 |
| Percentage supported by government | 14.9% | 8.7% | 9.1% | 11.1% | 12.7% | 8.9% | 7.2% | 6.5% | 9.1% |
| Increase in home mortgages | $ 21.9 | $ 40.2 | $ 57.4 | $ 54.4 | $ 40.0 | $ 41.6 | $ 69.3 | $ 99.5 | $105.3 |
| Supplied by federal and federally sponsored agencies | 7.9 | 4.3 | 6.2 | 15.2 | 21.0 | 11.8 | 10.3 | 23.7 | 30.2 |
| Percentage supplied by government | 35.8% | 10.8% | 10.8% | 27.9% | 52.5% | 28.4% | 14.9% | 23.8% | 28.7% |

[a]Includes FFB loans to the U.S. Postal Service and to the TVA.
[b]HEW-guaranteed loans held by SLMA; FHA/VA guaranteed loans held by mortgage pools, FNMA, GNMA and FHLMC; FmHA-guaranteed loans held by mortgage pools.

Sources: Table 11-1; Table 11-2; *Federal Reserve Bulletin*; Board of Governors of the Federal Reserve System, *Flow of Funds Accounts*.

There is no reason to suppose that such programs cause different flows than would occur if all lending and loan insurance were privately financed. If this argument could be made about all federal loan guarantees, then it would not be necessary to consider guarantees when assessing the impact of government credit activity. However, defaults are not rare under all programs.

We have already noted the increasing importance of federal programs that guarantee high-risk debt even though defaults are expected; the intent of these programs is to provide a subsidy in the form of government payments for defaults. In these cases, it seems likely that the guarantees will divert credit to those who would not otherwise receive it, and that income distribution and resource allocation will be different than they would be in the absence of the program. Thus, the ideal procedure in assessing the government's role in these credit markets would be to weight the guarantees according to the degree of subsidization and to add the weighted guarantees to direct loans and pools in order to derive a measure of federal credit activity. In the absence of a valid weighting system, Table 11-3 provides totals, including guaranteed loans held by private agencies and totals excluding all guarantees.

It seems clear that all guarantees cannot simply be added to direct credit and pools in tabulating the government's share of credit generated. For example, in periods of massive agency acquisitions of loans, the lending agencies purchase large volumes of guaranteed loans. Since most of the loans thus purchased were insured under VA or FHA programs having little subsidy value, it is unlikely that the original insurance diverted much credit to housing or was responsible for spending that would not otherwise have occurred. Consequently, these purchases can best be treated as an exchange of government credit for private credit, despite the prior federal guarantees. Thus, if forced to choose between the extremes of including or excluding all guarantees, we would regard *direct* federal credit as the better measure of the federal share.

## Federal Credit Programs and Sector Spending

It is tempting to conclude from Table 11-3 that federal credit programs are of major significance to output and resource allocation. However, these data do not prove that federal credit is important for real economic activity. The remainder of this chapter discusses this question, although it should be emphasized that only tenuous and tentative conclusions can be reached because the theoretical relationships are complex and the empirical evidence available at this time is inconclusive.[19]

Four reasons for the existence of federal credit programs were given earlier: alleviation of economic recessions, correction of market imperfections leading to misallocation of resources, encouragement of sectors providing external economies, and redistribution of wealth. An assessment of the programs' effectiveness necessarily centers on these problems. Do the programs alleviate recessions? Do they improve the allocation of resources? Do they promote activities that embody external economies? Do they redistribute income and wealth in a desirable way? The first question can be restated: Do federal credit programs affect total GNP? The other three questions represent different aspects of a single issue: Do federal credit programs cause productive resources to be shifted from one sector of the economy to another? If they do not, the impact on resource allocation, external economies, and income distribution will be minimal at best. This section considers the latter question; the next section considers the impact of federal lending agencies on GNP.

Federal programs designed to channel credit to a sector of the economy will increase economic activity and output in that sector only if they meet two conditions: (1) the program must succeed in increasing the quantity or reducing the cost of credit to the sector; and (2) economic activity in the sector must be sensitive to changes in credit conditions. Although the following discussion relates primarily to the housing industry, most of the arguments apply to any other industry that might benefit from federal programs.

*Cost and Quantity of Credit* Federal credit programs are numerous and diverse but, basically, they attempt to influence credit to favored economic sectors in only two ways. The first method provides the familiar services of financial intermediaries—portfolio diversification, maturity trans-

[19] For a further discussion of some of the issues raised in this section, see Chapter 13.

formation, and size flexibility. The second offers a direct subsidy.

By acting as an intermediary, a federal agency, such as Fannie Mae, attempts to make the mortgage market more efficient and more attractive to ultimate savers, especially those that might not normally participate in the mortgage market. If successful, these efforts should increase credit flows in the mortgage markets. Whether the existence of federal intermediaries has the intended effect is a difficult theoretical and empirical question. It does appear, however, that the extent of monopolistic barriers in the financial system is critical to this issue. If such barriers are common, addition of a new intermediary should help break down impediments to credit flows, thereby increasing credit availability and reducing its cost. In contrast, if credit markets are competitive, the government can affect allocation only by offering a subsidy. However, creation of a subsidy is almost unavoidable in any government-sponsored credit operation. An agency financing such an operation borrows with the explicit or assumed backing of the U.S. government. Because the federal government has the ability to command the resources needed to pay its debts, its debt instruments have no default risk. Hence, an agency that borrows with federal backing has lower interest costs. Some of the cost savings are passed on to those who borrow from the agency, thereby providing an implicit subsidy. Of course, the agency can also provide an additional explicit subsidy by lending at rates below its own costs, paying for the difference out of direct Treasury appropriations.

Does availability of federally subsidized credit inject funds into a sector that would otherwise go elsewhere? Certainly a subsidy of any type should encourage consumption and production in the favored area. Credit subsidies are no exception: a reduction in interest rates for certain kinds of loans will encourage institutions and individuals to borrow from the agency providing the subsidy. If the agency specifies the purposes for which its loans can be spent, spending in the favored areas should be encouraged. However, there are several reasons for doubting that a dollar of lending by federal agencies increases the availability of credit to a sector by the same amount.

First, it is possible that subsidized borrowing merely replaces unsubsidized credit that would have gone to the favored sector anyway. All subsidy programs aid intramarginal participants in the subsidized market, but credit programs are especially prone to do this. Individuals or institutions that are able and willing to borrow at unsubsidized rates will naturally take advantage of the subsidy. Unless the agency deliberately seeks to exclude them, they will be preferred to marginal borrowers for obvious reasons. Many credit programs, in fact, make no attempt to give special preference to marginal borrowers. In the case of housing, for example, large amounts of funds are provided to those who would have purchased houses anyway; smaller amounts go to those who could not otherwise afford a house. Hence, the effect of such programs on housing starts may be small.[20]

The second reason for doubting the ability of federal credit agencies to inject new funds into a sector is that they raise a high proportion of their funds by selling agency securities to the public—and most of the public is unfamiliar with the agencies' functions. Individuals and institutions that are knowledgeable about an agency are likely to be active in the same markets the agency serves and may acquire agency debt at the expense of direct loans in the market. For example, buyers of FNMA securities are likely to be institutions active in housing lending themselves, for they are most familiar with FNMA operations. If so, the additional funds FNMA supplies to the housing market may come from funds that would have gone into housing in the first place. Of course, no one would claim that 100 percent of FNMA's funds are diverted from direct housing loans. Because of its preferred risk status, FNMA (and the other credit agencies serving housing) issue securities attractive to investors who do not normally make housing loans. In fact, these agencies, especially GNMA and FHLMC, have gone to great lengths to tailor their obligations to the preferences of those who do not make mortgage loans, thereby increasing the likelihood that their agencies' funds will not be raised

[20] For example, Von Furstenberg found that the moderate subsidies provided under the Emergency Housing Acts of 1974 and 1975 had only a modest effect on housing starts. See George M. Von Furstenberg, "Distribution Effects of GNMA Home Mortgage Purchases and Commitments Under the Tandem Plans," *Journal of Money, Credit and Banking* (August 1976).

at the expense of direct housing loans.[21] An estimate of the sources of agency funds is provided by the Treasury in its periodic surveys of agency security ownership. At the end of November 1978, about 25 percent of the FHLB's securities outstanding were held by commercial banks, mutual savings banks, life insurance companies, and savings and loan associations.[22] Among financial institutions, these four are the leaders in mortgage lending. Unfortunately, the Treasury survey does not provide a complete assessment of the extent to which the FHLB raises funds from mortgage lenders themselves. For example, more than half the FHLB securities were held by "other investors," a category that includes the financial institutions not reporting in the survey. Thus, the proportion of securities held by these four institutions could be anywhere from 30 percent to 60 percent of the total. Since the "other" category also includes individuals who could be providing deposits to mortgage lenders, the figures suggest that mortgage lenders could supply a considerable percentage of funds to FHLB.[23] A similar situation exists at FNMA. Of FNMA's outstanding securities, about 30 percent were reported held by the same four types of institutions and more than 40 percent were held by "others." Consequently, FNMA, too, appears to raise a substantial proportion of its funds from institutions that might otherwise make mortgage loans themselves.

Third, many federal credit programs operate through private lending institutions rather than dealing directly with ultimate borrowers, and in these cases there is no guarantee that the entire benefit of the subsidy is passed on to the final borrower. This problem is especially serious for FNMA, GNMA, FHLB, and the other sponsored agencies that do not deal with individual borrowers. Thus, if the FHLB's advances to the savings and loan associations are used to rebuild liquidity or to acquire financial investments other than mortgage

loans, much of the rationale for the programs is defeated. The fact that S&Ls raised their liquidity ratios in the spring of 1975 when the FHLB was especially active in providing advances to S&Ls is evidence that such lender behavior may seriously limit the impact of federal lending programs.[24]

Recent empirical studies based on large-scale econometric models of the housing market support these theoretical contentions that agency actions may not significantly increase total credit flows. For example, the models indicate that FNMA purchases of FHA-VA mortgages from private institutions have little effect on the total housing market.[25] The basic reason is that institutions appear to reduce their holdings of mortgages by an amount at least equal to the purchases of FNMA. Apparently, then, agency purchases do not succeed in offsetting declines in mortgage demand during poor housing-market conditions. In addition, FNMA deals with mortgage bankers who, in turn, deal with life insurance companies and other institutons having alternative outlets for their funds. As mortgage credit expands and yields on mortgages decline, these institutions shift to other financial investments and FNMA purchases, in fact, allow them to do so. In effect, FNMA shifts mortgages from the private sector to the public sector without increasing the total supply. FHLB advances to savings and loan associations appear to have a greater effect on the mortgage market than actions of the other agencies. The basic reason is the financial structure of savings and loans: they are less free to shift from mortgages to other investment outlets.

---

[21]This is the rationale for the complicated pass-through securities described earlier.

[22]*Treasury Bulletin*, January 1979.

[23]In a recent study it was estimated that between 15 and 50 percent of securities issued by the FHLB System were acquired by individuals at the expense of savings accounts during the tight-money years of 1966 and 1969. See Peter Fortune, "The Effect of FHLB Bond Operations on Savings Inflows at Savings and Loan Associations: Comment," *Journal of Finance* (June 1976).

[24]See Von Furstenberg, "Distribution Effects of GNMA Home Mortgage Purchases and Commitments Under the Tandem Plans."

[25]Dwight M. Jaffee, "An Econometric Model of the Mortgage Market," in *Savings Deposits, Mortgages, and Housing*, eds. Edward M. Gramlich and Dwight M. Jaffee, Lexington Books, Lexington, Mass., 1972, especially 170–174; and Eugene A. Brady, "An Econometric Analysis of the U.S. Residential Housing Market," in *National Housing Models*, ed. R. Bruce Ricks, Lexington Books, Lexington, Mass., 1973. This conclusion is supported by Francisco Arcelus and Alan H. Meltzer, "The Markets for Housing and Housing Services," *Journal of Money, Credit and Banking* (February 1973). They point out that while the reduction of mortgage debt effected by agency purchases does encourage housing starts, this result is offset by other events. The sale of bonds by the agencies raises the general level of interest rates and increases the level of government (and agency) debt, both of which discourage housing starts.

Thus, infusions of funds from the FHLB System are more likely to be recycled into the mortgage market.[26]

*Response of Sector Spending to Credit Conditions* Even if the funds supplied to a sector are raised from sources outside the sector itself and can be directed to borrowers who would not have borrowed without aid, little impact on real spending will occur unless spending in the sector is at least somewhat sensitive to credit conditions. Otherwise, a great deal of money could be used for subsidies and yet have little or no effect on spending. Furthermore, it is necessary to distinguish between long-run sensitivity and short-run sensitivity. Even if it can be shown that a crash program to aid housing finance in a difficult time (such as that mounted by GNMA, FNMA, and FHLB in 1974) does increase spending in the sector during the period of the program, there is no assurance that the spending was not "borrowed" from future spending—spending that would have taken place without the program. In other words, the programs might affect the timing of spending but not the total amount spent over time. A number of studies of housing finance have found that the long-run demand for housing is determined by income, relative prices, the rental rate of housing services, and demographic factors, such as the size and age structure of the population. Financial variables seem to affect short-run behavior only.[27]

In summary, our evidence shows that the ability of federal credit programs to direct economic resources to favored sectors seems to be less impressive than the size of the programs would indicate. The programs' effectiveness depends on their ability to increase the availability of credit or to reduce its cost, and on the sensitivity of sector spending to changes in credit availability and cost. Unless credit markets have significant monopolistic barriers, the only way credit programs can affect credit conditions is to offer a subsidy. But there are three reasons to suspect that credit subsidies are inefficient methods for changing credit conditions faced by a sector of the economy: (1) subsidized borrowing may replace unsubsidized credit that would normally flow into the sector; (2) federal agencies may raise their funds from individuals and institutions that would supply credit in the desired direction anyway; and (3) many federal credit programs operate through private lending institutions, which may fail to pass the full value of their subsidies on to the ultimate borrower. If federal programs do succeed in reducing the cost of credit to a sector, there will be no effect on spending unless spending is sensitive to credit terms. Empirical evidence indicates that spending is sensitive to credit terms in the short run, but there are also indications that short-run increases in spending occur at the expense of later spending. If federal credit programs have little effect on spending in particular sectors, then such programs will have little ability to reallocate resources, encourage activities with external economies, or redistribute income.

## Federal Credit Programs and Total GNP

One question remains: does an increase in sector spending stimulated by a credit subsidy increase total spending in the economy or does it come at the expense of spending in other sectors? The point at issue here is that subsidies are not manna from heaven; someone must provide them. If individuals and institutions are taxed, forced to borrow at rates above the market, or otherwise compelled to pay for the subsidy, they may well reduce their own spending. In that case, the increase taking place in the subsidized sector comes at the expense of a decrease in other sectors. No increase in total spending results. In other words, credit intermediation or subsidies provided through government agencies might not be efficient in increasing total output even if they resulted in reallocation of resources from one sector of the economy to another. The few published empirical studies of the subject indicate that federal agencies' effects on GNP are indeed weak.[28] Of course, no one is arguing that

[26]See Jaffee, "An Econometric Model of the Mortgage Market."

[27]See James Kearle, Kenneth Rosen, and Craig Swan, "Relationships Between the Mortgage Instruments, the Demand for Housing and Mortgage Credit: A Review of Empirical Studies," *New Mortgage Designs for Stable Housing in an Inflationary Environment,* Federal Reserve Bank of Boston, Boston, 1975.

[28]See Von Furstenberg, "Distribution Effects of GNMA Home Mortgage Purchases and Commitments Under the Tandem Plans"; and Kearle, Rosen, and Swan, "Relationships Between the Mortgage Instruments, the Demand for Housing and Mortgage Credit."

subsidies have no effects whatever; subsidies always benefit someone, and the beneficiaries are likely to change their spending habits.

One might argue that it would be better to achieve increases in housing output during a business downturn—without significant opportunity costs—by putting unemployed resources to work rather than by forcing output reductions in other sectors. This would certainly be true if the housing sector always behaved in the same way as the economy. However, housing starts turned down long before the economy moved into the 1974 recession, for example; in general, housing has had some tendency to move counter to the cycle in the past. The reason for this probably has lain in the short-run sensitivity of the industry to credit conditions: in inflationary times, when interest rates were high and rising, housing demand fell off, causing production in the industry to decline before the rest of the economy turned down.[29] Under such conditions, it may not have been desirable to stabilize the housing sector at all since it acted as a built-in stabilizer and the focal point of monetary policy. Thus, federal policy toward housing until recently faced a dilemma: should agencies help stabilize housing, or should their concern lie with the economy as a whole?

## Conclusion

Since 1916, when the first significant federal lending program was established, the federal government's role in credit markets has expanded to the point where it is now a dominant force in some of these markets. Although federal programs affect all parts of the credit system, the bulk of the activity is confined to five sectors of the economy: housing, agriculture, education, transportation, and foreign trade. Small businesses in all sectors also receive benefits. These programs were established partly in response to the public's conviction that the private capital markets were not providing enough

[29]In the past the effects of tight money have been compounded by withdrawals of savings from S&Ls and other mortgage lending institutions. In the business cycle that peaked early in 1980 the withdrawal problem was less severe and mortgage lending was sustained somewhat longer, albeit at high interest rates, by the existence of money market certificates of deposit issued by S&Ls, mutual savings banks, and commercial banks at high and rising interest rates.

credit to these areas. The Great Depression reinforced these attitudes since, at that time, the credit system seemed to be in complete disarray. However, the end of the Depression did not remove all the causes for discontent. The basic issue was, and still is, should the government change the allocation of credit determined in private markets? The usual case for intervention is that government can alleviate recessions, correct imperfections in the market, encourage activities that have values transcending economic rewards, and redistribute income. All four justifications have been used at one time or another in support of existing and proposed government credit programs.

The role of federal credit agencies in the financial system is significant: at the end of 1978, they had provided $296 billion in direct credit to the private sector and guaranteed $211 billion of private credit. However, these magnitudes do not necessarily prove that federal credit programs either add to gross national product or even reallocate credit to the favored sectors. Extension of credit cannot have the same effect as a gift or a purchase of goods and services. In fact, if no subsidy is involved, federal credit programs probably have no effect on the economy at all beyond that provided by private financial institutions. Some of the largest programs offer only the implicit subsidy of passing on the government's lower borrowing costs to their private-sector customers. Even if a significant subsidy is offered, there are many possibilities for the effects to be dissipated before they reach the intended beneficiary. They include the following: the program will benefit many who would have borrowed and spent without any subsidy, and so provides no stimulus to spending beyond that induced by the income transfer; government credit agencies sell many of their securities to institutions making loans in the area to be subsidized or to individuals with deposits in such institutions; some programs aid lending institutions and not ultimate borrowers, allowing the institutions to use the funds for liquidity or other purposes not related to credit aid; sector spending may not be sensitive to changes in credit conditions; and increased spending in a sector receiving credit aid may come at the expense of spending in other sectors, resulting in no increase in GNP. Empirical studies of federal credit in the housing sector suggest that the effects of the programs, while tangible, are still quite small given the size and subsidization of the programs. The housing sector should be especially affected by credit programs since the largest programs operate in this sphere, the most highly subsidized programs benefit this sector, and real spending in the sector is supposedly most sensitive to credit conditions.

## Questions

1. Why do federal credit programs exist?
2. What are the major sources of funds for government credit programs? What factors influence the use of particular sources by a given agency?
3. What are the major uses of funds for government credit programs? Does it matter how the government provides credit?
4. How can the government aid private borrowers without raising or using funds at all?
5. What is a federally sponsored agency? An off-budget agency? Why are programs put into such agencies?
6. Some people argue that federal credit agencies should assist general monetary policy, not counteract it. Do these agencies counteract monetary policy? If so, what would be the consequences of forcing them to follow the Federal Reserve's general policies?
7. Why doesn't a dollar of federal loans have the same effect on the economy as a dollar of federal spending or transfer payments?
8. What factors weaken the impact of federal credit on GNP?
9. What is a mortgage pool? Should the mortgages in the pool and the securities issued against them be included in the balance sheets of the agencies that sponsor the pools?
10. What is the FNMA-GNMA Tandem Plan? Explain how tandem plans can reduce the apparent size of federal spending and the federal budget deficit.
11. The federal program that exhibits the most variability in uses of funds is the FHLB System's advances to savings and loan associations. Why does program activity vary so much?
12. What impact do you expect the Federal Financing Bank to have on federal credit programs?

## Selected Bibliography

Arcelus, Francisco, and Allan H. Meltzer. "The Markets for Housing and Housing Services." *Journal of Money, Credit and Banking* (February 1973).

Board of Governors of the Federal Reserve System. *Ways to Moderate Fluctuations in Housing Construction.* Washington, D.C., 1972.

Bosworth, Barry, and James Duesenberry. "A Flow of Funds Model and Its Implications." In *Proceedings of the Monetary Conference.* Federal Reserve Bank of Boston, Boston, 1973.

Fair, Ray C. "Disequilibrium in Housing Markets." *American Economic Review* (May 1972).

First Boston Corporation. *Handbook of Securities of the United States Government and Related Agencies.* New York, 1978.

Fortune, Peter. "The Effects of FHLB Bond Operations on Savings Inflows at Savings and Loan Associations: Comment." *Journal of Finance* (June 1976).

Gibson, William F. "Protecting Homebuilding from Restrictive Credit Conditions." *Brookings Papers on Economic Activity,* 3 (1973).

Gramlich, Edward M., and Dwight M. Jaffee. *Savings Deposits, Mortgages and Housing: Studies for the Federal Reserve-MIT-Penn Econometric Model.* Lexington Books, Lexington, Mass., 1972.

Kearle, James, Kenneth Rosen, and Craig Swan. "Relationships Between the Mortgage Instruments, the Demand for Housing and Mortgage Credit: A Review of Empirical Studies." *New Mortgage Designs for Stable Housing in an Inflationary Environment.* Federal Reserve Bank of Boston, Boston, January 1975.

Penner, Rudolph G., and William L. Silber. "The Interaction Between Federal Credit Programs and the Impact on the Allocation of Credit." *American Economic Review* (December 1973).

Ricks, R. Bruce. *National Housing Models.* Lexington Books, Lexington, Mass., 1973.

Schwartz, Harry S. "The Role of Government-Sponsored Intermediaries in the Mortgage Market." *Housing and Monetary Policy.* Federal Reserve Bank of Boston, Boston, October 1970.

U.S. Department of Housing and Urban Development. *Annual Report,* various issues.

U.S. Federal Home Loan Bank Board. *Annual Report,* various issues.

———. *The Federal Home Loan Bank System.* Washington, D.C., 1971.

U.S. Federal National Mortgage Association. *Annual Report,* 1978.

———. *Background and History.* Washington, D.C., 1973.

U.S. Office of Management and the Budget. *The Budget of the U.S. Government,* with *Appendix* and *Special Analyses,* various issues.

U.S. Senate. *Committee on Appropriations Hearings.* Department of Housing and Urban Development and Certain Independent Agencies Appropriations. 94th Cong., Second Sess., Part 4.

Von Furstenberg, George M. "Distribution Effects of GNMA Home Mortgage Purchases and Commitments Under the Tandem Plan." *Journal of Money, Credit and Banking* (August 1976).

# III

# The Demand for Loanable Funds

# 12

# Business Investment Demand

Traditionally, business is said to "invest" when it makes expenditures for plant, equipment, and inventories. These are the types of expenditures most macroeconomists associate with business investment, and these are the categories of data reported as business investment in the National Income Accounts. However, these are not the only categories of expenditures regarded as investment by many businesses. In addition to spending for physical assets—the inventory, plant, equipment hardware—the capital-budgeting systems of some firms review selected expenditures for "services" from which significant future benefits will be derived. These services may be as diverse as a special training or educational campaign, a switch in product distribution procedures, or purchases of mineral exploration rights, undeveloped patents, or contracts with special people. Thus, the term *investment* or *capital expenditure* should not be limited to the purchase of physical assets, such as factories or machines. Instead, investment should be viewed as any use of present resources that will help the production process to provide output in future periods. As a practical matter, of course, only significant expenditures are considered investments by firms and subjected to capital-budgeting analysis, although what is defined as significant may differ substantially from firm to firm.

Naturally, any definition is in part arbitrary and a line must be drawn somewhere. If economic relationships did not change, the location of the line probably would not matter very much, but modern economies do change. In particular, the service sector of the American economy has become so much more important over the past two decades than it had been that it is not clear how much longer we can continue to ignore it in the National Income Accounts and still provide reasonable explanations for fluctuations in business investment. Table 12-1 illustrates some of these definitional difficulties by summarizing expenditure categories for different groups and indicating whether or not they are regarded as investment by the group itself and by the National Income Accounts.[1]

---

[1] Some economists have tried to broaden the concept of investment to include the capitalized present value of the stock of services expected to be released in future production periods. Thus, labor might have both a current wage rate and a capitalized value (to be depreciated in

**Table 12-1 Investment-Type Expenditures as Viewed by the Investing Sector and by the National Income Accounts**

| | Is it considered investment by | | | |
|---|---|---|---|---|
| Capital Expenditure Category | Households (A) | Government (B) | Firms (C) | National Income Accounts |
| Short term assets | | | | |
| Fluctuations in inventory | no | no | no | yes (C) |
| Fluctuations in other current asset requirements | no | no | no | no |
| Permanent changes in level of current asset requirements | no | no | yes | no |
| Long-term real assets | | | | |
| Land, plant, houses, etc. | yes | yes | yes | yes (A,C) |
| Equipment | no | yes | yes | yes (A,C) |
| Consumer durable goods (cars, etc.) | yes | seldom | corporates: no sm. firms: yes | no |
| Services | | | | |
| Development of systems | no | yes | yes | no |
| Purchase of services with multiperiod benefits (education, advertising, etc.) | yes | seldom | sometimes | no |
| Financial assets | | | | |
| Purchase of existing financial instruments (stocks, bonds, etc.) | yes | yes | yes | no |

Several things can be noted from Table 12-1. First, items that most of us as consumers regard as investments from the viewpoint of household expenditures are not included in the National Income Accounts private-sector investment data. The exception is spending for housing. Second, none of what the government—at any level—might regard as investment from a decision-making viewpoint is included in the NIA total. Thus, government money spent to build either a new power plant or a new highway is not classified as investment in the NIA Accounts. Third, much of what some firms regard as capital expenditures, such as long-term changes in current assets or spending for research and development, is excluded from the NIA investment total. Finally, one item firms almost never analyze as a capital project—fluctuations in inventories—is included in the government investment totals.[2] In sum, the aggregate investment data in

the National Income Accounts attempt to report net new investment for structures (houses and plant facilities), for physical equipment used in production by private firms, and for inventory changes by private firms.

Because of these difficulties, it may be useful at this point to summarize definitions of certain terms used in this chapter. *Investment,* any use of present resources to help a production process provide output in future periods, has already been defined. *Business investment* is the National Income Accounts measure of aggregate investment by private firms. It is equal to gross private domestic investment less fixed investment in residential structures. Thus, business investment is the sum of expenditures by private firms for plant, equipment, and changes in business inventories. Business investment is a process that leads to a change in the *stock* of physical capital for the firm. It is important to remember that theories about business investment (how decisions are made to increase or reduce existing capital) are not always the same as theories about the total stock of capital (how much capital

---

future production periods) associated with special attributes. This broadened concept is not reflected in data showing current aggregate business investment. One possible exception is in the treatment of professional sports. A baseball team, for example, can buy and sell players' contracts and treat the players as a depreciable asset.

[2] Firms do analyze inventory behavior, however. The techniques have come to be known as operations-research

approaches to inventory modeling. The approach is a limited optimization procedure that relies very much on the computer for both analysis and ongoing control.

should be used in the first place and why the stock of capital differs from country to country). *Capital expenditure* is any investment made by the firm that is subject to capital-budgeting analysis. Generally, this includes, but is not limited to, large expenditures of the kinds that make up the business investment component of the National Income Accounts. This concept, however, is broader than NIA business investment. It also includes spending for new systems of operation, major new marketing programs, the acquisition of other firms, permanent additions to net working capital, and so forth. *Total claims* is the value—measured variously as *book value,* current *market value,* or equilibrium *economic value*—of all funds supplied to the firm. Creditors supply debt, usually reported as current liabilities or long-term debt or the capitalized value of leases. Stockholders supply equity, measured as *net worth* (the balance-sheet book value) or as *shareholder firm value* (the current market price of the stock times the number of shares outstanding).

The remainder of this chapter is divided into three main parts: (1) some theories about aggregate business investment; (2) some inferences about investment and economic fluctuations revealed by actual macro investment data for the United States in recent decades; and (3) discussion of what the data on actual macro sources of funds reveal about the financing of capital expenditure by U.S. firms. Following these discussions is a brief concluding section and, following that, an appendix which explores in greater detail the investment decisions in the individual firm.

## Theories About Aggregate Business Investment

Modern theories of investment by individual firms (discussed in more detail in the appendix to this chapter) are based on the notion that obtaining capital for the firm is a two-stage process. First, physical assets that provide a flow of services (returns) over time are purchased.[3] Second, financial capital (money) is obtained either from stockholders or creditors to pay for the current expenditures on physical capital. Contrast this with obtaining

[3]As we have seen, these "physical" assets might include services, patents, and so forth. Also, "purchased" might be broadened to include leases and other arrangements, which are not, strictly speaking, purchases.

labor. Labor is hired (workers are not usually paid ahead of time), products are made for sale at the end of the production period, and workers are paid their wages. The actual "stages" of this process are described in Figure 12-1.

Basic theory assumes that the total cost of physical capital is paid immediately. Thus, if the firm needs 100 units of physical capital costing $20,000 per unit, it pays the supplier $2 million now, paying with financial or money capital. But the total cost of *money* capital is never paid immediately. Since the benefits (the cash flows) attributed to the physical capital units will be realized only over a number of production periods, the money could be returned only over those future periods. This type of split-contract procedure for obtaining capital permits us to evaluate the worth of capital in a new way. Instead of looking directly at marginal product in a period relative to total costs (including money costs) for that period, we examine marginal benefits over and above all costs *except* money costs to see if this remainder at least covers money costs. Of course, in the end, the two types of analysis must be the same. This marginal benefit above all costs except money costs can be translated into a relative measure called the *marginal efficiency of capital* (*MEC*).

### Marginal Efficiency of Capital

In financial theory, the MEC, which is a yield or net rate of return above costs, is also known as the *internal rate of return on investment.* Investment is made to obtain a series of future cash flows. The cost of these inflows is the current outlay for equipment, plant, and so forth, and the future series of cash outflows, say, for wages, electricity, and so on. The yield on such investment outlays is the rate that will equate the present value of the inflows to the present value of the outflows. For example, suppose a machine costs $1,000 (immediate cash outflow) today and another $300 in wages and other operating expenses to be paid at the end of a year (obviously, very tolerant employees!). The realized benefits from using the machine (some combination of reduced expenses or increased revenues from greater production) will be $1,400 at the year's end, at which time the machine is assumed to be worthless. These flows will create an internal rate of return of 10 percent. That is, the outlay of $1,000

**Figure 12-1   The Role of Financial Capital in a Simple Production Model of the Firm**

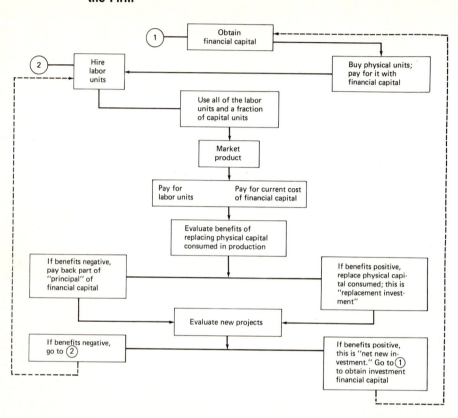

will have been recouped (full depreciation implies return of investment) and a return of 10 percent *on* investment for the year will have been earned.

This investment is only worthwhile, however, if the cost of financing the outlay—the price of financial capital—is less than the 10 percent internal rate of return. In other words, if the MEC is greater than the cost of financial capital (in a certain world, this would be the interest rate), the investment will be profitable and ought to be made. Thus, given the interest rate, the number of investments undertaken will depend on the investment opportunities facing the firm. However, golden opportunities are necessarily limited in number; that is, in general, projects are more abundant at low, rather than at high, yields. For a society where no firm is dominant, any particular firm will usually have a large number of investment opportunities at yields equal to the cost of financial capital.[4] All opportunities, when arrayed in cumulative order of promised internal rate of return, will almost invariably portray a schedule of diminishing marginal efficiencies.

A possible MEC schedule is shown in Figure 12-2. Also shown in the same diagram is a possible cost of financial capital (let us call it the *marginal cost of funds* or MCF). It is important to remember that Figure 12-2 is a representation of opportunities *at the firm level*. This has important consequences, for it means that (with the exceptions to be noted later) a firm does not determine its marginal cost of

----

[4]Two examples: the firm could buy its own securities, in effect "retiring" some of its own financial capital. Or, the firm could invest in the physical capital of other similar firms—in effect be the supplier of financial capital for other firms' attractive projects and the "manager" of the production functions of those particular project divisions.

### Figure 12-2 The Marginal Efficiency of Capital and the Marginal Cost of Funds for the Firm

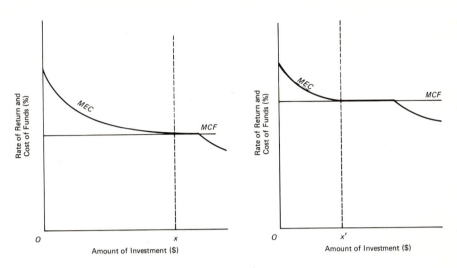

funds; the MCF is "given" by the marketplace. Also, the firm will generally have a *large* number of opportunities to invest at rates equal to the MCF. For any particular firm, this will be true even if the marketwide MCF increases! Most firms will desire to invest in all projects where MEC > MCF and some projects that return just enough to cover their cost of funds. For example, one firm might select *x* as the amount to invest given the relationship in Figure 12-2(a) or *x'* given the higher MCF in Figure 12-2(b). Increases in the interest rate (if that is the MCF) may significantly affect the number of golden opportunities perceived and, hence, the business manager's expectations, but for any particular firm, there will always be a large number of potential opportunities at about the MCF. Clearly, investments returning less than the MCF should not be made.[5]

Actually, economists interested in MEC curves rarely bother to analyze the investment opportunities available to the individual firm. Interest has focused on aggregate investment demand and hence on the aggregate MEC curve. The aggregate MEC curve may look quite different from the curves for any of the firms making up the total

demand. This is directly analogous to the fact that the firm's demand curve in a perfectly competitive industry is dramatically different from the industry's curve. It will be recalled that the firm's perceived product demand curve in a perfectly competitive industry is perfectly elastic [see Figure 12-3(a)]. But the product demand curve for the industry as a whole will have some slope; it may even have some elastic and some inelastic regions [see Figure 12-3(b)]. Actually, it is possible for every firm to be operating in the elastic region of its own demand curve, and yet have the industry operating in the inelastic region of the aggregate product demand curve. Exactly the same sort of thing is possible for the aggregate MEC curve.

In effect, in an aggregate marginal-efficiency-of-capital curve, many opportunities of *individual* firms are netted out of the curve. For example, investment opportunities are counted only once, so we do not count again a firm's opportunity to purchase the real assets of another firm. Also, traditionally, the opportunity to purchase existing financial assets is not considered. Finally, there is some ambiguity about concurrent derivative investments—it may become profitable to build a new power plant, for example, if, and only if, a new chemical plant is actually going to be built. In sum, the aggregate MEC curve is at best an approximation of the private-sector rate-of-return expec-

---

[5]The macroeconomic implications of this fact are explored further in Chapters 21 and 22.

**Figure 12-3 Firm-Perceived and Industry-Perceived Product Demand Curves in a Perfectly Competitive Industry**

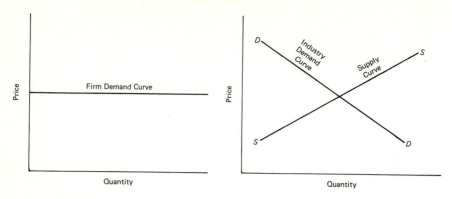

tations for net new real investment; but it is expected to be downward sloping as indicated in Figure 12-4.

## Acceleration Theories

Despite the variable empirical nature of aggregate MEC elasticity, it has become customary to assume that the aggregate MEC schedule is inelastic in the equilibrium region—that is, that relatively small expansion in aggregate private investment entails relatively large declines in expected rate of return. From this it follows that relatively large declines in interest rates are needed when national policy demands greatly expanded investment. The result is that for narrowly circumscribed changes in interest rates, corporate investment demand will appear unresponsive to corporate finance. Under these conditions, what is investment demand responsive to? The answer is, to *shifts* in the MEC curve— that is, to changes in the profitability of investment brought about by increased demand for the firm's output. In such a model, the cost and availability of funds do not affect the demand for investment funds. Rather, the demand for investment funds reacts to such "real" events as increases in real incomes and changes in tastes for the product, as well as to unpredictable innovations. In effect, to assume that investment return schedules are inelastic and that finance costs (interest rates) are infinitely elastic, is to attribute corporate investment demand to the acceleration process.

Pure acceleration theory sees investment as responsive only to shifts in derived demand (MEC) and totally insensitive to the cost of funds (MCF). Once we allow any elasticity to the MEC schedule, however, the question of shape or relative slope, steep or flat, as well as shifts in position of both the MEC and MCF curves, become relevant to the investment decision. Let us examine complications of the pure acceleration theory in more detail.

Figure 12-5 shows the pure acceleration case, where the MEC schedule is completely inelastic. In this case a decline in interest rates will induce no increase in the volume of investment ($a = b$). More investment will occur only through a shift in

**Figure 12-4 The Aggregate Marginal Efficiency of Capital**

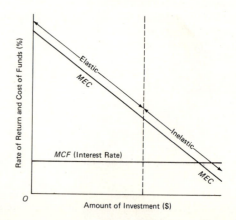

**Figure 12-5   The Pure Accelerator Case**

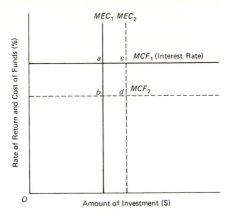

**Figure 12-7   The Case of the Relatively Elastic MEC Schedule**

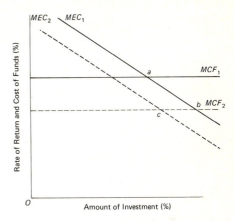

the MEC curve to the right (for example, to $c$, which can be attained without interest rate cuts; however, $d$ is no better than $c$).

A more realistic example is shown in Figure 12-6, where the MEC schedule is slightly responsive to the cost of funds. However, shifts in the MEC curve may overwhelm movements along the curve as interest rates decline. If, as is usually assumed, funds will be cheaper only when demand for the firm's output has softened, the shift in the MEC curve to the left will more than outweigh the small shift down the original MEC schedule in response to lower finance costs (investment ends up less at

**Figure 12-6   The Case of the Relatively Inelastic MEC Schedule**

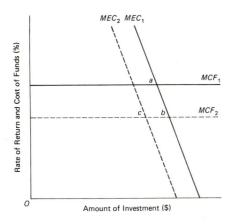

$c$ than at $a$, despite the lower interest rates). This makes investment appear unrelated to lower interest rates.

In contrast, Figure 12-7 shows that if the MEC schedule is relatively elastic, a decrease in finance costs (equal to that in Figures 12-4 and 12-5) would induce a relatively large increase in investment demand (from $a$ to $b$)—so large, indeed, that even a shift to the left of the MEC curve (equal to that in Figure 12-5) might not completely offset that effect (compare $c$ to $a$). Still, because of the leftward shift of MEC, aggregate investment appears less responsive to interest rate changes than it really is. However, provided that the MEC schedule is relatively elastic, interest rates clearly affect the investment decision despite the assumption that finance is available at a fixed cost regardless of quantity demanded. In this case, one can rule out the influence of the interest rate only by assuming that it cannot be lowered for institutional reasons.[6]

An additional complication of the pure acceleration theory is that the power of MEC shifts to affect investment demand may be lessened by the

[6]Or because "liquidity trap" conditions—that is, an infinitely elastic demand for money—prevail. These conditions, in turn, require the unlikely combination of deep depression and policy paralysis witnessed in 1932–1934. For analysis of the liquidity trap hypothesis, see the discussion in Thomas M. Havrilesky and John T. Boorman, *Monetary Macroeconomics,* AHM Publishing Company, Arlington Heights, Ill., 1978.

increased cost of financing that extra investment. To illustrate, in Figure 12-8 starting out at point *a,* if the MEC schedule shifts upward and to the right, investment demand will increase all the way to *b* with constant finance costs, but only to *c* if costs of finance rise with volume demanded. Furthermore, if monetary and fiscal policy shifts financial costs and, therefore, the MCF schedule to higher levels, it is possible to offset the shift in the MEC curve completely—see point *d,* where investment demand is back again at the *a* level. Note that a simple rise in the cost of perfectly elastic borrowed funds sets back investment demand only to *e,* a smaller effect than occurs with a shift in the rising MCF curve.

In other words, if funds are available only at rising costs, it restricts the power of shifts in the MEC schedule to influence investment demand. And, as we saw before, investment demand may change without any shifts in the MEC curve, if the MEC is responsive to changes in finance costs.

Thus, a real or nonfinancial theory of corporate demand for funds—an accelerator model—implies that only final demand-induced shifts in MEC affect corporate investment demand significantly. In contrast, what we might call the financial theory of corporate demand for funds allows MEC shifts but also, by introducing variable or less than perfectly elastic cost-of-funds schedules, it limits the effects of MEC shifts on investment demand. Nevertheless, it recognizes that, given some elasticity of the MEC schedule, shifts in the cost of funds can cause significant changes in corporate investment demand, even without shifts in the MEC curve. In other words, corporate investment and the corporate demand for funds is a function of the MEC *and* the MCF; so long as the MEC exceeds the MCF, investment will prove profitable and should be adopted. The precise volume of corporate financial demand depends, then, on both the position and shape of the MEC schedule and the position and slope of the MCF schedule.

## The Rising Marginal Costs of Finance

Thus far we have considered the reasons why the MEC curve is certainly downward-sloping and variably elastic, but we have not explained why the MCF schedule is upward-sloping and less than perfectly elastic. In brief, the answer is that not all

**Figure 12-8  The Case of the Rising MCF Schedule**

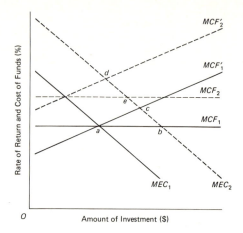

funds are borrowed and, even assuming that they were, risk (and, hence, cost) varies directly with the amount of borrowing.

To draw the marginal-cost-of-funds schedule as a horizontal line is to assume that funds are available in any quantity at constant cost. However, such a supply-of-funds curve not only assumes pure and perfect competition, it assumes certainty as well. Worse yet, given certainty conditions, the entire business "problem" is assumed away. In any case, it would be inconsistent to allow for "shifts in expectations" (that is, uncertainty) to affect the MEC schedule and not to allow for the effects of uncertainty on the cost-of-funds curve as well.

In short, there is no business problem and, hence, no problem of business finance and capital markets unless we admit business uncertainty into the model. Having introduced business risk, however, *financial* risk inevitably follows if funds are borrowed, for, while the returns are uncertain, the cost (interest payment) is certain. If business risk exists—some possibility that return expectations will be disappointed—borrowed funds will be available only at increasing costs for increasing amounts, because financial risk rises as the proportion of borrowed to total funds rises. Note that once risk is admitted, the distinction between debt and equity sources of funds becomes significant. Under *certainty* conditions, when funds are available without limit at "the" interest rate, the reward to owners cannot differ from that to creditors. Under conditions of *uncertainty*, however, and given the residual nature of the ownership claim, equity suppliers will "require" a higher rate of return than will creditors. Thus, the marginal-cost-of-funds schedule necessarily rises as additional funds are borrowed or as other (nondebt) sources are tapped for funds.

It follows that, if the MCF is a rising curve, corporate investment demand depends on the cost and availability of funds as well as on the MEC. And the MCF schedule is, in part, determined by the nature and state of the capital markets. In other words, corporate investment demand is only partially explained by the *real* forces of final demand versus current capacity. Not only are there non-accelerator factors that influence the shape and position of the MEC schedule, there are financial factors, acting through the MCF curve, that, in part, determine the equilibrium volume of investment demand. For example, an accelerator-induced upward shift in the MEC schedule is thwarted in whole or in part by the fact that additional funds are available only at higher cost. However, forces that shift the MEC curve in one direction may tend to induce "sympathetic," or facilitating, shifts in the MCF schedule as well. In any case, corporate investment demand in an uncertain environment is vitally affected by corporate financial conditions.

Business risk is present when expected returns can be analyzed as a probability distribution rather than as a point statistic. For our purpose, we can assume that the effect on the MEC curve downward of introducing business risk is simply to shift the entire MEC curve downward and to the left (see Figure 12-9). That is, expected returns are reduced when uncertainty is considered. The so-called certainty equivalent of an uncertain average expected return of 5 percent is less than 5 percent, even when the expected dispersion around the average 5 percent is normally distributed. This is so because it is usually assumed that business executives (and the stockholders whom they represent) are risk averters. For example, it is assumed that a project promising 5 percent certainty is preferable to a project also promising an average of 5 percent but having equal probabilities of earning 4 percent or 6 percent. Aversion to risk implies that unpredictable fluctuations are disliked, *per se,* and are

**Figure 12-9  The MEC Schedule Discounted for Risk**

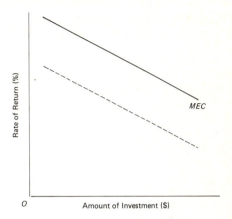

discounted accordingly. This is not merely a consequence of a basic asymmetry in risk taking, namely, that great gains are only great gains, but great losses may involve the "risk of ruin." Of more general and continuing importance is the fact that, in most situations, people behave as though the value (or utility) of a chance to add substantially to one's wealth is not so great as the satisfaction that would have to be forgone in the event of the equal probability of a loss of the same number of dollars. In short, risk aversion simply means that equal odds on substantial gains or losses are viewed unfavorably. Hence, to convert uncertain expected returns to certainty equivalents involves a reduction, or discount, of the average expected return. Thus, the MEC curve shifts to the left to allow for business risk.

It is more important, however, to stress the effects of introducing uncertainty on the MCF schedule. When business risk is introduced, distinctions between the cost of equity and debt funds, as well as between internal and external sources of finance, become significant. When returns are certain, these distinctions cannot exist, for limitless funds can yield nothing but a reward for forgoing liquidity—a pure (time-preference) rate of interest. Once returns are uncertain, however, the return offered on equity must promise to exceed that on debt to offset the additional risk-bearing of the equity share. And, once the concept of debt limits arises, given that retained earnings are, by definition, finite and limited, the cost of *external* equity finance must be separately considered, and it will necessarily be greater than the cost of internal equity funds. In short, when business risk is present, the MCF is a rising curve, at least beyond the point where the firm must go outside for funds. Thus, the capital market—the place where external funds are obtained—becomes an important force in determining corporate investment demand.

## Other Theories of Business Investment

Thus far, this chapter has tried to sketch the following conjectures about business investment and its relation to other macroeconomic variables:

1. To invest in real capital immediately, firms purchase money capital. The money capital is "repaid" over a number of periods as the real capital is utilized. At the margin, firms will not make additional investment unless the MEC is higher than the cost of financial capital.
2. The marginal efficiency of capital of a project is an index (a number called the internal rate of return) reflecting business expectations about the time-distributed benefits of a project relative to all the costs except the cost of financing.
3. If business expectations are more or less given (for example, the aggregate MEC curve is fixed) with regard to real investment opportunities, the level of periodic net new investment becomes primarily a function of the marginal cost of funds. That is, changes in the interest rate level will have an important effect on investment. On the other hand, if business expectations about perceived benefits from a given set of real projects were to change, the MEC curve would shift. Thus, an increase in output (caused by a shift in consumption, in tax patterns, or whatever) should induce a change in the rate of investment, causing further changes in output and investment—the familiar multiplier-accelerator process. A similar shift in expectations leading to forecasts of increased costs associated with an investment would lead to a reduced rate of investment. Most macroeconomists believe that these shifts in expectations are a bigger determinant of fluctuations in business investment than shifts in the cost of funds. There is less agreement on the relative importance of reve-

nue-cost expectations versus the cost of funds in determining the long-run level of net new investment.

There are two other issues that need discussion. One issue, technology, is an important determinant of long-run shifts in the level of investment. The second issue, inventory policy, concerns some short-run fluctuations in business investment.

If the level of aggregate real capital is primarily determined by the production functions available to society, then business investment—the replenishment and alteration of real capital stock—may depend significantly on the rate of *innovation* associated with production functions. Again, production functions are to be broadly construed to incorporate the possibility of new products, new types of labor, new marketing-distribution systems. (Some of those changes, however, may be more easily analyzed as firm-directed efforts to alter the demand function.) Several decades ago, the economist Joseph Schumpeter developed a theory of innovations. He suggested that most of the really significant fluctuations in net business investment could be related to the rate of innovation.[7] Innovation is considered to be basically profit motivated and to have a large element of chance. Innovation may be due to discovery (a new class of customers, a better-educated labor force, for example), to invention (microchip electronics, laser beam surgery, among others), or to a new synthesis of existing factors put together by some entrepreneur (private nursing homes, electronic video games, to name only two). Whatever the source, after its acceptance, the bulge in new investment will fall back to replacement-level investment as the extraordinary profit opportunity is exhausted. The implication of this type of focus is that policies directed toward shifting output or interest rate levels will be only marginally successful in altering business investment. To obtain significant shifts, one must devise investment policies that create a climate for innovation and the entrepreneurship necessary to develop those innovations.

An economist today is more likely to identify himself as a Keynesian disciple or a monetary economist than as a Schumpeterian economist. So, at least in terms of the competition of ideas for

---

[7]See Joseph Schumpeter, *Business Cycles,* McGraw-Hill Book Company, New York, 1939. Vol. 1, Chap. 3.

broad economic viewpoints, Schumpeter is not a winner in the United States and Great Britain. This is not surprising. From a policy viewpoint, it seems to be easier to influence the money supply or to alter government expenditures to stimulate consumer and/or investment demand than it is to attempt to increase (or decrease) the flow of applications to the patent office. Still, there is enough truth to the power of innovation that it cannot be ignored in discussing long-term business investment cycles or differential growth rates across countries with different cultures.[8]

While innovations tend to take time to work their way through the system, *inventory* adjustments are essentially short-run phenomena. As we have already noted, changes in the stock of inventories are a component of the National Income Accounts total for business investment. In fact, if we look at changes in the quarter-to-quarter flow of business investment during many periods, changes in inventory investment dominate. Thus, a theory to explain fluctuations in aggregate business investment must explain fluctuations in both business fixed investment and in inventory levels.

It is not surprising that macroeconomists have tended to rely on inventory models that focus on the relationship between business investment and aggregate real output (accelerator-type models). The simpler versions of the model suggest that, other things being equal, investment is proportional to expectations about output. In the simplest case, for example, inventory would be maintained as a fixed proportion of expected output. As output is expected to grow (the economy does better), inventories will be increased and, with some lag, so will other business investment. The money spent to produce these investment goods is, of course, income to the workers. Since most of this worker income will be spent on consumption, leading to higher expectations about output, the familiar multiplier process begins. Given some time differentials between expectations and actual realizations, and some feedback on investment demand from the induced consumption, it is possible to simulate the

whole multiplier-accelerator process.[9] As we have seen, however, accelerator models leave little room for financial costs.

Unfortunately, this macro business-investment scenario is only a crude approximation of the actual process in today's business corporation. The previous section suggests that business fixed investment is determined primarily by the marginal efficiency of capital and the marginal cost of funds. Fluctuations in investment may be related to output expectation changes, but it is also possible that they are related to changes in the relative cost of real capital and to financial costs. For most firms, though, inventory management is completely separate from this type of capital-budgeting analysis. Most firms would not consider inventory adjustments a part of the "business investment" decision at all.

Even the simplest inventory models seldom relate the level, or changes in the level, of inventory to output as a simple proportionate multiplier. And the models do allow for financial costs by allowing for an opportunity carrying cost of inventories. The most famous basic inventory model for finished goods suggests, in fact, that, holding other things constant, the level of inventory should be a function of the square root of output; hence, fluctuations in these inventories should be related to the square root of expected fluctuations in output. Table 12-2 summarizes one version of this model.[10] As the example indicates, if the firm expects output to double, the new ordering level for inventory will go up by less than 50 percent. Of course, the frequency of placing orders at the higher level would increase to reflect the higher output level. This reflects the fixed cost of ordering versus the variable cost of carrying inventories. The higher the financial cost of capital, the more frequent the order placing and the smaller the average inventory level. Contrast these results with a simple proportional model. In example (a) in Table 12-2, the inventory/output ratio is 0.10. If the ratio were maintained, inventory would double in (b) to a 200-

---

[8]For an interesting thousand-year perspective that looks at major systematic innovations in Western society and their relation to inflation, see the essay by David Warsh and Lawrence Minard in *Forbes,* November 15, 1976.

[9]A terse description of this process can be found in the classic book by R. G. D. Allan, *Mathematical Economics,* The Macmillan Company, New York, 1960.

[10]For the derivation of such models, see a basic corporate finance or operations research textbook, for example, James Van Horne, *Financial Management and Policy,* Prentice-Hall, Englewood Cliffs, N.J., 1977.

**Table 12-2  Basic Inventory Model (Simple EOQ or Economic Order Quantity Model)**

$$I^* = \sqrt{\frac{2 \cdot q \cdot \phi}{p \cdot r}}$$

$I^*$  = number of units of inventory to order when needed

$q$  = units expected to be sold during the period

$p$  = price the units will be sold for (assumed to be a simple mark-up of costs)

$\phi$  = dollar cost of placing an order for more inventory (not the cost of the inventory, but the fixed "overhead")

$r$  = a rate of charge for holding inventory; includes the financial cost of capital and wastage or other charges that vary as a function of the amount of inventory held

Example:
$q$ = 1,000 units per period

$p$ = \$100

$r$ = 10%

$\phi$ = \$50

Therefore

$$I^* = \sqrt{\frac{2 \cdot 1000 \cdot \$50}{\$100 \cdot 10\%}} \qquad \text{(a)}$$

= 100 units per order

If $q$ is expected to double to 2,000 units per period, the new amount that a firm would order each time would be

$$I^* = \sqrt{\frac{2 \cdot 2000 \cdot \$50}{\$100 \cdot 10\%}} \qquad \text{(b)}$$

= 144 units per order

In case (a), a firm would reorder inventory 10 times per period, whereas in case (b) a firm would place a new order about 14 times per period.

unit per order level and the frequency of ordering per period would remain at 10. Few large firms today would use so simple a model.

It can be shown that for the Economic Order Quantity (EOQ) model outlined in Table 12-2 the relative growth in desired inventory levels is equal to the square root of the relative growth in expected output. For small changes, this comes closer to a proportional relationship. If output is expected to increase by 10 percent, for example, the desired inventory level would be about 5 percent higher. This is still a big difference in a forecasting sense.

Many large corporations now have inventory management systems considerably more complex than the system suggested by this basic model. Large firms today operate on-line computer systems, which are tied in with inventory models that consider various lags and a variety of costs—including the probability and cost of running out of inventory or ending up with too much.

What do these new trends in inventory analysis and management at the firm level imply about the aggregate behavior of inventory fluctuations? To date, economists are not completely sure. There seems to be some evidence that inventory fluctuations have moderated relative to output fluctuations in some periods. But this has been partially masked in recent years by the sharp shifts in expectations about the rate of inflation, which can have a significant effect on the desired level of both raw material and finished-goods inventories. And, of course, not all firms follow efficient inventory-management policies. There are still a great many companies that "reorder when the bin is empty," that "double the size of the inventory order when sales go up 50 percent," or that follow similar rules of thumb.

We close this section by reminding the reader that fluctuations in inventory levels are only one part of current-asset or working-capital management. Even more dramatic changes have occurred in the models and systems used to manage "cash" and accounts receivable over the past two decades. But fluctuations in these accounts are not a part of the NIA business investment data (and, of course, are usually not part of an individual firm's capital-budgeting analysis). It is not clear that economic analysis has been well served by combining in one figure private-business fixed investment and changes in the level of inventories.[11]

**Macro Investment Data**

The first part of Table 12-3 summarizes post–World War II trends in private domestic investment. The remarkable thing to note about the long-run trend is that gross private domestic investment has re-

[11]We cannot entirely blame the government statisticians for any misuse or misinterpretation of the aggregate investment figure. They always publish and identify the underlying components. See, for example, any issue of the *Survey of Current Business*.

**Table 12-3(a)  Gross Private Domestic Investment (data are annual flows in billions of dollars)**

| | 1947 | 1950 | 1955 | 1960 | 1965 | 1970 | 1975 | 1976 | 1977 | 1978 |
|---|---|---|---|---|---|---|---|---|---|---|
| Structures | $ 7.5 | $ 9.5 | $ 14.5 | $ 18.0 | $ 26.0 | $ 37.5 | $ 53.0 | $ 56.0 | $ 64.0 | $ 82.0 |
| Producers' durable equipment | 15.5 | 18.0 | 24.0 | 29.5 | 45.0 | 63.0 | 96.0 | 106.0 | 126.5 | 140.0 |
| Change in business inventories | −.5 | 7.0 | 6.0 | 4.0 | 9.5 | 4.0 | −11.5 | 13.5 | 15.5 | 15.5 |
| Total | $ 22.5 | $ 34.5 | $ 44.5 | $ 51.5 | $ 80.5 | $104.5 | $137.5 | $175.5 | $206.0 | $237.5 |
| Residential structures and equipment | 11.5 | 20.0 | 24.0 | 25.0 | 31.0 | 36.5 | 51.5 | 68.0 | 92.0 | 107.0 |
| Gross private domestic investment | 34.0 | 54.5 | 68.5 | 76.5 | 96.5 | 141.0 | 189.0 | 243.5 | 298.0 | 344.5 |
| Gross national product | $233.0 | $286.0 | $399.0 | $506.0 | $688.0 | $982.5 | $1,529.0 | $1,706.5 | $1,887.0 | $2,106.5 |

**Table 12-3(b)  Nonfinancial Business Sources and Uses of Funds (data are annual flows in billions of dollars)**

| | 1947 | 1950 | 1955 | 1960 | 1965 | 1970 | 1975 | 1976 | 1977 | 1978 |
|---|---|---|---|---|---|---|---|---|---|---|
| **USES** | | | | | | | | | | |
| Capital expenditures | $ 21.2 | $ 40.8 | $ 45.0 | $ 52.1 | $ 84.8 | $107.9 | $127.6 | $175.5 | $212.0 | $242.1 |
| Net acquisition of financial assets | 10.4 | 17.2 | 17.2 | 2.3 | 21.3 | 17.2 | 38.4 | 48.5 | 52.9 | 79.7 |
| Total | $ 31.6 | $ 58.0 | $ 62.2 | $ 54.4 | $106.1 | $125.1 | $166.0 | $224.0 | $264.9 | $321.8 |
| **SOURCES** | | | | | | | | | | |
| Internal saving | $ 18.1 | $ 25.4 | $ 39.2 | $ 47.2 | $ 70.3 | $ 79.6 | $138.7 | $163.1 | $177.4 | $190.1 |
| New equities | 1.1 | 1.3 | 1.7 | 1.4 | .0 | 5.7 | 9.9 | 10.5 | 2.7 | 2.6 |
| Bonds | 2.8 | 1.6 | 2.8 | 3.5 | 5.4 | 19.8 | 29.8 | 25.3 | 24.5 | 23.3 |
| Mortgages | 2.2 | 2.8 | 3.7 | 4.4 | 9.2 | 13.3 | 16.4 | 22.7 | 36.9 | 43.5 |
| Other | 10.5 | 22.4 | 17.7 | 5.0 | 29.9 | 15.7 | 14.3 | 22.5 | 50.1 | 76.7 |
| Discrepancy | −3.1 | +4.5 | −2.9 | −7.1 | −8.7 | −9.0 | −43.1 | −20.1 | −26.7 | −14.4 |

Sources: Economic Report of the President; Board of Governors of the Federal Reserve System, *Flow of Funds Accounts*.

mained a very stable fraction of gross national product throughout this period—between 14 and 15 percent of GNP can be attributed to gross private domestic investment. During this period, the fraction of GNP that can be attributed to the manufacturing sector stayed relatively constant at about 23 percent, while that fraction attributed to the service-finance sectors rose from about 23 percent to about 28 percent. The underlying structure of the economy has changed in other ways as well, yet there is still a ratio of about $8.50 of GNP output for every dollar of gross private business investment.[12]

Producers' durable equipment—the machinery and tools necessary to run industry—is the largest component of private domestic business investment, ranging from 50 to 70 percent of the total, and averaging 60 percent in recent years. The most variable component of private domestic business investment over the three decades is, however, the fluctuations in business inventories. That change alone often accounts for more than half the year-to-year fluctuations in private business investment.

### Recent Business Cycles and Business Investments

One can get some indication of how business investment has fluctuated with business cycles over the past two decades from Table 12-4. Table 12-4 reports cumulative changes in major GNP sectors, in terms of 1972 dollars, for five recession periods and five expansion periods. The periods are dated peaks to trough (recessions) or troughs through next eight quarters (expansions), according to cycle definitions of the National Bureau of Economic Research.

Table 12-4 reveals that declines in real GNP in the past three decades have been short and generally moderate. Even the 1973–1975 decline (the largest in the post–World War II period) was only about 5 percent of real GNP. In current-dollar terms, GNP has hardly declined at all, as the year-end GNP figures in Table 12-4 suggest. The first part of Table 12-4 (recession periods) separates the cumulative changes in real GNP during recessions into their major components. As can be seen, that

part of gross private domestic investment known as the change in inventory investment (which is largely a change in business inventories) accounts for most of the change in real GNP, especially in the more recent recessions.[13] In effect, the recessions could almost be characterized as periods when businesses decided to adjust their inventory positions or their rate of production. Of course, these changes were brought about by some event. Infrequently, the event might be a change in tastes, where all at once everybody decides they do not like big cars, fancy clothes, or canned foods. More likely, however, the event is simply a working out of the accelerator principle—where a decrease in the rate of consumption, or even a decrease in the rate of *growth* in consumption, leads to a shift in business expectations. This shift, or sharply rising interest rates, leads to a cutback in inventory accumulation and, somewhat later, to a reduction in business fixed investment.

Pessimism in business expectations, whether induced by real demand shifts or higher costs of funds, is probably the key factor in moderate business recessions. In every one of the five recessions cited, real private domestic business investment declined. In three of those recessions, real personal consumption was actually increasing, though at a slower rate than normal. Residential construction was mixed, and the patterns seen here may be undergoing long-run structural changes as mobile homes and multifamily dwellings grow relatively faster than single-family homes. Government expenditures appear to be very volatile but tend to be smoothed out because of lags with the rest of the business cycle.

The impact of positive expectations can be seen in the first eight quarters of the five recovery periods. Private domestic business investment is positive and has a multiplier of between three and four in relation to real GNP. The change in inventories is again the largest component of changing business investment, which continues to be large and positive. Even in the first eight quarters, the real-dollar value of the personal consumption increase was about $55 billion compared to the less than $10 billion increase during the shorter average reces-

---

[12]See Table B-5, p. 189, in the 1979 edition of the *Economic Report of the President*.

[13]The inventory investment figures in Table 12-4 include some items (primarily agriculture commodities) that were not included in the "change in business inventories" figures in Table 12-3(a).

**Table 12-4(a)   Cumulative Changes in Major GNP Sectors in Five Recession Periods (percent of change in real GNP)**

|                                                        | 1953.2–1954.2 | 1957.3–1958.1 | 1960.1–1960.4 | 1969.3–1970.4 | 1973.4–1975.1 | Average Share |
|--------------------------------------------------------|---------------|---------------|---------------|---------------|---------------|---------------|
| Cumulative change Real GNP                             | −100.0        | −100.0        | −100.0        | −100.0        | −100.0        | −100.0        |
| Personal consumption                                   | +8.7          | −18.8         | +57.6         | +93.3         | −13.9         | +25.4         |
| Residential construction                               | +4.4          | −2.7          | −56.5         | +4.2          | −22.8         | −14.7         |
| Business fixed invest.                                 | −4.9          | −26.5         | −17.6         | −76.7         | −22.1         | −29.5         |
| Inventory invest.                                      | −45.1         | −47.1         | −202.3        | −83.3         | −56.3         | −86.8         |
| Net exports                                            | +13.6         | −21.1         | +45.9         | +7.5          | +8.8          | +10.9         |
| Government                                             | −76.7         | +16.2         | +72.9         | −45.0         | +6.3          | −5.3          |
| Addendum:                                              |               |               |               |               |               |               |
| Change in real GNP (billions of 1972 dollars)          | −20.6         | −22.3         | −8.5          | −12.0         | −81.5         | −29.0         |

**Table 12-4(b)   Cumulative Changes in Major GNP Sectors in Five Recovery Periods (percent of change in real GNP)**

|                                                        | 1954.2–1956.2 | 1958.1–1960.1 | 1960.4–1962.4 | 1970.4–1972.4 | 1975.1–1977.1 | Average Share |
|--------------------------------------------------------|---------------|---------------|---------------|---------------|---------------|---------------|
| Cumulative change Real GNP                             | 100.0         | 100.0         | 100.0         | 100.0         | 100.0         | 100.0         |
| Consumption                                            | 61.1          | 48.3          | 49.7          | 64.9          | 64.6          | 57.7          |
| Residential construction                               | 4.9           | 12.3          | 7.3           | 15.6          | 12.2          | 10.5          |
| Business fixed invest.                                 | 16.8          | 7.1           | 8.3           | 12.9          | 5.5           | 10.1          |
| Inventory invest.                                      | 15.5          | 26.3          | 11.7          | 5.7           | 18.7          | 15.6          |
| Net exports                                            | 4.0           | −0.5          | −3.4          | −1.3          | −5.9          | −1.4          |
| Government                                             | −2.3          | 6.5           | 26.4          | 2.2           | 4.9           | 7.5           |
| Addendum:                                              |               |               |               |               |               |               |
| Change in real GNP (billions of 1972 dollars)          | 61.9          | 77.3          | 73.9          | 130.8         | 135.7         | 95.9          |

Source: Federal Reserve Bank of San Francisco, *Economic Review* (Spring 1977), 14–22.

sion period. And, in most cases, the recovery periods lasted longer than eight quarters.

Actually, the relationship between business investment decisions and business cycles is quite complex. It is certainly true that firms adjust their working capital positions sometime after an expansion is well established. On the current asset side, this may mean a slowdown in the growth of inventories and accounts receivable and a slight expansion of cash reserves. On the current liabilities side, it may mean a stabilization of accounts payable or some increase, and a decrease in bank loans or term loans outstanding. But these are more or less regularized operating decisions that reflect expectations about current business decisions. The expectations must persist for a time before capital-budgeting decisions about structures, producers' durable equipment, and "permanent" changes in working capital are significantly affected. What

may be more important in the short run is that the onset of a recession can seriously affect the perceived sources of funds. Earnings decline so, to the extent dividends are stabilized, earnings retained for reinvestment in the business decline. Banks may become somewhat stricter in providing term loans, and corporations do not care to sell as much new stock when the stock market is declining. Thus, declines in capital spending result from a combination of perceived increases in costs of obtaining capital and perceived declines in opportunities for profitably investing that capital.

## Major Sector Differences

Not all sectors of the economy grow uniformly, nor do they have the same requirements for capital funds. Growth in gross national product by broad industry sectors is summarized in Table 12-5. Table

**Table 12-5(a)  Gross National Product by Industry (in billions of 1972 dollars)**

|  | 1950 | 1955 | 1960 | 1965 | 1970 | 1975 | 1977 |
|---|---|---|---|---|---|---|---|
| Gross national product | $533.5 | $654.8 | $736.8 | $925.9 | $1,075.3 | $1,202.3 | $1,332.7 |
| Agriculture | 29.1 | 31.9 | 32.2 | 33.0 | 34.3 | 37.0 | 38.3 |
| Contract construction | 29.3 | 38.2 | 46.1 | 57.0 | 57.1 | 49.8 | 56.9 |
| Manufacturing | 131.3 | 165.8 | 172.0 | 235.1 | 260.6 | 277.1 | 322.3 |
| Transportation and utilities | 39.6 | 49.4 | 58.0 | 74.3 | 95.1 | 113.5 | 124.0 |
| Wholesale and retail trade | 87.6 | 103.2 | 117.9 | 148.6 | 178.4 | 206.2 | 227.9 |
| Finance and real estate | 64.4 | 82.0 | 101.9 | 127.2 | 152.9 | 182.3 | 204.0 |
| Services | 59.4 | 67.5 | 82.2 | 101.2 | 124.7 | 145.2 | 159.0 |
| Government | 75.4 | 95.4 | 107.2 | 127.4 | 152.0 | 162.7 | 165.7 |
| Other | 17.5 | 21.4 | 19.4 | 22.1 | 20.4 | 28.6 | 34.5 |

**Table 12-5(b)  Gross National Product by Major Type of Product (in billions of 1972 dollars)**

|  | 1950 | 1955 | 1960 | 1965 | 1970 | 1975 | 1977 | 1978[p] |
|---|---|---|---|---|---|---|---|---|
| Gross national product | $533.5 | $654.8 | $736.8 | $925.9 | $1,075.3 | $1,202.3 | $1,332.7 | $1,385.1 |
| Durable goods | 84.4 | 112.9 | 111.6 | 152.6 | 179.1 | 219.8 | 248.0 | 257.8 |
| Nondurable goods | 166.5 | 195.7 | 221.2 | 257.7 | 300.0 | 328.2 | 351.6 | 360.8 |
| Services | 206.0 | 257.6 | 310.7 | 389.1 | 477.2 | 560.1 | 602.9 | 627.2 |
| Structures | 66.0 | 80.9 | 89.0 | 115.3 | 114.6 | 104.0 | 121.3 | 128.8 |

[p]Preliminary.

Source: *Economic Report of the President, 1979.*

12-5(a) separates GNP into industry-type sectors; Table 12-5(b) decodes the same GNP totals into final product categories.

In terms of the constant 1972-dollar figures, GNP in the 1950–1977 period more than doubled. (Of course, in current-dollar terms, GNP in this period increased more than 6.6 times.) The smallest sector increase is the 33 percent rise attributed to agriculture. The largest increase is the more than 300 percent increase attributed to the finance and real estate component. Almost as large an increase is attributed to the transportation and utilities groups, followed by the professional services groups. The dramatic nature of this trend can be seen more clearly in the broad final product categories of Table 12-5(b). Goods that are "services" increased almost 300 percent, while all the rest—the physical goods categories—increased only about 190 percent. And, as can be seen in Table 12-5(a), most of this increase was not in government-provided services. We have in this century become one of the few industrialized countries in the world where the production of services is overtaking the importance of the production of goods.

These trends may have important implications for business expenditures in the future. Some types of services, such as transportation or communications, are capital intensive and regularly make huge business investments. But others, such as banks, law firms, and hospitals, do not usually make significant capital expenditures. It is possible that relative growth of the service sector generally may have some mitigating influences on the fluctuations in business inventories and investments.

In the next section we look at business sources of funds to see if there have been secular changes in how capital is raised that relate to long-term changes in the relative components of GNP.

**Trends in Corporate Sources of Funds**

Table 12-6 summarizes annual data for sources of funds for nonfinancial business firms. Since aggregate sources must equal aggregate uses of funds, the previous discussion of how uses (business investment) varies with the business cycle applies also to aggregate fund sources. As can be seen in

**Table 12-6   Relative Sources of Funds for Nonfinancial Business (percentages)[a]**

| Year | Internal | New Equities | Bonds | Mortgages | Other | Total[b] |
|------|----------|--------------|-------|-----------|-------|----------|
| 1947 | 52 | 3 | 8 | 6 | 31 | $34.7 |
| 1948 | 60 | 2 | 10 | 5 | 23 | 42.0 |
| 1949 | 89 | 2 | 9 | 10 | (10) | 29.4 |
| 1950 | 47 | 2 | 3 | 5 | 43 | 53.5 |
| 1951 | 60 | 4 | 7 | 5 | 24 | 47.7 |
| 1952 | 77 | 6 | 12 | 5 | 0 | 39.5 |
| 1953 | 80 | 5 | 9 | 6 | (3) | 39.9 |
| 1954 | 84 | 4 | 9 | 6 | (3) | 39.9 |
| 1955 | 60 | 3 | 4 | 6 | 27 | 65.1 |
| 1956 | 72 | 4 | 6 | 5 | 13 | 55.2 |
| 1957 | 76 | 4 | 11 | 4 | 5 | 55.6 |
| 1958 | 75 | 4 | 10 | 8 | 3 | 55.6 |
| 1959 | 69 | 3 | 4 | 8 | 16 | 69.0 |
| 1960 | 77 | 2 | 6 | 7 | 8 | 61.5 |
| 1961 | 70 | 3 | 7 | 10 | 10 | 68.6 |
| 1962 | 71 | 0 | 6 | 11 | 12 | 76.8 |
| 1963 | 67 | 0 | 5 | 11 | 17 | 86.0 |
| 1964 | 68 | 1 | 4 | 10 | 16 | 93.0 |
| 1965 | 61 | 0 | 5 | 8 | 26 | 114.8 |
| 1966 | 63 | 1 | 9 | 8 | 19 | 119.8 |
| 1967 | 67 | 2 | 13 | 8 | 10 | 115.7 |
| 1968 | 57 | 0 | 9 | 8 | 26 | 140.2 |
| 1969 | 55 | 2 | 8 | 8 | 27 | 148.0 |
| 1970 | 60 | 4 | 15 | 10 | 11 | 134.1 |
| 1971 | 55 | 7 | 12 | 14 | 12 | 163.6 |
| 1972 | 54 | 6 | 7 | 18 | 15 | 193.7 |
| 1973 | 48 | 3 | 5 | 14 | 30 | 227.7 |
| 1974 | 50 | 2 | 10 | 12 | 26 | 218.0 |
| 1975 | 66 | 5 | 14 | 8 | 7 | 209.1 |
| 1976 | 67 | 4 | 10 | 9 | 9 | 244.1 |
| 1977 | 61 | 1 | 8 | 13 | 17 | 291.6 |
| 1978 | 57 | 1 | 7 | 13 | 23 | 336.2 |

[a]See Table 12-3 for actual dollar amounts.
[b]Totals in billions of dollars.

Source: Board of Governors of the Federal Reserve System, *Flow of Funds Accounts.*

Table 12-3(b), the most variable component on the sources side is the "Other" component, which reflects net changes in bank loans, trade credit, and other working-capital adjustments. In contrast, the dollar aggregate "Internal saving" (which includes earnings retained in the business and noncash depreciation charges—revenue-generated funds available for investment) is remarkably stable. The total declines only slightly in recession years and increases moderately in every other year.

One may get a clearer understanding of the *relative* variation in fund sources from looking at Table 12-7, which is based on Table 12-6. There are several things to note here. First, internal fund sources have almost always constituted at least half of all fund sources as defined. Indeed, this source comes close to accounting for two-thirds of funds raised. (If the "Other" account were excluded and we focused on just the long-term fund sources, the internal sources would be more than 70 percent of the total most years.) Of the internal sources at the aggregate level, two-thirds might come from capital consumption allowances ("Depreciation flows") and one-third from undistributed profits (Retained earnings"). In recent years, about 40 percent of net income as reported to shareholders has been paid out as dividends and the other 60 percent (the undistributed profits) retained for reinvestment in the firm. Of course, these fractions vary from industry to industry. In capital-intensive industries where

**Table 12-7  Average Relative Funds Sources for the Period 1947–1978**

| | | |
|---|---|---:|
| Internal | | 65% |
| Depreciation flows | 40% | |
| Retained earnings | 25% | |
| New equities | | 3 |
| Bonds | | 8 |
| Mortgages | | 8 |
| Other debt | | 16 |
| Total | | 100% |

Source: Calculated from Table 12-6.

profits are low (for example, railroads) or are constrained by regulation (utilities), depreciation will be a higher fraction of internal sources than for the typical manufacturing firm. Financial corporations and service-sector firms, with relatively little fixed capital, must rely more heavily on undistributed profits for internal sources of funds.

It may be surprising to find that the sale of new stock constitutes such a small fraction of total fund sources. This particular source has not, in recent decades, amounted to even 10 percent of all funds used in any given year. In some years, net new equity financing is almost zero as a relative source, and it is seldom above 5 percent of total sources. (This is consistent with the theory reviewed more fully in the appendix to this chapter, which suggests that the perceived marginal cost of new stock financing is higher than any other source of new capital.)

One of the more surprising features of the distribution of aggregate fund sources is its relative stability over long periods of time. Although there are cyclical influences, there do not appear to be any real secular trends or fluctuations in the percentages reported in Table 12-6. There is an apparent increase in the relative use of mortgages as a fund source, but this may relate as much to accounting and definitional changes as to real changes. It is also true that, after a year or two of relying on high other-fund sources (short-term funds), there appears to be a shift back into permanent capital sources. However, fund shifts over the business cycles of the past three decades have not followed any simple, observable pattern. A more or less unique story must be told to explain patterns of fund sources for each of the five recession and recovery periods described in Table 12-4.

That is to say, from an explanatory or predictive viewpoint, we would be about as well off projecting the average figures each year as trying to explain year-to-year variations. Average relative sources for the thirty-year period are given in Table 12-7.

### Financial Structure Trends

Data on aggregate corporate capital structures over the past half-century and more indicate that the major corporate financial ratios—the debt/equity and payout ratios—are, indeed, quite stable. There does seem, however, to be a slight upward drift in the internal/external finance ratio.

For these findings to be consistent, the relative *composition* of external finance must have shifted toward debt and away from common stock sufficiently to match the rise in internal equity. There has also been a shift from preferred stock to bonds, plus a shift from long-term to short-term debt within the debt total itself. Note that these shifts, both in the overall role of external finance and in its composition, imply a relative secular decline in the role of the capital market in financing corporate investment requirements.

Another way to view these changes in the composition of external finance is to note that the role of security issuance as a means of financing corporations has been declining in importance. The absolute decline in preferred stock outstanding as well as the relative decline of common stock has not been fully offset by the slight relative (though large absolute) increase in the use of bonds as a source of external finance. Actually, it has been shorter-term debt that has soared. However, the capital markets are still of crucial importance to particular industries and to all industries at particular times.

It should be noted that utilities, with their heavy (three-fifths) dependence on external finance and slight use of short-term debt, are the bread and butter of the investment banking or security underwriting business. Two-thirds of all stock issues and one-half of all bond issues in the postwar period have been in the form of utility stocks and bonds, although utilities have raised only one-seventh of total corporate funds since World War II. On the other hand, in financing 70 percent of their requirements internally, industrials sold little stock (one-sixth of all issues) but did float about one-half of all new bond issues. Without the utilities, therefore, stock flotation would be negligible and the bond market would be much smaller. Security flotations are crucial only to the financing of the utility sector, except at the peak of a boom, at which time industrial bond issues rise sharply.

One of the issues that must be faced over the next two decades is what will happen to these ratios as the United States becomes increasingly a service-sector economy. Private service-sector firms now have relatively little access to the major capital markets. Since there are few ''assets'' in such firms, creditors are reluctant to supply debt capital unless they receive some sort of third-party guarantee. Another trend that could alter these ratios is the development of foreign capital markets. Multinational firms using those capital markets may find the institutional constraints quite different (for example, Japanese firms have higher debt/equity ratios than American firms).

The capital markets, especially the bond markets, retain their critical importance in the financing of corporations during a boom. More important, the capital markets are of continuing significance to new and growth corporations. But such functions may be thought of as ''marginal,'' even if crucial, in these cases. The capital markets are of continuing significance to all corporations, however, because this is where the prices of outstanding equities are determined, and equity prices—the principal component in measuring stockholders' welfare—not only reflect earnings retention but also are the gauge by which financial management scales its efforts. In short, the capital markets are still of the greatest importance to the corporate investment decision even when new funds are not being raised in those markets.

## Conclusion

Investment demand, important in the explanation of both economic growth and economic fluctuations, has a *real* demand component, depending on the accelerator process and the pressures on capacity, and a *financially* conditioned component, depending on the cost of finance, given the expected returns from investment. An eclectic theory of investment demand—an accelerator-residual funds theory—provides an understanding of both the cyclical and secular behavior of business investment and its financing. In effect, this eclectic theory is a profit theory, in which business investment demand is fundamentally dependent on capacity but is subject to a variety of important financial constraints as well. These financial factors can be expressed in terms of the shape and position of the marginal-cost-of-finance schedule.

When investment data are classified into utility and manufacturing sectors, cyclical and secular patterns demonstrate the usefulness of the eclectic theory of investment demand. Utilities do not experience the cylical variability of residual funds or the need for synchronization of the supply of funds with the demand for funds that is typical of manufacturing industry, nor do they have the averison to debt and to external finance generally found in nonregulated industries. The financial ratios, although stable, are quite different for regulated and nonregulated businesses. And the acceleration principle, which explains plant and equipment expenditures in electric utilities quite well, does *not* do so for manufacturing or for total business investment where financial constraints, namely the supply of and demand for funds, play a crucial role.

Overall, corporate financial ratios tend to be secularly stable. Nevertheless, a slight secular upward drift can be observed in the internal finance ratio and a sharp shift in the composition of the declining external finance portion. However, the aggregate debt/equity ratio seems stable at around 30 percent, as does the dividend payout ratio at around 50 percent. A variety of real (investment opportunity) and financial (cost of capital) factors account for the relative rise in internal finance and for the shift in proportions within external finance from stock to debt and, within debt, from long term to short term. But, after all these changes are accounted for, what has kept the debt/equity ratio secularly stable? The answer seems to lie in the fact that the rise in *internal* equity finance has tended to offset the decline in *external* equity financing.

Despite the secular stability of the principal financial ratios, however, there has been a substantial decline in the use of securities as a share of total corporate sources of finance. Thus, the relative use of preferred stock has declined very sharply; the relative use of common stock has fallen somewhat less, but still substantially; and bond issuance has also decreased relatively, although not by very much. In short, despite the overall structural stability of corporate financing patterns, the role of the capital markets and investment banking in corporate finance has declined relatively, especially since the 1920s. However, during cyclical upswings, the capital markets are crucially important in financing operations and, as gauges against which financial managers can measure their performance, the capital markets still remain significant.

### Appendix: Investment Decisions for the Firm

Investment decisions of the firm were examined briefly in the body of this chapter, but the purpose there was to study theories of aggregate business investment. The purpose of this appendix is to look at investment and financing decisions of the firm in somewhat more detail, although, necessarily, the treatment still must be brief. This appendix proceeds from the capital-expenditure decision to the financial-structure decision and concludes with a review of financial-structure data—capital structure in practice.

In analyzing the investment-financing process at the firm level, it is customary to consider three principal uses of funds: capital expenditures, net working capital, and dividend payments. The sources of funds for these various uses include internal sources—earnings retained in the business from current net income flows and cash flow-throughs arising because of charges for noncash outlays (depreciation)—and the usual external sources of funds—finance credit, bank loans, new stock or bond financing, and so forth. It is important to remember that while, by definition, sources and uses of funds totals must match, particular sources do not necessarily match particular uses. Receipts from the sale of a new bond issue may end up financing increased inventory, or a new plant, or as part of this quarter's dividend payment. This is true at the firm level, and it is also true for aggregate sources and uses, such as the totals in Table 12-3(b).

The essence of the firm's investment decision may be seen graphically in Figure 12-10. This figure portrays investment opportunities for a very simple firm that operates in a two-period world—the present and the future. Distances on the horizontal axis represent amounts available for consumption by the firm's owners in the present; distances on the vertical axis represent amounts available in the future. Thus, for example, point A represents a combination of $600 of consumption in the present and

$0 in the future. In contrast, point E represents $660 of future consumption and $0 of present consumption. Point C represents $660 of future consumption and $400 today.

Suppose now that the sources of income for the firm add up to $600 in the present (point A). The firm has a number of choices it can make with respect to the uses of this income. One is the point A choice of consuming all $600 of the income in the present period and $0 in the future. However, this may not be the best choice because the owners may not prefer all consumption to take place in the present.

A second choice is to lend some of the present funds in the capital market, in effect giving up some present consumption in exchange for more future consumption. In Figure 12-10 this trade-off is illustrated by the line AE, the financial market's opportunity line, which shows the relationship between present and future consumption available in the capital markets. As can be seen, the trade-off in

**Figure 12-10    Investment Opportunities for the Firm in a Two-Period World**

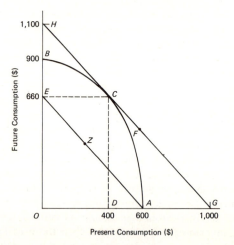

this example is available at a rate of 10 percent. In other words, starting at A with $600 of possible present consumption and $0 of future consumption, the firm could move along line AE by investing funds in securities offering a return of 10 percent. As a result, the firm can achieve for its owners any desired combination of present and future consumption along the line (for example, point Z). If the firm moves all the way to point E (lending all $600), the result is $660 of future consumption and $0 of present consumption.

The firm's third choice is productive investment in capital equipment, which also offers a trade-off between present and future consumption. This alternative is illustrated by the curved line AB, which is known as the production possibilities curve; it indicates the rate of trade-off of present for future consumption. However, unlike the line AE, the slope of AB is changing constantly as the firm moves along it. For the first $200 of investment (that is, decline in present consumption equal to AD), the return in the form of additional future consumption is very high (namely, $DC = OE$, or $660). But note that the last $400 of potential investment (DO) returns only $240 (EB), a much lower rate of return. Thus, the slope of the production possibilities curve AB at any point is a simple measure of marginal efficiency of capital. As the slope of AB flattens, the project return (MEC) declines, and the projects are ranked so that the projects with highest returns will come first (near A) and the lowest return project comes last (near B).

Therefore, for any firm with access to the capital markets, there are two types of opportunities for both the firm and its shareholders. The first is the financial market's opportunity line, which gives trade-offs between the present and the future at a given rate—the so-called cost of capital. In Figure 12-10 the cost of capital is drawn as a 10 percent rate. The other opportunity is the chance of return through real capital usage illustrated by the production possibilities curve AB. The rational economic unit will want to expand wealth by moving along curve AB as far as point C, where MEC just equals the cost of capital (10 percent in this example). Or, to say this another way, the wealth-maximizing firm makes all investments whose internal rate of return is higher than the firm's cost

of capital.[14] At point C the firm has maximized the value of the firm for existing stockholders. This can be seen by drawing line HG through point C and parallel to AE. This financial market opportunity curve is analogous to AE, but it shows the possible combinations of present and future consumptions when optimal productive investment has been undertaken. As one can see, maximum present value (possible present consumption) of $1,000 results. The preferred combination of present versus future consumption is obtained by moving along HG by borrowing and increasing present consumption (the range of combinations CG) or by lending and increasing future consumption (the range of combinations CH). Any of the combinations along HG are maximum-wealth combinations because they are consistent with maximum present value.

## The Cost of Capital

So far we have been using the term *cost of capital*, as it relates to a firm, without defining precisely what it is or how to estimate it. We have assumed a perfect capital market, where business firms have been able either to borrow or to lend at a single rate called the cost of capital. The truth of the matter is that it is a very complex issue and neither finance theorists nor practitioners agree on all the answers. Here we try to outline some of the issues and give a first-round approximation of how you might attempt to estimate the overall cost of capital.

Most agree that the cost of capital for a firm is an *opportunity cost* measure used in helping the firm make marginal-investment decisions. In particular, the cost of capital is that minimal rate of return on new investment such that the value of the firm to *the existing owners* will not decline if the new investment is made. This is not the same as the supply price of capital. For example, the supply price of debt to the firm is basically the interest rate paid on the bonds. The firm may have

---

[14]There are complexities in using internal rate of return (and in finding the tangency point in real capital markets) that are beyond the scope of this brief section. For a discussion of these issues, see J. Hirshleifer, *Investment, Interest, and Capital,* Prentice-Hall, Englewood Cliffs, N.J., 1970.

a \$5 million project in mind that could be financed by selling bonds at 8 percent yield. The marginal cost of capital to the firm of financing this project is not 8 percent. In a country such as the United States, where interest is a tax-deductible expense and where a firm might be in an effective 40 percent income tax bracket, the marginal cost of *debt* capital might be something like 6 percent. [Note that the firm's after-tax bond interest rate would be 8% $(1 - .40) = 4.8\%$, not 6%. The 6% calculation is derived from assumptions about cost of capital theory that require more advanced treatment than we can provide here.] That is, the project should be accepted if it is expected to generate a return higher than 6 percent. Consequently, this cut-off rate for debt-financed investments is not even directly dependent on the prevailing interest rate! The answer might be the same whether the firm had to pay 9 percent or 7 percent on its bonds. To repeat, the cost of capital is not necessarily the supply price of a particular type of capital. The cost of capital is another type of measure: it is the minimally acceptable rate an investment financed by a particular type of capital must earn if the value of the firm to the existing owners (the holders of its common stock) is not to decline.

The cost of capital does vary from firm to firm. Traditional theories relate this variation to relative risk differences among firms. The more risky an investment opportunity appears to be, the higher the expected-return premium investors will demand. Thus, the return for an investment in an all-equity firm can be conceptually defined as:

$\epsilon$ = return demanded by stockholders in an all-equity (unlevered) firm

= $f$ (the pure rate of interest, inflation premium, marketability risk, real operating risk)

The first three elements of the function are associated with all financial securities. The pure rate of interest can be approximated by the return on a comparable government security—say, a long-term government with a current yield-to-maturity of 6 percent—to which a premium for risk can be added. Since private firms are generally assumed to be riskier than the federal government in our country, $\epsilon$ would have an additional risk premium—say, 2 percent—making the total return demanded about 8 percent.

In general, stockholders' expected return will be even higher because stockholders are exposed to an additional risk—the risk of financial leverage. The ''returns'' to stockholders (the earnings of the firm) are a residual after everybody else has been paid. Since bondholders are paid before stockholders, it seems reasonable that the return expected by stockholders will be somewhat higher than the return expected by the bondholders. And the return expected by the stockholders may increase as their exposure to financial risk (usually measured as the firm's debt/equity ratio) increases.

$k$ = return demanded by stockholders in any firm

= $f$ ($\epsilon$, financial risk)

As a continuation of the previous example, if $\epsilon$ is 8 percent and the financial risk premium added something less than 1 percent to the total expected by stockholders, $k$ would be around 9 percent.

Earnings are the flows generated by the firm for the stockholder owners. Not all income is distributed immediately in most cases. Some may be distributed as dividends, and the rest is reinvested in the firm to generate higher future earnings and dividends. The present value of these future expected dividend increases is theoretically (and actually, in most cases) captured now by an increase in the market price of the stock. So stockholders realize the earnings returns generated for them as dividends distributed and as capital-gains returns on the shares of stock they hold.

In highly competitive, efficient capital markets, individuals can hold portfolios of securities of different firms and diversify away the firm's unique operating risks.[15] This is directly analogous to the principle of insurance at work. But since earnings and, hence, dividend and stock prices of firms in the economy have some tendency to move together, not all risk can be diversified away. What this means is that the return demanded by shareholders in any firm might alternatively be described as:

$k = f$ (pure rate of interest, inflation premium, $\beta_i$)

where $\beta_i$ is a risk index that measures the relationship between the returns on security $i$ and the returns on all other securities.

[15]See Chapter 24.

One form of the relationship, called the capital asset pricing model[16] (which can be derived only under some restrictive sets of assumptions), suggests the following types of relation for return on security $i$:

$$k_i = r^* + \beta_i(R_M - r^*)$$

where $r^*$ is a risk-free inflation-adjusted return on some security (say, a special government bond), and $R_M$ is the return expected on a market-basket portfolio of all other securities. As an example, $r^*$ might be about 6 percent, $\beta_i$ about 1.3, and the market return $R_M$ about 9 percent. Then the expected $k$ for firm $i$ would turn out to be about 10 percent.

The overall cost of capital—the marginal opportunity cost that is an index of the minimal acceptable return on a new project—may be taken as a weighted average cost *to the firm* of various sources of capital, where the weights are the marginal or desired proportions of different capital types (bonds, common stock, retained earnings, and so forth) for the firm.[17]

Although the marginal costs of particular capital sources differ, it should not be assumed at the firm level that the overall cost of capital changes as additional funds are acquired. For example, once an appropriate capital structure is determined, the cost of capital will usually change only if the firm alters its relative capital structure, the perceived risk of the firm's investment changes, or the general level of interest rates changes. Thus, at the firm level, the cost of capital as a function of the magnitude of capital raised should have a positive slope only in the following cases: (1) the additional capital raised alters capital structures—for example, by increasing leverage to the point where bankruptcy risk (and hence, firm risk to all suppliers of funds) increases; (2) the firm is investing in riskier projects as more of them are undertaken, so that fund suppliers' required returns are higher; or (3) what the firm does is correlated with what other firms are doing, so that aggregate firm demand is increasing. Of course, we would expect the *aggregate* (all firm) MCF schedule usually to be increasing for the reasons described in the body of this chapter. So long as funds suppliers perceive higher rates of investment to be somewhat riskier, and the supply of funds available to firms is limited by consumption (utility) preferences, the aggregate MCF (that is, the supply price of capital) will be upward sloping.

## Capital Structure of Firms

So far we have seen that firms make capital-budgeting decisions by (1) analyzing the future cash flows before financing considerations for a project, and (2) adjusting those cash flows for risk and time pattern by discounting at the cost of capital. But what determines the type of financing that will be used for these long-term investments?

For certain projects, specific institutional factors may play a dominant role in the type of financing used. Thus, a firm building a new tire plant in a particular section of the country may get partial financing for the expansion from some state development agency. Or a bank may agree to arrange lease financing for a particular type of equipment. However, in the long run, the capital structure of a firm is not due to an aggregation of what are, more or less, chance particular decisions but is due to a planned financial-structure policy.

In that long run, there seem to be three important factors in determining typical capital structure. The first is the perceived liquidity of the assets required for the conduct of business. As an extreme example, consider a firm whose assets are almost all government bonds. It is likely that creditor-supplied capital for such a firm could be very high relative to equity-supplied capital. In fact, we do find in the United States that banks and some other types of financial services firms that are perceived to have readily marketable assets have total debt/equity ratios of almost 15:1 or higher, as compared to 1:1 or lower for many manufacturing

---

[16]See Chapter 24.

[17]This is just a first approximation to the cost of capital. Projects that change the risk of the firm or that have only finite lives require more complex computations of the cost of capital. Note these are costs to the firm, not rates demanded by the supplier of capital; thus, the measured cost of debt is the after-tax cost to the firm, not the yield-to-maturity demanded by bondholders. Although we can "measure" the cost of debt this way, this is not the true marginal cost of debt since the value of stockholders' equity is affected by any change in relative debt utilized. That is, $k$ may increase as debt used increases, so that the true marginal cost of debt is not only the after-tax interest cost but also the increase in $k$.

firms.[18] Attitudes about asset liquidity are institutionally determined and persist for long periods of time, but are not always the same from country to country. Thus, industrial firms in Japan tend to have higher debt/equity ratios than similar firms in the United States.

A second factor in determining capital structure relates to operating risk. Other things being equal, creditors will supply more debt to those firms they perceive as having stable operating income. The most obvious example is probably a regulated, noncompetitive industry, such as electric utilities. Whereas the "asset liquidity" factor may determine whether total debt/equity ratios are closer to 15:1 or 5:1, the "operating-income risk" factor may determine whether the debt/equity measure is closer to 2:1 or 0.5:1. Banks or other institutions are known to change their attitudes somewhat about acceptable levels of operating risk depending on their optimism about business conditions.

The third factor determining capital structure is, of course, the relative price of various sources of capital. Since obtaining more credit exposes stockholders to greater financial risk, the marginal costs of different types of capital are a function of both the yield on risk capital required by a supplier group, and how the use of that capital affects the value of the firm to the existing shareholders. This is, of course, the *cost of capital* concept explored earlier.

It is, in fact, true that the typical business corporation generally is reluctant to go outside the firm to obtain funds for expansion. *All* corporations are reluctant to finance externally beyond the proportions deemed appropriate by the customs of the firm or the industy or by the working rules of the institutional sources of external finance. This reluctance is exhibited in numerous surveys of business leaders' opinions and behavior as well as in capital structure data.[19]

Management generally is reluctant to go outside the firm for funds because it prefers to avoid dependence on the impersonal capital (and money) markets with the "discipline" and unpredictable costs involved. (One can be rationed or priced out of a tight capital market.) More specifically, corporate management is reluctant to go outside to borrow (at least beyond the norm) because of its so-called aversion to debt. Another factor is the rising cost of debt as borrowing increases. On the other hand, its reluctance to go outside for equity funds (that is, to sell new stock) stems both from the aversion to being judged by an impersonal capital market, or loss of full control, and from the high cost such external equity financing might entail.

### Financial Structure Trends

As we pointed out earlier, data on aggregate corporate capital structures over the past half-century and more indicate that the major corporate financial ratios—the debt/equity and payout ratios—are, indeed, quite stable. There appears, however, to be a slight upward drift in the internal/external finance ratio.

As we noted, for these findings to be consistent, the relative *composition* of external finance must have shifted toward debt and away from common stock sufficiently to match the rise in internal equity. We also find a shift from preferred stock to bonds and, within the debt total itself, from long-term to short-term debt. These shifts, both in the overall role of external finance and in its composition, imply a relative secular decline in the role of the capital market in financing corporate investment requirements.

Corporate financial management desires to keep the two principal financial ratios stable. However, this analysis suggests neither a secular rise in internal finance nor structural shifts in external finance. The explanation for the decline in external finance and for changes in its composition is to be found, rather, in secular shifts in the costs of finance and in the risks associated with investment opportunities. Let us now examine these trends more closely.

Taken as the ratio of dividends to corporate profits after taxes, the payout ratio averaged about 50 percent during the past four decades (with cyclical variability ranging from 35 percent to 65 percent). The ratio of dividends to total cash flow (net profits *plus* depreciation) showed even less cyclical dis-

---

[18]We are referring to total debt (current liabilities and long-term debt) here. The firm's production function determines the relative amount of working capital and fixed capital required.

[19]For example, the proportion of debt-to-equity. In this connection, see G. Donaldson, *Corporate Debt Capacity,* Harvard Business School, Boston, 1961.

persion over this period, while averaging some 30 percent.

The debt/equity-plus-debt ratio for all corporations also has remained close to 30 percent since the turn of the century. Taking such reasonably uniform periods as 1901–1929, 1930–1958 and 1947–1977, one finds that equity finance provided 68.2 percent, 69.7 percent, and 58.2 percent of total sources of corporate funds, respectively (see Table 12-8).

The overall stability of these ratios has not been impaired by various shifts in the importance of industry sectors and their financing patterns, for the shifts appear to have been offsetting. For example, since 1920 debt has been substituted for equity to a slight degree in the capital structure of industrials (presumably, this has been due to decreased business risk in the postwar period) but, for the railroads, the opposite trend has developed due to *increased* business risk. This slight increase in the debt ratio of industrials does not appear in the stable debt ratio for *all* corporations since the decreasing importance of the regulated industries with their high average debt/equity ratio overshadows the effect of the industrials' rising, but relatively low, debt/equity ratio.

The ratio of internal-to-total finance for all corporations does appear to show a slight secular rise from 55 percent (1901–1912) to 65 percent (1952–1967), but it has fallen back to 60 percent over the past decade (1968–1977). The question that comes to mind is how the internal ratio could have risen over time when both the payout and debt ratios remained stable. The answer is that the proportion of external equity financing has been reduced. Business has taken advantage of higher and more stable earnings in the postwar period to shift from external to internal finance, and, thus, to reduce its overall financing costs.

*The Decline in External Finance and the Shift in Its Composition* Not only has there been a relative decline in external equity—that is, the sale of common stock—as a source of finance (matching the corresponding rise in internal equity finance), but there also has been a relative decline *within* external finance in the use of preferred stock and a matching rise in the use of debt. *Both* of these shifts away from stock issues as sources of funds parallel our evolution from a relatively unstable, low-tax economy to a high-employment, high-tax economy!

Perhaps the two greatest changes in the financial environment over the past thirty years have been the sizable increase in the role of income taxation and the disappearance of depressions or even deep or frequent recessions. The sharp increase in *personal* income taxation in the post-1940 years has increased the cost of acquiring equity funds externally rather than internally, for funds plowed back are not subject to personal income tax (although their fruits are subject to capital gains tax). Meanwhile, the new relative profit stability resulting from the mastering of depressions and prolonged recessions has made internal finance both more reliable and more abundant. (But recent inflation—rapid and unanticipated—may have begun to impair business capacity to finance internally.) Also, the

**Table 12-8  The Ratio of Equity Sources to Total Sources of Funds in All Nonfinancial Corporations, 1901–1977 (in billions of dollars)**

|  | *1901–1929* | *1930–1958* | *1947–1977* |
|---|---|---|---|
| Total sources | $202.2 | $581.6 | $2,618 |
| Common stock | 22.7 | 34.4 | 103 |
| Internal sources | 115.2 | 371.3 | 1,556 |
| Total equity sources | 137.9 | 405.7 | 1,659 |
| Total equity sources including preferred | 146.0 | 410.7 | 1,719 |
| Ratios |  |  |  |
| Equity to total sources | 68.2% | 69.7% | 58.2% |
| Equity plus preferred to total sources | 72.2% | 70.6% | 65.7% |

Sources: R. Lindsay and A. W. Sametz, *Financial Management: An Analytical Approach*, rev. ed., Richard D. Irwin, Homewood, Ill., 1967, p. 362; A. W. Sametz, "Trends in the Volume and Composition of Equity Finance," *Journal of Finance* (September 1964); *Statistical Abstract of the United States for 1978.*

sharp increase in *corporate* income taxation has increased the cost of raising "fixed" charge funds via preferred stock as compared with debt, while the added risk of debt over preferred stock has been offset by decreased "business" risk in the postwar economy.

As a result, the role of both new common and preferred-stock issues has declined since 1946. Common stock's share in *total* sources of finance has fallen from 14 percent in the 1920s to 5 percent in the 1950s to 3 percent in the 1960s. In the decade of the 1970s it moved back toward the 5 percent level. Common-stock issues, which comprised some one out of every four dollars raised by new sales of corporate securities from 1900 to 1929, fell to one out of every six dollars by 1950–1959. And, in the sixties, new common-stock issues declined further, yielding only one out of every seven dollars raised by the sale of all new security issues, most of which have consisted of the sale of bonds (see Table 12-9). However, in the 1970s, common stocks' share revived to the levels of the 1950s.

Preferred stock, which in 1926 supplied 7 percent of *total* sources of funds, saw its share fall to less than 1 percent by the end of the 1960s. As a percentage of *external* financing, its share has declined from 18 percent in the 1920s to 6.5 percent in the 1970s (see Table 12-9).

One final observation may be in order on the composition of external finance. Although debt has been replacing preferred stock in the capital structure, it has been not long-term but short-term (that is, nonsecurity issue) debt that has risen most sharply. The 30 percent debt-to-total-sources ratio in 1926 consisted of 7 percent preferred, 12 percent bonds, and 11 percent short-term debt; by the mid-1960s, however, the respective percentages were 1 percent, 14 percent, and 15 percent. Note, then, that the cost-induced shift from preferred stock to debt expanded short-term debt even more than it expanded long-term debt as a source of funds. Only with the financial crisis of 1974–1975 was the role of short-term debt reversed as business tried to "fund" this debt.

The substitution of bank and trade credit for open-market or bonded debt can be attributed to both monetary and real factors. Thus, there is some evidence that short-term rates have declined relative to long-term rates in the twentieth century, although this was not true during the financially disruptive mid-1970s. More important, however, is the fact that current assets, as a percentage of total business assets, have risen secularly as the regulated industries have declined in importance, while inventories and short-lived real assets (for example, equipment) have increased in importance. In the

**Table 12-9  All New Security Issues, by Type, for Selected Years (in billions of dollars)**

| Type of Security | 1920–1929 | 1950–1959 | 1960–1969 | 1970–1977 |
|---|---|---|---|---|
| Common stock | $ 8.6 | $ 16.3 | $ 20.0 | $ 58.0 |
| Preferred stock | 7.5 | 6.2 | 4.5 | 17.0 |
| Bonds | 23.8 | 75.0 | 115.5 | 229.7 |
|    Total security issues | $ 39.9 | $ 97.5 | $140.0 | $ 304.7 |
| Common stock / Total securities | 22% | 17% | 14% | 19% |
| Preferred stock / Total securities | 18% | 6% | 3% | 6% |
| Bonds / Total securities | 60% | 77% | 83% | 75% |
|    Total | 100% | 100% | 100% | 100% |
|    Total sources (internal and external) | $110 | $320 | $660 | $1,365.1 |

Sources: Lindsay and Sametz, *Financial Management*; Securities and Exchange Commission, Statistical Releases; "Trends in the Volume and Composition of Equity Finance"; *Statistical Abstract of the United States for 1978*.

latter connection, it should be recalled that a goodly portion of short-term assets is financed automatically by short-term liabilities.

## Questions

1. How is *investment* defined for purposes of the National Income Accounts? How would you alter this definition when considering the role of investment in: (a) economic growth; (b) business fluctuations; (c) social welfare?
2. Distinguish between real and financial investment demand for both the short run (one business cycle) and the long run (secular trends).
3. What is the marginal efficiency of capital? What factors determine the shape of the MEC schedule for the firm? For the economy?
4. Is it possible for firms to be operating in the elastic portion of their MEC schedules, yet have the aggregate schedule such that the economy as a whole is operating in the inelastic region of the aggregate MEC schedule?
5. What types of risks may affect the marginal cost of funds? Could the MCF curve ever be a declining schedule?
6. Contrast investment in an industry that has been dominated by "innovation" with investment in an industry that seems to fit the pattern for accelerator-model strategies.
7. Under what circumstances might a business consider an inventory decision to be a capital-budgeting decision rather than a working-capital decision? Would the use of a capital-budgeting analytical framework (say, internal rate of return or net present value) lead to different conclusions about inventory policy than the use of short-run inventory models?
8. "Real, rather than financial, factors dominate utility investment as contrasted with the situation in manufacturing investment." Discuss this statement. What are the implications for theories of investment demand? For the capital market? For governmental countercyclical policy?
9. Once uncertainty and business risk are introduced, the MCF may be a rising cost curve, and distinctions between the cost of equity and debt funds as well as distinctions between internal and external sources of funds become significant. Why?
10. All sources of corporate finance have both out-of-pocket and imputed costs. Explain in detail. Distinguish between the opportunity cost "marginal cost of capital" and "returns" demanded by the various types of suppliers of capital to the firm.
11. Can you find any relationship between "changes in business inventories" and "capital expenditures" in Table 12-3?
12. If 80 percent of gross national product were derived from service-sector industries in the year 2100, how would business investment change? Would the type of pressures put on the capital markets shift?
13. Contrast the capital structure of a bank with the capital structure of an oil company. Why do they differ? Would the average cost of capital for a bank necessarily be different from the average cost for an oil company?
14. "The relative role of capital markets in financing corporate investment requirements has declined secularly." What is the evidence for this assertion? What factors might reverse the relative decline in securities issuance? Why do capital markets remain of crucial importance to financial managers despite the long-run decline in the use of new securities to finance corporate investments?
15. Which of the considerations in business investment would also apply to public-sector (government) investment? MEC? MCF? Constrained financial structure?

## Selected Bibliography

Anderson, W. H. L. *Corporate Finance and Fixed Investment.* Harvard University Press, Cambridge, Mass., 1964.

Brittain, J. A. *Corporate Dividend Policy.* The Brookings Institution, Washington, D.C., 1966.

Donaldson, G. *Corporate Debt Capacity.* Harvard Business School, Boston, 1961.

Fama, E. F., and M. H. Miller. *The Theory of Finance.* Holt, Rinehart and Winston, New York, 1972.

Ferber, R., ed. *Determinants of Investment Behavior.* Columbia University Press, New York, 1967.

Goldsmith, R. W. *The Flow of Capital Funds in the Postwar Economy.* Columbia University Press, New York, 1965.

Hickman, B. G. *Investment Demand and U.S. Growth.* The Brookings Institution, Washington, D.C., 1965.

Kopcke, R. W. "The Behavior of Investment Spending During the Recession and Recovery, 1973–76." *New England Economic Review* (November 1977).

Kuh, E. *Capital Stock Growth.* North Holland Publishing Co., Amsterdam, 1963.

Kuznets, S. *Capital in the American Economy: Its Formation and Financing.* Princeton University Press, Princeton, N.J., 1961.

Lindsay, R., and A. W. Sametz. *Financial Management: An Analytical Approach,* rev. ed. Richard D. Irwin, Homewood, Ill., 1967.

Meyer, J. R., and R. R. Glauber. *Investment Decisions, Economic Forecasting and Public Policy,* Harvard University Press, Cambridge, Mass., 1964.

Miller, M. H., and F. Modigliani. "Some Estimates of the Cost of Capital to The Electric Utility Industry 1954–1957." *American Economic Review* (June 1966).

Myers, S. C. "Applications of Finance Theory to Public Utility Rate Cases." *Bell Journal* (Spring 1972).

"Prospects for the Credit Markets in 1980." Salomon Brothers, New York, 1980.

Sametz, A. W. "Trends in the Volume and Composition of Equity Finance." *Journal of Finance* (September 1964).

Sharpe, W. F. *Portfolio Theory and Capital Markets.* McGraw-Hill Book Company, New York, 1970.

Taggart, R. A., Jr. "A Model of Corporate Financing Decisions." *Journal of Finance* (December 1977).

Tobin, J., and W. Brainard. "Assets, Markets and the Cost of Capital." Cowles Discussion Paper 427 (March 1976).

# 13

## The Demand for Mortgage Credit

The mortgage market has absorbed more private savings in the last quarter century than the corporate, municipal, and U.S. government sectors of the securities markets combined. As shown in Table 13-1, the volume of mortgage funds raised in U.S. credit markets of the economy between 1951 and 1978 totaled over a trillion dollars.

In recent years the growth rates of other kinds of credit have also been large, but the mortgage market still remains the biggest single capital market in American finance. Despite this, the characteristics and operations of mortgage markets are probably less well known and understood by financially knowledgeable people than the more visible corporate and government capital markets. In large part, this is because there is much less trading in outstanding mortgages, when one compares them with other types of securities, and the market tends to be dominated by specialized, institutional lenders.

Technically, a mortgage is different from other financial instruments because of the nature of the asset that secures the loan. A mortgage loan is simply a debt secured by a lien on real property (such as land or buildings) rather than on personal property (automobiles, furniture, and the like) or the general credit of the borrower. Thus, the demand for mortgage loans is related to both the production of real property, such as new homes and business buildings, and the refinancing of existing real properties.

Unlike most other types of long-term debt, mortgages almost always call for repayment on a regular, periodic basis (amortization), usually in monthly instalments. These instalments include repayment of principal as well as interest charges. In contrast, corporate debt securities require payment of interest income periodically (usually every six months), but the principal need not be repaid until the maturity date of the security. Also, mortgage loans typically can be repaid in full at any time at the option of the borrower and, in fact, a significant number of loans are prepaid each year—due primarily to the sale of the mortgaged property. Under the usual terms of a corporate or government security, however, the borrower is generally not permitted to pay off investors and cancel the debt until the maturity date is reached. Since mortgage loans can be and are often prepaid, the net change in mortgage debt outstanding during any given year

**Table 13-1  Debt Funds Raised in U.S. Credit Markets by Private Domestic Nonfinancial Sectors, 1951–1978 (in billions of dollars)**

| Period | Mortgages | U.S. Government Securities | State & Local Obligations | Corporate Bonds |
|--------|-----------|---------------------------|---------------------------|-----------------|
| 1951–1955 | $ 56.5 | $ 13.1 | $ 21.6 | $ 17.5 |
| 1956–1960 | 75.4 | 6.3 | 24.9 | 24.7 |
| 1961–1965 | 116.3 | 23.3 | 29.5 | 25.9 |
| 1966–1970 | 136.6 | 38.4 | 44.0 | 69.6 |
| 1971–1975 | 325.3 | 145.5 | 77.5 | 87.0 |
| 1976–1978 | 364.2 | 179.5 | 67.7 | 63.9 |
| Total, 1951–1978 | $1,074.3 | $406.1 | $265.2 | $288.6 |

Source: Board of Governors of the Federal Reserve System, *Flow of Funds Accounts.*

is not an accurate measure of the total volume of mortgage lending activity taking place during the year. For this reason, it is important to look at more than the net increase in mortgage credit outstanding; the volume of new mortgage credit must be examined as well.

A wide variety of real properties are used to secure mortgage loans, and this gives rise to a wide variety of mortgage instruments. Mortgage loans may be classified according to whether they are secured by residential, nonresidential, or farm properties. Residential loans may be further classified as to whether the property is a single-family dwelling or a multifamily dwelling. Nonresidential properties financed by mortgages include office buildings, retail stores, churches, schools, hospitals, and industrial properties.

In addition, mortgage funds may be obtained from a wide variety of lenders, but not all lenders are active in the market for all types of loans. Lenders tend to specialize. For example, the majority of residential mortgage loans are made by the nation's thrift institutions, while commercial banks and life insurance companies are more heavily oriented toward nonresidential mortgage loans.

Prior to the mid-1960s, the mortgage market was for the most part private, in the sense that the government sector was largely inactive as a supplier of mortgage credit. After 1966, however, governmental involvement grew substantially. Federal credit agencies and federally sponsored mortgage pools became important conduits for channeling funds to mortgage credit.

In addition, an increasingly active secondary market for mortgage instruments has been developing in recent years. In the secondary market,

mortgage loans or securities backed by mortgages are transferred from one lender to another, either because one lender wants to reduce holdings of mortgage instruments or, as in the case of mortgage bankers and some other lenders, mortgage loans are originated with the expectation of eventual sale to another holder. Thus, the origination and servicing of mortgage loans for other investors has become an important activity for mortgage-market organizations.

## Residential and Nonresidential Mortgage Demand

We have seen that mortgage loans may be classified as to whether they are secured by residential, nonresidential, or farm properties. As shown in Table 13-2, between 1951 and 1978, residential mortgage flows exceeded $700 billion compared to commercial mortgage flows of about $200 billion and farm mortgage flows totaling $76 billion. Within the residential mortgage category, more than six times as much mortgage money was used to finance the purchase of one-to-four-family homes (including condominiums) as went to finance multifamily residential structures, such as apartments. Thus, the most important mortgage credit markets are closely related to the nation's housing markets, and it is to this area that we now direct our discussion.

### Housing and Mortgage Demand

The demand for mortgage credit is closely related to the demand for housing services and to the supply of housing. It is important, therefore, to un-

**Table 13-2  Mortgage Flows by Principal Type, 1951–1978 (in billions of dollars)**

| Period | 1–4 Family Home Mortgages | Multifamily Residential Mortgages | Commercial Mortgages | Farm Mortgages | Total Mortgages[a] |
|---|---|---|---|---|---|
| 1951–1955 | $ 43.1 | $ 4.2 | $ 6.9 | $ 3.0 | $ 57.2 |
| 1956–1960 | 53.7 | 7.3 | 14.1 | 3.8 | 78.9 |
| 1961–1965 | 78.5 | 17.4 | 22.1 | 8.4 | 126.4 |
| 1966–1970 | 77.1 | 21.9 | 30.1 | 8.6 | 137.7 |
| 1971–1975 | 193.1 | 40.5 | 73.8 | 21.1 | 328.5 |
| 1976–1978 | 270.2 | 19.3 | 55.3 | 25.1 | 370.0 |
| Total, 1951–1978 | $715.7 | $110.6 | $202.3 | $70.0 | $1,098.7 |

[a]Mortgage totals shown here are greater than those reported in Table 13-1 as a result of the inclusion of mortgage flows in the financial sector.

Source: Board of Governors of the Federal Reserve System, *Flow of Funds Accounts*.

derstand how the housing and mortgage markets interact.

Three types of participants in the housing and mortgage markets may be identified:[1] demanders of housing services and of funds with which to finance housing purchases; suppliers of new houses and of improvements to existing ones (builders and remodelers); and suppliers of funds for use in financing housing purchases. The collective behavior of these three groups determines the volume of housing construction and purchases and the amount of mortgage lending that takes place in the economy during any given period of time.

*Demand for Housing Services*  A variety of economic and demographic factors influences the demand for housing services. These factors include the price of housing services, the relative prices of other goods and services, the level and distribution of income and wealth among the population, and consumer tastes and preferences. Among the more important demographic factors are the size and age distribution of the population, the rate of household formations, and the rate of removals from the housing stock during some period.

The price of housing services reflects both land and construction costs as well as the costs of owning and operating the housing units. On average, construction costs of single-family units are substantially above those of apartment units, which makes total residential construction expenditures

[1]This is the approach taken by Ray C. Fair in describing housing and mortgage markets. See his article, "Disequilibrium in Housing Models," *Journal of Finance* (May 1972).

sensitive to the composition of housing starts. The average contract value (construction cost) for single-family units was $44,000 in 1977 compared with $26,260 for multifamily units. The principal factor accounting for this difference is average size per unit: single-family units averaged 1,720 square feet versus 938 square feet for multifamily units. It might be expected that land costs per unit would be higher for single-family than for apartment units since a single-family home has more square feet of land than the average apartment. However, many apartments are constructed in densely populated areas where land costs are high, while new single-family houses are typically built on the suburban fringe where land costs are relatively low. Firm figures are not available, but rough estimates suggest that land costs, on the average, are somewhat higher for single-family units. The price of housing services also reflects costs of maintaining and operating the housing unit. Thus, the demand for housing services will be affected by expenses for utilities, insurance, and real estate taxes as well as for maintenance and other expenses in general.

The demand for housing services, including the demand for purchased housing units, is influenced by the amount of wealth held and income earned by individuals, households, and businesses. Wealth is relatively more important with regard to the purchase as compared to the rental of housing units, since funds for making down payments (equity investment) are usually provided out of wealth holdings. Income serves as a budget constraint on housing expenditures. In 1960, according to a Department of Commerce survey of consumer expenditure patterns, about 36 percent of the typical household budget was devoted to housing expenses. In 1973, however, after improvements in the standard of living, changes in taxes and preferences, and movements in relative prices, it was found that households typically spend 41 percent of their incomes on housing.

One reason that households may be willing to spend a greater proportion of their incomes on housing services is that the attractiveness of owning a residence for investment purposes has increased in recent years as the price of many homes (both new and used) have been appreciating at rates that are some 2–3 percent greater than the rate of inflation. Thus, while homeowners derive utility from the housing services they consume each month, they also benefit from the real return on their investments.

Changes in the income and wealth distribution of the population will also produce changes in the demand for housing services. If wealth and income become more concentrated among a fewer number of households, presumably fewer housing units will be purchased, but these units will be higher in quality and price. If income and wealth become more uniformly distributed across households, relatively more households will be in a position to buy housing units, and more housing units will be purchased.

There has been concern recently over whether there is a widening "affordability gap"—whether fewer and fewer households are financially able to purchase housing. The evidence of the affordability gap is very sensitive to the data used in making comparisons over time and the time period chosen. For example, for the period 1965–1975, per capita disposable personal income rose some 108 percent while the median sales price of new homes rose 71 percent. However, the Department of Commerce's housing index, which takes into account financing costs, maintenance costs, and tax and insurance costs, as well as purchase costs, rose about 111 percent. If, however, one considers median family disposable personal income, rather than per capita disposable personal income, the increase between 1965 and 1975 was on the order of 81 percent. Thus, the question of whether housing is becoming more expensive relative to income growth depends on the category of income considered and on the dimension of home ownership cost considered. If households are willing to spend a greater proportion of their income on housing, as the previously cited Department of Commerce statistics suggest, the demand for home ownership can remain relatively strong despite rapid increases in home prices and home ownership costs.

A variety of demographic factors influence the volume and type of housing services demanded. For example, young families, old families, and poorer families are less likely to live in owner-occupied (largely single-family) dwellings. (See Tables 13-3 and 13-4.) Consequently, the demand for single-family housing will tend to grow relative to the demand for other types of housing as the proportion of households whose head is neither young nor old increases and as real incomes rise. For the United States, the number of families whose head is between 25 and 44, the prime home-buying ages, is expected to increase during the 1980s, as shown in Table 13-5. Thus, the demand for single-family housing is expected to increase strongly over the next fifteen years. The number of households consisting of people 65 years and older is also expected to rise, which indicates a strong demand for housing for the elderly.[2]

As mentioned previously, the demand for housing services is closely linked to the demand for funds with which to finance housing purchases. While the purchase of a housing unit may not require mortgage financing, in the vast majority of cases such financing is obtained. Thus, the demand for mortgage credit, and hence the demand for housing services, is influenced by the availability of mortgage money and the terms obtainable by the borrower. These terms include interest costs (contract rate plus fees or points charged), the loan-to-value ratio, and the length of the amortization period.

In theory, as the cost of mortgage credit rises, the demand should fall. An increase in the loan-to-value ratio (the ratio of the amount borrowed to purchase the housing unit to the purchase price of the unit) will lower the size of the down payment necessary to make the purchase, but monthly payments will be higher. To the extent that down payments are a constraint to buyers, an increase in the

[2]A more detailed treatment of the nation's future housing needs appears in the monograph, *The Nation's Housing: 1975–1985*, by B. J. Frieden and A. P. Solomon, published by the Joint Center for Urban Studies of the Massachusetts Institute of Technology and Harvard University, April 1977.

**Table 13-3  Percentage Distribution of Owner-Occupied vs. Renter-Occupied Housing Units by Household Income, 1970 and 1977**

| Income | 1970 | | 1977 | |
| --- | --- | --- | --- | --- |
| | Owner-Occupied | Renter-Occupied | Owner-Occupied | Renter-Occupied |
| Less than $3,999 | 49.9% | 50.1% | 43.2% | 56.8% |
| $4,000–$6,999 | 51.5 | 48.5 | 51.0 | 41.0 |
| $7,000–$9,999 | 61.3 | 38.7 | 53.1 | 46.9 |
| $10,000–$14,999 | 72.6 | 27.4 | 61.7 | 38.3 |
| $15,000–$24,999 | 80.5 | 19.5 | 75.8 | 24.2 |
| $25,000 or more | 84.5 | 15.5 | 87.7 | 12.3 |

Source: U.S. Department of Commerce, Bureau of the Census, *Annual Housing Survey: 1970 and 1977.*

**Table 13-4  Percentage Distribution of Owner-Occupied vs. Renter-Occupied Housing Units by Age of Head of Household, 1970 and 1977**

| Age of Head of Household[a] | 1970 | | 1977 | |
| --- | --- | --- | --- | --- |
| | Owner-Occupied | Renter-Occupied | Owner-Occupied | Renter-Occupied |
| Under 25 | 26.0% | 74.0% | 35.4% | 64.6% |
| 25–29 | 48.3 | 51.7 | 56.6 | 43.4 |
| 30–34 | 65.7 | 34.3 | 74.5 | 25.5 |
| 35–44 | 76.7 | 23.3 | 82.5 | 17.5 |
| 45–64 | 80.8 | 19.2 | 86.8 | 13.2 |
| 65 and over | 78.4 | 21.6 | 83.2 | 16.8 |
| All | 70.7 | 29.3 | 77.1 | 22.9 |

[a]Refers to 2-or-more-person households that have a male head, wife present, and no nonrelatives.

Source: U.S. Department of Commerce, Bureau of the Census, *Annual Housing Survey: 1970 and 1977.*

**Table 13-5  Projections of Change in Households by Age of Head, 1978–1995 (in thousands)**

| Age of Head | 1970–1978 | 1978–1985 | | 1985–1990 | | 1990–1995 | |
| --- | --- | --- | --- | --- | --- | --- | --- |
| | | High | Low | High | Low | High | Low |
| Under 25 | +233 | +125 | +25 | −5 | −122 | +97 | −44 |
| 25–34 | +642 | +641 | +472 | +439 | +181 | +14 | −243 |
| 35–44 | +145 | +621 | +552 | +703 | +584 | +561 | +409 |
| 45–54 | +48 | −4 | −48 | +388 | +319 | +737 | +623 |
| 55–64 | +170 | +87 | +77 | −102 | −109 | −17 | −22 |
| 65 and over | +341 | +394 | +335 | +427 | +347 | +324 | +234 |

Source: U.S. Bureau of the Census.

loan-to-value ratio should tend to increase the demand for mortgage funds, while a decrease in the ratio would have the opposite effect. Finally, as the length of the amortization period is increased, the amount of the required monthly payment declines for a mortgage with a given contract rate and of a given size. Thus, an increase in the length of the amortization period should have a positive impact on the demand for mortgage credit; a decrease should have the opposite effect.

An illustration of the terms of a mortgage and their impact on the size of the monthly payment required to amortize the mortgage is given in Table 13-6. When the loan-to-value ratio is increased from 50 percent (Case 1) to 80 percent (Case 2), the monthly payment required to purchase a $40,000

**Table 13-6    An Illustration of the Relationship Between Mortgage Terms and Required Monthly Payments**

|  | Case 1 | Case 2 | Case 3 | Case 4 |
|---|---|---|---|---|
| Purchase price | $40,000 | $40,000 | $40,000 | $40,000 |
| Amount borrowed | $20,000 | $32,000 | $20,000 | $20,000 |
| Down payment | $20,000 | $ 8,000 | $20,000 | $20,000 |
| Loan-to-value ratio | 50% | 80% | 50% | 50% |
| Contract interest rate | 9.0% | 9.0% | 9.0% | 9.25% |
| Term | 25 years | 25 years | 29 years | 25 years |
| Monthly payment | $167.84 | $268.54 | $162.03 | $171.28 |

Source: H. Robert Bartell, Jr., and H. Prescott Beighley.

house rises from $167.84 to $268.54. Similarly, if the loan-to-value ratio is unchanged at 50 percent and the length of the amortization period is increased from 25 years to 29 years, the size of the monthly payment declines from $167.84 (Case 1) to $162.03 (Case 3). And if the contract rate on a 25-year mortgage with a loan-to-value ratio of 50 percent is increased from 9.0 percent to 9.25 percent, the monthly payment increases from $167.84 (Case 1) to $171.28 (Case 4).

The typical loan-to-value ratio probably varies between new single-family homes and apartments, but it is difficult to determine which type of property is more liberally financed. Apartment units generally are built for investment purposes, and investors are inclined to minimize their equity in the property so as to maximize returns on investment and to minimize the size of potential capital losses. To the extent that lenders are optimistic concerning the future value of residential income properties, they will be generous in appraisals and

will lend the maximum percentage allowed. The principal mortgage lenders—savings and loan associations, commercial banks, savings banks, and life insurance companies—are regulated institutions, and one element of regulation is the maximum loan-to-value ratios permitted on mortgage loans. The maximum loan-to-value ratios of the major lending institutions on single-family dwellings are higher than those on apartments, as are the average ratios on actual loans made. However, it is sometimes asserted that lenders are more liberal in appraising multifamily properties. If this is so, the lower loan-to-value ratios reported on income properties may be misleading.

In any given year, a large proportion of real estate transactions involves the transfer of existing homes rather than the sale of new ones. As shown in Table 13-7, for one- to four-family homes financed with long-term mortgages between 1970 and 1977, 2½ existing homes were financed for every new home financed. The dollar volume of loans

**Table 13-7    Volume of 1–4 Family Homes Financed by Long-Term Mortgage Loans, 1970–1977**

| Year | Loans Closed (in billions of dollars) | | | Dwelling Units Financed[a] (in thousands of units) | | |
|---|---|---|---|---|---|---|
|  | New Homes | Existing Homes | Total Homes | New Homes | Existing Homes | Ratio |
| 1970 | $12.6 | $ 23.0 | $ 35.6 | 536.8 | 1250.4 | 2.33 |
| 1971 | 20.5 | 37.3 | 57.8 | 818.6 | 1815.2 | 2.22 |
| 1972 | 25.8 | 50.0 | 75.8 | 779.2 | 2272.2 | 2.92 |
| 1973 | 28.0 | 51.2 | 79.2 | 996.6 | 2233.3 | 2.24 |
| 1974 | 24.1 | 43.4 | 67.5 | 810.4 | 1771.0 | 2.19 |
| 1975 | 24.7 | 53.3 | 78.0 | 741.7 | 1945.3 | 2.62 |
| 1976 | 22.2 | 54.5 | 76.7 | 618.4 | 1828.9 | 2.96 |
| 1977 | 44.4 | 112.9 | 157.3 | 1096.3 | 3253.6 | 2.97 |

[a]Estimated by dividing dollar amount of loans closed by average loan amounts obtained from Federal Home Loan Bank Board.

Source: Department of Housing and Urban Development.

originated to finance existing homes was also greater than that to finance new homes in each of the seven years.

The transfer of existing properties typically gives rise to an increase in the demand for mortgage credit because the value of existing homes has tended to increase over time, the old loan has been reduced by amortization payments, and the old loan may have been made when permissible loan-to-value ratios were lower. The loan to the new buyer is, therefore, usually greater than the seller's outstanding mortgage balance. Suppose, for example, that someone purchased a home in 1973 for $35,000 with a 75 percent loan (75 percent loan-to-value ratio). They would have taken a $26,250 loan and made a $8,750 down payment. Assuming the loan had a 30-year maturity and carried an 8.25 percent interest rate, after six years the loan balance would have been paid down to $24,698. If the house was sold in 1980, seven years after the purchase, for $50,000 (a not unlikely possibility) and the new loan was for 80 percent of the selling price, or $40,000, there would be a net increase in mortgage demand of $15,302 ($40,000 − 24,698).

In this example, the increase in mortgage demand arose because of refinancing resulting from the resale. The turnover, or resale, of existing homes does not occur uniformly over time but is related to trends in population mobility, higher income levels that encourage homeowners to trade up to obtain more desirable accommodations (or, infrequently, to trade down), and the availability of credit. When mortage money is tight, the turnover of existing properties slows down; people interested in buying homes simply wait for the return of more favorable financing terms before completing their purchase.

Mortgage demand can also arise through refinancing even if no home transfer takes place. In recent years, many homeowners have taken advantage of rising equities (caused by higher home prices and past repayments) and more liberal loan-to-value ratios and have refinanced their homes using the proceeds for such non–real-estate expenditures as automobiles, vacation trips, college expenses, and the like. To some extent, this merely substitutes mortgage credit for other types of consumer credit. However, since mortgage rates are generally lower than consumer credit rates, and since the terms of repayment on mortgages are

more liberal, some people who might not otherwise borrow are encouraged to do so by the availability of refinancing mortgage loans.

Existing residential income properties, such as apartment buildings, are usually resold or refinanced for different reasons than owner-occupied dwellings. The primary motive for owning income properties is to produce a return on invested funds. As the owner's equity rises over time through regular loan repayments and increasing property values, that owner's financial leverage declines. By selling or refinancing the property, the owner can recapture a portion of that equity for reinvestment at a possibly higher return elsewhere. Also, since much residential income property is held by wealthy individuals who use the depreciation on the property as a deduction against ordinary income for tax purposes—and since resale may create a higher depreciable base and, therefore, greater tax deferral for a new owner than for the old one—turnover of existing properties is encouraged.

Repayments on existing loans provide a supply of funds that can be used to make additional mortgage loans. Amortization constitutes a relatively stable source of funds to mortgage lenders because amortization payments are contractual, and continued nonpayment is cause for foreclosure on the loan. Unless economic conditions deteriorate very badly and incomes drop severely, most homeowners can be expected to make their monthly mortgage payments on time. Some slowdown is noticeable when unemployment rises, however, and many lenders are willing to postpone payments under such extenuating circumstances.

Voluntary, unscheduled prepayments on loans tend to fluctuate more widely over the business cycle than do amortization payments. We have already noted that changes in the cost and availability of credit affect the level of activity in real estate markets. When housing sales slow down, so do prepayments.

Prepayments are sometimes made even when the mortgaged property is not sold. A homeowner may wish to prepay a portion of the loan from liquid savings in order to reduce interest costs. For example, if a homeowner has a savings account earning 5¼ percent and a mortgage loan costing 8¼ percent, that individual can, in effect, earn an additional 3 percent by using the savings account to reduce the mortgage loan. As might be expected, voluntary prepayments tend to rise during periods of low interest rates, when alternative uses of savings produce low returns relative to mortgage costs. Offsetting this, to some extent, is the fact that low interest rates generally coincide with higher rates of unemployment, and high unemployment can reduce the amounts available for voluntary prepayment. On balance, however, most mortgage lenders observe a slowdown of repayments in periods of high interest rates and a speedup as rates decline.[3]

*Supply of Housing Services*  The supply of housing services depends on the behavior of both the construction and financial sectors of the economy. With regard to the construction sector, the supply of housing services depends on homebuilders' expectations concerning the profitability of building and selling housing units. Builders must take into account construction costs, which include the costs of materials and labor as well as the cost of short-term credit needed to finance construction. In addition, builders must also consider the probability of selling the newly built housing unit at a profit within a relatively short period of time. Vacancy rates and the availability and cost of mortgage financing strongly influence builders' assessments of the likelihood of attaining a given level of sales. The difference between construction and financing costs and the price at which the finished product is expected to be sold determines the builder's expected profitability. The greater the expected profitability, the greater the supply of housing units per unit of time.

In addition to construction factors, homebuilders consider the availability of funds to finance newly produced housing units. Builders will hesitate to build new units if they think that prospective purchasers will find it difficult to obtain mortgage funds. Moreover, a builder's ability to obtain short-term financing for construction activities depends

on whether the builder can obtain commitments from lenders guaranteeing the availability of mortgage funds once construction is completed. During periods of tight money, such commitments are difficult to obtain and, consequently, the volume of construction declines, often quite sharply.

## Nonresidential Mortgage Demand

Mortgage loans on nonresidential and farm properties, while much smaller in the aggregate than home mortgage loans, are still an important component of mortgage lending. Such loans accounted for approximately one-quarter of all long-term mortgage loans originated between 1970 and 1977, as shown in Table 13-8.

Just as residential mortgage demand is largely determined by the demand for residential housing units, nonresidential mortgage demand is derived ultimately from the possible investment return from industrial and commercial properties. While detailed information about the composition of commercial and industrial properties financed by mortgage loans is not readily available, information is available on the value of new construction put in place in the United States annually. This gives some indication of the relative importance of various types of nonresidential construction activity. Private and public construction outlays for 1977 are summarized in Table 13-9.

Not all categories of the nonresidential construction expenditures shown in Table 13-9 give rise to mortgage demand (as is the usual case with private residential properties). For instance, public-sector construction generates no mortgage demand because government units do not ordinarily finance expenditures with mortgage credit. Likewise, if an electric utility builds an atomic power plant and finances the plant by selling $100 million of bonds secured by a mortgage on the plant, the $100 million does not constitute "mortgage debt" as one generally thinks of the term. Ordinarily, the $100 million would be classified as a business loan, not as mortgage credit, even though the loan is secured by a lien on real property. For this reason, the public utility sector is generally excluded when one considers the "mortgage market" and the "demand for mortgage credit." Life insurance companies and private pension funds, the largest holders of public utility securities, would consider the hypo-

---

[3]A recent study of mortgage prepayments to a sample of savings and loan associations found that the rate at which mortgages are prepaid is directly related to the number of housing starts and inversely related to the age of the mortgage, the difference between the current mortgage rate and the original contract rate, and total population. See Maurice E. Kinkade, "Mortgage Prepayments and Their Effects on S&Ls," *Federal Home Loan Bank Board Journal* (January 1976).

**Table 13-8 Originations of Long-Term Mortgage Loans by Type, 1970–1977 (in billions of dollars)**

| Year | 1–4 Family Homes | Multifamily Residential | Non-residential | Farm Properties | Total[a] |
|------|------------------|-------------------------|-----------------|-----------------|----------|
| 1970 | $ 35.6 | $ 8.8 | $12.5 | $ 3.0 | $ 59.9 |
| 1971 | 57.8 | 12.5 | 19.4 | 4.1 | 93.8 |
| 1972 | 75.9 | 15.4 | 24.5 | 5.8 | 121.6 |
| 1973 | 79.1 | 14.0 | 27.4 | 7.1 | 127.6 |
| 1974 | 67.5 | 12.3 | 24.0 | 7.7 | 111.5 |
| 1975 | 77.9 | 10.7 | 24.2 | 7.8 | 120.6 |
| 1976 | 76.7 | 8.4 | 17.3 | 7.5 | 109.9 |
| 1977 | 157.3 | 14.4 | 34.4 | 12.1 | 218.2 |

[a] Figures reported here are gross originations, whereas those reported in Tables 13-1 and 13-2 are net figures in which loan repayments have been netted out.

Source: Department of Housing and Urban Development, Office of Policy Development and Research.

**Table 13-9 Value of New Construction Put in Place in the United States in 1977 (in billions of dollars)**

| | | |
|---|---:|---:|
| Private Construction | | $134.8 |
| Residential buildings | $81.0 | |
| Nonresidential buildings | 28.7 | |
| Farm nonresidential | 2.7 | |
| Public utilities | 21.1 | |
| Other private | 1.3 | |
| Public construction | | 37.8 |
| Total construction | | $172.6 |

Source: U.S. Department of Commerce.

thetical $100 million issue to be a part of their bond portfolios, not their mortgage portfolios.

A similar situation arises with many, but not all, industrial properties. If the Ford Motor Company builds an assembly plant in Atlanta and finances the project with a bond issue secured by the facility, is this counted as mortgage debt? As in the utility case, the bonds, even though they are "mortgage bonds," would be classified as industrial bonds and included with business loans, not real estate loans. On the other hand, if a small manufacturing company is established in Atlanta and the firm finances its required real estate by a loan secured by the property, the loan would probably be classified as a mortgage loan. The primary difference between the two loans is that the loan to the Ford Motor Company is secured, in reality, more by the general credit strength of the corporation than by the physical property, whereas the loan to the small, new company is secured more by the property than by the creditworthiness of the firm as a whole. Industrial properties, then, are sometimes financed through securities backed principally by the general credit of the firm, and sometimes by mortgages in the traditional sense of the word.

Commercial properties—retail and service establishments and office buildings—are, like residential construction, usually financed with mortgage credit. Good statistics on the percentage of commercial development that is financed with mortgage debt are not available, but it is probable that mortgage funds are considerably more important for commercial than for industrial development. The owners of the commercial properties—investors who own shopping centers, retail stores, and office buildings, as well as retailers who own their premises—generally do not have the financial strength of manufacturing firms, which means that they must rely on mortgage credit to a greater extent. Further, commercial properties are typically not as specialized as industrial properties, making commercial properties easier to dispose of in the event of default and foreclosure on the loan. This fact makes it easier to separate the value of the real estate from the value of the enterprise as a whole, and this enhances the value of commercial property as loan collateral.

Farm properties, like commercial and residential properties, are generally financed with mortgage credit. Individual farmers do not have the financial strength of industrial firms, so they generally use secured credit. In addition, farm land and buildings are not specialized—in the sense that they can be used by more than one farmer—so these properties make relatively good collateral. The net result is that mortgage credit is used extensively in the agricultural sector.

Generalizations such as those made about public utilities and industrial, commercial, and farm properties are simply not possible for the other types of nonresidential properties. Churches, private schools, hospitals, and the like are financed sometimes with mortgage credit, sometimes by donations. When mortgage loans are used, in some cases the loan is made primarily on the strength of the real estate and, in other cases, it is made on the basis of guarantees either by a sponsoring agency, such as a national church organization, or by a group of wealthy individuals. The safest generalization one can make with regard to this type of property is that generalizations are unreliable.

An alternative to mortgage financing exists in the sale-and-leaseback arrangement. During the 1930s, Safeway Stores and several other retail chains pioneered this new method of financing real estate. Suppose a firm, such as Safeway, decides to construct a new building, then sell it to a financial institution and, simultaneously, lease it back under a long-term contract. Certain tax and other considerations might make such an arrangement more satisfactory than conventional mortgage loan financing both to Safeway and to the financial institution. As a consequence, sale-and-leasebacks have been gaining importance in recent years. This device is used frequently for industrial plants, department stores, office buildings, and shopping centers.

Technically, the volume of sale-and-leaseback financing is not included as mortgage debt. Rather than owning a promise-to-pay secured by a building, as in a mortgage loan, the financial institution owns the building outright. However, in either a sale-and-leaseback or a mortgage, the user of the building has a long-term contract giving him use of the building, and the lender has a long-term, noncancellable promise calling for a specified annual payment. A great deal of similarity exists between sale-and-leaseback arrangements and mortgage lending, and both must be recognized as important means of financing nonresidential real estate.

## Construction Cycles and the Supply of Mortgage Credit

Construction outlays exhibit a strong cyclical pattern. For residential construction this pattern, until very recently, has been countercyclical, rising during the latter stages of a general business contraction and the early part of the ensuing expansion, and then turning down well in advance of the business cycle peak. The consistency of this countercyclical pattern over a long period of time has led the National Bureau of Economic Research to classify housing starts as a leading indicator of business-cycle turning points.[4] Commercial and industrial construction moves in more general conformity to the business cycle. For both the residential and nonresidential construction sectors, however, the amplitude of fluctuations greatly exceeds that for economic activity as a whole, as is true for most forms of capital investment.

The difference in cyclical timing between residential and nonresidential construction derives from their relative sensitivity both to interest rates and to the availability of financing. Typically, as economic activity expands to the point where capacity is strained, the demand for long-term funds rises abruptly—a result of the well-known accelerator effect of rising consumption on investment. This results in shortages of funds and rising interest rates, a development that is frequently abetted by tighter monetary policy.

Corporations and other business-type borrowers are less sensitive to high interest rates in making construction plans and may have better access to sources of funds than do homebuyers and homebuilders. Commercial and industrial enterprises predicate construction programs on long-run profit potential and are, therefore, less likely to cut back on these programs when demand for output is strong. For homebuyers, on the other hand, current interest costs are very important, and the purchase of a new home is highly postponable in the short run. Thus, housing sales react more sharply to changes in interest rates and in credit availability.

## Mortgage Credit and Housing Cycles

If we consider only the housing market, forgetting temporarily the financial sector, we can say that equilibrium is reached when the price and quantity of housing units are such that a positive number of

---

[4]An exception to this may turn out to be the recovery from the 1974–1975 recession, when the upturn in housing construction did not precede the upturn in the overall economy, but was coincidental to the moderate growth experienced by the economy during 1975 and 1976.

vacancies exist (that being the amount needed to meet the normal requirements of market turnover) and such that there is at that price an equality between quantity demanded and quantity supplied. As in any typical economic market, disequilibrium can occur; nonetheless, if price and quantity are free to adjust, equilibrium will be restored. Thus, as this adjustment process takes place, housing production will speed up and slow down and, perhaps, too many new units will be produced in a given time interval with the result that they are sold at a loss.

So far, we have seen that the financial sector influences housing production through the cost of mortgage credit and the cost of short-term funds. There is, however, another important link between the mortgage and housing markets that we must also consider. During periods of tight money, when savings flows to lending institutions are adversely affected, mortgage credit may be rationed. This means that mortgage rates do not rise sufficiently to clear the mortgage market, with the result that the mortgage market enters a state of disequilibrium. This process of rationing affects both the demand for credit, as lenders require large down payments or shorter amortization periods or both, and the supply of new housing units as builders are unable to secure commitments for final mortgages in order to qualify for short-term financing. Consequently, both construction activity and mortgage lending decline in volume. Although recent changes in financial regulations, including scheduled phase-out of interest rate ceilings on deposits at savings and loan associations, commercial banks, and mutual savings banks, are intended to mitigate this problem, it seems unlikely that cyclicality in mortgage markets will be eliminated entirely.

Credit rationing may be viewed as a decrease in the supply of mortgage credit. In Figure 13-1 the volume of mortgage credit per period is related to the mortgage interest rate through a demand schedule $D_m$ and a supply schedule $S_m$. During periods of tight money, lenders may, for example, lower the maximum acceptable loan-to-value ratio, causing the supply schedule to shift to $S'_m$. If the mortgage interest rate were allowed to rise to its market-clearing level, $i'$, the volume of mortgage lending would drop by $v - v'$. If, however, the mortgage rate is maintained at $i$, the volume of mortgage lending will drop by a larger amount, $v - v''$. The gap $v - v''$ represents the excess demand for mort-

**Figure 13-1  Demand and Supply of Mortgage Credit**

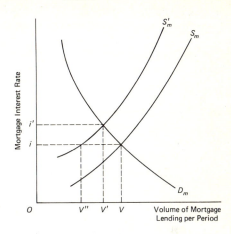

gage funds associated with interest rate $i$ occurring as a result of the rationing of mortgage credit.

A sharp reduction in the availability of mortgage credit will mean that lenders will not grant builders as many mortgage commitments as they would like, and so builders will not be able to obtain as much short-term construction financing as they would like. Generally, builders are not as concerned with the cost of credit as they are with its availability. To builders, short-term credit costs are costs they may be able to pass on to the buyer. The cost of long-term mortgage credit will, however, affect builders insofar as they may be unable to sell their newly built homes to buyers at their desired prices.

### Empirical Research on Mortgage Credit and Housing Cycles

Up to now the discussion of mortgage credit and housing activity has been largely theoretical. However, in order to determine the relative importance and significance of those factors that influence either the demand for mortgage credit or housing construction, we must look to the results of empirical tests.

A number of researchers have investigated the relationship between residential mortgage credit demand and selected economic and demographic factors. For the most part, the flow of mortgages is used as the dependent variable. Studies vary, however, according to whether they use gross or net mortgage flows and according to the type of property financed by the mortgage (for example, single- versus multifamily) and the type of mortgage instrument (for example, FHA, VA, or conventional). A vast majority of the studies have used the mortgage interest rate as the price variable in the demand for mortgages schedule.[5] And, for most studies, the mortgage rate is the only element of the mortgage instrument that is considered. Several researchers have experimented with other mortgage variables—such as the loan-to-price ratio and the length of the amortization period—but they have not been able to produce results that conform to theory and to accepted statistical procedures. One would, for theoretical reasons, expect other mortgage factors besides the interest rate to influence the demand for residential mortgages. The fact that researchers have failed to confirm empirically the existence of such a strong relationship probably does not mean that one does not exist, but that problems of model specification and measurement of variables have not been adequately resolved. Once this is done, however, researchers are likely to find empirical confirmation that the loan-to-value ratio and the amortization period do, in fact, influence the demand for mortgage credit.

One reason for the lack of strong, consistent empirical results in studies of the demand for mortgage credit may well be problems associated with the length of the period during which adjustment is presumed to occur. For example, factors that affect the demand for mortgage credit in the short run might well be absent, or behave very differently, in the long run. Suppose, for example, an increase in the loan-to-value ratio is observed. This change will likely increase the demand for mortgage credit in the short run, but how long will this effect last? Furthermore, how is this increase in the demand for mortgage credit related to the demand for new housing units? Will equilibrium occur at a new (higher) stock of housing units and outstanding mortgage debt or will equilibrium be attained at the present level of the housing stock, but with the

adjustment process occurring at a faster rate? In any event, it is important to consider carefully both the long-run and the short-run implications of empirical models of the demand for mortgage credit. And it is equally important to avoid drawing long-run conclusions from models having a short-run focus.

While some studies have focused on the demand for mortgage credit, others have sought to measure the impact of key explanatory variables, such as price and availability of credit, on the volume of housing starts. A variety of measures of credit availability, including the loan-to-value ratio, the length of the amortization period, savings flows to financial institutions, and measures of mortgage acquisitions and commitments, have been used in attempts to explain housing starts. And most of these studies conclude that both cost and the availability of credit are important determinants of *short-run* fluctuations in housing activity.[6] In contrast, one recent study concludes that there is no empirical basis for the view that availability matters.[7] However, a number of researchers have criticized this study, arguing that the authors did not appropriately distinguish between the long and short run.[8] In the short run, credit rationing and credit availability appear to cause cyclical fluctuations in housing activity. This does not, however, rule out the possibility that over longer periods of time the availability of mortgage credit has little influence on the equilibrium size of the housing stock.

One would expect that the prevailing mortgage rate and the number of housing starts to be in-

---

[5] For a recent review and summary of relevant empirical works, see James Kearl, Kenneth Rosen, and Craig Swan, "Relationships Between the Mortgage Instruments, the Demand for Housing and Mortgage Credit: A Review of Empirical Studies," in *New Mortgage Designs for Stable Housing in an Inflationary Environment,* eds. F. Modigliani and D. Lessard, Federal Reserve Bank of Boston Conference Series No. 14, Boston, January 1975.

[6] See Kearl, Rosen and Swan, "Relationships Between the Mortgage Instruments, the Demand for Housing and Mortgage Credit," for a review of recent empirical research on the factors that influence housing activity and the demand for mortgage credit.

[7] See F. Arcelus and A. H. Meltzer, "The Markets for Housing and Housing Services," *Journal of Money, Credit, and Banking* (February 1973), 78–89.

[8] See, for example, Craig Swan, "The Markets for Housing and Housing Services: A Comment," *Journal of Money, Credit, and Banking* (November 1973) and the reply to Swan's comment by Arcelus and Meltzer. Swan's debate with Arcelus and Meltzer is also discussed by Robert H. Edelstein and Irwin Friend, "The Allocative Efficiency of the Private Housing Finance Sector," *Resources for Housing,* Proceedings of the First Annual Conference, Federal Home Loan Bank of San Francisco, December 9–10, 1975.

versely related since, other things being equal, monthly payments will be higher at higher mortgage rates. Moreover, individuals are likely to postpone the purchase of a house and builders are less likely to start new construction if rates are expected to fall in the future. Observed interest rate elasticities of housing starts have been found to be between −0.3 and −2.78, with most estimates falling between −1 and −2.[9] An elasticity factor of −1 should mean that a 1 percent rise in the mortgage rate (from, say, 8 percent to 8.08 percent) would cause housing starts to fall by 1 percent.

Housing starts appear to move in the same direction as loan-to-value ratios; reported elasticity estimates range from +1.18 to +5.61.[10] In view of the relative high elasticity estimates, it appears that if the loan-to-value ratio is decreased as a means of rationing credit, housing starts will decline substantially. It should be noted that a higher loan-to-value ratio implies lower down payments but higher monthly payments. Thus, there is a "down-payment effect" as well as a "monthly payment effect" when the loan-to-value ratio is changed. These two effects work in opposite directions. The empirical finding of a positive relationship between housing starts and the loan-to-value ratio suggests that the down-payment effect dominates the monthly payments effect.

## Sources of Mortgage Credit

Since the availability of credit is such an important determinant of construction and real estate activity, it is necessary to include a section on the supply of mortgage credit in a well-rounded discussion of the demand for mortgage funds. Our treatment is brief, however, since the supply of mortgage credit from various financial intermediaries is discussed more fully in Part II of the text.

### The Relative Importance of Different Mortgage Lenders

A breakdown of the relative importance of various lenders in the residential and nonresidential mort-

gage markets appears in Table 13-10. Savings institutions are clearly dominant in the residential mortgage market, accounting for over one-half of the total increase in outstanding mortgages from 1951 to 1978. There is no similar dominance in the nonresidential markets, but savings institutions and life insurance companies are the most important lenders.

Another dimension of the supply of mortgage funds should also be considered. The ultimate source of much of residential mortgage credit is personal savings. If personal savings is low, then the supply of residential mortgage credit will ordinarily be low. A high level of personal savings does not, however, necessarily mean that a large supply of funds will be available for residential mortgage lending. If, for example, most personal savings is channeled into the equities market, this does very little for the mortgage market. Even if a large share of savings is placed in financial intermediaries, it is very important to the residential mortgage market whether the funds go primarily to commercial banks and life insurance companies or to savings and loan associations and mutual savings banks. If the bulk of the savings is channeled to the former institutions, the residential mortgage market does not fare all that well. This last point is illustrated in Table 13-11. During the period 1966–1978, life insurance companies, commercial banks, and mutual savings banks made smaller percentages of their increases in funds available to the housing market than did savings and loan associations, which directed virtually all of their net flows into this market. Clearly, it makes a great deal of difference to the residential mortgage market where personal savings flow.

### Characteristic Lending Practices of Intermediaries

It is also useful to consider the lending practices of the primary intermediaries—savings and loan associations, life insurance companies, mutual savings banks, and commercial banks. The first point to be noted is the difference among the lenders with regard to their use of government-guaranteed or insured-lending programs (FHA-VA) versus conventional mortgage loans (those not supported by government). Frequently, lenders prefer to use conventional financing on loans secured by prop-

---

[9]See Kearl, Rosen, and Swan, "Relationships Between the Mortgage Instruments, the Demand for Housing and Mortgage Credit" for a review of interest rate elasticities obtained from recent empirical studies.

[10]*Ibid.*

Table 13-10 Annual Residential (R) and Nonresidential (NR) Mortgage Flows by Principal Type of Lender, 1951–1978 (in billions of dollars)

| Period | Savings Institutions[a] | | Commercial Banks | | Life Insurance Companies | | Finance Companies | | REITs | | Households | | Government[b] | | Other[c] | |
|---|---|---|---|---|---|---|---|---|---|---|---|---|---|---|---|---|
| | R | NR | R | NR | R | NR | R | NR | R | NR | R | NR | R | NR | R | NR |
| 1951–1955 | $ 23.8 | $ 3.3 | $ 5.6 | $ 1.7 | $9.2 | $ 4.0 | $ .92 | $ (.09) | — | — | $ 1.4 | $ 3.6 | $ 2.0 | $ .8 | $ .2 | $ .3 |
| 1956–1960 | 37.0 | 1.4 | 4.1 | 3.5 | 7.2 | 5.0 | .24 | .03 | — | — | 2.8 | 6.7 | 4.7 | 2.0 | 1.0 | 1.2 |
| 1961–1965 | 59.7 | 17.5 | 11.2 | 9.4 | 4.7 | 13.5 | 2.8 | (.1) | -.1 | — | .1 | 2.3 | .1 | 1.8 | 2.0 | 2.4 |
| 1966–1970 | 38.4 | 14.2 | 12.2 | 11.1 | (2.9) | 17.3 | 1.9 | 1.0 | .6 | 3.3 | 7.0 | 3.7 | 18.3 | 8.5 | 1.3 | 1.7 |
| 1971–1975 | 126.8 | 23.2 | 36.9 | 26.1 | (5.5) | 20.3 | .4 | 1.5 | 3.6 | 3.9 | 12.3 | 6.8 | 60.9 | 10.8 | (1.4) | 1.2 |
| 1976–1978 | 159.3 | 14.5 | 52.2 | 24.5 | (3.8) | 20.5 | 1.2 | (.2) | (3.4) | (3.8) | 21.1 | 13.3 | 70.6 | 10.3 | 0.8 | 1.6 |

[a]Includes savings and loan associations, mutual savings banks, and credit unions.
[b]Includes general funds of state and local governments, U.S. government, government-sponsored credit agencies, and federally sponsored mortgage pools.
[c]Includes private pension funds, state and local government retirement funds, and other insurance companies.

Source: Board of Governors of the Federal Reserve System, *Flow of Funds Accounts.*

**Table 13-11   Percentage of Net Inflows of Funds Invested in Residential Mortgages, 1966–1978**

| | Savings & Loan Associations | Mutual Savings Banks | Commercial Banks | Life Insurance Companies |
|---|---|---|---|---|
| 1966 | 92.5% | 103.9% | 8.0% | 57.5% |
| 1967 | 78.5 | 61.5 | 12.9 | 34.1 |
| 1968 | 100.0 | 65.1 | 9.6 | 27.2 |
| 1969 | 131.1 | 96.4 | 6.2 | 22.6 |
| 1970 | 73.7 | 40.0 | 2.7 | 22.6 |
| 1971 | 81.4 | 39.8 | 17.5 | 8.7 |
| 1972 | 89.6 | 52.9 | 22.3 | 11.0 |
| 1973 | 98.5 | 107.6 | 22.9 | 28.6 |
| 1974 | 79.3 | 64.7 | 17.8 | 31.8 |
| 1975 | 71.6 | 20.7 | 12.4 | 14.8 |
| 1976 | 87.0 | 31.2 | 22.1 | 8.7 |
| 1977 | 90.6 | 58.0 | 27.9 | 17.2 |
| 1978 | 85.4 | 81.9 | 24.7 | 25.3 |

Source: Board of Governors of the Federal Reserve System, *Flow of Funds Accounts.*

erties located in the lenders' immediate operating area but use FHA-VA loans on properties located at a distance from the lenders' home offices. Savings and loan associations, with their strong local orientation, operate mainly with conventional loans. Life insurance companies, since they generally operate nationally out of a single home office, use government-supported loans to a greater extent. Mutual savings banks typically use conventional financing for loans made in their immediate operating areas but use government-supported mortgages for loans made at greater distances. Commercial bank practices are similar to those of mutual savings banks although they purchase loans from outside their local areas less frequently than do mutual savings banks.

Savings and loan associations operate primarily in the residential, rather than the nonresidential, market. S&Ls were created to supply funds for the construction and purchase of homes—with the idea of improving the nation's housing stock. As a consequence, legal restrictions have been placed on their nonresidential mortgage-lending activities although these restrictions have been reduced somewhat by federal law in 1980 to enable S&Ls to withstand better cyclical pressures felt in mortgage markets. Mutual savings banks likewise are relatively active in the residential mortgage market. However, while S&Ls tend to concentrate on single-family home loans, mutual savings banks are more active in lending on multifamily units. Again, this reflects different regulations and also the fact

that mutual savings banks are concentrated in the metropolitan areas of the Northeast where apartments are relatively more important. Both life insurance companies and commercial banks are more active in nonresidential than residential mortgage lending. This reflects the fact that banks and insurance companies serve both households and businesses, whereas S&Ls and mutual savings banks are much more oriented toward household financing.

Differences among lenders also exist with regard to the terms on the loans that they make. Selected characteristics of conventional mortgage loans made during 1977 by four major types of lenders are shown in Table 13-12.

The terms on mortgage loans made by mortgage companies (often referred to as mortgage bankers) stand out compared to those made by other types of lenders largely because these loans are intended to be sold to final investors at some later point in time. Accordingly, they are more likely to be originated in areas of the country that are relatively short of capital. As Table 13-12 shows, loans originated by mortgage companies tend to have the highest contract rates and initial fees and charges, the longest term-to-maturity, and the highest loan-to-price ratio. On the other hand, commercial banks tend to have the lowest loan-to-price ratios on originated mortgages and also the shortest term-to-maturity. Thus, borrowers who obtain mortgage financing from commercial banks generally have to make larger down payments and agree to pay off

**Table 13-12  Average U.S. Interest Rates and Other Characteristics of Conventional First Mortgage Loans Originated on Existing Single-Family Homes, by Major Types of Lender, 1977**

| Lender | Contract Interest Rate (percentages) | Initial Fees and Charges (percentages) | Term to Maturity (in years) | Loan-to-Price Ratio (percentages) | Purchase Price (in thousands of dollars) |
|---|---|---|---|---|---|
| Savings and loan associations | 8.86% | 1.32% | 26.6 | 76.8% | $46.9 |
| Mortgage companies | 8.89 | 1.44 | 29.6 | 86.3 | 45.6 |
| Commercial banks | 8.77 | 0.81 | 21.9 | 67.5 | 50.2 |
| Mutual savings banks | 8.57 | 0.46 | 25.4 | 80.0 | 51.6 |

Source: Federal Home Loan Bank Board.

the loan faster than if they obtain financing from some other type of lender.

Savings institutions tend to fall in between commercial banks and mortgage companies with respect to term-to-maturity and loan-to-price ratio. Mutual savings banks appear to have lower initial fees and charges than other lenders and also lower contract rates. Differences in lending rates and fees are probably due more to geographical factors than to institutional differences. Most mutual savings banks are located in the northeastern states where mortgage rates for all lenders tend to be below the national averages.

## Credit Terms on Nonresidential Loans

Unlike the residential sector of the mortgage market, good statistics on the credit terms—interest rate, loan-to-value ratio, life of loan, and loan fee—are unavailable for nonresidential mortgages. However, statements in the literature, confirmed by an informal survey conducted by the authors, suggest that terms in the nonresidential sector are generally (1) more diverse—there is less concentration of terms because the properties and the borrowers are more diversified—and (2) less liberal—maturities tend to be shorter, loan-to-value ratios lower, and loan fees and interest rates somewhat higher, except when the borrower is a very strong company. Another difference is that, while virtually all residential loans are fully amortized, a substantial proportion of commercial and industrial loans are either not amortized or not fully amortized.

Experience has shown nonresidential mortgage loans to be somewhat riskier, on average, than residential loans. Nonresidential loans have experienced higher foreclosure rates in the past, and losses on foreclosed properties have been higher

on nonresidential than on residential properties. The primary reason for this difference is that commercial and industrial properties tend to be much more highly specialized than residential properties in the sense that these buildings are suitable to only a few types of business occupants. Thus, if these businesses experience financial difficulty, the value of the securing property may decline below the original cost. Further, business properties frequently become obsolete more rapidly than do well-constructed residential properties. These factors lead to the conclusion that nonresidential mortgages are generally somewhat riskier than residential loans and this, in turn, leads to the differential terms on the two types of loans.

## Mortgage Markets

It is important for analytical purposes to distinguish between primary and secondary markets for mortgages. So far the discussion has been chiefly concerned with primary mortgage markets, those markets in which long-term mortgage loans are originated. When a borrower, such as a home buyer or investor, acquires a mortgage to finance the purchase of real property, the borrower and the lender act together to create the mortgage. To the lender it is an asset; to the borrower a liability. Once the mortgage has been created, it may be bought and sold in the marketplace just as other financial assets are bought and sold. Lenders may buy and sell mortgage assets for a variety of reasons, some of which we will now discuss in detail. In our discussion, the term *secondary market for mortgages* includes all transfers of mortgages from one lender to another.

The dollar volume of secondary market purchases by all types of lenders between 1970 and

**Table 13-13   Annual Secondary Market Purchases of Mortgage Loans, 1970–1977 (in millions of dollars)**

| Year | 1–4 Family Homes | Multifamily Residential | Nonresidential | Farm Properties | Total Properties |
|------|------------------|-------------------------|----------------|-----------------|------------------|
| 1970 | $13,406 | $1,027 | $ 776 | $1,199 | $16,408 |
| 1971 | 18,293 | 1,274 | 1,154 | 952 | 21,673 |
| 1972 | 25,075 | 1,821 | 1,418 | 991 | 29,305 |
| 1973 | 22,573 | 2,144 | 1,960 | 892 | 27,569 |
| 1974 | 23,046 | 2,388 | 2,245 | 1,270 | 28,949 |
| 1975 | 31,931 | 3,150 | 2,109 | 1,464 | 38,654 |
| 1976 | 31,070 | 1,866 | 1,453 | 910 | 35,299 |
| 1977 | 54,839 | 4,195 | 2,250 | 1,809 | 63,093 |

Source: Department of Housing and Urban Development.

1977 is given in Table 13-13. As one can readily see, the majority of these purchases involved mortgages on one-to four-family homes.

Secondary markets play a very useful role in the economy by facilitating the flow of capital from sectors and areas that have capital surpluses to those that have capital deficits. For example, homebuilding and the demand for mortgage funds are presently stronger in the western and southern regions of the country than in other parts of the nation. In order to meet the needs of local borrowers, lenders in western states may sell some of their mortgage loans from their loan portfolios to buyers in other areas of the country. This will, in effect, enable these lenders to make additional local mortgage loans, thereby satisfying to a greater extent the capital needs of their region. Funds to purchase these mortgages presumably come from areas that would not be able to employ the capital at a rate of return equal to the rate available outside those areas. One should note, however, that any barriers that affect free capital flows hinder the operation of secondary mortgage markets. In the past, for example, the existence of usury ceilings, which placed upper limits on mortgage interest rates, tended to impede the smooth interregional flow of mortgage funds. As market rates rose above the usury ceiling rates, regional disparities occurred among mortgage rates.[11] To eliminate the kinds of problems that developed in some states, including capital outflows, Congress in 1979 and 1980 passed acts overturning all interest rate ceilings on residential mortgage loans unless re-enacted by the states before April 1, 1983.

In addition to facilitating the flow of mortgage capital, secondary markets also serve to increase the liquidity and marketability of mortgage loans, thereby making them relatively more attractive to lenders. Both originators and holders of mortgage assets will be more willing to enter the market if there is sufficient breadth and depth to enable exchange to occur without significant loss in value to the seller. In other words, highly liquid secondary markets are desirable in the sense that sellers who seek liquidity can sell mortgages quickly and easily without incurring capital losses. Greater liquidity increases the relative attractiveness of mortgage lending and may increase total availability of mortgage funds.

In recent years, a number of private and public institutions and agencies have sought to make mortgage instruments more attractive to broad classes of investors. In addition to developing a wider range of alternative instruments for mortgage investors, there have been attempts to make mortgage instruments more uniform. This is desirable since product uniformity is an important element in any successful secondary market.

While it is difficult to measure precisely the extent to which development of a stronger, more active secondary market for mortgages has contributed to the overall economic efficiency of the nation's housing finance system, it is possible to obtain some insight into the matter by comparing market yields on mortgage loans with yields on

[11]The impact of usury ceilings is discussed in P. K. Robins, "The Effects of State Usury Ceilings on Single Family Homebuilding," *Journal of Finance* (March 1974); and J. R. Ostas, "Effects of Usury Ceilings in the Mortgage Market," *Journal of Finance* (June 1976). Empirical evidence on the adverse effects of usury ceilings is presented in both studies.

other capital market securities. Since the risk of default on most loans sold in the secondary market is virtually nil, owing to the existence of public insurance programs (FHA and VA) and to private insurers, a mortgage holder faces essentially two nondefault types of risks: marketability risk and liquidity risk. As the secondary markets become more highly developed, mortgage holders become increasingly certain of being able to convert mortgages quickly and easily into cash, without loss of capital. Consequently, the rate of return they require to hold mortgages will decline relative to the return on alternate capital market instruments for which highly developed secondary markets already exist.

### Private-Sector Secondary Market Participants

Private-sector purchasers of home mortgages in the secondary market include commercial banks, mutual savings banks, savings and loan associations, mortgage companies, and other lenders, including insurance companies. With the exception of mortgage companies, these financial institutions ordinarily use funds acquired as savings to purchase mortgages for investment (income-earning) purposes.

Mortgage bankers typically play a different role. They often originate mortgages for the purpose of holding them only until a suitable investor is found. In a sense, these mortgage companies "warehouse" mortgages that have been originated recently; they then sell from this inventory at a later time. One might question whether such transactions are really secondary market transactions

since they involve the origination of mortgages. In a sense, the importance of these mortgage companies is understated in Table 13-14 since purchases of mortgages by mortgage companies are only a small part of their overall operation.

Of all the private-sector home mortgage purchasers, savings and loan associations were the largest buyers between 1970 and 1977, as shown in Table 13-14. The other types of purchasers varied from year to year in terms of relative importance.

In the earlier stages of development, private secondary markets brought buyers and sellers of mortgages together on an informal basis. Personal contacts were very important. More recently, private mortgage insurance companies have sought to bring interested parties together, largely as a means of attracting customers to purchase insurance. These private insurers also serve to facilitate the flow of relevant market information among interested parties and to support educational programs designed to better equip market participants.

The Automated Mortgage Market Information Network (AMINET) was established in recent years to provide a means of communicating relevant secondary market information electronically to interested parties. This system, sponsored by a number of private trade associations along with several government agencies, should enhance the performance of the secondary markets.

### Public-Sector Secondary Market Participants

While involvement of the public sector in secondary mortgage markets has been comparatively recent, the impact has been substantial. As shown in

**Table 13-14   Percentage Distribution of Secondary Market Purchases of Home Mortgage Loans by Lender Group, 1970–1977**

| Year | Commercial Banks | Mutual Savings Banks | Savings & Loan Assns. | Mortgage Companies | Federal Credit Agencies | Federally Supported Pools | Other Lender Groups |
|---|---|---|---|---|---|---|---|
| 1970 | 3.85% | 10.51% | 25.36% | .33% | 40.11% | 13.67% | 6.08% |
| 1971 | 6.18 | 10.27 | 36.26 | 2.21 | 20.38 | 21.57 | 3.13 |
| 1972 | 4.14 | 10.80 | 37.87 | 5.69 | 19.91 | 18.97 | 2.62 |
| 1973 | 4.21 | 8.88 | 23.97 | 6.30 | 33.67 | 19.02 | 3.95 |
| 1974 | 1.60 | 4.50 | 20.90 | 4.0 | 38.10 | 27.33 | 3.46 |
| 1975 | .74 | 3.54 | 22.44 | 2.46 | 33.64 | 34.94 | 2.24 |
| 1976 | 2.54 | 4.88 | 26.47 | 4.67 | 23.65 | 36.47 | 1.32 |
| 1977 | 3.12 | 5.54 | 23.59 | 5.63 | 42.11 | 42.11 | 1.98 |

Source: Department of Housing and Urban Development.

Table 13-14, with the exception of 1971 and 1972, federal agencies and mortgage pools have accounted for more than half of all secondary market purchases of home mortgages. Three federal agencies are dominant in secondary market activities: the Federal National Mortgage Association (FNMA, or Fannie Mae), the Government National Mortgage Association (GNMA, or Ginnie Mae), and the Federal Home Loan Mortgage Corporation (FHLMC, or Freddie Mac). These agencies have contributed greatly to the overall development of secondary mortgage markets, both by innovation with regard to financial instruments and mechanisms and by efforts to standardize the mortgage instrument.

The Federal National Mortgage Association was established in 1968 as a government-sponsored, stockholder-owned organization and was given the responsibility of maintaining a secondary market for government-insured (FHA and VA) mortgages.[12] In 1970, FNMA was given the power to make a secondary market in conventional mortgage loans.

The Government National Mortgage Association differs from FNMA in that it is a wholly owned corporation of the U.S. government, functioning as part of the Department of Housing and Urban Development. GNMA is involved in a variety of housing finance programs, which are largely directed to low and moderate-income families. For example, under the recent Tandem Plan, GNMA may act with FNMA and FHLMC to make mortgage loans at below-market interest rates available to qualified borrowers. FNMA and FHLMC agree to buy these mortgages at below-market rates from the lending institution if that institution agrees to charge a below-market rate to the borrower. FNMA or FHLMC is the final holder of the mortgage, and the discount (difference between the current market rate and the below-market rate) is absorbed by GNMA.

GNMA also guarantees securities that are backed by government-insured or guaranteed mortgages.[13] The mortgages are pooled, and a security

is issued against them. Repayments on loans in the pool are used to pay off the security. Under a pass-through arrangement, the investor receives monthly payments of principal and interest obtained from mortgages in the pool. As shown in Table 13-14, these federally sponsored pools have become increasingly important over the past several years.

The Federal Home Loan Mortgage Corporation, created in 1970, purchases mortgages from savings and loan associations, commercial banks, mutual savings banks and, more recently, mortgage bankers. FHLMC purchases whole mortgage loans as well as loan participations. The purchase of residential mortgages from originating lenders is financed by issuing mortgage-backed securities, private debt placements, and participations issued against large pools of mortgages.

The stated purpose of the public sector's involvement in mortgage markets is to promote national housing goals by directing financial capital into the housing finance system. While federal programs have no doubt accomplished this over the past seven or so years, it can be argued that their intervention has not been without cost to society.[14] One line of reasoning maintains that the contribution of these agencies is vastly overstated since the capital they have required from the private sector to finance mortgage purchases might well have gone into mortgages through private institutions anyway, thereby reducing the need for government intervention.

In view of the instability in present-day financial markets, some involvement at the federal level in the nation's housing finance system is probably warranted. But federal programs should be flexible and sensitive to the financial functioning of the economy so that their initial positive impact is not subsequently outweighed by negative factors.

## Inflation, Housing, and Mortgage Credit

It was pointed out above that demographic factors play an important role in the long-run demand for residential housing. As shown in Table 13-5, the number of households whose head is between 25

---

[12]The FNMA was originally chartered in 1938 as a corporation of the federal government. In 1954, it became a federal agency and, as a result of the Housing Act of 1968, it was established as a quasi-public corporation (see Chapter 11).

[13]The FHLMC and the Farmers Home Administration also guarantee mortgage pools.

[14]See, for example, Kenneth J. Thygerson, *The Effect of Government Housing and Mortgage Credit Programs on Savings and Loan Associations,* United States Savings and Loan League, Occasional Paper Number 6, 1973.

and 44 years old is expected to increase substantially over the next decade, and if these households behave in the future as they have in the past, there should be a corresponding growth in the demand for owner-occupied (largely single-family) dwellings. In the short run, however, the cost and availability of mortgage credit, together with other costs of home ownership, combine to influence strongly the demand for housing. The extent to which potential demand is realized depends on the extent to which would-be purchasers are able to meet downpayment requirements and to secure mortgage financing terms that meet their income characteristics and satisfy their spending preferences.

During the 1970s, a number of factors made it more difficult for households to purchase housing. One of the most important factors was the rise in the cost of mortgage financing. Between 1965 and 1979 the average annual mortgage contract rate rose from 5.74 percent to more than 10 percent. During the same period, the median price of a newly built home also grew sharply. Taken together, these increases in median purchase price and mortgage contract rate meant that the required monthly mortgage payment associated with owning the median-price home rose at a rate substantially higher than the consumer price index during these years.

## Mortgage Rates During Periods of Instability and Disintermediation

The increase in mortgage rates can be traced to two factors: lenders require extra compensation for anticipated higher rates of inflation over the life of the mortgage as well as for taking risks associated with operating in a financial environment that has experienced relatively great amounts of instability in recent years. With regard to the latter point, there have been several periods of tight money and high interest rates during the past decade. These "credit crunches" have caused savings outflow, or disintermediation, problems for financial institutions, especially those that specialize in mortgage lending.

Thrift institutions rely primarily on savings deposits as a source of funds with which to make mortgage loans but, in the past, the maximum rates that institutions could pay on these deposits were determined by federal regulatory authorities. When general market rates on competing instruments, such as Treasury bills and commercial paper, exceeded these deposit rate ceilings, depositors tended to withdraw or add less to their savings balances and to increase their purchases of higher-yield securities. This process, referred to as disintermediation, reduced the availability of mortgage funds, driving mortgage rates upward. Both the reduced availability of funds plus the higher borrowing costs served to curtail realized housing demand. The instability problem was especially severe in thrift institutions because they typically lent funds for long periods of time at fixed interest rates, but borrowed them for shorter periods at rates that changed more frequently. This mismatch in the maturity structure of assets and liabilities accentuated problems of instability in these institutions and also produced greater variation in the flow of funds to mortgage credit.

In response to problems of this kind in mortgage markets, Congress and the regulatory authorities instituted a number of changes beginning in 1978. In 1978 somewhat greater flexibility in deposit rates was granted to depository intermediaries, when money market certificates of deposit, with rates fluctuating with Treasury bill rates, were permitted beginning June 1. Further flexibility was permitted in 1979 and Congress decided in 1980 to eliminate all ceilings by 1986. Because fluctuating deposit rates could cause difficulties for institutions with inflexible asset structures, however, Congress and the regulators also took some actions on the asset side.[15] Beginning in 1980, federally insured savings and loans are allowed to hold up to 20 percent of assets in consumer loans and corporate debt securities. The ability to acquire assets with maturities shorter than those of mortgages and liabilities with longer maturities should serve to reduce swings in the supply of mortgage funds. This should, in turn, help to diminish fluctuations in construction activity and housing markets. Furthermore, lenders were permitted to make greater use of mortgages in which the interest rate can be adjusted up and down in relation to market rates of interest, the so-called variable-rate mortgage.

---

[15]Most of these changes affecting both assets and liabilities of S&Ls are contained in the various titles of the Depository Institutions Deregulation and Monetary Control Act of 1980, Public Law 96-221.

## Inflation and the Cost of Home Ownership

We have seen that inflation has an unfavorable impact on the demand for housing financed through mortgage credit since current inflation, as well as the anticipation of continued inflation, results in higher borrowing costs for home buyers. Moreover, fluctuations in the rate of inflation tend to contribute to fluctuations in construction activity.

As the anticipated rate of inflation increases, the mortgage interest rate rises and annual (and monthly) payments increase. This is because the interest rate has two components: a pure rent on the use of money required by lenders to put their funds into mortgage loan assets rather than into some other instrument, and an inflation premium required by lenders to protect them against anticipated erosion in purchasing power. If, for example, the current real rate of interest is 3 percent and prices are expected to rise by 5 percent annually, the nominal interest rate would probably be around 8 percent.

Under conditions of inflation, the stream of mortgage payments on a traditional, fully amortized, level-payment mortgage declines in real value over the life of the mortgage. This is because payments are made in dollars that are worth less and less in real terms. For illustrative purposes, consider a 25-year, $30,000 traditional mortgage. Assume the contract interest rate of 8 percent is based on a real rate of 3 percent and anticipated inflation of 5 percent. As shown in Table 13-15, the real value of the mortgage payment in terms of purchasing power will decline from $220.51 at the end of the first year to $68.30 at the end of 25 years if the inflation rate is 5 percent. The relationship between the real value of the monthly mortgage payments over time is shown graphically in Figure 13-2. If there is no inflation, the real value of the periodic payments would be $126.48, as shown by the horizontal line on the graph.

Now suppose a higher rate of inflation is anticipated, say 7 percent. The contract rate rises to 10 percent and nominal monthly payments rise to $272.61. In this case, real payments are initially higher than they were at the 5 percent inflation rate, but they decline more sharply over time as the effects of a greater rate of inflation become dominant. As shown in Figure 13-2, the effect of

**Figure 13-2  The Impact of Inflation on the Stream of Real Mortgage Payments**

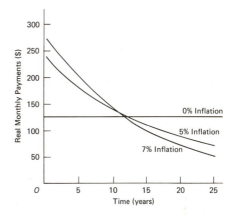

an increase in the inflation rate serves to tilt the real payments stream more sharply.[16]

It should be noted that if the value of the mortgaged asset (house) increases over the life of the mortgage at a rate corresponding to the rate of inflation, the *real* costs to the borrower are the same for both of these payment streams. They are also the same as the real costs that would exist under conditions of no inflation. The reason that real costs are equal for different inflation rates is that the inflation premium, which finances the purchase of the asset, will be recovered through the eventual gain in value of the asset. In fact, it might be argued that inflation may even lower the real cost of home ownership since interest expenses are fully deductible for income tax purposes whereas capital gains on residences are taxed at a capital gains tax rate.[17]

Inflation does, however, increase the nominal costs of home ownership even if the real costs are unaffected. Typically, home buyers must meet mortgage payments out of current income and lend-

[16]This tilt effect is discussed in greater detail in Donald Lessard and Franco Modigliani, "Inflation and the Housing Market: Problems and Potential Solutions," in *New Mortgage Designs for Stable Housing in an Inflationary Environment,* eds. Modigliani and Lessard.

[17]Under present law, capital gains taxes due on the sale of a residence are deferred if the proceeds of the sale are reinvested in another residence of the same or greater value within one year of the sale. Additional time is given if the new residence is to be constructed.

**Table 13-15  The Impact of Inflation on the Stream of Real Mortgage Payments**

| Year | Nominal Monthly Payment When Inflation Is: | | Index When Inflation Is: | | Real Monthly Payment When Inflation Is: | |
|---|---|---|---|---|---|---|
| | 5% | 7% | 5% | 7% | 5% | 7% |
| 1 | $231.54 | $272.61 | $1.05 | $1.07 | $220.51 | $254.78 |
| 5 | 231.54 | 272.61 | 1.28 | 1.40 | 180.89 | 194.72 |
| 10 | 231.54 | 272.61 | 1.63 | 1.97 | 142.05 | 138.38 |
| 15 | 231.54 | 272.61 | 2.08 | 2.76 | 111.32 | 98.77 |
| 20 | 231.54 | 272.61 | 2.65 | 3.87 | 87.37 | 70.44 |
| 25 | 231.54 | 272.61 | 3.39 | 5.43 | 68.30 | 50.20 |

Source: H. Robert Bartell, Jr., and H. Prescott Beighley.

ers typically place upper limits on the proportion of current income that may go for mortgage expenses. Thus, as mortgage rates rise in anticipation of higher inflation rates, the amount of housing households can afford will decrease, given that spending for housing is limited by the level of current income and the proportion of current income that may be channeled to housing.

### Inflation, Instability, and the Mortgage Instrument

An argument may be advanced along the lines that the traditional, fully amortized, level-payment, fixed-rate mortgage is not well suited to the problems of instability and inflation. While lenders have traditionally relied on this type of mortgage instrument, there is at present a move toward the use of alternative mortgage instruments. A wide variety of alternative instruments have been proposed, and a smaller number are already available to borrowers in various parts of the country. Thus, some comments about the usefulness of various types of mortgage instruments in dealing with problems of instability and inflation are in order.[18]

The variable-rate mortgage (VRM) has been proposed as an alternative mortgage instrument. The adoption of VRMs could substantially alleviate, if not eliminate, problems associated with maturity mismatches in assets and liabilities. The main feature of this mortgage instrument is that the interest rate applied to the borrower's outstanding balance is not fixed over the life of the loan but may move up or down depending on the changes that occur in a designated reference rate. If the reference rate is tied to an instrument whose maturity is comparable to that of the mortgage, the spread between the cost of new funds and the return on mortgage assets would remain largely unchanged over the interest rate cycle. This would mitigate swings in the volume of loanable mortgage funds. In the absence of ceilings on deposit rates, lenders could raise both the rate paid on borrowed funds (deposits) and the rate earned on mortgage assets, thereby assuring a more stable flow of funds during tight money periods.

Under the traditional mortgage, the burden of interest rates is essentially borne by new borrowers. At today's higher interest rates, new borrowers are in a sense subsidizing previous borrowers who originated their mortgage loans when interest rates were lower. This subsidization of below-market interest rate borrowers would be eliminated if the current market interest rate were applicable to all loans in the portfolio.

In effect, the VRM transfers some of the risk in lending for long periods of time from the lender to the borrower. The justification for such a transfer of risk lies in the fact that lenders have experienced greater degrees of instability in interest rates and in saving flows during the past decade. If they are to provide a steady stream of funds for financing housing in the future, especially after elimination of deposit rate ceilings, some of this risk must be eliminated or transferred to others.

In order to implement the VRM, the reference rate must be specified. Numerous possibilities exist

---

[18]See, for example, Richard A. Cohn and Stanley Fischer, "Alternative Mortgage Designs," in *New Mortgage Designs for Stable Housing in an Inflationary Environment,* eds. Modigliani and Lessard. See also David L. Smith, "Reforming the Mortgage Instrument," *Federal Home Loan Bank Board Journal* (May 1976).

with regard to term-to-maturity and type of the reference instrument. Statutory limitations may be imposed limiting the frequency with which rate changes may occur and the magnitude of each change may be constrained, as may the total permissible change during the life of the mortgage. For example, in California lenders must lower loan rates when the reference rate falls; they may raise rates when it rises. But rate increases cannot be made more frequently than every six months and no increase can be greater than ¼ percent. The adjusted mortgage rate cannot exceed the original rate by more than 2½ percent.[19]

In practice, changes in the interest rate on a mortgage may be made by changing the amount of the periodic payment, the term-to-maturity, or both. For example, a lender could raise a borrower's mortgage rate by extending the terms of the mortgage, leaving the amount of the monthly payment unchanged. Alternatively, the lender could leave the term-to-maturity unchanged and increase the size of the monthly payment. Finally, the lender could do both—increase the monthly payment and lengthen the term.

One shortcoming of the VRM is that the borrower cannot count on a stable payments-to-income ratio. It is possible, however, to modify the standard VRM to permit a stable payments-to-income ratio. Such an instrument is, by necessity, more complex in design.

While the variable-rate mortgage alleviates lenders' problems with mismatched asset and liability maturities, it does not eliminate the unfavorable effects of inflation on the time path of real mortgage payments. One type of mortgage instrument that appears to take into account anticipated inflation is the graduated-payment mortgage (GPM). Under this type of mortgage instrument, monthly payments increase in size, presumably as the income of the borrower increases over time. If payments increase over time at a rate equal to the inflation rate, the tilt effect in the stream of real mortgage payments is eliminated. Monthly payments are all equal to one another in terms of real purchasing power, although different in nominal terms. Moreover, as long as income grows at the same rate as inflation and as the monthly mortgage payments, a stable payments-to-income ratio exists for the borrower.

The main feature of this instrument is that families whose income is expected to grow can afford to purchase more housing today out of a given current income than they could with a traditional fixed-payment mortgage. This is an important consideration in a housing market where prices and home ownership costs are rising rapidly. Also, for buyers who are unable to make a sufficiently large down payment to obtain a traditional mortgage with affordable monthly payments, the GPM is an attractive option. A home of a given value may be financed with a smaller down payment and a larger mortgage if the borrower is able to meet increased monthly payments out of increased income.

An important point here is that the GPM involves negative amortization in the early years of the loan. If, for example, the borrower's income does not keep up with the rising monthly payments and that individual is forced to sell his home, the borrower may be required to repay the lender an amount greater than the original amount of the loan. A problem could arise if the market value of the home does not rise as fast as the outstanding balance of the loan.

One alternative mortgage instrument, which is very different in concept from the other instruments, warrants discussion. This is the reverse annuity mortgage. Under a reverse annuity mortgage, the borrower is paid a fixed annuity (fixed monthly payment) based on the borrower's equity in the mortgaged property. Such an arrangement would be attractive to retired homeowners who have built substantial equity interests in their homes and who desire additional funds to supplement retirement income. The borrower would not be required to repay the loan; after the borrower's death, his estate would repay the loan.

## Discrimination and Redlining

In underwriting a mortgage loan, that is, making credit judgments and setting terms, lenders consider a wide range of information about the borrower and the property that will secure the loan. This information is usually contained in an application, credit reports on the potential borrower,

[19]In 1979 the Federal Home Loan Bank Board authorized federally chartered S&Ls nationwide to offer mortgages on which rates will vary with the cost of money. For a discussion of the use of VRMs in California, see Mark J. Reidy, "VRMs in California: The Early Experience," *Federal Home Loan Bank Board Journal* (March 1976).

verification of employment and income, and an appraisal report on the property. In assessing this information, loan underwriters have had a tendency to use rules of thumb and stereotypes as a means of compressing all the various information items into a decision as to whether to make the loan and on what terms. Examples of such rules of thumb and stereotypes include the following: monthly loan payments, including principal, interest, real estate taxes, and insurance, should not exceed 25 percent of the borrower's monthly income; a working wife's income is less stable than her husband's; people with a history of frequent job changes are bigger risks than those employed for a long time with the same employer; real estate values are lower in neighborhoods subject to racial or ethnic change; houses in older neighborhoods are worth less than comparable houses in newly developed areas.

In recent years, lenders have been challenged and, in some cases, required to reexamine these rules of thumb and stereotypes to show that their underwriting decisions truly reflect the risk elements in a loan. The major impetus for this reexamination has been a shift in emphasis in civil rights activities from equal opportunity in education and employment to equal opportunity in access to housing and credit. Lenders are now being asked to disclose where and to whom they are making loans so that it is possible to determine whether they are discriminating in their lending decisions against certain legally protected groups, such as women and minority persons, and against areas where such persons might live. Discrimination against areas is often called "*redlining*," a term derived from the alleged practice by lenders of drawing a red line around an area on a map and refusing to make loans in that area or making loans on less favorable terms than in non-redlined areas.

Review of the data provided by lenders under the federal Home Mortgage Disclosure Act and similar state and local statutes indicates that few, if any, areas are entirely devoid of lending activity, but some areas appear to obtain less than their "fair share" of loans. Lenders have asserted that the low levels of lending in some areas reflect a lack of demand for loans in these areas rather than discriminatory lending policies. Antiredlining activists charge that the lack of demand is attributable to lenders discouraging applicants and to the perception by potential applicants that lenders will not make loans in certain areas. With the passage in 1977 of the Community Reinvestment Act, Congress has placed an affirmative responsibility on lenders to meet the reasonable credit needs of the communities they serve or, in other words, to stimulate demand rather than to respond passively to requests for credit.

It is unlikely that any increase in demand for mortgage credit due to lenders' efforts under the Community Reinvestment Act will have a major impact on aggregate mortgage demand. The impact is likely to be a shift of some demand from new housing in the suburbs to older housing in more central urban areas and a shift from investors who own rental housing to homeowners.

### Mortgage Credit and Public Policy

The goal of providing suitable housing for broad segments of the population has received considerable attention in the past decade. Public-sector intervention in the market for financing residential housing has taken a variety of forms. Subsidies have been granted for the construction of low-income housing. Special tax treatment has been given to the purchasers of newly built homes. Special legislative and regulatory consideration has been given to the nation's thrift institutions as the major suppliers of funds for residential mortgages. Federal mortgage loan-insurance programs (FHA and VA) have operated for many years to encourage lenders to make mortgage loans. Federal agencies have played a growing role both in providing funds for mortgage lending and in facilitating the exchange of mortgage assets in secondary markets.

One important issue is the question of the extent to which the nation's financial system—its institutions, markets, and instruments—should bear the burden of promoting society's housing goals. Some argue that regulation should not force the financial system to promote the nation's housing goals. These observers prefer direct subsidies or tax credits to regulation since they are less inflationary, do not warp financial institutions, and bring market forces into play in pursuing the nation's goals. Some people argue that direct subsidies are more easily identified and, thus, their value in supporting housing goals is more readily determined.

In the past, the government has provided tax and other incentives to encourage the growth of specialized savings intermediaries as a means of channeling funds into housing markets. While these institutions have doubtless contributed to the growth of the housing industry, their uniqueness and the fact that monetary policy has been used to contain inflation (with the result that wide swings in interest rates and saving flows have occurred) have certainly lessened any favorable impact of these specialized institutions. The real question is whether we are better off continuing to promote specialized institutions or whether it would be better to promote housing policies through some other, more direct, means. There is probably more agreement for lessening the emphasis on specialized thrift and home financing institutions than there is on how fast the change should come about. Thrift institutions and their supporters in the housing industry foresee a long period of adjustment to new powers and responsibilities if the home finance business is to be spared severe dislocations. Others argue that the nation's financial markets have substantial flexibility and could absorb any disruptions quickly. Congress compromised somewhat on this issue when it allowed a six-year phaseout of interest rate ceilings on deposits.

In any event, the performance of the nation's housing and mortgage markets will be strongly influenced in the years ahead by government policies, both direct policies aimed at specific housing goals and indirect policies that are an integral part of the package of broad economic policies implemented by the federal government. It is hoped that these policies will foster an equitable distribution of the nation's housing resources and mortgage capital.

## Conclusion

Mortgage loans are unlike most other types of long-term debt in that they are secured by a lien on real property and call for repayment of both principal and interest on a regular, periodic basis. Between 1961 and 1978, mortgage credit accounted for 53 percent of all debt funds raised in U.S. credit markets by the economy's private domestic nonfinancial sectors.

The bulk of mortgage lending involves financing the purchase of single-family and multifamily residences. The demand for residential mortgage credit depends on the demand for housing services, which, in turn, depends on a variety of economic and demographic factors, including the following: the price of housing services, the relative prices of other goods and services, the level and distribution of income and wealth among the population, consumer tastes and preferences, the size and age distribution of the population, the rate of household formation, and the rate of removals from the housing stock.

The supply of housing services depends on the behavior of both the construction and financial sectors of the economy. The rate of construction activity depends on homebuilders' expectations as to the profitability of building and selling housing units as well as on the anticipated availability of funds to finance construction and purchase of the units. During periods of tight money, when financing is difficult to obtain, the volume of construction declines—often sharply.

Mortgage loans on nonresidential and farm properties accounted for approximately one-quarter of all mortgage loans originated between 1970 and 1978. Real estate owned by large industrial and commercial enterprises is usually financed by non-mortgage types of debt, such as capital notes and debentures, whereas real estate owned by smaller firms is often financed by mortgage loans.

On the basis of recent empirical studies, the demand for mortgage credit appears to be inversely related to the mortgage interest rate and seemingly unrelated to the length of the amortization period and the loan-to-value ratio. Fluctuations in housing activity, measured in terms of the volume of housing starts, appear to be strongly influenced by the cost and the availability of credit, more so in the short run than in the long run.

Secondary markets in mortgage instruments have become increasingly important in recent years. These markets play a very useful role in facilitating the flow of housing capital from areas that have capital surpluses to those that have capital shortages.

High inflation rates have affected the costs of home ownership in recent years and have led to the development of alternatives to the standard, fixed-rate, level-payment mortgage. Variable-rate mortgages and graduated-payment mortgages are two such instruments that serve to enhance the flow of funds to housing at times when there is considerable instability in the economy's financial markets.

The government sector has become increasingly involved in the nation's housing and mortgage markets in recent years. Additional funds have been channeled into housing through the operation of agency mortgage pools, and legislation has been enacted to deal with discrimination in lending practices.

## Questions

1. Residential construction activity appears to be more sensitive than corporate activity to fluctuations in the cost and availability of credit. Why do you suppose this is true? In your answer, distinguish between business demand for (1) working-capital loans, and (2) loans for fixed-asset financing.
2. Which would you expect to be more sensitive to variations in credit terms: apartment or single-family-home construction? Explain.
3. Both loan amortization payments and prepayments constitute sources of funds for relending in the mortgage market. Amortization payments are quite stable, but prepayments are highly volatile. Why do you suppose this instability in the prepayment component exists? When would you expect prepayments to be high? To be low?
4. What is meant by a mortgage loan "commitment"? How would expectations about future levels of savings flows and interest rates affect the level of new commitments?
5. Differentiate between consumption and investment with regard to housing purchases.
6. How do high rates of inflation influence the following:
   a. the demand for residential mortgage loans
   b. the demand for nonresidential mortgage loans
   c. the supply of residential housing
   d. the type of mortgage instrument sought by borrowers
7. Explain how each of the following factors influences mortgage lending practices of savings and loan associations, banks, and life insurance companies:
   a. geographic location of lender
   b. legal restrictions
   c. cost of origination
   d. sources of funds for lending
8. Would you expect to find a stronger tendency toward uniformity of terms in a sample of residential or nonresidential mortgage loans? Why?
9. Discuss the relationship between the demand for residential mortgage credit and
   a. a tendency toward larger, higher quality homes;
   b. a shift in the ratio of apartment starts to single-family housing starts;
   c. an increase in the construction cost index;
   d. an increase in the value of raw land.
10. Discuss how the Federal Home Loan Bank System influences the housing and mortgage markets.
11. Compare the secondary mortgage market to the market in outstanding issues of common stock and U.S. Treasury securities.
12. Compare the process of originating mortgages with the new issues market for corporate and municipal bonds.

## Selected Bibliography

Arcelus, Francisco, and Allan H. Meltzer. "The Markets for Housing and Housing Services." *Journal of Money, Credit, and Banking* (February 1973).

——."A Reply to Craig Swan." *Journal of Money, Credit, and Banking* (November 1973).

Carliner, Geoffrey. "Income Elasticity of Housing Demand." *Review of Economics and Statistics* (November 1973).

Cohn, Richard A., and Stanley Fischer. "Alternative Mortgage Designs." *New Mortgage Designs for Stable Housing in an Inflationary Environment*, eds. F. Modigliani and D. Lessard. Federal Reserve Bank of Boston Conference Series No. 14, January 1975.

De Leeuw, Frank. "The Demand for Housing: A Review of Cross-Section Evidence." *Review of Economics and Statistics* (February 1971).

Edelstein, Robert H., and Irwin Friend. "The Allocative Efficiency of the Private Housing Finance Sector." *Resources for Housing,* Proceedings of the First Annual Conference, Federal Home Loan Bank of San Francisco, December 9–10, 1975.

Fair, Ray C. "Disequilibrium in Housing Models." *Journal of Finance* (June 1972).

Friend, I., ed. *Study of the Savings and Loan Industry.* Federal Home Loan Bank Board, Washington, D.C., July 1969.

Kearl, James, Kenneth Rosen, and Craig Swan. "Relationships Between the Mortgage Instruments, The Demand for Housing and Mortgage Credit: A Review of Empirical Studies." *New Mortgage Designs for Stable Housing in an Inflationary Environment*, eds. F. Modigliani and D. Lessard. Federal Reserve Bank of Boston Conference Series No. 14, January 1975.

Kinkade, Maurice E. "Mortgage Prepayments and Their Effects on S&Ls." *Federal Home Loan Bank Board Journal* (January 1976).

Lessard, Donald, and Franco Modigliani. "Inflation and the Housing Market: Problems and Potential Solutions." *New Mortgage Designs for Stable Housing in an Inflationary Environment*, eds. F. Modigliani and D. Lessard. Federal Reserve Bank of Boston Conference Series No. 14, January 1975.

Meltzer, A. H. "Credit Availability and Economic Decisions: Some Evidence from the Mortgage and Housing Markets." *Journal of Finance* (June 1974).

Ostas, James R. "Effects of Usury Ceilings in the Mortgage Market." *Journal of Finance* (June 1976).

Stansell, Stanley R., and James A. Millar. "An Empirical Study of Mortgage Payment to Income Ratios in a Variable Rate Mortgage Program." *Journal of Finance* (May 1976).

Swan, Craig. "The Markets for Housing and Housing Services: A Comment." *Journal of Money, Credit, and Banking* (November 1973).

Tucker, Donald P. "Financial Innovation and the Mortgage Market: The Possibilities for Liability Management by Thrifts." *Journal of Finance* (May 1976).

# 14

# Consumer Credit Demand

Although the Flow of Funds Accounts clearly show the household sector to be a net lender in financial markets (usually through financial intermediaries), households still borrow substantial volumes of funds both for housing (mortgage credit) and for other purposes (consumer credit). Both forms of household credit have shown extraordinary growth in the twentieth century; consumer credit alone rose from about $0.5 billion outstanding at the turn of the century to more than $340 billion outstanding in early 1979. While consumer credit is extended in a variety of forms, most of it is instalment credit repayable in two or more payments. At the end of 1978 more than 80 percent of consumer credit outstanding was classified as instalment credit.

Most observers agree that consumer credit provides two important economic benefits. First, it makes the purchase of large durable goods easier for many families by enabling them to change the time pattern of saving and expenditures. Rather than postponing the purchase of durable goods, like automobiles, until they can accumulate sufficient liquid assets (a difficult task for some families), consumers can use credit to purchase the durables first, saving for them afterward by making instalment payments while using the goods. Second, there is little doubt that development of consumer credit markets has contributed to the growth of major durable goods industries. Without consumer credit it seems unlikely that the automobile and appliance industries today would occupy the same relative positions among American businesses. Nevertheless, despite the apparent importance of consumer credit for both consumers and for the growth of important industries, rapid increases in consumer indebtedness concern both economists and policymakers. This concern has tended to center around two major issues, which may be described, in general terms, as the cyclical issue and the consumer-protection issue.

Essentially, the cyclical issue concerns the possibility that availability of consumer credit may initiate or accentuate cyclical tendencies in the macroeconomy. According to one theory, sometimes referred to as the *burden theory*, early in a cyclical upswing optimistic consumers are able to borrow freely and buy consumer goods ahead of saving, thereby propelling the economy upward on the strength of additional consumption demand. However, according to this hypothesis, after some years of such spending, the accumulated "burden" of consumer debt causes consumers to slow their spending as both their optimism and their ability to make more instalment payments wane. Thus, in this view, the consumers' debt burden intensifies the cyclical downturn and calls into question the overall usefulness of consumer credit to the macroeconomy.[1]

In contrast to the burden theory is the idea that, while consumer credit does have an effect on business cycles, its impact is actually countercyclical. According to this hypothesis, when lenders and sellers are willing to extend favorable credit terms during a recession, consumers can increase major purchases. As a consequence, the consumer sector is then in a position to lead the economy out of the recession. Then, after some years of expansion, consumers' "prudence" prevents most of them from becoming overextended or unduly "burdened." This prudence limits excessive spending that might result in the onset of recession. In this view, consumer credit does not play a major part in causing a recession, but rather it smooths the tendencies toward cyclicality that are produced elsewhere in the economy. Whatever the correct view or combination of views, however, it seems reasonable to conclude that consumer credit provokes some cyclical responses, if only because the consumer sector is so large.

The second issue, the consumer-protection issue, involves the actual conditions and practices that prevail in markets where credit is extended to consumers. According to some observers, the inherent imbalance in market power and understanding between lenders and borrowers in consumer credit markets means that the government must play a role in helping consumers protect their own interests. Extreme adherents to this position argue that virtually every aspect of consumer credit markets should be carefully regulated by governmental officials, including even, on occasion, a consumer's right to borrow at all. Those who take the opposite view argue that competition in the marketplace protects consumers most efficiently and, because consumer credit markets are quite competitive, there is little need for government intervention. Obviously, the strength of either of these views hinges to a large extent on the degree of market competitiveness, which is not an easy question to analyze. Because most observers believe that consumer credit markets are neither perfectly competitive nor perfectly monopolistic, they tend to recommend roles for both competition and government. The result appears in recent years to be a simultaneous increase in both competition and regulation. Competition seems increasingly to be forcing financial institutions to attract new customers by making their products more attractive, while government protection is expanding as well.

This chapter examines the factors influencing consumers' demand for nonmortgage credit. Following this discussion, it will be possible to examine further both the cyclical issue and the consumer-protection issue. Before turning to these problems, however, it seems reasonable, first, to devote some attention to the types and suppliers of consumer credit.[2]

## Types and Suppliers of Consumer Credit

Consumer credit can be classified in a number of ways, such as method of extension and repayment (noninstalment credit, closed-end instalment credit, and open-end or revolving instalment credit) or institutional source of the credit (banks, finance companies, credit unions, and so forth). In the past, published statistics on uses of the funds (automobile credit, repair and modernization loans, and the like) were provided monthly by the Federal Reserve System, which collects and publishes statistics on consumer credit, but these classifications were dropped in 1978. It appears that recent changes in credit markets (such as the increase in unsecured revolving credit) have made it increasingly difficult to collect accurate statistics on purposes of loans, with the result that the Federal Reserve no longer publishes this classification. Still, it is possible to talk about purposes of consumer loans, even if collecting accurate statistics

---

[1] The burden theory seems to gain the greatest number of adherents, and to achieve the greatest media coverage, near business cycle peaks when analysts are expecting the onset of a downturn and are looking for possible explanations. See, for example, articles in the *Wall Street Journal,* August 28, 1978, and *Business Week,* October 16, 1978.

[2] Further information about the suppliers of consumer credit can be found in Chapter 10.

is difficult. Common types of consumer (nonmortgage) credit include automobile credit, home repair and modernization loans, mobile home credit, credit for other consumer goods (including furniture and appliances), and personal loans for such things as taxes, educational and medical expenses, and for consolidating and refinancing other debts. This section of the chapter examines consumer credit classified according to method of extension and repayment and according to institutional source. The next section of the chapter examines why consumers take on debts.

Noninstalment credit refers to consumer credit due to be repaid in a single payment or on an irregular basis. At the end of 1978 there was $64.3 billion outstanding in this kind of credit, a large sum but less than one-quarter of total instalment credit. Noninstalment credit consists of three major components: charge accounts, service credit, and single-payment loans. *Charge accounts* represent balances owed to retailers for purchases of various goods. Typically, charge accounts are payable upon receipt of a bill or within a short period, such as 30 or 90 days. This kind of account has declined in relative importance in recent years as many retailers have given up their own credit plans in favor of accepting bank credit cards, such as Master Card and Visa. However, many department stores and furniture stores, as well as small neighborhood merchants, maintain charge-account plans. Formerly, the Federal Reserve System also classified balances on oil-company credit cards as charge accounts. Beginning in 1971, though, balances on oil company credit cards have been reclassified as instalment credit.

*Service credit* consists of amounts owed by consumers to professional practitioners and institutions (such as doctors, lawyers, and hospitals) and to suppliers of services that do not demand immediate payment (for example, electric and telephone utility companies). *Single-payment loans* are made directly to individuals by banks, insurance companies, and other institutions for a variety of purposes, including medical expenses, education, and payment of taxes. Often these loans are made to individuals with assets like stocks and other securities that can be pledged as collateral for the loan. Frequently, single-payment loans are the lowest-cost consumer credit available. Rates can be relatively low because this kind of credit is usually

offered on a fully collateralized basis and, since monthly payments are not required, simplified processing procedures can be employed. Loans offered by life insurance companies using the cash value of policies as collateral are usually made on a fixed-interest-rate basis.[3] In contrast, single-payment loan arrangements with banks may involve a fluctuating interest rate that depends upon the bank's cost of funds over time.

*Closed-end instalment credit* is a very common consumer credit arrangement, in which a specified amount of credit is advanced for a certain length of time and is repayable in a certain number of payments. Automobile credit is the largest and best example. On a standard automobile contract a certain amount of credit is advanced (purchase price and fees less trade-in and down payment), a finance charge is calculated, and the total of the two is divided equally into a specified number of monthly payments. Although variations exist, most closed-end instalment contracts involve a single extension of credit and incorporate a fixed number of payments. Most consumer credit arrangements of any size—such as contracts to purchase automobiles, mobile homes, large amounts of furniture or appliances, or large personal loans—are made on a closed-end instalment basis.

*Open-end instalment* or *revolving credit* involves a prearranged line of credit where timing of both extensions and repayments are at the option of the credit user, within the limits of the agreement. Familiar examples are check-credit or overdraft-checking plans at banks, which allow the account holder to write checks for more than the balance in the checking account (the difference constituting a loan), and credit advanced through use of revolving credit cards. In both cases, decisions about the amount and timing of credit advances are left to the account or card holder; repayments are also made at the speed preferred by the debtor, as long as some agreed minimum payment is provided. Revolving credit-card credit is made available by both retail stores and banks, and revolving loan credit is extended by both banks and finance companies.

[3]Many observers of credit markets regard life insurance policy loans as a withdrawal of savings represented by the policyholder's equity (albeit at an interest cost to the policyholder) rather than as a true debt. Largely for this reason, policy loans are not included in statistics on consumer credit published by the Federal Reserve System.

In recent years, revolving credit has grown increasingly popular with consumers, presumably because of its convenience and flexibility.

Table 14-1 provides a distribution of the various types of consumer credit outstanding at the end of selected years. Table 14-1 shows that instalment credit has grown relative to noninstalment credit, reaching more than four-fifths of the total in 1978. The other noteworthy structural change is the rapid increase in revolving credit in recent years, the amount outstanding at year-end multiplying more than ninefold between 1970 and 1978. It seems likely that this category will continue to grow in the future, although possibly at a slower rate, as consumers continue to react to the convenience afforded by this form of credit and as financial institutions gain more experience in the area. It appears from Table 14-1 that between 1970 and 1978 revolving credit grew at the expense of both closed-end instalment credit for nonautomotive purposes and noninstalment credit. Since both closed-end instalment credit and some kinds of noninstalment credit require separate trips to the financial institution and new credit negotiations each time credit is extended, it seems reasonable that consumers often would prefer revolving credit. Creditors also seem more willing to extend this kind of credit in recent years as they have become more experienced with its risk-related features and as computers and other technological advances make the necessary record keeping easier and less expensive.

Table 14-2 shows the institutional sources of consumer instalment credit outstanding at the end of selected years (noninstalment credit is excluded from the table). It is obvious that not only have commercial banks been the dominant source of consumer instalment credit for many years, but they also have tended to increase their market share over time. At the end of 1978, banks held $136.2 billion of consumer instalment credit, about half of the total. Credit unions have exhibited the fastest growth among major creditors, however; and they held about one-ninth of all consumer instalment credit at year-end 1978.[4] In the past three decades banks and credit unions have tended to increase their market shares largely at the expense of finance companies and retail outlets. Banks and credit unions are, generally, the lowest-cost credit sources among the four major creditor groups, which gives them an advantage in a competitive environment and may well explain their growth. Still, for a variety of reasons, many consumers appear to prefer the credit plans offered by retailers and finance companies (especially for smaller amounts of credit), and so the outstandings of these institutions have continued to grow absolutely, if not relatively. An additional reason for the loss of market share among retailers is the tendency of smaller retailers in recent years to discontinue their own credit plans in favor of accepting bank credit cards. The effect of this change shows up, of course, as a relative loss of market share for retail firms and a relative gain for commercial banks.

## Consumers' Demand for Credit

As pointed out in the last section, consumers use credit for many purposes. Traditionally, the prime reason has been financing major durable goods, such as automobiles, but other uses have also been common. In the inflationary environment of the 1970s it was not surprising that consumers used credit, even for smaller purchases. If consumers postponed purchases until they had cash available, the prices of the desired goods would probably have been higher. Finance charges are deductible for income tax purposes anyway, at least for taxpayers who itemize their deductions.

It has long been known that certain segments of the population are more likely to use consumer credit than others. Young married couples, for example, especially those with small children, use substantial amounts of consumer credit. Older, re-

---

[4]It seems possible that credit unions may not be able to grow as rapidly in the future as competitive conditions change in the markets for consumer deposits, the primary source of funds for credit unions. For many years credit unions had an advantage in competing for rate-sensitive consumer deposits because, according to existing regulations governing interest rate ceilings on deposits, credit unions could pay higher rates than other institutions. This advantage suffered substantial erosion in the latter 1970s as competing institutions were allowed to offer higher deposit rates, as for example on "money-market certificates," whose maximum rates are tied to open-market Treasury bill rates. All interest rate ceilings on deposits at competing institutions are scheduled to be phased out by 1986 under provisions of the Depository Institutions Deregulation Act of 1980.

### Table 14-1 Types of Consumer Credit

| | Amount Outstanding (in billions of dollars) | | | | Percentage of Total Amount Outstanding | | | |
|---|---|---|---|---|---|---|---|---|
| | 1950 | 1960 | 1970 | 1978 | 1950 | 1960 | 1970 | 1978 |
| Instalment credit | $15.5 | $45.0 | $105.5 | $275.6 | 60.5% | 69.2% | 73.7% | 81.1% |
| Revolving credit | — | — | 5.1 | 47.1 | — | — | 3.6 | 13.8 |
| Automobile credit | 6.0 | 18.1 | 36.3 | 102.4 | 23.4 | 27.8 | 25.4 | 30.1 |
| Other (closed-end) credit | 9.5 | 26.9 | 64.1 | 126.1 | 37.1 | 41.4 | 44.8 | 37.1 |
| Noninstalment Credit[a] | 10.1 | 20.0 | 37.6 | 64.3 | 39.5 | 30.8 | 26.3 | 18.9 |
| Total consumer credit | 25.6 | 65.0 | 143.1 | 339.9 | 100.0 | 100.0 | 100.0 | 100.0 |

[a]Includes single-payment loans at banks, savings and loan associations, and mutual savings banks, charge accounts, and single-payment medical and service credit.

Source: Board of Governors of the Federal Reserve System.

### Table 14-2 Sources of Consumer Instalment Credit

| | Amount Outstanding (in billions of dollars) | | | | Percentage of Total Amount Outstanding | | | |
|---|---|---|---|---|---|---|---|---|
| | 1950 | 1960 | 1970 | 1978 | 1950 | 1960 | 1970 | 1978 |
| Commercial banks | $ 6.6 | $18.7 | $ 48.7 | $136.2 | 42.6% | 41.6% | 46.2% | 49.4% |
| Finance companies | 5.3 | 15.4 | 27.6 | 54.3 | 34.2 | 34.2 | 26.2 | 19.7 |
| Credit unions | 0.6 | 3.9 | 13.0 | 45.9 | 3.9 | 8.7 | 12.3 | 16.6 |
| Retailers[a] | 2.9 | 6.3 | 13.9 | 24.9 | 18.7 | 14.0 | 13.2 | 9.0 |
| S&Ls | 0.1 | 0.6 | 1.5 | 8.4 | 0.6 | 1.3 | 1.4 | 3.0 |
| Gasoline companies | — | — | — | 3.2 | — | — | — | 1.1 |
| Mutual savings banks | — | 0.1 | 0.9 | 2.7 | — | 0.2 | 0.8 | 1.0 |
| Total | $15.5 | $45.0 | $105.5 | $275.6 | 100.0% | 100.0% | 100.0% | 100.0% |

[a]Includes automobile dealers.

Source: Board of Governors of the Federal Reserve System.

tired couples and unmarried individuals generally are much less likely to be in debt. Younger married couples often have not had sufficient time to accumulate a volume of liquid assets with which to acquire the durables and other necessities associated with forming a household. Often, it appears, consumers opt for credit so that they may actually use the durables while the funds to pay for them are accumulated in the form of instalment payments. Older couples tend not to purchase sizable amounts of durable goods as frequently as families in the formative stages and so, typically, they do not use as much consumer credit.

Table 14-3 provides some information about consumer credit users from a survey sponsored by the banking regulatory agencies in the summer of 1977. The survey found that at that time half of American households were using various forms of consumer credit—excluding credit-card and mortgage credit—which is roughly the same proportion found in similar surveys undertaken in the 1960s.[5] Obviously, however, credit use is not distributed evenly throughout the population. The proportion of credit-using families is quite small among families where the head is retired. The proportion rises sharply among families with younger heads, though, and includes about three out of every four families where the head is less than 45 years old, married, and has children.

Occasionally, the view is heard that consumer credit, especially instalment credit, is a low-income or lower-middle-income phenomenon. Actually, survey findings reveal that instalment credit is found more often among middle-income and upper-

[5]See Thomas A. Durkin and Gregory E. Elliehausen, *The 1977 Survey of Consumer Credit,* Board of Governors of the Federal Reserve system, Washington, D.C., 1978.

**Table 14-3 Percentage of Families with Instalment Debt Within Various Population Groups in 1977**

| Life-Cycle Stages of Family Heads | Percentage with Instalment Plan |
|---|---|
| Under 45 years | |
|   Unmarried, no children | 46 |
|   Married | |
|     No children | 65 |
|     Youngest child under 6 years old | 77 |
|     Youngest child 6 years old or over | 75 |
| 45 years old and over | |
|   Unmarried, no children | |
|     Head retired | 13 |
|     Head in labor force | 32 |
|   Married | |
|     Children under 19 years old | 65 |
|     No children under 19 years old | |
|       Head retired | 21 |
|       Head in labor force | 42 |
| Any age, unmarried, has children under 19 years old | 50 |
|   All families | 50 |

| Family Income | Percentage with Instalment Debt |
|---|---|
| Less than $3,000 | 21 |
| $3,000–4,999 | 31 |
| $5,000–7,499 | 41 |
| $7,500–9,999 | 56 |
| $10,000–14,999 | 58 |
| $15,000–19,999 | 66 |
| $20,000–24,999 | 68 |
| $25,000 or more | 58 |
|   Income not ascertained | 28 |
|   All families | 50 |

Source: Thomas A. Durkin and Gregory E. Elliehausen, *The 1977 Survey of Consumer Credit,* Board of Governors of the Federal Reserve System, Washington, D.C., 1978.

middle-income households. Instalment credit at financial institutions is often less available to lower-income families because of the risks perceived by the potential lenders. Also, low-income families include many retired workers living on pensions. Many of the latter may have financial assets available and so may not require credit for purchases. Also, these people are less likely to be acquiring the large volumes of durable goods and other purchases associated with new household formations

of younger people. In any case, the second part of Table 14-3 shows that consumers in all income categories employ instalment credit, but its use appears to be more frequent in the middle- and upper-income categories. Probably most interesting is the high proportion of consumers with incomes of $20,000 or more who were using instalment credit. More than three families in five in this relatively high income bracket were found to be instalment credit users.

Table 14-3 probably even understates, to some extent, the use of consumer credit by higher-income families because it refers only to traditional forms of consumer instalment credit and excludes credit cards. It is difficult to incorporate credit cards into a table like Table 14-3, because credit cards are used as substitutes for cash and checks as well as for instalment-credit purposes. This definitional problem, and the fact that most credit-card transactions are relatively small in comparison to the typical instalment loans, suggests that they be examined separately. Nevertheless, substitution of credit-card credit for other forms of instalment credit by at least some consumers probably means that Table 14-3 understates the proportion of consumers in all income classes who use instalment credit. One conclusion is clear, though: consumer instalment credit is widely used by members of the public, especially by middle- and higher-income families.

Table 14-4 provides information on the use of various kinds of credit cards within family income groups. Like traditional forms of consumer credit, credit-card use is well distributed across income categories, but card use also rises with income. More than 60 percent of American families were at least occasional users of credit cards in 1977 (up from 50 percent in 1970), with retail store cards used by about half of all families and bank credit cards used by 35 percent. Both of these individual categories were up substantially from the prior survey in 1970, from 45 percent for retail cards and 16 percent for bank cards. Only families using gasoline cards declined relatively in the 1970s, from 33 percent of families surveyed in 1971 to 31 percent in 1977.[6]

[6]Further information on card holding and use may be found in Durkin and Elliehausen, *The 1977 Survey of Consumer Credit.*

**Table 14-4  Percentage of Families Using Various Kinds of Credit Cards in 1977 Within Various Income Categories**

| | Use Any Card | Use Bank Card | Use Retail Card | Use Travel and Entertainment Card | Use Gasoline Card |
|---|---|---|---|---|---|
| Less than $3,000 | 22 | 8 | 15 | —[a] | 10 |
| $3,000–4,999 | 24 | 5 | 18 | —[a] | 10 |
| $5,000–7,499 | 33 | 10 | 25 | 1 | 13 |
| $7,500–9,999 | 49 | 22 | 44 | 2 | 18 |
| $10,000–14,999 | 63 | 29 | 50 | 2 | 28 |
| $15,000–19,999 | 73 | 46 | 62 | 6 | 32 |
| $20,000–24,999 | 82 | 56 | 73 | 10 | 50 |
| $25,000 and more | 90 | 68 | 77 | 25 | 63 |
| All families | 60 | 35 | 50 | 7 | 32 |
| Note: Have cards but do not use or use not ascertained | —[b] | 4 | 4 | 1 | 3 |

[a]Less than 0.5 percent.
[b]Depends on card type.

Source: Thomas A. Durkin and Gregory E. Elliehausen, *The 1977 Survey of Consumer Credit*, Board of Governors of the Federal Reserve System, Washington, D.C., 1978.

A variety of factors has been suggested as important in influencing the aggregate demand for consumer credit.[7] Among these are some we have already mentioned—including the impact of life cycle and age structure of the population and the rise in aggregate income over time—but also including some other variables. Prominent within the latter group are consumers' liquid assets available for alternative financing; the prices and technological changes of durable goods, which might make them more or less attractive as outlets for expenditures; and existing stocks of both durable goods and consumer credit. Any new study of the aggregate demand for consumer credit would undoubtedly have to examine carefully the role of inflation and inflationary expectations in the 1970s in increasing consumers' willingness to change their time pattern of spending and to pay tax-deductible interest and finance charges.

The most important concern of economists and policymakers in the area of consumer credit in the latter 1970s was the debt-burden issue mentioned earlier. Relying on aggregate measures, such as total consumer debt, and on ratios of debt and repayments to aggregate disposable income, many observers concluded that consumers' debt burdens had reached an all-time high. While the view was by no means unanimous, the high ratios of debt and repayments to income strongly suggested the possibility of a spending slowdown—clearly a matter of concern because of the size of the consumer sector in total spending.

Table 14-5 provides information about the growth of consumer and mortgage credit in the period 1960–1978. The first column lists the average amounts of consumer credit (instalment and non-instalment) outstanding in the fourth quarter of each year, and the second column lists the corresponding volumes of household mortgage credit. Column 3 records the rate of liquidations (repayments) of consumer instalment credit, and column 4 lists mortgage liquidations. Each of these columns

[7]See, among other sources, William C. Dunkelberg and Frank P. Stafford, "Debt in the Consumer Portfolio: Evidence from a Panel Study," *American Economic Review* (September 1971); Helen Manning Hunter, "A Behavioral Model of the Long-Run Growth of Aggregate Consumer Credit in the United States," *Review of Economics and Statistics* (May 1966); John B. Lansing, E. Scott Maynes, and Mordechai Kreinin, "Factors Associated with the Use of Consumer Instalment Credit," in *Consumer Instalment Credit*, ed. Board of Governors of the Federal Reserve System, Part I, Vol. 2, Washington, D.C., 1957; Frederic S. Mishkin, "What Depressed the Consumer: The Household Balance Sheet and the 1973–75 Recession," *Brookings Papers on Economic Activity* (Number 1, 1977); and James F. Smith, *The Demand for Instalment Credit Since 1948: A Dynamic Stock-Adjustment Approach*, Unpublished Ph.D. dissertation, Southern Methodist University, 1971.

**Table 14-5  Consumer and Mortgage Credit Outstandings and Liquidations: Amounts and Ratios to Disposable Personal Income, 1960–1978**

| Year | Billions of Dollars | | | | Relative to Disposable Personal Income | | | | |
|---|---|---|---|---|---|---|---|---|---|
| | Consumer Out. | Mortgage Out. | Consumer Liq. | Mortgage Liq. | Consumer Out. | Mortgage Out. | Consumer Liq. | Mortgage Liq. | Consumer plus Mortgage Liq. |
| 1960 | $ 64 | $137 | $ 48 | $13 | 18.1% | 39.1% | 13.6% | 3.8% | 17.4% |
| 1961 | 66 | 150 | 51 | 15 | 17.8 | 40.2 | 13.7 | 4.0 | 17.7 |
| 1962 | 72 | 164 | 54 | 16 | 18.6 | 42.0 | 13.9 | 4.1 | 18.0 |
| 1963 | 81 | 180 | 60 | 17 | 19.6 | 43.6 | 14.5 | 4.1 | 18.6 |
| 1964 | 91 | 198 | 67 | 19 | 20.2 | 44.1 | 14.9 | 4.2 | 19.1 |
| 1965 | 101 | 214 | 75 | 20 | 20.6 | 43.8 | 15.3 | 4.1 | 19.4 |
| 1966 | 107 | 229 | 80 | 20 | 20.5 | 43.7 | 15.4 | 3.9 | 19.2 |
| 1967 | 113 | 241 | 88 | 21 | 20.2 | 43.2 | 15.8 | 3.8 | 19.5 |
| 1968 | 124 | 258 | 94 | 22 | 20.6 | 42.9 | 15.6 | 3.7 | 19.3 |
| 1969 | 134 | 276 | 102 | 24 | 20.6 | 42.4 | 15.7 | 3.7 | 19.3 |
| 1970 | 139 | 291 | 111 | 26 | 19.9 | 41.4 | 15.9 | 3.7 | 19.6 |
| 1971 | 156 | 318 | 131 | 28 | 20.5 | 41.9 | 17.2 | 3.7 | 21.0 |
| 1972 | 175 | 359 | 142 | 33 | 20.9 | 42.9 | 17.0 | 3.9 | 20.9 |
| 1973 | 201 | 406 | 157 | 36 | 21.4 | 43.3 | 16.8 | 3.8 | 20.6 |
| 1974 | 211 | 441 | 164 | 40 | 20.7 | 43.4 | 16.2 | 4.0 | 20.1 |
| 1975 | 220 | 479 | 179 | 46 | 19.5 | 42.5 | 15.9 | 4.1 | 20.0 |
| 1976 | 245 | 540 | 197 | 53 | 20.1 | 44.2 | 16.1 | 4.3 | 20.4 |
| 1977 | 286 | 634 | 229 | 64 | 21.0 | 46.6 | 16.8 | 4.7 | 21.5 |
| 1978 | 337 | 738 | 266 | 78 | 22.1 | 48.4 | 17.5 | 5.1 | 22.6 |

Source: Board of Governors of the Federal Reserve System.

is then divided by disposable personal income (DPI), at fourth-quarter annual rates, to produce a series of burden ratios shown in columns 5 through 8. The last column, column 9, which combines columns 7 and 8, shows the combined ratio of consumers' instalment-debt repayments and mortgage repayments relative to disposable personal income. This ratio, and the ratio to DPI of the instalment component alone, are reproduced in Figure 14-1.

Table 14-5 and Figure 14-1 show the reasons for concern about debt burden in the latter 1970s. Consumer and mortgage credit rose steadily through the decade, as did debt-burden ratios. By year-end 1978, not only had the amounts of credit outstanding reached all-time highs, but so had the debt-burden ratios. A number of *caveats* must be considered, however, before using this information as evidence that consumers acted imprudently.

One *caveat* is that inflation has tended to distort many statistical series. In an inflationary environment, growth rates of some economic variables tend to accelerate, not because of behavioral changes in the economy, but because the monetary unit declines in value. Sales of the same physical number of automobiles, for example, with the same proportion financed and the same relative proportion of purchase prices paid as down payments and trade-ins, generate larger dollar amounts of credit. This occurs because the dollar has declined in value in relation to the car or, in other words, more dollars are needed to buy an automobile. This means that the growth rate of consumer debt can increase even if both population and consumers' behavior remain the same.

Careful examination of this argument about growth rates shows that it may partly explain growth in absolute amounts of debt, but not in terms of the debt-burden ratios. The ratios are derived by dividing debt by disposable personal income, which is also subject to inflationary trends. The increase in the ratios over time indicates that something more is happening than just inflation—a larger portion of income actually is devoted to debt repayment. This seems to be the reason for concern among economists and policymakers, but even this fact must be examined closely before concluding that debt is becoming more burdensome.

Figure 14-1 shows clearly that the content of the instalment credit series has changed over time. Beginning in 1971, oil-company credit was moved into instalment credit. Not including oil-company credit in instalment credit would lower the ratio, and the later 1970s would not appear as high in relation to the 1960s. In addition, small retailers have gradually

**Figure 14-1   Household Debt Burden (Repayments Relative to Income)**

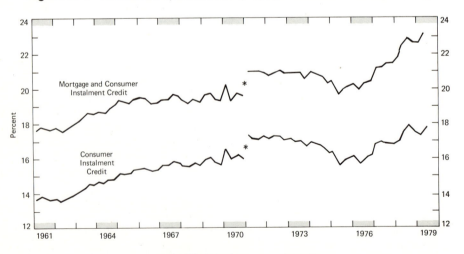

\* Discontinuity reflects inclusion of oil company credit-card credit after 1970.
Note: Consumer credit repayments are for instalment credit (noninstalment repayments unavailable). Prepayments are included, as well as scheduled payments of principal and interest.

Source: Board of Governors of the Federal Reserve System.

abandoned their charge account plans in favor of bank credit cards. Charge accounts are not counted as instalment credit in the consumer credit figures released by the Federal Reserve, but bank card credit is included, even though some of this credit is used to replace charge accounts. It is not possible to remove the charge-account component from the instalment-credit series, even if its inclusion distorts trends over time to some extent. Some experts have contended that the exclusion of charge-account credit counted as instalment credit would lower the debt-burden ratio by more than a percentage point.[8] If it were possible to remove both charge-account credit on bank credit cards and the oil-company credit inconsistency from the instalment-credit series, the debt-burden ratios might appear no higher, and might even be lower, than they were in the mid-1960s. This hypothesis does not offer a ready answer as to whether or not consumers act prudently. It does, however, suggest that debt levels in 1978 do not warrant drastically different conclusions about the future course of consumer spending than they did in earlier years.

Other influences should also be evaluated. For example, changing population trends can have an impact on the amount of debt generated without necessarily implying a behavioral change. The rapid increase in the 1970s in the number of family heads in the family-forming and debt-using 25–35-year-old age bracket undoubtedly had an effect of this kind. Also, consumers' assets, including liquid assets such as savings accounts, have risen along with debt, possibly making debt less burdensome. Furthermore, in the 1970s, many families had more than one income earner, which means at least part of family income might be protected even if one earner should face reduced hours or unemployment in a recession. All of these considerations must be evaluated in studying the debt-burden issue.

## Consumer Credit Protection

The issue of common protection in the credit area concerns the proper role of government in influencing both the range of consumer choices available in the marketplace and the terms and condi-

tions under which the choices can be provided. Traditionally, this issue has been a matter of state concern, although the role of the federal government has been increasingly important since 1968.

States have regulated most aspects of consumer-credit transactions, but probably the most important regulations have been in the areas of rate (price) ceilings and right-of-entry into the market. Most states instituted these regulations when they attempted to eliminate the evils associated with illegal lending ("loansharking") prevalent in the latter half of the nineteenth century and early twentieth century by creating a legal, but carefully regulated, market for consumer credit.

Generally speaking, consumer credit is an expensive kind of credit for financial institutions to extend. Relatively small amounts of credit are involved (in comparison with business credit and loans to governmental bodies) and, since instalment repayment is usually involved, credit-checking and loan-processing costs loom large in relation to the amount of credit. This means that finance rates must be high in comparison with other forms of credit before financial institutions will be willing to make these loans. Often, in the past, the higher rates necessary to attract funds into consumer credit conflicted with interest rate ceilings established by the laws of the various states. The result was widespread illegal lending, often at extremely high interest rates, accompanied by harsh and abusive collection and other practices.

In response to the loanshark conditions found in many places in the early part of the twentieth century, states began to legislate exceptions to their general interest-rate ceilings around 1910 and allowed regulated lenders, such as finance companies, banks, and credit unions, to extend credit to consumers at legal rates that covered their production costs. States controlled entry by allowing only chartered financial institutions or licensed finance companies to lend legally at the higher rates.[9] Credit extended by retail outlets had a somewhat

[8] See, for example, the statement of William C. Dunkelberg before the House Budget Committee Task Force on Inflation, United States House of Representatives, June 27, 1979.

[9] For discussion of the historical aspects of rate ceiling and entry regulations, see David H. Rogers, *Consumer Banking in New York*, Columbia University Press, New York, 1975, and references contained there. For further discussion of the economic issues associated with rate ceilings on consumer credit, see National Commission on Consumer Finance, *Consumer Credit in the United States: The Report of the National Commission on Consumer Finance*, Government Printing Office, Washington, D.C., 1972.

different historical and legal background, but the essential principle is the same: if they follow various state requirements, lenders can charge relatively high finance rates (high, at least, in relation to well-known interest rates like Treasury bills and the prime rate for business loans). In general, retail credit is subject to less state regulation than loan credit at financial institutions, but most states do regulate retail credit in some ways.

Federal consumer protection in the credit area began with passage of the Truth-in-Lending Act, Title I of the Consumer Credit Protection Act of 1968.[10] Since 1968 the federal government has enacted a series of additional consumer credit regulations including the Fair Credit Reporting Act (1970), the Fair Credit Billing Act (1974), the Real Estate Settlement Procedures Act (1974), the Federal Trade Commission Improvement Act (1975), the Home Mortgage Disclosure Act (1975), the Consumer Leasing Act (1976), and the Fair Debt Collection Practices Act (1977). In some cases, individual states have enacted similar laws either before or after the federal initiative, but these federal laws are fundamentally different from the main, historical thrust of state regulation. States have been primarily interested in regulating the price of the service and the type of lenders that may offer consumer credit. In contrast, at the federal level, the main emphasis centers on the content and quality of the service itself. Especially important at the federal level has been the requirement that creditors make certain kinds of information readily available to consumers. Most of the federal laws mentioned earlier included sections designed to ensure that lenders made disclosures of various kinds. For some acts, of course, especially Truth-in-Lending, Home Mortgage Disclosure, Real Estate Settlement Procedures, and Consumer Leasing, disclosure is their main purpose.

Although it is difficult to evaluate all the impacts of government regulation in the consumer-credit area, it is safe to conclude that the various kinds of regulations are quite controversial. It is widely believed that rate ceilings at the state level limit the availability of consumer credit for higher-risk borrowers and those demanding small amounts of credit.[11] The controversy arises because some observers believe rate ceilings should be high enough to allow credit to be widely available, and competition should be encouraged to prevent price gouging by creditors. Other observers, apparently having little faith in competition, believe that such a policy results only in higher profits for creditors. Beyond this, some people advance the argument that some higher-risk borrowers would be "better off" without credit anyway, and so higher rate ceilings are not needed. Because the essentials of this argument run deeper than economics and involve fundamental philosophies of the role of government in society, economic analysis on the extent of competition in the markets seems unlikely to provide a solution.

Consumer credit regulation at the federal level has, if anything, proven to be even more controversial than state regulation. Even the basic purpose and coverage of the laws have been subject to continuous interpretations and changes. The Truth-in-Lending Act was amended on a number of occasions between 1969 and 1979, and a major reform proposal was enacted in 1980. The Real Estate Settlement Procedures Act was revised substantially within a year of initial passage, and the scope of coverage of the Equal Credit Opportunity Act was broadened significantly within a few months of its effective date in October 1975. Most observers maintain that these laws have provided a variety of benefits to consumers. Quantitative measurement of benefits is difficult, however, since every consumer has different needs and different capacities for assimilating and using information disclosures. One thing seems clear, though: compliance with many of the complex rules has been both difficult and costly for creditors. One report by a government commission concluded that continuous changes in disclosure forms required by Truth-in-Lending alone caused immense costs for creditors. According to the commission, if forms could be approved for a period as short as one year, the savings would be approximately $600 million.[12] While neither benefits nor costs of consumer

---

[10]Public Law 90-321. During World War II, the late 1940s, and the Korean War period, the federal government instituted a program of credit controls (Regulation W), but these controls on down payments, maturities, etc., were undertaken for macroeconomic stabilization purposes rather than specifically for protection of individual consumers.

[11]See National Commission on Consumer Finance, *Consumer Credit in the United States*.

[12]Commission on Federal Paperwork, *Consumer Credit Protection*, Government Printing Office, Washington, D.C., 1977.

protection can be measured with precision, sums such as this, resulting from only one aspect of one law suggest, at least, that consumer-protection benefits are not free.

## Conclusion

In conclusion, it seems likely that consumer credit will continue to expand along with population growth and increases in income. Growth will probably take place in an increasingly competitive environment, however, so market shares of firms, as well as whole industries, might be expected to change. Technological advances, including electronic funds transfers, promise even greater upheavals in the future. Whether consumer-protection regulations are able to provide benefits to consumers without restricting innovations remains to be seen.

## Questions

1. Explain some economic benefits provided by consumer credit.
2. How could one's assessment of the competitiveness of consumer credit markets affect one's position on the need for government regulation of consumer credit?
3. Explain how different kinds of consumer credit might be classified. Which kinds of consumer credit appear to be growing in importance?
4. Explain why different kinds of consumer credit might carry different annual percentage rates of finance charge.
5. Explain why consumer credit use is more likely among some segments of the population than among others.
6. What is meant by *open-end* or *revolving credit*? Which population groups appear to use this kind of credit most?
7. What is meant by the debt-burden issue? Explain some of the problems in using aggregate statistics to evaluate this issue.
8. Explain why rate ceilings contributed to illegal lending in the nineteenth century and describe how states responded to protect consumers from abuses of this kind.
9. Contrast the main thrusts of consumer-protection regulations of consumer credit at the state level and at the federal level.
10. What are some of the controversial elements of consumer-credit regulation at the state and the federal levels?

## Selected Bibliography

Commission on Federal Paperwork. *Consumer Credit Protection*. Government Printing Office, Washington, D.C., 1977.

Dunkelberg, William C., and Frank P. Stafford. "Debt in the Consumer Portfolio: Evidence from a Panel Study." *American Economic Review* (September 1977).

Durkin, Thomas A., and Gregory E. Elliehausen. *The 1977 Survey of Consumer Credit*. Board of Governors of the Federal Reserve System, Washington, D.C., 1978.

Hunter, Helen Manning. "A Behavioral Model of the Long-Run Growth of Aggregate Consumer Credit in the United States." *Review of Economics and Statistics* (May 1966).

Lansing, John B., E. Scott Maynes, and Mordechai Kreinin. "Factors Associated with the Use of Consumer Credit," in *Consumer Instalment Credit,* ed. Board of Governors of the Federal Reserve System, Part I, Vol. 2, Washington, D.C., 1957.

Mishkin, Frederic S. "What Depressed the Consumer: The Household Balance Sheet and the 1973–75 Recession." *Brookings Papers on Economic Activity* (Number 1, 1977).

National Commission on Consumer Finance. *Consumer Credit in the United States: The Report of the National Commission on Consumer Finance*. Government Printing Office, Washington, D.C., 1972.

Rogers, David H. *Consumer Banking in New York*. Columbia University Press, New York, 1975.

Smith, James F. *The Demand for Consumer Instalment Credit Since 1948: A Dynamic Stock-Adjustment Approach*. Unpublished Ph.D. dissertation, Southern Methodist University, 1971.

# 15

# The Demand for Agricultural Credit

Although the relative importance of agriculture in the economy has declined in recent years, it is still one of the largest industries in the United States in terms of output and employment. It seems paradoxical that the nation with the most advanced financial institutions in the world should have difficulty meeting the financial needs of one of its major industries. Yet many people who speak for agricultural interests contend that this is indeed the case. Their claims are not without foundation: the marked rise in government activity in farm finance in recent years clearly indicates that the public and their elected representatives find the performance of private lenders deficient in some respects. Given that profound changes in technology and in the structure of agriculture have increased the financial needs of the industry and are likely to continue to do so, the performance of the financial system in this area is of serious concern to everyone, not only in the United States, but also in the rest of the world.

This chapter offers a discussion of the major factors affecting agriculture's credit needs and of the financial system's ability to supply those needs. The first section briefly reviews the profound changes in the nature of farming. An analysis of the farm sector's demand for credit follows. The third section focuses on the markets and institutions supplying credit to agriculture. The final section considers the adequacy of the financial system to meet the financial requirements of this rapidly changing business, which now appears indispensable to the physical, political, and economic well-being of the world.

## Recent Developments in Agriculture

The decline in agriculture's relative importance in the economy is well known. In 1930, nearly one-fourth of the nation's population lived on farms; in 1978 less than one person in twenty did so. In 1930, 8.0 percent of total gross national product originated in agriculture; by 1978, the sector's share had fallen to less than 3 percent (see Table 15-1).[1] This process is similar to that experienced by other nations that have entered the stage of advanced in-

[1] That agriculture's share of population fell much more than its share of output indicates the significance of technical change in the industry.

**Table 15-1  Trends in Farm Output, Population, and Acreage**

| | Farm Output[a] (in billions of dollars) | GNP Originating in Agriculture (in billions of dollars) | Farm Income[a] (in billions of dollars) | Agriculture's Share | | Average Farm Size (in acres) |
| | | | | GNP[a] (percentages) | Population (percentages) | |
|---|---|---|---|---|---|---|
| 1930 | $30.9 | $22.9 | $18.2 | 8.0% | 24.9% | 157 |
| 1935 | 30.4 | 22.9 | 19.3 | 8.8 | 25.3 | 155 |
| 1940 | 35.6 | 24.7 | 21.2 | 7.2 | 23.2 | 175 |
| 1945 | 40.0 | 25.8 | 22.5 | 4.6 | 17.5 | 195 |
| 1950 | 43.1 | 26.9 | 21.6 | 5.0 | 15.3 | 216 |
| 1954 | 46.0 | 28.3 | 22.0 | 4.6 | 11.8 | 242 |
| 1959 | 50.9 | 28.2 | 22.5 | 3.9 | 9.4 | 303 |
| 1964 | 55.2 | 29.2 | 23.4 | 3.3 | 6.8 | 352 |
| 1969 | 61.3 | 29.9 | 23.7 | 2.8 | 5.1 | 390 |
| 1974 | 65.3 | 32.0 | 25.0 | 2.6 | 4.4 | 388 |
| 1975 | 65.9 | 33.7 | 24.9 | 2.8 | 4.2 | 391 |
| 1976 | 66.6 | 32.4 | 23.2 | 2.5 | 3.9 | 394 |
| 1977 | 70.1 | 34.4 | 25.2 | 2.6 | 3.6 | 397 |
| 1978[b] | 71.0 | 34.2 | 24.9 | 2.4 | N.A. | 400 |

N.A. = Not Available.
[a] Output, GNP, and income data are in constant 1972 dollars.
[b] Preliminary.

Sources: *The National Income and Product Accounts of the United States*; *Survey of Current Business*; *Agricultural Statistics*.

dustrial development: the labor force needed by the rapidly expanding nonfarm sectors is supplied by migration from the rural areas.[2] Technical change in the farm sector enables it to increase output enough to feed the rest of the population despite the shrinking agricultural labor force.

Agriculture's relative decline has not occurred at a steady rate. Economic recession tends to slow the process or even reverse it. During the depression of the 1930s, the farm sector's share of both output and population rose temporarily. In comparatively mild recessions, such as 1954 and 1974, agriculture increased its share of output but not its share of population. It is not hard to explain these responses to economic contractions. The income elasticity of demand for agricultural products is low: when national income declines people concentrate their spending reductions on postponables, such as consumer durables and entertainment, and maintain expenditures on food, shelter, and other "necessities," which are less subject to discretionary variation. In deep depressions, farm output is swelled by subsistence farmers who are unable to find work elsewhere. A small plot of land is capable of providing minimum amounts of food and shelter through the direct efforts of the farmer and his

[2] For further discussion, see Edward F. Denison, *Why Growth Rates Differ: Postwar Experience in Nine Western Countries*, The Brookings Institution, Washington, D.C., 1967.

family. This may be a better alternative than trying to market specialized skills in a depressed economy.

Factors other than the business cycle seem to have been at work since 1969, slowing the decline in agriculture's importance in the economy. The sector's share of GNP has not decreased at all since 1969, and its share of population has fallen much more slowly than it had in the period 1930–1969. Part of this is due to the fact that the sector cannot shrink forever. It is hard to see how our food needs can be met with many fewer resources devoted to food production. Recent changes in the world food situation also seem to call for increased food output by the United States. While phenomena of the early 1970s—extension of the Sahara Desert, failure of the monsoon in India, and disastrous harvests in the Soviet Union, for example—may not recur (at least not all at once), the experience has suggested that American agriculture may be a key factor in world affairs. It is quite possible that the American farmer may be the main line of defense against mass starvation and economic collapse. This possibility has led policymakers to reassess the conventional wisdom that high prices and output restrictions are in the best interests of the country in general and of farmers in particular.

Not only has agriculture's role in society and the economy undergone profound changes, but so has the sector's internal structure. Table 15-2 shows

**Table 15-2   Selected Inputs, 1930–1978**

| | Structures and Equipment[a] | Equipment[a] | Structures[a] | Labor[b] | Land[c] |
|------|------|------|------|------|------|
| 1930 | $26.0 | $ 9.8 | $16.2 | 22,921 | 990 |
| 1935 | 20.2 | 7.4 | 12.8 | 21,052 | 1,055 |
| 1940 | 20.4 | 9.4 | 10.9 | 20,472 | 1,065 |
| 1945 | 21.0 | 11.2 | 9.8 | 18,838 | 1,142 |
| 1950 | 36.4 | 21.6 | 14.8 | 15,137 | 1,161 |
| 1954 | 41.9 | 24.3 | 17.6 | 13,310 | 1,158 |
| 1959 | 43.5 | 23.5 | 20.1 | 10,301 | 1,124 |
| 1964 | 47.1 | 24.2 | 23.0 | 8,194 | 1,110 |
| 1969 | 56.0 | 30.0 | 26.0 | 6,196 | 1,107 |
| 1974 | 62.8 | 34.1 | 28.8 | 5,178 | 1,084 |
| 1975 | 64.6 | 35.4 | 29.2 | 4,990 | 1,063 |
| 1976 | 66.3 | 36.6 | 29.7 | 4,807 | 1,059 |
| 1977 | 67.4 | 37.1 | 30.3 | 4,650 | 1,055 |
| 1978 | 68.4 | 37.5 | 30.8 | 4,431 | 1,052 |

[a]Billions of 1972 dollars.
[b]Millions of manhours.
[c]Millions of acres.

Sources: *Survey of Current Business,* August 1976 and April 1976, "constant-dollar net stocks of fixed nonresidential business capital"; *Agricultural Statistics,* 1979.

amounts of selected inputs used in farming since 1930. The net stock of farm buildings and equipment has more than doubled since that year. Much of this growth, however, occurred shortly after World War II; expansion of capital has been relatively slow since the 1950s. The breakdown of capital between buildings and equipment reveals several interesting features. For one thing, equipment has expanded much faster than plant, a characteristic that holds true for other sectors of the economy as well. In addition, the stock of plant reached its depression low later than did the stock of equipment. The stock of buildings continued to fall throughout World War II. This was due to the fact that farmers, like everyone else, were forced to cut back on maintenance and replacement during the war.

Table 15-2 also reveals that the quantity of labor used in agriculture has declined sharply since 1930. The decrease accelerated immediately after World War II as special wartime needs disappeared. Significant reductions have persisted to the present day. The amount of land used in farming has been relatively stable. Increases in acreage were recorded until 1950, no doubt in response to the pressures of war and depression. Since 1950, land in farms has declined steadily but slowly. Postwar technical changes have not reduced the need for

land in the way they have reduced the need for labor.

An interesting fact revealed in Tables 15-1 and 15-2 is that farm output has increased steadily since World War II despite a significant decline in labor input and a slight decrease in land input. Increases in capital are partly responsible, but capital has not increased enough to provide the entire explanation. Important contributions have been made by inputs not shown in the tables, such as pesticides and fertilizers. Actually, as Table 15-1 demonstrates, farmers have been using intermediate goods of all types (goods used as inputs for a further stage of production) to a much greater extent in recent years. The difference between total farm output and GNP originating in agriculture is almost entirely accounted for by expenditures on intermediate goods. These expenditures increased from one-fourth of total output in 1930 to approximately one-half in 1978. This trend, too, is interrupted by deep depression: the entire decrease in farm output between 1930 and 1935 was due to a reduction in expenditures on intermediate goods. Mild recessions do not seem to have that effect.

A second major factor in the relative decline of the traditionally emphasized inputs—land, labor, and capital—is the growing importance of input-augmenting technical advances, such as improved strains of plants and animals. Nor can one ignore the improvement in the most important input—the farmer. More farmers are realizing that a strong back and a willingness to work hard are no longer sufficient for success in agriculture. They are now taking advantage of the numerous advances in technology, finance, marketing, and management. Their business skills are comparable to those found in other lines of business.

Changes in farm output are no less important than changes in inputs. Basically, the individual farm has become more specialized. Fewer farmers are engaged in subsistence agriculture, attempting to provide most of their needs on their own land. Instead, they are producing for the market and purchasing needed goods in the market. This development is indicated by significant reductions in farm products consumed on the farm and by the wholesale disappearance of very small producers. Between 1960 and 1974, the total number of farms fell by 29 percent, while the number of farms with sales of less than $2,500 declined 63 percent.

These changes in farm input and output have encouraged the formation of larger individual units of production in order to achieve maximum efficiency. The average farm in 1978 was two and one-half times as large as the average in 1930, having increased from 157 acres to 400 acres.[3] The heavy use of plant and equipment, fertilizers, pesticides, and other inputs create expenses that cannot be carried by small units.

Where is the farm sector likely to go from here? While the decline in agriculture's share of GNP is not likely to continue, there seems to be no end in sight for the changes in the sector's structure. The concentration of land into larger units is not likely to be reversed despite the political rhetoric in favor of the family farm. The vast majority of production will be done by these large units. The small farm will not disappear, but most will survive only because of off-farm earnings by family members.

It is interesting that government policy, which is ostensibly designed to protect small operations, actually has promoted the concentration of resources into larger units. The basic reason is that federal support has not taken the form of income transfers to marginal farmers. Instead, the government has offered price supports (which help large producers

more), subsidized credit (which is of greatest value to large-scale borrowers), and tax benefits (which attract investment by the wealthy). Unless a major change in the direction of policy occurs, the government is not likely to save the family farm.

One controversial issue is the role of corporations in agriculture. Many people fear the possibility that farm output will be dominated by a few large corporations. As yet, the corporate form of ownership is not significant and shows no signs of becoming so. There is certainly nothing about the developments in agriculture that require use of incorporation; sizable businesses have been and can be run as partnerships or proprietorships. However, the large investment needed to operate successfully as a commercial farmer may exceed the fund-raising capacity of a single individual or family. The managerial skills required may also be too much for one person. The corporation has always been a solution for these problems, and it is not impossible that it may take over in agriculture. However, even if the threat (or opportunity) is real, its advent seems far in the future. It is also necessary to remember that not all corporations are giants: most corporations existing in agriculture are closely held (that is, they have ten or fewer shareholders). Many are actually family farms.

Another possible development, also viewed with alarm by many people, is vertical integration of the industry. The farmer, though nominally independent, would be tied by contract to a single food processor, which would buy his entire output. The farmer would be little more than an employee of the processor. Poultry and some fresh vegetable markets are now dominated by these arrangements, but there is no sign of its spreading to other farm products.

Although farms are getting larger, there is no particular evidence that the larger farms are dominating the industry or even increasing their share of it. On January 1, 1963, the largest 4.1 percent of all farms held 24.2 percent of total farm assets. On January 1, 1974, the largest 4.1 percent held 22.8 percent of total farm assets.[4] The share of the largest farms actually decreased in those eleven years. Of course, many small farms have disappeared, and the survivors are much larger. But the fear that

[3]See Table 15-1.

[4]Table 15-4.

the industry will be dominated by a handful of giants seems to have little basis in fact at the present time.

Yet another alternative is the combination of independent farmers into cooperatives, which would negotiate collective agreements with processors in much the same way that labor unions bargain collectively with business firms. Milk production in some parts of the country is organized in this way. The economic and political clout that such cooperatives can hold was revealed in one of the many scandals that beset the Nixon administration. That one of President Carter's first acts was to redeem a campaign promise by raising milk price supports suggests that the power of these cooperatives is a force to be reckoned with.

Although the future structure of agriculture cannot be predicted in detail today, some characteristics seem almost certain to be part of that structure. Even the slightest acquaintance with agriculture impresses on one the conclusion that agriculture has undergone a profound transformation that is not yet complete. In many respects the process resembles what took place in other sectors decades ago: a shift from small family businesses to larger, more complex units run by teams of experts. There can be no doubt that the financing of agriculture must change, even as the financing of business changed. It is likely that there will be many parallels between changes in agricultural finance in the future and business finance in the past. With this in mind, we now turn our attention to the problems of financing an agricultural sector in transition.

## Financing Agriculture

### Financial Structure

The basic financial structure of the farm sector may be ascertained from the balance sheets presented in Table 15-3. It should be emphasized that the data contained therein are subject to important limitations. Because most farm business is unincorporated, it is not possible to separate farmers' business accounts from their personal accounts. Items such as "Household equipment" are obvious enough, but most are not easily disentangled. The data in Table 15-3 include both business and personal accounts. Furthermore, the data are incom-

plete. Reported financial assets include only three categories: deposits and currency (actually, bank deposits), U.S. savings bonds, and investment in cooperatives. Claims on all other financial institutions and all marketable securities are omitted, as are accounts receivable. Because of these omissions, Table 15-3 overstates the relative importance of physical assets and understates financial assets. Even with this *caveat* in mind, however, the relative unimportance of financial assets to total assets is striking. In 1930, 12 percent of total assets were financial, while in 1979 only 5 percent were financial. Considering that more than half the increase in financial assets during this period took the form of equity in cooperatives, the significance of even that 5 percent is reduced. When farmers borrow from credit cooperatives, such as production credit associations, they are required by law to purchase stipulated amounts of stock in these organizations. Such financial investment is partially involuntary and does not necessarily indicate a preference for financial over real assets.

Because of the incomplete data for financial assets, too much emphasis should not be placed on the *precise* figures given for the relative share of financial assets in the total. However, the general conclusion that financial assets are relatively unimportant is not likely to be vitiated. It is certainly consistent with the conventional wisdom that farmers tend to be land rich and cash poor.

Looking at the asset structure somewhat differently, one can see that farmers, like most business executives, prefer to reinvest their earnings in their own businesses in the form of real assets. However, farmers appear to do this to a much greater extent than do other businesspeople. Thus, physical assets constituted some 35 percent of the total assets of all manufacturing corporations in 1978 as compared to 95 percent for all farms.[5] No doubt, the profound changes in agriculture outlined previously account for much of the difference between agriculture and manufacturing as well as for the change in agriculture since 1950. Many farmers feel relentless pressures toward modernization and mechanization that force virtually all cash flows to be used for additions to physical capital.

[5] Data for manufacturing are from Federal Trade Commission, *Quarterly Financial Report*. The ratio for the smallest asset size category, less than $5 million, is 27.6 percent. This may be a more relevant comparison.

**Table 15-3  Balance Sheet of Agriculture, 1950–79[a] (in billions of dollars)**

| | 1950 | 1960 | 1970 | 1971 | 1972 | 1973 | 1974 | 1975 | 1976 | 1977 | 1978 | 1979 |
|---|---|---|---|---|---|---|---|---|---|---|---|---|
| **ASSETS** | | | | | | | | | | | | |
| Real estate | $ 75.3 | $130.6 | $206.9 | $215.0 | $231.5 | $260.6 | $325.3 | $368.5 | $416.9 | $483.8 | $525.8 | $599.5 |
| Livestock and poultry | 12.9 | 15.3 | 23.5 | 23.7 | 27.3 | 34.1 | 42.4 | 24.6 | 29.5 | 29.1 | 32.0 | 51.3 |
| Machinery and motor veh. | 12.2 | 22.7 | 32.3 | 34.4 | 36.6 | 39.3 | 44.2 | 55.7 | 65.0 | 71.9 | 77.7 | 84.3 |
| Crops | 7.6 | 7.7 | 10.9 | 10.7 | 11.8 | 14.5 | 22.1 | 23.3 | 21.3 | 22.0 | 24.9 | 27.4 |
| Household equipment | 8.6 | 9.6 | 9.8 | 10.3 | 10.8 | 11.9 | 12.3 | 14.0 | 14.2 | 14.4 | 16.4 | 19.2 |
| Total physical assets | 116.6 | 185.9 | 283.4 | 294.1 | 318.0 | 360.4 | 446.3 | 486.1 | 546.9 | 621.2 | 676.8 | 781.7 |
| Deposits and currency | 9.1 | 9.2 | 11.9 | 12.4 | 13.2 | 14.0 | 14.9 | 15.1 | 15.6 | 16.0 | 16.3 | 16.8 |
| U.S. savings bonds | 4.7 | 4.7 | 3.7 | 3.6 | 3.7 | 4.0 | 4.2 | 4.3 | 4.4 | 4.4 | 4.4 | 4.8 |
| Investment in co-ops. | 2.1 | 4.2 | 7.2 | 8.0 | 8.8 | 9.7 | 10.8 | 12.1 | 13.3 | 14.2 | 15.5 | 16.9 |
| Total financial assets | 15.9 | 18.1 | 22.8 | 39.6 | 25.7 | 27.7 | 29.9 | 31.5 | 33.3 | 34.6 | 36.2 | 38.5 |
| Total assets | $132.5 | $204.0 | $306.2 | $333.7 | $343.7 | $388.1 | $476.2 | $517.6 | $580.2 | $655.8 | $713.0 | $820.2 |
| **LIABILITIES AND EQUITY** | | | | | | | | | | | | |
| Real estate debt | $ 5.6 | $ 12.1 | $ 29.2 | $ 30.3 | $ 32.2 | $ 35.8 | $ 41.3 | $ 46.3 | $ 51.1 | $ 56.7 | $ 63.7 | $ 72.3 |
| Land Banks | .9 | 2.3 | 6.7 | 7.1 | 7.9 | 9.1 | 10.9 | 13.4 | 16.0 | 18.5 | 21.4 | 24.6 |
| FmHA | .2 | .7 | 2.3 | 2.4 | 2.6 | 2.8 | 3.0 | 3.2 | 3.4 | 3.7 | 4.0 | 4.1 |
| Life insurance cos. | 1.2 | 2.2 | 5.7 | 5.6 | 5.6 | 5.6 | 6.0 | 6.3 | 6.7 | 7.4 | 8.8 | 10.2 |
| Banks | .9 | 1.5 | 3.5 | 3.8 | 4.2 | 4.8 | 5.5 | 6.0 | 6.3 | 6.8 | 7.8 | 8.6 |
| Individuals and others | 2.4 | 4.7 | 11.0 | 11.4 | 11.9 | 13.4 | 15.9 | 17.4 | 18.7 | 20.3 | 21.7 | 24.8 |
| Other debt | 6.8 | 12.8 | 23.9 | 24.2 | 27.0 | 29.6 | 32.8 | 35.6 | 39.8 | 46.1 | 55.6 | 65.2 |
| Banks | 2.0 | 4.8 | 10.3 | 11.1 | 12.5 | 14.3 | 17.2 | 18.2 | 20.2 | 23.3 | 25.7 | 28.3 |
| P.C.A.s | .4 | 1.4 | 4.5 | 5.3 | 6.1 | 6.6 | 7.9 | 9.6 | 10.8 | 12.2 | 13.5 | 15.0 |
| Other held by | | | | | | | | | | | | |
| FICBs | .1 | .1 | .2 | .2 | .2 | .3 | .3 | .4 | .4 | .4 | .4 | .5 |
| FmHA | .3 | .4 | .8 | .8 | .8 | .8 | .9 | 1.1 | 1.8 | 1.9 | 3.1 | 5.8 |
| CCC | 1.7 | 1.2 | 2.7 | 1.9 | 2.3 | 1.8 | .8 | .3 | .3 | 1.0 | 4.5 | 5.2 |
| Nonreporting creditors | 2.3 | 4.9 | 5.3 | 4.8 | 5.0 | 5.8 | 5.9 | 6.0 | 6.3 | 7.3 | 8.4 | 10.4 |
| Total liabilities | $ 12.4 | $ 24.8 | $ 53.0 | $ 54.4 | $ 59.1 | $ 65.3 | $ 74.1 | $ 81.9 | $ 90.9 | $102.8 | $119.3 | $137.5 |
| Equity | $120.1 | $179.2 | $253.2 | $279.3 | $284.6 | $322.8 | $402.1 | $435.7 | $489.3 | $553.0 | $573.7 | $682.7 |
| Debt-to-asset ratio | 9.4% | 12.2% | 17.3% | 16.3% | 17.2% | 16.8% | 15.6% | 15.8% | 15.7% | 15.7% | 16.7% | 16.8% |

[a]Data are for January 1 of each year.

Source: U.S. Department of Agriculture, Economic Research Service, *Balance Sheet of the Farming Sector*.

Another fundamental characteristic of agricultural finance revealed by Table 15-3 is that the overwhelming majority of assets are financed by equity rather than by credit. Only 16.8 percent of assets were financed by debt at the beginning of 1979. By way of contrast, only about 50 percent of the assets of manufacturing corporations were financed by stockholders at the end of 1979. One reason for this difference is that farmers can invest through their own direct labor in clearing land, adding buildings, and expanding livestock herds. Another possible explanation is that farmers have less favorable access to credit markets.

The debt-to-asset ratios reported in Table 15-3 have not been constant through time. The ratio rose rapidly between 1950 and 1970 (actually, it reached a peak in the late 1960s) before declining somewhat to its present level. The impressive increase before 1970 is easy to explain, but what accounts for the later decrease? The likely explanation is found in the rapid inflation of the 1970s. The value of farm land, the most important asset of the sector, rose so fast that farmers could not borrow enough to keep up! This suggests that the financial strength and borrowing capacity of agriculture are very favorable, in contrast to the widespread view that insists that farmers are treated as second-class citizens by financial institutions.

These figures might cause one to wonder why so much is made of the agriculture credit problem when the sector seems to rely so little on outside financing. Part of the answer lies in the tendency of outsiders to provide the *marginal* dollar. Farmers traditionally have borrowed only when they had to, when some critical need such as a major capital improvement could not be adequately financed from internal sources. Under such conditions, the 15–20 percent financed externally is of vital importance to the industry.

Furthermore, the balance sheet for the sector as a whole obscures the fact that many individual cases may differ radically from the average. Past surveys of agricultural finance have shown that farms with debt tend to be larger in terms of assets and sales than farms without debt. Most of the farm debt is owed by relatively few of the borrowers.[6]

Table 15-4 provides information about the finances of large farms. At the beginning of 1978, the large operations had, on the average, a debt ratio of 19.5 percent, above the 16.7 percent for all farms. It is also interesting to note that these large farms owed 38.7 percent of all farm debt.

### Demand for Credit

It seems that farm debt is concentrated in the hands of relatively few borrowers, and the borrowers are the larger and more productive members of the industry. Thus, the ability of the financial system to provide credit to agriculture is a far more important issue than is suggested by aggregate data.

Furthermore, it seems likely that agriculture, especially its larger units, will become increasingly dependent on credit for financing. There are several reasons for this. Foremost, no doubt, is the technological revolution described earlier. The replacement of labor by other inputs brings the farmer into closer contact with the financial system. Much farm labor can be supplied directly by the farmer and the farm family without incurring financial outflows. On the other hand, pesticides, fertilizer, machinery, and other important inputs cannot be produced directly on the farm. As a result, they must be purchased from the outside, creating a cash outflow. Such purchases create a need for intermediate-term (one-to-five-year) credit, for the production and sale of the output thus generated occur one to five years after the expenditures for the inputs.

The reduced use of home-produced food and fiber has also increased the dependence of farmers on financial transactions. Purchase of basic consumption goods from the outside establishes competing uses for the cash flow of the enterprise.

The farmer's dependence on the weather has always encouraged the use of credit. Most crops are seasonal in nature, requiring heavy outlays in the spring when the ground is prepared for planting,

---

[6]J. H. Atkinson, "A New Look at the Farm Debt Picture," *Federal Reserve Bulletin* (December 1962),

summarizes the 1960 Sample Survey of Agriculture. The surveys of 1960, 1966, and 1970 are compared in J. Bruce Hotel, Robert D. Reinsel, and William D. Crowley, "Debt Status of U.S. Farm Operators and Landlords by Economic Class, 1960, 1966, 1970," *Agricultural Finance Review* (April 1976).

**Table 15-4  Comparative Balance Sheets of "Large" Farms[a] and All Farms (in billions of dollars)**

|  | January 1, 1963 | | January 1, 1974 | | January 1, 1978 | |
|---|---|---|---|---|---|---|
|  | "Large" Farms | All Farms | "Large" Farms | All Farms | "Large" Farms | All Farms |
| **ASSETS** | | | | | | |
| Real estate | $35.9 | $144.3 | $ 72.2 | $325.3 | $176.2 | $525.8 |
| Livestock and poultry | 4.2 | 17.3 | 12.9 | 42.4 | 11.5 | 32.0 |
| Machinery and motor vehicles | 4.8 | 23.5 | 7.2 | 44.2 | 22.2 | 77.7 |
| Crops | 2.3 | 9.3 | 3.6 | 22.1 | 10.1 | 24.9 |
| Household equipment | 1.1 | 9.0 | 2.6 | 13.3 | 3.2 | 16.5 |
| Total physical assets | 48.3 | 203.4 | 98.5 | 447.3 | 223.2 | 676.8 |
| Deposits and currency | 2.9 | 9.2 | 4.9 | 14.9 | 5.4 | 16.3 |
| U.S. savings bonds | .6 | 4.4 | .9 | 4.2 | 0.7 | 4.4 |
| Investments in co-ops. | 1.9 | 5.1 | 4.2 | 9.5 | 7.4 | 15.5 |
| Total financial assets | 5.4 | 18.7 | 10.0 | 28.6 | 13.5 | 36.2 |
| Total assets | $53.7 | $222.0 | $108.5 | $475.9 | $236.7 | $713.0 |
| **LIABILITIES AND EQUITY** | | | | | | |
| Real estate debt | $ 3.6 | $ 15.2 | $ 14.9 | $ 41.3 | $ 23.5 | $ 63.6 |
| Other debt: CCC | .6 | 2.1 | .1 | .8 | 1.7 | 4.5 |
| Other debt: excluding CCC | 5.1 | 14.2 | 14.8 | 32.1 | 21.0 | 51.1 |
| Total liabilities | $ 9.3 | $ 31.5 | $ 29.8 | $ 74.1 | $ 46.2 | $119.3 |
| Equity | $44.4 | $190.6 | $ 78.8 | $401.8 | $190.5 | $593.7 |
| Debt-to-asset ratio | 17.3% | 14.1% | 27.4% | 15.6% | 19.52% | 16.73% |

[a]"Large" farms in 1963 and 1974 are those that rank in the top 4.1 percent in terms of sales. In 1963, this included all farms with sales in excess of $40,000; in 1974, all farms with sales in excess of $100,000. In 1978 this category included all farms with sales of $100,000 and over.

Source: U.S. Department of Agriculture, Economic Research Service, *Balance Sheet of the Farming Sector.*

and producing cash inflows primarily during a short harvesting season. Farmers are heavily dependent on seasonal financing to bridge the gap between their peak revenues and expenses. Recent developments in agriculture are likely to increase the need for seasonal financing: highly mechanized operations tend to specialize in one or two crops. Reduction of the seasonal patterns through output diversification is less likely.

Another matter of considerable importance in farm finance is the transfer of farms from one owner to another. Few new owners are able to purchase their farms without substantial outside financing. Table 15-5 presents data on the number of transfers of ownership per 1,000 farms, with detailed information on the cause of the transfers.

The number of farms that have changed hands because of foreclosures of mortgage loans has declined steadily since the Great Depression, as has the number of farms transferred through tax sales. This trend obviously reflects the generally improved financial health among the survivors in the industry. Voluntary transfers, on the other hand, exhibit a pronounced tendency to increase during periods of economic prosperity and decrease during

recessions. A postwar peak was recorded in 1974, a year of unprecedented prosperity in agriculture. These fluctuations are still another example of the tendency, noted earlier, for the migration of farmers out of the industry and the consolidation of their holdings into larger units to slow down during economic downturns.

The level of "Other sales" also has a slight procyclical variation. This category includes many intergenerational transfers, and the data do not do justice to the problems such transfers create in agricultural finance. Most farms are not corporations and suffer the same problems as other proprietorships and partnerships in providing for orderly change in ownership. By the time the farmer's successor has paid the inheritance tax and bought out the co-heirs, he will be saddled with a substantial debt even if the previous owner had managed to rid the farm of debt in his own lifetime. Thus, the process of changing operators of a farm requires repeated use of external financing. This has always been one of the more vexatious pressures on farm finance, and it is likely to become more of a problem. As farms increase in size, it will become more difficult for an operator to liquidate all debt within

**Table 15-5   Farm Ownership Transfers, 1930–1978**

| | Number of Transfers per Thousand Farms | | | | |
|------|-----------|-------------|-----------|-------------------------|-------|
| | *Voluntary* | *Foreclosures* | *Tax Sales* | *Other Sales*[a] | *Total* |
| 1930 | 23.7 | 15.7 | 5.1 | 17.0 | 61.5 |
| 1940 | 30.3 | 12.5 | 3.3 | 16.7 | 62.8 |
| 1950 | 37.0 | 1.4 | .4 | 13.4 | 52.2 |
| 1960 | 30.7 | 1.6 | .6 | 14.2 | 47.1 |
| 1970 | 27.8 | 1.6 | — | 12.0 | 41.4 |
| 1974 | 41.2 | .9 | — | 16.2 | 58.3 |
| 1975 | 32.3 | 1.3 | — | 14.2 | 47.8 |
| 1976 | 28.1 | 1.5 | — | 13.1 | 42.7 |
| 1977 | 28.0 | 1.4 | — | 13.6 | 43.0 |
| 1978 | 26.9 | 2.0 | — | 12.8 | 41.7 |

[a]Includes inheritances and gifts, administrators' and executors' sales, and miscellaneous or unclassified sales.

Source: U.S. Department of Agriculture, *Agricultural Statistics.*

a lifetime. The possibility of a permanent debt suggests the use of the corporate form of organization. Relief from the inheritance tax is also a possibility.

Some indication of the magnitude of agriculture's need for credit is given by Table 15-3. Between 1950 and 1979, real estate debt in the farm sector rose $66.7 billion, with $22.1 billion occurring in the last three years. Non–real-estate debt grew $58.4 billion over this period, of which $25.4 billion came in the last three years. The debt-to-asset ratio rose from 9.4 percent to 16.8 percent. The magnitude of agriculture's immediate past and probable future credit needs has caused many observers to become concerned about the burden of farm debts. Is the sector threatening to outstrip its capacity to service debt? Of course, pessimists have questioned the wisdom of the borrowing tendencies of the entire economy for many years, and nothing disastrous has happened yet. In the case of agriculture, the increase in debt has been especially large while farm incomes have grown relatively slowly. The concern about ability to repay debt seems more to the point for that sector, and the question deserves some study.

A farmer's capacity to service debt derives basically from three sources: farm income, off-farm income, and unrealized capital gains on farm assets. The first is the best known, and those who predict trouble for farm debt often consider this source alone. Certainly, farm income has not been robust in recent years. Since 1950, total liabilities of the sector have increased more than tenfold (from $12.4 billion to $137.5 billion), while farm income has increased only slightly (from $14.1 bil-

lion in 1950 to $18.3 billion in 1977).[7] Another measure of debt capacity, the rate of return on equity, presents a similar picture. Table 15-6 shows the ratio of income to equity since 1960. While returns have improved substantially following 1960, they are not comparable to those found in other lines of business. It is not very likely that the unusual set of circumstances that pushed up farm incomes in 1973 will recur. It should be emphasized, of course, that average rates of return do not necessarily reflect returns to the larger farms,

**Table 15-6   Ratio of Income to Equity in Agriculture (percentages)**

| *Year* | *Ratio* |
|--------|---------|
| 1960 | 2.7% |
| 1965 | 4.5 |
| 1970 | 3.5 |
| 1971 | 3.4 |
| 1972 | 5.2 |
| 1973 | 10.1 |
| 1974 | 6.5 |
| 1975 | 5.6 |
| 1976 | 3.8 |
| 1977 | 3.7 |

Source: U.S. Department of Agriculture, *Balance Sheet of Agriculture.*

[7]The income figure is somewhat misleading, for the 1977 income is shared by far fewer farms. The decrease in the number of farms has allowed income per farm to almost quadruple (from $2,417 in 1950 to $11,772 in 1978). The picture is more favorable, but the ratio of income-to-debt still falls. Data are taken from the *Economic Report of the President,* U.S. Government Printing Office, Washington, D.C., 1979.

which are the ones that borrow the most and produce the most output. It is likely that rates of return to these farms are comparable to those earned in other lines of business, and no recourse to "psychic income" is needed to explain the continued existence of a substantial farm sector.

Off-farm earnings by farmers have become increasingly important to the total income of farm families and is a factor in agriculture's ability to bear its debt load. Since 1950, off-farm income has more than tripled, and today it is nearly 50 percent of total personal income received by the farm population. This has to be good news for lenders, for not only is total income raised, but income stability is improved by off-farm income. Actually, this income is all that keeps many small farms in business. As one would expect, it is much more important to small farmers than to large ones.

Capital gains on farm assets is often overlooked as a source of support for debt, but it is difficult to overestimate its importance. It is not hard to see why rising values help potential borrowers; real estate is frequently pledged as collateral for loans, and assets are security for liabilities, even if they are not specifically pledged. It is not difficult to prove that asset values, especially land values, have increased enormously in recent years. According to Table 15-3, the value of farm real estate has risen from $75.3 billion to $599.5 billion between 1950 and 1979. Table 15-2 shows that the physical quantity of land in farms has actually declined slightly during that time. Thus, more than 100 percent of the increased value is due to rising prices of land. The result is confirmed by data on land prices, given in Table 15-7. In 1950 the price index was 41.5 (1967 = 100), and by 1978 it had soared to 308. The rate of inflation was in excess of 7 percent per year. If this rate is added to the returns on equity shown in Table 15-5, the yields on investment in agriculture look more respectable. It is also interesting to note that the $524 billion increase in the book value of farm real estate between 1950 and 1979 was greater than the total income received by farmers from farm operations throughout that period. It is these figures, more than anything else, that show agriculture's financial strength to be greater than one would suspect if one considered only the income data.

It may seem paradoxical that the value of farm land should rise sharply while farm income lags behind income available in other sectors of the economy. In theory, the value of an asset should be the present value of the income earned from that asset. If income is depressed, asset values should be depressed. A number of factors are probably at work pushing up the value of farm land. General price inflation, fueled by inflationary monetary and fiscal policies, will affect all asset values, including farm land. The long-range outlook for farm income is not particularly bleak, as explained at the beginning of the chapter, and these expectations may be capitalized into farm land prices. Off-farm income also increases the purchasing power of farm families. Government programs to raise and stabilize farm income may be capitalized. Urban expansion may have a marginal effect, but relatively few farm areas are in the path of such expansion. More important may be the purchase of marginal farm land by urbanites seeking a place to "get away from it all." Technical change in farm production and the consequent rise in the optimum size of farms has been suggested as a possible cause, but consolidation of farms into larger units does not automatically increase the net demand for land. It is true that efficient operators need more land, but inefficient operators leaving the industry do not need land at all. However, some empirical studies have indicated that consolidation is indeed a factor in the rising prices of land.[8]

The relationship between prices paid by farmers and prices received has always been a bellwether of the state of the farm economy. In late 1972 the index of prices received moved ahead of that for prices paid, indicating that farmers enjoyed good profit margins in the mid-1970s. If these trends had continued, income from farm operations would have contributed to the debt capacity of agriculture. Unfortunately for farmers, these favorable trends did not last very long.

## Supply of Credit

Is the present system for supplying funds to agriculture adequate for accommodating the continuing changes in the farm sector? Dissatisfaction with the

[8] For a brief discussion of these models, see Marvin Duncan, "Farm Real Estate Values—Some Important Determinants," *Monthly Review,* Federal Reserve Bank of Kansas City (March 1977).

**Table 15-7   Farm Indices, 1930–1978**

| Year | Plant and Equipment Prices | Land Prices | Livestock Prices | Output | Income | Prices Paid | Prices Received |
|------|---------------------------|-------------|------------------|--------|--------|-------------|-----------------|
| 1930 | 26.2 | 26.0 | 35.4 | 36.3 | 34.3 | N.A. | N.A. |
| 1940 | 29.4 | 19.0 | 28.8 | 29.8 | 28.2 | N.A. | N.A. |
| 1950 | 55.5 | 41.5 | 75.6 | 76.2 | 78.3 | N.A. | N.A. |
| 1960 | 68.3 | 68.5 | 68.7 | 73.2 | 65.2 | 88 | 94 |
| 1970 | 94.9 | 118.5 | 87.8 | 87.0 | 83.5 | 112 | 110 |
| 1971 | 99.7 | 124.5 | 86.2 | 89.3 | 80.6 | 120 | 113 |
| 1972 | 104.5 | 136.5 | 100.0 | 100.0 | 100.0 | 125 | 125 |
| 1973 | 114.9 | 160.0 | 134.9 | 143.7 | 161.0 | 144 | 179 |
| 1974 | 131.2 | 196.0 | 122.0 | 146.8 | 141.1 | 164 | 192 |
| 1975 | 144.3 | 220.5 | 127.2 | 148.6 | 141.9 | 180 | 185 |
| 1976 | 176.0 | 254.5 | 70.7 | 150.8 | 120.5 | 191 | 186 |
| 1977 | 200.6 | 289.5 | 85.0 | 159.2 | 129.1 | 202 | 183 |
| 1978 | 217.0[a] | 308.0[a] | N.A. | 183.4 | 166.6 | N.A. | N.A. |

N.A. = Not Available.
[a]Preliminary

Sources: U.S. Department of Agriculture, *Agricultural Statistics*; *Survey of Current Business*.

system is a venerable tradition in U.S. politics, having been expressed by agrarian movements over the last century. Federal government activity in these credit markets appeared early and continues to play a significant role in farm finance. Before we describe the credit system, a few special characteristics of agriculture that present opportunities and problems to potential lenders require attention.

A major problem to lenders arises from the size of farms. Most farms are very small, a few are very large, and the industry seems to be moving from a small-unit system to a large-unit one. Each of these factors creates a headache for lenders. Because most farms are small, much of the industry shares many of the typical financing problems faced by small business in general. Loans to such units are usually small in size, and since costs are no different for small loans than for large, either interest rates must be comparatively high or the net profits per dollar of loan will be comparatively small. Even more important is the fact that a small business may be an unknown entity to a lender. The skill of the entrepreneur as technician, salesperson, and financial manager is of paramount importance, but it can be ascertained by the prospective lender only on the basis of personal contacts. What is more, since the personal finances of a single proprietor cannot always be separated from his business finances, knowledge of at least part of the borrower's personal affairs is unavoidable. Thus, if a small borrower applies for a loan to finance inventory,

the lender must be able to determine whether the proceeds will be used for the stated purpose or diverted to personal use. Even if such personal knowledge is available, this inseparability of the farmer's household and business affairs makes evaluation of the latter difficult.

These characteristics encouraged a financial system consisting primarily of small lenders operating on the basis of close personal contacts. The system worked reasonably well, for farmers could rely on their lenders to offer flexible arrangements with a minimum of formality. The danger was that credit activities tended to be confined to the one or two institutions with which the requisite personal relationship had been established. Such a system exhibited little competition among lenders and did nothing to encourage innovation. It was also likely to be ill-prepared for major changes in the structure of agriculture.

A financial system designed to serve small borrowers is bound to have many problems meeting the needs of large operators. Many lenders lack the resources needed to finance a modern, highly efficient operation. A more serious problem is that the old way of doing things made many lenders insufficiently flexible to cope with or take advantage of economic change.[9] But, in a market economy, if established institutions do not adjust, new ones will

[9]One example of this was revealed by the 1966 survey of bank loans to agriculture. Only one-third of the rural

take their place. To some extent, this has happened in agricultural finance. We will discuss these changes later.

The weather creates special difficulties for agricultural lenders. In addition to requiring special seasonal financial arrangements, uncertainties caused by weather increase risk. If normal weather patterns are interrupted by drought, floods, hail, or other abnormalities, expected revenues may fail to materialize. The lender must be prepared at the very least to carry a seasonal debt through another growing season—and must face the possibility that the farmer will be unable to repay at all. The fragmentation of the loan market into numerous small lending areas compounds this problem. An institution serving a small geographical area will find that the soundness of all its loans depends on the same general set of circumstances. If these circumstances prove unfavorable, the lending institution can be put in financial jeopardy and this may throw the entire local financial system into disarray. Fortunately, the increasing size and complexity of financial affairs in agriculture has forced a gradual breakdown in the barriers that have prevented free flow of farm credit from one section of the country to another. Competition from federal agencies has also been a factor in creating a national credit market for agriculture.

Inelastic demand for farm products coupled with erratic supply shifts generate more severe price fluctuations than those ordinarily faced by other industries. Because the industry is competitive rather than oligopolistic, farmers are not in a position to mitigate these fluctuations by means of tacit collusion on output and price decisions.[10] This situation can lead to serious financial reverses if output prices fall after farmers have committed themselves to production at high input prices. Rational planning of production and its financing, therefore, is difficult.

Agriculture requires long-term mortgage financing because of the increasing pressure to enlarge farms despite rising land prices. The necessity of acquiring expensive and long-lived capital equipment adds to the burden. Because a farm requires a long time to earn the money to repay these debts, farm mortgages tend to carry longer maturities than do mortgages in other economic sectors. This presents a difficult problem to lenders: the low income-to-debt ratio of a newly financed farm further increases the risk faced by creditors.

All of these special requirements and problems force lenders to acquire a thorough knowledge of the farm business. Given that conditions vary substantially in different parts of the country, extensive understanding of local conditions is mandatory. This presented no particular problem as long as most farms were small enough to be served by local lending institutions that were prepared to do business on the basis of close personal relationships. However, as farms and their credit needs have grown, they have strained the capabilities of the old system. Unfortunately, they were not quite ready to enter the national money markets either. Most nationwide financial institutions prefer to deal in large transactions on an impersonal basis and avoid loans requiring them to serve a large group of small- to medium-sized borrowers with a host of special characteristics. Both private and government-supported lending institutions are adjusting to the new financial needs of agriculture. The federal government has taken the lead in these developments, and its role in agriculture has expanded enormously. While it is true that most federal agencies were established to subsidize farm borrowing, another important purpose was, and continues to be, to end the dependence of the farmer on local financial sources.

We are now ready to examine the specific institutions supplying credit to agriculture. It is convenient to separate mortgage lending from short-term lending, as is done in Table 15-3.

*Sources of Mortgage Credit* The major suppliers of farm mortgage credit, in order of their importance as of the beginning of 1979, were individuals and others (34 percent of total mortgage credit), Federal Land Banks (34 percent), life insurance companies (14 percent), commercial banks (12 percent), and the Farmers Home Administration or

---

banks were paying the maximum allowable rate on passbook savings accounts, while one-half of all banks did. Those rural banks that acknowledged difficulty in meeting loan requests did not pay significantly higher rates than those that did not. Evidently, many banks were not making a serious effort to expand loan capacity. See ''Bank Financing of Agriculture,'' *Federal Reserve Bulletin* (June 1967).

[10]Government support for farm prices is partly designed to provide this capability to agriculture.

FmHA, (6 percent).[11] The relative importance of these institutions has changed considerably over the years. In 1919, individuals held roughly 69 percent of all farm mortgages, banks and insurance companies about 14.5 percent each, and Federal Land Banks the rest. The Depression occasioned a considerable redistribution of mortgage holdings from private lenders to the federal government. Insurance companies held their own; unlike banks and individuals, they were not dependent on local conditions for their own financial health. But the share of individuals and others fell to 34 percent, and that of banks to about 10 percent. The slack was taken up by federal agencies, whose share rose to over 40 percent. These agencies were heavily involved in refinancing farm debt in an effort to keep the farm sector from being devastated by the economic conditions of the times.

With the advent of war and postwar prosperity, farmers repaid much of their debt to the federal agencies, and borrowed mainly from private sources. This occurred primarily because, at that time, the private lenders had more flexible lending arrangements. Another possible reason may have been that the federal programs were initially established to relieve distress. Many farmers may have felt the need to liquidate these loans in order to prove to others—and to themselves—that they no longer required government assistance. In any case, the share of farm mortgages held by government agencies (mainly Federal Land Banks and the Farmers Home Administration) fell to just under 20 percent by 1950. Individuals and others held 42.9 percent, life insurance companies 21.4 percent, and banks 16.1 percent.[12] Since then, the government's share has risen substantially, mainly at the expense of insurance companies and individuals. A closer look at each of the lender types may reveal some reasons for the changes in market shares.

Most mortgage loans made by individuals involve direct financing of the buyer by the seller of the land. The usual reason for the arrangement is the inability of the buyer to come up with a down payment large enough to satisfy an institutional lender. Most sellers are willing to accept deferred payment if the alternative is no sale at all. The arrangement may take the form of a second mortgage, with the first mortgage held by an institution, or full financing by the seller. Land contracts, with the seller holding title until enough payments have been made to furnish a down payment for a standard mortgage, are common. They reduce risk for the seller and can spread the profits on the sale over enough years to make an appreciable difference in his or her capital gains tax. The seller also has the advantage of keeping some of the money invested at a favorable rate of interest. Unless financial institutions drastically change their lending standards, seller financing will always be a major source of farm mortgage credit. On the other hand, the changes in the structure of agriculture are making farm loans more attractive to institutions, and their share is likely to increase somewhat.

The second-ranking supplier of farm mortgages, the Federal Land Bank System, is part of a larger organization called the cooperative Farm Credit System. The System includes twelve Federal Land Banks, twelve Federal Intermediate Credit Banks, twelve Banks for Cooperatives, and a Central Bank for Cooperatives. The country is divided into twelve Farm Credit districts, each of which contains one of the three institutions. The System is supervised and examined by the Farm Credit Administration, an independent agency of the federal government. The System is financed primarily by borrowings from the public; the funds raised are disbursed through loans to the farm sector.[13]

The Federal Land Banks provide loans secured by first mortgages on farm and rural real estate to borrowers whose eligibility is established by law. Farmers and ranchers, rural residents,[14] and farm-related businesses are eligible. Maturities are from 5 to 40 years, the amount may be up to 85 percent of the market value of the property used as security, and rates are set according to the interest costs borne by the land banks. The banks are experimenting with variable-rate mortgages, contracts that allow the interest rate on a loan to be raised or lowered during the life of the loan as market rates change. Since the banks are privileged borrowers in the financial markets, interest costs can

---

[11]Table 15-3.
[12]Table 15-3.

[13]The components of the Farm Credit System are federally sponsored agencies. Their finances are discussed in Chapter 11. See also the annual reports of the System.
[14]Each land bank may have up to 15 percent of its loan volume outstanding in mortgages on rural homes.

be lower than those required by private lenders. It is not unusual for farmers to borrow from a private lender and refinance with a land bank as soon as they meet the eligibility requirements. The lower rates and longer maturities are attractive to borrowers. The land banks' loan maturities are the longest in the industry; in fact they originated the long-term, amortized mortgage loan. Their flexibility and willingness to experiment with new programs and procedures would make them a major factor in real estate lending even without federal sponsorship and backing.

The land banks do not deal directly with farmers. Instead, they work through some 550 local organizations called Federal Land Bank Associations. These associations are credit cooperatives: they are owned and operated by their farmer-borrowers. Each borrower is required to buy stock in the association, and is given an equal voice with all other borrowers in the association's affairs, including one vote in the selection of the board of directors.[15] The associations, like the land banks, are nonprofit organizations and are authorized to distribute in the form of dividends all earnings not accumulated into loss reserves. They are also exempt from all income taxation. As federally chartered institutions they are exempt from state usury laws, a privilege which gave them an enormous advantage over private lenders when credit was tight. This advantage came to an end when Congress and some states enacted remedial legislation in 1974.

In general, Federal Land Bank Associations behave like private lenders. They are managed by professionals, and they make loans only to sound credit risks after an independent appraisal of the property to be mortgaged.[16] Though they are nonprofit, they are expected to pay their own expenses. They are not in business to subsidize marginal or submarginal borrowers, but to tap the national credit markets and channel the money to agriculture on a sound business basis. It has been presumed, of course, that the private credit system has for some reason been unwilling to do this. Later

we will discuss the impact of this and other federally sponsored credit agencies on farm finance.

Once the dominant institutional lender in the farm mortgage market, life insurance companies have sharply curtailed their role. The basic reason is that they have no fundamental commitment to farm lending, and competing uses of funds have proven more attractive. Farm mortgages never were a large part of insurance companies' investment portfolios; in 1978 they represented less than 3 percent of the total investments of the companies.[17] Insurance companies hold these mortgages because they have reasonable yields given their risk and they are useful for diversifying financial investment portfolios. If yields are higher elsewhere, as they were before relief from state usury ceilings was obtained, insurance firms will move funds out of agricultural lending. Unlike land bank associations or commercial banks, insurance companies have no regulatory or geographic reasons to remain in farm lending. In addition, when high market interest rates increase the demand for low-interest policy loans, insurance companies must obtain funds from somewhere to meet these obligations. Compared to commercial or multifamily projects, farm loans have a short lead time between loan commitment and loan disbursement. Thus, it is relatively easy to curtail farm loans.

Because farm mortgage loans are desirable investments, it is likely that insurance companies will always play a significant role in that market. However, the nature of these loans and of the companies will impart special characteristics to the companies' activities. One problem is that insurance companies, unlike other institutional lenders, do not have loan offices in the field. As a result, they tend to concentrate on large loans made to the more substantial operators. They also rely on locally based institutions to act as brokers on their behalf. This gives the local institutions an opportunity to meet the needs of borrowers whose financial requirements are too large for the local bank to handle.

---

[15]Rural home borrowers purchase nonvoting certificates, not stock. The aim is to keep control of the associations in the hands of bona fide farmers.

[16]Although the associations approve and service the loans, the land banks disburse the funds and hold the mortgage notes.

[17]Board of Governors of the Federal Reserve System, *Flow of Funds Accounts, 1949–1978*; American Bankers Association, *Agricultural Lending: Sources of Funds*. Though farm mortgage loans are a small part of total lending by insurance companies, the companies are still the third-ranking supplier, with 13.6 percent of total farm mortgages.

Because of these characteristics, as well as the need for specialized personnel if a major effort in this market is to be undertaken, most agricultural loans held by insurance companies are concentrated in the hands of a few companies. About 87 percent of all farm mortgage loans outstanding are held by eight companies.[18]

Commercial banks have traditionally concentrated their lending on short maturities. They do make mortgage loans, but rarely do maturities exceed 15 years. The short maturities prevent the amounts from being very large; the average mortgage loan made by a bank is smaller than that made by any other lender group.[19] The small amounts make it difficult for banks to finance acquisitions of entire farms. Most of their loans are for "add-on" acreage, that is, purchase of additional land by an ongoing operation. Further discussion of bank lending to agriculture will be deferred to the section on short-term credit.

The Farmers Home Administration is part of the U.S. Department of Agriculture. It has become a major factor in credit markets; recent legislation has broadened its scope far beyond farm business. It is a significant factor in rural housing and also provides development loans. Its farmer-oriented programs include long-term mortgage loans as well as short- and intermediate-term production loans. Although it is the least significant mortgage lender in agriculture, its activities are important to those it does serve. FmHA is the only lender that offers subsidized credit. Maturities are long, up to 40 years, and interest rates are below market rates. Access to its credit is limited to those who are unable to obtain funds from another source on reasonable terms. It is especially attractive to the beginning farmers and to those operating marginal family farms. A loan limit of $100,000 ensures that only small operators will be able to use FmHA as a credit source. If farmers prosper, they are expected to seek financing from conventional sources. For this reason, FmHA is not truly a competitor for private lenders.

FmHA also guarantees loans made by private sources. The guarantee enables borrowers, who would not normally be able to do so, to obtain private credit. The agency prefers guarantees to direct loans since the guarantees involve no cash outflow unless default occurs. Restrictions on access to the program are the same as those for direct loans.

FmHA will participate in loans with private lenders. Each lender may be responsible for its own share of the risk, or on occasion FmHA will agree to subordinate its own claim to that of the private lender. Such arrangements are attractive to private institutions because they enable them to make loans that otherwise would be too risky. The agency's participation, even if not subordinated, reduces risk because of the availability of FmHA personnel to supervise the loan and advise both borrower and lender on technical matters.

A farmer desiring credit from the FmHA may apply at one of the many county offices. The local officials will determine eligibility and disburse the loan. If the borrower would prefer a loan participation, the farmer can apply at a private credit institution and the institution can make arrangements with the federal agency.

*Sources of Short- and Intermediate-term Credit*
The major suppliers of nonmortgage credit, in order of their importance as of the beginning of 1979, were commercial and savings banks (with 43 percent of the total), Production Credit Associations (23 percent), nonreporting lenders—mainly individuals, merchants, and dealers—(16 percent), the Farmers Home Administration (9 percent), private lenders whose loans have been acquired by the Federal Intermediate Credit Banks (1 percent), and the Commodity Credit Corporation (8 percent).[20] As is the case with mortgage debt, the relative importance of these lenders has changed considerably over the years. Before the Depression, banks and nonreporting lenders dominated short-term credit. At that time, the FmHA, the Commodity Credit Corporation, and the Production Credit Associations did not exist; the Federal Intermediate Credit Banks were in their infancy[21] and

[18]American Bankers Association, *Agricultural Lending: Sources of Funds,* Washington, D.C., 1976.

[19]A large loan amount coupled with a short maturity would make the monthly payment too large for most farmers to bear.

[20]Table 15-3.

[21]The FICBs were established in 1923 and the land banks in 1916. PCAs were started in 1933 to encourage use of the FICBs.

were having difficulty getting their programs off the ground. The Depression brought substantial government participation in the market, which was reduced somewhat during the prosperous war and immediate postwar years. In 1950, nonreporting lenders held about a third of the debt, the CCC a quarter, and banks just under 30 percent.[22] In the last twenty-five years, commercial banks and PCAs have increased their share, largely at the expense of nonreporting creditors and the CCC.

Commercial banks have always been a key factor in the supply of short-term credit for agriculture. Most of their loans are for operating expenses and mature annually or, in the case of livestock or other output with a longer production cycle, at the end of the cycle. Banks also supply intermediate-term (1-to-5-year) credit for equipment, livestock, or other needs. They have the advantage of close proximity to their customers, detailed first-hand knowledge of individual businesses and local affairs, and the capacity to offer a wide range of financial services. They are willing to make small loans with very flexible terms suitable for individuals in vastly different circumstances. But banks, too, have their problems, and there is no assurance that they will always dominate short-term credit in agriculture.

Most of the banks' difficulties in meeting farm credit needs arise from their small size. As of December 31, 1975, banks with less than $25 million in deposits held 55.5 percent of all farm real estate loans held by banks and 52.8 percent of the non–real-estate debt held by banks, but controlled only 13.8 percent of total deposits in the System.[23] Many rural banks find their legal loan limits pressed by the needs of the increasingly numerous large farming operations. National banks and nearly all state banks are prohibited from lending more than an amount equal to 10 percent of their capital and surplus to a single borrower. Given that the average capital-to-asset ratio for banks with deposits between $10 million and $25 million is 7.8 percent, even a bank with $25 million in deposits cannot

lend more than $195,000 to a single borrower. The larger farms can easily borrow this much. A $10 million bank can lend only $78,000, an amount that is not large at all by today's standards. Total liabilities of agriculture were $137.5 billion at the beginning of 1979, divided among about 2.4 million farms. The average debt per farm was $57,292. The full debt load of a farm not too much bigger than average would strain the resources of a small bank.

Legal limits aside, the rapid expansion of farm credit demand creates problems for banks. Because they tend to be confined to relatively small geographic areas, their internal lending resources are limited to whatever their community can provide. The general tendency has been for credit demand to grow faster than the lending resources of the banks. The difference is met by liquidation of securities portfolios and increasing loan-to-deposit ratios, but the process cannot continue forever.

Fortunately, commercial banks do have the opportunity to raise funds from outside. Nearly all banks have a correspondent relationship with a large city bank. One aspect of that relationship is the willingness of the large bank to participate in loans that are beyond the resources of the small bank. The small bank originates the loan, makes the appropriate credit checks, and services it for its duration. The correspondent puts up a share of the principal in exchange for a share in the income. Participations may also be arranged with insurance companies, Production Credit Associations, and the Farmers Home Administration. The FmHA can be used only if the borrower meets the standards set by the agency for its programs. A difficulty with life insurance companies, as we have already seen, is their tendency to pull out of the farm credit markets rather abruptly if credit conditions tighten. Correspondent banks may also do this.

Under the Monetary Control Act of 1980, all commercial banks, member and nonmember, may use the Federal Reserve's seasonal borrowing privilege and this may prove helpful. Using this privilege, a bank may obtain credit for 90 days, far beyond the usual maturity of member-bank borrowings. To qualify, a bank must lack access to national money markets and must have an identifiable seasonal pattern of funds flows.

Larger banks are becoming more interested in agricultural loans. In addition to their correspon-

---

[22] Table 15-3.

[23] Federal Deposit Insurance Corporation, *Assets and Liabilities of Commercial and Mutual Savings Banks, December 31, 1975.* See also Mary Hamlin, "Bank Lending to Agriculture," *Monthly Review,* Federal Reserve Bank of Kansas City (November 1975).

dent relationships, they are also making direct loans. Some have established farm-loan subsidiaries in their holding-company systems. Naturally, they are interested in the largest and most creditworthy borrowers. More and more farms are large enough to attract the interest of these banks.

In general, banks are beginning to keep up with the trends in agriculture. They are shedding their stodgy, ultraconservative attitudes and are showing a willingness to meet—and even beat—the increasing competition from government and private sources. If they succeed in tapping national markets for funds while keeping their advantage with respect to local knowledge, they should have no trouble holding their own in farm finance.[24]

Production Credit Associations are the major competition for banks in the short-term loan business for agriculture. PCAs, like Federal Land Bank Associations, are government-sponsored credit cooperatives. Their voting stock is held by farmers and other eligible holders who are active borrowers. The borrowers elect the boards of directors of the associations, which in turn hire professional managers. PCAs are exempt from all income taxes, but they escape the federal income tax only if they return income to farmers in the form of patronage refunds. Though they are nonprofit organizations, their operations are self-supporting. Decisions are made strictly on a businesslike basis, and no subsidized credit is offered.

Production Credit Associations make loans of up to 7 years' maturity. Most are single-payment or amortized, but a few are line-of-credit arrangements. The ability to buy seed, pesticides, fertilizer, feed, and so forth, as needed, without having to draw separate notes for each transaction is a major advantage for borrowers. Line-of-credit financing is used more by larger operations, but PCAs tend to serve larger farms than do commercial banks. Perhaps a reason for that is that there are about 450 PCAs with about four times that number of offices, far fewer than the number of rural banking outlets. PCAs cover a larger territory and are in a better position to select the best credit risks.

Farmers, ranchers, producers and harvesters of aquatic products, rural homeowners, and certain farm-related businesses are eligible to borrow from PCAs. Only 15 percent of loans outstanding can be for rural housing. Most of the loans are for production of agricultural or aquatic products. All borrowers must buy stock in their PCA, but only active borrowers who are farmers, ranchers, or producers or harvesters of aquatic products hold voting stock.

Production Credit Associations are financed primarily by funds advanced from Federal Intermediate Credit Banks. The FICBs, like Federal Land Banks, are part of the Cooperative Farm Credit System and are classified as federally sponsored agencies. They issue their own securities to the public and are financially independent of the federal government. FICBs also discount intermediate-term farm paper held by commercial banks and other lenders. PCAs will participate in loans originated by private lenders. Many banks are reluctant to enter participation agreements with PCAs because the borrower must still buy stock in the PCA. This gives the association an opportunity to win the farmer's entire loan business,[25] which was probably not hard to do before banks obtained partial relief from state usury ceilings in 1974.[26] As federal agencies, PCAs were exempt.

Nonreporting lenders consist mainly of merchants and dealers. Some individuals also provide short-term credit. Suppliers of big-ticket items, such as tractors and other equipment, offer financing arrangements. Many have a captive finance company or an arrangement with a financial institution whereby the institution buys paper originated by the dealers. Suppliers of other goods also offer credit but on a less formal basis. Dealer credit is expensive and tends to attract somewhat less desirable credit risks than does bank or other institutional credit. It is not surprising that nonreporting lenders have declined in importance since 1950. More farmers qualify for credit from institutions, and more are sophisticated enough to seek out such credit.

---

[24]An example of aggressive marketing is the line-of-credit financing system described in *Banking* (April 1974).

[25]American Bankers Association, *Agricultural Lending: Sources of Funds*.

[26]The Financial Amendments Act of 1974 authorized national banks to charge 5 percentage points above the Federal Reserve discount rate on business and agricultural loans of $25,000 or more. Competitive pressures encouraged some states to provide relief for state banks. A similar act was passed in 1979 in response to the high interest rates that year.

The Farmers Home Administration offers short- and intermediate-term credit as well as real estate credit to farmers. As is the case for mortgage loans, FmHA's short- and intermediate-term loans are available only to those unable to obtain credit at reasonable terms from conventional sources. Those who qualify receive a subsidized interest rate. Strict limits on loan size ensure that only family farms benefit from the program.

It is debatable whether the Commodity Credit Corporation is a lending agency at all. It operates the farm price-support program, and its main function is to subsidize the income of farmers. Farmers may apply for a short-term loan, against which they pledge their crops. The crops are valued at the legal support price. The farmers are free to sell the crop in the market and retire the loan, but if market prices do not rise above the support price they may turn the crop over to the CCC with no liability for the deficiency. That the loans are nonrecourse is some justification for not treating CCC operations as credit transactions at all; surely a loan that is repaid only at the option of the borrower deserves different treatment. On the other hand, credit *is* granted by the government, and the subsidy involved in the repayment is fundamentally no different from other subsidized loan operations. In recent years, changes in the price-support program have reduced the subsidy element, and more farmers have repaid in cash.

There is no possibility that the CCC programs could become self-supporting. The agency is part of the U.S. Department of Agriculture, and its expenses are financed by regular appropriations from the Treasury.

*The Role of Government in Farm Credit* Table 15-8 shows the increase in farm debt since 1950 and the proportion of that increase supplied by the government. The federal government has always played a major role in supplying credit to agriculture: if CCC loans are included, the U.S. government has never supplied less than about one-fourth of the total except for short periods. At times the proportion has been over 60 percent. The federal government was a more significant factor in the 1960s than in either the 1950s or 1970s. Much of the difference is due to different government policies in those three decades. The annual data for the 1970s reveal a pronounced cyclical pattern. Dependence on government sources dropped sharply during 1972 and 1973, but rose substantially during the tight-money year of 1974. Evidently, farmers will seek federal credit if private credit is hard to get. It would be easy to conclude that the farm sector would be driven to the brink of insolvency if the federal government did not come to its aid in periods of tight credit.

Chapters 11 and 13 suggested that public credit for housing may have relatively little impact on the housing market. The reasons for this include the tendency of mortgage lenders and their depositors to use money that might go into housing anyway to purchase the securities of the federal credit agencies, the possibility that those who borrow from the government could and would borrow from the

**Table 15-8   U.S. Government's Share of Farm Debt (in billions of dollars)**

|  | Change in Total Debt | Supplied by U.S. incl. CCC | Supplied by CCC | U.S. Share | U.S. Share excl. CCC |
|---|---|---|---|---|---|
| 1950–1960 | $ 6.5 | $ 2.5 | $(0.5) | 38.5% | 42.9% |
| 1960–1970 | 17.1 | 11.0 | 1.5 | 64.3 | 60.1 |
| 1970 | 1.1 | 0.5 | (0.8) | 45.5 | 68.4 |
| 1971 | 4.7 | 2.2 | 0.4 | 46.8 | 41.9 |
| 1972 | 6.2 | 1.5 | (0.5) | 24.2 | 29.9 |
| 1973 | 8.8 | 2.4 | (1.0) | 27.3 | 38.7 |
| 1974 | 7.8 | 4.2 | (0.5) | 53.8 | 60.3 |
| 1975 | 9.0 | 4.7 | 0.0 | 52.2 | 52.2 |
| 1976 | 11.9 | 5.0 | 0.7 | 42.0 | 36.1 |
| 1977 | 16.5 | 9.2 | 3.5 | 55.8 | 34.5 |
| 1978 | 18.2 | 8.3 | 0.7 | 45.6 | 41.8 |

Source: Table 15-3.

private sector if government funds were not available, and the lack of response of the long-run demand for housing to credit conditions. Chapter 11 argued that there are probably no artificial barriers to home mortgage borrowing that could be broken down merely by the introduction of a new credit source. Can the same be said for agriculture?

Unfortunately, no significant empirical studies on the response of the farm sector to government programs exist. A few general comments on the similarities and differences between housing and agriculture are useful. First, the sectors are alike in that most government credit assistance is unsubsidized. This means that little effect can be expected unless artificial barriers to private lending exist. Do they? In the past, when commercial banks dominated institutional lending to agriculture, such barriers may well have existed. The banks were small, operated in a small area with little support from the outside, and enjoyed varying degrees of monopoly power over their markets. It is very possible that the federally assisted agencies provided funds to agriculture that the sector would not have gotten otherwise. Changes in agriculture and in rural banking have brought the sector into the mainstream of our financial markets, and the government agencies may have little marginal impact today. Second, the housing and agriculture sectors share the characteristic of being supported by federally assisted agencies, which issue securities to the public and hope to divert credit from general markets to a specific sector. The farm-related agencies, like the housing-related ones, probably issue securities that appeal most to those who might operate in the sector anyway. But agriculture has one advantage: it is more specialized and more concentrated geographically. Hence, the possibility exists that the sector does not yet have access to *all* sources of funds and that an effort to tap those sources would increase the total funds available to the sector. These issues cannot be resolved in the absence of empirical research, but it does seem possible that agriculture is not yet fully integrated into the financial system and that government efforts to channel funds to it can be successful.

## Conclusion

This review of farm finance reveals that agriculture is increasingly being drawn into the financial mar-

kets. Although about 85 percent of farm assets are financed by equity, the averages presented in Table 15-3 conceal important differences among farms. It appears that external financing is used most heavily by the most dynamic members of this rapidly evolving industry. Therefore, sufficient credit at reasonable cost must be available if the remarkable changes in farm techniques that have already occurred are to proceed smoothly. The capacity of the sector to service debt appears to be adequate. Income from farming has improved in recent years, though returns are low compared to those available in other sectors. The reason for optimism lies in the trend toward off-farm earnings and rising farm real estate values. Inflated values of farm land have substantially increased the borrowing capacity of agriculture. Inflation in the 1970s was rapid enough to cause the debt-to-asset ratio for agriculture to fall.

Will agricultural finance institutions be able to meet the sector's credit needs? Farming is a highly specialized, risky business. This characteristic, plus the small size of the average farm in the past, led to financial arrangements based on personal understandings between borrower and lender. The lenders were small and not particularly dynamic; not all were ready for the transformation of the sector. Government credit institutions were established to tap the national financial markets, and private institutions have learned to do the same thing. At this time farmers have a choice of institutions that cater to somewhat different clientele but that still compete directly with one another. Perhaps it can be said that agricultural finance is finally catching up with agricultural technology.

## Questions

1. What consequences has the technical revolution in agriculture had on agricultural finance?
2. If land and labor inputs into agriculture are declining in absolute terms, why is farm output rising?
3. What percentage of farm assets are financed by farm owners themselves? How does this figure compare with those for other industries? Can you explain the concern about availability of external funding?
4. What factors determine agriculture's capacity to service debt? Are these factors moving in a favorable direction?
5. What factors are likely to increase the need for outside financing for agriculture in the future? Are any

particular lenders likely to be especially favored by these developments?

6. If rates of return on equity are low in agriculture, why are farm land prices rising so rapidly?

7. What are the major sources of short-term and long-term credit to agriculture?

8. Use original sources of data to calculate the percentage of farm credit supplied by government or government-sponsored agencies. What reasons are apparent for recent trends?

9. Why does the decline in agriculture's share of the economy tend to be arrested in economic recessions?

10. Do federal agencies really increase the total amount of credit available to agriculture?

## Selected Bibliography

Amercian Bankers Association. *Agricultural Lending: Sources of Funds*. Washington, D.C., 1976.

Board of Governors of the Federal Reserve System. "A New Look at the Farm Debt Picture." *Federal Reserve Bulletin* (December 1962).

———. "Bank Financing of Agriculture:" *Federal Reserve Bulletin* (June 1967).

———. *Flow of Funds Accounts*. Washington, D.C., 1979.

Council of Economic Advisors. *Economic Report of the President*. Washington, D.C., 1979.

Denison, Edward F. *Why Growth Rates Differ: Postwar Experience in Nine Western Countries*. The Brookings Institution, Washington, D.C., 1967.

Federal Reserve Bank of Kansas City. "The Role of Financial Management in Agriculture." *Monthly Review* (July-August 1972).

———. "A Dispersed or Concentrated Agriculture? The Role of Public Policy." *Monthly Review* (March 1975).

———. "Bank Lending to Agriculture." *Monthly Review* (November 1975).

———. "Farm Real Estate Values—Some Important Determinants." *Monthly Review* (March 1977).

Hotel, J. Bruce, Robert D. Reinsel, and William D. Crowley. "Debt Status of U.S. Farm Operators and Landlords by Economic Class, 1960, 1966, 1970." *Agricultural Finance Review* (April 1976).

U.S. Department of Agriculture. *Agricultural Statistics*.

———. *Balance Sheet of Agriculture*, and *Supplement 1*.

U.S. Department of Commerce. *The National Income and Product Accounts of the United States, 1929–1974*, various issues.

———. *Survey of Current Business*, various issues.

U.S. Farm Credit Administration. *Annual Report of the Farm Credit Administration and the Cooperative Farm Credit System*, 1979.

U.S. Federal Trade Commission. *Quarterly Financial Report for Manufacturing, Mining and Trade*, various issues.

# 16

## Loanable Funds in the State and Local Government Sector

State and local governments borrow for three basic reasons. First, it is often difficult to finance expenditures for real assets from internal sources because the outlays are "lumpy"; that is, they are large relative to the overall yearly governmental budget. Examples of this sort of expenditure would include such projects as school buildings, roads, and sewer facilities. Outlays for these projects tend to be concentrated in the relatively short period of time when construction is in progress, so that revenues from internal sources may simply be insufficient. The supply of nonfinancial funds—taxes, user charges, and federal grants—tend to be fixed or highly inelastic in the short run. Real assets might be financed by reducing expenditures on current projects; but, again, since a large portion of current expenditures—salaries, maintenance expenses, and so on—is relatively fixed or nondiscretionary in the short run, the supply of funds from this source also tends to be inelastic. For this reason the governmental unit issues long-term debt to finance real assets that cannot be purchased with internal funds alone.

Second, the governmental unit may wish to shift the cost of capital projects to future beneficiaries. In this case, the governmental unit will borrow even if nonfinancial funds are available to meet the real-asset expenditure. Principal and interest charges are then paid out of *future* taxes and user charges.

Third, short-term borrowing is used in financial planning. Tax-anticipation notes are used to bridge the gap between current expenditures and expected tax revenues. Bond-anticipation notes finance construction expenditures; after the capital project is completed, the notes are retired with the proceeds of a long-term debt issue.

Certain periods, namely 1906–1930 and 1956–1978, have been characterized by borrowing for these three reasons. During these times, outstanding state and local debt increased at an average annual rate of slightly over 8.0 percent. In addition, unique circumstances have had a temporary effect from time to time on the demand for loanable funds. The most notable periods of "disorderly" finance were the Depression, World War II, and the immediate postwar period. Since 1955, state-local debt outstanding has increased at approximately the same rate as total private debt—somewhat faster during the earlier period, 1955–1960, and somewhat more slowly since then. State and local government liabilities represent about 9 percent of total nonfinancial credit-market debt outstanding.

## Demand for Loanable Funds

In a narrow sense, state-local borrowing is related to the sector's demand for real assets since, in most cases, these governmental units cannot legally borrow to finance current expenditures. It is conceptually impossible, however, to identify specific sources of funds that will be used for specific purposes. Quite simply, a sector's demand for loanable funds occurs because total expenditures exceed nonfinancial revenues. One cannot say that the deficit was "caused" by real-asset spending in excess of the sector's saving, because if the sector had made fewer current expenditures, for example, it could have allocated more current revenue to finance real assets.

We can narrow the identification problem, however, if we exclude from the discussion for a moment current receipts, current expenditures, and debt retirement in the income statement. The remaining sources of funds are saving ($\Delta NW$)—that is, the excess of internal funds over current expenditures—and net borrowing ($\Delta L$). These funds are allocated to spending on real assets ($\Delta RA$) and financial assets ($\Delta FA$). These four components, which comprise the balance-sheet portion of the complete sector sources and uses of funds statement,[1] provide the identity

$$\Delta NW + \Delta L \equiv \Delta RA + \Delta FA \qquad (16\text{-}1)$$

where, for convenience, we denote $\Delta FA$ as comprising both money and other financial assets.

We can rearrange Equation (16-1) to provide the following function:

$$\Delta L = (\Delta RA + \Delta FA) - \Delta NW \qquad (16\text{-}2)$$

Using this arrangement, we can view net borrowing as the residual that results from the decision to make real and financial asset expenditures in excess of saving in the current year. Equation (16-2) emphasizes that, in any given year, three sets of factors can affect the demand for loanable funds: (1) the net internal generation of funds ($\Delta NW$); (2) the

[1]See Chapter 2 for a full discussion of flow of funds statements.

net demand for financial assets ($\Delta FA$); and (3) the net demand for real assets ($\Delta RA$). Real-asset spending certainly affects the size of the deficit, but so do other factors that influence saving and the amount of net spending on financial assets.

The state and local government sector's annual spending for real assets generally exceeds its saving, but saving *plus* net borrowing is usually *larger* than spending on real assets. This means that this sector tends to accumulate financial-asset balances. Only *some* of these assets are later used for real-asset spending. Let us now examine each of these components of the demand for loanable funds in more detail.

### The Effect of Saving on Net Borrowing

The proportion of total expenditures that is financed with net internally generated funds (saving) is affected by such things as tax rate and user-charge structures, the income elasticity of these structures, the political willingness to change rate levels, the amount of federal intergovernmental grants, and changes in relative prices and the overall price level.

Table 16-1 summarizes the sector's relative reliance on these net internally generated funds—saving—for selected time periods. The periods chosen were unaffected by major wars or the Depression. As one can see, total state-local saving represents a growing proportion of total funds available for spending on real and financial assets (column 1). This trend of the "internal financing ratio" $\Delta NW/(\Delta NW + \Delta L)$ is generally representative of both state and local governmental units (columns 2 and 3).

The secular bias toward relatively more internal financing by the state-local sector may reflect an explicit choice by consumer-voters, who express these preferences through elections, lobbying and log-rolling activities, and the formal structure of tax and debt referendum-limitation laws. Thus, the decline in the overall success rate for state-local bond referendums in recent years may be interpreted as evidence that voters prefer less debt financing. The percentage approved in bond elections, measured by dollar amount or by number of issues, was generally 70–75 percent during 1957–1967. The average approval rate has since declined to about 60 percent. In addition, voter pressure to

**Table 16-1  State and Local Government Allocation of Sources of Funds, for Selected Time Periods[a] (percentages)**

| Selected Time Periods | $\dfrac{\Delta NW}{(\Delta NW + \Delta L)}$ | | | State $\Delta L$ |
|---|---|---|---|---|
| | State-Local (1) | State (2) | Local (3) | $\dfrac{\text{State } \Delta L}{\text{Total } \Delta L}$ (4) |
| 1900–1915 | 53.3 | 53.2 | 53.3 | 2.2 |
| 1923–1930 | 64.9 | 76.1 | 61.3 | 16.5 |
| 1953–1962 | 68.3 | 78.0 | 60.9 | 29.8 |
| 1963–1972 | 73.0 | 81.3 | 65.1 | 33.6 |
| 1973 | 77.3 | 83.9 | 70.7 | 35.2 |
| 1974 | 73.4 | 80.3 | 67.9 | 32.7 |
| 1975 | 73.1 | 69.8 | 75.4 | 46.8 |
| 1976 | 70.7 | 63.4 | 78.6 | 65.0 |
| 1977 | 77.4 | 83.8 | 71.9 | 33.4 |

[a]$\Delta NW$ = saving; $\Delta L$ = net borrowing.

Source: William E. Mitchell, "Demand and Supply of Loanable Funds for the State-Local Sector," in *Understanding Capital Markets: The Financial Environment and the Flow of Funds in the Next Decade,* eds. A. W. Sametz and P. Wachtel, D. C. Heath, Lexington, Mass., 1977, Chap. 9.

establish debt referendum and limitation laws (discussed later) indicates their preference for a higher internal financing ratio.

The preferences of government officials also influence the choice of financing methods. Government officials may be able to produce political benefits for themselves from such choices, and they have some discretion in choosing alternative policies. They do have an incentive to produce benefits in the current period through *borrowing* for public projects. This shifts the tax cost to the future. Producing "costless" benefits is an age-old political strategy. Similarly, there is little incentive to generate and accumulate funds in anticipation of future capital expenditures because government officials often cannot internalize the possible benefits of that type of capital budgeting: they would be producing short-term costs—taxes—and no short-term benefits. For this reason, we may assume some bias *toward* borrowing in the absence of effective controls. On balance, however, voter activity—the impact of voting, lobbying, and other methods of influencing decision making—have apparently limited the potential bias of government officials toward borrowing. In addition, uncertainty and lack of knowledge of financial markets may incline government officials, particularly those from the numerous small governmental units, toward internal financing.

Two additional factors have influenced state-local governments' ability to finance real assets internally. First, all of the *relative* growth in state-local nonfinancial revenue during the last two decades can be attributed to federal intergovernmental grants. The decline in the share of gross borrowing has been almost exactly offset by the growth in federal grants, while the share of revenue generated by state-local taxes and user charges has stayed approximately constant.[2] The relative growth in federal grants as a source of revenue has increased the sector's *ability* to finance internally, and since, on balance, these revenues have been used as a substitute for borrowing rather than as a net addition to funds, it also indicates a *willingness* to finance internally. In other words, if net borrowing had increased at previous rates, the subsequent growth in grant revenue would have supported a higher level of total expenditures than actually occurred.[3] Second, saving in the short run depends partly on changes in the price level. When prices

[2] For a discussion of trends in sources and uses of funds, see William E. Mitchell, "Demand and Supply of Loanable Funds for the State-Local Sector," in *Understanding Capital Markets: The Financial Environment and the Flow of Funds in the Next Decade,* eds. A. W. Sametz and P. Wachtel, D.C. Heath, Lexington, Mass., 1977, Chap. 9.

[3] The familiar and unanswerable question, of course, is, in the absence of increased grant revenue, would tax

are relatively constant, governmental units can achieve their target level of saving for spending on real and financial assets. When prices change rapidly, however, changes in nonfinancial revenues lag behind changes in nonfinancial expenditures because of the inelastic nature of many current expenditures. Thus, for example, as prices rise rapidly, current expenditures rise relative to current revenues, saving falls, and the deficit [$(\Delta RA + \Delta FA) - \Delta NW$] must be financed with relatively more borrowing.

Price-level changes and grant-revenue growth help to explain the short-run divergence of the internal financing ratio during 1973–1976 from the long-run trends outlined earlier. The marked reduction in the state government ratio (column 2) is associated with extremely high rates of inflation during these years. Conversely, the local government ratio (column 3) *increased* during this time period. It is likely that the unusually high increase—72 percent from 1973 to 1976—in federal-to-local grants substituted for borrowing, thus offsetting the price-level effect for local governments. In addition, turmoil in the tax-exempt securities market during these years forced a number of local governments to cut back temporarily on planned borrowing. These events were associated with the celebrated financial difficulties of New York City and a number of other central cities, located principally in the Northeast Corridor.

## The Effect of Financial-Asset Spending on Net Borrowing

Governments acquire financial assets for transaction balances and as reserves for future real-asset spending. State-local demand for money and near-money assets has been proportional to total expenditures in the past, averaging about 3½ percent in recent years. Period-to-period fluctuations in the acquisition of financial assets reflect the accumu-

lation or disposition of funds in relation to the timing of real-asset spending.

One question merits attention: will the demand for financial assets for transaction purposes continue to be proportional to total expenditure growth in the future? The state-local sector generally appears to hold excessive cash balances.[4] In the private sector, minimizing idle cash balances has a visible payoff in the form of higher profits. In contrast, a high degree of liquidity in the public balance sheet could convey an impression of safety in the handling of public funds and could, as a result, be a visible "output" for government officials.[5] This may change, however. The recent development and widespread use of financial management techniques in the private sector tend to highlight its absence in the public sector. Growing sophistication among voters may give public-sector managers an incentive to introduce financial management programs, and to reduce idle cash balances.

If we assume that net borrowing is a residual—that is,

$$\Delta L = (\Delta RA + \Delta FA) - \Delta NW \qquad (16\text{-}3)$$

then we can see that reducing financial-asset expenditures releases more saving for spending on real assets and decreases the relative reliance on net borrowing. Due to the arbitrage factor between tax-exempt and taxable yields, however, there is less incentive to conserve on the securities component of financial-asset balances for state-local units than for private decision-making units. As a result, financial innovation will proceed less quickly than it has in the private sector.

[4]An optimal cash balance can be measured by the amount of cash necessary to minimize forgone interest earnings and the cost of substitution between cash and other financial assets. Estimates for excess cash balances are provided in Martin E. Judd, "A Note on Idle Cash Balances of State and Local Governments: A Worsening Situation," *Nebraska Journal of Economics and Business* (Spring 1976), 59–63.

[5]Government officials have an incentive to minimize inputs to "invisible" output—activities that cannot be effectively measured. See, for example, Cotton M. Lindsay, "A Theory of Government Enterprise," *Journal of Political Economy* (October 1976), 1061–1077; Louis DeAlessi, "Implications of Property Rights for Government Investment Choices," *American Economic Review* (March 1969), 13–24.

revenue or borrowing have increased or would the level of expenditures have declined in the overall budget allocation? For a discussion of the impact of grants on expenditures, see Edward M. Gramlich and Harvey Galper, "State and Local Fiscal Behavior and Federal Grant Policy," *Brookings Papers on Economic Activity* (1973), 15–65.

## The Effect of Real-Asset Spending on Net Borrowing

State and local government demand for loanable funds is positively related to fluctuations in real-asset spending, but growth in real-asset spending has not led to proportionate changes in net borrowing. This decrease in the propensity to borrow is attributable, in part, to the declining importance of real assets in the overall budget and to changes in the composition of real-asset spending.

Spending on real assets has declined as a percentage of total general expenditures (*EXP*) for the state-local sector. The *RA/EXP* ratio averaged 26 percent in the 1950s and 19 percent in the 1970s. This change reflects, in part, a shift in demand from capital goods to services. For example, expenditures for the construction of roads and schools are declining—at least in relation to other expenses— while road maintenance and teachers' salaries are increasing. Moreover, it is now common practice to require developers to make necessary improvements—streets, sidewalks, storm and sanitation sewers—and include these costs in the price of the building.[6] This reduces state and local expenditures and financing for these facilities. Finally, price-level increases appear to affect labor costs more than material-input costs.[7] If labor inputs are inflexible in the production of state-local output, this could help explain the relative increase in the current-expenditure share of uses of funds in recent years. The secular decline in the *RA/EXP* ratio has reduced the ''lumpiness'' of the overall budget. The flow of real-asset spending is now smaller relative to the flow of total sources of funds. Therefore, capital expenditures can be more easily financed through discretionary intra- or interperiod shifts in funds between current and real-asset spending.

Several changes in the composition of real-asset spending have also affected the demand for loanable funds.[8] First, spending on school buildings has declined as school enrollments have fallen, and there has been slower growth for spending on highways, housing and redevelopment, conservation, and hospitals—categories that have typically accounted for heavy net borrowing. Second, the more rapid current and expected future growth in expenditures for sewer systems, mass transit, and water-supply projects are not likely to result in proportionate increases in net borrowing because of substantial federal grants for these projects.

## The Effect of Interest Rates on Net Borrowing

Interest rates can affect borrowing decisions in three ways. First, high interest rates increase the cost of capital projects. Borrowing and spending are postponed. Second, when interest rates are high, legal interest-rate limitations can effectively restrain borrowing. Third, state-local units appear to adjust their borrowing plans to movements in actual rates relative to their estimate of expected future rates. Thus, for example, rising yields may, at times, be associated with more borrowing if it is generally expected that rates will rise even further.[9]

On balance, state-local demand for loanable funds is negatively related to cyclical interest rates. Generally, 6–10 percent of planned borrowing is shifted from periods of high interest rates to periods

[6]Lennox L. Moak, *Administration of Local Government Debt*, Municipal Finance Officers Association, Chicago, 1970, p. 11.

[7]This evidence is based on a study of New York City for 1965–1972. See David Greytak, Richard Gustely, and Robert J. Dinklemeyer, ''The Effects of Inflation on Local Government Expenditures,'' *National Tax Journal* (December 1974), 583–598.

[8]See Barry Bosworth, James S. Duesenberry, and Andrew S. Carron, *Capital Needs in the Seventies,* Brookings Institution, Washington, D.C., 1975, pp. 35–36; David J. Ott, Attiat F. Ott, James A. Maxwell, and J. Richard Aronson, *State-Local Finances in the Last Half of the 1970s,* American Enterprise Institute for Public Policy Research, Washington, D.C., 1975, p. 94; and Tax Foundation, *The Financial Outlook for State and Local Government to 1980,* New York, 1973, p. 94.

[9]This latter point and a bibliography of debt-management literature is contained in Paul F. McGouldrick, ''The Effect of Credit Conditions on State and Local Bond Sales and Capital Outlays Since World War II,'' in *Public Facility Financing,* Joint Economic Committee, Washington, D.C., 1966, pp. 299–321. See also, John E. Petersen, ''Response of State and Local Governments to Varying Credit Conditions,'' *Federal Reserve Bulletin* (March 1971), 209–232; and Paul Schneiderman, ''Planned and Actual Long Term Borrowing by State and Local Governments,'' *Federal Reserve Bulletin* (December 1971), 977–987.

of low rates. Planned borrowing shortfalls were as large as 12 percent during the credit crunch of 1966. In 1970 the combination of legal interest-rate ceilings and historically high interest rates reduced planned borrowing by 28 percent. Since 1970 a number of states have revised or eliminated these ceilings.

The effect of high interest rates on borrowing[10] depends on the availability and cost of alternative financing sources. In 1970, for example, the 28 percent reduction in planned borrowing only reduced planned real-asset spending by approximately 5 percent.[11] Revenue-expenditure gaps are financed principally by short-term borrowing, by drawing down assets in bond funds, and by liquidating other financial-asset holdings.

State-government demand for loanable funds is negatively related to both fluctuations in cyclical interest rates and to the stock of financial assets available for real-asset spending. In contrast, local-government borrowing is only moderately influenced by cyclical interest rates and is unaffected by the stock of financial assets. Most local governments do not maintain large financial-asset balances, and they are not as likely as state governments to substitute between real and financial assets for timing purposes.[12] A large stock of financial assets, a higher internal financing ratio, and a lower *RA/EXP* ratio give state governments more flexibility than local governments to time debt issues over an interest rate cycle. These interperiod shifts between spending on financial and real assets reduce cyclical fluctuations in the demand for loanable funds.

The interest elasticity of borrowing is also related to the type of expenditure being financed. Primary and secondary education, along with water and sewer projects, tend to be quite insensitive to changes in interest rates, while administrative facilities, transportation, health, and welfare projects

appear to be postponable. Borrowing by state governments and *large* local governments is more highly interest-elastic than borrowing by small local governments, in part, because these latter units typically account for most of the interest-insensitive projects mentioned.

## Summary: A Model of the Demand for Loanable Funds

Based on the foregoing discussion, it appears that there is a propensity to finance real assets *internally* whenever possible and this tendency has increased over time. The growing desire and/or ability of the sector to finance internally can be attributed to several factors: a relative increase in the state-government share of total sector activity (since state governments have a higher propensity and/or ability to finance internally); a larger share of federal grants, which have been substituted for borrowing; and a secular decrease in the *RA/EXP* ratio. On occasion, this trend is reversed for a time, and there is a relative shift toward external financing. This reversal appears to be related to three factors that affect budgetary flexibility in the short run: (1) higher-than-average rates of inflation that reduce the sector's nonfinancial revenue relative to current expenditures; (2) high (or rising) *RA/EXP* ratios, which cause relative shifts toward more external financing; and (3) rising interest rates and the unavailability of alternative sources of funds to finance real-asset spending. Simply put, whenever prices rise rapidly *or* the *RA/EXP* is high and rising *or* interest rates are low and falling, there is a relative cyclical increase in net borrowing as a percentage of total discretionary sources of funds.[13] Changes in tax rates take time to formulate, propose, and enact, particularly when increases must be approved by referendum. Also, governmental units frequently have legal tax limitations that must be altered through the often lengthy process of legislative review. In the short run, therefore, borrowing is a more flexible source of funds. The larger debt accumulation is amortized out of higher *future* tax revenues. Over a longer planning horizon, however, state and local governmental units

[10]Reasons for borrowing shortfalls that are unrelated to interest rates include referendum defeats, high construction costs, legal problems, federal grant delays, debt limitations, and planning-administrative underwriting difficulties.

[11]Petersen, "Response of State and Local Governments to Varying Credit Conditions," pp. 217–218.

[12]Michael D. Tanzer, "State and Local Debt in the Postwar Period," *Review of Economics and Statistics* (August 1964), 237–244.

[13]See Mitchell (1977), "Demand and Supply of Loanable Funds for the State-Local Sector," pp. 147–154.

can overcome technical rigidities and more nearly achieve their target financing plans. They can eliminate revenue-expenditure lags, raise tax and user-charge rates, levy new taxes, and develop new sources of revenue. The extent to which state and local governments substitute borrowing for internal finance in the short run depends in part on prevailing interest rates, alternative sources of funds, and their ability and/or willingness to postpone capital projects.

## Supply of Loanable Funds

Tax exemption[14] is most profitable to three sectors: commercial banks, households, and fire and casualty insurance companies. In 1978 these three sectors held 90 percent of outstanding tax-exempt securities (Table 16-2). Nonprofit institutions, including state and local governments, private pension funds, and thrift institutions, pay little or no income taxes and, therefore, generally find the higher yields on taxable securities more profitable.

### Commercial Banks

At the end of 1978, commercial banks held 43 percent of the tax exempts outstanding, representing about 10 percent of their total financial assets. Tax exempts are purchased by commercial banks for a number of reasons.

1. In many cases, the transaction is equivalent to a business or consumer loan because the bank considers the governmental unit as a bank customer. Thus, for practical purposes, the bank considers these financial assets to be in its loan portfolio rather than its securities portfolio.
2. Often a commercial bank is the sole bidder for a local issue. Since the vitality of the local government is important to a bank's overall profitability, the bank may purchase the bonds to maintain good community relations, even if the net return is less than on a comparable business loan.

3. Commercial banks hold tax exempts as liquidity reserves.
4. They also participate in tax exempts through their role as investment bankers by maintaining an inventory and making a secondary market in securities they have underwritten.
5. They also use tax exempts as legally required security against state and local government bank deposits.

The increase in commercial bank participation in tax exempts during the last several decades is attributable to the banks' ability and willingness to attract a large and growing share of loanable funds. Amendments to Regulation Q since 1957 have allowed commercial banks to offer more competitive rates on time deposits, thus increasing their *ability* to attract loanable funds. Commercial banks also have increased their *willingness* to bid for higher-cost funds in recent years, accepting lower profit margins in order to maximize total net income. Given some positive spread between after-tax earnings on tax-exempt versus taxable securities, there is a smaller percentage decline in net income from tax-exempt securities as funds are shifted into higher-cost time deposits. This encourages a relative portfolio shift toward tax-exempt securities.[15] Commercial bank time deposits have increased substantially after each amendment to Regulation Q, and this has been matched by relative increases in their holdings of tax-exempt bonds.

The commercial bank share of tax-exempt bonds outstanding has declined somewhat from the early 1970s. There are at least three reasons for this change. First, when loan demand is slack, excess reserves are used to acquire tax exempts. Then, as economic conditions improve, loan demand rises and funds available for tax exempts decline. Thus, the change may be attributed, at least in part, to a cyclical portfolio shift. Second, more profitable new alternatives may be displacing some tax exempts in commercial bank portfolios. For example, the growth of bank holding companies provides investment outlets (such as leasing affiliates) that may yield more than tax exempts on a net-tax basis. Third, the growth of foreign branches of large U.S.

---

[14]The origin and economic impact of tax exemption is discussed in the section, "Tax Exemption and Public Policy."

[15]McGouldrick, "The Effect of Credit Conditions on State and Local Bond Sales and Capital Outlays Since World War II," p. 309.

**Table 16-2 Ownership of Tax-Exempt Securities Outstanding as a Percentage Distribution, for Selected Years[a]**

| Year | Commercial Banks | Households, Personal Trusts, and Nonprofit Organizations[b] | Fire-Casualty Insurance Companies | State-Local Governments | Thrift Institutions[c] | Life Insurance Companies | Nonfinancial Corporate Business |
|------|------|------|------|------|------|------|------|
| 1978 | 43.3% | 25.7% | 21.4% | 2.8% | 1.6% | 2.2% | 1.3% |
| 1976 | 44.7 | 30.7 | 15.8 | 3.5 | 1.5 | 2.4 | 1.4 |
| 1970 | 48.6 | 32.6 | 11.8 | 3.0 | 0.2 | 2.3 | 1.5 |
| 1965 | 38.7 | 36.8 | 11.3 | 4.8 | 0.3 | 3.5 | 4.6 |
| 1960 | 25.0 | 44.1 | 11.4 | 10.1 | 0.9 | 5.1 | 3.4 |
| 1950 | 21.1 | 43.8 | 4.2 | 14.7 | 0.4 | 5.0 | 2.1 |
| 1940 | 18.0 | 47.0 | 1.5 | 19.0 | 3.0 | 9.5 | 2.5 |
| 1930 | 13.2 | 52.7 | 2.2 | 19.2 | 4.9 | 3.3 | 3.8 |
| 1920 | 11.5 | 48.8 | 2.6 | 19.2 | 9.0 | 3.8 | 5.1 |
| 1913 | 10.9 | 39.1 | 2.2 | 19.6 | 17.4 | 4.3 | 6.5 |
| 1902 | 9.1 | 27.2 | 4.5 | 27.3 | 27.3 | 4.5 | 4.5 |

[a]1902–1950 fiscal years; 1960–1978 annual years. Data for 1902–1950 were estimated by a separate source and are not strictly comparable with later years.
[b]Includes minor amounts of holdings by brokers and dealers. Data for 1902–1950 also include minor amounts held by the U.S. government, corporate pension trust funds, and international accounts.
[c]Only mutual savings banks until 1968. Thereafter, savings and loan associations began acquiring small amounts of tax exempts. By 1976, the latter held 0.5 percent of outstandings.

Sources: For 1902–1950, U.S. Treasury, *Annual Report of the Secretary of the Treasury,* U.S. Government Printing Office, Washington, D.C., 1964. For 1960, Board of Governors of the Federal Reserve System, *Flow of Funds Accounts, 1946–1975,* Washington, D.C., December 1976. For 1965–1976, Board of Governors of the Federal Reserve System, *Flow of Funds Accounts Assets and Liabilities Outstanding, 1965–1976,* Washington, D.C., December 1977. For 1978, Board of Governors of the Federal Reserve System, *Flow of Funds Accounts, 1949–1978,* Washington, D.C., December 1979.

banks provides foreign tax credits that reduce the need for other tax-sheltered income.[16]

## Household Sector

The household sector has decreased its relative share of tax-exempt holdings in the last several decades. An interesting characteristic of this sector is the large number of individuals who do not purchase state-local securities when it appears to be profitable for them to do so on an after-tax basis relative to the yields on taxable securities. Part of this behavior is attributable to households' demand for assets with capital-gains possibilities as an alternative tax-sheltering device. In addition, there are implicit costs, such as knowledge constraints and market-and-search costs that offset the explicit gains from tax exemption. Given these portfolio preferences, individuals' demand for state-local securities is sensitive to the tax-exempt–taxable-yield differential; the controlling variables are the effec-

[16]Frank E. Morris, *Statement . . . Before the Committee of Ways and Means,* U.S. House of Representatives, Washington, D.C., February 23, 1973 (mimeographed).

tive marginal tax rate applicable to the individual investor, alternative tax-shelter sources, and yields on substitute securities. On the upturn of a business cycle, for example, equity yields generally fall in relation to tax-exempt yields. Since the household sector is sensitive to the relative yields on substitute securities, its demand for tax exempts rises while commercial bank demand falls. Thus, the conditions that cause banks to decrease demand for tax exempts (improving economic conditions, rising loan demand) cause households to *increase* demand for tax exempts (because of the large yield differentials between tax-exempt and taxable securities—especially equities).

Several factors will probably combine to produce a growing supply of loanable funds to the state-local sector by households. First, the demand for tax-sheltered income increases as real *or* nominal income rises and pushes more individuals into higher marginal income tax brackets. This effect is augmented by the growing use of income taxation by state governments. Second, alternative tax shelters are declining for individuals. The introduction of a minimum income tax and changes in tax rules for real estate, farm operations, cattle raising, and so on, have reduced tax-sheltering alternatives. The future "supply" of tax shelters depends, in part, on whether the rate of elimination by Congress can keep pace with the birth of ingenious new devices. Third, the intermediation function (risk pooling, professional management, and economies of scale) of tax-exempt-bond investment funds and common trusts should increase household demand for tax exempts. Tax-exempt-bond funds, first introduced in 1961, have grown rapidly in recent years. The Tax Reform Act of 1976, which allows these bond funds to be organized as corporations rather than as limited partnerships, has widened the tax-exempt market considerably for middle-income investors.

### Fire and Casualty Insurance Companies

State-local securities provide important tax shelters for this sector, as these companies are subject to the standard corporate tax rate. Tax exempts also provide necessary liquidity and income stability to an industry that experiences rather wide year-to-year swings in income.

### Other Sectors

Life insurance companies have reduced their tax-exempt holdings for several reasons. The 1959 revision of the tax laws lowered their average effective marginal tax rate to about 20 percent.[17] This change has widened the after-tax yield differential between taxables and tax exempts. In addition, there has been an overall trend in this industry toward holding a larger proportion of higher-risk, higher-yielding assets in their portfolios. Marginal tax rates vary widely between companies, however, so there is some demand for tax sheltering. Moreover, the *average* tax-exempt–taxable-yield differential does not accurately reflect the actual yields available to purchasers, particularly among the large and growing supply of higher-yielding

nonguaranteed tax-exempt bonds.[18] Life insurance companies are quite sensitive to yield differentials and thus are willing and able to buy high-risk, high-yield tax exempts.

The demand for tax-exempt securities by state and local governments, particularly public pension funds, is conditioned by important legal and political constraints. Pressure to achieve higher rates of return on earning assets has led to a relaxation of restrictions on eligible investments, so that corporate bonds, mortgages, and common stock now constitute a growing proportion of their portfolios. There are still important constraints, however, that bear on any strategy of income maximization. These include legislative-legal controls, routine public screening of portfolio operations, and political pressure to allocate local public funds to local public projects. (New York City's experience in the mid-1970s represents an extreme example of the latter point.)

Mutual savings banks specialize in the acquisition of mortgages, although they now also purchase small amounts of high-yield nonguaranteed bonds. Savings and loan associations began acquiring small amounts of tax exempts in 1968. By 1977 their holdings were one-half as large as those of mutual savings banks. The demand for tax-exempt securities by these institutions depends on saving inflows, mortgage lending opportunities, and competitive forces in the thrift market.

## Market Characteristics

### Bond Underwriting Process

Once a governmental unit has decided to borrow and has obtained the necessary authorization, it invites bids on a bond issue. For most general obligations and two-thirds of nonguaranteed bonds, investment bankers submit sealed bids for the issue. The winning bidder, determined by the lowest *net interest cost* (NIC),[19] is awarded the right to

---

[17]David J. Ott and Allan H. Meltzer, *Federal Tax Treatment of State and Local Securities,* The Brookings Institution, Washington, D.C., 1963, p. 47; also Elizabeth H. Bancala, "Life Insurance Companies," *Public Facility Financing,* Joint Economic Committee, Washington, D.C., 1966, p. 370.

[18]Nonguaranteed or "revenue" bonds are payable solely from pledged sources of revenue; they do not constitute an obligation against other resources of the political unit if pledged sources are insufficient. General-obligation bonds are backed by the taxing power of the governmental unit.

[19]Net interest cost (NIC) is computed as the ratio of all interest payments promised by the bond contract (net of

underwrite the issue. Often a number of investment bankers combine to form an underwriting syndicate in order to spread the risk for large issues, share pricing ideas, and achieve diverse selling potentials. A syndicate is managed by one firm or co-managed by several firms, and others are invited to participate in the group. The winning bidder either retains the bonds as a financial investment, "reoffers" them to ultimate lenders, or "wholesales" them to nonsyndicate dealers at a small discount from the public reoffering price. About one-third of nonguaranteed bonds and a small percentage of general obligations are handled on a negotiated basis, whereby the NIC is set by direct bargaining between a single investment banker or syndicate and the borrower. One would expect competitive bidding to result in lower borrowing costs for most issues, but many projects, particularly those financed with nonguaranteed bonds, have unique characteristics that require extensive financial consultation with an investment banker. Negotiated pricing compensates the bank or syndicate for the advisory services through larger underwriter spreads and *may* result in lower overall borrowing costs than if the issue had been offered through competitive bidding. An important feature of the underwriting process is that once the issue is awarded to the low bidder, the underwriter assumes the risk of ownership. State-local bonds are rarely placed privately or sold on an agency basis (where the risk of underwriting is borne by the borrowing unit).[20]

## Interest-Cost Determinants

The ultimate borrowing cost (NIC) to the governmental unit is derived as a residual in the pricing process. The investment dealer (or syndicate) first estimates the reoffering bond price at which the entire issue can be sold to ultimate lenders. The dealer then decides on an underwriting spread (price) that will provide compensation for distribution costs, market risk, and profit. The bid price to the borrowing unit is then determined by subtracting the underwriting cost from the reoffering price, and NIC is the ratio of interest payments to the accepted bid price.

The interest cost for a new state-local security is determined by three sets of factors: (1) market and institutional characteristics; (2) borrower characteristics; and (3) issue characteristics.[21] Some variables affect only the reoffering bond price, while others primarily affect underwriter spreads, and some variables that relate to differential risk affect both. The latter situation occurs because, during the distribution period, the underwriter assumes capital market risk. Thus, market and specific security characteristics that produce greater risk will require larger compensatory underwriter spreads.

*Market and Institutional Characteristics* An important determinant of borrowing cost is the market rate of interest, which reflects levels of (and changes in) the pure rate of interest, an inflation risk premium, and a capital-market risk premium. Borrower and underwriter uncertainty (risk) also produces higher borrowing costs. As market interest rates become more volatile, for example, average borrowing costs rise.[22]

---

any premium or plus any discount of the face amount of the issue from the offering price) to the principal. The NIC formula does not provide for discounting interest payments to a present-value basis, which reflects the higher cost of interest paid during the early years of a serial-maturity bond issue. For a discussion of technical distortions resulting from the NIC formula, see George G. Kaufman, "Improved Bidding Constraints on Municipal Bonds Sold Competitively by NIC," *Governmental Finance* (February 1975), 40–43.

[20]John E. Walker, "Municipal Bond Underwriting," *Public Facility Financing,* Joint Economic Committee, Washington, D.C., 1966, pp. 173, 176.

[21]Recent studies include the following: "Interest Cost Effects of Commercial Bank Underwriting of Municipal Revenue Bonds," *Federal Reserve Bulletin* (August 1967); Reuben A. Kessel, "A Study of the Effects of Competition in the Tax-Exempt Bond Market," *Journal of Political Economy* (July–August 1971), 706–738; William P. Smith, *Commercial Bank Entry into Revenue Bond Underwriting,* Comptroller of the Currency, Washington, D.C., 1968; Michael H. Hopewell and George G. Kaufman, "Commercial Bank Bidding on Municipal Revenue Bonds: New Evidence," 1975 (mimeographed); Gene Laber and Arthur A. Bayer, "Community Characteristics and the Net Interest Cost of Local Debt: Recent Experience in Vermont," *Quarterly Review of Economics and Business* (Autumn 1971), 47–54; and K. Larry Hastie, "Determinants of Municipal Bond Yields," *Journal of Financial and Quantitative Analysis* (June 1972), 1729–1748. See also Chapter 24 of the text for a general discussion of yield differentials.

[22]On this latter point, see Hopewell and Kaufman,

Tax exemption and the influence of tax laws are important institutional determinants of borrowing costs. Other institutional factors periodically exert a strong influence on borrowing cost. These factors include regulatory laws, customs, and liquidity needs, all of which constrain the free flow of loanable funds between substitute securities.

The degree of underwriter competition (number of bids) affects borrowing costs through its impact on both reoffering prices[23] and underwriter spreads. The evidence suggests that the number of bids varies inversely with risk. Risk is measured by average maturity, credit rating, market uncertainty (for example, interest rate volatility), type of security (general obligation or nonguaranteed), and size of issue (marketability or liquidity risk).[24]

*Borrower Characteristics* These variables, which reflect the probability of default risk, have two dimensions: ability to pay, and willingness to pay. A past default could represent an inability to meet debt-servicing requirements *or* an unwillingness to raise taxes to meet financial obligations. Agency credit ratings attempt to provide an ordinal or ranking index of inherent investment quality—the prospective incidence and magnitude of default risk. The prominent rating companies, Moody's and Standard and Poor's, assign individual ratings on the basis of such factors as times-interest-earned, lien position, capital structure, intended use of funds, and growth and stability of the local economy. Credit ratings are widely used as a surrogate

for investment quality by investors. Consequently, credit ratings are inversely related to borrowing costs.[25] In addition, investors discriminate between like-rated nonguaranteed issues by purpose of issue. High-risk projects (such as housing, dormitory, recreation, and toll road projects) require higher interest rates than low-risk projects (sewer, water, and nonuniversity school facilities).[26]

Willingness to pay is represented by the governmental unit's past record of financial responsibility. It has been found, for example, that a unit's borrowing cost is inversely related to the ratio of its collected-to-billed taxes.[27] The reasoning behind the use of the "collection ratio" as an index of willingness is as follows: units that make a diligent effort to collect taxes will make a similar effort to meet their own financial commitments.

*Issue Characteristics* Average maturity, type of security, indenture provisions, and size of issue provide a third set of factors that affect borrowing cost. These specific issue characteristics affect reoffering prices and underwriter spreads through their relationship to differential risk. State-local interest rates vary positively with average maturity. (The risk-maturity relationship is discussed in Chapter 23.) Nonguaranteed bonds require higher risk premiums than comparable general obligations. This effect occurs, in part, because, for similar projects, the ones financed with nonguaranteed bonds are assigned lower credit ratings than projects with general-obligation backing. Due to call-risk exposure for the lender, the inclusion of a call provision in the bond indenture raises borrowing cost. Issue size and interest rates are inversely

---

"Commercial Bank Bidding on Municipal Revenue Bonds."

[23]Reuben Kessel applies George Stigler's economics-of-information theory to explain the impact of competition on reoffering bond prices. When submitting bids, the several underwriters or syndicates incorporate their (incomplete) knowledge of the price that potential investors will be willing to pay for an issue: "the larger the number of bids submitted, the greater the probability of discovering the underwriter in possession of the knowledge of who will pay the most for a prospective issue; this is apt to be the underwriter who submits the winning bid" (Kessel, "A Study of the Effects of Competition in the Tax-Exempt Bond Market," 728–729). See also George J. Stigler, "The Economics of Information," *Journal of Political Economy* (June 1961), 213–225.

[24]The effect of underwriter competition on general-obligation and nonguaranteed interest rates is discussed in the section, "Commercial Bank Underwriting and Public Policy."

[25]Thus, it is possible that credit ratings partially *determine* interest rates rather than merely measuring and ranking the relative risk of bond issues. See Richard R. West, "Bond Ratings, Bond Yields, and Financial Regulation: Some Findings," *The Journal of Law and Economics* (April 1973), 159–168. Recent evidence, however, suggests that agency credit ratings can systematically predict financial loss at most two to four years in the future. See James S. Ang and Kiritkumar A. Patel, "Bond Rating Methods: Comparison and Validation," *Journal of Finance* (May 1975), 631–640.

[26]Hopewell and Kaufman, "Commercial Bank Bidding on Municipal Revenue Bonds."

[27]Laber and Bayer, "Community Characteristics and the Net Interest Cost of Local Debt," 48. Willingness to pay is also reflected in agency credit ratings, but it is not possible to isolate the effect.

related for two reasons. First, smaller issues receive fewer bids so that borrowing cost, by issue size, is affected by underwriter competition. Second, marketability (liquidity risk) varies inversely with issue size and with the amount of debt outstanding by the issuer.[28]

## Legal Restraints on Borrowing

### Origin of Legal Debt Limitations

Around 1820, state governments began issuing significant amounts of debt to finance transportation and other public works. The highly successful Erie Canal in upstate New York was financed in this manner; it was soon followed by debt-financed projects in other states. By 1843, however, 53 percent of state-government debt outstanding was in default! Some of the transportation ventures proved to be financially unsuccessful or only marginally successful. The long recession of 1837–1839 created the additional pressure that triggered the defaults. During this protracted economic decline, project revenues fell while high fixed costs, including debt-servicing costs, remained constant. Defaulting state governments were unable (or unwilling) to meet these project deficits with general-fund revenues. The broad political reaction to this experience was enactment of legislation that placed permanent restrictions on the debt-incurring powers of state legislatures.

This sequence of events—that is, widespread defaults during a recession by overextended governmental units, followed by the passage of additional legal debt limits—was to be repeated three more times in the following century. Most of the subsequent defaults involved local governments.[29] Legal limitations with varying degrees of restrictiveness are now provided in state constitutions and statutes.

### Evading Debt Limitations

Following the passage of each new set of laws, government officials devised methods of bypassing these constraints whenever the demand for loanable funds reached legal limits. Instead of pressing for revision or repeal, it apparently has been politically expedient to develop extralegal means to bypass the laws. Two principal financial innovations have been used to evade debt limitations.[30] Early attempts usually took the form of shifting financial responsibility to less restricted or unrestricted governmental units within the state. For example, municipality debt limitations impinged on financing the great surge in the demand for local-government capital facilities in the early 1900s and again after World War II. As a result, school and special districts were created to assume operational and financial responsibility for these functions.[31] Statutory "authorities" (for ports, marinas, water, power, and conservation projects and government office buildings, for example) and lease-financing techniques are two post–World War II variations of this financial innovation. After World War II, unrestricted nonguaranteed debt was also employed as a means of bypassing legal limits. State courts ruled that since nonguaranteed debt did not place the burden of risk of default on taxpayers, such borrowing was not restrained by legal debt limitations. The use of nonguaranteed debt, however, cannot be attributed *entirely* to the evasion of restrictive general-obligation debt limitations. Nonguaranteed debt also can be used to shift the locus of risk from taxpayers to other economic

[28]See Hastie, "Determinents of Municipal Bond Yields," 1732–1734. On the characteristics and cost of marketability, see William L. Silber, "Thinness in Capital Markets: The Case of the Tel Aviv Stock Exchange," *Journal of Financial and Quantitative Analysis* (March 1975), 129–142; Seha M. Tinic and Richard R. West, "Competition and the Pricing of Dealer Services in the Over-the-Counter Stock Market," *Journal of Financial and Quantitative Analysis* (June 1972), 1707–1727; Seha M. Tinic, "The Economics of Liquidity Services," *Quarterly Journal of Economics* (February 1972), 79–93; J. Ernest Tanner and Levis A. Kochin, "The Determinants of the Difference Between Bid and Ask Prices on Government Bonds," *Journal of Business* (October 1971), 375–379; and Harold Demsetz, "The Cost of Transacting," *Quarterly Journal of Economics* (February 1968), 33–53.

[29]For a historical discussion of debt limitations, see A. M. Hillhouse, *Municipal Bonds: A Century of Experience,* Prentice-Hall, New York, 1936; and B. U. Ratchford, *American State Debts,* Duke University Press, Durham, N.C., 1951.

[30]See William E. Mitchell, *The Effectiveness of Debt Limits on State and Local Government Borrowing,* New York University, Institute of Finance, New York, 1967.

[31]Morris A. Copeland, *Trends in Government Financing,* Princeton University Press, Princeton, N.J., 1961, Chap. 5.

units.[32] Taxpayers may wish to transfer all of the project costs, including potential default costs, to the beneficiaries of the services supplied by the facility. With nonguaranteed debt financing, the cost of potential default—the larger interest risk premium—is shifted to beneficiaries through higher user charges and fees for consuming the services of the public good.

Similarly, taxpayers may be willing to assume the risk of default for general-obligation debt up to a prescribed limit (as provided in the existing debt-limitation legislation), after which the risk of default for *further* debt is shifted from taxpayers to bondholders through nonguaranteed financing. If debt-limitation legislation is solely intended to limit the issuance of this additional debt, then the higher interest cost of using nonguaranteed debt is a voluntary payment made from general fund revenues by taxpayers to bondholders. Taxpayers choose to make this payment in order to shift risk of default to the latter group.

### Effectiveness of Debt Limitations

After controlling for different population and income levels, on a statewide basis, those states with relatively restrictive limitations have issued just as much *total* (general obligation plus nonguaranteed) debt as less restricted or unrestricted units. Thus, debt limits apparently have not restricted total debt issuance.[33] Nor has the relative *absence* of legal limits in some states led to a greater reliance on debt financing. It is evident that governmental units have nullified the laws by some combination of shifting financial responsibility, exploiting the legal flexibility provided by such devices as special referendums and constitutional amendments to exceed limits, and/or using unrestricted nonguaranteed debt.

State-local *general-obligation* debt *is* lower in states with more restrictive limits, so that circumvention methods other than nonguaranteed debt have not completely offset the limitations. However, as noted above, nonguaranteed debt *has* off-

set the shortfall in general-obligation financing. Therefore, if the primary reason for legal debt limitations is to protect current and future taxpayers against overissuance of total debt by government officials, this objective has not been achieved in those states with relatively restrictive limits. On the other hand, if the intent of such legislation is solely to limit the issuance of general obligation debt—that is, to shift the locus of risk—then we may conclude that legal limitations have been successful. In the latter case, the existence of more or less restrictive limitations in the several states is assumed to reflect voters' preferences for locus-of-risk debt financing, not their preferences for internal versus external financing. The correct answer most likely falls somewhere between these two extreme models of intended effects for legal limits. All states with very restrictive limitations substitute, to some extent, nonguaranteed for general-obligation debt.

## Tax Exemption and Public Policy

### Tax Exemption as a Grant

Tax exemption originated with the doctrine of reciprocal immunity between sovereign governments—the states and the federal government. Taxation of another government's securities was considered unconstitutional. Many authorities believe that the Sixteenth Amendment removed this condition. In the absence of a court test, however, it is uncertain if tax exemption is protected by the Constitution or whether Congress could alter the institution by statute.[34] In any case, Congress provided for tax exemption by statute in 1913.

There is broad political consensus that the federal government should provide some financial assistance to state and local governments. Regardless of its constitutionality, exempting state-local bond interest from federal income taxation is one way of doing this. Since bond purchasers are interested in after-tax yield and state-local government securities are exempt from federal income taxes, interest rates offered on these securities will be lower than on comparable taxable debt. Abstracting from risk and liquidity differences, the

[32]A. James Heins, *Constitutional Restrictions Against State Debt*, University of Wisconsin Press, Madison, 1963, pp. 56–60.

[33]Mitchell, *The Effectiveness of Debt Limits on State and Local Government Borrowing*, pp. 42–44; Thomas F. Pogue, "The Effect of Debt Limits: Some New Evidence," *National Tax Journal* (March 1970), 45–47.

[34]For a history of the tax exemption issue, see Robert P. Huefner, *Taxable Alternatives to Municipal Bonds: An Analysis of the Issues*, Federal Reserve Bank of Boston, Boston, 1973.

relationship between taxable and nontaxable debt can be expressed as:

$$i_e = i(1 - t) \qquad (16\text{-}4)$$

where $i_e$ and $i$ are tax-exempt and taxable interest rates, respectively, and $t$ is the market-clearing marginal tax rate. The lower interest yield on tax exempts is acceptable to the market because the difference is "paid" by the federal government in the form of taxes forgone, which can be considered a financial intergovernmental grant.[35]

Tax exemption is an inefficient grant mechanism, however, because the forgone federal tax revenue is currently larger than the interest saving that accrues to state-local borrowers.[36] This occurs because the income tax rate structure is progressive and the state-local demand for loanable funds exceeds the supply of funds available from the group that is in the highest marginal tax bracket. Figure 16-1 describes these conditions.[37] The horizontal axis measures dollars of loanable funds. The vertical axis measures the equilibrium tax-exempt/taxable "yield ratio," which is an alternative way of expressing the equilibrium yield relationship. Thus, rearranging Equation (16-4), we obtain:

$$\frac{i_e}{i} = (1 - t) \qquad (16\text{-}5)$$

[35] The individual states also exempt from state income taxes those bonds issued by their own governmental subdivisions.

[36] See, for example, Susan Ackerman and David Ott, "An Analysis of the Revenue Effects of Proposed Substitutes for the Tax Exemption of State and Local Bonds," *National Tax Journal* (December 1970), 397–406; Robert P. Huefner, "Municipal Bonds: The Costs and Benefits of an Alternative," *National Tax Journal* (December 1970), 407–416; Peter Fortune, "The Impact of Taxable Municipal Bonds: Policy Simulations with a Large Econometric Model," *National Tax Journal* (March 1973), 611–624; and Peter Fortune, "Tax-Exemption of State and Local Interest Payments: An Economic Analysis of the Issues and an Alternative," *New England Economic Review* (May–June 1973), 3–31.

[37] Figure 16-1 is a steady-state, long-run equilibrium model. Except for tax exemption, it assumes that tax-exempt and taxable securities are perfect substitutes. It also does not consider interest elasticity of the demand for loanable funds. Finally, it holds the aggregate demand and supply of funds constant. The model and subsequent analysis follow Fortune, "Tax-Exemption of State and Local Interest Payments."

Since the demand for loanable funds (or the supply of tax-exempt bonds, designated $D$ in Figure 16-1) is constant at any point in time, it is assumed to be independent of the yield ratio.[38] The kinked supply schedule for loanable funds (or demand for tax-exempt bonds, designated $S$ in Figure 16-1) reflects marginal tax rate circumstances at three different levels of demand. The highest marginal income tax rate is assumed to be 70 percent and thus, from Equation (16-5), the lowest equilibrium yield ratio will be 30 percent. At $D_1$, the state-local demand for loanable funds exactly equals the total supply of funds available from the highest marginal-tax-bracket group for financial assets with these risk/return characteristics. As the demand for funds exceeds the supply from investors in the 70 percent marginal tax bracket, tax-exempt yields must rise relative to taxable yields if they are to induce investors in the lower marginal tax bracket into the state-

**Figure 16-1  The Effect of the Tax Exempt/Taxable Yield Ratio on the Efficiency of Tax Exemption as a Financial Grant**

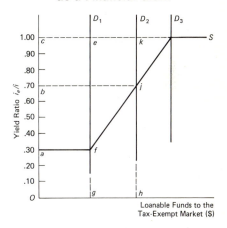

Source: Adapted from Peter Fortune, "Tax-Exemption of State and Local Interest Payments: An Economic Analysis of the Issues and an Alternative," *New England Economic Review* (May–June 1973), 21–31.

[38] A vertical demand schedule relating loanable funds to the yield ratio assumes that state-local and private goods are not close substitutes in the choice process. Consequently, the derived demand for financing these goods is not sensitive to changes in relative prices (interest rates in this case).

local securities market.[39] When demand increases to $D_2$, the yield ratio rises to 70 percent. However, the relatively higher tax-exempt interest rate is paid to all new investors regardless of their tax bracket. Consequently, intramarginal buyers above the market-clearing marginal tax rate at $D_1$ receive a "consumers' surplus"—that is, a rate of return above the rate necessary to attract loanable funds from these sources. At $D_3$ and beyond, comparable tax-exempt and taxable securities will have equivalent yields (see also footnote 42).

The size of the consumers' surplus, which measures the degree of allocative inefficiency, is shown in Figure 16-1.[40] If state-local securities were not tax exempt, the yield ratio would equal 1.00. Thus, for demand level $D_1$, the area $acef$ multiplied by $i$ is the amount of interest-cost saving accruing to the state-local sector because of tax exemption. Interest paid by state-local governments is $(0afg)(i)$. Consumers' surplus is zero and the grant is efficient. The entire federal grant—that is, forgone tax revenue—accrues to state-local governments as lower borrowing costs. At $D_2$, state-local

interest saving is $(bcekj)(i)$, but federal income tax forgone is $(ackjf)(i)$. Thus, consumers' surplus is $(abjf)(i)$.[41] For a given supply schedule $S$, as demand rises above $D_1$, consumers' surplus—and thus allocative inefficiency—increases. At the limit ($D_3$), the yield ratio equals 1.00; the grant mechanism is completely inefficient at the margin.[42] In 1976, tax exemption reduced federal income tax revenue by $3.5 billion. Thus, estimated consumers' surplus retained by state-local bondholders was $1.3 billion.[43]

In the long run, the relative efficiency of the grant mechanism depends partly on whether the demand for funds shifts by more or less than the supply of funds. During the early 1950s, the yield ratio increased from 70 percent to 90 percent, reflecting the relatively high annual growth (12 percent) in state-local demand for funds (see Figure 16-2). With lower annual growth rates since 1957, the yield ratio has returned to about 70 percent.

The yield ratio is also affected by supply-side factors. The somewhat lower yield ratio since 1965 is due in part to a relative increase in corporate yields. This effect reflects a higher default-risk premium caused by rising debt-to-resources ratios for the corporate sector.[44] The rising yield ratio in 1969 is generally attributed to uncertainty produced by congressional attempts at that time to alter the tax

[39]We could also view the relatively higher tax-exempt yield as the price necessary to attract more of the funds of top-bracket investors from alternative uses that presently produce risk/return characteristics that are preferable—in a utility-maximizing sense—to those offered by tax-exempt securities. Thus, a rising yield ratio does not necessarily mean that lower-tax-bracket investors are purchasing the additional bonds.

[40]Some writers in this field contend that a portion of the consumers' surplus is allocatively efficient because a liquidity premium is necessary to compensate investors for a thin tax-exempt secondary market. Thus, the federal government subsidy to investors maintains an efficient and viable market for state-local securities. See Frank E. Morris, "The Case for Broadening the Financial Options Open to State and Local Governments—Part II," *Financing State and Local Governments,* Federal Reserve Bank of Boston, Boston, 1970, p. 126; also, Roland I. Robinson, *Postwar Market for State and Local Government Securities,* Princeton University Press, Princeton, N.J., 1960, pp. 99–100. One study argues that the requisite subsidy to investors varies directly with a sector's demand for funds relative to the total supply of funds. See John G. Gurley and Edward S. Shaw, "Financial Intermediaries and the Saving-Investment Process," *Journal of Finance* (May 1956), 257–276.
Note that we refer only to the *additional* consumers' surplus originating with the interaction of the progressive tax rate structure and the tax-exemption institution. To the extent that the supply of loanable funds is positively related to interest rates, consumers' surplus exists for both tax-exempt and taxable securities.

[41]If income tax rates were proportional rather than progressive, consumers' surplus originating from tax exemption would be zero. With a constant $t$ in Equation (16-2), the yield ratio would also be a constant; in other words, the supply-of-loanable-funds schedule would be a horizontal line throughout.

[42]If tax-exempt and taxable assets are perfect substitutes (except for the impact of the progressive tax-rate structure), their relative yields will change in response to shifts in demand. Beyond $D_3$, the progressive-tax-structure effect disappears and the yield ratio remains constant. If the assets are not perfect substitutes, part or all of the elasticity of the supply schedule could be altered. Differential default risk and institutional constraints are supply-side factors that would alter the elasticity of $S$. Under the demand conditions assumed in Figure 16-1, a change in the yield ratio originating from the supply-of-funds side will alter the efficiency of the grant mechanism *only if* the elasticity of $S$ over the relevant range is changed. A parallel shift of $S$ changes the yield ratio but leaves the size of consumers' surplus unchanged.

[43]Frank E. Morris, "The Taxable Bond Option," *National Tax Journal* (September 1976), 356–359.

[44]See Mitchell "Demand and Supply of Loanable Funds for the State-Local Sector," pp. 171–173.

**Figure 16-2  The Relationship of the Tax Exempt/Taxable Yield Ratio to Demand and Supply Conditions**

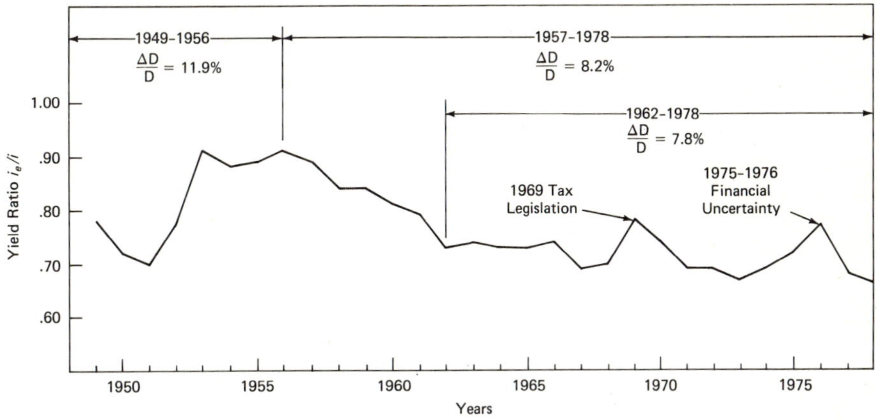

Notes: Yield ratios refer to state-local and corporate Baa-rated yields.
$\Delta D/D$ = average rate of change in state-local debt outstanding.

exemption law. The rising yield ratio during 1975–1976 reflected, in part, market uncertainty caused by financial difficulties of some units in the state-local sector, particularly New York City. As these uncertainties abated in 1977, the yield ratio returned to its historical level.

### The Taxable Bond Option

The straightforward solution to the foregoing problem, congressional repeal of the tax-exemption provision, is not politically feasible. State and local government officials prefer the tax-exemption form of grant because, unlike the majority of federal grants, it is open-ended and free of federal controls. The governmental unit itself decides when and how much to borrow, and for which projects. The grant is provided immediately at the time of borrowing. State and local government officials, therefore, are reluctant to give up this perquisite. State and local governments represent a powerful lobby, and they stand unified on this issue.[45] Moreover, the federal

interest subsidy has become an institution vested with an historical tradition—the American people, on the whole, believe it is appropriate. In view of the political difficulties of repeal an alternative plan—the taxable bond option—has been proposed. Under this plan,[46] if a state or local government chooses to issue taxable bonds, it receives a direct interest subsidy from the federal government. The subsidy rate, $s$, is some percentage of the borrowing rate. As the subsidy rate exceeds a particular marginal tax rate, this will induce some substitution of taxable for tax-exempt bond issuance. This effect is demonstrated in Figure 16-3. Assume that the equilibrium yield ratio before the subsidy is 70 percent and that $D_1$ represents the total demand for funds, all of which is initially represented by issuance of tax exempts. A subsidy of 30 percent or less would provide no incentive for issuers to substitute taxable for tax-exempt bonds, since that is the present marginal subsidy rate provided by the market. A subsidy of 50 percent, however, is higher than the market subsidy of 30 percent, so state-local governments will begin

[45] As one observer put it, "Very few Congressmen would be willing to take the political risk of standing for the elimination of a doctrine that appears to protect local independence and initiative and to lower the cost of local government." Alan Rabinowitz, *Municipal Bond Finance and Administration,* Wiley-Interscience, New York, 1969, p. 118.

[46] Other proposals, such as subsidizing purchases by pension funds or by an urban development agency that functions as a financial intermediary, would have similar results. See Harvey Galper and John Petersen, "An Analysis of Subsidy Plans to Support State and Local Borrowing," *National Tax Journal* (June 1971), 205–234.

to issue taxable bonds. New issues of *tax exempts* will decline to $D_2$. The distance between $D_2$ and $D_1$ represents the issuance of state-local *taxable* securities. As the supply of tax exempts declines, their interest rates will fall relative to taxables, inducing marginal investors to purchase the higher-yielding (after-tax) taxable securities. How far will tax-exempt yields fall relative to taxable yields? To the point where the market subsidy is again equal to the federal government subsidy. Thus, the equilibrium yield ratio in Figure 16-3 also can be stated in terms of the federal subsidy rate $s$:

$$\frac{i_e}{i} = (1 - s) \qquad (16\text{-}6)$$

When we compare Equation (16-5) with Equation (16-6), we see that the equilibrium condition for the yield ratio is $t = s$. All investors with *marginal* tax rates above the subsidy rate will continue to buy tax exempts; those below will buy taxable state-local or corporate securities. As the subsidy rate increases, consumers' surplus declines. At $D_3$ in Figure 16-3 (a subsidy rate of 70 percent), a yield ratio of 30 percent would produce an allocatively efficient grant.[47]

Some students of public finance see additional benefits in a program of federal subsidies. For example, they argue that because taxable bonds will widen the market for state-local securities, particularly for long-term bonds, overall interest costs for the sector will decline. Also, with a taxable bond subsidy program, they expect the market inefficiency produced by the cyclical supply shifts of commercial banks to be reduced. As the banks sell tax exempts, for example, $S$ in Figure 16-3 shifts upward along $D_1$, tax-exempt yields rise, and the yield ratio rises. With a taxable bond option, on the other hand, as $S$ shifts upward, state-local governments will substitute relatively more taxable bond issues. Tax-exempt borrowing declines to, say, $D_2$, the yield ratio stays constant, and interest rate variability declines.

The taxable bond option is considered to be politically feasible because it does not directly challenge the vested interests in the present market-subsidy program. Opposition remains, however, because there is always the suspicion (with histor-

**Figure 16-3  The Effect of Federal Interest Rate Subsidies on State-Local Taxable Bond Issuance**

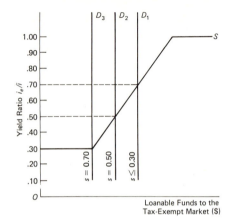

Source: See Figure 16-1.

ical justification) that once it establishes a direct subsidy program, Congress will eventually want more control over the decisions that concern borrowing and capital expenditures. Current proposals have attempted to defuse this objection by making the subsidy payments automatic and without discretionary control and by retaining tax-exempt borrowing as an option. Political opposition also comes from some segments of the investment banking industry which believes that it will be at a competitive disadvantage in marketing taxable securities.[48] Some observers also question the significance of cyclical interest-rate variability that is supposedly introduced by commercial banks' portfolio behavior. As we have discussed, the demand for tax exempts by the household sector is generally inverse to that of commercial banks, and thus provides a stabilizing influence on tax-exempt interest rates. Finally, some students question whether a taxable security option would significantly help the state-local sector. Most nonbank institutional investors are partially or wholly tax exempt and, as such, are potential investors in state-local *taxable* bonds. It is argued, however, that life insurance companies, private pension funds, and mutual funds are primarily interested in equities or debt

---

[47] At a subsidy rate of 70 percent, however, the program would be quite costly. This issue is discussed later.

[48] Fortune, "Tax Exemption of State and Local Interest Payments," 27.

securities with equity "kickers." Public pension funds also are moving in this direction. Thrift institutions specialize in mortgages, and educational and charitable institutions are not important suppliers of loanable funds.[49] If the supply of loanable funds with respect to the yield ratio is inelastic, overall interest costs (gross of subsidies) will be higher, offsetting somewhat the efficiency of the grant.

The *net* U.S. Treasury costs for a particular program are interest-subsidy payments and associated costs *minus* additional tax revenues gained from the new taxable state-local bonds.[50] The ultimate cost depends on the marginal-tax-rate structure, the supply of loanable funds available at each marginal tax bracket, and the elasticities of the underlying demand and supply of loanable funds.[51]

[49]Arthur Levitt, "The Case for Broadening the Financial Options Open to State and Local Governments: Discussion," in *Financing State and Local Governments,* Federal Reserve Bank of Boston, Boston, 1970, pp. 148–149.

[50]There are three types of costs incurred by the federal government from the taxable bond option plan. First, the net cost of the subsidy payments is

$$\sum_{i=1}^{n} (s - t_i)B_i$$

where $t_i$ and $B_i$ are, respectively, the marginal tax rate and the dollar volume of the $i$th investor who switches to taxable state-local securities (see Galper and Petersen, "An Analysis of Subsidy Plans to Support State and Local Borrowing," 622). If state-local debt issuance is somewhat interest elastic, then as the sector's net interest cost declines under the subsidy program, its debt volume will increase. This will displace other taxable security issuance (recall the model's assumptions). Thus, the cost of the program will be higher since subsidy payments will increase, but federal tax revenue will be unchanged after the substitution between the two types of taxable securities.

In a separate development, commercial banks are making use of new tax-sheltering devices. See, for example, Ralph C. Kimball, "Commercial Banks, Tax Avoidance, and the Market for State and Local Debt Since 1970," *New England Economic Review* (January–February 1977), 3–21. Even without the impact of the taxable bond option on tax-exempt yields, use of these new devices will raise interest costs to state-local governments and raise subsidy costs for the federal government. The taxable bond option will only exacerbate these effects. Second, as taxable interest rates rise, federal government borrowing costs will increase. Finally, there are administrative costs in operating the new program.

[51]For estimates of net costs, see Galper and Petersen, "An Analysis of Subsidy Plans to Support State and Lo-

## Commercial Bank Underwriting and Public Policy

The Glass-Steagall Banking Act (1933) prohibited commercial banks from underwriting corporate securities and state-local nonguaranteed obligations. The act had two principal objectives. First, it sought to reduce the potential for conflict between the underwriting and fiduciary functions of commercial banks. Banks serve as financial advisors and portfolio managers and, as such, *could be* biased toward securities they hold as an underwriter or dealer, regardless of their appropriateness for specific financial investment objectives. Second, banks allegedly have a competitive edge, vis-à-vis nonbank underwriters, since they control the principal source of funds used to finance underwriting operations. In addition, through their fiduciary operations and purchases of securities for their own investment account, commercial banks constitute an important segment of the buyers' market for securities.

The Glass-Steagall Banking Act led to the creation of a separate investment banking industry. Since its enactment, banks have dominated the underwriting of general-obligation issues and, due to some liberalization of the act, they have participated in a small, but growing, proportion of nonguaranteed underwriting.

The volume of nonguaranteed debt issued was small when the act was passed, but it has since grown to represent over 40 percent of the state-local new-issues market. Predictably, the commercial banking industry has intensified its efforts to eliminate the underwriting prohibition. Industry representatives contend that the additional competition would lower NIC for nonguaranteed issues. Several studies have concluded that for like-rated general-obligation and nonguaranteed bonds, the latter received fewer bids and paid higher interest rates because of larger underwriter spreads.[52]

Also, predictably, nonbank underwriters have mounted a spirited defense of the law that insulates them from bank competition. They have argued

cal Borrowing," and Fortune, "Tax Exemption of State and Local Interest Payments."

[52]See references in the section, "Interest Cost Determinants."

that the original objectives of the act—avoiding conflict of interest and bank domination—have contemporary significance. They contend that, due to strategic advantages of commercial banks, repeal would ultimately lead to domination of the industry by a few large banks, resulting in *less* competition and *higher* interest costs for the state-local sector. Moreover, they have criticized the research design of the studies that connected lack of competition in the nonbank underwriting industry with higher interest rates for nonguaranteed issues. They contend that like-rated bonds are not necessarily homogeneous with respect to risk and marketability; higher interest rates on nonguaranteed issues reflect additional default and liquidity risk, not lack of competition in underwriting.

After controlling for average maturity, quality rating, and so on, nonguaranteed yields do average 13 basis points (.13% or 13 hundredths of 1 percent) higher than comparable general obligations receiving the same number of bids. As noted above, the market discriminates among like-rated nonguaranteed bonds according to the source of revenues for amortizing the issue. By further controlling for risk by purpose of issue, the introduction of bank eligibility eliminates the interest-cost differential between nonguaranteed and general-obligation bonds. This evidence supports the contention that additional competition leads to lower borrowing costs. The position is weakened, however, by low levels of statistical significance in the tests, which increases the possibility that the conclusions are spurious.[53] Also, the number of bids is not always an accurate measure of the degree of competition. The formation of syndicates reduces the *number* of bidders, but may enhance the financial strength of such groups, thus *increasing* bidding competition. Moreover, although nonguaranteed bonds average one bid fewer than comparable general obligations, past experience indicates that bank eligibility for underwriting certain types of nonguaranteed issues has not increased the number of bids. Banks have tended to join existing syndicates rather than to form additional ones. Apparently, bank participation in a bidding syndicate increases its competi-

tiveness (lowers NIC) through the addition of the banks' unique marketing advantages and capital financing capabilities to the group.[54]

Legislation designed to provide bank entry into nonguaranteed bond underwriting has been recommended to Congress on numerous occasions.[55] Although a number of influential groups support amending the act, the basic law has remained intact.[56] Since the advantage of lower borrowing cost through greater competition has not been conclusively established, the uncertainty of the subsequent impact on the overall competitiveness of the industry has been an important barrier to change.

The argument that the entry of commercial banks into this field would cause underwriter concentration assumes that larger banks would offer higher prices (lower NIC) to state-local governments until the nonbank underwriting firms disappear and, further, that subsequent reentry would somehow be blocked. Only then could banks gain monopoly profits. However, it seems likely that so long as nonbank underwriting firms still exist for the distribution of corporate securities, costs of reentry into the state-local segment of the industry will probably be minimal, thus precluding monopoly pricing by banks. Even if banks were allowed to underwrite corporate securities and eventually eliminated nonbank competition, bank domination could only be maintained by continuing to offer lower borrowing costs since entry-reentry costs are generally low for financial institutions.

The conflict-of-interest argument is similarly weak. It suggests that the quality of the banks' fiduciary function is reduced when banking and

---

[53]Hopewell and Kaufman, "Commercial Bank Bidding on Municipal Revenue Bonds."

[54]Ibid.; Kessel, "A Study of the Effects of Competition in the Tax-Exempt Bond Market," 734–736.

[55]A chronological history for 1933–1967 is outlined in Rabinowitz, *Municipal Bond Finance and Administration,* Chap. 8. A recent compilation of arguments is contained in U.S. Senate, Committee on Banking, Housing, and Urban Affairs, "Hearings before a subcommittee of the Senate Committee on Banking, Housing, and Urban Affairs," *Trading in Municipal Securities,* 93rd Cong., 2nd Sess., May 6–8, 1974. See also Richard R. West, "Should Commercial Banks Be Allowed to Underwrite Municipal Revenue Bonds?" *National Banking Review* (September 1965), 35–44.

[56]These include the Federal Reserve System, the U.S. Treasury, the Hunt Commission, and the Municipal Finance Officers Association.

underwriting functions are combined in one firm.[57] But the financial services industry is very competitive. Bad advice sells at a discount, so that few banks would have an incentive to engage in such practices.

In summary, there is little support on the grounds of allocative efficiency for maintaining the present law. Banks may possess unique skills in the production of underwriter services, such that they would dominate in a freely competitive environment. If so, the issue of maintaining a legal monopoly that is costly (that is, allocatively inefficient) must be justified on other grounds, such as subjective judgments about the desirability of obtaining a particular distribution of income between bank and nonbank underwriters. This choice will be decided through the political decision-making process.

## Conclusion

The demand for loanable funds by the state-local sector has generally increased in nominal terms at about 8 percent per year. Over the long run, the sector has decreased its relative reliance on external financing. The growing desire and/or ability to finance internally is attributable to several factors: a relative increase in the state-government share of total sector activity; an increase in federal grants that can substitute for borrowing; a shift to a more income-elastic revenue structure; and a secular decline in the propensity to borrow per dollar of real-asset spending. The ability of state-local governments to achieve their target internal-financing proportions is periodically impaired. High rates of inflation and/or a high and rising $RA/EXP$ ratio reduces budgetary flexibility, resulting in temporary shifts toward relatively more external financing.

The overall sector's borrowing is somewhat interest elastic over the cycle. Interest sensitivity is attributable, for the most part, to state governments and large local units. Most local governments lack the necessary budgetary flexibility to time bond issues over an interest rate cycle. Shortfalls in borrowing do not lead to equivalent reductions in real-asset spending. Interim financing is employed to maintain real-asset spending when borrowing shortfalls occur.

Three sectors—commercial banks, households, and fire and casualty insurance companies—provide most of the loanable funds to state and local governments. These sectors have high marginal tax rates; consequently, after-tax state-local yields are higher than those on comparable taxable securities. Commercial banks hold over 40 percent of these outstandings, although their share declined somewhat between 1970 and 1978. This decline was due, in part, to cyclical substitution between loans and tax-exempt securities and, in part, to the use of alternative tax-sheltering devices. The household sector's participation has declined since 1960 as investors have sought higher-yielding equity outlets. Their future participation is likely to increase as the supply of alternative tax shelters declines and the intermediary services of bond funds and common trusts widen the market for tax-exempt securities.

The interest cost for a new state-local security is determined by three sets of factors: (1) market and institutional characteristics; (2) borrower characteristics; and (3) issue characteristics. Given the pure rate of interest and institutional characteristics, levels of, and changes in, interest costs vary according to differential default, capital market, and inflation risks. Risk premiums affect interest costs through their influence on both reoffering bond prices and underwriter spreads.

Legal debt limitations reflect a political response to past debt-related financial difficulties. Through the use of innovations, such as shifting financial responsibility and issuing nonguaranteed debt, these laws have been effectively "repealed." On a statewide basis, governmental units with relatively restrictive debt limitations have issued just as much debt as less restricted or unrestricted units. This suggests that the sector's total demand for loanable funds has not been constrained by legal debt limitations.

Tax exemption of state-local interest income is a type of intergovernmental grant. The grant mechanism is inefficient, however, because not all of the monies accrue to the intended recipients. This occurs because the income tax structure is progres-

---

[57]A "conflict of interest" charge also can be made against those nonbank financial institutions, such as the large brokerage firms, that have both underwriting and brokerage operations.

sive and the state-local demand for loanable funds exceeds the supply of funds available from investors in the highest marginal tax bracket. Since repeal of tax exemption is not politically feasible, a taxable bond subsidy program has been proposed as a viable alternative. This program is expected to reduce borrowing costs for state-local governments and increase the progressivity of the tax structure. The additional cost of the new subsidy program is unknown at the present time.

The Glass-Steagall Banking Act prohibited commercial banks from underwriting corporate securities and most state-local nonguaranteed obligations. The commercial banking industry, among others, would like Congress to repeal the act. It contends that the additional competition will lower borrowing costs for state and local governments. Opponents of repeal, including nonbank underwriters, contend that repeal will ultimately lead to bank domination and monopoly pricing. Given the present structure of the industry, however, it appears unlikely that repealing a law that restricts competition will lead to *less* competition.

## Questions

1. "Net borrowing can be viewed as a residual resulting from the decision to make real and financial asset expenditures in excess of saving in the current year." Explain this statement. What is the significance of viewing net borrowing in this manner?
2. Outline and briefly explain the reasons suggested in the text that the state-local sector has increasingly substituted internal for external financing over time. Why do rapidly changing prices affect the sector's ability to achieve its targeted internal-external financing proportions in the short run?
3. Is state and local government borrowing sensitive to cyclical interest rates? Explain your answer.
4. "Since legal debt limitations are effectively bypassed, they should be repealed." Discuss this statement critically.
5. Why is the market for state-local securities dominated by three sectors? Why might this pattern of flow of funds change in the future?

6. Why does the cost of underwriting state-local securities vary according to differential risk?
7. Why can we view the tax-exempt status of state-local bonds as a type of intergovernmental grant?
8. Why is tax exemption said to be an inefficient grant?
9. Outline the principal objectives and characteristics of the proposed *taxable bond option* plan.
10. Critically examine the case for and against the Glass-Steagall Banking Act provision that prohibits commercial banks from underwriting corporate securities and state-local nonguaranteed obligations.

## Selected Bibliography

Bosworth, Barry, James S. Duesenberry, and Andrew S. Carron. *Capital Needs in the Seventies*. Brookings Institution, Washington, D.C., 1975.

Copeland, Morris A. *Trends in Government Financing*. Princeton University Press, Princeton, N.J., 1961.

Hillhouse, A. M. *Municipal Bonds: A Century of Experience*. Duke University Press, Durham, N.C., 1936.

Mitchell, William E. "Demand and Supply of Loanable Funds for the State-Local Sector," in *Understanding Capital Markets: The Financial Environment and the Flow of Funds in the Next Decade,* eds. A. W. Sametz and P. Wachtel. D. C. Heath, Lexington, Mass., 1977, Chap. 9.

Moak, Lennox L. *Administration of Local Government Debt*. Municipal Finance Officers Association, Chicago, 1970.

Ott, David J., Attiat F. Ott, James A. Maxwell, and J. Richard Aronson. *State-Local Finances in the Last Half of the 1970s*. American Enterprise Institute for Public Policy Research, Washington, D.C., 1975.

*Public Facility Financing*. Joint Economic Committee, Washington, D.C., 1966.

Rabinowitz, Alan. *Municipal Bond Finance and Administration*. Wiley-Interscience, New York, 1969.

Ratchford, B. U. *American State Debts*. Duke University Press, Durham, N.C., 1951.

Robinson, Roland I. *Postwar Market for State and Local Government Securities*. Princeton University Press, Princeton, N.J., 1960.

Tax Foundation. *The Financial Outlook for State and Local Government to 1980*. Tax Foundation, New York, 1973.

# 17

# Federal Government Demand

Private economic choices are constrained by the scarcity of economic resources—labor, wealth, income. Every time a manufacturer chooses to produce or not to produce, or a banker to lend or not to lend, or a consumer to buy or to save, a separate decision is made on how best to allocate the limited resources of the individual or firm. Governments operate under somewhat different rules.

Government decisions—like private decisions—rest upon a comparison of costs and benefits, but they are measured according to a different calculus. The federal government's domestic spending power, in particular, is neither created nor limited by its economic productivity, but by its vast powers to tax and borrow. The power to tax extends as far as the voters will permit. The power to borrow, in turn, reflects (at least until recently) a widely accepted assumption that the public will always vote whatever taxes are needed to maintain complete assurance that the government will meet all payments—including both interest service and principal—due its creditors on schedule.[1] Because of the confidence in the scope and use of the federal taxing power, and because few citizens would emigrate to another country to escape that power (or go to prison à la Thoreau), U.S. Treasury securities have enjoyed the highest credit standing in the world.

In this chapter our concern is not with the process by which the fiscal decisions of the U.S. government are made, but with their consequences—which determine whether the government will be a borrower or a lender in the credit markets. These consequences usually have relatively little influence on the spending and taxing decisions. Because of the premier status of Treasury securities, prevailing credit market conditions are not likely to be an important limiting factor in the political process that molds federal budgets. The government may pay some attention, it is true, primarily at budget time, to the possible impact of federal operations

[1]It would, of course, be impossible to pay off all the debt at once without resorting, on the one hand, to Draconian tax increases or, on the other, to the printing press for money. As long as interest payments are made regularly, however, it is possible to refinance the principal amounts as they fall due. Moreover, in the event of some disastrous financial crisis, the Treasury could meet its nominal obligations by borrowing from the Federal Reserve System, an escape hatch not available to private debtors.

on interest rates and credit availability. But, most of the time, the Treasury's relationship to the credit markets grows out of legislatively mandated revenues and outlays. That is why the Treasury—when it is in deficit, which is usual—is labeled a *necessitous* borrower: unlike a private firm or household, it lacks the option of controlling its borrowings by altering its operating plan to increase receipts or to reduce spending. Once legislative decisions have frozen revenues and outlays, the Treasury's demand schedule for funds becomes virtually inelastic with respect to interest rates. In the language of the government securities market, where outstanding Treasury obligations are bought and sold in amounts averaging over $10 billion a day, the Treasury is said always to get its money first, while other borrowers must be content with the leftovers.

The Treasury is by far the largest single borrower and debtor in our credit markets. The total of U.S. government and federal agency securities outstanding in the hands of the public at the end of 1978 came to $798 billion, equal to over one-fifth of the aggregate of all loans, mortgages, bonds, and other debt instruments outstanding in the United States. A private loan or security sale of $300 million is large; a Treasury debt operation of $2 billion is routinely small. The mere mechanics of keeping afloat such a huge debt, most of it concentrated in short maturities (Table 17-1), is a major task.

## The Budget

Analysis of the government's financial impact on the economy takes the federal budget as its point of departure. The president submits the budget to Congress each January or February. The budget provides updated spending, revenue, and borrowing estimates for the fiscal year in progress ending September 30, as well as detailed projections for the next fiscal year (and, frequently, information pertinent to later fiscal years as well). The budget thus represents a forecast running over eighteen months into the future. As such it necessarily is based on a host of assumptions that are bound to be at least somewhat inaccurate. In order to prepare the budget, the government must forecast the rate of national production and income, for it is the course of the economy that will largely determine the yield of income, profits, excise and other taxes, as well as the size of certain federal outlays, such

as unemployment insurance or farm price-support payments. It is also necessary to predict the cost and availability of items the federal government buys, ranging from paper clips to the services of millions of civilian employees and soliders all the way to intercontinental missiles. Of course, the figures also assume the willingness of Congress to ratify the legislative programs, often including changes in tax laws or rates, that underlie or are submitted in the budget.

In Congress, under procedures adopted in the mid-1970s, a somewhat parallel process occurs. The House and Senate each has a Budget Committee. These committees review the administration's submissions and, in consultation with other committees, arrive at budget recommendations that may differ from the president's. By the time the new fiscal year begins on October 1, these committees must issue a series of joint congressional resolutions that delineate spending and revenue targets, which are legislatively binding on the executive—and on Congress as well. They bind Congress in the sense that no member may subsequently offer any spending or tax proposal that would increase the deficit (or reduce the surplus), unless these committees approve a new joint budget resolution. These new procedures reflect an effort by Congress to force itself to view the budget as a whole. This is in marked contrast to its previous method of piecemeal treatment, which tended to produce undisciplined expenditure aggregates.[2]

Table 17-2 gives a summary of the 1979 budget request submitted by President Carter in February 1978. The top section, "Budget authority," shows the amounts Congress is asked to vote or has already voted in the past. The appropriate committees consider *authorizations* that set limits for particular types of expenditures. These authorizations must traverse the usual legislative process, which culminates in their being signed by the president.

[2]For discussion of many issues that must be considered as Congress makes the budget, see *The 1979 Budget—Setting National Priorities*, The Brookings Institution, Washington, D.C. (or later editions of this annual volume). See also George P. Shultz and Kenneth W. Dam, *Economic Policy Beyond the Headlines*, Stanford Alumni Association, Stanford, Calif., 1977, Chaps. 2 and 3. The mechanics of the budget process are summarized in *The Budget of the United States Government, Fiscal Year 1978*, Government Printing Office, Washington, D.C., pp. 222–231.

**Table 17-2   The Budget (in billions of dollars)**

| | Fiscal Years | | |
| --- | --- | --- | --- |
| | 1977 Actual | 1978 Estimate | 1979 Estimate |
| Budget authority (largely appropriations) | | | |
| Available through current action by Congress | | | |
| Enacted or pending | $317.5 | $318.9 | $ — |
| Proposed or to be requested | — | 8.5 | 366.9 |
| Available without current action by Congress | 206.9 | 235.3 | 264.8 |
| Deductions for offsetting receipts[a] | (59.2) | (59.8) | (63.6) |
| Total budget authority | 465.2 | 502.9 | 568.2 |
| Total budget | | | |
| Receipts | 356.9 | 400.4 | 439.6 |
| Outlays | 401.9 | 462.2 | 500.2 |
| Budget surplus or deficit | (45.0) | (61.8) | (60.6) |
| Deficit of off-budget federal entities | (8.7) | (11.5) | (12.5) |
| Total deficit | (53.7) | (73.4) | (73.1) |
| Borrowing from the public | 53.5 | 66.0 | 73.0 |
| Other means of financing | .2 | 7.4 | .1 |
| Outstanding debt, end of year | | | |
| Gross federal debt | 709.1 | 785.6 | 873.7 |
| Held by the public | 551.8 | 617.8 | 690.8 |
| Outstanding loans, end of year | | | |
| Direct loans—on budget | 68.2 | 76.1 | 80.4 |
| Direct loans—off budget | 32.7 | 43.8 | 56.8 |
| Guaranteed and insured loans[b] | 183.9 | 200.4 | 223.6 |
| Government-sponsored enterprise loans[c] | 98.9 | 115.2 | 130.1 |
| Total, direct, guaranteed, and enterprise loans | 383.7 | 435.5 | 490.9 |

[a]These consist of interfund and intragovernmental transactions and proprietary receipts from the public.
[b]Excludes loans held by government accounts and government-sponsored enterprises.
[c]Net of loans between government-sponsored enterprises and between such enterprises and federal agencies. Government-sponsored enterprises include the Banks for Cooperatives, Federal Intermediate Credit Banks, Federal Land Banks, Federal Home Loan Banks, Federal Home Loan Mortgage Corporation, Federal National Mortgage Association, and Student Loan Marketing Association.

Source: *The Budget of the United States Government, 1979.*

No money may be *obligated* (or spent), however, until an *appropriations* bill for the expenditure has run a similar legislative gamut. The Office of Management and Budget then has the responsibility for monitoring the actual spending process in the various disbursing agencies.

The next section of Table 17-2 shows the actual amounts expected to be received and disbursed and the budget surplus (the last one occurred in fiscal 1969) or deficit. The Treasury must finance, however, not only budget deficits but also the net disbursements of certain "off-budget" federal agencies and credit programs whose outlays, by law, are not considered part of the budget.[3] The sum of

any budget deficits and any off-budget net outlays determines the approximate amount of borrowing and growth in the accumulated debt (shown in the third section of Table 17-2). Some of the securities that the Treasury issues to finance the debt may eventually be purchased by the Federal Reserve System or placed with certain agencies that are considered part of the federal government itself. Such borrowing is excluded in arriving at the fiscal 1978 figures of $66 billion and $617.8 billion, respectively, estimated as *borrowing from the public* and *debt held by the public* at fiscal year-end (that is, September 30, 1978).

---

[3]These agencies are the Federal Financing Bank, Rural Electrification and Telephone Revolving Fund, Rural Tel-

ephone Bank, Pension Benefit Guaranty Corporation, Exchange Stabilization Fund, Postal Service Fund, and U.S. Railway Association.

**Table 17-1  Maturity Structure of the Marketable Federal Debt, as of June 30 (in billions of dollars)**

| Years to Final Maturity | 1978 Amount | 1978 Percentage | 1977 Amount | 1977 Percentage | 1970 Amount | 1970 Percentage | 1960 Amount | 1960 Percentage | 1951 Amount | 1951 Percentage |
|---|---|---|---|---|---|---|---|---|---|---|
| One year or less | $220.7 | 46% | $212.0 | 49% | $105.5 | 45% | $ 70.5 | 38% | $ 43.9 | 32% |
| Over 1 to 5 years | 174.3 | 36 | 144.5 | 34 | 89.6 | 39 | 72.8 | 40 | 46.5 | 34 |
| Over 5 to 10 years | 44.4 | 9 | 46.0 | 11 | 15.9 | 7 | 20.2 | 11 | 8.7 | 6 |
| Over 10 to 20 years | 14.9 | 3 | 11.6 | 3 | 10.5 | 5 | 12.6 | 7 | 29.9 | 22 |
| Over 20 years | 23.4 | 5 | 17.1 | 4 | 11.0 | 5 | 7.7 | 4 | 8.8 | 6 |
| Total | $477.7 | 100% | $431.1 | 100% | $232.6 | 100% | $183.8 | 100% | $137.9 | 100% |
| Average maturity | 3 yrs. 3 mos. | | 2 yrs. 10 mos. | | 3 yrs. 8 mos. | | 4 yrs. 4 mos. | | 6 yrs. 7 mos. | |

Note: Excludes savings bonds and other nonmarketable issues.

Sources: *Federal Reserve Bulletin; Treasury Bulletin.*

**Table 17-3  Federal Receipts and Expenditures in the National Income Accounts (in billions of dollars)**

| Description | 1977 Actual | 1978 Estimate | 1979 Estimate |
|---|---|---|---|
| **RECEIPTS** | | | |
| Personal tax and nontax receipts | $165.5 | $185.5 | $195.6 |
| Corporate profits tax accruals | 57.4 | 63.1 | 69.7 |
| Indirect business tax and nontax accruals | 24.6 | 28.5 | 34.8 |
| Contributions for social insurance | 116.5 | 133.7 | 151.3 |
| Total receipts | 364.0 | 410.8 | 451.4 |
| **EXPENDITURES** | | | |
| Purchases of goods and services | $140.7 | $158.4 | $171.6 |
| Defense | (92.0) | (99.8) | (108.1) |
| Nondefense | (48.7) | (58.6) | (63.5) |
| Transfer payments | 169.7 | 184.2 | 201.8 |
| Domestic ("to persons") | (166.5) | (180.7) | (198.0) |
| Foreign | (3.2) | (3.5) | (3.8) |
| Grants-in-aid to state and local governments | 66.0 | 77.0 | 81.6 |
| Net interest paid | 29.3 | 34.5 | 39.8 |
| Subsidies less current surplus of government enterprises | 6.1 | 9.5 | 9.2 |
| Total expenditures | 411.8 | 463.6 | 504.0 |
| Deficit | (47.8) | (52.8) | (52.6) |

Source: *Special Analyses—Budget of the United States Government, Fiscal Year 1979*, p. 46.

All parts of the budget (as well as its total size) exert significant influence on the economy and, therefore, on its financial markets. As it is conventionally presented, however, the budget is designed chiefly to meet the government's accounting and control needs and is not necessarily in the most useful form for economic or financial analysis. Those economists who prefer to interpret economic developments mainly through the National Income Accounts (which focus on GNP, national income, and their composition) frequently employ the so-called National Income Accounts (NIA) presentation of the budget (Table 17-3). This differs from the presentation in Table 17-2 mainly in that more outlay and revenue items are entered on an accrual rather than cash basis (which alters their timing) and federal credit programs are excluded (because they involve transactions other than purchases of goods and services or transfer payments). Another sometimes useful version of the budget is the so-called high-employment or full-employment budget, which reestimates the budget to show how receipts might be greater and expenditures lower at given levels of unemployment. One may argue that large deficits at times of high unemployment

are tolerable or even desirable as long as the budget structure is such that a return to full employment brings the budget into balance or surplus. The same objective—the effort to distinguish quantitatively the effect of the economy on the budget from the budget's influence on the economy—leads to the calculation of measures of "fiscal thrust" that endeavor to quantify this distinction.[4]

Analysis of the federal government's impact on the flow of funds and on financial markets over any given interval requires two major adjustments to the budget. First, changes in the Treasury's cash position must be considered. The Treasury main-

[4]See Michael Levy, *The Federal Budget: Its Impact on the Economy,* The Conference Board, New York, 1976; and Federal Reserve Bank of St. Louis, *Federal Budget Trends* (quarterly). See also Chapter 29 of the text.

Examine the most recent budget document or at least the short summary, *The Budget in Brief,* that accompanies each federal budget. In the 1979 budget, data for the National Income Accounts basis and for credit programs are contained in Special Analyses B and F, respectively. These and other analyses (running up to P) are published in a separate volume called *Special Analyses—Budget of the United States Government.*

tains large balances at the Federal Reserve and commercial banks to cover differences in timing between receipts and expenditures.[5] Outlays tend to bunch up early each month (reflecting mainly payment of Social Security benefits), while many major tax receipts flow in after mid-month (such as after the April 15 individual and corporate income tax deadline). Running down the Treasury's balances temporarily reduces borrowing needs; building them up makes it necessary to borrow more than the amount needed to meet immediate expenditure requirements.

One other major adjustment is needed to move from the budget to the government's demand for credit. Analysts must take full account of the government's huge participation in credit and credit-guarantee programs (see the bottom block of Table 17-2). While some of these programs do appear in the budget, many do not. Within the government, there is an entity called the Federal Financing Bank, one of the off-budget agencies referred to in Table 17-2, that serves as the conduit for channeling Treasury funds to many of the lending agencies in question. In housing and agriculture, however, which are the chief beneficiaries of federally backed credit programs, most governmental lending is done by quasi-independent agencies which issue their own securities to the public, are outside the budget, and are largely exempt from budgetary review. Their borrowing is not included in "borrowing from the public," as defined in Table 17-2. Whenever the private credit situation tightens, borrowers draw on these federal lending institutions more heavily and they, in turn, must increase their security issuance. When private credit sources are cheap and abundant, the agencies' role diminishes.

Chapter 11 is devoted to a detailed discussion and analysis of government credit agencies. Here we focus almost exclusively on the influence of the Treasury's own borrowing on the economy and on the financial markets. Keep in mind, however, that not only are other federal agencies sizable borrowers but that the government and its agencies are also major lenders and guarantors in most credit markets.

## Types of Treasury Debt

With so large a quantity of debt to keep afloat, the Treasury has, over the years, resorted to issuing many different types of securities through many different marketing techniques. Most of the debt is marketable—that is, it takes the form of fixed-interest securities that holders can freely buy and sell in the secondary market. Over one-third of the debt, however, consists of nonmarketable issues, comprising primarily U.S. savings bonds sold to individuals and special securities sold under certain conditions to foreign as well as state and local governmental buyers.

The marketable debt embraces Treasury bills, notes, and bonds. Bills are discount securities with an original maturity of less than a year. Three- and six-month bills are auctioned weekly; 52-week bills every four weeks; and special bills (often maturing shortly after major tax-payment dates when the Treasury has cash available for debt retirement) from time to time. Auction bids take the form of an offer to pay, say, $98,500 for $100,000 of three-month bills (which happens to correspond to an annual discount of 6 percent). The Treasury goes down the list and accepts bids until the amount of the offering is exhausted. The total amount offered (at this writing, close to $6 billion each week) is usually, but not necessarily, what is needed to "roll over" the previously issued Treasury bills that are maturing. Securities dealers and other sophisticated financial institutions (and sometimes the Federal Reserve and its foreign central-bank clients) play the major role in the auctions. The successful bidders include some institutions that plan to keep the bills and others that will act as "wholesalers" in distributing them to smaller buyers around the world. The discount rates on new bills established in the weekly competitive bidding and published in Tuesday's newspapers are one of the chief indexes of money-market conditions.[6]

---

[5]Most balances at commercial banks take the legal form of overnight loans to the banks. Banks pay the Treasury a rate of interest related to the Federal Funds rate (which is the interest rate for overnight loans between banks).

[6]Small buyers are allowed to enter a noncompetitive bid up to $500,000 that will be honored at the average bid of the auction. Governmental bidders, foreign and domestic, have the same privilege but have no restrictions on the size of the bid insofar as they are bidding to replace maturing holdings. All bills and much of other Treasury and agency debt, it may be noted, are on a "book entry" basis; ownership and transfers are recorded through computer entries. Actual securities are no longer issued.

Treasury notes, defined as obligations with original maturity of one to ten years, and Treasury bonds, which have lifespans longer than ten years, are called *coupon* issues. In contrast to bills, on which interest is discounted in advance, notes and bonds pay a stipulated annual rate of interest in two semiannual instalments. Coupon issues are usually auctioned like bills: Figure 17-1 reproduces the official offering-and-results summaries for one such financing. An alternative to the auction method is a subscription offering: the Treasury advertises a given amount of a new issue for subscription at a stipulated price. Normally there is a sizable oversubscription; small subscribers may have their requests allotted in full, while larger subscriptions are prorated. The major problem with such fixed-price offerings is that several days must elapse between offer and allotment. If there is a drop in the market during this time, the price may be unrealistic and the offering may fail. In order to avoid such an outcome, the Federal Reserve is more or less obligated to try to maintain interest rates on an "even keel" during that period. These attempts may involve supplying extra funds to the economy at a time when monetary policy calls for restraint. The Treasury shifted most of its borrowing from the subscription to the auction technique primarily to avoid these difficulties.

The Treasury has virtually total discretion as to how to conduct its borrowing operations and frequently modifies its procedures. Federal agencies also have wide discretion and generally use marketing techniques that differ from the Treasury's. Most of the agencies make an effort to follow a regular schedule so that potential investors can anticipate the times at which certain types of securities will be on offer.[7]

## The Government Securities Market

The existence of marketable Treasury securities implies the existence of an active secondary market in these instruments. Indeed, the ready salability of government securities is a key source of their prime standing as liquid reserve assets. This salability is provided by a highly efficient and competitive over-the-counter market. At the core of the market are more than thirty "primary" dealers, consisting mainly of the dealer departments of major investment or commercial banking firms. This "wholesale" market is located in New York City, but it is linked by telephone and telex to major customers and smaller dealers throughout the world.[8]

In recent years, the volume of transactions of the primary dealers (who report statistics to the Federal Reserve Bank of New York) has been averaging over $10 billion a day. Most of this volume involves Treasury bills and other short-term securities. Still, despite this enormous turnover, it is only on rare occasions that a dealer finds large buy and sell orders that exactly match as to particular issue, quantity, and price. To be sure, a dealer may find that another dealer has a buy order to match a sell order (or vice versa). For the most part, however, competitive forces will compel a dealer to buy securities from a client and to hold them in the expectation of later resale or to sell the client securities borrowed from some institution in the expectation of being able to "buy them in" advantageously later (a "short" sale).[9]

In these markets where the minimum round-lot transaction ranges from $100,000 for long-term bonds to $1 million for Treasury bills, dealers depend on their virtually automatic and massive borrowing ability to finance the inventories that may have to be carried to bridge purchases and sales spaced through time. The dealers' creditworthiness derives from the premier quality of the government securities that serve as collateral, the unquestioned integrity of their word as to prices and

---

[7]See Margaret E. Bedford, "Recent Developments in Treasury Financing Techniques," *Monthly Review,* Federal Reserve Bank of Kansas City (July–August 1977).

[8]The various Treasury, agency, and money market securities, and the dealer market, are described in the biennial *Handbook of Securities of the United States Government and Federal Agencies,* 28th ed., 1978, published by The First Boston Corporation, one of the principal dealer firms.

[9]Of course, dealers hope to make a profit by having the market move in their favor over this "bridging" interval. It should be emphasized that the function of dealers is to move market prices so as to express as closely as possible the continual changes in market evaluation on the part of buyers and sellers (including the dealers themselves). Dealers stabilize prices only insofar as they absorb in their inventory random fluctuations in buy and sell orders and insofar as they make it possible for large amounts to be bought or sold, whichever way the market is moving.

**Figure 17-1**

# FEDERAL RESERVE BANK
## OF NEW YORK
Fiscal Agent of the United States

May 19, 1980

## RESULTS OF TREASURY'S MAY QUARTERLY FINANCING

*To All Banking Institutions, and Others Concerned,*
*in the Second Federal Reserve District:*

The following statement was issued by the Treasury Department:

Through the sale of the three issues offered in the May financing, the Treasury raised approximately $3.6 billion of new money and refunded $9.6 billion of securities maturing May 15, 1980. The following table summarizes the results:

| | *9¼%* *Notes* *(Series K-1983)* | *10¾%* *Notes* *(Series B-1989)* | *10%* *Bonds* *(Bonds of 2005-2010)* | *Non-marketable Special Issues* | *Total* | *Maturing Securities Held* | *Net New Money Raised* |
|---|---|---|---|---|---|---|---|
| | | | *New Issues* | | | | |
| Public | $3.5 | $2.0 | $2.0 | — | $ 7.5 | $4.0[1] | $3.5 |
| Government Accounts and Federal Reserve Banks | 3.0 | 1.3 | 1.0 | $0.3 | 5.6 | 5.6 | — |
| Foreign Accounts for Cash | 0.1 | 0.1 | — | — | 0.2 | — | 0.2 |
| TOTAL | $6.6 | $3.4 | $3.0 | $0.3 | $13.2 | $9.6 | $3.6 |

Details may not add to total due to rounding.

[1] Comprised of $1.7 billion of maturing notes and $2.3 billion of maturing cash management bills.

In addition, the Treasury has released the following detailed results for each offering:

### RESULTS OF AUCTION OF 3¼-YEAR TREASURY NOTES
(Notes of Series K-1983)

The Department of the Treasury has accepted $3,506 million of $10,212 million of tenders received from the public for the 3¼-year notes, Series K-1983, auctioned today [*May 6*]. The range of accepted competitive bids was as follows:

Lowest yield .................. 9.28%
Highest yield .................. 9.35%
Average yield.................. 9.32%

The interest rate on the notes will be 9¼%. At the 9¼% rate, the above yields result in the following prices:

Low-yield price................ 99.816
High-yield price .............. 99.623
Average-yield price............ 99.706

The $3,506 million of accepted tenders includes $1,057 million of noncompetitive tenders and $2,411 million of competitive tenders from private investors, including 5% of the amount of notes bid for at the high yield. It also includes $38 million of tenders at the average price from Federal Reserve Banks as agents for foreign and international monetary authorities in exchange for maturing securities.

In addition to the $3,506 million of tenders accepted in the auction process, $3,000 million of tenders were accepted at the average price from Government accounts and Federal Reserve Banks for their own account in exchange for maturing securities, and $102 million of tenders were accepted at the average price from Federal Reserve Banks as agents for foreign and international monetary authorities for new cash.

(Over)

**Figure 17-1** (Continued)

**HIGHLIGHTS OF TREASURY
OFFERINGS TO THE PUBLIC
IN MAY 1980 FINANCING**

**SECURITIES TO BE ISSUED MAY 15, 1980**

| | **3¼-Year Notes** | **9½-Year Notes** | **30-Year Bonds** |
|---|---|---|---|
| **Amount Offered:** | | | |
| To the public . . . . . . . . . . . . . . . . . . | $3,500 million | $2,000 million | $2,000 million |
| **Description of Security:** | | | |
| Term and type of security . . . . . . . . | 3¼-year notes | 9½-year notes | 30-year bonds |
| Series and CUSIP designation. . . . . . | Series K-1983 (CUSIP No. 912827 KR2) | Series B-1989 (CUSIP No. 912827 KC5) | Bonds of 2005-2010 (CUSIP No. 912810 CP1) |
| Maturity date . . . . . . . . . . . . . . . . . . | August 15, 1983 | November 15, 1989 | May 15, 2010 |
| Call date. . . . . . . . . . . . . . . . . . . . . . | No provision | No provision | May 15, 2005 |
| Interest coupon rate . . . . . . . . . . . . . | To be determined, based on the average of accepted bids | 10¾% | To be determined, based on the average of accepted bids |
| Investment yield . . . . . . . . . . . . . . . . | To be determined at auction | To be determined at auction | To be determined at auction |
| Premium or discount . . . . . . . . . . . . | To be determined after auction | To be determined after auction | To be determined after auction |
| Interest payment dates . . . . . . . . . . . | February 15 and August 15 (first payment on February 15, 1981) | November 15 and May 15 | November 15 and May 15 |
| Minimum denomination available . . | $5,000 | $1,000 | $1,000 |
| **Terms of Sale:** | | | |
| Method of sale . . . . . . . . . . . . . . . . . | Yield auction | Price auction | Yield auction |
| Accrued interest payable by investor . . | None | None | None |
| Preferred allotment . . . . . . . . . . . . . | Noncompetitive bid for $1,000,000 or less | Noncompetitive bid for $1,000,000 or less | Noncompetitive bid for $1,000,000 or less |
| Payment by non-institutional investors. . . . . . . . . . . . . . . . . . . . | **Full payment to be submitted with tender** | **Full payment to be submitted with tender** | **Full payment to be submitted with tender** |
| Deposit guarantee by designated institutions. . . . . . . . . . . . . . . . . | Acceptable | Acceptable | Acceptable |
| **Key Dates:** | | | |
| Deadline for receipt of tenders . . . . . | **Tuesday, May 6, 1980, by 1:30 p.m., EDST** | **Wednesday, May 7, 1980, by 1:30 p.m., EDST** | **Thursday, May 8, 1980, by 1:30 p.m., EDST** |
| Settlement date (final payment due from institutions) | | | |
| a) cash or Federal funds . . . . . . . . | Thursday, May 15, 1980 | Thursday, May 15, 1980 | Thursday, May 15, 1980 |
| b) readily collectible check . . . . . . | Monday, May 12, 1980 | Monday, May 12, 1980 | Monday, May 12, 1980 |
| Delivery date for coupon securities . . . | **Friday, May 23, 1980** | **Thursday, May 15, 1980** | **Wednesday, May 28, 1980** |

**Figure 17-1** (Continued)

## FEDERAL RESERVE BANK
## OF NEW YORK
Fiscal Agent of the United States

$$\begin{bmatrix} \text{Circular No. } \textbf{8816} \\ \text{May 1, 1980} \end{bmatrix}$$

## TREASURY ANNOUNCES MAY QUARTERLY FINANCING

*To All Banking Institutions, and Others Concerned,*
*in the Second Federal Reserve District:*

The following statement was issued yesterday by the Treasury Department:

The Treasury will raise about $3,500 million of new cash and refund $1,712 million of notes and $2,326 million of cash management bills maturing May 15, 1980, by issuing $3,500 million of 3¼-year notes, $2,000 million of 9½-year notes and $2,000 million of 30-year bonds. The 9½-year notes will be an addition to the 10¾% notes of Series B-1989 originally issued November 15, 1979. The public currently holds $1,981 million of the outstanding 10¾% notes.

The $1,712 million of maturing notes are those held by the public, including $38 million held, as of today, by Federal Reserve Banks as agents for foreign and international monetary authorities. In addition to the public holdings, Government accounts and Federal Reserve Banks, for their own accounts, hold $5,553 million of the maturing notes that may be refunded by issuing additional amounts of new securities. Additional amounts of the new securities may also be issued to Federal Reserve Banks, as agents for foreign and international monetary authorities, to the extent that the aggregate amount of tenders for such accounts exceeds the aggregate amount of maturing notes held by them.

Printed on the reverse side is a table summarizing the highlights of the offerings. Copies of the official offering circulars will be furnished upon request directed to our Government Bond Division (Tel. No. 212-791-6619). In addition, enclosed are copies of the forms to be used in submitting tenders.

This Bank will receive tenders at the Securities Department of its Head Office and at its Buffalo Branch up to 1:30 p.m., Eastern Daylight Saving time, on the dates specified on the reverse side of this circular as the deadlines for receipt of tenders. *All competitive tenders,* whether transmitted by mail or by other means, must reach this Bank or its Branch by that time on the specified dates. However, for investors who wish to submit noncompetitive tenders and who find it more convenient to mail their tenders than to present them in person, the official offering circular for each offering provides that *noncompetitive* tenders will be considered timely received if they are mailed to this Bank or its Branch under a postmark no later than the date preceding the date specified for receipt of tenders.

Bidders submitting noncompetitive tenders should realize that it is possible that the average price may be above par, in which case they would have to pay more than the face value for the securities.

**Payment with a tender may be in the form of a personal check, which need not be certified, an official bank check, or a Federal funds check (a check drawn by a commercial bank on its Federal Reserve account). All checks must be drawn payable to the Federal Reserve Bank of New York;** *checks endorsed to this Bank will not be accepted.* **Payment may also be made in cash or in Treasury securities maturing on or before the issue date of the securities being purchased.**

Recorded messages provide information about Treasury offerings and about auction results: at the Head Office — Tel. No. 212-791-7773 (offerings) and Tel. No. 212-791-5823 (results); at the Buffalo Branch — Tel. No. 716-849-5046. Additional inquiries regarding these offerings may be made by calling, at the Head Office, Tel. No. 212-791-6619, or, at the Buffalo Branch, Tel. No. 716-849-5016.

ANTHONY M. SOLOMON,
*President.*

(Over)

**Figure 17-1**  (Continued)

## RESULTS OF AUCTION OF 10¾% 9½-YEAR TREASURY NOTES
### (Notes of Series B-1989)

The Department of the Treasury has accepted $2,000 million of $3,992 million of tenders received from the public for the 10¾% 9½-year notes, Series B-1989, auctioned today [*May 7*]. The range of accepted competitive bids was as follows:

|          | *Price*   | *Approximate Yield* |
|----------|-----------|---------------------|
| High ............... | 106.10[1]  | 9.75%  |
| Low ............... | 104.84     | 9.95%  |
| Average ........... | 105.27     | 9.88%  |

[1]Excepting two tenders totaling $4,000,000.

The $2,000 million of accepted tenders includes $201 million of noncompetitive tenders and $1,799 million of competitive tenders from private investors, including 28% of the amount of notes bid for at the low price.

In addition to the $2,000 million of tenders accepted in the auction process, $1,300 million of tenders were accepted at the average price from Government accounts and Federal Reserve Banks for their own account in exchange for maturing securities, and $55 million of tenders were accepted at the average price from Federal Reserve Banks as agents for foreign and international monetary authorities for new cash.

## RESULTS OF AUCTION OF 30-YEAR TREASURY BONDS
### (Bonds of 2005-2010)

The Department of the Treasury has accepted $2,000 million of $3,648 million of tenders received from the public for the 30-year bonds auctioned today [*May 8*]. The range of accepted competitive bids was as follows:

| | |
|---|---|
| Lowest yield ................. | 10.08% |
| Highest yield ................. | 10.18% |
| Average yield................. | 10.12% |

The interest rate on the bonds will be 10%. At the 10% rate, the above yields result in the following prices:

| | |
|---|---|
| Low-yield price................ | 99.248 |
| High-yield price ............... | 98.322 |
| Average-yield price............. | 98.876 |

The $2,000 million of accepted tenders includes $182 million of noncompetitive tenders and $1,818 million of competitive tenders from private investors, including 55% of the amount of bonds bid for at the high yield.

In addition to the $2,000 million of tenders accepted in the auction process, $976 million of tenders were accepted at the average price from Government accounts and Federal Reserve Banks for their own account in exchange for securities maturing May 15, 1980.

ANTHONY M. SOLOMON,
*President.*

quantities—though given over the telephone verbally rather than in written form—and, last but not least, the concern of the Treasury and Federal Reserve System in preserving the market for government securities. It is probably not unusual for a dealer firm to be able to run a Treasury-bill inventory position of fifty times its capital.[10]

Any significant impairment of the government securities market's ability to handle large transactions at reasonably continuous prices is a traumatic experience for the economy because it calls into question the solvency of the many institutions that, in effect, hold substantial parts of their working balances and reserves in Treasury obligations. There have been a number of brief panics in the market, generally resulting from an unanticipated (or unexpectedly severe) tightening of monetary policy. The most notable of these panics occurred in May 1953, June 1958, August 1966, and May 1970 (during the Cambodian crisis). In these and other lesser instances, however, the Treasury and/or the Federal Reserve intervened to support the market by purchasing securities or supplying credit to market participants. The existence of this backstop is the ultimate source of the confidence of investors all over the world in U.S. government securities, and it has prevented many incipient money market crises from ever reaching a pitch such that official intervention was needed.

These considerations illustrate a proposition of great significance. Theoretically, monetary policy can be made as tight as necessary to achieve the desired economic result. As a practical matter, however, the public possesses a huge quantity of near-monies, including such assets as savings accounts and government securities, which it counts on being able to convert into money (demand deposits or currency) in the event of a money or credit shortage. While a sufficiently tight monetary policy can prevent such conversion, for example, by destroying the ability of government securities dealers to borrow to finance their positions, to do so would cause a cataclysmic destruction of confidence in financial instruments and the institutions

that issue them. Thus, monetary policy cannot be as decisive a short-term anti-inflationary instrument as might otherwise be supposed.

## Ownership of the Treasury Debt

Although the U.S. Treasury pays the lowest interest of any American borrower,[11] owners of Treasury securities are found all over the globe. U.S. government securities owe their popularity to their unparalleled safety as to income and principal, and to the promptness and low cost at which large amounts may be bought or sold in the over-the-counter markets. Treasury obligations, especially those with short maturities, are an ideal secondary-reserve asset.[12]

From the Treasury's point of view, this has advantages and drawbacks. The major advantages are, of course, a large demand for its securities and a relatively cheap cost of borrowing. The disadvantage is that, in many cases, Treasury obligations are bought not for their own sake, so to speak, but as a haven for temporary or precautionary balances. As soon as the liquidity of the public is squeezed or alternative investments, such as business and consumer capital goods or other-than-Treasury securities become more attractive, widespread selling of government securities is apt to develop and new offerings can be lodged only at sizable interest-rate concessions. Rises in Treasury interest rates drive up the interest rates that all borrowers must pay, since Treasury security yields serve as the benchmark from which other rates are calibrated upward.

A substantial volume of Treasury securities is owned by the Federal Reserve banks, which have acquired them in open-market operations over the years. Still another chunk is owned by various Treasury trust funds. Profit, loss, and liquidity considerations play virtually no part in the financial investment decisions of these holders. To the extent that Treasury obligations are acquired by other governmental agencies and the Federal Reserve,

---

[10]Banks and corporations are the major source of such financing, most of which takes place on an overnight basis. The Federal Reserve may also lend to dealers, at its option, in the form of a repurchase agreement.

[11]Except for the special case of state and local bodies, which pay a lower rate because interest on their securities is exempt from the federal income tax.

[12]Primary reserves are those required by law; secondary reserves are those dictated by prudence or lack of attractive financial investment alternatives.

the public is spared the task of having to decide at what interest rates it will forgo other uses of its funds in order to purchase government securities. Intragovernmental debt placement is, therefore, essentially irrelevant to the flow of funds. If all governmental financial activities were consolidated (used a single checking account, so to speak), it would be unnecessary for governmental entities to sell securities to each other. We may look at these government activities in the same way we look at the business activities of large corporations: the internal debts and claims generated by the divisions of a large private corporation cancel each other out when we consider the firm as a whole.

What is important from the standpoint of economic activity and credit markets is the remaining and major part of the debt—known as the *publicly held debt* (Table 17-4). The growth of the total publicly held debt depends, of course, on the size of the budget deficits and the needs of federal credit programs. Its distribution among various classes of owners depends on the terms of the securities of-

fered and their competitiveness with alternative uses of funds available to the potential buyers.

The household sector is a steady source of demand for the Treasury's nonmarketable savings bonds, which are designed to be attractive to individuals. Savings bonds may be bought from the Treasury and turned in for cash at any time, but they may not be transferred from person to person. The rate of interest earned depends on how long an investor holds them. While interest rates on savings bonds are low relative to some other savings instruments, they offer the advantages of automatic extension and the deferral of taxes on interest income until such time as the bonds are turned in.

Individuals (including personal trust funds) also hold a lesser, but considerable, amount of marketable Treasury obligations, many of them bought during periods of tight money, as in 1969–1970 and 1973–1975 when the government was forced to offer higher interest rates than depository institutions were paying on savings accounts. The label *disin-*

**Table 17-4  Ownership of Treasury and Federal Agency Debt (in billions of dollars)**

| Year End | Total Publicly Held[a] | Commercial Banking | Nonbank Financial Institutions | Foreign, Mainly Official | Corporate Nonfinancial Business | State and Local Governments | Households |
|---|---|---|---|---|---|---|---|
| 1946 | $205.5 | $ 76.5 | $ 42.9 | $  1.9 | $12.8 | $ 5.1 | $ 66.3 |
| 1950 | 197.2 | 64.5 | 36.8 | 3.1 | 17.9 | 6.7 | 68.2 |
| 1955 | 207.4 | 65.2 | 34.0 | 5.8 | 21.6 | 11.5 | 69.3 |
| 1960 | 214.2 | 63.9 | 34.4 | 10.6 | 16.9 | 14.5 | 74.0 |
| 1965 | 232.6 | 66.0 | 38.7 | 13.2 | 8.8 | 18.9 | 82.0 |
| 1970 | 277.6 | 76.4 | 41.2 | 19.7 | 9.5 | 25.5 | 107.2 |
| 1975 | 453.6 | 119.5 | 72.2 | 66.5 | 14.7 | 28.3 | 152.8 |
| 1977 | 601.7 | 138.5 | 119.9 | 109.6 | 10.4 | 46.1 | 177.2 |
| 1978 | 681.3 | 139.0 | 137.9 | 137.8 | 4.1 | 58.6 | 203.8 |
| | | | *Percentage of Total* | | | | |
| 1946 | 100% | 37% | 21% | 1% | 6% | 2% | 32% |
| 1950 | 100 | 33 | 19 | 2 | 9 | 3 | 35 |
| 1955 | 100 | 31 | 16 | 3 | 10 | 6 | 33 |
| 1960 | 100 | 30 | 16 | 5 | 8 | 7 | 35 |
| 1965 | 100 | 28 | 17 | 6 | 4 | 8 | 35 |
| 1970 | 100 | 28 | 15 | 7 | 3 | 9 | 39 |
| 1975 | 100 | 26 | 16 | 15 | 3 | 6 | 34 |
| 1977 | 100 | 23 | 20 | 18 | 2 | 8 | 29 |
| 1978 | 100 | 20 | 20 | 20 | 1 | 9 | 30 |

Note: Includes issues of federal agencies and sponsored corporations (totaling $158.4 billion at year-end 1977), as well as direct Treasury debt. Details may not add to totals because of rounding.

[a]That is, excluding securities owned by the Federal Reserve and U.S. government accounts.

Source: Board of Governors of the Federal Reserve System, *Flow of Funds Accounts*.

*termediation* describes the process in which the public withdraws funds from savings accounts to invest in higher-yielding federal obligations.

Most other Treasury securities are owned by various domestic and foreign financial institutions, primarily American commercial banks. The initial purchases in bulk by domestic financial intermediaries were made during World War II, when budget deficits mushroomed and few other financial investment outlets were available. While commercial banks later replaced many of these holdings with loans and private-sector securities, large purchases resumed in the 1970s when huge budget deficits and the attendant Treasury security offerings again became commonplace. In general, financial institutions tend to liquidate government securities when the private economy is expanding. They replenish their holdings at other times (generally periods of business stagnation and recession) when expansionary monetary policies create deposits and other sources of funds that exceed suitable lending opportunities in the private sector.

Nonfinancial corporations also greatly enlarged their holdings of (mainly short-term) government securities during World War II, but they reduced their holdings subsequently as business uses for the funds expanded and tax payment schedules were speeded up. In recent years privately issued money market paper, such as commercial paper and bank time certificates of deposit, has become more competitive with short-term Treasury securities. Nevertheless, as corporate liquidity surged after 1974, investment in government securities increased sizably.

State and local governments and foreigners (mainly official institutions) are the only major investor classes whose holdings of government securities have shown an essentially uninterrupted uptrend. In the case of state and local governments, investment in short-term government securities offers public authorities, of which there are many thousands, a means to earn interest on short-term working balances. Public bodies also own billions of nonmarketable Treasury securities representing reinvestment, as defined by Internal Revenue Service regulations, of funds obtained through so-called advance refundings of their own tax-exempt issues. State and local employee pension funds, one of the most rapidly growing types of financial intermediaries, used to invest largely in long-term Treasury bonds. Since the 1960s these public pension funds have been acquiring corporate bonds and stocks for the most part. They nevertheless remain important participants in the government bond market.

Foreign official buyers also have become a major source of demand for U.S. Treasury securities. Most noncommunist countries hold large parts of their foreign-exchange reserves in short- and medium-term interest-bearing dollar obligations, chiefly U.S. government securities. These reserves have been growing rapidly, reflecting the large external deficits of the U.S. In the 1960s and early 1970s, the main dollar outflow was to other industrial countries. A small part of the Treasury debt sold to these foreign official authorities consisted of nonmarketable issues carrying exchange-rate guarantees or denominated in foreign currency. After the huge oil-price increase of 1974, some of the oil-producing countries also became major buyers of Treasury securities. In the mid- and late 1970s, the central banks of several countries—notably Germany, Japan, and Great Britain—bought up billions of dollars in the foreign exchange markets in an effort to slow the appreciation of their own currencies. They placed the proceeds in U.S. Treasury securities.[13]

## Treasury Borrowing and Its Impact on Interest Rates and the Economy

In theoretical treatments of the effect of Treasury borrowing, it is especially important to specify what one is holding constant and what one allows to vary. This task is difficult enough when using mathematics or diagrams; it is even harder without these aids. That is why popular or journalistic treatments of the subject more often than not are inaccurate. The introductory discussion here is strictly verbal. Some elementary diagrams may be found in the appendix to this chapter. Fuller theoretical analysis is deferred to Chapters 22 and 29. The student is urged to review this section after studying those chapters.

Changes in the Treasury's necessitous demand for funds often have profound consequences for financial flows and interest rates. After all, the Treasury's activities are hardly those of the ordi-

[13]See Chapters 18 and 30.

nary, obscure borrower. They are, instead, huge in size, well publicized, and highly visible. Large swings in the federal deficit are apt to affect private as well as total saving and investment and may even deflect Federal Reserve policy from its plan, with major repercussions on GNP and inflation.

Other things being equal (which they rarely are), an increase in the Treasury's deficit will expand total lending and spending and raise interest rates and GNP.[14] Conversely, a reduction in the deficit will reduce interest rates and GNP. The Treasury's added demand for credit (that is, its sale of new securities) bids up interest rates. The higher rates have two simultaneous effects. First, they elicit some dishoarding of previously idle money balances held by the public, thereby expanding the total quantity of loanable funds. Second, they ration out of the market marginal private borrowers who are unable to afford the higher interest rate. Thus, the Treasury's borrowing (and, thereby, some of its spending) is financed partly at the expense of private would-be borrowers and partly by the public's dishoarding in response to the rise in the interest rate.

Aggregate borrowing and spending, public and private, has been lifted. Because Treasury spending is up more than private spending is down, nominal GNP is now larger. At the new GNP, the Treasury's deficit, as well as the public's propensity to spend, lend, save, and hoard, are presumably different than they were before. The whole process now repeats itself, but new quantities are involved.

The extent to which the Treasury's deficit increases GNP and interest rates depends (1) on the responsiveness of the supply of funds—the public's dishoarding—as interest rates become more attractive, and (2) on the degree of resistance offered by private credit demand as it is "crowded out." If dishoarding and private credit demand are interest-rate elastic, rates will rise less; if they are inelastic (quantities offered and demanded respond little to changes in interest rate), rates must rise sharply.

Thus far we have assumed that federal and private credit demands are independent. But this is generally not the case. Indeed, one often finds that federal and private credit demands are almost me-

chanical mirror images of one another. For example, whenever the public must make large tax payments, thereby reducing the Treasury's credit requirements, corporations and households will almost surely become larger borrowers in the credit market. When, on the other hand, the government is borrowing to make large payments to the public, the recipients are likely to use some of the funds to avoid borrowing or to repay debt. Private credit demand will fall.

A similar but more complex and important relationship also holds on a cyclical basis. When the economy and private credit demands are expanding, federal tax revenues tend to rise more rapidly, while certain outlays—such as unemployment insurance payments—decline. Thus, the budget deficit shrinks.[15] However, even though federal demand subsides, total credit demand will probably expand. In business recessions, conversely, declining private activity typically reduces private borrowing by more than the increased federal borrowing necessitated by diminishing tax revenues. Total credit demand falls.

The responses of the private sector are highly significant to the ultimate impact of Treasury borrowing on interest rates, the distribution of credit, and economic activity. A larger budget deficit, and the various changes in government spending or taxation that produce it, may affect the incentives for private spending and borrowing. In the United States of the 1930s, for example, when deliberate deficit spending was novel, the business community allegedly was frightened into curtailing its investment activity. In the modern inflation-conscious world, by contrast, growing government deficits are more generally seen as harbingers of credit stringency. They are, therefore, signals for private borrowers to speed up their borrowing in order to "beat" the expected rise in interest rates.[16]

[14]See the appendix to this chapter for a limiting exception.

[15]In the language of Chapter 29, the actual deficit shrinks, while the high-employment surplus or deficit, or the fiscal thrust, may remain unchanged or may conceivably even grow larger.

[16]In the late 1960s and early 1970s, larger deficits also tended to speed up private spending because the private sector believed that the deficits would lead to stronger business and higher prices. More recently, after the inflation and bankruptcy debacle of the mid-1970s, the public seems more inclined to believe that inflationary consequences of budget deficits will quickly overwhelm any stimulus to real output.

## Interaction Between Fiscal and Monetary Policy: Illustrations

Thus far, we have been discussing mainly the interactions between federal and private credit *demand*. But there is an even more important interaction with the credit *supply,* in particular that pivotal part of the supply represented by the Federal Reserve's creation of money. The Federal Reserve's response to changes in federal borrowing and their consequences is, technically speaking, the ultimate determinant of the results.

Any large increase in credit demand, private or official, boosts interest rates and draws credit away from "weak" borrowers (in the United States the housing industry stands out as an example). Capital losses are incurred by bondholders.[17] Nobody likes high or rising interest rates. Thus, the Federal Reserve comes under political pressure to finance at least some of the excess credit demand by the creation of new money. Because the Treasury's borrowing is almost always the most visible source of the congestion in the credit market, and because the Federal Reserve normally buys Treasury obligations in its routine open-market operations, the political pressure is apt to be strongest at times of Treasury financing. To the extent the Federal Reserve acquiesces by allowing bank reserves—and hence the quantity of money—to expand more quickly, the supply of funds increases to match the demand, so that interest rates are at least temporarily prevented from rising in response to the Treasury's borrowing. In this way, the public's desire to have its cake and eat it, too, creates its own fulfillment in a higher GNP and—especially if the economy is near full employment—in a rise in the price level.[18] The process becomes especially pernicious and self-aggravating once it is widely understood. This happens because Federal Reserve's actions immediately trigger inflationary expectations and anticipatory borrowing and commodity price increases. This process explains the widely held view that budget deficits are in and of themselves inflationary.

During World War II and until June 1951, the Federal Reserve did in fact undertake to "peg" the prices of government bonds, that is, to buy up any oversupply at a fixed price, just as some crop prices are supported by official buying. The consequences were remarkably similar. Bonds piled up in the Federal Reserve "warehouse," and every purchase created new bank reserves that served as the basis for further additions to the money supply. The Federal Reserve had indeed become an "engine of inflation." Recognizing that this policy was fueling inflation, the Federal Reserve wanted to allow the oversupply of bonds to depress their prices, but such a policy change was opposed by the Treasury and others who feared disruption of the government securities market and objected to higher interest rates. The bitter conflict, involving President Truman as well as Congress, was resolved by the Treasury–Federal Reserve "accord" of March 1951, which largely freed the Federal Reserve to pursue an independent monetary policy without particular regard to the level of interest rates.[19]

More subtle political interplay between fiscal and monetary policy persists, however, and presumably always will. In the inflationary circumstances of 1966–1968, for example, the Federal Reserve strongly urged the administration and Congress to take the politically difficult step of increasing taxes. If taxes were raised, it was hinted, credit conditions would ease and interest rates decline. A 10 percent income tax surcharge was finally put into effect in mid-1968. At that point, however, partly to make good on its vague commitment to lower interest rates and partly because it feared that the tax in-

---

[17]When new bonds are issued at higher rates than prevail on outstanding bonds, the latter must fall in price if they are to remain salable. If today, for example, $1,000 will buy an 8 percent bond, then owners of yesterday's 7 percent bonds will have to accept less than $1,000 if they wish to sell them. The longer the term of the bond (the longer its owner is to be saddled with an inferior interest rate), the greater will be the capital loss.

[18]See Chapter 21.

[19]This issue is discussed extensively in Joint Committee on the Economic Report, U.S. Congress, *Monetary Policy and the Management of the Public Debt,* Government Printing Office, Washington, D.C., 1952. A succinct and flavorful description of the economic and political issues, as well as of the negotiations, is given by Allan Sproul (in 1951, President of the Federal Reserve Bank of New York) in "The Accord—A Landmark in the First Fifty Years of the Federal Reserve System," *Monthly Review,* Federal Reserve Bank of New York (November 1964). Oddly enough, the official conducting the negotiations from the Treasury side (while Secretary Vinson was ill) was Assistant Secretary William McChesney Martin, who subsequently became chairman of the Federal Reserve Board.

crease might represent economic "overkill," the Federal Reserve eased monetary policy. This relaxation, in effect, encouraged and enabled the public to up its borrowing. The public was thus able to replace the funds it was losing through higher taxes and thereby to maintain and even increase its spending. In this way the fiscal year from July 1, 1968 to June 30, 1969, the last time the federal budget was in surplus, also became a year of intense inflation and, after the Federal Reserve recognized its error, of sharply rising interest rates.

Partly to escape the recurrent political controversies centering on interest rates, the Federal Reserve adopted in 1970 a policy (which received additional emphasis in 1979) of focusing its own and the public's attention primarily on targets for monetary growth. The policy has been remarkably successful in deflecting criticism of rising interest rates.[20] This new approach led to an analytically interesting and practically important debate in regard to the counterrecessionary income tax rebate of spring 1975. Congress had passed a $10 billion tax rebate and Social Security "bonus" to be paid during May and June. It was obvious that the rebate would, at least temporarily, sharply raise the public's demand for money balances, as recipients chose to deposit some of the windfall in their checking accounts. If the Federal Reserve freely supplied additional bank reserves to underpin the rise in deposits, the money stock was sure to rise at what the authorities deemed, and the Congress seemed to agree, was a highly inflationary pace. But, if the Fed failed to supply reserves, interest rates might rise sharply as the Treasury borrowed in the market the huge chunk of credit it needed to pay the rebate. In that case, the expansionary impact of the tax rebate on the economy would be greatly diluted and the intent of Congress apparently frustrated.

The central bank chose a middle course.[21] It permitted part of the initial bulge in Treasury borrowing and money supply to be accommodated at stable interest rates, but then it raised interest rates so that not all the money supply increase would be permanent. This episode once again highlighted the critical role of monetary policy in determining the outcome of fiscal initiatives. New monetary policy operating procedures announced in October 1979 re-emphasized the importance of meeting monetary rather than interest rate targets, as will be explained further in Chapter 28.

## "Crowding Out"

The debate over the impending budget deficit for the fiscal year 1975–1976—some officials publicly warned of a figure as high as $100 billion—generated concern in some quarters that federal borrowing might "crowd out" private credit demand from the marketplace and, thereby, impede or halt recovery from the recession. A review of this issue provides an opportunity to summarize the conclusions of this section.[22]

Under conditions of full employment, the superimposition of additional, inelastic federal credit demands does indeed displace private borrowing. Presuming that the Federal Reserve does not increase the supply of money and credit to match the additional borrowing by the Treasury, interest rates must rise until enough private borrowing is eliminated—crowded out—to make room for the new Treasury borrowing. As long as the Federal Reserve limits the increase in the quantity of money to less than the enlargement of the federal deficit, the Treasury will gain access to additional real purchasing power. Since existing real resources are already fully employed, it is clear that resources can be freed for government usage only by diverting them from the private sector.

In 1975, however, unemployment and idle industrial capacity were widespread. Because of the weakness of the economy, private credit demand had diminished while the federal deficit had ballooned. Nevertheless, some economists argued that the deficit was raising interest rates and crowding out private borrowers to such an extent that economic recovery would have been faster (and less inflationary) had the deficit been smaller.

But how could the government reduce the Treasury deficit and borrowing? To be sure, it could have raised taxes, but in the prevailing recession

---

[20]See Chapter 28 for a description of current monetary policy techniques.

[21]For an evaluation of the difficulties from the Federal Reserve's point of view, see Board of Governors of the Federal Reserve System, *62nd Annual Report* (1975), pp. 52–54.

[22]For a further discussion and analysis of "crowding out," see Chapter 29.

that would have further lowered personal disposable incomes and/or business profits and weakened the financial condition of the private sector. Or, as an alternative to higher taxes, government spending could have been curtailed. Insofar as such reductions diminished government purchases of goods and services, however, that also would tend to lower employment and incomes in the private sector. And if the government spending cuts fell on transfer payments to households, the public's ability to buy the products of business would be impaired. Thus the measures—higher taxes or lower government spending—needed to shrink the deficit very likely would have intensified the recession. The conclusion is that total borrowing and GNP were very probably higher as a result of the enlarged government deficit.

Why only *probably*? Why can't we be certain? Again we must look to the role of the Federal Reserve. In a recession, the private demand for credit normally falls sharply. If there is no offsetting increase in federal credit demand, and if the Federal Reserve continues to adhere strictly to a policy of sustaining stable monetary growth at a pace appropriate to prosperity, interest rates will plummet. As a practical matter, however, central banks have always been reluctant to allow sharp declines in, or exceptionally low levels of, interest rates, among other reasons because such developments may lead to speculative disturbances as well as to serious weakness in the foreign exchange position of the currency in question. One can also argue that once interest rates fall below some low level, further declines no longer stimulate private credit use: in such circumstances, there may exist a so-called liquidity trap. It has also been said that monetary policy is "pushing on a string." This is not the place to debate the particular merits, if any, of this argument. Suffice it to say that in the absence of an enlarged federal credit demand to moderate the decline in interest rates by "filling in" for (in contrast to "crowding out") a reduced private demand, the Federal Reserve would probably have settled for less growth in money and credit than it originally intended or that in fact took place. And if so, the GNP would have been lower, too.

In 1975 and 1976 the Federal Reserve did indeed undershoot its announced monetary growth targets—notwithstanding federal budget deficits of $45.1 billion in 1974–1975 and $66.5 billion in 1975–1976.[23] Nevertheless, the economy recovered strongly and inflation slowed down.

Once stimulative measures take hold, however, and the economy revives, the crowding-out argument regains its force. In 1977–1978, as the economy moved closer to full employment, monetary growth came to exceed the Federal Reserve's targets. This was presumably allowed to occur because the monetary authorities were reluctant to give free rein to the pressures for higher interest rates—pressures that were due in part to the large federal deficits. The inflationary consequences were prompt and severe.

Much of the widely expressed concern about crowding out seems to fail to distinguish sharply enough between the business-cycle aspects of the problem and the long-run political issues. For those who wish to limit or reverse the long-run growth of government spending, lending, taxing, and borrowing, *any* crowding out of the private sector should be avoided at all times, whether in expansion or recession. Such a point of view justifies limits on the federal deficit even during recessions. Its proponents believe that any enlargement of the federal deficit at the expense of the private sector appears to be irreversible—at least over the long run. It is still the case, however, that an increase in the federal deficit during a recession will, in general, raise business activity, employment, and profits. The issue is whether, and to what extent, this particular medicine should be administered.

In sum, the effects of fiscal policy can be very difficult to predict. Much depends on the spending, saving, borrowing, hoarding, and pricing responses of the public. In a technical sense, the last word always rests with monetary policy, but the makers of monetary policy, like everyone else, are subject to conflicting pressures and goals that condition their response to fiscal actions.

[23]Increases in federal debt held by the public were considerably larger: $50.8 billion in 1974–1975 and $83.4 billion in 1975–1976.

## Appendix: Diagrammatic Interpretation of the Impact of Treasury Borrowing

In Figure 17-2, the $D_{lf}$ schedule represents the demand (over some time period) for loanable funds by ultimate borrowers, including the government. The supply of loanable funds is represented by $S_{lf}$. Supply and demand intersect at $A$, giving an equilibrium interest rate $OR_1$, and total borrowing $OQ_1$.[24] Now suppose the Treasury's net borrowing increases by an amount $Q_1X(=AB)$. Since the Treasury, as a necessitous borrower, must get all the funds it needs no matter how high the added demand pushes rates, the new demand curve $D'_{lf}$ is parallel to $D_{lf}$, the distance between them corresponding to $AB$.[25] The new equilibrium is at $C$, corresponding to a higher interest rate $OR_2$ and a new, larger quantity of loanable funds, $OQ_2$.

At the new equilibrium, the Treasury meets its needs $EC$ ($= AB = Q_1X$) partly at the expense of private borrowers, who ration themselves because of the higher cost of credit to only $OH$ (as compared with $OQ_1$ previously). These borrowers must, therefore, curtail their spending. The rest of the Treasury's needs are met, however, by the public's dishoarding in response to the higher interest rates, in this instance $Q_1Q_2$. GNP will ultimately rise, through the autonomous expenditure multiplier, by a multiple of $Q_1Q_2$. We see that $Q_1Q_2$ represents the extent to which the net new spending by the Treasury occurs without reducing spending by anyone else. The recipients of these Treasury payments now have additional income, some or all of which they may respend for other goods and services, the sellers of which thus gain new income, and so on, expanding GNP by more than the initial increment $Q_1Q_2$.[26]

Let us suppose (Figure 17-3) that private demand was more elastic but hold everything else the same. Private borrowers would be rationed out more quickly by rising credit costs, and the rise in total

[24]The interest rate is, of course, used as a proxy for the total cost of credit, which may well include many nonrate aspects.

[25]This implies that the additional amount ($AB$) borrowed by the Treasury is perfectly interest inelastic. Recall p. 350.

[26]Note that we have said nothing about how the rise in GNP is divided between higher prices and higher real output. For a more formal treatment of this process, and its limiting factors, see Paul A. Samuelson, *Economics,* 10th ed., McGraw-Hill Book Company, New York, 1976, Chap. 12.

**Figure 17-2  The Impact of an Increase in Treasury Borrowing**

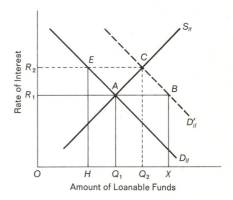

**Figure 17-3  The Impact of an Increase in Treasury Borrowing with an Elastic Demand Schedule**

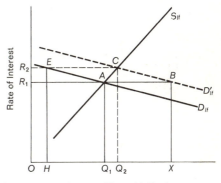

borrowing $Q_1Q_2$, and hence in GNP, would be smaller. The same would be true if, given the same demand as in Figure 17-2, the supply of funds being saved or dishoarded in response to rising interest rates were less elastic (Figure 17-4). Indeed, if supply were totally inelastic, GNP would not rise at all.[27] Thus, the frequently stated view that a government deficit is *necessarily* expansionary or in-

[27]Actually, GNP might even fall if the supply curve were backward sloping, as might be the case if rising rates caused people to hoard more money in expectation of yet higher rates to come or if savers had a fixed goal of future (retirement) income so that they would need to save less if interest rates rose.

**Figure 17-4 The Impact of an Increase in Treasury Borrowing with an Inelastic Supply Schedule**

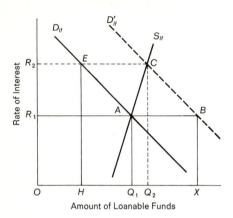

**Figure 17-5 Shifts in the Supply and Demand Schedules for Loanable Funds**

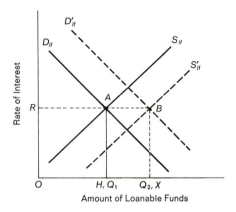

flationary (and vice versa for a surplus) is not correct.

Finally, Figure 17-5 illustrates a case in which an increase in the demand for funds ($D_{lf}$ shifts right to $D'_{lf}$) is "accommodated" by an increase in the supply—that is, by additional monetary creation fostered by the Federal Reserve. An increment to the money stock of $HQ_1Q_2X$ is exactly enough to finance the additional credit demand at stable interest rates. Such a combination of increased budget deficit and rising money stock is powerful expansionary and/or inflationary medicine.

## Questions

1. Look up a post–1980 U.S. budget and see how the actual outcome for 1979 and 1980 differed from the estimates shown in Table 17-2. What explains the discrepancies?
2. How might the economy and interest rates respond to an increase in the Treasury's deficit? How would this response differ if the enlarged deficit were due to (a) increased spending; (b) lower tax revenues reflecting a business recession; or (c) a reduction in income tax rates?
3. How might the responses to a reduced deficit differ under conditions of full employment and recession?
4. How might the responses differ if a budget surplus were used to increase the Treasury's deposit balances rather than to retire maturing debt obligations?

5. If the Treasury were to sell more marketable securities to individuals by paying more attractive interest rates, what might be the impact on other credit markets in which individuals participate directly or indirectly?
6. In times of credit stress, federal credit agencies that lend to housing and farm credit institutions face increasing loan demands, as normal sources of funds to these sectors are pinched. These agencies then issue short-term securities to raise money to lend to savings and loan associations and other institutions. To some extent, this is a self-defeating procedure. Explain.
7. Treasury bills are now available only in book-entry form and plans call for eventually eliminating all actual issuance of Treasury securities. This means that such securities will in effect be registered in the name of owners or their nominees. They will no longer be available in *bearer* form, that is, unidentified as to owner. How, if at all, do you suppose this may affect interest rates on these securities?
8. The larger the U.S. balance-of-payments deficit, the easier it is to finance the budget deficit. Explain.
9. The Federal Reserve owns an immense inventory of government securities and never has to worry about profit, loss, income, or financing. Why should it not take over the functions of the government securities dealers?

## Selected Bibliography

The Brookings Institution. *Setting National Priorities* (1980 or later). Washington, D.C.

*The Budget of the United States Government* (1980 or later). Government Printing Office, Washington, D.C.

The First Boston Corporation. *Handbook of Securities of the United States Government and Federal Agencies and Related Money Market Instruments,* 28th ed., New York, 1978.

Levy, Michael. *The Federal Budget: Its Impact on the Economy, Fiscal 1977, Number 2.* The Conference Board, New York, 1976.

Shultz, George P., and Kenneth W. Dam. *Economic Policy Beyond the Headlines.* Stanford Alumni Association, Stanford, Calif., 1977.

# 18

# Foreign Investment

The preceding chapters concern, for the most part, the flow of *domestic* saving into *domestic* investment. This chapter examines one aspect of financial relations between the United States and the rest of the world, namely, international financial investment. Under general conditions, the international flow of funds increases investor utility by expanding the set of investment opportunities. For example, U.S. investors may benefit from selecting foreign investments with unusually high expected returns over domestic investments with lower returns. In addition, investors can obtain diversification gains when the expected return on foreign investment is weakly correlated with returns on domestic investments. From a larger macroeconomic viewpoint, foreign investment is likely to increase world welfare. By allowing countries to smooth their intertemporal consumption/investment decisions, international financial flows should permit higher levels of world consumption, trade, and welfare.[1]

Over the past ten years the nature of the formal system of international financial markets and the behavior of prices on these markets have changed dramatically. The quiet and stability of exchange markets, associated with the 1944 Bretton Woods agreement, effectively ended with the 1967 pound sterling devaluation. After many interim arrangements and U.S. dollar devaluations in 1971 and 1973, the formal, pegged exchange-rate system was abandoned in favor of a system of managed floating exchange rates, the rules governing which are still evolving. Over this period both the magnitude and volatility of monetary and real shocks increased, contributing to double-digit inflation, wage and price controls, and record postwar unemployment. These shocks hit the rest of the world with varying strength and at different times—which contrib-

---

[1] In many ways, the importance of an international capital market for a single country is analogous to the importance of any financial market for an individual investor. When a financial market exists in a domestic economy, an individual agent is not constrained to set current expenditure equal to current income. Similarly, in an open economy, an individual country is not constrained to have current expenditure equal to domestic output. A country with domestic output greater (less) than current expenditure runs a balance-of-trade surplus (deficit). The surplus (deficit) country then accumulates (runs down) financial claims issued by the rest of the world.

uted to the uncertainty of international financial markets.[2]

In spite of increased volatility in international markets, the foreign sector became more important in the United States during the post–World War II years. Exports of goods and services as a percentage of GNP grew from 4.9 percent in 1950 to 6.4 percent in 1970 and 9.7 percent in 1978.[3] The stock of U.S. direct foreign investment increased by 123 percent over the 1970–1978 period; annual income from these direct investments more than tripled from $11.8 billion to $43.5 billion over the same period.[4] In addition, U.S. lending to foreigners, which had been depressed by exchange controls, expanded sharply in 1974 when these controls were dropped. In 1974, foreign issuers raised $15.3 billion in the U.S. market (or 8.1 percent of the yearly total); up from only $6.2 billion (or 3.0 percent) in 1973.

Total foreign lending to the U.S. has remained highly variable in recent years. Over the nine years 1970–1978, total foreign sources of funds to U.S. credit markets averaged 9.7 percent but ranged between 4.2 percent (or $4.2 billion) in 1970 to 15.8 percent (or $53.8 billion) in 1977.[5] The international flow of funds data for this period are summarized in Table 18-1. It can be observed that when U.S. imports exceed U.S. exports, foreigners have excess funds—which they often relend in the U.S. credit market. This "recycling" of the U.S. trade deficit (largely the result of petroleum imports) appeared to peak in 1977. The importance of a properly functioning capital market that allows a country to finance a trade imbalance is clear.

In part because of U.S. capital controls associated with the increased volatility of this period, two external market sectors experienced enormous recent growth. Eurocurrency deposit liabilities increased at a rate in excess of 30 percent per year as did the assets of overseas branches of U.S. banks. These figures are *prima facie* evidence that U.S. capital controls succeeded in shifting inter-

national financial activity away from the United States, rather than suppressing the activity itself.

The purpose of this chapter is twofold. First, the chapter describes a theory of international capital movements. Of critical importance for international financial flows are the relative prices of foreign money, bonds, and equities in terms of their (U.S.) counterparts and the behavior of these prices over time. However, real factors are also important and the chapter shows how structural factors influence financial flows. Second, the chapter describes the historical flow of financial funds between the United States and the rest of the world. Because these financial flows are many-faceted, it is helpful to classify some flows—for example, private versus official flows, direct investment versus portfolio flows, long-term versus short-term flows, and on-shore versus offshore markets—in order to trace this history and identify impacts on particular components of U.S. markets.

The next section presents theoretical issues concerning international capital movements. The text then reviews aggregate foreign investment flows, broken down according to several criteria. The chapter then summarizes the U.S. international investment position (or stock position), after which the relationship of Eurocurrency markets to the U.S. financial market is discussed. An analysis of the internationalization of capital markets and the outlook for the future concludes the chapter.

## A Theory of International Capital Movements

Ideally, one would like to analyze international capital movements in the context of a general equilibrium macroeconomic model. In this way, one could predict the total impact of both real and monetary variables on international capital flows. For example, assume that U.S. residents decide to buy more German automobiles. To pay for the imports, either U.S. residents reduce their holdings of Deutsche marks, or German residents agree to hold U.S. debt.[6] In the latter case, the trade flow clearly gives rise to a capital market transaction.

---

[2]The evolution of the current international financial system is thoroughly analyzed in Thomas D. Willett, *Floating Exchange Rates and International Monetary Reform*, American Enterprise Institute, Washington, D.C., 1977.

[3]*Economic Report of the President*, 1980.

[4]*Ibid*.

[5]*Ibid*.

[6]The debt could be denominated in U.S. dollars, Deutsche marks, or any other *numeraire*. The important point is that the debt represents a claim against U.S. residents for payment of the imports. The example is not

**Table 18-1 Total Funds Raised in U.S. Credit Markets by Nonfinancial Sectors, 1970–1978 (in billions of dollars)**

| Year | 1970 | 1971 | 1972 | 1973 | 1974 | 1975 | 1976 | 1977 | 1978 |
|---|---|---|---|---|---|---|---|---|---|
| Total funds raised | $100.6 | $153.5 | $176.0 | $203.8 | $188.8 | $208.1 | $272.5 | $340.5 | $400.3 |
| Borrowers—users of funds | | | | | | | | | |
| U.S. government | 11.9 | 24.9 | 15.1 | 8.3 | 11.8 | 85.4 | 69.0 | 56.8 | 53.7 |
| Private domestic nonfinancial sectors | 86.0 | 123.5 | 156.9 | 189.3 | 161.6 | 109.5 | 182.8 | 271.4 | 314.4 |
| Foreign | 2.7 | 5.2 | 4.0 | 6.2 | 15.3 | 13.2 | 20.7 | 12.3 | 32.3 |
| Lenders—sources of funds | | | | | | | | | |
| Private domestic nonfinancial sectors | 63.4 | 85.9 | 116.4 | 140.7 | 116.5 | 137.8 | 166.2 | 197.7 | 217.0 |
| Foreign | 4.2 | 23.1 | 15.5 | 9.3 | 28.6 | 11.7 | 23.0 | 53.8 | 46.5 |
| Other | 33.0 | 44.5 | 44.1 | 53.8 | 43.7 | 58.6 | 83.3 | 89.0 | 136.8 |
| Foreign (lenders − borrowers) | 1.5 | 17.9 | 11.5 | 2.9 | 13.3 | (1.5) | 2.3 | 41.5 | 14.2 |
| Balance of merchandise trade | 2.6 | (2.3) | (6.4) | 0.9 | (5.3) | 9.0 | (9.4) | (31.1) | (33.7) |

Source: *Economic Report of the President,* 1980.

If one allows for growth or economic development, one can establish other linkages between real variables and international capital flows. For example, a young, underdeveloped country with promising investments (for example, the United States in 1776) may import capital and issue debt. The young debtor country runs a balance-of-trade deficit. As the investments become profitable, excess real output is generated and sold in the export market to pay for debt service and to retire the initial debt. If the investments continue to be profitable, the country will accumulate wealth. Once the country retires its initial debt and holds some of its wealth as foreign investment, one may call the country a mature creditor.[7]

A less general theory of international capital movements predicts that, in the absence of intervention or market imperfections, flows of funds will be from countries with relatively low *expected* rates of return (for a given level of risk) to countries with relatively high expected rates of return (for a given level of risk).[8] A more detailed description of international capital movements depends on the exchange rate system, the predictability of exchange rate changes, and investors' attitudes toward risk, since these conditions affect the calculation of expected return and risk.

Assume for the moment that the world consists of two countries and two currencies, permanently linked by fixed exchange rates. In this case, the two countries behave as though they were two regions within a single nation having a single currency. An international flow of funds in response to yield differences between countries increases the total (domestic plus foreign) supply of loanable funds in the recipient country and decreases the supply of loanable funds in the investing country. The international lending has two noteworthy results. First, world income increases as capital is transferred from low-return to high-return investments. World aggregate expenditure also increases. Second, after the capital flows, the structure of interest rates is identical in the two countries. The increase in the supply of funds in the recipient country will tend to increase the availability of credit and lower interest rates, while the reduction of the supply of funds on the domestic market in

valid under pure floating exchange rates where the spot rate adjusts fully to reflect the increased demand for Deutsche marks.

[7]It helps to expand the analogy between a country's growth cycle and an individual's consumption-investment cycle. If a steel worker loses his job because changes in technology reduce his comparative advantage, the steel worker will maintain consumption by running down savings or borrowing and will retrain by making new investments in human capital, perhaps to become a computer programmer. Similarly a mature creditor country such as the United States may temporarily lose its comparative advantage in its export goods. The country may run a balance-of-trade deficit and incur debts to the rest of the world. Policy in the country during the adjustment period may be directed toward reallocating resources to restore the country's comparative advantage in trade.

[8]In a portfolio model of international capital flows, covariance risk is also an important factor. For a given level of expected returns, funds will flow toward investments that reduce the total risk of the portfolio.

the investing country will lead to tighter credit conditions and raise interest rates.[9]

Even this highly simplified theory does not rule out the possibility of two-way capital flows when several different financial assets exist. Suppose country A specializes in the production of a short-term asset (a U.S. Treasury bill, for example) and country B issues only long-term assets (such as a U.K. perpetuity or "consol"). If investors from both countries desire to hold portfolios containing both assets, then capital flows from A to B and from B to A may occur simultaneously. Similarly, if country A dominates the higher-risk equity market while country B has a more developed bond market, two-way capital flows will result if investors desire a diversified portfolio of available assets.[10]

Now consider a case where the exchange rate between the two national currencies is flexible. However, investors know the magnitude and date of the exchange-rate change with certainty. The pending exchange rate change affects the expected rate of return from foreign investment, but not the risk, since all aspects of the exchange rate change are known with certainty. As in the first example, capital will still be attracted to the country with the higher expected rate of return for a given risk. However, the nominal foreign rate of return must be decreased (or increased) to reflect the known devaluation (or upward revaluation) of the foreign currency. As a result, the structure of nominal interest rates in the two countries will converge until the difference in interest rates equals the expected change in the exchange rate.

Finally, consider a case where the expected magnitude and timing of exchange rate changes are not known with certainty. What effect does this uncertainty have on the volume of international capital flows? The answer depends on investors' attitudes toward foreign-exchange risk. The next section argues that if investors are risk averse, they will demand a premium for bearing a foreign exchange risk. This premium will reduce the volume of international capital flows. Therefore, expected real rates of return will not equalize across countries, as in the earlier examples. However, if some investors are risk neutral, the volume of international capital flows will be unaffected by exchange risk.

### Foreign Exchange Risk

The principal difference between foreign lending (or borrowing) and domestic lending (or borrowing) is the necessity, in the former case, for either the lender or the borrower to convert his own national currency into that of the other. The rate, or price, for an immediate exchange of one nation's currency for that of another is called the *spot exchange rate*. Currently, the foreign exchange value of the U.S. dollar vis-à-vis the currencies of most major industrial countries is determined in a system of managed floating exchange rates.[11] Under this system, market forces (that is, the interaction of private demand and supply of foreign exchange) are generally left free to determine the spot exchange rate. However, from time to time, a government central bank may transact in the market to smooth (that is, to "manage") what it views as unnecessary or undesirable short-term fluctuations in the exchange rate.

Foreign exchange risk arises from the possibility of an unexpected change in the exchange rate between the time a loan is made and the time that it is repaid. On any foreign investment, the necessity of exchanging one currency for another exposes *both* parties to the risk of loss as a result of an unfavorable movement in the rate of exchange between the two currencies.[12] For example, let us

---

[9] The portion of the adjustments in financial markets and interest rates that will occur in each country depends, to a considerable extent, on their relative size. Theoretically, the determinants will be the elasticities of demand and supply of funds in each country; the lower the elasticities, the larger the interest rate change. Small financial markets normally have lower elasticities.

[10] For discussion of a case where differential taxes lead to simultaneous two-way flows, see Maurice D. Levi, "Taxation and 'Abnormal' International Capital Flows," *Journal of Political Economy* (June 1977).

[11] The foreign exchange value of the U.S. dollar vis-à-vis the currencies of smaller nations is maintained within a narrow range by official central-bank intervention. Other industrial countries adhere to different exchange-rate systems. For example, each country in the European Economic Community (EEC) agrees to peg its currency to that of the other members. However, all EEC currencies are floating vis-à-vis the U.S. dollar. For a summary of the current foreign-exchange market arrangements, see International Monetary Fund, *28th Annual Report of Exchange Market Restrictions,* Washington, D.C., 1978.

[12] The situation is strictly analogous to inflation risk in a domestic financial market. Suppose an investor lends funds at a 10 percent nominal rate when a 5 percent

suppose that a Canadian provincial government floats a bond issue in the New York securities market. The American buyers of the bonds will desire to pay in U.S. dollars; the Canadian province will desire to receive Canadian dollars. Assume that the flotation costs and nominal interest rates do not depend on the currency of denomination and, furthermore, that the spot rate is expected to remain at $1.00 per Canadian dollar. Arbitrarily, it is decided that the bonds will be denominated in U.S. dollars.[13] The Canadian borrower will receive the proceeds in this form and will then convert them into Canadian dollars on the foreign exchange market. Interest and principal will be paid to American bondholders in U.S. dollars, necessitating the periodic conversion of Canadian dollars into U.S. dollars as such payments are made.

Between the time that the initial U.S. dollar proceeds of the bond issue are sold by the Canadian borrower and the time when U.S. dollars are purchased to make repayment, an unanticipated change in the spot exchange rate may occur. Suppose the spot rate for the Canadian dollar rises to $1.11 (the U.S. dollar depreciates). In this case, the Canadian borrower is better off because he now requires only $C.90 to repay each $1.00 of debt. The U.S. lender, however, is worse off since he could have charged a higher interest rate on the loan. On the other hand, if the spot rate for the Canadian dollars falls to $.90, the situation is reversed: the Canadian borrower is worse off because he now must raise $C1.11 to repay each $1.00 of debt, and the U.S. lender is better off because each $1.00 repaid commands a greater purchasing power over Canadian goods than he had anticipated. The example illustrates that the two-sided nature of foreign exchange risk could drive a wedge between borrowers and lenders and reduce the volume of international capital flows. The critical point in the example is that the change in the exchange rate is unanticipated and, therefore, not reflected in the price and other terms of the international loan arrangement.

The risk of loss (and gain) attached to short-term investments is often eliminated by hedging in the *forward foreign exchange market.* The forward market, like any futures market, is simply a market in foreign currencies for delivery at specified future dates. Thus, the Canadian borrower in the earlier example could have denominated the debt in U.S. dollars, received the proceeds, and converted them into Canadian dollars, *at the same time* purchasing U.S. dollars for delivery on the date the bonds matured. The price of U.S. dollars for future delivery in terms of the Canadian dollar (the forward exchange rate) is set in the forward contract and is known on the date that the bonds are initially sold. Thus, the Canadian borrower could have hedged, or *covered,* his exchange risk.

Under most circumstances, international capital flows will increase when forward cover is available at low cost. The cost of forward cover is best viewed as an opportunity cost. In the previous example, if the Canadian covers the U.S. dollar liability, he purchases U.S. dollars at the forward rate. If he remains uncovered, the Canadian meets his U.S. dollar liability by purchasing U.S. dollars at the future spot rate. Therefore, the cost of forward cover depends on the relationship between the forward rate and the future spot rate. When these two rates are equal, the cost of forward cover is zero.[14] As a theoretical matter, if investors form rational expectations of the future spot rate and are risk neutral, the cost of forward cover will be differentially close to zero. In this case, the presence of foreign exchange risk will not reduce the volume of international capital flows.[15] This result cannot

---

inflation rate is anticipated. The expected real rate of return is 5 percent. If the actual inflation rate is higher (lower) than 5 percent, the lender realizes an unanticipated loss (gain) in real purchasing power. The situation is, of course, the reverse for borrowers.

[13] For an analysis of the currency-contract decision, see Stephen P. Magee, "Currency Contracts, Pass-Through and Devaluation," *Brookings Paper on Economic Activity,* No. 1 (1973); and Stephen P. Magee, "U.S. Import Prices in the Currency-Contract Period," *Brookings Paper on Economic Activity,* No. 1 (1974).

[14] An alternative formulation concludes that the cost of forward cover is equal to the percentage difference between the forward rate and the *current* spot rate. This formulation represents more of a sunken cost than an opportunity cost. For further discussion, see Rita M. Rodriguez and E. Eugene Carter, *International Financial Management,* Prentice-Hall, Englewood Cliffs, N.J., 1976; and David K. Eiteman and Arthur I. Stonehill, *Multinational Business Finance,* Addison-Wesley Publishing Company, Reading, Mass., 1973.

[15] For a rigorous proof, see D. P. Baran, "Flexible Exchange Rates, Forward Markets, and the Level of Trade," *American Economic Review* (June 1976).

happen without a group of speculators who provide forward cover at no cost and a group of international investors who are willing to accept fair gambles.

As a practical matter, however, well-developed forward markets exist primarily for the industrial currencies and for maturities not longer than three years. Therefore, a large number of international investments cannot be hedged.[16] In addition, international investors may be risk averse. Where this is the case, the investors (if their investments are denominated in foreign currency) generally will require a premium rate of return over what they could get on a comparable domestic financial investment in order to compensate for the risk of loss due to exchange rate changes. If the investment is denominated in the lender's currency, the borrowers will be willing to pay a slightly lower return, due to the risk of exchange rate change, than they would if they were borrowing in their own currency. These tendencies, of course, mean that the international flow of funds will be smaller, and that interest differentials will be larger, than would be the case if there were no foreign exchange risk.

Finally, we must consider the case where international investors are risk preferrers. One way for investors to take on more risk is by speculating in forward contracts.[17] Investors who can predict the future spot rate more accurately than the aggregate of other forward market participants may make sizable speculative profits. We should distinguish two cases.

First, under pegged exchange rates, speculators face primarily a "one-way" risk. For example, in October 1967, the British pound sterling was pegged at $2.80. Ninety-day forward contracts were heavily supported by the Bank of England and traded at $2.76. Speculators who sold pounds forward made enormous percentage profits when, in the following month, the pound devalued to $2.40. The speculators assumed little risk since there was essentially no possibility that the future spot rate would be above $2.82 (the upper support limit effective under pegged rates). In cases such as this one, speculative capital flows may be much greater than the amount predicted by more basic economic factors.

Contrast this situation to a second case where exchange rates are freely floating. Suppose the forward price of Canadian dollars is $1.00. If the future spot rate is equally likely to be $.95 or $1.05, speculators face a "two-way" risk, which may discourage them from taking open forward positions. In this case there will be "insufficient" speculation. A reduction in international capital flows will result because there are fewer forward contracts available for hedging purposes.

## Departures from the Theoretical Assumptions

Our analysis of international capital flows thus far has abstracted from transaction costs, taxes, exchange controls, and political risk. In reality, investors make decisions based on expected returns after adjusting for risk, taxes, and transaction costs. Therefore, no analysis of international capital flows that excludes these factors can correctly classify the incentive for capital flows.

The simple model of covered interest arbitrage has provided a popular and useful framework for relaxing the perfect-capital-market assumptions. Simply stated, the covered interest arbitrage model assumes that an investor who begins with $1 faces two alternatives: (a) a domestic investment that yields the rate $i$; or (b) a foreign investment constructed by buying foreign currency in the spot market at time $t$ (and price $S_t$), purchasing a foreign

---

[16] The fact that interest rates and forward rates tend to adjust to reflect anticipated exchange rate changes suggests that the market provides a built-in hedge for financial investments. For investments in real plant, equipment, and inventory, purchasing-power parity theory suggests that price-level changes associated with exchange rate changes also provide a built-in hedge for nonfinancial assets. Therefore, the existence of a forward market is not critical for hedging foreign exchange risk. For more on these issues, see Robert Z. Aliber and Clyde P. Stickney, "Accounting Measures of Foreign Exchange Exposure: The Long and Short of It," *Accounting Review* (January 1975).

[17] An important issue of current research is whether foreign exchange risk is analogous to systematic risk or unsystematic risk in the sense of portfolio theory. For discussion, see Bruno H. Solnik, *European Capital Markets*, D. C. Heath, Lexington, Mass., 1973; F. Z. A. Grauer, R. H. Litzenberger, and R. E. Stehle, "Sharing Rules and Equilibrium in an International Capital Market and Uncertainty," *Journal of Financial Economics* (June 1976); and Bruno H. Solnik, "Testing International Asset Pricing: Some Pessimistic Views," *Journal of Finance* (May 1977). See also Chapter 24 of this text for a discussion of the concepts of systematic and unsystematic risk.

asset (with return $i^*$), and converting the foreign currency back to domestic currency in the forward market at time $t$ (and price $F_t$). Assuming the foreign and domestic assets are similar in all respects and differ only because of currency of denomination, the two alternatives, (a) and (b), will return the same dollar amounts when Equation (18-1) is satisfied.

$$\$1(1 + i) = \frac{\$1(1 + i^*)F_t}{S_t} \qquad (18\text{-}1)$$

By rearranging terms, we get the *interest rate parity condition*:

$$\frac{F_t - S_t}{S_t} = \frac{i - i^*}{1 + i^*} \qquad (18\text{-}2)$$

which is plotted in Figure 18-1 as line $XX$.

The interest rate parity condition is significant because it represents one simple equilibrium condition for the foreign exchange market. If prices (of $F_t$, $S_t$, $i$, and $i^*$) are aligned so that interest rate parity does not hold, one can demonstrate that a risk-free profit opportunity exists. These opportunities will provide the incentive for capital flows that will eliminate the profit opportunity. For example, at point $P_1$ the forward premium $(F_t - S_t)/S_t$ exceeds the interest differential $(i - i^*)/(1 + i^*)$. The reader can calculate that investment (b) is more attractive than investment (a) and there will be a U.S. capital outflow. The covered arbitrage outflow can be broken down into four separate transactions:

1. Sell U.S. security.     ($i$ adjusts higher)
2. Buy sterling currency     ($S$ adjusts higher) spot.
3. Buy U.K. security.     ($i^*$ adjusts lower)
4. Sell sterling currency     ($F$ adjusts lower) forward.

These transactions set economic forces in motion so that prices adjust and point $P_1$ moves closer to parity line $XX$. Similarly, at a point like $P_2$, investment (a) is more attractive than investment (b), which will lead to a U.S. capital inflow and a reverse set of transactions:

1. Sell U.K. security.     ($i^*$ adjusts higher)
2. Buy U.S. dollar spot.     ($S$ adjusts lower)
3. Buy U.S. security.     ($i$ adjusts lower)
4. Sell U.S. dollar forward.     ($F$ adjusts higher)

Given the perfect-capital-market assumption, all observations should fall along line $XX$, which

would remove all risk-free incentives for capital flows.

In two articles published in the mid-1970s, Frenkel and Levich developed a covered interest arbitrage model that explicitly accounts for transaction costs.[18] In their model, transaction costs lead to a neutral band, within which the expected profits from covered arbitrage flows do not exceed transaction costs. Empirical tests of this model suggest that the markets are highly efficient in setting prices so that risk-free profit opportunities in excess of transaction costs are quickly bid away.

Levi introduced taxes into the covered arbitrage model.[19] In the real world, profits on forward contracts may be taxed at a capital gains rate ($t_k$) while interest receipts qualify for the ordinary income tax rate ($t_y$). On an after-tax basis, Equation (18-2) becomes

$$\frac{F - S}{S}(1 - t_k) = \frac{i - i^*}{1 + i^*}(1 - t_y) \qquad (18\text{-}3)$$

or

$$\frac{F - S}{S} = \frac{i - i^*}{1 + i^*} \cdot \left(\frac{1 - t_y}{1 - t_k}\right) \qquad (18\text{-}4)$$

For arbitrary tax rates, $t_y = 0.5$ and $t_k = 0.25$, the slope of the interest parity line is reduced to 0.67. A point like $A$, which indicated a profitable capital flow from foreign to domestic markets before taxes, now suggests that the opposite flow will be profitable after taxes. Levi's model further suggests that if residents of the domestic country face $t_y = t_k$ (line $XX$) and residents of the foreign country face $t_y = 0.5$ and $t_k = 0.25$ (line $YY$), then point $A$ will foster two-way capital flows between the countries. In this case, the presence of unequal tax rates across countries may lead to instability in international capital markets.

The issues of exchange controls and political risk have been addressed by Aliber, Dooley, and Dooley and Isard.[20] Aliber reported that the inter-

[18]Jacob A. Frenkel and Richard M. Levich, "Covered Interest Arbitrage: Unexploited Profits?" *Journal of Political Economy* (April 1975); and Jacob A. Frenkel and Richard M. Levich, "Transaction Costs and Interest Arbitrage: Tranquil Versus Turbulent Periods," *Journal of Political Economy* (November-December 1977).

[19]Levi, "Taxation and 'Abnormal' International Capital Flows."

[20]Robert Z. Aliber, "The Interest Rate Parity Theorem: A Reinterpretation," *Journal of Political Economy* (November-December 1973); Michael P. Dooley, "Note

**Figure 18-1 International Capital Flows and Interest Rate Parity**

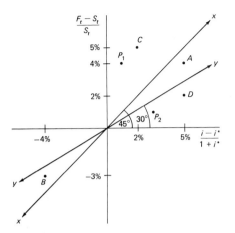

est parity Equation (18-2) holds more closely when arbitrage is between Euromarket assets rather than domestic or onshore assets.[21] One explanation for this finding is that Euromarket assets are more comparable in terms of risk, while onshore assets (for example, U.S. and U.K. Treasury bills) may differ in terms of political risk. Dooley stressed that it is important to distinguish between the cost of known capital controls in place and the risk premium that may be demanded because of the uncertainty about changing capital controls in the future. Dooley and Isard analyzed the time series of onshore and offshore interest rates on Deutsche mark assets. The authors concluded that most of the interest rate differential can be explained by

known economic factors and, therefore, little variation can be attributed to uncertainty concerning future governmental policies.

The kinds of restrictions that a government may exercise over foreign investment by its nationals range from complete prohibition—approached by some of the exchange control systems in developing countries—to mild tax disadvantage or even selective controls—such as the U.S. Foreign Investment Control program instituted in 1968. Between these extremes are such devices as requiring government approval either for all foreign investments or for certain types of foreign investment.

Some of the developed industrial nations have adopted measures to encourage certain kinds of private foreign investments by their citizens in particular areas. These involve such items as government guarantees against loss due to expropriation or revolution, preferred tax treatment for income on foreign investment, and subsidized loans to private foreign investors in certain areas or industries.

The restrictions and requirements imposed by recipient countries on foreign investment also vary greatly. Some induce capital inflows—examples include tax holidays and guarantees that repatriation of earnings will be permitted. Perhaps more important are measures requiring certain behavior by foreign-owned companies. These measures may be undertaken for a variety of reasons: to maintain domestic control over strategic industries, to protect existing institutions, or to avoid the "colonial" implications arising from loss of control of domestic resources, among others. The measures employed may consist of limits on the repatriation of capital funds in the future, the remittance of earnings to the parent company, and so forth.

In the postwar period, the major trend has been toward removing restrictions over international capital flows and increasing the incentives for specific kinds of investments in certain areas. With this relaxation of controls, the volume of international investment has increased significantly.

In sum, the basic forces shaping the international flow of capital funds are those "real" variables that govern the expected returns on real capital. At the same time, transaction costs, taxes, and exchange controls are important variables that may reinforce or repress the normal flow of funds. In addition, foreign exchange risk may dampen the international flow of funds and further segment international capital markets. It should also be noted that while

on Interest Parity, Eurocurrencies and Capital Controls," *International Finance Discussion Papers,* No. 80, Board of Governors of the Federal Reserve System, Washington, D.C., February 1976; and Michael P. Dooley and Peter Isard, "Capital Controls, Political Risk, and Deviations from Interest-Rate Parity," *Journal of Political Economy* (April 1980).

[21]A *Euromarket asset* is an asset denominated in a currency other than that generally used in the host country or controlled by the host country's monetary authorities. For example, either a U.S. dollar-denominated deposit issued by a London or Singapore bank or a Swiss franc-denominated bond traded in Luxembourg or Hong Kong satisfy this definition. Further discussion of this market is found in the section, "Special International Markets and Institutions."

historically there have been severe governmental restrictions on the free movement of funds across national frontiers, these have been progressively relaxed in the postwar period.

## Types of Foreign Investment

The essential purpose of financial investment in a foreign country is to transfer purchasing power from a resident of one nation to a resident of another. Thus, U.S. investment abroad involves the use of current U.S. saving, dishoarding, and new bank credit to finance spending—directly or indirectly—in another country. The opposite holds true with respect to foreign investment in the United States.

This section examines four broad categories of foreign financial investment for which data exist. First, however, we will briefly define each category.

The acquisition of, or addition to, a foreign business with funds from *an American parent company* (a company that owns 25 percent or more of the foreign firm) is defined as *direct investment* for balance-of-payments purposes. This type of foreign investment has been the most important in terms of volume in recent years—except for 1974 and 1976. Since direct investment involves a high degree of ownership and control of a foreign enterprise, this type of foreign investment is particularly conducive to the international transfer of technical and managerial talent.

*Portfolio investment* includes the purchase of bonds and stocks of foreign companies, the latter involving a minor equity interest. Investment in foreign securities is further subdivided into *new issues* (whether actually issued in the U.S. or in foreign financial centers) and *trade in outstanding securities* (that is, seasoned securities). In addition, *term loans* to foreigners made by bank or nonbank financial institutions are generally included in the portfolio investment category. As a rule—and in the ensuing discussion—items with an original duration of over one year (namely, long-term securities or loans) are included in foreign portfolio investment. All new issues or loans of less than one year, on the other hand, are included in short-term foreign investment.

Formally, *short-term foreign investment* involves the acquisition by an American resident of any foreign-issued financial asset with an original maturity of one year or less. Note that this category encompasses a broad group of assets: demand deposits; time deposits at commercial banks and other financial institutions; and a wide range of open-market paper, including foreign short-term government securities, bankers' acceptances, and short-term loans.

*Government capital transfers* may be included in these categories or excluded and treated as a separate item. In this chapter, the discussion separates private from government foreign investment, primarily because the motives associated with government investment are highly political (and hopefully humanitarian), while those governing private capital movements are essentially economic. The decision to include both loans and grants or only loans in government foreign investment is a matter of analytical preference. In the United States, the Balance of Payments Accounts consider grants as unilateral transfers and, therefore, as a current government expense. However, for economic purposes there is little difference between a soft loan and a grant. We will consider both loans and grants as government capital transfers.

For every category of U.S. investment abroad (that is, of foreign demands for U.S. funds), there is a category covering the same type of flow in the opposite direction. Thus, there is direct foreign investment in the United States, the purchase of U.S. securities by foreigners, and—most important—the acquisition of U.S. short-term financial instruments by foreigners.

## Aggregate Foreign Investment Since 1960

In the last two decades international flows of capital have grown greatly. Private U.S. foreign investment has increased steadily over the period with a significant decline only in 1977. U.S. government capital outflows have also shown substantial increases. The percentage increase in foreign capital flows to the United States swamps the growth in the previous two categories; however, this growth is from a smaller base and has been highly erratic. The annual amounts of these capital flows are illustrated in Figures 18-2, 18-3, and 18-4.

## Figure 18-2 The Flow of Private U.S. Funds for Foreign Investment, 1960–1977–1978

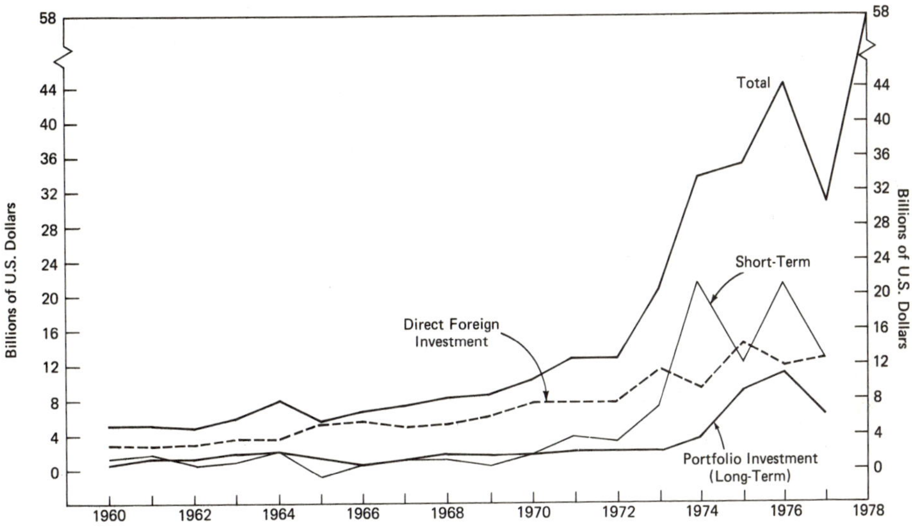

Source: *Survey of Current Business* (June 1978).

The gross annual outflow of U.S. private funds (Figure 18-2) increased from $5 billion in 1960 to nearly $44 billion in 1976 and $57 billion in 1978.[22] Until 1973 the increase principally resulted from direct foreign investment flows. After 1973 both short-term and long-term portfolio flows surged upward. The dramatic change in the composition of U.S. capital flows is the result of two factors: (1) the increased volatility in the foreign exchange market and the general downward drift in the value of the dollar; and (2) the relaxation of U.S. capital controls at the start of 1974, which enabled foreigners to borrow more in the U.S. and American residents and financial institutions to lend more abroad. U.S. portfolio investments increased fairly consistently in the postwar years, reaching a peak of almost $2 billion in 1964. Thereafter, the U.S. government, for reasons of balance-of-payments policy,[23] imposed the Interest Equalization Tax

and the Voluntary Foreign Credit Restraints programs as well as a highly restrictive domestic monetary policy. The result was a sharp decline in foreign portfolio investment. These policy measures and their effects are examined later in this chapter. Short-term foreign investment has shown more marked variation, especially in recent years, as a result of uncertainty concerning the expected rate of change in exchange rates.

Figure 18-3 shows U.S. government capital outflows (net of repayments) over the same period. After a decline in the early 1950s to approximately $2 billion annually following the elimination of Marshall Plan grants, a prolonged increase in loans beginning in 1960 raised total government capital outflows until a peak was reached in 1974 of over $10 billion. Comparing Figures 18-2 and 18-3 shows

---

[22] The figures are reported in nominal terms. It is important to remember that the U.S. Consumer Price Index increased by more than 110 percent over the sample period.

[23] The Interest Equalization Tax was a tax on the purchase price of long-term foreign securities (and bank loans) acquired by Americans. It, in essence, lowered the

effective annual yield on these securities. This yield was reduced from 1 percent, in the period 1963–1968, to 0.57 percent in 1969. The Voluntary Foreign Credit Restraints program was strengthened after its initial enactment, and a part of it became mandatory in 1968. The program attempted to limit foreign lending by U.S. banks and financial institutions and to suppress the rate of direct investment abroad. On January 1, 1974, all of these controls were abolished.

**Figure 18-3  U.S. Government Grants and Long-Term Loans to Foreigners, 1960–1977**

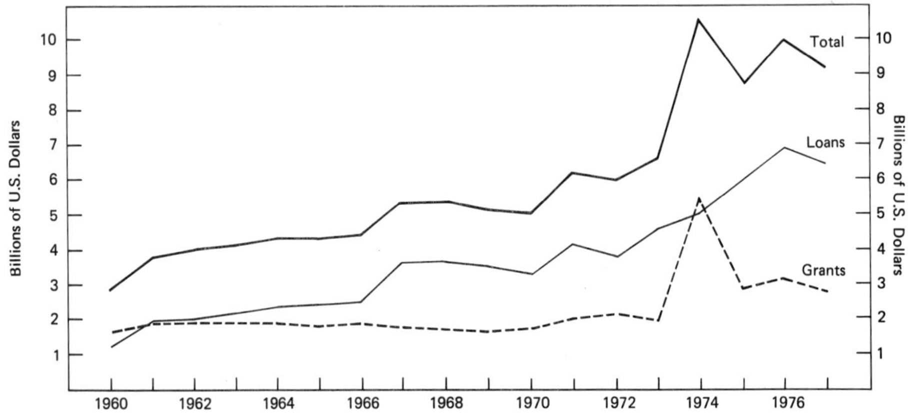

Source: *Survey of Current Business* (June 1978).

that the private sector has been a more important source of capital funds to the rest of the world than have government aid programs and, furthermore, the relative importance of private-sector flows has increased substantially.

Figure 18-4 plots the various components of foreign investment in the United States. The most outstanding feature is how strongly short-term investment dominates the total. Long-term foreign investments in the United States have been relatively small, never exceeding $1.2 billion per year, while short-term funds from foreigners had fluctuated to as high as $19 billion in 1974. A comparison of foreign investment in the United States and U.S. investment abroad demonstrates that there is some truth to the notion that the "United States finances its long-term foreign investment with foreign short-term funds"—that is, that the United States acts like a financial intermediary.[24] However, since the dollar devaluation in 1973, foreign direct investment in the United States has increased substantially to record highs. The large increases have sparked debate concerning future restrictions on this kind of investment. Short-term foreign investment flows to the United States have

been extremely volatile since 1967 reflecting (1) the increased short-run variation in exchange rates, and (2) the enormous build-up of liquid funds in the oil-exporting (OPEC) countries.[25]

For the entire postwar period, a cursory comparison of total U.S. investment abroad (private plus government) with total private investment in the United States indicates a sizable, and growing, net flow of funds from the United States (that is, a net foreign demand for U.S. funds) except in 1968 and 1969. The traditional explanation for the net outflow—a sizable current account (export) surplus and the loss of international reserves—was valid over most of the period. The United States ran a current account surplus in every year between 1960 and 1978 except 1971–1972 and 1977–1978; in the latter years, the deficit reached record amounts.[26] Similarly, U.S. international reserves declined steadily from $19.4 billion in 1960 to $13.2 billion in 1972. Since 1972 the U.S. reserves have risen

[24]This aspect is considered in more detail in Chapter 30.

[25]Frenkel and Levich, in "Transaction Costs and Interest Arbitrage," argue that the pound sterling devaluation in November 1967 marks the changeover from a quiet peg period to a turbulent peg period (1968–1969). The analysis suggests that there may have been a structural change in the system, even though the formal organization of the exchange-rate system remained unchanged.

[26]*Economic Report of the President*, 1979, p. 294.

**Figure 18-4    Flow of Foreign Funds for Investment in the United States, 1960–1977**

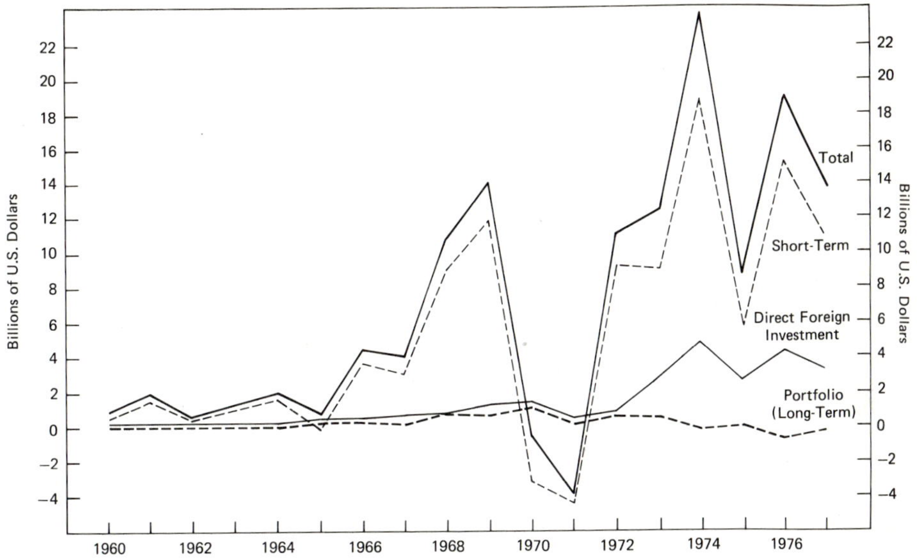

Source: *Survey of Current Business* (June 1978).

(to approximately $18 billion in 1978),[27] reflecting intervention agreements in the foreign exchange market and rises in the price of gold. By the 1980s, however, with managed floating exchange rates, current account deficits will in large measure have to be matched by net capital inflows to the United States.

## U.S. Direct Investment

This section examines the causes and characteristics of U.S. investment in foreign business concerns. Foreign direct investment in the United States is described later.

U.S. direct investment has been the largest component of U.S. foreign investment in the postwar period (see Figure 18-2). Furthermore, outflows of funds for direct investment more than doubled from the 1960s to the 1970s. During the 1960s, direct investment was the largest and also the fastest-

[27]International Monetary Fund, *International Financial Statistics*, Washington, D.C., 1979.

growing type of U.S. foreign investment. As noted earlier, changes in exchange rate expectations and exchange controls altered the relative attractiveness of foreign investments in the 1970s, increasing the attractiveness of portfolio investments.

The structure of direct investment outflows by geographic area and by industry groups is illustrated in Tables 18-2 and 18-3. The tables show the average outflow of funds for direct investment for recent subperiods, with the percentage distribution for area and industry. The final columns in Tables 18-2 and 18-3 show the distribution of the total stock of U.S.-owned foreign enterprises at the end of 1978. The figure reflects the net results of all previous direct investment outflows, retained foreign earnings, valuation adjustments, and depreciation.

Table 18-2 shows that average total outflows to all areas has increased more than 40 percent from each subperiod to the next. This increase has extended to all areas although the increases for Latin America and Europe are especially high. Traditionally Canada has been the major recipient of U.S.

**Table 18-2  U.S. Direct Foreign Investment by Geographic Area**

| | Average Annual Outflow from the United States | | | | | | | | Stock of U.S. Direct Investment, Year-End 1978 (book value) | |
| | 1967–1970 | | 1971–1973 | | 1974–1976 | | 1977–1978 | | | |
| Area | (in millions of dollars) | (percentages) | (in millions of dollars) | (percentages) | (in millions of dollars) | (percentages) | (in millions of dollars) | (percentages) | (in millions of dollars) | (percentages) |
|---|---|---|---|---|---|---|---|---|---|---|
| ALL AREAS | $5,922 | 100% | $8,611 | 100% | $11,977 | 100% | $15,636 | 100% | $168,081 | 100% |
| Canada | 1,326 | 22 | 1,509 | 18 | 2,795 | 23 | 1,721 | 11 | 37,280 | 22 |
| Europe | 2,216 | 37 | 4,333 | 50 | 5,884 | 49 | 7,265 | 46 | 69,669 | 41 |
| Other developed countries | 590 | 10 | 956 | 11 | 966 | 8 | 1,232 | 8 | 13,792 | 8 |
| Latin America | 802 | 14 | 1,174 | 14 | 2,351 | 20 | 4,287 | 27 | 32,509 | 19 |
| Other developing countries | 988 | 17 | 639 | 7 | 20 | — | 1,289 | 8 | 14,831 | 9 |

Source: *Survey of Current Business.*

**Table 18-3  U.S. Direct Foreign Investment, by Industry**

| | Average Annual Outflow from the United States | | | | | | | | Stock of U.S. Direct Investment, Year-End 1978 (book value) | |
| | 1967–1970 | | 1971–1973 | | 1974–1976 | | 1977–1978 | | | |
| Industry | (in millions of dollars) | (percentages) | (in millions of dollars) | (percentages) | (in millions of dollars) | (percentages) | (in millions of dollars) | (percentages) | (in millions of dollars) | (percentages) |
|---|---|---|---|---|---|---|---|---|---|---|
| ALL INDUSTRIES | $5,922 | 100% | $8,611 | 100% | $11,977 | 100% | $15,636 | 100% | $168,081 | 100% |
| Petroleum | 1,465 | 25 | 1,732 | 20 | 1,587 | 13 | 2,263 | 14 | 33,302 | 20 |
| Manufacturing | 2,577 | 44 | 4,440 | 52 | 5,564 | 46 | 6,523 | 42 | 74,207 | 44 |
| Other | 1,879 | 32 | 2,438 | 28 | 4,826 | 40 | 6,850 | 44 | 60,572 | 36 |

Source: *Survey of Current Business.*

direct investment funds, but in recent years it has received declining portions of new investment outflows and by 1978 it accounted for only 22 percent of U.S. direct investment. Europe and other developed countries together accounted for almost 50 percent of the total volume of U.S. investment, with the remaining 28 percent spread throughout Latin America and other developing countries.

The flow of new investment in the period 1967–1978 was dominated by flows to developed countries, particularly to Europe. The growth in the rate of outflows to the European Economic Community (EEC), spurred by expectations of rapidly expanding European markets and the prospect of a high common external tariff, was phenomenal—from roughly 10 percent of annual flows in the early 1950s to nearly 50 percent of annual flows in the 1970s.

Table 18-2 also indicates that the fraction of U.S. direct investment going to other (less developed) countries has fallen from roughly 40 percent in the 1950s to 30 percent in the 1960s to 20 percent in the early 1970s (with some recovery toward the end of the decade). This changing pattern of capital flows has occurred during a period that placed great emphasis on the importance of accelerated development by the poorer nations.

The declining share of U.S. direct investment going to underdeveloped areas reflects in part the changing industrial structure of direct investment outflows, as can be seen in Table 18-3. Historically, U.S. direct investment has been dominated by investment in foreign enterprises—especially oil and natural resource-connected enterprises—that complemented the resources of American parent companies. Since the 1950s this picture has changed radically, with new outflows in manufacturing and the service industries increasing in importance, while new petroleum investment has declined. Thus, by the end of 1978, manufacturing enterprises accounted for 44 percent of total direct investment, petroleum accounted for 20 percent, with the remaining 36 percent comprising investments in financial companies, trade, communications, and other service companies. The increase in the relative importance of direct investment in manufacturing enterprise is consistent with the increase in the importance of outflows to Europe, where most direct investment is of this type.

Direct investment outflows from the United States are, overwhelmingly, for the purpose of building new, or expanding existing, operating facilities of foreign subsidiaries of American parent companies. Typically less than 10 percent of U.S. direct investment outflows are for the acquisition of existing foreign companies. There are, nevertheless, a few U.S. holding companies that specialize in such ventures and some individual acquisitions are indeed sizable. The percentage of funds spent for this type of investment has increased in recent years.

Figure 18-5 shows the sources and uses of funds by foreign affiliates of American parent companies over the period 1966–1972. Of total funds employed by such companies, U.S. direct investment funds represent a small share. In 1968, when mandatory Foreign Direct Investment Program (FDIP) controls were established, the absolute amount and relative share of external funds from U.S. sources declined substantially. The FDIP and the Interest Equalization Tax were intended to reduce the outflow of capital from the United States in order to improve the U.S. balance of payments. Figure 18-5 suggests that U.S. foreign affiliates were able to tap foreign sources of funds so that total sources of funds continued to rise over the period. As for the uses of funds, plant and equipment expenditures account for roughly 65 percent of the total while additions to inventories and working capital account for the remainder.

In recent years, the total earnings of U.S. direct investments have exceeded $15 billion annually. Of this total, the percentage remitted to American parent companies in the form of dividends has declined from about 65 percent to about 55 percent over the last ten years. In part, this reflects the relaxation of balance-of-payments policies that systematically attempted to persuade U.S. companies to improve their individual balance of payments.

It was argued earlier that after one considers differences in risks, including foreign exchange risks, the expected rate of return (after taxes) on alternative foreign investments is a major factor in determining the volume and direction of foreign investment. Although actual past earnings cannot serve as an indicator of the expected rate of return, they are valuable indicators of the performance of foreign operations relative to domestic ones. Figure

**Figure 18-5  Sources and Uses of Funds of Foreign Affiliates of U.S. Companies, 1966–1972**

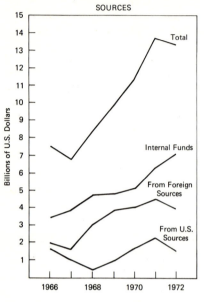

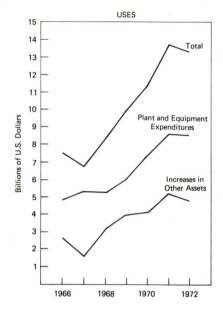

Source: *Survey of Current Business* (July 1975).

18-6 shows the rate of return on book value for U.S. domestic manufacturing industries and for U.S. direct foreign investment subsidiaries. As can be seen, the correlation of domestic and foreign returns appears to be very strong between 1969 and 1977. The impact of the 1970 U.S. minirecession appears to have been stronger on U.S. returns; however, the deeper 1974–1975 recession appears to have had a larger impact on foreign yields. In the final period, the rates of return on U.S. and foreign investment differ by less than 1 percent. It was during this period that the big surge of foreign investment into the United States occurred (see Table 18-4).

Ultimately, the factor that influences the flow of foreign direct investment is simply the expected rate of profitability on foreign investment relative to domestic investment. In the early postwar period, the U.S. market was large, stable, mature, and dominated by oligopolistic firms, but foreign markets were in a much greater state of flux and the prospective growth in those markets was greater. Under the circumstances it could have been expected that U.S. companies would expand

their foreign operations very rapidly. This was true of companies in the extractive sector, the manufacturing sector, and the services—especially financial—as well. By the early 1970s, however, international conditions had changed. The U.S. market looked more attractive, and the expectation of faster growth in sales, less governmental involvement in company decision making, and a substantial depreciation of the dollar, all made investment in facilities in the United States *relatively* more attractive for *both* foreign firms and for American firms. These factors are reflected in the higher growth of foreign direct investment in the United States and the slowing of the increase in U.S. direct investment abroad during the post-1972 period as compared with the earlier postwar period.

## U.S. Long-Term Portfolio Investment[28]

Earlier we observed that U.S. foreign portfolio investment underwent a relatively sustained expan-

[28]The term *portfolio investment* is used here to include new issues of foreign securities in the United States (less

**Figure 18-6    Returns on Manufacturing Investments**

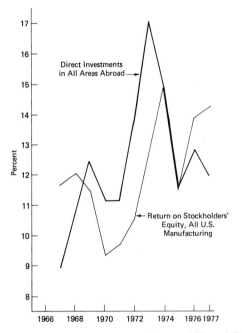

Sources: *Survey of Current Business* (August 1977); and *Economic Report of the President, 1979.*

sion in the early postwar period. But, from a level of more than $2 billion in 1964, portfolio flows declined to only $0.5 billion in 1966. This period coincided with the advent of U.S. capital controls. Over the next seven years, portfolio flows grew back toward the $2 billion level. After controls were relaxed in 1974, portfolio flows surged to nearly $12 billion in 1976, then declined sharply in the following year.

Annual rates of foreign portfolio investment in certain subcategories for various periods since 1950 are shown in Table 18-5. The single dominant item has been purchases of new issues of bonds and stocks, which have increased in each period and have accounted for well over half of total portfolio investment since 1961. New issues, which fluctuated near $1 billion through the 1960s, expanded

dramatically to more than $7 billion in the period 1975–1977.

Long-term foreign lending by U.S. banks also increased fairly steadily until 1966, when repayments actually exceeded extensions by $300 million as a result of extremely tight credit conditions and high interest rates in the United States. Repayments continued to exceed new lending for the next four years through the 1969–1970 credit crunch. Banks became net long-term foreign lenders again in 1971 and showed substantial increases over the period 1972–1977 (see Table 18-5). Foreign lending by nonbanks had been relatively minor until the late 1960s, at which time it averaged $393 million per year. By 1977, however, foreign lending by nonbanks had declined substantially. Similarly, the flow of funds from the purchase (or sale) of outstanding foreign securities has been relatively small compared to new security issues or bank loans. It also has been highly variable, shifting from a net outflow in the early 1960s to a sizable inflow in 1964–1966, and back again to a record net *sale* of outstanding foreign securities over the period 1972–1977 (see Table 18-5).

The sizable U.S. capital outflow for portfolio investment would imply that expected borrowing costs in the United States are lower. For the foreign borrower there are three main components in the cost of borrowing: (1) the nominal interest charge; (2) the unanticipated exchange rate change; and (3) the flotation fees and transaction costs of bringing a new issue to the market. As we discussed earlier, borrowers can reduce the risk of unanticipated exchange rate changes by buying forward contracts to offset their liability position in foreign currency. For long-term borrowing where complete forward contracts are not available, the comparison of nominal interest rates becomes more important. Until the mid-1960s, U.S. domestic interest rates were lower than those in every major industrial country except Switzerland (where the government carefully controls foreign capital issues on the domestic capital market). Since the mid-1960s, U.S. nominal interest rates have risen substantially, especially vis-à-vis rates in Germany, Japan, and Switzerland.[29]

[29]For a detailed empirical analysis of holding-period yields in international bond markets, see Robert Z. Aliber, *Exchange Risk and Corporate International Finance,* Macmillan & Co., Ltd., London, 1978.

redemptions), term loans to foreigners by U.S. banks and other residents, and net purchases of outstanding foreign securities by Americans. Foreign securities include issues of international organizations, such as the International Bank for Reconstruction and Development (World Bank), in the U.S. money and capital markets.

**Table 18-4  Foreign Direct Investment in the United States**

|  | Average Annual Inflow to the U.S. (1977–1978) | | Stock of Direct Investment in the U.S., Year-End 1978 | |
|---|---|---|---|---|
|  | (in millions of dollars) | (percentages) | (in millions of dollars) | (percentages) |
| All areas | $5,030 | 100% | $40,831 | 100% |
| Canada | 129.5 | 3 | 6,166 | 15 |
| U.K. | 783.5 | 16 | 7,370 | 18 |
| Other Europe | 3,083 | 61 | 20,525 | 50 |
| Japan | 755 | 15 | 2,688 | 7 |
| All others | 279 | 6 | 4,081 | 10 |
| All industries | $5,030 | 100% | $40,831 | 100% |
| Petroleum | 982 | 20 | 7,885 | 19 |
| Manufacturing | 1,834 | 36 | 16,289 | 40 |
| Trade | 1,381 | 27 | 8,884 | 22 |
| Insurance | 322 | 6 | 2,759 | 7 |
| Other | 510 | 10 | 5,013 | 12 |

Source: *Survey of Current Business*.

**Table 18-5  Types of Long-Term Portfolio Foreign Investment by the United States (annual average outflows in millions of dollars)**

|  | 1950–1955 | 1961–1968 | 1969–1971 | 1972–1974 | 1975–1977 |
|---|---|---|---|---|---|
| New issues of securities less redemptions | $132 | $ 909 | $1,079 | $1,183 | $7,057 |
| Net purchases of outstanding foreign securities | 75 | 1 | 36 | (152) | (229) |
| Net long-term foreign lending by U.S. banks | 73 | 155 | 53 | 1,141 | 1,823 |
| Net long-term foreign lending by U.S. nonbanks | 45 | 137 | 393 | 371 | 112 |
| Total | $325 | $1,202 | $1,561 | $2,543 | $8,763 |

Source: *Survey of Current Business*.

The fact that borrowing occurred at the higher U.S. rates in recent years does not necessarily reflect irrationality on the part of foreign borrowers. First, foreign borrowers in the United States generally obtain U.S. dollars, which are universally acceptable in international commerce. If the borrowers had borrowed domestically and then purchased the dollars with their local currency proceeds, they might have had to pay a premium. Second, in the 1970s the rise in foreign borrowing on U.S. financial markets, where nominal interest costs were higher than those prevailing in other foreign markets, might reflect an expectation that the U.S. dollar would depreciate on the foreign exchange market in the long term. The foreign borrowers, as indicated earlier, would thus be able to repay the dollar-denominated loans in cheaper dollars (in terms of their own currency). The importance of this factor, although impossible to determine, was no doubt significant in the 1975–1978 period.

Perhaps most important, if foreign borrowers in the United States had actually floated their debt at home, the interest spread in favor of home borrowing might well have disappeared or have actually turned to favor the United States. Borrowing in the United States reduces the demand for funds (and, therefore, interest rates) in the borrower's own country below what it would have been had the flotations been made at home. The impact of this U.S. borrowing on local interest rates depends on the elasticity of supply of local funds; the lower the elasticity of supply, the greater the reduction in local interest rates as a result of a given amount of U.S. borrowing.

There is good reason to believe that the elasticity of supply of funds in many foreign countries is quite low. If this is true, then a switch by foreign borrowers in the United States to their local capital markets would cause a relatively large increase in foreign interest rates. However, the ability of the huge U.S. capital market to absorb easily a sizable amount of foreign portfolio issues—that is, a high elasticity of supply of funds in the United States—implies a negligible change in U.S. interest rates due to foreign borrowing. Thus, the observation of an *ex post* spread favoring local borrowing, rather than U.S. borrowing, is not necessarily indicative of a similar *ex ante* spread.

Furthermore, official government agencies in many foreign countries regulate the timing and size of new bond issues. Those borrowers who are not permitted to float an issue locally may turn to the United States, thereby removing a source of demand for funds from the local market and permitting local interest rates to remain below those in the United States while, at the same time, foreign borrowers are floating bonds in New York City.

The elasticity of supply of funds depends, to a considerable extent, on the relative size of capital markets—that is, on the volume of new issues, the frequency of transactions, the number and financial soundness of market participants, and so forth.

With respect to these factors, U.S. financial markets are unsurpassed. Table 18-6 gives one rough indication of the relative size of capital markets. Although this is not a precise comparison because the data among countries are not strictly comparable, it does indicate the rough order of magnitude as measured by new issues of securities and the market value of existing securities. Using the former measure, the U.S. market appears to be at least twice as large as that of the capital markets of the other countries listed in Table 18-6. Using the latter measure, the market value of listed securities in the U.S. clearly outdistances other industrial countries. Thus, the notion that a large volume of borrowing by a foreign institution may take place in the U.S. market because funds are available, while they are not readily available in a foreign market, contains considerable truth—but this factor is of declining importance as continental European markets and the Euromarkets become more sophisticated and acquire greater depth.

Although interest costs are the most important of all borrowing costs, underwriting spreads, legal fees, local security taxes, and so forth, are also important. Little in the way of reliable information

**Table 18-6  Relative Size of U.S. and Foreign Financial Markets, Selected Measures (in billions of dollars)**

| | United States | Japan | United Kingdom | Germany | Canada | Switzerland | France | Euromarket | World Total |
|---|---|---|---|---|---|---|---|---|---|
| Money supply, end of 1977[a] | $342.5 | $253.3 | $ 45.1 | $ 93.9 | $25.4 | $31.6 | $110.1 | — | — |
| Quasi-money, end of 1977[a] | 529.8 | 405.2 | 48.5 | 276.1 | 61.3 | 57.8 | 102.1 | 383.4[b] | — |
| Average annual issue of stocks and bonds, 1972–1974[c] | 56.9 | 27.4 | 3.6 | 14.7 | 4.1 | 3.3 | 6.6 | 5.2[d] | — |
| 1975–1977 | 134.3 | 55.7 | 15.9 | 30.0 | 8.7 | 7.6 | 9.8 | 15.1[d] | — |
| Market value of listed securities, 1978[e] | 817.1 (54.0%) | 275.2 (18.2%) | 101.3 (6.7%) | 68.5 (4.5%) | 57.8 (3.8%) | 35.0 (2.3%) | 34.4 (2.3%) | — | 1,514.3 (100.0%) |

[a]International Monetary Fund, *International Financial Statistics*, 1978.
[b]Estimated gross amount of Eurocurrency deposits as reported in Bank for International Settlements, *Annual Report*, 1978.
[c]Calculated from data in OECD, *Financial Statistics*, 1978.
[d]Bank for International Settlements, *Annual Report*, 1978.
[e]Capital International, *Perspective* (1978), Geneva, Switzerland. Percentage in parentheses.

is available on the relative "flotation" costs in various countries, but such data as are available indicate that such costs are lower in the United States and Switzerland than in other countries.[30] It has been estimated that the average U.S. flotation cost on foreign issues in 1958 was 2.75 percent of the net proceeds of the issue and 1.7 percent for domestic issues.[31] As the machinery for handling foreign issues abroad has improved and the Eurobond market for international issues has developed, this spread has probably narrowed. It is also probable, however, that flotation costs in the United States still are relatively low internationally. This is evidenced by the fact that many international borrowers in foreign capital markets use American underwriters, and a significant percentage of foreign public flotations in the United States have been acquired by foreign purchasers. Indeed, over 25 percent of foreign public new issues in New York were purchased by foreigners from 1975 to 1977.

In sum, the traditional advantages of foreign portfolio borrowing in New York, including acceptability of the dollar proceeds, freedom from government intervention through foreign borrowing, and the ready availability and lower cost of U.S. credit, still generally prevail, but such relative advantages declined significantly in the middle and later 1960s. This is at least partly reflected in the decline in average portfolio investment in 1964–1967, as noted previously. (See Figure 18-2.) Tight credit conditions in the United States pushed interest rates to postwar highs in the late 1960s while, at the same time, credit conditions were easing in some continental European countries. As a result, the interest-cost advantage favoring the United States disappeared in a number of cases. In addition, U.S. capital controls instituted for balance-of-payments purposes retarded U.S. portfolio investment directly.

After these controls were relaxed, the volume of new foreign issues spurted to record high levels. The U.S. financial markets remain very large, even compared to the Euromarkets. If the level of U.S. regulation remains low, it seems likely that the U.S.

market will continue to purchase a large volume of long-term foreign securities.

## The Supply of U.S. Government Funds to Foreigners

Another major source of U.S. funds for foreigners is the various programs carried out by the U.S. government. As can be seen in Figure 18-3, U.S. government funds available to foreigners in the form of grants and long-term loans have grown to more than $9 billion in recent years, roughly equal to the gross outflow from private long-term investments.

While private capital outflows respond to financial incentives, which can ultimately be subsumed under expected rates of return, the factors governing the volume of government funds made available are a complex mixture of political, humanitarian, and—sometimes—economic motives. As a result, a strictly economic interpretation of U.S. foreign-aid programs is inadequate, and any careful appraisal of the causes and effects of aid programs and the mechanisms by which funds and other resources (for example, military hardware or surplus agricultural commodities) are transferred abroad is almost impossible. Such an analysis is definitely beyond the scope of this chapter. What follows, therefore, is but a brief description of the major government programs that supply funds to foreigners.

The amounts plotted in Figure 18-3 cover only the *dollar* outflows under U.S. government economic-aid programs. In addition to these, other programs involve resource transfers in other forms. The entire economic-aid program, and the relative importance of the various components for the period 1966–1978, is shown in Table 18-7.

The major category to show a trend toward upward growth between periods has been credits repayable in dollars, while the other major category, grants, declined relatively in the 1966–1978 period. Dollar credits rose from 48 percent of total aid in 1966 to 61 percent in 1978, while grants declined from 41 percent to 29 percent over the same period. The remaining categories taken together account for only 10 percent of the total. The category labeled "Subscriptions to international organizations" primarily covers U.S. dollar capital subscriptions to local or international development banks, such as the Inter-American Development

[30]Peter B. Kenen, "Towards an Atlantic Capital Market," *Lloyds Bank Review* (July 1963), 20–22.

[31]Paul Meek, "United States Investment in Foreign Securities," in *U.S. Private and Government Investment Abroad,* ed. Raymond F. Mikesell, University of Oregon Press, Eugene, 1962.

**Table 18-7  Distribution of Net U.S. Government Foreign Economic Aid (in millions of dollars)**

| | 1966 | 1967 | 1968 | 1969 | 1970 | 1971 | 1972 | 1973 | 1974 | 1975 | 1976 | 1977 | 1978 |
|---|---|---|---|---|---|---|---|---|---|---|---|---|---|
| Total | $4,676 | $5,227 | $5,358 | $5,032 | $5,036 | $6,041 | $5,808 | $7,180 | $9,935 | $8,831 | $9,956 | $9,187 | $10,746 |
| Grants | 1,910 | 1,802 | 1,707 | 1,644 | 1,734 | 2,045 | 2,174 | 1,938 | 5,475[a] | 2,893 | 3,146 | 2,775 | 3,152 |
| Credits repayable in dollars | 2,248 | 2,665 | 3,028 | 2,861 | 2,788 | 3,772 | 3,436 | 3,972 | 4,245 | 5,268 | 5,793 | 5,507 | 6,573 |
| Credits repayable in foreign currency | 354 | 776 | 559 | 432 | 199 | 156 | 80 | 281 | 223 | 24 | 45 | 38 | 26 |
| Subscriptions to international organizations | (101) | 194 | 127 | 184 | 234 | 246 | 271 | 373 | 538 | 654 | 1,102 | 870 | 867 |
| Other | 265 | (210) | (65) | (89) | 81 | (178) | (153) | 616 | (546) | (8) | (130) | (3) | 128 |

[a]Includes extraordinary U.S. government transactions with India; see "Special U.S. Government Transactions," *Survey of Current Business* (June 1974).

Source: *Survey of Current Business.*

Bank and the International Finance Corporation. This total does not, however, include funds raised by floating bonds of the International Bank for Reconstruction and Development (World Bank) in the U.S. capital market. These bonds are acquired by private entities and are included in the totals for private portfolio investment discussed in the preceding section.

There are three major programs under which the U.S. government provides resources directly to foreigners: the Foreign Assistance Act of 1961, which established the Agency for International Development (AID); the Export-Import Bank; and grants or sales of surplus agricultural commodities for local currencies under Public Law 480. The last is not of direct concern here because it does not involve an outflow of dollars. Rather, PL-480 permits the sale of U.S. agricultural commodities, which have been acquired by the U.S. government under the farm price-support program, in exchange for the currency of the recipient. The currencies acquired in such a manner may then be disposed of in a number of ways, including maintenance of U.S. government missions in the country, grants to the foreign government to cover its expenditures, and so forth. This program has become sizable in recent years with the value of commodities sold approaching $1.5 billion per year. Ultimate U.S. financing of these sales involves U.S. Department of Agriculture payments to farmers for the supported commodities, a current government expenditure financed by tax revenues or borrowing.

More relevant for our purposes are the net grants and long-term low-interest dollar loans[32] made under the auspices of AID. This represents the largest dollar component under the U.S. economic aid program, as seen in Table 18-7, and includes "project" aid—that is, dollars made available for specific expenditures associated with a particular capital project—and to a lesser extent "program," or general, aid, which is not earmarked for a specific project.[33] The credit component is generally made on liberal

terms, with 15- to 40-year maturities, lower-than-market interest rates, and fairly long grace periods before interest and amortization payments start. The credit component will, barring default, eventually result in a net return flow of dollars to the U.S. government.

Whether AID funds are made available through grants or loans, the overwhelming proportion must be spent directly on U.S. goods (in other words, on U.S. exports). This "tying" of foreign aid stems from the U.S. balance-of-payments problem and is designed to reduce the net "foreign exchange cost" of the aid programs. The funds channeled through AID to foreign governments or private investors are raised in the United States through government tax receipts and borrowing. The impact on U.S. capital markets of this supply of dollars to foreigners is, therefore, indirect and manifests itself through federal government financing.

The Export-Import Bank is a government corporation established in 1934 to stimulate U.S. exports. Its primary function still remains the financing of U.S. exports, although in the 1960s the government established a variety of other programs, including repayment guarantees on export loans made by private lenders and participation with some private insurance companies in a scheme to insure against political risks in export financing.[34]

The Eximbank may make long-term loans to foreigners: (a) to finance U.S. exports associated with a particular project, and (b) for balance-of-payments emergencies to maintain a foreign country's imports from the United States. The usual export loans (and guarantees) are for short duration. The volume of Eximbank financing increased considerably in the 1970s, reaching an average outflow (net of repayments) of nearly $2.2 billion in the period 1973–1976, as compared with only $500 million per year in the decade 1956–1965. By 1978 the bank had total liabilities of $12 billion, of which $1 billion was in capital stock subscribed to by the U.S. government, and $7.8 billion represented borrowing authority in U.S. securities markets.[35]

---

[32]AID has a number of other foreign-aid and technical-assistance functions apart from its loans and grants. However, the latter is of primary concern here. For other components of the credit programs of AID and the Export-Import Bank, see Chapter 11.

[33]See Raymond F. Mikesell, *Public International Lending for Development,* Random House, New York, 1966.

[34]For a review of these programs, see Marina Whitman, *Government Risk-Sharing in Foreign Investment,* Princeton University Press, Princeton, N.J., 1965. Programs of the Export-Import Bank are also discussed in Chapter 11.

[35]*U.S. Statistical Abstract,* 1979, p. 867.

Eximbank loans are made at lower than commercial rates and the project loans may extend from five to twenty years. Increased lending, in general, requires a flotation of Eximbank bonds in the U.S. capital market. Thus, this institution is a nonbank financial intermediary whose use of funds is directed solely to foreign borrowers (or foreign affiliates of U.S. firms) and whose main source of funds is bonded debt to American lenders.

Besides these major programs, U.S. government policies include a myriad of programs that may involve small flows of funds to foreigners or affect the flow of private funds for foreign investment. For example, U.S. tax treatment of the earnings of foreign subsidiaries has affected foreign capital outflows; government insurance against political risks has tended to increase foreign investment; and a host of other measures may directly or indirectly alter the incentives for foreign investment.

### Short-Term Capital Outflows and Inflows[36]

The emphasis thus far has been on U.S. long-term private and official capital outflows—that is, on the foreign demand for U.S. funds or the U.S. supply of funds to foreigners. This emphasis seems reasonable because foreign investment in the United States in these categories has been minimal, while the foreign demand for U.S. funds has been sizable. Short-term international capital movements pose a different problem. The gross flows in *both* directions have been sizable since 1960. Figure 18-4 suggests that short-term capital historically has dominated the total inflows of foreign funds. Figure 18-2 illustrates that through the entire 1960s, short-term capital was a small part of total U.S. capital outflows. However, beginning in 1973, short-term U.S. outflows expanded sharply to surge ahead of U.S. direct foreign investment and long-term portfolio flows.

Table 18-8 reports the gross flow of U.S. short-term investment abroad (shown as foreign assets) and the gross flow of foreign short-term funds to the U.S. (shown as liabilities to foreigners) over

[36]These consist of cash, demand deposits, time deposits, and marketable instruments of one year or less to original maturity. Marketable U.S. government securities, regardless of maturity, are considered short term.

the period 1968–1977. The data trace out a highly volatile path, which we interpret as a response to four fundamental events:

1. the fourfold increase in the price of oil in 1973–1974 and the subsequent massive balance of payments surplus accrued by the OPEC countries
2. the U.S. (and worldwide) recession in 1974–1975 and the spotty recovery toward growth in 1976–1977
3. the major dollar devaluations in 1971 and 1973 before the move toward generalized (and managed) floating exchange rates
4. the removal of U.S. capital controls in 1974

To begin with the fourth event, U.S. short-term outflows appeared to make a quantum adjustment in 1974 to a higher level. While U.S. short-term outflows have been volatile over the 1974–1977 period, the average value is significantly higher than in earlier periods covered by controls.

The massive oil price increases in 1973–1974 led to a balance-of-payments surplus approaching $40 billion in the OPEC countries. Since OPEC consumption did not increase proportionately and real investment projects were not immediately available, the OPEC surplus was "recycled" into short-term financial assets, primarily in Euromarkets and U.S. financial markets. The large OPEC surplus in 1974 and its continuing (although smaller) surpluses in later years contributed to the peak in foreign short-term inflows in 1974.

The worldwide pattern of real GNP also helps to explain short-term capital flows. If saving is a positive function of income, then foreign capital flows to the United States should be positively related to foreign growth. Table 18-9 reports the growth rate in real GNP for the United States and Europe in the 1974–1978 period. The pattern of private short-term inflows (Figure 18-4) clearly follows the pattern of the European real growth rate. For the United States, a similar explanation is also suggested. U.S. short-term outflows decline and rise in 1975–1977, roughly following the U.S. real growth rate. In 1974, U.S. short-term outflows expanded despite the negative U.S. growth rate, suggesting that the lack of U.S. capital controls dominated the market.

Finally, but not of least importance, we must mention the role of exchange rate changes and ex-

**Table 18-8  Private International Short-Term Capital Flows (in millions of dollars)**

| | 1968 | 1969 | 1970 | 1971 | 1972 | 1973 | 1974 | 1975 | 1976 | 1977 |
|---|---|---|---|---|---|---|---|---|---|---|
| U.S. short-term foreign assets | | | | | | | | | | |
| U.S. banks | $ 105 | $ 867 | $1,122 | $ 2,368 | $ 2,199 | $5,047 | $18,333 | $11,175 | $19,006 | $10,676 |
| Nonbanks | 982 | (298) | 10 | 1,061 | 811 | 1,987 | 2,747 | 991 | 2,254 | 1,841 |
| Total | 1,087 | 569 | 1,132 | 3,429 | 3,010 | 7,034 | 21,080 | 12,166 | 21,260 | 12,517 |
| U.S. short-term liabilities to foreigners | | | | | | | | | | |
| Nonbank | 759 | 91 | 902 | (15) | 221 | 737 | 1,934 | (87) | 422 | 993 |
| Bank | 3,799 | 8,726 | (6,321) | (6,661) | 4,605 | 4,475 | 16,008 | 908 | 10,759 | 6,346 |
| Nonofficial total | 4,558 | 8,817 | (5,419) | (6,676) | 4,826 | 5,212 | 17,942 | 821 | 11,181 | 7,339 |
| Official total | (3,101) | (554) | 7,637 | 27,615 | 9,734 | 4,456 | 8,481 | (3,301) | 563 | 814 |
| Grand total | 1,457 | 8,263 | 2,218 | 20,939 | 14,560 | 9,668 | 26,423 | (2,480) | 11,744 | 8,153 |
| Net (liabilities − assets) | 370 | 7,694 | 1,086 | 17,510 | 11,550 | 2,634 | 5,343 | (14,646) | (9,516) | (4,364) |

Source: *Survey of Current Business*.

**Table 18-9 Growth Rates in Real National Product, 1974–1978 (percentage change)**

|  | 1974 | 1975 | 1976 | 1977 | 1978 |
|---|---|---|---|---|---|
| United States | −1.4% | −1.3% | 5.7% | 5.3% | 4.4% |
| European Community | 1.7 | −1.8 | 5.0 | 2.3 | 3.1 |

Source: *Economic Report of the President,* 1980.

pectations in determining short-term capital flows. It was argued earlier that in an efficient financial market, nominal interest rates will be set so that expected real rates of return are equalized across investments with similar risk properties. Profit-maximizing private investors will move capital in the direction of high expected real returns.

It is tempting, then, to argue that private foreign investors anticipated the first dollar devaluation (on August 15, 1971), and that this factor was responsible for the massive outflow of foreign short-term funds in 1970 and 1971. It may then seem anomalous that foreigners accumulated dollar balances in 1972 and 1973 prior to the second dollar devaluation (in March 1973). If foreign investors did correctly anticipate the exchange rate change, then other factors must be responsible for their decision to increase dollar-denominated assets. One such factor was that OPEC countries (especially in 1973) were already experiencing increasing current surpluses in their balance of payments and several of them had consistently held a large share of their liquid assets in dollars. Another is that many foreigners did not accurately anticipate the 1973 move to floating rates. Since we cannot directly observe investor expectations, it is extremely difficult to test hypotheses concerning investor rationality.

We have observed that both short-term capital flows and rates have been volatile during the period of floating exchange rates.[37] Policymakers must decide whether the relationship between the two variables reflects causality (in either direction) or simply a response to other, underlying causal variables. In the first scenario, we may picture a world with a large pool of interest-sensitive funds. If investor expectations are not firm, capital flows that change interest rates slightly may lead to a

large wave of subsequent capital flows. Alternatively, if investors respond to a set of fundamental variables, exchange rates and capital flows will have low volatility when underlying variables are also stable. The issue of stabilizing versus destabilizing capital flows is an important component in the debate between pegged and floating exchange rates. Clearly this issue is well beyond the scope of our discussion, but the recent volatility in exchange markets and capital flows continues to generate concern and it will be an important issue for future research.[38]

In Table 18-8, the change in U.S. short-term liabilities has been divided into official and nonofficial liabilities. "Official" foreign holdings are deposits in U.S. commercial banks, U.S. government securities, and other short-term dollar investments made by foreign monetary authorities. Such holdings are part of the international reserves of the countries that hold them and represent the "reserve currency" status of the U.S. dollar.[39] Dollars were available to official institutions in sizable amounts throughout the 1960s and 1970s, consistent with the U.S. balance-of-payments deficit. As Table 18-8 indicates, the accumulation of foreign official dollar holdings has followed a highly volatile course over the decade 1968–1977—ranging from a peak inflow of $27.6 billion in 1971 to outflows of more than $3.0 billion in 1968 and 1975.

This volatility in part reflects the fact that managers of official portfolios face the same sorts of decisions as private investors. Under floating exchange rates, managers can reduce their exposure to risk by holding assets diversified across a number of currencies. Following this reasoning, at the

[37] For a graph of recent exchange rate behavior, see Chapter 30.

[38] The recent experience with flexible rates is described in Willett, *Floating Exchange Rates and International Monetary Reform.* The classic argument favoring flexible exchange rates is Friedman's "The Case for Flexible Exchange Rates," in *Essays in Positive Economics,* ed. Milton Friedman, University of Chicago Press, Chicago, 1953. In contrast, Kindleberger argues for a pegged rate system in Charles P. Kindleberger, "The Case for Fixed Exchange Rates 1969," *The International Adjustment Mechanism,* Federal Reserve Bank of Boston (1970). A thorough discussion of the issues related to tests of stabilizing versus destabilizing speculation may be found in Steven W. Kolhagen, "The Identification of Destabilizing Foreign Exchange Speculation," *Journal of International Economics* (August 1979).

[39] For a more extended analysis of these points, see Chapter 30.

onset of generalized floating in 1973, managers of portfolios with a high dollar concentration would have had an immediate (stock) demand for non-dollar assets and reduction in the ongoing (flow) demand for dollar assets in the future. To emphasize the other half of the two-parameter (mean-variance) model, managers would continue to switch official assets in response to expected value gains. But, as emphasized in Chapter 30, the more important factor involved with the expansion of U.S. liabilities to foreign official institutions is the "management" of floating exchange rates. As countries with rising (strong) currencies attempt to limit or avoid those rises, they buy dollars on the foreign exchange market. These dollars become short-term foreign investments in the United States and account for most of the observed changes since 1973.

### The International Investment Position of the United States

A country's international investment position represents its international ownership of assets at a point in time. It, therefore, represents the accumulation of all past capital flows.[40] As a consequence of the capital flows described in the preceding section, there has been a secular increase in the total stock of foreign assets owned by Americans as well as an increase in the stock of U.S. assets owned by foreigners.[41]

The total stock of outstanding U.S. foreign investments and foreign investments in the United States, as well as their components, is shown in Table 18-10. The total stock of U.S. foreign assets has grown dramatically—more than doubling between 1958 and 1967 and then more than tripling between 1967 and 1978. To gain a perspective on these numbers, the U.S. Consumer Price Index is also included in Table 18-10. In the period 1967–

---

[40]The international investment position in international accounting is analogous to the balance sheet in corporate accounting. Similarly, the Balance of Payments Accounts, which represent a flow per unit of time, are analogous to a corporation's profit statement.

[41]In addition to current investment flows, the international investment position is affected by retained earnings by foreign subsidiaries, changes in the valuation methods applied to direct investments, changes in exchange rates, and the like.

1978, U.S. price inflation was greater than 90 percent as compared with 15.5 percent in the previous period. Therefore, in real terms, the increase in the U.S. asset position was roughly 180 percent in the 1967–1978 period compared with 90 percent in the 1958–1967 period. Foreign investment in the United States grew by about 90 percent in the period 1958–1967 and by 1978 increased to more than four times the level in 1967.

The difference between the U.S. ownership of foreign assets and the foreign ownership of U.S. assets is defined as the *net U.S. creditor position*. In nominal terms, the net U.S. creditor position rose steadily over the sample period (the largest percentage increase being in the period 1958–1967), reaching $63.9 billion in 1976. However, in 1977 the U.S. net creditor position declined to $53.1 billion as a consequence of the U.S. balance-of-payments deficit and the massive return flow of foreign dollar funds for investment in the United States. Furthermore, if we consider the effect of inflation, the net U.S. creditor position appears further eroded. In real terms, the value of net U.S. claims on foreigners was smaller in 1975–1978 than in 1967.

Trends in the components of the international investment position are also of interest. Throughout the postwar period, as suggested earlier, foreign assets of the U.S. private sector have increased faster than those of the government sector. The growth rate for private short-term U.S. foreign assets has been much greater than the growth rate for private long-term U.S. assets. Despite this trend, in 1977 nearly 70 percent of private U.S. foreign assets were long term. Conversely, foreign investments in the United States have been concentrated in short-term instruments. Nearly all the growth in foreign short-term claims on the United States in the period 1967–1977 can be attributed to increased foreign holdings of U.S. government securities. This increase primarily represents the recycling of the enormous OPEC surpluses and the accumulation of dollars by foreign central banks in the process of keeping their currencies from rising in price. The growth in foreign direct investment in the United States has also accelerated. In fact, for the period 1967–1975 the percentage increase of foreign direct investment in the United States exceeded that for U.S. direct foreign investment abroad.

**Table 18-10   The International Investment Position of the United States, End of Year (in millions of dollars)**

|  | 1950 | 1958 | 1967 | 1975 | 1976 | 1977 | 1978 |
|---|---|---|---|---|---|---|---|
| U.S. assets abroad—total | $32,844 | $59,449 | $122,292 | $295,113 | $347,174 | $382,985 | $450,050 |
| Private assets | 19,004 | 41,118 | 93,287 | 237,070 | 282,418 | 314,105 | 377,185 |
| Long-term | 17,488 | 37,630 | 81,442 | 174,393 | 198,800 | 217,971 | 245,731 |
| Direct investment | 11,788 | 27,409 | 59,267 | 124,050 | 136,809 | 149,848 | 168,081 |
| Foreign dollar bonds | 1,692 | 3,931 | 9,666 | 25,328 | 34,704 | 39,329 | 42,184 |
| Other foreign securities | 2,641 | 3,650 | 6,351 | 9,585 | 9,453 | 10,110 | 11,238 |
| Other long-term | 1,367 | 2,640 | 6,158 | 15,430 | 17,834 | 18,684 | 24,228 |
| Short-term | 1,516 | 3,488 | 11,845 | 62,677 | 83,399 | 96,134 | 131,454 |
| U.S. government foreign assets | 13,840 | 18,331 | 29,005 | 41,817 | 46,008 | 49,566 | 54,215 |
| Long-term | 13,518 | 16,192 | 23,545 | 39,822 | 44,138 | 47,770 | 52,277 |
| Short-term | 322 | 2,139 | 5,460 | 1,995 | 1,870 | 1,796 | 1,938 |
| Foreign assets in the U.S.—total | 19,712 | 36,106 | 69,613 | 220,482 | 264,569 | 310,600 | 373,345 |
| Long-term | 7,997 | 16,394 | 31,962 | 80,718 | 92,549 | 94,310 | 96,262 |
| Direct investment | 3,391 | 6,115 | 9,923 | 27,662 | 30,770 | 34,595 | 40,831 |
| Corporate stocks | 2,925 | 8,305 | 15,511 | 35,313 | 42,866 | 39,704 | 42,007 |
| Bonds (excluding U.S. gov't.) | 181 | 455 | 2,159 | 10,025 | 11,964 | 13,209 | 13,424 |
| Other long-term | 1,500 | 1,519 | 4,369 | 7,718 | 6,949 | 6,802 | —a |
| Short-term and U.S. government securities | 11,715 | 19,712 | 37,651 | 139,764 | 172,020 | 216,290 | 271,960 |
| Private | 6,512 | 10,931 | 22,901 | 26,210 | 30,004 | 33,359 | 41,580 |
| Government | 5,203 | 8,781 | 14,750 | 113,554 | 142,016 | 182,931 | 230,380 |
| Net U.S. creditor or debtor position—total | 13,132 | 23,343 | 52,679 | 58,405 | 63,860 | 53,071 | 63,178 |
| Government | 8,637 | 9,550 | 14,255 | (71,737) | (96,008) | (133,365) | (176,165) |
| Private | 4,495 | 13,793 | 38,424 | 130,142 | 159,868 | 186,436 | 239,343 |
| Long-term | 23,009 | 37,428 | 73,025 | 133,497 | 150,389 | 171,431 | 201,746 |
| Short-term | (9,877) | (14,085) | (20,346) | (75,092) | (86,751) | (118,360) | (138,568) |
| U.S. Consumer Price Index | 100.0 | 120.5 | 139.2 | 223.6 | 236.5 | 251.2 | 271.3 |

aThe distinction between long- and short-term liabilities is discontinued for some data in 1978. In this table, these are reported as short-term private.

Sources: *Survey of Current Business*; *International Financial Statistics*.

The net creditor position of the United States can also be broken down into its components, as shown at the bottom of Table 18-10. The net credit position, $63 billion in 1978, appears to be based entirely in the private sector and in long-term assets. Classified in terms of the government sector or in terms of short-term assets, the United States is a net debtor to the rest of the world.

This structure of foreign assets and liabilities indicates that the United States has acted as a financial intermediary for the rest of the world. Much the same as any deposit-type financial intermediary, net short-term liabilities have been issued (on the United States) in the form of foreign accounts at U.S. banks, foreign holdings of U.S. government securities, and so forth, while the United States has acquired even greater net amounts of long-term foreign assets.[42] The data suggest, however, that the nominal value of the U.S. creditor position declined in 1977 and the real value of the U.S. creditor position declined sharply during the decade 1969–1978.[43]

[42]The net acquisition of foreign assets was paid for by U.S. goods and services (a net current account surplus) and U.S. gold losses.

[43]It should be noted that the real value of many U.S. investments declined by a similar magnitude over the same decade. For example, the Dow-Jones Industrial average remained roughly constant while the Consumer Price Index nearly doubled.

## Special International Markets and Institutions

So far we have examined some theoretical issues concerning international capital markets and have studied in some detail international capital flows. This section examines some special institutions and markets that have become important parts of international finance. In particular this section will describe the two sectors of the international capital markets—the domestic (or onshore) sector and the external (offshore or Eurodollar) sector—and analyze their interrelationships.

### Onshore Markets and Covered Interest Arbitrage

*Arbitrage* is the sale of one asset and the simultaneous purchase of a close substitute at a lower price (or purchase of the same asset in another market at a lower price) in order to profit from the price difference. Arbitrage has, of course, the effect of tending to drive the prices of substitutes closer together, because the sale will tend to lower the price of the asset that is sold and raise the price of the asset that is bought. Consequently, arbitrage and arbitrageurs tend to minimize price differences for close substitutes in financial markets and to make the markets more efficient.

One kind of arbitrage, covered interest arbitrage, is an important mechanism that links domestic financial markets among countries. An example will make the operation explicit. Suppose interest rates on 90-day U.K. Treasury bills are 1.0 percent higher than those for 90-day U.S. Treasury bills. Americans will sell their U.S. Treasury bills, use the proceeds to buy pounds on the spot market, and immediately buy U.K. Treasury bills. Since the Americans want to avoid the risk of holding pounds, they will simultaneously sell their anticipated pound receipts (for U.S. dollars) in the 90-day forward market. These four transactions tend to reduce the interest differential between U.K. Treasury bills and, simultaneously, to increase the discount on 90-day forward pounds. When the interest differential in favor of U.K. Treasury bills equals the forward discount on pounds, the incentive for a covered outflow of funds disappears.[44]

[44]This equality is also known as the interest rate parity

Empirical research on covered interest arbitrage has concentrated on securities traded in onshore markets, for the simple reason that, until the 1960s, these were the only markets in existence. This body of research suggested that large covered interest differentials did persist during the postwar period among Treasury bills in the United States, United Kingdom, Canada, and elsewhere. Many explanations for these deviations relied on transaction costs, exchange controls, or the suggestion that the two financial assets were not similar in all aspects of risk.[45] The development of offshore markets provided a unique opportunity to explore the possible differences in risk.

### Offshore Markets—Determination of the Rate Structure

Offshore markets, external markets, and Eurocurrencies markets describe the same phenomenon—a marketplace for financial assets denominated in a currency other than that generally used in the host nation and not controlled by the local monetary authorities. For example, a U.S. Treasury bill traded in New York is in the onshore market, but U.S. dollar deposits in a bank in London, Zurich, or Singapore are in the offshore market. A bond denominated in Deutsche marks, issued by Volkswagen, and traded in Frankfurt is in the onshore market, but a similar DM bond issued and traded in London, Paris, or the Bahamas is in the offshore market. Typically, onshore markets are characterized by a high level of government regulation or the threat of government regulation, especially concerning the international transfer of capital. In contrast, offshore markets are characterized by a relative absence of regulation. In this situation,

condition. See the section "Departures from the Theoretical Assumptions" and Figure 18-1.

[45]Frenkel and Levich, "Covered Interest and Arbitrage" and "Transaction Cost and Interest Arbitrage," report that transaction costs can explain a high percentage of covered interest differentials, especially during quiet periods. The concept of political risk is developed in Aliber, "The Interest Rate Parity Theorem." For a survey of other issues in interest rate parity theory, see Lawrence H. Officer and Thomas D. Willet, "The Covered Arbitrage Schedule: A Critical Survey of Recent Developments," *Journal of Money, Credit and Banking* (May 1970).

pricing in offshore markets is more likely to reflect pure market forces.

Empirical research suggests that the interest parity condition is extremely robust in offshore markets. In fact, most traders explicitly use interest parity theory when quoting prices. For example, if one-year Eurosterling deposits in Zurich are quoted at 8 percent and one-year forward sterling is at a 2 percent premium vis-à-vis the U.S. dollar, then the trader should be willing to quote one-year Eurodollar deposits at about 10 percent.

Up to this point, the chapter has delineated the relationship between onshore markets and the relationship between offshore markets. In both cases covered interest arbitrage is a factor, although empirical studies have noted the importance of controls and transaction costs in the relations between onshore markets. With this information as background, this section can now explore the interrelationship between onshore and offshore markets.[46] To begin, consider the U.S. domestic financial market. The demand ($D$) and supply ($S$) curves for this market are illustrated in Figure 18-7. Commercial bankers in this market require a spread to cover their business expenses and provide a profit. The spread determines a unique equilibrium where the lending rate is $R_L$, the deposit rate is $R_D$, and the size of the market is $Q$. Now assume that a new market for U.S. dollar-denominated balances opens in London. Americans will supply dollars to the offshore market only if they are compensated for bearing the extra costs and risks associated with London. Since Americans can earn $R_D$ with minimum cost and risk in the onshore market, the supply curve to the offshore market ($S'$) is hinged at $R_D$. Similarly, in the absence of capital controls, no borrower would travel to London to pay a higher price for money. Therefore, the demand curve for offshore funds ($D'$) must be hinged at $R_L$. The size of the offshore market ($Q'$), the offshore lending rate ($R_L'$) and the offshore deposit rate ($R_D'$) are determined once the spread required by offshore commercial bankers is known.

[46]The general outline of the following discussion is based on Robert Z. Aliber, "Attributes of National Monies and the Independence of National Monetary Policies," in *National Monetary Policies and the International System,* ed. R. Z. Aliber. University of Chicago Press, Chicago, 1974.

**Figure 18-7 Euro-Rate Determination, with No Capital Controls**

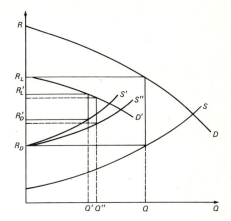

Figure 18-7 suggests several important results. First, in the absence of capital controls, the offshore market exists only because its spread is smaller than the spread in the onshore market. It is clear that the size of the offshore market is inversely related to the spread. A number of fundamental factors explain the smaller spread in offshore markets. First, the Euromarket is a wholesale market, which typically operates in units of $1 million and services large and well-known clients. Second, Eurobanks are largely unregulated. They can hold smaller reserves than onshore banks, and the reserves they do hold can be in the form of interest-bearing assets rather than in a zero-interest-rate Federal Reserve account.

Figure 18-7 also illustrates the normal relationship between onshore and offshore interest rates, that is, $R_L > R_L' > R_D' > R_D$. The offshore market survives by driving a wedge into the onshore financial market; it provides a similar financial service at a lower price. The interest rate differentials $(R_L - R_L')$ and $(R_D' - R_D)$ provide a measure of the benefits received by borrowers and depositors. Finally, Figure 18-7 illustrates a case where American depositors lower their assessment of offshore risks. The supply curve shifts to the right ($S''$) and the offshore market expands to $Q''$. The difference between onshore and offshore lending rates increases, while the difference between offshore and onshore deposit rates decreases.

**Figure 18-8   Euro-Rate Determination, with Interest Rate Ceiling**

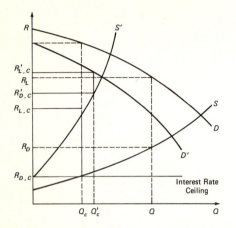

In our scenario, domestic capital controls led to a contraction in the onshore market. Since a large number of profitable projects were left without financing, investors entered the offshore market and were willing to pay the higher rate $R'_{L,C}$. The analysis also suggests that the offshore market is larger as a direct result of the control program ($Q'_C > Q'$). This scenario is a reasonable description of the U.S. experience with capital controls. During periods of the U.S. "credit crunch," the Eurocurrency markets tended to expand significantly with Eurodollar rates exceeding onshore rates. This analysis suggests that the primary impact of capital controls was to shift the location of market activity rather than to significantly reduce the total volume of loanable funds.

Now consider a case, illustrated in Figure 18-8, where the U.S. financial market is subject to regulation. In the preregulation situation, the size of the onshore market is $Q$ and the size of the offshore market is $Q'$ following the reasoning in the earlier model. Suppose the domestic regulation takes the form of an interest rate ceiling on domestic deposits, so that $R_{D,C} < R_D$, and the subscript ($C$) indicates the presence of the ceiling or a similar control. Now assume that the interest rate ceiling is effective. This means that domestic deposits are reduced and the size of the onshore market falls to $Q_C$.[47] If the size of the lenders' spread remains the same, then the lending rate with the deposit rate ceiling is $R_{L,C}$. In response to the shortage of loanable funds in the onshore market, demand shifts to the offshore market. Suppliers (depositors) of funds are also encouraged to shift funds offshore. The new supply and demand curves for offshore funds ($S'_C$ and $D'_C$) increase the size of the offshore market to $Q'_C$. As a consequence of the controls, both offshore interest rates exceed the onshore rates.[48]

$$R'_{L,C} > R'_{D,C} > R_{L,C} > R_{D,C}$$

### Growth of the Eurocurrency Market

Table 18-11 presents a summary of the growth in the Eurocurrency market.[49] During the period 1968–1978, the total external liability position of European banks grew at an annual rate in excess of 30 percent. By far the largest share of the Eurocurrency market is denominated in U.S. dollars; the second largest share is denominated in Deutsche marks. The secular trend seems to be toward a smaller U.S. dollar share and a larger DM share. In part, this may reflect a decline in the prominence of the U.S. dollar because of increased exposure to exchange risk and inflation risk. In this regard, it is interesting that after the two major U.S. dollar devaluations in 1971 and 1973, the U.S. dollar share of the offshore deposit market declined significantly.[50]

---

[47]We assume that the volume $Q_C$ allows sufficient economies of scale so that the spread remains constant and $R_L - R_D = R_{L,C} - R_{D,C}$.

[48]Implicitly, it is also assumed that U.S. capital controls are present to prevent borrowing onshore at $R_{L,C}$ and depositing offshore at $R'_{D,C}$.

[49]Further analysis on the growth of the Euromarket is presented in E. Wayne Clendenning, *The Euro-Dollar Market,* Clarendon Press, Oxford, 1970; Ronald I. McKinnon, "The Eurocurrency Market," *Essays in International Finance,* No. 125, Princeton University, Princeton, N.J., 1977; and Gunter Dufey and Ian H. Giddy, *The International Money Market,* Prentice-Hall, Englewood Cliffs, N.J., 1978.

[50]In Table 18-11, the real growth in the Euromarket and the real decline in the U.S. dollar share in 1971 and 1973 is overstated somewhat because the U.S. dollar was used as the *numeraire.* If the entries in Table 18-11 are restated in terms of Deutsche marks (which appreciated from 4.0 DM/$ at the end of 1968 to 2.105 DM/$ at the end of 1977), the estimated rate of growth of the market is greatly reduced.

**Table 18-11 External Liability Position of Reporting European Banks (in millions of dollars with percentage of total in parentheses)**

| Year | U.S. $ | DM | Swiss Franc | Other | Total |
|------|--------|-----|-------------|-------|-------|
| | | | Currency of Denomination | | |
| 1968 | $ 26,870 (79.7) | $ 3,010 (8.9) | $ 2,290 (6.8) | $ 1,540 (4.6) | $ 33,710 |
| 1969 | 46,200 (81.5) | 4,640 (8.2) | 4,030 (7.1) | 1,850 (3.3) | 56,720 |
| 1970 | 58,700 (78.0) | 8,080 (10.7) | 5,720 (7.6) | 2,790 (3.7) | 75,290 |
| 1971 | 70,750 (72.4) | 14,630 (15.0) | 7,760 (7.9) | 4,580 (4.7) | 97,720 |
| 1972 | 96,730 (73.3) | 19,540 (14.8) | 8,810 (6.7) | 6,850 (5.2) | 131,930 |
| 1973 | 131,380 (68.4) | 32,020 (16.7) | 17,160 (8.9) | 11,540 (6.0) | 192,100 |
| 1974 | 156,430 (70.9) | 34,380 (15.6) | 18,290 (8.3) | 11,670 (5.3) | 220,770 |
| 1975 | 189,470 (73.2) | 39,940 (15.4) | 15,290 (5.9) | 13,970 (5.4) | 258,670 |
| 1976 | 230,040 (74.1) | 47,230 (15.2) | 15,880 (5.1) | 17,500 (5.6) | 310,650 |
| 1977 | 272,880 (71.2) | 64,970 (16.9) | 20,870 (5.4) | 24,720 (6.4) | 383,440 |
| 1978 | 348,590 (68.2) | 93,080 (18.2) | 27,890 (5.5) | 41,250 (8.1) | 510,810 |

Source: Bank for International Settlements, *Annual Report* (June 1979).

The Eurocurrency market has grown in other dimensions as well. First, the Euromarket began with only one currency of denomination (U.S. dollars) but has grown to include most other major currencies. Second, the first Euromarket activity was based in London, but now the market has expanded to include Paris, Zurich, Frankfurt, the Bahamas, and Singapore. Third, the Euromarket was initially a market for very short-term deposits. Now, quotations on one-year (or longer) Eurodeposits are readily available on most currencies.

Table 18-12 summarizes the sources and uses of funds for the Eurocurrency market. For most of the last decade, the United States has been a net user (borrower) of Eurocurrency deposits. However, in the three years 1976–1978, the United States became a net source (lender) of Eurocurrency funds, which may reflect an increase in the perceived risk/return ratio for supplying offshore funds. Non-European developed countries and Eastern European countries are major users of Eurocurrency funds, reflecting the lack of development of domestic financial markets in these areas.

The OPEC countries stand out clearly as the major supplier of funds to the Eurocurrency market. However, the gross share of funds from OPEC appears to be fairly constant since 1974.

Recent activity in the international bond market is reported in Tables 18-13 and 18-14. The total volume of issues has risen from $7 billion in 1971 to $35 billion in 1978. The majority share (roughly one-half to two-thirds) of Eurobonds was denominated in U.S. dollars with the remainder denominated primarily in Deutsche marks. In most years, nearly one-half of all foreign issues have been placed in the United States; the majority of the remaining issues have been placed in Switzerland.

The distribution of new issues across borrowers is presented in Table 18-14. Borrowing by the United States has declined from 20 percent of the total in 1971 to only 5 percent in 1978. European issues have expanded to offset the U.S. decline. We note that while most U.S. and European issues are placed in the Euromarket, most Canadian and institutional issues are placed in foreign (onshore) markets, primarily the United States.

**Table 18-12  Estimated Sources and Uses of Eurocurrency Funds (in billions of U.S. dollars)**

| | Year | United States | Europe | Other Developed[a] | Eastern Europe | Offshore Banks[b] | OPEC[c] | Other | Total |
|---|---|---|---|---|---|---|---|---|---|
| Uses | 1969 | 16.8 | 15.0 | N.A. | N.A. | N.A. | N.A. | 12.2 | 44.0 |
| | 70 | 13.1 | 24.0 | N.A. | N.A. | N.A. | N.A. | 19.9 | 57.0 |
| | 71 | 8.3 | 32.8 | N.A. | N.A. | N.A. | N.A. | 29.9 | 71.0 |
| | 72 | 9.6 | 38.9 | N.A. | N.A. | N.A. | N.A. | 43.5 | 92.0 |
| | 73 | 13.2 | 51.3 | N.A. | N.A. | N.A. | N.A. | 67.5 | 132.0 |
| | 74 | 18.2 | 61.5 | 38.6 | 10.1 | 26.7 | 3.5 | 18.4 | 177.0 |
| | 75 | 16.5 | 63.0 | 46.0 | 15.9 | 35.6 | 5.3 | 22.7 | 205.0 |
| | 76 | 18.2 | 74.4 | 54.6 | 20.8 | 40.8 | 9.6 | 28.6 | 247.0 |
| | 77 | 21.0 | 99.2 | 61.3 | 23.8 | 43.7 | 15.6 | 35.4 | 300.0 |
| | 78 | 24.6 | 136.0 | 59.3 | 31.4 | 55.0 | 24.3 | 44.4 | 375.0 |
| Sources | 1969 | 4.1 | 21.7 | N.A. | N.A. | N.A. | N.A. | 18.2 | 44.0 |
| | 70 | 4.5 | 27.7 | N.A. | N.A. | N.A. | N.A. | 24.8 | 57.0 |
| | 71 | 6.1 | 32.4 | N.A. | N.A. | N.A. | N.A. | 32.5 | 71.0 |
| | 72 | 6.9 | 35.2 | N.A. | N.A. | N.A. | N.A. | 49.9 | 92.0 |
| | 73 | 9.5 | 51.5 | N.A. | N.A. | N.A. | N.A. | 71.0 | 132.0 |
| | 74 | 11.9 | 67.8 | 27.2 | 5.1 | 17.8 | 29.1 | 18.1 | 177.0 |
| | 75 | 15.4 | 79.5 | 28.2 | 5.4 | 21.8 | 34.6 | 20.1 | 205.0 |
| | 76 | 18.8 | 86.7 | 31.8 | 6.4 | 30.1 | 45.2 | 28.0 | 247.0 |
| | 77 | 24.9 | 108.6 | 35.0 | 6.4 | 33.2 | 54.0 | 37.9 | 300.0 |
| | 78 | 37.0 | 142.5 | 39.2 | 8.8 | 45.4 | 54.7 | 47.4 | 375.0 |
| Net | 1969 | +12.7 | −6.7 | N.A. | N.A. | N.A. | N.A. | −6.0 | N.A. |
| | 70 | +8.6 | −3.7 | N.A. | N.A. | N.A. | N.A. | −4.9 | N.A. |
| | 71 | +2.2 | +0.4 | N.A. | N.A. | N.A. | N.A. | −2.6 | N.A. |
| | 72 | +2.7 | +3.7 | N.A. | N.A. | N.A. | N.A. | −6.4 | N.A. |
| | 73 | +3.7 | −0.2 | N.A. | N.A. | N.A. | N.A. | −3.5 | N.A. |
| | 74 | −6.3 | −6.3 | +11.4 | +5.0 | +8.9 | −25.6 | +0.3 | N.A. |
| | 75 | +1.1 | −16.5 | +17.8 | +10.5 | +13.8 | −29.3 | +2.6 | N.A. |
| | 76 | −0.6 | −12.3 | +22.8 | +14.4 | +10.7 | −35.6 | +0.6 | N.A. |
| | 77 | −3.9 | −9.4 | +26.3 | +17.4 | +10.5 | −38.4 | −2.5 | N.A. |
| | 78 | −12.4 | −6.5 | +20.1 | +22.6 | +9.6 | −30.4 | −3.0 | N.A. |

N.A. = Not Available.
[a]Includes Canada and Japan.
[b]Offshore banking centers located in Bahamas, Bermuda, Cayman Islands, Hong Kong, Singapore, and others.
[c]Oil-exporting countries including Algeria, Indonesia, Iran, Kuwait, Saudi Arabia, and others.

Source: Bank for International Settlements, *Annual Reports*.

## Growth of International Banking

During the 1960s and early 1970s, international banking activity grew at a dramatic pace. Statistics on the international activity of U.S. banks are presented in Table 18-15. The number of U.S. banks with overseas branches expanded from only eight to well over one hundred banks. The assets of these overseas branches amounted to $175 billion in 1975.

Several reasons for this high growth rate can be cited. First, international trade and the activity of U.S. multinational firms expanded sharply during the period. U.S. banks followed their customers overseas in order to maintain or strengthen their competitive position. Second, the enormous growth of the Euromarket occurred during this period. U.S. banks established branches overseas to compete in this unregulated market and to minimize the adverse impact of U.S. capital controls and restrictive U.S. monetary policies. Finally, changes in Federal Reserve Board regulation made it easier for U.S. banks to establish overseas operations. In 1966, the Federal Reserve Board authorized the direct acquisition of foreign subsidiaries by the parent bank. Formerly, the acquisition of overseas subsidiaries could be made only through Edge Act banks, that is, through subsid-

**Table 18-13  International Bond Issues, by Type, Currency, and Location (in millions of U.S. dollars with percentage of total in parentheses)**

| Year | Eurobond Issues | | | | Foreign Issues | | | |
|------|-------|--------|-------|-------|-------|---------|-------------------|---------------------|
| | Total | U.S. $ | DM | Other | Total | In U.S. | In Switzerland | In Rest of World |
| 1971 | $ 3,760 | $ 2,240 | $ 860 | $ 660 | $ 3,350 | N.A. | N.A. | N.A. |
| | | (59.6) | (22.9) | (17.6) | | | | |
| 1972 | 6,490 | 3,860 | 1,240 | 1,390 | 4,230 | N.A. | N.A. | N.A. |
| | | (59.5) | (19.1) | (21.4) | | | | |
| 1973 | 4,600 | 2,890 | 1,000 | 710 | 5,310 | $ 1,490 | $1,540 | $2,280 |
| | | (62.8) | (21.7) | (15.4) | | (28.1) | (29.0) | (42.9) |
| 1974 | 4,520 | 3,080 | 650 | 790 | 7,790 | 3,590 | 990 | 3,210 |
| | | (68.1) | (14.4) | (17.5) | | (46.1) | (12.7) | (41.2) |
| 1975 | 10,520 | 4,920 | 3,100 | 2,500 | 12,300 | 6,850 | 3,530 | 1,920 |
| | | (46.8) | (29.5) | (23.8) | | (55.7) | (28.7) | (15.6) |
| 1976 | 15,370 | 10,000 | 2,820 | 2,550 | 18,930 | 10,630 | 5,440 | 2,860 |
| | | (65.1) | (18.3) | (16.6) | | (56.2) | (28.7) | (15.1) |
| 1977 | 19,480 | 12,340 | 5,220 | 1,920 | 16,610 | 7,670 | 4,960 | 3,980 |
| | | (63.6) | (26.4) | (10.1) | | (48.6) | (30.1) | (21.3) |
| 1978 | 15,870 | 7,650 | 6,540 | 1,680 | 20,800 | 6,160 | 7,060 | 7,580 |
| | | (48.2) | (41.2) | (10.5) | | (29.6) | (33.9) | (36.4) |

N.A. = Not available.

Source: Bank for International Settlements, *Annual Reports.*

**Table 18-14  International Bond Issues by Borrowing Country or Area (in millions of U.S. dollars)**

| | 1971 | 1972 | 1973 | 1974 | 1975 | 1976 | 1977 | 1978 |
|---|------|------|------|------|------|------|------|------|
| **United States** | | | | | | | | |
| Eurobond | $1,110 | $ 2,030 | $ 820 | $ 110 | $ 310 | $ 410 | $ 1,300 | $ 1,320 |
| Foreign issue | 280 | 240 | 500 | 80 | 140 | 30 | 220 | 370 |
| **Western Europe** | | | | | | | | |
| Eurobond | 1,720 | 2,490 | 2,080 | 1,460 | 4,880 | 5,740 | 9,010 | 5,360 |
| Foreign issue | 600 | 590 | 960 | 1,490 | 3,150 | 5,110 | 5,060 | 5,950 |
| **Canada** | | | | | | | | |
| Eurobond | 210 | 370 | 200 | 440 | 1,150 | 3,000 | 1,950 | 830 |
| Foreign issue | 640 | 1,140 | 1,010 | 1,960 | 3,410 | 6,080 | 3,430 | 4,020 |
| **Rest of the world[a]** | | | | | | | | |
| Eurobond | 590 | 1,140 | 610 | 470 | 2,670 | 3,120 | 4,740 | 5,530 |
| Foreign issue | 350 | 400 | 790 | 890 | 1,580 | 2,410 | 3,060 | 4,850 |
| **International institutions** | | | | | | | | |
| Eurobond | 130 | 460 | 890 | 2,040 | 1,510 | 3,100 | 2,480 | 2,830 |
| Foreign issue | 1,480 | 1,860 | 2,050 | 3,370 | 4,020 | 5,300 | 4,840 | 5,610 |
| **Total issues placed** | | | | | | | | |
| Eurobond | 3,760 | 6,490 | 4,600 | 4,520 | 10,520 | 15,370 | 19,480 | 15,870 |
| Foreign issue | 3,350 | 4,230 | 5,310 | 7,790 | 12,300 | 18,930 | 16,610 | 20,800 |
| Grand total | 7,010 | 10,720 | 9,910 | 12,310 | 22,820 | 34,300 | 36,090 | 36,670 |

[a]Including developed countries and Eastern European countries.

Source: Bank for International Settlements, *Annual Reports.*

## Table 18-15 Overseas Branches of U.S. Banks

| Year | No. of Banks with Overseas Branches[a] | No. of Overseas Branches[a] | Assets of Overseas Branches (in billions of dollars)[b] |
|---|---|---|---|
| 1960 | 8 | 131 | $ 3.5 |
| 1965 | 13 | 211 | 9.1 |
| 1969 | 53 | 459 | 41.1 |
| 1970 | 79 | 536 | 52.6 |
| 1971 | 91 | 583 | 67.1 |
| 1972 | 108 | 627 | 77.4 |
| 1973 | 125 | 699 | 118.0 |
| 1974 | 125 | 732 | 151.9 |
| 1975 | N.A. | N.A. | 175.9 |
| *Compound Rate of Growth* | | | |
| 1960–1969 | 23.4% | 14.9% | 31.5% |
| 1969–1975 | 18.7 | 9.8 | 27.4 |
| 1960–1975 | 21.7 | 13.1 | 29.8 |

N.A. = Not available.
[a]Overseas branches include branches of member banks in U.S. possessions and territories as well as in foreign countries.
[b]Branch assets include interbranch balances.

Source: *Financial Institutions and the National Economy* (FINE) Study, Committee on Banking, Currency and Housing; House of Representatives (June 1976), p. 812.

iaries of banks formed solely for the purpose of international banking.

The growth of international banking has had an important impact on U.S. financial markets. Table 18-16 reports that in 1975 foreign branches accounted for 15.4 percent of total commercial bank assets. This percentage is more than double the figure for 1970. This suggests that a larger percentage of the U.S. money supply is not in the direct control of the Federal Reserve Board, which may weaken the ability of the Federal Reserve to control monetary aggregates. If foreign operations are riskier than domestic operations, then the stability of U.S. banks may be reduced. However, it could also be argued that international banking results in a diversification gain and allows the possibility of avoiding costly capital controls. Finally, it should be pointed out that international banking may, in effect, expand the role of the Federal Reserve as the lender of last resort. For example, if a London branch of a U.S. bank fails, the Federal Reserve is not legally responsible for supporting the branch and minimizing the adverse impact in the offshore market. However, from a practical or political view-

point, it seems unlikely that the Federal Reserve would risk the possibility of an offshore banking crisis that could, in turn, damage the U.S. commercial banking system.[51]

## The Internationalization of Capital Markets

A basic trend in the postwar period, which has been implied in preceding sections of this chapter, has been toward the "internationalization" of capital markets. At the end of World War II, national capital markets either did not exist in some countries or were isolated by strict exchange controls. The international transfers of funds that did occur (such as U.S. aid for reconstruction) were largely determined by government decision and not by market allocation.

Over the last three decades, the gradual relaxation of controls over foreign payments and the return of confidence in foreign investments have permitted private capital to respond to international economic forces. The ways in which this sustained, and at times rapid, internationalization of financial markets has been manifest are many and diverse. Some of them have already been discussed. One result has been to tie the financial markets of the major industrial countries closer together in many, often subtle, ways. Lenders and borrowers have been provided with a broader range (although still severely limited in certain cases) of alternative uses and sources of funds *outside* their country of residence. The ability of lenders to *substitute* foreign financial assets for domestic ones, and for borrowers to *substitute* foreign sources of funds for domestic sources, inevitably reduces the independence of financial market conditions and interest rates for any one country from those prevailing in other capital market centers.

When the linkages between financial markets are complete, we define the markets as *integrated*. A condition of market integration is that the real rate of return is equalized across assets with similar risk. A further condition is that the risk/return relationship is equalized across financial markets. Financial markets within the United States (or any

[51]See *Financial Institutions and the National Economy* (FINE) Study, Committee on Banking, Currency and Housing, House of Representatives (June 1976), p. 911.

**Table 18-16  Assets of Foreign Branches and Domestic Offices of All Insured Commercial Banks in the United States (in billions of dollars)**

| Year | Foreign Branches | Domestic Offices | Total | Foreign as Percentage of Total |
|------|------|------|------|------|
| 1970 | $ 47.4 | $572.7 | $ 620.1 | 7.6% |
| 1971 | 61.3 | 635.8 | 697.1 | 8.8 |
| 1972 | 80.0 | 732.5 | 812.5 | 9.8 |
| 1973 | 121.8 | 835.2 | 957.0 | 12.7 |
| 1974 | 151.8 | 919.4 | 1,071.2 | 14.2 |
| 1975 | 175.9 | 964.9 | 1,140.8 | 15.4 |
| | | *Compound Rate of Growth* | | |
| 1970–1975 | 30.0% | 11.0% | 13.0% | 15.2% |

Source: FINE Study.

unified currency area) should appear to be integrated because of the large volume of funds ready to remove any potential arbitrage profits. For example, if similar U.S. Treasury bills traded at 94 in New York and 95 in San Francisco, traders would buy the bills in New York and sell them in San Francisco until prices equalized. For another example, if the structure of prices were such that the premium for bearing risk on the New York Stock Exchange was 10 percent (per unit risk) and 12 percent (per unit risk) on the American Stock Exchange, then investors would prefer stocks on the American Stock Exchange. Investors would sell stocks on the New York exchange and buy stocks on the American exchange until, in equilibrium, the risk premium was equalized across the two exchanges. A critical assumption behind both of these examples is that capital is mobile between markets and that investors are rational and free to react quickly to exploit available profit opportunities. An important consequence of market integration is that capital will be invested in projects with the highest expected rates of return and resources will be allocated according to an optimal economic calculus.

An important question for this section is whether these sufficient conditions hold for international capital market integration. In other words, is there a sufficient volume of funds that is free to move in response to an expected profit opportunity or disequilibrium situation?

A further interesting question concerns the correct model for testing international capital market integration. Suppose, for example, that the U.S. risk-free interest rate is 5 percent and the expected return on the market portfolio of risky assets is 15

percent (implying a 10 percent U.S. market risk premium). Suppose also that the risk-free interest rate in France is 10 percent and the expected return on the French market portfolio is 25 percent (implying a 15 percent risk premium in *French franc terms*). If the expected depreciation of the French franc vis-à-vis the U.S. dollar is 5 percent, are the two capital markets in equilibrium or are profit opportunities available, similar to our example of the New York and American stock exchanges? One argument that avoids this tricky question of international market integration is the following. Suppose that 10-year French-franc bonds are fairly priced (that is, in equilibrium or integrated) vis-à-vis one-month French franc bonds and that 10-year U.S. dollar bonds are fairly priced vis-à-vis one-month U.S. dollar bonds. If covered arbitrage is active and links the two short-term rates, then, by transitivity, we could argue that the term structures and the schedules of risk premiums in the two markets are integrated.

Empirical studies that test for international capital market integration have not been conclusive— in part because of the difficulties in specifying the appropriate test.[52] Studies showing the advantages and importance of international portfolios are more numerous and successful. The classic article by

[52]For a study that was unable to reject the hypothesis that the risk-return relationship is equal across major industrial countries, see Tamir Agmon, "The Relations Among Equity Markets: A Study of Share Price Co-Movements in the United States, United Kingdom, Germany and Japan," *Journal of Finance* (September 1972). For a discussion of this study, see Michael Adler and Reuven Horesh, "The Relationship Among Equity Markets: Comment," *Journal of Finance* (September 1974).

MacDougall demonstrated the *expected value gains* for investors and the welfare gains for an open economy that result from international investment.[53] More recent studies by Grubel, Levy and Sarnat, and by Solnik have documented the *diversification gains* that result from holding many international assets in a single portfolio.[54] Since asset returns are not perfectly correlated across countries, portfolio managers gain by selecting their *n* securities from the world market, rather than from any single market. Lessard has attempted to quantify the potential diversification gains for managers in various countries.[55] For example, an Italian manager who holds a portfolio of 200 Italian securities may feel that this is a well-diversified portfolio. However, if securities are priced in an integrated, worldwide market, the Italian market portfolio may contain considerable diversifiable risk. Lessard calculates that if the Italian portfolio manager were to hold a well-diversified portfolio of securities selected from all world markets with total risk equal to the original pure Italian portfolio, the expected return would increase by about 6 percent. For a large country such as the United States or a small country with security returns that are strongly correlated with the world market, the loss from not diversifying across international markets is much smaller—only a fraction of 1 percent.

To take advantage of the gains associated with freedom of capital movements, a number of institutional changes have occurred that have sped the process of "internationalization." First, the growth of foreign direct investment owes much to the development of the *multinational corporation* with subsidiaries in a number of countries. Often the foreign subsidiaries, which are large companies themselves, are creditworthy in their own right.

However, with the explicit or implicit guarantee of the subsidiary's debt by the American (or foreign) parent company, the subsidiaries have access to the local capital market. Furthermore, the funds borrowed in one market by one subsidiary may sometimes be transferred by the parent company to other arms of the multinational firm. As a result, the transferral of funds *within* the firm may, in fact, involve the *international* transfer of funds. And, in taking advantage of intrafirm mobility, the multinational corporation has access to a number of national capital markets. It can shop about for the best borrowing terms. Borrowing is then more responsive to relative financial market conditions in various countries as a result of the sizable increase in international direct investment.

Closely associated with this is the rapid increase in *commercial banking connections* among countries. Whereas in the early postwar period the typical international banking arrangement was that of the foreign correspondent, large U.S. and foreign commercial banks have now established extensive worldwide networks of branches.[56] Branches of foreign banks not only increase the competition for customers in the local money and capital markets and, thereby, tend to improve practices and efficiency, but they also facilitate the international movement of funds by providing a worldwide marketing network for the home office. They also facilitate the transfer of funds deposited in one national market to a borrower in another country, thereby increasing the mobility of funds as well as tying national financial markets closer together.

Another major aspect in the internationalization of financial markets is the development of extensive offshore operations—in Eurocurrency deposits,

[53]G. D. A. MacDougall, "The Benefits and Costs of Private Investment from Abroad: A Theoretical Approach, *Economic Record* (March 1960).

[54]See Herbert G. Grubel, "Internationally Diversified Portfolios: Welfare Gains and Capital Flows," *American Economic Review* (December 1968); Haim Levy and Marshall Sarnat, "International Diversification of Investment Portfolios," *American Economic Review* (September 1970); and Bruno H. Solnik, "Why Not Diversify Internationally Rather Than Domestically?" *Financial Analysts' Journal* (July-August 1974).

[55]Donald R. Lessard, "World, Country, and Industry Relationships in Equity Returns," *Financial Analysts' Journal* (January-February 1976).

[56]Data on U.S. international banking activity were reported in the preceding section. According to the *American Banker* (March 23, 1979), 278 foreign banks were represented (by branches, agencies, representative offices, subsidiaries, or affiliates) in the United States in 1978. The expansion of foreign banking activity was encouraged, in part, because foreign banks were not subject to federal regulation regarding interstate branching, reserve requirements, or retail deposit insurance. The International Banking Act of 1978 requires foreign banks to insure domestic deposits with the FDIC, gives the Federal Reserve the authority to set reserve requirements on foreign banks with assets greater than $1 billion, and forbids interstate branching in the future. Foreign banks' interstate branches that were opened before the act became law can remain in place.

Eurobonds, Eurocredits, and Eurosecurities. Data on several characteristics of offshore markets are found earlier in this chapter. As noted in those discussions, U.S. firms have borrowed considerable sums in European capital markets since 1965, especially in 1968, by issuing dollar-denominated bonds. This has been one result of the U.S. government's encouraging American firms to borrow abroad and of foreign subsidiaries to borrow locally so as to improve the U.S. balance-of-payments position. Indirectly, this may also have stimulated the development of more efficient European capital markets as a result of increased volume and the injection of U.S. and U.K. investment-banking techniques.

The future internationalization or integration of financial markets depends heavily on the nature of future capital controls or other barriers (for example, exchange rate uncertainty) that impede the mobility of capital. The experiment with controls in the 1960s—beginning with the Interest Equalization Tax in 1963 and extending through the mandatory foreign credit restraint program in 1968—did not provide a viable long-term solution to the U.S. balance-of-payments deficit. The structural causes of the deficit persisted and private institutions (such as the Euromarkets) expanded to provide financing alternatives. The two U.S. dollar devaluations in 1971 and 1973 moved the international system closer to equilibrium. For this reason, among others, U.S. capital controls were removed in 1974 in time to aid the recycling of the enormous OPEC surplus. A current proposal under consideration, creation of an offshore banking center in New York City, may suggest a relaxation of barriers to U.S. competition in financial markets—an attempt to redress one of the side effects of earlier controls. Recent legislation to regulate foreign banking activity in the United States does not represent a real threat to market integration. U.S. banks depend heavily on international markets.[57] Any attempt to regulate the U.S. activity of foreign banks too heavily could easily result in retaliation. U.S. banks constitute a major force in international banking, so it seems clear that the United States'

interest cannot lie in any legislation that would restrict the international integration of financial markets.

## Conclusion

Since this chapter covers considerable ground, it may be useful to summarize the major points. The chapter has been organized around two general themes: first, the description of a theory of international capital movements; and second, a description of the historical data on financial flows between the United States and the rest of the world. The theoretical discussions assert that a rigorous model of international capital movements should be set in the context of a general equilibrium macroeconomic model. Models of this kind, which are necessary for analyzing the total impact of both real and monetary disturbances on international capital flows, are beyond the scope of this chapter. Therefore, the link between trade flows or real economic growth and capital flows was merely noted. In a partial equilibrium model, the incentive for international capital movements depends on the difference between the expected foreign return and the expected domestic return adjusted for the expected exchange rate change. The anticipated exchange rate change is, therefore, an important factor, which influences the expected return on a foreign investment. The unanticipated exchange rate change, in like manner, is an important component in the risk of foreign investment. An investor can eliminate foreign exchange risk by covering in the forward market, which leads to the classic model of covered arbitrage flows and the interest rate parity theorem. The interest rate parity model illustrates the impact of taxes, transaction costs, exchange controls, and differential risk measures (of onshore and offshore financial assets) on covered arbitrage flows. Certainly other real variables play a role, at least to the extent that they determine the variables in the interest rate parity model—domestic and foreign interest rates and spot and forward exchange rates. The final section of the chapter noted that portfolio factors may also influence international capital flows as investors desire diversification gains.

Empirical observations have been generally consistent with the theory and have also illustrated several striking events and trends. First of all, for-

[57] For example, only 18 percent of First National City Bank's 1977 after-tax earnings came from domestic operations. Many other U.S. banks rely heavily on overseas operations. *Financial Times of London, World Business Weekly* (January 15–21, 1979), 29.

eign investors have become a more important element in U.S. financial markets. This corresponds to the long-run growth trend in the rest of the world and to the recent U.S. balance-of-trade deficits, which have required substantial foreign financing. These trends, however, do not imply unhealthy foreign influence or domination of U.S. financial markets. Competition in U.S. financial markets is still extremely keen, and foreigners who willingly hold U.S. dollars and dollar-denominated assets provide a service to the United States. They help to smooth U.S. consumption by financing cyclical trade deficits.

The discussion also pointed out the differences in the composition of U.S. assets abroad and foreign assets in the United States, as well as changes in the composition over time. The United States is a net creditor on the private and long-term accounts, while it is a net debtor on government and short-term accounts. In part, this illustrates the comparative advantage of U.S. short-term credit markets and instruments, which are well developed vis-à-vis the rest of the world. Throughout the chapter the need to adjust for price inflation was emphasized when observations occurring over a long time series were analyzed. In this regard, the recent decline in the U.S. net creditor position, expressed in real terms, was noted. This decline reverses a long-standing trend.

Finally, a concluding remark should be made about three major events that marked this period: the move to generalized floating exchange rates in 1973, the relaxation of U.S. capital controls in 1974, and the continuing development and maturation of the offshore capital markets. Under floating exchange rates, foreign investments exhibit more of the characteristics of two-way risk. Correspondingly, international capital flows are more sensitive to anticipated exchange rate changes, especially in the short run. The data do suggest that short-term flows in particular have become more variable under floating exchange rates. Not investigated was whether floating exchange rates have added an additional risk factor that reduces the *level* of international capital flows. It should be added that, to the extent that exchange rates are left to float freely (rather than with official management), the burden of balance-of-payments adjustment is placed solely on the private sector, either through exchange rate changes or private credit markets, rather than

through official assets. The removal of U.S. capital controls in 1974 ended a ten-year experiment in the use of controls to affect capital flows and the balance of payments. The data clearly indicate that foreign borrowers, both long term and short term, returned heavily to the U.S. market in 1974, but future developments will depend on market forces. The removal of most controls should signal that onshore and offshore interest rates will maintain the normal theoretical relationship indicated in Figure 18-7. Finally, the offshore market itself has emerged as a major factor in an international capital market. The world's largest banks and financial institutions have become international in scope, following globally integrated strategies. While it may be convenient to measure international capital flows between onshore markets, the offshore market has grown too large to be ignored simply because it does not fit neatly into a model of capital flows between countries.

## Questions

1. What are the basic differences between domestic financial investment (the acquisition of financial assets) and foreign investment?
2. What does positive net foreign investment imply about the relationship between a country's gross saving and its capital investment? Between its aggregate demand and aggregate output?
3. In what ways can flexible exchange rates, uncertainty, and expectations affect international capital flows?
4. Consider points *A, B, C,* and *D* in Figure 18-1. When no taxes are present, do these points correspond to potential U.S. dollar outflows or inflows? Why? When taxes exist ($t_y = 0.5$ and $t_k = 0.25$), do these points suggest U.S. dollar outflows or inflows? Why?
5. Name the various types of foreign investment. What are the distinguishing characteristics of each?
6. Describe briefly the trends in various types of U.S. foreign investment since 1960.
7. What has been the geographical and industrial pattern of U.S. direct investment abroad since 1958? What are some possible explanations for these patterns?
8. What kinds of debt instruments change hands as a result of an international short-term capital movement? Discuss the variation in short-term capital flows since 1973. What factors affect the international flow of short-term capital?

9. Describe the international investment position of the United States. How has it changed since 1950? In what sense can the United States be called a "financial intermediary" for the rest of the world?

10. What are the indications of greater "internationalization" of financial markets in the industrial countries? What are some of the effects of this trend toward internationalization?

## Selected Bibliography

Adler, Michael, and Reuven Horesh. "The Relationship Among Equity Markets: Comment." *Journal of Finance* (September 1974).

Agmon, Tamir. "The Relations Among Equity Markets: A Study of Share Price Co-Movements in the United States, United Kingdom, Germany and Japan." *Journal of Finance* (September 1972).

Aliber, Robert Z. "The Interest Rate Parity Theorem: A Reinterpretation." *Journal of Political Economy* (November-December 1973).

———. "Attributes of National Monies and the Independence of National Monetary Policies." In *National Monetary Policies and the International System,* ed. R. Z. Aliber, University of Chicago Press, Chicago, 1974.

———. *Exchange Risk and Corporate International Finance.* Macmillan & Co., Ltd., London, 1978.

———, and Clyde P. Stickney. "Accounting Measures of Foreign Exchange Exposure: The Long and Short of It." *Accounting Review* (January 1975).

Baron, D. P. "Flexible Exchange Rates, Forward Markets and the Level of Trade." *American Economic Review* (June 1976).

Clendenning, E. Wayne. *The Euro-Dollar Market.* Clarendon Press, Oxford, 1970.

Dooley, Michael P. "Note on Interest Parity, Eurocurrencies and Capital Controls." *International Finance Discussion Papers,* No. 80. Board of Governors of the Federal Reserve System, Washington, D.C., February 1976.

———, and Peter Isard. "Capital Controls, Political Risk and Deviations from Interest-Rate Parity." *Journal of Political Economy* (April 1980).

Dufey, Gunter, and Ian H. Giddy. *The International Money Market.* Prentice-Hall, Englewood Cliffs, N.J., 1978.

Eiteman, David K., and Arthur I. Stonehill. *Multinational Business Finance.* Addison-Wesley Publishing Company, Reading, Mass., 1973.

Frenkel, Jacob A., and Richard M. Levich. "Covered Interest Arbitrage: Unexploited Profits?" *Journal of Political Economy* (April 1975).

———. "Transaction Costs and Interest Arbitrage: Tranquil Versus Turbulent Periods." *Journal of Political Economy* (November-December 1977).

Friedman, Milton. "The Case for Flexible Exchange Rates." In *Essays in Positive Economics,* ed. Milton Friedman. University of Chicago Press, Chicago, 1953.

Grauer, F. Z. A., R. H. Litzenberger, and R. E. Stehle. "Sharing Rules and Equilibrium in an International Capital Market and Uncertainty." *Journal of Financial Economics* (June 1976).

Grubel, Herbert G. "Internationally Diversified Portfolios: Welfare Gains and Capital Flows." *American Economic Review* (December 1968).

Kenen, Peter B. "Towards an Atlantic Capital Market." *Lloyds Bank Review* (July 1963).

Kindleberger, Charles P. "The Case for Fixed Exchange Rates, 1969." *The International Adjustment Mechanism.* Federal Reserve Bank of Boston (1970).

Kohlhagen, Steven W. "The Identification of Destabilizing Foreign Exchange Speculation." *Journal of International Economics* (August 1979).

Lessard, Donald R. "World, Country and Industry Relationships in Equity Returns." *Financial Analysts Journal* (January-February 1976).

Levi, Maurice D. "Taxation and 'Abnormal' International Capital Flows." *Journal of Political Economy* (June 1977).

Levy, Haim, and Marshall Sarnat. "International Diversification of Investment Portfolios." *American Economic Review* (September 1970).

MacDougall, G. D. A. "The Benefits and Costs of Private Investment from Abroad: A Theoretical Approach." *Economic Record* (March 1960).

McKinnon, Ronald I. "The Eurocurrency Market," *Essays in International Finance,* No. 125. Princeton University, Princeton, N.J., December 1977.

Magee, Stephen P. "Currency Contracts, Pass-Through and Devaluation." *Brookings Papers on Economic Activity,* No. 1 (1973).

———. "U.S. Import Prices in the Currency-Contract Period." *Brookings Papers on Economic Activity,* No. 1 (1974).

Meek, Paul. "United States Investment in Foreign Securities." In *U.S. Private and Government Investment Abroad,* ed. Raymond F. Mikesell. University of Oregon Press, Eugene, 1962.

Mikesell, Raymond F. *Public International Lending for Development.* Random House, New York, 1966.

Officer, Lawrence H., and Thomas D. Willett. "The Covered Arbitrage Schedule: A Critical Survey of Recent Developments." *Journal of Money, Credit and Banking* (May 1970).

Rodriguez, Rita M., and E. Eugene Carter. *International Financial Management.* Prentice-Hall, Englewood Cliffs, N.J., 1976.

Solnik, Bruno H. *European Capital Markets*. D. C. Heath, Lexington, Mass., 1973.

——. "Testing International Asset Pricing: Some Pessimistic Views." *Journal of Finance* (May 1977).

——. "Why Not Diversify Internationally Rather Than Domestically?" *Financial Analysts Journal* (July-August 1974).

Whitman, Marina. *Government Risk-Sharing in Foreign Investment*. Princeton University Press, Princeton, N.J., 1965.

Willett, Thomas D. *Floating Exchange Rates and International Monetary Reform*. American Enterprise Institute, Washington, D.C., 1977.

# IV

# The Money and Capital Markets

# 19

# The Capital Market

The capital market is a market for financial assets other than money or near-monies. Such a market is often quite properly called an exchange, for the essential function of this market is to facilitate the purchase and sale, or exchange, of long-term claims or securities.

Since exchange presupposes some specialization and standardization, the capital market, in fact, consists of many separate, but interrelated, markets of varying degrees of organization, such as the New York Stock Exchange and the over-the-counter markets for government securities and corporate and muncipal bonds.

It is customary, and logical as well, as we shall see in the following chapter, to consider the money market—the market for near-money financial assets or claims, such as 90-day Treasury bills and negotiable time certificates of deposit—quite separate from the capital market. In fact, the money market proper might better be named the "near-money market," since money is exchanged for close money substitutes. Of course, the market in which money is exchanged for real assets rather than for financial assets is called the commodity market, or the market for goods and services. But the capital market is the network of facilities that provides for the transfer of long-term claims and funds.

The bulk of trading in the capital market is in outstanding securities; only a simple reshuffling of owners is involved. No new issues or additional saving takes place; instead, wealthholders are readjusting their desired asset mix of cash and securities. The analytical emphasis of economists is usually on trading in new issues, for placing such primary securities involves net new saving (and investment) or the transfer of funds from surplus to deficit units. However, the secondary trading market is of crucial importance. First, active, ongoing markets are indispensable to the effective marketing of new issues. Second, trading in outstanding securities is important in its own right because ease of asset shifts facilitates wealthholders' constant efforts to optimize the satisfactions derived from their portfolios.

Thus, the capital market, the network of facilities for transferring long-term claims, provides a means for readjusting a given stock of financial assets and liabilities as well as a means for augmenting the flow of loanable funds—that is, for adding to the stock of financial assets (and liabilities). By performing both of these financial functions efficiently, the capital market enhances the economy's real wealth and income.

That an efficient capital market has such beneficial effects is intuitively demonstrated through what may be called the "terms of trade" approach. All freely chosen transfers presuppose that both parties to the exchange benefit: otherwise, the trade would not take place. The proposition holds, of course, whether the claims are exchanged for other claims (financial-asset readjustment) or new saving is exchanged for new claims (financial-asset increment). When existing financial assets are exchanged, presumably the wealthowners (or households) concerned improve their "portfolio satisfaction" in the process. However, when current saving is exchanged for new financial assets, there is another gain: the real assets behind the claims gravitate toward the best bidder, that is, the one who, presumably, provides their most productive employment. This benefits the economy as a whole, by expanding its productive potential in the fullest manner.

The rest of this chapter develops these ideas. The next section discusses the nature of capital markets and the reasons they are important for developed economies. The following two sections examine the structure of the capital markets in the United States and study their recent performance. The remainder of the chapter analyzes market efficiency.

## The Nature of Trading in the Capital Market

### The Origins of the Capital Market

Capital markets arise for three important reasons:

1. They allow gains to be made through economic specialization.
2. They allow for interpersonal differences in consumption time preferences.
3. They allow for interpersonal differences in attitudes toward risk.

Let us look at each of these reasons briefly before examining in more detail the gains from trade.

Looking at the first reason, clearly if there were no differences among economic units and if all units were self-sufficient, all finance would be internal. There would be no capital or other financial markets. However, differences in personal tastes, talents, and opportunities require specialization for efficiency, and specialization, of course, must be accompanied by exchange. Generally, in our society, specialists in supplying real assets (businesses) also tend to be net suppliers of financial assets; households, on the other hand, tend to specialize in demanding financial assets. Such specialization would develop even in a riskless society owing to personal preferences with respect to work and leisure and different opportunities. These imbalances associated with specialization are usually measured in terms of net saving versus investment, or surpluses versus deficits. Recall that although actual saving and investment are always of equal size in the aggregate, some sectors, or parts of the totality, may well be net savers and lenders while other sectors are net borrowers. Thus, households (or consumers) as a group are net savers, or net purchasers of financial assets; business firms (producers) are net borrowers, or suppliers of financial assets.[1]

Second, even if current saving and investment were to balance in all sectors individually, as well as in the aggregate, there would still be a capital market, for all units would still desire to trade in existing financial assets as their tastes changed, say, during the course of the life cycle. A secondary capital market would exist, then, even if the primary market atrophied. In any case, the primary market depends heavily on the existence of a functioning secondary market. In short, interpersonal differences and the resulting specialization ensure that financial assets will be created (by deficit units), and that those financial assets will be actively traded.

The third and, perhaps, the most important reason for formation of capital markets is the existence of interpersonal differences in attitudes toward risk. In general terms, risk involves the probability of loss and, more precisely, the extent to which returns in practice will diverge (as measured by the standard deviation) from their expected values. As Chapter 24 shows, risk may be reduced by forming a diversified portfolio but, beyond this, the process of reducing nondiversifiable, or market, risk involves reducing returns. In general, both risk and

[1]See Chapter 1.

expected return rise as one moves from saving in the form of money to saving in other financial assets and, finally, to investing in real assets. Obviously, each wealthholder must make a choice with regard to the risk/return trade-off, but there is no reason why choices made by all economic units need necessarily be the same. Note that people's attitudes or *preferences* toward risk and return, as well as *actual* risk and return, are influential in the decision-making process.

In sum, the capital market—trading in long-term claims or securities—has its origins in people's differing saving propensities, time preferences, and attitudes toward risk. Saving-investment imbalances within the various sectors lead to new issues, that is, to the development of the primary capital market. On the other hand, variations in risk and time preference lead to adjustment of outstanding financial assets, to the development of a secondary capital market. The existence of a secondary, or trading, market facilitates new issues, for liquidity is then provided to the supplier of new funds. However, it should be noted that all capital markets necessarily originate as new-issue markets, from which point forward trading in outstanding securities may develop.[2]

## The Gains From Trade: Capital Market Efficiency

The origins of the capital market are apparent in individual differences in perceptions of and attitudes toward risk and information. However, as in all trading, the swap of claims for money or claims for claims presumably benefits all parties to the exchange, and the "better" the various segments of the capital market, the greater the individual gains. But, as stated in the introduction to this chapter, when current saving is exchanged for financial assets, the economy as a whole also benefits.

In understanding how the economy benefits from exchange, we must first recognize the basic fact of scarcity: that real resources (means) are limited relative to competing uses (ends). Clearly, then, the basic aim in all economic problems is to get the most out of our limited resources—to "economize"

[2]See Chapter 24 for further discussion of the concept of risk.

on them and to direct them to their most efficient uses.

There are two broad ways of promoting economic welfare in a world of scarcity:

1. Arrange ends in order of decreasing desirability so as to allocate resources to these ends in that order until the resources run out. This allocational efficiency assures that resources are put to their best uses since not all uses can be satisfied.

2. Whatever ends are chosen for priority, they should be met with the least expenditure of scarce resources. This operational efficiency assures that, given the list of priorities, we can then proceed as far down that list as is possible given our limited resources.

A competitive capital market is important for the economy because it encourages both kinds of efficiency. It encourages allocational efficiency when it directs saving flows to the best investment returns for a given level of risk. If there were no risk, funds would best be allocated when the interest rate was uniform in all uses. Since risk does exist in the real world, however, funds are best allocated when return differentials are just sufficient to offset risk differentials among uses. Thus, in measuring the degree of allocational efficiency in capital markets, we can study risk differentials.

A competitive capital market promotes operational efficiency when the allocation of funds is carried out at least cost, in other words, with minimal costs of transfer. This operational efficiency can be measured in terms of flotation costs, brokerage charges, and the ability of the capital market to generate economies of scale. Alternatively, operational efficiency can be gauged by the degree of trading risk as measured by the narrowness of the bid-ask spread or the stability of the security's equilibrium price under trading pressures of size and timing. *Measurement* of both allocational and operational efficiency are discussed later in this chapter.

Both allocational and operational efficiency of the capital market depends on the competitiveness of the market in marshaling and redirecting funds. If, in this market, funds tend to be allocated to the highest bidder by least-cost financial intermediation, both kinds of efficiency are likely to exist. There are relatively few studies of the financial industry, but the general impression from those that are available seems to be that financial industry is more competitive in structure and performance than is industry proper. That is, as measured by size and number of firms and homogeneity of product, the financial industry appears relatively competitive in structure; as measured by profitability and ease of entry and exit, it would also seem to be fairly competitive. We consider some additional evidence on these matters at a later point.

Economies of scale also are relevant to this discussion of capital market efficiency. Generally, the capital market may be thought of as an organized intermediary between ultimate lenders and borrowers. Such intermediation, naturally, develops economies of scale via both specialization and diversification. Indeed, intermediation could not operate at a profit unless it could carry out financial operations at a lower transfer cost than individuals can. So long as economies of scale are developed without an equally parallel development of offsetting monopoly power (say, via size), the economy gains.

However, a dynamic capital market does more than simply promote optimal allocation of given funds; it also stimulates additional saving (and investment). In the very process of obtaining the best compositional flow of funds, a well-functioning capital market is raising the marginal utility, or usefulness, of saving and lowering the marginal cost of finance. By widening savers' choices, both risk averters and risk takers are encouraged to save more, for the effect of these capital market pooling operations is to increase the rate of return available for a given risk. Similarly, through the implicit diversifying operations of the capital market, higher rates of return are possible without decreasing somebody's liquidity. In sum, an effectively competitive capital market not only makes for optimal use of a pool of existing funds but it also tends to augment the size of that pool by lowering the required rate of return on investment and by raising the rate of return on saving for given risk classes.

## Competition in the Capital Market

Note that the capital market need not be perfectly competitive to induce these results. Indeed, a perfect market in which a single interest rate prevails everywhere is an impossible market, for it assumes no risk differentials and no transaction costs. How-

ever, so long as the future is unknown and knowledge is imperfect, there will be multiple rates and costs in the capital market even though this market may be quite competitive.[3] In fact, one sign of a developing, competitive, capital market may well be a narrowing of yield differentials and falling transaction costs.[4] However, to assume the absence of all yield differentials is to assume away the prime task and gain of the capital market, namely, to provide economic units with efficient means of coping with an uncertain future despite imperfect current information and varying attitudes toward risk.

It remains, of course, to ascertain the degree of competitiveness of the capital market of the United States. We attempt to do so later in terms of the level and behavior of interest rates and their differentials, as well as transaction costs. In other words, in terms of the behavior of prices in the capital market, are the various sectors of the market broad, deep, and resilient? For performance, in terms of costs and prices, is a fundamental test of competitiveness in the secondary capital market. In the primary capital—or new issues—market, performance also involves flotation costs (including investment bankers' spread) and, in general, ease of access (that is, entry) into such markets. Flotation costs are examined for overall trends as well as for various offering sizes. One would expect that developing competitiveness in a primary capital market would be marked by falling costs and by a narrowing of the cost differentials against smaller issues.

In general, transaction costs—the difference, for example, between the borrowing rate and the lending rate—fall as a competitive market evolves owing to the development of economies of scale and of competitive pressures. Increasing scale on the issuing or marketing side (that is, on the side of the investment banker, government, or giant corporations) does not appear to have brought monopoly power in its wake owing to the simultaneous rise of financial intermediaries representing ultimate lenders. Indeed, the growth of those lenders' coun-

---

[3]See George J. Stigler, "Imperfections in the Capital Market, *Journal of Political Economy* (June 1967), 287–292.

[4]This essentially long-run effect should be distinguished from the fact that, in the short run, imperfections undeniably exist in the U.S. capital market. In this connection, see Chapters 23 and 24.

tervailing power, as represented by such financial intermediaries as insurance companies, pension funds, and mutual funds, appears to have outstripped the power of the selling side.

However, the rise of private placements (direct offerings of new securities by issuers to large buyers without resort to public sale) does curtail the volume of trading in the capital market insofar as these private sales could have been successfully offered publicly. But, in general, the rise of financial intermediaries and their professional portfolio management has, in all probability, caused a rise in the volume of securities trading in the latter's search for optimal performance records. And it is trading volume, above all, that characterizes a highly developed, competitive capital market. For example, despite the fact that continental European capital markets handle a considerably greater relative volume of new issues than do U.S. markets, they are considered underdeveloped markets because of the paucity of secondary trading.[5] It is interesting to note that highly developed secondary markets in corporate stocks are indispensable in the shift to internal finance from new issues; capital gains earned via retained earnings must be "salable" if stockholders are to acquiesce to their plowback. And, more generally, instant transferability, or quick and cheap marketability of securities, is a fundamental prerequisite to raising large amounts of funds directly from ultimate lenders. The mass of households require that their limited saving be available, essentially on demand, to meet precautionary, or simply planned, future expenditures of such personal saving. Given the "thinness" of their capital markets, continental European savers traditionally obtain that "liquidity" primarily via deposits.

Thus, the single most revealing characteristic of a nation's capital market is the breadth, depth, and resiliency of the *trading* in that market. In the United States, the substitution of internal for external finance by large corporations has depended initially on the development of external markets. Furthermore, the substitution of institutional for individual trading has also been dependent on the existence of "thick" markets (institutional trading has itself contributed to the development of such

markets). In addition, the intermediation process has increased the volume of trading by utilizing the net savings of individuals who would not trade directly in securities. Finally, even the rise in the proportion of negotiated, or direct, security trades (or exchanges) off the open market is fundamentally dependent on the existence—and the alternative—of the firm quotations from trades *on* the open market.

A market is said to have *depth* when there are both sell and buy orders above and below the last market price. If those orders are in volume and from diverse investor groups, the market has *breadth* as well. And *resiliency* exists when new orders pour in to take advantage of a price break. In sum, a market with all three of these characteristics is a market of small price changes and large quantity turnover. It is a highly competitive market.

Broad, deep, resilient markets are also low-cost, high-information markets. That is, proxies for trading conditions are transaction costs: flotation costs, commissions, bid-asked spreads, and the like. Such costs tend to be lower in "thick" markets owing to competitive pressures and economies of scale.

This is not to say that a good capital market is necessarily a low-risk market—quite the contrary. A great advantage of such a market is that the whole range of risk taking is available both in terms of credit or default risk and in terms of money or interest-rate risk. The fewer the gaps in the maturity and risk classes, the greater the opportunity for wealthholders to find a risk-return combination that is best for them. And, to come full circle, the closer to their preference they can come, the better the composition of saving (and allocation of investment) and the greater the volume of saving (investment). Thus, it is not risk but risk for a given return (or cost and trading profit) that is minimized in a thick capital market.

## The Structure and Functioning of the Capital Market

### Introduction: Capital Market Instruments and Institutions

If we are to evaluate the performance of the capital market—that network of facilities by which long-term funds are raised and allocated or through

[5] Organization for Economic Cooperation and Development (OECD), *Capital Markets Study,* Vol. 3, *Functioning of Capital Markets,* Paris, 1968; and OECD *Financial Statistics* (April 1975 and December 1977).

**Table 19-1   The Capital Market for Businesses, Government, and Households**

|  | Businesses | Government | Households |
|---|---|---|---|
| Internal finance | Retained earnings | Taxes | Disposable income saved |
| External finance | | | |
|   Short-term | Short-term loans from banks | Short-term bills and notes | Consumer loans |
|   Long-term | Stocks and bonds | Government bonds | Mortgage loans |
| Relevant instruments (securities) | Corporates | Governments | Mortgages |
| Relevant institutions | Commercial banks, investment bankers | Federal Reserve banks, government agencies | Contractuals: pension funds, insurance companies<br>Depositories: MSBs, S&Ls, CBs, CUs |

which financial assets are readjusted—we must examine the structure and functioning of its various components. Although we generalize about the efficiency of the U.S. capital market as a whole, we find our evidence for these generalizations in the functioning of the separate markets for corporates, governments, and mortgages—instruments which, however, are linked through their comparative returns and normal differentials. We can demonstrate the competitive cohesiveness of the capital market by examining the various financial institutions involved in the several sectors of the capital market as well as by studying the financial instruments themselves. Whatever the variety of detail provided, however, the essential question is: How effectively does the capital market allocate funds to their best real use at least real cost?

The framework for this section is shown in Table 19-1. We will examine the demand for funds in terms of the securities issued, and will look at the supply of funds in terms of who purchases them. Data are given for the various intermediaries as they participate in the different segments of the capital market and for the instruments in terms of their owners. A final summary of these data affords a view of the development and overall size of the U.S. capital market. In effect, we are now considering this market as the market for trading in "durable" financial instruments—stocks, bonds, and mortgages—instruments for necessary permanent financing beyond what can be provided internally.

### Structure of the U.S. Capital Market

During the postwar period, the total of long-term securities (and all credit market *debt,* including short-term debt) has expanded at the same rate as total output and real assets—roughly tenfold. The relationship between GNP and these overall financial flows is remarkably stable at about 1.7, that is, for every dollar increase in GNP, debt tends to rise by $1.70. This stable relationship is useful for *forecasting* overall financial flows;[6] and while it cannot be used to forecast sector or particular security flows, the overall relationship serves as the average measure against which to compare the growth of individual segments of the capital markets.[7]

Table 19-2 lists the five major components of the capital market and compares the total volume of securities outstanding in each segment in 1946, and their distribution among holders, with the corresponding totals in 1978. Table 19-2 shows that the capital market mix has undergone some sharp changes over the period. The government securities market, which was the largest sector in 1946, now is equaled by the corporate bond market and is smaller than the mortgage and equity markets.

---

[6] For example, if GNP is forecast to be $3.25 trillion in 1985, capital market debt is forecast to be $5.5 trillion. Note that total flows of funds are always larger than GNP or expenditures because the former includes spending for financial assets plus net capital gains as well as spending for goods and services.

[7] See Chapters 25–27 for discussions of forecasting.

**Table 19-2  Capital Market Instruments Outstanding, Classified by Holder, 1946 and 1978 (in billions of dollars)**

| | 1946 | 1978 | Change, 1946 to 1978 |
|---|---|---|---|
| U.S. government bonds[a] | $161 | $ 471 | 2.9× |
| Savings institutions | 14 | 53 | |
| Insurance and pensions | 28 | 62 | |
| Commercial banks | 50 | 97 | |
| Other institutions | 8 | 37 | |
| Individuals | 60 | 145 | |
| Foreign | 1 | 77 | |
| State and local government bonds | 15 | 263 | 17.5× |
| Commercial banks | 4 | 126 | |
| Insurance (nonlife) | 1 | 62 | |
| Other | 4 | 28 | |
| Individuals | 6 | 75 | |
| Corporate bonds | 28 | 422 | 15.1× |
| All banks | 4 | 29 | |
| Insurance | 14 | 180 | |
| Pension funds | 1 | 129 | |
| Individuals | 8 | 68 | |
| Other | 1 | 16 | |
| Mortgages | 42 | 1,173 | 27.9× |
| Commercial banks | 7 | 214 | |
| Savings institutions | 12 | 531 | |
| Insurance and pensions | 7 | 118 | |
| Other | 2 | 203 | |
| Individuals | 14 | 106 | |
| Total long-term debt | 246 | 2,329 | 9.4× |
| Corporate stock | 111 | 1,086 | 9.8× |
| Insurance | 3 | 55 | |
| Pension funds | 1 | 141 | |
| Investment companies | 1 | 31 | |
| Other | 3 | 8 | |
| Individuals | 103 | 851 | |
| Total | $357 | $3,415 | 9.7× |
| Notes | | | |
| Short-term governments | $ 70 | $ 210 | 3× |
| Total credit market debt (short-term and long-term) | $316 | $2,539 | 8.0× |
| Gross national product | $210 | $2,128 | 10.1× |

[a]Total privately held and excluding all short-term issues.

Source: Board of Governors of the Federal Reserve System, *Flow of Funds Accounts*.

Note, however, that while new issues explain the mortgage expansion, the equity expansion is explicable mainly in terms of earnings plowback and increased price/earnings multiples. In other words, it is primarily the result of forces in the secondary and not in the new-issues primary market. The relatively small expansion in federal government debt has taken place chiefly in the short- and inter- mediate-term end of the market. But it is state and local government debt, not federal government debt, that has expanded greatly over the last generation.[8] Capital market securities outstanding in 1978 of $3,400 billion are fairly evenly distri-

[8]Over the last decade, the rates of increase in various forms of debt have been more parallel, all rising approx-

buted among three subsets: all bonds, mortgages, and equities, each with about $1,100 billion outstanding.

Not only has the mix of total outstanding securities changed; so, too, has the mix of holders. Today U.S. government securities are held less by private financial institutions and individuals and more by government itself through federal agencies such as the Social Security Administration and the Federal Reserve System. In 1946, 90 percent of outstanding U.S. government marketable securities was in private domestic hands; today, only 70 percent is so held. Thus, for example, the Federal Reserve System holds more than $100 billion. This drift has reduced trading in the government bond market per billion dollars of outstanding Treasuries, for government agencies as investors rarely sell net from portfolio, and depository and private insurance institutions generally hold close to minimal requirements. Foreign holdings—the only really rapidly growing holder of government bonds—is another sector not noted for rapid turnover of its portfolio.

___

imately twofold. But, even for this period, the rates of increase of *private* debt (business and households) exceeded that of government debt, whether federal or state/local. (It was the market value of equity that increased hardly at all.)

### Capital Market Investments (in billions of dollars)

|  | 1967 | 1974 | 1976 | 1978 |
|---|---|---|---|---|
| **Debt** | | | | |
| Federal government | $ 167 | $ 258 | $ 348 | $ 471 |
| State and local | 114 | 208 | 237 | 263 |
| Corporate bonds | 150 | 281 | 355 | 422 |
| Mortgages | 382 | 742 | 889 | 1,173 |
| Total debt | $ 813 | $1,489 | $1,829 | $2,329 |
| **Equity** | | | | |
| Corporate stock | 887 | 601 | 990 | 1,089 |
| Total securities outstanding | $1,700 | $2,090 | $2,819 | $3,415 |

*Sources:* See Table 19-1.

It is only by the mid-1970s that federal debt rises at rates even equal to that of the private sectors. Over this recent period, federal debt rose by a striking one-third, but *total* securities outstanding rose by one-third also; total debt rose by almost one-fourth.

Fortunately for the financing of state and local governments, the principal demanders of tax exempts—commercial banks and wealthy individuals—are stronger demanders today than they were in 1946. This demand results from high corporate and personal income tax levels and relatively high yields. Together, commercial banks and individuals own about three-fourths of these securities outstanding.

Owing to the phenomenal growth of contractual saving in the postwar period, the corporate bond market has developed into the most institutionalized market of all the capital market segments. This growth came through life insurance companies at first and later through private and public pension funds. These intermediaries now hold almost 80 percent of all corporates outstanding. On the other hand, owing to the lack of tax privileges, individuals have lost more of the small interest they previously had in corporate debt. The mortgage market is similarly institutionalized and owes its phenomenal growth in the postwar period to the surge of individuals' desires to hold much of their saving in the form of deposits as well as in contractual form. Thus, nine-tenths of all privately held mortgages are held by commercial banks, nonbank depository intermediaries, and life insurance companies.

Again individuals are important as holders (they own over 75 percent) of all common stock outstanding. However, institutional holders currently are heavier *traders* in stock (one-half of the total) than are individuals. Nevertheless, stocks, along with municipals, are those segments of the capital market of greatest direct significance to the individual. Of course, the fastest-growing holders of equities are private noninsured pension funds and mutual funds. Together, thus far, even they hold only about one-sixth of all stock outstanding.

### Comparative Rates of Return

The five markets mentioned—namely, the government, municipal, and corporate bond markets, the mortgage market, and the equities market—are, of course, interrelated in terms of their comparative rates of return. Interest yields on publicly marketed bonds tend toward standard risk differentials. For example, not only do all government securities carry lower rates than corporate bonds of comparable maturity, but within the corporate sector rates vary according to the credit rating of the issuer. Furthermore, all bonds tend to offer a lower return (lower risk) than equities. For example, corporate debt tends to have a similar *yield* to equities over the long run, but when capital gains are added to the long-run return on equity, the latter return averages 4.0–4.5 percent more than corporate bonds (see Table 19-3). Presumably, equities—at least in the eyes of their owners—must bear substantially more risk than corporate debt does: that is, the variability as well as the average rate of return on equities is greater than that on debt.

In general, rate differentials develop as required to attract capital to sectors of differential risk. The bidding for funds may be viewed as a process that requires additions to a basic risk-free rate to compensate for additions to the riskiness of the alternative uses. (See Table 19-4 and Figure 19-1.)[9] In general, all yields tend to rise and fall together in response to shifts in aggregate demand for funds relative to aggregate supply. However, the differ-

**Table 19-4 Attracting Capital via Rate Differentials: 1977 Averages**

| | |
|---|---|
| The base rate | 5.0–5.5% = Treasury bill rate |
| Plus liquidity risks and transaction costs | 2.0–2.5% |
| Treasury bond rate | 7.5% |
| Plus business debt differentials Aaa industrials differential over Treasuries | 0.3% |
| Aaa bond rate | 7.8% |
| Baa differential over Aaa | 0.8% |
| Baa bond rate | 8.6% |
| Plus equity risk differential over debt | 4.0–4.5% |
| Expected return on equity | 12.6–13.1% |
| Average | 12.3% |

Sources: J. H. Lorie and M. T. Hamilton, *The Stock Market: Theories and Evidence,* Richard D. Irwin, Homewood, Ill., 1973, pp. 21 and 48; I. Friend and M. E. Blume, "The Demand for Risky Assets," *American Economic Review* (December 1975), 919; R. G. Ibbotson and R. A. Sinquefield, "Stocks, Bonds, Bills and Inflation: Year by Year Historical Returns," *Journal of Business* (July 1977), 317; and A. W. Sametz and P. Wachtel, "The Financial Environment and the Flow of Funds over the Next Decade," in *Understanding Capital Markets*, Vol. 2, Heath-Lexington Books, Lexington, Mass., 1977, Chap. 9, pp. 167 ff.

**Table 19-3 Rates of Return on Capital Market Instruments, Selected Dates (percentages)**

| | 1946 | 1965 | 1977 |
|---|---|---|---|
| Long-term bonds | | | |
| U.S. governments | 2.2 | 4.2 | 7.5 |
| Municipals (prime) | 1.6 | 3.1 | 5.5 |
| Corporate Aaa | 2.5 | 4.5 | 8.0 |
| Corporate Baa | 3.2 | 5.6 | 8.7 |
| FHA mortgages | 4.2 | 5.1 | 9.1 |
| Long-run average interest rate | | 4.0–4.5[a] | 8.0[b] |
| Equity | | | |
| Dividend yield | 3.9 | 3.0 | 4.5 |
| Capital gains | 3.0 | 8.0 | 0.0 |
| | 7.0 | 11.0 | 4.5 |
| Long-run average return on equity | | 9.0[a] | 12.0[b] |

[a] 1926–1965.
[b] 1965–1977.

Sources: Salomon Brothers and Hutzler; *Historical Statistics of the United States,* Series X 330; Joint Economic Committee, *Economic Indicators.*

[9] See also Chapter 24.

entials, or spreads, do narrow and widen among classes of securities, depending on the degree to which demand and supply in particular sectors are subject to unique forces. For example, the differential of corporate bonds over state-local (municipal) bonds may widen during a period of investment boom and tight money (see Figure 19-2). On occasion, the supply of corporate securities (corporate demand for funds) may soar as business seeks funds in great quantities in the open market. If the flow of funds to life insurance companies (the principal purchasers of corporates) is sluggish, the demand for corporate bonds may be weak. When these events occur simultaneously, the result is a wider spread.

Changing supply and demand pressures cause rate differentials *within* the corporate sector to vary during the waves of expansion and contraction of the economy. Typically, the risk differential widens

**Figure 19-1   Yields of Long-Term Treasury, Corporate, and Municipal Bonds**

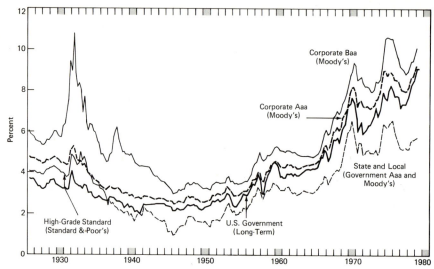

Source: Board of Governors of the Federal Reserve System, *1979 Historical Chart Book.*

**Figure 19-2   Interest Rate Differentials, 1977–1979**

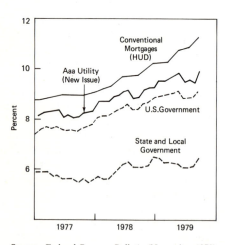

Source: *Federal Reserve Bulletin* (November 1979).

as rates rise toward the peak of a boom when demands for funds are heavy, funds are scarce, and overall risks are increasing (a downturn is expected). For example, during the boom and financial crisis of 1969–1971, the differential between Baa and Aaa corporate bonds widened to 2 percentage points as compared to an average differential of 1 percent or less. Baa bonds were sold to yield 11 percent (Aaa at 9 percent) as compared to recent rates of 9 percent and 8 percent respectively (see Figure 19-3).

The yield differential of mortgages over corporates may narrow considerably during periods of tight money when most interest rates are rising sharply (see Figure 19-2). Part of this is due to the lagged responses of mortgage yields (because of administrative restrictions and administered prices) compared to more flexible open-market rates during such periods; part is also due to a fall-off in net inflows to thrift institutions during tight money periods combined with the impact of higher yields on the demand for mortgages by marginal borrowers. (The costs of long-lived investments, such as homes, increase significantly as mortgage rates rise.)

Obviously, then, the institutional demand for U.S. governments, corporate bonds, and mortgages is as significant as the supply of those instruments in determining the various interest rates and their differentials. In the case of municipals, while monetary conditions and the demand from commercial banks is crucial, the role of individuals is also very important.

**Figure 19-3  Corporate Bond Yield Differentials**

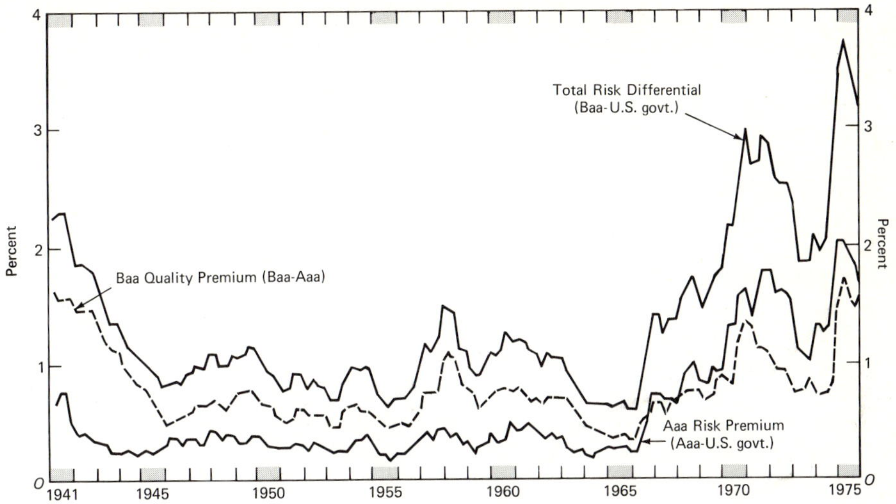

Source: Federal Reserve Bank of San Francisco, *Economic Review* (Summer 1976).

Of course, changes in the demand for equities (supply of funds to equity markets) are the dynamic force affecting stock prices (and equity yields) since changes in the supply of new issues are relatively small and, in any case, unresponsive to equity price changes.[10] Here, too, although individual holdings dominate, trading variability depends largely on (contractual) institutional demand. Although the relationships between equities and debt instruments depend on factors other than comparative yields, it is nonetheless true that, given risk preferences and corporate earnings, a rise in interest rates will depress stock prices—that is, raise equity yields—as investors shift from stocks to bonds. In other words, a rise in, say, corporate interest rates leads, not only to a rise in Treasury and other rates, but also to an increase in equity yields.

In this whole process, the entire rate structure moves up and down more or less together. At the same time, however, the differentials among rates

[10]For example, increased demands for stocks leading to increased prices for stocks do not call for increased "output" of stocks. The supply of outstanding stocks may be assumed to be constant while the demand for outstanding stocks is quite volatile, depending as it does on expected stock market prices or on future earnings per share and earnings multipliers.

in *different* sectors of the capital market vary with both demand and supply factors. Of course, interest rates in different sectors of the capital market do not move in perfect synchrony because the various financial instruments are not perfect substitutes for one another and because there are barriers among the various sectors of the capital market. Issuers of securities differentiate their product by specifying various (noninterest) terms of borrowing, and many investors are restricted in their portfolio choices either by law or custom. Shifts in the supplies of various new securities offered, in attitudes toward risk, and in transaction costs all may affect interest rate differentials, especially in the short run, that is, before the markets have time to adjust fully to the changes. However, despite the segmentation of markets that makes these shifts and lags possible, one is still impressed with the rough correspondence of interest rate movements across all segments of the capital market. Depending on one's approach and aims, one may view the integration of the various sectors of the capital market as constantly being restored or constantly being disrupted.

Just as rate differentials based on risk differences vary over time, so do rate differentials based on maturity differences. Although, on average, for the same credit risk, the longer instrument will carry a positive differential to allow for the added liquidity risk, interest differentials between long and short debt (that is, term-structure differentials) vary depending on whether rates are low and expected to rise or high and expected to fall. During booms when all rates are high, short rates may *exceed* long rates (given equal risk) because rates are expected to fall and high-paying long-term debt is eagerly bid for (see Figure 19-4 and Chapter 23).

Just as there cannot be a single interest rate in an uncertain environment, so there cannot be a single capital market. But the overall effectiveness of capital market activities requires not only that risk and other differences be accommodated but that the various segments thus created move in the direction of integration. Efficiency requires that a wide variety of financial channels be available *and* that they be interconnected. However, just as the variety offered can be wide, without being infinite, so can the interconnections be close, without necessarily being perfect.

There are appreciable differences in viewpoints as to the significance for the economy of the extent of imperfections within and among the various sectors of the capital market in the short run. On the other hand, there is considerable agreement that those imperfections have been breaking down over time. To the extent that imperfect knowledge has been a factor, the information explosion is relevant. Furthermore, the deregulation movement, the secular trend toward freeing financial institutions (for example, depository institutions and life insurance companies) from portfolio and other constraints, has proceeded at an accelerated pace over the last decade. Finally, the barriers between financial markets have been further breached in recent years by innovations in financial instruments, such as by negotiable time certificates of deposit, and by computer hook-ups and cathode-ray-tube displays.

## Understanding Changing Capital Markets

### Capital Markets During Recession and Financial Crises, 1970–1977

The traditional cyclical shifts in capital market flows and interest rates were not of much help in understanding the financial patterns of the 1970s.

Ordinarily the recession or contraction phase of the business cycle is marked by declines in aggregate flows of funds because the contraction of business and consumer borrowing is greater than the increase in government (deficit) spending and mortgage loans. But the *recession* of 1973–1974 was marked by a spurt of inflation—largely due to nondomestic events, such as the rise of oil prices and the worldwide grain shortage; and the recession was accompanied by a financial crisis that culminated, in 1974–1975, in historical peaks in interest rates. As a result, the flows of funds in 1974–1977 reflected not just the slow recovery of the economy but also the gradual winding down of inflation as well as the continuing financial conservatism that follows from financial scares or brushes with financial stringency, if not bankruptcy. Thus, the data for 1975–1977 show:

1. There was a rise in aggregate flows of funds—a mark of real economic recovery—but also a *decline* in interest rates, especially short-term rates (see Figures 19-1 and 19-4 and Table 19-5). Interest rates did not rise during the expansion because the *inflation* premium built into interest rates fell even though money became increasingly tight. (See Chapter 22 for a discussion of the inflation premium.)

2. Federal government debt soared, as it usually does when countercyclical fiscal policy is employed against recession, but corporate securities (both stock and new bond issues) also *rose* despite weak business investment requirements. Business use of the capital markets swelled to take advantage of relatively low long-term interest rates as inflation's rate of increase slowed down. Reflecting the scare of 1974–1975 credit stringency, business increased its use of the capital markets to lengthen or "fund" business debt in order to reduce the liquidity and solvency threats of too much short-term debt and high debt/equity ratios. Municipal issues also rose even though the financial crisis hit with special and unaccustomed force in the municipals market—with New York City threatening bankruptcy. This made municipals less attractive, and rates were actually higher in 1976 than in 1974 (Table 19-5).

3. Mortgage debt, following tradition, expanded rapidly in the early stages of the recovery. However, untraditionally, mortgages did not fall off in 1977 (well into the expansion) because short-term interest rates did not rise as tradition predicts. The

**Figure 19-4 Maturity Yields, 30-Day Commercial Paper and 30-Year AAA Utilities**

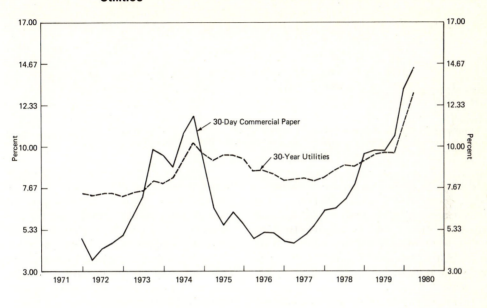

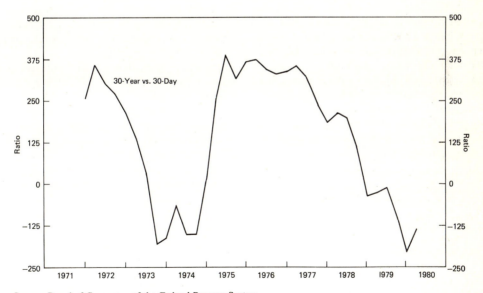

Source: Board of Governors of the Federal Reserve System.

**Table 19-5  Interest Rates—Money and Capital Markets, 1974–1978**

|  | 1974 | 1975 | 1976 | 1977 | 1978 |
|---|---|---|---|---|---|
| **Money market rates:** | | | | | |
| Federal Funds | 10.51 | 5.82 | 5.05 | 5.54 | 7.94 |
| U.S. Treasury 3-month bills | 7.84 | 5.80 | 4.98 | 5.27 | 7.19 |
| **Capital market rates** | | | | | |
| Government notes and bonds | | | | | |
| U.S. Treasury 20-year bonds | 8.05 | 8.19 | 7.86 | 7.67 | 8.48 |
| State/local Bond Buyer Series | 6.17 | 7.05 | 6.64 | 5.68 | 6.03 |
| Corporates | | | | | |
| Aaa utility bonds—new issues | 9.33 | 9.40 | 8.48 | 8.19 | 8.96 |

Source: *Federal Reserve Bulletin* (December 1979).

result was that the traditional period of "disintermediation" did not take place in that year.[11] (The differential between short rates at 6.5 percent and mortgages at 9 percent did not narrow via rising short rates, so mortgage lending continued to be profitable and savers continued to find deposit rates attractive at thrift institutions.)

Thus, the traditional financial expansion path of 1974–1977 was altered by the double-digit inflation and financal crisis that preceded the expansion. As a result interest rates generally fell during the expansion despite increased credit demand and flows. However, the principal takers of specific instruments did follow the traditional patterns. For example, pension funds and insurance companies took most of the corporate securities and depositories took most of the mortgages, with U.S. government securities widely distributed and municipal bonds and notes divided among commercial banks, nonlife insurance, and individuals.

## Capital Markets During Inflationary Expansion, 1976–1980

After a decade marked by successive waves of inflation—price levels doubled over the decade 1966–1976 and financial crunches with wild swings in interest rates (between 4 percent and 12 percent), the capital markets seemed to have settled into new norms in 1976. By that year, the flows of funds in capital markets were more than twice the size of those in 1965, although the economy had not grown

in real terms at a rapid rate, and interest rates, on average, were about 3 percent higher than they were in the pre-1966 period. The higher interest rates after 1965 may be explained by market adjustment to higher inflation rates: over the period 1926–1965 inflation averaged about 2 percent a year; but since 1965, it has averaged more than 5 percent and has been increasing secularly. (See Chapter 22 for further discussion of financial market adjustment to inflation.) Increasing inflationary expectations during 1979 and early 1980 culminated in March and April 1980 in the highest interest rates ever seen in this country.

The one market that had not adjusted to higher inflation by early 1980 was the stock market. Inflation raised required yields on stocks just as it did on bonds. However, because businesses by early 1980 had not been able to adapt fully to the new inflationary trends, after-tax earnings and dividends did not keep pace with inflation. The result was a decline in stock prices. Only after inflation has stabilized and business has adapted its own pricing and tax structure to the newly established rate of inflation, will stock prices rise. Simplified parallelism would require stocks to earn a rate of return of 16.5 percent, or to sell at six times earnings, for investors to be willing to purchase them when high-grade bonds are paying 12 percent. (See Table 19-4 where a corporate-bond-rate/stock-return differential of 4–4.5 percent is found.) The 16.5 percent required return on equity when anticipated inflation runs at 9 percent can also be shown to be an extrapolation of the 9.3 percent long-run return on stock between the years 1926–1965, a period during which inflation grew at a rate of about 2 percent per annum.

[11] Recall that disintermediation, until very recently, was usually triggered by rising open-market short-term interest rates (say, for CDs or Treasury bills), which attracted funds away from savings depositories.

## Contrasts to the Credit Crunches of the 1960s

The high-interest rate periods of the 1960s were more traditional in that they developed as a consequence of deliberate Federal Reserve policy to curb a demand-pull boom that threatened to get out of hand. But the sharpness of the curbs, and later the beginning of more rapid inflation, resulted in sharp increases in interest rates.

*Credit Crunch I: 1965–1966*  The 1965–1966 credit crunch had two classic causes with the leading element being the sharp increases in government long-term borrowing, a consequence of increased war expenditures and the failure to raise taxes. Second in importance was the surge in corporate bond offerings as business sought to finance an investment boom during a period of tight money when commercial banks were unable to make loans in the amounts required.

With this outpouring of governments and corporates, interest rates rose, not merely because of the large influx of supplies of such securities, but also because it was necessary to attract the public's savings or, in other words, the individual buyer, as well as the traditional institutional buyers. As rates on the open market rose, state and local governments held back, or withdrew, new issues to await a time of cheaper finance. The sharpest slump, on the other hand, occurred in new mortgages marketed, not merely due to the falling away of demand that accompanied high rates but, more importantly, because the typical buyers of mortgages—the nonbank depository intermediaries—had lost the deposits of individuals who now employed those funds to purchase securities (corporates and governments) directly. These shifts in the composition of new issues and in financial disintermediation were quite pronounced between 1965 and 1966, although the aggregate capital flows for the two years differ but slightly. Note that the sharp shifts in 1965–1966 flows hardly affect the overall picture as reflected in the totals of the various classes of *outstanding* securities in those years. The upsetting increase in long-term government securities only raised the total outstanding at that time from $165 billion to $169.5 billion. Nonetheless, these securities constitute one-fourth of all long-term debt securities, and the increase was more than one-tenth of all new long-term funds raised in 1966. The decline by $4.4 billion in the amount of new mortgages issued in 1966 as compared to 1965 seems small relative to the $299 billion outstanding at the year's beginning, but this was about a 20 percent decline in new issues as compared to 1965. Nonbank deposit-type intermediaries' purchases of mortgages fell by almost half and the residential building industry was severely depressed. All this, even though total mortgages outstanding rose from $499 billion to $520 billion instead of to a more normal $525 billion. A quick look at municipals in 1965–1966 shows that the difficulty there was almost exclusively due to the fact that commercial banks—a principal demander—stopped buying municipals when they found themselves short of funds to lend to their business customers.

Perhaps most striking, though not significant for the 1965–1966 credit crunch, is the triviality of new stock issues vis-à-vis outstanding equities even in a period when there is a great temptation to sell new issues of stock. By and large, annual new issues of equities comprise less than 1 percent of those outstanding, whereas for all debt other than federal, annual new issues tend to average some 10 percent of those outstanding. The usual trends in the equities area were barely affected by the frantic capital market activity. Intermediaries continued to acquire equities faster than new issues were augmenting the supply, with the result that individuals as a group remained net sellers of equities. However, prices in the equity markets were affected by the very sharp rise in interest rates. As a result of this, and for other reasons, stock prices declined by 20 percent in 1966.

This sequence—surging expansion of federal government and corporate issues in the capital markets and contractions of municipals and mortgage issues, rising interest rates, and disintermediation—is the classic scenario for economic expansion checked by tight monetary rather than fiscal policy.

*Credit Crunch II: 1968–1969*  These years marked the beginning of the decade-long battle with inflation and financial crisis. The surging interest rates of mid-1968 and mid-1969 cannot be attributed to either federal or corporate expenditure expansion. For fiscal 1969, the government budget actually showed a moderate surplus. However, a major factor allowing the increase in interest rates to continue from mid-1968 to mid-1969 was the hesitancy and delay of the government's tax policy and the consequent build-up of inflationary expectations in the economy. Monetary policy, which had been eased when the income tax surtax was first enacted in mid-1968, tightened severely late in 1968 and this posture of monetary stringency continued through 1969 in an attempt to counteract the hesitancy and short-run ineffectiveness of fiscal policy. In short, the credit crunch of 1968–1969 occurred despite reduced sales of net new government securities in the latter year (see Table 19-6). Private demands for funds took up much of the slack as businesses and consumers, noting the sharpest increase in commodity prices in twenty years, hurried to borrow so that they might spend before prices went even higher.

However, the surge in interest rates was not due primarily to increased demand for funds as in Credit Crunch I; rather, it was more the result of reduced supplies of (bank) funds and the persistence of inflationary expectations. Interest rates, especially short-term rates, continued to rise in 1969 as a result of tightening monetary policy, but even before that they had been rising despite a relative balance in the supply and demand for funds. Lenders were now requiring a "premium" against inflationary erosion of fixed-income securities, and borrowers were willing to pay such a premium to acquire the funds and to spend them in anticipation of further price increases. For example, when prices rise at a rate of 5 percent a year (as they did between mid-1968 and 1969) and are expected to continue to rise at that rate rather than the customary 2 percent, interest rates of 7+ percent are the

"real" equivalent of the old 4+ percent. Thus, the immediate impact of reduced supplies of bank credit (tight money) was to raise interest rates still further, even though the object, and eventual outcome, of such restrictions on the supply of money and credit inevitably would be a slowing down of the boom and a reduction in the demand for funds and inflationary pressures, including lower interest rates.

For our purpose here, the main point is that the flow of funds from mid-1968 to mid-1969 did not exhibit the pressures (seen in 1965–1966) that would lead one to expect soaring interest rates. Inflationary psychology and lags in the execution and effectiveness of fiscal and monetary policies, factors not highlighted by flow of funds data for this period, were the villains.

Although the rate of increase in interest rates in 1968–1969 was fully the equal of 1965–1966, structural shifts in the flow of funds were smaller and less violent and the effects of financial intermediaries appeared to be neither as large nor as shocking. The stable demands from nonfinancial business on the securities markets in 1968–1969 and the reduced demands of the federal government in 1969 shielded the mortgage and municipal markets from the kinds of abrupt declines in funds that they had experienced in 1966. However, interest rates on mortgages and municipals rose very sharply indeed. During 1969, it was the commercial banking system rather than the nonbank depository institutions that suffered the sharpest rate of decline in loanable funds. Rather than the degree of disintermediation manifested in 1966, there was the more traditional or orthodox commercial bank squeeze. This shift in emphasis was quite conscious on the part of the monetary authorities. Thus, for example, the ceiling on the rates that commercial banks could pay for short-term negotiable certificates of deposit was not raised as competing short-term open market rates rose. At the same time, nonbank deposit-type intermediaries were given additional powers to issue savings certificates. As a result of commercial banks' inability to bid savings funds away from S&Ls and mutual savings banks, mortgage funds—the principal use of funds by these nonbank intermediaries—did not suffer as badly as in Credit Crunch I. However, although funds were more available to finance building construction, mortgage rates still rose very sharply.

**Table 19-6  Flow of Funds in the Capital Market, Net New Issues and Acquisitions, 1968–1969 (in billions of dollars)**

|  | 1968 | 1969 |
|---|---|---|
| U.S. government bonds | +$16.0 | +$ 4 |
| State and local securities | + 11.0 | + 10 |
| Corporate bonds | + 13.0 | + 13 |
| Mortgages | + 25.4 | + 24 |
| Corporate stock | + 0.4 | + 2 |
|  | +$85.8 | +$53 |
| Bank loans, excl. mortgages | (+$21.0) | (+$15) |

Source: *Federal Reserve Bulletin.*

It is also interesting to note the upsurge in new issues of common stocks during Credit Crunch II as compared to Credit Crunch I. This was attributable, in part, to the very high cost of corporate debt (Aaa interest rates reached 9 percent) and to the length of the business boom and the heavy borrowing associated with it, which finally appeared to have raised corporate debt/equity ratios to cautionary heights. Nonfinancial corporations further retreated from these extended debt limits by making over 20 percent of new (1968) debt convertible into common stock.

In sum, although federal government demand for funds was not at pressure levels after mid-1968, the second credit crunch in the late 1960s was felt in the capital market and interest rates soared. This time, however, they were fueled by the dynamics of the inflationary process and by the severe restrictions imposed on bank credit by the Federal Reserve System in response to the former, as well as to the hesitancy and short-run ineffectiveness of fiscal policy after the huge increase in government borrowing in the preceding fiscal year. In many ways the experience in 1979–1980 paralleled the events of a decade earlier.

### Financial Forecasting in a Fragile Financial Environment

Although it is useful to utilize the traditional relationships to forecast the post–financial-crisis period, it is well to remember that traces of the causes and the effects of the 1970–1975 years of financial turmoil are still with us, and they are likely to remain important in the foreseeable future. Most of them—including changes in monetary policy, hastened financial deregulation, and fears of financial crisis—result in increased variability of rates of return and higher required equilibrium rates of return on financial assets. In other words, required rates of return are higher in this post–financial-crisis era than before it. One of the consequences, beyond the greater difficulty of forecasting interest rate shifts, is that until profit rates readjust upward, the volume of investment (and thus the strength of expansion) is likely to be restrained.

The increased volatility of interest rates, which is discussed further in Chapter 28, results from the shift to a monetary policy that is centered on stabilizing the money supply and from a policy of

pressing financial deregulation as rapidly as possible. Setting firm money-supply targets (rather than interest rate targets) allows interest rates to shift as required by the aggregate monetary goal or requirements. Also, relaxing Regulation Q ceilings on time deposits may help induce fluctuations in short-term rates and hence in bond (and stock) prices. Add to this floating (rather than pegged) exchange rates and interest rate fluctuations become worldwide. Whatever the beneficial effects on efficiency via increased price-system allocation of funds, the harmful effects via increased money or market risk should be recognized.

Increased credit or default risk is an inevitable result of the experience of financial crisis and it results in higher equilibrium yields. Threatened mass or major bankruptcies and even credit stringencies demonstrate that in the "new," more flexible monetary and financial environment, sudden lack of available funds "at any price" or soaring interest rates (even if temporary) can drive firms into financial difficulty. As a result, lenders today require a higher premium and stockholders require higher yields.[12]

All the effects combine to make for bond and stock markets where prices fluctuate more sharply, thus widening the capital gain–capital loss possibilities and, therefore, the risk of buying capital market instruments.

Although the effects on the real economy—to lower the level of investment and thus real output and prosperity in general—are of first importance and, obviously, not favorable, increased risk may have some secondary benefits. For example, to the extent that increased risk reduces pressures on industrial capacity, it might simultaneously reduce inflationary pressures. It might also improve our ability to forecast financial flows and interest rates in an otherwise more volatile financial environment.

### The Efficiency of the Capital Market: Introduction

As we noted earlier, allocational and operational efficiencies promote economic welfare in a world of scarce resources. Competitive capital markets

---

[12]Recall that stock market price breaks have averaged ±30 since 1966, and the overall average market price index in early 1980 was no higher than it was more than a decade earlier.

help establish both kinds of efficiency. An earlier section proposed a number of ways of measuring the degree of competition and efficiency: what remains now is to examine capital market competition and efficiency in more detail.

## Testing Capital Market Efficiency

Although it has been common practice in economic textbooks to state that the securities market exemplifies a competitive market, little direct evidence has been developed. By and large, competitive results have been presumed to follow from competitive structure, and the structure itself has seemed competitive in comparison to the structure of industry. Thus, the large number of brokers and dealers (sellers), the homogeneity of the product sold (the bond or stock), and the relative ease of entry have appeared more likely to assure competitive performance in finance than in industry. But, in fact, securities trading tends to be channeled through a relative handful of specialists or dealers, the instruments themselves have become increasingly differentiated, and such trading is quite closely regulated. This is not to imply that the capital market is noncompetitive—only that any test must concentrate on performance rather than merely assume performance from structure.

The capital market can be said to perform optimally when competitive pressures cause net saving to be allocated to those activities promising the best return and when all capital market transactions are carried on at minimal transaction costs. Although direct substantial evidence on the overall quality of allocational and operational efficiency is difficult to develop, there is some evidence based on comparative markets. As in the case when comparing rate differentials, when gauging competitive forces in the capital market one can stress either the overall competitiveness evident or the particulars of rigidities and lack of competition between and within certain segments of the market.[13]

We have already alluded to the fact that yield differentials tend to be responsive to shifts in demand/supply conditions in those markets. Even when, as in the mortgage market, these characteristics do not apply very well, what with rate ceilings in the past, portfolio restrictions, and absence of a large secondary market for conventional mortgages, such competition as does exist among the four major mortgage-making institutions tends to offer some assurance. The mortgage market aside, given the thousands of securities actively traded by thousands of institutions and millions of individuals, the general conclusion is that prices in such "thick" markets by and large tend to serve the required "rationing" effect rather well; that is, that bidders for funds appear able to obtain them if they are willing to pay the price. However, ideal allocation requires that the differential paid be no more than is appropriate to the additional risk entailed. And ideal operation requires that the transaction be carried out at least cost. We will turn to analysis of and evidence on these matters after first examining, briefly, the way that capital market securities are traded.

## Some Details on Capital Market Structures: Exchange and Over-the-Counter Markets

Although some capital market debt is generated by direct negotiation between borrower and ultimate lender (mortgages and directly placed bonds), most capital markets tend to be dealer markets; that is, markets are made by traders investing funds in inventories of securities offered for sale at a "spread" over their purchase price. This is true both for underwriters selling new issues in the so-called primary market and for market-makers in the secondary markets. Securities are bought and sold by the dealers either over the counter (that is, directly with other dealers or buyers and sellers, but not through an organized exchange) or through a securities exchange. On an exchange, only securities that meet specific qualifications are listed for trading. Markets in those stocks are "made" by specialists who run a continuous auction on the floor of the exchange, with prices set between the highest bid and the lowest offer, or by competition between buyers and sellers. These dealers stand ready to take and meet orders of floor brokers at specific prices. However, it is only through member brokerage firms that the public buys securities, paying a commission for the service. Listed securities tend to have thick markets, price quotations are readily available (continuous taping of trans-

---

[13]Actions of the government designed to encourage market efficiency are discussed in Chapter 32.

actions are summarized in newspapers), and one pays "list" price plus brokerage. Examples of organized exchanges are the New York Stock Exchange, the American Stock Exchange, the various regional stock exchanges, and the New York Bond Exchange. While most of the value (over three-fourths) and the bulk (over two-thirds) of the trading of all stock outstanding is in listed securities comprising, perhaps, 5,000 different stocks,[14] a great number of smaller corporate equities and those of large commercial banks and life insurance companies, as well as all new issues, are traded over the counter (OTC). For bonds the opposite is normally the case; except for large corporate issues, the market is largely over the counter.

OTC markets are made by dealers in various securities; they are negotiated, not auction, markets. When a financial firm stands ready to buy or sell a security at given prices, it is making a market. Indeed, the OTC market is simply the schedules of bid and asked prices. The OTC wholesaler-dealer profits from the spread between bid and asked prices and, unlike the broker, runs the risk of price fluctuations between transactions since the dealer carries inventories. The retailer who buys from the wholesaler to meet the public's specific demands charges a "markup" over the wholesale price rather than a fixed brokerage fee when selling to the public. Prices of actively traded OTC securities are obtainable from "pink" sheets (and are reprinted in the financial section of some newspapers). These show the bid-asked quotations as reported to the National Quotation Bureau by the leading dealers in each stock.[15] But the publicity of trading and transactions is slight compared to that of the organized exchanges. Furthermore, the transaction costs for OTC common stock tend to average about 5 percent of the value of the securities, as compared with 1 percent to 2 percent on listed securities.[16] However, such costs are not necessarily profit indicators since trading OTC, on the average, is in small-scale trades and low turnover per issue. Although 70 percent of OTC trading volume is in stocks, OTC markets are the only markets for municipals and U.S. governments and are a major market for corporate bonds.

## Allocational Efficiency

### Returns on New Issues Versus Outstanding Issues

Before the development and testing of the capital asset pricing model (see the next section and Chapter 32), most tests of allocational efficiency were made by seeing whether new issues offered the same return as outstanding issues having equivalent risk.

If we think of allocational efficiency as the capital market's capacity to keep rates of return on comparable investments equivalent, we are setting up conditions under which funds necessarily flow to their most profitable uses. To test the "efficiency" of new common-stock issues, one could compare the performance of such issues in terms of price experience and rates of return with comparable outstanding issues; efficiency would then call for closely similar performance. That is, allocational efficiency is provided in the new-issues market when, in that market, equivalent rates of return (or costs of financing) and equal access to funds are achieved for comparable investment opportunities. Under these conditions, funds flow to the best profit/risk outlets. This is what Friend and Longstreet found: "There is no evidence to support the assumption that investment in unseasoned securi-

---

[14]Note, however, that the New York Stock Exchange (NYSE) with 1,536 listed stocks accounts for 90 percent of the value of listings on all exchanges, and the value of trades in NYSE stock also accounts for about 90 percent of total trades on all exchanges plus over-the-counter (OTC).

[15]Technological change in computers and communications systems has led to the development of automated communications networks that not only transmit quotes and trade volume (information) instantly but have capabilities for automatic execution. An example is the National Association of Security Dealers Automatic Quotation System (NASDAQ) for OTC.

[16]For example, in mid-1977, Merrill Lynch's commission rate was 2 percent of the value of a 100-share order of a stock selling at $30 per share, that is, $60. The fee was less on higher-priced shares and greater for less than 100-share lots. Massive institutional orders are hotly competed for and may be traded for fees well under 1 percent. Note that while transaction costs for institutional trades on Exchange stocks have fallen by about one-third below the fixed schedules specified by the Exchange before May 1975, transaction costs for small traders (that is, households) is little different from "fixed"-rate times; if anything, their costs are higher. (For further detail see the section on operational efficiency below, and Chapter 32.)

ties . . . produced a higher average (long-run) rate of return than seasoned securities of the same general class.''[17] From their tests they concluded that investors apparently did not require a higher long-run (1958–1963) return on new than on outstanding securities of the same risk class.

Evidence based on the "hot" new-issue decade of the 1960s appears to show, however, that new issues of unseasoned industrial equity securities were underpriced,[18] that is to say, that issuers paid too high a spread and that purchasers obtained bargains and/or investment bankers made excess profits. However, this underpricing was rapidly corrected within one month's market trading activity and the period of the 1960s may have been unique.[19] Moreover, the potential allocational inefficiency applied only to equities; there is strong evidence of competitive pressures in new flotations of corporate bonds and, above all, of government bonds (as discussed later).

Thus, if there is some allocational inefficiency in the equity markets, it is minor and confined to industrial rather than utility issues, for selected periods, and for brief times within those periods. In short, if there is some monopoly or inefficient dissemination of information, it is with respect to the new-issues market; numerous, careful studies have demonstrated the efficiency of secondary markets with little dissent.[20]

We may generalize, then, that the stock market generates differentials only as risk differs and this, of course, is what efficient allocation requires.[21]

[17]Irwin Friend and J. R. Longstreet, "Price Experience and Return on New Stock Issues," in *Investment Banking and the New Issues Market,* World Publishing Company, Cleveland and New York, 1967, Chap. 8.

[18]R. G. Ibbotson, "Price Performance of Common Stock New Issues," *Journal of Financial Economics* (September 1975), 235–272. For counterevidence, see George Stigler, "Public Regulation of the Securities Markets," *Journal of Business* (April 1964), 117–143.

[19]Obviously, this implies that during such periods there can be no shortage of equity or risk capital, at least for corporations large enough and willing to issue stock. So long as new, unseasoned issues can be sold at no greater (and even less) cost than comparable outstanding stock, new issues may be too "hot" or overvalued, but they are easy to sell. In effect, there is discrimination in favor of risk capital.

[20]See Chapter 32.

[21]However, for other views and tests, see W. J. Baumol, *The Stock Market and Economic Efficiency,* Fordham University Press, New York, 1965, especially Chap. 3.

Note, too, and we will return to this matter shortly, that in the short run, new equity issues cause little disturbance in the market—the market is effectively broad, deep, and resilient—and that the costs of flotations average well under 10 percent of proceeds.

Although the "stock allocation" tests are limited in terms of sample size, period covered, and so on, and are subject to different interpretations, similar results were obtained in an independent study of the bond market. The question raised was: "Do securities of essentially equal quality sell for similar yields whether they are direct placements or publicly offered securities, whether they are mortgages or bonds, whether they are in California or New York, whether they are seasoned or newly issued, and so forth?" In a perfect market the answer would be "yes." One author chose to test the perfection of the bond market by comparing yields on new versus seasoned issues because, in this case, it is easier to establish equivalence of risk class, or homogeneity, among the securities considered. It was found that the bond market is nearly perfect in that: "The yield spread between a new issue and similar bonds outstanding tends to disappear within about three months from date of issue."[22] Flotation costs also consistently provide evidence that "spreads" on new issues are higher, the greater the risk characteristics of the security. For example, the larger the issue, the smaller the spread. All this is evidence of efficient allocation in that entrepreneurs would find equal access to new funds at comparable costs, and the potentially most profitable (or otherwise most attractive) investments would be able to bid funds away from investments offering lower rates of return.

But most evidence with respect to market efficiency applies to the secondary markets for outstanding equities.[23] It is generally accepted that these markets for stock are efficient in that current stock prices reflect all information available and are determined under competitive conditions. The efficient allocation of *internal* funds—optimal cap-

[22]Joseph W. Conard, *The Behavior of Interest Rates,* University of California Press, Berkeley, 1966, pp. 117–118.

[23]See E. F. Fama, "Efficient Capital Markets: A Review of Theory and Empirical Work," *Journal of Finance* (June 1970), 383–417. And for a convenient summarizing of empirical findings, see J. H. Lorie and M. T. Hamilton, *The Stock Market: Theory and Evidence,* Richard D. Irwin, Homewood, Ill., 1973, pp. 70 ff.

ital-budgeting decisions—require efficient stock prices as one input.

## The Capital Asset Pricing Model and Efficient Capital Markets

One can test the efficient market hypothesis to determine within the context of the capital asset pricing model whether or not security prices are efficient in the sense that such prices are determined by competitive forces and tend toward that competitive equilibrium.

According to financial theory, in an efficient market "a security's price will be a good estimate of its investment value, that is, the present value of its future prospects as estimated by well-informed and clever analysts. . . . Major disparities between price and investment value will be quickly noted by alert analysts who will seek to take advantage of their discoveries."[24] This capital asset pricing model suggests that in an efficient market, return is directly and linearly related to risk that cannot be diversified away, that is, market risk or risk related to fluctuations in the market as a whole (see Chapter 24). Since the unique (or nonmarket) risk of any single stock can be offset by making it part of a portfolio, such risk is not rewarded. However, overall market risk must be rewarded by a return that exceeds the risk-free return, for example, the rate on Treasury bills.

Since, in an efficient market, one cannot systematically outguess the market, the individual sets the risk level by picking the proportion of risk-free instruments in his or her investment portfolio rather than by trying to pick particular stocks for that portfolio. Having set the preferred risk level by the risk-free proportion, the investor then "buys" the market (for example, an index fund—unless he or she has "inside" or "special" information).

Further, *individual* stocks will be priced to reflect their individual differences in market risk from that of the overall market portfolio. If a stock's variability matches that of the overall market, its beta is said to be 1.0, and it will sell to have an excess return (excess over the risk-free rate) equal to the return on the entire market minus the risk-free rate. If a stock's variability exceeds that of the market—it rises and falls more than the market—

its beta will exceed 1.0 and its excess return will be proportionately greater than the average market rate.

Thus, the expected value of the *excess* return on a security in efficient markets is:

$$B (R_M - R_F) \qquad (19\text{-}1)$$

where
$B$ or beta = responsiveness to market portfolio
$R_M$ = return on the market portfolio
$R_F$ = risk-free return

and the *total* return on an individual stock is:

$$R_F + B (R_M - R_F) \qquad (19\text{-}2)$$

or the total reward for risk.

For example, suppose beta for a particular stock is 0.5—if the market is expected to rise (fall) by 10 percent, this security is expected to rise (fall) by only 5 percent. It is a defensive, less than average risk, stock.

Suppose also that the Treasury bill rate is 7 percent and the market portfolio is expected to return 13 percent. Under these conditions this security can be expected to return 10 percent: 7% + 0.5(13% − 7%). The risk-free rate of 7 percent is an illiquidity and inflation premium, and 3 percent is the premium for risk.[25]

For purposes of the discussion in this chapter, the important theoretical conclusion is that in an efficient market, returns on securities must be a linear function of risk. Consequently, market efficiency can be tested by examining whether returns on securities reflect all available information about risk.

Repeated tests show that equity returns equal the risk-free rate (that is, the Treasury bill rate) plus an extra differential to cover the market (undiversifiable) risk of the particular equity, which is above or below the return on the equity market as a whole, depending on comparative variances as measured by beta.[26] Empirical tests do demonstrate that investors in equities cannot reasonably expect to outperform the market; but that is the

[24]W. F. Sharpe, *Investments,* Prentice-Hall, Englewood Cliffs, N.J., 1978, pp. 23–24.

[25]For greater detail on the Capital Asset Pricing Model (CAPM), see Chapter 24.

[26]Among the empirical studies are: F. Black, M. Jensen, and M. Scholes, "The CAPM: Some Empirical Tests," in *Studies in the Theory of Capital Markets,* ed. M. Jensen, Frederick A. Praeger, New York, 1972; M. Blume, "Betas and Their Regression Tendencies," *Journal of Finance* (June 1975), 785–796; B. Rosenberg and

same as saying that stock prices are efficient in the sense that they reflect all generally available information, including risk. This is an important demonstration of the *allocative* efficiency of equity markets.

However, that testing process has been largely applied to stock prices and, in any case, does not apply to trading or transaction costs. In short, the efficient market test is a test of allocational efficiency, not operational efficiency; it clearly applies to equity markets, but applies to debt markets only by implication. Furthermore, it examines the capital markets from the viewpoint of the investor in outstanding stocks rather than the issuer of new equity or debt. Nevertheless, it does provide better evidence than we have ever had that stock market differential returns reflect risk differentials. And that is the prime test, if not the sole test, of the allocational efficiency of financial markets.

## Operational Efficiency

As in tests of allocational efficiency, one is not able to prove directly and conclusively that transaction costs are minimal for a given quality of service. However, evidence suggests that transaction costs in the secondary market are not very large. Also, it can be shown that *flotation costs* on new corporate issues tend to vary with risk and size differentials rather than with underwriters' "market power." For example, for common stock, underwriters' spreads vary inversely with issuer size, size of offering, and offering price; the latter is an especially good proxy for risk or issue quality, for it does not reflect economies of scale as the other "size" factors do.[27] Furthermore, it can be demonstrated that flotation costs have fallen secularly (that is, since the 1920s) as a result of rising competitive pressures as well as reduced services and, for much of the period (up to 1960), lower interest rates. Also, flotation costs in this country are low

relative to such costs in other countries. We will examine the evidence on flotation costs in more detail after first examining secondary markets.

Until 1975, brokers' commissions and dealers' spreads in transferring outstanding securities were not likely to be least-cost prices, given the structure of exchanges and fixed-rate schedules.[28] But there was a similar lack of hard evidence of this absence of competitive pressure. If commissions were above competitive cost levels, presumably this would show up in the profits of commission houses, but this has been denied, although the high and rising price of a seat on the New York Stock Exchange (NYSE) up to 1970 seems to indicate some monopoly value.

However, since May 1975, when the Securities and Exchange Commission ordered that commission rates for listed securities be negotiated rather than follow a fixed schedule of charges, rates have fallen, on average, with rates on block (institutional size) sales falling sharply, while rates on small transactions (200 shares or less) have remained stable or have even risen a bit. For example, overall security firms' commission incomes fell 5–10 percent, institutional rates fell 30–35 percent, and individual fees rose 2 percent over the year ending April 1976.[29]

The consequences of this increased competitiveness extended far beyond simple cuts in costs to carry out security transactions. Other consequences include:

1. Institutional (not full-line) brokerage houses went out of business or merged. It has been estimated that the number of firms in the industry has fallen by about 25 percent. (The number of New York Stock Exchange member firms fell from 646 to 505 between January 1968 and May

J. Guy, "Prediction of Beta from Investment Fundamentals," *Financial Analysts Journal* (May-June 1976), 60–72 and (July-August 1976), 62–70; and W. Sharp and G. Cooper, "Risk Return Classes of NYSE Common Stocks 1931–1967," *Financial Analysts Journal* (March-April 1972), 46–54.
[27]See M. Mendelson, "Underwriting Compensation," in Friend and Longstreet, *Investment Banking and the New Issues Market,* Chap. 7.

[28]Commissions plus transfer taxes averaged about 2 percent of securities sales price.
[29]Securities and Exchange Commission, "The Effect of the Absence of Fixed Rates of Commissions," August 1976 and May 1977. For individual purchasers of less than 200 shares, commissions rose from 2.03 percent of principal value; for institutional purchases of 1,000–10,000 shares, rates fell from 1.28 percent to 0.94 percent. (Ibid., p. 15). For background analysis of commission rates and prices, see I. Friend and M. E. Blume, "Competitive Commissions on the New York Stock Exchange," *Journal of Finance* (September 1973), 795–819; and R. R. West and S. M. Tinic, *The Economies of the Stock Market,* Frederick A. Praeger, New York, 1971, Chaps. 4–5.

1975; between May 1975 and May 1978, the number declined further to 465.)[30] Increased volume of trading and rising stock prices in 1978 eased this process.

2. The Third Market—firms competing by trading in listed securities off the Exchange floor—has diminished sharply as rates fell for trading on the exchanges.

3. The decline in fees was accompanied by a decline in services performed by brokerage houses for their customers.

Thus, the total impact of unfixing rates on the industry and its customers is complex, but the immediate impact to cut institutional costs and to increase operational efficiency overall is clear.

It is also clear that "monopoly" power in the industry has fallen, as measured by the price of seats on the New York Stock Exchange. However, as measured by concentration ratios—an oligopoly power measure—the largest twenty-five firms in the industry accounted for 54 percent of total securities revenues in 1977; in 1972, the proportion was 31 percent. In recent years, the price of a seat on the NYSE has fallen precipitously from a peak of $515,000 in 1969 to $200,000 by 1973 to a low of $40,000 in November 1976.[31] At year-end 1977, a seat sold for $65,000. While the decline toward $200,000 in 1973 would seem to be the result of the fall in trading volume and increased back-office costs after the mid-1960's bull market, the further decline since then can be attributed to the increased competitiveness injected by the SEC's requirements, effective May 1975, of competitive commissions. Between 1975 and 1978, the SEC exerted increasing pressure to establish a National Securities Market System in which the NYSE's power would be further reduced by such things as the lifting of Rule 390—a rule that restricted NYSE members to trading in listed securities only on the floor of the Exchange. It is the removal of not just the price restrictions but also the trading restrictions that is effectively curbing NYSE monopoly power. Reduced prices of seats—that is, privileges to trade on the Exchange—thus mirror more than the fall in commission rates.

[30]See Carol J. Loomis, "The Shakeout on Wall Street Isn't Over Yet," *Fortune* (May 22, 1978), Table on p. 61.
[31]New York Stock Exchange, *Fact Book*, 1978, pp. 58 and 80.

No comparably major structural shift has taken place in transaction costs on *new* issues, that is, flotation costs, for these charges have always been set by negotiation rather than according to a fixed schedule. However, there is evidence that transaction costs here, too, have been subject to secular competitive pressures.

Flotation costs are measured as the spread, or difference, between the price of the security to the investor (say $100) and the price received by the issuer (say $95) or net proceeds; in this case, the spread is $5 (or 5 percent), which is divided among the investment banking community, that is, among the originators, underwriters, and distributors of the security.

Data on spreads (Tables 19-7 and 19-8) demonstrate a few things. First, the inverse relationship between spread and size of issue (or offering price) reflects the lesser risk of larger issues as well as economies of scale. Second, the downward trend in spreads on issues of all sizes reflects, on the one hand, the increased competitiveness in markets and, on the other, a decrease in services offered and costs incurred, with some offset since 1969 due to higher interest rates. This evidence seems consistent with the hypothesis of operational efficiency.

In addition, of course, numerous *qualitative* factors affect spreads, but they are difficult to quantify

**Table 19-7 Underwriters' Spread as a Percentage of Gross Proceeds for Public Offerings of Corporate Securities, Selected Periods, 1925–1972**

| Size of Issue | 1925–1929 | 1940s | 1963 | 1972 |
|---|---|---|---|---|
| **Debt** | | | | |
| Small < $1M | 5.7% | 5.1% | 4.7% | 4.5% |
| Large > $20M | N.A. | 1.8 | 0.8 | 0.8 |
| **Common stock** | | | | |
| Small < $1M | N.A. | 17.0 | 9.0 | 12.0 |
| Large > $20M | N.A. | 9.0 | 4.3 | 3.0 |

N.A. = Not Available.

Source: I. Friend, et al., *Investment Banking and the New Issues Market,* World Publishing Co., Cleveland and New York, 1967, pp. 408–409; V. Carosso, *Investment Banking in America,* Harvard University Press, Cambridge, Mass., 1970; and SEC, *Cost of Flotation of Registered Securities, 1963–1965,* Washington, D.C., 1970; and *1971–1972,* Washington, D.C., 1974.

**Table 19-8  Estimates of Average Total Cost of Flotation of Corporate Securities by Various Methods (as a percentage of gross proceeds)**

| Method | Bonds | Preferred Stock | Common Stock |
|---|---|---|---|
| Private negotiation | 1.1%[a] | 1.9% | 11%[c] (public offering) |
| Competitive bidding | 0.6 | 1.5 | — |
| Direct placement | 0.4[b] (finders fee) | 0.8 (all stock) | 6.7 (privileged subscription) |

[a]S. L. Hayes III, "Investment Banking: Power Structure in Flux," *Harvard Business Review* (March-April 1971), 137, shows that this negotiated bond spread is typically divided up as follows: $2/10$ to manager, $3/10$ to underwriter, and $5/10$ to selling group.

[b]J. Connolly, "Is the Syndicate Bid on the Way Out?" *Institutional Investor* (May 1976), 39–42, shows that this type of negotiated stock spread is typically divided up as follows: $2/10$ to manager, $2/10$ to underwriter, and $6/10$ to selling group.

[c]E. Shapiro and C. R. Wolf, *The Role of Private Placements in Corporation Finance,* Harvard University Press, Cambridge, Mass., 1972, demonstrate that the differential between a negotiated and a privately placed bond sized $10 to $20 million would be about 0.6 percent in favor of the broker/agent fee arrangement in contrast to the more expensive dealer/underwriter arrangement.

Sources: R. Lindsay and A. W. Sametz, *Financial Management, An Analytical Approach,* rev. ed., Richard D. Irwin, Homewood, Ill., 1967, p. 462; SEC, *Cost of Flotation of Registered Issues, 1971–1972,* Washington, D.C., 1974.

or to generalize about aside from the type of security offered and the degree of services performed by the investment bankers. Qualitative factors include the industry of the issuer and the previous trading record, if any, of the company's securities and whether it is traded on an exchange. For example, securities floated by utilities with active secondary markets will have relatively low flotation costs. These costs will be still lower if the security floated is a bond rather than a stock and if it is privately placed with an institution rather than offered to the general public.

Although it has not been possible to remove the economies-of-scale effect, nor the reduced-service-cost effect on spreads, it does seem that spreads differ primarily because of risk differentials and are under greater competitive pressure today than in times past.

For common-stock issues, flotation costs (Tables 19-7 and 19-8) far exceed commission costs, with large negotiated underwritings averaging 3 percent spreads (versus under 1 percent commission costs for larger buyers of outstanding stock). The flotation costs of *large* stock issues are far lower than for small stock issues (over 12 percent) but far higher than for large new-bond issues (under 1 percent). Note, too, that flotation costs for stocks have fallen over the last three decades far more than flotation costs for bonds; indeed, over a long period the sharpest declines were for small stock issues.

Within each security class, flotation cost at all times is lower for issues that are not marketed publicly (negotiated underwritings) but, instead, are placed directly with institutions or existing security holders. And issues that are publicly bid for

in open competition have lower costs than issues arranged by negotiations with investment bankers. The full package of investment banking services include origination or financial advice, underwriting or assumption of risk, and distribution or selling effort; private placement eliminates the latter two services (and costs), while competitive bidding puts pressure on spreads, which are reduced either by curtailed investment bankers' profits or by curtailed services and costs.

Operational efficiency can be implied also from the vast *turnover* of outstanding securities in these markets (see Table 19-9). Of course, "thin" markets also impair allocational efficiency by discouraging efforts to float new securities. However, easy and cheap shifting of existing securities (and of financial assets in general) among holders is important to consumer welfare. A striking difference between the United States and the financial markets of other developed nations is the lack of thick secondary markets in the latter. Transaction costs in thin markets, whether measured by bid-asked spreads, or by commissions, tend to be relatively high.

Some indicators of depth-breadth-resiliency in the capital market are shown in Table 19-9. Note especially that one-half of the value of outstanding securities turn over each year—only the corporate bond market is relatively sluggish owing to the long-term nature of investor interest and to private placements, which tend to stay put until maturity. New issues account for one-ninth of all sales—important in all segments of the capital market except the stock market. The absolute dollar amounts of trading are very great, adding up to $824 billion

**Table 19-9  Annual Sales of Securities Compared to Total Outstanding and New Issues, 1976**

| | Billions of Dollars | | | Ratios | |
|---|---|---|---|---|---|
| | Sales | Outstand-ings | New Issues | Sales/Out-standings | Sales/New Issues |
| U.S. government bonds (> 1 year) | $624 | $ 190 | $47 | 3:1 | 13:1 |
| Listed corporate bonds | 5 | 145 | 30 | 1:29 | 1:6 |
| Corporate stock | 195 | 854 | 11 | 1:4 | 18:1 |
| Totals | $824 | $1,189 | $88 | 1:1.5 | 10:1 |
| Ratio to personal saving ($66 billion) | 12:1 | | 1.7:1 | | |
| Ratio to GNP ($1,707 billion) | 1:2 | 1:1.4 | | | |

Sources: *Federal Reserve Bulletin* (April 1977); New York Stock Exchange, *Fact Book*, 1977; *Statistical Abstract*, 1977.

annually, or $3 billion each trading day. If we had included the short-term government securities market, *daily* total trading would exceed $10 billion.

## The Capital Market and the Money Market

Any separation of the money market from the capital market must be arbitrary, although it is the custom to draw the line at a maturity of one year. However, the true distinction between, say, Treasury bills, on the one hand, and bonds, on the other, is a risk difference and usually a transaction-cost difference. The potential lender has three choices: to hold money, to buy short-term claims (for example, bills), and to buy long-term claims (for example, bonds). So long as transaction costs are exceeded by the short-term interest rate, the individual buys bills and forgoes the holding of money. Thus, the lender's choice between bills and bonds depends on whether the expected extra return is worth the extra risk.

From the borrower's point of view, it is also a question of transaction costs and risk "costs"; presumably, one borrows in the cheapest manner. If, for example, the funds are needed for a short period, transaction costs will be minimized by tailoring a loan so that it will mature within the same short period. So long as the short rate is below the long rate and, in the postwar period, this usually has been the case, it will pay to borrow "short." But, if the need is long term, the transaction costs of renewing the loan or issuing new bills may be great enough to offset the lower rate and to call for selling bonds.

Short-term claims and the money market exist, then, because they meet the felt needs of surplus and deficit units. Lenders (especially regulated institutions) have a permanent liquidity requirement, and some individuals insist upon a lump sum of irreproachable liquidity. This aversion to risk depresses average short rates below "longs," other things being equal, and thereby provides borrowers with a least-cost motivation for supplying short-term claims against themselves. Moreover, some borrowers have predictable short-term needs (just as some lenders have only temporary surpluses) and may want to avoid the risk and transaction costs of refunding bonds when the funds are no longer needed (available). All these factors, in effect, segment the market for loanable funds into loosely distinct (near) money and capital markets. Although interest rates on "longs" and "shorts" are intimately interrelated, the segmented nature of some of the demand for, and supply of, funds permits the rates on occasion to move in opposite directions just as risk conditions occasionally cause short rates to exceed "longs."

However, one must not make too much of the exceptions. Just as we noted that all long rates tend to move up together over time, keeping their distances from each other by amounts that roughly reflect their risk differentials, so, too, do short rates tend to lead. This happens because the Federal Reserve executes its open-market operations largely in the Treasury-bill market. However, if bill rates rise and risk conditions are little changed, lenders will shift from "longs" to "shorts" to reap the higher return and borrowers will issue relatively more long-term securities, in the process depressing bond prices and, thereby, raising long-term market rates.

Thus, although both the money and the capital markets serve equally well to provide the external finance required to channel funds from savers to investors (beyond investors' internal funds), the money markets are, in an important sense, a "temporary" source of funds.

This is not to say that there are no permanent users of short-term funds (the Treasury and industrial business, for example) but that, in many cases, short-term sources are utilized at a time when access to the long-term methods is too costly in terms of either transaction costs or interest rates. And, of course, this essential tie between the two markets is exhibited by the term or maturity structure of interest rates.[32]

In the next chapter, we turn to the variety of specialized instruments and institutions that have been developed to meet the short-term financial needs of lenders and borrowers in what we call the money market. We will see that many of the financial institutions we have discussed in the capital market also serve the money market. The banking system and dealers in government securities, in particular, play a leading role in welding the money and capital markets together. And all of those net demanders of long-term funds, such as governments, business firms, and households, are also demanders of short-term funds and occasionally, if not regularly, have developed money-market instruments to serve their needs.

## Conclusion

The capital market—the network of facilities for transferring long-term claims—provides a means for readjusting a given stock of financial assets and liabilities as well as a means for augmenting the flow of loanable funds (that is, adding to the stock of financial assets and liabilities). By performing both of these financial functions efficiently, the capital market enhances the economy's real wealth and income.

The benefits of exchange in the capital market are explicable in terms of gains from specialization as well as in terms of interpersonal differences with respect to time preference and risk. Specialization

[32]See Chapter 23.

ensures that financial assets will be created by deficit units and that such assets will be actively traded among surplus units. Saving-investment imbalances within the various sectors thus lead to new issues, or to the development of the primary capital market. On the other hand, variations in individual attitudes toward risk and time preference lead to adjustment of outstanding financial assets, or to the development of a secondary capital market. If there were no risk, funds would best be allocated when the rate of interest was uniform in all uses. Since risk does exist in the real world, however, funds are best allocated when return differentials are just sufficient to offset risk differentials among uses. Such allocational efficiency of funds in the capital market is a prerequisite to efficient allocation of real resources in the economy.

The capital market promotes efficient use of resources when allocation of funds is carried out at least cost, or with minimal costs of transfer. This operational efficiency can be measured in terms of flotation costs, brokerage charges, and the ability of the capital market to generate economies of scale.

An effectively competitive capital market not only makes for optimal use of a pool of existing funds as such funds are attracted to the highest bidders, but also tends to augment the size of that pool by lowering the required rate of return on investment and by raising the rate of return on saving for given risk classes. In other words, performance in terms of costs and prices is a fundamental test of competitiveness in the secondary capital market. In the primary capital (new-issues) market, performance also involves flotation costs, including investment bankers' spreads and ease of access (that is, entry) into such markets.

In general, the most revealing characteristics of a nation's capital market are the breadth, depth, and resiliency of trading in that market. A market with all three of these characteristics exhibits small price changes and large quantity turnover. It is both an orderly and a busy market; returns in such a market reflect differential risks.

Over the entire postwar period, the capital market (and all financial assets) has expanded approximately tenfold, as has GNP or total output. However, the capital market mix has undergone some profound changes. For example, in contrast to federal government debt, corporate long-term debt has expanded one and one-half times as rapidly as GNP, with business short-term debt increasing even more quickly. Not only has the mix of total outstanding securities changed, so, too, has the mix of holders. For example, corporate debt is now largely in the hands of pension funds and life insurance companies.

Shifts in supplies of various new securities offered, changes in attitudes toward risk, and alterations in transaction costs all may affect interest rate differentials, especially in the short run (in other words, before markets have time to adjust fully to these changes). Despite the segmentation of markets and inflation, however, one is still impressed by the rough correspondence of interest rate movements across all segments of the capital market.

The credit crunches of 1966 and 1969 illustrate how changes in monetary and fiscal policies cause short-run shifts in the structure of the capital market and in comparative interest rates, as well as revealing their more obvious impacts in reducing the overall availability of credit and in raising its average cost.

The inflationary spurts and the financial crises of 1970 and 1974–1975 illustrate the resiliency and responsiveness of the capital markets. But the strains imposed on the system resulted in sizable changes in the size and composition of financial flows. And the increased uncertainty and risk have added to the difficulties of forecasting capital market flows and interest rates. Moreover, difficulties in designing and implementing the appropriate monetary, fiscal, and financial policies increased during this past turbulent financial decade, which was also plagued by contradictory antistagflation policy requirements.

Although the capital market performs optimally when competitive pressures cause net saving to be allocated to those activities promising the highest returns and when transaction costs are minimized, substantial direct evidence on the quality of allocational and operational efficiency for the market as a whole is difficult to develop. However, there is some evidence based on comparative markets. The stock market seems to generate differentials only as the degree of risk differs, and this is what efficient allocation requires. That the capital markets are efficient is also suggested when similar investment opportunities find equal access to new funds at comparable costs, and when the potentially more profitable investments are able to bid funds away from others offering lower rates of return, one may presume that the capital market is allocating funds optimally.

As in tests of allocational efficiency, one is not always able to prove directly and conclusively that transaction costs are minimal for a given quality of service in the capital market. One can show, however, that flotation costs on new corporate issues tend to vary with risk and size differentials, and this is evidence of the operational efficiency of the capital market. So, too, is evidence that transaction costs have been falling secularly while restrictive price and trading rules have been lifted.

In general, the real wealth and output of the U.S. economy depend, to an important degree, on the efficiency of its capital market.

## Questions

1. What are the beneficial effects of exchange in the capital market in both monetary and in real terms? What are the prerequisites of such a capital market?
2. Distinguish among the following: (a) money and capital markets, (b) primary and secondary markets, (c) surplus and deficit units, (d) operational and allocational efficiency, and (e) the flow of loanable funds and saving.
3. Compare and contrast the relative degree of risk of real and financial assets, including money.
4. "The capital market has its origins in people's differing saving propensities, time preferences, and attitudes toward risk." Discuss this statement.
5. How do we measure efficiency in the capital market? And how do efficient capital markets contribute to efficiency in the real economy? What means are available to sustain those features that characterize efficient capital markets?
6. An increasingly competitive capital market is characterized by "a narrowing of risk differentials and falling transaction costs," but to assume the complete absence of such differentials and costs is to "assume away the prime task and gain of the capital market." Explain this statement and discuss it critically.
7. In the United States, the substitution of internal for external finance of large corporations depended initially on the development of the external (corporate securities) market. Explain.
8. Describe the principal shifts in the (instrumental and institutional) mix of the capital market since the end of World War II. To what factors do you attribute

these shifts? What further shifts do you predict for this decade? What are the bases for your predictions?

9. What are the basic causes of the rate differentials among the five principal capital market instruments? What causes these differentials to narrow (or widen) at various times? Provide some realistic illustrations in your answer in addition to an overall analysis in terms of supply and demand.

10. Despite the upward secular trends of mortgage and municipal debt, cyclical forces in the upswing inhibit these various capital market issues. Discuss critically.

11. How do we determine whether the capital market is operationally efficient, that is, performing with minimal transaction costs? Allocationally efficient, that is, allocating funds to activities promising the best returns? Can you suggest possible efficiency tests beyond those considered in this chapter?

12. Why is it generally agreed that the mortgage market is the least efficient sector of the capital market both in operational and in allocational terms? Explain in some detail.

13. The competitive performance of the capital market can be tested in terms of costs and prices in both the primary and secondary markets. Evaluate the performance of the U.S. corporate bond or stock market in these terms.

## Selected Bibliography

Altman, E. I., and A. W. Sametz. *Financial Crises*. John Wiley and Sons, New York, 1977.

Bankers Trust Company. *The Investment Outlook* (Annual). New York, 1977.

Baumol, W. J. *The Stock Market and Economic Efficiency*. Fordham University Press, New York, 1965.

Bloch, E., and A. W. Sametz. "A Modest Proposal for a National Securities Market System and Its Governance." *Monograph Series in Finance and Economics,* New York University, 1977-1.

Board of Governors of the Federal Reserve System. *Flow of Funds Accounts, 1946–1975*. Washington, D.C., 1977; and Quarterly Supplements.

Conard, Joseph W. *The Behavior of Interest Rates*. University of California Press, Berkeley, 1966.

Duesenberry, J. S. "Criteria for Judging the Performance of Capital Markets." In *Elements of Investments—Selected Readings*, eds. H. K. Wu and A. J. Zakon. Holt, Rinehart and Winston, New York, 1965.

Fama, E. F. "Efficient Capital Markets: A Review of Theory and Empirical Work." *Journal of Finance* (June 1970).

Fand, D. "Financial Regulation and the Allocative Efficiency of Our Capital Markets." *National Banking Review* (September 1965).

Fisher, L., and J. H. Lorie. *A Half Century of Returns on Stocks and Bonds*. The University of Chicago Press, Chicago, 1977.

Friend, I., et al. *The Over-the-Counter Securities Market*. McGraw-Hill Book Company, New York, 1958.

———. *Investment Banking and the New Issues Market*. World Publishing Company, Cleveland and New York, 1967.

———, and M. E. Blume. "Competitive Commissions on the New York Stock Exchange." *Journal of Finance* (September 1973).

Goldsmith, R. W. *Financial Institutions*. Random House, New York, 1968.

———. *The Flow of Capital Funds in the Postwar Economy*. Columbia University Press, New York, 1965.

Gurley, J. G., and E. S. Shaw. *Money in a Theory of Finance*. The Brookings Institution, Washington, D.C., 1960.

Hamilton, J. L. "Competition, Scale Economies and Transaction Costs in Stock Markets." *Journal of Financial and Quantitative Analysis* (December 1976).

Hazard, J. W., and J. Christie. *The Investment Business* (A Condensation of the SEC's Special Study). Harper & Row, Publishers, New York, 1964.

Ibbotson, R. G. "Price Performance of Common Stock New Issues." *Journal of Financial Economics* (September 1975).

Lorie, J. H., and M. T. Hamilton. *The Stock Market: Theory and Evidence*. Richard D. Irwin, Homewood, Ill., 1973.

Loomis, Carol J. "The Shakeout on Wall Street Isn't Over Yet." *Fortune* (May 1978).

Moore, B. J. *An Introduction to the Theory of Finance—Assetholder Behavior Under Uncertainty*. The Free Press, New York, 1968.

New York Stock Exchange. *Fact Book*.

Organization for Economic Cooperation and Development. *Financial Statistics* (April 1975 and December 1977).

———. *Capital Markets Study*. Paris, 1967–1968.

Polakoff, M. E., and A. W. Sametz. "The Third Market—the Nature of Competition for Listed Securities Traded Off-Board." *The Antitrust Bulletin* (January–April 1966).

Robbins, S. *The Securities Markets*. The Free Press, Glencoe. Ill., 1966.

Salomon Brothers. *An Analytical Record of Yields and Yield Spreads*. New York, 1975.

Sametz, A. W. *Prospect for Credit Markets in 1977*. Heath-Lexington Books, Lexington, Mass., 1978.

———. *Prospects for Capital Formation and Capital Markets*. Heath-Lexington Books, Lexington, Mass., 1978.

————, and P. Wachtel. "The Financial Environment and the Flow of Funds over the Next Decade." In *Understanding Capital Markets,* vol. 2, eds. Sametz and Wachtel. Heath-Lexington Books, Lexington, Mass., 1977.

Securities and Exchange Commission. "The Effect of the Absence of Fixed Rates of Commissions" (August 1976).

————. *Report of the Special Studies of Securities Markets,* House Document No. 95, 88th Cong., 1st Sess., Government Printing Office, Washington, D.C., 1963, Parts 1–5.

Sharpe, W. F. *Investments.* Prentice-Hall, Englewood Cliffs, N.J., 1978.

Stigler, George J. "Public Regulation of the Securities Markets." *Journal of Business* (April 1964).

————. "Imperfections in the Capital Market." *Journal of Political Economy* (June 1967).

Wachtel, P., A. W. Sametz, and H. Shuford. "Capital Shortage—Myth or Reality?" *Journal of Finance* (May 1976).

West, R. R., and S. M. Tinic. *The Economics of the Stock Market.* Frederick A. Praeger, New York, 1971.

# 20

# The Money Market

The money market is a market for financial assets that are close substitutes for money and that mature in one year or less. Its basic function is identical to that of the capital market, namely, to maximize the satisfaction of financial asset holders (lenders) and debt issuers (borrowers). This function is performed through the exchange of already existing financial claims in the secondary market as well as through the exchange of money for new financial claims. The money market, however, differs from the capital market in that it deals solely with near-money instruments. This makes it a minimum-risk market.

Investors in any securities are subject to two major risks: a money risk, and a credit risk. The *money risk* stems from the fact that, as interest rates rise, the prices on outstanding debt securities decline. The prices of money market securities, however, cannot decline very much in response to a rise in interest rates since repayment of principal at maturity will take place in the near future. Thus, money market instruments are subject to far less money risk than are capital market securities.

*Credit,* or *default, risk* stems from the possibility that the borrower will not be able to meet periodic interest payments nor to repay the principal when due. Here, of course, there is some risk accruing to money market instruments, just as is true of long-term securities. However, since investors in the money market generally limit their purchases to the obligations of prime-quality borrowers, credit risk in this market is minimal compared to credit risk in the capital market. A main desire of purchasers of money market obligations is to acquire financial assets with maximum liquidity which quickly can be converted into money without the risk of *undue* losses; hence, they will never knowingly sacrifice the "moneyness" of their assets for such higher yields as may be available on riskier securities.

Interest rates in the money market fluctuate far more markedly than longer-term capital market yields. When the entire structure of interest rates moves up and down, short-term interest rates move further and faster than long-term interest rates. During very tight credit conditions and, therefore, at high levels of interest rates as in mid-1979, money market rates tend to rise above capital market rates, resulting in a downward-sloping yield curve. Similarly, when loanable funds are abundant

**Figure 20-1  Short-Term Interest Rates (Monthly Averages of Daily Figures)**

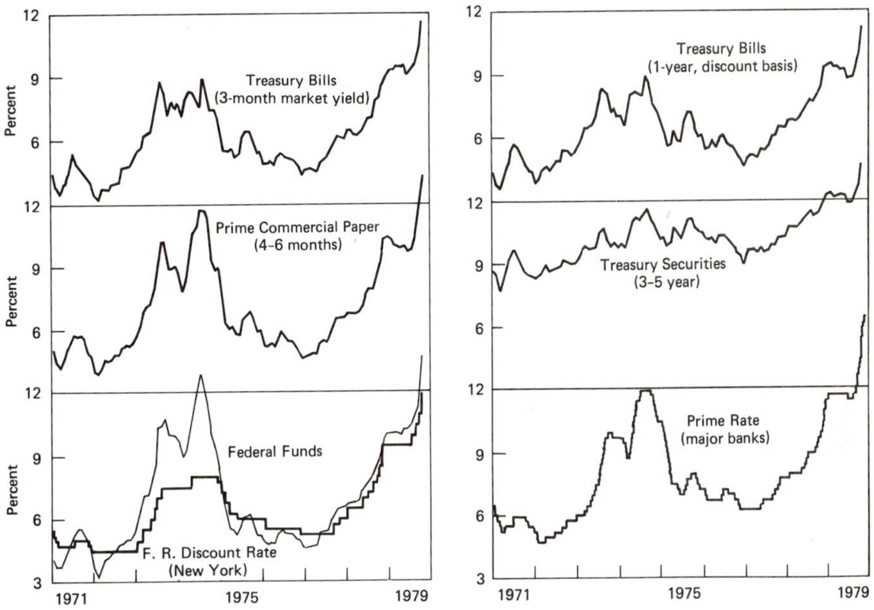

Source: Board of Governors of the Federal Reserve System, *1979 Historical Chart Book*.

and the structure of interest rates is low, short-term interest rates tend to be much lower than capital market yields, resulting in an upward-sweeping yield curve.[1]

Over time, money market rates tend to move up and down in tandem (see Figure 20-1) since the various segments of the market are closely interrelated through arbitrage. However, within the rate structure, there are considerable variations in the frequency and amplitude of changes in individual interest rates, depending on the flows of money market funds to particular sectors. And, since the government is the most important single borrower in the money market, a large proportion of the changes in the structure of money market rates are caused by Treasury debt management and related Federal Reserve open-market operations.

In the mid-1970s, interest rates on a wide variety of securities, including short-term Treasury obligations, became unusually volatile, by historical standards. Large and *unexpected* changes in yields posed serious problems for many groups of borrow-

ers and lenders, including money managers of financial institutions and corporate treasurers, who were affected by the inverse fluctuations in securities prices. In response to this increase in yield volatility, a futures market in financial assets developed, first (in 1975) for mortgage-backed certificates issued by the Government National Mortgage Association and later (in 1976) for three-month Treasury bills. This new market offers money managers of financial as well as nonfinancial corporations an opportunity to reduce their risk exposure to unexpected changes in the value of their asset portfolios or their liability costs, implicit in interest fluctuations, by buying and selling futures contracts. Through such hedging, money managers can transfer to speculators some of the risks connected with unanticipated interest rate changes. While a futures market in financial assets is of little use during periods of stable economic and monetary conditions, when interest rates change slowly and smoothly, this market is a significant addition to the central money market in times of considerable international and domestic financial uncertainties, such as were experienced in much of the 1970s. During such periods it offers money managers, who

[1]See Chapter 23 on the term structure of interest rates for various explanations of this phenomenon.

are inherently risk-averters, opportunities for partially shifting yield-related risks to others.[2]

While fluctuations in money market rates are a natural consequence of changes in underlying supply and demand conditions in the loanable funds market, there is little doubt that the money market is an extremely efficient market in which transaction costs are low and which offers considerable depth, breadth, and resilience. We shall return later to the question of the efficiency of the money market and also compare it to the capital market.

## Location and Organization

The money market is informally organized, as compared either to the equity market for most listed securities or to the commodity exchanges. It consists of many dealers who buy securities for their own positions and sell from their inventories when trades take place. Their profits result, then, not from serving as commission brokers but rather from the trading spreads between their bid and asked prices and any capital appreciation that may take place while holding the securities. In addition, since well over 95 percent of the funds employed by money-market dealers are borrowed, they also profit, whenever possible, from a positive carry. *Positive carry* is the spread between the interest cost of the money they borrow and the yields they earn on the securities they hold in their positions.

Although trading in the American money market takes place almost completely by telephone, the market is still centered in New York City. The various dealers in the money market are tied to each other by direct telephone lines over which each one may contact others hundreds of times daily. In this way, the dealers maintain constant touch with selling and buying quotes. If one dealer feels that another's prices are out of line with the market, he will immediately make a purchase from, or sale to, still a third dealer to take advantage of the differential. This type of arbitrage serves to keep the prices of different money market instruments virtually uniform among the various dealers.

Investors also contact various dealers to obtain the best prices[3] and this, too, helps even out price differentials, since the dealers whose asked prices are too high, for example, will immediately find their sales slackening until they lower their prices. Because dealers are constantly in contact with investors all over the nation and investors, in turn, are channeling their requests to New York, the money market there becomes the locus of marginal adjustments between the supply of, and demand for, funds throughout the nation. Also, because the government securities dealers themselves must finance their position with borrowed funds, they are continually searching throughout the country for the excess funds of banks, nonfinancial corporations, and others at the lowest possible interest cost to them. This process further helps to bring funds into New York and to even out interest rate differentials for similar securities among the various geographical areas.

Payment for securities traded in the money market is as simple as the process of obtaining quotations via the telephone, for the vast bulk of payments are made with Federal Funds, that is, funds in deposit accounts of the Federal Reserve banks. The Federal Reserve simply is ordered to move funds from the account of one customer's bank to the bank of the dealer, or vice versa. Even the physical transfer of securities is simplified by the availability of safe-keeping facilities in New York City banks, so that no nationwide shipping of negotiable securities need take place. The bulk of the transactions in U.S. government and federal agency securities among the large banks, the government securities dealers, and the Federal Reserve banks is now handled through a telegraphic arrangement and a book-entry custody system operated by the Federal Reserve Bank of New York. Almost all marketable government securities, and most of the agency securities as well, exist only in

[2]For details, see Wallace H. Duncan, "Treasury Bill Futures—Opportunities and Pitfalls," *Review,* Federal Reserve Bank of Dallas (July 1977), and "Hedging Interest Rate Fluctuations," *Business Conditions,* Federal Reserve Bank of Chicago (April 1976). The futures market in certificates issued by the Government National Mortgage Association ("Ginnie Mae") is located on the Chicago Board of Trade, while the market in Treasury bills was developed on the International Monetary Market, a division of the Chicago Mercantile Exchange. Other futures markets were established in 1977 for 90-day commercial paper and 1-year Treasury bills, 4-year Treasury notes, as well as long-term Treasury bonds.

[3]Joseph Scherer, "Institutional Investors in the Government Securities Market," in Joint Treasury–Federal Reserve Study of the U.S. Government Securities Market, *Staff Studies,* Part 1 (1970), pp. 59–60.

book-entry form. This transfer and custody system has greatly reduced the cost and risk of physical handling and has increased the speed with which transactions are completed.

## Changes in the Mix of Money Market Instruments

The New York money market today, as thirty years ago, continues to be dominated by federal government obligations (Table 20-1), but both the mix and the maturity range of these and other money market instruments have changed drastically since the end of World War II. Thus, in 1946, Treasury bills and other short-term government securities were practically the only instruments available in the money market. Negotiable time certificates of deposits issued by commercial banks were nonexistent, the Federal Funds market was still in an embryonic state, and the amounts outstanding of bankers' acceptances and commercial paper were minute.

Since then, the volume of short-term Treasury obligations has continued to increase, both in absolute terms and relative to long-term governments. Short-term marketable government securities rose about 80 percent between 1946 and 1968 and more than doubled in the following decade; they now represent approximately half the volume of all marketable governments, compared to one-third in

**Table 20-1  Major Money Market Instruments Outstanding,[a] End of 1946, 1968, and 1978 (in billions of dollars)**

|  | 1946 | 1968 | 1978 |
|---|---|---|---|
| Federal government marketable securities | $60.5 | $108.6 | $228.5 |
| Bankers' time certificates of deposit[b] | — | 23.5 | 97.0 |
| Bankers' acceptances | 0.2 | 4.4 | 33.7 |
| Commercial and finance company paper | 0.6 | 20.5 | 83.7 |
| Security credits to brokers and dealers by banks | 1.5 | 6.4 | 11.0 |
| Federal Funds and RPs | — | 6.7 | 41.3[c] |

[a] Instruments with maturities under one year.
[b] Certificates of deposit issued by large banks in denominations of $100,000 or more.
[c] Federal Funds sold and securities resale agreement as reported by all insured commercial banks as of September 30, 1978.

Sources: Board of Governors of the Federal Reserve System, *Flow of Funds Accounts*; and *Federal Reserve Bulletin*.

1946. Consequently, the *average* maturity of the federal government's marketable debt held by private investors of more than $356.5 billion has fallen from over four years at the end of 1968 to about three years in 1978. This has been a result of the need to finance the large federal budget deficits in the 1970s and the statutory limit on the coupon rate for longer-term Treasury securities.[4] Consequently, most of the increase in government debt over the last three decades has taken place in shorter maturities.

While the money market continues to be dominated by federal government obligations, the *rate of growth* in other money market instruments has surpassed even that of short-term governments during this period. Thus, commercial paper has increased tremendously, primarily because of the growth in the short-term debt of finance companies and, in recent years, of bank holding companies. Also, since the early 1960s, commercial banks have issued sizable amounts of negotiable certificates of deposits to compete for funds supplied by the nonfinancial business sector; and a very active Federal Funds market has evolved in which commercial banks can make marginal adjustments of their liquidity position without necessarily resorting to the discount window of the Federal Reserve. At the same time, the maturity range of near-money instruments has widened. For example, finance companies offer commercial paper that matures on any day specified by the purchaser (the lender), from "over-the-weekend" paper to paper with a maximum maturity of 270 days.[5] Also, in recent years, there have been nearly one hundred different

[4] The Public Debt Act of 1942 prescribed a limit of 4¼ percent on the coupon rate for Treasury bonds but left the Treasury the discretion to sell bills, certificates, and notes at any price or rate. The statutory 4¼ percent limit has been modified repeatedly by Congress in recent years. In 1967, for example, Congress lengthened the maximum maturity of notes from five to seven years. Since notes are not subject to the 4¼ percent ceiling, this in effect permitted the Treasury freely to sell securities of up to seven years' maturity. The maximum maturity of notes was further extended to ten years in 1976. Also, in 1971 the Treasury was authorized to issue up to $10 billion in bonds exempt from any interest rate limitation; this was raised to $12 billion in 1976.

[5] Under the Securities Act of 1933, paper maturing beyond 270 days must be registered with the Securities and Exchange Commission (SEC), which effectively limits the maturity of commercial paper to 270 days or less.

short-term government and government-agency obligations available daily, all maturing within one year and having little or no credit risk. Many of the short-term notes issued by different government-sponsored agencies resemble private commercial paper, and some notes are placed through dealers, like some of the commercial paper issued.

Despite these vast changes in the volume and composition of short-term debt instruments, the government sector has continued to dominate not only the *stock* of outstanding securities but also the *flows* of funds in the money market in most years (Table 20-2). Notice that the annual changes in net new issues (that is, net of repayment) of government and other money-market instruments can be substantial. Thus, the net swing of federal government marketable securities was more than $25 billion and that of bankers' time certificates of deposit was a huge $38.6 billion between 1974 and 1975.

Let us now turn to a brief survey of the major actors in the money market: the suppliers and users of funds. Following this review, we can discuss in some detail the instruments used in the market before studying the role of money market dealers and assessing the efficiency of the money market in the final sections of the chapter.

## Principal Suppliers and Users of Funds

### Commercial Banks

Commercial banks look to the money market both as a repository for their secondary reserves and as a place to raise additional funds to meet a decline in deposits or an increase in loan demand. All banks now have reserves in the form of cash in vault and deposit balances at the Federal Reserve as required by law. However, these primary reserves must be maintained behind the banks' deposits; when deposits decline, the banks can utilize only that portion of their primary reserves that initially backed the individual deposit to help meet the funds outflow. Thus, if the reserve requirement is 12 percent, on the average, for demand deposits and a bank loses $100 of deposits, only the $12 behind the $100 of deposits are freed to help meet the outflow. The remaining $88 must come from some other source, and often this source is a secondary reserve of

short-term securities, which can be sold quickly for cash with little risk of capital loss. Similarly, if loan demands increase, a bank needs to have liquid funds available to meet these requests. Rather than keep funds in non–interest-yielding cash, banks hold them in money-market instruments. Consequently, the secondary reserves of banks become a prime source of funds for the money market; they are held mainly in the form of short-term governments, and especially in Treasury bills.

The relative importance of commercial banks as holders of Treasury bills and other short-term government debt declined sharply during the 1960s and 1970s. In 1946 the banking system was primarily a government-financing sector with large holdings of highly liquid federal debt;[6] as business and household demands on commercial banks increased during the prosperous postwar years, though, the banks' relative holdings of government securities declined in favor of higher-yielding primary securities issued by the business and household sectors.

### Nonfinancial Business Sector

Corporations may hold liquid assets in the form of money market instruments for several reasons. First, funds that are now available but will have to be disbursed at some future time, such as on dividends or tax dates, are frequently placed in money market obligations. Second, funds obtained from the sale of long-term obligations are frequently put into money market instruments until the necessary investment expenditures associated with the sale of such obligations take place. In fact, this constitutes one of the several direct links between the capital market, in which the corporate securities have been floated, and the money market, in which the proceeds of the security issue are temporarily placed. Third, corporations keep precautionary balances in short-term money-market paper. These balances are then available in those cases where emergency needs for funds develop or where unexpected opportunities arise for which funds are necessary.

[6]At that time, the government yield curve was pegged at levels ranging from three-eighths of 1 percent for Treasury bills with 91-day maturity to 2½ percent for the longest-dated securities. Thus, bank holdings of government debt were, in fact, equivalent to interest-bearing excess reserves.

**Table 20-2   Flow of Funds in the Money Market, 1974–1978[a] (in billions of dollars)**

|  | 1974 | 1975 | 1976 | 1977 | 1978 |
|---|---|---|---|---|---|
| Federal government marketable securities[b] | $ 3.1 | $28.5 | $36.1 | $ 9.6 | $18.1 |
| Bankers' time certificates of deposit | 18.4 | (14.3) | (13.6) | 9.0 | 10.8 |
| Bankers' acceptances | 9.6 | 0.6 | 4.5 | 2.9 | 8.3 |
| Commercial and finance company paper[c] | 7.9 | (1.8) | 3.6 | 12.1 | 18.6 |
| Security credit to brokers and dealers[d] | (1.9) | 2.2 | 5.6 | 1.0 | 2.7 |
| Security RPs by banks | (2.2) | 0.2 | 2.3 | 2.2 | 7.5 |
| Short-term state and local government paper | 2.4 | (3.0) | (3.8) | 1.4 | 3.2 |

[a]Net new issues of money market instruments with maturities under one year.
[b]Held by private investors (transition quarter included in 1977).
[c]Including paper issued by bank holding companies and real estate investment trusts (REITs).
[d]Funds made available by commercial banks and foreign bank agencies.

Sources: Board of Governors of the Federal Reserve System, *Flow of Funds Accounts*; *Federal Reserve Bulletin*; *Treasury Bulletin*.

## Nonbank Financial Intermediaries

Insurance companies, savings banks, savings and loan associations, pension funds, and other nonbank financial intermediaries hold some money market instruments to meet either predictable future payouts or unexpected cash needs. In addition, these institutions will at times purchase money market instruments when they expect future increases in long-term rates. Should these higher rates (lower bond prices) materialize, the nonbank financial intermediaries will realize better long-term investment results by keeping investable funds temporarily in short-term securities.

## State and Local Governments

This sector is both a borrower from and a lender to the money market. Local municipalities and some state governments borrow directly through short-term tax-exempt notes issued in anticipation of revenue from taxes or proceeds of long-term bond issues and indirectly through so-called Project Notes sold regularly by municipal agencies related to urban renewal and local housing. State and local governments also invest in the money market for some of the same reasons as do other suppliers of short-term funds; for example, tax receipts and proceeds from the sale of state and municipal bonds frequently are not needed for immediate disbursements and, consequently, are temporarily placed in highly liquid earning assets.

## Rest of the World

The United States is a net long-term lender to the rest of the world, but it is a net borrower of short-term funds from foreigners.[7] Foreign governments and central banks hold interest-earning dollar assets as well as demand deposits. Nonofficial (nongovernmental) foreign suppliers of funds to the New York money market can sell their dollar claims to their own central bank, but they frequently prefer to retain their dollar-earning assets since they may later need dollar exchange for expenditures on American goods and services or because they are convinced that American securities offer a better combination of risklessness, income, and liquidity than do local money market obligations.

Both official and nonofficial foreign earners of dollar exchange hold large claims on the United States in the form of non–interest-earning commercial bank demand deposits, partly as working balances and partly because these funds can be redeposited through the channels of the Eurodollar market at higher interest rates than comparable yields on U.S. Treasury bills or other money market paper.

The American money market is a reserve center in which foreign governments and central banks hold their external reserves. These reserves may initially have been earned in Deutsche marks, French francs, or English pounds and subsequently

[7]In this connection, see Chapter 18.

exchanged for American dollars for financial investment in American money market instruments. Most of the foreign official money market investments in the United States are in short-term government securities and bankers' acceptances; whereas foreign commercial banks and nonfinancial corporations tend to invest in negotiable time certificates of deposit and commercial paper, including finance company paper.

### The Federal Reserve System

Finally, the Federal Reserve holds a large volume of short-term governments to facilitate its open-market operations. Indeed, the Federal Reserve is the largest single holder of short-term federal debt, reflecting its substantial role in the money market. The Federal Reserve System is responsible for maintaining an orderly money market in which funds are shifted smoothly and changes in the allocation of the market's instruments take place without major yield upsets. To accomplish this, the Federal Reserve Bank of New York carries out defensive or compensating open-market operations, frequently buying and selling Treasury bills simultaneously but dealing differently with various subsectors of the market. The Federal Reserve may also wish to exert pressure on the money market in order to achieve a desired impact on the domestic economy. In this case, it undertakes dynamic open-market operations, some of which involve massive intervention through purchase or sale of Treasury bills. The Federal Reserve, consequently, must possess a large inventory of short-term governments to accomplish both its compensating and its dynamic open-market role.

### Some Users of Money Market Funds

While money market lenders generally are of one mind, namely to gain some income on surplus funds while retaining sufficient liquidity for future needs, money market borrowers have various motives for tapping the market. For example, some of the funds drawn out of the money market by short-term borrowers are, in turn, used for long-term lending. Thus, large commercial banks began selling negotiable time certificates of deposit (CDs) in 1961 to raise additional funds. They did this because they considered the marginal cost of issuing the securi-

ties to be well below the rates of return that could be earned from investing these funds in the long-term markets. The banks were borrowing short and lending long and, therefore, presumably incurring an illiquidity risk in order to gain a favorable yield spread. However, they believed that they would always be able to obtain fresh short-term funds as outstanding CDs matured, even if higher rates had to be offered, and for this reason they believed that this particular form of financial intermediation actually could be carried on without undue risk of a liquidity crisis.

Other money market borrowers, such as the Treasury and some finance companies, borrow in the money market because their need for funds at the time (or at least for some of their funds) can be met more cheaply or easily in this market than in the capital market. These borrowers, therefore, alternate between the money market and the capital markets; for them there is no special reason to remain money market borrowers when yield and availability considerations move in favor of the longer-term market.

There are also borrowers whose need for funds vary considerably on a daily basis and who, therefore, must borrow in the money market. Such borrowers include commercial banks, which borrow the excess reserves of other banks in the Federal Funds market to meet temporary reserve deficiencies. Also, dealers in equities and debt instruments, including government securities dealers, who have frequent and often wide fluctuations in their securities positions, use the money market as a source of funds on a daily basis.

Finally, there are borrowers, notably the users of the bankers' acceptance market, whose need for funds is discontinuous and lasts for a period longer than a day or week but less than a year. This may be the time required to ship coffee from Brazil to New York and sell it in the coffee market. The money market is the natural source of short-term finance for such borrowers.

Thus, the reasons for borrowing funds from the money market are more varied in nature than are the reasons for supplying funds. Yet the money market operates under fairly fixed ground rules because the suppliers of funds are relatively uniform in motivation. Since risklessness and liquidity are of prime importance to money market investors, borrowers tend to tailor their obligations as much

**Table 20-3  Major Money Market Instruments Outstanding, 1967–1978 (in billions of dollars)**

| Year | Treasury Bills | Other U.S. Governments Less Than One Year | Certificates of Deposits[a] | Commercial Paper — Finance Paper[b] Dealer Placed | Commercial Paper — Finance Paper[b] Directly Placed | Nonfinancial Companies | Accept-ances | Brokers' Loans[c] | Federal Funds[d] |
|------|------|------|------|------|------|------|------|------|------|
| 1967 | 69.9 | 35.5 | 20.3 | 2.8 | 12.2 | 2.1 | 4.3 | 9.1 | 0.7 |
| 1968 | 75.0 | 33.6 | 23.5 | 4.4 | 14.0 | 2.8 | 4.4 | 12.0 | 1.2 |
| 1969 | 80.6 | 37.6 | 10.9 | 6.5 | 20.7 | 5.4 | 5.5 | 6.5 | 3.8 |
| 1970 | 87.9 | 35.5 | 26.1 | 5.5 | 20.4 | 7.1 | 7.1 | 7.2 | 1.6 |
| 1971 | 97.5 | 21.6 | 34.8 | 5.3 | 20.6 | 6.2 | 7.9 | 9.8 | 2.6 |
| 1972 | 103.9 | 26.6 | 44.5 | 5.7 | 22.1 | 7.0 | 6.9 | 13.5 | 5.1 |
| 1973 | 107.8 | 33.8 | 64.5 | 5.5 | 27.2 | 8.4 | 8.9 | 5.1 | 12.0 |
| 1974 | 119.7 | 28.3 | 93.0 | 4.6 | 31.8 | 12.7 | 18.5 | 7.6 | 9.8 |
| 1975 | 157.5 | 42.2 | 82.9 | 6.2 | 31.3 | 10.9 | 18.7 | 10.1 | 10.2 |
| 1976 | 164.0 | 47.0 | 65.9 | 7.3 | 32.5 | 13.3 | 22.5 | 11.4 | 19.2 |
| 1977 | 161.1 | 69.6 | 77.4 | 8.9 | 40.4 | 15.7 | 25.5 | 11.5 | 19.7 |
| 1978 | 161.7 | 66.8 | 100.0 | 12.3 | 51.6 | 19.7 | 33.7 | 11.0 | 15.1 |

[a]Negotiable certificates of deposits issued by large banks in denominations of $100,000 or more.
[b]Paper issued by financial companies, such as sales, personal, and mortgage finance companies; factoring, finance leasing, and other business lending companies; and paper issued by bank holding companies (bank-related paper).
[c]Loans made by banks to brokers and dealers for purchasing and carrying securities.
[d]Net purchases by leading money market banks.

Sources: Board of Governors of the Federal Reserve System, *Flow of Funds Accounts*; *Federal Reserve Bulletin,* various issues; and U.S. Department of the Treasury, *Bulletin,* various issues.

as possible to fit investor preferences. And, since the substitutability of practically all types of money market obligations is high from the point of view of risk—there is little difference between, say, bank CDs and finance company paper—money market borrowers tend to concentrate on the maturity dimension of their debt instruments. With this in mind, let us now turn to a brief description and analysis of the major money market instruments. (Amounts of the major instruments outstanding at year-end for the period 1967–1978 may be found in Table 20-3.[8])

## Money Market Instruments

### Government Obligations

These securities are the direct debt of the U.S. Treasury. They are sold to help finance the deficit, or gap, between the Treasury's expenditures and its receipts from taxes and other sources. Short-

term money market instruments may be issued by the Treasury to finance short-term deficits arising from lack of perfect synchronization between the time when specific expenditures are made and the dates when tax collections to cover these expenditures take place. In addition, short-term Treasury securities finance a large part of the permanent public debt, in which case maturing money market obligations are "rolled over," or refunded, with new short-term borrowing.

The basic debt instruments of the U.S. Treasury are bills, notes, and bonds. By far the most important single instrument is the Treasury bill, which is issued in a variety of maturities and denominations. Treasury bills amount to about 40 percent of total U.S. government marketable debt, are the most widely held liquid instruments, and are the principal securities used in Treasury and Federal Reserve debt management and in the execution of monetary policy through open-market operations. Bills with maturities of 91 days (13 weeks) and 182

[8]For a more detailed description of the various instruments, see First Boston Corporation, *Handbook of Securities of the United States Government and Federal Agencies and Related Money Market Instruments,* 28th ed., New York, 1978; Timothy Q. Cook, *Instruments of the Money Market,* 4th ed., Federal Reserve Bank of

Richmond, Richmond, Va., 1977; William A. Hawk, *The U.S. Government Securities Market,* Harris Trust & Savings Bank, Chicago, 1974; and Federal Reserve Bank of Cleveland, *Money Market Instruments,* 3rd ed., 1970.

days (26 weeks) are auctioned weekly, and an auction of 365-day (52 weeks) bills is held once a month. Short-term cash-management bills, also known as Federal Funds bills, with maturities usually ranging from 9 to 20 days were first introduced in 1975. These cash-management bills are used to bridge temporary cash shortfalls without resorting to more costly longer-term borrowing (91-day bills, for example) or to borrowing from the Federal Reserve, which was often done in the past.

Treasury bills are issued at a discount in five denominations ranging from $10,000 to $1 million. Bids, or tenders, in the weekly auctions may be on a competitive or noncompetitive basis. Competitive tenders are made by large investors, such as the large commercial banks, which are in close contact with the money market. Small investors—individuals, nonfinancial businesses, and smaller financial institutions—normally make noncompetitive bids. These tenders are accepted in full (usually up to $500,000) at the average price; only a varying proportion of the competitive bids is accepted.[9] Thus, the small investors submitting noncompetitive tenders avoid the risk of bidding too low and thereby losing their chance to buy; they also avoid the risk of bidding too high for bills that could have been acquired at a lower price. Most tenders received each week are noncompetitive, although the dollar volume of competitive bids is far greater.

While Treasury bills, including cash-management bills, are sold at a discount that establishes the yield to maturity, all other marketable Treasury obligations are coupon issues. These include Treasury notes with maturities from one to ten years and Treasury bonds with maturities of more than ten years.[10] The Treasury regularly issues 2-year, 4-year, and 5-year notes, which are typically held by commercial banks outside the money-market centers. Treasury bills are, of course, strictly money market instruments, but even notes and bonds become money market obligations when they have only a year or less until redemption. In

recent years, for example, one-fourth of the outstanding note issues have had a remaining maturity of one year or less.

Since bills, notes, and bonds are general obligations of the U.S. government, and since the federal government has the lowest credit risk (that is, it has no risk of default) of all participants in the money market, its obligations offer a lower yield to the investor than do other securities of comparable maturity. Yield spreads, or differentials, among money instruments are, therefore, generally measured in terms of the going rates on short-term Treasury securities.

### Negotiable Time Certificates of Deposit

Generally known as CDs, these are short-term securities with specific maturity dates and coupon yields issued by commercial banks to tap surplus funds available in the money market. The regulatory authorities consider them to be bank time deposits and to rank equally with all other bank deposits as a claim on bank assets in case of liquidation or default. They are called "negotiable" certificates because they can be sold to another investor (negotiated) before their maturity date.

Commercial banks have been extremely successful in selling CDs.[11] At the end of 1963, or only two years after the first certificates were issued, the volume of CDs outstanding was second only to short-term Treasury securities in the money market. CDs continued to grow rapidly during the 1960s and the early 1970s, except in years when interest rate ceilings under the Federal Reserve's Regulation Q prevented the banks from competing effectively with other money market instruments. However, all such interest rate limitations were suspended in 1973, and the volume of outstanding

---

[9]See Table 20-6.

[10]Treasury *certificates of indebtedness* with maturities of less than one year have not been issued since the mid-1960s; and the so-called *tax-anticipation bills* (TABs), designed to attract funds that corporations accrue for income tax purposes, were discontinued in late 1974. See Margaret E. Bedford, "Recent Developments in Treasury Financing Techniques," *Monthly Review,* Federal Reserve Bank of Kansas City (July-August 1977).

[11]The bank certificate of deposit has existed in various forms for decades and has been used by banks in many countries to attract time deposits. However, the *negotiable* bank certificate of deposit is an American financial innovation—one that has been emulated abroad. The transfer of this new financial technology was initially made by London branches of American banks which began to issue dollar-denominated certificates to their customers in the mid-1960s. They were quickly followed by some of the overseas and foreign banks, and a few years later the British banks started to issue sterling-denominated certificates.

CDs had increased to $100 billion by the end of 1978.[12]

The denominations of negotiable CDs range from $100,000 to several millions of dollars, depending on the size of both the issuing bank and the liquidity needs of the customer. The normal round-lot trading unit is $1 million in the secondary market, where the small denominations are not easily traded. Maturities range from 30 days to 18 months, but most maturities are less than 4 months. Certificates are often dated so that they mature on days when corporate taxes or dividends have to be paid. The interest rate paid on the certificate's par value will vary depending on the size of the issuing bank, the denomination of the certificate, and the length of time until maturity.

The demand for bank certificates of deposit is dominated by nonfinancial corporations. This is not surprising since, from the beginning, the CD was designed to attract corporate liquid balances in competition with other money market instruments. Corporate treasurers often keep their holdings of CDs in a fairly constant relationship to their investment in short-term government securities; frequent changes in corporate cash requirements are then adjusted through their holdings of Treasury bills, in which there is a very active secondary market with low transaction costs, while second-line liquidity requirements are met through the certificate market. Other major investors include state governments and agencies, commercial banks, foreign central banks and governments, some wealthy individuals, and a number of institutional investors, such as mutual funds, insurance companies, and dealers who make a market in CDs and, therefore, accumulate inventories of certificates.

## Bankers' Acceptances

Bankers' acceptances are short-term business liabilities with maturities of 30–270 days, employed to finance the shipment of commodities between countries as well as the shipment of some specific goods within the United States. Such liabilities be-

come bankers' acceptances when the debt instrument is endorsed by a bank of stature, which, in turn, makes the bank primarily liable for payment on maturity. This bank endorsement adds sufficient credit quality to the paper to make it generally acceptable as a prime money market instrument that can be sold immediately in the money market.

Frequently, however, the acceptance-creating bank will purchase (discount) its own acceptance and thus become the ultimate investor financing the transaction.[13] In this case the bank earns not only the acceptance commission but also the discount. In addition, the bank holds a financial claim that, unlike a conventional loan, is highly marketable and can be sold to an acceptance dealer at any time.[14] For this reason, acceptances purchased by banks form part of the banks' secondary liquidity reserves.

While commercial banks are major investors in bankers' acceptances, more than half of the volume outstanding is held by nonbank financial institutions, nonfinancial corporations, and foreign central banks. To these investors, acceptances represent a first-rate money market instrument and one of the safest forms of short-term investment.

The use of acceptance financing grew dramatically in the 1970s, and the volume of outstanding bankers' acceptances increased from a range of $5–$7 billion during 1970 to more than $40 billion at the end of 1979. This has been closely associated with the growth of foreign trade and, in particular, with the growth of American acceptance financing of trade between foreign countries. These "third-country" acceptances now represent well over 55 percent of the total. For example, much of Japan's foreign trade with countries other than the United States is denominated in U.S. dollars and financed

[12]Issued in denominations of $100,000 or more by large commercial banks reporting weekly to the Federal Reserve. See Board of Governors of the Federal Reserve System, *Federal Reserve Bulletin*, Washington, D.C., Table 1.30: "Large Weekly Reporting Commercial Banks."

[13]More than 80 percent of the acceptance portfolios of banks engaged in the acceptance business consists of their own acceptances. Such bills held by accepting banks amounted to 23 percent of all acceptances outstanding at the end of 1978.

[14]Moreover, most acceptances are eligible for rediscount or for purchase from the Federal Reserve under the rules contained in Regulations A, D, and H of the Board of Governors of the Federal Reserve System. See Ralph T. Helfrich, "Trading in Bankers' Acceptances: A View from the Acceptance Desk of the Federal Reserve Bank of New York," *Monthly Review*, Federal Reserve Bank of New York (February 1976). See also Jack L. Hervey, "Bankers' Acceptances," *Business Conditions*, Federal Reserve Bank of Chicago (May 1976).

by drafts accepted by American banks, mostly located in New York City or in San Francisco. This is, of course, yet another indication of the increasing internationalization of the U.S. money market.

## Commercial Paper

Commercial paper[15] consists of unsecured promissory notes issued by financial and industrial companies to raise short-term funds from money-market lenders. This paper is guaranteed solely by the name of the borrowing firm and is not backed by the pledge of any specific assets. However, borrowers generally maintain back-up lines of credit with banks equal to the amount of paper outstanding. Since, in addition, only companies of unquestionable credit standing are able to sell their paper in the money market, commercial paper is considered a high-quality money market instrument.

Among the principal borrowers in this segment of the money market are the leading *sales finance companies*, such as General Motors Acceptance Corporation and CIT Financial Corporation, which continually issue *finance company paper* to raise funds in order to lend to instalment credit borrowers at higher interest rates. All of this paper is sold directly by the borrower to the money-market investor through the borrower's own market organization, thus circumventing the commercial-paper dealers. This arrangement is less costly to the borrower with a large amount of paper outstanding and almost daily issuance of new paper. Finance company paper is commonly sold on a discount basis, with maturities ranging from 3 to 270 days but frequently tailored to the lenders' specifications. Most paper has an initial maturity of 60 days or less. In addition to the approximately forty large finance companies, which account for practically all of the directly placed paper, smaller sales finance, personal loan, and business finance companies sell their notes through commercial-paper dealers who then, in the majority of cases, assume the responsibility for placing the notes with ultimate investors.[16]

While the finance companies dominate the commercial-paper market, both in terms of directly placed and dealer-placed paper,[17] a number of industrial firms—typically large, highly regarded corporations in textiles and food-manufacturing industries, construction, services, wholesale and retail trade—sell what is sometimes referred to as *industrial paper* to help finance special or seasonal needs for funds. Such paper is sold through commercial-paper dealers rather than directly to the investor, with issuance on a discount basis and maturities ranging usually from 3 to 120 days. While the dealer does not formally guarantee the paper, its handling of the paper nevertheless amounts to a de facto guarantee that the borrower possesses a very high credit rating.[18] However, the collapse of the Penn Central in June 1970, at a time when this huge transportation company had nearly $100 million worth of commercial paper outstanding, significantly influenced investor attitudes. Instead of merely relying on implicit dealer guarantees for dealer-placed paper, investors became much more involved in scrutinizing the financial soundness of the potential borrowers. Another consequence of the Penn Central collapse was to reduce the relative importance of dealer-placed paper issued by smaller and less well-known companies.

The shift to larger issuing firms of commercial paper has been accompanied by the emergence of

---

[15] For additional discussion of commercial paper, see Evelyn M. Hurley, "The Commercial Paper Market," *Federal Reserve Bulletin,* Board of Governors of the Federal Reserve System, Washington, D.C. (June 1977).

[16] While the outright sale of notes to the dealer is the most common method of placing paper indirectly in the market, some borrowers use an arrangement often referred to as "bought as sold"; the borrowing firm receives the proceeds of the sale, minus dealer commission, only after the sale has been made. Under this arrangement the market risk is shifted from the dealer to the borrower.

[17] Finance company paper, including paper placed through dealers, accounts for approximately 75 percent of the volume of outstanding paper. More than 80 percent of all finance paper is placed directly. Board of Governors of the Federal Reserve System, *Federal Reserve Bulletin,* Washington, D.C., Table 1.33.

[18] Moody's Investors Service, Standard & Poor's Corporation, and Fitch Investors Service together rate over 700 issuers of commercial paper. Many borrowers are rated by two services, which makes their paper more readily acceptable by dealers—who are required, under a Securities and Exchange Commission ruling of July 1977, to write down their inventory value of commercial paper issued by borrowers who are rated by only one of the three services. Hurley, "The Commercial Paper Market," 529. Paper with a given rating (say, P-1, A-1, or F-1) is sold at a yield that, in part, depends on the rating of the issuer's long-term bonds.

public utilities and bank holding companies as large-scale borrowers in this market. Public utilities were attracted to the market during periods characterized by large differences between the cost of bank credit—the traditional source of short-term borrowing—and cost of funds raised in the commercial-paper market. Even when the cost of bank funds declined as credit availability eased, these utilities often remained in the commercial-paper market in order to preserve investor contacts. Bank holding companies entered the commercial-paper market in the late 1960s when their bank subsidiaries encountered increasing difficulties in selling certificates of deposit because of restrictive rate ceilings on these deposits under Federal Reserve Regulation Q. However, after the Federal Reserve Board imposed reserve requirements on funds raised by banks and affiliates in the commercial-paper market (which raised the effective cost of such borrowing) and subsequently removed Regulation Q ceilings on large denomination CDs, the participation of bank holding companies in the commercial-paper market leveled off. By the end of 1978, the so-called bank-related paper amounted to approximately $16 billion, or about 20 percent of all commercial paper outstanding.

## Federal Agency Securities

Several government-sponsored agencies in recent years have issued short-term notes that in many respects resemble commercial paper. Such notes typically are issued through dealers, mostly investment banking houses, which are also active in the commercial-paper market. These federal government-sponsored agencies were established by the U.S. Congress to undertake various types of financing without tapping the public treasury. In order to do so, the agencies have been given the power to borrow money by issuing securities, generally under the authority of an act of Congress. The Treasury rarely guarantees such agency securities directly; however, these securities are highly acceptable and marketable for several reasons, not least because many are exempt from state, municipal, and local income taxes and a few are even exempt from federal income tax. Nevertheless, agency securities must offer a higher yield than direct Treasury debt of the same maturity to find money-market buyers, partly because these

securities are not general obligations of the Treasury.

The main agency borrowing institutions are five privately owned, government-sponsored corporations, two of which are primarily engaged in providing funds for the mortgage and home-building markets, while the other three corporations provide farm credit. The *Federal National Mortgage Association* (Fannie Mae) issues short-term discount notes tailored to the maturity needs of investors in much the same fashion as commercial paper, and with maturities ranging from 30 to 270 days. These discount notes are made attractive to individual investors as well as to institutions by their denominations from $5,000 to $1 million.

The *Federal Home Loan Bank System,* consisting of twelve Federal Home Loan banks, issues, in addition to long-term bonds, coupon notes with maturities up to one year, which appeal to both individual and institutional investors. It also issues consolidated discount notes with maturities from 30 to 360 days at the discretion of the investor. The latter are similar to commercial paper and attract mostly institutional investors.

The *Farm Credit System* embraces thirty-seven institutions[19] engaged in long-term as well as seasonal lending to farmers, stockmen, and cooperative associations. The Farm Credit System as a whole sells consolidated discount notes with maturities from 5 to 150 days. These notes are similar to those issued by the Federal Home Loan Bank System and compete with regular commercial paper for the attention of institutional investors. They provide interim finance between bond issues and supplemental borrowing from other short-term sources such as commercial banks.[20]

[19]Twelve Federal Land Banks, twelve Federal Intermediate Credit Banks, twelve Banks for Cooperatives, and a Central Bank for Cooperatives.

[20]In addition to government-*sponsored* corporations, which normally are privately owned, some federally *owned* agencies have access to the money market for interim financing. For example, Public Housing and Urban Renewal Project Notes are regularly issued in maturities varying from 3 to 12 months. These notes are exempted not only from state and local taxes but also from federal income tax, and they are available in denominations of $1,000 and up. Most of these federally owned agencies, such as the Export-Import Bank, the Postal Service, the Tennessee Valley Authority, and the U.S. Railway Association, now obtain most of their funds from the Federal Financing Bank, which was established in

## Short-Term Tax-Exempt Securities

Short-term tax-exempt securities are general obligations of the issuing state and municipal governments and are typically tax or revenue anticipation notes (TANs or RANs). Frequently, they are sold in anticipation of proceeds of long-term bond issues (BANs) under borrowing authority granted by the voters. Notes may vary in maturity from a few days to a year, but most notes sold at competitive bidding have 6-month and 1-year maturities.

The tax-exempt feature of state and local government securities makes them attractive investments for nonfinancial corporations and commercial banks, which are taxed at the standard corporate rate. In addition, a high degree of marketability is assured by an active secondary market comparable to the market for short-term federal agency securities. In the case of tax or revenue and bond anticipation notes, the general credit standing of the issuing local government is rated by Moody's, and the rating determines the yield basis on which new notes are sold.

## Federal Funds[21]

Transactions in the Federal Funds market take place between banks and involve the purchase (borrowing) or sale (lending) of bank reserves on deposit at Federal Reserve banks. The demand for Federal Funds comes from banks, which on any given day may need temporary reserves to meet their reserve requirements; the supply of Federal Funds arises because other banks on the same day may have reserves in excess of their requirements. The transactions are negotiated either directly between participating banks or through several Federal Funds brokers in New York City operating to bring together the borrowers and lenders of funds.

The bank with excess reserves instructs its Federal Reserve bank to transfer the funds from its reserve account to the account of the borrowing bank, which, in turn, gives the lending bank its own check plus one day's interest for the funds. The account of the lending bank is debited and that of the borrowing bank is credited on the day of the loan; on the following day, the transaction is automatically reversed as the borrowing bank's check is cleared. Most transactions in the Federal Funds market are such one-day, unsecured, so-called straight transactions; *secured* one-day Federal Funds transactions are used mostly by smaller banks and are, in dollar volume, much less important. In a transaction of this type, the bank purchasing (borrowing) Federal Funds places U.S. government securities in a custody account for the seller (lender) for one day until the funds are repaid.[22]

A large volume of reserves is moved about daily within the banking system by means of the Federal Funds market. For example, the group of forty-six major banks reporting Federal Funds transactions to the Federal Reserve System on a daily basis showed average *daily* net interbank transactions of $15 to $25 billion during 1978.[23]

The Federal Funds rate fluctuates frequently and widely, and its volatility became more pronounced in the 1970s. In the very short run, it often exhibits exaggerated swings on those days when the reserve period for banks ends and banks with excess reserves immediately turn to the Federal Funds market as lenders.[24] Over the longer run, fluctuations in the Federal Funds rate are highly correlated with

---

1974 to consolidate the financing of a variety of federal agencies and other borrowers whose obligations are guaranteed by the federal government. For further discussion of the lending agencies sponsored or owned by the federal government, see Chapter 11.

[21]See Parker B. Willis, *A Study of the Market for Federal Funds,* prepared for the Steering Committee for a Fundamental Reappraisal of the Discount Mechanism Appointed by the Board of Governors of the Federal Reserve System, Washington, D.C., 1967. See also C. M. Lucas, M. T. Jones, and T. B. Thurston, "Federal Funds and Repurchase Agreements," *Quarterly Review,* Federal Reserve Bank of New York (Summer 1977).

[22]The closely related repurchase agreement is typically used in Federal Funds transactions with government securities dealers. See the following section for further discussion.

[23]Net interbank transactions are the difference between gross purchases and gross sales. For the forty-six large member banks, gross purchases typically exceed gross sales by a factor of three or four. The data are weekly averages of *daily* figures and are published in the *Federal Reserve Bulletin.*

[24]Required reserves currently are computed on the basis of average daily deposits held during a weekly reserve period two weeks prior to the reporting week. The statement of reporting week runs from Thursday through Wednesday. Excess reserves averaging up to 2 percent of required reserves may be carried forward to the subsequent settlement period. Consequently, banks tend to dispose of their excess reserves at whatever interest they can get at the end of the reserve period, and the Federal Funds rate will often dip sharply on Wednesdays.

other money market rates, such as the 3-month Treasury bill yield, since the Treasury bill and Federal Funds markets are, to some extent, alternative media for adjusting reserve positions and obtaining new funds to meet loan demand. However, the Federal Funds rate tends to be above more often than below the bill rate because the Federal Funds market is superior to the bill market for *quick* adjustment to changes in the individual bank's reserve position. In other words, Treasury bills, while good, are not perfect substitutes for Federal Funds.

## Dealer Loans and Repurchase Agreements

An important but highly specialized function of the money market is to finance the limited number of large dealers in U.S. government securities. This financing takes the form of short-term bank loans, or *call loans,* collateralized by the securities that are being financed[25] and *repurchase agreements* involving the actual sale of securities to the lender by the borrowing dealer who, simultaneously, makes a commitment to repurchase the securities at the same price plus interest.

Call loans are usually arranged on a daily basis, and the bulk of these loans are made by a small number of New York City banks. More important than call loans in the financing of nonbank government securities dealers is the repurchase agreement (sometimes referred to as an RP or RePo). Such contracts, involving the sale of securities (usually other money market instruments) and a simultaneous agreement to repurchase the securities at a future date, are made with nonfinancial corporations as well as with commercial banks. Agreements with fixed maturities may range from one day to several weeks, even months. Some repurchase agreements have no fixed maturity dates and, consequently, are demand obligations similar to call loans; they can be terminated at any time at the option of either the borrower (the securities

dealer) or the lender (for this transaction, generally a bank outside New York City).

Short repurchase agreements are also concluded with the Federal Reserve as part of the System's open-market operations in the government securities market. Such transactions always involve Federal Funds (''immediate'' or same-day money) and provide additional reserves to the market in periods of temporary reserve shortages and relatively large dealer inventories. However, they are designed to provide additional reserves for a limited time only; this makes it unnecessary for the Federal Reserve, with a few days' interval, to buy and sell outright large blocks of securities, which could have an undesirable effect on interest rates and expectations in the money market. When repurchase agreements are used by the Federal Reserve, money-market participants know that the reserve injection will be temporary. The reverse repurchase agreement, or the matched sale-purchase transaction, is also used by the Federal Reserve, in this case to absorb reserves temporarily. The Federal Reserve sells securities to the dealers and concurrently makes a commitment to repurchase the securities at a future date. Both repurchase agreements and matched sale-purchase transactions are always initiated by the Federal Reserve, and the rate is set through competitive bidding by the dealers.[26]

## Government Securities Dealers[27]

As has already been noted, government securities represent the largest single component of the money market, with some thirty government securities dealers forming the hub of this market. They participate in the primary distribution of Treasury obligations and make secondary markets by selling and buying outstanding issues for their own accounts, thereby giving scope and diversity to the whole range of the government securities market. Since practically all the dealers do some trading in the entire spectrum of maturities, ranging from the shortest Treasury bill to the longest gov-

[25]Call loans are also made to dealers in other than U.S. government securities, as well as to brokerage firms, to finance their customers' position of securities purchased or carried on margin. The call-loan market today is a minor segment of the money market, whereas it was the largest and most active component of the money market in the late 1920s when bank loans to brokers and dealers were extensively used to finance transactions at the New York Stock Exchange.

[26]Federal Reserve Bank of New York, *Quarterly Review* (Spring 1977), 41–43.

[27]See *Report* on the Joint Treasury–Federal Reserve Study of the U.S. Government Securities Market, Board of Governors of the Federal Reserve System, Washington, D.C., 1969; and *Staff Studies*—Part 1 (1970), Part 2 (1971), and Part 3 (1973). See also Hawk, *The U.S. Government Securities Market.*

ernment bond, they tend to form a bridge between the money market and the capital market for the government sector. Moreover, since most of the dealers also trade in government agency obligations, corporate securities, mortgages, and other long-term marketable debt, their arbitrage over both the maturity range and the risk spectrum is a key element in adjusting the yield structure in the financial markets to changes in the supply of, and demand for, loanable funds. In other words, dealer arbitrage contributes to the allocational efficiency of the financial markets and, thus, the dealers play an important role in the saving-investment process.

The daily volume of dealer transactions in government securities is large by any standard. In 1978, for example, transactions averaged more than $10 billion per day, while the total market value of sales effected in stocks on all registered securities exchanges in the United States averaged less than $1 billion daily in that year.[28] By far the largest volume of transactions takes place in short maturities, which is not surprising since short-term money market instruments are principally means of holding liquid balances and, consequently, are expected to turn over rapidly. The large transaction volume also reflects the highly elastic conditions in the market for short-term Treasury obligations as compared to the market for long-term governments. The reaction of dealers and others to small price changes on Treasury bills and other money market instruments is quick and massive.

The essence of the dealer function is to clear the market by buying and selling securities for the dealer's own account; the broker, on the other hand, arranges transfers between buyers and sellers. The large government securities dealers are usually ready to sell or buy any amount of short-term Treasury obligations at their quoted asked and bid prices.[29] They may, on the other hand, be reluctant to "stand on their market" (to buy and sell at their quoted bid and ask prices) for large amounts of longer-dated governments for which the market is relatively thin. An individual dealer may not be willing to buy such a large volume of longer-term securities until he or she has disposed of part or all of the offered securities to other dealers or to customers. In this respect, the dealer acts as a broker rather than as a dealer.

In order to perform the dealer function adequately, the government securities dealers hold inventories, or *positions,* of practically all outstanding government maturities as well as many government agency issues and corporate securities. Since the largest volume of transactions takes place in shorter maturities, the dealers need larger inventories of these maturities. Positions tend to be highest when yields are high and securities prices are expected to increase. This is due both to the dealers' stabilizing function in the government securities market—buying at falling and selling at rising prices—and to a speculative element in their portfolio management—taking a long position in anticipation of higher prices in the immediate future.

The average inventory turnover is very high, as might be expected. In 1978, for example, the entire dealer position in government securities turned over nearly four times *daily,* on the average.[30] The turnover ratios for longer maturities generally are much higher than for money market obligations. For example, while securities with less than one year until maturity turned over approximately two and-a-half times a day in 1978, those securities maturing in from one year to five years turned over much more rapidly on the average. The reason for the differences in turnover is, in part, that most dealers will hold only a bare minimum of those securities with the highest price risk. However, it should be noted that the data represent *averages*

[28]Securities and Exchange Commission, *Statistical Bulletin* (February 1978).

[29]Money market quotations are given on a discount or yield basis, while longer-term securities are quoted in prices. For example, a 90-day issue of Treasury bills may be quoted 4.64 "bid" and 4.60 "asked," which means that the dealer is willing to buy 90-day bills at a price that would yield him 4.64 percent for the holding period, and to sell the same bills at a price that would yield 4.60 percent to the buyer. A 4-year Treasury note may be quoted 101.20 "bid" and 101.28 "asked," which means that the dealer is willing to pay 101-20/32nds (equal to

$101.62½ per $100 face value) for such notes and to sell them at 101-28/32nds (equal to 101.87½ per $100 face value). See the discussion of dealer quotations in the following section, "The Efficiency of the Money Market."

[30]In 1978 the average daily transaction volume of dealers in all maturities of government securities was $10.3 billion, and the average daily dealer position in all maturities was $2.6 billion. Board of Governors of the Federal Reserve System, Washington, D.C., *Federal Reserve Bulletin,* various issues, Tables 1.44 and 1.45.

for all major dealers in the government securities market and that the distribution of long-term securities is uneven relative to the distribution of Treasury bills and other short-term governments.[31]

The U.S. government securities dealers are constantly in search for funds to finance their inventory of securities as well as funds for other users.[32] Without extensive borrowing, the bulk of which is on a day-to-day basis, the dealers would be unable to make a market in government securities. Their need for finance varies considerably from one day to the next, within the year, and over the course of the business cycle, depending on the variations in dealer positions. These variations are, of course, very much influenced by the Federal Reserve's open-market operations, and it is partly through the nonbank dealers' search for funds that monetary-policy actions through the open market are transmitted to the banking system and beyond.

More than 95 percent of the dealers' total sources of funds are borrowed. Commercial banks are an important source of funds, accounting for 25 to 50 percent of the total in recent years. Most of bank financing is in the form of collateral loans, which are part of what bankers report as "loans to brokers and dealers"; about half of these loans are made by banks in New York City. Nonfinancial corporations are a major source of funds in years

characterized by large corporate cash balances in search of temporary financial investment. (Corporate sources have been less important recently than they were in the early 1960s.[33]) Most of the nonfinancial corporate funds are obtained under repurchase agreements, which are attractive to corporations because the maturities can be tailored to the corporate payments schedule.

The thirty-odd reporting U.S. government securities dealers are by no means a homogeneous group of financial firms. For the twelve bank dealers the performance of the dealer function in the government securities market is only a part, and not even a major part, of their business. The other dealer firms vary considerably in size and in their emphasis on different types of activities in the financial markets. However, one activity is common to all government dealers: all are engaged in making a market in Treasury bills and other short-term government obligations.

## The Efficiency of the Money Market

Undoubtedly, the short-term market for government obligations is more efficient than any other financial market in the United States. Among other things, an efficient credit market possesses *depth,* with actual and potential orders both above and below the market price; *breadth,* with a large volume of orders coming from widely divergent investor groups; and *resilience,* with orders to buy and sell pouring into the market to take advantage of sharp and unexpected fluctuations in prices or yields. In other words, such a market features highly price-elastic supply and demand conditions; that is, relatively small price changes bring forth a large volume of orders to buy or to sell. While the institutional structure of the government securities market would seem, at first glance, to dispel the notion of market efficiency since it is characterized by a relatively small number of dealer firms with entry closely regulated, in point of fact practically *all* of the thirty-odd government securities dealers are in active competition with each other trading

[31]This may also reflect a higher degree of dealer concentration in longer than in shorter obligations for some dealers. See *Report* of the Joint Treasury–Federal Reserve Study of the U.S. Government Securities Market, pp. 26–27. In mid-1978, there were a total of thirty-four government securities dealers reporting transactions, positions, and quotations to the Federal Reserve Bank of New York. Twelve were bank dealers (namely, large commercial banks that also perform the dealer function), and twenty-two were nonbank dealers, mostly investment banking firms. The Federal Reserve System's open-market operations are also conducted through these thirty-four dealers.

[32]The dealers hold "accounts receivable" in the form of securities sold but not yet delivered (payments due from customers). Dealers also borrow securities to sell short or to complete a transaction, and cash deposits in favor of lenders of securities are normally required in such transactions. Finally, some nonbank dealers carry investment accounts for long-term capital gains. These accounts are separated from the trading positions. See William G. Colby, "Dealer Profits and Capital Availability in the U.S. Government Securities Industry," in Joint Treasury–Federal Reserve Study of the U.S. Government Securities Market, *Staff Studies,* Part 3 (1973), pp. 102–110.

[33]In 1961–1962 nonfinancial corporations provided a daily average of 40–45 percent of dealer financing, compared to an average of 22 percent during the three years from 1976 to 1978. See *Federal Reserve Bulletin,* various issues.

daily in *huge* amounts of Treasury bills and similar Treasury obligations.[34]

There is little need to discuss the *allocational efficiency* of the money market[35] since investors in money market instruments are concerned primarily with liquidity and only secondarily with earnings. Differentials in those yields at which Treasury bills with identical maturities are traded cannot exist for more than a few minutes because dealer firms are constantly in touch with each other and with their customers. Yields established on new 3-month Treasury bills on the day of their weekly auction are usually identical to yields on outstanding 6-month Treasury bills with three months to maturity. Rates on the large money-market banks' time CDs with the same maturity, but issued by different banks, are also practically identical. These rates will tend to be above the Treasury bill rates for the same maturities, but the difference between the certificate rate of return and the yield on Treasury bills will merely reflect the slight differences in risk between the two securities.

While questions of allocational efficiency lose some of their importance in a market for low-risk money substitutes that are in demand primarily for their liquidity rather than for their yields, the degree of *operational efficiency* is of interest in comparing the short-term with the long-term market for loanable funds. The more operationally efficient market, of course, is the one in which transactions are carried on at lower costs as measured, for example, in terms of dealers' spreads. Again, we shall focus here primarily on government securities since, by so doing, we can ignore credit risk differences and concentrate on variations of dealers' bid and asked prices as an index of the relative efficiency of the various segments of the market for Treasury obligations.[36]

Most dealers publish daily quotation sheets, giving bid and asked yields for Treasury bills. Prices

on government securities other than bills are stated in thirty-seconds of a point.[37] The spreads between bid and asked prices typically range from two thirty-seconds to four thirty-seconds of one point for outstanding securities with less than one year until maturity; from four thirty-seconds to eight thirty-seconds of one point for securities with maturities between one and five years; and from eight thirty-seconds to one point for longer-term governments.

The quoted bid and asked prices are not necessarily commitments to buy and to sell *any* amount of government securities at those prices. The large dealers stand ready to transact practically any amount in most of the shorter maturities at the quoted prices; that is, their effective supply and demand schedules are almost infinitely elastic, and the difference between those schedules is the spread. However, dealer commitments in longer securities may bear little relationship to the quoted prices, which must be considered optional except for small-lot transactions. Furthermore, the daily quoted spreads by government securities dealers are outside quotations, while *inside* spreads, applicable to interdealer or large-lot transactions, are normally considerably narrower. The inside-market spread is frequently narrowed to 1/64 of a point and sometimes to 1/128 of a point, or about $78 on a $1 million dollar transaction.[38]

Table 20-4 summarizes differences between bid and asked prices as percentages of the market's bid prices for all U.S. government securities other than Treasury bills on a randomly chosen date. It clearly indicates that the spreads widen as we move from shorter to longer maturities of government obligations. These differences in average spreads obviously are related to dealer positions in U.S. government securities. Large dealer positions in short maturities are associated with narrow spreads, and relatively thin positions in longer maturities are reflected in wider spreads. The same picture emerges when we take the dollar equivalents of the

---

[34]For a description of the trading activities of the government securities dealers, see Hawk, *The U.S. Government Securities Market,* pp. 1–6, 63–70.

[35]For a discussion of allocational efficiency in the capital market, see Chapter 19.

[36]For a systematic and thorough study of market performance, see Louise Ahearn and Janice Peskin, ''Market Performance as Reflected in Aggregative Indicators'' in Joint Treasury–Federal Reserve Study of the U.S. Government Securities Market, *Staff Studies,* Part 2 (December 1971).

[37]A point is 1 percent of the *face value* of the security. One point on a $1 million bond is therefore $10,000, and one thirty-second of one point in this case is $312.50. See also footnote 29.

[38]See Tilford C. Gaines, *Techniques of Treasury Debt Management,* The Free Press, Glencoe, Ill., 1962, pp. 206–207; also Ahearn and Peskin, ''Market Performance as Reflected in Aggregative Indicators,'' p. 134.

### Table 20-4 Quoted Spreads on U.S. Notes and Bonds, March 2, 1977

| Maturities | Issues | Range of Spreads as Percentage of Bid Prices[a] | Difference in Range | Dollar Equivalent of Average Spread[b] |
|---|---|---|---|---|
| Less than 1 year | 17 | 0.1222%–0.1249% | 0.0027% | $1,250.00 |
| From 1 to 5 years | 47 | 0.0624%–1.1057% | 1.0433% | 2,234.04 |
| More than 5 years | 29 | 0.1205%–1.4011% | 1.2806% | 6,271.55 |

[a]Decimal equivalents of spreads quoted in 1/32nds as percentages of closing bid prices.
[b]The average dollar difference between quoted bid and asked prices for a $1 million transaction. Computed as the sum of the spreads, stated in 1/32nds of a point, multiplied by $312.50 (1/32 of $10,000, see footnote 37), and divided by the number of issues in each maturity group.

Source: Federal Reserve Bank of New York, Market Statistics Division, *Composite Closing Quotations for U.S. Government Securities*, March 2, 1977.

differences between bid and asked prices (Table 20-4). The average spread for shorter maturities is one-eighth of 1 percent of the face value, or $1,250 per $1 million transaction, as compared to an average of close to three-fifths of 1 percent for the longer maturities, or $6,300 per $1 million transaction. The quoted spreads also fluctuate considerably over time, partly in response to changes in dealer positions. For example, when government securities dealers increase their inventories of long-term securities—perhaps they expect falling interest rates—and the quoted spreads narrow, this indicates an improvement in the operational efficiency of the market for these securities. Thus, interest rate expectations play an important role among the determinants of dealers' position policy and the operational efficiency of the market, as measured by dealer spreads.[39]

Treasury bills are quoted on a discount basis (Table 20-5). The difference between bid and asked rates of discount (that is, the spread on this kind of money market instrument) usually varies between 3 and 10 basis points (0.03 to 0.10 percent) for the middle range of maturities, depending on market conditions and attractiveness of individual maturity dates. For example, on March 2, 1977, a 90-day

[39]See Ira O. Scott, Jr., *Government Securities Market*, McGraw-Hill Book Company, New York, 1965, pp. 123–131; also, *Report* of the Treasury–Federal Reserve Study of the U.S. Government Securities Market, p. 28. Note, however, that quoted dealer spreads do not always reflect the *actual* trading spreads in the market. As mentioned previously, trading spreads are also a function of timing and size of transactions. See also Kenneth D. Garbade and William L. Silber, "Price Dispersion in the Government Securities Market," *Journal of Political Economy* (November 1976).

Treasury bill was quoted at a bid discount rate of 4.64 percent and an asked rate of 4.60 percent. The spread was 4 basis points, and the dealer would have earned a *gross* profit of an even $100 if he had bought and sold simultaneously $1 million of such Treasury bills.[40]

As can be seen from Table 20-5, the spread in terms of rates of discount widens (the price equivalents narrow) as we approach the maturity date. This inverse relationship between spread and maturity on Treasury bills is not an indication of thin markets with a lower degree of operational effi-

[40]The market price of a Treasury bill can be computed from the rate of discount (r) by using the following formula:

$$d = F \times r \times \frac{t}{T}$$

where $d$ is the *dollar* amount of discount, $F$ is the face value ($) of the Treasury bill, $t$ is the number of days to maturity, and $T$ is 360, which is the number of days in the "bill-year." The market price of the Treasury bill is $F - d$. Using as an example the 90-day Treasury bill mentioned in the text, we can compute the *dollar* amount of discount (d) on the basis of the quoted bid rate as follows:

$$d = \$1,000,000 \times 0.0464 \times \frac{90}{360} = \$11,600$$

The price at which the dealer would have *bought* Treasury bills of this maturity on March 2, 1977, is $F - d$, or $1,000,000 - $11,600 = $988,400. Likewise, the dollar amount of discount can be computed based on the quoted asked rate, and the price at which the dealer would have sold Treasury bills of this maturity on that date was $988,500. The dealer's gross profit is, of course, the difference between the price paid and the price received for a simultaneous purchase and sale, or, on this particular date, $100 on a $1 million transaction.

## Table 20-5 Closing Quotations for Treasury Bills, March 2, 1977

| Issue | No. Days to Maturity[a] | Bid | Asked | Yield[b] |
|---|---|---|---|---|
| 3/8/77 | 4 | 4.54 | 4.32 | 4.38 |
| 3/10/77 | 6 | 4.54 | 4.32 | 4.38 |
| 3/17/77 | 13 | 4.51 | 4.27 | 4.34 |
| 3/24/77 | 20 | 4.48 | 4.26 | 4.33 |
| 3/31/77 | 27 | 4.47 | 4.27 | 4.34 |
| 4/5/77 | 32 | 4.50 | 4.36 | 4.44 |
| 4/7/77 | 34 | 4.50 | 4.38 | 4.46 |
| 4/14/77 | 41 | 4.51 | 4.41 | 4.49 |
| 4/21/77 | 48 | 4.58 | 4.48 | 4.57 |
| 4/28/77 | 55 | 4.58 | 4.48 | 4.57 |
| 5/3/77 | 60 | 4.64 | 4.54 | 4.64 |
| 5/5/77 | 62 | 4.63 | 4.55 | 4.65 |
| 5/12/77 | 69 | 4.65 | 4.57 | 4.67 |
| 5/19/77 | 76 | 4.66 | 4.58 | 4.69 |
| 5/26/77 | 83 | 4.65 | 4.59 | 4.70 |
| 5/31/77 | 88 | 4.67 | 4.59 | 4.71 |
| 6/2/77 | 90 | 4.64 | 4.60 | 4.72 |
| 6/9/77 | 97 | 4.70 | 4.62 | 4.74 |
| 6/16/77 | 104 | 4.71 | 4.65 | 4.78 |
| 6/23/77 | 111 | 4.73 | 4.65 | 4.78 |
| 6/28/77 | 116 | 4.74 | 4.68 | 4.82 |
| 6/30/77 | 118 | 4.74 | 4.68 | 4.82 |
| 7/7/77 | 125 | 4.80 | 4.72 | 4.87 |
| 7/14/77 | 132 | 4.80 | 4.76 | 4.91 |
| 7/21/77 | 139 | 4.84 | 4.76 | 4.92 |
| 7/26/77 | 144 | 4.85 | 4.77 | 4.93 |
| 7/28/77 | 146 | 4.84 | 4.78 | 4.94 |
| 8/4/77 | 153 | 4.89 | 4.81 | 4.98 |
| 8/11/77 | 160 | 4.89 | 4.83 | 5.01 |
| 8/18/77 | 167 | 4.91 | 4.85 | 5.03 |
| 8/23/77 | 172 | 4.91 | 4.83 | 5.01 |
| 8/25/77 | 174 | 4.91 | 4.85 | 5.04 |
| 9/1/77 | 181 | 4.91 | 4.87 | 5.06 |
| 9/20/77 | 200 | 5.00 | 4.90 | 5.10 |
| 10/18/77 | 228 | 5.06 | 4.98 | 5.19 |
| 11/15/77 | 256 | 5.12 | 5.04 | 5.26 |
| 12/13/77 | 284 | 5.16 | 5.08 | 5.32 |
| 1/10/78 | 312 | 5.20 | 5.14 | 5.39 |
| 2/7/78 | 320 | 5.21 | 5.17 | 5.44 |

[a]Counted from the day of delivery, March 4, 1977.
[b]Yields are based on asked rates and are for delivery on March 4, 1977.

Source: Federal Reserve Bank of New York, Market Statistics Division, *Composite Closing Quotations for U.S. Government Securities,* March 2, 1977.

ciency in the shorter maturities; it merely stems from the technical price-yield-maturity relationship for all *discounted* instruments.[41] The quoted bid and asked discounts in Table 20-5 for the *entire*

maturity range of Treasury bills on that day yielded an average dollar equivalent spread of $239.40 per $1 million transaction, with a low of $24.42 for the 4-day Treasury bill and a high of $631.12 for the 284-day Treasury bill. Furthermore, twenty-one of the thirty-nine issues outstanding on March 2, 1977, were quoted at rates of discount yielding a dollar equivalent spread of less than $200 per $1 million transaction. If operational efficiency of a financial market can be adequately measured by the differences between bid and asked discounts, as quoted by dealers, the efficiency of the market for U.S. Treasury bills is unequaled.[42]

The concept of flotation costs, as used in connection with the capital market, is not applicable to the money market where most instruments are issued at a discount, which establishes the yield until maturity. However, we may gain some insight into the efficiency of the auction market for *new* Treasury bills, in which the government securities dealers play a crucial role, by considering the very close range of prices bid for the regular weekly issues of 3-month and 6-month Treasury bills (Table 20-6). At a typical auction selected for illustration, there was a difference between the highest and the lowest bidders of only 13 cents per $1,000 worth of 3-month Treasury bills. The extreme closeness of the tenders, which is a persistent feature of the auction market for Treasury bills, provides additional evidence of the highly developed communication links and efficiency that characterize this segment of the money market.

## Conclusion

In this chapter we have explored the sources and uses of short-term funds. We have seen that the money market is considerably more homogeneous than the capital market because borrowers' short-term debt preferences are relatively close to lend-

---

[41] For example, if a dealer wanted to establish a spread for the shortest maturity in Table 20-4 that would yield the same gross profit in dollars on a $1 million transaction

as the gross profit given by the four basis point spread for the 90-day Treasury bill in the table ($100 per $1 million transaction), the spread between the bid and asked rates of discount would have to be 90 *basis points*.

[42] See also Ahearn and Peskin, "Market Performance as Reflected in Aggregative Indicators," in which market performance is measured by volume of trading, turnover, dealer positions, frequency of small and large daily price changes, and dealer spreads. Garbade and Silber, "Price Dispersion in the Government Securities Market," tested hypotheses concerning price dispersion in the context of the Treasury securities market.

**Table 20-6 Auction Prices for Treasury Bills, January 28, 1980**

|  | Prices Bid | Discount Rate |
|---|---|---|
| 13-week Treasury bills | | |
| Highest bids | $96.965 | 12.007% |
| Average | 96.957 | 12.038 |
| Lowest bids | 96.952 | 12.058 |
| 26-week Treasury bills | | |
| Highest bids | $94.019 | 11.831% |
| Average | 94.011 | 11.846 |
| Lowest bids | 94.003 | 11.862 |

Note: This average price is weighted by volume. Total bids amounted to $6.40 billion for the 13-week bills and $5.42 billion for the 26-week issue. The Treasury accepted 50 percent and 59 percent of the bids, respectively, including noncompetitive bids of about $790 million for the 13-week issue and $474 million for the longer bills. The noncompetitive bids were accepted in full at the average price.

Source: *Wall Street Journal*, January 29, 1980.

ers' liquid-asset preferences. Credit risk, as well as money risk, is substantially lower in the money market than in the capital market. The government is more directly involved in the money market than in the capital market, through the operations of the Federal Reserve System and the large-scale borrowing on short maturities by the Treasury. Moreover, many of the participants in the money market are simultaneously borrowers and lenders, an institutional feature that closely ties together the various segments of this market. It is an extremely efficient market in which transaction and flotation costs are very low and in which considerable depth, breadth, and resilience prevail. Also, money markets are more closely linked internationally than are capital markets; a large part of world trade is financed through the organized money market—markets that also accommodate payments for services and enable dealers and speculators in foreign currencies to adjust their portfolios in response to their expectations about possible changes in exchange rates. The internationalization of the money market in the United States is also reflected in the very substantial increase in foreign ownership of U.S. government debt since the early 1970s. Foreign holdings of government securities exceed 20 percent of total publicly held Treasury debt, and, apart from the Federal Reserve System, foreigners have become the largest single group of investors in Treasury bills, now being even more important than U.S. commercial banks.

Conceptually, as well as practically, however, it is not possible to make a sharp distinction between the money market and the capital market. Short-term funds are borrowed to finance the purchase and carrying of capital market obligations, and long-term securities eventually become money market instruments as they approach maturity. Dealers in government securities make a market in private capital market instruments as well as in short-term and long-term Treasury obligations, and some investors are willing, at times, to switch their funds out of one market and into the other. Consequently, interest rates in both markets bear more than an accidental relationship to each other. The *degree* of interrelatedness of the yield structure *between* the money and capital markets, and *within* the latter, as well as some of the suggested explanation of such interrelations, form the subject matter of the following four chapters.

## Questions

1. There are only a few countries in which an effective money market exists. Discuss some major prerequisites for the development of an organized money market.
2. What are the properties of money market instruments? Why are these instruments often referred to as "near-money" or "money substitutes"? Do they substitute for all of the functions of money?
3. What features distinguish bank certificates of deposit from finance company paper? Bankers' acceptances from certificates of deposit? Commercial paper from finance company paper? Treasury bills from short-term federal agency paper?
4. Why is federal agency paper said to possess many of the features of commercial paper?
5. Using various issues of the *Federal Reserve Bulletin* or a recent issue of the *Treasury Bulletin*, prepare a table showing annual changes in short-term government securities for a period of six to eight years. What are some reasons for the variations from year to year?
6. Why are some of the participants in the money market simultaneously borrowers and lenders?
7. What are some of the bridges connecting the money market with the capital market? What is the significance of these links?
8. Why is the concept of allocational efficiency much more important for the capital market than for the money market?
9. In what ways may we measure operational efficiency in the money market? Operational efficiency in the capital market? Why do we want to measure the efficiency of a financial market?

10. In what ways may an efficient money market affect the positions and slopes of the supply and demand schedules for loanable funds?

11. A Treasury bill with 120 days until maturity is quoted 4.74 percent "bid" and 4.66 percent "asked." Using the formula given in footnote 40, compute the dealer spread in dollars on a $1 million transaction. You may also use a table called "Dollar equivalent of 0.01 percent discount per $1 million," which is found in most investment manuals.

12. An 8¼ percent government bond maturing during the years 2000–2005, is quoted 104.14 "bid" and 104.30 "asked." Compute the dealer spread on a $1 million transaction in dollars. You may use a table called "Decimal equivalents of 32nds and 64ths per $100," found in most investment manuals.

## Selected Bibliography

Ahearn, Louise, and Janice Peskin. "Market Performance as Reflected in Aggregative Indicators." In Joint Treasury–Federal Reserve Study of the U.S. Government Securities Market, *Staff Studies,* Part 2 (1971).

Bedford, Margaret E. "Recent Developments in Treasury Financing Techniques." *Monthly Review.* Federal Reserve Bank of Kansas City (July-August 1977).

Board of Governors of the Federal Reserve System. *Reappraisal of the Federal Reserve Discount Mechanism.* Washington, D.C., 1968. Studies include: Robert C. Holland and George Garvy, "The Redesigned Discount Mechanism and the Money Market" (1968); David M. Jones, "A Review of Recent Academic Literature on the Discount Mechanism" (1968); Delores P. Lynn, "Reserve Adjustments of the Eight Major New York City Banks During 1966" (1968); Parker B. Willis, "A Study of the Market for Federal Funds" (1967); and "The Secondary Market for Negotiable Certificates of Deposits" (1967).

Colby, William G. "Dealer Profits and Capital Availability in the U.S. Government Securities Industry." In Joint Treasury–Federal Reserve Study of the U.S. Government Securities Market, *Staff Studies,* Part 3 (1973).

Duncan, Wallace H. "Treasury Bill Futures—Opportunities and Pitfalls." *Review.* Federal Reserve Bank of Dallas (July 1977).

Federal Reserve Bank of Chicago. "Hedging Interest Rate Fluctuations." *Business Conditions* (April 1976).

Federal Reserve Bank of Cleveland. *Money Market Instruments*, 3rd ed. Cleveland, Ohio, 1970.

Federal Reserve Bank of Richmond. *Instruments of the Money Market*, 4th ed., Timothy Q. Cook. Richmond, Va. 1977.

First Boston Corporation. *Handbook of Securities of the United States Government and Federal Agencies and Related Money Market Instruments*, 28th ed. New York, 1978.

Gaines, Tilford C. *Techniques of Treasury Debt Management*. The Free Press, Glencoe, Ill. 1962.

Garbade, Kenneth D., and William L. Silber. "Price Dispersion in the Government Securities Market." *Journal of Political Economy* (November 1976).

Hawk, William A. *The U.S. Government Securities Market*. Harris Trust and Savings Bank, Chicago, 1974.

Heebner, A. G. *Negotiable Certificates of Deposits: The Development of Money Market Instruments*. Institute of Finance, Graduate School of Business Administration, New York University, New York, 1969.

Helfrich, Ralph T. "Trading in Bankers' Acceptances: A View from the Acceptance Desk of the Federal Reserve Bank of New York." *Monthly Review*. Federal Reserve Bank of New York (February 1976).

Hervey, Jack L. "Bankers' Acceptances." *Business Conditions*. Federal Reserve Bank of Chicago (May 1976).

Hurley, Evelyn M. "The Commercial Paper Market." *Federal Reserve Bulletin*. Board of Governors of the Federal Reserve System, Washington, D.C. (June 1977).

Joint Treasury–Federal Reserve Study of the U.S. Government Securities Market, *Report*. Board of Governors of the Federal Reserve System, Washington, D.C., 1969. *Staff Studies,* Part 1 (1970), Part 2, (1971), Part 3 (1973).

Lucas, C. H., M. T. Jones, and T. B. Thurston. "Federal Funds and Repurchase Agreements." *Quarterly Review*. Federal Reserve Bank of New York (Summer 1977).

Myers, Margaret G. *The New York Money Market, Origins and Development*. Columbia University Press, New York, 1931.

Nichols, Dorothy M. *Trading in Federal Funds*. Board of Governors of the Federal Reserve System, Washington, D.C., 1965.

Polakoff, Murray E., and William L Silber. "Reluctance and Member Bank Borrowing: Additional Evidence." *The Journal of Finance* (March 1967).

Scherer, Joseph. "Institutional Investors in the Government Securities Market." In Joint Treasury–Federal Reserve Study of the U.S. Government Securities Market, *Staff Studies,* Part 1 (1970).

Scott, Ira O., Jr. *Government Securities Market*. McGraw-Hill Book Company, New York, 1965.

Selden, Richard T. *Trends and Cycles in the Commercial Paper Market*. National Bureau of Economic Research, New York, 1963.

Tanner, J. Ernest, and Lewis A. Kochin. "The Determinants of the Difference Between Bid and Ask Prices on Government Bonds." *Journal of Business* (October 1971).

# V

# Interest Rates: Level and Structure

# 21

# A Basic Theory of Interest Rate Determination: The Theory of Liquidity Preference

Previous chapters of this book have provided both a broad introduction to the saving-investment process and a closer analysis of the causes of financial flows. This chapter and the next combine these elements to arrive at an overview of the financial system by examining some theoretical structures used by economists to study how financial markets interact with the rest of the economy. In particular, these two chapters look at macroeconomic frameworks used in the analysis of interest rates. Much of the rest of the book builds on and elaborates parts of the theories outlined in these chapters. This chapter examines interest-rate determination using constructs derived ultimately from the work of John Maynard Keynes in the 1930s. Today these constructs form the basis of much of macroeconomic theory. Primarily a static theory, Keynes's analysis of financial asset holding, first developed in *The General Theory of Employment, Interest, and Money,* has become an important framework for interest rate analysis. This framework is known as the *theory of liquidity preference.* Chapter 21 reviews the skeletal outlines of liquidity-preference theory and leads up to a second theoretical construct, the *loanable funds theory,* which is the main subject of Chapter 22. The loanable funds theory has the same behavioral foundation as liquidity preference, but it is more relevant to analysis of financial markets and institutions.

## Some Important Preliminary Concepts

Possibly the most important questions studied by economists are the major macroeconomic questions about the determinants of income, output, the price level, and economic growth. Economists study numerous other problems ranging from causes of historical events to demand for municipal social services, but the fundamental macroeconomic questions receive more attention than any others. In order to analyze determinants of these variables and the interactions among them, economists build theoretical structures called models. These *models* are abstract representations of economic realities; economists hope they have enough theoretical and empirical content to make them useful for analysis and prediction.[1] The models

[1] For discussion of some fundamental methodological principles in model building, see E. Nagel and Paul

have various degrees of complexity depending on their purpose. Simple models for descriptive or illustrative purposes may consist of a short verbal passage, a graph, or a single equation. Other models may consist of hundreds of simultaneous difference equations, which can be solved only with the aid of large electronic computers. All the models, though, have the common characteristic that they are statements (or hypotheses) about the relationships among two or more variables. Models used in macroeconomic analysis include all the major policy variables that economists want to predict and policymakers want to influence. In addition, macroeconomic models often contain intermediate variables, including interest rates. Policymakers do not necessarily believe these variables are important in themselves, but they may have important interactions with the main policy variables.

As a first step in introducing macroeconomic interest rate models in this chapter, it is useful to clarify a few important concepts that we will discuss further later on. The first concept is the distinction between equilibrium and disequilibrium. *Equilibrium* is, of course, a state of rest among variables. It is caused either by an absence of forces necessitating changes or by a perfect balance of opposing forces resulting in an unchanging relationship. An example is the equilibrium price that clears any market. The equilibrium price is the price at which supply forces just balance demand forces and eliminate any tendency for the market price to vary. Any change in either supply or demand causes a *disequilibrium* (that is, absence of equilibrium) that lasts until market price and quantity exchanged both vary sufficiently to balance supply and demand again. At the new price there will again be a stationary equilibrium unless new forces again unbalance the market.

A second important distinction is the one between statics and dynamics. *Statics* in economics is the study of stationary equilibria. It involves analysis of equilibrium positions after all causal forces have run their course. *Comparative statics*

is the comparison of equilibrium positions. It involves comparison of equilibrium values of variables before and after changes take place. The Keynesian investment multiplier is a familiar example. The multiplier is found by solving

$$\Delta Y = m \Delta I_a \qquad (21\text{-}1)$$

for $m$, where $\Delta I_a$ is the change in autonomous investment and $\Delta Y$ or $Y_2 - Y_1$ is the change in equilibrium income. The multiplier compares the equilibrium values of income before and after a change and expresses the change in terms of the change in autonomous investment that caused income to vary. Solving for $m$ gives

$$m = \frac{(Y_2 - Y_1)}{\Delta I_a} \qquad (21\text{-}2)$$

The multiplier is a comparative static concept.

*Dynamics* is the study of changes. Statics analyzes stationary relationships and comparative statics looks at the relationships before and after changes, but dynamics studies the changes themselves. Important questions of dynamics include:

1. Order: What occurred first? What second?
2. Time: How long did each take?

Specification of a fully dynamic theoretical model is usually considerably more complex than specification of a static model. A static model requires only behavioral relationships or functions that suggest the direction and magnitude of changes in variables when a disequilibrium occurs. This is often difficult enough in itself, but the difficulty pales in comparison to the problems of constructing a dynamic model in which the disequilibrium behavior of all market participants must be modeled as well.

A simple example illustrates the distinction between statics and dynamics. Imagine that Figure 21-1 is a model of the market for coffee. Coffee demand is given by $D_1D_1$, which is a negative function of price. Supply is given by $S_1S_1$, a familiar supply curve that is a positive function of price. The market clears at price $P_1$ with quantity $Q_1$ exchanged in the market. Suppose population growth increases coffee demand to $D_2D_2$ with no corresponding change in the supply relationship. Now the equilibrium price is $P_2$ (higher than $P_1$) and the amount demanded and supplied is $Q_2$ (also higher). The points $P_1Q_1$ and $P_2Q_2$ are examples of stationary equilibria; comparisons between them are examples of comparative statics.

---

Samuelson, "Assumptions in Economic Theory," *American Economic Review* (May 1963); also, Milton Friedman, "The Methodology of Positive Economics," in Milton Friedman, *Essays in Positive Economics,* University of Chicago Press, Chicago, 1953.

**Figure 21-1  The Market for Coffee**

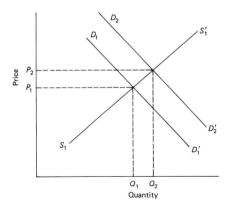

Much—but not everything—can be learned from comparative statics. One familiar comparative-static inference is market elasticity—the comparison of the percentage change in quantity exchanged to the percentage change in price. In the coffee example, existence of two sets of price-quantity observations and knowledge that the change was caused by a shift in demand allows one to estimate elasticity of supply,

$$\frac{(Q_2 - Q_1)/Q_1}{(P_2 - P_1)/P_1}$$

Nothing, however, can be said about order or timing of events. Did price or quantity change first? How long did the changes take? Theoretical analysis of the dynamics would require proper specification of disequilibrium behavior of market participants. In the coffee example this might not be too difficult. It would be possible to hypothesize that the demand shift would cause a shortage at the old price, which would cause prices to rise. Producers seeing higher prices would respond, after a lag, by expanding the quantity supplied until the market again cleared. The problem would be specification of the determinants of the lag. The lag could be variable in length and might depend upon a great many factors, including magnitude and speed of the prior price change and amount of producers' excess capacity. Specification of the lag structure is a severe problem in building dynamic models. Frequently, lags cannot be specified by theoretical means and empirical methodologies must be employed. Variable lags simply mean the behavioral determinants are not adequately understood. Most

macroeconomic models make the same prediction about the direction of impact of a change; the remaining (and possibly more important) question is the length of time that change will take, that is, the dynamics of the change. We will return to this point later.

**Traditional Macroeconomic Models**

One of Keynes's significant contributions was his insistence that monetary changes (the main province of the "macroeconomist" before his time) be analyzed only in the context of a complete economic system. The system itself might have a number of parts, but interaction of all parts would have to be considered before any interpretations or predictions could have validity. For this reason, the rest of this chapter is devoted to outlining a Keynesian model of the macroeconomy. While this outline does not do justice to the extent of work that has been done on each part of the Keynesian model, it is a useful introduction. The rest of this book is devoted to further study of one part of the macroeonomic model—the part concerned with financial markets.

Partial Equilibrium I: The Market for
Goods and Services

The first section of our macroeconomic model is the market for goods and services. This section (and, for that matter, all sections) of the model consists of three parts: a demand relation, a supply relation, and a relation that specifies the equilibrium condition in the market—that supply equals demand. Complexity of the supply and demand relations in Keynesian macroeconomic models varies depending on the uses of the model, but the equations always take the same general form. Total demand for goods and services consists of the sum of consumption demand ($C$), investment demand ($I$), government demand ($G$), and net demand for exports ($EXP$). In symbols, total or aggregate demand can be expressed as:

$$D = C + I + G + EXP \qquad (21\text{-}3)$$

where the meanings of $C$, $I$, $G$, and $EXP$ are those just given. For analytical convenience we must assume away the existence of the foreign sector for the moment (a not too unreasonable assumption for the American economy, where the foreign sector is relatively small in relation to the economy as a whole). Equation (21-3) then becomes:

$$D = C + I + G \qquad (21\text{-}4)$$

where $D$ is still aggregate demand.

The other side of the market, the supply of goods and services, is represented by income. Ultimately, those who supply basic resources in the forms of labor, capital, and materials do so in order to earn income. In a complex economy, the suggestion that market supply equals income involves a large number of convenient assumptions about human motivations and about the efficiency of labor and resource markets. Nevertheless, for the purposes of this chapter, it does not seem unreasonable to assume that resources are supplied because they provide income for suppliers. Using $S_G$ for market supply of goods and services and $Y$ for income received, then

$$S_G = Y \qquad (21\text{-}5)$$

Equilibrium in the market for goods and services occurs (as in any market) when supply equals demand. From Equations (21-4) and (21-5), the equilibrium condition in the market for goods and services is given by

$$Y = C + I + G \qquad (21\text{-}6)$$

Since recipients of income have only three possible uses of income, consumption spending ($C$), saving ($S$), and payment of taxes ($T$), Equation (21-6) can be expanded and simplified to

$$C + S + T = C + I + G \qquad (21\text{-}7)$$

and

$$S + T = I + G \qquad (21\text{-}8)$$

Equation (21-8) shows that there is equilibrium in the market for goods and services when saving plus payment of taxes equals investment plus government spending. This equation, however, is merely definitional. It is merely an expansion of the definition of equilibrium: that supply of goods and services equals demand. As a definition, it is not particularly useful for analytical purposes since it provides no information about disequilibrium behavior and, by itself, suggests nothing about how a disequilibrium might occur.

The problem is that the market for goods and services is not always in equilibrium. Saving and investing in the economy are not necessarily done

by the same people, and, consequently, at the start of any period savers' and investors' plans may differ. Furthermore, government may not formulate taxing and spending plans at the same time or with the motivation of balancing the budget. As a result, there is no reason to expect that nonspending plans of savers and taxpayers, at the beginning of any period, will exactly match the investing plans of investors and the spending plans of government. In other words, the fact that there are many economic agents interacting to determine macroeconomic quantities allows the possibility of disequilibrium causing pressures for macroeconomic quantities to change. This highlights another of Keynes's major contributions. He hypothesized some behavioral relationships among macroeconomic variables that suggested both how a disequilibrium might occur and what the resulting changes might be. These hypotheses give some analytical meaning to the income-expenditure relationships in Equations (21-6) and (21-8). Although crude in their pure Keynesian form, these relationships provide behavioral content and predictive value to the goods-market section of standard macroeconomic models. In this way, they form the basis of modern, more complex models, and for this reason we turn to them now.

*The Consumption Function and the Multiplier* Probably the most famous Keynesian behavioral hypothesis is the consumption function, outlined in Chapters 8–10 of the *General Theory,* which he used to explain consuming and saving behavior. Simply stated, the consumption function is the behavioral hypothesis that consumption spending is a function of income. Although Keynes himself did not attempt to derive his hypothesis from basic assumptions, such as utility maximization, economists in the forty-plus years since publication of the *General Theory* have subjected the hypothesis to intense theoretical and empirical study.[2] For our purposes, however, what we need is a simple statement of the function for use in our outline of the structure of traditional Keynesian macroeconomic

[2]Some of the basic theoretical analysis is found in Franco Modigliani and Richard Brumberg, "Utility Analysis and the Consumption Function," in *Post-Keynesian Economics,* ed. Kenneth K. Kurihara, Rutgers University Press, New Brunswick, N.J., 1954; and Milton Friedman, *A Theory of the Consumption Function,* Princeton University Press, Princeton, N.J., 1957. Review of these and other theoretical and empirical studies

theory. Equation (21-9) satisfies this need; it suggests, simply, that consumption is a proportional function of income

$$C = C(Y) = bY \qquad (21-9)$$

where $b$ is the proportion of income that is consumed. In this proportional form, $b$ is both the average propensity to consume—the ratio of consumption to income $(c/Y = bY/Y = b)$—and the marginal or incremental propensity to consume $(dc/dY = b)$.

The consumption function hypothesis in Equation (21-9) provides behavioral content to the expenditure Equation (21-6) and makes it analytically useful. Assume, for expositional simplicity, that government revenues just equal spending and, consequently, that Equation (21-6) can be simplified to

$$S = I \qquad (21-10)$$

Now, suppose that during some time period investors plan to invest more than savers plan to save. The result is a disequilibrium in the economy as new investment intentions cause total planned aggregate demands for goods and services (consumption plus investment demand) to exceed planned aggregate supply. The consumption function hypothesis suggests the disequilibrium behavior of income recipients and proposes a solution to the disequilibrium. Let us see how the consumption function does this.

Investment spending in excess of planned saving provides new income to suppliers of resources. Under the consumption function hypothesis, a portion $b$ of this new income is spent, and the remainder $1 - b$ is saved. However, the changes do not stop there. The newly induced consumption spending *also* provides income to someone, part of which, again, is spent as consumption and part of which is saved. Theoretically, these cycles of income, spending, and saving will continue until income has risen sufficiently so that planned saving again equals planned investment and the disequilibrium is eliminated. The necessary total change in income is found by solving the difference form of the expenditure Equation (21-6).

$$\Delta Y = \Delta(C + I + G) \qquad (21-11)$$

Substituting

$$\Delta Y = \Delta(bY + I + G) \qquad (21-12)$$

and solving

$$\Delta Y = \frac{1}{1 - b}\Delta(I + G) \qquad (21-13)$$

Assuming no change in government spending during the period (that is, $\Delta G = 0$), then Equation (21-13) reduces to the investment multiplier

$$\Delta Y = \frac{1}{1 - b}\Delta I \qquad (21-14)$$

Equation (21-14) shows how a behavioral hypothesis such as $C = bY$ has provided a solution to the development of a disequilibrium: income will change by $1/(1 - b)$ times the size of the disequilibrium, thereby encouraging a sufficient change in savings to eliminate the disequilibrium. That savings will change by the same amount as investment can be shown by solving for $S$.

$$\Delta S = (1 - b)\Delta Y$$
$$= (1 - b)[1/(1 - b)]\Delta I = \Delta I \qquad (21-15)$$

Thus, the disequilibrium will be closed when income has risen sufficiently so that planned saving again equals planned investment. The analysis does *not* show, however, how long it will take to close the disequilibrium. That would require specification of the time behavior of market participants: for example, how long does it take for income recipients to react?

In sum, the consumption function provides behavioral content to the income-expenditure identity. Armed with this hypothesis, it is possible to suggest the outcome of the development of a spending disequilibrium. In the example, the change in income that results from the disequilibrium will equal $1/(1 -$ Marginal Prospensity to Consume) times the size of the original disequilibrium. The quantity $1/(1 - b)$ is called the investment multiplier, a comparative static concept. As noted before, the multiplier expresses the change in income in terms of the investment (or government spending) disequilibrium. It is not a dynamic concept and has no time content attached to it.[3]

of the consumption function may be found in intermediate and advanced textbooks in macroeconomics, such as William H. Branson, *Macroeconomic Theory and Policy,* Harper & Row, New York, 1972.

[3]Changes in income through a multiplier process are produced by a variety of spending changes, such as changes in investment, government spending, or taxes. In a more complex model, beyond the scope of this chap-

Figure 21-2 shows a graph of the consumption function and the multiplier relation. In Figure 21-2, income is graphed on the horizontal axis and expenditures or components of aggregate resource demand are graphed vertically. The 45° line from the origin is the locus of equilibria: at any point along this line planned spending $(C + I + G)$ just equals income. Also passing through the origin is a proportional consumption function $C = bY$, whose slope, $b$, is the average and marginal propensity to consume with $0 < b < 1$. Investment and government spending, $I$ and $G$ respectively, are assumed not to be functions of income and are graphed as horizontal lines. Summing the components of spending gives the aggregate spending curve $C + I + G$, which is parallel to the consumption function. Equilibrium occurs at income level $Y_0$, which satisfies Equation (21-8).

Suppose, for some reason, investors' plans changed and they decided to invest $I_1 > I_0$. The resulting spending disequilibrium would cause income to rise until a new equilibrium income level $Y_1$ was reached, which again satisfied Equation (21-8). The change in income $Y_1 - Y_0$ would equal $1/(1 - b)\Delta I$. The remaining question, however, is: what caused investment to change? To answer this question we must turn to the investment function.

*The Investment Function* The investment function is a behavioral hypothesis about the second part of the income-expenditure equation, Equation (21-6). Like the consumption function, it gives behavioral content to this income-expenditure relation and suggests what happens as determinant variables change. Unlike the consumption function, however, the investment function is not a Keynesian invention—although Keynes did discuss it. Instead, the investment function is derived ultimately from the work of Irving Fisher, the great American economist of the first half of the twentieth century.[4]

---

ter, the multiplier may assume a more complex form, but the concept is always the same. The multiplier is always the relationship between the change in income and the size of the spending disequilibrium that caused income to change. For discussion of more complex multipliers, see Branson, *Macroeconomic Theory and Policy*, or Thomas M. Havrilesky and John T. Boorman, *Monetary Macroeconomics*, AHM Publishing Company, Arlington Heights, Ill., 1978, Chap. 11.

[4]See Irving Fisher, *The Theory of Interest*, The Macmillan Company, New York, 1930.

**Figure 21-2 The Consumption Function and the Multiplier**

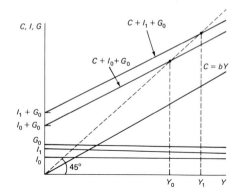

Investment in any time period, $I_t$, is the net change in the capital stock, $K$. Like income it is a flow concept indicating an amount per unit of time. In time period $t$, investment is given by

$$I_t = \Delta K_t = K_t - K_{t-1} \qquad (21\text{-}16)$$

This equation shows that investment is simply the change in the capital stock. It seems reasonable, therefore, to start our discussion of investment with a brief analysis of capital usage.

As a first step in studying capital use, it is important to make clear the distinction between financial and real capital. Financial capital refers to savings that are held in the form of financial assets, including currency, deposits, and bonds. In contrast, real or physical capital is a physical object—such as a factory, a machine, or even a service like education—which exists in the present but provides a stream of returns over time. According to one definition:

> Capital goods are intermediate productive commodities, valuable not for their own sakes, but only insofar as they represent the potentiality of generating the consumption goods that are the fundamental objects of choice. Real capital is thus coordinate with labor, the other main class of productive commodity.[5]

Economic agents employ physical capital because, through capital usage, it is possible to trans-

[5]Jack Hirshleifer, *Investment, Interest, and Capital*, Prentice-Hall, Englewood Cliffs, N.J., 1970, p. 154.

form presently available resources into a flow of returns in the future. Productive machinery is a good example. Present resources are used to purchase or build the machines, but the return is in the form of a stream of inflows in the future. Whenever the *present value* of this stream of returns is greater than the present resources expended, the *net* present value of the asset is positive and rational (wealth-maximizing) economic agents will use present resources as capital.[6]

Equation (21-17) is the equation for the net present value of a capital asset. Using $C$ for present cost, $R_t$ for return in period $t$, and $i$ for the borrowing rate, then:

$$NPV = -C + \frac{R_1}{(1+i)^1} + \frac{R_2}{(1+i)^2} + \cdots + \frac{R_n}{(1+i)^n}$$

(21-17)

Thus, the net present value of an asset is the sum of the present values of the returns from each time period minus the present cost. Using this equation, one can examine the determinants of the optimal amount of capital and see how they are important for the theory of investment. For this purpose, it is necessary to introduce the concept of the *marginal efficiency of capital* (MEC).

The marginal efficiency of capital is a special rate of discount, $r$, that can be used in Equation (21-17). It is the rate of discount that just causes the present value of the return stream to equal the present cost. Thus, this special discount rate marks the dividing line. Whenever the borrowing rate is *less than* the marginal efficiency of capital, net present value is greater than zero. In contrast, if the borrowing rate is *greater than* the MEC, then net present value is less than zero. This illustrates the importance of MEC. As long as MEC is greater than the cost of borrowing (the rate of interest), it is rational for economic agents to borrow resources to purchase and employ more real capital assets because $NPV > 0$. Put another way, as long as the marginal efficiency of capital is greater than the rate of interest, wealth is expanded by borrowing and using more real capital. The last unit of capital that should be employed is the one at which the mar-

ginal efficiency of capital just *equals* the rate of interest.

Now we must ask, how much capital is this? In other words, what is the relationship between *amount* of capital and MEC, the discount rate that just makes the net present value of the last unit of capital equal zero? The *law of fixed factors* (also called the *law of diminishing returns*) suggests an answer. According to this law, as a variable factor is increased against a fixed factor, the productivity of the variable factor declines.[7] In this case, this means that for higher levels of the capital stock with fixed amounts of labor and materials, the productivity of capital diminishes. In terms of Equation (21-17), this means that as the capital stock is increased, the $R$s decline. Since the marginal efficiency of capital is the discount rate which makes Equation (21-17) equal zero, the MEC also declines as capital increases. Graphically, this is shown in the first part of Figure 21-3.

With this information about the shape of the relation between the amount of capital and its marginal efficiency, it is now possible to say something about the shape of the demand curve for capital in terms of the rate of interest. Since optimal capital accumulation occurs when the marginal efficiency of capital equals the market rate of interest ($i$), it is possible to substitute $i$ for $r$ in Figure 21-3 and derive the demand curve for optimal capital in terms of the rate of interest. Now the negatively sloped curve represents the relation between the rate of interest, $i$, and *optimal* capital $K^*$. Since capital is optimal when $i = r$, this curve is exactly the same as the previous one except for the change in labels. (The new labels for the axes are shown in parentheses in the first panel of Figure 21-3.) This is not investment demand, which concerns changes in the capital stock. The left side of Figure 21-3 simply becomes the demand curve for optimal capital in terms of the rate of interest.

Having looked at the demand curve for capital stock, it is now possible to look at demand for *investment*—that is, the demand for changes in the capital stock. As a first step, at any point in time given the rate of interest, $i$, it is possible to compare

---

[6]Much of the field of finance involves analysis and elaboration of this point.

[7]For further discussion, see any text in microeconomic theory, such as C. E. Ferguson and J. P. Gould, *Microeconomic Theory,* 4th ed., Richard D. Irwin, Homewood, Ill., 1975, Chap. 5.

### Figure 21-3 The Marginal Efficiency of Capital and the Marginal Efficiency of Investment

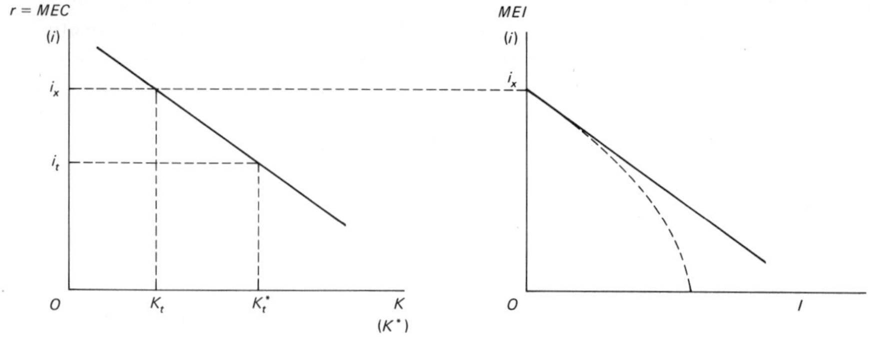

optimal capital $K^*$ with existing captal stock $K_t$ and determine whether there is a capital deficiency. Only if $K_t$ is *less then* $K^*$ is there a positive demand to increase the capital stock—a positive investment demand. Put somewhat differently, given some rate of interest, $i$, if economic agents see profitable investment opportunities, then current capital stock is not optimal. Capital deficiency and positive investment demand are analogous concepts. Only when $K_t < K^*$ is there a positive investment demand. Most simple macro models essentially assume a capital deficiency and corresponding positive investment demand. This assumption is made because, in a growing economy, there usually is a capital deficiency, if for no other reason than growth in the supply of labor. As labor grows, more capital goods can be employed profitably. The result is a shift to the right in the marginal efficiency of capital schedule (Figure 21-3) as the MEC equates the $R$s in Equation (21-17) with zero at higher levels of capital stock.

The remaining question is the amount of investment in a time period, assuming the existence of a capital deficiency. It would seem as if the amount of profitable investment could be derived from the demand schedule for optimal capital and the current rate of interest. Unfortunately, it is not quite that simple. The left half of Figure 21-3 contains a demand curve for optimal capital. Current interest rate $i_t$ suggests optimal capital $K_t^*$ which is greater than current capital stock $K_t$ or, in other words, that there is a capital deficiency. In fact, at any interest rate below $i_x$—the interest rate at which current capital stock would be optimal—there is a

capital deficiency. It would seem that this is sufficient information to derive the investment demand curve. The intercept is $i_x$, and for $i_t < i_x$, optimal investment demand $I_t^*$ should equal $K_t^* - K_t$. This investment demand curve is depicted as the solid curve in the right-hand side of Figure 21-3.

The problem is that capital deficiency is a stock concept, a certain *level* which equals $K^* - K_t$. In contrast, investment is a flow—the *change* in a stock in a given period of time. Optimal investment in a period may not equal the capital deficiency simply because it may not be possible to eliminate the deficiency in this period of time either for physical or for cost reasons. It is therefore useful in discussing investment demand to introduce another important concept, the *marginal efficiency of investment*.

The marginal efficiency of investment (MEI) is the discount rate, $r$, which, applied to the flows from a particular *investment* project, will just make the net present value of the project equal zero. It is the value of $r$ that just satisfies Equation (21-18):

$$0 = -C + \frac{F_1}{(1 + r)^1} + \frac{F_2}{(1 + r)^2} + \cdots + \frac{F_n}{(1 + r)^n}$$

$$(21\text{-}18)$$

where $C$ is the present cost of the project and $F_1$ to $F_n$ are the flows from the project for $N$ periods. It is easy to see that the MEI is closely analogous to the MEC although MEI is concerned with investment and MEC is concerned with a unit of the capital stock. As long as the marginal efficiency of investment is greater than the rate of interest, it is rational to invest further; in other words, substituting the rate of interest, $i$, into Equation (21-18) will produce a positive net present value for the project. The difference between MEC and MEI is that the MEI, because it involves investment in a specific time period, is subject to institutional constraints. These constraints arise because as investment in a time period increases, production bottlenecks may occur in capital goods industries and increasing costs may be associated with rapid deployment of new investment goods. In terms of Equation (21-18), this means that $C$ rises as investment increases in a time period. The result of rising initial costs is falling MEI as investment increases. This is shown by the dashed curve in the right-hand portion of Figure 21-3. This curve shows that as a capital deficiency results in more rapid investment, the cost of the capital project rises and the marginal efficiency of the investment falls. As Figure 21-3 shows, it may not be possible to fill the capital deficiency in one time period.

More important for our purposes than the investment time period is the functional relation between investment and the rate of interest. Figure 21-3 suggests that as long as the rate of interest falls, investment demand will increase, even if it does so at a decreasing rate because of rising costs. Assuming, then, the existence of a capital deficiency in the first place, this means that investment is a negative function of the rate of interest. This investment function is given by Equation (21-19):

$$I = I(i), \quad dI/di < 0 \qquad (21\text{-}19)$$

In sum, optimal investment is determined in two steps. In the first step, determination is made whether there is a capital deficiency. As long as the marginal efficiency of capital is greater than the rate of interest, it is profitable to employ more capital. In the second step optimal investment is evaluated. In this case, as long as the marginal efficiency of *investment* is greater than the rate of interest, it is profitable to continue to invest. Substituting the market rate of interest for MEI produces a demand curve for optimal investment. The important aspect of investment demand is that it is a negative function of the rate of interest. Thus, the investment function provides behavior content to a second part of the income-expenditure equation [Equation (21-6)].

*Government Spending and Fiscal Policy* The third component of aggregate demand for goods and services seen in Equation (21-6) is government spending, $G$. Governments spend for a variety of reasons including education, defense, social projects, and other economic goals. The important point about government spending for purposes of constructing our simple macroeconomic model, however, is that determinants of government policy are "exogenous" to the model—in other words, they are determined by forces outside the model. Government expenditures for final goods and services ($G$) are largely determined by legislative action and political decisions rather than by variables internal to the model, such as the rate of interest or the level of income. For this reason, it is possible to assume that government spending is simply an amount determined by the political processes and to say nothing more about its behavioral determinants. In terms of Equation (21-6) and Figure 21-2, government spending can be denoted as $\overline{G}$, a quantity independent of income or the rate of interest.

*Market Equilibrium* Now that behavioral determinants of consumption, investment, and government spending have been examined (however briefly), it is possible to say something more about market equilibrium. From Equation (21-6), we know that the definition of equilibrium in the goods and services market is that expenditure equals income. Substituting the consumption function from Equation (21-9), the investment function from Equation (21-19), and exogenous government spending $\overline{G}$ into Equation (21-6), produces the following expression for equilibrium:

$$Y = bY + I(i) + \overline{G} \qquad (21\text{-}20)$$

Solving for equilibrium income leaves a function in $b$, $i$, and $\overline{G}$:

$$Y = \frac{I(i) + \overline{G}}{(1 - b)} \qquad (21\text{-}21)$$

Assuming government spending is fixed at $\overline{G}$, then Equation (21-21) shows that equilibrium income depends on the level of investment, and investment, in turn, is a function of the rate of interest. This means that equilibrium income is indeterminate unless the rate of interest is known—Equation (21-21) is a single equation, but even if $\overline{G}$ and $b$ are determined, it still contains two unknowns, $i$ and

*Y*. For each rate of interest there is a different optimal level of investment and a different equilibrium income at which $C + I + G = Y$. Graphically these relations are shown in Figure 21-4.

The first panel of Figure 21-4 shows an investment demand curve similar to the one in Figure 21-3. Optimal investment levels $I_0$, $I_1$, and $I_2$ correspond to interest rates $i_0$, $i_1$, and $i_2$. In the second panel, investment spending corresponding to the three hypothetical interest rate levels is added vertically to consumption spending in a graph that resembles Figure 21-2. These three levels of investment spending produce three equilibrium income levels, $Y_0$, $Y_1$, and $Y_2$, one for each hypothetical rate of interest. Thus, it can be seen that there is a series of combinations of the rate of interest and the level of income at which spending equals income and the goods market is in equilibrium. These combinations are plotted in the third panel of Figure 21-4, which shows that they trace out a negatively sloped curve. This curve is usually called the *IS* curve because, for any of the combinations of *i* and *Y* exhibited, investment (plus government spending) equals savings (plus taxes).

## Partial Equilibrium II: The Market for Financial Assets

As we have seen, the market for goods and services involves flows of income, consumption, investment, and total spending. The next step is to examine the holding of assets. We have already noted that when income is received, only two things can be done with it: either it can be spent (in the form of consumption or payments to the government), or it can be saved and held in some asset form. This section of the chapter looks at asset holding as the second major part of our macroeconomic framework. Following this examination, it will be possible to combine equilibrium in asset holding with equilibrium in spending on goods and services to say something about conditions of general equilibrium in the macroeconomic system as a whole.

Assets can be classified into two general groups. The first of these, real assets, makes up the economy's capital stock. In our macro model, demand for these "productive" or real assets is included in analysis of the market for goods and services. As we have seen, the demand for real capital depends on the rate of interest and the marginal efficiency

of capital. Although this involves many simplifications, this formulation is not unreasonable for our purposes. If a growing economy is assumed, demand for additional capital assets is summarized in the marginal efficiency of investment schedule— the demand for *investment* in terms of the rate of interest. The holding of other assets—*financial* assets, such as money and bonds—is in need of further analysis.

There are many kinds of financial assets, including cash (currency and coins), deposits at banks and nonbanks, and many kinds of securities, such as government bonds, corporate bonds, and money market instruments. Like real assets, financial assets provide their holders with a return that makes holding the financial assets attractive. The return can take a variety of forms, including a financial return, such as interest or capital gains, but the return may also be in nonfinancial form, such as convenience or other useful characteristics.[8] Money is one kind of financial asset that is held for reasons beyond the financial return it provides. The theory of the demand for this particular financial asset is one of the oldest branches of economics, dating to at least the sixteenth century.[9] We now direct our attention to some theories of the market for money.

Money is a financial asset that serves as a store of value like other financial assets, but it has a unique role in that it also serves as a medium of exchange. Financial assets can be divided into two groups, then: those which serve as a medium of exchange (money), and those which do not (for convenience we can call this group bonds). This division has the interesting implication that if there are two general classes of financial assets (money and bonds), then supply-demand equilibrium in the holding of one of them (for example, money) means that there is simultaneously supply-demand equilibrium in the holding of the other one (bonds). In other words, if people are not satisfied with the proportion of their financial assets that they are holding in the form of money, then simultaneously they are not satisfied with the proportion held in

---

[8]Ultimately decisions to hold any asset or not are made in the way that maximizes utility. This point is discussed further in Chapter 24.

[9]See, for example, Edwin Dean, *The Controversy Over the Quantity Theory of Money*, D. C. Heath, Lexington, Mass., 1965, which discusses, among other things, a sixteenth-century view of money demand.

**Figure 21-4  The Market Equilibrium for Goods**

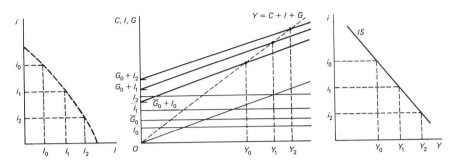

bonds. If the portion of their financial asset portfolio held in money is too large, this is the same thing as saying that the portion held in nonmoney is too small.[10] The important point is that talking about the asset market in terms either of money or bonds does not exclude the other form of financial asset. Usually the market for financial assets is described in terms of the demand for money (liquidity preference theory) rather than in terms of the demand for bonds (loanable funds theory), but the market could be described in terms of either. In this chapter we look at the market for financial assets in the familiar way—in terms of the demand for money. In the next chapter we examine the alternative—loanable funds theory—which serves as the framework for much of the book.

*The Supply of Money*  The market for financial assets can be analyzed in the same way as the market for anything else: there is a supply relation, a demand relation, and a market-clearing relation—the equality of supply to demand. This chapter concentrates on the latter two relations; further discussion of money supply is found in Chapter 5.

Analysis of money supply is a difficult problem by itself. Even the definition of money is a subject of considerable controversy. Money frequently is defined as currency and demand deposits, but other, broader, definitions are also proposed. Some monetary economists even suggest that it is not possible to define money at all without resort to empirical methodologies. For them money is whatever does money's work, and this can only be known by studying data.[11] For our purposes, this controversy is not too important; money can be defined simply as a financial asset that can be held, but which is also acceptable as a medium of exchange. We will assume it is under the control of the monetary authorities, not too unreasonable an assumption at least over a time period long enough to allow the authorities a chance to act.

One important money-supply distinction must be made at this time, however—the distinction between nominal and real money stocks. The nominal stock of money is the number of units (say, dollars) included in all the financial assets that satisfy the definition of money. For example, if money is defined as currency and demand deposits, then the nominal money stock is simply the total of the two, which we can call $M_s$. In contrast, the *real* money stock is the nominal stock adjusted for changes in the price level, in other words, real purchasing power. If $M_s$ is the nominal stock and $P$ the price index, then the real money stock is $M_s/P$. Only if

[10]This is an example of the operation of Walras's law, named after the nineteenth-century economist Leon Walras, an early student of equilibrium systems. Simply stated, Walras' law says that if all submarkets but one are in equilibrium (supply equals demand), then the last submarket must also be in equilibrium. One submarket cannot be in disequilibrium alone; it can only exhibit excess supply or demand in terms of something else. In the example here, saying that a portfolio contains too much money for its given size is the same thing as saying it contains too few bonds—either bonds and money are simultaneously in equilibrium in relation to each other or simultaneously in disequilibrium.

[11]For discussion of some of these points, see, for example, Dwayne Wrightsman, *An Introduction to Monetary Theory and Policy,* 2nd ed., The Free Press, New York, 1976.

the price level does not change will the real and nominal stocks be the same over time.

*The Demand for Money* As mentioned before, the question why people hold some of their assets in the form of money has a long history in economic thought. Before Keynes, the demand for money was part of a larger theory known as the *quantity theory of money,* although the quantity theory was also concerned with wider questions, such as the determinants of spending and causes of price fluctuations.

According to the classical quantity theorists, money was held because of the services it provided, but chief among these services was its usefulness in facilitating trade and exchange. In a world where people interact, and buy and sell goods and services, a medium of exchange greatly simplifies trade. Goods and services do not have to be exchanged directly for other goods and services as they do in a barter economy. Similarly, people do not have to exchange their own labor directly for goods or services, which they might have to exchange further in order to satisfy their needs. Instead, people are paid in money, and they buy and sell goods and services for this convenient financial asset. As long as all transactions do not take place simultaneously, and as long as it is not completely costless to hold nonmoney assets that can be converted instantly into money when needed, there will be a positive demand for money balances to facilitate transactions. In the theoretical structure of the classical economists where uncertainty was not explicitly considered, this demand for money for transaction purposes constituted the total demand for money.

Since money is held only for transaction purposes, it seemed reasonable to the classical economists that the quantity of money demanded would be related in some way to the volume of transactions. Using income as a proxy for the volume of transactions, this leads to a money demand equation of the following forms:

$$M_D = M_D(PY) \quad \text{or} \quad \frac{M_D}{P} = M_D(Y) \quad (21\text{-}22)$$

where the first form is the demand for nominal money balances and the second is the demand for real money balances. In both cases, money demand is assumed to increase with higher income—at

higher income more money is needed simply for transactions.[12] In the first case, the demand for nominal money is also higher at higher prices since there is more "work" for money to do in facilitating transactions at higher prices. The second form shows, however, how *real* money demand is not affected by prices—it is solely a function of real income. In mathematical terms this means that the derivatives of the demand for nominal money are positive with respect to prices and real income; the derivative of real money demand with respect to real income is also greater than zero.

$$\delta M_D/\delta Y > 0, \ \delta M_D/\delta P > 0, \ \delta\left(\frac{M_D}{P}\right)\!\!\Big/\delta Y > 0,$$

$$\delta\left(\frac{M_D}{P}\right)\!\!\Big/\delta P = 0 \quad (21\text{-}23)$$

In the *General Theory,* Keynes rejected the notion that money is held solely to facilitate transactions. Instead he formulated his analysis of money demand in terms of money's two primary functions—as a medium of exchange and as a store of value—and he brought uncertainty explicitly into the analysis. It is important to note how he did this.

According to Keynesian theory, money is held to facilitate spending and, on occasion, as a hedge against uncertain and changing future bond prices. Looking first at the former use, Keynes suggested, as the classical economists had done, that money is a convenient asset for simplifying transactions. Still, money provides no explicit return or a return lower than that available on alternative financial assets and, consequently, it does not seem reasonable to hold money for transaction purposes unless some further conditions are also true. The first condition is that receipts and expenditures are not perfectly synchronized. If all inflows were received and all payments made at exactly the same instant,

---

[12]This discussion does not do justice to the diversity of classical thought on money demand, much of which ultimately concerns the functional form of $M_D$. Nevertheless, this money demand function does include the essence of both the American school of the quantity theory of money, founded by Irving Fisher of Yale University, and the Cambridge school, founded by A. C. Pigou of that university, as long as it is assumed that real income, $Y$, is a reasonable proxy for both transactions and wealth. For further analysis of the classical quantity theory of money, see Dean, *The Controversy Over the Quantity Theory of Money.*

then one would not need to hold money. The second condition is that it is costly to switch back and forth continuously between money and other assets. These "brokerage costs" (such as the opportunity cost and inconvenience of time spent in transferring asset forms) increase the relative attractiveness of money holding. The result is that money will be held to facilitate transactions even if money provides a lower (or nonexistent) explicit return.

The next question is *how much* money will be held for transaction purposes. Following the classical economists, it seems reasonable to assume that transactions demand for money is related to the volume of transactions to be undertaken. Since income seems to be a good proxy for transactions, this means that transactions demand is a positive function of income. For this reason, Equation (21-22), the classical demand for money, can be used to represent transactions demand in a system that allows other motives for holding money. Keynes himself was fairly crude in his formulation of the transactions demand, essentially applying a quantity theory approach. As in Equation (21-22), the transactions demand for money is a positive function of the level of income. Arguments have been advanced since the *General Theory* about the functional form of the transactions demand (linear or not), but this controversy goes beyond the current discussion.[13] For present purposes it is sufficient to conclude that there is a demand for money balances for transaction purposes and that it is positively related to the level of income. As with the classical demand for money, money demand for transaction purposes can be expressed in terms of demand for nominal or real balances.

$$M_D^T = M_D^T(PY) \qquad \text{or} \qquad \frac{M_D^T}{P} = M_D^T(Y) \quad (21\text{-}24)$$

The second motive for holding money is the precautionary or contingency motive. The precautionary motive concerns the unknown or uncertain; the public simply desires, according to this hypothesis, to hold sufficient monetary assets to meet unexpected expenditures or exceptional opportunities. Like transaction balances, the amount of money

that the public wishes to hold for precautionary purposes will vary directly with the level of income. Abstracting again from the question whether this motive for holding money is a strictly linear function or not, the precautionary motive for holding money may be expressed in the following simple functional form. Again, as with transactions demand and the classical total-money demand, it may be expressed in nominal or real terms.

$$M_D^P = M_D^P(PY) \qquad \text{or} \qquad \frac{M_D^P}{P} = M_D^P(Y) \quad (21\text{-}25)$$

Because both transactions and precautionary demands are functions of the same thing, it is possible to combine them into one function—which is often referred to simply as the "transactions demand" for money. This is simply a modification of the definition to include both transactions and precautionary demands together. In nominal and real terms,

$$M_D^T + M_D^P = M_D^{T+P}(PY)$$

or

$$\frac{M_D^T}{P} + \frac{M_D^P}{P} = \frac{M_D^{T+P}}{P}(Y) \qquad (21\text{-}26)$$

The third motive for holding money, the speculative or asset demand for money, concerns the second primary function of money. The transactions and precautionary motives for money holding arise from the usefulness of money as a medium of exchange. In contrast, the speculative demand arises from the usefulness of money as a store of value, especially when there is uncertainty about the future price of bonds. In particular, the speculative demand arises from the belief of asset holders that the current prices of alternative assets (bonds) are too high and, consequently, that they are likely to fall. If bond prices do fall, then bondholders will sustain capital losses. When such expectations exist, bonds are less attractive as a store of value, and this suggests the possibility of an asset demand for money in addition to transactions and precautionary demands.

The question is, under what circumstances will there be a positive speculative demand for money? Holding money normally incurs an opportunity cost (forgone return) because the explicit return on money holding is less than the explicit return on

[13] For further discussion of the transactions demand for money, see Wrightsman, *An Introduction to Monetary Theory and Policy,* Chap. 7, and the references there.

bonds.[14] However, as has been seen, "brokerage costs" of asset transfers still make money holding rational for transactions and precautionary needs. The question, then, is: when is additional money holding rational for purely speculative reasons? It seems that the answer is that speculative money holdings are rational whenever the opportunity cost (loss of return) on holding money is less than the expected capital loss on holding bonds. Expressed equivalently but in different words, money holding for speculative purposes is rational whenever the forgone interest on bonds *not* purchased is less than expected capital losses if bonds *are* purchased. In the opposite case—when the forgone return on bonds is expected to be *greater* than the likely capital loss—bonds are more attractive.

The final question, then, is: when are these conditions true? It seems that the former condition—that the return forgone is less than the capital loss expected and money is preferable—is more likely when interest rates are low (that is, when bond prices are high). The opposite case, that the forgone return is *greater* than probable losses and bonds are preferable, is more likely when interest rates are high (when bond prices are low). This means, then, that the speculative demand for money is a function of the rate of interest, greater when interest rates are low and less when interest rates are high.[15] Graphically, this relation is shown in Figure 21-5.

Thus, in Keynesian theory, the total demand for money is the sum of the three components: the transactions demand, the precautionary demand, and the speculative demand.

$$M_D = M_D^T(Y)P + M_D^P(Y)P + M_D^S(i)P \quad (21\text{-}27)$$

or in real terms

$$\frac{M_D}{P} = \frac{M_D^T}{P}(Y) + \frac{M_D^P}{P}(Y) + \frac{M_D^S}{P}(i) \quad (21\text{-}28)$$

The total demand for money in real terms is shown graphically in the upper panel of Figure 21-6.

[14] The explicit return on money holding may be greater than zero.

[15] For a more detailed discussion of the speculative demand, see Harry G. Johnson, *Macroeconomics and Monetary Theory*, Aldine Publishing Company, Chicago, 1972; and Wrightsman, *An Introduction to Monetary Theory and Policy*.

**Figure 21-5  The Speculative Demand for Money**

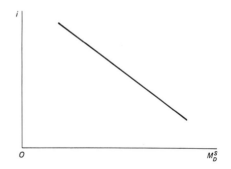

At any *given* level of real income, the speculative demand for money causes total money demand to be greater at lower interest rates. This is shown by the curve farthest to the left in the first panel of Figure 21-6. The distance *OA* represents transactions and precautionary money demand at hypothetical real income level $Y_1$. At some high rate of interest, $i_H$, speculative demand is 0 because everyone expects bond prices to rise and anticipates capital gains; consequently, total money demand consists of transactions and precautionary demands only. Below $i_H$, speculative demand is also positive, and this is reflected in a total money demand curve that slopes outward to the right as interest rates decline below $i_H$.

Total money demand also increases, however, as real incomes rise. This is shown by the second and third curves in the first panel of Figure 21-6, which represent total money demand at higher real income levels $Y_2$ and $Y_3$ with corresponding higher transactions and precautionary components. In effect, there is a family of demand curves for real money balances, one curve for each level of real income. At any given interest rate, real money demand is greater at higher real income. Since, at a given income level, money demand is also greater at lower rates of interest, then total real money demand is a positive function of real income and a negative function of the rate of interest. In mathematical terms

$$\delta\left(\frac{M_D}{P}\right)\Big/\delta Y > 0 \qquad \delta\left(\frac{M_D}{P}\right)\Big/\delta i < 0 \quad (21\text{-}29)$$

*Market Equilibrium*  Figure 21-6 also shows graphically the condition for market equilibrium:

**Figure 21-6  Equilibrium in the Market for Financial Assets**

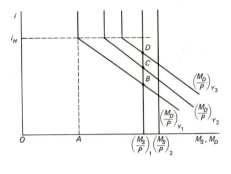

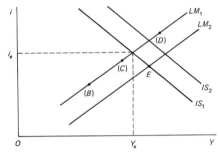

upper-sloping curve. This curve is called the *LM* curve because any point on it is a combination of the rate of interest and the level of real income at which the demand for money (liquidity preference, or *L*) equals the supply of money (*M*). Any of these combinations produces equilibrium in the market for financial assets.

### General Macroeconomic Equilibrium

In sum, we now have developed two sets of combinations of *i* and *Y* that produce an equilibrium in a part of the economic system. The first set, an inversely related series of *i* and *Y* combinations plotted as the *IS* curve in the second panel of Figure 21-6, produces equilibrium in the market for goods and services. The second set, this time positively related to one another, provides equilibrium in the holding of financial assets; this set is the positively sloped *LM* locus, which is also plotted in the second panel of Figure 21-6. We know, however, that the people who make decisions in one market are the same people who make decisions in the other. Thus, there is only one combination of *i* and *Y* that gives simultaneous equilibrium in both markets. Graphically, this general equilibrium is that combination of the rate of interest and the level of income at which *IS* = *LM*. Only at this combination of *i* and *Y* are supply and demand of goods and services in simultaneous equilibrium with supply and demand for financial assets. In the second panel of Figure 21-6, the general equilibrium combination is given by $i_e$ and $Y_e$.

A problem with the apparent simplicity of the *IS* and *LM* relations is that many other important relations are summarized in only two equations or curves. For example, the *IS* relation includes the consumption function, the demand for investment, and government expenditures, too; all of which interact in forming the *IS* equilibrium locus. Similarly, the *LM* relation hides the supply of money and multiple components or determinants of money demand; all of these factors affect the *LM* locus. A change in any of these underlying relationships will change the summary relations and the general equilibrium combination. An example or two should make this clear.

Suppose a general equilibrium combination is given by $Y_e$ and $i_e$, but this general equilibrium income is less than a full employment level of in-

that money demand equal money supply. The real supply of money, $M_S/P$, is given by the vertical line $(M_S/P)$.[16] Market equilibrium occurs at points *B*, *C*, and *D*, which indicate equality of supply and demand. Each of these points represents a combination of the rate of interest, *i*, and the level of real income, *Y*, at which there is equilibrium in the market for financial assets. These equilibrium combinations of *i* and *Y* are plotted against one another in the second panel of Figure 21-6 and trace out an

[16]This representation of the money supply as independent of the rate of interest is consistent with an assumption that the monetary authorities (the Federal Reserve System) can control the stock of money. In a model with a more rigorous development of a money supply function, it might be found that money supply is a positive function of the rate of interest; this would alter the equilibrium locus but it would not fundamentally alter the components of the framework. Also, assuming that the Federal Reserve can control the stock of money essentially assumes that prices are invariant so that a change in nominal money is converted into real money. As we will see, this assumption may be entirely unrealistic and must be removed under conditions of full employment.

come. Suppose the government decides to undertake further spending plans as a means of increasing employment. The additional spending constitutes an upward shift in autonomous government spending in Figure 21-2 causing equilibrium income to be higher for every rate of interest. Transferred to Figure 21-6, this represents a shift to the right in the *IS* curve to $IS_2$. A new equilibrium is now indicated at higher *Y* and *i*.[17]

Using another example, the government might prefer a tax reduction to a spending change as a way of raising equilibrium income. If, for example, taxes were lowered by providing tax rebates, this might cause consumption spending to be higher at every level of income in Figure 21-2 and again cause the *IS* curve to shift to the right. Assuming away, temporarily, any impacts due to increased government borrowing to finance the rebates, then this case, too, will result in higher general equilibrium levels of both *i* and *Y*. However, both cases assume constancy in the other parts of the model. Any additional changes will cause further impacts on the summary *IS* or *LM* relations.

Another possibility is an increase in the supply of money. Both of the previous examples, the first involving spending changes and the second concerned with tax changes, have involved constant levels of financial assets. Suppose now, however, that the monetary authorities decide to increase the supply of money. In the first panel of Figure 21-6, this involves a rightward shift in the real money stock from $(M_S/P)_1$ to $(M_S/P)_2$. As can be seen from the first panel of Figure 21-6, given the money demand function represented by the three curves, the new financial-asset-holding equilibrium will occur at lower rates of interest for every level of income. In terms of the second panel of Figure 21-6, this means that the *LM* curve shifts downward to the right to $LM_2$. Corresponding to this new curve is a new general equilibrium combination of *i* and *Y* at a higher level of income but at a lower rate of interest.

These three examples illustrate some important aspects of *IS-LM* analysis that should be remembered. A first point is that *IS-LM* analysis concerns changes that occur as a result of movement from one equilibrium to another. Equilibrium positions are being compared; therefore, review of *IS-LM* changes involves comparative-static analysis. Nothing is said about the time path. In the case of the monetary increase, for example, the rightward shift in the *LM* curve reveals only that the new equilibrium will be at lower *i* and higher *Y*. Nothing in the analysis suggests, however, whether the interest rate will decline quickly or slowly, or whether it will decrease continuously or have intervening upward phases until it reaches the new equilibrium level. Only a fully dynamic analysis would reveal whether the rate declines abruptly or slowly or whether it might not fluctuate upward and downward along its downward path. A second point that should be recalled is that equilibrium predictions, or even predictions about the likely direction of movement of affected variables, depend on assumptions concerning the behavior of the other parts of the model. If any of these assumptions do not hold for any reason, or if more than one change occurs simultaneously, then, clearly, an analysis that ignores the necessary interactions can lead to erroneous conclusions.

## Partial Equilibrium III: Aggregate Supply of Resources

This discussion of changes in underlying factors—including investment demand and the supply of money—that cause changes in the summary *IS* and *LM* curves implicitly has assumed that all impacts on income are on real income with no changes in prices. In fact, nothing has yet been said even about the possibility of price changes despite their frequent occurrence. So far, the analysis has assumed both that prices are constant and that real output can change either positively or negatively, assumptions that may not always be realistic. This section of the chapter examines these assumptions more carefully and ultimately discusses the circumstances surrounding the case where output is not flexible, particularly not upwardly flexible. As will be seen, this is the case when price level increases are likely to occur.

[17]Government deficits, of course, have to be financed in some way: either through higher taxes, borrowing, or monetary increases. Since each of these methods of financing also has an impact on either *IS, LM,* or both, more than one shift in the curves may be necessary before a new general equilibrium position is reached.

On occasion, production (and, consequently, real income) may be constrained by limited availability of real productive resources. If prices can vary, then any attempt by economic agents to produce more than the maximum allowed by the resource constraint will nean higher prices rather than larger output. In terms of the *IS* and *LM* curves in Figure 21-6, assume that $Y_e$ is also the income and output level associated with resource full employment. Then, shifts in either *IS* or *LM* that cause the intersection to occur at any income level greater than income level $Y_e$ will result merely in higher prices, not in more output or income.

The idea that there may be some kind of production constraint in the macroeconomy suggests that we must examine a third market, the market for productive resources, when we construct a macroeconomic theoretical structure. As with the other markets—the market for goods and services and the market for financial assets—this market may be studied by looking at the supply relation, the demand relation, and the equilibrium equation of supply to demand. Together these three relations determine the condition of the market and its impact on the other sectors. Since labor, particularly skilled labor, is the productive factor most commonly in short supply as economic activity advances—in other words, labor has the greatest inelasticity of supply at the margin—the resource market most often is examined in terms of the supply and demand for labor. This means simply that labor, especially skilled labor, is the economic resource that ultimately creates a production constraint limiting output.

*The Demand for Labor*   Assume for purposes of analysis, that output in the economy in physical terms is characterized by a two-factor production function

$$Q = Y = Q(N,K) \qquad (21\text{-}30)$$

where $Q$ is real output, $N$ is employment of labor, and $K$ is the capital stock. If, at some given point in time, the capital stock is fixed at level $\overline{K}$, then Equation (21-30) reduces to a one-factor production function

$$Q = Q(N,\overline{K}) \qquad (21\text{-}31)$$

Since, according to the law of diminishing returns, the marginal product of a variable factor dimin-

ishes, this means that the marginal physical product of labor, $\delta Q/\delta N$, decreases as more labor is employed.[18] These functions are shown in Figure 21-7 where the top panel is the production function and the bottom panel is the marginal productivity of labor, which slopes downward to the right. In mathematical terms,

$$Q = Q(N,\overline{K}), \qquad \delta Q/\delta N > 0, \qquad \delta_2 Q/\delta N^2 < 0 \qquad (21\text{-}32)$$

Now, the demand for labor by business firms depends on its price, the wage rate that must be paid, $W$. Business firms will be unwilling to pay employees more than the market value of their marginal product, but if competitive labor markets exist and if business firms hope to hire and retain employees, they will be unable to pay labor less than its marginal product either. What this means is that in an environment of competitive labor mar-

**Figure 21-7   The Market for Resources**

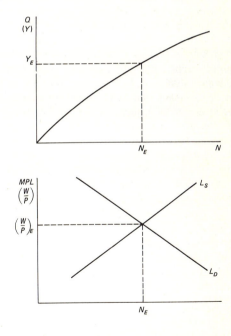

kets business firms will continue to hire labor until the market value of its marginal product $P \cdot MPL$ just equals the necessary wage rate $W$.

$$P \cdot MPL = P \cdot \delta Q / \delta N = W \qquad (21\text{-}33)$$

Dividing both sides by the average price level of output, $P$, this means that firms will hire labor until its marginal physical product is equal to the real wage, $W/P$.

$$MPL = \delta Y / \delta N = \delta Q / \delta N = W/P \qquad (21\text{-}34)$$

Taken together, Equations (21-32) and (21-34) say that since the marginal product of labor declines as employment increases (assuming constant capital stock and technology), then the real wage, $W/P$, must also decline before business firms will hire additional employees. Consequently, substituting the real wage into the lower panel of Figure 21-7 produces the demand curve for labor in terms of its real price, $W/P$. As can be seen, the demand curve for labor is an inverse function of labor cost, similar to typical demand curves.

$$L_D = L_D\,(W/P), \quad dL_D/d\left(\frac{W}{P}\right) < 0 \quad (21\text{-}35)$$

*The Supply of Labor* It is reasonable to assert that the supply of labor is also a function of the real wage rate, in this case, though, a positive function. This means that more labor will be supplied only at increasingly higher wages, not a surprising proposition. In mathematical terms, this relation is expressed by Equation (21-36) and shown graphically by the supply of labor curve $L_S(W/P)$, which slopes upward to the right in the lower panel of Figure 21-7.

$$L_S = L_S(W/P), \quad dL_S/d\left(\frac{W}{P}\right) > 0 \quad (21\text{-}36)$$

Any point along this labor supply curve denotes a "full employment" supply of labor for the corresponding real wage. Any "unemployment" along the curve is simply voluntary; in other words, an unwillingness to work except at higher real wages.

*Market Equilibrium* The remaining step is to specify the equilibrium condition in the labor market, the condition that supply equals demand.

$$L_S = L_D \qquad (21\text{-}37)$$

Graphically, this solution is given by the intersection of $L_S$ and $L_D$ in the lower panel of Figure 21-

7. The intersection of these curves determines the equilibrium real wage rate $(W/P)_E$ and the full employment amount of labor that can be employed and is willing to work, denoted by $N_E$.[19] Now, given this level of employment and the production function in Equation (21-31), maximum output is also determined; it is $Y_E$ in the upper panel of Figure 21-7. This presents a second case for our macroeconomic model summarized by the *IS* and *LM* curves of Figure 21-6.

Thus, standard *IS-LM* analysis presents two cases: first, the case examined above where there is no production constraint that limits further production and income; and second, the case just reviewed where production cannot increase further because of a resource constraint. Let us now look at this second situation by assuming that a production constraint prevents real income $Y$ from rising above income level $Y_E$. Assume also that prices can rise. Now changes in any of the underlying relationships, such as the investment function or the supply of money that would suggest equilibrium $Y$ greater than $Y_E$, simply cannot be attained. Instead, prices will rise as producers attempt to bid needed resources away from one another. An example is shown in Figure 21-8 where *IS*, and *LM*, suggest equilibrium income $Y_E$, which is also the full employment income $Y_F$. Suppose, however, that the monetary authorities decide for some reason to increase the supply of money above the level that produced $LM_1$. *IS* and the new, hypothetical, $LM_2$ intersect at $Y > Y_F$, an income level that cannot be produced. Producers attempt to expand production (either because of the effect of lower interest rates on investment or because of other more direct effects of increased money supply on spending). Because of this, prices begin to rise as producers try to bid limited resources away from one another. What happens? Rising prices decrease the real money stock $M_S/P$, causing the *LM* curve

[19]As can be seen clearly in Figure 21-7, involuntary unemployment, $L_S > L_D$, is a disequilibrium condition caused by a wage rate that is too high for the given marginal productivity of labor and willingness to work. Because it is a disequilibrium condition, it seems reasonable to conclude that pressures for change will exist. However, because of the widespread belief among the public that market forces in this area act too slowly in relation to the human misery provoked by unemployment, labor markets have become important areas for government economic-policy initiatives.

### Figure 21-8  Full Employment and Rising Prices

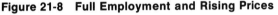

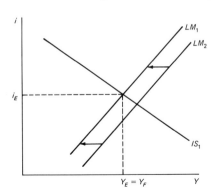
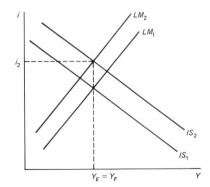

to shift backward to the left. Equilibrium returns when the real money stock has returned to its former level and $IS = LM$ at $Y_F$. We know that the real money stock must return all the way to its former level (and the $LM$ curve shift all the way back) because otherwise the rate of interest suggested by the model would be too low and the hypothetical income level could not be achieved given the resource constraint. As long as conditions in the system suggest an interest rate below $i_E$ and an income level greater than $Y_E$, prices will continue to rise.

The second panel of Figure 21-8 suggests another example, also similar to one examined earlier, but now there is a resource constraint. Suppose that government policymakers decide to undertake additional spending programs, but this time they do it under conditions of full employment (that is, at income level $Y_E = Y_F$ in the second panel of Figure 21-8). The impact of the new spending program (assuming no other changes) is shown by a shift of the $IS$ curve to new, hypothetical, $IS_2$. Equilibrium income suggested by this curve, however, cannot be produced. The result again is rising prices and, again, a decrease in the real money stock and leftward movement of the $LM$ curve. Equilibrium returns when $LM$ has shifted to $LM_2$. As can be seen, price changes induced by new government spending results in a higher equilibrium rate of interest, $i_2$.

In sum, conditions that suggest an equilibrium level of output and income greater than the level that can be produced with given resources results in rising price levels. Rising prices cause the real

money stock to decline and interest rates to rise above the levels the model would suggest in the absence of price changes. The sequential nature of these changes illustrates some important features of $IS$-$LM$ analysis. A first important point is that equilibrium analysis such as this involves the interaction of many markets and forces. Any predictions based on such models must specify properly the relationships among many variables and numerous subcomponents of the model. A second point is that, because there are so many interactions, changes in any of the variables in the model may affect more than one part of the model. Third, $IS$-$LM$ analysis says nothing about the length of time involved in any of the changes. It is a static or comparative model and reveals nothing about the time path of the changes. This seems especially important when considering price changes, which may require a long time to work themselves out fully.[20]

### Conclusion

In conclusion, this chapter has provided, in broad skeletal outline, the framework of an economic model of the macroeconomy. While this simple model cannot provide all the answers about the causes and impacts of economic events, it is a useful first step in understanding macroeconomic forces. The next step, elaboration of the interaction

[20] For further, more detailed, analysis of inflation using the $IS$-$LM$ framework, see Havrilesky and Boorman, *Monetary Macroeconomics*, especially Chaps. 13–15.

of financial markets with the macroeconomic model, forms the subject matter of the next chapter.

## Questions

1. Explain clearly the distinctions between equilibrium and disequilibrium and between statics and dynamics.
2. Define marginal efficiency of capital and marginal efficiency of investment. Explain how these concepts are related to optimal capital and optimal investment, respectively.
3. Graph the consumption function and the investment function. Show how they interact in determining equilibrium income.
4. Explain briefly the concept of *Walras's law* and explain why it might be important in studying financial asset holding.
5. Explain the concepts of the *transactions demand for money* and the *speculative demand for money.*
6. Using graphs, explain the concept of the *total demand for money* and its components. Show graphically how money supply and money demand interact to determine equilibrium conditions in the market for financial assets.
7. Show graphically how an increase in government spending might affect the macroeconomy. How might the results differ if the government decided to finance the increase in spending by increased taxation?
8. Show graphically how an increase in the supply of money might affect the macroeconomy. What does the *IS-LM* model tell us about the length of time it would take for these changes to occur?
9. Explain how the demand for labor and the supply of labor interact to form a potential constraint on total output.
10. Suppose that the government should undertake additional spending at a time when the macroeconomy is operating at full employment. Explain some of the effects we might expect to see. Use graphs in your presentation.

## Selected Bibliography

Branson, William H. *Macroeconomic Theory and Policy.* Harper and Row, New York, 1972.

Dean, Edwin. *The Controversy Over the Quantity Theory of Money.* D. C. Heath, Lexington, Massachusetts, 1965.

Ferguson, C. E., and J. P. Gould. *Microeconomic Theory,* 4th ed. Irwin, Homewood, Illinois, 1975.

Fisher, Irving. *The Theory of Interest.* New York, MacMillan, 1930.

Friedman, Milton. "The Methodology of Positive Economics." In Milton Friedman, *Essays in Positive Economics.* University of Chicago Press, Chicago, 1953.

————. *A Theory of the Consumption Function.* Princeton University Press, Princeton, New Jersey, 1957.

Havrilesky, Thomas M., and John T. Boorman, *Monetary Macroeconomics.* AHM Publishing Co., Arlington Heights, Illinois, 1978.

Hirshleifer, Jack. *Investment, Interest, and Capital.* Prentice-Hall, Englewood Cliffs, New Jersey, 1970.

Johnson, Harry G. *Macroeconomics and Monetary Theory.* Aldine Publishing Company, Chicago, 1972.

Keynes, John M. *The General Theory of Employment Interest and Money.* Harcourt Brace, New York, 1936.

Modigliani, Franco, and Richard Brumberg. "Utility Analysis and the Consumption Function," in *Post-Keynesian Economics,* ed. Kenneth K. Kurihara. Rutgers University Press, New Brunswick, New Jersey, 1954.

Nagel, E., and Paul Samuelson. "Assumptions in Economic Theory." *American Economic Review* (May 1963).

Wrightsman, Dwayne. *An Introduction to Monetary Theory and Policy*, 2nd ed. The Free Press, New York, 1976.

# 22

# Loanable Funds Theory and Interest Rate Determination

This chapter, like the previous one, attempts to explain how "the" rate of interest is determined. According to traditional Keynesian macroeconomic theory, as Chapter 21 demonstrates, interest rates are determined simultaneously with other macroeconomic variables, such as the levels of income, consumption, investment, employment, and prices. However, as early as Chapter 1, we noted that interest rates are also bound up with the supply of and demand for loanable funds. According to the thumbnail sketch in Chapter 1, the price that clears the market for loanable funds is also called "the" equilibrium rate of interest.

The purpose of this chapter is to show the connection between the traditional general equilibrium theory of interest rate determination, which is discussed in Chapter 21, and loanable funds theory, outlined in Chapter 1, which serves as the overall framework of this book. We shall see that, rather than being opposing theories of interest rate determination, liquidity preference theory and loanable funds theory are actually complementary. For this reason, even if there were no other reasons, it seems important to examine loanable funds theory. However, as we shall also see, loanable funds theory is useful for analyzing the role of financial markets in the determination of interest rates. Financial markets are present in liquidity preference theory, but this role is not always clear since financial asset holding is summarized in terms of the supply of and demand for money. Loanable funds theory makes the role of financial markets more explicit.

In this chapter we will continue to discuss interest rates in terms of "the" rate of interest, which abstracts completely from credit or default risk (long-term government bonds, for example) and from those costs involved in the handling of such securities as this rate represents. Actually, of course, we do not find "the" rate of interest in financial markets. What we do find, as we pointed out in Chapters 19 and 20, are many different interest rates reflecting, in part, the different characteristics of various types of money and capital market instruments. Such instruments differ from one another with respect to maturity, risk, transaction costs, differential tax status, and so forth, Chapters 23 and 24 systematically take into account many of these attributes in the analysis of such rate differentials. In so doing, however, they will be working at a somewhat lower level of abstraction than we propose to do here.

## Loanable Funds—A Flow Theory

Unlike the analysis in the previous chapter, loanable funds theories of the rate of interest are not usually presented in static terms. Rather than examining the reasons why economic units hold money or bonds at a point in time, as in static analysis, the loanable funds approach studies why during a period of time people lend or borrow. Unfortunately, as we shall see, examining loanable funds theory in flow terms presents some analytical difficulties. Nevertheless, because of the importance of flows in determining the time path of interest rates between equilibria, we want to examine the cause and nature of these flows.

## The Supply of Loanable Funds[1]

The supply of loanable funds during some period of time consists of several basic elements:

1. that part or flow of current saving per period of time ($S$) which is loaned out rather than hoarded ($H$)
2. net increments in the total amount of credit per unit of time supplied by the banking system

Since banks typically pay for increases in the volume of bank credit—the making of loans and the acquisition of securities—incurring additional liabilities against themselves in the form of demand deposits, we can think of such credit changes as changes in the money supply ($\Delta M$).[2] Therefore, the supply of loanable funds ($S_{lf}$) is equal to $S - H + \Delta M$. We now turn to a more detailed discussion and analysis of each of these components.

## The Rate of Saving and Its Determinants

Throughout the book, aggregate saving has been defined as the difference between GNP, or national income, and consumption expenditures ($S = Y - C$). Just as the supply of loanable funds can be broken down into its basic components, so can we break down aggregate saving in terms of the basic sectors of the economy, namely, households, business firms, and governmental units. For reasons that will become apparent later, however, we will omit government saving from the supply side and include it with the demand for loanable funds.

Net personal saving ($S_p$) is the difference between the disposable personal income of households after their payment of personal income taxes ($Y_d$) and the amount spent by them for consumer goods ($S_p = Y_d - C$). The saving is "net" rather than "gross" because we have already, in effect, subtracted consumer borrowing for the purchase of durable goods from gross saving. In other words, for the household sector as a whole we have already taken account of the fact that, for some households, expenditures for consumer goods exceed their disposable personal income—that is, they have dissaving or negative personal saving ($-S$)—while, for others, disposable personal income is greater than their consumption expenditures—their personal saving is positive ($S_p$). The difference between the two represents net personal saving for the sector as a whole.[3]

Gross business saving ($S_b$) is defined as depreciation allowances plus net business income after the payment of business taxes and the disburse-

---

[1]Parts of this and the two succeeding sections draw heavily on some basic ideas incorporated in H. H. Liebhafsky's interest theory in his book, *The Nature of Price Theory*, Dorsey Press, Homewood, Ill., 1963.

[2]Since, in discussing loanable funds, we are dealing with flow rather than with stock concepts (that is, we are interested in changes over time rather than with results at a point in time) and since, unlike saving which is a flow, the amount of money at any given moment is a stock concept, one way of transforming the latter into a flow variable is simply to take its first difference between any two points in time.

[3]In the Flow of Funds Accounts, unlike the National Income Accounts, consumer purchases of durable goods are treated as an act of investment rather than as a consumption expenditure (Chapter 2, Appendix). If we had followed the accounting concepts and terminology of the former, we could have subtracted household investment from personal saving to arrive at excess saving by this sector. We could have done the same for the business and governmental sectors so that, for the economy as a whole, such consolidation would have left us with our surplus and deficit sectors, or ultimate lenders and borrowers. That we have deliberately chosen not to net out such differences between internal saving and investment for the household and business sectors represents nothing more than a concession to conventional methods of presenting loanable funds theory.

ment of dividends $(Y_b)$.[4] *Net* business income is identical with what is also called retained earnings.

These paragraphs represent nothing more than a set of definitional and *ex post* equalities. As such, they tell us nothing about the reasons why our basic sectors save. Let us now turn to some explanations for such saving.

According to the classical and neoclassical economists, the volume of saving desired by the public required the existence of a positive rate of interest. It was also thought to rise with a rise in interest rates. The higher the interest rate, the greater would be the amount of saving desired by the public, other things being equal. The lower the rate of interest, the less would be the quantity of saving desired by the public. The rationale for such a positive-sloping saving schedule lay in the basic assumption that, other things being equal, people preferred present goods to future goods. Therefore, people could be induced to abstain from consuming all of their current income—to save—only if such an act of abstention provided greater consumption in the future.[5] The higher the rate of interest, the greater would future consumption be relative to current consumption foregone and the greater would be the volume of saving. Thus, the aggregate supply schedule of saving, as depicted in Figure 22-1, shows a positive correlation between these two variables with no saving at a zero rate of interest. Furthermore, for most of the classical and neoclassical economists, the supply of saving and the supply of loanable funds were one and the same thing, with saving being used to acquire primary securities in the money and capital markets.

While it seemed obvious to the classical and neoclassical economists that saving varied directly with the rate of interest and, moreover, was highly interest elastic, this conclusion was predicated on certain basic assumptions. For one thing, as we have seen, economists believed that people had a positive time preference such that, for example, if

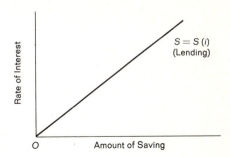

**Figure 22-1  The Aggregate Supply of Saving and Loanable Funds**

the typical person had a choice of equal incomes this year and the next, or a larger income this year accompanied by a correspondingly smaller income next year, that person would choose the latter pattern. However, many frugal people tend to overvalue rather than undervalue future to present income. This, in turn, implies that such people may be willing to save out of current income even at a zero rate of interest. As has been stated elsewhere, and by a firm believer in neoclassical theory, there is no proof that society as a whole tends to discount future relative to present consumption, at least in real terms.[6]

Another basic assumption of the classical and neoclassical economists was the postulate of a positive-sloping saving function at a given level of income represented by full employment of all resources. Suppose, however, that a full employment level of income represents only one possibility, with various levels of underemployment also being possible. Then it seems common sense that the ability to save as well as the amount saved are primarily functions of the level of income rather than of the rate of interest. No matter how enticing interest rate levels may appear by themselves, aggregate saving will be very low, or nonexistent, at income levels approximating bare subsistence. We know, for example, that interest rates are very high in the capital-scarce developing nations, even as compared to our own in recent years. Nevertheless, the volume of domestic saving in such countries is pitifully low relative to saving here. Conversely, in a country with very high income levels

[4]Since business expenditures for consumer goods are, by definition, equal to zero, it follows that $S_b$ and $Y_b$ must always be equal to one another.

[5]For a discussion of what must be included in the phrase "other things being equal," see Appendix 22-2 at the end of this chapter. This appendix is designed for those students who may desire a somewhat more sophisticated version of the positive time preference argument. The appendix elucidates the argument using a geometric example involving indifference curve analysis.

[6]George Stigler, *The Theory of Price,* 3rd ed., The Macmillan Company, New York, 1966, p. 280.

like our own, saving probably would be positive even at a zero rate of interest. The pronounced differences in saving obviously are primarily related to significant differences in income levels rather than to interest rates.

Of course, none of this negates the assertion that a return on saving is preferred to no return, or that higher yields are preferred to lower yields. Rather, it stresses the fact that people do not save primarily to obtain a return on their saving. However, once the volume of saving is more or less given by the level of income, the forms in which such saving is held (that is, whether in the form of money or in the form of higher-yielding financial assets) is obviously affected by the rate of interest. In fact, this is a major reason for distinguishing between the supply of savings and the supply of loanable funds. While saving is an essential source of loanable funds, it is not basically responsive to changes in interest rates. On the other hand, the supply of loanable funds—which includes that portion of current saving not hoarded, as well as changes in bank credit—is responsive to interest rate changes, as later sections of this chapter make evident.

Finally, even if one, for the sake of argument, were to go along with the classical and neoclassical notions of saving as being not only dependent on, but also an increasing function of, the rate of interest, such a contention would still be open to some controversy. Thus, some individuals might wish to save in order to acquire a fixed amount of wealth in the future. To the extent that interest rates rose, to that extent such individuals would be enabled to save less currently to meet their future wealth goals. Similarly, while an increase in the rate of interest might lead, according to this approach, to the substitution of future for current consumption, it seems only fair to point out the other side of this coin, to wit, that this might be more than offset by such an improvement in future income prospects resulting from the interest rate change as would lead to current saving being less than before the rate change. In other words, for those prepared to accept such an argument, one could point out that at sufficiently high and rising interest rates, the net result might be a backward-sloping supply curve of saving.[7]

Given these criticisms of the classical and neoclassical theories of interest, how would one depict the relationship between aggregate saving (*S*) and the rate of interest? As Figure 22-2 shows, positive saving probably would take place even at a zero rate of interest in an economy such as our own given the motivations for saving that we have just mentioned and given the ability to save. However—and as a minor concession to neoclassical theory—the saving schedule can be drawn as being highly, if not completely, interest inelastic, that is, basically unresponsive to moderate interest rate changes. Moreover, apart from the slope, or curvature, of the saving schedule, a change in the value of one of the parameters (for example, an increase in the level of income from *Y* to *Y'*) will result in a shift to the right in the saving schedule such that, at each rate of interest, the amount of saving desired will increase by *RS*.[8]

## Hoarding and Dishoarding and Their Determinants

As already suggested, the classical and neoclassical economists were mistaken in assuming that the supply of saving constituted the total supply of

**Figure 22-2   The Aggregate Supply of Saving**

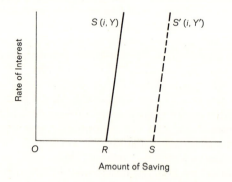

---

of future for current consumption induced by these higher and rising rates. For an analysis and discussion of income and substitution effects resulting from price changes, see any standard text in price theory, such as Stigler, *The Theory of Price*, pp. 63–68.

[8] There is no reason to assume that a shift in the position of the saving schedule will also involve a change in its slope. Therefore, the *S*(*i, Y*) and *S'*(*i, Y'*) schedules are so drawn as to be parallel to one another.

[7] Less saving would result because the income effect of such higher interest rates would outweigh the substitution

loanable funds.[9] In addition to the supply of saving, banks may add to the supply of loanable funds by net increments in their loans and other financial investments ($\Delta M$). Also, in a money- and credit-using economy, account must be taken of the fact that, at any given moment of time, the amount of money that people desire to hold (a desired stock of cash holdings) can diverge from the amount that they do hold (an actual or *ex post* stock). The difference between desired and actual money holdings may be defined as hoarding (a flow), or

$$H = M_D - M_S \qquad (22\text{-}1)$$

where $M_D$ represents the desired holdings and $M_S$ the actual amount available for holding.

While we shall shortly discuss the determinants of the desire to hoard, we can say at this point that if $H$ is positive, or if the amount of cash balances people desire to hold is greater than the amount they actually do hold, hoarding will take place. Conversely, if $H$ is negative, or if the amount of money held exceeds desired cash balances, dishoarding will occur. Assuming, for the moment, no changes in the money supply ($\Delta M$), hoarding would imply a subtraction from current saving such that the supply of loanable funds ($S_{lf}$) would be less than the supply of saving. On the other hand, if dishoarding occurred—and still assuming no change in the money supply—this would mean that, in addition to current saving, people would be putting to work previously accumulated saving that they had been holding in the form of idle cash balances. As a result, the supply of loanable funds during the period would exceed the supply of saving out of current income. In order to ascertain whether hoarding or dishoarding will take place, decreasing or increasing the supply of loanable funds out of saving, we must now analyze the relationship between desired and actual money balances and the determinants of each.

As we saw in Chapter 21, there are three basic motives for desiring to hold money ($M_D$): the transactions, the contingency or precautionary, and the speculative motives. The demand for transaction balances ($M_D^T$) refers to the fact that the public

wishes to hold money temporarily for the purpose of financing needed expenditures on goods and services as they arise between income payments. Since there is a lack of synchronization between flows of income and outlays for goods and services, the public must keep sufficient money balances to bridge the gap. Some of the long-run determinants affecting the transactions demand for money are:

1. the payment habits of the community
2. the degree of vertical integration in the production process
3. the development of the financial system of a country

To the extent that the public is paid biweekly instead of monthly, for example, money will be sitting idle for a shorter period of time, on the average, with the result that the same level of spending will be attainable with smaller transaction balances and, hence, with a smaller supply of money (the velocity of money will rise). In short, a speedup in the payment habits of the community tends to reduce the transactions demand for money. Similarly, the greater the degree of vertical integration of productive processes carried on within firms and, therefore, the smaller the number of separate firms each carrying their own cash balances, the smaller will be the transactions demand to finance the entire process. Furthermore, as the financial system of a country develops and attains maturity, it becomes simpler for the public to obtain credit instead of holding larger cash balances to bridge the income-outlay gap. Such developments, therefore, will result in a lower transactions demand for money.

In addition to these, a basic determinant for holding transaction balances is the level of income. While the institutional determinants described change very slowly over time, changes in the level of income are subject to significant short-run as well as long-run changes. Assuming that the institutional variables are constant in the short run, the quantity of money demanded for transaction purposes will vary directly with the level of income. Thus, Figure 22-3 indicates that, as the level of income increases, the quantity of money required for transaction purposes also increases. Should the institutional determinants that we have described change, the result would be a shift in the schedule for transaction balances.

[9]An exception to this statement may be found in the writings of the Swedish economist Knut Wicksell. See his *Lectures in Political Economy,* Vol. 2, George Routledge and Sons, London, 1934.

**Figure 22-3 The Transactions Demand for Money**

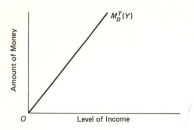

Unlike the transactions motive—which pertains to the known, or certain, rhythm of income and outlays—the precautionary motive ($M_D^P$) concerns the unknown or uncertain. The public desires to hold sufficient money to meet unexpected expenditures, which may be the result either of emergencies or exceptional opportunities. For example, when going on vacation it would be foolhardy indeed to budget for known expenditures without allowing for the possibility of the car breaking down, accident and illness, and so forth. Like the transactions motive, the amount of money that the public wishes to hold for precautionary purposes will vary directly with its level of income. Figure 22-3, therefore, can serve as a proxy for the contingency as well as the transactions demand for money.[10]

The third motive for wishing to hold money, namely, the speculative motive ($M_D^S$), concerns the desire of the public to hold cash in order to take advantage of an anticipated fall in the prices of securities, or conversely, of a rise in their interest rates. Since we are dealing with "the" interest rate, this is tantamount to saying that the public desires to hold cash balances so as to take advantage of an expected fall in the price of, for example, long-term government bonds or an increase in their yield.[11] Obviously, the more people expect the interest rate to rise in the future, the greater will be the demand for idle cash balances currently. But this still leaves

unresolved the basic question as to what causes such expectations in the first place.

One way of handling this problem is by considering what people conceive to be a "normal range" of rates. Whether a rate is thought to be high or low is primarily a function of the public's recent experience. Thus, if the rate of interest has fluctuated recently in a range of 7 to 9 percent, the fact that it is now at 10 percent will lead to the expectation of a decline in the rate to a more normal level. Consequently, the public will exchange idle speculative balances for bonds in order to take advantage of the high yield as well as the anticipated capital gain that may be realized when the rate declines and the price increases. Conversely, should the current yield be 5 percent, the public will sell bonds and hold cash since it expects the rate to rise in the future. Also, if the rate does increase as anticipated, those still willing to hold bonds instead of money will be faced with a decline in the prices of the bonds and the possibility of capital losses. The avoidance of potential capital losses as well as lower yields will accelerate the substitution of money for bonds. At yields very much above the normal range, it might well be expected that the demand for speculative balances would be close to zero. Conversely, at extremely low rates, the demand for idle cash balances might well be infinitely elastic.[12] Consequently, as depicted in Figure 22-4, the speculative demand for money varies inversely with the rate of interest, rising as the interest rate declines and falling as the rate of interest rises.[13]

---

[10] Figure 22-3 is drawn so as to suggest that changes in the demand for transaction and contingency balances are proportional to changes in income. To the extent that this is not so (for example, desired cash balances for these purposes may be subject to economies of scale), the slope depicting these relationships would be nonlinear in character.

[11] The speculative demand for money is also discussed in Chapter 21.

[12] For a critique of the notion that there can ever exist an infinite demand for speculative balances, see Don Patinkin, *Money, Interest, and Prices: An Integration of Monetary and Value Theory,* 2nd ed., Harper & Row, New York, 1965.

[13] Many economists who accept the notion of an asset demand for money have serious reservations about, or reject outright, speculation as the source of this demand. Instead, other reasons are put forth as to why the demand for idle balances may respond to changes in the interest rate. Some of these reasons include the size distribution of individual wealthholdings and transaction, and other, costs of buying and selling securities, as well as the degree of aversion to risk and the lack of consensus as to the direction of the change in the rate of interest. Since these reasons do not alter the nature of the inverse relationship between the demand for idle balances and the rate of interest, there is no need, for our purposes, to pursue them in great detail. For an interesting review of these

**Figure 22-4 The Speculative Demand for Money**

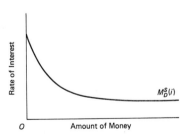

**Figure 22-5 The Total Demand for Money**

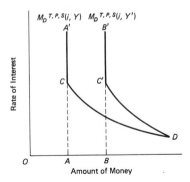

Given the total demand for money represented by the transactions, contingency, and speculative motives, what will the functional or behavioral relationship between the rate of interest and this total demand look like? The answer is provided in Figure 22-5, which is the same as the first panel of Figure 21-6 in the previous chapter. As we have already noted, both the transactions and the contingency demands for money are functions of the level of income rather than of the rate of interest. Another way of stating the same thing is by saying that these demands for cash are infinitely interest inelastic. Thus, in Figure 22-5, that segment of the schedule for the total demand for money represented by the transactions and precautionary demands is labeled $A'A$ and is parallel to the vertical, or interest rate, axis. It shows that, regardless of the level of rates, the amount of money desired to satisfy these motives will be equal to $OA$. Obviously, $OA$ is a positive amount which depends on the level of income, $Y$. That segment of the curve labeled $CD$ represents the speculative demand for money and varies inversely with the rate of interest. Hence, the position and slope of the

total demand for money schedule is given by $A'D$. Suppose now that there is an increase in the level of income from $Y$ to $Y'$. The result will be a rightward shift in the demand curve for money since the public will now desire to hold more transactions and contingency balances than before at each rate of interest. Hence, the new demand for money schedule represented by an increase in income from $Y$ to $Y'$ will be $B'D$ instead of $A'D$ as formerly. In sum, changes in the level of income will shift the whole demand for money curve, while changes in the rate of interest will change the quantities demanded via movements along a given demand curve.

In contrast to our rather lengthy discussion of the determinants of the demand for money, we shall say very little concerning the money supply.[14] For our purposes, it is sufficient to state that the money supply can be taken as an exogenous variable substantially under the control of the Federal Reserve System. Therefore, at any given point in time, the supply of money is a fixed amount, which does not vary with changes in the rate of interest.[15]

issues, see Gardner Ackley, *Macroeconomic Theory,* The Macmillan Company, New York, 1961, pp. 182–184. On the other hand, see John G. Gurley and Edward S. Shaw, *Money in a Theory of Finance,* The Brookings Institution, Washington, D.C., 1960, pp. 70–71, for a discussion of a possible diversification demand for money resulting from the growth of near-money substitutes created by nonbank financial intermediaries. The significance of the latter development lies in its potential for causing instability in the asset demand schedule for money. The importance of this will be stressed later in the chapter when we discuss the role of financial intermediaries in loanable funds theory

[14]For a detailed analysis and discussion, see Chapter 5.

[15]We probably are simplifying somewhat in representing the supply curve of money as being perfectly interest inelastic. To the extent that the Fed does take account of interest rates in deciding on the quantity of reserves it will make available to the banking system (such reserves providing the base for bank credit), to that extent the money supply schedule will respond, in some measure, to interest rate changes. Also, it should be noted that with the recent advent of NOW accounts and share drafts as part of the basic money supply, the public's desire to substitute such interest-bearing cash balances for time

**Figure 22-6 The Supply and Demand for Money**

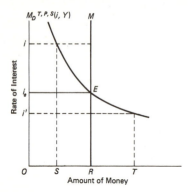

This—along with the schedule of the demand for money—is shown in Figure 22-6 as a line parallel to the vertical axis.[16]

We are now in a position to relate what is happening in the money market, as seen in Figure 22-6, to the problem of hoarding and dishoarding and their impacts on the supply of loanable funds during the same period of time. At the equilibrium rate of interest represented by $i_e$, the amount of money the public desires to hold is just equal to the money supply ($OR$), or to the amount that they actually do hold. (Note that at any given point in time, the quantity of money outside banks—that is, the money supply—must be identical with the amount of money actually held by the public since money cannot escape being held by someone.) As we have already seen, the difference between what the public desires to hold in the way of cash balances, and what it does hold, is equal to hoarding or dishoarding, depending on whether this difference is positive or negative. At $i_e$, however, the amounts desired and actually held are equal, or the difference between the two is zero, so no hoarding or dishoarding occurs. Consequently, there is no change in the supply of loanable funds at $i_e$ that arises from changes in hoarding.

However, let us now turn to the relationship between desired and actual holdings of money at interest rate $i'$. At $i'$ we observe that the amount of cash balances the public desires to hold ($OT$) is greater than the amount it actually does hold ($OR$). This holds true for all rates of interest below $i_e$. In other words, for all rates of interest less than $i_e$, the difference between the quantities of money desired to be held, and the amounts actually held, will be positive, and hoarding will occur. Conversely, at interest rate $i'$. At $i'$, we observe that the amount of ($OS$) is less than the amount actually held by the public ($OR$). This relationship holds true for all rates of interest above $i_e$. In other words, for all rates of interest greater than $i_e$, the difference between the amounts of money the public desires to hold and the quantities actually held will be negative, and dishoarding will occur.

Figure 22-7 relates zero, positive, and negative hoarding to the supply of saving and the supply of loanable funds (still assuming that there are no changes in the money supply).[17] At interest rate $i_e$, which corresponds to the same equilibrium rate of interest found in Figure 22-6, no hoarding or dishoarding occurs, or $H$ is equal to zero. Therefore, the difference between the saving supply potentially available to be loaned out $S(i, Y)$, and that part of it which is hoarded $[S(i, Y) - H(i, Y)]$, is equal to zero at interest rate $i_e$. In other words, at $i_e$ both schedules are equal to one another and they intersect. Thus, the potential volume of saving available to be loaned out, or to acquire securities, is, in fact, the actual quantity of saving that will be employed in this manner ($i_e E$). The supply of saving and the supply of loanable funds represented by $[S(i, Y) - H(i, Y)]$ will be equal.

As we have already seen in Figure 22-6, at interest rate $i'$, desired cash balances are greater than actual balances and hoarding occurs. Interest rate $i'$ in Figure 22-7 corresponds to the same rate as in Figure 22-6. Hoardings in both cases are also equal, amounting to $RT$ in Figure 22-6 and $AB$ in Figure 22-7. Thus, at $i'$, the difference between the volume of saving ($i'B$) and hoarding ($AB$) is equal to the supply of loanable funds ($i'A$).

---

deposits can lead to *shifts* in the money supply schedule, if not directly affecting the *slope* of that schedule.

[16]We have here assumed that the money supply and the demand for money are independent of one another. Only in this way can we ascertain whether changes in the interest rate are a function of changes in money demand or supply.

[17]If there are no changes in the money supply then, in effect, $S - H$ represents the total supply of loanable funds per period of time since, of course, $\Delta M = 0$, and the total supply of loanable funds is defined as $S - H + \Delta M$.

**Figure 22-7    The Relationship of Hoarding and Saving to Loanable Funds**

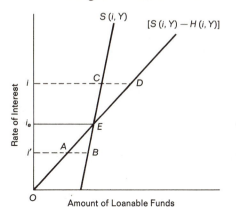

Finally, as seen in Figure 22-6, at interest rate $i$, the quantity of money balances desired by the public is less than the cash balances they actually hold. Consequently, dishoarding occurs. Interest rate $i$ in Figure 22-7 corresponds to the same rate as in Figure 22-6. Dishoardings in both cases are equal, amounting to $SR$ in Figure 22-6 and $CD$ in Figure 22-7. Thus, at $i$, the volume of current saving, $iC$, is supplemented with dishoarding of idle cash balances out of past saving, $CD$, so that the supply of loanable funds during the period is greater than the volume of saving by $CD$. Obviously, changes in the level of income would result in shifts both of the saving and $[S(i, Y) - H(i, Y)]$ schedules since the value of this parameter influences the position of both schedules.

## Changes in the Money Supply and Loanable Funds

Until now we have ignored changes in the money supply, or $\Delta M$, as one of the major sources of loanable funds. The acquisition of additional securities by the banking system is a function of its excess reserves and these, in turn, are more or less determined by central-bank policy. As in our previous discussion of the stock of money, we can take changes in that stock, or flows, as being exogenously determined by Federal Reserve policy. To whatever extent there are changes in the money supply from one period to the next, there will be corresponding shifts in the $\Delta M$ schedule.

Figure 22-8 presents a complete picture of the supply of loanable funds with $\Delta M$ being added to saving and hoarding or dishoarding. The $\Delta M$ schedule is drawn parallel to the vertical axis since it is assumed to be a function of central-bank policy; it does not respond primarily to changes in the rate of interest. $\Delta M$ is equal to $OG$. The schedule $[S(i, Y) - H(i, Y) + \Delta M]$, or the aggregate supply of loanable funds ($S_{lf}$), is depicted as being parallel to the $[S(i, Y) - H(i, Y)]$ schedule since the difference between them is a constant equal to $\Delta M$.[18] At $i_e$, $S(i, Y)$ is equal to $[S(i, Y) - H(i, Y)]$, with the total supply of loanable funds being greater than both by $EF$, which is equal to $OG$, or $\Delta M$. At $E_1$, since $AB = BE_1 = \Delta M$, and $BE_1$ also equals $H$, $\Delta M = H$. Therefore, $\Delta M - H = 0$, and the supply of loanable funds must be equal to saving since $\Delta M$ and $H$ just offset one another, enabling the $S_{lf}$ and $S(i, Y)$ curves to intersect at $E_1$. Also, at that point, both $\Delta M$ and $H$ are greater than zero.

## The Demand for Loanable Funds

Just as the supply of loanable funds comprises several basic components, so does the demand for loanable funds during some period of time. First of

**Figure 22-8    The Supply of Loanable Funds**

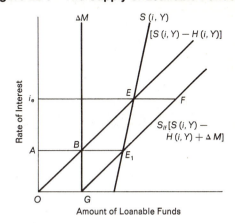

[18]Whether a change in the money stock in fact leads to an equivalent, less than equivalent, or nonexistent shift in the loanable funds schedule really depends on what the public desires to do with the additional money balances. This problem is discussed at some length later in the chapter.

all, we have the demand for loanable funds by such ultimate borrowers as business firms. The latter need funds for investment purposes; that is, they wish to acquire new plant and equipment as well as to add to their inventories and, normally, such demand exceeds their internal sources of saving. Second, there is the demand by government, including federal, state, and local units. Previously, in discussing the components of aggregate saving, we deliberately omitted governmental saving from the supply of loanable funds since such saving typically is negative. Governmental units as a whole usually spend more for final goods and services ($G$) than their net income, or revenue, arising out of tax receipts minus transfer payments ($S_g = G - T_n$).[19] Therefore, since most governmental units usually are faced with budgetary deficits ($-S_g$, or $G > T_n$) rather than budgetary surpluses ($S_g$, or $G < T_n$) and, since governmental units normally have to borrow to finance such differences between their incomes and expenditures ($B_g$), we believe that it is advisable to add this net difference to the demand side for loanable funds.[20]

A third demand for loanable funds arises from the household sector, which wishes to borrow to finance expenditures on durable goods. However, we have already taken account of such consumer borrowing, or dissaving, by subtracting it from gross personal saving to arrive at net personal saving for the sector as a whole. Unlike the government sector, aggregate net personal saving invariably has been positive and so we have added it to the supply of loanable funds.[21]

The final demand for loanable funds, hoarding ($H$), was already taken account of when we decided to place it on the supply side in the form of a deduction from saving ($S - H$). Again, this is simply a matter of preference and convenience rather than of logical necessity. Thus, we can now picture our final results as having been derived in the following manner:

$$S + T_n + \Delta M = I + G + H \quad (22\text{-}2)$$
$$S - H + T_n + \Delta M = I + G \quad (22\text{-}3)$$
$$S - H + \Delta M = I + (G - T_n) \quad (22\text{-}4)$$
$$S - H + \Delta M = I + B_g \quad (22\text{-}5)$$

or

$$S_{lf} = I + B_g \quad (22\text{-}6)$$

Furthermore, the sum of private investment demand ($I$) and government borrowing ($B_g$) constitutes the net demand for loanable funds, or

$$I + B_g = D_{lf} \quad (22\text{-}7)$$
$$\therefore S_{lf} = D_{lf} \quad (22\text{-}8)$$

Equations (22-2) through (22-8) represent nothing more than a set of definitional and *ex post* equalities. We now turn to a brief analysis of the determinants of investment demand and government borrowing[22]—just as we have previously done for $S$, $H$, $\Delta M$—since we are interested in the factors determining their behavior.

## Investment Demand and Its Determinants

Any business decision involving potential investment must, at the same time, also take account of several other possible alternatives, to wit, purchases of outstanding or newly issued debt instruments, and purchases of secondhand real assets—used machinery, for example. Only when new capital goods are purchased, however, will there be investment by others, so that there is a net increment to the capital stock.[23] For such a decision to take place, however, the newly produced capital

---

[19] Transfer payments are payments to the public for which a current productive service is not received in return as, for example, old age assistance. Consequently, transfer payments are not part of GNP.

[20] If we desired to do so, we could just as well have left $S_g$ on the supply side even if it turned out to be negative. In that case we would have deducted this amount from the total supply of loanable funds without showing it on the demand side. Or, instead of taking the net difference between $T_n$ and $G$ ($=S_g$) and placing it either on the supply or demand side, we could simply have added $T_n$ to the supply side as a gross source of loanable funds and $G$ to the demand side as a gross use of loanable funds. Our decision to place $S_g$ ($=B_g$) on the demand side is a matter of preference rather than of logic.

[21] Furthermore, not only is net personal saving positive but even if we subtracted from it intermediate- and long-term consumer borrowing in the form of instalment credit and home mortgages, for example (the Flow of Funds

Accounts treats both housing expenditures and the purchase of consumer durables as investment by households), the household sector would still remain, on balance, a surplus sector financing such typically deficit sectors as business firms and government.

[22] Further details on consumer, business, and government demand are provided in Chapters 12–18.

[23] The total value of newly produced capital goods is known as gross investment. Some of these recently pro-

goods must be expected to yield a higher rate of return than the other alternatives. This is true whether the business firm uses its own internally generated saving or borrows, since even self-financed investments involve an opportunity cost inasmuch as these funds could have been used to purchase financial assets or secondhand real assets having their own rates of return. In sum, what is involved is a comparison of the rates of return of different types of assets, and this is a function of time and uncertainty about the future returns.

As we saw in Chapter 21, investors continue to invest during a time period as long as the rate of interest is less than the marginal efficiency of investment. When the anticipated future earnings from an investment are discounted by the current rate of interest, the result is the present value of the asset. Thus,

$$NPV = -C + \frac{F_1}{1+i} + \frac{F_2}{(1+i)^2} + \cdots + \frac{F_n}{(1+i)^n}$$

$$(22\text{-}9)$$

where $NPV$ is the net present value of the asset (the net current value of all the future earnings); $F_1 \cdots F_n$ is the expected money inflows above expenses (prospective annual returns) in years 1, 2, to the last year of the asset's life; $i$ is the market rate of interest, and $C$ is the present cost of the asset. So long as the net present value of the capital good ($NPV$) is positive, it will be profitable to continue to invest. This amounts to saying that so long as the rate of interest is less than the marginal efficiency of investment, or the internal rate of return, the inducement to invest will continue. Conversely, when the rate of interest is greater than the marginal efficiency of investment—when the value of the capital good is less than its cost—such investment will not take place. Equilibrium will be reached when investment is extended to that point where the marginal efficiency of investment and the interest rate are equal, or where the present value is equal to the replacement cost of the capital good.[24]

duced capital goods will be used as replacements for that part of the stock of capital goods used up in the productive process. The remainder constitutes net investment.

[24]Chapter 21 examines these relationships in more detail. Obviously, most small businesses do not explicitly undertake analyses of the type suggested here, although implicitly they are considering these factors.

**Figure 22-9   Investment Demand Schedule**

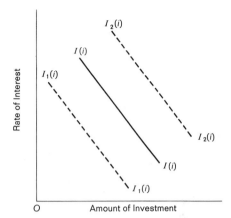

At any given time, there exists a large array of potential investment projects in the economy. As we saw in Chapter 21, if the rate of interest falls, some additional investment will be undertaken because the net present value of more projects is positive. Therefore, it follows that investment is a function of the rate of interest, increasing as the interest rate declines. As Figure 22-9 makes clear, the investment demand schedule is negative sloping, which indicates the inverse relationship between such demand and the rate of interest.[25]

[25]There is still a great deal of controversy in the theoretical and empirical literature surrounding the degree of elasticity of the investment demand schedule, or just how responsive investment is to changes in the rate of interest. It seems fair to say that, while no general consensus has emerged as yet, most of the disputants consider the rate of interest to be of generally minor importance compared to other relevant variables that influence investment decisions through their impacts on such investment costs and expected annual returns. Changes in the values of these variables, discussed later, can cause shifts in the investment demand schedule (see dashed $I$ schedules in Figure 22-9), which may overwhelm movements along the curve resulting from changes in the rate of interest. In other words, the fact that the interest rate may be of minor importance in investment decisions does not imply that the investment demand schedule is interest inelastic. Even if it were highly elastic, its effects might still be overwhelmed by the instability of the schedule (shifts of the curve). Chapter 12 discusses this matter more fully.

## Federal Government Borrowing and Its Determinants

While investment demand during some time period is responsive to changes in the rate of interest—the only question being the degree of its interest elasticity—the same cannot be said of federal government borrowing ($B_f$), or the relationship of $T_{nf}$ and $G_f$. Given the structure of tax rates, $T_{nf}$ is primarily a function of the level of gross national product, or $Y$. Similarly, federal government expenditures for final goods and services ($G_f$) are determined by legislative action rather than by changes in the rate of interest. Thus, fiscal policy, which may be defined as the relationship of federal government revenues to expenditures, is basically independent of the rate of interest.[26] It is, in fact, a political decision. As seen in Figure 22-10, $B_f(Y)$, therefore, is drawn parallel to the vertical axis. When it is added to the investment demand schedule, the combined result is a demand schedule $[I(i) + B_f(Y)]$ parallel to $I(i)$ since the difference between the two represents $B_f$, a constant, at any given level of income. Should the level of income change, both the $B_f$ schedule and the $I + B_f$ curve will also shift, and by the same amounts, since the former is affected by the level of income while the latter is composed, in part, of borrowing by the federal government.

## State and Local Government Borrowing and Their Determinants

Unlike borrowing by the federal government ($B_f$), which is perfectly interest inelastic, the timing of state and local government borrowing, or $G_{s/l} - T_{ns/l}$, is affected, to some degree, by changes in the rate of interest. The volume of such borrowing decreases as interest rates rise.[27] In terms of our

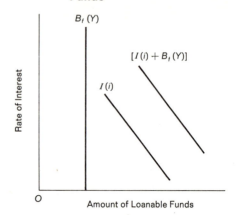

**Figure 22-10  Federal Government Borrowing and the Demand for Loanable Funds**

model, this implies that when state and local borrowing ($B_{s/l}$) is added horizontally to borrowing by the federal government ($B_f$) to give us borrowing for all governmental units ($B_g$), the result is not only a schedule to the right of $I(i)$ and $B_f(Y)$ but also one where the difference between the total demand for loanable funds curve ($D_{lf} = I + B_g = I + B_f + B_{s/l}$) and $I + B_f$ varies with changes in the rate of interest.

This can be seen in Figure 22-11, depicting the behavioral relationship between the total demand for loanable funds schedule and the rate of interest. Should the level of income change, both the $B_{s/l}$ and $D_{lf}$ schedules will shift since the former, like $B_f$, is also affected by the level of income, while the latter, as we have already shown, is partially composed of borrowing by state and local governments as well as borrowing by the federal government.

## Loanable Funds and Interest Rate Determination

Given our discussion of the components making up the supply of and demand for loanable funds, as well as the determinants of each of these components, we are finally in a position to tackle the problem of interest rates within the period of time under consideration. Figure 22-12 indicates that the loanable funds, or securities, market presumably will be in equilibrium at $E_1$ since, at interest $i_1$, the supply of, and demand for, loanable funds during

---

[26]This does not mean that debt management, or managing the composition of the federal government debt, is also independent of the rate of interest. For example, given a budgetary deficit arising out of $G_f > T_{nf}$, government debt managers will still attempt to finance such a deficit as cheaply as possible.

[27]In this connection, see Paul F. McGoldrick and John E. Petersen, "Monetary Restraint and Capital Spending by Large State and Local Governments in 1966," *Federal Reserve Bulletin* (July 1968). For a much more detailed discussion and analysis of this whole matter as well as the relationship between interest rates and capital expenditures by state and local governments, see Chapter 16.

**Figure 22-11  All Government Borrowing and the Demand for Loanable Funds**

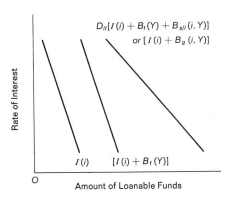

**Figure 22-12  The Loanable Funds Market and the Equilibrium Rate of Interest**

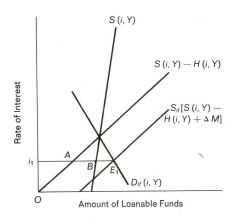

the period will be equal. While this is true, it represents, at best, only a partial and unstable equilibrium since, simultaneously, there is disequilibrium between intended saving, on the one hand, and planned investment plus the difference between governmental expenditures for final goods and services and governmental net revenue, on the other, or disequilibrium in what Chapter 21 referred to as the commodity or goods market. Similarly, disequilibrium exists in the relationship of $\Delta M$ and $H$. Thus, at $E_1$, $S(i, Y) = i_1 B$ while $I + B_g = i_1 E_1$. In other words, intended saving at given income level $Y$ is less than intended investment and $G - T_n$ by $BE_1$. Furthermore, at $E_1$, $\Delta M = AE_1$ while $H = AB$. Therefore, $\Delta M > H$ by $BE_1$. Consequently, although point $E_1$ may indicate something about the current status of interest rates, further changes will follow.

From Chapter 21 we know that when $I + B_g > S(i, Y)$, or when aggregate demand is greater than the value of all final goods and services, one result will be an increase in the level of income. We also know that when there is an excess supply of money $(\Delta M > H)$, it must be spent either directly for goods and services or employed in the purchase of securities, leading to a rise in the price of the latter or a fall in the rate of interest. Since investment, for example, is a function of the rate of interest, a decline in the rate will result in an increase in the quantity of investment demanded and, consequently, will lead to an increase in the level of income. Therefore, even though at $E_1$ the supply of, and demand for, loanable funds are equal, disequilibrium in the other markets results in an in-

crease in income. With the increase in income, the $S(i, Y)$ schedule will shift to the right, the $[S(i, Y) - H(i, Y)]$ schedule will also shift to the right—but not by as much, since part of saving will be hoarded with the increase in income—and, therefore, since two of the three components comprising the supply of loanable funds will shift rightward while the other remains constant—$\Delta M$ is exogenously determined—the aggregate supply schedule will also shift to the right. On the demand side, given the change in income, there will be no shift in desired investment since, in our simple model, investment demand is a function of the rate of interest but not of the level of income. However, $B_g$ is responsive to income levels since, as we have already seen, one of its components, namely, $T_n$, is positively correlated with the level of income. But as $T_n$ increases relative to $G$—which is autonomous—the budgetary deficit, or $G - T_n$, will decrease leading to a decline in $B_g$ at each rate of interest. In sum, the demand for loanable funds schedule will shift to the left while the supply schedule shifts rightward. The overall result, as depicted in Figure 22-13, will be an increase in the level of income and a decline in the rate of interest from $i_1$ to $i$.

Two important questions arise, however, about this conclusion regarding the path of interest rates. The first question is: under what conditions will the new rate, $i$, constitute a stable and general equilibrium rate so that there will be no tendency for further shifts in our schedules? The second question is: how long will the necessary changes take? Let us examine each of these questions.

**Figure 22-13 Equilibrium in the Loanable Funds Market**

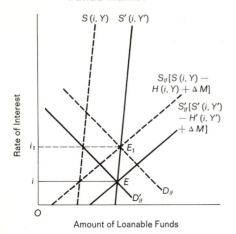

Amount of Loanable Funds

From what we have already said, we can infer, in answering the first question, that if $i$ is to be such a rate it will have to equate, not only demand and supply in the loanable funds market, but also—and simultaneously—demand and supply in the commodity and money markets as well.[28] Since there is more to this statement than meets the eye, however, let us examine carefully the precise conditions necessary for simultaneous equilibrium in all three markets.[29]

As we noted in Chapter 21, income, from the expenditure point of view, may be defined as

$$Y = C + I + G \qquad (22\text{-}10)$$

On the other hand, from the uses, or allocational, point of view,

$$Y = C + S + T_n \qquad (22\text{-}11)$$

or

$$S + T_n = I + G \qquad (22\text{-}12)$$

or

$$S = I + (G - T_n) \qquad (22\text{-}13)$$

or

$$S = I + B_g \qquad (22\text{-}14)$$

This equation represents the necessary condition for income equilibrium, or equilibrium in the commodity (goods) or income market.

Equilibrium in the securities, or loanable funds market, on the other hand, has already been defined as

$$S - H + \Delta M = I + B_g \qquad (22\text{-}5)$$

If we now subtract from this our equilibrium equation for the commodity market, we obtain the following:

$$
\begin{aligned}
S - H + \Delta M &= I + B_g \qquad &(22\text{-}5)\\
-S \phantom{- H + \Delta M} &= (I + B_g) \qquad &(22\text{-}14)\\
\hline
- H + \Delta M &= 0 \qquad &(22\text{-}15)
\end{aligned}
$$

Equation (22-15) shows that the sum of dishoarding and changes in the money supply must be equal to zero.[30] Alternatively, we can say that, since

$$-H + \Delta M = 0 \qquad (22\text{-}15)$$
$$\therefore \Delta M = H \qquad (22\text{-}16)$$

But, as we have seen previously,

$$H = M_D - M_S \qquad (22\text{-}1)$$

or

$$H + M_S = M_D \qquad (22\text{-}17)$$

and, under conditions of monetary equilibrium, the amount of money people desire to hold must be

---

[28] This also presupposes equilibrium in two other markets, namely, the domestic market for human resources, or labor market, and the foreign exchange market. For an analysis of the conditions necessary for general equilibrium in an "open economy," that is, an economy featuring not only domestic transactions but also transactions with the rest of the world, see Appendix 22-1 at the end of this chapter.

[29] Such conditions have been a source of much confusion and controversy in the literature. See, for example, S. C. Tsiang, "Liquidity Preference and Loanable Funds Theories, Multiplier and Velocity Analysis: A Synthesis," *American Economic Review* (September 1956), 539–564; "Liquidity Preference and Loanable Funds Theories of Interest: Comment," by Gardner Ackley, and "Reply" by S. C. Tsiang, *American Economic Review* (September 1957), 662–678; Ackley, *Macroeconomic Theory*, pp. 201–207; Warren L. Smith, "Monetary Theories of the Rate of Interest: A Dynamic Analysis," *Review of Economics and Statistics* (February 1958), 15–21; Liebhafsky, *The Nature of Price Theory*, pp. 374–381; and Paul B. Trescott, *Money, Banking, and Economic Welfare*, 2nd ed., McGraw-Hill Book Company, New York, 1965,

pp. 224–235. Patinkin's work cited earlier (see footnote 12) certainly has done much to resolve this controversy with its insistence on analyzing the problem within a general, rather than a partial, equilibrium framework.

[30] See Liebhafsky, *The Nature of Price Theory*, pp. 379–380.

equal to the amount that they do hold (the stock of money), or

$$M_S = M_D \qquad (22\text{-}18)$$

Therefore, substituting into Equation (22-17), we get,

$$H + M_D = M_D \qquad (22\text{-}19)$$

or

$$H = 0 \qquad (22\text{-}11)$$

But

$$\Delta M = H \qquad (22\text{-}16)$$

and, since

$$H = 0 \qquad (22\text{-}20)$$

then,

$$\Delta M = 0 \qquad (22\text{-}21)$$
$$\therefore \Delta M = H = 0 \qquad (22\text{-}22)$$

By way of summation, then, in depicting the adjustment from what was previously a disequilibrium position at $E_1$ (as seen in Figure 22-12 or the dashed lines in Figure 22-13) to the general equilibrium position found at $E$ in Figure 22-13, desired saving must be equal to desired investment plus $B_g$ and, simultaneously, the sum of changes in the money supply and dishoarding must not only add up to zero but each, in turn, must be equal to zero. Given equilibrium in these two markets, it follows that there must also be equilibrium in the loanable funds market.[31]

We can see from our discussion that these conditions for equilibrium in the market for loanable funds are nothing more than the macroeconomic general equilibrium conditions discussed in Chapter 21. In other words, the equilibrium condition for flows during a time period is that at least at some point in time supply equals demand in all markets simultaneously. One way this might come about is the case illustrated in Figure 22-13 and Equations (22-10) to (22-22). In this case, at a point in time, the supply of money, $M_S$, is unchanging ($\Delta M = 0$) and income is at its equilibrium level, $Y'$.[32] This income level provides the equilibrium supply of loanable funds in Figure 22-13. Therefore, Figures 22-12 and 22-13 make the same prediction about

the direction of the path of interest rates following an increase in the supply of money (downward, assuming unemployed resources) as the static analysis of Chapter 21.

The loanable funds framework for analyzing flows during a time period is, thus, one way in which we might examine interest rate determination. However, as we have seen, while the equality of lending and borrowing intentions may tell us something about the current status of interest rates (Figure 22-12), their equality does not necessarily indicate a general equilibrium or the absence of further change. In fact, a variety of further changes may continue to affect interest rates. As long as supply and demand are not equal in all markets simultaneously and the economy is continuing to adjust along its path between Figure 22-12 and Figure 22-13, interest rates could be changing. Figure 22-13 represents one case of simultaneous equilibrium in all markets—the static equilibrium case illustrated in Chapter 21, in which all fluctuations have run their course and quantities are no longer changing. We see from this that static analysis is not independent of the broader dynamic analysis, it is simply a special case. Much can be learned from this case, including the direction and magnitude of changes, although nothing can be said about the timing of changes. Unfortunately, the alternatives to static equilibrium analysis and comparative statics (namely dynamic analysis and comparative dynamics) are very complex and difficult. While these analyses are beyond the scope of this chapter, we can mention some of the problems encountered in them.[33] Then we can examine briefly the impact of expectations of inflation on market rates of interest.

One important problem of any dynamic analysis is specification of the disequilibrium behavior of market participants. For example, Figure 22-8 shows that hoarding or dishoarding is an important part of the supply of loanable funds. However, the amount of hoarding or dishoarding was derived in Figures 22-6 and 22-7 as the difference between money supply and money demand without saying anything about the length of time the hoarding or dishoarding might take. Clearly, if all the changes took place in one day, we would find an impact on

---

[31] Equilibrium in any two of the three markets must mean equilibrium in the remaining one, since the variables that make up the securities market also encompass the commodity and money markets.

[32] Technically, income is a flow, but we are speaking about its level or rate of flow at some point in time.

[33] For more detail see Ackley, *Macroeconomic Theory*, pp. 201–207.

financial markets dramatically different from the case of hoarding-dishoarding over twenty-five years. In terms of Figure 22-8, rapid hoarding-dishoarding would make $H(i, Y)$ a dominant element in the short-run path of interest rates. In contrast, if hoarding-dishoarding were very slow, then the total supply of loanable funds would be dominated in the short run by saving and changes in the money supply. In this case, $[S(i, Y) - H(i, Y)]$ in Figure 22-8 and Figure 22-12 would be very close to $S(i, Y)$, and $S(i, Y)$ and $\Delta M$ would be the dominant elements in interest rate determination.

A second, closely related problem is the question of speed of adjustment of other variables to adjustments in the financial sector. Movement from Figure 22-12 to Figure 22-13 involves adjustments in investment, income, saving, taxes, and hoarding. Since each of these adjustments may take time, their adjustment periods are important in analyzing the movements of interest rates.

In conclusion, a fully dynamic theory of interest rate determination is difficult indeed. Besides specification of changes that might occur, the disequilibrium behavior of economic units must also be specified before anything can be known from theory about the order or timing of events. In part because of the difficulty of dynamic analysis and the inherent plausibility of many different dynamic behavioral assumptions, economists make use of various kinds of empirical methodologies in studying interest rates and their movements over time.[34] In the next section of this chapter we will examine an important recent development (with much older foundations) in interest rate theory that has both dynamic and empirical elements.

## Interest Rates in an Inflationary Economy

In recent years it has become increasingly clear to economists that since inflation and inflationary expectations can have an important influence on market interest rates, they must be included in any theory of interest rate determination. Inflation is important because it seems unlikely that lenders would be willing to lend at the same interest rate in an inflationary environment as they might if they expected stable prices. In the former case, the pur-

chasing power of the sum of money loaned would decline over the life of the loan—certainly not an attractive prospect for the lender (although it might be especially attractive to borrowers who could repay in cheaper dollars). For this reason it seems that lenders expecting inflation would demand some kind of purchasing-power protection before they would be willing to lend on the same terms as they would under stable prices. Let us see how this demand for purchasing-power protection might be incorporated into our analysis of interest rate determination.[35]

At the outset, it is important to note that neither general equilibrium liquidity preference theory (Chapter 21) nor equilibrium loanable funds theory (such as Figure 22-13) allows analysis of the impact of inflation while prices are still changing. Inflation was examined briefly in Chapter 21, but that chapter was devoted to static analysis. Both the causes and effects of inflation could be studied, but not the inflationary process itself. One needs a dynamic analysis to study fully the impact of inflation on interest rates while prices are changing and are expected to change more. The difficulties of dynamic analysis have already been noted, but some simple assumptions about the behavior of lenders and borrowers in an inflationary environment can provide valuable insights into the movements of market interest rates.

Suppose that the economy can be represented by our loanable funds model (Figure 22-12). Assume also, however, that both borrowers and lenders are concerned about the potential changes in purchasing power of dollars loaned if the price level should change during the term of a loan. In particular, lenders want to protect themselves against potentially *rising* prices of goods and services that might result in loans being repaid to them in dollars of reduced purchasing power. Borrowers, in contrast, would fear periods of *falling* prices when repayment in more valuable dollars would be required.

In order to incorporate the desire for protection from purchasing-power changes, we must recognize the distinction between the *real* rate of interest and the *nominal*, or market, rate. The real rate of interest is the return in real purchasing power that

---

[34] In this context see Chapters 25 and 26.

[35] This discussion draws upon theories of interest rates first developed by Irving Fisher. See Irving Fisher, *The Theory of Interest*, The Macmillan Company, New York, 1930.

is necessary to compensate potential lenders enough to make them willing to part with resources and lend them (thereby deferring their own spending).[36] In contrast, the nominal rate of interest is the sum of the real rate and the premium necessary to maintain constancy in purchasing power.[37] To use an example, if lenders and borrowers were willing to exchange resources at a real rate of interest of 3 percent per year but prices were expected to rise at a 5 percent annual rate, the necessary nominal interest rate would be 8 percent. Expressed in general terms and assuming that the expected rate of change in the price level is known with certainty,[38]

$$i_n = i_r + \dot{P} \qquad (22\text{-}23)$$

where $i_n$ is the nominal rate of interest; $i_r$ is the real rate of interest; and $\dot{P}$ = the expected rate of change of prices.

Equation (22-23) suggests that when prices are expected to rise, the nominal rate is above the real rate; if prices are expected to fall, the nominal rate is below the real rate. In an inflationary environment it seems that borrowers would be willing to pay a nominal rate higher than the real rate because they know they will be repaying in cheaper dollars and because the value of the assets they purchase with borrowed funds should increase along with the commodity price level. This willingness of borrowers to pay a higher nominal rate, along with the lenders' requirement for a return exceeding the real rate, will create the conditions for borrowers and lenders to strike a bargain for resource transfers at a nominal interest rate above the real rate. The opposite would be true in a deflationary environment.

The difficulty for interest rate analysis is that future price movements are not known with certainty, and expectations of market participants are

undoubtedly a complex function of past experiences. Furthermore, it is likely that these expectations are subject to change as more experience is gained. The result is not only a divergence of nominal (market) interest rates from real rates, but a divergence that is subject to variations over time. This is indeed a difficult problem for analysts.

Reconciliation of this discussion about the divergence of nominal, or market, interest rates from real rates with traditional liquidity preference theory (Chapter 21) is not difficult once one recalls that liquidity preference theory involves static analysis. In contrast, the discussion here concerns events within a period of time when prices are changing and are expected to change further. Clearly, this is not a static analysis—it involves events *between* the static equilibria of Chapter 21. An example should make this clear.[39]

Suppose that the monetary authorities desire an expansion of the supply of money. In Chapter 21 we saw that this would mean equilibrium at a lower interest rate (assuming available unemployed resources), although we had no way of knowing how long the changes might take. In this chapter, too, we concluded that an increased money supply would lower interest rates, in this case because there would be an increase in the supply of loanable funds. Our question concerns the time path of interest rates. Do they proceed directly to their new (lower) levels, or might there be some intervening phases? To answer this question, we can employ the distinction between the nominal and real rate of interest.

Imagine that at the beginning of the period under discussion there is equilibrium in financial markets (the supply of and demand for money are equal, as are the supply of and demand for loanable funds). Equilibrium occurs at interest rate $i_E$, which is illustrated as point A in Figure 22-14. Now, suppose that there is an increase in the supply of money. Within some length of time, this increase in the supply of loanable funds will lead to a reduction in interest rates (point B in Figure 22-14). As we have seen, however (Figure 22-12), this is not an equilibrium position for the economy. Lower interest rates will, after some lag, encourage more invest-

[36] The necessity for a positive real rate of interest arises ultimately from the assumption of positive time preference—that present resources are preferable to future resources. This matter is explored in more detail in Appendix 22-2.

[37] The "premium" may be negative if prices are expected to fall.

[38] Equation (22-23) is an approximation of the relation $i_n = i_r + \dot{P} = i_r\dot{P}$, which takes into account the declining purchasing power of the real return as well as the principal of the loan. If either $i_r$ or $\dot{P}$ is small, then $i_r\dot{P}$ is small and can be ignored.

[39] Fuller discussion may be found in William E. Gibson, "Interest Rates and Monetary Policy," *Journal of Political Economy* (May-June 1970).

**Figure 22-14   The Time Path of Interest Rates**

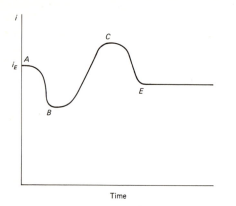

ment and, through a multiplier process, bring about higher levels of income. Higher income, in turn, will increase the transactions demand for money resulting in a *higher* interest rate as wealthholders attempt to exchange bonds for money. Thus, as the impact of the change in money supply works its way through the economy, there will be, first, a declining-interest-rate phase and, second, a rising-interest-rate phase. How far market interest rates rise depends on the impact of greater investment (and higher income) on prices. If inflation occurs, market (nominal) rates can diverge from real rates and rise beyond the initial equilibrium rate (point *C* in Figure 22-14). Eventually, assuming no further shocks to the economy, interest rates can fall to their new equilibrium level as inflationary expectations subside and the nominal rate again equals the real rate (point *E* in Figure 22-14, which corresponds to *E* in Figure 22-13 and *E* in Figure 21-6). How long this process takes is an interesting empirical issue.

In sum, price changes and expectations of further price changes pose difficulties for analysis of interest rates. While it is possible to reconcile changes in price expectations with the liquidity preference model of Chapter 21, these changes can be illustrated more easily in the loanable funds framework. In this case, the faster the expected rate of price increase, the greater the demand for funds at any interest rate (the schedule shifts to the right) and the smaller the supply (the supply schedule shifts to the left in Figure 22-12). As a result, the faster the expected rate of inflation, the higher is the interest rate. However, whether one employs the

loanable funds or the liquidity preference model, the problem of predicting interest rates is still most difficult for the reasons cited in this section (see also Chapters 25 and 26).

## Financial Intermediaries and Loanable Funds Theory

What is the role, if any, of financial intermediaries in loanable funds theory? We have seen in Chapters 1 and 2 that surplus units with excess saving—such as households, business firms, and government—are the ultimate suppliers of loanable funds.[40] To the extent that such excess saving is employed to acquire the indirect securities of financial intermediaries rather than used directly to purchase primary securities, intermediaries merely play the role of brokers or middlemen in rechanneling loanable

---

[40]Thus, Figure 1-1 in Chapter 1 indicated that only ultimate lenders were in a position to *create* loanable funds. The monetary system (that is, the commercial banks, the Federal Reserve System, and the U.S. Treasury) as well as nonbank financial intermediaries are merely the conduits through which part of such excess saving was transferred to ultimate borrowers. This process followed from the fact that the earlier analysis was based on the National Income and Flow of Funds Accounts and that these accounts, in turn, deal exclusively with realized, or *ex post*, magnitudes. Thus, in the National Income and Flow of Funds Accounts, the only economic units capable of saving and, therefore, of supplying loanable funds are units with incomes greater than their expenditures on current and capital account—namely, those units with incomes greater than their consumption and investment expenditures. (To the extent that this applies also to commercial banks and nonbank financial institutions as *business firms,* to that extent—but to that extent *only*—do they also supply loanable funds.) In a planned, or *ex ante,* sense, however, it may be possible for commercial banks and other financial intermediaries *to add* to the supply of loanable funds by creating additional liabilities against themselves—that is, by borrowing—which, at the same time, do not draw the excess saving of surplus units out of financial markets. Under these circumstances, the supply of loanable funds will be *augmented.* This chapter, which analyzes in detail equilibrium conditions in the loanable funds market, necessarily deals with behavioral relations that involve *ex ante* magnitudes rather than *ex post* accounting identities, such as are to be found both in the National Income and Flow of Funds Accounts. Consequently, the analysis and discussion in this section point out just what conditions must be present if financial intermediaries are to be in a position to augment the supply of loanable funds.

funds to deficit units, or ultimate borrowers. Their existence, presumably, does not affect the aggregate volume of loanable funds. Supposedly, the one financial institution that is potentially unique in its ability to increase the supply of loanable funds is the banking system. As pointed out earlier and in Chapter 2, banks can borrow by creating liabilities against themselves in the form of demand deposits, or money. In creating new money, banks at the same time acquire primary securities—presumably without, in any way, drawing loanable funds away from surplus units. Hence, so the argument runs, banks are different from other financial intermediaries in "creating" credit, or adding to the supply of loanable funds.[41]

It is now time to examine the validity of this argument more carefully. Let us begin with the banks. To the extent that the banking system has excess reserves it can, if it so desires, initially add to its outstanding loans and other claims and, in the process, create new money.[42] But does this necessarily imply an increase in the supply of loanable funds? The answer very largely depends on what other economic units desire to do with the additional money. It must always be remembered that banks, like any other suppliers of goods or credit, are restrained, in the last analysis, by the demand for such goods or credit.

Let us begin with an admittedly extreme illustration in order to make the argument clear. Suppose that the banking system does have excess reserves and, furthermore, wishes to employ them in the acquisition of additional primary securities. Presumably, it can do this by creating additional liabilities against itself in the form of money. But now let us assume that, concurrent with the increase in the stock of money, the public desires to hold idle a sum of money equal to the additional money issued by the banking system. In other words, its desire to hold money has increased. Consequently, since hoarding is the difference between the amount of money desired to be held and the amount

actually held, we can say that hoarding has increased. Hence, the final result will be no net addition in the flow of loanable funds because the potential increase in the supply through the creation of additional money ($\Delta M$) has just been offset by an equivalent increase in hoarding ($H$). Also, since there is no change in the supply of loanable funds, there will be no changes in the equilibrium rate of interest and level of income.

Having indicated how the banking system may be constrained by the public's demand for money, let us proceed now with a somewhat more realistic example. Starting from a position of equilibrium, as before, let us assume that the public does not wish to hold any of the additional money at the prevailing rate of interest and level of income. In other words, there is no change in its desire to hold money. As a result, the amount of money the public desires to hold will now be less than the quantity it actually does hold. Consequently, $H$ will be negative and dishoarding will occur. The result of the addition to the supply of money under these circumstances will be an equivalent increase in the supply of loanable funds as well.[43] Given the initial disequilibrium introduced by the increment to the money stock (see position $E_1$ in Figure 22-12, or the dashed lines in Figure 22-13), the money will be used, at least partially, to acquire additional securities, thereby raising their prices and lowering the rate of interest. Moreover, since desired investment is a function of the rate of interest, a lower interest rate will mean additional investment and a higher level of real or money income. The latter, in turn, will mean a shift to the left in the demand for loanable funds schedule since the need for government borrowing will decrease as $T_n$ rises relative to $G$. At the same time, an increase in the level of income will lead to an increase in desired saving since saving is primarily a function of the level of income. Finally, at the new point of equilibrium, $E$, depicted in Figure 22-13, income will be higher, the rate of interest will be lower, and, si-

---

[41]This is why earlier in the chapter (Figure 22-12), the supply of loanable funds schedule, or $[S(i, Y) - H(i, Y) + \Delta M]$, was drawn as parallel to the $[S(i, Y) - H(i, Y)]$ curve with the difference between them equal to the constant $\Delta M$.

[42]For a discussion of the process by which this takes place, see Chapter 5, "The Supply of Money and Bank Credit."

[43]The most realistic example is probably one where part of the increase in the money supply is employed to acquire additional goods and securities, with the remainder being hoarded. Hence, the final result will be *some net increase* in the supply of loanable funds since the increase in the money supply will be greater than the public's desire to hold all such additional cash balances at the prevailing level of interest rates.

multaneously, there will be equality in the loanable funds, commodity, and money markets.[44]

We have now seen that the banking system as well as the surplus units can create loanable funds, but the former can do so only as long as there exists a disequilibrium between the amount of money supplied and the quantity of it demanded by the public. But we know that, apart from banks and the monetary authorities, other financial institutions cannot increase their liabilities by issuing money.[45] Hence, it would seem as if the only method available to them to increase their liabilities would be to attract some of the public's net current saving and this, as we have already seen, certainly would not add to the supply of loanable funds. It would appear, then, that nonbank financial intermediaries are, indeed, nothing more than middlemen in the saving-investment process and that only banks are unique in their ability to increase the supply of loanable funds.

But now let us take a closer look. Cannot nonbank intermediaries increase their liabilities by causing, in the same manner as banks, a disequilibrium to emerge between the amount of money supplied and the amount demanded by the public? Again, as in the case of banks, it must be recalled that there exists not only a supply but also a demand function for the liabilities of such institutions. Let us, for example, take the case of nonmonetary liabilities supplied by institutions other than commercial banks. Such liabilities in the form of time

**Figure 22-15**

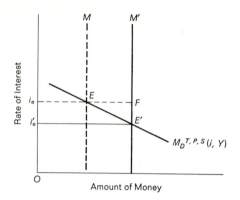

deposits and savings shares may be very close substitutes for money. Suppose, as a result of a change in public preferences among liquid assets and/or an increase in the rates paid on these near-monies, the public is induced to substitute some of these indirect securities for previously held idle cash balances.[46] In other words, the public now desires to hold less money relative to the existing supply of money than it did previously. The result will be dishoarding.[47] As the nonbank depository institutions acquire funds in this manner, they, in turn, will use the proceeds for the acquisition of additional primary securities. Consequently, the supply of loanable funds will increase. As in the case of our bank illustration, the result will be a decrease in the rate of interest and an increase in the level

---

[44]In general equilibrium, of course, both the sum of changes in the money supply and dishoarding must not only add up to zero, but each, in turn, must be equal to *zero*. Let us once more visualize this, but this time think in terms of Figure 22-15, which shows the stock of money and the desire to hold that stock. At the old monetary equilibrium, *E,* the stock of money is given and the amount desired to be held is equal to the amount actually held. Hence, $\Delta M = H = 0$. Now let us assume an increase in the stock of money from *M* to *M'*. The difference between the two is $\Delta M$, or $\Delta M = M' - M$. Assuming no change in the desire to hold money at the former equilibrium rate of interest, $i_e$, dishoarding will now be equal to *EF*. Consequently, the rate of interest will decline as the excess money is used to purchase securities. But, as the rate of interest declines, the amount of cash the public desires to hold increases. Finally, at *E'*, the quantity of money desired to be held will be equal to the new stock of money. At this point, $\Delta M$ will be equal to *zero*, as will *H*. Hence, at *E'*, $\Delta M = H = 0$.

[45]As in Chapter 5, the term *banks* is being used to denote all institutions that can issue monetary liabilities.

[46]Strictly speaking, this model is at a somewhat lower level of abstraction than our earlier one where the choice was only between holding money and bonds. However, the growth and proliferation of financial intermediaries does extend the range of asset options available to the public. We could have taken account of near-monies earlier in the analysis without, in any way, changing the propositions made.

[47]Figure 22-16 depicts the new situation by showing no change in the stock of money but a *shift* to the left in the desire to hold money. Consequently, at each rate of interest the quantity of money desired to be held will be less than previously. At the former equilibrium rate of interest, $i_e$, dishoarding will be equal to *AE*. Once the new equilibrium rate, $i'_e$, is attained, however, dishoarding will be equal to zero. Also, $\Delta M$ is equal to zero since the money supply has remained constant. Consequently, at the new equilibrium rate we find once again that $\Delta M = H = 0$.

of income until a new general equilibrium is achieved.[48] While banks, *by increasing the money supply,* can add to the supply of loanable funds by creating a disequilibrium between the supply of money and the quantity desired to be held by the public, nonbank financial intermediaries can do the same thing *through lowering the demand for money* relative to the existing money stock. In principle, therefore, both bank and nonbank intermediaries—in addition to surplus units—are potential creators of loanable funds. In this matter they can affect the rate of interest, real income, and the price level.[49]

## Appendix 22-1: Loanable Funds Theory in an Open Economy*

The theory presented in the body of this chapter is sufficiently general in nature so as to encompass both domestic and foreign transactions in loanable funds. On a somewhat lower level of abstraction, however, it is important to distinguish between domestic and foreign flows of funds. On this level, therefore, loanable funds theory as previously discussed in this chapter becomes applicable only to a "closed economy," that is, an economy in which transactions with the rest of the world are ignored

**Figure 22-16**

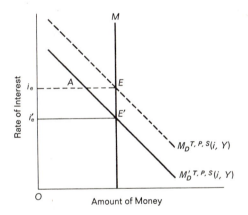

$M_D^{T, P, S}(i, Y)$

$M_D'^{T, P, S}(i, Y)$

[48]Like the shift to the right in the supply of loanable funds curve shown in Figure 22-12, which results from an increase in the money supply, there also will be a rightward shift in that schedule as a result of the public's substitution of nonbank intermediary claims for money. The significance of introducing the availability of interest-yielding money substitutes created by these intermediaries lies in the fact that the demand for liquidity is no longer viewed as synonymous with the demand for money (see the previous discussion of the determinants of the demand for money). Attention, thereby, is directed not to the elasticity of the money demand schedule but to possible *shifts* in it due to the growth in the near-monies of nonbank intermediaries. This, in turn, may be translated as shifts in the loanable funds schedule emanating from this source.

*This appendix extending the analysis in the main body of the chapter to those conditions necessary for equilibrium in an "open economy" was written by Professor Robert Hawkins of New York University.

[49]Whether or not the liabilities of nonbank intermediaries are, indeed, close substitutes for money resulting, therefore, in shifts in the loanable funds schedule or, what amounts to the same thing, in increases in income velocity, is basically a question of fact rather than of theory. On the theoretical level, opinion on this issue in the past has been more or less divided. See, for example, Gurley and Shaw, *Money in a Theory of Finance,* Chap. 6; Richard Thorn, "Nonbank Financial Intermediaries, Credit Expansion, and Monetary Policy," *Staff Papers,* International Monetary Fund, November 1958; Ezra Solomon, "The Issue of Financial Intermediaries," *Proceedings of the 1959 Conference on Savings and Residential Financing,* U.S. Savings and Loan League, May 7 and 8, 1959; Joseph Aschheim, "Commercial Banks and Financial Intermediaries: Fallacies and Policy Implications," *Journal of Political Economy* (February 1959); James Tobin, "Commercial Banks as Creators of 'Money,'" in *Banking and Monetary Studies,* ed. Deane Carson, Richard D. Irwin, Homewood, Ill., 1963; W. L. Smith, "Financial Intermediaries and Monetary Controls," *Quarterly Journal of Economics* (November 1959); and Arthur Burns, "Statement Before Congress," *Federal Reserve Bulletin* (March 1975). Nevertheless, several econometric findings indicate rather conclusively that some nonbank intermediary liabilities, such as savings and loan shares and deposits of mutual savings banks, are, indeed, very good money substitutes. See, in this connection, T. H. Lee, "Substitutability of Non-Bank Intermediary Liabilities for Money," *The Journal of Finance* (September 1966); Lee, "Alternative Interest Rates and the Demand for Money: The Empirical Evidence," *The American Economic Review* (December 1967); and V. K. Chetty, "On Measuring the Nearness of Near-Moneys," *The American Economic Review* (June 1969). For some earlier empirical findings, which are criticized by Lee and Chetty in their articles, see E. L. Feige, *The Demand for Liquid Assets: A Temporal Cross-Section Analysis,* Prentice-Hall, Englewood Cliffs, N.J., 1964; and M. J. Hamburger, "The Demand for Money by Households, Money Substitutes, and Monetary Policy," *Journal of Political Economy* (December 1966). For a recent survey of find-

or are assumed not to exist. Such, of course, is not the case in the real world. Even for the United States, which carries out a relatively small proportion of transactions with the rest of the world, the absolute magnitudes are sizable.

In order to transform our more general formulation into one that explicitly takes account of external transactions, consideration must be given not only to foreign sources and uses of loanable funds but also to payments for exports and imports of goods and services. However, both foreign borrowing and lending, and payments for exports and imports, normally involve transactions in the foreign exchange market.[50] Therefore, the latter represents an equilibrium requirement in addition to the three noted in the body of this chapter. Thus, as will be shown, general equilibrium in an "open economy" requires equilibrium not only in the loanable funds, money, and commodity markets but *also,* and *simultaneously,* equilibrium in the foreign exchange market.

## Foreign Uses and Sources of Funds

In the absence of strict government control or prohibition, there will always be some foreign borrowing in the United States (that is, a foreign demand or use of funds) and some foreign lending to U.S. citizens and businesses. This will be the case simply because of the existing channels of trade and communication; some foreign borrowers know of available credit in the United States that is more attractive than sources at home while, at the same time, some American borrowers for some reason may prefer to use foreign sources of funds. Normally there will be lending to, and borrowing from, the rest of the world within the same time period.

In terms of loanable funds theory, the rest of the world is both a source of demand for, and a supplier of, funds to the U.S. loanable funds market. This is in addition to the domestic sources of supply and demand already identified in this chapter. The volume of current loanable funds made available by foreigners to the United States will depend, among other things, on the relative rates of interest. The supply of foreign funds in the U.S. market will be greater the higher the U.S. rate of interest is relative to foreign interest rates. As long as foreign rates are constant, a higher U.S. rate will increase the incentive (reduce the disincentive) to lend in the United States as opposed to the foreign market. Similarly, the higher U.S. rates are relative to foreign rates, the stronger will be the inducement for American borrowers to seek foreign funds. Thus, the (gross) foreign supply of funds to the United States is a positive function of the difference between U.S. and foreign interest rates.

The opposite line of reasoning applies to the foreign demand for U.S. funds. The lower U.S. lending rates are relative to foreign rates, the greater will be the amount of U.S. funds foreign borrowers will desire. Similarly, the higher foreign rates are relative to U.S. rates, the greater will be the inducement to American lenders to seek out foreign, as opposed to domestic, borrowers. As a result of both forces, the (gross) foreign demand for U.S. loanable funds is an inverse function of the United States–foreign interest rate differential.

Let us assume, for the sake of clarity, that foreign interest rates are constant, thus making variations in the U.S. rate equal to variations in the difference between U.S. and foreign rates. We could then show the gross foreign supply and gross foreign demand for U.S. loanable funds as additions to the domestic supply and demand functions found in this chapter. For simplicity, however, we shall deal only with the *net* foreign demand for loanable funds, which is the gross foreign demand for U.S. funds minus the gross foreign supply of funds.[51] Thus, net foreign demand will be positive

---

ings, see Edgar L. Feige and Douglas K. Pearce, "The Substitutability of Money and Near-Monies: A Survey of the Time Series Evidence," *Journal of Economic Literature* (June 1977).

Finally, the *theoretical distinction* between bank and nonbank intermediaries insofar as their potential ability to affect the supply of loanable funds is concerned does not lie in whether the former has a *greater quantitative* impact on the supply of loanable funds than does the latter but simply in whether they are *qualitatively similar* inasmuch as both can elicit disequilibrium between desired and actual money balances held by the public.

[50]The foreign exchange market, as the name implies, is that market in which one national currency (more precisely demand deposits denominated in a national currency unit) is exchanged for another national currency. The rate at which one nation's currency exchanges for that of another is the *exchange rate*.

[51]This is the same type of treatment accorded to hoarding and dishoarding in the body of this chapter.

when gross demand exceeds supply and negative when gross supply exceeds demand.

When foreign rates are assumed constant, net foreign demand is related negatively to U.S. interest rates. This must clearly be so since gross demand is negatively related while gross supply is positively related to U.S. interest rates.

The schedule $F(i)$ in Figure 22-17 represents this relationship between the net foreign demand for U.S. loanable funds and the U.S. interest rate. If the U.S. interest rate is below $i_0$, such as at $i_a$, foreigners will borrow more in the United States than Americans borrow abroad, and the difference between the two (volume represented by $OA$) will be the net foreign demand for U.S. loanable funds.

If, on the other hand, the U.S. interest rate is above $i_0$, such as $i_b$, foreigners borrow less in the United States than Americans borrow abroad by the amount $OB$. This is a negative net foreign demand for U.S. funds, or put somewhat differently, it represents a net supply of loanable funds to the U.S. market. At $i_0$, of course, the quantity demanded of U.S. funds by foreigners exactly equals the quantity supplied to the U.S. market by foreigners so that the *net* foreign demand is zero.

The net foreign demand must be added to the other sources of demand (investment and net government borrowing) in Figure 22-11. This addition is seen in Figure 22-18 where $I + B_g$ represents the sum of desired domestic investment and government demand for loanable funds and $F(i)$ represents

## Figure 22-17   Net Foreign Demand for U.S. Loanable Funds

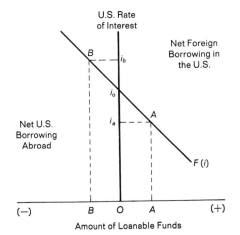

U.S. Rate of Interest

Net Foreign Borrowing in the U.S.

Net U.S. Borrowing Abroad

$F(i)$

(−)   B   O   A   (+)

Amount of Loanable Funds

## Figure 22-18   The Demand for Loanable Funds in an Open Economy

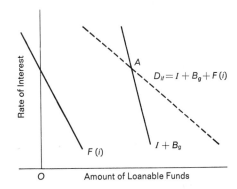

$D_{lf} = I + B_g + F(i)$

$F(i)$   $I + B_g$

O   Amount of Loanable Funds

the net foreign demand shown in Figure 22-17. The horizontal sum ($D_{lf}$) of the two thus gives the total (domestic and foreign) demand for funds in an open economy. At any level of U.S. interest rates below that represented by point $A$, foreign borrowers will be removing more funds from the U.S. market than foreign lenders are supplying—the typical case—as represented by the distance between the $I + B_g$ and $D_{lf}$ curves, which is equal to the distance of $F(i)$ from the vertical axis. At points above $A$ (that is, at high U.S. interest rates) there is a net foreign supply, or a negative net foreign demand, for U.S. funds.

### Equilibrium in an Open Economy[52]

The adjustment processes and the conditions of equilibrium in the loanable funds market in an open economy are very similiar to those in a closed economy. The supply of loanable funds is the same in each case, that is:

$$S_{lf} = S(i, Y) - H(i, Y) + \Delta M \qquad (22\text{-}24)$$

And, as we have just seen, the demand for loanable funds, including net foreign demand, can be expressed as

$$D_{lf} = I + B_g + F(i) \qquad (22\text{-}25)$$

[52] The theoretical formulation here owes much to various contributions of R. A. Mundell made in a different context. Most relevant is his "Capital Mobility and Stabilization Policy Under Fixed and Flexible Exchange Rates," *Canadian Journal of Economics and Political Science* (November 1963), 475–485.

For equilibrium to occur, the interest rate must adjust so as to equate the total demand for loanable funds ($D_{lf}$) with the total supply of loanable funds, as shown in Equation (22-26).

$$[S(i, Y) - H(i, Y) + \Delta M] = I + B_g + F(i) \quad (22\text{-}26)$$

However, the desired $S_{lf} = D_{lf}$ is a necessary, but not a sufficient, condition for equilibrium. It was previously noted that in a closed economy two additional conditions must be fulfilled. These are that *ex ante* saving equal *ex ante* investment plus net government borrowing, so as to equate the supply and demand for real output; and that hoarding and changes in the money supply both be equal to zero for equilibrium to exist in the money market. To repeat these two *closed-economy* conditions in algebraic form:

$$S(i, Y) = I + B_g \quad \text{(goods market)}$$
$$H(i, Y) = \Delta M = 0 \quad \text{(money market)}$$

If one or more of these conditions are not met, forces will be set in motion that will change $i$, $Y$, or both, and hence $S$, $I$, $H$, until the conditions are met.

In the open-economy model, however, the market for real output must include sales to foreigners and purchases from foreigners. Thus, the national product identity becomes

$$Y = C + I + G + X - M \quad (22\text{-}27)$$

where $X$ stands for exports of goods and services and $M$ stands for imports of goods and services.[53] The current account balance in the Balance of Payments is $X - M$. Recalling Equation (22-11)—which is the same for an open economy—we have

$$Y = C + S + T_n \quad (22\text{-}11)$$

This equation shows the allocation or uses of income ($Y$). However, since in the National Income and Flow of Funds Accounts, uses of income must be equal to sources of income, then it must follow that

$$C + S + T_n = C + I + G + X - M \quad \begin{matrix}(22\text{-}11)\\(22\text{-}27)\end{matrix}$$

[53]To be more precise, in the U.S. National Income Accounts definitions, $X$ is the value of current output (goods and services) sold to foreigners plus any unrequited transfers of foreign income to Americans. Likewise, $M$ includes the total transfer of current income to foreigners, either for the purchase of goods and services or as a unilateral transfer.

Since we previously defined $B_g$ as $(G - T_n)$ [Equations (22-13); (22-14)], if we now subtract Equation (22-11) from Equation (22-27), we get

$$S = I + (X - M) + B_g \quad (22\text{-}28)$$
$$(X - M) = S - (I + B_g) \quad (22\text{-}29)$$

Equation (22-29) shows clearly that for equilibrium to occur in an open economy, the *ex ante* net foreign balance on current account ($X - M$) must be equal to the difference between domestic saving ($S$) and domestic investment plus the government deficit ($I + B_g$). Put differently, as in Equation (22-28), domestic saving must cover the sum total of investment demand, net sales of output to foreigners, and net government deficits. Only if this is true will total production of output at current prices be exactly sufficient to fulfill the demand for the output from the various sources.

To summarize these three necessary conditions for equilibrium reflecting the external sector, we have

$$S - H + \Delta M = I + B_g + F(i)$$
$$\text{(loanable funds market)} \quad (22\text{-}26)$$
$$S = I + B_g + (X - M)$$
$$\text{(goods market)} \quad (22\text{-}28)$$
$$\Delta M = H = 0$$
$$\text{(money market)} \quad (22\text{-}22)$$

These three conditions, as expressed, are represented in Figure 22-19. They are necessary conditions, but for full equilibrium one additional condition must be met. This condition relates to

**Figure 22-19  Loanable Funds Market Equilibrium in an Open Economy**

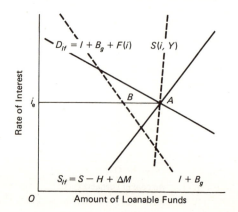

equilibrium in the foreign exchange market, or the balance of payments.

If the money-market condition in Equation (22-22) is met, then Equation (22-26) becomes

$$S = I + B_g + F(i) \qquad (22\text{-}30)$$

but

$$S = I + B_g + (X - M) \qquad (22\text{-}28)$$

Therefore, subtracting Equation (22-28) from Equation (22-30) yields

$$0 = F(i) - (X - M) \qquad (22\text{-}31)$$

or

$$F(i) = X - M \qquad (22\text{-}32)$$

That is, for balance-of-payments (or foreign-exchange-market) equilibrium, the *ex ante* current account $(X - M)$ surplus (deficit) must equal the net foreign demand for (supply of) funds on the U.S. loanable funds market. When all four of these conditions are met—Equations (22-26), (22-28), (22-22), and (22-32)—both internal and external equilibrium exists.

In Figure 22-19, $S_{lf}$ and $D_{lf}$ represent the total supply and demand functions for U.S. loanable funds. In addition, we show separately the domestic component of the demand for loanable funds $(I + B_g)$ and the saving component $(S)$ of total supply. Equilibrium occurs at interest rate $i_e$ and

the total flow of loanable funds into investment, net government borrowing, and net foreign investment is $i_e A$. Thus, the distance

$$i_e A = S_{lf} = D_{lf} \qquad (22\text{-}33)$$

and the loanable funds market is cleared at $i_e$. In addition, at point $A$, the saving function $(S)$ intercepts the total $S_{lf}$ function, implying that $-H + \Delta M = 0$. This, in turn, was shown previously to imply that $H = \Delta M = 0$, suggesting that the money market is also cleared at $i_e$.

Points $A$ and $B$ are, respectively, on the total $D_{lf}$ function and the domestic demand for funds function. They differ by the amount of foreign demand for funds, $F(i) = BA$. Similarly, at point $A$, the distance

$$i_e A = S \qquad (22\text{-}34)$$
$$i_e B = I + B_g \qquad (22\text{-}35)$$
$$BA = X - M \qquad (22\text{-}36)$$

By adding, we see that the horizontal distance

$$i_e A = i_e B + BA = S = I + B_g + (X - M) \qquad (22\text{-}37)$$

This indicates equilibrium in the market for goods and services. Finally, $AB$ represents both $F(i)$ and $(X - M)$, fulfilling the final condition for general equilibrium, that of equilibrium in the balance of payments.

## Appendix 22-2: Positive Time Preference, the Rate of Interest, and the Supply of Saving

As the body of this chapter points out, most classical and neoclassical economists have accepted the notion that the typical individual prefers present to future consumption. However, this myopia for present over future goods is not necessarily independent of the *time pattern of income flows*. Therefore, to isolate the subjective time preferences of the "neoclassical individual" from the time pattern of that individual's income flows, the illustration that follows assumes that current income and expected future income are equal. Given the classicists' belief in a positive time preference among individuals, it follows that such psychological propensities can be overcome only by offering people a premium for abstaining from the consumption of all their current income (that is, saving) in the form of an interest return. The higher the interest rate,

the greater would be the amount of saving undertaken by the public.[54] In other words, the higher the rate of interest, the greater would future consumption be relative to current consumption foregone and the greater would be the volume of saving. At each rate of interest, equilibrium would be established at the point where the interest rate and the opportunity cost of foregoing present consumption—the public's subjective time preference between current and future consumer goods—were equal. In terms of modern indifference curve analysis, this can be illustrated as follows:

[54]A critique of this approach is to be found in the main body of the chapter. This appendix is primarily concerned with translating the classical and nonclassical notions of the determinants of saving by use of a geometric example involving the use of indifference curves.

In Figure 22-20(a), the horizontal axis depicts current consumption while the vertical axis represents future annual consumption. $I_1$, $I_2$, and $I_3$ represent three of the indifference curves of the household. The fact that $I_3$ is above and to the right of $I_1$ and $I_2$ indicates that the total utility to the household derived from being at any point on the $I_3$ curve is greater than the utility it obtains from being at any point on the $I_1$ or $I_2$ schedules. This is so because, on $I_3$ as compared to $I_1$, for example, the household will always enjoy a greater amount of future consumer goods at the same level of current consumption, or it will enjoy the same amount of future consumption while having more consumer goods in the present. By way of specific illustration, given the same current consumption out of income at points $F$ and $J$ on $I_1$ and $I_3$ respectively, future annual consumption will be greater at $J$ than at $F$.

The fact that the indifference curves are negative sloping merely points out a familiar characteristic of such schedules, namely, that all points on an indifference curve provide the same total utility or satisfaction. Furthermore, the fact that the curves are convex to the origin, with a slope numerically greater than unity at their intersection with a line having a 45° slope extending from the origin, indicates that as more and more of current consumption is forgone out of current income—saved—it will have to be compensated for with greater and greater amounts of future consumption if total utility is to remain constant.[55] In other words, the marginal rate of substitution of future for current consumption—represented by the slope of the indifference curve—becomes increasingly greater the more future consumption is substituted for current consumption.

As previously explained, in order to isolate the classical and neoclassical notions of positive time preference for current versus future consumption goods from income patterns through time, we have assumed equal incomes for the household in both the current and following years. Therefore, as shown in Figure 22-20(a), $OY_1 = OY_2$. Assuming further that the household has no accumulated wealth, it will have a consumption possibility, or

[55]If the indifference curve had a slope of $-1$ along a 45° line, this would imply that an individual had a neutral time preference between current and future consumer goods.

**Figure 22-20(a)  A  Household's Preferred Combination of Current Consumption and Increases in Future Annual Consumption**

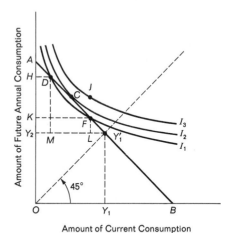

budget, line, $AB$, given by the present discounted value of its two years' incomes, or

$$\text{Present Value} = Y_1 + \frac{Y_2}{1 + i} \quad (22\text{-}38)$$

where $i$ is the current rate of interest. For a given set of incomes, therefore, the consumption possibility line may be written,

$$Y_2 = (1 + i)(\text{Present Value} - Y_1) \quad (22\text{-}39)$$

At one extreme, the household can consume all of its current income ($OY_1$) plus the present discounted value of its future income, or $Y_1B$. In other words, it currently can consume $OB$. At the other extreme, it can consume none of its current income and save all of it for future consumption, in which case its future consumption will be equal to its future income ($OY_2$) plus $Y_2A$, the latter representing all current income saved multiplied by 1 + i. In other words, the following year the household can consume $OA$. In between these two extremes, the budget line indicates that the household can spend its income on any one of a variety of alternative combinations of current and future consumer goods. The slope of $AB$ represents the ratio of the price of current consumption to future consumption. Thus, we see that $OA$ is necessarily larger than $OB$, the difference between the two being the amount of interest.[56] To the extent that the household gives up one unit of current consumption—saves—to that extent it can acquire one-unit-plus of future consumption, the additional amount acquired being a function of the specific rate of interest.

Given an income of $OY_1$, current consumption at point $F$ will be $KF$, or $Y_2L$, and current saving will be $LY_1'$. The foregoing of current consumption equal to $LY_1'$ will mean that future consumption will equal $OK$, with $Y_2K$ being larger than $LY_1'$. On the other hand, at point $D$, current consumption will be equal to $Y_2M$ (= $HD$) and current saving will be equal to $MY_1'$. Current saving of $MY_1'$ will, in turn, mean future consumption of $OH$, with $Y_2H$ greater than $MY_1'$. However, neither points $D$ nor $F$ represent equilibrium positions for the household since, at both points, $I_1$ intersects $AB$. The household can maximize its utility or satisfaction, therefore, by moving to the highest available indifference curve, which in this case must be at point $C$. At $C$, the consumption-possibility line just touches—but does not cross—the indifference curve, $I_2$, and this is the highest curve the household can reach. Thus, the household is in equilibrium where the slope of the consumption-possibility line is exactly equal to the slope of the indifference curve, $I_2$, or the subjective time preference of the household.

Figure 22-20(b) shows the impact of a change in the rate of interest on the consumption-saving decisions of our representative household. As in Figure 22-20(a), equilibrium before the change in the interest rate is at point $C$, with current consumption equal to $Y_2V$ and saving equal to $VY_1'$. Given an increase in the market rate of interest so that the budget line shifts from $AB$ to $BK$, points $R$ and $T$ on $I_2$ now intersect the new consumption-possibility curve. Therefore, the household can increase its total utility by moving from point $C$ on $I_2$ to point $U$ on $I_3$, at which point the new market rate of interest and subjective time preferences between present and future consumer goods are once again equal to each other. At this new point of tangency, current consumption will be less than previously, or $Y_2S$ as compared to $Y_2V$. Conversely, saving out

[56]The *rate* of interest, therefore, must be equal to

$$\frac{AO - OB}{OB}, \quad \text{or} \quad \frac{OA}{OB} - 1$$

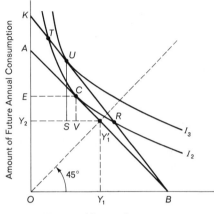

**Figure 22-20(b)   The Effect of a Change in the Rate of Interest on the Consumption-Saving Decisions of a Representative Household**

of current income will now be greater than before the increase in the interest rate, rising from $VY_1'$ to $SY_1'$. If we now go on to sum up the amount of saving desired by all households at varying rates of interest (changing the slope of the budget line accordingly), we obtain the neoclassical aggregate supply schedule of saving depicted in Figure 22-1.

## Questions

1. What are the major elements making up the supply of loanable funds? The demand for loanable funds?
2. Why is saving basically a function of the level of income rather than highly responsive to changes in interest rates?
3. Define *hoarding* and *dishoarding*. Why are hoarding and dishoarding responsive to interest rate changes?
4. Define the *marginal efficiency of capital*. What determines the slope of the investment demand schedule? What are some of the determinants of shifts in the investment demand schedule?
5. Why does *general* equilibrium assume simultaneous equilibrium in the domestic securities, commodity, and money markets?
6. How may commercial banks augment the supply of loanable funds? How may nonbank depository intermediaries add to the supply of loanable funds?
7. Why is it highly unlikely that a financial intermediary, such as private pension funds, would augment the supply of loanable funds?

8. What is the difference, if any, between changes in the money supply and loanable funds?
9. In an "open economy," *general* equilibrium assumes not only simultaneous equilibrium in the domestic securities, commodity, and money markets but also equilibrium in the balance of payments. Explain.
10. Why is dynamic analysis essential in studying the impact of inflationary expectations on changes in interest rates?

## Selected Bibliography

Ackley, Gardner. "Liquidity Preference and Loanable Funds Theories of Interest." *American Economic Review* (September 1957).

———. *Macroeconomic Theory.* The Macmillan Company, New York, 1961.

Aschheim, Joseph. *Techniques of Monetary Control.* Johns Hopkins Press, Baltimore, Md., 1961, Chap. 7.

Burns, Arthur. "Statement Before Congress." *Federal Reserve Bulletin* (March 1975).

Cacy, J. A. "Alternative Approaches to the Analysis of the Financial Structure. *Monthly Review,* Federal Reserve Bank of Kansas City (March 1968).

Chetty, V. K. "On Measuring the Nearness of Near-Moneys." *American Economic Review* (June 1969).

Culbertson, John M. "Intermediaries and Monetary Theory." *American Economic Review* (March 1958).

Feige, E. L. *The Demand for Liquid Assets: A Temporal Cross-Section Analysis.* Prentice-Hall, Englewood Cliffs, N.J., 1964.

——— and Douglas K. Pearce. "The Substitutability of Money and Near-Monies: A Survey of the Time Series Evidence." *Journal of Economic Literature* (June 1977).

Gibson, William E. "Interest Rates and Monetary Policy." *Journal of Political Economy* (May-June 1970).

Gurley, John G., and Edward S. Shaw. *Money in a Theory of Finance.* The Brookings Institution, Washington, D.C., 1960.

Klein, Benjamin. "Competitive Interest Payments on Bank Deposits and the Long-Run Demand for Money." *American Economics Review* (December 1974).

Lee, T. H. "Alternative Interest Rates and the Demand for Money: The Empirical Evidence." *American Economic Review* (December 1967).

———. "Substitutability of Non-Bank Intermediary Liabilities for Money." *Journal of Finance* (September 1966).

Liebhafsky, H. H. *The Nature of Price Theory.* Dorsey Press, Homewood, Ill., 1963, Chap. 15.

Patinkin, Don. *Money, Interest and Prices: An Integration of Monetary and Value Theory,* 2nd ed. Harper & Row, New York, 1965.

Smith, Warren L. "Financial Intermediaries and Monetary Controls." *Quarterly Journal of Economics* (November 1959).

———. "Monetary Theories of the Rate of Interest: A Dynamic Analysis." *Review of Economics and Statistics* (February 1958).

Solomon, Ezra. "The Issue of Financial Intermediaries." *Proceedings of the 1959 Conference on Savings and Residential Financing,* U.S. Savings and Loan League, May 7 and 8, 1959.

Thorn, Richard. "Nonbank Financial Intermediaries, Credit Expansion, and Monetary Policy." *Staff Papers,* International Monetary Fund, November 1958.

Tobin, James. "Commercial Banks as Creators of 'Money.'" In *Banking and Monetary Studies.* Ed. Deane Carson. Richard D. Irwin, Homewood, Ill., 1963, Chap. 22.

Trescott, Paul B. *Money, Banking, and Economic Welfare,* 2nd ed. McGraw-Hill Book Company, New York, 1965, Chap. 9.

Tsiang, S. C. "Liquidity Preference and Loanable Funds Theories of Interest: Reply." *American Economic Review* (September 1957).

———. "Liquidity Preference and Loanable Funds Theories, Multiplier and Velocity Analysis: A Synthesis." *American Economic Review* (September 1956).

# 23

# The Term Structure of Interest Rates

In ordinary conversation, people often talk about "interest rates" being high or low, much as they might talk about the price of shoes or baseball tickets. Such reference to interest rates or shoe prices in the plural recognizes that despite discussions of *the* interest rate in Chapters 21 and 22, as a practical matter there are as many interest rates as there are types of different credit transactions. Interest rates, like the "price of shoes," is an abstraction representing thousands of differing price tags. Differing costs of raw material, design, and production; differing elements of risk to buyer and seller; and disparate conditions of sale all make for corresponding variations in price, whether the product in question is shoes or credit.

This chapter concerns just one dimension of the pricing of credit: the influence of differing terms to maturity—the term structure of interest rates. Some loan contracts are made for very brief terms—often only overnight in the money market. Others, like mortgages or the bond issues of industrial corporations or governments, may specify a repayment date twenty years, thirty years, or even longer in the future. Indeed, some British government bonds, called *consols,* are to pay interest in perpetuity and never to be redeemed.

For each different contract duration, the market may, and normally does, choose to establish a different interest rate; and these interest rates, in turn, fluctuate from day to day (or even from minute to minute in the bond markets). Usually, long-term interest rates are higher than short-term interest rates, but the spread varies substantially. Sometimes short-term rates even rise above long rates—and for very good reason, as will be seen later.

As a practical matter, it is extremely difficult—perhaps even logically impossible—to disentangle the influence of term to maturity from the many other factors that determine the interest rate on any given credit contract. Nevertheless, one can approximate the influence by comparing interest rates on substantially identical loan contracts that differ among each other *only* with respect to term to maturity. Any difference in rate then presumably reflects solely the difference in length of contract.

For just this reason, most empirical research on the term structure has focused on the interest rates of U.S. government obligations, precisely because these are viewed as carrying negligible default risk whether they are short or long term; because they are outstanding in large quantities spanning a wide range of maturities; and because they are heavily traded in an active marketplace that continually establishes up-to-the-instant quotations summarizing the preferences of an extremely wide-ranging, diverse, and sophisticated investing public. Both student and researcher should keep in mind, however, that owing to a host of tax and other technicalities and market imperfections as well as differences in term, no two issues of U.S. Treasury securities are genuinely identical from the investor's point of view. Moreover, results of empirical studies of interest rates on Treasury securities need not hold for other interest-bearing obligations, because the maturity distribution and total quantity of Treasury borrowing, in sharp contrast to that of private issuers, is not set so as to minimize interest expense and risk. The supply and composition of Treasury debt are largely interest inelastic (see Chapter 17). To complicate matters further, interest rates on Treasury bonds and other forms of debt influence each other, so that the "pure" term structure of interest rates may be unobservable.

## Yield Curves and Theories of the Term Structure

Interest-bearing securities, such as marketable Treasury obligations, carry a *coupon* interest rate fixed at the time of issue—for example, the 8 percent notes due August 15, 1986, are to pay their holders $4 per $100 of face value every February 15 and August 15 (adding up to $8 each year) through August 15, 1986. However, the *price* at which these securities may be bought or sold in the marketplace varies continually in response to market conditions, in the same way that stock prices vary. This means that market yields can vary. If, for example, the Treasury currently has to place 9 percent coupons on new issues of notes due in 1986, then any owner of the old 8 percent notes outstanding who wished to sell them would have to accept less than $100 ("par") to find a buyer. Conversely, if new issues carry only 7 percent coupons, the higher rate on the old 8 percent notes would command a premium and the price of the old notes would rise to exceed par. This return, which includes the stream of coupons and also amortizes the price discount or premium on the bond over the bond's remaining life, is called *yield to maturity*; normally it differs from the coupon rate. Yield to maturity and price vary inversely: a higher price means a lower yield to the buyer; a lower price, on the other hand, raises the yield. To a reasonable approximation, the yield to maturity of an already outstanding bond may be regarded as the coupon rate that a new security issued at par would have to carry in order to be acceptable in the market. As a result, the terms *interest rate* and *yield* are used more or less interchangeably in the literature as well as in the marketplace.

The formula by which the yield to maturity of a bond is calculated is

$$P = \sum_{t=1}^{N} \frac{C}{(1 + r)^t} + \frac{F}{(1 + r)^N} \qquad (23\text{-}1)$$

where $P$ is the price of the bond, $C$ is the amount of the coupon, $F$ is the final payment (face amount) repayable at maturity, $t$ stands for the number of years running up to the total number of years to maturity $N$, and $r$ is the yield to maturity. Thus $r$ is that discount rate which, when applied to all the scheduled future payments of principal and interest stipulated in the bond contract, equates the present value of these payments to the current price of the bonds. As the formula shows, the price of a bond ($P$) and its yield ($r$) vary inversely. The longer the maturity (the more terms on the right hand side of the formula), the greater the effect of a given change in yield on the price (and, conversely, the less the impact of a change in $P$ on $r$). For the owner of the bond actually to earn the yield to maturity, however, the formula demands that he or she be able to reinvest each future coupon payment at precisely that yield. If it is possible to reinvest at a higher average rate, the owner will end up earning more than the indicated yield to maturity; but if the owner must reinvest at a lower rate, earnings will be less.

In practice the yield to maturity is found by referring to yield tables, or it can be quickly obtained on suitably equipped calculators. On the 8 percent notes described earlier, for example, the yield as of September 5, 1978, was 8.30 percent at the prevailing offered price of 98$^9$/$_{32}$. Had the price been 97, the yield would have been 8.53 percent; for a price of 99, it would have been 8.17 percent.

**Figure 23-1  Yield Curves of Selected Maturities of U.S. Government Obligations, 1958–1974**

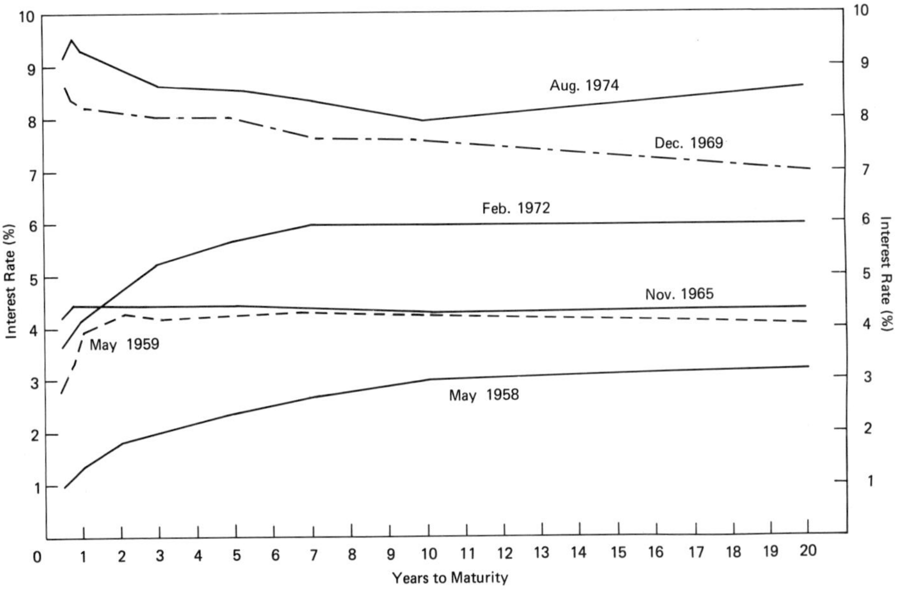

Source: The First Boston Corporation, Fixed Income Research.

## The Yield Curve

For any class of fixed-interest securities, we may visualize a *yield curve* that relates interest rates and term to maturity. Such a curve shows the prevailing yield to maturity for all relevant maturities. From a slightly different perspective, such a curve may be viewed as the cost of issuing new securities at different maturities—that is, as the prevailing *term structure of interest rates,* which is the subject of this chapter.

Figure 23-1 depicts the *yield* curves of selected maturities of U.S. government obligations near some watershed dates in recent financial history. The curves relate yields on these securities to their maturities.[1] Clearly a great diversity of shapes is to

be observed. Figure 23-2 illustrates, for parts of 1975 and 1976, the variety of yield curves that may prevail even within one year. Generalizations that describe the trend of interest rates simply as "up" or "down" suppress some of the most interesting aspects of interest rate behavior.

the plotting. Given also the unavoidable need for interpolation in the charting, the true term structure at any time can only be approximated, often by rather subjective judgments. Differences of opinion about such judgments have created serious problems in evaluating the results of empirical studies. The curves shown in the charts here are based on so-called constant-maturity yields estimated by the Federal Reserve and the U.S. Treasury.

For a discussion of, and a possible technique for dealing with, the theoretical issues that arise in estimating the term structure from the actually prevailing yield curve, see J. Huston McCulloch, "Measuring the Term Structure of Interest Rates," *Journal of Business* (January 1971), 19.

[1]Because of tax considerations and market imperfections, many securities have yields lying far off the presumed true yield curve. Such securities are omitted from

**Figure 23-2  Yield Curves of Selected Maturities of U.S. Government Obligations, 1975–1976**

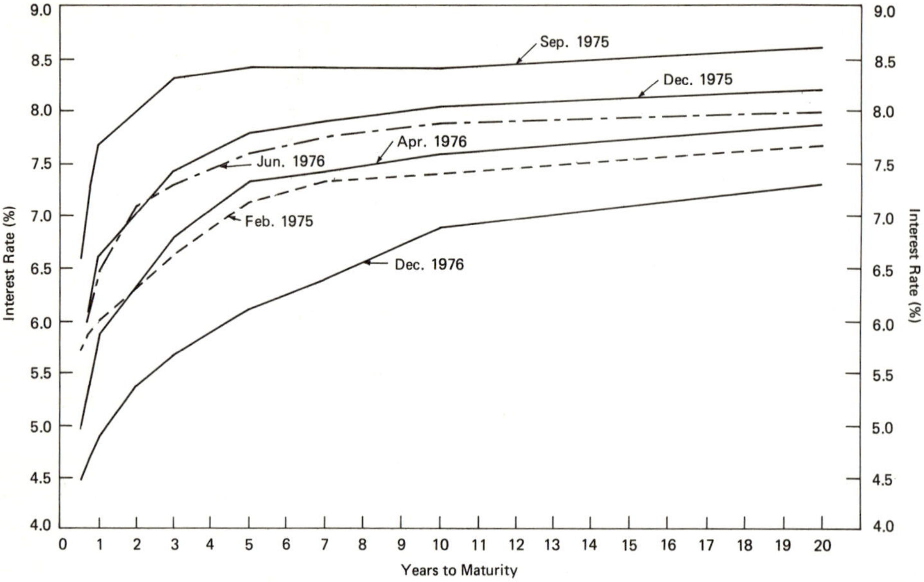

Source: The First Boston Corporation, Fixed Income Research.

## The Expectations Hypothesis

Assuming that 30-year Treasury bonds and 30-day Treasury bills are indeed regarded as equally free of default risk, why should their yields differ? Why isn't the yield curve a horizontal straight line?

Suppose, only for the moment, that the buyers of the obligations are all speculators with essentially unlimited resources. Note that there is no prescribed span over which any speculator must stay invested. An individual may invest for thirty years (or any other span) by continually "rolling over" short Treasury bills; alternatively, it is possible to invest for thirty days (or any other span thirty years or shorter) by buying 30-year bonds and selling them at selected times. Such mythical speculators would be indifferent between (say) 6 percent 30-day Treasury bills and 6 percent 30-year Treasury bonds (both priced at par) if, and only if, they expected the total return over the years to be the same on either security (after proper adjustment for compounding, discounting, and so forth). If

they did not expect the return to be the same, clearly they would buy the security offering the higher expected return, and the market yields of the two securities could not remain identical. Indeed, they rarely are.

What this hypothetical example illustrates is that, at the most fundamental level, the yield curve is a curve and not a flat line because people do *not* expect interest rates in the future to remain the same as they are today. They have learned from experience, some of which is reflected in the analysis presented in the preceding chapters, that interest rates (and, equivalently, bond prices) can and do fluctuate. Thus, it makes sense for a longer-term investor to buy 5 percent Treasury short-term bills today in preference to 6 percent bonds, despite the lower return, if the investor expects 7 percent bonds to be available tomorrow. And it makes sense to buy 5 percent long-term bonds in preference to 6 percent bills, if the investor expects bond yields on new issues soon to drop to 4 percent.

Stated more generally, the yield curve must reflect market opinion in such a way that the expected return to any specified date in the future will be the same no matter what sequence of investment is chosen.[2] If the yield curve shows, for example, that a 10-year security purchased today yields 7 percent, then the expectations underlying the curve as a whole must be such as to render it a matter of indifference whether one invests for ten years by buying a 5-year security and planning to buy another 5-year security thereafter; or buying a 2-year security and then an 8-year security; or, for that matter, buying a 12-year bond with the intention of selling it after ten years (by which time it will have shortened to a 2-year bond).

A logically equivalent but simpler statement of this "theorem" is that the observed yield today to any specific date in the future must be equal to the average (the geometric average to allow for compound interest) of the succession of expected short-term rates over that interval. That is to say, the observed 2-year rate is the average of today's 1-year rate and the 1-year rate expected to prevail a year from now. Today's 5-year rate is the average of the currently observed 1-year rate and the 1-year rates expected to prevail two, three, and four years hence. Or, identically, the 5-year rate must equal, for example, the average of the currently ruling 2-year rate and the 3-year rate expected to prevail two years hence.

We have now implicitly introduced a crucial new concept—the *holding-period return*. Suppose we wished to invest for a year and observed that today's yield curve showed 1-year securities available at 5 percent and 2-year securities at 6 percent. Why not buy the 2-year issue, collect 6 percent interest for one year, and sell after that year?

Would we be able to earn 6 percent for the year rather than the 5 percent indicated by the yield curve? Not at all. What the yield curve implies is that when we go to sell our 2-year security next year (by then it will have shortened to 1-year paper), the market will not pay us par ($100), but only $99. Thus the dollar we have gained on coupon income we lose on the sale, and our net *holding-period return* for the year is the same 5 percent we would have obtained had we bought a 1-year maturity.

What about the person to whom we sell our 6 percent security (with one year left to run) at $99? A year later (two years from now), this buyer will have gotten 6 percent interest and $100 return of principal for a security for which he paid only $99. His *holding-period return* for the year will be 7 percent—six dollars of interest plus one dollar of "capital gain." Today's yield curve of 5 percent at one year, 6 percent for two years, thus expresses the market's expectation that the 1-year rate next year—the coupon a new 1-year issue priced at par would have to offer—will be 7 percent. Or, from another perspective, we may say that today's 6 percent 2-year rate is the average of this year's observed 1-year rate of 5 percent and next year's expected 1-year rate of 7 percent.

By analogous reasoning, and by matching various securities, one can derive a whole set of such expected future rates. Any yield curve that includes observations on securities that mature at frequent intervals in the future carries within it a more or less mechanically ascertainable set of *forward rates*, rates that presumably reflect the market's composite expectations as to the yield curves that will prevail long into the future.[3]

---

[2]There is a problem in defining how the market averages the opinion of various participants, particularly if they are unequal in size—which means that some opinions are, therefore, backed by more cash than others. The typical, but very artificial, assumption is that all participants have identical expectations. Alternatively, one may assume all participants have large (but not infinite) resources that free them of bankruptcy risk. (If anyone had infinite resources, that person's opinion would determine the price structure; if all had infinite resources, even one maverick could prevent a consensus.) Also, transaction and information costs are assumed to be zero. In fact, as we note later, these assumptions are clearly contrary to the facts—yet another obstacle in the way of verifying any particular theory of the term structure.

[3]The actual formula is

$$(1 + {}_tR_N) = \sqrt[N]{(1 + {}_tR_{N-1})^{N-1}(1 + {}_{t+N-1}r_1)}$$

where ${}_tR_1$ is the current 1-year rate, ${}_tR_2$ the 2-year rate, etc., and ${}_{t+1}r_1$ the implied 1-year forward rate at time $t + 1$ one year from now, ${}_{t+2}r_1$ the expected 1-year rate two years hence, and so on. The $R$s in this formulation, however, do not mesh well mathematically with the way yield to maturity is calculated in the marketplace. Significant differences in the calculated $r$s or in the actual holding-period return can result from differences in timing of interest receipts, differences in coupons, and differences in the interest rate at which interest earnings can be reinvested. Here is still another major source of difficulty in empirical studies. See Burton G. Malkiel, *The Term*

With this background, we may state somewhat more formally the principal elements of the *expectations hypothesis,* a traditional explanation of the term structure. The pure form of the hypothesis depends on a number of simplifying assumptions, most of which are not met in the real world. The most important are the following:

1. All securities are free of default risk or are at least identical with respect to any risk that payment of interest or principal may be defaulted.
2. There are no transaction costs, and bonds do not have any special tax or call features.
3. Investors are able to make accurate forecasts of future interest rates.
4. Investors are profit maximizers.
5. Investors have no specific maturity preferences for institutional or other reasons.

These assumptions imply that investors will choose to purchase the combination of securities that maximizes their expected holding-period yield. Since investors are assumed to be pure profit maximizers and, since it is further assumed that there are no costs associated with the purchase and sale of a security, investors will behave as arbitrageurs, buying combinations of securities that produce higher holding-period yields and selling those securities and combinations that produce lower yields. As a consequence of this arbitrage process, security prices will move so as to force the yield for any intended holding period to a level identical for each investor regardless of the combination of securities that individual holds. As long as yields on some combinations of securities remain unequal for a given holding period, arbitrage will continue in the bond market to force them into equality. As we have seen, this arbitrage process means that long-term yields will be an average of present and expected short-term yields. The expectations hypothesis in this pure form says nothing about relative supplies of securities of various maturities. Their quantities do not matter because, with the expected holding-period yields equal and certain,

investors view longs and shorts as perfect substitutes.

The expectations hypothesis presents a very simple rationalization of the term structure of interest rates and the shape of yield curves. If expected future short-term rates are above the current short-term rate, then the yield curve will slope upward. Similarly, if expected short rates are below the current short rate, the yield curve will slope downward. The yield curve will be flat if future short rates are expected to be the same as the current short rate.

The expectations hypothesis also makes it easy to understand the greater sluggishness of long yields as compared with shorts. People often change their minds about the outlook for short rates over the year or two immediately ahead without altering their view of what such interest rates might be ten, twenty, or thirty years in the future. Recall that prevailing long rates are essentially an average of expected short rates. Most of the time the public is apt to reevaluate expected short-term rates only for the nearby years. Perhaps only the timing as to when high and low short rates are expected may be altered, but not the average rate level. Such reconsideration may alter yields on some short-term securities materially, while affecting long-term yields little or not at all. Similar reasoning explains why the long end (often called the "tail") of the yield curve out beyond fifteen years or so is virtually always quite flat. People may have reason for anticipating large fluctuations in short-term interest rates in nearby years, but they have little or no basis today for expecting rates in (say) years 20, 21, and 22 to differ predictably from each other. As a result, even though the level of long-term rates may change sharply, the tail of the yield curve never has any sizable slope.

Various efforts have been made to examine empirically the future, or forward, rates implied by yield curves to see what can be learned about the expectations hypothesis. One immediate conclusion is that the "forecasts" contained within the yield curve often are wrong. A more interesting subject is how these implicit expectations respond to and are changed by actual market developments, which reveal their errors. To the extent that, as the evidence suggests, expectations (forward rates) are adjusted in a manner responsive to the error, the expectations hypothesis of the term structure of

*Structure of Interest Rates,* Princeton University Press, Princeton, N.J., 1966, pp. 21, 40–49; and Sidney Homer and Martin L. Leibowitz, *Inside the Yield Book; New Tools for Bond Market Strategy,* Prentice-Hall, Englewood Cliffs, N.J., 1972, especially Chaps. 1, 9, and 15.

interest rates is confirmed. However, there is still the basic difficulty, putting it in outrageously oversimplified terms, that rational persons may respond to a forecast error by taking the new data to indicate a changed world and radically revise all their forecasts. They may, on the other hand, view the new situation as merely an aberration from which there will eventually be a return to "normal." Or they may take any position in between. As a result, conclusive empirical verification of any particular expectations model is unlikely.

Putting it more formally, the prevailing term structure is the joint outcome of the way in which the public forms its expectations as well as of the way the market functions to express those expectations in bond prices and yields. To use the data to test the expectations hypothesis, it is necessary to presume a model of how the public forms its expectations; to study the formation of expectations, it is necessary to assume a market model. On the whole, empirical work has tended to the latter, generally assuming that the market functions according to a modified form of the expectations hypothesis and attempting on this basis to determine the behavior of expectations.[4]

It may be noted that, beginning in 1975, a number of organized futures markets in fixed-interest instruments have been established, on the model of traditional markets in commodity futures. In these markets, whose early growth has been spectacular, it is in effect the bets on the future—the forward rates we have just described—that are traded, rather than the securities themselves. This resembles commodity trading, where participants in the copper or grain futures markets do not expect ever to make or take actual delivery of the goods. The behavior of these new markets may in time provide a lode of more direct measurements of interest rate expectations and how they are formed.

## The Shape of the Yield Curve and the Liquidity Premium Hypothesis

A major puzzle with the expectations approach has been the fact that so much of the time long-term rates are higher than short-term rates. During the relatively infrequent and brief periods when short rates are higher than long rates, market participants tend to regard the situation as an anomaly. Moreover, when downward sloping, so-called inverse yield curves are observed, they rarely show nearly so steep a gradient as is often found when "normal" upward-sloping curves prevail.

The observed upward-sloping yield curve—rising rates as maturities become more distant—should mean that interest rates are expected to increase. It is true that in recent decades the trend of interest rates has been upward and that we have had more years of business expansion (generally associated with rising interest rates) than contraction (associated with falling rates). Nevertheless, and taking into account evidence from earlier periods, the preponderance of upward-sloping curves is probably excessive.

There are several explanations—by no means mutually exclusive—of this phenomenon. One reason for long-term rates being consistently higher than short-term yields may be simply that investors almost always see an increasing risk of default as the horizon recedes. This is surely the case for even the highest-grade private obligations. With respect to U.S. Treasury securities, as already mentioned, empirical term-structure studies assume an absence of credit risk, but market participants may, nevertheless, harbor some residual doubts as to the certainty of payment on 30-year obligations—doubts that do not trouble them with respect to the Treasury's short-term debt. To that extent, the higher rates on long-term securities may in part reflect higher perceived default risk rather than expectation of higher interest rates.

---

[4]The first major study along these lines was by David Meiselman, *The Term Structure of Interest Rates*, Prentice-Hall, Englewood Cliffs, N.J., 1962. Meiselman modified the pure expectations hypothesis, which had been criticized by others who pointed out that the implicit forward rates in the model did not conform to subsequent empirical yield structures, by introducing an error-learning component to demonstrate that incorrect market forecasts were subsequently altered to bring implicit forward rates in line with actual market rate changes. His conclusions and statistical results, however, have been criticized and modified by many subsequent investigators. The article by S. W. Dobson, R. C. Sutch and D. E. Vanderford, "An Evaluation of Alternative Empirical Models of the Term Structure of Interest Rates," *Journal of Finance* (September 1976), classifies and compares several subsequent studies. For a more recent effort to measure "unanticipated" interest rate changes, see J. Huston McCulloch, *The Cumulative Unanticipated Changes in Interest Rates: Evidence on the Misintermediation Hypothesis*, Working Paper No. 222, National Bureau of Economic Research, Cambridge, Mass., December 1977.

More generally, one should recall that the discussion thus far has postulated a market free of transaction costs and composed entirely of speculators with large resources and/or identical expectations. To enjoy huge resources means to be indifferent to equiprobable prospects of capital gain or loss. As soon as one's capital is limited, however, the possibility of large losses raises the specter of bankruptcy. Consequently, most economic units must be regarded as being to a greater or lesser degree *risk averse,* that is, more concerned with avoiding capital loss than with creating capital gain.

This has important consequences for the term structure of interest rates. As illustrated in Table 23-1, the mathematics of bond yields is such that the price impact of a change in yields increases sharply with the maturity of the security. The reason for this is intuitively easy to understand. Assume an investor has just bought some 6 percent securities at the ruling market price of par. Now, for whatever reason, rates on all new securities rise to 7 percent. Clearly the owner of a 1-year 6 percent security will suffer a smaller loss of price than the owner of a 20-year security, who is stuck with a low coupon for so much longer. Of course, should interest rates fall, the gains on long-term bonds would be greater but, in a world in which excessive losses can destroy an enterprise, it will take an *extra* yield inducement to entice investors to crawl out along the yield curve. Even though short *rates* usually (but not always!) move more than longs, *prices* on intermediates and longs almost always move more than prices on shorts.

A factor closely related to risk aversion in producing the typical upward slope in the yield curve

is the so-called liquidity premium that results from the market's apparent preference for owning short-term securities and aversion to issuing them. Not only are market participants limited in capital, but most of them are not in the business of speculation or arbitrage. The true speculator would be active as a lender or borrower at all conceivable maturities, whenever the market yield curve differed from his or her own forecast. In the real world, no such speculators exist. Most issuers of debt instruments—and issuers, in principle, should be just as sensitive as buyers to interest rate expectations in their choice of maturity—are not in the securities business at all. They are governments, business firms, and households whose main concern is with other matters. Business firms are justifiably sensitive to the dangers of bankruptcy courted by excessive short-term debt. Governments realize that excessive issuance of short-term securities on their part may create undue liquidity in the economy (although the fact that short borrowing is cheaper and more easily done in large quantity frequently has carried the day). Major household borrowing is almost always for multiyear periods, with installment repayment, since most households are rarely able to accumulate large lump sums in the short term. All in all, then, the economy probably does not borrow at short term as much as it might were interest rate expectations the sole basis for choice of debt maturity.

At the same time, for rather similar reasons, buyers probably demand more short-term securities than they "should." Many investors in fixed-interest securities tend to center on short maturities. Business firms investing temporary excess cash normally avoid the risk of major price change that attends long-term securities. They often feel that it does not pay to divert much capital or management time to pursuits that are peripheral to their main lines of business. Individuals surely have a preference for immediately accessible financial investments, such as savings accounts. Banks and other financial institutions are more inclined to be "speculative," but they, too, must be concerned about capital risk. This is especially true because of the short-term nature of most of their liabilities, which are withdrawable requiring little or no notice by household and other depositors. Pension funds and life insurance companies, on the other hand, because of the long range and relatively predictable

**Table 23-1  Price Effect on Bonds of Varying Maturity of a Rise in Interest Rates from 6 Percent to 7 Percent**

| Maturity | Price Decline (percentages) |
|---|---|
| Three months | 0.3% |
| One year | 0.9 |
| Two years | 1.8 |
| Five years | 4.2 |
| Ten years | 7.1 |
| Twenty years | 10.7 |
| Fifty years | 13.8 |
| Forever | 14.3 |

nature of their liabilities, tend primarily to longer-term investments. For these institutions their *income risk,* the danger that interest and other income may be insufficient to cover contractual obligations to pensioners and beneficiaries, is large relative to *market risk,* that is, the risk of capital loss due to forced sale at low prices. Consequently, they are attracted by the premium yields on long-term bonds.

In the aggregate, however, pension funds and life insurance companies notwithstanding, the financial participants in the world economy display a preference for acquiring short-term securities and some aversion to issuing them. In principle, such an imbalance affords profit opportunities to speculators but, in practice, no one has assembled the huge capital needed to exploit them. Indeed, presumably because of market risk, security dealers do not provide as ready market facilities in long bonds as in short paper. Transaction costs are high: not necessarily, perhaps, in relation to principal value, but usually in relation to, say, a year's interest income. The greater inherent risk in long-term maturities is compounded by the fact that at infrequent—but recurrent—times of market stress, holders may find large lots of long-term bonds unsalable at any reasonable price. This particular lack of marketplace "liquidity" is an additional factor contributing to the general preference for issuing long-term, but owning short-term, securities.

In sum, it can be shown that once one questions the assumption of certainty of interest rate forecasts made on the basis of the pure expectations hypothesis, a crucial outcome of the expectations hypothesis is also placed in doubt. If future interest rates are not known, investors will be unlikely to consider short-term securities perfect substitutes for long-term securities, even if their holding-period yields are the same. If this is so, arbitrage will not take place to produce equality between long-term rates and the geometric average of the current short rate and intervening expected short rates.

The liquidity-premium hypothesis argues that, notwithstanding the important role of expectations in determining the term structure, the existence of risk aversion will result in a preference for shorts over longs unless there is some compensation, namely, a liquidity premium. This premium is necessary because the default risk and market risk of shorts is less than that of longs; consequently, risk-

averting investors require a higher yield on longs than on shorts when they are otherwise indifferent between the two categories of securities.

Once investors' aversion to market risk is admitted as a factor shaping the yield curve, then its slope is subject to change as the degree of investors' risk aversion changes. An increase in risk aversion requires an increase in the liquidity premium and steepens the yield curve; conversely, a decline in risk aversion flattens the curve. More importantly, if investors no longer regard longs and shorts as perfect substitutes but, instead, prefer shorts to longs, then the maturity distribution of the outstanding securities becomes relevant. If the issues are predominantly longs, then a wider liquidity premium (that is, a steeper yield curve) will be needed to induce the risk-aversive market to hold the existing stock of securities. If the issues are mainly shorts, on the other hand, a flatter yield curve (narrower liquidity premium) will prevail. Thus, the liquidity-premium modification of the expectations hypothesis implies that the maturity (and other risk-relevant) characteristics of the stock of securities may be important determinants of the term structure.

Various investigators have noted and tried to quantify the bias of the market in demanding more and supplying fewer short-term securities than pure interest-rate considerations would dictate. In general the results have confirmed the existence of a liquidity premium, but its nature and dimensions remain a matter of controversy.[5]

### Market Segmentation

Borrowers and issuers are sometimes said to have preferred maturity "habitats," outside of which they may be wary of venturing. As already indicated, most financial institutions, and most types of borrowers, are at least somewhat specialized as to the classes of maturities they normally buy or sell. Such specialization, due presumably to economies resulting from division of labor, is reinforced by legal, regulatory, and accounting practices, as

[5]See, for example, Reuben Kessel, *The Cyclical Behavior of the Term Structure of Interest Rates,* Occasional Paper 91, National Bureau of Economic Research, New York, 1965, Chap. 3; and J. Huston McCulloch, "An Estimate of the Liquidity Premium," *Journal of Political Economy* (February 1975).

well as by tradition and habit, and motivated by lessons drawn from past financial crises.

The resulting inflexibility on the part of issuers and buyers of debt instruments with respect to their maturity preferences may at times produce a glut or scarcity of securities in a particular maturity class. For example, public utilities, which tend to do most of their borrowing in long-term bonds, might all at the same time decide to build major new generating plants. Such a decision would flood the bond market with an exceptional volume of new 25-year bonds. This action would raise long-term interest rates relative to shorts. Or, to take an opposite case, life insurance companies and pension funds, which, as already mentioned, prefer to buy long-term securities because their liabilities are highly predictable actuarially, sometimes find themselves with uninvested funds shortly before they must publish year-end statements. They may then become aggressive buyers of long-term bonds, driving the price up and the yield down.

If all market participants acted on the basis of interest expectations only, then any distortion of the yield curve resulting from such an abnormal situation in a particular maturity would be quickly arbitraged away by "bargain hunters." But if, in fact, bargain hunters are few and small relative to the huge—and allegedly inflexible—institutions that quantitatively dominate the market, then observed yield curves may rarely, if ever, accurately reflect the market's interest rate expectations. Instead, changes in the yield curve would result from changes in the supply and demand for securities in particular maturity *segments*, with developments in any one segment conceivably being largely independent of developments in others.[6]

In point of fact, of course, given sufficient inducement most "inhabitants" of any given segment can be enticed some distance into neighboring habitats. If such movements occur with sufficient promptness, they may well iron out the yield curve. To produce an expectations-dominated yield curve, it is not necessary for all market participants to be active in all segments of the market. A good deal of overlap will suffice. And there are participants, such as professional dealers and commercial banks, that do normally operate across the whole spectrum of maturities.

In the present state of knowledge, market observation clearly shows that virtually no investors or issuers regard longs and shorts as perfect substitutes and, thus, the relative supply and demand for such obligations must, at least at times, significantly affect the yield curve. And, indeed, unless they are adjusted for liquidity preference and segmentation, the implicit forward rates in the yield curve follow neither the course required by the pure expectations hypothesis nor the "random walk" required by the efficient markets hypothesis (the view that asset prices instantly incorporate all available information—see Chapters 19, 24, and 32.)

It has been suggested that liquidity preference, segmentation, and other possible sources of the discrepancy be viewed in a larger framework as aspects of a "term premium" needed to compensate lenders for the risks of maturity extension (or borrowers for shortening their issues). The risks in question, however, are not the familiar market risks of an economy with a well-understood mode of operation, but rather the risks of unforeseeable and unfathomable change that encumber all contracts—the more so the further these contracts extend into the future.[7]

Most market participants follow an eclectic approach. As occurs so often in financial markets, the influence of expectations on prices may well vary

[6]See, for example, John Culbertson, "The Term Structure of Interest Rates," *Quarterly Journal of Economics* (November 1957); Franco Modigliani and Richard Sutch, "Debt Management and the Term Structure of Interest Rates: An Empirical Analysis of Recent Experience," *Journal of Political Economy,* Supplement (August 1967); J. W. Elliott and M. E. Echols, "Market Segmentation, Speculative Behavior, and the Term Structure of Interest Rates," *Review of Economics and Statistics* (February 1976), and "Rational Expectations in a Disequilibrium Model of the Term Structure," *American Economic Review* (March 1976); and B. M. Friedman, *The Effect of Shifting Wealth Ownership on the Term Structure of Interest Rates,* Working Paper No. 239, National Bureau of Economic Research, Cambridge, Mass., February 1978.

[7]See Thomas J. Sargent, "Rational Expectations and the Term Structure of Interest Rates," *Journal of Money, Credit and Banking* (February 1972), 75; C. R. Nelson, *The Term Structure of Interest Rates*, Basic Books, New York, 1972; J. B. Michaelsen, *The Term Structure of Interest Rates,* Intext Educational Publishers, New York and London, 1973, particularly Chaps. 3 and 4; and Thomas F. Cargill, "The Term Structure of Interest Rates: A Test of the Expectations Hypothesis," *Journal of Finance* (June 1975), 761.

from time to time, depending on the ebb and flow in institutional habits and regulations, in the assurance with which the expectations are held, and in the penalties that investors perceive in case of error. Broadly speaking, it may be suggested that a given set of market expectations as to future states of the world includes much more than just a term-structure forecast. Among the many other dimensions is a general notion as to the amounts of various classes of securities expected to be issued and of the funds available for their purchase in the hands of various classes of investors. Thus, an unpredicted but apparently long-lasting change in relative supplies or sources of demand is likely to significantly alter the yield curve.

## Official Intervention in the Yield Curve

The debate between the "expectations" and "segmentation" approaches has strong practical relevance to Treasury debt-management policy and Federal Reserve open-market operations. Within a given configuration of monetary policy, can the authorities shape the yield curve to their liking? In practice, this usually means trying to hold long rates down, so as to promote housing and other investment, at times when short rates are moving up.

For several years after the 1951 Treasury–Federal Reserve "accord," [8] the Federal Reserve pursued, with few exceptions, an open-market policy of buying and selling "bills only," precisely to avoid exerting any influence on the term structure of interest rates. The concern was that making deliberate choices to operate in particular maturity sectors of the government debt would distort the market and lead back to the despised pre-1951 commitment to peg a specific structure of rates. This hands-off policy was roundly criticized by many economists and others, who believed it both desirable and feasible for the Federal Reserve to limit rises on long-term interest rates by buying long-term bonds.

The "bills only" policy was abandoned in 1960 in the effort to stimulate a stagnant domestic economy without intensifying a serious balance-of-payments problem that was producing large gold

[8]See Chapter 17.

losses. A combination of debt management and open-market operations was employed in the effort to "nudge" or "twist" the term structure of interest rates. The objective was to raise short-term yields so as to attract foreign funds into the United States money market. Meanwhile, long-term rates were to be kept low so as to promote private investment and domestic economic growth.

Ironically, many economists had by this time come to believe that expectations determined the yield curve regardless of the relative quantities of short- and long-term securities and, therefore, questioned whether such an "operation twist" could succeed. For a number of years, however, the government achieved its objective. Short rates did, in fact, rise while long rates remained stable—but it is unclear, and probably impossible to determine, whether this result was due primarily to governmental action or to other influences. One problem was that the Treasury, while going so far as to issue short-term debt to boost short-term interest rates even when it did not need the money, was at the same time appreciably lengthening the maturity of the debt in its other operations. Although the goal of lengthening the debt was in conflict with that of stabilizing long rates, both were accomplished. Evidently market forces were working in the same direction as the government and may have been principally responsible for the outcome.

Investors and borrowers tend to take for granted certain patterns of Treasury debt management. When these are unexpectedly and substantially altered, the public may revise its expectations of future interest rates to conform with the change. It is a rash market participant who assumes that the Treasury and the Federal Reserve, with their virtually unlimited resources, cannot at least temporarily achieve a rearrangement of the term structure of yields if they give that objective an overriding priority. But, as was true even in 1960–1964, control of the yield curve is an unlikely first priority of stabilization policy in peacetime. Whether any less-determined approach would succeed remains to be tested.

After the middle 1960s, the Treasury and Federal Reserve largely abandoned their efforts to regulate the yield curve. Although the authorities continue to play an active role in all maturity sectors, their current attitude is closer to the bills-only policy of the 1950s. The emphasis is on behaving in moderate and predictable fashion, thereby minimizing direct governmental influence on the term structure of yields.

## Cyclical Changes in Term Structure

Over the business cycle, the yield curve changes according to a fairly typical pattern, although the sequence is, of course, by no means precise. During recessions, there is usually a wide spread between short and long rates, that is, a steeply upward-sloping yield curve. Short-term rates are low, reflecting the weakness of the economy, but long-term rates tend to remain close to their expected long-run levels. The recession is regarded as temporary, and the yield curve and interest rates are expected to rise.

As economic recovery progresses, the yield curve does indeed flatten. Interest rates rise at all maturities, but short rates rise the most. As the boom nears its crest, the curve may become actually flat or even inverse. Sometimes a hump appears in the intermediate-maturity range: rates in the 5-year sector, say, may exceed both shorter- and longer-term yields. The credit market is tight, but perhaps investors also expect that the situation soon will ease and that interest rates, especially short rates, will fall. Meanwhile, short rates have not risen as much as they might because the demand for liquid—promptly cashable—assets is disproportionately great. As recession sets in, short rates fall more than longs, and the cycle is repeated.

What difference, if any, does all this make to the pace or distribution of economic activity? The effect of high or low (and rising or falling) interest rates on various industries is well understood, but does the relationship among rates on different maturities matter much?

The subject has not been intensively investigated, but it would appear that the consequences may be significant because of impacts on financial intermediaries. Almost by definition, depository institutions are in the business of borrowing short and lending long. When the profit spread is wide, that is, when the short rates at which they borrow are low relative to the long rates at which they lend, intermediaries (such as commercial and savings banks, savings and loan associations, and credit unions) are stimulated to lend more aggressively. They may ease nonrate credit terms, promoting activity in the credit-sensitive sectors of the economy. When short rates are high relative to returns on long-term investments, on the other hand, lending becomes unprofitable and is curtailed. In general, steep yield curves favor financial intermediation and the activities financed thereby (most notably the mortgage market and construction industry). Flat or inverse curves tend to eliminate the financial "middleman" and to favor spending by large governmental or corporate units, which can readily sell their debt obligations directly to the public. The loss of deposits, lending power, and incentive suffered by depository savings institutions in such circumstances is, in fact, labeled disintermediation.

"Playing the yield curve" is an important aspect of the management of the investment portfolios of financial institutions. Management is needed, for in the absence of countervailing measures, portfolios shorten with the passage of time. A large institution wishing to maintain a constant average maturity in a diversified bond portfolio faces a never-ending series of decisions as to when to buy, sell, or swap issues of various maturities to offset the passage of time and to profit from changes in the yield curve. One such technique is referred to as "riding the yield curve." Often the curve may have a "shoulder" point somewhere in the 2- to 7-year maturity range: a more or less pronounced kink, beyond which the curve is relatively flat, and short of which it is relatively steep. Buying securities with maturities just beyond the shoulder, in order to sell them at appreciably lower yield and higher price after a brief passage of time has shortened them, can be quite profitable. But sometimes the locus of the shoulder changes swiftly and unexpectedly. The expected profit may become a loss. Managing a portfolio requires close attention to such features as coupons, yields, tax treatment, callability and sinking funds, size and distribution of existing as well as potential new issues, timing and reinvestment of interest receipts, reliability of secondary markets, and many other technical matters beyond the scope of this chapter.[9]

## Conclusion

The behavior of bond-market participants and the yield curve seem, broadly speaking, to conform to the behavior postulated by the expectations hy-

[9]See Homer and Leibowitz, *Inside the Yield Book.*

pothesis, modified for risk aversion and liquidity preference as well as for various institutional peculiarities and market imperfections. But what shapes the expectations? Fully to explain or predict the yield curve requires an understanding of what explains the public's expectations of the future, a subject that involves deep epistemological difficulties. Isn't all available knowledge already discounted by the market? What, if anything, constitutes genuinely "new" knowledge, that is, a surprise? How much and how fast should rational persons react to surprises (if such exist) and how much do they or should they rely on habit? The subject of the term structure of interest rates is sure to fascinate scholars and practitioners alike, but it is most unlikely that anyone will discover a magic key that solves the mystery.

## Questions

1. For the yield curves shown in the Figures 23-1 and 23-2 calculate (very approximately) what structure of forward rates is implied.

2. Surveys indicate that market participants make specific interest rate forecasts only a year or two into the future. Why does or doesn't this contradict the expectations hypothesis of the term structure?

3. For decades long-term high-grade bond yields never rose above 5 percent. Since the late 1960s, however, they have been much higher. How do you suppose the formation of expectations was affected during and after the transition?

4. From World War II until 1970, there were few, if any, major bankruptcies. Since then, there have been several. How may this have affected the yield curve?

5. Since the U.S. Treasury does not need to fear its own bankruptcy, suppose it always borrowed at the lowest available interest rate (usually short-term). If this permanently flattened the yield curve, what might be the consequences for various financial intermediaries, for the flow of funds, and for the distribution of credit and spending?

6. In the preceding question, would it make a difference to the yield curve if such a borrowing policy were enacted into law? Why or why not?

7. Under the law, the Treasury may not issue bonds (defined as securities with ten or more years to maturity) at coupon interest rates over 4¼ percent, far below what the market requires. In recent years, however, the Congress has in effect superseded this interest rate ceiling by repeatedly giving the Treasury authority to issue limited amounts of new bonds free of any restriction on interest rates. What might be the effect on the yield curve, if any, if the 4¼ percent ceiling were reinstated (remember that the Treasury is not the only long-term borrower in the market)?

8. How can you explain a "shoulder" in the yield curve? A "hump"?

9. As a Treasury official, you are approached by a housing industry delegation urging you to reduce issuance of longer-term Treasury securities, so as to promote lower mortgage interest rates. What pros and cons must you consider and what decision might you recommend?

10. Just as there is a term structure of interest rates, there may also be said to be a risk structure, with obligors of good credit standing paying the lowest rates and those who are more default-prone paying higher rates. Applying arguments used to interpret the term-structure yield curve, what factors, cyclical and otherwise, might cause risk "yield curves" to steepen or flatten?

## Selected Bibliography

Conard, Joseph W. *Introduction to the Theory of Interest*. University of California Press, Berkeley, 1959.

Hickman, W. Braddock. *The Term Structure of Interest Rates: An Exploratory Analysis*. National Bureau of Economic Research, New York, 1943.

Homer, Sidney. *A History of Interest Rates*. Rutgers University Press, New Brunswick, N.J., 1963.

————, and Martin L. Leibowitz. *Inside the Yield Book; New Tools for Bond Market Strategy*. Prentice-Hall, Englewood Cliffs, N.J., 1972.

Kessel, Reuben. *The Cyclical Behavior of the Term Structure of Interest Rates*. Occasional Paper 91. National Bureau of Economic Research, New York, 1965.

Malkiel, Burton G. *The Term Structure of Interest Rates*. Princeton University Press, Princeton, N.J., 1966.

Meiselman, David. *The Term Structure of Interest Rates*. Prentice-Hall, Englewood Cliffs, N.J., 1962.

Michaelsen, Jacob B. *The Term Structure of Interest Rates*. Intext Educational Publishers, New York and London, 1973.

Nelson, Charles R. *The Term Structure of Interest Rates*. Basic Books, New York, 1972.

Van Horne, James C. *Financial Market Rates and Flows*. Prentice-Hall, Englewood Cliffs, N.J., 1978.

# 24

## A Portfolio Approach to the Determination of Yield Differentials

Chapters 21 and 22 considered interest rate determination in the context of a single interest rate. This is consistent with the original exposition of John Maynard Keynes, who considered the existence of only one type of asset with an explicit return (long-term bonds) and one type of asset with an implicit return (money).[1] In the Keynesian case, if the central bank increases the money supply, people find that the proportion of their holdings in long-term bonds is less than they desire. As Chapter 21 points out, they then attempt to shift some of their holdings from money to long-term bonds. This action causes the price of these bonds to increase and the yields of these bonds to decline. The decline in bond yields causes the interest rate at which corporations borrow funds to decline, thereby stimulating real investment, output, and employment. Thus, there is a clear relationship between monetary policy, the interest rate, and the economy as a whole. Similar results derive from loanable funds analysis, since an increase in the money supply adds to the supply of loanable funds relative to the demand for these funds, thereby forcing down the interest rate and increasing the volume of investment and GNP.

Chapter 23 extended this analysis by taking into consideration the existence of securities of different maturities issued by the same borrower. It showed the relationship between yields on long-term bonds and yields on short-term securities and the different theories purporting to explain the term structure of interest rates.

This chapter goes beyond the others inasmuch as it deals with the complete spectrum of yields on financial assets issued by different borrowers, ranging from the low yields on Treasury bills to the high yields on growth stocks. It looks at *portfolio theory*—that is, the conceptual device that provides a framework that can show how the yields of different types of financial assets are related to their risk attibutes.[2] Once this relationship between risk and return has been established, it is possible to

[1] J. M. Keynes, *The General Theory of Employment Interest and Money,* Harcourt Brace and Company, New York, 1936.

[2] For a comprehensive discussion of portfolio theory, see H. Markowitz, *Portfolio Selection,* John Wiley & Sons, New York, 1959; also, William F. Sharpe "Capital Asset Prices: A Theory of Market Equilibrium Under Conditions of Risk," *Journal of Finance* (September 1964), 425–442.

trace the impact of monetary policy on the risk and return structure of the entire spectrum of financial assets and see how a change in the supply of one type of asset changes, not only the risk and return of that particular asset, but also the risk and return of other assets as well. Thus, the purpose of this chapter is to examine portfolio theory to show how it is related to macroeconomic theory in the determination of market interest rates. The first part of the chapter studies the meaning of risk and shows how portfolio theory incorporates risk into the pricing of financial assets. The second part of the chapter examines the impact of changes in the supply of various financial assets on the level and structure of various asset yields.

## Portfolio Theory: Return and Risk

While Keynes assumed that there were only two financial assets (long-term bonds and money), it is obvious that in the real world there is an almost unlimited variety of financial assets. Furthermore, as Keynes well knew, the returns received from holding most of these assets over any time period is not known in advance with certainty. Thus, the best that can be done is to estimate an average expected return by assigning probabilities to possible returns and weighting each possible return by its probability. For example, let us begin our analysis by considering common stocks. Assume that security A may be purchased at the beginning of a period for $1,000. While its value at the end of the period is not known in advance, an estimate is made that it has a 25 percent probability of being worth $1,226.50 if the economy is in a boom period, a 25 percent probability of being worth $1,163.25 if the economy is in good shape, a 25 percent probability of being worth $1,036.75 if the economy is in fair shape, and a 25 percent probability of being worth $973.50 if the economy is in a recession. Now, using this information, the return that an investor would receive may be computed for each of the four possible end-of-period values as follows:

$$\frac{\text{Value of security A at end of period} - \text{Value of security A at beginning of period}}{\text{Value of security A at beginning of period}}$$

If, for example, the value of security A at the end of the period was $1,226.50, the investor's return would be:

$$\frac{\$1,226.50 - \$1,000}{\$1,000} = 22.65\%$$

In like manner, returns can be calculated for the other possible end-of-period values.

The returns for each of the four possible values of security A are listed in column 4 of Table 24-1. Column 6 of the table is used to determine the most likely return. The figures in column 6 are obtained by multiplying each return in column 4 by the probability of its occurrence; the sum of these numbers in column 6 equals the *expected* return on the investment. This "expected" return may be interpreted as the best estimate of what the return of the investment will be. In the example, the expected return for security A equals 10 percent. It is the average of all of the possible returns weighted by their probabilities.

*Risk* concerns the possibility that the investor may not actually achieve what was expected. An extension of the previous analysis permits us to compute measures of risk. One measure, known as the variance ($\sigma^2$), is simply the average squared difference between the possible returns and the expected return, weighted by the probability of each return. This calculation is found in Table 24-2.[3] The standard deviation, another common measure of risk, is the square root of the variance,

$$\sigma = \sqrt{\sigma^2}$$

For security A, the standard deviation is equal to the square root of 0.01, which equals 0.10.

## The Relation Between the Returns of a Particular Asset and the Return of Financial Assets as a Whole

Note in the example that the return on security A is a function of the state of the economy, although the economy assumed here is obviously a simplification. However, not only is security A's return a function of the state of the economy, but so are the returns of practically all other financial assets as well. This is an important point, because it means that there is a correlation between security A's return during a period and the return of all financial assets.

---

[3]For a discussion of this statistical measure, see T. Yamane, *Statistics: An Introductory Analysis,* 2nd ed., Harper & Row, New York, 1967.

**Table 24-1  Return Distribution for Security A**

| (1)<br>Value at<br>Beginning<br>of Period | (2)<br>State of<br>the Economy<br>During Period | (3)<br>Value at<br>End of<br>Period | (4)<br>Realized<br>Return<br>(3) − (1)/(1) | (5)<br><br><br>Probability | (6)<br>Realized Return<br>Times Probability<br>(4) × (5) |
|---|---|---|---|---|---|
| $1,000 | Excellent | $1,226.50 | .22650 | .25 | .056625 |
| $1,000 | Good | $1,163.25 | .16325 | .25 | .0408125 |
| $1,000 | Fair | $1,036.75 | .03675 | .25 | .0091875 |
| $1,000 | Poor | $ 973.50 | −.02650 | .25 | −.006625 |

$$\Sigma(\text{Probability} \times \text{realized return}) = 0.10 = E(r)$$

**Table 24-2  Calculation of Risk for Security A**

| (1)<br>State of the<br>Economy During<br>the Period | (2)<br><br>Realized<br>Return | (3)<br>Realized<br>Return<br>−E(r) | (4)<br><br>Square of<br>Column (3) | (5)<br><br><br>Probability | (6)<br>Column 4 Times<br>Probabilities<br>(4) × (5) |
|---|---|---|---|---|---|
| Excellent | .22650 | .12650 | .016 | .25 | .004 |
| Good | .16325 | .06325 | .004 | .25 | .001 |
| Fair | .03675 | −.06325 | .004 | .25 | .001 |
| Poor | −.02650 | −.12650 | .016 | .25 | .004 |

$$\sigma^2 = .010$$
$$\sigma = .10$$

In order to see this relationship more clearly, let us look at the return of all financial assets. Consider a portfolio of financial assets where the proportion invested in each asset is equal to the proportion that the total market value of that particular asset represents in relation to the total market value of all financial assets. Since the weight of each asset within the particular portfolio is identical to its weight in the overall market for financial assets, this portfolio has the same risk/return characteristics as the overall financial market; in other words, the return of this portfolio will always equal the weighted average return of all financial assets. For this reason this portfolio may be called the *market portfolio*.

For purposes of comparison, the market portfolio may be treated as another asset. In order to examine the relationship between security A and all financial assets (the market portfolio), a series of points may be plotted where security A's actual returns in a number of periods are measured on the vertical axis and corresponding market returns on the horizontal axis. Next, a line may be drawn with the closest possible fit to the series of points. This line is called the *characteristic line*.

The return of security A for a particular period can be expressed by an equation of the characteristic line:

$$R_{At} = \alpha_A + \beta_A R_{Mt} + \epsilon_{At} \qquad (24\text{-}1)$$

where $R_{At}$ is the return of security A during period $t$; $\alpha_A + \beta_A R_{Mt}$ is the expected return for security A during period $t$, based on the return of the market portfolio ($R_{Mt}$) during the period; and $\epsilon_{At}$ is the residual return of security A during period $t$.

As indicated in Figure 24-1, $\alpha_A$ is the intercept with the vertical axis. It represents the expected return on security A when the return on the market portfolio ($R_{Mt}$) is equal to zero. $\beta_A$, referred to as the Beta of security A, is the slope of the line and indicates the relative response of the return on security A to the market return. Consequently, the return *expected* on security A depends on the Alpha ($\alpha$) and Beta ($\beta$) coefficients and the actual return on the market portfolio as noted in Figure 24-1. The difference between the *actual* return on asset A and the *expected* return in a given period is referred to as the *residual return*. It is represented in Figure 24-1 by the distance between a given point and the characteristic line.

**Figure 24-1    Security A's Returns vs. Returns of the Market Portfolio**

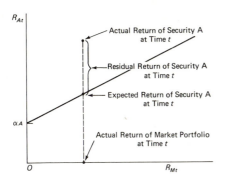

## Systematic Risk

Now, from Equation (24-1) we can readily see two reasons for security A having a particular return during that period:

1. the systematic relationship between the return of security A and the return of the market portfolio as captured by the $\beta$ coefficient
2. the residual return of security A (the part of security A's return that is not systematically related to the return of the market portfolio)

We can use the relationship in Equation (24-1) to distinguish between two types of risk: systematic risk and unsystematic risk. The *total* risk of a security is defined as the variance of its returns and, therefore, can be calculated by taking the variance of the left-hand side of Equation (24-1). This is the variance calculated in Table 24-2. Since this must be equal to the variance of the right-hand side of Equation (24-1), we have the following equation:[4]

$$\sigma_A^2 = \beta_A^2 \sigma_M^2 + \sigma_{\epsilon_A}^2 \qquad (24\text{-}2)$$

where $\sigma_A^2$ is the total risk for security A; $\beta_A^2 \sigma_M^2$ is the systematic risk of security A (that part related to market); and $\sigma_{\epsilon_A}^2$ is the unsystematic risk of security A (that part unrelated to market). As indicated in Equation (24-2), the systematic part of

the risk of a particular security ($\beta_A^2 \sigma_M^2$) is a function of two factors:

1. the risk of the overall market for financial assets ($\sigma_M^2$)
2. the $\beta$ of the particular security

The fact that there is risk in the overall market for financial securities is illustrated by the nonconstant returns of the market portfolio in Figure 24-1. Since the risk of the overall market for financial assets is the same regardless of the specific security considered, the only way for securities to have different levels of systematic risk is through different Betas.

One other comment on Beta is useful at this point. Beta is often referred to as an indicator of a security's volatility. Securities with Betas greater than one are considered highly volatile in that their prices are more responsive than average to general market movements. Conversely, securities with Betas lower than one are said to be less volatile than the average security.

## Unsystematic Risk

So far we have discussed only systematic risk. For many securities, unsystematic risk (risk that is unique to that specific security and not related to the risk of the group of financial assets as a whole) is a far larger component of total risk than is systematic risk. This results from the fact that many events have a significant impact on the return of a specific asset without their having a significant impact on the return of the overall group of financial assets. For example, suppose the particular security is the common stock of an oil company that discovers a new oil well during a period. The price of this security may increase as investors anticipate higher future profits and dividends. This event, which is independent of systematic factors in the economy, will cause the asset to have a high return during the period (causing its return to be above the characteristic line). A negative event will have the opposite effect.

A single security will tend to have a relatively large amount of unsystematic risk. However, the inclusion of additional securities to form a portfolio will tend to reduce unsystematic risk, that is, the residual returns of the single-security portfolio. This is due to the fact that often when one security in the portfolio has positive residual returns (re-

[4]It may be noted that the variance of the constant such as $\beta_A$ times a variable such as $R_m$ equals the constant squared times the variances of the variable ($\beta_A^2 \sigma_m^2$). This explains the derivation of the first term on the right-hand side of Equation (24-2).

turns greater than those predicted by the characteristic line), the other securities have negative residual returns (returns less than those predicted by the characteristic line) and vice versa. As the number of securities within the portfolio is increased, the residual returns of all the securities in the portfolio tend to cancel each other out (the unsystematic risk approaches zero). Thus, since it is possible to diversify away unsystematic risk by including many securities, unsystematic risk is often called diversifiable risk, while systematic risk (not capable of being diversified away by holding many securities) is called nondiversifiable risk.[5]

Because in a portfolio with a sufficient number of assets investors can diversify away all of the unsystematic risk of a particular asset, they should be concerned with a security's systematic risk. Similarly, the relevant risk of a portfolio is a function of the weighted average of the systematic risk of each of the assets in the portfolio and not a function of the total risk of each of the assets.

### Risk Aversion

Although we have defined risk, we still have not discussed how it enters into the decision-making process. Most people are averse to risk. In other words, they will voluntarily take on more risk only if they receive a reward for doing so in the form of a greater expected return.

We can illustrate risk aversion graphically by considering all positions that offer a particular investor the same level of satisfaction—one utile (unit) of utility. These positions are represented by all the points on curve $U_1$ in Figure 24-2. The point where curve $U_1$ intersects the vertical axis is the riskless return that gives the investor one utile of utility. In order for the investor to maintain the same level of satisfaction when entering riskier positions, the investor has to be given a greater expected return (illustrated by greater expected returns for higher risk levels on curve $U_1$). Since the investor is indifferent among all of the positions that lie on curve $U_1$ (all the positions are equally

[5] For an empirical examination of the effect of diversification on the reduction of unsystematic risk, see J. L. Evans and S. H. Archer, "Diversification and the Reduction of Dispersion: An Empirical Analysis," *Journal of Finance* (December 1969).

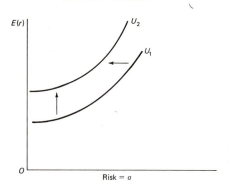

**Figure 24-2  Indifference Curves Between Risk and Return**

attractive, or unattractive), this curve is called an indifference curve.

In order to receive a higher level of satisfaction, an investor must move to positions offering either higher returns for the same level of risk or the same return with lower levels of risk. This is accomplished by moving from indifference curve $U_1$ to indifference curve $U_2$ as depicted in Figure 24-2. The implication of the possibility of such a move is that some positions are clearly superior to other positions. A position having the same expected return as a second position but entailing less risk is superior to the second position (dominates the second position). Similarly, a position having the same risk as another position but entailing greater expected return dominates the second position. This principle can be generalized. Any risk-averse investor, regardless of the exact shape of the indifference curve, will prefer portfolios that dominate to those that are dominated. Thus, among all possible portfolios, any portfolio will be eliminated from consideration for investment if there is another portfolio having the same or higher expected return but lower risk or having the same or less risk but greater return. When all possible portfolios are depicted in risk/return space, as in Figure 24-3, the set of portfolios that are not dominated by other portfolios is called the *efficient frontier*. Any risk-averse investor will select a portfolio from among those on the efficient frontier.

We can now apply some of the relationships that have been established through the efficient frontier to the risk/return attributes of individual securities.

## Figure 24-2   The Efficient Frontier

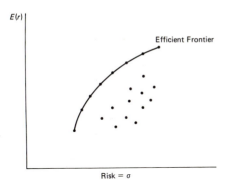

Recall that, in a well-diversified portfolio, the contribution that an individual security makes to the risk of the portfolio is related, not to the security's total risk, but to its systematic risk. In order for assets to enter portfolios that are on the efficient frontier, their expected return must be directly related to their systematic risk.

### The Security Market Line

We have argued for the existence of a positive relationship between volatility ($\beta$) and expected return. As noted above, both securities and portfolios can be characterized by their levels of volatility and return. Let us be more precise about the exact nature of the relationship between these variables. In order to do this, we will assume the existence of two assets: a riskless security (such as a Treasury bill), and a market portfolio (an asset that duplicates the performance of the group of financial assets as a whole). We will then examine the relationship between them.

Assume that the expected return of the riskless security is 5 percent. Since the riskless security has a constant return, there can be no relationship between its return and the group of financial assets as a whole. Consequently, its Beta is equal to zero. Assume that the expected return of the market portfolio is 10 percent, which is an average of the returns on all securities. Since the market portfolio has a risk and volatility equal to the average for all financial assets, its Beta is one.

Consider now an investor who places half his holdings in the riskless asset and half his holdings in the market portfolio. The expected return of this investor's portfolio is equal to the average of the riskless rate and the expected return of the market portfolio (7.5 percent). The relative volatility of this portfolio (the Beta) is equal to the average of the relative volatility of the riskless asset and the relative volatility of the market portfolio (0.5).[6]

Next, consider a second investor who holds many different assets each of which has a relative volatility of 0.5. The relative volatility of this investor's portfolio is equal to the relative volatility of the first investor's portfolio. Since the sole determinant of the systematic risk of each of the portfolios is its relative volatility and since each of the two portfolios has the same relative volatility, then each must have the same systematic risk. As explained earlier, because unsystematic risk can be diversified away, the only risk of concern to investors is systematic risk. Since, in this example, the two portfolios have the same level of this risk, they also must have the same expected return (7.5 percent).

Suppose this is not the case, and the expected return of the first investor's portfolio was greater than the expected return of the second investor's portfolio. The second investor would sell the portfolio and buy a portfolio similar to that of the first investor in order to achieve a higher expected return without additional risk. The sale of the second investor's portfolio would reduce the prices of the assets in the portfolio and thereby increase the expected return of those assets.[7] This would occur until the second investor's portfolio and the first investor's portfolio have an identical expected return (7.5 percent) when an equilibrium is reached. The result is that in equilibrium all assets with a relative volatility of 0.5 will have an expected return equal to the average of the expected return of a portfolio of assets, half of which have a relative

[6]The expected return of a portfolio of assets is equal to the average of the expected returns of each of the assets in the portfolio weighted by the proportion of the portfolio of each asset. The relative volatility of a portfolio is equal to the average of the relative voltality of each of the assets in the portfolio weighted by the proportion of the portfolio of each asset.

[7]When the price of an asset increases (decreases) and the expected cash flow that the asset provides remains constant, the expected return of the asset declines (increases).

volatility of zero while the other half have a relative volatility of 1.

We can now place the three assets we discussed on a graph, where the expected return of the security is depicted on the vertical axis and the relative volatility is depicted on the horizontal axis (see Figure 24-4). The first security is the asset with the zero relative volatility. Since this security is riskless, we designate its return as the riskless rate, $R_F$. In our example it is 5 percent. The second asset is the market portfolio that has relative volatility equal to one and expected return equal to the expected return of the group of financial assets as a whole (in our example this is 10 percent). The third asset has a relative volatility of 0.5 and an expected return of 7.5 percent. Note that after all three assets are placed on a graph, a straight line may be drawn through them. This line depicting the relationship between expected return and relative volatility is called the *security market line*.[8] Although thus far we have focused primarily on riskless Treasury bills and risky common stocks, the risk/return relationship as represented by the security market line is valid for other assets as well.

### Introduction of Additional Financial Assets

Our analysis until now has been concerned with the determination of risk/return relationships in the markets for Treasury bills and common stocks. Viewing a security in a portfolio context, it has become evident that the price (or what is the same thing in our example, the expected return) of a security is a function of the security's risk as measured by the systematic relationship between the security's return and the return on a market portfolio comprised of all securities. In order to use the portfolio framework to examine the impact of the government and the private sectors on the structure of interest rates and the economy, it is necessary to broaden the framework to include assets other than common stocks and Treasury bills. Let us begin by considering how money is incorporated into an individual's portfolio.

[8] That the relationship between expected return and relative volatility must be linear is shown in Sharpe, "Capital Asset Prices."

**Figure 24-4   The Relationship Between Expected Return and Relative Volatility ($\beta$) of Assets**

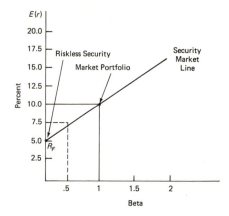

A riskless asset, as defined above, is one for which the monetary return during the next period is known. In our example, the return on riskless Treasury bills is known to be 5 percent. The riskless asset that has the greatest impact on the economy is money. Disregarding changes in purchasing power, it is evident that holding money, like holding Treasury bills, has no risk. If a dollar is maintained as a demand deposit in a commercial bank for one year, we can count on withdrawing that dollar at year's end or any other time we choose. Remember, however, that Treasury bills provide the same end-of-period certainty plus a positive explicit return, 5 percent in our example. For many years the explicit return on money has been zero, although, as we have seen, the recent introduction of NOW accounts and other new kinds of liabilities by financial intermediaries has made changes in this area. Still, money has been held despite its low explicit return. At first glance, it might appear that Treasury bills provide a higher return for the same risk and, therefore, would be preferred to (would dominate) money. If this were so, the theory of investor behavior discussed earlier would suggest that investors are irrational in holding money since, by switching to Treasury bills, they could receive a greater return without increasing risk.

As Chapters 21 and 22 point out, however, money—unlike Treasury bills or common stocks—is held for reasons other than its monetary return.

One of the primary reasons for holding money is the transactions motive. If an individual's portfolio consisted only of Treasury bills and equity securities, each time that individual wished to purchase an item that person would have to sell one or more of those securities. Accompanying that purchase would be a transaction cost. Moreover, it would take some time and effort to receive the cash, causing inconvenience and possibly a time lag between desired possession of the good and actual possession.

As illustrated so far, the portfolio framework represents all assets in terms of return and risk. This was sufficient for Treasury bills and common stocks, since it was assumed that investors' utility for these assets was based solely on those attributes. However, the utility of money is not only related to its return and risk but also to its value as a medium of exchange. How can we introduce this factor into the analysis? The answer is by referring to the nonmonetary utility provided by money as an *implicit return*. Thus, the return on money has both an explicit and an implicit component. The total return on money may be measured by equating it to the explicit monetary return on another asset that provides, at the margin, the same utility to its holder. Because money is riskless, the total (explicit plus implicit) marginal return on the amount of money held by an individual should equal the marginal return on other riskless assets. To illustrate this point, consider the following simple example.

Let us assume a financial world where only two assets exist: money and Treasury bills. And let us further assume that an individual with $130,000 considers the following portfolio optimal: $30,000 of money and $100,000 of 1-year Treasury bills yielding a return of 9 percent. In other words, given that the individual has only $130,000, this combination provides the greatest total utility. Alternatively, we can state that the marginal utility for each asset is equal. Since the investor is indifferent between holding the last dollar in money or in Treasury bills, we can assume that the last dollar held in money must be providing the investor with the same return as the last dollar in Treasury bills. Thus, this return is implicit in the investor's behavior. If the marginal utility of money were greater than the marginal utility of Treasury bills,

the implicit return on money would be greater than 9 percent, say, 13 percent or some other amount greater than 9 percent. A rational investor in this situation would sell Treasury bills to increase his or her stock of money and, thereby, achieve a portfolio that offered greater total utility. In equilibrium, however, where the individual is satisfied with the portfolio held, the implicit marginal return of money must equal the explicit return of other riskless assets.

This example suggests another important difference between the implicit return on money and the return on assets previously considered—Treasury bills and common stocks. Assuming that purchases by one investor do not affect market price, then an investor may acquire any amount of any stock without influencing the return or risk expected from that investment. In other words, marginal return is constant, regardless of amount purchased. Furthermore, the same return is provided to all investors on each dollar of financial investment in a given stock.

In contrast, the implicit marginal return on an additional dollar of money is not constant for an individual. Instead it is influenced both by that individual's transaction needs and the size of his or her holdings. Because the usefulness for transaction purposes of an additional dollar in money balances probably declines as the balances increase, the marginal return on money is generally considered to be a monotonically decreasing function, that is, the implicit return of an additional dollar maintained in cash declines as the level of money held increases. This is depicted in Figure 24-5. Thus, if the individual in our example increases the level of money in his or her portfolio, because the money provides a greater implicit return than the 9 percent return of the Treasury bills, the marginal utility of each additional dollar converted from Treasury bills to money will decrease. The individual would continue to sell Treasury bills until the marginal utility of money just equals the marginal utility of Treasury bills. At this point the individual's portfolio is in equilibrium and, therefore, the implicit return of money would be 9 percent. This is indicated in Figure 24-5 by the intersection of the two curves.

In sum, we can say that an individual holds stocks of money such that the total marginal return

**Figure 24-5** **Determination of the Optimal Level of Money in an Individual's Portfolio**

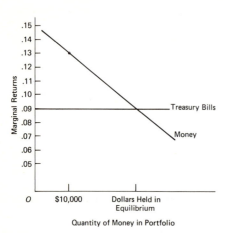

Quantity of Money in Portfolio

**Figure 24-6** **The Security Market Line with Nonequity Securities**

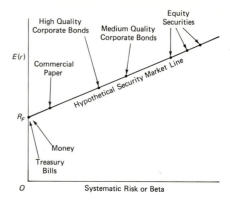

on money (explicit and implicit) equals the explicit return on other riskless assets. In terms of risk/return space, money is coincident with Treasury bills, as depicted in Figure 24-6. Point $R_F$ in Figure 24-6 similarly represents other riskless assets, such as savings deposits and savings and loan shares. The total return on these assets also has both explicit and implicit components. The explicit interest rate yielded by these near-money assets may be less than that provided by Treasury bills, although, of course, it will typically be greater than the return on money. In equilibrium, the differences between the Treasury bill rate and that explicit return must equal the implicit return. Again, the implicit return results from the smaller transaction costs associated with these deposits, their liquidity, and their availability in convenient denominations in comparison to other assets. In equilibrium, then, the total return on all riskless assets will be identical for the rational individual and may be depicted by point $R_F$. For a particular asset, $R_F$ may include implicit as well as explicit components. If an event occurs that causes returns to differ, an individual should react by substituting the higher-return asset for the lower-return asset until all riskless assets in that individual's portfolio are once again in equilibrium. As will be explained shortly, this adjustment process permits us to analyze the impact of government policy on yield structure. Before proceeding to this, however, let

us introduce risky assets other than common stocks into the individual's portfolio. This is depicted in Figure 24-6. These nonequity risky financial instruments also may be represented in risk/return space. Just to the right of our riskless asset, for example, we would find commercial paper and bankers' acceptances. The investor in these instruments historically has received a somewhat higher return on them in comparison with short-term government bonds as compensation for a slightly greater risk exposure. Long-term liabilities of the private sector, such as corporate bonds, generally provide still higher yields. Of course, yields on particular bond issues also differ, reflecting different levels of risk; lower quality issues offer higher returns in order to compensate investors for the greater risk level. Figure 24-6 depicts all these assets in risk/return space.

### The Impact of the Supply of Various Financial Assets on the Level and Structure of Yields

#### The Impact of Monetary Policy on the Level and Structure of Interest Rates

Now that we have examined the essentials of portfolio theory, it is possible to use this framework to analyze the impact of changing supplies of financial assets on the structure of interest rates. In order to analyze the impact of monetary policy, let us assume that the structure of yields for the economy as a whole is represented at a given point in time by Figure 24-6. We assume that the financial markets are in equilibrium so that all participants in these markets are inactive: demanders of financial assets are comfortable at the margin with the risk/return trade-offs that exist among financial assets, and, therefore, there is no pressure to sell one asset in exchange for another. Also, suppliers of financial assets have raised sufficient capital in view of their cost of funds and their investment opportunities. Let us now explore the adjustment process that occurs in the financial markets when the quantity of money is changed. Our concern is with the effects of changes in the money supply on the yields of other financial assets.

Consider the impact of a purchase of Treasury bills by the Federal Reserve System from the private sector. The sales and purchases of securities by the Federal Reserve System, unlike those of most investors, can influence the market prices of assets because of the size of the transaction. Assume that the private sector is one individual, hereinafter referred to as 1. The Federal Reserve's demand for Treasury bills will place upward pressure on the price of these instruments, which is to say that Treasury bill yields will tend to fall. Also, as purchases are made, 1 will receive additional money from the Federal Reserve equal in value to the purchase price of the Treasury bills.[9] This additional money, as explained earlier, will have lower marginal utility for the holder than the money previously held. Thus, the implicit return on money, like the yield of the Treasury bills, falls when the supply of money increases. This means that, during the equilibration process, there will be adjustments until there is a new, lower, riskless return.

More important for our purposes is the adjustment that takes place in other asset yields in response to changes in the riskless rate. Remember that prior to the Federal Reserve's purchase of bills, 1 was satisfied with the risk/return relationship among all securities. Now the immediate effect of the purchase is that the riskless return is lowered. Because 1's utility for financial assets is a positive function of return, a smaller return on the riskless asset, *ceteris paribus,* will make holding this asset less desirable relative to others. Accord-

ingly, 1 might demand fewer Treasury bills and more commercial paper. This change in demand for commercial paper causes its price to rise and yield to fall. Simultaneously, 1 would desire to purchase other financial assets as well, including corporate bonds and equity securities because these would now be yielding an excessive risk-adjusted return relative to Treasury bills and commercial paper. If the supply of securities remains constant, therefore, we would expect all yields to fall in adjusting to the Fed's open-market operation. In Figure 24-7, this is depicted graphically by the lower efficient set of risky assets and security market line. For the same levels of risk that existed prior to the Fed's action, all securities would yield smaller returns.

The net result, therefore, as in Keynesian and loanable funds analysis, is that when the money supply increases, yields decline. By examining the effects across individual securities, however, the portfolio approach provides a broader framework for examining changes in the *entire structure* of interest rates rather than merely one interest rate in particular. Keynesian and loanable funds theory either implicitly assume that all financial assets provide the same yield or abstract from the problem of yield structure by assuming only two financial assets, namely, money and long-term, riskless, government bonds. In contrast, portfolio theory is able to discuss the relationship of changes in the yield on any asset to the yields of all other assets. We now turn to an analysis of the impact of changes

---

[9]See Chapter 5 for a discussion of the mechanics of monetary policy and how Federal Reserve open-market operations increase bank reserves and, in a second step, money.

**Figure 24-7 The Impact of Federal Reserve Purchase of Securities on Security Market Line (SML)**

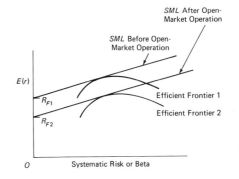

in the supply of financial assets other than money on the structure of yields.

## Impact of Changes in the Supply of Corporate Bonds on the Structure of Interest Rates

In this section, we consider the impact of changes in the supply of risky assets. For the sake of simplicity, let us first assume that there are only two types of risky assets: corporate debt and equities. Points $D$ and $E$ in Figure 24-8 denote the expected return and risk on each of these assets in equilibrium. Once again, $R_F$ represents the riskless return. From earlier sections of this chapter, it is evident that by combining two risky assets such as $D$ and $E$, the supplier of funds may obtain any combination of risk and return represented by the locus of points on a line between points $D$ and $E$. The curvature of the line depends on the relationship between the returns of the two assets, but some risk/return combination will be available to the investor as long as the demand and supply functions of all assets do not change. We will now examine what ensues when the supply of one of these assets—for example, corporate debt—increases.

The immediate effect of an increase in supply would be a reduction in bond prices and an increase in yields. At this juncture, however, the financial markets would not be in equilibrium. Investors would not be satisfied with their portfolios. The higher rates on bonds relative to equities will tend to make investors want to reduce their holdings of equities and invest more heavily in debt instruments. This desire on the part of investors to adjust their portfolios in response to the higher bond yields will result in downward pressure on equity prices and rising yields. The portfolio adjustment process would continue until once again each investor is satisfied with his or her portfolio and the demand and supply for the two assets are in equilibrium. The amount of the change in yields depends on investors' preferences for risk and return, the substitutability of the two assets, and institutional factors.

The structure of yields would change in other ways as well. The higher rates offered on risky assets would stimulate individual suppliers of funds to want to reduce their holdings of riskless assets. Consequently, the net result of the initial increase in the supply of bonds would be that all rates increase. After these and similar adjustments among all assets, a new efficient frontier would result. This is depicted by line $D'E'$.

In sum, an increase in the supply of debt securities and the resulting increase in bond yields cause an increase in all alternative yields. The exact change in yields will depend on the substitutability among assets and the preferences of the suppliers of funds. However, the net result must be that more bonds are held, and that while the yields of all assets increase, if there are no perfect substitutes for bonds, there is a greater relative increase in bond yields.

## Figure 24-8 The Impact of an Increase in the Supply of Corporate Debt

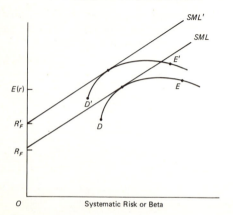

## Interaction with the Real Sector

In previous sections of this chapter, the relationship among interest rates on various securities has been examined without regard to activity in the real sector of the economy. However, determination of interest rate structure and equilibrium in the financial markets both affects and is affected by activities in the real sector. For this reason, it is clear that the portfolio decisions of an individual economic unit are more complex than indicated so far. In particular, funds are allocated among real capital assets and consumption as well as to financial assets.

In order to introduce real assets into the portfolio framework, let us assume for the moment that the consumption of an economic unit in a particular period is made prior to that unit's capital investment decision and, therefore, that the former can be regarded as fixed for present purposes. The consumption decision is treated in greater detail later.

Now it is evident that physical assets may be held for investment purposes. For example, an individual's portfolio may comprise money, common stock, and real estate. As with financial assets, individuals often invest in real estate and other tangible assets to obtain diversified portfolios that best satisfy their risk/return preferences. In such instances, the same principles of diversification and portfolio selection may be applied to investments in real assets. Recognizing this, physical assets, such as real estate or capital equipment, can be represented in Figure 24-6.

In some cases, however, individuals hold physical assets for the services they provide, rather than for their monetary return. For example, the value of tangible assets, such as consumer durables or homes, is not based only on the monetary return and related risk provided to its owner, but rather on the utility related to the services they offer. Like money, these assets may be thought of as yielding a total return that has explicit and implicit components. Such assets will be purchased provided that the utility they afford exceeds that of alternative investments, including both financial assets and real assets that provide only monetary returns. In allocating available funds among money, other financial assets, real assets that provide monetary returns, and other nonmonetary real assets, the individual will attempt to make that allocation that provides the greatest total utility.

Within this broader perspective, let us reconsider the determination of interest rate structure. Assume that initially equilibrium exists in the economy as a whole. In terms of our portfolio framework, this means that for each economic unit the marginal utilities provided on all real and financial assets in its portfolio are equal. Under these conditions there would be no reason for any unit to readjust its asset holdings. Now suppose there is a shift in the supply of a particular financial asset.

For example, assume that the Federal Reserve reduces the reserve requirement on demand deposits held at commercial banks. As discussed in Chapter 5, the banks' portfolios will no longer be in equilibrium. In particular, reserves will be overrepresented relative to other assets. In order to balance their portfolios, banks may purchase Treasury securities and make additional loans, in the process increasing the money supply. As a result of the banks' actions, pressure will be exerted on the structure of interest rates.

First, interest rates on Treasury bills will decline since, in order to stimulate the public to sell its securities, the banks must be willing to pay higher prices to the sellers of the bills. Secondly, in order to increase their loan portfolios, banks must induce the public to borrow more by lowering interest rates. As explained earlier, these immediate reactions will cause readjustments throughout the financial markets, creating downward pressure on all rates and causing other economic units to increase their holdings of money. But now let us shift our attention to the reaction in the real sector.

The increase in money holdings and the lower rates on securities and loans will cause individuals to desire to readjust their portfolios with respect to real assets. Because the return on financial assets, including money, has decreased without any concomitant changes in risk, the risk/return opportunities on real assets—which, as yet, remain unchanged—become relatively more attractive. That is, initially for equal levels of risk, real assets will dominate (afford higher returns than) financial assets. Accordingly, units will desire to hold a greater proportion of their portfolios in physical assets. The result will be a tendency for market participants to exchange financial assets for real assets. As the latter's prices are bid up (their returns fall), the desire to substitute physical assets for financial assets will decline.

There also will be other forces at work prompting further investment in physical assets and, ultimately, a return to equilibrium. Because of the increase in money holdings and lower interest rates, the marginal utility provided by consumption will initially exceed that provided by financial assets. The result will be a greater demand for consumer goods. This change in demand could lead to greater consumer spending, which, if translated into greater business profits, would mean higher returns on capital goods. This, in turn, would produce an additional incentive for market participants to substitute capital assets for financial assets in their portfolios.

To continue to identify reactions in the real sector, it is useful at this point to relax an assumption implicit in the previous analysis. It has been assumed that the supply of financial assets other than money remains fixed. There is, however, a crucial link between the supply of financial assets and the demand for real assets in investors' portfolios. Greater investment in capital goods by business firms necessitates greater financing. To a small extent, business firms may finance their capital goods expenditures by reducing cash and other financial securities in their portfolios or by cash generated by current operations. For the most part, however, increased capital expenditure is financed by issuing new financial liabilities. In terms of the present scenario, this would be wise for two reasons:

1. Interest rates have fallen because of the Federal Reserve's action making it relatively less expensive to raise funds.
2. The return on capital investment has increased because of higher product prices, which resulted from increased consumer demand.

Thus, additional investment in capital goods and the issuance of new financial liabilities would be expected.

It should be recalled that the debt instrument issued by any participant in the financial markets is, at the same time, the asset of another participant holding that instrument. Thus, in our example, the financing of additional capital expenditures through the issuance of corporate bonds would increase the supply of financial assets. To induce suppliers of funds to increase the proportion of corporate bonds in their portfolios, other things being equal, business firms must offer a return higher than that on comparable securities in existence at the time. This would create a tendency for corporate bond rates to rise, inducing higher rates throughout the money and capital markets, as explained earlier.

We have come full circle. Summarizing what has occurred: in response to a lower reserve requirement, market participants initially adjusted their portfolios of financial assets. The result was a downward shift in the structure of interest rates.

Consumption and investment in real assets became relatively more attractive uses of funds. Higher prices of capital goods stimulated additional capital-goods creation financed by the issuance of financial assets. The greater supply of financial assets caused upward pressure on interest rates. As the process continues, the following pressures will tend to produce a new equilibrium position:

1. Capital goods will become less desirable as: (a) more consumer products are produced and returns fall; and (b) the cost of financing increases.
2. Financial assets will become more desirable as: (a) yields on securities rise; and (b) returns on capital assets fall.

Equilibrium will again exist when the portfolio preferences of each participant are matched with the new supply of financial assets and real assets. The net result will be that returns on securities, on average, will have fallen relative to the returns on real assets. As a consequence, the proportion of assets held (a) in money will increase; (b) in securities will decrease; and (c) in capital goods will increase.

In sum, the structure of interest rates in the economy is determined by the portfolio decisions of all economic units. Each unit operating independently seeks a mix of assets and liabilities that provides a risk-adjusted return that maximizes its total utility. All participants continually adjust their portfolios in response to changes in preferences and shifts in the prices of financial and real assets. It is because of these portfolio adjustments that the general level and structure of interest rates change.

## Institutional Sources of Yield Differentials

In developing a general theory to explain interest rate structure, we have made several implicit assumptions. In doing so, however, we have neglected many institutional factors that bear upon the determination of interest rate differentials. Some of these factors can easily be incorporated into the earlier analysis without modifying the theory. To introduce other factors, however, portfolio theory must be extended. The purpose of the following discussion is twofold: (1) to identify the principal institutional factors that influence yield differentials, and (2) to relate these factors to the general theory.

As is shown in the discussion that follows, contrary to the previous analysis, all assets with the same rate of return and systematic risk are not perfect substitutes for each other. Many institutional factors cause such assets to be less than perfect substitutes and, therefore, to be priced differently (to provide different yields). For purpose of discussion, the principal institutional factors have been divided into market imperfections and legal and institutional constraints.

## Market Imperfections

*Differences in Marketability* Implicit in the security market line is the assumption that all assets are equally marketable (liquid); that is, each asset represented may be sold in an identical short period of time without incurring a significant loss in value. In reality, this is not the case. For some assets a strong secondary market does exist, permitting the purchaser of the asset to sell it quickly before its maturity date. For example, in the case of U.S. government bonds the lender (purchaser of the bonds) can sell some or all acquired holdings to someone else via the secondary market. The lender may incur a capital loss or realize a gain, but most of the principal can be recovered. In general, listed corporate securities can be resold as quickly, although the price is more uncertain. Many types of mortgages and loans, however, have little or no secondary market.

Generally, the more marketable the asset, other things being equal, the lower the rate of interest that the supplier of funds will be willing to accept. Thus, interest rate differentials among securities may be caused by differences in marketability as well as by differences in systematic risk.

*Transaction Costs* Another factor that influences the structure of interest rates but that has not yet been considered is transaction costs. There are transaction costs associated with both the purchase and sale of assets. Such costs occur both at the time that the asset is first issued (at the time of the primary market transaction) and at the time of transactions in the secondary market.

Considering the primary market first, it may be noted that some types of loans cost more to arrange

than others, and this differential must be reflected in the rate charged. Some instruments cost virtually nothing to create. Large finance companies, for instance, issue commercial paper (essentially IOUs), which they sell directly to business firms with temporary excess funds. A multimillion dollar transaction requires only a telephone call between issuer and buyer and the typing of a few numbers onto a small preprinted piece of stationery resembling a check. By way of contrast, some other transactions—for example, long-term bank loans—may need to be individually negotiated at great length and often require complex, legally documented agreements, which lay down rules of financial conduct that the borrower must observe over the life of the loan. (Obviously, the lender must also exercise steady surveillance to ensure that the rules are obeyed. The cost of all this can easily run into thousands of dollars.) The size of the transaction is also an important rate determinant. In every type of lending, a small loan almost always involves more processing expense per dollar loaned than a large loan. Costs of inspection and appraisal, credit investigation, legal advice, and clerical handling are not much less for a $75,000 home mortgage than for a $1 million mortgage on an apartment building. The same principle also applies to trading in the secondary market for equity securities where the odd-lot, smaller-than-standard transaction bears a penalty. Thus, transaction costs vary by type of security and by size of transaction.

In general, the smaller the transaction and issuance costs, the greater the ability of economic units to adjust their asset holdings to an overall change in economic conditions and to changes in the market for one type of asset vis-à-vis the markets for other assets. If transaction costs in secondary markets were totally prohibitive, no adjustments would take place at all when economic conditions changed. This, of course, would lead to great disparities along the security market line. Smaller transaction costs cause smaller, although at times significant, disparities.

*Taxes* Our earlier analysis assumed that either (1) we live in a no-tax world, or (2) all market participants are taxed in the same manner for every dollar of income. In the latter case, we could unequivocally state that a dollar of pre-tax return implies a certain percentage of that dollar return after tax for all market participants no matter what their income. Neither of these assumptions, of course, is true.

For instance, commercial banks and other profit-making financial institutions must pay corporate income taxes. Mutual institutions, such as savings banks and many life insurance companies, are taxed to a varying degree, but less heavily than commercial banks. Pension funds pay no federal taxes. Capital gains are taxed more lightly than coupon-interest income. Corporations may deduct interest payments as a cost, like wages, but they must pay dividends on their stocks out of after-tax profits. Banks and certain other institutions may deduct capital losses from income for tax purposes to an unlimited extent but pay only the capital gains tax on security profits. This enables them to reduce taxes by certain techniques of trading in fluctuating bond markets, even when the capital gains and losses balance out. Interest income from municipal bonds is exempt from federal tax, and income on U.S. Treasury securities from state income taxes. And all this, of course, is far from a full list of important tax considerations.

The immunity to federal tax of the interest income from municipal bonds explains why municipal bond yields can be much lower in reality than corporate bond yields, which are not exempt. It explains why commercial banks are often large buyers of municipal bonds, but buy few corporate bonds, on whose income they are taxed. Conversely, pension funds, which are not taxed, naturally choose the higher yield on corporate bonds over the low yields on municipals. One could cite many similar, though perhaps less dramatic, instances of tax-related investment decisions.

However, the significant points are that (1) assets with the same before-tax yield and risk are not necessarily perfect substitutes in a portfolio of a particular market participant and, therefore, (2) the difference in before-tax yields among assets may, in part, be explained by our complex tax structure.

*Other Market Imperfections* Finally, in a financial structure that encompasses so many varied "submarkets" and participants, one should expect to find yield differentials that reflect market imperfections resulting from such factors as lack of perfect information, monopoly, and even local or personal relationships.

For instance, to adjust one's portfolio to changing economic conditions, one must first recognize the changes. The amount of time that elapses before the general market recognizes changes in economic conditions, and the disparity of access to information among economic units, may affect yield differentials and the equilibrium adjustment process. As a result, sometimes virtually identical instruments may carry significantly different interest rates.

### Legal and Institutional Constraints

Market participants may not view assets and liabilities with identical risk/return characteristics as perfect substitutes for reasons other than market imperfections. Legal and institutional constraints on the behavior of economic units as well as tradition have a tendency to segment markets and to make assets and liabilities less substitutable.

For example, many demanders and suppliers of funds are limited in terms of geography, type of instrument they may create or hold, and degree of credit risk to which they may expose themselves. A prime illustration of this is afforded by savings and loan associations, whose financial investments are primarily local residential mortgages. There are many other examples. A business executive will usually find it easier to get a short-term than a long-term loan, but the executive's employees will generally find it to be the other way around. Many pension funds are allowed to buy only the higher-quality bonds, but many insurance companies (which are also in the pension business) buy primarily the medium grades.

On the liability side, most credit to the business sector comes from commercial banks. Established firms, of course, borrow directly from the banks. For less creditworthy companies, borrowing from suppliers (trade credit), factors, and finance companies are the major—and much more expensive—alternatives. However, these "substitute bankers," in turn, depend heavily on the banks for their own financing, so that bank funds are still being loaned, albeit indirectly.

Governments are even more inflexible than business firms in their borrowing. Their expenditures and receipts are mandated by law, and they may often depart from initial estimates since program costs and tax-base forecasts are subject to inevitable error. If there is a default, it must be financed promptly, at any cost.

Practically all governmental borrowing is done in the open market. Because interest on state and local securities, as mentioned earlier, is exempt from federal income tax, these instrumentalities can borrow at relatively low rates—so long as there is sufficient demand from certain insurance companies, wealthy individuals, and commercial banks to whom the tax-exemption feature is valuable.

In addition to business and government, many individuals are substantial borrowers. Debt is incurred primarily in the form of instalment loans for the purchase of cars and other consumer durables and mortgages to finance homebuying. Demand for consumer credit appears relatively insensitive to interest rates, and the market's rationing proceeds chiefly through variations in down payments and maturities (which affect the size of monthly amortization payments). Consumer credit rates have been very "sticky," but mortgage rates move somewhat more freely.

Of course, on a net basis the household sector is a saver rather than a borrower. But much of the saving is reloaned to other households via savings banks and savings and loan associations. When they have ample funds, mortgage rates and terms tend to ease. At such times, moreover, borrowing by business firms is often sluggish, so that commercial banks, life insurance companies, and other lenders to business may also have funds available for mortgages. On the other hand, as thrift institutions become "tight" and occasional lenders withdraw, mortgage rates and terms stiffen.

The primary function of financial intermediaries is to borrow from some for the purpose of lending to others. Such organizations have the task of borrowing in the cheapest market and relending in the market that offers the highest return. In principle, they should, therefore, be more flexible in responding to market forces than are the ultimate borrowers and lenders, and they should move in quickly to help iron out any rate differentials not justified by the fundamental considerations outlined earlier.

On the basis of practice and law, however, some of these institutions are much more specialized in the markets they serve than are others. Thus savings banks and savings and loan associations must get most of their funds from savings accounts and put most of their funds into mortgages—at least at

the present time. But this is atypical. Large finance companies, for example, though fairly specialized in consumer and certain types of business lending, nevertheless draw their funds from a broad spectrum of sources. Insurance-type intermediaries—life companies and pension funds—are, of course, specialized in their sources of funds. But they are more versatile in lending those funds.

The most mobile financial intermediary, however, is the commercial bank, and this mobility has greatly increased in recent years with the growth of time deposits. Commercial banks can obtain funds from a great variety of sources, domestic and foreign, and they have the most diversified lending and investing opportunities: short- and long-term business loans, government or municipal bonds, consumer credit, mortgages, and so forth. When market conditions and official regulations permit banks to offer competitive rates on time and savings deposits, the banking system becomes an engine for smoothing out yield differentials, as individual banks quickly bid for the cheapest sources of funds and lend or acquire securities where returns are the most attractive. The enormous growth of commercial banks in the 1960s and 1970s has undoubtedly contributed to a marked reduction in yield spreads among many financial instruments of differing maturity and risk.

However, if one of the various money and capital submarkets created by legal and institutional constraints becomes chronically over- or undersupplied with funds (or securities), yields may find themselves out of line with those in other markets. To be sure, such disparities create pressures for redefining the boundaries of the operations of institutions to allow borrowers or lenders to do their business in other and greener pastures. Nevertheless, often many years may pass before law and habit are substantially altered. In sum, yield spreads among different assets of the same maturity reflect differences in constraints on market participants that have been established by law and regulation.

The underlying trend in financial markets over the past generation has been toward breaking down the market imperfections and reducing the constraints that separate the various financial assets. Money has been allowed to flow more readily among the various markets. On the whole, this may have tended to make the general level of rates more volatile, since disturbances in any one market are transmitted more quickly to all the others. But, by the same token, it has probably tended to narrow yield spreads among the markets, as borrowers and lenders have been able to take advantage more quickly of those markets offering a "better buy."

It should be recognized, however, that rapid changes in financial practice are often blocked or moderated by law. As a result, some institutional changes occur very gradually: the slow and cautious freeing, state by state, of public pension funds to purchase common stocks, for example. Others remain pent up until the dam breaks under overwhelming pressure and change occurs with a rush. The prohibition of competitive interest payments on time deposits by commercial banks, dating from the 1930s when government desired to minimize interbank competition in order to reduce bank failures, began to be rescinded in the 1960s. Almost immediately, large banks took advantage of their new freedom to bid for additional funds with which to step up their lending and security purchases. Since then, the growth of large banks has greatly accelerated, with interest-bearing time deposits the chief source of new funds. And, with the passage of the Depository Institutions Deregulation and Monetary Control Act, enacted in 1980, all banks as well as federally insured savings and loan associations and mutual savings banks can issue interest-bearing demand deposits in the form of NOW accounts, with federally insured credit unions being allowed similar privileges in the form of share drafts.

Sometimes, however, new dams are built to cushion or prevent change. Thus, in mid-1966, Congress feared that the competition from commercial banks might drain other depository institutions of their savings accounts. It therefore enacted new legislation empowering the regulatory agencies to control rather minutely the savings interest rate structure of savings and loan associations and savings and commercial banks.[10] Similarly, balance-of-payments difficulties produced new regulations in the 1960s that greatly restricted the latitude for lending abroad and for purchasing

foreign securities. The foreign lending restrictions were phased out in the 1970s, and interest rate ceilings on savings accounts are scheduled to be phased out by 1986.

The trend, which apparently prevails, toward reduction of market imperfections has several roots. Perhaps the most important has been the heightening of competition nurtured by the fantastic improvement in communications. Cheap and lightning-fast, the long-distance telephone and telegraph have gone far to integrate the whole industrial world into a single financial market. Even the smallest borrower or saver now has the option of driving to the shopping center on the other side of town, if locally offered financial services or rates are unsatisfactory, or of trading via telephone or wire on securities exchanges all over the globe. While sizable differentials in interest rates persist in different regions of the United States, especially for mortgages and consumer loans, forces are clearly at work tending to break these down. Through various new techniques, financial assets, such as mortgages and receivables, are now, in effect, regionally or nationally salable to a much greater extent than previously, although the secondary markets still leave a great deal to be desired.

In the course of rapid economic change, some types of borrowers have outgrown their traditional fields of financial investment. For example, state and local jurisdictions, including such diverse bodies as school and sanitation districts, hospitals, and highway and airport authorities, would have been hard put to place all the bond issues needed to finance their burgeoning expenditures if only wealthy investors were attracted by the tax-exempt feature of municipal securities. As it has turned out, however, the success of commercial banks in exploiting their greater freedom to bid for deposits has provided these institutions with funds for the purchase of many more municipal bonds than before. Banks have also increased their penetration of other long-term markets, including those for mortgages, consumer instalment loans, and long-term business loans, formerly thought to be not quite suitable for large-scale bank participations. Similarly, the rapid growth of pension funds has led successively to a broadening of their investment scope, initially often restricted to governmental securities, to encompass other bonds, mortgages, and common stock.

[10]Once more, however, this dam has broken with the passage of the Depository Institutions Deregulation Act of 1980, which provides for phasing out Regulation Q ceilings for all commercial banks and thrift institutions by 1986.

In sum, the trend has been toward reduction of market segmentation, increased substitutability of assets, and narrowing of yield differentials. A stone thrown into any part of the credit lake causes ripples throughout the whole financial structure more directly and promptly than in the past.

## Comparison of Yields

Before concluding our discussion of institutional sources of yield differentials, it is important to note that because of technical differences among assets, it is often difficult to compare yields directly.

For example, the nominal rate on bank loans is often less than the true rate of return to the lender. Whether interest is deducted from the loan in advance (in which case the rate quoted is a "discount" rather than an interest rate) or payable later, whether the loan is repayable in instalments or in a lump sum, whether the borrower must maintain a "compensating" balance or not—these are all factors that can greatly alter effective rates of return.

Also, depending on market conditions, the presence of a sinking fund, call protection, or variations in the terms on which such calls may be made will significantly influence quoted yields in the bond market. A *sinking fund* requires the issuer to buy up stated portions of the issue prior to maturity; this may raise its price as the amount outstanding declines. *Callability* refers to the right often retained by the borrower to prepay the issue, which might be exercised if interest rates fall and it becomes advantageous to re-fund at a lower rate. The *call price* refers to the price at which the issuer is entitled to "buy back" the bond before maturity.

In addition, risk differentials may be compensated for in other ways than through rate of return alone. Sometimes the interest rate is not free to vary. For example, until they were overturned by federal law in 1980, many states had "usury laws" for mortgages, and many states still have rate ceilings on other consumer loans. Often these maxima are less than what the market would command. In that case, other terms, such as closing fees, repayment schedules, or minimum-balance requirements must be adjusted if the lender is to find the loan worthwhile. In auto loans, for example, the size of the down payment and the term to maturity can often be set more flexibly than the interest rate.

Finally, the nature of the collateral may be an important consideration. Loans secured by U.S. government securities carry lower rates than do loans where the value of the collateral may be uncertain, questionable, or difficult to realize.

All of these factors tend to make different assets less than perfect substitutes and thus are examples of factors that cause the general theory presented earlier to be less than a complete explanation of observed yield differentials.

## Conclusion

This chapter examined the determinants of interest rate structure in terms of portfolio theory. The first section of the chapter set forth the fundamental principles of portfolio theory. That part of the risk of a particular asset that is independent of the risk of financial assets as a whole was shown to be unimportant to the investor because it can be diversified away by holding a portfolio of assets. As a result, asset yields are related only to their systematic risk.

The development of this and other portfolio principles established the basis for assessing the impact of the government and private sectors on the structure of interest rates. Unlike earlier Keynesian and loanable funds approaches, which either implicitly assume that all financial assets provide the same yield or abstract from the problem of yield structure by assuming only two financial assets, the portfolio approach permitted us to examine the relationship of changes in the yield on any asset to the yield on all other assets. Similarly, the theory permitted an examination of how each market participant adjusts his or her portfolio in response to changes in the supply and demand for assets by other market participants. Extending this analysis, we were able to understand the determinants of changes in the general level and structure of interest rates.

The final section of the chapter discussed several institutional factors that tend to interfere with a perfectly efficient equilibrium process. It was shown that institutional considerations often cause assets with the same rate of return and systematic risk to provide different yields and, therefore, the theory to be less than a perfect description of reality. Nevertheless, portfolio theory appears to be the broadest and most useful framework available to examine interest rate structure.

## Questions

1. Suppose people become more risk averse. What would happen to the spread in expected return between high-Beta and low-Beta securities?
2. Suppose foreigners buy a large amount of Treasury bills. What would happen to the spread in expected return between high-Beta and low-Beta securities?
3. How will a corporation's decision to finance expansion through the issuance of corporate bonds instead of stock affect the Beta of the company's stock?
4. What effect will the issuance of a large amount of corporate debt have on the expected return of stock?
5. Suppose U.S. investors decide to invest more heavily in foreign securities. What effect will this have on the expected return of U.S. securities?
6. Does the saying, "Don't put all your eggs in one basket," make sense if eggs in all baskets have an equal probability of breaking? Explain your answer.
7. Assuming investors can freely diversify, would there be any motivation for a corporation to diversify its operations among many different industries? Explain your answer.
8. What effect might an increase in required reserves initially have on the risk and expected return of a bank's assets? How might the bank adjust to this?
9. Is throwing darts against the stock market page of the *Wall Street Journal* a superior way to select a low-risk portfolio than selecting stocks of a particular industry group? Explain your answer.
10. What effect would the elimination of tax exemption for municipal bonds have on the expected return of municipal bonds and corporate bonds?

## Selected Bibliography

Evans, J. L., and S. H. Archer. "Diversification and the Reduction of Dispersion: An Empirical Analysis." *Journal of Finance* (December 1969).

Keynes, J. M. *The General Theory of Employment Interest and Money.* Harcourt, Brace and Company, New York, 1936.

Markowitz, H. *Portfolio Selection.* John Wiley & Sons, New York, 1959.

Robichek, A. A., R. A. Cohn, and J. L. Pringle. "Returns on Alternative Investment Media and Implications for Portfolio Construction." *Journal of Business* (July 1972).

Sharpe, William F. "Capital Asset Prices: A Theory of Market Equilibrium Under Conditions of Risk." *Journal of Finance* (September 1964).

Tobin, J. "A General Equilibrium Approach to Monetary Theory." *Journal of Money, Credit and Banking* (February 1969).

———. "Liquidity Preference as Behavior Towards Risk." *Review of Economic Studies* (February 1958).

Yamane, T. *Statistics: An Introductory Analysis,* 2nd ed. Harper & Row, Publishers, New York, 1967.

# VI

# Forecasting Financial Flows and Interest Rates

# 25

# Sources and Uses of Funds Analysis

Interest rate forecasts have gained increased attention during the years of high and widely fluctuating rates since the mid-1960s. Earlier, after World War II, when interest rates were still relatively low following the secular decline of the 1920s and 1930s, only a relatively small group of business and financial market participants and observers took much cognizance of interest rate forecasts. Even though there were obvious cyclical movements in interest rates and the trend was unmistakably upward, the subject did not stir much interest beyond the business and financial community. In the late 1960s, however, interest rates began to fluctuate widely, soaring to heights not seen before in this century, as shown in Figure 25-1. With interest rates in the headlines, today there is a large group of savers and investors who pay close attention to interest rate developments and forecasts.

Ever since World War II, the tools and methods for forecasting interest rates have been developing and expanding. Interest rate forecasts have always been made implicitly, if not explicitly, in borrowing and lending transactions by investors and in industry and commerce as well. Many of these forecasts are based on assumptions that the current level or the current trend will continue. Before World War II, when the concept of the gross national product was first being developed and statistically measured, the data were simply not available for preparing an organized interest rate forecast based on macroeconomic variables, including an outlook for spending in the major areas of the economy. After World War II, however, the Department of Commerce began to report the National Income Accounts regularly, thereby providing a framework for studying and forecasting economic developments.

In the early post–World War II years, the interest rate forecasting undertaken by economists rested—as it still does today—on an assessment of the outlook for business activity. In their development of an interest rate outlook, economists of that time also relied on the assumption that the Federal Reserve was able to control interest rate movements and that it would tighten or ease credit in line with fluctuations in economic activity. In effect, interest rate forecasters concentrated on the economic outlook and the probable Federal Reserve responses, under the dictum that "as business goes, so go interest rates."

**Figure 25-1   Long- and Short-Term Interest Rates**

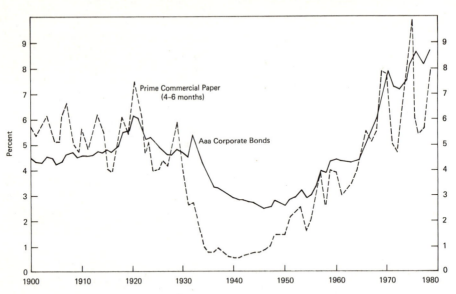

Sources: Standard and Poor's Corporation (for corporate bonds) and Board of Governors of the Federal Reserve System (for prime commercial paper).

## The Flow of Funds and the Residual

In the 1950s and through the early 1960s, financial economists began to utilize the growing body of statistical data on credit market flows available in the Federal Reserve Flow of Funds Accounts and from other sources. The statistics covered the amounts of mortgages, securities, and loans outstanding, on the one hand, and the asset holdings of investor groups, such as banks, insurance companies, pension funds, and savings and loan associations, on the other. Net changes in these amounts represented the supply (changes in investor holdings) and demand (changes in outstanding mortgages, loans, and securities) for funds in the credit markets as a whole.[1] Projections of credit

[1]Net changes in outstanding amounts consist of the gross amounts issued and purchased less retirements and other payoffs and sales. Net rather than gross amounts are used, because mortgages, securities, and loans are acquired from the proceeds of funds provided through retirements and sales, as well as from net new funds (savings, etc.). Furthermore, while there are figures for the gross amounts of corporate and municipal bonds and mortgages issued, such statistics are not available for loans, nor are statistics available covering the ownership of gross amounts issued. Thus, even if it were desirable,

market flows could then be based on an underlying outlook for economic activity and Federal Reserve policy, but they would necessarily reflect a host of other subsidiary assumptions.

Originally, financial economists had hoped to come up with summations, which would compare the projected demands for funds against the projected supplies, as in loanable funds theory, and to determine the price (or interest rate) that would clear the market from these summations. It soon became apparent, however, that statistics on *anticipated* demands and *anticipated* supplies were not available and that it was impossible to construct such schedules accurately. Thus, analysts had to settle for projections on an *ex post* rather than an *ex ante* basis, that is, projections of the magnitudes of the demands that would actually be financed rather than of the magnitudes that would be desired.

This did not mean, however, that analysts could not utilize the flow of funds projections to measure

it has always been impossible to measure the demand for loans and the supply of all credit instruments from gross amounts.

the impact of demands for funds on interest rate movements. Economists could do this by studying the impact of the "noninstitutional" supplies of funds—by analyzing movements in the residual or household section. In other words, since the projections of fund flows were made on an *ex post* basis, it was clear that the supply of funds actually placed had to equal the demand for funds, or the funds actually raised. The demand side could be totaled up. On the supply side, however, there were no statistics for the volume of funds supplied by individuals and a large group of institutions, including nonprofit associations, trust funds, and miscellaneous investors, as well as some institutional investors. (Some of these statistics gradually became available.) However, because supply necessarily equaled demand, it was still possible to derive the volume of funds supplied by these groups as a residual.

Analysts noticed that the amount of funds supplied by the residual sources varied widely from year to year and that the variations were related to fluctuations in economic activity and the consequent size of the demand for funds. Because the credit markets were primarily institutional markets, it seemed reasonable to suppose that institutions would preempt most of the available supply of funds in years of slack demand when interest rates were relatively low. There would be little need for more funds from the residual sector. Conversely, in years of high levels of economic activity and heavy demand for funds, institutions would not be able to supply sufficient funds to meet all of the demand, and interest rates would have to rise in order to entice the residual sector to buy directly in the credit markets rather than placing funds in the market indirectly through savings institutions.

In the 1950s and first half of the 1960s, the residual analysis worked reasonably well, with some qualifications,[2] but it was never considered to be a magic key to forecasting interest rates. As a residual, it was subject to all of the errors in the projections from which it was derived. Nevertheless, the residual is still useful as a factor in assessing the outlook for interest rates from the flow of funds.

With growing use of flow of funds projections in the 1960s, it became evident that supplemental benefits accompanied familiarity with the flow of funds. For example, improved grounding in flow of funds analysis leads to a better understanding of interrelationships in the financial markets. Furthermore, knowledge of the relative magnitude of the flows of funds and of developing changes or shifts enables the analyst to assess the importance of particular developments, not only with respect to impending interest rate changes, but also with respect to potential effects on the economy as a whole.[3] Flow of funds analysis and projection also bring into focus the areas where innovations are being introduced in the financial markets. Finally, this kind of analysis provides insight into the interactions of the financial markets and the real economy, although much more work remains to be done.

## Interest Rates and Inflation

In the late 1960s, a critical factor, which, on occasion, diminished the effectiveness of the residual analysis, was introduced into the economy. When the use of flow of funds was first being developed, and even after analysts were becoming more sophisticated in its use, the rate of inflation—because of its relative stability—had been almost completely ignored as a factor to be assessed in projecting the outlook for interest rates. In the late 1960s, though, as interest rates mounted along with prices, the tendency for interest rate movements roughly to parallel movements in prices, albeit with different leads and lags, became noticeable. This had been the case over long spans of time in the past, as Figure 25-2 shows. As prices rise, investors, particularly long-term investors, tend to demand higher interest rates to protect their investments against the expected erosion of purchasing power from inflation.

---

[2]These were spelled out by Sally S. Ronk, *The Sources and Uses of Funds Approach to Analysis of Interest Rate Developments,* unpublished Ph.D. dissertation, Graduate School of Business Administration, New York University, 1965, Chap. 13.

[3]It is interesting to speculate as to whether the course of developments leading to the Great Depression might have been different if the magnitude of the effect of stock market credit on the flow of funds had been fully understood in 1929. See, for example, Charles P. Kindleberger, *The World in Depression, 1929–1939*, Penguin Press, 1973, pp. 113–114, 117–118.

**Figure 25-2   Interest Rates and Prices**

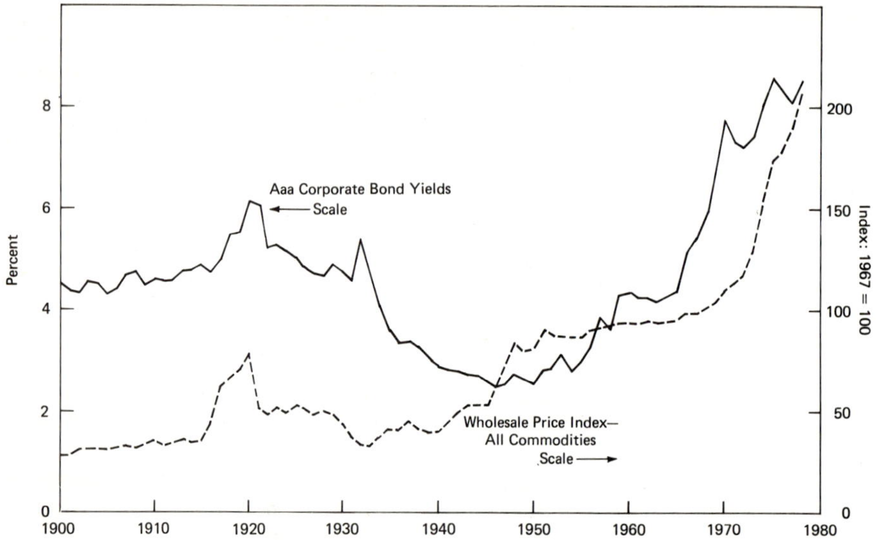

Sources: Standard and Poor's Corporation (for corporate bond yields) and Bureau of Labor Statistics (for wholesale prices).

As a result, the "real rate of return" and "inflation premium" analysis, first propounded by Irving Fisher in the 1920s, was revived.[4] Basically, Fisher's interest rate theory rested on concepts of the productivity of capital on the demand side and time preference and risk (or impatience and opportunity in relation to income) on the supply side to explain the real rate of return and, through a money-prices equation, to explain the inflation premium. As expectations of continuing inflation become embedded in the public's consciousness, recognition of the importance of the inflation premium in the assessment of the probable course of interest rates becomes more widespread, although any one method of measuring exact quantities for the inflation premium, inflationary expectations, and the real rate of return has not been accorded general acceptance.[5] Another element, over and above the

flow of funds and its underlying outlook for economic developments and for Federal Reserve policy, was thus introduced into the analysis of interest rate prospects.

**Judgment in Financial Forecasts**

The flow of funds technique for analyzing interest rate prospects still rests, ultimately, on subjective projections of the flow of funds, which, in turn, are based on assumptions—often subjective—regarding economic developments, price movements, and Federal Reserve policy. The interest rate outlook that evolves from these ingredients cannot, in any case, be precise as to the extent of specific movements in rates and yields—and, consequently, as

[4]Irving Fisher, *The Theory of Interest,* The Macmillan Company, New York, 1930.

[5]Researchers have investigated several methods, using different variables and different time lags between price changes and interest rate changes. See, for example, William P. Yohe and Denis S. Karnovsky, "Interest Rates and Price Level Changes, 1952–69," *Review,* Federal

Reserve Bank of St. Louis (December 1969); T. J. Sargent, "Commodity Price Expectations and the Interest Rate," *Quarterly Journal of Economics* (February 1970); Martin S. Feldstein and Otto Eckstein, "The Fundamental Determinants of Interest Rates," *Review of Economics and Statistics* (November 1970); and William E. Gibson, "Interest Rates and Inflationary Expectations: New Evidence," *The American Economic Review* (December 1972).

to spreads between different types of yields—but it necessarily relies on analytical judgment as to the probable trends indicated. In recent years, in the effort to be more precise, forecasters have increasingly utilized econometric techniques to develop models to forecast interest rates. These systems incorporate variables—sometimes through proxies—for important elements in the flow of funds as well as for the fundamental events and policies affecting economic development, price movements, and Federal Reserve policy.[6] Progress on such models is moving forward rapidly, but so far econometric models, which themselves are based in part on variables that depend on judgment, are still in the developmental stage and have not yet been proved to perform any better than the forecasts of qualified analysts relying on their own best judgment and experience.[7] At the present time, therefore, judgment is still a necessary underlying ingredient for forecasting interest rates.[8]

The flow of funds projections themselves are developed through a melding of assumptions—based on the professional judgment of qualified analysts—

[6] The major large-scale econometric models of the economy now include subsidiary or integrated equations that generate interest rates, to wit, the models produced by the private forecasting services, such as Chase Econometric Association, Inc., Data Resources, Inc., and Wharton Econometric Forecasting Associates, Inc. Smaller-scale models have been developed by the Federal Reserve Bank of St. Louis and several other individuals and organizations (for example, by Lacy H. Hunt in *Dynamics of Forecasting Financial Cycles,* Contemporary Studies in Economic and Financial Analysis, Graduate School of Business Administration, New York University, JAI Press, Greenwich, Conn., 1967). The following chapter contains a more detailed description and analysis of such models and their use in interest rate forecasting.

[7] One researcher found substantial errors in publicly announced interest rate forecasts of both long- and short-term rates, without noticing, or at least mentioning, any distinction between those developed from econometric models and those developed judgmentally. See Donald R. Fraser, "On the Accuracy of Interest Rate Forecasts," *Business Economics* (September 1977).

[8] This does not mean to imply that the judgmental forecaster does not utilize econometric techniques for sectoral analysis in formulating the projections for individual flows of funds to verify a trend, set parameters, and determine the degree of association or of cyclicality and amplitude of fluctuation. These include not only the conventional statistical-type analyses, such as regressions and trends, but also the newer types of techniques, such as Box-Jenkins, all of which are helpful in contributing to the most likely results, based on past experience.

of varying degree regarding the probable behavior of borrowers and lenders. The forecaster developing a set of flow of funds projections must iterate and reiterate many of the flows in order to obtain the sought-after balance, on an internally consistent basis, between funds raised and funds supplied for each sector and for the total. Often, after the projections for the various individual flows are assembled, the projection for the behavior of one series will prove to be inconsistent with the behavior attributed to another variable. The forecaster will then have to modify one or both of the projections.

The leap from an internally consistent set of flow of funds projections to an interest rate forecast also relies on a large measure of judgment, or "feel," which depends on wide knowledge of the past behavior of the numerous and many-faceted series involved under varied conditions as well as on recognition of the underlying factors causing these conditions and of the effects of inflationary and other expectations.

The interest rate forecaster using the flow of funds method is, therefore, still practicing an *art* rather than a *science.* A set of flow of funds projections is usually presented in a straightforward-enough fashion, and in enough detail, to permit the user also to practice the art by altering any projection that does not appear reasonable. In addition, by providing a clear format for tracking actual developments as they occur, a set of flow of funds projections enables the user, as well as the forecaster, to modify the original projections and update the interest rate forecast as new information becomes available. Thus, the flow of funds framework for forecasting interest rates permits users, as well as those who construct the projections, to formulate alternative forecasts and, thereby, provides a useful service to the financial community.

### Framework for Flow of Funds Analysis

Summaries of sets of flow of funds projections presented by interest rate forecasters are usually divided into two parts: one part consists of a summary of the various demands for funds, and the other a condensation of the institutional sources of funds. Typically, at least two periods are shown, one a record of historical flows and the other a projection for the future. This summary approach is used in preference to a presentation of a complete one-period matrix, because the detail required for the different types of borrowing and lending makes a complete matrix unmanageable in size unless it is all compressed to an extent that makes the detail insufficient for analytical purposes.[9] Also, for interest rate forecasting, it is desirable to be able to discern readily the areas of demand or supply that are likely to increase or decrease and the magnitude of the changes in prospect that can augment or diminish pressures in the financial markets.

In the various compilations used by flow of funds forecasters, however, the detail included in their summaries is not uniform. Thus, no one figure for total funds raised, similar to the gross national product in the National Income Accounts, is universally accepted. In addition, many of the components of demand or supply are not standardized. The variations usually arise because of differing concepts as to what measures of borrowing and lending influence interest rates. For example, demands for funds on the part of financial institutions, which usually finance other borrowings by business or consumers, are sometimes excluded from summaries on the grounds that they represent double counting of the basic demand for financing. Other frameworks exclude direct purchases of mortgages and loans by the federal government and agencies as not contributing to market pressures on interest rates, since they are financed by the sales of federal government and agency securities already included. Still others exclude some of the smaller and less significant loan categories, which are conceived of as not falling within the market process.

For purposes of illustration, Tables 25-1 and 25-2 show a framework for flows of funds through the credit markets, which includes all of the net bor-

rowing through various types of credit instruments and all of the net lending by the different groups for which statistical series are available.[10] It will be noted that the data in Tables 25-1 and 25-2 cover calendar years, which is usual for a formal set of flow of funds projections. Although the rapid changes in market conditions during recent years have led some forecasters to present projections of half-year flows, the volatility of credit flows makes projection of shorter time periods difficult and tenuous.[11]

On the demand side of Tables 25-1 and 25-2, the various types of credit instruments are listed, as in the usual flow of funds summary format, as representing the purpose for which the funds are raised, rather than as representing users of funds. Either of the two formats might have been employed, though. Even aside from amounts, the flow of funds is three-dimensional, since it covers not only "how much," but also "who borrows from whom for what purpose." Thus, the demand side could alternatively be couched in terms of a second demand

---

[9]The complete flow of funds matrix (outlined in Chapter 2) allocates hoarding, saving, and investment, as well as borrowing and lending, to broad sectors. The interest rate forecaster, on the other hand, is interested in covering only the borrowing and lending portions. However, in compiling a set of flow of funds projections, analysts use large-sized matrices (with credit instruments on one side and lenders or borrowers across the top) for balancing out the totals for the individual items of funds raised and supplied over a period. The matrix thus becomes an integral part of the iterative process through which the forecaster achieves a reasonable and balanced set of projections, given the underlying assumptions and corollary trends.

[10]This format includes security credit, which is credit extended by banks, brokers, and customers to finance security purchases by individuals, foreign investors, and brokers and dealers. It also includes corporate stocks, which are usually included by flow of funds forecasters as "credit instruments," or borrowing and lending in the loanable funds framework, on the grounds that corporations can choose to finance in the market at long term through either debt or equity issues and that investors have a similar choice for the placement of investment funds. However, net trade credit (receivables less payables) is omitted, as is usual, on the grounds that the credit so extended does not represent a borrowing operation; it is entered into in the normal course of business transactions. For any one sector, the net outstanding can be either trade credit or trade debt. When all sectors are considered, the total volume of trade credit on the books of various creditors should theoretically match the total volume of trade debt on the books of debtors, but time lags in the statistics produce a discrepancy.

[11]Seasonally adjusted data are available, but current seasonal-adjustment techniques—which have to deal with the complication of negative numbers, that is, numbers representing declines in credit outstanding over a period—are not completely satisfactory. In addition, even when seasonally adjusted, quarterly credit flows still tend to be quite volatile. Another impediment to their use is that market participants who, of course, do not undertake financing on a "seasonally adjusted" basis, will not place reliance on seasonally adjusted numbers, especially when they see that demand is actually impinging on supply, even though the seasonally adjusted numbers show that supply is ample.

# Table 25-1 Funds Raised in U.S. Credit Markets, 1968–1978 (in billions of dollars)

| | 1968 | 1969 | 1970 | 1971 | 1972 | 1973 | 1974 | 1975 | 1976 | 1977 | 1978 |
|---|---|---|---|---|---|---|---|---|---|---|---|
| **Long-term funds** | | | | | | | | | | | |
| Mortgages | | | | | | | | | | | |
| Home | $ 17.5 | $ 18.1 | $ 15.0 | $ 30.6 | $ 43.8 | $ 44.9 | $ 33.3 | $ 41.4 | $ 65.4 | $ 99.5 | $105.5 |
| Multifamily | 3.4 | 4.9 | 6.9 | 9.7 | 12.8 | 10.4 | 6.9 | — | 1.9 | 7.3 | 10.2 |
| Commercial | 6.7 | 5.8 | 7.2 | 9.9 | 16.8 | 19.1 | 15.3 | 11.2 | 13.6 | 18.4 | 23.3 |
| Farm | 2.2 | 1.8 | .8 | 2.4 | 3.6 | 5.5 | 5.0 | 4.6 | 6.1 | 8.8 | 10.2 |
| Total | 29.8 | 30.7 | 29.9 | 52.6 | 77.0 | 79.9 | 60.5 | 57.2 | 87.1 | 134.0 | 149.2 |
| Corporate securities[a] | | | | | | | | | | | |
| Corporate bonds | 14.4 | 13.8 | 23.3 | 23.5 | 18.4 | 13.6 | 23.9 | 36.4 | 37.2 | 36.1 | 31.5 |
| Corporate stocks | .6 | 5.2 | 7.7 | 13.7 | 13.8 | 10.4 | 4.8 | 10.8 | 12.9 | 4.8 | 3.6 |
| Total | 15.0 | 19.0 | 31.1 | 37.2 | 32.1 | 24.0 | 28.7 | 47.1 | 50.1 | 40.8 | 35.1 |
| Total long-term funds | 44.8 | 49.8 | 61.0 | 89.8 | 109.1 | 103.9 | 89.2 | 104.3 | 137.1 | 174.8 | 184.3 |
| **Government securities** | | | | | | | | | | | |
| U.S. government | $ 10.5 | $(1.2) | $ 12.9 | $ 26.0 | $ 14.3 | $ 7.9 | $ 12.0 | $ 85.8 | $ 69.1 | $ 57.6 | $ 55.1 |
| Federal agencies | 6.9 | 7.4 | 8.8 | 4.9 | 9.3 | 20.4 | 22.2 | 12.3 | 19.0 | 26.7 | 40.1 |
| State and local governments | 9.5 | 9.9 | 11.2 | 17.4 | 14.7 | 14.7 | 16.5 | 15.6 | 19.0 | 29.2 | 30.1 |
| Total | 26.9 | 16.1 | 32.9 | 48.3 | 38.3 | 43.0 | 50.7 | 113.7 | 107.1 | 113.5 | 125.3 |
| **Short-term funds[b]** | | | | | | | | | | | |
| Business credit | | | | | | | | | | | |
| Open-market paper | $ 4.2 | $ 12.4 | $ 2.1 | $ (.1) | $ 1.7 | $ 8.3 | $ 17.5 | $ (1.5) | $ 7.4 | $ 14.4 | $ 25.4 |
| Bank loans | 12.7 | 15.7 | 5.6 | 7.6 | 21.9 | 42.3 | 34.4 | 15.6 | (2.4) | 22.4 | 34.5 |
| U.S. government loans | .4 | .4 | .8 | .6 | .3 | 1.2 | 2.3 | 3.0 | 2.9 | 4.1 | 7.8 |
| Federal agency loans | 1.2 | 4.8 | 2.3 | (2.0) | .8 | 8.5 | 9.3 | (2.4) | .3 | 6.4 | 14.6 |
| Finance company loans | 2.2 | 5.0 | .4 | 1.3 | 4.2 | 5.0 | 4.8 | 2.1 | 5.4 | 10.3 | 8.3 |
| Security RPs & Federal Funds | .6 | 2.6 | (2.2) | 1.0 | 2.5 | 12.9 | (5.2) | (2.5) | 5.2 | 4.6 | 9.2 |
| Total | 21.4 | 40.9 | 8.9 | 8.4 | 31.3 | 78.2 | 63.1 | (17.0) | 18.7 | 62.3 | 99.7 |
| Consumer credit | 10.0 | 10.4 | 5.9 | 13.1 | 17.1 | 23.8 | 10.2 | 9.4 | 23.6 | 35.0 | 49.9 |
| Security credit | 6.6 | (6.7) | (.8) | 3.8 | 8.7 | (7.9) | (5.0) | 3.6 | 13.2 | 4.4 | (.1) |
| Foreign loans | | | | | | | | | | | |
| Bank loans | (.5) | (.2) | (.3) | 2.1 | 2.9 | 2.8 | 4.7 | 3.7 | 6.6 | 1.6 | 15.8 |
| U.S. government loans | 2.2 | 2.1 | 1.3 | 1.8 | 1.5 | 1.7 | 1.5 | 2.8 | 3.3 | 3.0 | 3.8 |
| Total | 1.7 | 1.9 | 1.0 | 3.9 | 4.4 | 4.5 | 6.2 | 6.5 | 9.9 | 4.5 | 19.6 |
| **Other loans** | | | | | | | | | | | |
| U.S. government loans | | | | | | | | | | | |
| To sponsored agencies | .2 | (.3) | — | — | — | — | .7 | .9 | (.4) | (1.2) | — |
| To state & local governments | .3 | .7 | .1 | .4 | .3 | .3 | .7 | .2 | 2.0 | .2 | (1.5) |
| Total | .5 | .5 | .1 | .4 | .3 | .3 | 1.4 | 1.1 | 1.6 | (1.0) | (1.5) |
| Loans to households | | | | | | | | | | | |
| Bank loans | 2.5 | 1.3 | 1.1 | 2.5 | 2.9 | 6.5 | (.8) | (2.0) | 2.2 | 8.2 | 2.7 |
| U.S. government loans | .5 | .5 | .4 | .4 | .4 | .2 | .5 | .6 | .5 | .6 | 1.2 |
| Policy loans | 1.2 | 2.5 | 2.2 | 1.0 | .9 | 2.2 | 2.7 | 1.6 | 1.4 | 1.7 | 2.6 |
| Total | 4.2 | 4.3 | 3.7 | 3.8 | 4.2 | 8.9 | 2.5 | .1 | 4.0 | 10.4 | 6.5 |
| Total other loans | 4.8 | 4.8 | 3.8 | 4.2 | 4.6 | 9.2 | 3.8 | 1.2 | 5.6 | 9.5 | 5.1 |
| Total short-term funds | 44.5 | 51.3 | 18.8 | 33.4 | 66.1 | 107.8 | 78.4 | 3.6 | 71.0 | 115.7 | 174.2 |
| *Total funds raised* | $116.2 | $117.1 | $112.7 | $171.5 | $213.5 | $254.7 | $218.3 | $221.7 | $315.2 | $404.0 | $483.8 |

Note: Figures in this and the following flow of funds tables have been rounded and may not add to totals shown.

[a]Including foreign securities.

[b]Including bank term loans and long-term federal credits.

Source: Board of Governors of the Federal Reserve System, *Flow of Funds Accounts,* May 1979.

**Table 25-2  Funds Supplied to U.S. Credit Markets, 1968–1978 (in billions of dollars)**

| | 1968 | 1969 | 1970 | 1971 | 1972 | 1973 | 1974 | 1975 | 1976 | 1977 | 1978 |
|---|---|---|---|---|---|---|---|---|---|---|---|
| *Savings institutions* | | | | | | | | | | | |
| Contractual-type: | | | | | | | | | | | |
| Life insurance companies | $ 8.7 | $ 8.6 | $ 9.0 | $ 11.8 | $ 13.2 | $ 15.9 | $ 15.2 | $ 18.8 | $ 26.6 | $ 29.4 | $ 33.9 |
| Private pension funds | 5.9 | 6.2 | 6.8 | 7.5 | 6.5 | 7.8 | 8.1 | 13.8 | 12.5 | 15.5 | 12.4 |
| State & local retirement funds | 4.7 | 5.6 | 6.3 | 6.5 | 8.2 | 9.1 | 9.2 | 11.6 | 13.4 | 12.8 | 16.0 |
| Fire & casualty insurance co's. | 2.7 | 2.6 | 4.8 | 6.2 | 6.6 | 5.8 | 4.1 | 6.6 | 13.4 | 14.4 | 14.2 |
| Total | 21.9 | 23.0 | 26.9 | 32.0 | 34.6 | 38.6 | 36.7 | 50.8 | 66.0 | 72.1 | 76.5 |
| Deposit-type: | | | | | | | | | | | |
| Savings and loan associations | 9.7 | 9.6 | 12.2 | 28.4 | 35.7 | 28.3 | 21.4 | 36.0 | 52.5 | 65.7 | 60.3 |
| Mutual savings banks | 4.5 | 3.2 | 4.2 | 10.0 | 10.3 | 5.4 | 3.0 | 10.8 | 13.0 | 12.1 | 9.5 |
| Credit unions | 1.5 | 2.1 | 1.4 | 2.0 | 2.9 | 3.6 | 2.7 | 5.4 | 6.0 | 7.3 | 8.5 |
| Mutual funds | 3.5 | 2.6 | 1.7 | .4 | (1.8) | (2.0) | — | .3 | (.7) | (1.5) | 1.7 |
| Total | 19.1 | 17.5 | 19.4 | 40.8 | 47.0 | 35.3 | 27.1 | 52.4 | 70.8 | 83.7 | 80.0 |
| Total savings institutions | 41.1 | 40.5 | 46.3 | 72.8 | 81.6 | 73.9 | 63.8 | 103.2 | 136.8 | 155.8 | 156.5 |
| *Banking* | | | | | | | | | | | |
| Federal Reserve banks | $ 3.7 | $ 4.2 | $ 5.0 | $ 8.9 | $ .3 | $ 9.2 | $ 6.2 | $ 8.5 | $ 9.8 | $ 7.1 | $ 7.0 |
| Commercial banks | 40.1 | 17.6 | 36.6 | 51.3 | 75.4 | 83.4 | 62.2 | 29.7 | 65.2 | 86.4 | 118.5 |
| Total | 43.8 | 21.8 | 41.6 | 60.2 | 75.6 | 92.6 | 68.3 | 38.3 | 75.0 | 93.5 | 125.5 |
| *Business* | | | | | | | | | | | |
| Nonfinancial business | | | | | | | | | | | |
| Corporate | $ 3.1 | $ 1.2 | $ (.8) | $ 6.4 | $ 2.6 | $ 8.2 | $ 1.9 | $ 11.4 | $ 11.5 | $ (2.9) | $ 3.3 |
| Nonfarm noncorporate | .4 | .4 | .6 | .4 | .5 | .9 | .7 | .8 | 1.2 | 1.4 | 1.5 |
| Total | 3.5 | 1.6 | (.2) | 6.9 | 3.1 | 9.2 | 2.7 | 12.3 | 12.6 | (1.5) | 4.8 |
| Financial business | | | | | | | | | | | |
| Finance companies | 5.2 | 8.6 | 2.2 | 5.2 | 9.4 | 11.5 | 5.0 | 1.4 | 8.8 | 18.1 | 18.3 |
| Security brokers & dealers | 3.3 | (3.0) | 1.2 | 1.3 | 4.3 | (3.4) | (3.2) | 3.0 | 8.6 | 1.2 | (1.6) |
| Real estate investment trusts | .8 | 1.2 | 1.9 | 2.3 | 4.2 | 5.6 | .2 | (4.8) | (3.8) | (2.4) | (1.0) |
| Total | 9.3 | 6.7 | 5.2 | 8.8 | 17.8 | 13.7 | 2.0 | (.4) | 13.5 | 16.9 | 15.7 |
| Total business | 12.8 | 8.3 | 5.0 | 15.7 | 20.9 | 22.9 | 4.7 | 11.9 | 26.2 | 15.4 | 20.4 |
| *Government* | | | | | | | | | | | |
| U.S. government | $ 5.2 | $ 3.1 | $ 2.8 | $ 2.8 | $ 1.8 | $ 2.8 | $ 9.7 | $ 15.1 | $ 8.9 | $ 11.8 | $ 18.6 |
| Federal agencies | 3.8 | 9.4 | 11.1 | 5.2 | 9.2 | 21.4 | 25.6 | 14.5 | 20.6 | 26.9 | 46.0 |
| State and local governments | 1.8 | 5.3 | (.2) | (2.3) | 7.8 | 7.8 | 3.8 | 3.4 | 14.7 | 26.4 | 23.1 |
| Total | 10.8 | 17.9 | 13.7 | 5.7 | 18.9 | 32.0 | 39.1 | 33.0 | 44.3 | 65.1 | 87.7 |
| *Foreign* | $ 2.7 | $ .9 | $ 11.1 | $ 27.2 | $ 10.9 | $ 3.3 | $ 11.7 | $ 10.9 | $ 17.9 | $ 42.2 | $ 40.2 |
| *Households* (residual) | $ 5.1 | $ 27.8 | $ (4.9) | $(10.1) | $ 5.6 | $ 30.1 | $ 30.7 | $ 24.5 | $ 15.1 | $ 31.9 | $ 53.6 |
| *Total funds supplied* | $116.2 | $117.1 | $112.7 | $171.5 | $213.5 | $254.7 | $218.3 | $221.8 | $315.2 | $404.0 | $483.8 |

Source: Board of Governors of the Federal Reserve System, *Flow of Funds Accounts,* May 1979.

dimension—in terms of the sectors that are doing the borrowing, to wit, nonfinancial business, households, government, financial business, and foreign. Indeed, analysts who are examining the economic effects of borrowing by various sectors often do study that type of summary framework. For the study of the impact of the flows of funds on financial markets and interest rates, however, the particular types of credit instruments are more directly related to market demand in particular markets and to analysis of market behavior and of interest rates.

The highly developed and efficient set of institutional arrangements in the U.S. credit markets, whereby funds are channeled from saving to investment, works through financial transactions made by means of credit instruments, which are originated and traded in separate markets and, thereby, differ in their market effects. For example, both home mortgages and consumer credit finance the household sector, while both corporate stocks and bank loans to business finance nonfinancial business, each with varying impacts on particular markets and on other credit instruments and, therefore, on the markets as a whole.[12]

On the supply side, the lending institutions are classified into sectors, such as savings institutions (the name used in Table 25-2 for nonbank financial intermediaries), banking, business, and government and, within these sectors, into broad groups having similar sources and uses of funds. The single number, shown in Table 25-2, for each institutional group represents the total of credit instruments of all types absorbed by that group. Not only does its composition vary according to the type of business and investment powers and proclivities of each group, but the year-to-year totals vary because of the diverse liability structures of the various institutions. For example, even among nonbank financial intermediaries, insurance-type intermediaries (insurance companies and pension funds, called *contractual-type* savings institutions in Table 25-2) receive their funds from regular payments for long-term insurance and pension contracts, while nonbank depository intermediaries (called *deposit-type* savings institutions in Table 25-2) garner funds irregularly from the public through passbook or fixed-term deposits or through purchases of redeemable shares (in the case of mutual funds). This has resulted in a more stable inflow of funds for insurance-type intermediaries than for depository intermediaries, although the instability of the latter has been somewhat mitigated by the introduction in June 1978 of large ($10,000 minimum) money market certificates and, since then, by smaller-denominated certificates, which are tied to market

rates. Nevertheless, the essentially diverse nature of the liabilities, as well as the investment powers, and proclivities, of each group has resulted in widely different patterns of investment. Thus, projections of the total funds supplied in the summary table still depend on an analysis of the sources and uses of funds of each institutional group.

In the analysis of the sources and uses of funds of the financial intermediaries—savings institutions and banks—the uses of funds, that is, their net investment in credit market instruments, become sources of funds to the credit markets in the summary tables (see Tables 25-1 and 25-2, for example). By the same token, their sources of funds (that is, net additions to their deposits, reserves, or mutual funds shares) are not counted as credit instruments in a credit market flow of funds framework, but constitute funds that enter the credit markets after they have been invested in credit market instruments.

The credit flows shown in summary Tables 25-1 and 25-2, therefore, do not cover a complete statement of all funds raised or supplied; rather, they cover only those funds represented by credit instruments: securities, mortgages, and loans. Thus, funds raised by financial intermediaries, changes in cash balances, and miscellaneous financial claims are omitted. In contrast, the Federal Reserve Flow of Funds Accounts contain a summary table that not only incorporates funds raised in the credit markets but also adds in deposits of financial intermediaries, insurance and pension reserves, security credit, and miscellaneous assets—such as trade debt and profit taxes payable—to obtain a total for funds allocated to sectors as assets, as shown in Table 25-3.

This treatment harks back to the very origin of the Federal Reserve Flow of Funds Accounts, which were then based on the pioneering efforts of Morris A. Copeland in the 1940s and 1950s.[13] Copeland had envisaged developing aggregate measures of money flow transactions. His focus was not on financial flows *per se* but on the flow of funds matrix or social-accounting aspects provided by a systematic and comprehensive set of interlocking nonfinancial and financial accounts, covering all

---

[12]The effort to assess where the pressures are arising makes it desirable for commercial bank loans—which are made to many different borrowing groups for a variety of purposes—to be disaggregated into broad categories. These categories include loans to business, foreign loans, and loans to households as well as into the bank share of mortgage loans, open-market paper, consumer credit, and security credit (see Table 25-9).

[13]Morris A. Copeland, *A Study of Money Flows in the United States,* National Bureau of Economic Research, New York, 1952.

**Table 25-3 Total Claims and Their Relation to Total Financial Assets, 1978 (in billions of dollars)**

| | |
|---|---:|
| *Total credit market funds raised, all sectors, by type* | |
| Total funds raised | $490.8 |
| Investment company shares | (1.1) |
| Other corporate equities | 3.6 |
| Debt instruments | |
|     U.S. government securities | 95.2 |
|     State & local obligations | 30.1 |
|     Corporate & foreign bonds | 31.5 |
|     Mortgages | 149.2 |
|     Consumer credit | 49.9 |
|     Bank loans N.E.C. | 53.0 |
|     Open-market paper & RPs | 42.5 |
|     Other loans | 36.9 |
| *Total claims and their relation to total financial assets* | |
| Total funds raised (from preceding) | $490.8 |
| Other liabilities | |
|     Official foreign exchange | .2 |
|     Treasury currency & SDR certificates | .5 |
|     Deposits at financial institutions | 155.1 |
|         Demand deposits and currency | 27.2 |
|         Time deposits at banks | 68.7 |
|         Deposits at savings institutions | 59.2 |
|     Life insurance reserves | 9.0 |
|     Pension fund reserves | 60.7 |
|     Security credit | (.1) |
|     Trade debt | 59.2 |
|     Profit taxes payable | 3.6 |
|     Noncorporate, proprietors' equity | (31.4) |
|     Miscellaneous | 82.5 |
|     Interbank claims | 23.2 |
| Total liabilities above | $853.3 |
| Floats not included in assets | |
|     Demand deposits | |
|         U.S. government | (1.7) |
|         Other | (.5) |
|     Trade credit | (5.6) |
| Liabilities not allocated as assets | |
|     Treasury currency | — |
|     Profit taxes payable | (.4) |
|     Miscellaneous | 13.3 |
| Total allocated to sectors as assets | $848.2 |

Source: Board of Governors of the Federal Reserve System, *Flow of Funds Accounts.* May 1979.

receipts, expenditures, and financial transactions involving the transfer of money (with the exception of "technical" transactions, such as interbank settlements). However, such a complete study has never been implemented.

After the Federal Reserve undertook the development of a flow of funds system in the early 1950s, the concept and coverage were narrowed to saving, investment, and net changes in financial assets and liabilities. At the present time, however, the Federal Reserve has discontinued publishing both a matrix and totals for saving and investment in the summaries of its Flow of Funds Accounts. Instead, as in the case of the private forecasters, its summaries focus on credit market flows.

**Comparison of Summaries of Projections of Credit Flows**

The Federal Reserve Flow of Funds Accounts provide complete sources and uses of funds statements for investing groups and for credit instruments, beginning in 1946 for annual data and in 1952 on a quarterly basis. The statements also show gross saving, gross investment, and net financial investment for most investing groups, along with some of the relationships between financial flows and output and income for the economy, as measured by the National Income Accounts. The data, which are seasonally adjusted as well as unadjusted, are collected from many government and private sources and are made available to the public on a timely basis; for example, preliminary data for the first quarter of 1979 were available as of May 15, 1979. It should be noted, however, that the preliminary data, which are necessarily based on incomplete information, are subject to substantial revision, as are, from time to time, the older data when the basic series are revised.[14] In addition, once a year, the year-end financial assets and liabilities outstanding are published.[15] However, the projections of the flows of funds, which the Federal Re-

[14]These data are published in truncated form in the *Federal Reserve Bulletin,* but appear in complete detail in the publications, which are regularly circulated and available to interested users, of the Flow of Funds Section, Board of Governors of the Federal Reserve System, 20th & Constitution Ave., N.W., Washington, D.C., 20551.

[15]The outstanding amounts as of year-end can be adjusted by quarterly flows to estimate the outstanding amounts of assets and liabilities on quarterly dates. Caution should be observed, however, with respect to using outstanding common stock holdings as benchmarks, since the year-end amounts are quoted at market value, while the flows are corrected for changes in market value.

serve prepares for internal consumption, are not released to the public.

Several prominent financial institutions regularly prepare and circulate projections of flows of funds through the U.S. credit markets.[16] Some of these sets of projections are confidential or proprietary, but several are made widely available to the financial community. Most of the projections that are disseminated are on a calendar-year basis and are issued very early in the year for which the projections are made. However, most institutions maintain updated projections for internal use, and some of these updates are circulated.

Often users of these various flow of funds projections express confusion because of differences in the amounts of the total for funds raised and of the residual. The differences are attributable in large part, of course, to the varying concepts of the appropriate measures of credit market pressures, discussed earlier, but a minor part of the reason for the differences is that some of these institutions compile their own data, which may be conceptually different from, or not available from, the data used by the Federal Reserve from its sources. Also, as new data become available, making it possible to increase the coverage (which increases the total of funds raised or shrinks the size of the residual), some private forecasters have adopted the change sooner than others. In any one year, therefore, the amounts for total demands or for the residual shown in the various sets of projections should not be treated as absolutes, but only as indications of the pressures arising from the various credit flows, which each projection computes on the same basis from year to year.

The most widely circulated of these published projections is that of Salomon Brothers, published at least annually for many years.[17] The Salomon Brothers summary, shown in Table 25-4, does not provide all-inclusive coverage, as does Table 25-3. Nor does it follow a concept of excluding nonfinancial flows; rather, it is confined to a concept of *net demand,* by which it means that federal government and agency participation in the credit markets, both on the supply and demand sides, other than direct borrowing, is netted out as not contributing to interest rate pressures. In addition to federal government and agency loans, mortgages, and holdings of securities, Federal Reserve holdings of Treasury and agency securities and state and local government sinking-fund holdings of state and local securities are omitted from the summary, along with corporate stocks, security RPs (repurchase agreements) and Federal Funds, policy loans of life insurance companies, and nonbank security credit. Thus, the scope of Table 25-4 is very abbreviated, but the categories of demand omitted are generally shown in supporting tables, which cover the various demands for funds and investor groups.

The exclusions on the demand side in the Salomon Brothers summary are probably undertaken because of the firm's emphasis on the bond markets.[18] However, the movements in the residual are not greatly affected by the exclusions, because the items omitted are also excluded on the supply side of the summary table, where most of the institutional groups are covered. On the supply side, in fact, the size of the residual is lower in the Salomon summary than it would otherwise be, because of the inclusion of several important investing groups not generally covered separately by either the Federal Reserve Flow of Funds Accounts or other private forecasters; these consist of foundations and endowments, municipal bond funds, and closed-end corporate bond funds.

Another important set of flow of funds projections, which has been regularly circulated since 1955, is that prepared by the American Council of Life Insurance (formerly the Life Insurance Association of America), as shown in Table 25-5. The total demand for funds shown in this summary is

[16]The institutions include the American Council of Life Insurance, Bankers Trust Company, the Chemical Bank, Merrill Lynch Economics, Inc., Morgan Guaranty Trust Company, New York Life Insurance Company, Prudential Insurance Company, Scudder, Stevens & Clark, and Salomon Brothers.

[17]The Salomon Brothers study originally projected gross flows of investment funds and the funds available to meet them, in an effort to arrive at an *ex ante* basis (Salomon Brothers and Hutzler, "Memorandum to Portfolio Managers," unpublished manuscript, New York, February 7, 1950), but, beginning in 1956, Salomon Brothers switched to a net basis.

[18]Sidney Homer, who became responsible for the Salomon study in 1962—after pioneering flow of funds analysis while at Scudder, Stevens & Clark—is a student of bond and money rates (in fact, he characterizes himself as a "bond man") and prepared the monumental *A History of Interest Rates,* Rutgers University Press, New Brunswick, N.J., 1963.

**Table 25-4  Summary of Supply and Demand for Credit (in billions of dollars)**

| | Annual Net Increases in Amounts Outstanding | | | | | | | Amounts Outstanding 12/31/78 |
|---|---|---|---|---|---|---|---|---|
| | 1973 | 1974 | 1975 | 1976 | 1977 | 1978 | 1979 | |
| **NET DEMAND** | | | | | | | | |
| Privately held mortgages | $ 68.7 | $ 42.8 | $ 40.2 | $ 72.3 | $110.4 | $116.7 | $109.0 | $ 999.9 |
| Corporate & foreign bonds | 14.2 | 29.1 | 39.1 | 39.1 | 37.9 | 34.5 | 37.5 | 442.5 |
| Subtotal long-term private | 82.9 | 71.9 | 79.3 | 111.4 | 148.3 | 151.2 | 146.5 | 1,442.4 |
| Short-term business borrowing | 53.0 | 57.3 | −15.0 | 13.3 | 45.6 | 74.6 | 95.8 | 451.7 |
| Short-term consumer borrowing | 30.0 | 14.2 | 12.0 | 35.0 | 48.6 | 55.5 | 47.1 | 417.1 |
| Subtotal short-term private | 83.0 | 71.5 | −3.0 | 48.3 | 94.2 | 130.1 | 142.9 | 868.8 |
| Privately held federal debt | 21.6 | 26.9 | 83.3 | 71.8 | 74.4 | 71.9 | 74.7 | 681.9 |
| Tax-exempt notes and bonds | 14.1 | 14.5 | 16.3 | 17.1 | 31.1 | 28.3 | 25.0 | 301.4 |
| Total net demand for credit | 201.6 | 184.8 | 175.9 | 248.6 | 348.0 | 381.5 | 389.1 | 3,294.5 |
| **NET SUPPLY**[a] | | | | | | | | |
| Thrift institutions | $ 36.0 | $ 25.6 | $ 53.4 | $ 69.0 | $ 81.5 | $ 78.6 | $ 65.1 | $ 670.7 |
| Insurance, pensions & endowments | 19.5 | 29.8 | 40.2 | 51.0 | 65.2 | 69.9 | 76.0 | 592.8 |
| Investment companies | 2.1 | 1.9 | 3.7 | 4.6 | 5.7 | 7.5 | 8.7 | 35.3 |
| Other nonbank finance | 17.9 | 5.1 | −4.4 | 7.9 | 15.1 | 11.9 | 15.1 | 146.1 |
| Subtotal nonbank finance | 75.5 | 62.4 | 92.9 | 132.5 | 167.5 | 167.9 | 164.9 | 1,444.9 |
| Commercial banks[b] | 77.6 | 59.8 | 31.0 | 64.0 | 88.4 | 109.0 | 111.5 | 1,002.8 |
| Business corporations | 3.1 | 8.9 | 12.1 | 8.7 | 4.9 | 2.8 | 5.5 | 95.7 |
| State & local government | 3.3 | 1.2 | 3.4 | 4.9 | 11.9 | 15.2 | 9.0 | 70.3 |
| Foreign[c] | 4.4 | 16.2 | 4.6 | 15.2 | 37.5 | 37.4 | 31.9 | 187.8 |
| Subtotal | 163.9 | 148.5 | 144.0 | 225.3 | 310.2 | 332.3 | 322.8 | 2,801.5 |
| Residual (mostly household direct) | 37.7 | 36.3 | 31.9 | 23.3 | 37.8 | 49.2 | 66.3 | 493.0 |
| Total net supply of credit | 201.6 | 184.8 | 175.9 | 248.6 | 348.0 | 381.5 | 389.1 | 3,294.5 |
| | Percentage Growth in Outstandings | | | | | | | |
| Total credit | 11.5% | 9.5% | 8.2% | 10.7% | 13.5% | 13.1% | 11.8% | |
| Government | 7.0 | 7.6 | 16.7 | 12.9 | 13.6 | 11.3 | 10.1 | |
| Household | 12.8 | 6.6 | 5.6 | 11.0 | 14.6 | 13.8 | 11.0 | |
| Corporate | 11.4 | 16.0 | 3.9 | 8.1 | 11.9 | 13.9 | 14.9 | |
| Long-term | 13.5 | 11.2 | 8.2 | 11.3 | 14.3 | 19.8 | 14.0 | |
| Short-term | 9.9 | 8.0 | 8.2 | 10.2 | 13.0 | 11.5 | 9.8 | |
| Held by nonbank finance | 10.1 | 7.6 | 10.5 | 13.6 | 15.1 | 13.1 | 11.8 | |
| Commercial banks | 13.5 | 7.2 | 4.4 | 8.7 | 11.0 | 12.2 | 11.1 | |
| Foreign | 6.1 | 21.1 | 4.7 | 15.6 | 33.2 | 24.9 | 17.0 | |
| Household direct | 13.6 | 11.5 | 9.1 | 6.1 | 9.3 | 11.1 | 13.5 | |
| Economic correlations | | | | | | | | |
| Growth in real GNP | 5.5 | 1.4 | 1.3 | 5.7 | 4.9 | 3.8 | 2.6 | |
| Nominal GNP | 11.6 | 8.1 | 8.2 | 11.2 | 11.0 | 11.6 | 11.0 | |

[a]Excludes funds for equities, cash, and miscellaneous demands not tabulated above.
[b]Includes loans transferred to books of nonoperating holding and other bank-related companies.
[c]Includes U.S. branches of foreign banks.

Source: Salomon Brothers, New York.

considerably larger than that of Salomon Brothers—almost as large as that shown in the illustrative framework (Tables 25-1 and 25-2). On the demand side (uses of funds), this summary excludes security RPs and Federal Funds and security credit other than that extended by banks, as well as Federal Home Loan Bank System advances to savings and loan associations; but these differences are relatively minor in their effects on the total. In addition, several of the categories, such as U.S. gov-

**Table 25-5   Sources and Uses of Funds in the United States Money and Capital Markets, 1973–1979 (in billions of dollars)**

|  | 1973 | 1974 | 1975 | 1976 | 1977 | 1978 | 1979e |
|---|---|---|---|---|---|---|---|
| **SOURCES OF FUNDS** | | | | | | | |
| Life insurance companies | 15.9 | 15.6 | 19.0 | 26.6 | 29.1 | 33.2 | 34.8 |
| Noninsured pension funds | 7.6 | 7.9 | 12.8 | 11.0 | 15.6 | 13.9 | 19.9 |
| State and local retirement funds | 9.1 | 9.3 | 11.8 | 13.1 | 15.5 | 18.7 | 20.9 |
| Savings and loan associations | 27.2 | 18.1 | 37.0 | 51.5 | 63.3 | 58.5 | 52.6 |
| Mutual savings banks | 4.7 | 3.4 | 10.9 | 12.6 | 11.6 | 8.6 | 3.9 |
| Commercial banking | 81.3 | 64.5 | 31.6 | 66.1 | 90.0 | 125.9 | 125.0 |
| Federal Reserve banks | 9.2 | 6.1 | 8.5 | 9.9 | 7.2 | 7.0 | 4.5 |
| Federal loan agencies | 13.3 | 26.5 | 29.9 | 28.4 | 32.3 | 49.7 | 64.1 |
| Nonfinancial corporations | 9.4 | 14.3 | 14.3 | 17.0 | 12.8 | 15.8 | 34.8 |
| Fire and casualty companies | 5.8 | 4.1 | 6.7 | 13.5 | 18.7 | 18.0 | 19.5 |
| Real estate investment trusts | 5.6 | 0.2 | (4.9) | (3.7) | (2.4) | (1.0) | (0.4) |
| Mutual funds | (2.0) | (0.2) | 0.4 | (0.8) | (1.5) | 1.8 | 11.5 |
| Foreigners | 3.4 | 11.7 | 10.8 | 18.0 | 42.1 | 40.1 | (8.3) |
| Individuals and others | 50.2 | 38.0 | 37.2 | 40.6 | 55.7 | 70.0 | 72.8 |
| Total sources | 240.7 | 219.4 | 226.0 | 303.8 | 390.0 | 460.0 | 455.5 |
| **USES OF FUNDS** | | | | | | | |
| Corporate and foreign bonds | 13.6 | 23.9 | 36.4 | 37.2 | 36.1 | 31.6 | 30.0 |
| Corporate stocks | 10.4 | 4.8 | 10.8 | 12.9 | 4.8 | 4.7 | 6.5 |
| State and local govt. issues | 15.0 | 17.2 | 16.3 | 17.7 | 23.9 | 26.7 | 23.5 |
| Federal government issues | 7.8 | 12.0 | 85.8 | 69.1 | 57.6 | 55.1 | 36.5 |
| Federal agency issues | 20.4 | 22.0 | 12.3 | 19.0 | 26.7 | 40.1 | 46.0 |
| Mortgages | | | | | | | |
| Residential | 55.3 | 40.2 | 41.4 | 67.3 | 106.8 | 115.5 | 117.0 |
| Nonresidential | 24.6 | 20.3 | 15.8 | 19.7 | 27.2 | 33.5 | 42.0 |
| Consumer credit | 26.0 | 9.9 | 9.7 | 25.6 | 40.6 | 50.6 | 43.0 |
| Commercial paper | 6.5 | 7.9 | (1.8) | 3.6 | 11.3 | 17.3 | 27.0 |
| Business loans | 47.9 | 49.5 | (11.9) | 9.6 | 38.2 | 53.7 | 65.5 |
| All other loans | 13.3 | 11.3 | 11.2 | 22.1 | 16.9 | 31.2 | 18.5 |
| Total uses | 240.7 | 219.4 | 226.0 | 303.8 | 390.0 | 460.0 | 455.5 |

Note: The uses of funds measure the net changes in outstanding loans and securities; the sources of funds measure the net changes in ownership. Because of rounding, components may not add to totals shown.

e — Estimated.

Source: American Council of Life Insurance, Washington, D.C.

ernment issues (which include some U.S. government loans) and business credit, differ; while nonbusiness loans of banks and others are lumped into the fairly large category "all other loans." The supply side does not segregate credit union, security broker and dealer, and U.S. and state and local government takings of credit instruments; this tends to enlarge the residual (individuals and others), with the result that the ACLI residual is much larger than that shown in Table 25-2.

When utilizing the various flow of funds projections, it is helpful to understand the major causes of the differences in the size of the totals of demands for funds and of the residual. The two examples given here should alert the reader, however, to the fact that what is important is that the various

systems furnish users with projections that can compare behavior today with behavior in the past, on a consistent basis, and that provide insights into the probable trend, if not the magnitude, of the likely change in interest rates for the period projected.

## Projecting Sources and Uses of Funds by Sector

The volume of financing in any one period is related to the volume of spending and saving in the economy, but the relationship is far from precise. Similarly, Federal Reserve policy affects the volume of spending and saving, but only indirectly and imperfectly, through influencing the cost and availability of funds borrowed by the economic sectors to finance investment projects or consumption.[19] Thus, the starting point for a set of projections of sources and uses of funds statements for credit instruments and investor groups is usually an economic projection of the components of the gross national product (the spending, income, and saving) of the various sectors. Also, it is necessary to formulate a specific Federal Reserve policy.[20]

However, the sources and uses of funds statements of the various sectors underlying a flow of funds summary contain many items that are only very indirectly and remotely related to the GNP magnitudes.[21] It is in these areas where the flow of funds analyst must make corollary assumptions—some of which depend on noneconomic variables—by drawing on his or her accumulated fund of knowledge regarding past trends and current developments. Even so, when such corollary assumptions are made regarding demands for funds, the supply of funds available for a specific credit instrument may not be consistent with the size of the demand projected, so that one or both of the original assessments may need to be scaled down or expanded in the process of iteration. The following discussion deals with the essential factors in the process of building up and modifying the interlock-

---

[19] In the real world, of course, financing availability has repercussions on, and can change the course of, spending. Under present methods of projecting the volume of financing, such feedbacks are just beginning to be identified. Thus, for forecasting purposes, they usually need to be assumed at the outset in connection with the general assumption on Federal Reserve policy underlying the economic outlook.

[20] For an economic outlook, the assumption of Federal Reserve policy can be stated within a broad range: from relative ease to very restrictive. However, for a flow of funds projection, the assumption of Federal Reserve policy must be specific as to the degree of tightness or ease in order to obtain the size of the increase in bank deposits and bank credit anticipated.

[21] It should be pointed out that, when some of the spending by one sector represents a transfer of assets from another sector, the total volume of funds raised or supplied is not affected as, for example, when corporate business buys used plant and equipment from noncorporate business or when institutional investors buy common stocks from individuals. In the latter case, the transaction appears as an increase in the holdings of common stock of the institutional investor and a decline in such holdings of individuals.

ing sources and uses of funds statements, which underlie each of the items in the summary tables.

## Corporate Sector

Some of the large cyclical magnitudes in the sources and uses of funds statement of the nonfinancial corporate sector—plant and equipment, inventories, and internal funds—can be determined through a cut-and-dried computation of the nonfinancial corporate share of the corresponding variable in the GNP. Only two items of spending on physical assets—foreign investment and oil leases—must be derived from different source material on the basis of likely developments in those fields. Internal funds tend to finance a higher percentage of spending on physical assets in recovery years than in recession or boom years. For example, in 1974 the proportion was 56 percent whereas, in 1976, it was over 90 percent and had fallen back to 70 percent by 1978. However, nonfinancial corporations must cover other requirements, such as net trade credit (since their trade credits—accounts receivable—usually exceed their trade debts). The sources and uses of funds of nonfinancial corporations are shown in Table 25-6.

Furthermore, the financing undertaken by nonfinancial corporations to meet liquidity requirements must be considered. The analysis of liquidity requirements involves the projection of liquidity and debt ratios. For this purpose, balance sheet (or outstanding) amounts of both liquid assets (deposits, short-term securities, and other short-term credit instruments) and current liabilities (open-market paper, bank loans, finance company loans, U.S. government loans, trade debt, and miscellaneous) must each be totaled. Thus, the projections of acquisitions of liquid assets and of short-term debt are worked out in tandem, using as guides corporate psychology and liquidity preferences, the relative advantages of lending and borrowing in various markets, and the behavior of other borrowers and lenders.

After juggling all of these considerations (and bearing in mind that securities issued by utilities are more directly related to plant and equipment spending than in other industries), the forecaster is in a position to formulate projections, not only for the various types of credit market instruments

**Table 25-6    Sources and Uses of Funds of Non-financial Corporations, 1978 (in billions of dollars)**

| SOURCES OF FUNDS | |
|---|---|
| Internal sources | |
| Retained profits[a] | $ 34.0 |
| Depreciation and depletion[b] | 107.6 |
| Profit tax liability | 1.8 |
| Total | 143.4 |
| Funds raised in credit markets | |
| Mortgages | 23.4 |
| Corporate bonds | 20.1 |
| Corporate stocks | 2.6 |
| Corporate tax-exempt bonds | 3.2 |
| Open-market paper | 3.9 |
| Bank loans | 27.9 |
| Finance company loans | 8.3 |
| U.S. government loans | 1.7 |
| Total | 91.2 |
| Miscellaneous liabilities | 3.5 |
| *Total sources of funds* | $238.1 |
| USES OF FUNDS | |
| Physical assets | |
| Plant and equipment | $173.1 |
| Residential structures | 3.8 |
| Foreign investments | 3.8 |
| Mineral rights from U.S. government | 2.0 |
| Inventories | 16.8 |
| Total | 199.6 |
| Credit market instruments | |
| U.S. government securities | (6.6) |
| Federal agency securities | .7 |
| State & local government securities | .2 |
| Open-market paper | 1.7 |
| Security RPs | 6.1 |
| Consumer credit | 1.1 |
| Total | 3.3 |
| Other assets | |
| Demand deposits & currency | 5.0 |
| Time deposits, including CDs | 2.0 |
| Net trade credit | 6.3 |
| Miscellaneous | 6.1 |
| Total | 19.4 |
| *Total uses of funds* | $222.3 |
| Discrepancy (sources less uses) | $ 15.8 |

[a]Undistributed profits less inventory profits (inventory valuation adjustment).
[b]Including capital consumption adjustment to allow for replacement rather than book value of depreciation.

Source: Board of Governors of the Federal Reserve System, *Flow of Funds Accounts*, May 1979.

raised, but also for those purchased (incidentally, the total for the latter constitutes the funds supplied to the credit markets shown in summary Table 25-6).

### Federal Sector

The prospective receipts, expenditures, and deficit of the federal government are spelled out officially in the January and mid-year reviews of the federal budget. The Congressional Budget Office publishes revised estimates from time to time.[22] However, analysts usually keep close track of current federal income and outgo, often modifying even the latest official estimates.[23] The federal government's financing requirements depend not only on the budget deficit but also on the financing needs of the Federal Financing Bank and other off-budget lending, as well as on changes in the cash position of the Treasury and other means of financing. Thus, in order to project a sources and uses of funds statement for the federal government, it is useful to keep track also of the burgeoning amounts of federal direct loans and loan guarantees, most of which are now financed through Treasury securities, either within the budget or through the Federal Financing Bank.[24]

In addition to the direct lending of the federal government, the sponsored federal agencies, such as the Federal National Mortgage Association and

[22] *The Budget of the United States Government, Fiscal Year,* Government Printing Office, Washington, D.C., is issued in January to cover the fiscal year in progress (now ending September 30) and the following fiscal year. The estimates are modified, because of the course of events and congressional action, by the Office of Management and Budget in a mid-year review. Also, the Congressional Budget Office issues periodic reports entitled, "Congressional Budget Scorekeeping Report," which show the current state of congressional action on the budget. (Congressional Budget Office, U.S. Congress, Washington, D.C.).

[23] Current federal income and outgo can be followed from the "Monthly Treasury Statement of Receipts and Outlays of the United States Government," Bureau of Government Financial Operations, Department of the Treasury, Washington, D.C.

[24] See ibid., Table IV, for means of financing. Federal government direct and guaranteed lending, by type of loan, is laid out in detail for fiscal years in Special Analysis "E" of the budget, along with projections. Quarterly data are available from the *Treasury Bulletin.*

the Farm Credit Administration, raise funds through direct market borrowings to make housing or agricultural loans. Those borrowings are treated, in the illustrative flow of funds framework, as part of the demand for funds; the lending is treated as part of supply. In order to follow developments on the sources and uses of funds of federal agencies, one must keep track of government programs and developments in the housing and agricultural fields.[25]

## State and Local Governments

The projections for state and local government borrowing and purchases of credit instruments begin with projections of state and local government receipts and expenditures (including construction expenditures), which are covered in the basic economic projections. State and local governments borrow at long term to finance construction projects, but they also borrow at both short and long term for other purposes, such as to meet liquidity requirements or to refund outstanding issues in advance of their due dates when a significant saving on the interest paid is involved.

The relationship between state and local government bond borrowings and construction expenditures, while useful to examine, is subject to great variation, so that considerations involving the probable size of refunding, including advance refunding, the nature and composition of unusual expenditures, or financing arrangements (such as bonds backed by single-family housing mortgages) and liquidity requirements must be weighed. State and local governments tend to build up their liquidity even when they are running deficits, but the build-up is larger when they are running surpluses and rises with the size of the surplus. Thus, the determination of state and local government borrowings, by type, and their acquisitions of credit instruments are other areas where the forecaster must resort to corollary assumptions, which draw on knowledge of current market conditions or other developments in the field. The sources and uses of funds of state and local governments are shown in Table 25-7.

[25]Data on borrowing and lending of sponsored agencies can be obtained periodically from the *Treasury Bulletin* or from the institutions themselves.

## Table 25-7 Sources and Uses of Funds of State and Local Governments, 1978 (in billions of dollars)

| SOURCES OF FUNDS | |
|---|---:|
| Credit market borrowings | |
| Bonds | $ 26.8 |
| Notes | .2 |
| Total | 27.0 |
| U.S. government loans | −1.5 |
| Total | 25.5 |
| Other liabilities (trade debt) | 1.0 |
| Total sources of funds (financial liabilities) | $ 26.5 |
| USES OF FUNDS | |
| Credit market instruments | |
| Mortgages | $ 1.0 |
| U.S. government securities | 17.1 |
| Federal agency securities | 4.1 |
| State & local government securities | .9 |
| Total | 23.1 |
| Other assets | |
| Demand deposits & currency | −1.5 |
| Time deposits | 7.8 |
| Taxes receivable | 1.2 |
| Total | 7.5 |
| Total uses of funds (financial assets) | $ 30.6 |
| Net financial investment (financial assets less financial liabilities) | $ 4.1 |
| Less general fund surplus or deficit (−)[a] | 11.2 |
| Discrepancy | −7.1 |
| Memoranda | |
| Receipts[a] | $328.1 |
| Expenditures[a] | 299.8 |
| Total surplus or deficit (−) | 28.4 |
| Social insurance funds (state & local retirement, etc.) | 17.2 |
| General funds | 11.2 |

Note: Details may not add to totals because of rounding.
[a]National Income Accounts basis.

Source: Board of Governors of the Federal Reserve System, *Flow of Funds Accounts,* May 1979.

## Consumer Credit

Another major sector for which projections depend on the underlying economic assumptions, at least indirectly, is that of consumer credit. Projections of the various types of instalment credit extended—automobile, mobile home, revolving (including credit cards and check credit), and other (including personal loans)—are generally related to the amounts of the appropriate types of consumer spending in the GNP. It is then necessary to estimate repayments through examining their trend and behavior in comparison with consumer credit extensions over time in the past.[26] From the totals of the various types of new credits extended and repaid, net changes in instalment credit can be computed and, along with projections of noninstalment credit, can be consolidated into the one figure for consumer credit used in a summary table on the demand side. On the supply side, consumer credit is provided by finance companies, commercial banks, some savings institutions, and nonfinancial business. The volume so provided is worked into, and may be modified by, the constraints provided by the sources and uses of funds for each of these separate groups.

## Consumer Sector

The consumer or household sector, as a whole, can be analyzed in connection with the basic economic assumptions for income, spending, saving, and investment, and a total for the net increase in the financial assets of individuals obtained. Personal saving in the National Income Accounts can be translated into the Flow of Funds Accounts as consisting of the net increase in financial assets of individuals plus their net investment in consumer durables, less the net increase in their debts (also in government insurance and pension reserves as well as in capital gains and dividends). Thus, from an estimate for personal saving (NIA basis) and spending on consumer durables (less depreciation), together with the already determined projections for the net increase in mortgage and consumer debt (and a few minor debt items, including a statistical discrepancy), it is possible to determine a projection of the net increase in financial assets.[27]

The projected net increase in financial assets can be distributed among the various types of financial assets, including demand deposits, time deposits, insurance and pension reserves, and mutual fund shares, as well as credit market instruments and miscellaneous assets. The projected net changes in

demand deposit holdings of individuals can be based in broad terms on the money supply assumptions used, while the portion allocated as an inflow of funds to nonbank financial intermediaries (time deposits, insurance and pension reserves, and mutual fund shares) depends on assumptions regarding any pickup or slowdown in the rates of growth of the various types of institutions, as well as on any possible disintermediation, and competitive or other special (regulatory or other) trends and developments underway. The balance, after miscellaneous assets have been determined, represents the direct contribution of the consumer sector to the credit markets (net purchases of credit instruments). Through this method, the total contribution to the financial markets of the household sector, either through financial intermediaries or through direct purchases of credit market instruments, is related indirectly to the economic background.

## Nonbank Financial Intermediaries

The analysis of the consumer sector provides a start for the projections of the sources and uses of funds of the nonbank financial intermediaries. The listing of these institutions in Table 25-2 (called *savings institutions* in the table) begins with life insurance companies, and that group will be used as an example, since space does not permit a complete description of the assumptions needed for projecting the sources and uses of funds of each group.

Sources of funds of life insurance companies consist mainly of additions to insurance and pension reserves, which will already have been obtained in the process of distributing the net increase in financial assets of individuals. Miscellaneous liabilities and current surplus can be projected on a trend basis, with modifications for any cyclical, inflationary, or competitive movements underway. The sources and uses of funds of life insurance companies are shown in Table 25-8.

On the uses side, life insurance companies have wider investment powers and opportunities than any other type of nonbank intermediary. In addition to purchasing mortgages—on income-producing properties in particular—they acquire stocks, bonds, government securities, and commercial paper and make policy loans. They also purchase

---

[26]In this assessment, the use of an econometric technique known as the Almon distributed lag is appropriate.

[27]The Salomon Brothers study, cited earlier, contains such a table in somewhat modified form.

**Table 25-8  Sources and Uses of Funds of Life Insurance Companies, 1978 (in billions of dollars)**

| SOURCES OF FUNDS | |
|---|---:|
| Life insurance reserves | $  8.7 |
| Pension fund reserves | 17.6 |
| Miscellaneous liabilities | 8.7 |
| Current surplus | 4.0 |
| Total sources of funds | $ 39.0 |
| **USES OF FUNDS** | |
| Credit market instruments | |
| Mortgages | $  9.2 |
| Corporate bonds | 17.4 |
| Corporate stocks | .7 |
| U.S. government securities | (.5) |
| Federal agency securities | 2.4 |
| State & local government securities | .2 |
| Open-market paper | 1.9 |
| Policy loans | 2.6 |
| Total | 33.9 |
| Other assets | |
| Plant and equipment | 2.3 |
| Demand deposits & currency | — |
| Miscellaneous assets | 1.8 |
| Total | 4.1 |
| Total uses of funds | $ 38.0 |
| Discrepancy (sources less uses) | $  1.0 |

Source: Board of Governors of the Federal Reserve System, *Flow of Funds Accounts,* May 1979.

large amounts of plant and equipment, as when John Hancock or Prudential builds big towers.[28] The investment pattern of life insurance companies varies with their differing choices under changing circumstances. As a consequence, projecting their specific net new investments requires an up-to-date examination of current trends and of their past and probable inclination for future participation in each area.

## Foreign Sector

Currently, one of the large investing groups supplying funds to the U.S. credit markets is the foreign sector. The net financial investment of foreigners (their total financial assets owned less their

[28]Although, in the past, some life insurance companies have undertaken other real estate investments through housing projects, their current participation in the real estate business is almost universally confined to lending.

financial liabilities owed in this country) represents the net surplus or deficit on current account (net exports in the National Income Accounts) plus a statistical discrepancy. From the net financial investment, gross totals for financial assets and liabilities can be projected; these are then disaggregated, according to current trends, into various types, including the following: purchases of bonds and stocks and deposits in banks, on the asset side; and foreign bonds and stocks raised in the United States and loans from U.S. banks, on the liability side. Nevertheless, the net provides a constraint to the size of both totals.

## Commercial Banks

A key group for projection purposes is commercial banks. The projections for sources of funds of the commercial banking sector (which includes holding companies and other affiliates) depend heavily on the assumption regarding Federal Reserve policy for determination of the increase in demand and time deposits. (Incidentally, a sources and uses of funds statement is also needed for the Federal Reserve.) However, commercial banks have developed and utilize several nondeposit sources of funds, such as sales of debentures, commercial paper, security RPs, and Eurodollars, in addition to the funds that they obtain through sales of stock and retained profits. The sources and uses of funds of commercial banks are shown in Table 25-9.

On the uses side, the demands for bank loans emanating from the business and consumer sectors have already been obtained in the course of the analysis of those sectors. Vault cash and reserves are, of course, related to deposits (after allowing for any change in reserve requirements). Also, investment in plant and equipment and in miscellaneous assets can be trended. Security holdings and the remaining asset and liability items are then treated, as in the case of nonfinancial corporations, by examining options open to the banks in the light of liquidity considerations, in the course of which one can work out a reasonable balance between supply and demand.

## Mortgage Financing

The mortgage sector provides an illustration of how the amount of spending on current production does

**Table 25-9 Sources and Uses of Funds of Commercial Banks,[a] 1978 (in billions of dollars)**

| SOURCES OF FUNDS | |
|---|---:|
| Credit market borrowings | |
| Corporate bonds | $ .2 |
| Corporate stocks | .2 |
| Open-market paper | 4.3 |
| Security RPs & Federal Funds | 7.0 |
| Total | 11.7 |
| Deposits | |
| Demand | 21.0 |
| Time | 68.7 |
| Total | 89.7 |
| Other | |
| Federal Reserve & Eurodollar borrowing | 12.5 |
| Interbank claims | 13.6 |
| Miscellaneous liabilities, including F.R. float | 24.9 |
| Current surplus | 3.7 |
| Total | 54.8 |
| Total sources of funds | $156.2 |
| USES OF FUNDS | |
| Credit market instruments | |
| Mortgages | $ 35.0 |
| Corporate bonds | (.2) |
| U.S. government securities | (6.3) |
| Federal agency securities | 7.0 |
| State and local government securities | 7.8 |
| Open-market paper | (1.3) |
| Loans to nonfinancial business | 32.9 |
| Loans to financial business | 1.6 |
| Foreign loans | 15.8 |
| Consumer credit | 26.9 |
| Security credit | (3.4) |
| Other loans | 2.7 |
| Total | 118.5 |
| Other assets | |
| Plant and equipment | 4.2 |
| Vault cash and reserves | 6.0 |
| Interbank claims | 13.6 |
| Other | 20.8 |
| Total | 44.6 |
| Total uses of funds | $163.1 |
| Discrepancy (sources less uses) | $ (6.9) |

[a]Including affiliates, holding companies, Edge Act corporations, agencies of foreign banks, and banks in U.S. possessions.

Source: Board of Governors of the Federal Reserve System, *Flow of Funds Accounts,* May 1979.

not directly or even necessarily indicate the volume of financing. The relationship between spending on new construction in the GNP accounts and mortgage financing is far from stable from year to year and, indeed, has gradually shifted toward a larger percentage of mortgages per construction dollar over the years. Twenty-five years ago, net new single-family mortgages amounted to about 50 percent of total new single-family construction; multifamily mortgages to 30 percent of multifamily construction; and commercial mortgages to 15 percent of commercial construction. By 1978 the percentages had more than doubled to 116 percent, 65 percent, and 37 percent, respectively.

The instability of the relationship from year to year is due to changes in the rate of turnover of properties and the leads and lags between construction and financing over relatively short periods, when real estate is picking up or slowing down. It may also be caused by shifts in the composition of construction, for example, as between multifamily and single-family housing. The trend toward larger and even excess percentages of mortgages to construction may be ascribed to a number of factors: rising land prices and values of resales, higher loan-to-value ratios, easier mortgage availability, and a tendency to raise funds through mortgages for purposes other than to meet construction expenditures or purchase a property, as well as the current effort to use housing investment as an inflation hedge.

In assessing the outlook for mortgages, all of these factors need to be taken into consideration. The factors affecting mortgages have differing impacts with respect to the various types of mortgages, so that separate projections should be made for home, multifamily, commercial, and farm mortgages. As a start, the GNP accounts are based on estimates of new construction of each type. Home mortgages cover not only new single-family units but also mortgages on existing homes and on condominiums in apartment buildings, so that projections of mortgages in these areas need to take account of an adjustment for this, as well as for the differential impact of turnover, land costs, and resale prices. Projections for the other classes of mortgages require similar considerations.[29]

[29]The ratio of mortgages to construction can be projected by weighting these factors based on the analyst's best judgment. A desirable check on these results can be achieved through a regression analysis of the relation-

The specific availability of funds to each institutional group is also of importance in the net generation of mortgages. After the initial projections for the total of net new mortgages issued of each type have been made on the basis of basic demands, these projections may not agree with the totals that have been developed from the sources and uses of funds projections for each group. It is then necessary to undertake the process of iteration, making reasonable adjustments where they appear necessary.

The foregoing explanation does no more than highlight the various types of methods used for projecting demands and supplies in the many sources and uses of funds statements backing up a summary. As the explanation has progressed, it has become increasingly evident that the accounts are almost completely interlocking. A projection of commercial mortgage purchases in the sources and uses of funds table of life insurance companies will also be needed in the table on commercial mortgages and may affect purchases by other sectors or may even affect total purchases of commercial mortgages. Thus, the first round of projections results in a system of checks and balances between one item and another; it may turn out that a factor has been overlooked or that a different corollary assumption would be more appropriate. Hopefully, this process of iteration through trial and error eventually leads to the desired, internally consistent, and integrated picture of financial flows.

## Interpreting Projections

Little would be gained for the reader by critiquing or rehashing past projections.[30] It would be useful instead to describe how to read a set of projections, assuming perfect foresight. How would a set of

accurate flow of funds projections lead you to the conclusion that interest rates would behave as they actually do?

### The Residual as an Indicator

First, it is useful to look at some of the measures that can be developed from flows of funds that give clues to the general financial environment and to the probable trend of interest rates. One measure, movements in the residual, has already been mentioned. The annual movements in the amount of the actual residual and in the average auction yield on 3-month Treasury bills are shown in Figure 25-3. Short-term Treasury bills are used in this context as representative of the general trend of interest rates. One *caveat,* however, is that the greater volatility of short-term rates than of long-term rates, shown in Figure 25-1, makes it necessary to forecast the two types of rates separately. However, the following discussion will center on short-term rates.[31]

Figure 25-3 shows that the movements in the annual averages of yields on 3-month Treasury bills tended to follow the pattern of the residual during the calendar years 1952–1978.[32] Although there were exceptions, in periods when the residual declined, interest rates also declined, and vice versa. In almost every case, when large and abrupt changes occurred in the amount of the residual,

[31]Short-term Treasury bill yields are sometimes affected by special factors and may fluctuate at slightly—but not significantly—higher or lower levels than the "general market." Also, the use of annual averages for interest rates obscures interim changes over the course of a year but, for most years, the change from year-end to year-end conforms with the change in the annual average. The exceptions were years of abrupt changes toward year-end, when rates fell as a recession was developing (1953, 1957, and 1974) or rose as one was ending (1961 and 1972). Even so, the changes in the averages are generally more representative of developments than are the year-end to year-end changes.

[32]The statistical tests referred to in the following footnotes, such as the coefficients of determination showing the degree of relationship between variables ($R^2$), covered annual data. On a quarterly basis, the leads and lags and "noise" make the statistical relationships less precise, but the general tendency shown by the annual averages is still visible. Also, where applicable, the regressions were adjusted to correct for regular patterns in the unexplained portion of the association between the variables (or autocorrelation).

ships, based on the effects of loan-to-value ratios, trend variables, prices, and general availability of financing. This is one of the areas where statistical and econometric techniques are very useful.

[30]Although a study comparing sets of projections of flow of funds with the actuals was made covering the years 1953–1963 (Ronk, *The Sources and Uses of Funds Approach . . . to Interest Rate Developments,* pp. 159–267), no definitive recent studies have been circulated. An obstacle to the comparison lies in the frequent revisions in the basic data from which the projections were made.

**Figure 25-3   The Residual and Interest Rates**

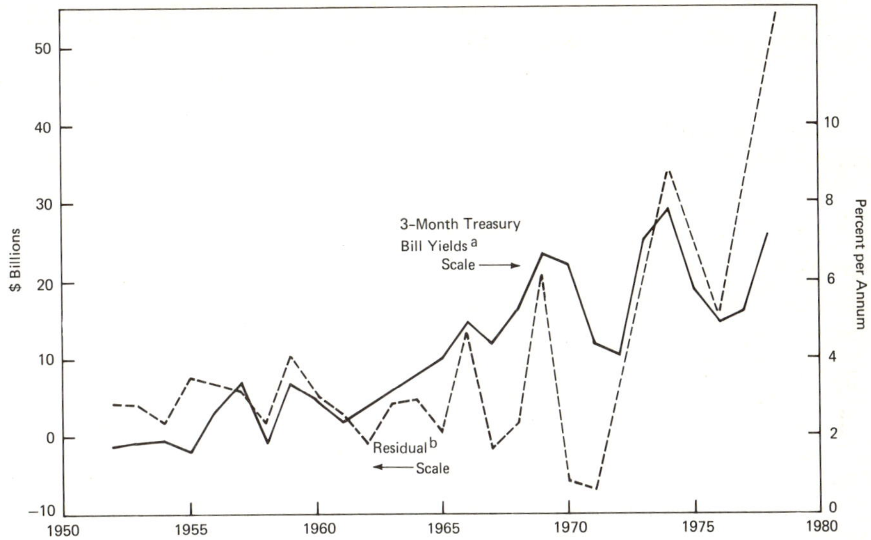

[a]Annual averages of auction rates.
[b]Funds supplied to credit markets by noninstitutional sources (individuals and others).

Sources: Department of the Treasury and Board of Governors of the Federal Reserve System.

they were accompanied by shifts in Treasury bill yields in the same direction. For the exceptions during the twenty-seven-year span—when interest rates rose even though the residual declined (1956, 1957, 1962, and 1965) or interest rates declined even though the residual rose (1972)—the changes in both the residual and interest rates were almost invariably moderate. Thus, it appears that the residual is a significant indicator of the direction, but not of the amount, of change in Treasury bill yields.[33] (However, in recent years with the growth of specialized investing groups, such as municipal

bond funds and corporate bond funds, which act as intermediaries for individuals but are not identified separately in the statistics, a higher floor than formerly has been placed under the size of the residual.)

The general behavior described above is true not only of the size of the residual itself but also of the residual as a percentage of GNP and of funds raised.[34] The latter two measures place the residual into perspective with the huge increases in the economy and in the volume of funds raised in recent years. Thus, the residual, if it can be gauged

[33]Figure 25-3 shows the general similarity in movements pictorially, but gives an exaggerated impression of the relative degree of change in the dependent variable (Treasury bill yields) associated with the independent variable (the residual). This is because the scales used in Figure 25-3 roughly coincide with the amplitude of the fluctuations in each variable. Statistically, the whole period 1952–1978 showed a somewhat better fit ($R^2$ of .79) than did the more recent period 1966–1978 ($R^2$ of .48), when the financial structure was undergoing change and interest rates fluctuations became much more volatile. Nevertheless, a regression of changes in Treasury bill yields on changes in the residual over the whole period 1952–1978, which—because of the greater volatility of

data showing year-to-year changes rather than outstandings—would be expected to produce very low $R^2$s, yielded relatively good results ($R^2$ of .42). As for changes in direction, the equation predicted nine out of the twelve turning points, thereby reinforcing the conclusion that the residual is more useful for predicting the direction of change in Treasury bill yields than for the amount of change.

[34]The regressions for these two variables against Treasury bill yields—as well as for changes in either variable and/or in Treasury bill yields—also produced high $R^2$s, as was the case for the regressions for the amount of the residual.

correctly, is a good tool for forecasting the direction of change in short-term interest rates.

Another clue to the type of prospective financial environment indicated by a set of flow of funds projections consists of the lead time between the movements in the residual and in funds raised as a percentage of GNP. Figure 25-4 shows the residual as a percentage of funds raised and the funds raised as a percentage of GNP. Figure 25-4 shows Treasury bill yields as well.

The funds raised as a percentage of GNP have increased over the years 1952–1978 in tandem with the growth of intermediation and the greater propensity to borrow for investment and consumption spending. Nevertheless, the percentage has fluctuated cyclically around the rising trend. However, the peaks in the funds raised as a percentage of GNP have usually occurred a year before the peaks in the percentage of funds supplied by the residual and the accompanying peaks in interest rates. Similarly, the lows in the funds raised as a percentage of GNP usually preceded the lows in the percentage of funds supplied by the residual or in interest rates.[35] The tendency for the residual—and interest rates—to peak after the percentage of funds raised to GNP has peaked is probably attributable to the tendency for demands for funds to build up to a point where they outrun institutional supplies, thus necessitating heavier residual purchases and higher interest rates before demands are cut back.

## Year-by-Year Analysis

Examining the clues we have mentioned can facilitate the interpretation of a set of flow of funds projections. Nevertheless, a close look at the composition and nature of demands, on the one hand, and of supplies, on the other, is also required. Too often, analysts concentrate on the demand side, but it must be remembered that the supply side is equally important. To illustrate the factors that caused the peaks and valleys in interest rates during

[35] Thus, the ratio of funds raised to GNP forecast the direction of change in short-term interest rates for the following year in seventeen of the eighteen years in the 1961–1978 period. A regression of Treasury bill yields on the percentage of funds raised to GNP, adjusted for autocorrelation, produces an $R^2$ of .63 for the period 1952–1978, but this is improved to an $R^2$ of .76 by lagging the percentage of funds raised to GNP by one year.

the turbulent years 1968–1978, a thumbnail sketch of the credit flows that were important in each year follows. (Refer back to Tables 25-1 and 25-2 for summaries of the actual flows. Note that the following discussion generally refers to the types of funds raised [demands] and of funds supplied under the nomenclature shown in Tables 25-1 and 25-2.)

At the start of 1968, interest rates were below the levels of the previous peak, having receded after the first "credit crunch" of 1966 and the slower growth of 1967. Demands for mortgages, bank loans to business, and consumer credit all increased substantially during the year, for a sharp step-up in total funds raised to a new peak in relation to GNP. A tax increase to finance the Vietnam War was accompanied by an easier monetary policy, which stimulated the economy and raised demands, but the funds supplied by savings institutions increased concomitantly as did those supplied by business and government. As a result, although the residual did rise, it remained so small, at $5.1 billion, or 4.4 percent of funds raised, as to indicate little upward pressure on interest rates. Yet the average rate on 3-month Treasury bills pushed up by about 1 percentage point as prices started to escalate. This is where the effect of inflation and inflationary expectations overrode supply-demand pressures in influencing interest rates.

During the boom in 1969, an accurate set of flow of funds projections would have augured tighter credit markets and higher interest rates. As the economy overheated and business credit demands mounted, mortgage growth stopped and consumer credit leveled off, while other types of borrowings were also curtailed. At the same time, the thrift institutions were hit by severe disintermediation, and bank credit expansion was radically reduced. Therefore, although the volume of total funds raised held at about the 1968 level (and declined in relation to GNP), the residual rose to a new record of $27.8 billion, or 23.7 percent of funds raised. The situation was so extreme that the interest rate forecaster using an accurate set of flow of funds projections would have been able to foresee the much higher interest rates, which did, indeed, materialize.

In addition a special situation developed in the municipal bond market in 1969. There had been, historically, a tendency to cut back new issues of state and local bonds, together with mortgages,

**Figure 25-4  Funds Raised as a Percentage of GNP, the Percentage of the Residual to Funds Raised, and Interest Rates**

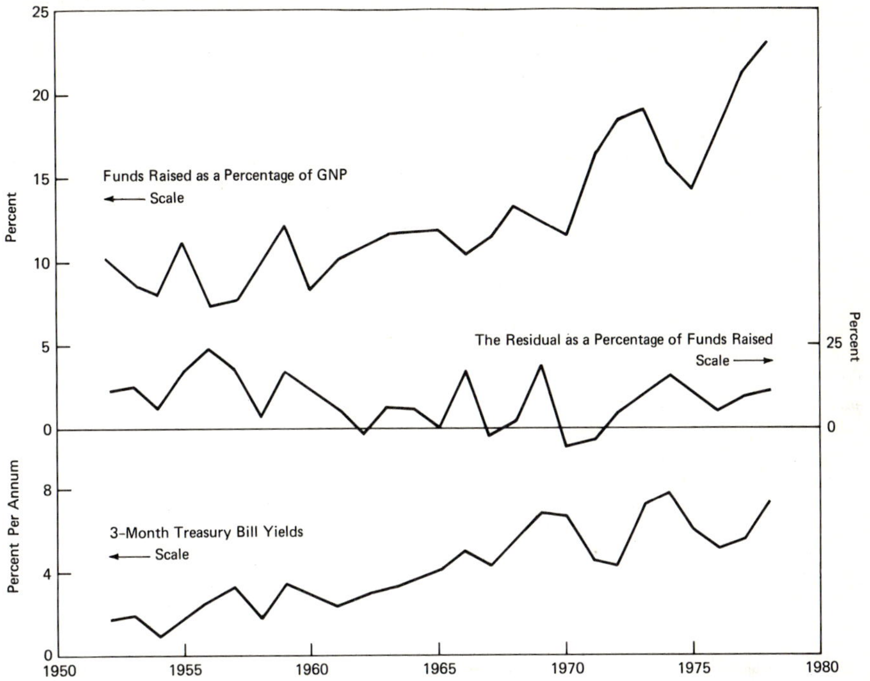

Sources: Department of the Treasury and Board of Governors of the Federal Reserve System.

when business had high loan demands and was able to bid away the available funds. This time, however, additional pressure for impending legislative changes (which appeared to threaten tax exemption) unsettled the municipal bond market. As a result, municipal bond yields rose from about 65 percent of corporate bond yields to 71 percent on an average basis. The interest rate forecaster would have had to recognize this special situation in order to forecast municipal bond yields that year.

In the recession year 1970, the movement of interest rates was also relatively easy to forecast, given the correct figures on flows of funds. As business activity declined, business credit demands contracted severely. Although some of the slack was taken up by higher Treasury cash borrowings—as the Treasury's position turned to deficit—and by higher corporate bond offerings—as corporations stepped in to begin redressing their liquidity—total funds raised declined both in amount and in relation to GNP. On the supply side, how-

ever, flows to savings institutions and bank credit expansion picked up. Thus, the amount of funds supplied by the residual plummeted to a negative figure; that is, residual holders on balance sold credit instruments to institutions. The rapid decline in the residual in 1970 was almost a sure sign that interest rates would head down, but here again, persistently high inflationary expectations kept interest rates from falling by as much as the underlying supply-demand situation might have warranted.

In 1971 and 1972 mounting demands for funds would have misled those interest rate forecasters relying mainly on the demand side of the credit market equation to project interest rates. In fact, before price controls were instituted in August 1971, rates had indeed risen. After inflation slowed down, the government adopted a stimulative tax program. Monetary policy as well as federally imposed price controls began to take effect, and interest rates actually declined through 1971 and into 1972. Even though demands for funds—especially mortgages and state and local government bonds—mounted further, supplies of funds zoomed, as flows to savings institutions and bank credit expansion soared. As a result, the residual became even more negative in 1971 and rose to only a moderately positive level in 1972.

In the years 1973 and 1974, the economy was buffeted by external shocks from the huge food and oil price increases, which, when combined with the overheating and attendant shortages of high and rising economic activity, resulted at times in double-digit annual rates of increase in the wholesale and consumer price indexes. In this adverse environment, mortgage, consumer, and municipal credit demands were progressively curtailed; at the same time, business credit demands soared and business liquidity was squeezed. Also, heavy disintermediation set in again. Throughout most of 1973, the Federal Reserve largely accommodated the swollen credit demands, permitting a record expansion in bank credit, before bearing down heavily to curtail credit in late 1973 and 1974. The result was a mounting residual, which skyrocketed to $30.1 billion in 1973 and $30.7 billion in 1974, reaching 14.1 percent of funds raised. These stresses were accompanied by a rise in interest rates to previously unprecedented levels in 1974. It is safe to say that, before the character and effects of the external shocks had been realized, neither flow of funds analysts nor other types of interest rate forecasters could have fully appreciated—and certainly did not forecast—the concatenation of special events which led to the then historic peaks in interest rates.

The recession, which began in the fall of 1974 and lasted into the spring of 1975, was short-lived but very deep. The cutback in the total volume of funds raised from the 1973 high of $254.7 billion to $218.3 billion in 1974 resulted from some diminution of private demands later in the year as well as from the curtailment of funds from tight credit. The volume of funds raised as a percentage of GNP declined from the high of 19.5 percent in 1973 to 15.5 percent in 1974, thus presaging the subsequent drop in interest rates.

In 1975 the total volume of funds raised leveled off at around $221.7 billion, thus slipping further to 14.5 percent of GNP, as the recovery was not vigorous enough to push demands up by very much.

This was true despite the massive federal deficits, which ballooned federal cash borrowing from the public from $12.0 billion in 1974 to $85.8 billion in 1975. Also, corporate liquidity-building caused corporate bond borrowings to reach a new peak of $36.4 billion in 1975, compared with $13.6 billion and $23.9 billion, respectively, in the two previous years. However, as the result of heavy liquidation of business borrowings and only modest expansion in consumer and other short-term credit, short-term funds outstanding barely grew. At the same time, a mammoth surge of funds to savings institutions and stepped-up purchases of credit instruments by business provided ample funds—despite the meager expansion of bank credit—thereby belying the fears that the massive federal deficits would "crowd out" other borrowings. As a result, the averages of short-term rates showed substantial declines for the year. Long-term rates, on the other hand, while settling back from the 1974 peaks, were under pressure from the exceptionally large corporate and Treasury borrowings and remained high, with their averages showing slight increases for the year. The flow of funds forecaster who had projected these swings in demand and supply was able to forecast the declining trend in short-term interest rates in 1975 and the failure of long-term rates to follow suit.

In 1976 the recovery was well established. Even though there was a temporary economic "pause" that autumn, real GNP grew by 5.9 percent, while the rate of inflation (as measured by the GNP deflator) slackened to 5.2 percent. Paced by revived mortgage activity, demands for funds mounted steeply. Net new corporate bond issues remained on a high plateau; Treasury demands, while falling off, still remained large; and short-term business credit demands picked up. The total volume of funds raised spurted to $315.2 billion, or 18.5 percent of GNP. However, flows to savings institutions continued to soar and bank credit expansion, which had been at a depressed level in 1975, more than doubled. Thus, despite the record volume of funds raised, the residual dropped markedly, to $15.1 billion, or only 4.8 percent of funds raised. It was not surprising, therefore, to flow of funds analysts that interest rates showed a decline for the year. In contrast, demand-oriented—or business-cycle—analysts had been calling for rates to increase with rising business activity.

The year 1977 opened with economic activity rebounding strongly from the slowdown in the second half of 1976 and with credit demands picking up further. Although the rate of increase in real GNP settled back as the year progressed, culminating in another economic "pause" later in the year—with the result that real GNP growth for the year subsided to 5.3 percent—credit demands forged ahead, reaching a new high of 21.3 percent of GNP. Demands for mortgage and consumer credit were especially strong, as housing activity and automobile sales gained momentum. Also, business demands for short-term credit, which had revived in 1976, accelerated. Total demands for credit rose at a somewhat slower pace than in 1976 (28 percent versus 42 percent) only because of a substantial fall-off in corporate long-term borrowings (bonds and stocks) and a further reduction in Treasury borrowing requirements.

On the supply side, however, institutional funds were not as readily available in 1977 as in 1976. The growth of both savings flows to nonbank financial institutions and bank credit slowed down, and corporate liquidity declined as corporations sold money market instruments. However, state and local governments, which were flush with surpluses, stepped in and bought money market instruments heavily. Perhaps most important, foreign investors acquired record amounts of U.S. credit instruments as the dollar weakened. Even so, the pressure of demands for credit against supply heightened, so that the residual more than doubled to $31.9 billion. In relation to funds raised, however, the residual, at only 7.9 percent, was far from a peak. As a consequence, the rise in short-term interest rates for the year was relatively moderate until later in the year, while long-term rates virtually leveled off.

The economic background for credit flows in 1978 was marked by fits and starts of activity, caused by a strong catch-up in the spring from the slowdown stemming from the rough winter weather and a speeding up again at the end of the year. Although real GNP for the year as a whole grew by less than in 1977, or by 4.4 percent, a substantial surge in inflation raised the growth of current-dollar GNP noticeably above the 1977 level. Credit flows also moved erratically during the year, as mortgage expansion dropped sharply and then revived; short-term business credit, after an early speedup, tapered down. In addition, the growth of both corporate and Treasury securities was once again smaller than in the previous year. All in all, total funds raised increased to a new high of 22.7 percent of GNP, reaching $483.8 billion, which was 20 percent above the previous year.

The contribution of nonbank financial institutions to the credit markets in 1978, however, barely held at the prior year's level. Despite continuing growth for insurance-type intermediaries and the burgeoning in money market certificates, money market funds, and Federal Home Loan Bank System advances to savings and loan associations, nonbank financial intermediaries as a group placed fewer funds in credit market instruments than in the year before. On the other hand, foreign investors continued their heavy placement of funds in the U.S. credit markets, while commercial bank credit expansion soared, even though the Federal Reserve acted to tighten credit progressively during the course of the year. Nevertheless, the institutional supplies of funds failed to meet the higher demands, with the result that residual investors were called on to place a record volume of funds— $53.6 billion, or 11.1 percent of funds raised—in the credit markets. Thus, correct projection of supply and demand factors would have pointed to a sharp rise in interest rates during 1978, even without the drastic action of November (which included raising the discount rate by one percentage point) to stem the large outflow of dollars abroad. Over the year, 3-month Treasury bill rates averaged 7.22 percent and reached 9.12 percent for the month of December.

## Conclusion

The financial markets make up a complex system. Correctly forecasting the flow of funds requires intimate knowledge of the whole system and its many-faceted interrelationships. Although flow of funds analyses and methods of projection are constantly being improved, there is still much room for further research and development of the empirical analysis that we have described, as well as development of its theoretical underpinnings. Not only is much more exploration needed regarding the relationships within the financial system, but our incomplete knowledge of the interactions between the financial system and the real economy should be enlarged as well.

Within the financial system itself, there are forces and trends underway that should be examined more thoroughly. For example, this discussion has centered on the concept of credit flows and has only touched on the relationships between asset and liability holdings and net worth in relation to financial flows and economic activity. One of the phenomena of the inflationary years of the 1970s has been an acceleration in the growth of debt outstanding in the economy. From 1952 through 1969, total credit market debt outstanding increased at a compound annual rate of 6.8 percent, but from 1969 through 1978 the annual rate of increase jumped to 12.3 percent. This is reflected in the rise in the ratio of credit market debt to GNP from 1.36 in 1952 to a temporary high of 1.55 in 1969, and to 1.74 in 1978. Does this mean that a larger debt structure is required to support GNP, or is it cause for alarm that debt is becoming top-heavy?

Flow of funds analysis has come a long way, far enough to be extremely useful in its present form as an analytical and forecasting tool. It nevertheless has much room for further development and improvement, and it will be interesting to see how flow of funds forecasting unfolds in the future.

## Questions

1. What impediments do interest forecasters face if they try to construct schedules covering the supply and demand for funds as they are conceived of in loanable funds theory? Explain.
2. Since supply equals demand in the flow of funds summaries, how can a set of flow of funds projections aid in forecasting interest rates? What supplemental benefits are there to flow of funds analysis?
3. A set of flow of funds projections depends on underlying assumptions. Explain in detail what assumptions are needed.
4. Describe the differences between the statistics used in a set of flow of funds projections and the statistics that would be used in the system of flows of funds or money flows as it was originally conceived by Morris Copeland. Draw up a skeleton framework for changes in assets distinguishing between the following:
   a. the types of flows of funds covered by interest rate forecasters

b. financial flows
c. money flows
5. What accounts for the differences between the amounts of total demands for funds and of the residual in the projections of the various forecasters?
6. In a flow of funds framework, what is the specific meaning of each part of the phrase: "who borrows from whom for what purpose?" In the statistics on flows of funds, what are the usual components of each part in that phrase?
7. What factors other than the basic amounts of spending on plant, equipment, and inventories must be considered in forecasting external borrowings (long and short term) of nonfinancial corporations? Elaborate.
8. What specific factors in the National Income and Output (GNP) Accounts are important for determining a projection of the flow of funds in the following sectors? Explain why.
   a. State and local government borrowing
   b. Household borrowing through consumer credit
   c. Changes in deposits at savings and loan associations and mutual savings banks
9. What major clues to prospective interest rate movements are available from a set of flow of funds projections? What are the limitations to these clues?
10. To familiarize yourself with flow of funds data, update Tables 25-1 and 25-2 and compare them with the behavior of interest rates. Prepare a brief explanation of how the actual flows in your update affected the actual interest rate movements.

## Selected Bibliography

Board of Governors of the Federal Reserve System. *Introduction to Flow of Funds*. Washington, D.C., 1975.

Butler, William F., and Robert A. Kavesh, eds. *How Business Economists Forecast*. Prentice-Hall, Englewood Cliffs, N.J., 1966.

Conard, Joseph W. *The Behavior of Interest Rates*. National Bureau of Economic Research, New York, 1971.

Freund, William C., and Edward D. Zinbarg. "Application of Flow of Funds to Interest Rate Forecasting." *Journal of Finance* (May 1963).

National Bureau of Economic Research. *The Flow of Funds Approach to Social Accounting*. Princeton University Press, Princeton, N.J., 1962.

Taylor, Stephen P. "Uses of Flow-of-Funds Accounts in the Federal Reserve System." *Journal of Finance* (May 1963).

# 26

# Econometric Models of the Financial Sector

Econometric models of the macroeconomy are a postwar phenomenon whose development coincided with the Keynesian revolution in macroeconomic thinking. Since early Keynesian thinking tended to de-emphasize the importance of the financial sector of the economy, it was given short shrift in most early modeling efforts. Only in the second generation of models that emerged in the late 1960s has the financial sector regained some importance, and only in the third generation of the 1970s are there finally some attempts to integrate the financial sector fully into macroeconometric models.

The specification of econometric models of major financial institutions and their relationships with the real sector of the economy is still under development. The subject is also the center of much controversy because of the increased monetarist emphasis in recent macroeconomic discussions The differences in approaches to monetary theory involve issues crucial to model specification, such as the level of aggregation and the channels of financial influences on the real sector. Although enormous progress has been made in model building over the last two decades, the task is far from complete.

The purpose of this chapter is, first, to explain what an econometric model is and what it can do. A hypothetical model is introduced in order to illustrate and explain the features and uses of macroeconometric models. Next, the characteristics of macroeconometric models are described, with particular emphasis on the financial sector. This is followed by a brief history of macroeconometric model builiding in the United States since its inception less than thirty years ago. Again, this section emphasizes developments in the financial sectors of the various generations of the models. The next section of the chapter continues this discussion with a more detailed review of the financial sectors of specific models.[1] These discussions should provide an introduction to, and brief explanation of, the scope, usefulness, and limitations of financial econometric modeling.

---

[1]This section is slightly more technical than the preceding sections. Students wanting only a simple introduction to modeling should find the earlier sections adequate.

## A Brief Explanation of Models

Macroeconomic theory provides the economist with a set of hypotheses regarding causality among economic variables. An econometric model is an empirical expression of these hypotheses. Construction of a model involves, first, the *specification* of relationships—which variables are included and in what way—and second, the *estimation* of the coefficients of the relationships—the numerical values associated with the relationships among the variables. A model can then be viewed as a set of simultaneous equations that relate economic variables to one another. Much of econonometrics is devoted to techniques for estimating coefficients in simultaneous equations systems,[2] but we will not discuss this complex issue. Our interest here is to familiarize the reader with the notion of a model and then to describe the uses of a model.

As we have indicated, analysis of which variables are included and which hypotheses determine the form of the model and of each equation is the lengthy process known as *specification of the model*. *Endogenous variables* are determined internally by the model. Typically, model equations include other variables—exogenous variables—that affect the model but that are determined outside the model. Exogenous variables may be policy variables, noneconomic phenomena, or simply economic phenomena that the model does not attempt to explain. Once the model structure is specified, behavioral relationships are estimated statistically. The regression techniques used can be quite complicated because of the statistical problems that arise in a system of simultaneous equations.

It is extremely important that a model structure be firmly based in economic theory. The would-be model builder draws on relationships suggested by economic theory in developing the specification. It is not sufficient simply to choose those variables

that are closely related to one another in the historical data. Instead, economic theory suggests those relationships that appear to indicate causality and they are then investigated statistically to arrive at a proper specification.[3]

There are also many practical problems faced by the model builder, particularly concerning the adequacy of data. Clearly reliable data are an important input into any modeling effort. Data are not always available very promptly. For a quarterly forecasting model, data that do not appear for several months after the end of the quarter are less useful than up-to-date data. In addition, many economic data series are released in preliminary form and are subject to substantial revision, sometimes years later. Finally, data are usually used in seasonally adjusted form, and although the standard seasonal adjustment procedures are highly sophisticated, they are on occasion unreliable. In financial econometric modeling, these data problems are often encountered with the flow of funds data on sectoral financial flows and asset stocks. Some financial data, such as interest rates, which are directly observed in financial markets are, by and large, free of these problems.

Once a model has been specified and the behavioral relations estimated, it is possible to supply values of the exogenous variables and to solve for the values of the endogenous variables that simultaneously satisfy the model equations. This is known as a model *solution*. Model solutions can be used for forecasting, for explaining historical developments, or for simulating the effects of alternative policies. These concepts of specification, estimation, and solution are illustrated with the following hypothetical example.

## A Hypothetical Model

Actual models are often very large and complicated. The number of variables can number in the hundreds and equations are often very complex,

---

[2] A simultaneous equation system is a model of two or more equations that express relationships among the variables. The model is termed simultaneous because some of the variables in one equation interact with variables in at least one other equation. Each equation is an exact algebraic relationship among variables. For example, if the relationship between variables $X$ and $Y$ is $Y = a + bX$, the coefficients of the equation are the parameters $a$ and $b$. Econometrics is the study of various procedures for obtaining numerical estimates of these coefficients from historical data on $X$ and $Y$.

[3] An implication of this emphasis on economic theory is that the serious model user should be familiar with the specification of the model. Unfortunately, it is often difficult to gain insights into the economic theory and empirical view of the world of a specific model from casual inspection of a complex and lengthy set of equations. In the third and fourth sections of this chapter, we attempt to convey the "flavor" of the economic theory of the financial sectors in some of the better known models.

reflecting complicated dynamic relationships. Nevertheless, a simple hypothetical example of a model structure will illustrate some of the problems encountered with a model and clarify some of the concepts. The model structure follows the Keynesian aggregate-demand approach of virtually all actual models. It has many features of a typical first-generation model and a discussion of the equations will clarify many model concepts. There are nine equations in the model; statistical coefficients are given by the letter $b$ and variables in capital letters are defined below. Definitions of exogenous variables are denoted by asterisks(*):

$$C = b_{10} + b_{11}(Y - T) \qquad (26\text{-}1)$$

$$I = b_{20} + b_{21}(RL - \pi^e) + b_{22}(Y - Y_{t-1}) \quad (26\text{-}2)$$

$$\frac{M}{P} = b_{30} + b_{31}Y + b_{32}RS \qquad (26\text{-}3)$$

$$RS = b_{40} + b_{41}RES + b_{42}RDIS + b_{43}(Y - Y_{t-1}) \qquad (26\text{-}4)$$

$$RL = b_{50} + b_{51}RS_{t-1} + b_{52}RL_{t-1} \qquad (26\text{-}5)$$

$$\pi = b_{60} + b_{61}(Y - YPOT) + b_{62}\pi^e_{t-1} \qquad (26\text{-}6)$$

$$\pi^e = \sum_{i=1}^{4} b_{7i}\pi_{t-i} \qquad (26\text{-}7)$$

$$\pi = 100 (P - P_{t-1})/P_{t-1} \qquad (26\text{-}8)$$

$$Y = C + I + G + (X - M) \qquad (26\text{-}9)$$

where

$$
\begin{aligned}
C &= \text{real consumption expenditures} \\
I &= \text{real investment expenditures} \\
G &= \text{real government expenditures*} \\
(X - M) &= \text{real net exports*} \\
Y &= \text{real gross national product} \\
T &= \text{real taxes*} \\
M &= \text{money supply} \\
P &= \text{price level} \\
RL &= \text{long-term interest rate} \\
\pi^e &= \text{expected inflation rate} \\
RS &= \text{short-term interest rate} \\
RES &= \text{bank reserves*} \\
RDIS &= \text{discount rate*} \\
\pi &= \text{inflation rate} \\
YPOT &= \text{potential GNP*}
\end{aligned}
$$

The model contains nine equations and nine endogenous variables. Six of the equations of the model are behavioral relationships that must be estimated statistically, and three are identities or definitional relationships (for $\pi^e$, $\pi$, and $Y$). The six exogenous variables include policy variables (for example, government expenditures) and economic phenomena outside the scope of the model (bank reserves, for example, are exogenous because the model does not include a banking sector). An explanation of the model structure follows.

Begin with Equation (26-9), the National Income identity relating GNP to its components. Two of the components (government expenditure, $G$, and net exports, $X - M$) are exogenous. The other two components (consumption and investment) are determined endogenously by the model in Equations (26-1) and (26-2), which are the behavioral equations for consumption and investment, respectively. These behavioral relationships follow specifications suggested by economic theory, but the precise form of each equation is decided on after extensive empirical investigation that compares the explanatory power of alternative forms.

The financial sector of the model is found in Equations (26-3), (26-4), and (26-5). Equation (26-3) is a behavioral equation for the demand for money, while Equation (26-4) is a reduced-form equation that summarizes both the supply and demand forces which determine interest rates. Ideally, economic theory indicates that the model should specify demand and supply equations for money; these would together determine the quantity of money and its price (the short-term interest rate, $RS$). However, it is often difficult to specify a supply function for financial securities without extensive modeling of the behavior of the institutions that issue the security (in this case the commercial banks). To avoid that task, most models until very recently have utilized an equation like Equation (26-4). It is often called a reduced-form, or rate-setting, equation because it summarizes the forces that determine interest rates. Equation (26-5) for the long-term interest rate is also a reduced-form type of relationship. Rather than specifying all the market forces, it presents a summary in the form of a relationship between the long-term and short-term interest rates. Relationships of this type are called the term structure of interest rates. This model assumes a fixed term structure given by the estimated relationship Equation (26-5).

The final sector of our model is the price sector. It includes one behavioral equation and two definitions. Equation (26-8) simply defines the inflation rate as the rate of change of the price level. Equation (26-7) defines a proxy for the expected rate of inflation, which is unobservable; it is assumed that the expected rate of inflation is a weighted average of past inflation rates. The weights ($b_{7i}$, $i = 1$, . . . , 4) cannot be estimated since $\pi^e$ is unobservable, so they must be chosen arbitrarily. Model builders faced with this type of problem will be guided by their view of what makes the most economic sense. Finally, the behavioral equation for the inflation rate, Equation (26-6), indicates that $\pi$ is determined by the gap between output and potential output (a measure of the degree of slack in the economy) and by the expected inflation rate.

Clearly the scope of this model is limited, since there is no wage and employment sector or foreign sector. However, every model builder must narrow the scope of the model at some level of detail and must treat certain economic phenomena as exogenous for the purposes of the model structure.

An important feature of the hypothetical model is that the structure is dynamic. Economic variables affect each other over time and, therefore, lagged values of the variables appear in a number of equations. When generating a model solution for the current time period, the lagged endogenous variables are treated as exogenous variables. That is, given particular values for the exogenous and lagged endogenous variables as well as coefficient estimates, the nine equations are solved for the values of the nine endogenous variables that satisfy the model.

Considerable testing of the model is likely to take place before a specific set of estimates is chosen. The simplest test is to examine single equation residuals (errors); that is, one wishes to see how well each behavioral equation explains the dependent variable with which it deals. Although the form of the equation is suggested by economic theory, testing is required to see that the form used actually explains behavior. A more sophisticated type of test involves solving the entire model. This could take the form of an *ex post* (after the fact) forecast. That is, the model is solved using actual values of the exogenous variables for some historical period. Then model forecasts can be compared to the actual known outcomes.

### Forecasting with the Model

The primary use of an econometric model like this one is to generate forecasts. For example, suppose that the most recently available data are for the fourth quarter of 1979 (written as 1979 IV) and we

would like to use the model to forecast the values of the endogenous variables for the four quarters of 1980. How do we proceed?

We can generate a model forecast by using predictions for the exogenous variables and solving the set of simultaneous equations. However, at this point we do not know what the values of the exogenous variables will be, and, consequently, we must use our best judgment. Clearly, the resultant model forecast will be only as good as these judgmental inputs. The model solution for 1980 I will use actual data for the lags since they are available but, for subsequent quarters, previously forecasted values have to be used for lagged values.

In practice, forecasting with econometric models usually involves even more judgmental elements. These are often necessary because a model structure estimated from prior historical data may not provide an entirely appropriate explanation of current behavior. Thus, it is common practice to adjust coefficients, most frequently the constant terms ($b_{10}$, $b_{20}$, . . . , $b_{60}$ in our example), in forecasting. For example, in examining the model performance for 1979, it might be apparent that the investment equation has been underpredicting. That is, given the actual values of all right-hand side variables, the predicted level of investment has been systematically less than the actual value. If this systematic error is expected to continue into 1980, the forecaster might adjust the constant term, $b_{20}$, appropriately to correct this problem. Constant-term adjustments are often made judgmentally after a systematic analysis of previous errors.

Although an econometric model imposes a formal structure on forecast activity, these judgmental elements are important. The forecaster's judgment enters in the determination of exogenous variables and in making constant-term adjustments. Furthermore, there is a great deal of interaction between the model and the forecaster. For example, after examining a model forecast solution, the forecaster might well reconsider predictions of exogenous variables. In the final analysis, a model forecast is a judgmental forecast with a structure that guarantees internal consistency.

### Simulation of the Model

Equally as important as the forecasting uses of a model is their use for simulation purposes. Of particular value are policy simulations. For example, what does the model tell us about the impact of government expenditures on the economy? The answer to this question will depend on the initial conditions, since, in a nonlinear, dynamic model such as this one, the effect of a change in one variable depends on the values of the other variables. Therefore, a policy simulation is really a comparison of two dynamic model solutions that differ only with respect to the policy change being examined.

Start, for instance, with a control solution for the period 1978 I to 1979 IV. The control solution uses actual values for exogenous variables and for lags prior to 1978 I. However, after 1978 I, model solution values are used for lags. This solution would be called a dynamic *ex post* simulation. Now we generate another solution that is identical in every way but one. The only difference is that in the second solution government expenditures in each quarter are $10 billion higher than the actual values. This is also a dynamic simulation—using model solution values for lags after 1978 I, but it differs from the control because of the continuous government expenditure "shock" of $10 billion of additional spending.

A comparison of the control and shocked solution values for the endogenous variables provides the model estimates of multiplier effects. For example, the impact multiplier of government expenditure on GNP is given by

$$\frac{Y'_{78I} - Y_{78I}}{G'_{78I} - G_{78I}}$$

where the primed variables are from the shocked solution and the unprimed from the control. The second-period multiplier is found by comparing shocked and control solution values for 1978 II. In this manner, the series of dynamic multipliers can be estimated. Remember that these multipliers are specific to our particular experiment, although moderate changes in the situation would not radically alter the pattern or size of the multipliers.

The dynamic multipliers are an important source of information derived from models. They provide specific estimates of the magnitude of the economy's response to policy change as well as estimates of the pattern of those responses over time. Suppose that in this example the dynamic multipliers show the following pattern: 0.8, 0.9, 1.2, 1.5, 1.4, 1.3, 1.2. This suggests that a sustained $10 billion increase in government expenditures leads

immediately to a $8 billion increase in GNP. Because of lagged responses, the effect increases to $15 billion after four quarters and then begins to level off somewhat. Both the estimated magnitudes and patterns of the multipliers are important in designing policy.

Simulations are also used to compare alternative scenarios. For example, a package of constant-term adjustments and estimates of exogenous variables that reflect the situation of an oil embargo can be used to generate one solution. This can then be compared to a control solution to gain some insights about the impact of an embargo on the economy.

Virtually all existing large-scale models are used for both forecasting short-run aggregate economic behavior and for simulating the effects of policy alternatives. Their performance in both areas has been studied for a number of years. Specifically, the forecast records indicate that, by and large, the models are as good as any other forecast technique—sometimes better, sometimes worse. The fact that models do not produce perfect forecasts is not surprising given the judgmental inputs into forecasting. The real value of econometric models lies in their ability to impose a framework on our thinking. They require modelers to maintain the consistency of relationships and enable them to obtain specific estimates of the relationships involved. It is important to remember that models cannot reproduce the real world. The real world does not feel constrained to obey the dictates of a particular model structure.

## Characteristics of Financial Sector Models

There are a number of characteristics of models of the financial sector that can be used to distinguish one model from another. These characteristics differ among the models of different generations and are important in determining the overall focus of the models. A number of features are especially important for our review of financial models.

### Degree of Disaggregation

Financial sector models can aggregate or disaggregate on two sets of variables: number of sectors, and number of financial assets. For example, an aggregated model, with respect to sectors, might lump all financial institutions together, while a disaggregated model would treat banks, savings and loan associations, and savings banks separately. With respect to financial assets, an aggregate model might use a single wealth variable, while a disaggregate model would treat various securities (such as government securities, corporate bonds, municipal bonds, and mortgages) separately. The latter aggregation decision then determines which interest rates enter the model endogenously. As financial models have developed over time, they have tended to become more disaggregated.

## Determination of Interest Rates

Theoretical models view interest rates as determined by the equilibrium condition "supply equals demand." For example, there are a series of demand equations for security $X$, a supply equation, and an equilibrium condition, $S = D$. Since the interest rate on security $X$ enters as an argument in the demand and/or supply equations, its value is determined at the level at which supply equals demand.

Econometric models of the financial sector only rarely determine interest rates in this way. Often only one interest rate, say, the Treasury bill rate, is determined by the supply-equals-demand condition in the market for (say) bank reserves. All other interest rates are determined by so-called reduced-form equations, which summarize the underlying economic phenomena without modeling market behavior. The reduced-form equations usually regress the other rates (for example, the long-term government bond rate or the corporate bond rate) against the "basic rate" plus some other variables (like the total supplies of certain categories of securities).

## Portfolio Adjustments

All models use a stock-adjustment type of specification for the demand and supply equations for financial assets. This approach stresses the gradual adjustment of portfolio composition from a position of disequilibrium (where actual stocks of an asset differ from a desired stock) to equilibrium. This is clearly a short-run consideration, although the short run can, of course, mean two or more years.

## Portfolio Constraints

Later-generation financial-sector models have also taken into account, in varying degrees, the total wealth and balance-sheet constraints. These constraints produce the condition that only $N - 1$ of $N$ equations for securities in a model are independent, since the balance-sheet components must add up to total wealth. The balance-sheet constraints also impose certain consistency requirements on the set of equations for each sector.[4]

Models take these constraints into account in different ways. Some models make one asset in each sector's portfolio a residual, whereas others estimate equations for all assets in a portfolio taking explicit account of the constraint in the estimation procedure. A forecast made without an explicit model must take the balance-sheet and wealth constraints into account by appropriate designation of a residual category of asset or liability.[5]

## Interaction Between Real and Financial Sectors

The relationship between real economic activity and the financial sector reflects a model's underlying approach to macroeconomics. The traditional question is how financial markets influence real economic activity. A number of possible channels of influence have been suggested, including interest rates (cost of capital), credit availability, and wealth. The models differ profoundly in their emphasis on different channels. The reverse channels or the impact of real activity on financial flows are also of interest. A major issue is: what type of financial flows are generated by particular categories of real expenditure? Does housing always

---

[4]These constraints are best explained by an example. Suppose that a given level of wealth will be held in $N$ assets. There cannot be $N$ independent demand equations because the $N$-predicted demands need not sum to the given level of wealth. If any $N - 1$ demand equations are estimated, the demand for the last asset can be obtained as a residual. It is simply the given level of wealth less the other estimated demands. Thus, there are only $N - 1$ independent demand equations to be estimated. It is best to omit an asset whose demand is institutionally fixed or is of little economic importance.

[5]These constraints were first discussed by William Brainard and James Tobin in "Pitfalls in Financial Model Building," *American Economic Review* (May 1968).

generate mortgage flows, or is the stock market a source of funds as well?

The emphasis on different channels reflects the underlying approach of the model builders to macrotheory as well as their views about the uses of the model. The monetarist revolution of the 1970s has led model builders to search much more actively for linkages between the real and financial sectors. If the model is designed for policy analysis, this leads to exhaustive work on the channels of monetary policy or the activities of government agencies.

## History of Financial Model Building

The great granddaddy of American econometric models is the Klein-Goldberger model. It is basically a Keynesian real-aggregate-demand model, which endogenously determines the major components of both the output and income sides of the income and product accounts as well as employment, prices, wages, and interest rates. No attempt is made to model the behavior of financial institutions, and the model includes only the bare bones of any financial relationships. A short-run interest rate is determined by exogenous policy and banking conditions. The long-term interest rate, determined by a term structure relationship, is then linked to the real sector through investment.

The Klein-Goldberger model, which appeared in 1955, is an annual model for the period 1929–1952 (excluding the war years) and includes fifteen behavioral equations. It set the pattern for later modeling efforts, such as those at the University of Michigan by Daniel Suits, at the Wharton School of the University of Pennsylvania by Lawrence Klein, and at the Office of Business Economics of the Department of Commerce. These first-generation quarterly econometric models appeared in the 1960s and are all similar to some extent. In the next section of this chapter we will discuss the financial sector of one of them: the OBE model.

Soon after these models appeared, it became apparent that the Keynesian demand emphasis of the first generation of models gave insufficient attention to the role of financial institutions in the economy. This was rectified, in part, by the financial model developed by Frank de Leeuw as part of the Brookings model project. This work appeared in 1965 and can be considered the granddaddy of financial models. De Leeuw's model of financial behavior was constructed as part of the *Brookings Quarterly Econometric Model of the U.S.*, and it was the first detailed specification of financial behavior. In contrast, the earlier models largely ignored the behavior of financial institutions. They generally relied on a simple determination of interest rates from exogenous policy influences and feedbacks from the real sector. The de Leeuw model, on the other hand, exhibits a completeness and sophistication that belies its status as a pioneer.

In the de Leeuw model, interest rates are determined in two stages. The Treasury bill rate is determined in the market for bank reserves. The bill rate is a variable in the bank excess reserve and borrowing equations; hence it is determined at the level required to bring about supply-equals-demand equilibrium. The long-term government bond rate is determined via a term structure equation; the private security yield is also determined via a "yield structure equation."

The de Leeuw model is highly aggregated, both across sectors (it aggregates nonbank deposit institutions and insurance claims) and by type of asset (it aggregates all private debt), although the behavior of the commercial banks within the financial sector is modeled explicitly. Since there is little disaggregation, the portfolio balance conditions are applied only sparingly. But it is in the overall consistency of the model that de Leeuw makes his most important contribution. The model stresses the importance of the legal prohibition of interest payments on three assets: reserves, currency, and demand deposits. Supplies and demands must be brought into balance without any variation in these three prices and, consequently, certain relationships must be dropped from the system.

A more detailed examination of the estimated equations in this model is no longer really worthwhile. The specifications are less sophisticated than those of second-generation models and the level of aggregation is too great. However, anyone building a financial model, or forecasting financial assets, should examine de Leeuw's overall approach; it is simple and instructive.

The second-generation models are much larger, primarily because of the advances in computer technology of the 1960s, and include much broader specifications of the financial sector. Examples of this genre are the Brookings model and the FRB-

MIT model named after its sponsors, the Federal Reserve Board and the Massachusetts Institute of Technology. The FRB-MIT model, which first appeared in 1968, has undergone several revisions and a change of name since its appearance; the financial sector of one version will be discussed in detail in the next section.

The overall philosophy of the FRB-MIT model is to develop the channels through which monetary policy affects real economic activity. The explanation of the details of the financial sector—which subsectors were developed and which were not—can better be understood with this in mind. Three channels are discussed: cost of capital, credit availability, and wealth. The cost-of-capital channel requires that the model include various interest rates on private securities: the corporate bond rate, the mortgage rate, and the dividend-price ratio. But none of these rates gets determined by supply-demand equilibrium conditions. Rather, the short-term Treasury bill rate gets determined in the market for bank reserves (as in de Leeuw's model), and various term structure and yield structure equations append all other rates to the model.

Even second-generation models, like the FRB-MIT model, are lacking in their treatment of the financial sector. Complete sectoral balance sheets are not specified. Furthermore, the models do not consider linkages between particular types of expenditure and specific financial flows. Stocks of financial assets (for example, corporate or government bonds outstanding) do not really affect interest rates, nor are they determined by interest rates. In the FRB-MIT model, the only rates that react to a model specification of underlying supply-demand forces are those in the Treasury bill and mortgage markets. All other rates are tied to the bill rate in one way or another. The reasons for these shortcomings are twofold. First, complete financial balance sheets were not viewed as essential to the short-term forecasting and policy-simulation uses of the second-generation models. Second, a full integration of the real and financial sectors requires a very difficult integration of the National Income and Product Accounts (NIPA) data on real sector activity with the saving and asset/liability balance sheets from the Flow of Funds (FOF) data.

In the last decade, third-generation models that provide a full integration have begun to emerge. These involve some conceptual advances and suggest others which are still under development. The models constructed by Barry Bosworth and James Duesenberry and by Patric Hendershott are well-known examples of this generation. These models first appeared in 1973 and will be discussed in some detail in the next section. Another important example is the model constructed by Data Resources, Inc. (DRI), a commercial forecasting service. It is a third-generation outgrowth of the Brookings model, which includes full integration of the NIPA and the FOF balance sheets for the household and corporate business sectors.

Hendershott's model, which has recently been presented in full, differs from the second-generation models in a number of respects. First, interest rates on different financial assets are determined by supply-demand equilibrium conditions in each market. This does not imply, of course, that the rates on (say) governments, mortgages, and corporates are determined independently. Rather, instead of being linked directly by a "yield structure" relationship, they are linked by cross elasticities of supply and demand (for example, the rates on all three securities appear in the demand for any one of these assets).

The second distinguishing feature of the Hendershott model is that specific attention is paid to how households and the nonfinancial corporate business sector finance their real expenditures. Different categories of real expenditures appear as independent variables in the equations determining the assets and liabilities of corporations and households. Thus, Hendershott is able to conclude that consumer durables, for example, are financed 50 percent by consumer credit, 25 percent by issuing mortgages, and 25 percent by drawing down financial assets. The approach is completely empirical, relying on the regression procedure to pick the most significant relationship between particular categories of real expenditures and financial flows. The model represents an interesting first pass at this issue, but it certainly requires further work.

The third feature of the model is the meticulous attention paid to satisfying the balance-sheet constraints. This is especially important in this model because it includes all assets in a sector's portfolio and, therefore, the balance-sheet constraints must be satisfied. Hendershott's model is estimated with a "stacking-technique" that imposes these constraints in the course of estimating equation coefficients—the technique will be described later. He also provides a fairly detailed disaggregation of both sectors and assets.

The Bosworth-Duesenberry model is also based explicitly on the Flow of Funds Accounts. However, the departure from traditional structural modeling activities is not as profound. Bosworth-Duesenberry suspend the portfolio balance conditions when standard specifications are empirically more appealing.

This brief history of model building would be incomplete without mention of another type of model that is very different from those discussed already. The previous discussion is devoted to structural models in which the model builder attempts to set out the relationships that represent the structure of the economic system. An alternative approach is to estimate a "reduced-form model," where the endogenous variables are expressed as functions of exogenous variables alone.[6] The motivation for estimating a reduced form is that the structural relationships might be too complex to specify so that reduced-form relationships are employed to forecast economic activity. Reduced-form models have the major drawback of telling us very little about how the economy operates. That is, if money supply is exogenous and GNP endogenous, a reduced-form equation will provide an estimate of the effect of money supply on GNP, but it fails to express any theory or provide any explanation about why the effect is present.

Reduced-form models are not widely used but have attained some notoriety from the most prominent example of the genre—the St. Louis Model, so named because the model was constructed in the late 1960s at the Federal Reserve Bank of St. Louis.[7] It gained its notoriety because, in the St. Louis model, the money supply was a more important determinant of GNP than was the case in structural models of that time. Thus, it was often used to bolster monetarist arguments and had a role in prodding other model builders to specify fully the channels of monetary policy.

## The Financial Sectors of Major Models

This section discusses the financial sectors of a few major econometric models, with examples taken from models of each generation. In the context of specific models, it will be possible to better illustrate the characteristics of models, their conceptual deficiencies, and their value in economic analysis and forecasting.

The first-generation model that we will discuss is the model constructed at the Office of Business Economics (now the Bureau of Economic Analysis of the Department of Commerce).[8] It illustrates the limitations of first-generation models and is presented here for that purpose.

### A First-Generation Model

The OBE model consists of thirty-six behavioral equations. Real GNP is broken down into thirteen components, nine of which are determined by behavioral relationships and four of which are exogenous (exports, government sectors, and two minor categories). There are also equations for the overall price deflator and wage rates. Price deflators for GNP components are related primarily to the overall deflator. The labor sector determines employment and manhours which, along with the wage rate, determine labor income. Corporate profits, as well as several other components of national income, are also determined endogenously.

Finally, there are four equations to the financial sector. Monetary policy is exogenous, and the two policy variables are excess reserves as a percentage of total reserves ($R$) and the Federal Reserve discount rate ($r_d$). The short-term interest rate is not the outcome of any equilibration of supply and demand for financial securities. Instead, the activities of the entire financial system are summarized by a single equation, which reflects the policy influences on the 4- to 6-month commercial paper rate ($r_s$):

$$r_s = 1.06 - .214R_{-1} + .977r_d \qquad (26\text{-}10)$$

The excess reserve variable clearly depends on the behavior of the commercial banking system, which is affected by economic activity. But for the pur-

[6]A structural model can be solved so that each endogenous variable is expressed as a function of the exogenous variables only. In a reduced-form model, we estimate the coefficients of this reduced form rather than the structural equations.

[7]See L. C. Andersen and K. M. Carlson, "A Monetarist Model for Economic Stabilization," *Monthly Review,* Federal Reserve Bank of St. Louis (April 1970).

[8]The complete specification of this model is available in M. Liebenberg, A. Hirsch, and J. Popkin, "A Quarterly Econometric Model of the United States: A Progress Report," *Survey of Current Business* (May 1966).

poses of this model, it is taken as exogenously determined. In a sense, we can conclude that the OBE model of 1965 had no financial sector.

The long-term interest rate is determined by a lagged response to $r_s$, and the mortgage rate by a lagged response to the long-term rate. The form of the lagged response is the same in both cases and is illustrated by the equation for the long-term rate ($r_L$, Moody's corporate bond rate):

$$r_L = .243 + .082r_s + .885r_{L-1} \qquad (26\text{-}11)$$

This type of lagged response is a very common approach to summarizing relationships among interest rates. The lag process can be clarified by an example. Assume that $r_s$ is 5 percent and that both $r_s$ and $r_L$ have not changed ($r_L = r_{L-1}$). Then $r_L =$ 5.68 percent. If $r_s$ increases to 6 percent in that quarter:

$$r_L = .243 + .082(6) + .885(5.68) = 5.76\% \quad (26\text{-}12)$$

And, in the next quarter,

$$r_L = .243 + .082(6) + .885(5.76) = 5.83\%$$

The long-term rate will gradually adjust to the change in $r_s$, until a steady state is reached, at which time $r_L = r_{L-1}$ is obtained:

$$r_L = .243 + .082(6) + .885\, r_{L-1} = 6.39\% \qquad (26\text{-}13)$$

Further discussion of the relationship between short- and long-run interest rates can be found in Chapter 23.

The final financial sector behavioral equation of the OBE model determines the level of liquid assets held by households from nominal consumption and $r_L$. Since financial balance sheets are not included in the model, no constraint relates the change in liquid assets to the implied saving flow.

This small number of financial variables is linked to real sector behavior at several points. Household liquid assets affect personal consumption expenditures on nonautomobile durables. Housing starts, which determine housing expenditure with a lag, are affected by the mortgage rate and excess reserves. Presumably, the latter variable is a crude proxy for the availability of mortgage funds. Interest rates do not enter the equation for nonresidential fixed investment because the model relies on survey data on investment expectations. Clearly, businesses' expectations are affected by financial conditions, but the survey data are exogenous to the model.

With the perspective of over a decade's additional developments in macroeconomics, it is easy to view the financial sector of this first-generation model as terribly naive. However, it reflects the thinking of the early 1960s, which placed little emphasis on the linkages between the financial and real sectors and viewed the operation of financial institutions as an element of disaggregation (akin to, say, an industrial breakdown of output) beyond the scope of an aggregate model.

To summarize, the bare-bones financial sector of the first-generation models includes the determination of a short-run interest rate by Federal Reserve policy:

$$r_s = f(\text{policy}) \qquad (26\text{-}14)$$

and a term structure approach to the determination of one or more long-term rates:

$$r_L = f(r_s) \qquad (26\text{-}15)$$

The first equation makes interest rates "policy determined." They cannot be viewed as truly exogenous, however, since the Federal Reserve surely reacts to business and financial conditions in setting policy.

This approach is inadequate because it makes no effort to include other market influences on interest rates (bank loan activity, for example) and it tells us very little about which Federal Reserve activities will affect interest rates and by how much. The second-generation models make an effort to rectify this problem.

## Second-Generation Models

Second-generation models expanded the financial sector by including an aggregate banking sector identity, which provides a framework for modeling Federal Reserve behavior.[9] For example, unborrowed reserves ($RU$) is the sum of free reserves ($RF$) and required reserves. Required reserves are determined by the reserve ratios and the stocks of demand and time deposits ($DD$ and $TD$, respectively):

$$RU = RF + k_D DD + k_T TD \qquad (26\text{-}16)$$

The required reserve ratios are exogenous policy variables, as is the supply of unborrowed reserves.

[9] The following illustrative model ignores many current real world complications.

The short-term interest rate, among other variables, affects the demand for free reserves and deposits, and will adjust so that the identity holds. In other words, second-generation models typically determine the short-term rate by the demand (from $RF$, $TD$, and $DD$) and exogenous supply of unborrowed reserves. Thus, the financial sector is closely linked to the Federal Reserve policy instruments. The model is completed by specifying the three demand equations, for example;

$$RF = f(r_d, r_s, DD) \qquad (26\text{-}17)$$
$$DD = f(GNP, r_s, r_{TD}) \qquad (26\text{-}18)$$
$$TD = f(GNP, r_s, r_{TD}, r_L) \qquad (26\text{-}19)$$

Free reserves are positively related to the Federal Reserve discount rate ($r_d$), positively related to the short-term rate and the scale or impact variable, $DD$. The demand for deposits is scaled to GNP and relevant interest rates.

So far the four equations of the model include three exogenous variables ($RU$, $r_d$, $GNP$) and six endogenous variables ($RF$, $DD$, $TD$, $R_s$, $r_L$, $r_{TD}$). As noted earlier, $r_s$ is viewed as the interest rate determined by supply and demand interaction in the money market. Therefore, to close the model, we add a term structure equation for the long-term rate and a supply function that determines how banks set the rate paid on time deposits:

$$r_L = f(r_s) \qquad (26\text{-}20)$$
$$r_{TD} = f(r_L, \frac{TD}{TD + DD}, r_{MAX}) \qquad (26\text{-}21)$$

where $r_{MAX}$ is the ceiling rate (an additional exogenous variable), and banks adjust to the long-term rate and a desired deposit mix.

This simple model can easily be expanded. For example, supply and demand functions for long-term securities can be substituted for the term structure equation and, in this case, the stock of long-term securities can be introduced as well (bank loan market, government securities, and so on). A major difference between the second-generation approach and the first-generation approach described earlier is that there are linkages between the real and financial sectors in both directions. In the above model, GNP affects interest rate determination in the financial sector and, at the same time, interest rates affect real sector behavior.

The most prominent example of this type is the model constructed by the Federal Reserve Board. Since its initial presentation in 1968, it has undergone several changes in name and is available in numerous versions with various levels of detailed disaggregation. The model is used extensively for forecasting and policy simulation by the Federal Reserve Board as well as for research on the effects of policy. We will discuss in some detail a version of the model which is readily available—the FRB-MIT-Penn model.[10]

The money market sector of the FRB-MIT-Penn model follows the model outlined above rather closely. There is a reserve identity and demand equations for currency, demand deposits, and free reserves. Each of these includes linkages to other financial markets as well as to the real sector. The complexity of these specifications is illustrated by the free reserves equation:

$$
\begin{aligned}
RF = {} & .66(1 - k_D)(RU - RU_{-1}) \\
& - .51 k_D (CL - CL_{-1}) \\
& - .35(\Delta k_T TD_{-1} + \Delta k_D DD_{-1}) \\
& + (.0011 + .0013 r_d - .0016 r_{TB}) \sum_{i=1}^{4} .25 DD_{-i} \\
& + .65 RF_{-1} \qquad\qquad (26\text{-}22)
\end{aligned}
$$

where new variables are the Treasury bill rate ($r_{TB}$), the endogenous rate that equilibrates the money market, and commercial loans ($CL$). The demand for free reserves increases when the supply of unborrowed reserves increases and decreases when the supply of loans increases. It responds both to changes in reserve requirements and to fluctuations in interest rates. Finally, note that its own lagged value appears in the equation, indicating a gradual adjustment of free reserves. Adjustment models of this type are very common in econometrics. It can be interpreted as a partial adjustment model:

$$RF - RF_{-1} = \lambda(RF^* - RF_{-1}) \qquad (26\text{-}23)$$

where $RF^*$ would in this case be the desired, or target, level of free reserves and in each quarter $RF$ changes to close some proportion ($\lambda$) of the gap between desired and actual free reserves. The coefficient of .65 on $RF_{-1}$ indicates that $\lambda = .35$.

The model includes supply and demand equations for some other securities as well, although not for all of them. Several additional interest rates are determined by term structure or yield structure relationships. These include the commercial paper rate (from $r_{TB}$), the corporate bond rate (from the

---

[10]This version of the model is presented in Bert Hickman, ed., *Econometric Models of Cyclical Behavior*, National Bureau of Economic Research, New York, 1972.

commercial paper rate), the mortgage rate (from the corporate bond rate), and the municipal bond rate (from the corporate bond rate and a demand proxy variable).

The commercial loan, commercial bank time deposit, savings and loan, and mutual savings bank deposit markets are all endogenous in this model. In each case, interest rates and deposits are both determined by a rate setting (supply) and a deposit demand equation. For example, look at the equations in (26-24) for deposits at S&Ls ($MSL$) and their interest rate ($r_{SL}$). The interest rate is determined by a lagged adjustment to time deposit and mortgage rates. The demand for real S&L deposits ($MSL/P_C$, where $P_C$ is the consumption deflator) is determined by the interest rate on these deposits and the rate on substitute assets and real household net wealth ($NW/P_C$), all with a lagged adjustment.

$$r_{SL} = -.12 + .07r_{TD} + .08r_M + .86r_{SL-1}$$

$$\ln \frac{MSL}{P_C} = -.20 + .004 \ln r_{TD} + .100 \ln r_{SL}$$

$$- .040 \ln r_{CB} + .05 \ln \frac{NW}{P_C}$$

$$+ .95 \ln \frac{MSL_{-1}}{P_{C-1}} \qquad (26\text{-}24)$$

Besides having a more fully developed financial sector, the FRB-MIT-Penn model also places increased emphasis on linkages between the real and financial sectors. These linkages include both wealth and interest rate effects on demand. For example, the model includes an equation that relates the dividend-price ratio on common stocks to current and lagged corporate bond rates and inflation rates. The dividend-price ratio and the real-sector determination of dividend income determine stock market wealth which, along with housing, durables stocks, and accumulated financial saving, determine household net wealth. Thus, financial sector disturbances affect stock prices, which determine net worth and consumption. The wealth effect is, therefore, an important link between the financial sector and consumption.

For plant and equipment expenditures, the cost of capital is the channel that links the financial sector to real demand. The cost of capital, determined by interest rates, is part of the rental value of capital (along with tax and depreciation variables). It, in turn, determines the target capital/output ratio, which determines new orders and, ultimately, expenditures.

The housing sector is modeled in a similar fashion. Interest rates determine the cost of capital, which determines housing starts. An additional financial influence on housing is the availability of mortgage funds (determined by net inflows into MSB and S&L deposits), which is endogenous to the financial sector.

As would be expected, simulation of this model indicates that the financial sector interacts with the real sector in many ways. For example, increased GNP drives up short-term rates quickly and long-term rates follow with a lag. Money demand rises sharply and then falls off in response to higher interest rates. Similarly, an increase in unborrowed reserves leads to a sharp decline in interest rates, which is reduced over time as the demand for money and free reserves responds with lags.

Policy effects on GNP are also relatively large in this model, although they do not begin to accumulate for several quarters. However, by the end of three years, the GNP multiplier of a change in unborrowed reserves is greater than 4. The government expenditure multiplier is about 3 at the end of three years.

Having reviewed the structure of the Federal Reserve model, we can now examine its major deficiency. As noted earlier, the model does not close the relationship between the real and financial sectors. For example, the income and product side of the model implies a level of net financial investment by the household sector. However, this figure is not related to the flows into various financial assets determined endogenously in the model. Third generation econometric models turn their attention to this problem and attempt to construct complete or closed models of the financial sector.

### Third-Generation Models

As noted, the two major drawbacks of the second-generation models are their failure to model supply and demand behavior for each security and the absence of a complete set of financial sector accounting identities. In the 1970s, model builders turned their attention to these issues and several models now provide complete or partial solutions to the problem.

The typical second-generation model generally does not always identify supply and demand functions for specific securities. As discussed earlier, these models often solve for quantity and price (the interest rate) by using a demand equation and a rate-setting equation. The rate-setting equations summarize term structure relationships and institutional determinants. These models apply the supply-equals-demand relationships to only a few securities, and they do not consider any financial accounting identities.

One approach taken by the more recent models is to increase the level of disaggregation (by sector and security) and then include the adding-up identities relating components and aggregates when solving the model. Examples of this approach are the Bosworth-Duesenberry model and the DRI model. We will outline the structure of the Bosworth-Duesenberry model and then describe some simulation results from the DRI model.

*The Bosworth-Duesenberry Model* The Bosworth-Duesenberry model financial sector equations are similar to those in second-generation models. For each financial security there is a sectoral demand (or supply) equation and a rate-setting equation. However, the model differs from its predecessors in a very important feature. The difference is that in the Bosworth-Duesenberry model financial asset and liability acquisitions of each sector are related to the sectoral income-expenditure surplus (savings) from the real or production side of the model. For example, from the National Income and Product Accounts, the business sector deficit is defined as: plant and equipment expenditures *plus* direct foreign investment, *less* retained earnings, foreign branch profits, inventory valuation adjustment, and capital consumption allowances. This deficit is financed by the excess of the increase in financial liabilities over the increase in financial assets. The model includes identities relating real-sector deficits to financial balance sheets for each sector (business, federal government, state and local government, foreign, household). In addition, there are financial balance sheets for commercial banking and nonbank intermediaries.

The existence of the balance-sheet constraint implies, as noted earlier, that for each sector the equation for one security is redundant. In general, the model considers four types of securities: deposit accounts, loans, liquid marketable securities, and long-term securities. The residual category includes a number of assets that lack a market-clearing price (trade credit, for example) and the statistical discrepancy between FOF and NIPA data.

There are several ways of estimating a portfolio model. Either constraints can be ignored or a technique for estimating systems of simultaneous equations can be used or the portfolio constraints can be used to imply coefficient restrictions. If constraints are ignored and individual asset equations are specified and estimated independently for all but one of the assets, there is an implied estimate for the residual that may or may not be sensible. Alternatively, a simultaneous estimation procedure that incorporates both demand equations and portfolio constraints can be used. However, unless one is confident of the structural specification of the whole model, there are a number of econometric pitfalls that make this procedure risky. A third approach to handling portfolio constraints is to impose them on the coefficient estimates of a restricted model. This is the approach used in the Hendershott model discussed later.

Bosworth-Duesenberry opt for the first procedure: equations are specified and estimated independently. The model builders are mindful of the implied coefficients for the residual asset in choosing their equations, but the constraints are not formally imposed for estimation purposes. Keep in mind that the portfolio constraints are fully operative in solving the model once it has been estimated.

While we will not go into further detail concerning the Bosworth-Duesenberry model, it is important to note that the model advances the state of the art by specifying relationships between real-sector deficits and financial saving. Another model that specifies these linkages, but for the business and household sectors only, is the DRI model. We will describe some results from this model in order to give some idea of the scope of financial detail now available in third-generation models.

*The DRI Model* The DRI model is revised every year. Recent versions have developed models of the FOF sectoral accounts for the household and nonfinancial corporate business sectors, as well as a model of mortgage flows from various lending institutions. That the model contains strong linkages between the real and financial sectors can be seen in the following discussion of its response to a monetary-policy shock.

We shall compare two ten-year dynamic simulations of the model that use 1963 as a starting point. The control simulation assumes that all exogenous variables grow along stable growth paths; all exogenous shocks in the historical data are eliminated. The second simulation differs by a particular policy shock—an additional $1 billion of non-borrowed bank reserves is injected by open-market operations and maintained at the higher level. What happens to the economy?

According to the model simulation, the Treasury bill rate drops immediately by 120 basis points and then slowly adjusts to a long-run equilibrium about 35 basis points below the control solution. The corporate bond rate declines initially by 50 basis points. After a year, the income effect of the expansionary monetary policy increases the bond rate. After three years, the inflation-expectations effect brings the rate to what it would be in the control solution.

Because the model includes equations for many flow of funds components, the interactions between the real and financial sector can be seen in great detail. The sharp initial drop in the Treasury bill and other money market rates makes savings deposits relatively more attractive because the yields on deposits are slower to react than are Treasury bill rates. Thus, deposit inflows to MSBs and S&Ls rise sharply for two years. Subsequently, as money market rates increase with stronger real activity (the income effect), deposit inflows level off. With the higher deposit flows, mortgage commitments increase and rates decline. After five quarters, housing starts are more than 200,000 greater than in the control solution. A stock adjustment process causes housing activity to return to the level of the control solution after some years.

In addition to the channel through the housing sector, the real and financial sectors are also linked through consumption and investment expenditures. The economic stimulation increases the value of household financial assets, which increases consumption demand through a wealth effect. On the investment side, the easy monetary policy decreases the rental price (or cost) of capital (through the corporate bond rate) and increases cash flow. These factors lead to increased investment demand. Producers' durable-equipment expenditures rise sharply (by about $1.5 billion) and then decline to the control solution level after about three and a half years.

The results of this policy simulation are, in many ways, similar to those found with the FRB-MIT-Penn model, which also places great emphasis on the mortgage markets. However, more financial flow detail is obtained from the DRI model. Also, there are some major differences in the channels of monetary policy effects—for example, the DRI model does not include the effects of capital gains on equities. In sum, the approach of the DRI and Bosworth-Duesenberry models is to correct the deficiencies of the second-generation models by broadening the scope of the model. As the number of securities is expanded, the model builders are also able to include some accounting identities. As an example, in the DRI model NIPA personal saving is related to the FOF saving flows for the household sector, with a few components exogenous. Such detail is not present in the various second-generation models.

*Hendershott's Financial Sector Model*  Another approach to financial sector modeling found in third-generation models represents a more radical departure from traditional structural specifications. This approach starts with a theoretical model of the demand and supply for each financial asset by each sector (including issuers). The balance-sheet constraints are used in obtaining coefficient estimates. All endogenous securities appear in at least two sectoral portfolio equations, that is, they appear in both asset demand and the issuer's supply equations. Thus, supply and demand equations are identified and supply-equals-demand equilibrium determines both the market-clearing quantity and the equilibrium interest rate.

Hendershott's model of the financial sector is the best known example of this approach. He treats the entire real sector as exogenous and models the financial behavior of about half a dozen real and financial sectors. For each sector, a system of portfolio-allocation equations is estimated. For a particular sector these equations determine the allocation of (exogenous) savings given interest rates. Interest rates are endogenous to the overall model because, after aggregating across sectors, the asset holders' demand for a security must equal the issuer's supply. When the overall model is solved with these aggregate accounting identities, interest rates are determined endogenously.

A major feature of the model is that each sector's system of portfolio allocation equations satisfies certain constraints suggested by theory. This can best be explained by an illustration.[11] Suppose that a particular sector allocates its saving ($S$) among two financial assets ($FA_1$ and $FA_2$) and financial liabilities ($FL$). Thus its balance sheet is:

| $FA_1$ | $FL$ |
|--------|------|
| $FA_2$ | $S$  |

Given the balance-sheet constraint ($FA_1 + FA_2 = FL + S$) and the exogeneity of saving, the set of demand and supply functions for financial assets and liabilities, respectively, must satisfy the following:

$$\frac{\delta FA_1}{\delta R} + \frac{\delta FA_2}{\delta R} - \frac{\delta FL}{\delta R} = 0 \qquad (26\text{-}25)$$

where $R$ is the interest rate on any asset or liability, and

$$\frac{\delta FA_1}{\delta S} + \frac{\delta FA_2}{\delta S} - \frac{\delta FL}{\delta S} = 1 \qquad (26\text{-}26)$$

In other words, these constraints imply that, for a given level of saving, an increase in the interest rate on, say, $FA_1$, which increases the demand for that asset, must lead to an offsetting decrease in the other asset or an increase in liabilities. The second condition indicates that any increase in saving is allocated exactly among financial asset increases or liability decreases.

Another set of constraints often considered in theoretical discussions is the symmetry constraint. That is, the effect on the demand for one asset (or liability) with respect to a change in the interest rate of a second should be the same as the effect on demand for the second asset of a change in the interest rate on the first. In our example:

$$\frac{\delta FA_1}{\delta R_{A2}} = \frac{\delta FA_2}{\delta RA_1}$$

$$\frac{\delta FA_1}{\delta RL} = \frac{-\delta FL}{\delta RA_1}$$

$$\frac{\delta FA_2}{\delta RL} = \frac{-\delta FL}{\delta RA_2} \qquad (26\text{-}27)$$

[11]The remainder of this section describes the theoretical advances made in some of the current research on financial modeling. The neophyte to the subject can skip this section without loss of continuity.

In general the three portfolio equations are:

$$FA_1 = b_1 R_{A1} + b_2 R_{A2} + b_3 R_L + b_4 S \qquad (26\text{-}28)$$
$$FA_2 = b_5 R_{A1} + b_6 R_{A2} + b_7 R_L + b_8 S \qquad (26\text{-}29)$$
$$FL = b_9 R_{A1} + b_{10} R_{A2} + b_{11} R_L + b_{12} S \qquad (26\text{-}30)$$

The constraints imply that

$$b_1 + b_5 - b_9 = 0 \qquad (26\text{-}31)$$
$$b_2 + b_6 - b_{10} = 0 \qquad (26\text{-}32)$$
$$b_3 + b_7 - b_{11} = 0 \qquad (26\text{-}33)$$
$$b_4 + b_8 - b_{12} = 1 \qquad (26\text{-}34)$$
$$b_2 = b_5 \qquad (26\text{-}35)$$
$$b_3 = -b_9 \qquad (26\text{-}36)$$
$$b_7 = -b_{10} \qquad (26\text{-}37)$$

Using the constraints, the system can be written as:

$$FA_1 = b_1 R_{A1} + b_2 R_{A2} + b_3 R_L + b_4 S \qquad (26\text{-}38)$$
$$FA_2 = b_2 R_{A1} - (b_7 + b_2) R_{A2} + b_2 R_L + b_8 S \qquad (26\text{-}39)$$
$$FL = (b_1 + b_2) R_{A1} - b_7 R_{A2} + (b_3 + b_7) R_L + (b_4 + b_8 - 1) S \qquad (26\text{-}40)$$

Least squares regression estimates of each equation will not provide coefficient estimates that satisfy these constraints. However, appropriate estimates can be obtained if the three equations are "stacked" or treated as a single system. That is, the system can be estimated as if it were a single equation with a dependent variable of $3T$ observations (where $T$ is the length of the sample period). The exact equation is:

$$\begin{bmatrix} FA_1 \\ FA_2 \\ FL + S \end{bmatrix} = b_1 \begin{bmatrix} RA_1 \\ 0 \\ RA_1 \end{bmatrix} + b_2 \begin{bmatrix} RA_2 \\ -RA_2 \\ RA_1 \end{bmatrix}$$

$$+ b_3 \begin{bmatrix} R_L \\ 0 \\ R_L \end{bmatrix} + b_7 \begin{bmatrix} 0 \\ -RA_2 \\ R_L - RA_2 \end{bmatrix}$$

$$+ b_4 \begin{bmatrix} S \\ 0 \\ S \end{bmatrix} + b_8 \begin{bmatrix} 0 \\ S \\ S \end{bmatrix} \qquad (26\text{-}41)$$

This procedure can be followed for each sector. The entire model then includes supply and demand equations for each security. For example, if the above sector represents the savings banks, its liability is accounts held by the household sector. But an asset demand equation for savings accounts appears in the household-sector portfolio-allocation equation. When the overall model is solved simultaneously, interest rates are endogenously determined at the level that equates supply and demand for each financial security.

Hendershott has estimated a financial-sector model that satisfies the constraints we have just discussed. It has been used to simulate the effects of real-sector shocks and policy changes on the financial system. The approach is clearly a theoretical advance, although it remains to be seen whether it is practical for an ongoing model of both the real and financial sectors. Some models would argue that it is overly ambitious in its attempt to model all financial flows. It is clear, nevertheless, that econometric models are moving in the direction of a more complete modeling of fund flows.

## Usefulness of Models

Econometric models, such as those discussed in this chapter, have been widely used for forecasting, policy analysis, and research for more than twenty years. It is therefore appropriate before concluding to discuss the usefulness of models. Some have been disappointed that models have not provided the panacea of foolproof forecasting and policy analysis. This view is, however, unrealistic. It is clear that our understanding of the workings of the economy has been increased by the availability of models and by the research efforts that go into model building.

Models are used for forecasting economic activity on a regular basis. The question that is often asked is whether they are better than other forecasting techniques. The answer is not simple. Judgmental short-run forecasts of aggregate measures of economic activity are often as accurate as model forecasts.[12] But this is not surprising since an *ex ante* model forecast includes important judgmental elements—the values of the exogenous variables and adjustments in the structural equations. In periods when there have been abrupt structural changes in economic relationships (such as the 1973–1974 oil crisis), models estimated from prior experience failed to capture these changes.

Why then are models important forecasting tools? The answer lies in their ability to impose consistency on the forecaster. The model guarantees that the different economic measures forecasted have consistent relationships to each other. Furthermore, the model imposes consistency over time as well. Thus, the forecast for the next quarter and subsequent quarters must be consistent with one another. The use of models has made the entire forecasting profession much more careful about internal forecast consistency.

The use of models for policy analysis was described earlier and cannot be overemphasized. Today, whenever a tax proposal of any kind is made, the immediate question that arises is: what will it do to the economy? Detailed responses are provided by the various econometric models. It is routine practice in government and business to use simulations from econometric models in both designing and evaluating policy.

Finally, econometric models play an important role in economic research. One of the major theoretical issues in macroeconomics in the 1970s centered around the role of the money supply. The issue often needs to be argued from empirical evidence, and that evidence is often provided by econometric models. A theory about the role of money will be substantiated by examining the predictive accuracy of a model that incorporates that role in its structure. Thus, models provide a forum for economic researchers to discuss their views.

## Conclusion

It is clear from this brief summary of econometric modeling of the financial sector that many major developments are as yet forthcoming. Nevertheless, the progress made in the last decade has been substantial.

The bare-bones financial sectors of the first-generation quarterly models that appeared in the 1960s are no longer found in econometric models. Although the financial sectors are not entirely satisfactory, third-generation models are grappling with many of these problems. The two major categories of problems under consideration are the linkages between the real and financial sectors and the integration of real and financial balance sheets.

The first issue is a source of much theoretical controversy about the role of the financial sector

[12] For a discussion of forecast accuracy, see Stephen S. McNees, "An Evaluation of Economic Forecasts," *New England Economic Review* (November/December 1975); and Stephen S. McNees, "The Forecasting Record for the 1970s," *New England Economic Review* (September/October 1979).

in macroeconomics. Economists differ in their views of the linkages, and a consensus view is likely to emerge very slowly. For example, recent empirical work on consumption behavior emphasizes the role of capital gains; work on the investment function has reopened the issue of whether long- or short-term interest rates determine investment.[13]

The second issue is more methodological. Almost every economist will agree that real-sector expenditure flows and financial flows should be integrated. However, satisfactory specifications of models that do so are difficult to develop. Improved specifications of financial behavior are required before fully integrated models are truly reliable.

A major remaining inadequacy of financial-sector models is their suitability for long-term forecasting. The specifications of the behavior of financial institutions are as yet too crude to provide forecasts for more than a few years into the future. Furthermore, institutional change takes place so rapidly in the financial sector that model builders have a difficult time keeping pace with developments. As yet no effort has been made to "endogenize" institutional change. In fact, models designed to explain long-run economic developments have bare-bones financial sectors like the first-generation models. Clearly, financial-sector models will continue to develop in many directions in the coming years.

## Questions

1. What is the relationship between saving from the National Income Accounts and the Flow of Funds and why is it important for financial-sector modeling?
2. Why do first-generation models generally conclude that monetary policy has little impact on the economy?
3. What is the major difference between the FMP model and the Bosworth-Duesenberry model?
4. Which models provide a behavioral explanation of the behavior of financial institutions and how do they do so?
5. What are the major uses of a "reduced-form model," and why are they less useful than structural models?

6. What is meant by a "dynamic simulation"? How would a dynamic simulation of the effect of a change in the discount rate be useful to policymakers?
7. Study the equations of the model presented—Equations (26-1) to (26-9)—and show the linkages between the real and financial sectors. Do the same thing for the OBE model equations (see the reference section for the source).
8. Why are econometric models of little use in forecasting the economic consequences of natural (such as droughts) and political (for example, war) disasters?
9. It is unlikely that econometric models will ever surpass the accuracy of market professionals and traders in explaining day-to-day variation in interest rates. Why?
10. Formulate the structure of an econometric model for one of the major financial sectors (for example, commercial banks or savings institutions) that explains its portfolio decisions. Be sure to specify which variables are exogenous, which are endogenous, and how the institution relates to the macroeconomy.

## Selected Bibliography

### Sources of models discussed

*Klein-Goldberger Model:*

Klein, L. R., and A. S. Goldberger. *An Econometric Model of the United States, 1929–1952.* North-Holland, Amsterdam, 1955.
Theil, H. *Principles of Econometrics.* John Wiley & Sons, New York, 1971.

*OBE Model:*

Hirsch, A. "Policy Multipliers in the BEA Quarterly Econometric Model." *Survey of Current Business* (July 1977).
Hirsch, A., M. Liebenberg, and G. Green. "The BEA Quarterly Econometric Model." National Technical Information Service (COM73-1114), 1973.
Liebenberg, M., A. Hirsch, and J. Popkin. "A Quarterly Econometric Model of the United States: A Progress Report." *Survey of Current Business* (May 1966).

*Brookings Model:*

Duesenberry, J. S., G. Fromm, L. R. Klein, and E. Kuh, eds. *The Brookings Model: Some Further Results.* American Elsevier, New York, 1969. See, in particular, "A Model of Financial Behavior" by F. de Leeuw, and "An Extension of the Monetary Sector" by S. Goldfeld.

[13]See Robert E. Hall, "Investment, Interest Rates, and the Effects of Stabilization Policies," and Fredric S. Mishkin, "What Depressed the Consumer? The Household Balance Sheet and the 1973–75 Recession," both in *Brookings Papers on Economic Activity*, Washington, D.C., 1977, pp. 61–104 and pp. 123–164, respectively.

———. eds. *The Brookings Quarterly Econometric Model of the United States*. North-Holland, Amsterdam, 1965.

### Federal Reserve Model:

Ando, A., F. Modigliani, and R. Rasche. "Equations and Definitions of Variables for the FRB-MIT-Penn Econometric Model." In *Econometric Models of Cyclical Behavior*. Ed. B. Hickman. National Bureau of Economic Research, New York, 1972.

de Leeuw, F., and E. Gramlich. "The Federal Reserve-MIT Econometric Model." *Federal Reserve Bulletin* (January 1968).

### Bosworth-Duesenberry Model:

Bosworth, B., and J. S. Duesenberry. "A Flow of Funds Model and Its Implications." In *Issues in Federal Debt Management*. Conference Series No. 10, Federal Reserve Bank of Boston, 1973.

### DRI Model:

Eckstein, O., ed. *Parameters and Policies in the U.S. Economy*. North-Holland Publishing Co., Amsterdam, 1976.

———, E. W. Green, and A. Sinai. "The Data Resources Model: Uses, Structure and Analysis of the U.S. Economy." *International Economic Review* (October 1974).

### Hendershott Model:

Hendershott, P. *Understanding Capital Markets*. Vol. 1, A Flow of Funds Financial Model. Lexington Books, Lexington, Mass.. 1977.

———, and R. C. Lemmon. "The Financial Behavior of Households: Some Empirical Estimates." *Journal of Finance* (June 1975).

### St. Louis Model:

Andersen, L. C., and K. M. Carlson. "A Monetarist Model for Economic Stabilization." *Monthly Review*, Federal Reserve Bank of St. Louis (April 1970).

### Other References

Brainard, William C., and James Tobin. "Pitfalls in Financial Model Building." *American Economic Review* (May 1968).

———. "Econometric Models." In *Methods and Techniques of Business Forecasting*. Eds. W. F. Butler, R. A. Kavesh, and R. B. Platt, Prentice-Hall, Englewood Cliffs, N.J., 1974.

Evans, M. K. *Macroeconomic Activity*. Harper & Row, Publishers, New York, 1969.

Hendershott, P. "Recent Developments of the Financial Sector of Econometric Models." *Journal of Finance* (March 1968).

Hickman, B. G., ed. *Econometric Models of Cyclical Behavior*. National Bureau of Economic Research, New York, 1972.

Kuh, E., and R. L. Schmalensee. *An Introduction to Applied Econometrics*. American Elsevier Publishing Company, New York, 1973.

McNees, Stephen K. "An Evaluation of Economic Forecasts." *New England Economic Review*, Federal Reserve Bank of Boston (November-December 1975).

———. "The Forecasting Period for the 1970s." *New England Economic Review* (September-October 1979).

Pindyck, R. S., and D. L. Rubinfeld. *Econometric Models and Economic Forecasts*. McGraw-Hill Book Company, New York, 1976.

Silber, W. L. *Portfolio Behavior of Financial Institutions*. Holt, Rinehart and Winston, New York, 1970.

# 27

# Financial Prerequisites for Economic Growth

The growth of the nation's economy stems from three interrelated sources: growth of the labor force, enlargement of the capital stock, and technological change that enhances productivity. Growth of the capital stock is, of course, the end result of the saving-investment process; net investment is simply another name for net additions to capital. National income accounting tells us that income saved is equal to resources available for investment, although we know that savers and investors in new real capital do not necessarily have to be the same people. The balance between saving and investment is maintained by the financial sector, which channels resources from surplus to deficit units through financial intermediaries and the capital markets. Our main interest in this chapter is in this financial activity, which channels resources toward real investment and thereby enables the capital stock and the economy to grow. For this reason, we examine in some detail the financial sector activities that are necessary to sustain a satisfactory level of real growth. The chapter looks at the role of the financial system in providing the wherewithal for growth and offers some projections of financial activity.[1]

This chapter begins with a discussion of capital shortages. We then turn to the savings-investment account for the real sector, proceeding from past trends to a projection consistent with a growing economy in the first half of the 1980s. Savings and investment projections for the real sector are then related to sectoral net financial investment. This important step moves the discussion to a flow of funds (FOF) context. Finally, we proceed to the overall matrix of fund flows by sector and security, that is, to a summary of the financing activity that provides the basis for growth.[2]

---

[1] The framework of the analysis in this chapter generally stresses the long run, that is, we are primarily interested in *long-run projections* of growth potential rather than forecasts of short-run—or cyclical—phenomena.

[2] Both the discussions and projections in this chapter draw heavily on the capital formation and financing project at the New York University Graduate School of Business Administration sponsored by the American Council for Life Insurance. The research results from the project are found in Arnold W. Sametz and Paul Wachtel, eds., *Understanding Capital Markets*, vol. 2, *The Financial Environment and the Flow of Funds in the Next Decade*, Heath-Lexington Books, Lexington, Mass., 1977. A summary of the projections is to be found in Arnold W.

## The Myth of a Capital Shortage[3]

In recent years, both business analysts and more academically oriented economists have been arguing about the prospects for a so-called *capital shortage*. Often the term is used interchangeably to refer to both inadequate resource availability for capital formation and to the inability of financial markets and institutions to allocate resources efficiently. Both aspects of the issue are related and will be discussed here. A later section makes some long-run projections for both the real and financial sectors. These projections show that normal long-run economic growth can evolve without inhibiting shortages in either the real sector or in the capital market.

### The Question of Resource Adequacy

The more polemical arguments center around the first of these issues: insufficient real-resource availability. Analysts who hold this position begin with a menu of desired investment projects, which can add up to 20 percent of GNP (gross investment has averaged around 15 percent of GNP). This shopping list is then compared to the amount of saving projected, and the comparison results in the enormous gap between saving and investment called the *capital shortage*. Of course, *ex post*, saving must always be equal to investment so that the shortage situation does not actually emerge. However, the alarm stems from the fact that the shopping list appears to be completely beyond reach unless policy actions are taken to increase the level of saving. Alarmists, therefore, reach the conclusion that some such policy action is necessary.

Before jumping to this conclusion, however, we should take a serious look at the impact of a "capital shortage." To begin with, it is interesting to

note that the very term *capital shortage* suggests an inability of the free market to produce an appropriate or socially desirable outcome. Second, the implication of this apparent market failure is that the government should intervene in the allocation process. Are these conclusions warranted? Let us look at them more closely.

The proportion of total output devoted to investment purposes in a market economy is determined by the rate of return to capital. The usual argument made in support of the capital shortage hypothesis is that the profitability of investment has been declining and, thus, there is little incentive to invest in capital goods. It is difficult to measure rates of profit and there is a great deal of controversy about whether rates of return have in fact declined secularly.[4] Nevertheless, a declining rate of return would suggest an abundance—rather than a shortage—of capital stock. As long as we expect investment to have diminishing marginal productivity, the real return will decline as capital becomes relatively more abundant. Consequently, it is erroneous to infer a capital shortage from declining rates of return.[5]

In what sense, then, can we argue that there is a capital shortage? The answer is that the capital stock that emerges from the market allocation process may well be less than socially desirable.[6] This could be because the reward to savers for deferring consumption—say, because of taxation of investment returns—is less than the value to society of additional capital. It is not possible to judge directly whether this is, in fact, the case. However, it is well known that the U.S. devotes less of its output to capital formation than most other industrial countries. In the long run, therefore, productivity and output will grow faster elsewhere. If our long-run growth potential is of concern, more capital formation should be taking place. However, it must

Sametz, *Prospects of Capital Formation and Capital Markets,* Heath-Lexington Books, Lexington, Mass., 1978. It should be emphasized that no attempt has been made to update the base year for the projections (1976) or the conclusions drawn therefrom, if for no other reason than to convey the complexity of attempting to forecast what at the time (1976) was a decade into the future.

[3]This section draws on Paul Wachtel, Arnold W. Sametz, and Harry Shuford, "Capital Shortages: Myth or Reality?" *Journal of Finance* (May 1976), 269–285; also, Sametz and Wachtel, eds., *Understanding Capital Markets,* vol. 2, Chap. 2.

[4]See Martin Feldstein and Lawrence Summers, "Is the Profit Rate Falling?" *Brookings Papers on Economic Activity,* The Brookings Institution, Washington, D.C., 1977.

[5]It is possible that increasing amounts of government regulatory activity have lowered rates of return. Government intervention in business activity may depress the profitability of investment and, consequently, result in a capital stock that is smaller than socially desirable.

[6]For a discussion of these problems, see Eli Shapiro and William White, eds., *Capital for Productivity and Jobs,* Prentice-Hall, Englewood Cliffs, N.J., 1977.

be remembered that in the short run this is possible only by reducing consumption or disrupting market allocations of resources.

Much existing government policy, although it is well motivated, tends to reduce the resources available for the capital formation necessary for economic growth. In particular, government deficits, although they finance many worthwhile activities, absorb savings that could otherwise be available to finance private capital formation.[7] This is an ever-present problem since the government, always a favored borrower, does not compete in the marketplace for capital.

If there is indeed a capital shortage, it is possible to induce more investment by a policy that increases the returns to capital. The policies that are often suggested involve reduced taxation of capital income. If government expenditure is to be maintained, the revenue loss will have to be recouped. Thus, in this case, reduced taxation of capital income represents a transfer of resources to the owners of capital. Should we increase the taxation of wage income in order to reduce the taxation of capital income? Of course, if such a policy is successful, investment will increase and so will total output, thereby making everyone better off. However, the empirical evidence on this issue is not at all clear. Reduction of corporate income taxes may be an important spur to growth or it may just be a shift of the burden of taxation away from those most able to pay. This issue is under debate today in the political sphere. There is an apparently growing consensus that reduced corporate income or capital gains taxes, although they reduce the tax burden of the wealthy, may be worthwhile as they can provide the necessary incentives for increased investment and real growth.

Alternative policy approaches involve increasing the returns to saving or direct interference in the allocation of resources. In the first instance, the most frequent suggestions involve further elimination of regulatory constraints in the financial sector.

[7] The decisions are often hard ones for society to make. For example, deficits in the Social Security System can absorb savings that would otherwise be allocated to investment. See "Social Security" by Alicia Munnel in *Setting National Priorities, the 1978 Budget,* The Brookings Institution, Washington, D.C., 1977. See also George von Furstenberg, "The Long-Term Effects of Government Deficits on the U.S. Output Potential," *Journal of Finance* (June 1978), 989–1001, for a technical discussion.

## Ability of Financial Markets to Allocate Resources

When we posed the problem of capital shortages, we noted that there are really two problems: (1) the adequacy of the total amount of capital formation, and (2) the ability of financial markets to allocate capital. This latter aspect is as complicated as the former because current market structures include a great deal of regulatory intervention in the allocation process.

A free market system provides an efficient allocation of resources because it finances investment projects in the order of their profitability. However, government policy affects the relative profitability of various activities either through favorable tax treatment, which increases the profitability of particular activities, or through government activity in the financial markets, which reduces financing costs for specific activities. These policies affect costs and returns of specific activities and influence the resultant allocation outcome. They include such diverse aspects of government policy as oil depletion allowances, interest rate ceilings, deductibility of interest payments, and government loan guarantees.

In promoting additional interference in the market allocation of financial resources, policymakers should weigh the trade-offs carefully. If we continue to promote certain favored activities—such as housing construction—we reduce the resources that are available for business capital equipment. The allocation of capital is already highly regulated, and it is not obvious that further intervention is desirable. If, for example, we extend government loan guarantees to the energy or automobile industry, we reduce financing costs and promote capital formation in that industry. However, we do so by removing some investment decisions from the competitive market for financial capital; we run the risk of encouraging inefficient, unproductive, or unnecessary projects. Before we take such a move, we should have a clear picture of national priorities.

Finally, we should note that many of the arguments made by the business community about the capital shortage problem are merely polemical. The business community often prefers government to bear some of the risks of investment activity by providing financing or favored tax treatment for certain activities. In any event, it is inevitable that through taxation, expenditures, and market interventions, the government will affect the operation of the capital markets in order to satisfy specific interest groups. It is necessary, therefore, to evaluate the gains and benefits of each activity that might distort the allocation of capital so that apparent capital "shortages" or distortions are kept to a minimum.

In sum, we might ask whether there is any merit at all to the capital-shortage arguments. It would be an overstatement to suggest that existing allocations are in every sense adequate and appropriate. Thus, discussions of capital shortages, even if erroneous, provide a useful forum for analyzing some important issues.[8]

## Approaches to Long-Term Financial Forecasting

The overall volume of finance is largely determined by the investment and saving activities of the nonfinancial sectors: businesses, households, and governments. What remains for the financial forecaster is to work out the detailed financial interrelationships that will satisfy both the demanders and suppliers of funds. That is, in addition to the consistency of saving-investment and borrowing-lending as a whole, there must be consistency, for example, between the specific supply of corporate bonds forecast to be offered for sale and the forecast demands for corporate bonds by individual and institutional buyers. Similarly, in addition to overall equality between demand and supply of mortgage funds, there must be consistency between the availability of funds in particular mortgage-making financial institutions and these institutions' demands for mortgages as part of their preferred portfolios. Such consistency between the financial and the real sectors in the particulars as well as in the aggregate—so that every column and every row of the flow of funds matrix matches, not just the end or total column and row—must be assured by the forecast methodology employed.

Whether the forecasting follows from fully defined *econometric* behavioral relationships (in the form of equations constrained so that, not only is there a use for each source, but for each financial instrument purchases equal sales) or from *judgmental* constraints on financial behavior, the basic information on financial behavior is found by studying *past* trends and patterns in the flow of funds.[9] It is in the *use* of these measured behavioral relationships that forecasting techniques differ. Since the real sectors are given exogenously, extrapolation of past financial behavior does not assure instrument-by-instrument or sector-by-sector equality. Only aggregate sources and uses are obviously equal. Balancing of all the particulars is assured in *econometric models* by building into the equations an interest rate factor that will rise or fall so as to bring about equality between supply and demand. In *judgmental* models, the equality is brought about "by hand"—that is, a first-pass matrix is generated that will certainly reveal imbalances that develop from confrontation of the given real sector flows with past financial patterns. In adjusting the financial flows to accomplish balance, the real flows are assumed unchanged; the necessary changes presumably are brought about by financial shifts and/or changes in interest rate differentials as required.

For our purpose—to gain preliminary insights into the functioning of financial markets—the judgmental approach is more revealing because employing this approach forces one to specify the shifts in financial flows and explain the reasonableness of each shift or financial innovation. However, if one is primarily interested in interest rate differentials, the econometric approach is more informative. (Indeed, *both* approaches are required for a full understanding of financial markets. Joint use of these methods provides informative checks through studying differences in flows forecast by the two approaches.) The judgmental method of financial forecasting shows how a given level of real economic activity can be financed, indicating necessary structural changes and necessary rate shifts in the process. Most such efforts, and this one is no exception, provide a limited matrix that forecasts the major financial flows. In essence, the financial structure is treated as the handmaiden of the real

---

[8] For further discussion, see Robert Eisner, "Capital Shortage: Myth and Reality," *American Economic Review* (February 1977), 110–115; and Leonall Andersen, "Is There a Capital Shortage: Theory and Recent Evidence?" *Journal of Finance* (May 1976), 257–268.

[9] For a more detailed discussion of forecasting techniques, see Chapters 25 and 26; for a discussion of the flow of funds, see Chapter 2.

sector. The basic tool in this exercise is the flow of funds matrix, to which we now turn.

The essential framework of any financial forecasting method is the flow of funds matrix that links the saving-investment data of the National Income and Product Accounts to the lending-borrowing activities associated with those "real" S-I activities. The potential use or value of the Flow of Funds (FOF) Account structure and data base is perhaps best described by the Federal Reserve:

> The matrix is an essential framework for both calculating and using financial market statistics on an economy-wide basis. . . . The explicit constraints of the system enforce a consistency of analysis not easily reached without the framework, particularly in questions at a macroeconomic level, where all market forces interacting with one another are to be accounted for. Such questions become operable only when the transactions involved have been stated within the matrix context on a complete basis but without double-counting.

Analysis of this kind can be applied to an actually expected set of developments by using the matrix structure as a device in forecasting or projecting the future, with the specific function of keeping individual parts of the forecast in touch with one another. The merit of such constrained system-wide forecasts is that each element can be tested by the plausibility of its counterparts in other areas of the matrix. The structure as a whole is reasonable only when all of its parts are reasonable. Whether the elements are derived econometrically from empirical models or put together judgmentally by hand, there is room in the procedure for successive approximations that approach the final result by working out the effects of each change on the rest of the structure and by then working back from the effects to revised versions of the initiating change.[10]

A flow of funds matrix can be constructed in terms of flows in a time period or, alternatively, in terms of the underlying stocks. Net flows in a time period augment the stock of assets or liabilities of

the demanding and issuing sectors, respectively. Thus, we can make projections based on relationships between the real sector and financial flows or on the real sector and financial assets and liabilities. In this chapter, we concentrate on the former approach because real-sector saving/investment behavior implies particular levels for funds flows. However, in making long-term projections, we should remember that flows accumulate over the years to a particular level for stocks. Consequently, it is important to evaluate the relationships between the stocks and real economic activity forecasts to see if they are feasible in the context of historical experience. For example, there is a surprising degree of historical stability in the ratio of total credit market debt to GNP; it has been rising slightly to about 1.5. It is then of interest to ask whether a flow projection implies any major change in the ratio.

Unfortunately, analysis of stocks involves a number of problems. For example, evaluation of projected asset and liability ratios requires that flows be forecast year by year for the entire projection period. Although important, this is a difficult task for long-term projections. Thus, the judgmental forecasts for 1985 presented below are not evaluated in the light of projected stock/flow ratios.[11]

Second, the cumulative effect of heavy business financing requirements extending over a decade or more may create serious constraints on the behavior of both the business sector and financial intermediaries. In fact, this approach is the source of most of the concern about developments over the last decade as well as a source of concern about the future. Analysts have traditionally expressed their misgivings about balance-sheet constraints on the business sector by analyzing a series of familiar ratios: for example, the ratios of internal to external financing, debt to equity, and short-term debt to long-term debt. The changes in these familiar stock ratios over the last decade are viewed with almost universal alarm. However, developments in corporate balance sheets in the early 1970s are fully understandable as the consequence of three fac-

[10]Board of Governors of the Federal Reserve System, *Introduction to Flow of Funds,* Washington, D.C., pp. 5–6. See also Chapter 25 of this book for further discussion of flow of funds forecasting.

[11]For some long-term forecasts that emphasize the asset and liability stocks rather than flows, see Patric Hendershott, "Long-Term Financial Forecasting with a Flow of Funds Model," in *Understanding Capital Markets,* vol. 2, eds. Arnold W. Sametz and Paul Wachtel.

tors—the tax treatment of dividend and interest payments, accounting conventions that do not reflect inflationary influences, and the impact of protracted recession on profits earned and retained. The deductibility of interest payments and a sluggish equity market are sufficient to explain the readiness of the business sector to emphasize debt financing. Furthermore, inflation increases the demand for external financing because depreciation allowances are less than replacement costs. The deleterious effects of inflation on the real value of depreciation allowances and on inventories, as well as the advantageous effect on financial liabilities, make the traditional cash-flow and balance-sheet analysis less useful.[12]

With this discussion as background, we can begin to construct our long-run financial analysis. We start with the saving-investment account from the National Income and Product Accounts (NIPA), which summarizes the allocation of resources to capital formation. This is then used as a basis for calculating the net financial investment of each sector. This summary of financial activity is further employed to construct an overall flow of funds matrix. The matrix is constructed judgmentally, considering those activities that are feasible in a given institutional context and suggesting the types of institutional innovations that are likely.

## A Financial Forecast

### Real-Sector Saving and Investment

Financial flows are ultimately determined by real-sector activity. The NIPA saving and investment account shows the amount and types of economic activity that need to be financed. Furthermore, the financial flows that emerge vary enormously with the mix of both saving and investment among their components.

The usual presentation of a saving-investment account can be found in Table 27-1.[13] On the investment side, the components are nonresidential

[12]For further discussion, see Chapter 12.
[13]The revision of the NIPA in 1976 changed the definitions of several important elements of the saving-investment account. Specifically, the capital-consumption adjustment was introduced to revalue historical cost depreciation to a replacement-cost basis. The new definitions are used here.

**Table 27-1   Saving and Investment as a Percentage of GNP**

|  | 1965 | 1976 | 1985 |
|---|---|---|---|
| Gross investment | 16.9 | 14.2 | 15.3 |
|   Gross private domestic | 16.3 | 14.3 | 16.0 |
|     Nonresidential fixed | 10.4 | 9.5 | 11.4 |
|     Residential | 4.5 | 4.0 | 3.8 |
|     Changes in inventories | 1.4 | .8 | .8 |
|   Net foreign | .6 | −.1 | −.7 |
| Gross private saving | 16.7 | 16.0 | 15.5 |
|   Personal saving | 4.4 | 3.9 | 4.7 |
|   Undistributed profits | 3.9 | 1.6 | 2.2 |
|     Retained earnings | 3.7 | 3.3 | 3.4 |
|     Inventory-valuation adjustment | −.3 | −.8 | −.6 |
|     Capital-consumption adjustment | .5 | −.9 | −.6 |
|     Capital-consumption allowance | 8.4 | 10.5 | 8.6 |
| Government surplus | .1 | −2.1 | −.2 |
|   Federal | .1 | −3.2 | −.3 |
|   State and local | 0.0 | 1.1 | .1 |
| Statistical discrepancy | .1 | .3 | 0 |

Source: *Survey of Current Business; Federal Reserve Bulletin*; and forecast by the author for 1985.

fixed, residential, inventory, and net foreign investment. As can be seen in Table 27-1, the first category, which represents an increase in the capital stock of American business, is only about two-thirds of the total. On the saving side, there is business saving (retained earnings, capital consumption allowances, and capital consumption and inventory valuation adjustments), personal saving, and government saving. The magnitudes and patterns of these real-sector flows in 1965 and 1976 are also shown in Table 27-1. These years are not associated with business cycle extremes, but the differences in the flows indicate the extent of variation in saving and investment typically experienced.

Table 27-1 also presents a long-run projection. This projection for 1985 should not be viewed as a specific outlook for that year but as a more general statement about the typical, or average, outcome to be expected in the first half of this decade. Thus, 1985 is assumed to be an idealized year, not buffeted by cyclical experiences. With this in mind, it is possible to discuss the general characteristics of the saving-investment projection.

A key variable is the forecast of gross investment. There has been a great deal of overall stability in this real-sector flow as a percentage of GNP in the past two decades. Still, there is surprisingly broad agreement among forecasters that the level will be higher in the future for reasons that will be discussed shortly. Most forecasts indicate that there will be a reallocation of more than 1 percent of total output toward the largest component of gross investment, namely, business fixed investment. Another group of forecasters call for even higher levels of investment, but these should probably be viewed as goal statements rather than forecasted outcomes. The increase in total gross private domestic investment (GPDI) is smaller than the increase in business fixed investment because most observers expect a continued decline in the proportion of GNP devoted to residential investment. The forecasters who project an increase in the proportion of GNP devoted to housing expenditures seem to be creating a potential imbalance between investment and saving.

It is almost certain that plant and equipment expenditures will constitute a larger part of GNP over the next decade than they have over the past 20 years partly as a consequence of mandated investment in pollution-abatement equipment, induced investment toward energy independence, and increases in the capital/output ratio of new investment. Indeed, it is this expected increase in required plant and equipment expenditures that triggered the fears of a capital shortage. However, there are some mitigating factors. Not only are pollution and energy investment projects being stretched out over time, but it is also clear that less capital-intensive projects are being developed. And there are expected structural shifts in the economy that will restrain investment in capital-intensive industries, for example, shifts in consumption patterns toward less energy-intensive goals. Rising interest rates may also restrain investment to the extent that any financing shortage threatens to develop. It still seems, though, that nonresidential fixed investment will tend toward a larger share of GNP as the economy moves into the 1980s.

Thus, our view of investment demand is that GPDI will be only a slightly larger fraction of GNP than in the past, although business fixed investment will increase. Studies of industrial requirements for new plant and equipment, the costs of new energy technologies, and the costs of environmental pro-

tection provide a forceful argument for some reallocation of GNP toward investment in business capital even if real output growth is small and financial markets do not provide a more favorable climate for intermediation of savings.[14]

As mentioned earlier, housing demand is another important component of aggregate investment. For a number of years it has been fashionable to argue that the housing needs of the country require an average level of construction that has rarely been met even in cyclical housing booms. As a result, it might appear that this country has suffered a perpetual housing shortage and this might portend continued heavy investment in this area. This view may not be correct, however, as shifting social priorities reduce the pressure for increased housing expenditures. In addition, declining population growth, an expected reduction in relative costs due to changes in construction technology, and an increased willingness to accept multifamily housing and smaller units may also ease constraints in the housing market.

The second critical real variable in the forecast is the NIPA surplus of the government sector. The net impact of government expenditures and taxation on the nation's resources is the most conjectural element of any forecast. It is feasible to project government resource requirements, but the net impact on the investment-saving balance is difficult to assess. Most forecasters view the historical federal government deficit to be an inevitable feature of the political-economic system, a view bolstered by recent history and the likely increased net costs of government redistributive activity (a national health insurance system, for example). On the other hand, it seems that government is responsive in the long run to the nation's needs, and it is not inconceivable that a government surplus of up to 1 percent of GNP will emerge in the future. We lean to the view that the growth of the government sector will be constrained somewhat more in the future and we also believe that public opinion and policy are already shifting in this direction.

Government dissaving can be a problem for the economy. The threat, of course, is the possibility that large government deficits can "crowd out"

[14]For an example of a forecast of long-term business investment needs, see Beatrice N. Vaccara, "Some Reflections on Capital Requirements in 1980," *American Economic Review* (February 1977), 122–127.

business by cutting into aggregate saving, thus reducing investment possibilities. The threat does not appear to reflect the reality, however. There is little evidence to suggest secularly rising dissaving by government. This is not to say that budget deficits will not reach historical peaks in absolute terms. But they are unlikely to increase significantly as a proportion either of GNP or of saving over the cycle as a whole. Furthermore, any increase in government dissaving would have to be very large to have a long-run impact, for government dissaving, on average, is but a small fraction of private saving. In short, the government deficit is unlikely to inhibit growth in the United States over the next decade by absorbing saving, nor can it be viewed as a source of capital.[15]

The third area of concern in our forecast is private saving. Personal saving rates are difficult to forecast under any circumstances, but recent experience has involved special problems. For example, after a decade of historically unprecedented high levels of personal saving, the rate dropped sharply in 1975. Our forecasts indicate that the apparent rise in saving rates is a permanent feature of the economy, however, and that recent experience is not typical of a new trend. This belief is based primarily on studies that attribute high savings to economic uncertainty, which is primarily inflation induced.

The long-term factors that are often cited as depressants of personal saving are demographic change and social security. It is thought that increases in the relative number of very young and aged households who save very little will depress saving. However, the major impact of these changes has probably been felt already. As for social security, it is argued that social security benefits reduce the need for private retirement saving. Again, social security coverage and benefits are not likely to be further improved, so that no further saving depressant is expected.

Our forecast is for business saving to follow historical norms. It is difficult, however, to predict magnitudes of the inventory-valuation and capital-

consumption allowances, which depend on changes in inflation rates. The relatively high levels shown for 1985 are consistent with a continuation of current inflation levels. As for capital-consumption allowances (depreciation), it is assumed that adjustments to the tax laws will keep them at their historical norm—a norm that has been surprisingly constant.

Both theory and experience suggest that household saving and business saving tend to move in offsetting directions. Well known is the remarkable historical stability of total private saving in the U.S., a propensity to save that averages about 15 percent of gross national product. The reasons why business and household savings exhibit compensating movements are less clear. Particular periods of offsetting behavior, however, can be quite convincingly explained through certain specific conditions or developments—recent inflationary trends, for example.

The principal cause of the decline in business saving—unanticipated and erratic inflation—is also a major cause of the rise in household saving. Unexpected inflation impairs business saving by reducing the real rate of return on net worth. Inflation does this as a consequence of:

1. the lag of prices behind costs, which cuts profit margins
2. the use of historical rather than replacement cost accounting for depreciation and inventories, which raises effective taxes on profits
3. increases in interest rates to match the rate of inflation, which raise the nonequity costs of capital
4. increases in dividend payouts to match rising interest rates

Still, until recently, unexpected inflation appeared to increase household saving. Economists cannot assume that householders suffer from the "money illusion" of failing to realize that their money incomes are eroded by rises in prices. Nor can analysts always expect them to sally forth to do battle with inflation through anticipatory purchasing. Instead, sometimes they react to the threat that unanticipated inflation poses to their future real personal income levels and to the value of their financial assets or past saving by increasing their rate of saving—in particular, by reducing borrowing to finance such consumer durables as automo-

---

[15] The large federal deficit in 1978 (2.3 percent of GNP) is viewed as a temporary phenomenon and not as a pattern set for the next decade. This is a result of stated government policy and the concern of policymakers (both Democrats and Republicans) with the arguments we have just noted.

biles and homes. Thus, while we forecast sluggish business saving relative to investment requirements, we also forecast above-trend household saving relative to household "investment" expenditures.

All this is not to say that the financial horizon is problem free, but the major difficulties are problems of *intermediation* of savings—of channeling them effectively from households to business. These projections require that the business/financial system be flexible and adaptive in rearranging the flows of funds through the system.

The channeling of funds from personal saving into business investment is of great importance, since an external financial gap above historical trends is forecast for the business sector over the next decade. Internal finance as a percentage of GNP for all nonfinancial corporations has remained stable at about 7 percent over the last two decades; however, corporate physical asset purchases rose from 7.5 percent in 1956–1965 to 9 percent of GNP in 1961–1975, thereby increasing the financing "gap" from 0.5 percent of GNP to 2 percent of GNP. A major question for the next decade is what will be the sources of corporate funding, or who will purchase the expected surge of stock and bond issues. Plainly, personal saving has to be channeled successfully, either directly or via intermediaries, into corporate securities.

### Financing Requirements

The patterns of real investment and saving just summarized have some immediate implications for funds flows in the economy. We can relate the real behavior of the business, household, and governmental sectors to financial flows by examining the net surpluses or deficits sector by sector and by asking how financial intermediaries and markets will have to channel resources among these sectors. Although this exercise does not represent a full flow of funds analysis of the supply and demand for credit, it is a useful intermediate step because it illustrates the demands on financial markets implicit in the real-sector forecasts. In fact, a given view of the real sector may or may not imply considerable strain in the financial markets.[16] In this

section, we discuss the financing requirements associated with the real sector's saving and investment account in Table 27-1. Sectoral statements of funds flows for the two most important sectors—households and nonfinancial corporate businesses—are shown in Table 27-2.

It is not a simple matter to relate the NIPA definition of saving to the sectoral flow of funds.[17] There are often important definitional differences as well as sizable discrepancies between the different calculations. The first part of Table 27-2 relates NIPA personal saving to the FOF household-sector saving account, while the second part of Table 27-2 shows the FOF sources and uses account for the nonfinancial corporate business sector. This is the most important business sector, but it does not include all the business activity in the overall saving-investment account of Table 27-1.[18]

The saving of the household sector is important because the sector's net financial investment is the surplus available to finance the net investment activities of the other sectors. It represents the resources that could be channeled, for example, toward business capital expenditures. Household net financial investment has averaged about 4.5 percent of GNP since the mid-1960s and is projected at about the same level in 1985. This outcome results largely from a forecast of moderate growth in housing and durable assets, accompanied by continued high levels of financial asset acquisitions.

The housing forecast implicit in the first part of Table 27-2 is based on a forecast of 2 million private housing starts in 1985. The durables forecast is largely shaped by the assumption that 1985 retail new car sales will total 10 million units. In effect, this assumes no real growth in the housing and automotive sectors. Increases in liabilities are not, however, expected to fall as home mortgages grow

---

[16]We should emphasize that this has always been the case. The ability to adjust to strain is a reflection of capital

market strength rather than a sign of instability or weakness. In fact, adjustment to apparent financial strain is important for maintaining an efficient allocation of real capital resources.

[17]For a detailed analysis of the relationship between NIPA saving and investment and net financial investment on an FOF basis, see George M. von Furstenberg, "Flow of Funds Analysis and the Economic Outlook," *Annals of Economic and Social Measurement* (Winter 1977), 1–25.

[18]Noncorporate, farm, and financial businesses are excluded.

**Table 27-2   Sectoral Saving as a Percentage of GNP**

|  | 1965 | 1976 | 1985 |
|---|---|---|---|
| **A. HOUSEHOLD SECTOR** | | | |
| Personal saving | 4.4 | 3.9 | 4.7 |
| + adjustments | .8 | 1.1 | 1.0 |
| + net investment on durables | 1.7 | 2.5 | 1.3 |
| = Net saving | 7.0 | 7.5 | 7.0 |
| − net physical investment | −4.1 | −4.5 | −3.4 |
| − discrepancy | 1.0 | 1.3 | 1.0 |
| = Net financial investment[a] | 3.9 | 4.3 | 4.6 |
| Net acquisition of financial assets | 8.5 | 9.9 | 8.2 |
| Demand deposits & currency & time deposits | 5.2 | 6.9 | 4.4 |
| Credit market instruments, corporate equities, other assets, & net investment in noncorporate business | .9 | −.1 | 1.2 |
| Life insurance & pension fund reserves | 2.5 | 3.1 | 2.6 |
| Net increase in liabilities | 4.6 | 5.6 | 3.6 |
| Home mortgage | 2.5 | 3.6 | 2.2 |
| Other | 2.1 | 2.1 | 1.4 |
| **B. NONFINANCIAL CORPORATE SECTOR** | | | |
| Total sources | 13.2 | 12.5 | 13.6 |
| Internal | 8.2 | 7.4 | 7.6 |
| Retained earnings[b] | 3.4 | 1.2 | 1.7 |
| Capital-consumption allowance | 4.7 | 6.2 | 5.9 |
| External | 5.0 | 5.1 | 6.0 |
| Bonds & equities | .8 | 2.1 | 2.4 |
| Bank loans | 1.5 | .1 | 1.2 |
| Other | 2.7 | 2.9 | 2.8 |
| Total uses | 11.9 | 11.6 | 12.5 |
| Capital expenditure | 9.0 | 8.2 | 9.9 |
| Plant & equipment | 7.5 | 7.3 | 8.7 |
| Residential | .4 | .1 | .4 |
| Inventories | 1.1 | .8 | .8 |
| Increase in financial assets | 2.9 | 3.3 | 2.6 |
| Discrepancy | 1.3 | 1.0 | 1.1 |

[a]Net acquisition of financial assets less net increase in liabilities.
[b]Includes capital-consumption and inventory-valuation adjustments.

Source: Calculated from Flow of Funds tables published by the Board of Governors of the Federal Reserve Board and forecast by the author for 1985.

vigorously. This is due, in part, to the refinancing of capital gains on the existing stock of housing.

The business sector tends to be the most important sector in any flow of funds framework, especially within a "capital shortage" context. The wide variety and large size of business sources of funds assures that business-sector financial forecasts have significant interactions with most of the other sectors of the economy.

In general, Table 27-2 indicates that little unusual pressure in financing business is expected. Although new security issues are likely to be substantial, they are projected to be only moderately greater than in 1976, and there are expected to be parallel increases in the demand for such securities. In short, there is no evidence of a lack of aggregate savings or even of business savings, but there *is* need to intermediate personal saving toward the permanent or long-term financing of capital formation. The lack of overall pressure is the combined result of forecasts of moderate increases in plant and equipment expenditures (an additional 1 percent of GNP at most), offset by reduced expenditures on residential housing and by revived business savings which, however, remain below historical peaks.

Another way of examining the issue is to concentrate on the "financing gap" of the nonfinancial corporate business sector, which is defined in the 1985 forecast shown in Table 27-2(B) as

| | |
|---|---|
| Capital expenditures | 9.9% |
| − Internal sources of funds | 7.6 |
| = "Financing gap" | 2.3 |
| + Discrepancy | 1.1 |
| = Net financial investment | 3.4% |

This gap has averaged almost 2 percent of GNP since the mid-1960s and is expected to maintain about the same relationship to GNP in 1985. (The other years shown in Table 27-2—1965 and 1976—are atypical in this respect. In both years the gap was much smaller [.8 percent of GNP] and financial asset increases larger than in most other years.) Nevertheless, the forecasted level of the financing gap is higher than the averages of the 1950s and early 1960s.

The remaining question with regard to business financing is: what institutions will take up these corporate securities? It seems likely that commercial banks will substitute purchases of long-term corporate debt for short-term corporate debt and thrift institutions will substitute corporates for mortgages. These trends are already underway. Also, contractual institutions, such as pension funds and insurance companies, will add to their portfolios of stock both out of new fund inflows and by substituting equities for other noncorporate long-term securities. Renewed interest in long-term corporate securities by households is dependent on the evolution of innovative instruments that provide cheap and attractive means of investing with maximum diversification and, thus, safety, such as index funds for equities, corporate bond funds, and price-indexed corporate bonds, for example. Other financial innovations may also arise; for example, improved secondary markets for corporate bonds, which would be particularly important in attracting individual and foreign funds—the latter is an increasingly important source of funds for long-term corporate securities.

The federal government's spending-saving impact on the 1985 economy is expected to be slight, according to our projections. This is not to say that the federal government's cyclical impact on the economy via monetary and tax policy, regulatory decisions, and choice of financial intermediation is not very important. Nevertheless, it is significant to note that the projections are not much influenced by expected government deficit spending (that is, dissaving) overall, after accounting for the net additions of financial assets (saving) by the federal government. Although federal deficits of up to 0.5 percent of GNP are likely to continue, the government also acquires financial assets, including Treasury debt. Thus, the net impact of the federal government as a whole on the availability of funds in the economy or on aggregate savings is not expected to be very great.

In this context, it is important to note that the share of federal debt outstanding as a proportion of total debt is likely to continue its long-term secular decline. For example, federal debt, which grew 50 percent between 1965 and 1975 (from $261 to $394 billion) is expected to increase by only one-third over the decade 1975–1985; as a consequence, other outstanding debt, especially private business and consumer debt, is expected to grow in relative importance. Indeed, there may be a relative shortage of federal debt instruments vis-à-vis the demand for such relatively riskless securities. What is forecast here is not a declining impact of the federal government on the economy but a low and stable impact on the aggregate funds available to finance required investment in other areas.

Our forecast of flows of funds between the United States and the rest of the world (ROW) over the next decade suggests that the United States will resume its role as a debtor nation. Substantial deficits on current accounts will be financed principally through purchases by foreigners of U.S. government bonds and corporate equities and by increased foreign holdings of short-term financial securities in the United States (such as bank deposits). In other words, the ROW sector is expected to reduce any potential for domestic capital shortages in the United States in the 1980s as it increases its portfolio investment here from the rough balance of the 1970s, thereby reducing this country's net direct investment abroad. Although the United States will remain an important net purchaser of foreign corporate bonds, foreigners are also expected to be important purchasers of U.S. corporate stock. Furthermore, the large expected takings of short-term marketable debt by the ROW, as well as its additional deposit holdings, will free U.S. lenders to provide larger corporate loans.

Net financial investment (NFI) by sector for 1965 and 1976 and the projection for 1985 are shown in Table 27-3. Net financial investment for each sector is the outcome of all the financial activity of the sector. Given NFI consistent with the sector's real activity, we can now turn to its implications in terms of particular financial assets acquired. Also, it will be possible to look across sectors to the amounts of each security demanded and supplied in the financial markets. What will emerge then will be a picture of the nature and scope of financial market activity that will be consistent with the real-sector growth scenario that we have described.

**Table 27-3 Net Financial Investment as a Percentage of GNP**

|  | 1965 | 1976 | 1985 |
|---|---|---|---|
| Household | 3.9 | 4.3 | 4.6 |
| Nonfinancial corporate business[a] | −2.1 | −1.8 | −3.4 |
| Other nonfinancial business | −1.3 | .2 | −1.9 |
| ROW | −.6 | −.4 | .6 |
| Government | −.5 | −3.3 | −.4 |
| Finance | .2 | .4 | .4 |

[a]Increase in financial assets less external sources of funds from Table 27-2(B).

Source: Calculated from Flow of Funds tables published by the Board of Governors of the Federal Reserve Board and forecast by the author for 1985.

## Financial Flows and Financial Structure

Given the saving and investment behavior of the "real" sectors and the necessity of lending and borrowing to finance part of real investment, the remaining questions concern the manner in which funds are supplied to the real sectors and, if intermediated, which intermediaries are involved. In addition, there are also the small "real" demands for funds by financial institutions, as businesses themselves, that have to be satisfied. In this section, we outline the specific patterns of financing that will channel funds toward the deficit sectors—particularly the business sector.

The overall flow of funds matrix provides an analytical framework that, unfortunately, is difficult to use. This is so because the matrix presentation implies, as noted earlier, a large number of constraints. For example, the total demands and supplies of funds must be equal. In addition, total funds raised must be the same, whether we aggregate across sectors or by financial instrument. This consistency is difficult to maintain because of imperfections in the measurement of funds flows. Consequently, the actual data include many approximations as well as discrepancies that most analysts ignore. Also, there are many examples of funds flows among the sectors for which no reliable reporting exists. An obvious example is trade credit. Furthermore, the size of these non-credit-market funds can be large and variable, but a complete analysis of flow of funds requires that they be considered, even though approximations may be necessary.[19]

A flow of funds matrix is presented in Table 27-4 for 1976 and in 27-5 for 1985 projections. Both Tables 27-4 and 27-5 show the sources and uses of funds for each financial instrument by issuing sector (demand or uses of funds) and purchasing sector (supply or sources of funds). These financial flows are consistent with the *net* financial investment shown in Table 27-3, which in turn is based on real-sector investment and saving in Tables 27-1 and 27-2.

The 1976 flows are in many respects atypical. The amount of funds raised in the credit markets, particularly by the federal government and the mortgage sector, was extraordinarily large. The financial markets were able to absorb this demand for funds with minimal interest rate pressures because of the business sector's relatively weak demand for funds in that year and because of the relatively abundant supply of funds from financial intermediaries and the foreign sector. The credit markets in 1976 reflected the rapid recovery of the real sectors from the 1973–1975 recession. The latter gave rise to a large federal deficit and substantial changes in corporate balance sheets during 1976. As a result, the total funds raised in 1976 relative to GNP (which was far below potential due to the recession) was very large—about 34 percent.

The projections for 1985 exhibit rather different patterns, which are evidently necessary because of the enormous differences in sectoral net financial investment between 1976 and 1985, as shown in Table 27-3.[20] Such differentials are essential if the business sector is to obtain the financing required for the growth in the capital stock implied in our real-sector projections as well as necessary to sustain economic growth in 1985. It should be recalled that these projections are based on some important assumptions, including the following:

1. The 1985 all-government net financial dissaving will be relatively small (about 0.4 percent of GNP) and the sale of governmental securities, especially federal government securities, will be small relative to customary demands for such securities.

2. The ROW sector will run a "surplus," that is, its net investment will approximate 0.6 percent of U.S. GNP in 1985. Among foreign saving

[19]Many analysts of the flow of funds restrict their study to those financial instruments that are traded in the credit markets. These are in general subject to less measurement error because the volume of new issues will be reported by a regulatory agency or through some organized market activity. Furthermore, most business and government financing is through the credit markets. Thus, for many purposes, it is possible to discuss financial activity without reference to an overall flow of funds matrix, although this is not the approach adopted here. An example of the credit market approach is the forecasts published by Salomon Brothers. See, for example, Henry Kaufman and James McKeon, "Prospects for the Credit Markets in 1978," Salomon Brothers, New York, 1977.

[20]For more detailed discussion of the patterns of financial flows in 1985 based on a similar set of projections, see Harry Shuford, "The Outlook for Financial Markets in 1985: A Flow of Funds Approach," in *Understanding Capital Markets*, vol. 2, eds. Sametz and Wachtel.

outlets in the United States, federal government securities will play a large role, rivaled only by purchases of equities and short-term loans and deposits.

The household sector has always been a net supplier of funds to the rest of the economy. The household surplus is channeled into the business or government sectors in a variety of ways. These include direct purchases of credit market instruments as well as indirect purchases through life insurance companies and pension funds, participations in various credit market asset funds, and through thrift institution flows (net of these lenders' mortgages). The projections for 1985 indicate that the flows through intermediaries "borrowing" from households are potentially large enough to absorb the long-term debt issues of the business sector. Arguments to the contrary are based not on the adequacy of aggregate flows but on the pattern of existing relationships. For example, it is suggested that corporate bond issues will be greater than the ability of traditional institutions (for example, life insurance companies) to absorb them. This, however, is not a relevant constraint; it merely suggests that pressures exist for innovative activities by the intermediaries serving the household sector and for the development of different financial instruments.

Thus, our views of household behavior—moderate housing demand and fairly high saving inflows—imply that the thrift institutions will be able to provide the necessary levels of intermediation for the mortgage market and may also emerge as a source of funds for the business sector. In addition, substantial supplies of funds will be channeled from the household to the business sector through traditional sources—life insurance companies and pension funds, for example.

Protracted and severely reduced flows of equity finance are incompatible with the real-sector assumption of sustained high levels of investment projected for 1985. That is, the impacts of inflation and/or recession that have depressed real corporate profits and, hence, retained earnings and stock market prices also depress expected returns and new business investment. But these cyclical events should not be extrapolated into the long-run forecasts. It seems far more likely that real recovery will take place and that the rate of inflation will be reduced or, alternatively, that business will learn

to adapt to inflationary pressures so as to neutralize the impact on real profit rates. This approach is used to generate the 1985 flows for the business sector. Business sources include substantial, although by no means unprecedented, new equity and bond issues as well as bank loans (included in other loans).

As for the financial sector, there are few significant changes postulated in the balance-sheet allocations of the major financial institutions. For commercial banks, the downtrend in holdings of U.S. government securities is projected to continue, while increases in holdings of state and local government securities and loans to corporate business are anticipated as offsets to this trend. The importance of deposits as the major source of funds for banks remains unchanged in these projections.

According to the projections in Table 27-5, the notable change at savings and loan institutions will be a shift from single-home to multifamily and commercial mortgages. Mutual savings banks will also undergo a similar shift, although the decline in anticipated home mortgages will be much more dramatic because their biggest gains are to be in the acquisition of corporate bonds. Credit unions also are expected to shift from the holding of U.S. government securities to favor an even more traditional outlet for loans, namely, the extension of consumer credit.

Life insurance companies are projected to continue their trend out of home mortgages and into claims on commercial and multifamily structures. Their investment in corporate shares is expected to remain near its recent high, although no increase in their relative share is anticipated. Non–life insurance companies are expected to do little that is new except to shift still further out of U.S. governments into corporate bonds. Private pension funds will likely revert back to their portfolio mix of the late 1960s; this will require a modest shift out of stocks into corporate bonds.

An alternative discussion of the projected FOF matrix for 1985 can be based on financial flows rather than on sectoral behavior. For example, we noted earlier that the supply of U.S. government securities should be relatively small (especially so when compared to the large deficits in 1976). The traditional demanders of these securities can, therefore, shift their attention elsewhere. For example, instead of demanding savings bonds house-

**Table 27–4(A)  Supply of Funds as a Percentage of GNP, 1976**

| Financial Instruments | House-hold | Nonfinancial Corporate Business | U.S. Govt. | State/Local Govt. | ROW | Other Business | Monetary Authorities | Fed. Agencies | Banks | Thrifts | Life Insur. & Pen. Funds | Other Financial | Total |
|---|---|---|---|---|---|---|---|---|---|---|---|---|---|
| U.S. govt. securities | -.1 | .6 | | .6 | .7 | | .6 | .2 | 1.2 | .6 | .6 | .1 | 5.2 |
| State/local securities | .2 | -.1 | | .1 | | | | | .2 | .1 | .4 | | .9 |
| Corp. & for. bonds | .2 | | | | .1 | | | | | .2 | 1.6 | .2 | 2.2 |
| Mortgages | .5 | | -.2 | .1 | | | | 1.1 | .8 | 2.9 | .2 | -.3 | 5.1 |
| Consumer credit | | .1 | | | | .1 | | | .7 | .4 | .2 | .2 | 1.4 |
| Other loans[a] | -.8 | .7 | 1.0 | | .8 | .1 | | | 1.7 | .4 | .2 | .3 | 4.4 |
| Corporate shares | -.2 | | | | .2 | | | | | | .8 | -.1 | .7 |
| Reserves | 3.1 | | | | | | | | | | | | 3.1 |
| Misc.[b] | .1 | 1.6 | .4 | .1 | .2 | | | | .3 | | | .3 | 3.1 |
| Deposits & currency | 6.9 | .4 | .2 | .1 | | | | | | -.1 | .1 | .1 | 7.8 |
| Total uses | 9.9 | 3.3 | 1.4 | 1.0 | 2.0 | .2 | .6 | 1.3 | 4.9 | 4.4 | 3.9 | .8 | 33.8 |

## Table 27-4(B)  Demand for Funds as a Percentage of GNP, 1976

| Financial Instruments | House-hold | Nonfinancial Corporate Business | U.S. Govt. | State/ Local Govt. | ROW | Other Business | Monetary Authorities | Fed. Agen-cies | Banks | Thrifts | Life Insur. & Pen. Funds | Other Financial | Total |
|---|---|---|---|---|---|---|---|---|---|---|---|---|---|
| U.S. govt. securities | | | 4.0 | | | | | 1.1 | | | | | 5.2 |
| State/local securities | | | | .9 | | | | | | | | | .9 |
| Corp. & foreign bonds | | 1.3 | | | .5 | | | | | | | .3 | 2.2 |
| Mortgages | 3.6 | .8 | | | | .6 | | | | | | | 5.1 |
| Consumer credit | 1.4 | | | | | | | | | | | | 1.4 |
| Other loans[a] | .1 | .8 | .2 | | 1.8 | −.6 | | | 1.5 | | .8 | | 4.5 |
| Corporate shares | | .6 | | | | | | | .1 | | .1 | −.1 | .7 |
| Reserves | | | .3 | | | | | | | | 2.9 | | 3.1 |
| Misc.[b] | .4 | 1.6 | .3 | | .1 | .1 | | | | | | .5 | 3.1 |
| Deposits & currency | | | | | .1 | | .6 | | 3.1 | 4.1 | | | 7.8 |
| Total sources | 5.6 | 5.1 | 4.8 | .9 | 2.5 | 0 | .6 | 1.2 | 4.7 | 4.1 | 3.8 | .7 | 34.0 |
| Net financial investment | 4.3 | −1.8 | −3.4 | .1 | −.4 | .2 | 0 | .1 | .1 | .2 | .1 | 0 | |

Note: Totals may not add up because of rounding off and the omission of flows that are less than .05 percent of GNP.
[a] Includes bank loans, commercial paper, and acceptances.
[b] Trade credit, security credit, profit tax liabilities, proprietors' equity, and miscellaneous unallocated assets and liabilities.

Source: Calculated from Flow of Funds tables published by the Board of Governors of the Federal Reserve Board and forecast by the author for 1985.

**Table 27-5(A)  Supply of Funds in 1985 as a Percentage of GNP**

| Financial Instruments | House-hold | Nonfinancial Corporate Business | U.S. Govt. | State/ Local Govt. | ROW | Other Business | Monetary Authorities | Fed. Agen-cies | Banks | Thrifts | Life Insur. & Pen. Funds | Other Financial | Total |
|---|---|---|---|---|---|---|---|---|---|---|---|---|---|
| U.S. govt. securities | 0.3 | .1 | | 0.1 | 0.3 | | 0.4 | | 0.2 | | | | 1.4 |
| State/local securities | 0.2 | | | | | | | | 0.5 | | 0.1 | 0.1 | 1.0 |
| Corp. & foreign bonds | 0.4 | | | 0.1 | | | | | 0.2 | 0.2 | 1.0 | 0.1 | 2.0 |
| Mortgages | 0.1 | | 0.1 | | | | | 0.7 | 0.9 | 1.6 | 0.5 | 0.1 | 4.0 |
| Consumer credit | | 0.1 | | | | | | | 0.5 | 0.2 | 0.3 | | 1.1 |
| Other loans[a] | 0.2 | 0.7 | 0.2 | | 0.4 | 0.1 | | 0.2 | 2.0 | | 0.2 | 0.2 | 4.2 |
| Corporate shares | | | | | 0.3 | | | | | | 0.8 | | 1.1 |
| Reserves | 2.6 | | | | | | | | | | | | 2.6 |
| Misc.[b] | | 1.3 | .3 | | .1 | | | | .2 | | | .1 | 2.0 |
| Deposits & currency | 4.4 | 0.3 | 0.2 | 0.4 | 0.2 | | | | | 0.1 | | 0.1 | 5.8 |
| Total uses | 8.2 | 2.6 | 0.8 | 0.7 | 1.3 | 0.1 | 0.4 | 0.9 | 4.5 | 2.1 | 2.6 | 1.0 | 25.3 |

**Table 27-5(B)  Demand for Funds in 1985 as a Percentage of GNP**

| Financial Instruments | House-holds | Nonfinancial Corporate Business | U.S. Govt. | State/Local Govt. | ROW | Other Business | Monetary Authorities | Fed. Agencies | Banks | Thrifts | Life Insur. & Pen. Funds | Other Financial | Total |
|---|---|---|---|---|---|---|---|---|---|---|---|---|---|
| U.S. govt. securities | | | 0.4 | | | | | 0.9 | | | | | 1.3 |
| State/local securities | | | | 1.0 | | | | | | | | | 1.0 |
| Corp. & foreign bonds | 1.6 | | | | 0.2 | | | | 0.1 | | | 0.2 | 2.1 |
| Mortgages | 2.2 | 0.9 | | | | 0.9 | | | | | | | 4.0 |
| Consumer credit | 1.1 | | | | | | | | | | | | 1.1 |
| Other loans[a] | 0.3 | 1.4 | 0.1 | | 0.4 | 1.0 | | | 0.5 | 0.1 | 0.2 | .3 | 4.2 |
| Corporate shares | | 0.8 | | | | | | | | | | .2 | 1.1 |
| Reserves | | | 0.3 | | | | | | | | 2.3 | | 2.6 |
| Misc.[b] | 1.3 | 1.3 | .2 | | .1 | .1 | | | | | | .3 | 2.0 |
| Deposits & currency | | | | | | | 0.4 | | 3.6 | 1.8 | | | 5.8 |
| Total sources | 3.6 | 6.0 | 0.9 | 1.1 | 0.7 | 2.0 | 0.4 | 0.9 | 4.3 | 2.0 | 2.5 | 1.0 | 25.3 |
| Net financial investment | 4.6 | −3.4 | −0.1 | −0.4 | 0.6 | −1.9 | | | 0.2 | 0.1 | 0.1 | 0.1 | 0 |

Note: Totals may not add up because of rounding off and the omission of flows that are less than .05 percent of GNP.
[a]Includes bank loans, commercial paper, and acceptances.
[b]Trade credit, security credit, profit tax liabilities, proprietors' equity and miscellaneous unallocated assets and liabilities.

Source: Calculated from Flow of Funds tables published by the Board of Governors of the Federal Reserve Board and forecast by the author for 1985.

holds can increase their deposits in thrift institutions. As a result, the depository institutions will have high levels of deposits, which can be allocated to the business sector since household demand for these funds (mortgages and consumer credit) is expected to be moderate.

An important feature of the projection is the substantial volume of new equity financing forecast to be forthcoming in 1985. It is all the more impressive since the underlying assumptions make no special allowances for encouraging equity purchases. Private pension funds are expected to reduce their holdings of corporate stocks, but this will be offset to some extent by a relative increase of corporate shares in the portfolios of state and local retirement funds. However, it is assumed that by the 1980s the household sector will cease to be a net seller of equities, although this depends on the rate of price appreciation of stocks. In any case, the acquisition of equities by either ROW or mutual funds could entirely offset household net sales of stock. Indeed, the foreign sector is projected to absorb 25 percent of the net new issues forecast for 1985.

The whole pattern of corporate finance is projected to show signs of change over the next decade. With corporate shares substituting for debt, the ratio of credit market borrowing to undistributed profits and new issues of stock should drop substantially relative to the 1960s and early 1970s, thereby easing some of the problems related to a higher degree of leverage. On the other hand, corporations will find that the relative gap between their capital outlays and internal funds will continue to grow. The increased availability of equity capital, however, will mean less reliance on debt to finance externally the historically high volumes of capital outlays.

In sum, it appears that there will not be severe pressure for a restructuring of existing patterns of financial activity over the next decade; there will, however, be selective pressures. For example, one needed innovation is the emergence of a rather strong and active secondary market in corporate bonds. This is necessary if corporate bonds are to become a true substitute in the eyes of many potential holders for longer-term government debt. The rise of mutual funds specializing in the acquisition of corporate bonds indicates that financial innovation in this area is well underway. Further changes may shortly be forthcoming as well. For example, relatively diminished construction expenditures, particularly for housing, may leave thrift institutions, especially mutual savings banks, with surplus funds available for lending to business. Another possibility may be federal "intermediation" to ease the direct demands in corporate debt markets. Federal financing of railroads, farming, and pollution-abatement expenditures has already emerged in the financial markets. The banking sector may also become a larger source of long-term credit via term loans and syndicated loan participations with smaller banks and nonbank investors. However, given the forecast of strength in the new issues market for stocks, it seems unlikely that extensive innovations or general federal support of corporate external financing will be required.

## Conclusion

In conclusion, our view of the future prospects of the capital markets predicates that real resource availability (capital shortages) will not be a problem; financial market stability will, nevertheless, require major structural developments by financial institutions. Although it is impossible to forecast financial innovation, we are confident that it will take place. In addition, the financial pressures on business that provide the climate for innovation are probably a desirable element inasmuch as they help to ensure an efficient allocation of resources through the capital markets. Business executives view these prospects with uneasiness—it makes their job harder—but financial markets without strain can lead to major long-run resource misallocations—misallocations that may well be one of the legacies of the 1960s. To avoid misallocation—this time, perhaps, underinvestment—financial innovations are evolving to cope with the impact of inflation in curtailing business saving and internal finance. There is ample evidence in recent experience that, given sufficient latitude by regulators, the financial system will be able to channel resources without massive federal intervention.

The analysis and discussion of trends in the financial markets in this chapter, however, should be viewed as merely suggestive. The explicit flow of funds forecasts but one way in which the financial markets could develop so as to sustain real-sector investment activity that is essential for growth. We can by no means be certain that such conditions will emerge. We can only conclude that there is a feasible financial-sector outcome consistent with the long-term growth potential of the economy.

It is surely true that a person who reads these forecasts in 1985 will find much that is amusing. At that time, errors of commission and omission should be painfully obvious. Some of the trends that have been confidently extrapolated into the next decade will certainly fail to materialize. Equally important, the reader in 1985 will probably have a difficult time finding any hint of some of the major financial developments that have been predicted as certain to take place.

If we reflect on previous prognostications, evidence of forecasting errors is easy to find. Thus, in the concluding chapter of his masterful study, published in 1961, Kuznets discusses the forces likely to influence patterns of capital formation and financing over an extended period. Kuznets concludes:

> Unless in the next few years the private sector can generate savings and capital formation in a greater proportion to a rising private product, the pressure of demand for goods upon the supply of savings will persist.[21]

Kuznets appears to have been alarmed by the prospect of a "capital shortage" as early as 1961, shortly before what turned out to be a decade of unprecedented capital growth. This gloomy prospect was avoided presumably because of the high rates of personal saving that actually took place, whereas Kuznets expected "rather low ratios of personal saving." As for the business sector, Kuznets forecast "a moderate rise in the share of internal financing"; instead, there have been large increases in internal financing since his analysis. Finally, in discussing patterns of finance, Kuznets argued that government policy was likely to determine any primary changes in these patterns, while more or less downplaying in his analysis what turned out to be a major avenue of accommodation, namely, the constructive responses of financial institutions to institutional needs.

[21]Simon Kuznets, *Capital in the American Economy: Its Formation and Financing,* Princeton University Press, Princeton, N.J., 1961, p. 457.

What then is the value of long-term financial projections? As can be seen, even the best forays into this type of analysis are fraught with risk and probable error. Still, when all is said and done, these analyses are valuable, not because they tell us what will transpire, but because they better prepare us for the surprises that are certain to evolve.

## Questions

1. Why is the term *capital shortage* puzzling to an accountant? Why is it puzzling to the market-oriented economist?

2. How does a free market determine the optimal size of the capital stock? Should society take account of any other considerations in determining capital policy? If so, to what extent is interference with market determination warranted?

3. What is the relationship between the National Income and Product Accounts and the Flow of Funds Accounts? Why is the relationship important for this chapter?

4. What is meant by a *judgmental projection* and how does it differ from an econometric forecast?

5. Is there a general consensus that business plant and equipment expenditures will be a larger proportion of GNP in the next decade than in the last? What are the projected sources of financing for 1985 (see Table 27-5)? How much of this financing is direct and how much takes place through intermediaries?

6. Examine the sources and uses tables for 1976 and 1985 and calculate the direct financing and intermediary financing of the household sector in each year.

7. It has been said that the oil-exporting nations helped the United States to conduct a fiscal policy that ended the 1973–1975 recession—a recession that those same countries helped induce. Evidence of this can be found in Table 27-4 by analyzing data on the supply and demand for funds in 1976. Explain this statement by pointing out the appropriate evidence.

8. Tables 27-4 and 27-5 indicate that each financial intermediary emphasizes a particular type of financing activity. What are they? What differences are found between 1976 and the forecast for 1985? Look up the flow of funds tables in the *Federal Reserve Bulletin* and see if similar patterns were prevalent in earlier periods.

9. It is possible that in 1985 business saving will be 1 percent more of GNP (because of higher depreciation allowances) and personal saving 1 percent less of GNP (because of lower flows into savings accounts). Recalculate the forecasted matrices for the supply and demand for funds (Table 27-5) under these assumptions.

10. How would a reduction in the taxation of capital gains affect the funds flows? Trace through its possible impact on household savings and corporate investment and from there to sectoral financing requirements.

## Selected Bibliography

Bosworth, Barry, James Duesenberry, and Andrew Carron. *Capital Needs in the Seventies.* The Brookings Institution, Washington, D.C., 1975.

Eisner, Robert. "Capital Shortage: Myth and Reality." *American Economic Review* (February 1977).

Sametz, Arnold W. *Prospects of Capital Formation and Capital Markets.* Heath-Lexington Books, Lexington, Mass., 1978.

Sametz, Arnold W., and Paul Wachtel. "The Financial Environment and the Flow of Funds over the Next Decade." In *Understanding Capital Markets,* vol. 2, eds. Sametz and Wachtel. Heath-Lexington Books, Lexington, Mass., 1977.

Shapiro, Eli, and William White, eds. *Capital for Productivity and Jobs.* Prentice-Hall, Englewood Cliffs, N.J., 1977.

von Furstenberg, George M. "Flow of Funds Analysis and the Economic Outlook." *Annals of Economic and Social Measurement* (Winter 1977).

Wachtel, Paul, Arnold W. Sametz, and Harry Shuford. "Capital Shortages: Myth or Reality?" *Journal of Finance* (May 1976).

# VII

# Public Policy

# 28

# Monetary Policy

There are four generally accepted economic objectives for the modern American economy: (1) price stability, (2) full employment, (3) adequate rates of economic growth, and (4) equilibrium in our international balance of payments.[1] To help meet these objectives the federal government engages in a variety of actions that are known collectively as federal economic policy. Each component of economic policy uses different methods in seeking to optimize the overall objectives and possibly is directed toward different aspects of the economy. Fiscal policy, for example, is concerned with the relation between taxation and government spending. Debt management policy is concerned with the form of government debt—its maturity structure and other characteristics.[2] Incomes policy is directed toward managing the relative levels of income of various economic agents—for example, the wages of labor and the profits of capital. Monetary policy, not surprisingly, is focused on money, although the thinking about just what monetary policy does has changed substantially over the years.

Monetary policy in the United States has been the responsibility of the Federal Reserve System since its establishment in 1913.[3] The Federal Reserve is a relatively independent branch of the government under the general direction of Congress. The Federal Reserve has had general responsibility for many activities (such as providing a nationwide system of check clearing, examining state-char-

---

[1]This is not the place for an extended discussion of each of these objectives. However, it should be noted that each involves conceptual and empirical problems peculiar to itself. Furthermore, policymakers are faced at times with situations where these objectives are conflicting rather than complementary. Thus, for example, attaining something approximating "full" employment may lead to wage and price inflation and disequilibrium in our balance of payments. Worse still, policymakers may find themselves faced simultaneously with high rates of unemployment, inflation, and an adverse balance of payments, as in 1973–1975. Confronted with such problems, policymakers may, at certain times, subordinate one or more objectives for others. Thus, in 1979 and 1980, the goal of full employment (however defined) was deliberately subordinated to the twin goals of curtailing inflation and inflationary expectations as well as achieving balance-of-payments equilibrium.

[2]Fiscal policy and debt management policy are discussed in Chapter 29.

[3]A more complete description of the Federal Reserve System is found in Chapter 5.

tered member banks, and acting as fiscal agent for the Treasury) that are not directly related to its function of formulating and executing monetary policy. The *raison d'être* of the Federal Reserve, however, is monetary policy.

As indicated in Chapters 21 and 22, monetary policy operates through financial markets. Beyond general agreement on this point, however, there are wide divergences of view concerning the specific channels of monetary influence on the economy. Economists and financial analysts disagree even about the objectives and strategies that should be pursued. And at the Federal Reserve itself, viewpoints have changed in recent years. Prior to the 1970s, the Federal Reserve supported the view that monetary policy should affect the cost and availability of credit. The central bank did not purport to control the cost of each type of credit, but it did see the purpose of monetary policy as attempting to influence some overall index representing the cost of credit. As a practical matter the Federal Reserve used the interest rate on short-term government securities and, to some extent, the long-term government bond rate as its index. It was primarily interested in preventing extreme short-run variations in these rates and in influencing significantly their longer-run direction as well as controlling the availability of credit.

During the 1950s and 1960s, a growing group of economists, led by Milton Friedman and loosely called *monetarists,* sharply challenged the "cost and availability of credit" view of monetary policy and argued that monetary policy should be directed toward determining the rate of growth of the money supply.[4] One reason advanced by the monetarists for focusing on the rate of growth of money rather than on interest rates was that monetary policy, in their view, was incapable of managing real (inflation-adjusted) interest rates anyway, except in the very short run. The contention was that while the Federal Reserve might, through its actions, affect nominal (market) interest rates for a time, subsequent activities of other economic agents would result in changes in the rate of inflation. Changes in the inflation rate would then alter nominal inter-

est rates, thus making interest rates an inadequate index of monetary policy.[5] Throughout the 1970s this view gained favor at the central bank as it adopted an approach to monetary policy that might be termed *practical monetarism.* The purpose of this chapter is to analyze and discuss some elements of this controversy over monetary policy by examining its objectives, strategies, and problems. First, however, it seems reasonable to discuss the principal instruments of monetary and credit control employed by the Federal Reserve System.

## The Instruments of Monetary Policy

Currently, the Federal Reserve employs five instruments of credit control with which it seeks to execute its monetary policy: (1) it engages in open-market operations in government securities; (2) it determines and executes discount policy; (3) it sets reserve requirements for bank and nonbank deposits within limits established by the Monetary Control Act of 1980; (4) it participates in determining maximum interest rates payable on bank time and savings deposits pending phase-out of ceilings by 1986; and (5) it establishes margin requirements for the carrying and purchase of securities. It is customary to divide these credit-control instruments into two groups: general tools, which presumably affect all financial markets and types of credit equally, and selective controls, which are intended to affect *specific* types of credit or *selected* areas of the economy. The first three instruments listed above are considered to be general tools, while the last two are regarded as selective credit-control instruments. We shall briefly discuss each of the general instruments.

### Open-Market Operations

Although open-market operations were initiated by the Federal Reserve in the 1920s, this instrument of monetary policy was formalized only in the 1930s as the responsibility of the monetary policy-making committee of the Federal Reserve System, namely, the Federal Open Market Committee (FOMC). The latter includes all seven governors of the Federal Reserve Board as well as five of the presidents

---

[4]See, for example, Milton Friedman, *A Program for Monetary Stability,* Fordham University Press, New York, 1960; and Friedman, "The Role of Monetary Policy," *American Economic Review* (March 1968).

[5]The economic theory behind this view was introduced in Chapter 22.

of the twelve Federal Reserve banks.[6] Current practice is for the FOMC to set policy guidelines for open-market purchases and sales of government securities roughly every four weeks, while the Manager of the Open Market Account (a Vice President of the Federal Reserve Bank of New York) has operational responsibility for effectuating daily the actual purchases and sales within those guidelines.[7]

These purchases and sales of U.S. government securities involve transactions between the Manager of the Account and some thirty-odd government securities dealers, a dozen of whom are money-market banks located in New York City and Chicago. Bids and offers by the Fed are solicited on a competitive basis so as not to unduly influence market prices. The slight margins of 1/64 to 1/128 of 1 percent between bid and offer prices often found at the short end of the government securities market (with only somewhat larger margins at the longer end) are ample testimony to the competitiveness and efficiency of this market.

As pointed out in Chapter 5, open-market purchases of government securities by the Fed can lead to a multiple increase in the money supply; conversely, open-market sales have the opposite effect. Although the impact of these purchases and sales is first felt in the New York money market, in time they produce a ripple effect on the reserve positions of banks throughout the country. By way of illustration, as New York City banks begin to lose reserves through their purchase of government securities from the Fed or through the purchase of these securities by nonbank dealers who keep their accounts with these money-market banks, the latter try to replenish their reserves by purchases in the Federal Funds market. One result is that other banks throughout the country selling their excess reserves to their New York counterparts soon begin to feel the pinch themselves so that the initial tightening impact in New York shortly begins to make itself felt throughout the country. The converse is true when the Fed engages in open-market purchases.

Open-market operations constitute the primary instrument of credit control employed by the Federal Reserve. Unlike discounting, where the initiative rests with the banks, or changes in reserve requirements, which can involve large and disequilibrating changes in bank portfolios and in financial markets, open-market operations can be finely tuned to the current objectives of monetary policy and quickly reversed should the Fed have initially miscalculated the impact of its operations on the money market. It is a continuous and flexible instrument in affecting reserve positions and, consequently, in determining the volume of credit and money that can be created.

## Discounting

There are two distinct aspects to Federal Reserve discount policy: (1) setting the discount rate, and (2) determining which institutions are eligible to borrow and under what conditions. Discounts are short-term loans (typically of two-weeks' duration) made by the Federal Reserve banks; the interest rate charged on such loans is the discount rate. Each of the twelve Federal Reserve banks ''sets'' its individual discount rate subject to the review and determination of these rates by the Federal Reserve Board in Washington. The U.S. Congress, through the Federal Reserve Act, and the Board, through its Regulation A, have established the types of securities that the borrowing institution must pledge as collateral and the various other conditions of the loan process.

In the early years of the Fed, discounting took the form of Federal Reserve bank purchases of member banks' short-term customer loans with recourse to the member bank in the event of the customer's default. In recent decades virtually all ''discounting'' has been in the form of ''advances'' of funds to a member bank on the bank's own promissory note, with government securities pledged as collateral. The Monetary Control Act of 1980 extended the discount privilege to nonmember banks and other institutions that offer either transaction accounts or nonpersonal time deposits. Advances occur only on the initiative of the borrowing institution; hence, the impact of discount policy on reserves relies on the ability of the Federal Reserve

[6]The structure of the Federal Reserve System is discussed in Chapter 5.

[7]Summaries of minutes of the FOMC meetings are published with approximately a one-month delay and may be found in the *Federal Reserve Bulletin*. From these minutes and directives issued to the Manager of the Open Market Account one can obtain some knowledge of the way in which monetary policy is decided.

to induce borrowers to request advances or on its ability to discourage advances when the latter are contrary to the current stance of monetary policy.

One way by which the Fed attempts to control the volume of discounting is through the pricing mechanism, that is, through the discount rate. To be effective, however, the discount rate must bear some relationship to the Treasury bill rate and the yield on Federal Funds. Thus, if the discount rate is set below the latter rates, it becomes relatively cheaper to borrow at the discount window than by selling government securities or purchasing Federal Funds, both close substitutes for discounting. Presumably, recourse to the latter will augment the reserve position of borrowing institutions, even if temporarily, and may lead to an increase in the money supply. On the other hand, recourse to the Federal Funds market or the sale of government securities merely redistributes reserves among the banks with no net additions to the reserve base. The result is the lack of any increment in the money supply from these sources although it may mean an increase in the velocity of money.

The second method by which the Fed attempts to control the volume of borrowing at the discount window is by rationing the quantity of credit. Put another way, the Fed is not content simply to rely on the pricing mechanism to determine the volume of discounting; rather, it supplements the latter through quantitative controls. The Foreword to Regulation A makes clear that discounting is a privilege rather than an automatic right and, furthermore, that such credit as is extended is primarily to be used by the borrowing banks for unanticipated cash drains or short-term seasonal needs rather than as a source of quasi-permanent capital by bank management through more or less continuous recourse to the discount window. Furthermore, borrowing is regarded as inappropriate when it is done to take advantage of a positive spread between the discount rate and the yields on securities that the banks can acquire or on the loan rates they charge their customers. In emphasizing its policies through "jawboning" or moral suasion and in applying them to specific loan requests, the Fed is in a position to reduce the aggregate amount of discounting that would otherwise prevail at any given discount rate.[8]

Many observers regard the discount window as a safety valve available to individual banks in times of need and, therefore, as an escape mechanism that tends to run counter to a tight monetary policy. From this point of view, open-market purchases of government securities tending to deplete reserves can be counteracted in part through additional borrowing at the discount window. Consequently, suggestions and countersuggestions have ranged from maintaining access to the discount window for those individual banks who, through no fault of their own, find themselves with temporary cash drains to the virtual elimination of discounting as a method for acquiring reserves.[9]

Any change in the discount rate is not only a cost phenomenon affecting the desire to borrow; it has also been interpreted as symbolic of Federal Reserve intentions concerning the direction of its policies. Presumably, an increase in the rate should alert members of the business and financial communities to the fact that the Fed will be tightening its monetary policy and should serve as a signal for cutbacks in bank loan demand. However, there have been times when the "announcement effects" of such changes have been perverse, prompting an acceleration of bank borrowing in order to forestall anticipated future declines in credit availability and higher loan rates. Again, suggested remedies have included abolition of the discount window or an automatic pegging of the discount rate to the weekly auction Treasury bill rate so that market uncertainty generated by discretionary changes in the discount rate can be eliminated.[10]

The discount rate, unlike open-market operations which are continuous in nature, is changed only at discrete time intervals. Nevertheless, it has

---

[8]For a full discussion of discounting, see Murray E. Polakoff, "Federal Reserve Discount Policy and Its Crit-

ics," in Dean Carson, ed., *Banking and Monetary Studies,* Richard D. Irwin, Inc., Homewood, Illinois, 1963; see also Board of Governors of the Federal Reserve System, *Reappraisal of the Federal Reserve Discount Mechanism,* Washington, D.C., 1971–1972.

[9]In the latter connection, see Friedman, *A Program for Monetary Stability.*

[10]Warren L. Smith, "The Discount Rate as a Credit-Control Weapon," *Journal of Political Economy* (April 1958), 174–175. Smith also advocated that the peg be such that the spread between the bill rate and the discount rate always be set in favor of the former by 1 percent or more. By so doing, presumably, the opportunity cost to the banks would favor the selling off of governments rather than the acquisition of additional reserves at the discount window. Historically, the discount rate has never been a

been altered far more frequently than have changes in reserve requirements. Traditionally, the discount rate has been changed in steps ranging from one-quarter to one-half of a percent in magnitude.[11] However, in November 1978, and again in 1979 and early 1980, the discount rate was raised by a full percentage point as part of major policy initiatives designed to reduce domestic inflationary pressures and maintain the value of the dollar abroad. (They have subsequently been lowered by a full percentage point several times, beginning with the onset of the recession in the spring of 1980.)

### Setting Reserve Requirements

During the 1930s the Federal Reserve Board was given authority by Congress to vary reserve requirements against member bank deposits. (Before then, these percentages were fixed by law.) The Monetary Control Act, enacted on March 31, 1980, improves the effectiveness of monetary policy by applying new reserve requirements set by the Fed not only to member banks but also to nonmember banks, savings banks, S&Ls, and credit unions that offer either transaction accounts (demand deposits, NOW accounts, automatic transfer service accounts, share draft accounts, accounts subject to telephone transfer, and all other accounts used for making payments or transfers), or nonpersonal time deposits. Under the act, reserve requirements on the first $25 million of an institution's transaction accounts is 3 percent; the initial requirement on remaining transaction accounts is 12 percent; and the initial requirement on nonpersonal time deposits is 3 percent. The new requirements will be phased in gradually, with the phase-in period depending in part on the present reserve status of the institution.[12] As of this writing, the mechanics of

calculating required reserve balances will remain the same as before the act was passed; namely, institutions subject to reserve requirements are not required to maintain minimum reserve balances on a daily basis; rather, average weekly reserves beginning each Thursday must equal average deposits two weeks prior to what is known as the "reserve settlement period."[13] Reserve requirements are changed infrequently, and the Federal Reserve gives reserve-holding institutions approximately two weeks' notice before the effective date of such changes, thereby permitting them to plan whatever portfolio changes are necessary.[14] Nonetheless, such changes in reserve requirements, even by as little as ¼ percent, involve changes in the composition of required and excess reserves of millions of dollars and are a clumsy instrument when compared to open-market operations.[15]

---

penalty rate in this country; that is, traditionally it has been at the lowest end of the spectrum of rates. For some, like Smith, this has encouraged profit-oriented banks to take advantage of positive spreads between it and other rates through borrowing at the discount window, in this manner circumventing the impact of a tight money policy.

[11]Between January 1, 1970 and December 31, 1979, the discount rate was changed thirty-five times, whereas reserve requirements were changed only seven times.

[12]As provided in the Monetary Control Act of 1980, reserve requirements for member banks will be phased down to the new reserve requirements over a period end-

ing about three and a half years after the September 1, 1980, effective date of the act. The amount of reserves a member bank must hold will be equal to the amount required under the old structure less ⅛ of the difference between that amount and the amount required under the new structure. Thereafter, at approximately six-month intervals after September 1, 1980, required reserves will be reduced by an additional ⅛ of this difference. As for nonmember institutions, they would be phased up to the new reserve requirement structure over an eight-year period. As of September 1, 1980, the required reserves of such institutions were equal to ⅛ of the requirement under the new structure. The amount of required reserves thereafter is to be increased by an additional ⅛ after each succeeding twelve-month interval following the September 1, 1980, effective date of the act. Finally, the act stipulates that reserve requirements are to be met with balances held directly with the Fed, balances held indirectly with the Fed on a pass-through basis, and vault cash. Depository institutions that are not members of the Federal Reserve System may hold reserve balances on a pass-through basis in a depository institution that maintains required reserve balances at a Federal Reserve bank, in a Federal Home Loan bank, or in the National Credit Union Administration Central Liquidity Facility.

[13]For institutions with reserve deficiencies under this lagged reserve accounting system, a penalty rate of 2 percent above the current discount rate is imposed by the Fed, subject to certain qualifications.

[14]There are also supplementary or marginal reserve requirements on certain "managed liabilities." See *Federal Reserve Bulletin* (January 1980), Table 1.15. Historical information on changes in reserve requirements may be found in the *Federal Reserve Bulletin* (July 1980), Table 1.15.

[15]By way of analogy, the difference between the two instruments could be compared to the use of a meat axe in undertaking a delicate brain operation vis-à-vis the use of a scalpel for this purpose.

## The Strategy of Monetary Policy

The Federal Reserve System, of course, attempts to use its policy instruments in a way that achieves its specific monetary policy objectives. These objectives are established by the Federal Open Market Committee so as to be consistent with the Committee's approach to economic policy generally. However, as pointed out in Chapter 5, the Federal Reserve does not directly control all of the variables associated with the monetary process. As a result, the System cannot meet its policy objectives directly; it must, instead, rely on intermediate "operating target" variables that are more closely under its control. These elements of the monetary policy transmission mechanism are outlined in Figure 28-1.

The overall plan for monetary policy established by the FOMC is often referred to as the "strategy" of monetary policy.[16] This overall plan has two important parts. The first part, often referred to as *long-term strategy,* consists of establishing monetary policy objectives (box 3 in Figure 28-1) that are consistent with broader economic policy objectives (box 4 in Figure 28-1). These monetary policy objectives involve establishing targets for the monetary variable or variables that the FOMC desires to influence.[17] In recent years, the long-term strategy of the FOMC has become evident in its policy statements each February that set target rates of growth in various definitions of the money supply for the coming year. These long-term growth rate targets for the money stock are established by first forecasting changes in the values of the several economic objectives and then attempting to determine the optimal rate of growth of the money stock thought to be consistent with these objectives. The procedure for relating changes in the economic ob-

jectives and growth rate targets for the money stock is as follows.

In preparing and implementing a long-term strategy, the FOMC through its staff first develops a forecast of GNP, employment, and prices for the coming year. These forecasts are updated quarterly for each meeting of the FOMC. The forecasting tool employed by the Fed is its own elaborate version of the quarterly large-scale econometric model of the U.S. economy developed by the Social Science Research Council, the Massachusetts Institute of Technology, and the University of Pennsylvania (SMP). The predictions of this model for the coming year are supplemented by the judgment of various members of the staff, and a resulting consensus forecast is presented to the FOMC. Using this information, along with data from other sources and their own judgments, the FOMC then decides on the growth rate target for the money stock. It should be pointed out that the individual estimates of the different members of the FOMC may vary because of different weights attached by each to changes in the various economic objectives or to their relative importance (for example, one member might attach a greater significance and weight to price stability than another member) and because of differing views regarding the structure of the economy (for example, divergent views on how well the SMP model replicates the economy). Thus, in effect, the long-run target rate of money stock growth is also a consensus target among FOMC members.

The second part of monetary policy strategy, often referred to as *short-term strategy,* consists of manipulating the monetary policy instruments on a day-to-day basis so as to achieve long-run money supply goals. Specifically, having selected its long-term strategy with respect to the targeted growth of the money stock, the FOMC must also plan the use of open-market operations and other policy instruments to meet its money growth target. Ultimately, this means setting an "operating target" for bank reserves or the Federal Funds rate (box 2 in Figure 28-1), since these are the variables immediately affected by Federal Reserve policy actions and most fully under its control. The operating target is chosen so as to be consistent with objectives for the money supply formulated as part of long-term strategy (box 3 in Figure 28-1). Short-term strategy also involves correcting unplanned

---

[16] See Raymond E. Lombra and Raymond G. Torto, "The Strategy of Monetary Policy," *Federal Reserve Bank of Richmond, Economic Review* (September/October 1975), 3–14.

[17] Because the FOMC cannot influence these variables directly with its policy instruments and because influencing these variables is not the ultimate goal of monetary policy (box 4 in Figure 28-1), these variables are often referred to as *intermediate target variables.* Also, goals for these variables are often referred to as *intermediate targets.* To avoid confusion with timing, the term *monetary policy objectives* is used in this chapter to describe box 3 in Figure 28-1, rather than the term *intermediate targets,* which might also be used.

### Figure 28-1  The Transmission of Monetary Policy

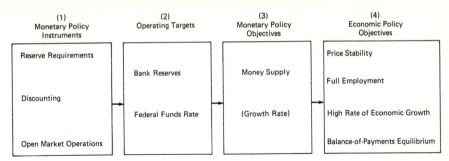

| (1)<br>Monetary Policy<br>Instruments | (2)<br>Operating Targets | (3)<br>Monetary Policy<br>Objectives | (4)<br>Economic Policy<br>Objectives |
|---|---|---|---|
| Reserve Requirements<br><br>Discounting<br><br>Open Market Operations | Bank Reserves<br><br>Federal Funds Rate | Money Supply<br><br>(Growth Rate) | Price Stability<br><br>Full Employment<br><br>High Rate of Economic Growth<br><br>Balance-of-Payments Equilibrium |

deviations in monetary growth rates. For example, if short-term changes in the money stock deviate from its long-run growth path, the FOMC will select from alternative short-term paths designed to return the money stock to its projected long-term path. The actual alternative selected will depend on how soon within the year the FOMC wishes to bring about the necessary adjustment between the two growth paths.

### Complications for Short-Term Monetary Policy Strategy

Choice of an operating target has caused difficulty for short-term monetary policy. From the early 1970s until October 6, 1979, the short-term monetary policy strategy of the Fed relied on maintaining, within relatively narrow bands, a targeted Federal Funds rate, whereas operating procedures after that date have concentrated on targeting the volume of bank reserves.[18] A brief analysis and review of the economic conditions prevailing before and shortly after the time the Federal Reserve changed its operating procedures reveals a central dilemma for this type of short-term monetary strategy: neither concentration on the Federal Funds rate as the operating target (the policy before October 6, 1979) nor concentration on bank reserves

[18]Given estimated income levels and targeted Federal Funds rates, the Fed felt that short-run money demand in the pre–October 1979 period was sufficiently stable and, therefore, predictable so that targeted money growth rates would fall within the limits set by it. Similarly, the post–October 1979 period concentrates on a presumably stable and predictable relationship between targeted reserve increases and a projected short-term growth path of the money stock.

(the policy after that date) is necessarily free from problems.

Essentially, the pre–October 1979 procedure employed by the Fed might be characterized as one that was demand driven. As may be seen from Figure 28-2, given the demand for bank reserves $DD$ (derived, ultimately, from the public's demand for money), the Fed would supply sufficient reserves $r_0 S_0$, so that the supply and demand for reserves (and for money) would be equal at the targeted Federal Funds rate, $r_0$. However, any upward shift in the demand for money, $D'D'$ (and, therefore, for additional reserves), would be met by the Fed's increasing the volume of reserves along what can be construed as an infinitely elastic supply curve, $r_0 S_0$. Thus, when the Fed pursued and maintained a targeted Federal Funds rate, bank

### Figure 28-2  Short-Run Federal Reserve Strategy

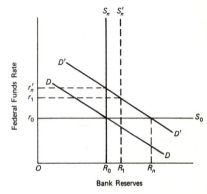

Source: Adapted from Raymond E. Lombra and Raymond G. Torto, "The Strategy of Monetary Policy," Federal Reserve Bank of Richmond, *Economic Review* (September/October 1975).

reserves and money stock growth became, in effect, demand driven. However, the demand for money (and reserves) was increasing at an unanticipated rate,[19] and the operating procedure employed by the Fed resulted, therefore, in larger than expected increases in reserves being supplied by it to member banks through open-market purchases of government securities. Consequently, monetary growth exceeded its targeted bands by wide margins, thereby contributing to price inflation.

The change in policy procedures on October 6, 1979, substituted for the demand-driven procedure operating techniques that are supply driven. As shown in Figure 28-2, a perfectly interest-inelastic supply curve of reserves (and money), $R_0S_n$, has been substituted for the perfectly elastic schedule $r_0S_0$. In this case, when the demand for reserves (and money) shifts upward to $D'D'$, the supply would still be maintained at $R_0S_n$, thereby forcing the Federal Funds rate upward from $r_0$ to $r_n$.[20] In this approach, the volume of reserves (and money) is held constant while the level of the Federal Funds rate is allowed to shift with changes in the demand for reserves (and money).

Unfortunately for Federal Reserve policymakers, the supply-driven policy is not free from difficulties either. One problem is that short- and long-term interest rates are much more volatile with this new policy. (As this was being written in mid-1980, Federal Funds rates, for example, had already fluctuated between 8 and 20 percent). Changes in money demand caused, say, by an increase in nominal income during a cyclical expansion might cause rapidly escalating interest rates that would be destabilizing for other sectors of the economy. Rapidly rising rates, in turn, could well cause severe problems for institutions like savings and loan associations or mutual savings banks whose sources of funds (liabilities) have shorter maturities than their uses of funds (assets). If rates

rise rapidly, as they did in late 1979 and early 1980, these institutions could face rapidly eroding profitability caused by the necessity of increasing their deposit rates to retain funds while being unable to raise rates on a large proportion of their mortgage portfolio, acquired at a time when mortgage yields were considerably lower. Also, with some open-market rates rising more rapidly than their deposit rates, some disintermediation would take place, causing a decline in mortgage loans and home construction. Volatile rates could also increase uncertainty among other sectors of the economy, with adverse effects on investment expenditures beyond the reductions attributable solely to high rates. The results could well be contractionary in nature leading to recession and unemployment.

A second kind of complication for short-term monetary policy arises because the relation between Federal Reserve policy actions and bank reserves is not precise in the short run, and fluctuations in reserves can occur even if the Fed should desire to hold reserves steady. As pointed out in Chapter 5, problems can develop because of changes in the "operating factors" affecting bank reserves, which the Federal Reserve does not control. These include discounting, changes in Federal Reserve float, fluctuations in foreign currency holdings, and changes in U.S. Treasury balances at the central bank and in other accounts not directly under its control. Increases in reserves due to discounting, for example, are likely to occur in response to Federal Reserve attempts to limit the growth of bank reserves, and so they reduce the ability of the Fed to predict precisely the effects in the short run of using its policy instruments. Changes in Federal Reserve float may be caused by random events, including power failures that slow the computerized processing of checks and even by bad weather. Precisely because of their random character, however, changes of this kind pose difficulties for monetary policy in the short run.

A third group of complications (also affecting the demand-driven policy) occurs because of an imprecise relation between changes in bank reserves and changes in the money supply—in other words, because of imprecision in the money multiplier. (However, changes in this area are also matters of long-run concern, and these complications cannot be classified solely as short-run complications.)

---

[19]Obviously, the Fed's forecasts of short-run money demand during this period were seriously deficient. For an analysis of the relationship of the demand for money, interest rates, and income levels, see Chapters 21 and 22.

[20]Actually, the perfectly inelastic reserve supply curve does shift to the right, say from $R_0S_n$ to $R_1S_n'$, in accordance with targeted rates of growth in bank reserves and the money supply. In the process, the Federal Funds rate rises from $r_0$ to $r_1$ rather than to $r_n$ as would be the case if no shift occurred in the reserve supply schedule.

The concept of the money multiplier was introduced in Chapter 5 and is reproduced here in Equation 28-1.

$$\Delta M = \Delta B \cdot \frac{(1 + c)}{(rr\% + c + nt\% + e)} \quad (28\text{-}1)$$

This equation states that the size of the change in the money supply, $\Delta M$, equals the size of the change in the monetary base, $\Delta B$ (which is bank reserves plus currency), times the money multiplier—the rest of the right-hand side of the equation. In this multiplier, $c$ is the public's desired ratio of currency to monetary deposits (including demand deposits and other transaction accounts), $rr\%$ is the required reserve ratio for monetary deposits, $t\%$ is the required reserve ratio for time deposits, $n$ is the public's desired ratio of time deposits to monetary deposits, and $e$ is the banks' desired ratio of excess reserves to monetary deposits. Thus, if $rr\% = .12$, $t\% = .03$, $n = 2$, $c = .25$ and $e = .04$, then the money multiplier in this illustration is 1.25/.47, or 2.66. This means that the money supply will increase by $2.66 for each increase in the monetary base of $1.00.

The complication for monetary policy is that all of the elements of the money multiplier depend, at least in part, on the behavior of economic agents outside the central bank. The nonbank public, for example, determines the relationship it desires between time deposits and monetary deposits ($n$), and between currency and monetary deposits ($c$). Commercial banks (in conjunction with potential borrowers) determine their desired excess reserve holdings ($e$). Even the values of $rr\%$ and $t\%$ depend on current shifts of deposits among classes of banks—at least during the transition period before all banks and other depository institutions have uniform reserve requirements on their monetary and nonpersonal time accounts as specified by the Monetary Control Act of 1980.[21] Further, the

growth of time deposits also affects the money multiplier. As was pointed out in Chapter 6, depositors respond to relative interest rates when allocating their savings. Thus, when the interest rates on time deposits rise along with a general upward movement of open-market rates, the public can be expected to shift some of its holdings of demand deposits into time deposits as well as into these other financial assets. For a given amount of total reserves or monetary base, the increase in money will be less when additional reserves are also required on nonmonetary (time) deposits. This may be seen in Equation 28-1. If $n$ (the public's desired ratio of time deposits to demand deposits) rises, the money multiplier declines.[22]

The demand for currency may also change sharply at certain times of the year, and may also exhibit long-term growth as income rises. Likewise, the volume of deposits among classes of banks may change rapidly and unpredictably as checks are written and deposited in banks still subject to different reserve requirements.[23] Thus, the Federal Reserve shares with other sectors of the economy those actions which determine the rate of growth of the money supply and must rely on predicting the activities of others in order to predict the relationship between its policy actions and the resulting effect on its monetary policy objectives.

---

[21]In estimates of the monetary base and the money multiplier published weekly by the Federal Reserve Bank of St. Louis, shifts in deposits among classes of banks have been handled by adjusting the monetary base rather than by changes in the money multiplier. This procedure (and, consequently, this version of the monetary base) is different from the calculations (and monetary base) of the Federal Reserve Board. In particular, the money multiplier calculated by the St. Louis Bank will appear more stable than the Board's multiplier, and its monetary base will appear less stable. For a discussion of the differences,

see Albert E. Buerger and Robert H. Rasche, "Revision of the Monetary Base," Federal Reserve Bank of St. Louis *Review* (July 1977); and Carl M. Gambs, "Federal Reserve Intermediate Targets: Money or the Monetary Base" Federal Reserve Bank of Kansas City *Economic Review* (January 1980).

[22]For recent estimates of the quantitative importance of these shifts as well as a theoretical discussion of them, see Richard D. Porter and Eileen Mauskopf, "Some Notes on the Apparent Shift in the Demand for Demand Deposits Function," Board of Governors of the Federal Reserve System, Washington, D.C., March 1978 (mimeographed).

[23]Figure 5-3 in Chapter 5 seemed to indicate that the money multiplier was fairly constant and predictable in the short run. However, the illustration was based on a different approach employed by the Federal Reserve Bank of St. Louis as compared to that of the Federal Reserve Board (see footnote 21). The former, unlike the latter, adjusts the monetary base for deposit shifts among classes of banks rather than allowing the shifts to affect the money multiplier, in this way obtaining a multiplier that appears somewhat more stable than the multiplier calculated by the Federal Reserve Board.

In sum, neither the demand-driven monetary policy in effect before October 1979, nor the supply-driven policy implemented at that time, is free from difficult problems. Although the Federal Reserve policymakers evidently believed a change would make monetary policy more effective in achieving overall economic objectives, it does not eliminate complications caused by fluctuations in bank reserves or the money multiplier. Of even greater significance is the possibility that the new policy will lead to greater volatility in market interest rates in the short run which, in turn, not only can cause special problems for some financial institutions and markets but may also lead to fluctuations in investment demand with resulting changes in income, employment, and prices.

### Problems of Long-Term Monetary Policy Strategy

Essentially, the problems of long-term monetary policy strategy, and, therefore, the efficacy of monetary controls, revolve around the linkages between monetary policy objectives (box 3 in Figure 28-1) and the ultimate economic objectives of price stability, full employment, growth, and balance-of-payments equilibrium (box 4 in Figure 28-1). These linkages were discussed in Chapters 21 and 22. However, they were not discussed within the context of the limits of monetary policy in successfully attaining the ultimate economic objectives. A major purpose of this section is briefly to assess some of these limits.

*Stability and Predictability of the Demand for Money* The triumph of "practical monetarism" in the 1970s, and especially after October 6, 1979, represents a triumph for Milton Friedman and for his followers in the Chicago School over those preaching the Keynesian gospel. It is a triumph for those who view monetary policy as being primarily concerned with changes in the rate of growth of the money stock over those basically concerned with the cost of credit (interest rates) and its availability.

Explicit in the Chicago School approach is the conviction that monetary policy can be highly effective in its impact on prices and nominal income because the demand-for-money function (and its

of money in the 1950s,[24] the monetarist position is that increases (decreases) in the quantity of money result in an excess supply of (demand for) money which, to a significant extent, is then used to purchase goods and services (rebuild money balances). In the process, prices and money income will be affected. Thus, the monetarist view of the way monetary policy works is much more simple and straightforward than the Keynesian view.

Although the stability of the demand for money *function* can be debated at great length, there is little doubt that, over the course of the business cycle, *velocity* does change and that the magnitude of such changes is difficult to predict. Consequently, even if the Fed was always able to meet its targeted rates of monetary growth, the linkage between its policy targets and such ultimate economic objectives as prices, money incomes, and the rate of unemployment could well contain sufficient slippages so as to prevent at any one time the successful achievement of those objectives.

There are many reasons why, in an empirical sense, the demand for money or velocity is unpredictable. Chief among these are high and rising interest rates which cause both households and business firms to economize on their cash balances, thereby producing a decrease in the demand to hold money or an increase in its velocity. Also, as we have already seen in Chapter 22, the competition of nonbank depository intermediaries with commercial banks may cause shifts in the public's demand for idle money balances vis-à-vis time deposits, resulting in changes in velocity and the supply of loanable funds as these balances become more active—that is, as they become dishoarded. In addition, financial innovations such as NOW accounts, telegraphic transfer of funds, share drafts, and automatic transfer services lead to declines in the demand for money narrowly defined to include only demand deposits and currency (M1-A). To the extent that the definition of the monetary aggregates is broadened to include these new forms

---

[24]Milton Friedman, ed., *Studies in the Quantity Theory of Money*, University of Chicago Press, Chicago, 1956. Latter-day Chicagoans do not see the demand for money as a simple, constant fraction of the level of national income but rather as a complex schedule influenced by interest rates, prices of goods and services, and expectations of future income.

of money as well as all types of close money substitutes, monetary policy is faced with a dilemma, since to encompass everything is to explain nothing. To predict the impact of monetary policy becomes increasingly difficult. This is an important reason why, as we have seen, the Fed was given permission by Congress in 1980 to impose uniform reserve requirements on NOW accounts and share drafts regardless of the institutions issuing them.

*Lags in the Effects of Monetary Policy* Another problem for the successful implementation of monetary policy in the long run involves the lags inherent in the monetary process. Not only is there overwhelming empirical evidence of the existence of such lags, but they are also highly variable from cycle to cycle. While we are primarily interested in this section with what has come to be called the "outside" lag, a short description of some of the other lags may not be irrelevant.

In order for monetary policy to be appropriate to the particular circumstances of the economy, a substantial amount of knowledge concerning the timing of monetary policy impacts is necessary. The period between the time of an event or state of the economy to which the Federal Reserve may wish to respond and the eventual response of the economy to the action taken by the Federal Reserve has been divided into the following segments for purposes of analysis: (1) a recognition lag, which is the time lapse between the occurrence of the event or state of the economy and the recognition of that occurrence by the Federal Reserve; (2) a decision lag, which measures the time between recognition on the part of the Federal Reserve and its responding use of the instruments of monetary policy; (3) an intermediate lag, which is a measure of the time lapse between the use of monetary policy instruments and the impact of that use on the supply of money or its rate of growth; and, finally, (4) the outside lag mentioned earlier, which measures the time lapse between the effect of policy on the money supply and the impact on the ultimate objectives such as the price level, GNP, and the unemployment rate. The recognition lag and decision lag are often referred to as the inside lag, since the length of that portion of the total lag depends almost entirely on the internal operation of the Federal Reserve in obtaining, processing, and utilizing information concerning the economy.

To illustrate the importance of these lags, consider the following example. Assume that the economy experiences a noticeable increase in the rate of unemployment. Assume further that if the Federal Reserve does nothing whatsoever, the rate of unemployment will increase for a time but then gradually decline until, in precisely two years, it will move back to an acceptable level. However, if the sum of the inside, intermediate, and outside lags is greater than two years, monetary policy actions designed to decrease the current rate of unemployment will not only begin to affect the economy too late to improve the situation but will be perverse in their impact. A perverse impact would result in this case since the Federal Reserve would be taking action to reduce unemployment, but the action would begin to be effective only when the unemployment rate was already so low that the action would be likely to precipitate inflationary pressures instead.

A further complication may arise if the intermediate and outside lags are distributed over considerable time periods. For example, if the Federal Reserve engages in open-market purchases to combat the unemployment problem just assumed, there would be some immediate increase in the money supply and bank reserves. However, the full multiple expansion process might take some time. Only after all of the impact is felt can the lagged effect be said to have occurred fully.

With respect to the recognition lag, the Federal Reserve does not have to wait until an event has occurred; it may predict that the event will occur in the future and take action based on that expectation. With a sufficiently accurate forecast of economic events, the recognition lag could become negative for that substantial portion of events which can be forecast. In the example already presented, if the Federal Reserve were able to forecast that an unacceptable unemployment rate was likely to occur in two years if no action were taken, it might take action now. If the intermediate and outside lags were on the order of two years, then the monetary policy action could be timely in its effect. Unfortunately, many events, such as oil embargoes, are quite difficult or impossible to forecast and, consequently, the recognition lag can never be negative for all events to which the Federal Reserve might wish to respond. Nevertheless, over time, improved forecasting techniques probably have reduced the average recognition lag by increasing that fraction of possible events which are subject to reasonably accurate forecasts.

The decision lag is a function solely of the way in which the Federal Reserve orders its activities. Currently, the Federal Open Market Committee meets every fourth week in Washington, and communicates more often through use of the telephone. The meetings probably are the best indicators of the end of the recognition lag and the beginning of the decision lag. Once the need for action is recognized, the delay before action is taken is probably quite short and cannot be reduced significantly.

The intermediate lag—the time lapse between Federal Reserve use of its policy instruments and a response in the availability of bank credit and the money supply—depends partly on the institutional structure of the financial system and partly on the behavior of the banks and the public. But there is, in addition, a methodological problem: the degree of aggregation of the data across banks and time significantly influences the estimates of the intermediate lag.[25] When one estimates the lag using data for individual banks, the lag appears to be slightly over three weeks. When the data for individual banks are aggregated, however, the lag is found to be more than five weeks. And when the aggregate data are converted from weekly data into monthly averages, the length of the lag appears to increase dramatically to nearly twenty-nine months. This is not the place to expound at length on econometric methods used to estimate the length of lags, but it does demonstrate the need to be sensitive to the statistical methods employed. More importantly, problems of this kind add to the complexities of analyzing monetary effects.

Most of the interest in measuring the impact of lags on the efficacy of monetary policy has concentrated on the outside lag, with the beginning of the lag identified by a money supply variable and the end of the lag identified by a production or price variable. A considerable amount of heat has been generated in the controversy over this lag, since the econometric techniques available for measuring

the lag do not indicate clearly the direction of the causal relationship. One is immediately tempted to identify an event that precedes another as its cause, but they may both have been caused by a third event with different lags. Furthermore, when the behavior of two events is cyclical—that is, recurring with some degree of regularity—either one may be considered the causal factor statistically. For example, if an economy experiences a marked increase in its rate of inflation and output every two years and also experiences a marked increase in its money supply every two years—with the events lagged precisely one year—one is at a loss to determine statistically whether increases in the money supply cause increases in prices and output after a one-year lag or whether increases in the latter cause an increase in the money supply over the same period. Tobin has shown that both are possible.[26] As a result, caution must be exercised before inferring causal relationships from the studies reported on briefly here.

With due cognizance of these caveats, let us now consider briefly some major estimates of the duration of the outside lag. Friedman's work provides a starting point. In the late 1950s, Friedman and several colleagues—particularly Anna Schwartz—developed long time series on the money stock of the United States and analyzed it to measure the outside lag.[27] They found that peaks in a measure of the money stock that includes time deposits at commercial banks preceded peaks in the business cycle (identified by the National Bureau of Economic Research) by an average of sixteen months while, measured from trough to trough, the lag averaged some twelve months. Furthermore, the eighteen cycles between 1870 and 1960 included lags between peaks varying between six and twenty-nine months. Thus, the lags appeared to be

[25]William R. Bryan, "Bank Adjustments to Monetary Policy: Alternative Estimates of the Lag," *American Economic Review* (September 1967).

[26]James Tobin, "Money and Income: Post Hoc Ergo Propter Hoc?" *Quarterly Journal of Economics* (January 1970).

[27]See in particular, Milton Friedman and Anna J. Schwartz, *A Monetary History of the United States, 1867–1960,* Princeton University Press, Princeton, N.J., 1963; J. M. Culbertson, "Friedman on the Lag in Effect of Monetary Policy," *Journal of Political Economy* (December 1960); and Friedman, "The Lag in Effect of Monetary Policy," *Journal of Political Economy* (October 1961).

long and variable. Other empirical studies, however, have shown a somewhat shorter outside lag.[28]

*Rules versus Discretion in Monetary Policy*
Problems in measuring, analyzing, and interpreting the lags associated with monetary policy have fueled the controversy over whether the central bank should attempt contracyclical monetary policy at all. Would not the economy be better served if the Federal Reserve were simply required to follow a relatively fixed rule with respect to the growth of the money stock rather than being allowed discretion to follow an activist policy as it does currently? Friedman, the best-known advocate of the fixed-rule position, has argued that the long and uncertain lag between policy action and its impact on the economy means, in effect, that discretionary monetary policy runs the great risk of being perverse. Consequently, he has recommended the elimination of the Fed's discretionary authority over monetary policy, substituting for it a rule for growth of the money supply at an average annual rate of 4 or 5 percent, a rate that would be altered, if at all, only at infrequent intervals.[29]

The argument for the imposition of a fixed rule has several serious drawbacks—notably, the inevitability of changes in the internal and external environments, the lack of constancy in what constitutes money as the financial sector rapidly evolves, and the inability to accurately predict fluctuations in velocity or the demand for money.[30] These and

other arguments have been ably stated in recent testimony before Congress by the current Chairman of the Federal Reserve System as follows:[31]

The suggestion has been made that this process (of attaining an appropriate restraint on growth of money and credit over time) could be speeded by setting out a specific target path for growth in the money stock over a number of years ahead. . . . In examining this question, members of the Federal Reserve Board remain of the view that there are decisive drawbacks to setting out so precise a growth target over so many years ahead. . . .

. . . Experience shows that many forces can affect the financial requirements of the economy at any time. Other governmental policies, institutional changes, exogenous shocks to the economy—emanating from both domestic and foreign sources—and changes in the public's money preferences can alter the relationship between money and economic performance. Rigid adherence to a fixed money stock path set for years ahead might therefore turn out to be inappropriate, something needlessly wrenching financial markets or unduly constricting our flexibility in responding to some cyclical or other disturbances. If, on the other hand, the targets are changed, or interpreted more flexibly, unnecessary confusion could arise, and the basic rationale would then be undermined.

. . . We must recognize that monetary control will always be imprecise. . . . Even the problem of specifying precisely the monetary variable that should be controlled over a period of years is a very knotty one; what serves as money in our rapidly changing financial system is far from a constant.

As previously indicated, several studies other than those of Friedman have shown the lags of monetary policy to be neither so long nor so variable as he suggests. However, they are sufficiently long and variable to warrant extreme caution on the part of the Fed. The evidence of their existence does tend to weaken the linkage between a discre-

[28]In this connection, see, for example, Beryl Sprinkel, "Monetary Growth as a Cyclical Predictor," *Journal of Finance* (September 1959); Thomas Mayer, "The Inflexibility of Monetary Policy," *Review of Economics and Statistics* (November 1958); John Kareken and Robert M. Solow, "Lags in Monetary Policy," in Commission on Money and Credit, *Stabilization Policies*, Prentice-Hall, Inc., Englewood Cliffs, N.J., 1963; and J. Ernest Tanner, "Lags in the Effects of Monetary Policy," *American Economic Review* (December 1969). For a novel method of measuring the combined intermediate and outside lags, and their distribution through time, see Gene C. Uselton, *Lags in the Effects of Monetary Policy*, Marcel Dekker, New York, 1974.

[29]Friedman, *A Program for Monetary Stability.*

[30]The observation by some adherents of the Chicago School that, in the face of unanticipated velocity changes, the rule could be altered so as to counteract these changes by appropriate revisions of monetary growth rates in effect destroys the efficacy of the argument, since varied responses to changing circumstances are the *sine qua non* of discretion.

[31]Statement by Paul A. Volker, Subcommittee on Domestic Monetary Policy, U.S. House of Representatives, November 13, 1979.

tionary monetary policy strategy and the attainment of the objectives of economic policy.

## Conclusion

In conclusion, monetary policy is one of the important, if not the most important, components of federal economic policy. The economic policies of the federal government are, of course, aimed at achieving the important objectives of price stability, full employment, adequate economic growth, and balance-of-payments equilibrium; they include fiscal policy and incomes policies in addition to monetary policy. Monetary policy has been the responsibility of the Federal Reserve System since its establishment in 1913, although the central bank's views about the channels of its influence have changed substantially over the years.

In carrying out its monetary policies the Federal Reserve uses a variety of policy instruments. Decisions concerning the use of those instruments are made by the System's central policymaking group, the Federal Open Market Committee (in the case of open-market operations) and by the Reserve banks, subject to review by the Federal Reserve Board (in the case of discount rate changes). Levels of and changes in reserve requirements are determined by the Federal Reserve Board within broad guidelines established by Congress.

In carrying out its monetary policy the Federal Reserve System faces a number of important problems. One problem concerns the necessity of establishing an overall plan or "strategy" for monetary policy that is consistent with major economic objectives. There are two aspects of this—long-term strategy and short-term strategy. Long-term strategy involves establishing a plan for monetary variables, such as a growth rate in the money supply, that is consistent with long-run economic objectives. Short-term strategy involves using the instruments of monetary policy in a way that produces changes in monetary variables in the directions and magnitudes called for by the long-term plan. Unfortunately, neither of these phases of monetary policy is free from a variety of complications which cause additional problems for the monetary managers. As a result, it seems unlikely that the art of "Fed watching" is likely to decline in popularity within the foreseeable future.

## Questions

1. Explain how each of the instruments of monetary policy might be used to influence important monetary variables.
2. Why may discounting in many cases counteract the impact on the economy of other Federal Reserve actions?
3. What is meant by the term *monetary policy strategy*? Explain the main parts of monetary policy strategy as carried out by the Federal Reserve.
4. Explain what is meant by *demand-driven* short-term monetary policy strategy. How does it differ from *supply-driven* policy?
5. Explain the reasons for the shift from a demand-driven policy to a supply-driven policy. What are the main difficulties associated with each of these kinds of short-term monetary policy strategy?
6. Explain how components of the money multiplier may cause complications for monetary policy.
7. Explain how changes in the demand for money may complicate monetary policy.
8. Distinguish between inside and outside lags in the effects of monetary policy and show the importance of studying lags.
9. Explain the reasons for the controversy over "rules versus discretion" in monetary policy.
10. Explain what is meant by the term *practical monetarism*. How is practical monetarism related to monetary policy?

## Selected Bibliography

Altman, E. I., and A. W. Sametz, eds. *Financial Crises.* John Wiley & Sons, New York, 1977.

Board of Governors of the Federal Reserve System. *Federal Reserve Bulletin.*

———. *Reappraisal of the Federal Reserve Discount Mechanism.* Washington, D.C., 1971–1972.

Bryan, William R. "Bank Adjustments to Monetary Policy: Alternative Estimates of the Lag." *American Economic Review* (September 1967).

Carson, Deane, ed. *Banking and Monetary Studies.* Richard D. Irwin, Homewood, Ill., 1963.

Cooper, J. Phillip. *Development of the Monetary Sector, Prediction and Policy Analysis in the FRB-MIT-PENN Model.* Lexington Books, Lexington, Mass., 1974.

Culbertson, J. M. "Friedman on the Lag in Effect of Monetary Policy." *Journal of Political Economy* (December 1960).

Eckstein, O., ed. *Parameters and Policies in the U.S. Economy.* North-Holland Publishing Co., Amsterdam, 1976.

Feige, Edgar L., and Douglas K. Pearce. "The Substitutability of Money and Near-Monies: A Survey of the Time-Series Evidence." *Journal of Economic Literature* (June 1977).

Friedman, Milton. "The Lag in Effect of Monetary Policy." *Journal of Political Economy* (October 1961).

———. *A Program for Monetary Stability*. Fordham University Press, New York, 1959.

———. "The Role of Monetary Policy." *American Economic Review* (March 1968).

———, and Anna J. Schwartz. *A Monetary History of the United States, 1867–1960*. Princeton University Press, Princeton, 1963.

Gurley, John G., and Edward S. Shaw. *Money in a Theory of Finance*. Brookings Institution, Washington, D.C., 1960.

Kareken, John, and Robert M. Solow. "Lags in Monetary Policy." In Commission on Money and Credit, *Stabilization Policies*. Prentice-Hall, Englewood Cliffs, N.J., 1963.

Lombra, Raymond E., and Raymond G. Torto. "The Strategy of Monetary Policy." Federal Reserve Bank of Richmond *Economics Review* (September-October 1975).

Polakoff, Murray E. "Federal Reserve Discount Policy and Its Critics." In *Banking and Monetary Studies*. Ed. Deane Carson. Richard D. Irwin, Homewood, Ill., 1963.

Porter, Richard D., and Eileen Mauskopf. "Some Notes on the Apparent Shift in the Demand for Demand Deposits Function" (mimeograph). Board of Governors of the Federal Reserve System, Washington, D.C. (March 1978).

Silber, William L. *Financial Innovation*. Lexington Books, Lexington, Mass., 1975.

———, and Murray E. Polakoff. "The Differential Effects of Tight Money: An Econometric Study." *Journal of Finance* (March 1970).

Sinai, Allan. "Credit Crunches—An Analysis of the Postwar Experience." In *Parameters and Policies in the U.S. Economy*. Ed. O. Eckstein. North-Holland Publishing Co., Amsterdam, 1976.

Tanner, J. Ernest. "Lags in the Effects of Monetary Policy." *American Economic Review* (December 1969).

Tinbergen, Jan. *On the Theory of Economic Policy*. North-Holland, Amsterdam, 1952.

Tobin, James. "Money and Income: Post Hoc Ergo Propter Hoc?" *Quarterly Journal of Economics* (January 1970).

U.S. Department of Commerce. *Survey of Current Business*.

Uselton, Gene C. *Lags in the Effects of Monetary Policy*. Marcel Dekker, New York, 1974.

Wonnacott, Paul. *Macroeconomics*. Rev. ed. Richard D. Irwin, Homewood, Ill., 1978.

Wrightsman, Dwayne. *An Introduction to Monetary Theory and Policy*. 2nd ed. The Free Press, New York, 1976.

# 29

# Fiscal and Debt-Management Policies

*Fiscal policy* refers to the use of government spending and taxing power to achieve macroeconomic objectives. It is a relatively recent development in government policy, receiving attention, for the most part, only since World War II. During his first presidential campaign, at the depth of the Great Depression, Franklin Roosevelt pledged to balance the federal budget if elected. As late as the 1937–1938 recession, President Roosevelt still attempted to contain and reduce the recession-induced budget deficits.[1] It is only since the end of World War II that a *passive* or *accommodating countercyclical* fiscal policy has become generally accepted practice in the United States. No postwar president or Congress has ever again attempted to curtail spending or to raise taxes during a recession in order to reduce a budget deficit caused by the "built-in stabilizers" of our economy.

An *active* or *discretionary* fiscal policy with a countercyclical as well as an economic-growth objective is of even more recent origin; it dates back to the New Economic Policy of the Kennedy-Johnson administrations in the first half of the 1960s. Moreover, its practice has been short-lived and erratic; it was not applied (for political reasons) during the crucial early inflationary phase of the Vietnam War. The concept of *discretionary* fiscal policy as such is not yet generally accepted; it was challenged in the early 1970s by the Nixon administration's reversion to a strictly *passive* fiscal-policy stance.[2]

## Passive Countercyclical Fiscal Policy: The Built-in Stabilizers

The economic and fiscal structure of modern industrialized nations provides a large degree of *passive* fiscal stabilization. *Built-in fiscal stabilizers*— the source of this *passive* stabilization—are defined as those government expenditures and receipts that move the government budget towards a larger deficit (or a smaller surplus) during an economic con-

---

[1] For an illuminating discussion, see Herbert Stein, *The Fiscal Revolution in America,* The University of Chicago Press, Chicago and London, 1969, Chap. 6.

[2] For a critical review of this reversion to an "automatic pilot" policy, see Michael E. Levy with Juan de Torres, Delos R. Smith, and Vincent G. Massaro, *The Federal Budget: Its Impact on the Economy,* The Conference Board, New York, 1971, 1972, 1973, especially fiscal 1972 ed., pp. 11–12; also fiscal 1973 and 1974 eds., pp. 11–12.

traction without any explicit policy decision or action. In the United States, during recessions or even during "growth recessions" (that is, periods of sluggish real growth well below the economy's potential), federal government spending is boosted countercyclically by enlarged payments for unemployment benefits, various welfare programs (for example, food stamps), and accelerated early retirement under social security provisions. Government receipts are reduced (or, at least, held down well below their "high-employment" level) mainly because of the interaction between declines, or slower gains, in personal income and the progressive rate structure of the individual income tax, eroding corporate profits, and reduced employment and consumption (which affect payroll and excise taxes).[3] Social security and excise taxes are also held down by higher unemployment and sluggish consumer spending. The resulting enlargement in the budget deficit (or reduction in the surplus) cushions, but does not arrest or reverse, the decline of the private sector's income during recessions, and it tends to restrain the pace of the subsequent recovery.

It is, therefore, important to distinguish the effects of passive fiscal responses of the built-in stabilizers from the effects of discretionary fiscal-policy actions. The former are designed to *reflect* and mitigate changes in economic activity, whereas the latter initiate or trigger such changes. Since changes in the *observed* federal budget surplus or deficit combine both passive and discretionary fiscal responses, such changes cannot serve as a suitable measure of countercyclical fiscal policies. Specifically, a large and growing budget deficit during a recession may reflect primarily the negative feedback from a weak economy or a combination of negative feedback and discretionary policies of fiscal stimulation. Similarly, a large and rising budget surplus during a period of high employment with inflation may merely reflect the positive feedback of the inflation (which, in the short run, tends to raise government revenues faster than government expenditures) or a combination of positive feedback and discretionary policies of fiscal restraint.

[3] For a detailed discussion of U.S. built-in stabilizers and estimates of their impact during the first four postwar recessions, see Wilfred Lewis, Jr., *Federal Fiscal Policy in the Postwar Recessions*, The Brookings Institution, Washington, 1962, especially Chaps. 2–3.

Consequently, the "full-employment budget surplus" (at times also referred to as the "high-employment surplus") has been used in the United States since the early 1960s as a simplified measure of fiscal policy designed to isolate discretionary fiscal policy from the effects of passive budget-feedback from changes in economic activity.[4] The full-employment surplus is estimated by computing both receipts and expenditures of a given budget program that could be expected to materialize if the economy were operating at full-employment output (GNP) consistent with price stability.

This is illustrated in Figure 29-1, where $RR$ represents budget receipts; $XX$, budget expenditures; and $BB$ the budget balance (all expressed as a function of GNP).[5] At full-employment output, $(F)$, receipts would be higher and expenditures somewhat lower than at the actual output level, $(A < F)$. The actual budget deficit $(B_a)$ would—as shown—be converted into a full-employment surplus $(B_f)$. More generally, the budget balance would shift upward, toward a smaller deficit, or a larger surplus, as the case may be. That is, $B_a < B_f$ for all $A < F$. This movement *along* the $RR$, $XX$, and $BB$ schedules as GNP rises from $A$ to $F$ reflects the feedback effect of the built-in stabilizers. Discretionary fiscal policy, by contrast, requires a *shifting* of the entire schedules.

## Discretionary Fiscal Policy

When comparing two budget programs for the same year (and at the same level of "price stability"), we consider the budget with the higher full-employment surplus to be fiscally more restrictive. When comparing budgets for different years, we should always measure their full-employment surpluses as a percentage of GNP in order to adjust for economic growth, which increases both GNP and the government budget over time. The larger

[4] For an extensive discussion and critical review of the concept of the high-employment surplus or deficit, see Michael E. Levy, *Fiscal Policy, Cycles and Growth,* The Conference Board, New York, 1963, especially Chap. 6 and Appendix to Chap. 6. For earlier developments and uses of this concept, see ibid., p. 82; also Stein, *The Fiscal Revolution in America,* Chaps. 9 and 16.

[5] As a simplifying device, all three functional relationships are shown in Figure 29-1 in linear form. In reality, these functions need not be linear.

**Figure 29-1**
**The Relationship Between the Actual and the Full-Employment Budget**

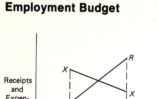

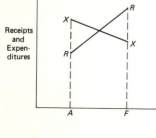

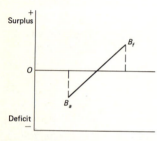

**Figure 29-2**
**Fiscal Stimulation**

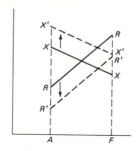

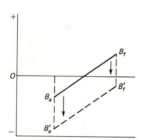

**Figure 29-3**
**Fiscal Restraint**

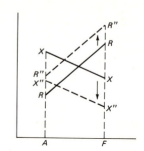

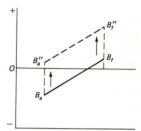

Source: Michael E. Levy, The Conference Board.

*relative* full-employment surplus is then taken to indicate a more restrictive fiscal stance.

In a depressed economy, additional fiscal stimulation may be provided either by cutting taxes (a downward shift from $RR$ to $R'R'$ in Figure 29-2), or by raising *discretionary* spending (an upward shift from $XX$ to $X'X'$), or by both. Such policies will reduce the full-employment surplus ($B'_f < B_f$ in Figure 29-2); they will increase the spending power of the private economy. Conversely, if the economy is suffering from excess aggregate demand and inflation, tax increases and/or reductions in *discretionary* spending will provide fiscal restraint. Such policies will increase the full-employment surplus ($B''_f > B_f$ in Figure 29-3).

This relationship between the full-employment budget surplus and discretionary countercyclical fiscal policy can be derived from the well-known Keynesian full-employment equilibrium condition, as pointed out in Chapter 21. In static Keynesian analysis, attainment or retention of full-employment GNP requires that *ex ante* full-employment

saving equal *ex ante* full-employment investment. If the government budget is measured in national income account terms (rather than in terms of the traditional, unified presidential and congressional budget),[6] then the full-employment budget surplus represents full-employment saving of the federal government. Static countercyclical fiscal policy requires that the federal government's full-employment saving, ($S_g^*$) be adjusted so as to balance any discrepancy at full employment between *ex ante* saving of the private sector ($S_p$) and of state and local governments ($S_{sl}$), on the one hand, and investment ($I$), on the other. Thus, an expanded

[6]The National Income Accounts budget uses accrual accounting (rather than cash accounting) for most transactions and excludes most lending and purely financial transactions that affect the composition of *existing* assets and liabilities (rather than current income). For further details and a reconciliation of the two budget concepts, see "Federal Transactions in the National Income Accounts," in *Special Analyses, Budget of the United States,* Government Printing Office, Washington, D.C. (annual).

static Keynesian equilibrium condition can be stated as follows (where starred symbols denote full-employment values):

$$S_p^* + S_{sl}^* + S_g^* = I^* \qquad (29\text{-}1)$$

By rearranging the terms of the expanded equilibrium condition, we can bring into sharper focus the role of discretionary countercyclical fiscal policy:

$$S_g^* = I^* - (S_p^* + S_{sl}^*) \qquad (29\text{-}2)$$

This formulation highlights the fact that the strength of investment and saving in the nonfederal sector (private, state, and local) determines whether it is appropriate for the federal government to run a surplus or a deficit in its full-employment budget. More specifically, when the traditional Keynesian deflationary or inflationary gaps are redefined with regard to the nonfederal sectors only, it becomes evident that a deflationary gap calls for an offsetting full-employment deficit, while an inflationary gap requires an offsetting full-employment surplus. The countercyclical fiscal-policy prescription becomes:

$$S_g^* \lesseqgtr 0 \text{ for } I^* \lesseqgtr (S_p^* + S_{sl}^*) \qquad (29\text{-}3)$$

It is clear from this policy prescription that it would be desirable to formulate fiscal-policy decisions on the basis of explicit estimates of full-employment investment and saving in the nonfederal sector. Unfortunately, few such estimates have been developed as a guide to fiscal policy, and there are serious estimating and reliability problems.[7] Moreover, *shifts* in the saving or investment functions are hard to detect as they occur; yet, such shifts are disruptions that may require changes in economic policy. As a practical matter, policymakers rely mainly on general economic indicators—such as the unemployment rate, the real growth rate of GNP, and the inflation rate—and on economic forecasts in order to assess the need for either greater fiscal stimulation or more fiscal restraint.

In recent years, with most industrialized countries suffering simultaneously from too much unemployment and excessive inflation, the static, neo-Keynesian, countercyclical policy described here has become inadequate. Experimentation with

new policy tools has come to supplement traditional countercyclical policies. At the macroeconomic level, new policy approaches include various forms of "incomes policies"; at a less aggregative level, increased emphasis is being placed on selective employment and training programs. Most forms of incomes policies have been effective, at best, in restraining inflation during relatively brief periods of time. Such policies are most promising when designed to de-escalate inflationary expectations during periods when the economy is not afflicted by excess demand. Increased emphasis on selective employment and training programs in the United States is of very recent origin, but it has gained growing support since the mid-1970s.

## The Full-Employment Budget Surplus Versus Fiscal Thrust as Measures of Fiscal Policy

So far, the full-employment budget surplus has served as a useful shorthand guide for the design and assessment of fiscal policy. We have said little, however, about the problems of estimating the full-employment surplus, which are considerable. Not only does one have to define the concept of full employment, but one must estimate revenues and expenditures that would materialize at this full-employment level. During the first half of the 1960s, full employment was defined pragmatically in terms of a 4 percent unemployment rate. Since then, the labor-force mix has changed drastically. There is now a much higher proportion of women, teenagers, and young adults in the labor force. Since these groups have traditionally above-average unemployment rates, the current "equivalent" unemployment rate (that is, adjusted for changes in labor-force mix) that corresponds to the 4 percent "full-employment rate" of the 1960s would be in the range of 4¾ to 5 percent, or possibly slightly higher.

When unemployment is far above the so-called full-employment rate (whichever way that term is defined), estimates of the *full-employment gap*—that is, the difference between the actual and the "would-be" full-employment budget numbers—become more and more tenuous. This problem is particularly severe for estimates of the *revenue gap*. For example, during the years 1975–1977, the

---

[7] For one early attempt, see Levy, *The Federal Budget*, Chap. 3.

unemployment rate remained above 7 percent with but a few brief exceptions. This meant that estimates of full-employment revenue gaps made during these years could not be tested and might have been far off the mark.

But a far more serious deficiency of the full-employment surplus as a measure of fiscal impact arises from the effects of inflation on the budget. In contrast to other feedbacks from the economy into the budget (that is, the more traditional built-in stabilizers), the current measures of the full-employment surplus do not include any means for neutralizing the feedback effects from inflation in the calculation. Specifically, in the short run, inflation tends to increase many federal government expenditures approximately in line with the overall inflation rate, to increase some expenditures more slowly, and to increase revenues at a faster rate. This inflation leverage of federal revenues is due mainly to the progressive nature of the personal income tax. (Taxpayers are shifted into higher marginal tax brackets.) Thus, in the short run, the feedback from inflation into the federal budget causes the deficit (actual, as well as full-employment) to decline, or the surplus to increase, as the case may be.

This is illustrated in Figure 29-4, where the original budget functions for an economy with "stable prices" are shown as: receipts (*RR*), expenditures (*XX*), the budget balance (*BB*), actual GNP (*A*), and full-employment GNP (*F*). Assume that the Federal Reserve engages in a highly expansionary monetary policy that generates a high rate of inflation. This inflation shifts all observed values and functions to higher levels (indicated by primed values in Figure 29-4). Since receipts are inflated at a faster rate than expenditures, the full-employment surplus is raised. Generally, a higher full-employment surplus is interpreted as indicating greater fiscal restraint; in our example, on the other hand, it is merely the *passive* result of a more inflationary monetary policy. Its value as a reliable measure of *discretionary* fiscal-policy action has been aborted by inflation.

This problem has long been recognized by the experts in this field, and several inflation adjustments for the full-employment surplus have been proposed.[8] Yet all these suggested solutions present serious conceptual and estimating problems and none has yet been adopted.

One other summary measure of fiscal policy has been developed in recent years that avoids many specific estimating problems, and most of the inflation-induced distortions, that impair the reliability of the full-employment surplus. This measure, termed *fiscal thrust,* consists of increases in *discretionary* budget expenditures plus any *structural* tax reductions (or minus any structural tax increases),

**Figure 29-4  Effects of Inflation on the Budget Structure and on the Full-Employment Surplus**

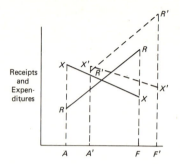

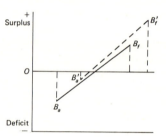

Source: Michael E. Levy, The Conference Board.

---

[8]For example, see President's Commission on Budget Concepts, *Report,* Government Printing Office, Washing-

ton, D.C., 1967, p. 21. Probably the best theoretical treatment of this problem, with a complex adjustment proposal, was presented by Edward M. Gramlich in "Measures of the Aggregate Demand Impact of the Federal Budget," in President's Commission on Budget Concepts, *Staff Papers and Other Materials Reviewed by the President's Commission,* Government Printing Office, Washington, D.C., 1967, pp. 438–440. The clearest exposition of the problem with numerical examples—and a complex "pragmatic" adjustment proposal—was presented by Arthur M. Okun and Nancy H. Teeters in "The Full Employment Surplus Revisited," *Brookings Papers on Economic Activity,* No. 1, Washington, D.C., 1970, pp. 90–96.

where "structural" tax changes are defined as changes in tax receipts due to changes in the tax base or rate. Note that all these changes are valued at the prevailing GNP level; therefore, fiscal thrust measures the initial autonomous expansionary impact of the federal budget to which a traditional Keynesian "multiplier" may be applied in order to assess its full effect on the economy.[9] Moreover, the specific components that make up fiscal thrust—that is, autonomous changes in expenditures and changes in the tax rates or bases of the various taxes—may be fed into modern econometric models in order to trigger a dynamic economic impact analysis.

Fiscal thrust excludes all feedback effects on the revenue side, whether caused by cyclical fluctuations, or by economic growth and inflation. Therefore, this measure avoids major distortions on the revenue side that afflict the full-employment surplus, including the difficulty of estimating the "revenue gap," that is, the difference between actual and full-employment revenue. There is also no need for estimating an "expenditure gap," since actual, rather than full-employment, increases in discretionary spending are included in the measure of fiscal thrust. The controversial issue of defining and measuring full-employment output is altogether avoided. For further comparison of the two fiscal impact measures, quarterly data for fiscal thrust and the full-employment surplus for recent years are provided in Table 29-1.

### Differential Impact Effects: The Balanced-Budget Multiplier

So far, the impact of fiscal policy on the economy has been assessed by means of simple summary measures, that is, the full-employment surplus or fiscal thrust. In its simplest form each measure gives equal weight to all types of budget expenditures and to all revenue effects that are included.

[9] The term fiscal thrust was coined by the present author, who has used this measure extensively and who developed first a consistent annual series and, more recently, a quarterly series. See Levy, The Federal Budget, annual editions since 1967; triannual since 1976, fiscal 1975, and subsequent editions. The best previous calculations and analysis along similar lines were contained in an article by E. Gerald Corrigan, "The Measurement and Importance of Fiscal Policy Changes," Monthly Review, Federal Reserve Bank of New York (June 1970), 133–145.

Thus, for example, a discretionary increase of $1 billion for public works is counted in exactly the same way as a $1 billion reduction in the income tax. Yet, extra spending differs from tax reductions in its initial impact (because tax changes affect saving as well as spending). Moreover, each specific type of spending or tax change is likely to have its own distinct dynamic multipliers and steady-state multipliers.[10] This means that each specific fiscal action has its own distinct time path of growing (or decaying) economic effects and its own distinct cumulative impact over time.

Modern econometric models are capable of simulating the dynamic time path of different fiscal actions and their final steady-state effect on the economy.[11] Even early static neo-Keynesian fiscal analysis recognized at least differences in fiscal impact between tax changes and changes in spending. This recognition took the form of the "balanced-budget multiplier" theorem, which stated in its earliest and simplest form that any spending increase that is matched by a tax increase of equal size will increase total income and output by the identical amount. This result is due to the fact that the spending multiplier exceeds the tax multiplier.

The balanced-budget multiplier can be readily derived from a simple Keynesian model:

$$Y = C + I + G \qquad (29\text{-}4)$$
$$C = a + b(Y - T) \qquad (29\text{-}5)$$
$$I = \bar{I} \qquad (29\text{-}6)$$
$$G = \overline{G} \qquad (29\text{-}7)$$
$$T = \overline{T} \qquad (29\text{-}8)$$

[10] Dynamic multipliers are period-by-period response rates of endogenous variables to exogenous shifts in parameters or flows. Thus, they measure response along the time path that leads ultimately to a new equilibrium position, whereas static multipliers measure the equilibrium response of the endogenous variables to exogenous changes. For estimates of dynamic multipliers for specific fiscal-policy changes, see, for example, Gary Fromm and Howard Taubman, Policy Simulations with an Econometric Model, The Brookings Institution, Washington, D.C., 1968, pp. 48–51.

[11] For example, see Fromm and Taubman, Policy Simulations with an Econometric Model; also Albert Ando and Stephen M. Goldfeld, "An Econometric Model for Evaluating Stabilization Policies," in Studies in Economic Stabilization, eds. Albert Ando, E. Cary Brown, and Ann F. Friedlander, The Brookings Institution, Washington, D.C., 1968, pp. 215–287; also Michael K. Evans and Lawrence R. Klein, The Wharton Econometric Forecasting Model, 2nd ed., University of Pennsylvania, Philadelphia, 1968, Chap. 5, pp. 50–69.

**Table 29-1   Measuring the Fiscal Impact of the Federal Budget (in billions of dollars)**

A. Actual and Full-Employment Budget

| | Actual Expenditures (1) | "Expenditure Gap" (2) | Full-Employment Expenditures (3) = (1) + (2) | Actual Receipts (4) | "Receipts Gap" (5) | Full-Employment Receipts (6) = (4) + (5) | Full-Employment Budget Surplus or Deficit (7) = (6) − (3) |
|---|---|---|---|---|---|---|---|
| **1974** | | | | | | | |
| I | $281.1 | $(0.2) | $280.8 | $275.6 | $ 7.0 | $282.6 | $ 1.8 |
| II | 293.7 | (0.4) | 293.3 | 286.1 | 7.5 | 293.6 | 0.3 |
| III | 306.0 | (0.9) | 305.1 | 297.9 | 7.1 | 305.0 | (0.1) |
| IV | 316.5 | (2.3) | 314.2 | 294.8 | 21.7 | 316.5 | 2.3 |
| **1975** | | | | | | | |
| I | 335.9 | (6.2) | 329.7 | 287.4 | 41.5 | 328.9 | (0.8) |
| II | 354.3 | (8.2) | 346.1 | 255.1 | 41.4 | 296.5 | (49.6) |
| III | 363.7 | (8.1) | 355.6 | 298.2 | 34.9 | 333.1 | (22.5) |
| IV | 374.5 | (7.7) | 366.8 | 307.0 | 35.3 | 342.3 | (24.5) |
| **1976** | | | | | | | |
| I | 376.3 | (5.8) | 370.5 | 318.6 | 23.5 | 342.1 | ( 8.4) |
| II | 375.8 | (4.8) | 371.0 | 329.4 | 20.5 | 349.9 | (21.1) |
| III | 387.5 | (5.2) | 382.3 | 335.5 | 20.8 | 356.3 | (26.0) |
| IV | 401.8 | (5.4) | 396.4 | 342.3 | 22.1 | 364.4 | (32.0) |
| **1977** | | | | | | | |
| I | 403.9 | (4.7) | 399.2 | 366.6 | 6.8 | 373.4 | (25.8) |
| II | 411.7 | (3.4) | 408.3 | 371.4 | 9.6 | 381.0 | (27.3) |
| III | 430.7 | (2.9) | 427.8 | 374.4 | 12.8 | 387.1 | 40.7) |
| IV | 444.1 | (2.6) | 441.5 | 385.5 | 11.6 | 397.1 | (44.4) |
| **1978** | | | | | | | |
| I | 448.8 | (1.9) | 446.9 | 396.2 | 17.7 | 413.9 | (33.0) |
| II | 448.3 | (1.3) | 447.0 | 424.7 | 3.8 | 428.5 | (18.5) |
| III | 464.5 | (1.3) | 463.2 | 441.7 | 5.0 | 446.7 | (16.5) |
| IV | 482.3 | 0.2 | 482.5 | 462.6 | (3.1) | 459.5 | (23.0) |
| **1979** | | | | | | | |
| I | 490.3 | (1.0) | 489.3 | 460.0 | 5.3 | 465.3 | (24.0) |
| II | 502.4 | (6.1) | 496.3 | 469.6 | 6.7 | 476.3 | (20.0) |
| III | 514.8 | (1.1) | 513.7 | 478.0 | 9.1 | 487.1 | (26.6) |
| IV | 526.8 | (1.2) | 525.6 | 488.0 | 11.2 | 499.2 | (26.4) |

where $Y$ = GNP, $C$ = consumption, $I$ = investment, $G$ = government expenditures, $T$ = taxes, $a$ = a constant term, and $b$ = the marginal propensity to consume. If we solve this model for $Y$, we get:

$$Y = \frac{a - b\overline{T} + \overline{G} + \overline{I}}{1 - b} \qquad (29\text{-}9)$$

If $\Delta G = \Delta T = \Delta B$ (where $\Delta B$ is the balanced change in the government budget), the effect on total income and output is derived from Equation (29-9) as follows:

$$\Delta Y = \frac{\Delta B - b\Delta B}{1 - b} = \Delta B \qquad (29\text{-}10)$$

For fairly simple economic models, the balanced-budget multiplier is always 1. For more complex economic models, it can be shown that the balanced-budget multiplier may be greater or smaller than 1, but it is always positive.[12] Spending changes exert a more powerful economic effect than tax changes, but the time path as well as the ultimate size of the economic impact depends on the *specific* spending program or tax change as well as the state of the economy at the time when the change in

[12] For a good sampling of the extensive literature on the balanced-budget multiplier, see the articles by H. M. Sommers and by W. A. Salant reprinted in Joseph Sherer and James A. Papke, eds., *Public Finance and Fiscal Policy*, Houghton Mifflin Company, Boston, 1966, pp. 336–361. A simulation of the balanced-budget multiplier for the U.S. economy by Ando and Goldfeld ("An Econometric Model for Evaluating Stabilization Policies," p. 252) yielded a first-year balanced-budget multiplier slightly greater than unity.

B. Measures of Fiscal Impact

| | Autonomous Expenditure Increases (+) or Reductions (−) (1) | Structural Tax Increases (+) or Reductions (−) (2) | Fiscal Thrust | | Changes in the Full-Employment Surplus | |
|---|---|---|---|---|---|---|
| | | | $ Billions (3) = (1) − (2) | As a % of GNP (4) | $ Billions (5) | As a % of GNP (6) |
| **1974** | | | | | | |
| I | $ 9.8 | $−4.4 | $14.0 | $1.02 | $ 2.1 | $0.15 |
| II | 12.8 | 0.2 | 12.4 | 0.89 | −1.5 | −0.10 |
| III | 14.5 | 2.8 | 11.7 | 0.82 | −0.4 | −0.03 |
| IV | 9.5 | 1.8 | 7.7 | 0.53 | 2.4 | 0.17 |
| **1975** | | | | | | |
| I | 13.4 | −4.4 | 17.8 | 1.23 | −3.2 | −0.22 |
| II | 22.4 | −39.1 | 61.5 | 4.11 | −18.8 | −3.26 |
| III | 11.7 | 28.7 | −17.0 | −1.09 | 27.1 | 1.73 |
| IV | 11.3 | 0.7 | 10.6 | 0.66 | −2.0 | −0.12 |
| **1976** | | | | | | |
| I | 2.8 | −3.4 | 6.2 | 0.38 | 3.9 | 0.22 |
| II | −2.7 | 0.1 | −2.8 | −0.17 | 7.3 | 0.54 |
| III | 14.7 | 1.9 | 12.8 | 0.74 | −4.9 | 0.28 |
| IV | 7.0 | 3.2 | 3.8 | 0.22 | −6.0 | 0.34 |
| **1977** | | | | | | |
| I | 2.1 | −4.0 | 6.1 | 0.33 | 6.2 | 0.34 |
| II | 9.0 | −2.5 | 11.5 | 0.62 | −1.5 | −0.08 |
| III | 18.4 | −3.7 | 2.1 | 1.15 | 13.4 | −0.70 |
| IV | 12.7 | 4.1 | 8.6 | 0.44 | −3.7 | −0.18 |
| **1978** | | | | | | |
| I | 5.1 | 0.3 | 5.6 | 0.28 | 11.0 | 0.53 |
| II | 0.3 | 0.2 | 0.1 | 0.00 | 14.5 | 0.69 |
| III | 14.1 | 4.7 | 9.4 | 0.44 | 8.0 | 0.09 |
| IV | 13.6 | 2.4 | 16.2 | 0.73 | −6.5 | −0.29 |
| **1979** | | | | | | |
| I | 7.1 | −14.6 | 21.7 | 0.95 | −1.0 | −0.04 |
| II | 11.3 | 1.5 | 9.8 | 0.42 | 4.0 | 0.17 |
| III | 14.0 | 1.3 | 12.7 | 0.54 | −6.6 | −0.28 |
| IV | 10.8 | 8.1 | 2.7 | 0.11 | 0.2 | 0.00 |

Sources: Federal Reserve Bank of St. Louis; Office of Management & Budget; Bureau of Economic Analysis; and The Conference Board.

fiscal policy is implemented (the so-called *initial conditions,* in econometric jargon). Considerations of initial conditions, dynamic time paths, and speed of economic adjustment may, at times, be more important to policymakers than simple ultimate steady-state effects.

Attempts to incorporate differential and dynamic fiscal effects into a simple measure of fiscal impact have included the weighting of full-employment revenue and "multipliers."[13] These efforts resulted in a concept of the weighted full-employment

surplus which was difficult to explain (since the size of the resulting numbers and their meaning defied common intuition).

By contrast, the autonomous expenditure increases and the structural tax changes (all valued at the prevailing GNP level) that comprise fiscal thrust are well-defined concepts that provide useful analytical information in and of themselves. Moreover, these measures may be introduced directly into econometric models, so as to trigger the dynamic and steady-state multipliers. Thus, if the fiscal sector of these models were adequately devel-

[13]See Richard A. Musgrave, "On Measuring Fiscal Performance," *Review of Economics and Statistics* (May 1964); Edward M. Gramlich, "The Behavior and Adequacy of the United States Federal Budget, 1952–1964," *Yale Economic Essays* (Spring 1966), 99–159, also 440–447, 459–464. Okun and Teeters ("The Full Employment

Surplus Revisited," p. 87), after reviewing these attempts at weighting, concluded: "It is surely more practical not to weight—and to remember this omission—than to negotiate the coefficients."

oped and reliable, the time path of the economic effects of each fiscal-policy action—such as an income tax reduction, or a social security tax increase—could be traced by introducing into the model its value (as estimated for the measurement of fiscal thrust) and running a simulation. Unfortunately, most current econometric models—even the most elaborate ones—have a relatively simple and underdeveloped fiscal sector, and simulations with alternate models yield, at times, mutually inconsistent results.[14]

### Financial Effects of the Budget: "Crowding Out"

Needless to say, specific changes in the tax structure, or in spending programs, differ not only with regard to their impact, their dynamic time path, and total cumulative income-generating effect, but also with regard to their respective effects on financial institutions and markets. For example, tax reductions that stimulate investment—such as investment tax credits or accelerated depreciation allowances—tend to increase the demand for equity capital, bonds, and commercial and industrial bank loans. Personal income tax reductions, by contrast, are mainly consumption-enhancing, but they do increase the savings flow into mutual savings banks and savings and loan associations. Thus, the impact of fiscal policy on financial institutions and markets depends not merely on the *degree* of fiscal stimulation or restraint, but also on its *specific makeup*.

So far, we have considered the direct impact and multiplier effects of fiscal policy that affect the income-generating process of the economy. We now turn to those financial effects of fiscal policy that affect the economy through changes in the size of the federal debt and the extent to which it is monetized. (Closely related liquidity effects, which derive from changes in the maturity structure of the debt, will be considered in the sections on debt-management policy.) Analysis of financial effects requires a switch in the budget accounting framework. For our previous analysis, the so-called National Income Accounts budget was most appropriate. (It uses "accrual accounting" for the most

part and eliminates federal lending as well as transactions in existing assets.) For the following analysis, cash-accounting budget concepts are far more appropriate.[15]

Any change in fiscal policy that is not a balanced-budget change (in terms of cash accounting) affects the financing needs of the government and, ultimately, the size of the federal debt.[16] Since stimulative fiscal policy tends to move the budget balance toward a deficit (see Figure 29-2), it tends to increase the borrowing needs of the government. If this increase in government debt is not financed by monetary expansion, it would *seem* simply to replace nonfederal (that is, private plus state and local) borrowing. Such an interpretation of what has come to be known as "crowding out" (of private borrowers) has had many prominent adherents in the financial community in recent years, despite its theoretical and empirical inadequacies.

Genuine crowding out should be associated with sharply rising interest rates as the government's demand for funds forces some private borrowers out of the market (since the government is *the* prime borrower and can always satisfy its demand for funds). This restraining financial effect of fiscal policy tends to offset at least some of its direct income-generating effects. Early in 1975, when the deficit of the unified budget was projected at $34.7 billion for fiscal 1975 and $51.9 billion for fiscal 1976 (actual deficits were $45.1 billion and $66.5 billion, respectively), Treasury Secretary Simon was joined by many financial conservatives in sounding the alarm over crowding out.[17] Similar concerns were voiced again in 1976 and 1977. Yet,

---

[14]In this connection, compare details of the results from the simulations by Evans and Klein with those from the simulations by Fromm and Taubman and by Ando and Goldfeld (see earlier references).

[15]Treasury statements on the federal budget are based on cash receipts and disbursements; the so-called unified budget includes net lending and is fairly close to cash accounting.

[16]Note that the size of the federal debt may remain unchanged in the short run as the Treasury adjusts its cash balance. Such an adjustment affects the money supply as commonly defined (excluding government deposits). In this connection, Musgrave's taxonomy of pure fiscal and pure liquidity effects (the latter subdivided into pure debt policy and pure monetary policy effects) may be helpful. See Richard A. Musgrave, *The Theory of Public Finance*, McGraw-Hill Book Company, New York, Toronto, and London, 1959, Chap. 22.

[17]For a review and an explanation of why these concerns were mistaken, see Michael E. Levy, "America's Economy at the Crossroads," *The Conference Board Record* (April 1975), 36–40.

throughout this entire period, there was no convincing evidence of any major crowding out, despite the fact that during the three fiscal years 1975–1977 the federal budget deficit was $45 billion or more each year.

What explains the stable or declining interest rates that prevailed throughout much of this period and the failure of crowding out to materialize? First, there is reason to believe that the Federal Reserve may have accommodated at least part of the financing for these large increases in federal debt. In doing so, the Federal Reserve would merely adhere to the rule that economic weakness and high unemployment should be remedied through coordinated expansionary fiscal and monetary policy.[18] Second, the more simplistic crowding-out views do not take into account one major consideration: in a relatively weak economy operating well below its full-employment potential, expansionary fiscal policy creates higher levels of national income and, hence, enhances private-sector saving. Under these circumstances, a considerable increase in federal borrowing may be financed from increased private saving before any crowding out of private investment occurs (particularly, as long as private investment demand remains depressed).

In a high-employment economy, on the other hand, large increases in the federal debt are likely to result in sharp interest rate escalations and a rapid crowding out of weaker borrowers (such as the housing market and state and local governments). This is particularly likely if the Federal Reserve adheres to a policy of monetary restraint (as it should in such an economic setting). Such crowding out is the consequence of a *perverse* fiscal policy, since an inflationary high-employment economy calls for fiscal restraint, which should reduce federal borrowing needs on two separate counts (see Figures 29-3 and 29-4).[19]

## Debt-Management Policy: Channels of Operation

So far, we have neglected any considerations of liquidity effects of federal borrowing, particularly

those resulting from changes in maturity structure. The traditional division of policy analysis places the analysis of these liquidity effects (or effects on interest rate differentials) under the heading "debt management" (but note that all policy effects reviewed in this chapter are closely interlinked).[20]

Debt management affects economic activity by inducing adjustments in financial assets held by the public. For example, if the Treasury decides to refinance a portion of the federal debt by issuing long-term bonds for maturing Treasury bills, long-term interest rates tend to rise and short-term rates to fall (unless longs and shorts are perfect substitutes). Such a change in rate structure is also associated with a change (reduction) in liquidity, since short-term debt is more liquid than long-term debt. The increase in long-term relative to short-term rates tends to restrain investment (since most investment is more sensitive to long-term interest rates) and consumption of durable goods; the reduction in liquidity is also likely to restrain other types of consumption.[21] The strength of these effects depends on the respective interest and liquidity sensitivity of the economy. The corresponding effects of shortening the maturity structure of the debt are, of course, the reverse and, therefore, are expansionary.

These general effects of debt-management policy are widely accepted. They form the basis for the

---

[18]Note, however, that the need simultaneously to combat excess inflation has put the Federal Reserve under severe constraints.

[19]In this connection, see also Musgrave, *The Theory of Public Finance*, especially p. 543.

[20]Ibid., Chap. 22.

[21]All medium- and large-sized econometric models include long-term interest rates in their investment equations for producer durables and for nonresidential construction. (As a rule, these interest rates enter by means of a "user cost" equation.) Interest rate differentials (for example, the difference between the Aaa bond rate and the commercial-paper rate) are incorporated into most equations for residential construction; consumer durables (such as automobiles and furniture) also tend to include either an interest rate differential or a liquidity variable. For the theoretical underpinnings and empirical application, see J. S. Duesenberry, G. Fromm, L. Klein, and E. Kuh, *The Brookings Quarterly Econometric Model*, Rand McNally & Company, Chicago, 1965, particularly Chaps. 2, 3 and 7; also Evans and Klein, *The Wharton Econometric Forecasting Model*, especially pp. 8–9 (Equations 4, 4a, 5, 5a, and 6), and pp. 23–28; also Saul H. Hymans and Harold T. Shapiro, *The Michigan Quarterly Econometric Model of the U.S. Economy*, Research Seminar in Quantitative Economics, The University of Michigan, Ann Arbor, revised November 1977 (mimeographed), especially Equations 15a, 15c, 21, 22, 23a, 24, and 26. See also Chapter 26 of this text.

traditional countercyclical debt-management prescription that the maturity structure should be shortened during recessions and lengthened during booms. (The feasibility and actual application of this prescription are reviewed in the last section of this chapter.) In order for these effects to occur, however, it is necessary that at least three basic conditions be met:

1. The term structure of interest rates must not be entirely independent of the relative supply of shorts versus longs. (At least one theory of the term structure postulates such independence.)[22]
2. There must be effective arbitrage between the market for governments and the market for private debt, so that the change in the term structure becomes diffused throughout the financial markets.
3. Investment demand must be at least somewhat elastic with regard to interest-rate changes and it must be more responsive to changes in long-term than in short-term rates.

The empirical work incorporated in major econometric models implies that investment in nonresidential structures and producers' durables is responsive to long-term interest rates.[23]

Consumption of durable goods (such as automobiles and furniture) and residential construction are usually viewed as responding primarily to either interest rate differentials or changes in liquid asset values. Most econometric models have included an interest rate differential between long- and short-term rates (or else a liquid-assets variable) in their equations for these GNP components.[24] Not only does a shift from short-term to long-term governments increase the interest rate differential and reduce liquidity, but the ensuing rise in long-term interest rates leads to sizable capital losses on bonds (while the offsetting decline of short-term rates has little impact on asset values). These combined effects of debt lengthening serve to restrain consumption, whereas debt shortening tends to stimulate consumption.

## Debt-Management Policy and Financial Intermediaries

Since debt management operates through changes in the relative supply of government securities of different maturity, its effects on financial intermediaries depend largely on the maturity structure and composition of their assets and liabilities. Institutions that have to operate mainly with a long-term asset structure—such as mutual savings banks—will be affected far more strongly than, say, commercial banks whose assets and liabilities are much more concentrated at the shorter end of the maturity spectrum. Intermediaries that hold a relatively modest proportion of their assets in government securities are less vulnerable than those who hold a more sizable proportion of governments (usually as a result of legal requirements).[25]

Moreover, since the various financial intermediaries specialize in serving distinct needs and sectors of the economy, the differential impact of debt-management policy will be communicated to these needs and sectors. Thus, a relatively strong impact on thrift institutions results in a strong effect on their main constituency, the mortgage and housing market. These institutional differences are, of course, neither inherent nor permanent. In fact, financial and legislative reforms that would reduce the distinctions between financial intermediaries and encourage more direct competition among them have been proposed repeatedly during the last two decades, culminating in the Depository Institutions Deregulation Act of 1980.[26] A recent, but

---

[22]A review and detailed discussion is provided in Chapter 23.

[23]In this connection, see references in footnote 21.

[24]Interest rate differentials have been used extensively in these equations (for example, in the Wharton and Michigan models); the early Brookings model used a liquid-assets variable.

[25]For a review of the relative size and maturity structure of government securities held by financial intermediaries and the determinants of these holdings, see Michael E. Levy, *Cycles in Government Securities*, vol. 1, *Federal Debt and Its Ownership*, and vol. 2, *Determinants of Changes in Ownership*, The Conference Board, New York, 1962 and 1965. For recent information, see the latest issue of the First Boston Corporation's *Handbook of Securities of the United States Government and Federal Agencies and Related Money Market Instruments*, New York, published biennially.

[26]See the following reports: Commission on Money and Credit, *Money and Credit: Their Influences on Jobs, Prices and Growth, Report*, Prentice-Hall, Englewood Cliffs, N.J., 1961; President's Commission on Financial Structure and Regulations, *Report*, Government Printing Office, Washington, D.C., December 1971; and Charles R. McNeill and Denise M. Rechter, "The Financial Institutions Deregulation and Monetary Control Act of 1980," *Federal Reserve Bulletin* (June 1980). See also

somewhat earlier, development was the joint action by the Federal Home Loan Bank Board, the Federal Deposit Insurance Corporation, and the Board of Governors of the Federal Reserve System permitting financial institutions to offer two new types of high-yield time certificates, effective June 1, 1978. The new *money market certificates* are 6-month issues with a minimum denomination of $10,000 and a maximum permissible yield tied to the average auction rate for the most recently issued 6-month Treasury bill.[27] Beginning in 1980 new 2½-year certificates with rates tied to Treasury bill rates were allowed for the first time. These new kinds of time deposits enabled the thrift institutions to compete effectively for funds in 1978–1980, as short-term interest rates soared to double-digit levels. Thus, a large-scale loss of funds (disintermediation) was avoided and the mortgage and housing markets remained remarkably buoyant for this advanced phase of the business cycle, at least until the extreme rates of early 1980.

## Debt-Management Policy: The Postwar Record

Macroeconomists traditionally recognize two major goals of debt management: to contribute to economic stabilization and growth, and to contribute to balance-of-payments equilibrium. The former goal became generally accepted in the United States in the 1950s. As explained earlier, it calls for debt shortening during recessions and debt lengthening during booms. The contribution of debt management to balance-of-payments equilibrium has usually taken the form of debt shortening in order to prevent short-term capital outflows (or promote inflows). This latter goal became generally accepted only in the 1960s.[28] Efficient debt management requires that these macroeconomic goals be

pursued with minimum interest cost to the Treasury.

The Treasury Department's own operating approach to debt management—while accepting the importance of macroeconomic goals—has always stressed as its "basic function" financing the budget deficit and refunding maturing obligations. In the last two decades, the Treasury Department has also attached increasing importance to "the maintenance and improvement of the debt structure," a euphemism for debt lengthening (and lately for "regularization" of coupon issues at specified quarterly or monthly dates).

If financing new debt and refinancing maturing debt at lowest cost were the primary objective of debt management, it could always be achieved by "monetizing" the debt (that is, through an expansion in the money supply). However, such a policy—often pursued by less-developed countries—creates powerful inflationary pressures, except during periods of massive unemployment. The goal of debt lengthening and regularization should be taken more seriously; it has received considerable professional support.[29] Frequent and unanticipated excursions by the Treasury into the financial markets are disruptive, constrain the timing of the Federal Reserve's monetary policy, and may, at times, result in unnecessarily high interest costs to the government.

Since the end of World War II, U.S. debt management has gone through four distinct phases. The first phase, from 1946 through 1960, was one of keeping interest costs down; the second, from 1961 to 1965, introduced balance-of-payment consider-

---

Chapter 31 of this text, Table 31-6, for a systematic review of the major provisions of all regulatory reform proposals of depository institutions for the two decades 1960–1980.

[27]The formula for determining the actual ceiling is somewhat complex, and it changes from time to time as all interest rate ceilings on deposits are phased out over 1980–1986. For the current ceilings, see the table on maximum rates payable on time deposits in the *Federal Reserve Bulletin*.

[28]For example, the Secretary of the Treasury, in his *Annual Report* for fiscal 1961, Government Printing Of-

fice, Washington, D.C., 1962, p. 30, stated: "Most recently, a whole new dimension has been added to debt management objectives by the emergence of international balance-of-payments considerations."

[29]See, for example, T. C. Gaines, *Techniques of Treasury Debt Management*, The Free Press of Glencoe, New York, 1962, especially Chap. 8; Milton Friedman, *A Program for Monetary Stability*, Fordham University Press, New York, 1960, pp. 52–65; Warren L. Smith, *Debt Management in the United States*, Study Paper for the Joint Economic Committee, U.S. Congress, 1960, especially Chap. 4; Herbert Stein, "Managing the Federal Debt," *The Journal of Law and Economics* (October 1958), 97–104; and Henry C. Wallich, "Public Debt Management and Economic Stabilization Policy," *United States Monetary Policy*, Second Duke Assembly, Durham, N.C., 1959, pp. 31–51. In this connection, see also the discussion earlier in this chapter.

ations; the third, from mid-1965 to mid-1971, was largely a time of impotence because of legislative constraints; and the most recent phase has stressed improved marketing techniques and the regularization of coupon issues.

In the early postwar period—mainly as the heritage of World War II financing—keeping down the interest cost on the government debt was an overriding objective of both monetary and debt-management policy. (One initial motivation was the desire to avoid inflicting large capital losses on individuals and institutions that had bought low-yielding government securities during the various patriotic war bond drives.) In any case, until the Treasury–Federal Reserve accord of March 3, 1951, the Federal Reserve was committed to a policy of supporting long-term government bonds at, or above, par and hence keeping interest rates low.[30] The 1951 "accord" enabled the Federal Reserve to pursue a more independent monetary policy aimed at the stabilization of aggregate demand, but full independence of monetary policy was reestablished only with the adoption of the bills-only doctrine in March 1953.[31] It consisted of a Federal Reserve commitment to conduct its open-market operations through purchases and sales of Treasury bills (except for brief corrections of "disorderly" market conditions), thus discontinuing any "pegging," or price support for longer-term maturities.

Following the 1951 accord, the Treasury, in turn, became the sole manager of the maturity structure of the federal debt and, hence, the only policy-making authority that could use debt management as a tool for minimizing costs. Subsequently, the proper coordination of monetary and debt-management policies for economic stabilization (or for other policy objectives) became again a policy issue. However, from 1951 through the end of 1960, the Treasury continued to manage its debt with low interest costs as its primary objective. This is evident from an analysis of cyclical changes in the maturity structure of the federal debt, as well as from changes in the term structure of interest rates over the course of the business cycle. According to traditional, countercyclical debt-management

policy, the maturity of the outstanding debt should be shortened during periods of contraction (in order to lower long-term interest rates, increase liquidity, and encourage investment and consumption) and lengthened during periods of inflation (in order to raise long-term rates, reduce liquidity, and discourage spending). From 1951 through 1960, however, Treasury financing followed the opposite course: lengthening the maturity structure of government debt during recessions and periods of monetary ease, when interest rates were low; shortening it during periods of inflation and monetary restraint, when interest rates were much higher and rising.[32] This pattern of debt management may be considered relatively "passive"; it was designed to keep the average interest cost on the federal debt down by lengthening the maturity structure of the debt only at those times when financial markets were willing to absorb medium- and long-term debt at interest rates only fractionally above those prevailing at the time.

Beginning in 1961, the preoccupation with minimizing interest costs waned as concern over the balance of payments and domestic economic expansion mounted. Policies for containing the balance-of-payments deficit called for higher short-term rates in order to keep capital from flowing out of the country, while policies designed to encourage domestic expansion required low long-term rates in order to encourage capital investment. The coexistence of these two policy objectives gave rise to the Federal Reserve's Operation Twist, an attempt to twist the term structure of interest rates by swapping Treasury bills for longer-term government securities. The aim of this policy was to raise the level of short-term rates while reducing long-term rates. However, the objective of buying long and selling short was not pursued vigorously. The Federal Reserve's Open Market Account revealed an extremely small amount of net purchases of bonds with a maturity in excess of five years. Moreover, the impact of these purchases was largely offset by the Treasury's efforts to lengthen the average maturity structure of the entire debt, which had shortened drastically since 1946. For this purpose, in June 1960, the Treasury introduced a new technique that was used frequently and with considerable success during the first half of the 1960s.[33]

---

[30] See Herbert Stein, *The Fiscal Revolution in America,* The University of Chicago Press, Chicago, 1969, Chap. 10.

[31] For a brief discussion of these deveopments, see Michael E. Levy, *Cycles in Government Securities,* vol. 1, The Conference Board, New York, 1962, pp. 17–20.

[32] Ibid., vol. 2, especially Charts 3-1, 3-2, and pp. 63–65.

[33] Advance refunding provides the bondholders (or

The actual behavior of short-term and long-term interest rates between 1961 and 1963 was consistent with the objectives of Operation Twist: short-term rates increased rather markedly during this period, while long-term rates remained fairly stable. However, rigorous tests of the success of Operation Twist led to the conclusions that the observed behavior of the term structure of interest rates during 1961 and 1963 could be explained primarily by expectation factors and certain institutional changes—particularly increases in Regulation Q—that were essentially unrelated to Operation Twist.[34] These results are not surprising in view of the fact that Operation Twist was not pursued vigorously and was often at crosspurposes with debt lengthening.

During the third phase of postwar debt management, from mid-1965 through mid-1971, the scope for either countercyclical or "twisting" debt-management policy was sharply limited by legislative constraints. The Second Liberty Bond Act of 1917—as amended by the Victory Liberty Loan Act of 1919—had included a 4¼ percent interest rate limitation on bonds issued by the federal government. Prior to 1965 (except for a brief episode during 1959–1960), long-term interest rates remained well below the level at which this interest rate limitation could serve as an effective constraint against the issuance of government bonds. However, when the Vietnam War was superimposed on an exuberant economy that, in mid-1965, approached full resource utilization, price stability gave way to rapidly escalating inflation and interest rates surged. By September 1965, the yield on long-term government bonds reached 4¼ percent, and it has exceeded this level ever since. Thus, the Treasury was effectively barred from issuing government bonds. Moreover, at that time, the longest permissible maturity for notes (which do not come

under the 4¼ percent limitation) was five years. In 1967, at the Treasury's request, Congress lengthened this maturity to seven years (followed by a subsequent extension to ten years). However, the full range of debt-management options was not restored until March 1971, when Congress authorized the issuance of up to $10 billion of bonds without regard to the 4¼ percent interest rate limitation.[35] Subsequently, the authorization for bonds exempt from the 4¼ percent interest limitation was raised first to $12 billion, and then, on June 30, 1976, to $17 billion. (But, as of mid-1980, Congress has rejected proposals for abolishing the rate limitation.)

The latest phase of debt management has emphasized improved marketing techniques and increasing reliance on coupon issues and their "regularization" in terms of quarterly and monthly "cycles." Moreover, since 1976, debt lengthening has become again a major objective of the Treasury's debt-management policy. These developments have occurred largely because of the need to finance extremely large and persistent budget deficits, beginning with fiscal 1975, in the face of continuing high inflation rates. Since the first auction of a coupon issue in fiscal 1970, the auction technique has been refined repeatedly and its use has been expanded. An end-of-quarter 2-year note cycle was introduced in October 1972; and in fiscal 1975, the basis was laid for a monthly 2-year note cycle with nine monthly issues. In fiscal 1976, further regularization of coupon issues was achieved by adding quarterly 4-year and 5-year note cycles to the monthly 2-year cycle with optimal "slotting." The 2-year notes mature at the end of each month, the 4-year notes at the end of each quarter, and the 5-year notes at the middle of each quarter. In order to achieve further debt lengthening, regular quarterly issues of long-term bonds and 7- to 10-year notes were added. In fiscal 1977–1979, further debt lengthening was achieved by deliberately paying down bills and raising large amounts of new cash in the coupon market. The result was a reversal of the ten-year decline in the average maturity of the privately held federal debt. This average maturity had declined from five years four months in June 1966 to two years four months in February 1976; by the end of fiscal 1979, it was up to three years seven months.

noteholders) with an opportunity to exchange their securities for new issues of longer maturity on attractive terms. Usually, advance refunding is applied to outstanding issues that are fairly close to maturity. For a review and assessment of the advance-refunding technique, see Thomas R. Beard, *U.S. Treasury Advance Refunding, June 1960–July 1964*, Board of Governors of the Federal Reserve System, Washington, D.C., 1966.

[34]See Franco Modigliani and Richard Sutch, "Innovations in Interest Rate Policy," *American Economic Review* (May 1966); also Levy, *Cycles in Government Securities*, vol. 2., p. 4.

[35]The first bond issued since 1965 was a 10-year bond in August 1971, followed by a 15-year bond in November. The first 7-year note had been issued in November 1967.

## Conclusion

Fiscal policy, the use of government spending and taxing power to achieve macroeconomic objectives, consists of passive components (the "built-in" stabilizers) and discretionary elements as well. Passive fiscal stabilization occurs in a modern industrialized economy because government tax receipts tend to vary directly with economic activity while government expenditures vary inversely, other things equal. The result is a government budget deficit that tends to rise automatically during recessions and decline relatively during economic expansions, even apart from any discretionary actions. Beyond these passive aspects of fiscal policy, taxes may be cut and expenditures increased during recessions as additional measures to stimulate the economy. However, the converse—namely, raising taxes and reducing expenditures during economic expansions—has often proven difficult for political reasons.

Because the size of the measured government sector budget surplus or deficit fluctuates automatically over the course of the business cycle, various additional measures have been proposed to reflect the impact of (and, possibly, the need for) additional fiscal responses. These measures include the "full employment budget" concept and a newer measure known as "fiscal thrust." However, beyond the direct impact of expenditure and tax changes on the economy through multiplier effects, fiscal policy may also have financial effects since government deficits must be financed in money and capital markets. Fears concerning the "crowding out" of private borrowers by the federal government in the mid-1970s proved unfounded as events unfolded, but substantial federal deficits in a high employment context could produce rapid increases in interest rates and the crowding out of weaker borrowers if such deficits should occur in the 1980s. Such a fiscal policy would actually be perverse, of course, since a high employment economy would call for budget surpluses rather than sizeable deficits.

Another financial aspect of fiscal policy consists of debt-management policy, or, in other words, Treasury management of the maturity structure of the federal debt. Changes in maturity structure of the debt may have impacts on the economy by affecting either long- or short-term interest rates, depending on the liquidity and interest sensitivity of the economy. For this reason the Treasury has devoted considerable attention to aspects of debt-management policy and has undertaken several notable policy changes over the past three decades. Since it seems unlikely that the future will prove less economically complex than the past, it is difficult to conclude that debt-management policy will cease to be a matter of concern in the years ahead. Undoubtedly, fiscal and debt-management policy will continue to require the careful attention of those charged with its formulation and execution.

## Questions

1. Distinguish between the built-in stabilizers and discretionary fiscal policy.
2. What are the general principles of countercyclical fiscal policy?
3. What is meant by "crowding out" effects of fiscal stimulation? Under what circumstances is substantial "crowding out" likely to occur?
4. Describe the main objectives of countercyclical debt-management policy.
5. What are the channels through which debt-management policy affects GNP?
6. Explain the differential impact of debt-management policy on financial intermediaries.
7. Explain the four major phases of postwar debt-management policy.
8. Explain why fears of "crowding out" proved unfounded during the mid-1970s.
9. Explain some of the problems encountered in using the size of the government budget surplus or deficit as a measure of fiscal policy.
10. Explain the concept of the "high employment surplus." What are some of the problems associated with constructing and using this concept?

## Selected Bibliography

Levy, Michael E. *Fiscal Policy, Cycles and Growth.* The Conference Board, New York, 1963.

Musgrave, Richard A. *The Theory of Public Finance.* McGraw-Hill Book Company, New York, 1959.

Scherer, Joseph, and James A. Papke, eds. *Public Finance and Fiscal Policy.* Houghton Mifflin Company, Boston, 1966.

Silber, William L. *Portfolio Behavior of Financial Institutions.* Holt, Rinehart and Winston, New York, 1969.

Tobin, J. "An Essay on Principles of Debt Management." *Fiscal and Debt Management Policies.* Prepared for the Commission on Money and Credit. Prentice-Hall, Englewood Cliffs, N.J., 1963.

# 30

# International Financial Policy

One concern of national monetary, fiscal, and debt-management policies is the nation's balance-of-payments position. Indeed, in recent years, it has become a primary focus of policy attention in the United States and several other industrialized countries. The international monetary system has undergone a major restructuring since 1971 and dramatic shocks to international payments and borrowing resulting from OPEC oil-price policy and other events have thrust international financial policy into the forefront of public awareness.

A country can purchase foreign goods, services, and investment only with the receipts of sales to foreigners or with its holdings of international reserve assets. Any one country's international reserves are necessarily limited. And certain types of policy actions, which would otherwise change the balance of payments, are often avoided because they conflict with national economic goals or are prohibited by international agreement. Since international reserves and liquidity (or borrowing capabilities) are limited, balance-of-payments equilibrium as a goal of national economic policy cannot be permanently avoided.

This goal and the means for achieving it are further complicated by the unique role which the United States has played in the international monetary system. This chapter attempts to outline the structure of the international monetary system and the United States' role within it. Emphasis is given to the problems and dilemmas in economic policy that the balance-of-payments and exchange-rate objectives create. The first section examines the nation as a spending unit, using the United States' experience in the postwar period as an example. Thereafter, the alternative mechanisms of balance-of-payments adjustment are outlined and the potential conflicts between the various measures for external balance and other domestic economic objectives are explored. The fourth and fifth sections describe the evolving international monetary system and the changing U.S. role in it.

## The Nation as a Spending Unit

In earlier chapters, households, business firms, and governments were classified as surplus or deficit spending units on the basis of whether *current income* (*Y*) *exceeded current expenditures* for consumption and real investment (*E*), or vice versa.

Differences between $Y$ and $E$ are possible because individual spending units are willing to change either their holdings or issuance of financial assets and liabilities. For all spending units taken together (that is, in a *closed* economy), current expenditures must equal current income. It follows, therefore, that the change in financial assets of surplus units must exactly offset the change in financial liabilities of deficit units.

A nation that is open to trade in goods and financial assets with the rest of the world may be analyzed in the same manner. For example, current expenditures by country A (an *open* economy) may exceed its current income if the rest of the world is willing to accumulate the liabilities of country A. Alternatively, current expenditures by country A may fall short of its current income if country A is willing to accumulate assets (claims) or reduce liabilities on the rest of the world. For the world, which is a closed economy, $Y$ must equal $E$, and net adjustments in financial asset and liability positions must sum to zero for all nations combined. But, for any one nation, this need not be the case; that nation may be either a net source (lender) of funds to the rest of the world or a net user (borrower).

To formalize the above, let $Y_A$ represent current national income for country A and let $E_D$ represent domestic national expenditure (domestic consumption plus domestic investment and domestic government expenditure, $C + I + G$). In an open economy, current national income is equal to domestic national expenditures plus the balance of trade (exports − imports). This is illustrated by Equation (30-1).

$$Y_A = E_D + (\text{Exports} - \text{Imports})$$
$$= (C + I + G) + (\text{Exports}-\text{Imports}) \quad (30\text{-}1)$$

Rearranging terms to form Equation (30-2), one sees that whenever a country has a positive trade balance (exports exceed imports), then current national income, $Y_A$, also exceeds domestic expenditures, $E_D$.

$$Y_A - E_D = \text{Exports} - \text{Imports} > 0 \quad (30\text{-}2)$$

This is the case of a surplus country: Its exports of goods and services exceed its imports (in other words, its national income exceeds its domestic expenditures) and it acquires financial assets (claims on foreigners). In contrast, a deficit country

is one whose imports exceed its exports (its domestic expenditures exceed its current national income) and it becomes a net debtor to other countries (which is to say, an issuer of liabilities to foreigners). In other words, the difference between current domestic output and income and domestic national expenditure is equal to the balance of trade in goods and services—that is, the current account in the balance of payments.[1]

Since expenditure decisions are made by decentralized units around the world, *ex ante* there is no assurance when expenditure plans are made that the constraints on the closed economy (that is, planned expenditure equal to planned output with no change in net financial assets) are satisfied in an open economy consisting of many diverse countries. To satisfy these constraints as *ex post* accounting identities, it may be necessary for the volume of exports and imports or relative prices, or both, to adjust. The nature of this "adjustment process" depends on the willingness of countries to hold the liabilities of other countries and on the type of exchange rate system linking national currencies.

If exchange rates between currencies are fixed, an excess of domestic expenditure over domestic production (a current-account deficit) may be "financed" by reducing net asset balances abroad or by increasing liabilities to foreigners. However, neither of these financing balances is unlimited. The assets it can draw on, in one sense a nation's "money balances," consist of its "international reserves" and its private foreign investments. Its *international reserve assets* are those assets that are generally acceptable to foreign central banks in official transactions and include monetary gold, foreign exchange (convertible currencies), the country's reserve position in the International Monetary Fund (IMF), and Special Drawing Rights (SDRs) issued by the IMF.[2] Private foreign investments

---

[1] In addition to exports and imports of goods and services, most nations also include net unilateral transfers in the current-account definition of the balance of payments. Unilateral transfers are normally small for most nations and do not change greatly from year to year. For convenience, one can denote the current-account balance as exports minus imports, as long as one understands that for analytical completeness it should include net unilateral transfers to foreigners.

[2] These items are included in the official definition of international reserves in reserve reports of the Interna-

consist of assets held abroad by nongovernmental bodies that might be used to purchase imports. All of these are finite, as is the willingness of foreigners to hold a country's liabilities. Typically, under a fixed exchange rate system, imbalances in payments and receipts with the rest of the world result in both international reserve flows and a willingness to hold liabilities, at least for a while; relative prices between countries would likely remain constant in the short run.

To illustrate, suppose country A has a current-account deficit (that is, $Y_A < E_D$ = Exports < Imports). Based on national income and balance-of-payments accounting identities, we know that the deficit will be equivalent to (financed by) the net flow of funds from the following sources:[3]

1. decreases in the country's international reserves, analogous to a decrease in cash balances
2. decreases in the home country's holdings of foreign financial assets
3. increases in liabilities to foreigners (borrowing abroad)

Note that *ex ante,* if one is to maintain the fixed exchange rate between the currencies, it is unlikely that private decisions will result in a current-account balance that is exactly offset by *private-sector* borrowing and lending abroad (items 2 and 3). The *ex post* equivalency of the current-account balance and the net flow of funds to finance it result from item 1—changes in the nation's reserve holdings—which acts as the residual-balancing item.

Under a system where exchange rates between currencies are completely free to change, the excess of domestic expenditure over domestic production leads to a different result. Assume as before that, at the current exchange rate, *ex ante* decisions in the country result in current expenditures in excess of current income.[4] This incipient current-account deficit ($Y_A < E_D$ = Exports < Imports) will be brought into balance in this case, too, by three forces:

1. a depreciation of the foreign exchange value of the home country's currency, which tends to change the spending patterns of local and foreign residents, so that exports increase (because they are less expensive for foreigners) and imports decrease (because they become more expensive in the home country)
2. decreases in the home country's holdings of foreign financial assets
3. increases in liabilities to foreigners

Note that under freely floating exchange rates, assuming foreigners do not suddenly seek to acquire the assets of country A, a depreciation of the home country's currency occurs rather than a decrease in its international reserves as occurred in the case of a fixed exchange rate system.[5] The use of international reserves to support exchange rates thus obviously depends on the type of exchange rate system employed by the country or the international monetary system. At the one extreme may be a complete lack of support of any specific exchange rate; this amounts to no intervention by the monetary authorities in the foreign exchange market. Under this system, private decisions relating to exporting, importing, and foreign lending and borrowing will be brought into equality by exchange rate adjustments. At the other extreme of complete fixity of exchange rates, any *ex ante* imbalance in the balance of trade (exports − imports)

---

[4]This refers to planned or *ex ante* expenditure and production. But *ex ante* expenditure and production are both dependent on the expected path of the exchange rate over the period and would vary with different levels of anticipated exchange rates.

[5]The means of keeping the exchange rate between currencies "fixed" is for the central bank of a deficit nation to use its international reserves to support (buy) its own currency on the foreign exchange market or for the monetary authorities of the surplus country to buy the deficit nation's currency on the foreign exchange market (that is, to sell its own currency on the foreign exchange market to keep its price from rising). This process is called *central-bank intervention* in the foreign exchange market. In the example of a free exchange rate, it is assumed that no central-bank intervention occurs and, thus, the exchange rate is free to adjust to private decisions to spend and invest.

---

tional Monetary Fund and are reported monthly for member countries in International Monetary Fund, *International Financial Statistics,* Washington, D.C.

[3]Increases in liabilities to foreigners occur when foreigners invest in long-term or short-term financial assets issued in the home country. The short-term liabilities to foreigners include foreign-owned demand deposits and bank notes as well as more conventional interest-bearing instruments, such as time deposits, CDs, Treasury bills, and the like. Increases in foreign financial assets of the home country would involve acquisitions of similar claims on foreigners by residents of the home country.

and net private foreign lending and borrowing must be made up by use of reserves through central-bank intervention on the foreign exchange market.

The international monetary system was predominantly a fixed exchange rate system from 1945 until 1971.[6] Since then, the system has evolved into a mixture of some degree of exchange rate flexibility along with a significant degree of exchange rate fixity and intervention. The evolution of the U.S. current balance and its international lending and borrowing is shown in Table 30-1. Note that for the postwar period, the United States had a current surplus, although this was finally reversed with a current-account deficit in 1977. But note also that U.S. lending and financial grants to foreigners, rather than simply acting as the balancing item, have consistently exceeded the current surpluses. In terms of the earlier example, although domestic expenditure has been less than domestic output ($Y_A < E_D$), the U.S. desire to acquire foreign financial (and real) assets has been even larger. This excess became particularly massive in the 1970s, averaging $46.8 billion annually from 1974–1978. Much of this is reflected in increased bank lending to countries needing funds to purchase oil in the aftermath of the massive oil-price changes of 1973–1974.

Although exchange rates between currencies were relatively fixed until 1971, the United States lost relatively few international reserves (less than $1 billion annually in most years) despite its chronic deficits caused by lending and grants abroad. Most of the excess of U.S. lending over the current surplus was balanced (financed) by U.S. borrowing from foreigners. Prior to the 1970s, most of that borrowing occurred through the financial markets, as foreign individuals and institutions sought to acquire U.S. (dollar-denominated) assets. But, in the 1970s, borrowing from foreign official institutions (mainly central banks) became the dominant source of change in U.S. liabilities to foreigners. This occurred through central-bank intervention in the for-

eign exchange market. In order to keep the dollar from depreciating (and their own currencies from rising in price in terms of the dollar) foreign central banks in surplus nations acquired dollars on the foreign exchange market and held those dollars as investments in United States financial instruments. Note that this occurred mainly *after* the fixed exchange rate system was abandoned in 1971. Thus, even though greater exchange rate flexibility has been evidenced since 1971, there have not been free exchange rate movements (that is, movements determined only by private market forces), and intervention with respect to the dollar has been much greater than prior to 1971.[7] Most of that intervention has been carried out by countries with balance-of-payments surpluses, and not by the United States, with its deficit.

## Balance-of-Payments Adjustment Policies

The United States has seen its net international liquidity decline rather drastically in the 1970s as short-term liabilities to foreigners have risen sharply, although international reserves have remained relatively stable. A nation with an overall deficit in its balance of payments may rectify that situation by reducing its current payments to foreigners or increasing its current receipts from foreigners (that is, to increase exports minus imports); or it may reduce net lending to foreigners. The methods used to do this are called balance-of-payments adjustment mechanisms.[8] Three alternative sets of policies and linkages may be utilized:

1. domestic monetary-fiscal policies to adjust the levels of domestic aggregate demand, money supplies, and interest rates relative to those abroad
2. changing, or allowing to change, the exchange rate between national currencies

[6] For a detailed description of the international monetary system with emphasis on the early days of the IMF, see Margaret de Vries, *The International Monetary Fund, 1946–1971*, International Monetary Fund, Washington, D.C., 1976. For more detail on the system since 1973, see Thomas D. Willett, *Floating Exchange Rates and International Monetary Reform*, American Enterprise Institute, Washington, D.C., 1977.

[7] See Richard K. Abrams, "Federal Reserve Intervention Policy," *Economic Review*, Federal Reserve Bank of Kansas City (March 1979), 15–23; also Stanley W. Black, *Floating Exchange Rates and National Economic Policy*, Yale University Press, New Haven, Conn., 1977.

[8] Extended examination of the international adjustment processes are found in standard international economics texts and in Robert M. Stern, *The Balance of Payments*, Aldine Publishing Company, Chicago, 1973.

**Table 30-1   U.S. Current Balance with the Rest of the World and Related Financial Flows in the Postwar Period (annual averages in billions of dollars)**

|  | 1947–1957 | 1958–1964 | 1965–1970 | 1971–1973 | 1974–1978 |
|---|---|---|---|---|---|
| Current surplus[a] | $3.5 | $3.6 | $ 5.5 | $ 3.7 | $ 4.7 |
| $(Y - E)$ = (Exports − Imports) |  |  |  |  |  |
| U.S. lending and financial grants to foreigners[b] | 4.8 | 6.8 | 12.5 | 21.3 | 46.8 |
| U.S. borrowing from foreigners:[c] Total | 0.8 | 2.7 | 6.8 | 21.1 | 40.1 |
| From private foreigners |  |  | 5.5 | 6.5 | 19.0 |
| From official institutions |  |  | 1.3 | 14.6 | 21.1 |
| Changes in U.S. international reserves | (0.2) | (1.1) | (0.4) | (0.8) | (0.9) |

[a]Current surplus is the value of exports of goods and services less imports of goods and services (excluding exports under military grants).
[b]Includes U.S. private long-term and short-term foreign investment, U.S. government loans to foreigners, U.S. government grants under aid programs, and remittances to foreigners.
[c]Includes short-term and long-term investment in U.S. assets by foreigners—official and nonofficial.

Source: *Survey of Current Business,* various issues.

3. instituting direct governmental controls over or impediments to foreign purchases and payments or providing nonmarket incentives for foreign receipts

### Adjustment by Financial Policy: Relative Inflation-Deflation

The "classical" procedure for eliminating a balance-of-payments imbalance or for restoring a nation's international liquidity position is to employ domestic financial policy to alter (relative to those abroad) domestic aggregate demand, price levels, interest rates, and money supplies. Thus, a country with a balance-of-payments deficit would employ restrictive monetary and fiscal policies so as to dampen aggregate demand, raise domestic interest rates in the short run, and reduce price inflation in the long run.

Changing aggregate demand—and real income—alters foreign expenditures relative to foreign receipts. A brief outline of this mechanism follows. Other things being equal, the level of exports is a function of the level of foreign aggregate demand and the competitiveness of exports in world markets—the prices of exported goods and services relative to prices abroad. The higher foreign national income and expenditures are—especially in the principal export markets of a country—the greater will be the demand for that country's exports. Similarly, the lower a country's costs and prices for its export goods relative to those pre-

vailing in foreign markets, the greater will be its export receipts.[9] Thus, either the existence of high levels of foreign economic activity or an increase in domestic prices that is low relative to foreign countries will tend to expand exports.

On the other hand, imports of goods and services are, other things equal, a function of *domestic* expenditures—or *domestic* income—and relative prices. High levels of domestic demand will tend to encourage imports in two ways. First, if households spend more on domestic consumer goods, it is likely that they will also spend more on imported consumer goods. Similarly, imported capital goods and raw materials will fluctuate with domestic investment spending. The net result is that spending for imports varies directly with total domestic spending, or aggregate demand. Second, since high levels of aggregate demand tend to be associated with rising price levels, relative prices among countries also depend, to some extent, on changes in domestic demand. Higher domestic prices relative to foreign prices will increase purchases of imported goods, and more foreign payments for imports will occur. Thus, suppressing domestic aggregate demand relative to that abroad through

[9]The latter is true only if the elasticity of demand for exports is greater than unity. Only then will the quantity of exports rise in greater proportion than prices fall, thereby increasing total receipts (in foreign exchange) for exports. Throughout this section, the assumption is made that demand elasticities for exports and imports exceed unity.

restrictive monetary and fiscal policies will tend to improve the current balance with the rest of the world (exports minus imports) due to a relative price effect as well as an income (or expenditure) effect.

For a country facing a balance-of-payments surplus, the appropriate expansionary policies which would tend to eliminate the surplus are the reverse of those we have just outlined. Higher money growth and lower interest rates will tend to expand domestic aggregate demand, raising the demand for imports and increasing domestic prices relative to foreign prices. This will tend to reduce the trade balance. Likewise, expansionary policies leading to lower interest rates should slow capital inflows or increase capital outflows.[10]

Restrictive monetary policies are generally associated with lower or slower-growing money supplies and higher domestic interest rates in the short run. And, although there are many factors that affect foreign investment (see Chapter 18), one factor is international interest rate differences.[11] To the extent that capital flows are responsive to interest rate differentials, increases (decreases) in in-

terest rates will, as long as other things are equal, decrease (increase) the international capital outflows. Thus, the capital account in the balance of payments may be (partly) adjusted by inducing changes in international interest rate differentials. The degree of responsiveness of capital flows to interest rate changes and the permanence of induced changes are still matters of debate.[12]

The avenues for influencing relative inflation-deflation are schematically shown in Figure 30-1, starting in the upper left-hand box. Aggregate demand, which can be influenced by monetary and fiscal policies, affects total spending and, indirectly, the level of prices. In addition, monetary and fiscal policies (both at home and abroad) influence international capital flows and, thus, the net capital-account balance. Movements in domestic variables relative to those abroad influence the current-account balance, which, when added to the interest rate effect on the capital account, yields the combined effects of the policies on the overall balance of payments.

It should be clear that balance-of-payments adjustment by relative inflation-deflation circumscribes the use of financial policy for domestic purposes.[13] It remains, however, the only means of realigning international price-cost relationships, in the event of persistent disequilibria, if exchange rate changes or direct controls are avoided. The principal role of international reserves is to permit the financing—without adjustment—of temporary balance-of-payments imbalances. In addition, adequate reserves may allow the process of adjustment by relative deflation-inflation to be carried out over an extended period so that absolute reductions in incomes or prices may be avoided, while the

[10]In the long run the simple quantity theory of money predicts that a higher growth rate in the money supply will result in both a higher inflation rate and a higher nominal interest rate (the Fisher effect), with no changes in any "real" economic aggregate variable. An anthology of papers describing this monetary approach is found in Jacob A. Frenkel and Harry G. Johnson, eds., *The Monetary Approach to the Balance of Payments,* Allen and Unwin, London, 1976. In addition, there, as elsewhere in this chapter, the longer-run feedbacks of one group of balance-of-payments items on other items are ignored. Especially important in this regard are the delayed feedbacks of interest and dividend earnings from foreign investment, induced exports to foreign subsidiaries, and the like, all of which involve effects on the current-account balance resulting from earlier capital-account outflows.

[11]Whether or not interest-induced capital flows are defined as a balance-of-payments adjustment is a matter of preference. Some economists view changes in the level of expenditures and prices (including the exchange rate) of one country vis-à-vis the rest of the world as the only fundamental means of adjustment. Capital flows induced by interest rate changes, export and import changes resulting from commercial and foreign payments policies, and so forth, would then be deemed "correctives," which can substitute for real adjustment only temporarily. See Fritz Machlup, "Adjustment, Compensatory Correction, and Financing of Imbalances in International Payments," in *Trade, Growth and the Balance of Payments,* eds. Robert E. Baldwin, et al., Rand McNally & Company, Chicago, 1965.

[12]For a review of some of the evidence, see Zoran Hodjera, "International Short-Term Capital Movements: A Survey of Theory and Empirical Analysis," *IMF Staff Papers* (November 1973), 683–741.

[13]Indeed, this is one of the arguments used against— and in favor of—the international gold standard. Under the gold standard, the policy prescriptions outlined in the text would presumably be implemented automatically, thus making balance-of-payments adjustment automatic regardless of the consequences for domestic prices, employment, or growth. For example, a deficit country would experience a loss of gold and the money supply would decrease, since its bank reserves would be tied directly to the gold stock. Thus, such a deficit would trigger "tight" financial conditions, thereby tending to eliminate the deficit.

## Figure 30-1   Basic Linkages in Balance-of-Payments Adjustment

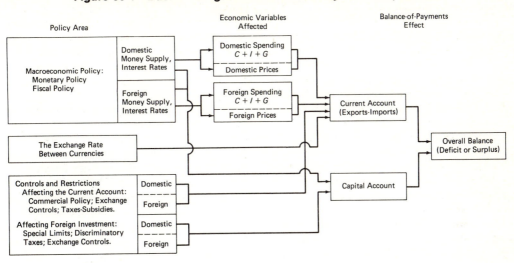

rates of increase of aggregate demand and prices relative to those abroad can be altered to induce long-run adjustment. All the same, the possibility of conflict between domestic economic goals and balance-of-payments adjustment is also present. These policy conflicts are discussed in a later section.

### Adjustment by Changes in the Exchange Rate

The exchange rate is the price of foreign currency in terms of the domestic monetary unit. A change in the exchange rate alters proportionately the prices of foreign goods in terms of the domestic currency and the prices of domestic goods in terms of the foreign currency. To illustrate, the U.S. dollar–Spanish peseta exchange rate was $0.014 = 1 peseta on July 11, 1977. The peseta was devalued by 20 percent (in peseta/dollar terms), to $0.012 on July 12, 1977. For an American, a Spanish item priced at 1,000 pesetas would have cost $14 on July 11, but only $12 on July 12 (assuming the Spanish exporter did not change the domestic currency price of his goods). As a result of the change in the dollar-peseta exchange rate, the United States would tend to import more from Spain and, assuming the U.S. demand for imports from Spain was price elastic, to pay more dollars for those imports. To generalize, a devaluation or depreciation of a

nation's currency tends to increase a nation's exports, whereas an appreciation tends to reduce its exports.

An opposite effect will occur for Spanish imports from the United States. An American export item valued at $14 would have cost a Spanish customer 1,000 pesetas before the peseta devaluation. But, after the devaluation, it would cost $14/$.012 or 1,167 pesetas. As a result, the imports of the devaluing country would tend to decline; the imports of an appreciating country would tend to increase.

This simple analysis predicts that a depreciation of a nation's currency will tend to improve its trade balance, producing a higher volume of exports and a lower volume of imports of goods and services.[14] These linkages are illustrated in the middle section of Figure 30-1. There are, however, some qualifications and extensions.

[14]The prediction that a currency depreciation will improve a nation's trade balance presumes that the "Marshall-Lerner conditions" hold which, in simplified terms, amounts to saying that the sum of the price elasticities of demand of the country's exports and imports exceeds unity. For elaboration, see Stern, *The Balance of Payments,* Chap. 5. Further, the impact of the change in relative prices on the trade balance presumes that the country's exports are not perfect substitutes for foreign products and/or that its import-competing production is not a perfect substitute for imports. That is to say, it is assumed that the country's trade does not consist only of homogeneous products. Prices for homogeneous products

First, is the price effect on the trade balance immediate or does it occur with a long lag? While there remains considerable controversy over that issue, there is a large body of opinion that the price elasticities of demand for exports and imports are much higher in the long run than in the short run.[15] Low short-run elasticities result from the fact that orders are already placed, and already-established supplier-customer relationships take time to reestablish with new sources of supply. Thus, in the short run, importers in a devaluing nation may continue to buy about the same volume of imports and pay more in terms of local currency for it. Likewise, the nation's cheaper exports (in terms of foreign currency) are not recognized by foreign customers immediately, and any change in volume occurs only after orders are placed and shipments made. Thus, it is believed that the time pattern of adjustment in the trade balance of a change in the exchange rate takes a "J" shape, deteriorating (toward deficit) immediately following the devaluation and then gradually improving in future periods as the effects of changes in the volume of exports and imports are felt.

Second, will changes in the trade balance be permanent or temporary? Our prediction, based on the simple analysis of the price effects of exchange rate changes, ignores indirect or induced adjustments in the domestic economy. There are several such second-order effects, which may tend to erode a part of the initial impact of the exchange rate change on the trade balance. One is that the devaluation may have an inflationary impact of its own on the local economy. Since the devaluation raises the domestic currency price of imports, consumer and wholesale prices rise approximately in proportion to the share of imported goods in the indices. This, in turn, raises the cost of production in industries using imported inputs and the inflationary impact is passed through to other industries, eventually raising the costs (and prices) of the country's exports, thereby undoing some of the positive effects of the devaluation on export volume.

In countries with significant monopoly elements in markets and where wages and other prices are "indexed" to the cost of living, there is also the possibility that the entire price structure would move up as a result of a currency devaluation, not just prices of those goods with imported components. To the extent that this occurs, and that the social and political system is not capable of breaking such linkages, the usefulness of adjusting exchange rates to effect balance-of-payments adjustments is substantially reduced.[16]

A third qualification to the positive aspects of a currency devaluation must be made because the current-account balance (exports − imports) is a part of the national income identity. A shift in the current-account balance in the balance of payments resulting from a change in the exchange rate activates the national income spending multiplier, raising the equilibrium level of income and the demand for imports. The rise in import demand, due to the higher level of income, is a further offset to the initial, positive, trade-balance effect of the devaluation.

Changes in exchange rates for balance-of-payments adjustment may come about in several forms, depending upon the type of international monetary system in existence at the time. At one extreme is a system in which exchange rates are "pegged" or fixed against some unit of account (or *numeraire*), such as gold or the U.S. dollar, and changed only by explicit governmental decision to change the level of the "peg," or "par value" of

---

cannot be different (or changed) from one country to another except for trade restrictions and transport costs. For most countries, trade in manufactured goods, which are differentiated, rather than in homogeneous products, is the rule rather than the exception. Thus, the capacity to change *relative* prices exists.

[15]For extensive discussion of these effects and empirical estimates of the responses of the U.S. trade balance, see Stephen Magee, "Currency Contracts, Pass-Through and Devaluation," *Brookings Papers on Economic Activity,* No. 1, 1973, pp. 303–325; and Peter Clark, "The Effects of Recent Exchange Rate Changes on the U.S. Trade Balance," *The Effects of Exchange Rate Changes,* U.S. Department of the Treasury, Washington, D.C., 1974.

[16]Some analysts believed that this situation existed in the United Kingdom in the late 1960s and early 1970s as money wage rates and unit labor costs quickly adjusted upward by the full proportion of pound sterling devaluations on a few occasions. This phenomenon has been variously called a "ratchet effect," a vicious circle, or a depreciation-induced wage-price spiral. The economic models of these processes are critically examined in Morris Goldstein, "Downward Price Inflexibility, Ratchet Effects, and the Inflationary Impact of Import Price Changes," *IMF Staff Papers* (November 1977), 569–613.

the currency. Such changes may be infrequent, and the range of permissible variation of the actual market price of foreign currencies around the par rate (or peg) may be quite narrow. In the periods between changes in the par rate, payments deficits and surpluses must be financed by changes in international reserves or balance-of-payments adjustment must be accomplished by other mechanisms. International reserves are expended or acquired in the process of maintaining the market exchange rate within the permissible band of fluctuation around the par rate.

More flexibility in the exchange rate may be achieved in two ways. One is to increase the frequency or ease the criteria for changing the pegged rate (or par value). In the postwar period prior to 1972, adjustments in pegged exchange rates were quite infrequent and occurred only when major disequilibria had emerged and persisted for some time in a nation's balance of payments. Such rigidities need not be the case, however, and frequent changes in par values are now the practice of several countries, such as Brazil and Peru.

Another means of achieving greater flexibility within a par-value system is to widen the bands of permissible variation in market exchange rates about the central "pegged" value. Prior to 1971, the permissible bands of flexibility were narrow (1 percent on each side of parity); from 1971 to 1973 there were wider bands of flexibility (2¼ percent on each side).

At the other extreme is a currency system without par values and without central-bank intervention to limit or influence market adjustment in the price of currencies. In such a system, the *ex ante* supply of foreign currencies from exports and capital inflows is continuously equated with the demand for foreign currencies for imports and capital outflows through adjustment in the price of foreign currencies. In such a "free market" exchange rate system, the balance of payments *automatically* adjusts *before* imbalances arise, although the amount by which the exchange rate must fluctuate is unsettled and could be quite large. Large and rapid changes in the exchange rate may be extremely disruptive for the local economy and, thus, a "free" exchange rate does not necessarily remove the "problem" of balance-of-payments adjustment. Thus far, no completely free market has been utilized in the major industrial countries.

It is also possible to have a system that has no par value for currencies but that includes central-bank intervention in the foreign exchange market of greater or lesser frequency and magnitude. On the one hand, such intervention to buy or sell foreign exchange may be limited, with an intent to smooth out short-run fluctuations and create "an orderly market."[17] On the other hand, the intervention could be sizable, with the intent to move or influence the level of the exchange rate in the longer term, or indeed, to keep the rate within a designated range decided on by the monetary authorities.[18] In the latter case, a nonparity exchange rate system behaves exactly like a par system, except that the parity is unofficial and unannounced.

Since adjustment would be automatic under a flexible exchange rate system, the need for and role of international reserves would be greatly reduced. One major advantage claimed for such a system is that it frees domestic monetary and fiscal policies from the goal of maintaining balance-of-payments equilibrium and permits them to concentrate on domestic economic goals. Changes in the exchange rate would bring about equilibrating changes in exports and imports and, thereby, make it unnecessary to use monetary and fiscal policies to deflate or inflate incomes and prices for the whole economy, as is required when the adjustment mechanism is relative inflation-deflation. As the following discussion indicates, this advantage may be limited.

Several arguments have been made against completely free exchange rates. First, in connection with international trade and investment transactions, flexible rates may increase the element of risk of a sizable change in the price of foreign currency between the time a debt is incurred and the time it is repaid. In addition, many bankers, and some economists, argue that free foreign ex-

[17]This was generally the policy of Canada during the earlier period of its floating dollar from 1950 to 1962. For the evidence, see G. Hartly Mellish and R. G. Hawkins, "The Stability of Flexible Exchange Rates—The Canadian Experiences," *The Bulletin,* No. 50–51, New York University, Institute of Finance, 1968. For more recent evidence, see Steven W. Kohlhagen, "The Identification of Destabilizing Foreign Exchange Speculation," *Journal of International Economics* (August 1979), 321–340.

[18]When this is done for domestic economic purposes, such as to keep export industries operating at capacity, as practiced in 1973–1977 by several countries, it is called "dirty floating."

change markets encourage the international flow of short-term capital (hot money) from one currency to another in a search for capital gains, increasing the volatility of free-market exchange rates. Furthermore, the danger exists that periodic swings in free exchange rates may result in costly reallocations of resources, which are subsequently reversed when the exchange rate moves in the other direction. A fixed rate, some of them argue, would avoid adjustment when balance-of-payments deficits (or surpluses) are temporary, by using changes in reserves to finance it. Flexible exchange rates, on the other hand, might provoke unnecessary and duplicative adjustment.

The force of these reservations is emphasized by the volatility of movements in market exchange rates in the mid-1970s and by the fact that most transactions in the foreign exchange market are "financial" in motivation. They are not made for the purpose of financing exports and imports or for long-term investment. Total turnover for 1977 in the foreign exchange markets has been estimated at $50 trillion, a number over twenty times the U.S. GNP, and twenty times larger than the value of international trade and long-term investment flows.[19] This suggests that there are eight or ten foreign exchange market transactions for each export, import, or foreign investment decision. It is this "financial overlay" of trading and speculation in foreign exchange that sets day-to-day exchange rates and serves as the filter (perhaps initiator) for "market" sentiment about the appropriate value of an exchange rate. This market sentiment may shift dramatically, producing significant short-run changes in free exchange rates.

Supporters of flexible rates (the absence of central-bank intervention in the foreign exchange market), on the other hand, contend that the market is usually responding to governmental actions or predicting what central-bank intervention postures will be for a particular currency. The market, they believe, would not be volatile and unstable if people were convinced that exchange rates would be free of manipulation by government.[20]

Thus, there are both theoretical and practical advantages and disadvantages attached to flexible exchange rates. To date, the fear that disruptive market conditions would occur if governmental intervention were completely absent has precluded an experiment with truly free floating exchange rates. But the practical difficulties of the semifloating system in existence since 1973 has convinced many that exchange rate adjustment is not a panacea for international adjustment problems.

### Adjustment by "Controls" over Payments and Receipts

A third broad category of adjustment measures, or corrective devices, for balance-of-payments purposes is direct government "controls and restrictions." This covers a broad spectrum of policy devices that may be employed directly to change import payments, export receipts, or capital movements. The avenues of influence and broad categories by type are shown in the lower segment of Figure 30-1. The more obvious forms of control for balance-of-payments purposes are tariffs, import quotas, and exchange-control systems that license and ration foreign exchange on a nonprice basis. In addition, taxes and subsidies designed to alter export receipts, and specific policies that tend to favor domestic as opposed to foreign suppliers, also must be included. Although these types of policies may, in many cases, have a rationale other than to affect the overall balance of payments, they are, nevertheless, sometimes used for that purpose. Finally, a wide range of measures has been designed to alter the flow of capital among countries, ranging from outright intergovernmental loans to discriminatory governmental taxation and to quantitative limitations on foreign investments. Such "foreign investment controls" were employed by the United States for balance-of-payments purposes from 1965 to 1974.[21] Many developing countries utilize con-

---

[19] This figure is based on an estimate of foreign exchange market turnover made by Citibank of New York and reported in "Choosing the World's Best Foreign Exchange Dealer," *Euromoney* (April 1979), 20.

[20] For an assessment of some of the related literature, see Steven W. Kohlhagen, "The Behavior of Foreign

Exchange Markets—A Critical Survey of the Empirical Literature," *Monograph Series in Finance and Economics*, No. 1978-3, New York University, Salomon Brothers Center for the Study of Financial Institutions, New York, 1978.

[21] For a more complete discussion of the U.S. capital controls, see Paul Schaffner, "The Balance of Payments Impacts of U.S. Capital-Control Programs: Evidence from Program Data and General Literature," Discussion

trols and restrictions of various sorts as a principal means of balance-of-payments adjustment.

The extensive variety and the complex economic arguments surrounding the use of direct action in balance-of-payments adjustment make a detailed analysis here impossible. Suffice it to say that these measures are often used for balance-of-payments purposes, but usually (at least ostensibly) only on a temporary basis. Furthermore, the goal of the IMF system and of its members is that such measures, in principle, are to be avoided.[22]

## The Balance of Payments and Domestic Economic Goals

### Cost of Adjustment and Conflicts in Goals

The foregoing suggests that any method of balance-of-payments adjustment is likely to carry some type of economic cost for the nation undertaking the adjustment—whether in deficit or surplus. Adjustment by relative inflation or deflation may give a surplus country unwanted inflation and less competitive export industries; it may give a deficit country lost output and higher unemployment as the economy contracts to cure its external deficit.

Exchange rate adjustments also carry economic costs. Whether by a discrete change of a pegged exchange rate or a market adjustment of a floating exchange rate, an increase in the price of foreign currencies brings out a reallocation of production from industries producing for the domestic market to industries producing for export or import competition. Such interindustry reallocations are costly and may involve temporarily idle resources or shortages. In addition, a country with a depreciat-

---

Paper No. 1, *U.S. Treasury Conference on Capital Control Programs,* Washington, D.C., December 1971.

[22]Indeed, the major international organizations—the General Agreement on Tariffs and Trade, the Organization for Economic Cooperation and Development, and the International Monetary Fund—all espouse "liberal" treatment of international commerce and payments and have as an objective the liberalization of controls for balance-of-payments purposes. As stated in the IMF *Articles of Agreement,* one of its purposes is "to assist in the establishment of a multilateral system of payments in respect of current transactions between members and in the elimination of foreign exchange restrictions which hamper the growth of world trade."

ing currency faces an additional source of inflation through higher-priced imports. This involves a change in its terms of trade so that each unit of domestic output buys fewer imports on world markets. Finally, exchange rate adjustments are costly because they bring about changes in the capital values of many assets denominated in foreign currencies, thus raising the perceived risk of international investment and no doubt affecting spending and saving decisions.

The economic costs of enforcing external balance by using direct controls and restrictions include a loss from misallocation of resources and the cost of the administrative apparatus to enforce and monitor compliance with the regulations. Not only do "controls" carry the danger of causing an inefficient allocation of economic resources, they may artificially bring about their own continuation by hiding the need for basic realignments in prices, incomes, or the exchange rate with the rest of the world. Controls are costly and difficult to administer. And they create major incentives to cheat— that is, to smuggle, to use "black markets," and the like. Efforts to avoid the controls are made by those who are restricted. Thus, to the extent that attempts at avoidance are successful, controls may tend to proliferate as governments try to prevent evasions and plug "loopholes."

Such, then, is the nature of the costs of balance-of-payments adjustment. The benefit of using any one mechanism of adjustment may be measured in terms of opportunity cost, involving the costs avoided by not having to use one of the other methods of adjustment. Thus, controls and restrictions are sometimes employed in order to avoid using deflation or devaluation. Taxation or restrictions on capital inflows have been used to avoid inflationary expansionist policies and appreciation of the nation's currency. In this sense, the benefit of restrictions is the lesser (perceived) cost of that method of adjustment as compared with the costs associated with alternative methods.

Countries may, of course, use international reserves to postpone or avoid any adjustment measures. Indeed, the principal economic functions of international reserves are to avoid costly adjustment to temporary shocks in the external balance and to slow down the pace of adjustment to permanent changes to allow time for the effects of adjustment measures to be felt in the balance of payments and foreign exchange market.[23] But there is also an opportunity cost of using international reserves. Aside from the fact that international reserves earn income, their current use means that they are not available to finance a potential external deficit in the future, when the need may be even greater.

Accumulation and holding of reserves by a surplus country involves an opportunity cost as well. This cost is the difference between the return on those international reserve assets and the social productivity of the capital formation that those reserves could finance. Another view of the same implicit opportunity cost is that if the surplus country's currency were revalued upwards, its terms of trade would improve, allowing each unit of its exported production to exchange for a greater volume of imports. There is, then, an economic cost of external surplus that a country must incur, although that cost is frequently viewed by the country as less than the cost involved in eliminating the surplus.

The ability to use international reserves to avoid (postpone) adjustment is, of course, limited by the amount of reserves a country holds and its capacity to borrow reserves from others. The combination of the two represents its *international liquidity*. The capacity to borrow obviously depends on the willingness of countries with external surpluses to lend (directly or indirectly) to deficit countries. Because the volume of international reserves is limited, and the willingness to lend also has limits, adjustment to disequilibria in the balance of payments cannot be postponed indefinitely, especially by deficit countries.

National policymakers thus face dilemmas and trade-offs in balance-of-payments adjustment policies. Countries have multiple economic goals—high employment, economic growth, price stability, preferred income distribution, and others—which are affected by the external balance. At the same time, the policies that can address the domestic objec-

---

[23] This relationship between international reserves and balance-of-payments adjustment costs is explored in more detail in B. J. Cohen, "Adjustment Costs and the Distribution of New International Reserves," *Studies in International Finance,* Princeton University, International Finance Section, Princeton, N.J., 1966; and Robert G. Hawkins and C. Rangarajan, "On the Distribution of International Reserves," *Journal of Finance* (June 1970), 881–891.

tives also influence the external balance. Since international reserves are limited, the external balance cannot ultimately be ignored.

A simplified view of these potential conflicts is summarized in Table 30-2. Table 30-2 demonstrates that, for any adjustment method, there are potential conflicts with at least some domestic economic (or political) objectives or group interests. No adjustment mechanism is without actual or perceived costs. Even the failure to adjust (by using reserve changes to substitute for adjustment) involves certain types of opportunity costs. The rejection of one or two adjustment processes implies that the nation—or nations collectively—chooses to avoid those costs to its national objectives, but it must be willing to accept the costs involved in the chosen alternatives. Obviously, national (or multinational) choices may shift over time as the magnitude or characteristics of balance-of-payments disturbances change.

As we noted earlier, until 1971 the postwar international monetary system utilized changes in exchange rates as a means of adjustment relatively infrequently. At the same time, the use of controls and restrictions (for balance-of-payments purposes) was reduced as exchange and investment controls were liberalized. These trends left more of the adjustment problem to relative inflation-deflation and to reserve changes, which placed particular stresses on the system. In the "currency float" period since 1973, different conflicts have become paramount.

## Domestic Economic Goals and Fixed Exchange Rates

For a nation that decides to keep the foreign exchange rate of its currency fixed, as most countries did from 1949 to 1971, the conflicts among the goals of balance-of-payments equilibrium and domestic economic objectives are explicit and predictable. Let one assume, along with a large body of economic literature, that the multiple domestic objectives of high employment, economic growth, price stability, and various income-distribution concerns can be summarized in one measure called *internal balance*. This term denotes the nation's desired choice of some attainable mix of inflation, unemployment, economic growth, and other elements in its portfolio of objectives. Departures from the de-

**Table 30-2 Domestic Objectives Potentially Affected by Alternative Balance-of-Payment Adjustment Mechanisms**

| Adjustment Mechanism | Domestic Policy Objectives in Possible Conflict with Adjustment Mechanism |
| --- | --- |
| Relative inflation/deflation | Price stability (for inflating country) <br> Economic growth (for deflating country) <br> Low levels of unemployment <br> Distribution goals: <br>   Performance of export and import–competing industries <br>   Concentration of unemployment in certain skills, occupations, or locations |
| Change in the exchange rate | Price stability (for depreciating country) <br> Full employment in export and import–competing industries (for appreciating country) <br> Distribution goals: <br>   Industry mix of output and employment; adjustment costs <br> Efficiency: <br>   Variable exchange rates may raise the risk of foreign trade and investment |
| Controls and restrictions | Efficiency: <br>   Benefits of liberal foreign trade and investment are compromised <br> Distribution goals: <br>   Some goups and industries dependent on open international commerce are harmed <br> Growth: <br>   Resources that could be producing output applied to monitoring compliance and avoiding control |
| Absence of adjustment: Finance the external imbalance by expending or acquiring international reserves | Economic growth (for surplus country): <br>   Reserves could be used to add to capital stock <br> Efficiency and distribution goals (for deficit country): <br>   Reserves used currently unavailable for future |

sired mix of target values are characterizied as recession or inflation. *Recession* denotes a situation in which unemployment is higher and economic growth lower than desired, while inflation is within the acceptable range. *Inflation* involves the opposite undesired mix of targets. Finally, let one suppose that monetary policy—operating through its influence on interest rates, the money stock, and the supply of credit—is the principal policy available to address domestic economic objectives *and* the balance-of-payments objective. Figure 30-1 shows the linkages of monetary policy to the overall balance-of-payments position; Figure 30-2 summarizes them again in a simple causal chain. Of course, the directions of change in the variables indicated would be the opposite for an expansionary monetary policy. While the size and the lag in the effect of policy actions remain matters of debate, the ultimate impact on the balance of payments depends also on the policy actions taken by the country's major trading partners. If the nation's trading partners simultaneously carry out contractionary monetary policies, the effects we have outlined are likely to be suppressed or completely undermined. This emphasizes the importance of *relative* inflation-deflation in Figure 30-1 and the importance of international coordination of policies in real life.

The possible dilemmas that policymakers may face with a fixed exchange rate system are illustrated in Table 30-3. Two domestic economic states are assumed, and each is associated with two possible situations in the external balance. To illustrate, combination I involves an internal recession with an external surplus. The necessary domestic financial policies are the same for both objectives— expansionary to increase output and reduce unemployment, to cope with internal recession; expansionary to lower interest rates, reduce capital inflows (or increase outflows), and to increase aggregate demand for imports, to deal with the external surplus. Likewise, the policy indications in combination II are consistent, calling for contractionary financial policies to cure domestic inflationary overheating of the economy as well as to reduce the external deficit. The monetary authorities would thus face no dilemma in those hypothetical states.

The dilemmas arise in combinations III and IV under a fixed exchange rate system. Combination

**Figure 30-2   Linkages of Monetary Policy to Overall Balance-of-Payments Position**

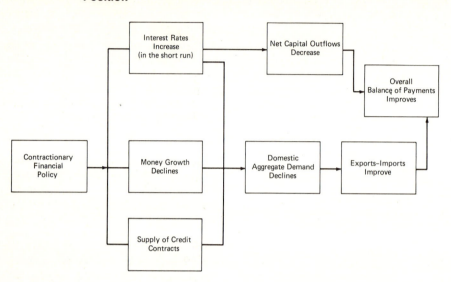

III pits a domestic recession calling for expansionary monetary policy against a balance-of-payments deficit that calls for contractionary policies. The country's course would depend on the strength of its commitment to the existing exchange rate, the level of its international reserves, its capacity to borrow from other countries, and several other economic and political variables. In the past, countries took a middle road, neither pursuing expansionary policies sufficiently to eliminate the recession nor restricting monetary growth enough to eliminate the deficit. At such times, "selective controls" over financial flows (or trade) tended to become (politically) attractive.

The opposite conflict situation—often faced by Japan and West Germany in the 1960s—is domestic inflation and a surplus in the balance of payments. The appropriate policy action for one objective compounds the other problem.

The 1960s witnessed substantial economic discussion about how a nation could avoid the dilemmas of the combinations shown in Table 30-3. It was suggested, by Mundell and others, that the assignment of available macroeconomic tools (monetary and fiscal policy) to the appropriate goal might accomplish both domestic and balance-of-

payments objectives simultaneously.[24] In a world of international capital mobility, the balance of payments should be more responsive to monetary policy (interest rate changes) than is domestic aggregate demand, while domestic target variables (output, employment) should be more responsive to fiscal policy than is the balance of payments. Thus, appropriate assignment in, for example, combination III would involve monetary policy moving in a contractionary direction to improve the external balance, and fiscal policy moving in an expansionary direction to accomplish domestic expansion.

In practice, however, such simple solutions have not been achieved. Fiscal policy has proven to be very cumbersome and inflexible as a cyclical policy tool. Changes in taxes and government spending

[24]The literature on the "assignment problem" is voluminous. See Robert A. Mundell, "The Appropriate Use of Monetary and Fiscal Policy for Internal and External Stability," *IMF Staff Papers* (March 1962), 70–76, for the original formal paper. The literature is reviewed in Marina von Neuman Whitman, "Policies for Internal and External Balance," *Special Papers in International Economics*, No. 9, Princeton University, International Finance Section, Princeton, N.J., 1970.

**Table 30-3 Possible Combinations of Domestic and Balance-of-Payments Conditions and Indicated Financial Policy Under Fixed Exchange Rates**

| Combination | State of the Domestic Economy | Monetary Policy Action for Internal Balance | State of the Balance of Payments | Monetary Policy Action for External Balance | Conflict or Consistency in Actions |
|---|---|---|---|---|---|
| I | Recession | Expansionary | Surplus | Expansionary | Consistent |
| II | Inflation | Contractionary | Deficit | Contractionary | Consistent |
| III | Recession | Expansionary | Deficit | Contractionary | Conflict |
| IV | Inflation | Contractionary | Surplus | Expansionary | Conflict |

simply cannot be made rapidly enough or in sufficient magnitude. In addition, this approach supposes that monetary and fiscal policies can be separated and used in significantly different ways. This also does not appear to be the case. If monetary policy reduces the supply of credit and money at the same time that the federal deficit is enlarged, government borrowing needs will preempt (crowd out) private borrowers unless the funds are supplied by foreign lenders. Thus, there is a serious question as to how effective fiscal policy can be for domestic objectives if monetary policy does not accommodate that policy.[25]

What is left, then, for countries which find themselves in combination III or IV situations? In the short term, a country in situation III may use monetary policy to expand the local economy and finance the external deficit with its international reserves or with liquidity borrowed from abroad. The combination IV country can accumulate international reserves and pursue contractionary monetary policy (which, however, pulls in more foreign funds to fuel domestic spending).

Ultimately, the costs of the dilemma tend to become even larger than the cost of using an alter-

native adjustment process. Thus, this sometimes leads to a change in the exchange rate and, in 1971–1973, it brought about the movement away from the very system of fixed exchange rates.

## Floating Exchange Rates and Domestic Financial Policy

As noted previously, one appeal of floating exchange rates is that domestic monetary policy may more actively pursue domestic economic objectives while the exchange rate adjusts to keep the external accounts in balance. In practice, this additional freedom has not been fully utilized and, in any case, may not be entirely effective. Under some conditions, floating exchange rates have complicated the attainment of domestic monetary policy objectives in spite of the fact that there is an additional channel of impact on domestic aggregate demand with a floating exchange rate.

When there are significant amounts of interest-sensitive international capital flows, a country pursuing expansionary monetary policy through faster growth in the money supply or through lower interest rates will find foreign investment outflows increasing, which, in turn, tends to make the nation's currency depreciate. The currency depreciation should (perhaps with a lag) bring about an improvement in the trade balance, which provides an additional stimulus to aggregate demand that would not exist under a fixed exchange rate system. In the extreme example of a small country that is unable to affect world interest rates and "perfect" international capital mobility, that nation would, under a fixed exchange rate system, be unable to use monetary policy to influence domestic credit conditions and interest rates at all. Any change in

[25] This is, of course, a part of the monetarist-Keynesian debate. For a diversity of approaches and views, see the papers by R. Dornbusch and P. Kouri, *Scandinavian Journal of Economics* (May 1976). Another aspect of this question is whether stabilization policy can be effective if people correctly anticipate future policies and adjust their behavior immediately. For more on the rational-expectations approach, see Thomas J. Sargent and Neil Wallace, "Rational Expectations and the Theory of Economic Policy," *Journal of Monetary Economics* (April 1976), 169–184; and William Poole, "Rational Expectations in the Macro Model," *Brookings Papers on Economic Activity*, No. 2, 1976, pp. 463–505.

domestic money and credit supplies would immediately be offset by international borrowing and lending, and monetary policy as a tool for achieving domestic objectives would be impotent. But with a flexible exchange rate, domestic demand would be affected through the change in the trade balance as a result of the exchange rate adjustment. Thus, it is argued by many that in a world of international capital mobility, monetary policy is more effective for domestic objectives with floating currencies than with fixed exchange rates.[26]

It should be remembered, however, that the adjustment in the currency itself may compromise some domestic objectives. To continue the example, a depreciation of the currency as a result of expansionary monetary policy raises the domestic currency prices of imports, and thus tends to be directly inflationary for the home country. For these and other reasons, floating currencies have not provided the degree of monetary freedom from balance-of-payments considerations that some advocates expected.

Flexible exchange rates are superior to fixed exchange rates in insulating a nation's domestic economy from economic and policy disturbances emanating from abroad. Again, however, floating currencies do not provide complete insulation, and only provide extra insulation at the cost of additional instability in domestic prices due to the flexing of the flexible exchange rate.

A simple example will illustrate. Suppose a nation's major trading partners experience a significant recession. Aggregate demand abroad declines; consequently, the demand for the home nation's exports declines as well. Under a fixed exchange rate system, the full decline in export demand would be translated into lower aggregate demand in the home country, thereby transferring the recessionary pressures from the trading partners to the home nation.

With a flexible exchange rate system, however, the decline in the demand for the home country's exports brings about a depreciation of its currency (an appreciation of the trading partners' currencies). This depreciation stimulates export demand. Thus, the combined impact on aggregate demand

in the home country is smaller with a flexible rate than with a fixed rate. On the other hand, the currency depreciation raises import prices and thus tends to be inflationary, an outcome that would not occur with fixed rates.

To summarize, any international adjustment process involves potential conflicts with one or more domestic economic objectives. Although floating currencies tend to insulate domestic aggregate demand from foreign disturbances more fully, they accentuate foreign influences on domestic price movements. The choice of adjustment process will involve trade-offs of costs and benefits. That choice will depend on the particular characteristics of a nation, especially its dependence on foreign trade. Small countries with great trade dependence tend to find exchange rate changes too disruptive to domestic prices and economic decisions, and often choose relative inflation-deflation as the preferred adjustment mechanism. Large countries with only small shares of total output dependent on foreign trade find exchange rate adjustment less disruptive to the local economy, while relative inflation-deflation policy for balance-of-payments purposes is viewed as too costly. Such countries more often choose exchange rate adjustment as the preferred mechanism.

### The International Financial System

The international financial system involves the rules, conventions, and practices of governments and international institutions in three areas. One involves the establishment of exchange rates among currencies and the nature of government obligations with respect to changing exchange rates. The second involves the conditions for employing the other mechanisms of adjustment—that is, relative inflation-deflation and direct restrictions over international payments. The third involves the definition and the obligations of acceptance and convertibility of international reserve assets. This section will briefly describe the system as it has evolved in the postwar period, and the following section will assess the changing role of the U.S. dollar in that system.

Since the end of World War II, the international monetary system has gone through three fairly distinct phases. Each phase has seen different emphasis placed on the alternative mechanisms of inter-

[26]For a review of these models, see Whitman, "Policies for Internal and External Balance"; also Black, *Floating Exchange Rates and National Economic Policy.*

national adjustment, as illustrated in Figure 30-1. In the early postwar period (up until 1958), many countries relied on controls over international payments to bring their external accounts into balance. There were a few important exceptions, such as the United States and Canada, but most of the major countries had elaborate exchange control systems in that period of "dollar shortage." The second phase, running from 1958 to 1971, was one in which relative inflation-deflation was relied on most heavily for adjustment. Controls over trade, payment, and capital movements were relaxed, and exchange rates were changed infrequently. Since 1971, exchange rate adjustments have increased considerably in importance as an adjustment process.

The role of the U.S. dollar in the international monetary system has changed significantly during the various postwar phases. Initially, it was a "scarce currency" that was made available to the reconstructing countries of Western Europe and Japan through governmental loans and grants under the Marshall and other aid plans. During the second phase, it was the principal source of growth in international reserves and liquidity, and a key currency serving as the principal international medium of exchange, unit of account, and store of value. In the 1970s, however, the dollar receded somewhat in relative importance, with unwanted dollar assets in foreign holdings becoming a problem for the system and with the dollar partially replaced by SDRs and other national currencies as units of account and in other functions of international money.

### The Bretton Woods System: 1946–1971

From 1946 to 1971, international financial arrangements were called the Bretton Woods System, after the New Hampshire resort where the negotiations were held in 1944. These negotiations resulted in the formation of the International Monetary Fund (IMF) and its sister institutions (the World Bank and International Finance Corporation), and the codification (in the "Articles of Agreement" of the IMF) of policy guidelines regarding exchange rates, reserves, and adjustment.[27]

[27]See de Vries, *The International Monetary Fund, 1946–1971*.

The framework established at Bretton Woods was designed to meet a number of specific ills associated with the gold exchange standard of the 1920s and the turmoil in international transactions of the 1930s.[28] First, it was believed that the international gold standard had proved unworkable because of conflicting domestic and international economic objectives, and that a shortage of monetary gold had led to the holding of a part of international reserves in the form of national currencies (the "gold reserve standard"), which facilitated currency crises and gold-price speculation. Second, the devaluations of currencies and the controls over foreign payments of the late 1930s, combined with the inevitably rigid exchange control systems of World War II, had resulted in many bilateral trade arrangements between countries which served to restrict and to distort the international flow of goods and services. Third, large short-term capital ("hot money") movements in the 1930s had continued in subsequent periods of floating exchange rates. It was thought that exchange rate flexibility may have contributed to these hot money flows and, therefore, that flexible exchange rates should be avoided under the new system.[29]

The salient features of the arrangements that resulted were (a) a system of pegged exchange rates among currencies; (b) a goal of free convertibility among currencies; and (c) a fund, or pool, of currencies and gold to supplement the international reserves owned by the member countries.

Under the Bretton Woods System, the United States pledged to exchange gold for dollars (or vice versa) with foreign central banks and the IMF at a fixed price of $35 per ounce. This was the only U.S. obligation to peg its dollar to gold or foreign currencies. All other IMF members agreed to maintain the price of their currency (either in terms of gold or U.S. dollars) within a 1 percent range of a fixed, par rate. The system of exchange rates was thus a *fixed exchange rate system* except for fluctuations of ±1 percent of the par rate. By purchasing or selling their national currency (for U.S. dol-

[28]A summary of the political and economic thinking that led to the Bretton Woods Agreement can be found in Willett, *Floating Exchange Rates and International Monetary Reform.*
[29]This view was forcefully made in Ragner Nurkse, *The International Currency Experience*, League of Nations, New York, 1944.

lars), a central bank kept its currency price within the permissible range. Under certain conditions of "fundamental disequilibrium" in the balance of payments, a nation was permitted (and sometimes encouraged) to change the par rate of its currency vis-à-vis the dollar. However, there was no formal provision for altering the par value of the dollar vis-à-vis gold, which remained at $35 per ounce until 1971.

In large measure the Bretton Woods System was a resounding success. As can be seen from Figure 30-3, exchange rates among the major currencies were relatively stable during the 1950s and 1960s. Par value changes were infrequent and, although these were sometimes preceded by substantial flows of "hot money" from weak to strong curren-

cies, the disruptions in the foreign exchange market were minor. More important, the stated objectives of the system were more or less achieved. As we have indicated above, exchange controls were gradually relaxed, and most industrial countries restored free convertibility between their currencies and the dollar for current payments in 1958 and 1959. Thereafter, there was a continued relaxation of controls over foreign investments so that, by the mid-1960s, most major industrial countries had relatively free international mobility of capital as well as unrestricted current-account transactions.

This was all accomplished in an environment in which international trade and investment expanded quite rapidly—faster than the economies of the major countries. All the same, most countries had relatively high rates of economic growth and low levels of unemployment in the 1950s and 1960s, consonant with the Articles of Agreement of the International Monetary Fund.

But, as noted earlier, these successes were facilitated by a continuing U.S. balance-of-payments deficit that fueled the expansion of international reserve holdings, in the form of dollar foreign exchange, of the major countries. This deficit, together with the relative rigidity in exchange rates and the reluctance to change the dollar price of gold, imparted considerable fragility to the system by the late 1960s, when U.S. liabilities to foreign central banks greatly exceeded U.S. holdings of international reserve assets. The convertibility of the U.S. dollar into gold then became impossible de facto; it was a major source of uncertainty for the system. At the same time, U.S. domestic economic policy was complicated by the inflationary excesses of its Vietnam involvement and, by the late 1960s and early 1970s, America's inflation rates were both high by world standards and accelerating. These trends culminated in the United States foreswearing its commitment of convertibility between gold and foreign official dollar holdings and encouraging floating exchange rates in August 1971. Thus, some of the critical obligations and guidelines of the Bretton Woods System were abandoned.

**Figure 30-3  Year-End Exchange Rates: Units of Foreign Currency per U.S. Dollar, 1953–1978**

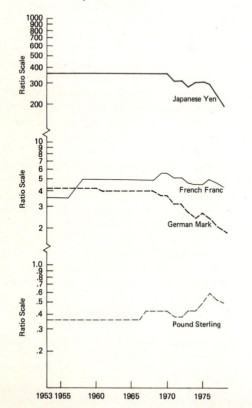

### The Evolving Post–Bretton Woods System

In the aftermath of the U.S. announcement, several currencies floated upward against the dollar (see

Source: International Monetary Fund, *International Financial Statistics.*

Figure 30-3) as international negotiations were conducted to reestablish the old system. The negotiations were completed in December 1971, and produced the Smithsonian Agreement. This agreement reestablished a pegged exchange rate system, with a 2¼ percent "band" of permissible market exchange rate variability on each side of the parity exchange rate. But the new par values were significantly adjusted, from the earlier levels, with the U.S. dollar devalued with respect to gold by approximately 10 percent, while other major currencies were revalued upward by varying amounts with respect to the dollar.

The restored system was to have a short life. After several speculative currency crises, continued disequilibrium in international payments, and new uncertainties posed by OPEC and its oil-pricing policies, par values were again abandoned in early 1973. These actions led to the demise of the Bretton Woods System as it had existed for over twenty-five years.[30]

### Exchange Rates

Within the system that has evolved and has gradually been institutionalized since 1973, each country may determine its exchange rate policy, and no member of the IMF has an obligation to maintain its exchange rate at any prescribed value against any other currency.

The IMF does, however, have an obligation to exercise surveillance over exchange rate practices of member countries, so as to facilitate international adjustment and avoid exchange rate manipulation to achieve domestic objectives at the expense of other countries' economic stability.

As a result, the exchange rate mechanism has been used much more frequently for balance-of-payments adjustment than it was in the earlier system, and fluctuations in exchange rates have been much greater. This is obvious with respect to the four currencies shown in Figure 30-3.

Although the current exchange rate system has been called one of "currency floats," not all currencies float against all others. Indeed, the current system is a complex mixture of fixed and floating exchange rates. In 1978, forty countries (most of

them relatively small) pegged their currencies to the U.S. dollar, maintaining actual transaction exchange rates within 2¼ percent of that pegged rate.[31] Thus, for international transactions between those countries and the United States, or with each other, the exchange rate is relatively fixed. However, since the dollar floats against some other major currencies, such as the Japanese yen, these countries find their currencies floating against the yen as well. Thus, they have a mixture of floating and pegged exchange rates.

Likewise, fourteen countries—mainly African ex-colonies—are pegged to the French franc, and four countries maintain a pegged rate with the pound sterling. At the other extreme, thirty-three countries maintain no obligations to keep their currencies within a specified range with any other currency, among them some of the world's largest trading countries, such as the United States, United Kingdom, Canada, and Japan.

About thirty countries peg their currencies to some opposite "basket" of foreign currencies, such as the SDR. This means that the actual market price of the nation's currency on the foreign exchange market is kept within a stated band of a weighted average of the price of several currencies in the "currency basket." Thus, if the dollar falls relative to the yen and West German mark, and each has equal weights in the basket of a fourth country, that country's exchange rate would remain unchanged, as measured against its par rate, while its market exchange rate would appreciate against the dollar and depreciate against the other two currencies.

The system is not, then, one of flexible exchange rates of all currencies against all other currencies. It is, rather, a system of "bloc floating" of dollar, French franc, and pound sterling blocs against each other; a few large free floaters against the rest; and a significant group of countries that utilize composite currency baskets as a basis for pegging their currencies. In 1979 the largest and most ambitious currency bloc was initiated. This was the European

---

[30]For a concise discussion of the events of this period, see Ronald I. McKinnon, "America's Role in Stabilizing the World's Monetary System," *Daedalus* (Winter 1978), 305–324.

[31]The obligations of member countries with respect to their exchange rates can be found in International Monetary Fund, *Annual Report, 1978,* Washington, D.C., 1978. A more general discussion of the obligations of members with respect to exchange rates in the reformed IMF is found in International Monetary Fund, *IMF Survey: The Fund Under the Second Amendment: A Supplement,* September 18, 1978.

currency unit, which is a major component of the European Monetary System.[32]

This agreement among the major European countries established a set of fixed parities among their currencies, with the obligation of maintaining market exchange rates within 2.25 percent of that parity, thereby providing a range of flexibility in exchange rates of 4.5 percent. Germany, France, the Netherlands, Belgium, Denmark, and Ireland adhere to this agreement. Italy has agreed to keep its currency within 6 percent of the parity rates. The intent is to lock together the currencies of the member countries, within narrow limits of permitted variability, and eventually for the system to have a common European currency. Although changes in parity rates are provided for, these are intended to be infrequent and to be used only under conditions of major disequilibrium within the system. The calculations of deviations in the market rates from parity are based upon the European Currency Unit (ECU), which is the system's unit of account, consisting of a weighted "basket" of European currencies.

In addition to its exchange rate arrangements, the European Monetary System involves the European Monetary Cooperation Fund, which is a pool of international reserves (mainly dollar assets) of about $30 billion. To create this pool, each member contributed 20 percent of its reserves to the fund in return for a credit entry in ECUs. This fund provides credits to deficit member countries so that they can support their currencies on the foreign exchange market in order to maintain the exchange rate structure. It is anticipated that the fund will evolve, through time, toward a true European central bank. The United Kingdom is a member of the European Monetary Cooperation Fund, but has not accepted the system's obligations with respect to exchange rates.

Since the system of limited flexibility in exchange rates was established in 1973, there have been significant movements in currency values, of a magnitude quite different from that under the earlier Bretton Woods System. This is clearly shown in Figure 30-3, but the movements after 1973 are shown more dramatically still in Figure 30-4. In Figure 30-4, the price of the various currencies is shown against a weighted average (on the basis of

[32]For a concise description, see International Monetary Fund, *IMF Survey* (March 19, 1979).

**Figure 30-4   Indices of Effective Exchange Rates, December 1972 to June 1979 (Monthly Averages of Daily Spot Rates)**

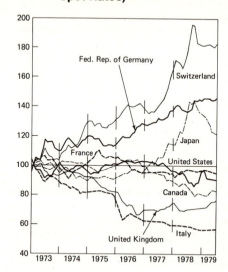

Note: First quarter 1973 = 100.

Note: The weights for calculating effective exchange rates are derived from the IMF's multilateral model.

Source: International Monetary Fund, *Annual Report*.

the trade patterns of the major countries) of the other currencies. The sustained appreciations of the West German mark and Japanese yen after 1975 are clearly indicated, as are the depreciations of the U.S. dollar, the Canadian dollar, the Italian lira, and the pound sterling. Figure 30-4 also shows the volatility in exchange rates, suggesting that the system of currency floats has witnessed substantial movements in currency values in one direction, later to be reversed. This, as suggested in earlier sections, has been a source of dissatisfaction with the system. This movement is caused by the free international mobility of a large pool of financial resources in conjunction with more fundamental variables of growth and inflation that are subject to frequent and unexpected changes.

In summary, the current international monetary system involves a diverse mixture of policies and obligations with respect to exchange rates. Many countries attempt to maintain a parity system for their currencies relative to another currency or basket of currencies. Others, including the United

States, Japan, and Great Britain, do not maintain the value of their currencies within any particular range of exchange rates with other currencies or a basket of currencies. Still others, however, including countries within the European Monetary System, are committed to a system of pegged exchange rates among their own currencies but do not seek a fixed rate of exchange between their currencies and the other major currencies, such as the U.S. dollar. Within this complicated system, exchange rate adjustments are a much more important mechanism for balance-of-payments adjustment than they were before 1973.

## Balance-of-Payments Adjustment

Despite the greater flexibility of exchange rates in recent years, they still do not fluctuate freely, and other methods of balance-of-payments adjustment are also used. A major method of adjustment employed by the advanced industrial countries is relative inflation-deflation. In periodic meetings—at the OECD in Paris, at the Bank of International Settlements in Basel, and at "economic summit" conferences of heads of state at various locations—the major countries confer on appropriate policies concerning prices, income growth, government budgets, and monetary policy. Indeed, targets are set for the growth in various aggregate economic indicators that reflect the balance-of-payments situation of the country and its domestic economic

conditions as well. Often, these targets are not achieved because of domestic political and economic pressures and because of the imprecise administration of policies.

Despite this international coordination of policies and frequent consultation among nations, and despite greater exchange rate flexibility, the system has experienced a major disequilibrium since 1970. This is amply demonstrated in Table 30-4, which shows various countries' cumulative balance-of-payments positions and exchange rate adjustments from 1970 to 1977 as well as their reserve holdings in the two years. Table 30-4 brings into focus the interrelationships between balance-of-payments positions, reserve changes, and exchange rate realignments.

Over the period indicated, the United States was obviously in a significant external deficit position, experiencing a $104 billion cumulative deficit on the "official transactions" balance. A major part of this can be attributed to the OPEC countries' surpluses resulting from the oil-price changes of 1973–1974. The oil-exporting countries had a cumulative balance-of-payments surplus of $67.5 billion in the same period. The almost 50 percent price increases imposed in 1979 will no doubt extend the OPEC surpluses into the 1980s.

Also shown in Table 30-4 are data for the major industrial countries with external surpluses. Almost one-half of the U.S. deficit over the period has its counterpart in the surpluses of three countries:

**Table 30-4  Cumulative Balance of Payments and Reserve Positions, 1970–1977 (in billions of SDRs)**

| | Cumulative Balance of Payments Deficit (−) or Surplus (+) (1970–1977)[a] | International Reserve Holdings | | | | Cumulative appreciation (+) or depreciation (−) of the currency vis à vis the dollar (percent) |
| | | Year-end 1970 | | Year-end 1977 | | |
| | | Amount | Percentage of World Total | Amount | Percentage of World Total | |
|---|---|---|---|---|---|---|
| United States | $−104.2 | $14.5 | 15.6% | $16.0 | 6.1% | — |
| United Kingdom | + 15.4 | 2.8 | 3.0 | 17.3 | 6.6 | − 30 |
| France | + 5.6 | 5.0 | 5.4 | 8.4 | 3.2 | + 17 |
| West Germany | + 28.8 | 13.6 | 14.6 | 32.7 | 12.4 | + 69 |
| Switzerland | + 7.8 | 5.1 | 5.5 | 11.4 | 4.3 | +107 |
| Japan | + 18.0 | 4.8 | 5.2 | 19.1 | 7.2 | + 48 |
| Major Oil Exporters | + 67.5 | 5.0 | 5.4 | 62.1 | 23.6 | — |

[a]Balance-of-payments surpluses or deficits are on an "official transaction basis" as shown in the IMF *Balance of Payments Yearbook*.

Source: Calculated from International Monetary Fund, *Balance of Payments Yearbook, Annual Report, 1978*; and *International Financial Statistics*.

West Germany, Japan, and Switzerland. In addition, the United Kingdom experienced a cumulative surplus (of $15 billion), with major surpluses in 1976–1977 after deficits in the earlier 1970s.

The balance-of-payments positions in Table 30-4 reflect two significant features of the international economy in the 1970s. The first is the massive redistribution of world income as a result of the quadrupling of oil prices in 1973–1974. This is reflected in the surpluses of the oil-exporting countries compared to the American deficit. Other countries, shown in Table 30-4, were able to adjust to the oil-price changes more rapidly and effectively than was the United States and were able to reestablish balance-of-payments surpluses. The United States, however, saw its oil import bill escalate from under $2.7 billion prior to 1972 to over $36 billion by 1977, dramatically enlarging its deficit. A similar situation arose in 1978, as Europe and Japan were able to absorb the new round of oil price increases better than was the United States.

The second feature of the international economy reflected in the structure of deficits and surpluses was the relatively higher U.S. inflation rates in the mid-1970s. In the 1970s, the United States inflation rate was consistently over 6 percent; in the 1960s, the rate of inflation was under 3 percent per year, on average. And, just as price adjustments may be used to adjust the balance of payments, relative inflation can cause deficits.

The last column in Table 30-4 shows the cumulative adjustment in the exchange rate of each country's currency against the dollar from 1970 to 1977. All of the major surplus countries saw their currencies appreciate against the dollar, some by large magnitudes. The pound sterling, reflecting the weakness of the currency prior to 1976, depreciated by 30 percent against the dollar. However, despite these major currency realignments, the deficits and surpluses shown in the first column were not avoided or removed. This suggests that central banks intervened in the foreign exchange markets to keep exchange rates from adjusting fully to changes in other economic variables.

The result of this intervention on the distribution of international reserves is shown in the middle columns of Table 30-4. Most dramatic, of course, was the growth of the official reserves of the oil-exporting countries, from about 5 percent of the world total in 1970 to over 23 percent in 1977. The other major surplus countries all had significant

increases in their reserves but could not quite maintain the same share of total world reserves as they had in 1970. Indeed, only the United Kingdom's share increased, while France experienced a significant decline in its share.

The United States, in its role as a reserve-currency nation, did not lose any international reserves despite running a cumulative balance-of-payments deficit of over $100 billion. This was possible for two reasons. First, the surplus countries supported the dollar on the foreign exchange markets in order to keep their currencies from appreciating too rapidly. Second, the OPEC countries, which received dollars for oil, added most of those dollars to their official reserves. Thus, the large disequilibrium in the international monetary system in the 1970s—with the United States as a large deficit country; OPEC with large surpluses; and West Germany, Japan, and other industrial countries also with surpluses—produced a major creation of international reserves. This occurred because nations were prepared neither to take the necessary relative inflation-deflation steps to allow the required exchange rate adjustments nor to impose the necessary restrictions to bring the system rapidly back into balance.

## International Reserves and Liquidity

International reserves constitute part of a nation's wealth and represent purchasing power over other nations' goods, services, or financial assets. They provide the means (directly or indirectly) to support the nation's currency on the foreign exchange market and, thereby, the means to finance balance-of-payments deficits. They thus permit a nation to slow down and stretch out balance-of-payments adjustment and even to avoid adjusting to minor and temporary disturbances.[33]

International liquidity is a broader concept than international reserves. For an individual nation, its liquidity includes, not only its international reserves, but also its capacity to borrow reserves from international organizations or other countries. A nation's liquidity may be impaired by its short-term liquid liabilities outstanding to other nations. Thus, while the United States has a modest amount

[33] A review of the economic literature on international reserves can be found in John Williamson, "International Liquidity—A Survey," *Economic Journal* (September 1973), 732–768.

of owned reserves, and a very large borrowing capacity, it has short-term liabilities to other countries of massive magnitude and is thus less liquid than might appear.

The creation and management of international reserves and liquidity is accomplished by a group of organizations centered in the IMF. The volume of international reserves outstanding cannot be closely controlled, because one element in those reserves—reserve currency holdings—depends on the structure of balance-of-payments imbalances and the willingness of countries to adjust to eliminate the imbalances. But the system of reserves and liquidity seeks to achieve a balance between adjustment and financing international imbalances and to provide an orderly means of extending balance-of-payments financing (liquidity) to countries that suffer balance-of-payments shocks which it would be too costly (or impossible) to adjust to in the short run.

As currently defined by the IMF, international reserves include a nation's monetary gold stock, its reserve position at the IMF (its automatic drawing—borrowing—rights), its holdings of Special Drawing Rights (SDRs), and its official holdings of reserve currencies (convertible foreign exchange holdings). The volume and composition of international reserves over the postwar period are shown in Figure 30-5. Figure 30-5 reflects several basic characteristics of the current system. First, gold has become relatively less important as a source of international reserves. Indeed, official gold holdings have declined since 1965. Gold is being phased out as an international monetary asset as the IMF and a few countries have sold some of their gold holdings on the private auction market. Second, while IMF automatic drawing rights and SDRs have gained importance as reserve assets since 1969, they still constitute less than 10 percent of total world reserves. Their absolute magnitudes rose as IMF quotas, upon which borrowing rights are based, were increased and as 9.4 billion SDRs were created (by agreement) in 1970–1972.[34]

The third, and most dramatic, facet of Figure 30-5 is the huge rise in total reserves and of official holdings of dollar-denominated assets beginning in

[34]For a detailed discussion of SDRs and their role in the system, see Douglas R. Mudd, ''International Reserves and the Role of Special Drawing Rights,'' *Review,* Federal Reserve Bank of St. Louis (January 1978), 9–14.

## Figure 30-5 The Volume and Composition of International Reserves, 1957–1978

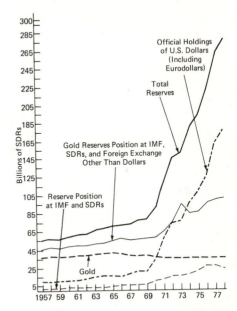

Note: On this graph, official gold holdings are valued at SDR 35 per fine ounce for the years 1971–1978. If instead this gold is valued at the London market price, the total value of gold rises from SDR 41.2 billion in 1971 to SDR 176.7 billion in 1978.

Source: International Monetary Fund, *Annual Report,* 1979, p. 47.

1970. The dollar component of world reserves rose from $21 billion in 1969 to $176 billion in 1978. In the current period of more flexible exchange rates, foreign holdings of dollars have risen by no less than $100 billion, reflecting the international imbalances shown in Table 30-4. Thus, the U.S. deficit, together with the slowness and reluctance of the system to adjust, combined with OPEC pricing policy, has fueled a huge growth in international reserves that may have little to do with the volume actually needed or used. Most of these reserves have been lodged with a relatively small group of oil-producing countries and a few surplus industrial countries. Other nations, especially developing countries that do not export oil, have not greatly increased their reserves, and many of them have suffered substantial shocks to their balance of payments as oil prices have risen. These shocks have accentuated their need for international liquidity and credit.

This need has been served both by private financial institutions and by international organizations,

mainly by the IMF. Short- and medium-term credits extended to developing countries by private financial institutions, especially commercial banks, expanded by over $100 billion from 1973 to 1976. Indeed, the volume of bank lending to developing countries rose so dramatically that observers voiced concern that banks were accepting too much "country risk" and that substantial defaults on the loans, and resulting impairment of bank solvency, was a major danger.[35] During this period, commercial banks had ample liquid funds available from OPEC nations, which redeposited their oil-dollar surpluses in Western financial markets, especially in the Eurodollar market. This heightened capacity to lend was matched by a swollen demand for loans from countries that suffered from increased oil import bills. The banks successfully served a major international financial intermediation function. The feared crisis in the international banking system did not materialize.

Although private financial markets played a major role in expanding international liquidity in the 1970s, significant measures were also taken to enhance official lending capabilities. The IMF makes "conditional" drawings (borrowings) available to member countries having balance-of-payments difficulties through its various "credit tranches," which are based on the member countries' quotas. This conditional liquidity more than doubled from 1970 to 1978. In addition, the IMF has established several special facilities beyond the regular credit tranches. These facilities are to assist the financing of particular types of balance-of-payments strains of member countries. They include the Extended Fund Facility (which provides IMF credits for periods beyond the normal three- to five-year period), the Compensatory Financing Facility (which provides credits to partially offset declines in export receipts), and the Buffer Stock Facility (which provides credits for member-country payments to establish buffer stocks under certain international commodity agreements). In addition, the IMF established an Oil Facility in 1974, which provided

additional lending capacity to finance adjustment to the 1973–1974 oil-price changes. The use of the combined credit facilities of the IMF rose from about $1.5 billion SDRs in 1973 to $14 billion SDRs in 1977.[36] Such increased use of IMF credit resources, of course, required increased quotas, but the IMF has also established an arrangement to borrow from member countries with balance-of-payments surpluses or with adequate reserves. This is done through the General Agreements to Borrow and the Supplementary Financing Facility.

International liquidity has, then, been dramatically expanded in the 1970s, as the monetary system has responded to the economic disequilibrium of the period. International reserves, narrowly defined, have grown rapidly in the wake of oil-price changes and the huge U.S. deficits. Much of the growth in reserves has come about because exchange rates have not been fully free to adjust. A large portion of reserve growth in the 1970s has thus been a result of disequilibrium rather than a planned expansion of "international money."

## The Changing U.S. Role

For much of the postwar period—until the late 1960s, in fact—the United States and the dollar played a unique role in the international monetary system.[37] As we have indicated in this chapter and in Chapter 18, the United States was a major "creditor" country, lending funds to the rest of the world, part of which was offset by the U.S. current-account surplus. The U.S. dollar was the "key" currency in the system. It served as an international medium of exchange in that it was readily accepted by the rest of the world in payment for goods, services, and financial assets. It was an international unit of account, as not only U.S. trade, but also trade and contracts between third countries, were denominated in dollars. And the U.S. dollar served as a store of value in that many foreign official institutions and private entities denominated their financial assets, including interna-

---

[35] On this point, see Stanley W. Black, "On Central Bank Intervention and the Stability of Exchange Rates," in *Exchange Risk and Exposure: Current Developments in International Financial Management*, eds. R. Levich and C. Wihlborg, Lexington Books, Lexington, Mass., 1980.

[36] For a general discussion of the use of IMF resources and the various facilities, see International Monetary Fund, *Annual Report, 1978*, pp. 62 ff.

[37] An extended discussion can be found in McKinnon, "America's Role in Stabilizing the World's Monetary System."

tional reserve holdings, in dollar instruments. The United States financial institutions and markets served a major intermediation function for the rest of the world as well. Foreigners held short-term dollar-denominated liquid assets in the United States, and Americans acquired long-term foreign assets through AID loans, purchases of long-term foreign bonds, and direct foreign investment by U.S. companies.

These unique roles for the dollar and for U.S. financial markets were the result of several characteristics. First, the dollar was viewed as a "strong" currency, unlikely to be devalued. It also had stable purchasing power since the U.S. inflation rate was low, on average, both in absolute terms and relative to other countries. Thus, dollar assets were viewed as superior stores of value, and the large U.S. financial markets were able to absorb foreign borrowing needs and depository requirements without disruption. Furthermore, the United States had no exchange controls over the convertibility of the dollar into other currencies (or into gold for foreign official holders), and almost no controls over foreign investments by Americans or investments by foreigners in the United States—nor was there a perceived likelihood of such controls. As a result of both these characteristics and the size of the United States economy, the dollar was widely sought after, both as an international reserve currency by foreign central banks and as a store of value and medium of exchange by the private sector. It was used to carry out intervention in the foreign exchange market by all countries and was the official unit of account of the IMF and of most other countries in international transactions.

By the late 1960s, however, this unique central role had begun to slip. The decline accelerated in the 1970s. First, the United States had an intractable balance-of-payments deficit, which pushed unwanted dollars into the hands of foreign central banks as they intervened in the foreign exchange markets in order to keep their currencies from appreciating (the dollar from depreciating). The convertibility of the dollar at a fixed price into other currencies or gold was thus called into question and finally abandoned in 1971. Second, the U.S. inflation rate rose to postwar highs in the late 1960s, and inflation accelerated in the 1970s. As a store of real value, dollar-denominated assets appeared less

attractive and less certain, despite the higher nominal yields caused by inflation. Third, the United States retrenched from its traditionally liberal policy of freedom over foreign investment. It imposed limits on bank lending to foreigners and foreign direct investment by U.S. companies; it also imposed an "interest equalization tax" on foreign securities acquired by Americans from 1965 to 1974.[38] This further compromised the attractiveness of dollar assets to foreign investors.

A fourth factor serving to erode the dollar's central role in the international financial system was the rapid rise of viable alternatives to the U.S. financial markets. The most important is the Eurocurrency market, which grew from less than $5 billion net deposits in 1960 to $600 billion in 1978.[39] The Eurocurrency market, of which Eurodollars represent about 70 percent of the total, is a banking market in time deposits and bank loans denominated in a currency other than the currency of the country in which the banks are located. The growth of the Eurocurrency system is largely the result of its relative lack of regulation. Reserve requirements are normally not required against such off-shore deposits, taxes are not imposed, and there are no interest rate ceilings. The principal location of the market is London, but other centers exist in Singapore–Hong Kong, Panama, Luxembourg, and other countries. The growth of the Euromarkets also received a major stimulus from U.S. imposition of foreign investment controls in the mid-1960s. American companies were, thereby, encouraged to borrow in the Euromarkets, and foreigners found it attractive to deposit funds there rather than in the United States because of higher yields, convenience, and perceived safety. In addition, the progressive relaxation of foreign investment controls by many other countries has contributed to the growth of this international money market. It provides an alternative asset—which can be denominated in U.S. dollars, if desired—for

[38]See Kaj Areskoug, "The Liberalization of U.S. Capital Outflows: International Financial Consequences," *The Bulletin,* No. 1976-2, New York University, Institute of Finance, 1976.

[39]An excellent description of the workings of the Euromarkets can be found in Gunter Dufey and Ian H. Giddy, *The International Money Market,* Prentice-Hall, Englewood Cliffs, N.J., 1978.

holders of liquid funds and a source of intermediate-term bank loans for borrowers. The importance of this new alternative is suggested by its huge size and rapid growth.[40] Thus, the earlier role of U.S. financial markets as a source of liquidity, free convertibility, and stability for foreign holders of funds is now being shared with international markets and with some national markets, such as those of Switzerland.

A fifth factor contributing to the decline in the international role of the United States dollar is the creation of the Special Drawing Right (SDR) and the introduction of the limited floating exchange rate system. When SDRs were first created in 1970, they were intended to supplement other forms of international reserves and add to world liquidity. Their value was equal to one U.S. dollar. However, when it became obvious that the dollar could decline (as well as rise) in price in terms of other currencies and gold, a new international *numeraire* (unit of account) was sought. This became the (weighted average) basket of major currencies in the SDR, and this has become the official international unit of account at the IMF and for transactions between central banks.

A final factor affecting the role of the dollar has been the massive transfer of financial wealth to the oil-exporting countries. Since oil payments to OPEC countries are normally denominated in dollars, these nations acquired huge amounts of investable dollars in the mid-1970s (estimated at over $60 billion in 1975 alone). Recipients have not always wanted to invest all of these funds in the United States, or even in the dollar segment of the Eurocurrency market, so they have become available on the foreign exchange markets, as other currencies are purchased to acquire investments in countries other than the United States. And, it appears that the investments in the United States made by the OPEC countries have tended to be predominantly short term in nature.[41] Thus, the abundance of dollars in OPEC hands, the higher oil-import bill of the United States, and the OPEC price increase have combined to provide a longer-term source of uncertainty and weakness of the dollar relative to other major currencies.

An immediate result of these factors is that the United States, viewed as a financial intermediary for the rest of the world, has become decidedly less liquid. This is suggested in Table 30-5, which shows U.S. foreign assets, by type, and foreigners' investments in the United States. As the first column of Table 30-5 shows, well over one-half of U.S. assets abroad have been long-term private investments. U.S. liabilities to foreigners, on the other hand, are overwhelmingly short term in nature, amounting to almost twice the magnitude of U.S. reserves ($19 billion at the end of 1977) and private short-term claims on foreigners ($96 billion). In contrast, U.S. long-term assets abroad are over twice as large as foreign long-term investments in the United States. Thus, while the United States, by financial institutional standards, remains quite solvent and is a net creditor country (its total foreign assets exceeded total foreign liabilities by $58 billion in 1977), it is nevertheless highly illiquid (in 1977, its short-term liabilities exceeded short-term assets (including reserves) by almost $100 billion).

The other two columns show the changes in the international investment position of the United States over the two decades 1957–1967 and 1967–1977. Note that over two-thirds of U.S. liabilities and assets were placed on the books during the 1967–1977 decade. This represents a very high rate of growth even after taking into account the effects of inflation on nominal values of new financial assets. The high growth rate reflects the continuing and accelerating internationalization of financial markets. Note also that while the U.S. *net* foreign investment position increased in both periods, there was only minor growth in the 1967–1977 decade. The deterioration of the liquidity position occurred mainly in the same period, with $180 billion being added to U.S. short-term liabilities (and government securities) while only $84 billion in private

[40]Data may be found in Bank for International Settlements, *Forty-ninth Annual Report,* Basel, 1979; and Dufey and Giddy, *The International Money Markets,* Chap. 3.

[41]While the OPEC investment patterns by currency and by country cannot be estimated with precision since considerable parts of the funds are managed elsewhere (Swiss banks, for example), U.S. data suggest the correctness of this statement. Similar conclusions have been reached by others. They can be found in Morgan Guaranty Trust Company, *World Financial Markets,* which contains periodic reports on OPEC's "petrodollar" flows.

**Table 30-5  The International Investment Position of the United States and Changes, by Type of Investments, 1957–1977 (in billions of dollars)**

| U.S. and Foreign Assets | Stock at End of 1977 | | Change | |
|---|---|---|---|---|
| | | | 1957–1967 | 1967–1977 |
| International reserves | $ 19.3 | | $(10.0) | $  4.5 |
| Gold stock | | 11.7 | (10.7) | (0.4) |
| IMF Automatic Drawing Rights | | 4.9 | (1.6) | 4.5 |
| Special Drawing Rights on IMF | | 2.6 | | 2.6 |
| Convertible foreign currencies | | 0.1 | 2.3 | (2.3) |
| U.S. government claims on foreigners | 49.6 | | 8.9 | 23.3 |
| Private short-term foreign assets | 95.8 | | 8.6 | 84.0 |
| Owned by U.S. banks | | 79.9 | | 71.3 |
| Owned by others | | 15.9 | | 12.7 |
| Long-term private assets | 216.6 | | 48.1 | 134.8 |
| Direct investment by U.S. companies | | 148.8 | 33.9 | 89.5 |
| Foreign corporate stock | | 10.1 | 4.7 | 4.9 |
| Foreign bonds | | 39.2 | 9.4 | 28.4 |
| Bank loans to foreigners | | 12.6 | | 8.7 |
| Other | | 5.9 | | 3.7 |
| Total foreign assets | $381.3 | | $ 55.6 | $247.0 |
| Total, excluding gold stock | $369.6 | | $ 67.9 | $247.4 |
| Net foreign investment position (excluding gold) | $ 58.4 | | $ 32.2 | $  5.8 |

| U.S. Liabilities to Foreigners (Foreign Investment in the U.S.) | Stock at End of 1977 | | Change | |
|---|---|---|---|---|
| | | | 1957–1967 | 1967–1977 |
| Short-term liabilities and U.S. government securities | $217.3 | | $17.5 | $179.6 |
| U.S. liabilities to foreign official institutions | 143.0 | | 7.7 | 121.9 |
| U.S. government securities | | 117.8 | | |
| Liabilities of private U.S. entities | | 25.2 | | |
| U.S. liabilities to nonofficial foreigners | 74.2 | | 9.7 | 57.6 |
| U.S. government securities | | 7.5 | | |
| Liabilities of private U.S. entities | | 66.7 | | |
| Long-term foreign investment in the U.S. | 93.9 | | 18.1 | 61.8 |
| Direct investment by foreign companies | | 34.1 | 4.2 | 24.2 |
| U.S. corporate stocks | | 39.7 | 9.4 | 24.2 |
| U.S. bonds | | 13.4 | 4.5 | 6.9 |
| Other long-term | | 6.7 | | |
| Total liabilities to foreigners | $311.2 | | $35.7 | $241.6 |

Source: *Survey of Current Business,* various issues.

short-term assets were added during the decade 1967–1977.

These factors, which are related to the deterioration in the international liquidity position of the United States, have brought about basic changes in the international role of the dollar. No longer is it the centerpiece of the international monetary system. Most of its functions are shared with other markets, instruments, and nations.

Perhaps the least erosion has occurred in the dollar's role as the currency of intervention in the foreign exchange market and as the vehicle currency for exchange market activity and international invoicing. But, even in this area, the monopoly of the dollar is no longer as complete as it once was. The European Monetary System and some other countries now utilize several currencies for intervention purposes.

The dollar shares its role as the unit of account with the SDR and, in Europe, the ECU. Official transactions among central banks are no longer denominated in dollars. Some private contracts, as well, now use other national currencies, such as the German mark or Swiss franc, and OPEC has threatened to denominate oil prices in a "currency basket," such as the SDR, if the dollar continues to depreciate significantly against other currencies.

Finally, the reserve-currency role, historically shared by the U.S. dollar, the pound sterling, and the French franc, has widened to include the German mark and the Swiss franc. Indeed, several smaller countries have attempted to reduce the amount of dollars in their reserve currency holdings and to diversify their reserve assets by holding several other currencies as well. Thus, the system is becoming a multiple-reserve-currency system as the risk of exchange fluctuations for any one currency is diversified away by central banks.[42] Closely related is the decline in the dollar as a store of value for foreign private investors. This role is now spread across the assets of several countries, as U.S. price performance and exchange rate stability have declined relative to some other countries.

## Conclusion

In the postwar period, most major industrial nations gradually relaxed their controls over international capital movements and current-account transactions. This has facilitated the integration of national financial markets, so that the financial markets and monetary policies of all nations are now much more interdependent than in earlier decades. At the same time, each nation still retains its own national monetary unit, tax system, central bank, and monetary authority—albeit each has more international interaction—and thus each country can have balance-of-payments disequilibrium with the rest of the world. Despite growing international financial integration, there are no world currency and automatic balance-of-payments adjustments.

Balance-of-payments adjustments are economically costly and often politically painful, whether accomplished by relative inflation-deflation, exchange rate adjustment, or direct governmental restrictions and controls. Each nation must eventually adjust, although international reserves and liquidity may be used to postpone or slow down the adjustment process. National policymakers are frequently faced with choices among international adjustment policies, each of which may conflict with or compromise one or more domestic economic objectives.

The international financial system comprises the rules and conventions of nations with respect to exchange rates, balance-of-payments adjustment, and international reserves and liquidity. Under the Bretton Woods System, which prevailed from 1946 to 1971, adjustments in exchange rates among currencies were used relatively infrequently for balance-of-payments adjustment. Restrictions on foreign payments were prevalent in most countries outside North America but were relaxed in the late 1950s and early 1960s. Relative inflation-deflation was often used as a balance-of-payments adjustment mechanism. During that period, the United States and the dollar played a central role, as the United States ran a persistent but manageable balance-of-payments deficit. This process allowed the rest of the world to have more surpluses than deficits and, thereby, to be less concerned about adjustment measures than would otherwise have been the case. The U.S. deficit also provided a source of international reserves and liquidity for the rest of the world in the form of dollar-denominated asset holdings. U.S. maintenance of convertibility between gold and dollars held abroad officially was the linchpin of fixed exchange rates and the gold exchange system.

By the early 1970s, the disequilibrium between the United States and other major industrial countries had gone on too long and was exacerbated by the degree of inflation taking place in the United States. U.S. deficits and the accumulation of unwanted dollars abroad, which accompanied those deficits, led to a dollar devaluation in terms of gold in 1971 and the abandonment of the U.S. pledge to maintain convertibility at a fixed price between the dollar and gold. The ensuing changes in OPEC oil prices in 1973–1974 and 1978–1979 placed additional stresses on the system and made imperative a major change from the pre-1971 fixed exchange rate and gold exchange standard.

[42]On this issue, see "Charting the Move Away from the Dollar," *World Business Weekly* (March 12, 1979).

The emerging system is one of much greater exchange variability, involving some aspects of freely floating exchange rates, some aspects of pegged currencies, and currency blocs. The IMF has assumed the role of enhancing international liquidity in order to deal with the large imbalances in an era of severe shocks stemming from inflation and higher energy prices. While exchange rates are more flexible, international adjustment has not been automatic. Indeed, the size of the U.S. imbalance vis-à-vis the surplus industrial countries has been greater under the new system than under the old. Also, hopes that floating currencies would better insulate national economies from economic events abroad have not been realized.

The 1970s have also witnessed a decline in the relative role of U.S. financial markets in total international finance. A growing number of currencies, assets, and institutions now share in the unit-of-account, medium-of-exchange, and store-of-value functions of international money—a role that the United States and the dollar held almost exclusively for twenty-five years. Given the economic performance (price movements and growth in real output) of the United States vis-à-vis the rest of the world, the continuing use of market power by OPEC, and the small likelihood of establishing a truly international central bank and returning to fixed exchange rates, it seems likely that the trends of the 1970s will persist for some time. Thus, while the dollar is still the world's preeminent currency—for transactions, for measuring value, and for holding, and while the U.S. financial markets are still the world's largest and most efficient—the dramatic advantage which the U.S. enjoyed in the 1950s and 1960s no longer exists. A world of truly multiple "key" currencies and financial markets is likely to continue to evolve.

The rapid internationalization of production and finance of the postwar period has made domestic economic performance and national economic policies more interdependent and interrelated. It has dramatized the conflicts between the need for effective balance-of-payments adjustment and financing, on the one hand, and domestic economic goals on the other. The international financial system is no longer neat and well defined; it is a system encompassing various types of exchange rate relationships and demonstrating little international control over reserve growth. However, the system has successfully coped with one major shock—namely, the massive increases in oil prices—and it continues to seek a means of adjusting to the erosion in the preeminence of the United States and the dollar. This process of accommodation is certain to be an important factor for some time to come.

## Questions

1. Describe the alternative balance-of-payments adjustment mechanisms, including the linkages that would make them effective.
2. It has been suggested that balance-of-payments adjustment, by both surplus and deficit countries, may be costly and may conflict with other national objectives. What is the nature of these costs and conflicts? Discuss them for each of the possible adjustment mechanisms.
3. For many purposes, a nation can be viewed as a household or a company with respect to financial flows. For a nation, what types of "flows of funds" with the rest of the world are available to offset differences between its current expenditure ($E$) and income ($Y$)? Explain.
4. What are the functions of international reserves and liquidity? Define each, and explain their components under existing international monetary arrangements.
5. Describe the international arrangements for determining exchange rates under the current (1980–1981) international financial system.
6. What is the International Monetary Fund and what are its functions?
7. The United States held a special role in international financial markets in the postwar period. Describe briefly the nature of that role.
8. How are international reserves created? Why and how did such a sizable increase in the 1973–1977 period occur?
9. The international monetary system was under substantial stress and disequilibrium in the mid-1970s. Describe the nature of the disequilibrium and the factors contributing to it.
10. National economies are quite interdependent, even for countries which export and import only small shares of their total output. A national economy may be affected either by economic events abroad or by the policies of foreign nations. Describe the linkages by which economic performance and economic policies by other countries may affect the economy of a nation. Do so for both fixed and flexible exchange rate systems.

## Selected Bibliography

Black, Stanley W. *Floating Exchange Rates and National Economic Policy*. Yale University Press, New Haven, Conn., 1977.

de Vries, Margaret. *The International Monetary Fund, 1946–1971*. International Monetary Fund, Washington, D.C., 1976.

Dufey, Gunter, and Ian H. Giddy. *The International Money Market*. Prentice-Hall, Englewood Cliffs, N.J., 1978.

Kohlhagen, Steven W. "The Behavior of Foreign Exchange Markets—A Critical Survey of the Empirical Literature." *Monograph Series in Finance and Economics,* No. 1978-3. New York University, Salomon Brothers Center for the Study of Financial Institutions, New York, 1978.

McKinnon, Ronald. "America's Role in Stabilizing the World's Monetary System." *Daedalus* (Winter 1978).

Mundell, Robert A. *International Economics*. The Macmillan Company, New York, 1971.

Stern, Robert M. *The Balance of Payments*. Aldine Publishing Company, Chicago, 1973.

Whitman, Marina von Neuman. "Policies for Internal and External Balance." *Special Paper in International Economics,* No. 9. Princeton University, International Finance Section, Princeton, N.J., 1970.

Willett, Thomas D. *Floating Exchange Rates and International Monetary Reform*. American Enterprise Institute, Washington, D.C., 1977.

Williamson, John. "International Liquidity—A Survey." *Economic Journal* (September 1973).

# 31

## Economic Efficiency, Public Regulation, and Financial Reform: Depository Institutions

Public policy toward the major depository institutions in the United States—commercial banks, saving and loan associations, mutual savings banks, and credit unions—harbors serious tension between the desire to promote competition and the apparent need to protect these institutions from the hazards that inevitably beset private enterprise. Those aspects of policy aimed at the promotion and maintenance of competition are supported by economic analysis and are consistent with political and legal tradition in the United States. Episodic experience, however, has persuaded policymakers that commercial banks and, in somewhat differing ways, the other depository institutions are affected with a public interest requiring government promotion and regulation. The result has been a mixed (some would say, confused) governmental purpose involving the encouragement of competition within a framework of regulation.

The framework itself, however, can hardly be viewed as stable. It has, over the last century, been altered by conscious intent in response to a succession of financial crises. In the last two decades, it has proved vulnerable to those dynamic forces generated in a free enterprise economy by the search for profit. Relatively unregulated institutions have seized the profitable opportunities created by restrictions on severely regulated institutions. The latter have innovated, circumventing old restrictions to meet the new competition. Regulatory agencies have been compelled to abandon old constraints in the interest of the institutions they regulate. The old regulatory framework, established in the Great Depression of the 1930s, has been passing; competition among commercial banks, and between commercial banks and other depository institutions, has intensified.

The passing from the old to the new has not, thus far, been a smooth transition. Some institutions, geared to the old restraints, have found it difficult to adjust to unplanned market developments. Other institutions have responded in an overaggressive fashion, ultimately creating serious difficulties for themselves and others. There has been a renewed experience with the problems of insolvency; particularly notable has been the failure of large banks. Attempts have been made to reformulate the regulatory structure in a comprehensive way. Moreover, the emergence of more intense competition, the erosion of the depression-determined regulatory framework, and the renewed concern with bank failure have been accompanied in recent years by technological advances, such as electronic fund transfer systems, that promise (or threaten, depending on one's point of view) drastic change in the way in which institutions operate and compete.

This chapter first indicates the foundation of both competitive and restrictive policies toward the depository institutions. The existing regulatory systems and their impact on competition and economic efficiency are then discussed. The revival of competitive policy in the last two decades is reviewed, along with the issues raised by bank failure. Finally, recent attempts at comprehensive and practical reform of the regulatory structure are evaluated.

## The Basis for Competitive Policy

The advantages of competition for financial intermediaries were briefly discussed in Chapter 1. We would expect competition among commercial banks and other depository institutions to result in the lowest possible costs and the offering of services at comparable competitive prices. Competitive prices imply the "right" amount of production—that is, at a point where the value obtained by the customer is just equal to the cost of producing it. Competition implies that borrowed funds are available to those businesses and consumers whose financial prospects make such competitively determined "prices" attractive. Loanable funds will tend to flow in the direction of their most essential (private) uses. Indeed, as this chapter discusses, there is ample evidence that the intensifying competition over the last fifteen years has tended to bring about lower "prices" for customers of depository institutions.

Regulation, however, can prevent competitive prices and bring about a misallocation of financial and real resources. Prohibitions and restrictions on the loans and investments of different groups of depository institutions tend to reduce the number of institutions competing for specific types of borrowers. Consider a local market in which there are three commercial banks, two savings and loan associations, and one credit union. If all could invest in business loans or in comparable mortgage loans there might be sufficient competition to assure that

rates on these types of loans in the local market approximated their costs. But if only the commercial banks can offer business loans, and only the S&Ls can offer mortgage loans, this result seems less likely. Rates or "prices" on business loans and mortgages may be too high, and there may be too little invested in both.

Even with larger numbers of banks and S&Ls in the market, specialization, coupled with interest rate restrictions on deposits, can preclude adjustments necessary to maintain a close relationship between rates and costs. Suppose business prospects improve relative to housing prospects, and the demand for business loans increases. Rates on business loans at commercial banks will rise. To some degree, profit-maximizing commercial banks will shift funds from other loans and investments, now less profitable, to business loans. But if the rates they can offer for new deposits are restricted by law, there will be no outflow of funds from the S&Ls. In effect, for long periods of time, too large a volume of funds may go to housing and too small a volume to business.

Quite separate from these economic arguments supporting competition, there has been in the United States a traditional concern about the dangers of concentrated financial power—particularly in the hands of commercial banks. The failure of both the First and Second Banks of the United States to secure charter renewals in the first decades of the nineteenth century was, in part, the result of this perceived danger. Demonstrating the same distrust of a centralized money power, Congress established the Federal Reserve System in 1913 as a regional system with twelve district banks as well as a board of governors in Washington, D.C.

Many state laws (as well as the National Currency Act of 1863) provided for virtual free entry into banking through the latter half of the nineteenth and during the first several decades of the twentieth centuries. The early banks in the United States had been organized under special acts of incorporation by Congress and by the state legislatures. After 1838, however, they were generally established by charters, which were issued by administrative officers to those who met the relatively simple conditions of general banking laws.

Within the framework of free entry and severe restrictions on branch banking (which were intended to restrain the growth of large banks), the unique structure of American banking evolved. Thousands of small local institutions were scattered throughout the country and a relatively few large banks were located in the principal metropolitan areas.

Other small depository institutions—mutual savings banks, building and loan (later, savings and loan) associations, and credit unions, with their mutual forms of organization—did not evoke the political and social concerns that surrounded commercial banks. Rather they were viewed as self-help, cooperative institutions engaged in socially beneficial enterprise. As they have developed in recent years into competitors of commercial banks, issues of competition and concentration have intruded on their own political and social underpinnings.

## The Basis for Regulation

Depository institutions are, nevertheless, highly regulated. With regard to commercial banking, regulation developed as it became clear that bank failure could destroy personal savings and going business concerns. Depositor losses were generally not insured until the 1930s. The loss of a banking relationship through failure could be calamitous for a small business concern. It was found, moreover, that the failure of one bank could lead to runs on other banks and plunge local communities, wider regions, and even the nation into financial distress.

For the most part, banking crises have interacted with general business contractions; banks proved particularly vulnerable during cyclical downturns as borrowers found it difficult to repay debt and depositors became concerned about the safety of their deposits. Bank failure, in turn, tended to intensify and prolong business contractions. Commercial banks provide a substantial portion of the money supply; and the collection of bank checks through the Federal Reserve and private clearing houses represents a major element in the payments mechanism. Sharp declines in the money supply and disruption in the payments mechanism resulting from bank failure have contributed to the severity of depressions.

As one student has noted, however, "It would be misleading . . . to suppose that impetus for bank regulation has come exclusively from customers of commercial banks." [1]

Many of the most restrictive banking laws have resulted from active lobbying by banks and by their trade associations. Although businessmen are inclined to praise free competition, the competitive environment they admire is usually one to be prescribed for an industry other than their own. [2]

There are still other reasons for regulation. The managers of depository institutions have extensive discretion over what is largely "other people's money." Such responsibility normally evokes public regulation to prevent mismanagement and fraud. Moreover, the important role played by savings and loan associations and mutual savings banks in residential mortgage markets and the "consumer-cooperative" purposes of credit unions are generally supported by government policy; such government support also typically evokes regulation.

## Regulatory Systems

The systems for regulating the several types of depository institutions are, in some ways, very similar. All provide for chartering and supervision under state and/or federal law. All institutions are subject to the regulatory authority of one or more governmental agencies. All must or may have their deposit or depositlike liabilities insured. Laws and regulation generally prohibit or limit certain lending and investing activities and certain kinds of liabilities (different ones for different types of institutions); restrict permitted balance-sheet items in one way or another; and restrict entry into the "industry" by new charters and entry into specific locations by new branch offices, mergers, and acquisitions. Interest rates on deposits and depositlike accounts have been restricted in the past, although rate ceilings on deposits are scheduled to be phased out by 1986 under provisions of the Depository Institutions Deregulation and Monetary Control Act of 1980 (DMCA). This far-reaching act, which will be mentioned repeatedly in the remainder of this chapter, is likely to lead to a dramatic inten-

[1] Ross M. Robertson, *The Comptroller and Bank Supervision: A Historical Appraisal,* Office of the Comptroller of the Currency, Washington, D.C., 1968, p. 7.
[2] Ibid.

sification of competition among depository institutions in the future. Nevertheless, differences in individual prohibitions and constraints still abound. We turn now to a more detailed specification of the several regulatory systems: first to commercial banking, which is the most complex, and then to the other depository institutions, which will be more briefly reviewed and compared.

## Commercial Banking

Commercial bank regulation is largely aimed at securing the solvency of banks. *Solvency* is often defined as a condition whereby a bank's assets are greater than its liabilities; *insolvency* would exist when capital has been completely extinguished. Solvency is impaired by noncollectible financial assets that must be written off against capital, by deposit losses that can be met only by selling financial assets at market prices below their book value, and by negative earnings that erode capital. The inability of a bank to meet contractual demands for funds by creditors—illiquidity—is tantamount to insolvency.

The determination that a bank is insolvent, however, is often a matter of judgment on the part of bank supervisors who determine which assets are "bad" and must be written off. The Federal Reserve, for example, can postpone or preclude declarations of insolvency by lending money to meet deposit outflows. In effect, a bank will be insolvent when the appropriate supervisory authority declares it to be insolvent.

For our present purpose, however, we need not consider all the complexities involved in a supervisory decision that a bank is insolvent. We need only view regulation as an attempt to prevent banks from getting into the kinds of trouble that might result in insolvency. To this end, a complex regulatory structure has developed in the United States. This structure is composed of:

1. a number of agencies having both independent and overlapping authority with regard to different groups of commercial banks
2. a set of explicit regulations based on federal and state banking laws
3. a procedure, the bank examination, for uncovering deviations from the laws or regulations and

other behavior or performance believed to be dangerous to bank solvency
4. a system of federal deposit insurance

We will discuss each of these elements in turn.

*The Agencies*   There are three federal bank regulatory agencies in the United States (the Comptroller of the Currency, the Federal Reserve, and the FDIC) and fifty state agencies. The authority of these agencies differs, depending on the specific function and class of bank.

Figure 31-1 attempts to summarize the division of regulatory responsibility and its overlapping nature. Nine types of authority are identified:

1. to charter new banks and to declare them insolvent
2. to authorize admission to Federal Reserve membership
3. to authorize admission to FDIC insurance
4. to examine
5. to require reports
6. to require reserves
7. to impose regulations
8. to give prior approval for mergers and branch offices
9. to authorize bank holding company formations and acquisitions and generally supervise and regulate operations under relevant statutes

Four classes of banks are indicated:

1. nationally chartered banks
2. state-chartered banks that are members of the Federal Reserve System
3. nonmember state banks that are insured by the FDIC
4. nonmember state banks not insured by the FDIC

The lines emanating from each regulatory agency indicate authority over the type of regulation to which they attach. So, for example, only the Comptroller of the Currency and state banking agencies can issue new bank charters—to "national" and "state" banks respectively. Likewise, only the Comptroller can declare a national bank insolvent, and only a chartering state agency can declare a state bank insolvent. On the other hand, supervisory responsibility, as indicated by the authority to impose regulations, require reports, and conduct examinations, involves considerable overlap. This

### Figure 31-1   The Tangled Web of Bank Regulation

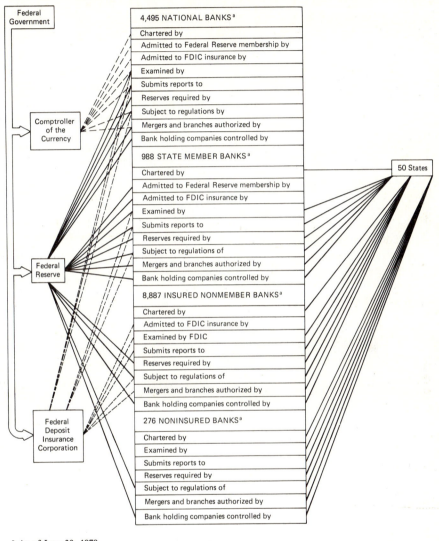

| Federal Government | 4,495 NATIONAL BANKS [a] |
| --- | --- |
| | Chartered by |
| | Admitted to Federal Reserve membership by |
| | Admitted to FDIC insurance by |
| Comptroller of the Currency | Examined by |
| | Submits reports to |
| | Reserves required by |
| | Subject to regulations by |
| | Mergers and branches authorized by |
| | Bank holding companies controlled by |
| | 988 STATE MEMBER BANKS [a] |
| | Chartered by |
| | Admitted to Federal Reserve membership by |
| | Admitted to FDIC insurance by |
| | Examined by |
| | Submits reports to |
| | Reserves required by |
| | Subject to regulations of |
| Federal Reserve | Mergers and branches authorized by |
| | Bank holding companies controlled by |
| | 8,887 INSURED NONMEMBER BANKS [a] |
| | Chartered by |
| | Admitted to FDIC insurance by |
| | Examined by FDIC |
| | Submits reports to |
| | Reserves required by |
| | Subject to regulations of |
| | Mergers and branches authorized by |
| | Bank holding companies controlled by |
| | 276 NONINSURED BANKS [a] |
| Federal Deposit Insurance Corporation | Chartered by |
| | Examined by |
| | Submits reports to |
| | Reserves required by |
| | Subject to regulations of |
| | Mergers and branches authorized by |
| | Bank holding companies controlled by |

50 States

[a] As of June 30, 1979.

Source: Adapted from Hearings on Financial Structure and Regulation, the Subcommittee on Financial Institutions of the Senate Committee on Banking, Housing, and Urban Affairs, 93rd Congress, 1st Session, Washington, D.C., 1973.

overlap results from the fact that the four classes of banks are not mutually exclusive. The Comptroller supervises all national banks. But all national banks must, by law, be members of the Federal Reserve System and be insured by the Federal Deposit Insurance Corporation. All state-chartered banks that are members of the Federal Reserve must also be insured by the FDIC. Thus, the Federal Reserve has some authority over national banks and the FDIC over member banks.

When chartering a national bank, the Comptroller of the Currency certifies to the Federal Reserve and the FDIC that their requirements have been met. Thus, the new national bank is effectively admitted to Federal Reserve membership and FDIC insurance by the Comptroller, as Figure 31-1 indicates. New state-chartered banks that have been granted membership in the Federal Reserve may obtain insurance by having the Federal Reserve certify to the FDIC that its requirements have been met. Thus, they are effectively admitted to insured status by the Federal Reserve, as Figure 31-1 indicates. State-chartered banks that do not become members of the Federal Reserve System may receive insurance by direct application to the FDIC.

Duplication of effort and potential conflict are avoided, to a degree, by a division of responsibility such that the Comptroller principally supervises national banks; the Federal Reserve, state member banks; and the FDIC, insured state nonmember banks. State agencies, of course, supervise all state-chartered banks as well.

Some banking laws divide federal responsibilities along the lines of principal supervision. Thus, all mergers among insured commercial banks must receive prior approval from one federal bank regulatory agency. The Comptroller decides in cases where the resulting bank will be a national bank; the Federal Reserve in cases where the resulting bank will be a state member bank; and the FDIC where the resulting bank will be an insured nonmember. Where resulting banks will be state chartered, state approval may also be necessary. On the other hand, holding-company formations, acquisitions, and operations are, at the federal level, entirely within the domain of the Federal Reserve.

The student need not bother to look for a simple underlying rationale for the existing distribution of regulatory responsibilities. The agencies themselves were established over the course of the past 115 years as ad hoc responses to financial crises. Their respective responsibilities and jurisdictions emerged in large part as a pragmatic political accommodation. There have been recommendations by respected commissions and bills in Congress for many years to rationalize the existing regulatory structure. Some movement was made along these lines with establishment of the Federal Financial Institutions Examination Council by the Financial Institutions Regulatory and Interest Rate Control Act of 1978 (FIRA). This council, composed of the Comptroller of the Currency and representatives of the Federal Reserve, the FDIC, the Federal Home Loan Bank Board, and the National Credit Union Administration, is charged with the responsibility of coordinating standards and methods of examining the financial institutions regulated by the respective agencies.

*Regulations* Regulation can be conveniently divided into four types: activity prohibitions; balance-sheet constraints; entry restrictions; and pricing restrictions.[3]

1. *Activity prohibitions.* Commercial banks have traditionally been viewed as providers of short-term loans to business and issuers of deposit liabilities withdrawable on demand. Their activities have always been more diverse than this, but expansion into new fields has typically been viewed (at least, initially) as dangerous to their liquidity and solvency.

Some types of investments have been completely prohibited. Investment in real estate was prohibited to national banks by the National Currency Act of 1863. Investment in corporate stock was similarly prohibited. In 1933, all insured banks were prohibited by the Banking Act of 1933 (the Glass-Steagall Act) from underwriting corporate stocks and bonds and acting as a broker in such securities.

2. *Balance-sheet constraints.* Banking law and bank supervision impose constraints on those activities in which commercial banks are permitted to engage. They are aimed, in large part (but not exclusively), at reducing the risks undertaken by banks through enforcing diversification, minimum capital requirements, and, to a degree, minimum liquidity standards.

Under federal and state laws, banks are typically required to meet certain capital requirements in order to be chartered. But these requirements, expressed in absolute dollar amounts, are usually minimum amounts. Supervisors will normally insist that a bank maintain some relationship between its capital and its total assets or some portion of them (for example, "risk assets"). The aim is to provide a cushion against bad loans and investments.

---

[3] This classification follows Franklin R. Edwards and James Scott, "Regulating the Solvency of Depositing Institutions: A Perspective for Reform," unpublished paper, 1976.

Reserve requirements were originally designed to insure minimum liquidity standards. A certain portion of assets were to be kept in "cash" or close substitutes. It is now generally recognized that reserve requirements contribute little to a bank's liquidity since what is *required* can be relied on to meet only a fraction of potential outflows of deposits. Supervisors, through the examination process, attempt to evaluate a bank's liquidity position and indicate certain minimum standards related to relevant risks.

The amount that a national bank may lend to a single borrower was limited by the National Currency Act of 1863. The amount member banks may loan to one of their own executive officers was limited by the Federal Reserve Act and amended by FIRA in 1978. Additional constraints abound in the banking laws, with differential applicability depending on the class of bank.

3. *Entry restrictions*. New entry into local banking markets occurs when an organizing group obtains a charter for a new bank, when an existing bank establishes a branch office in a new area, when a bank holding company obtains a charter for a new bank and then acquires it, or when a bank or bank holding company acquires an established bank in a new area. Each one of these entry possibilities requires regulatory approval of one kind or another.

As noted, a new bank may be chartered by either the Comptroller of the Currency or a state banking agency. Through much of our history, the Comptroller and the states had little discretion in denying applications for new charters. The National Banking Act stated that if, upon examination, "it appears that such association is lawfully entitled to commence the business of banking, the Comptroller *shall* give to such association a certificate . . . to commence such business." [4]

Since the establishment of the FDIC, it has been a practical necessity for most newly organized banks to be insured. In passing on an insurance application, the FDIC must consider, among other things, "the convenience and needs of the community to be served" and the "future earning prospects" of the bank. A state bank that becomes a member of the Federal Reserve System may receive insured status from the FDIC on certification

by the Board that it has considered these same factors. Similarly, a nationally chartered bank will become insured on certification to the FDIC by the Comptroller of the Currency.

Since the establishment of the FDIC, chartering-insurance decisions have, in effect, been integrated at the national level and also, for the most part, at the state level. The decisions of state agencies, the Comptroller, and the Federal Reserve have reflected the so-called "needs test" established under the FDIC Act. If one or more established banks appear vulnerable to additional competition, or if there is doubt as to the viability of the new bank itself, the charter application is likely to be denied. The measurement of "need" may take a variety of forms. Frequently, local area ratios, such as population-to-banks or population-to-banking offices, have been used to suggest whether the area "needs" a new charter or is already "overbanked."

It should be noted that the statutory language establishing the "needs test" leaves room for judgment and, therefore, discretion. Until the early 1960s all the agencies seem to have exercised their discretion to severely limit new charters. In the early 1960s, however, as we shall discuss, the Comptroller appeared to relax entry restrictions. [5]

New entry by established banks is restricted by federal law. The McFadden Act (1927, 1933) restricts national banks to branch offices in locations permitted within each state to state banks. Bank holding companies, where permitted by state law, are not currently permitted to acquire bank affiliates across state lines unless the state they enter specifically permits the entry of out-of-state bank holding companies. There are a number of multi-state bank holding companies that were established prior to the legal prohibition on such activities.

While a number of states permit branching throughout the state (statewide branching), many states limit branching locations (limited-branching states). Some states do not permit branching at all (unit-banking states). Multiple-bank holding companies are also prohibited in a number of states; however, they are permitted in some states that do

[4] 12 *U.S.C.* 27 (1970). (Emphasis added.)

[5] In a number of cases suit was brought by established banks, which claimed that the Comptroller had not met the statutory requirements. See, for example, *Webster Groves Trust Co.* v. *Saxon,* 370 F.2d 381 (1966); and *Warren Bank* v. *Camp,* 396 F.2d 52 (1968).

not permit branching, such as Colorado, Missouri, and Texas, and they provide a substitute for branching.

Beyond these specific federal and state prohibitions, all acquisitions and new branch offices must be approved by one or more regulatory agencies. The agencies possess considerable discretion in approving new branch offices and a lesser degree of discretion in merger and holding company approvals. The Bank Merger and Holding Company Acts require acquisitions to be evaluated on the basis of their competitive effects, among other things, as we shall discuss.

4. *Pricing restrictions.* Commercial banks began to pay interest on deposit accounts in the early part of the nineteenth century.[6] In each of the several financial crises during the latter part of the nineteenth and early part of the twentieth centuries, efforts were made, particularly by commercial bank clearing house associations, to restrict or prohibit the payment of interest on deposits by agreement or by law. Among other things, bankers felt that high interest payments would encourage banks to acquire riskier assets (with higher yields) to offset high costs. The clearing house associations of all twelve Federal Reserve bank cities agreed in 1920 to restrict the payment of interest on banker's balances to 2½ percent.[7] The growth of time and savings deposits in the 1920s also focused banker attention on what they considered to be excessive payments on this type of deposit.

The wave of bank failures in the 1929–1933 period produced, among other things, legislation to prohibit interest payments on demand deposits and to limit interest payments on time deposits. A maximum was to be established by the Federal Reserve for member banks and the FDIC for insured nonmember banks. The maximum for time and savings

deposits in 1935 was set at 2½ percent. Since 1935 maximums have been periodically revised upward, and under provisions of DMCA they are scheduled to be phased out entirely by 1986.

In the past, commercial banks, like other types of lenders, typically have been limited in the interest rates they could charge on personal, mortgage, and some other types of loans by state law. These restrictions were generally referred to as "usury laws." Their apparent purpose was to protect vulnerable bank customers from excessive charges, rather than to protect bank solvency. As part of DMCA, rate ceilings on business loans of more than $25,000 were relaxed (until July 1, 1983), regardless of existing state laws, unless specifically reinstated by individual states. Usury laws on residential mortgages were overturned (with no time limit) unless re-enacted by states before April 1, 1983. However, DMCA did not alter usury laws on other kinds of consumer credit, except on loans by federally chartered credit unions, where the ceiling was raised.

*Bank Examinations* Bank examiners are employed by the regulatory agencies to examine periodically banks within their jurisdictions. The examiners look for adherence to existing laws and regulations, make determinations of capital adequacy and liquidity positions, and evaluate management. They prepare reports on examined banks, which provide a basis for further investigation and recommendation if required. As mentioned previously, FIRA established an interagency council (the Federal Financial Institutions Examination Council) to work toward uniform examination standards.

*Deposit Insurance* One purpose of federal deposit insurance was to protect depositors, particularly small depositors, from the financial distress accompanying bank failure. A principal effect of deposit insurance has been to limit substantially the phenomenon known as the "bank run." In the nineteenth century and the early decades of the twentieth century, the failure of a weak bank often led to rumors about fundamentally sound banks and depositors would remove their funds as quickly as possible. But even healthy banks, operating on a fractional reserve basis, could not withstand such runs. Bank failure could, thus, reach epidemic proportions. Insurance has precluded the necessity of

---

[6]By the mid-1800s, large banks in New York had attracted substantial amounts of deposits from other commercial banks—so-called bankers or correspondent balances. By the end of the nineteenth century, interest was paid to large depositors, other banks, and on government deposits. See Charles M. Linke, "The Evolution of Interest Rate Regulation on Commercial Bank Deposits in the United States," *The National Banking Review* (June 1966).

[7]"The Impact of the Payment of Interest on Demand Deposits," A Study of the Staff of the Board of Governors of the Federal Reserve System, Washington, D.C., January 31, 1977.

concern among those depositors whose deposit accounts are insured.

*Conclusions* The bank regulatory system we have described has existed in the United States for a relatively short period. Many of the anticompetitive restrictions emerged in the early 1930s. Pricing and entry restrictions, with the exception of those involving bank mergers and holding company acquisitions, directly restrain competition; they were intended to do so as a way of minimizing bank failure. Activity prohibitions and balance-sheet constraints were, on the other hand, directly aimed at reducing the risks banks can accept in their day-to-day operations. These laws and regulations also restrain competition, and this has led to their erosion.

## The Regulation of Other Depository Institutions

As noted in a general way before, saving and loan associations, mutual savings banks, and credit unions are regulated in a similar fashion. This section briefly reviews the regulatory systems for these other depository institutions.

*Savings and Loan Associations* Like commercial banks, S&Ls may be chartered by an agency of the federal government, the Federal Home Loan Bank Board (FHLBB), or by the individual states. Federally chartered S&Ls must be members of the Federal Home Loan Bank System. State-chartered S&Ls may become members.[8] Table 31-1 indicates the membership composition of the FHLB System. Of the 4,723 S&Ls in the United States at the end of 1978, 4,154 were members of the FHLB System; only 569 were not.

The system was established in 1932 and is structured somewhat like the Federal Reserve. The FHLBB, located in Washington, D.C., has three members appointed for four-year terms by the president of the United States. Twelve regional banks, owned by their member associations, are governed by the FHLBB.

All federally chartered associations must have their deposits insured by the Federal Savings and Loan Insurance Corporation (FSLIC), a federal

**Table 31-1 Membership of FHLB System as of December 31, 1978**

| Type of Organization | Number |
|---|---|
| Savings & loan associations insured by FSLIC | |
| Federally chartered | 2,000 |
| State-chartered | 2,053 |
| Other state-chartered | 101 |
| Total savings & loan association membership | 4,154 |
| Mutual savings banks | 86 |
| Life insurance companies | 2 |
| Total membership | 4,242 |

Source: U.S. League of Savings Associations, *Saving and Loan Fact Book,* 1979.

agency that functions like the FDIC. Unlike the FDIC, which is an independent agency, the FSLIC is governed by the FHLBB. State-chartered associations that are members of the FHLB System may also be insured by the FSLIC. Of the 2,154 state-chartered member associations at the end of 1978, 2,053 were insured by the FSLIC. There were 670 state-chartered associations not insured by the FSLIC, but a number of these were insured by state-established agencies.[9] Members of the FHLB System account for over 98 percent of association assets; FSLIC-insured associations account for close to 98 percent. Thus, a "dual" system of chartering by both federal and state agencies also exists for S&Ls. But authority at the federal level is not fragmented among several independent agencies as is the case in commercial banking.

Activity prohibitions for S&Ls have been quite severe in the past. S&Ls' traditional purpose has been to finance home construction and ownership within a "local" area. S&Ls have been permitted by law and relatively simple regulation to make direct, amortized, long-term loans on the security of one- to four-family residential property within a relatively narrow geographic area around their home office. There have, however, been an abundance of permitted exceptions, and these have been widened substantially by DMCA in 1980, at least for federally chartered S&Ls. [Before DMCA, for example, S&Ls were able to invest in federally insured mortgage loan participations and mortgage-backed securities; they also made loans for mobile

---

[8]Membership in the Federal Home Loan Bank System is also open to mutual savings banks and life insurance companies.

[9]Massachusetts, Maryland, Ohio, and North Carolina provide for insurance of state-chartered S&Ls.

homes, home improvements, and for the purchase of some types of commercial and farm properties. Specific types of consumer loans, such as loans secured by passbook savings accounts and loans for educational purposes, were also permitted in the past. In 1980 DMCA allowed federally chartered S&Ls to invest up to 20 percent of their assets in consumer loans, commercial paper, and corporate debt securities.

In recent years, S&Ls have been permitted to offer a variety of certificate accounts in fixed amounts with fixed maturities; they have also been permitted to issue subordinated debentures. Associations have been authorized by DMCA to offer NOW accounts and telephone and automatic transfer accounts nationwide. For all practical purposes, these accounts are equivalent to interest-bearing checking accounts.

Balance-sheet constraints of the FHLBB include a required liquidity ratio,[10] a loan-loss-reserve requirement,[11] and a net-worth requirement.[12] These restrictions are aimed at protecting the solvency of associations. In the past, balance-sheet restrictions were also imposed in the form of maximum proportions of deposits that could be invested in mobile homes and other nonmortgage investments. These were aimed at limiting association departure from their traditional role. Following passage of DMCA in early 1980, these balance-sheet restrictions are being revised.

Entry restrictions on S&Ls are similar to those imposed on commercial banks. Under the provisions of the Home Owner's Loan Act of 1933, the Federal Home Loan Bank Board was authorized to charter federal S&Ls.

No charter shall be granted . . . unless in the judgement of the Board a necessity exists for such an institution in the community to be served, nor unless there is a reasonable probability of its usefulness and success, nor unless the same can be established without undue injury to properly conducted existing local thrift and home-financing institutions.[13]

In many states, parallel criteria for chartering have been established by the state. Some states condition the approval of a new charter on a commitment by the association to obtain deposit insurance. Provisions governing the application for FSLIC insurance by state associations do not specifically state a "needs test" but focus mainly on the character of management and all factors related to the financial condition of the association.[14]

The FHLBB can authorize branches for federally chartered associations. Branching for state-chartered associations is under the jurisdiction of the states. The policy of the FHLBB has been to authorize branches for federal S&Ls, except where the state has clearly established a flat prohibition against branches for all major competing depository institutions, not merely state-chartered S&Ls. Thus, federal and state restrictions on branching within a state may differ—unlike the case of commercial banking. In general, legal branching restrictions are less severe for S&Ls than for commercial banks. If a branch is to be acquired through merger, the FHLB Board must grant prior approval where the resulting association is to be a federally chartered association. A state agency will normally pass on mergers where the resulting association is state chartered.

Until 1966, S&Ls were not restricted in the interest they could pay on their accounts. The Interest Rate Adjustment Act of 1966 imposed Regulation Q-type maximums on S&Ls, as well as on mutual savings banks. The FHLBB was given the power to fix maximum rates paid on different types of accounts. DMCA established the Depository Institutions Deregulatory Committee (consisting of

[10]The FHLBB requires all member associations to meet a minimum "liquid asset" requirement defined as a given percentage of total savings deposits plus borrowing repayable within one year. Liquid assets include cash, demand deposits, and U.S. government and federal agency securities. The minimum requirement imposed has varied between 5 and 7 percent.

[11]The FSLIC requires insured associations to accumulate loan loss reserves equal to 5 percent of their total savings accounts.

[12]The FSLIC requires insured associations to have a minimum net worth, defined as general reserves, paid-in surplus, undivided profits and, for stock associations, the par value of its stock. The minimum itself is determined for each association on the basis of its assets.

[13]*U.S.C.* 1464(e) (1970), as quoted in K. E. Scott, "In Quest of Reason: The Licensing Decisions of the Federal Banking Agencies," *The University of Chicago Law Review* (Winter 1975), 241.

[14]Ibid., 272–273.

the Chairmen of the Federal Reserve, FDIC, FHLB Board, and National Credit Union Administration, and the Secretary of the Treasury and the Comptroller of the Currency) to supervise the phaseout of all interest rate ceilings on deposits mandated by the act by 1986. During the period 1966–1980, S&Ls and mutual savings banks were permitted to pay ¼ percent more interest on their deposits than were commercial banks for similar amounts and maturities. This ¼ percent differential, designed to aid the intermediaries heavily engaged in mortgage lending, was bitterly opposed by commercial banks for competitive reasons.

*Mutual Savings Banks* Mutual savings banks are chartered and generally supervised under state law in seventeen states—mostly the New England and Mid-Atlantic states. FIRA provided for federal chartering of mutual savings banks, and a number of institutions applied for federal charters from the FHLB Board in 1980. (As of August 1980, no federal charters had yet been approved.) Deposit insurance is available for federally and state-chartered mutual savings banks through the FDIC, and savings banks may become members of the FHLB System. At the end of 1978, 325 savings banks—70 percent of the total—were insured by the FDIC and 85 more—another 18 percent—were members of the FHLB System.[15] Federal regulation and supervision is, then, extended to most savings banks through FDIC and FHLB participation.

Most states limit mutual savings bank loans and investments to an "approved" list, normally including first mortgage loans on improved real estate and housing-related and "consumer-type" loans similar to those permitted S&Ls. Securities are normally restricted, but, unlike S&Ls before DMCA, high-quality utility and industrial bonds were permitted. Mutual savings banks obtain most of their funds from consumers' savings and time deposits, although some also offer checking accounts where permitted by law. DMCA authorized all mutual savings banks to offer NOW accounts to consumers and also authorized federally chartered

mutual savings banks to offer demand deposits to business, regardless of state law, where a commercial, corporate, or business loan arrangement exists. The act also authorized federal mutual savings banks to make commercial, corporate, and business loans, but not for more than 5 percent of the assets of the bank, and only within the state where the bank is located or within 75 miles of the bank's home office.

Balance-sheet constraints (and borrowing privileges) for the FHLB System members are similar to those described for S&Ls. The FDIC also imposes requirements for reserves and capital, as does state law.

New charter and branching restrictions vary from state to state; again restrictions are normally identical to those for S&Ls.

*Credit Unions* Credit unions may be chartered, supervised, and examined under federal law by the National Credit Union Administration (NCUA) or in accordance with differing provisions under state law. At the beginning of 1980, there were close to 13,000 federal credit unions and more than 9,000 state-chartered credit unions.[16]

Insurance for the principal credit union liability (credit union shares) is available through the NCUA. All federal credit unions must be insured, and state-chartered credit unions can apply for insurance to the NCUA. At the beginning of 1980, about 3,500 state-chartered credit unions had federal insurance. A substantial number of other state-chartered credit unions had share insurance under state-administered plans and through private insurance companies.

Until recently, federal credit unions have been restricted by law to relatively short-term loans, principally for personal expenditures and the purchase of consumer durables. In some states, longer-term loans have been permissible. Federal law and most state laws limit loans only to members and to other credit unions. For the most part, investments are restricted to U.S. government securities and federally insured accounts of S&Ls and mutual savings banks, though restrictions vary from state to state.

---

[15]National Association of Mutual Savings Banks, *National Fact Book of Mutual Savings Banks,* 1979. Mutual savings banks may also become members of the Federal Reserve System but, over the years, few have chosen to do so.

[16]National Credit Union Administration, *Annual Report,* 1979.

Amendments to the Federal Credit Union Act in 1977 have liberalized the lending authority of credit unions and have permitted the offering of new kinds of share accounts. Longer-term loans may now be made for residential mortgages, for mobile homes, and for home improvements. Share accounts with varying dividend rates, and certificate accounts with varying rates and maturities, are also permitted. Some federal credit unions had previously been permitted to issue credit union "share drafts"—checklike instruments payable through commercial banks—on an experimental basis. The 1977 legislation extended these powers, and DMCA permitted continuation of share drafts. Like deposit rate ceilings at other depository intermediaries, rate ceilings on credit unions' shares are to be phased out by 1986. As of 1980, maximum rates on loans by federal credit unions are limited to 15 percent.

As in the case of the other depository institutions, law and regulation also impose balance-sheet constraints. Loan loss reserves are required and limits are imposed on borrowing.

Entry restrictions are also imposed along familiar depository institution lines. The NCUA will issue a new organization certificate only after considering, among other things, the "economic advisability of establishing the proposed Federal credit union." The organization of a credit union also requires that the members have a "common bond," such as common employment, religious affiliation, or union affiliation. The required "common bond" may be viewed as a barrier to entry, as well as a constraint on lending.

## The Impact of Regulation

The regulation of depository institutions affects, among other things, structural characteristics of markets in which these institutions operate. Structure, in turn, has been found to affect prices charged and profits, that is, the performance of firms in these markets. This section examines several studies that illuminate the impact of regulation on structure, and of structure on performance.[17]

[17]It is also possible that regulation has important effects on the behavior of firms and, through behavior, on performance. Regulatory restrictions on competition may support anticompetitive motivations in oligopolistic markets.

## Restrictions on New Charters

The quantitative impact of the needs test for new banking charters has been studied by Peltzman.[18] He developed a model to predict the number of new charters that would have been granted in the absence of regulatory restrictions. In general form, the model may be characterized as follows:[19]

$$E_t = f(P_{t-1}, Z_t) \qquad (31\text{-}1)$$

where $E_t$ is the rate of new bank formation, that is, the number of new charters in year $t$ divided by the number of banks existing at the beginning of the year; $P_{t-1}$ is the expected rate of return adjusted for risk on capital invested in banking in period $t - 1$; $Z_t$ is all other variables that determine the rate of new bank formation. These include the rate of bank mergers ($M_t$), the rate of bank failures ($X_t$), the total stock of bank capital ($C_t$), and total deposits net of cash assets ($D_t$).

To this model he added a dummy variable to represent entry-restricting regulation ($R_t$).

$$E_t = f(P_{t-1}, Z_t) + kR_t \qquad (31\text{-}2)$$

Using data for the years 1921 to 1962, with the dummy variable $R_t$ taking on the value of 1 for the 1936–1962 period and 0 for the 1921–1935 period, Peltzman estimated the value of $k$ to be $-.579$.[20] The estimated value of $k$ suggests that new charters would have averaged about 58 per 10,000 banks *more* per year in the absence of the needs test. New charters did average about 60 banks per 10,000 per year over the period, so the calculated effect was to reduce new charters by about 50 percent. For the period as a whole, he calculates the

[18]Sam Peltzman, "Entry in Commercial Banking," *The Journal of Law and Economics* (October 1965), 11–50; and "Bank Entry Regulation: Its Impact and Purpose," *The National Banking Review* (December 1965), 163–177.

[19]This formulation is taken from Linda Edwards and Franklin Edwards, "Measuring the Effectiveness of Regulation: The Case of Bank Entry Regulation," *The Journal of Law and Economics* (October 1974), 446.

[20]The full equation containing this estimate is as follows:

$$E_t = .234 + 1.868 \log P_t - .047 X_t - .231 M_t$$
$$+ .619 \log D_t - 1.097 \log C_t - .579 R_t$$
$$R^2 = .871$$

loss in the number of new banks at about 2,200.[21] The impact of restrictions on new commercial bank charters after 1935 can, then, be characterized as important.

More recently, Edwards and Edwards have objected to Peltzman's approach on two grounds. Their first point is that the needs-test restriction of new charters tends to raise profit rates in banking and, therefore, results in an overestimate of the desired rate of bank formation and an overestimate of the regulatory coefficient $k$. Their second point is that the expected profit rate in any given period is a determinant of the degree of regulatory restriction under the needs test; in other words, banking regulators will measure "need" in a rough way by existing and expected profit rates. Thus, increasing profit rates, due in part to entry restrictions themselves, will tend to reduce the degree of restriction.

Peltzman's model, when modified to incorporate these two objections, provides a revised estimate for the regulatory effect. Rather than reducing new charters by about 2,000 over the period, the Edwards estimate that they were reduced by about 1,463.[22]

The regulatory impact of the needs test, therefore, may be quantitatively smaller than Peltzman originally estimated, but it is still important. There are several ways in which its effects may lead to higher prices to bank customers and diminished efficiency. In considering these avenues of influence, it is important to understand that commercial banks, as well as the other depository institutions, deal with large numbers of customers who are limited to doing business with institutions in their local areas. Important banking markets are characterized as local; they are approximated by "cities," "towns," "counties," and "standard metropolitan statistical areas" (SMSAs).

Limiting new charters tends to reduce the number of banks in local markets and increases the proportion of market assets or liabilities (for example, deposits) accounted for by the largest. Concentration, as represented by the percentage of market deposits held by the largest bank or largest two or three banks, is a characteristic of market structure that has been found to be directly associated with prices charged for banking services. In addition, restriction on new charters represents an important barrier to entry. High barriers, particularly in highly concentrated markets, permit banks to charge higher prices for their services.[23] Finally, the needs test itself (at least as characterized by Edwards and Edwards) implies that bankers might find it profitable to operate in inefficient ways. For example, it is generally acknowledged that many bankers were lethargic and inefficient in the conduct of their business for several decades following 1936. This apparent exchange of potential profit for a leisurely way of life might be partially explained as an attempt to persuade bank regulators that new entry is not warranted.

### The Effects of Concentration on Interest Rates

The level of concentration in local markets is determined by a number of factors. In addition to entry policies, concentration is affected by market

---

[21]He obtains this estimate by multiplying the estimated value of $k$ ($-.579$) by the number of existing banks in each year and cumulating. Edwards and Edwards object to this procedure, arguing that $-.579$ should have been multiplied by the number of banks that would have existed in the absence of regulation rather than the number in existence. Their recalculation yields a total of 2,378 additional banks that would have received new charters in the 1936–1962 period on the basis of Peltzman's analysis. See Edwards and Edwards, "Measuring the Effectiveness of Regulation," 451.

[22]Edwards and Edwards, "Measuring the Effectiveness of Regulation," 455.

[23]Barriers to entry are typically defined as structural characteristics of markets determining the extent to which established firms can maintain prices above competitive levels without attracting entry by new firms. Setting prices at such entry-discouraging levels is termed *limit pricing*. See Joe Bain, *Barriers to New Competition*, Harvard University Press, Cambridge, Mass. 1956. Regulatory barriers to entry in banking assume considerable importance because of high concentration in local markets and because other economic barriers are probably not very high. See Bernard Shull and Paul M. Horvitz, "Branch Banking and the Structures of Competition," *The National Banking Review* (March 1964), 305–312; and Gerald Hanweck, "Bank Entry into Local Markets: An Empirical Assessment of the Degree of Potential Competition via New Bank Formation," *Proceedings of a Conference on Bank Structure and Competition*, Federal Reserve Bank of Chicago, 1971, pp. 161–172.

size, economies of scale, and public policy toward mergers and acquisitions.

Until the 1960s, bank mergers were largely unregulated with regard to their impact on competition. A wave of mergers in the 1950s, including mergers of large banks in the same local areas (horizontal mergers), persuaded Congress to pass the Banker Merger Act of 1960. The act required the federal banking agencies to consider the competitive effects of mergers before approving them.[24]

Table 31-2 shows the average number of banks and the average percentage of deposits held by the largest banks in metropolitan areas in 1962 and 1974. The metropolitan areas are located in those states permitting statewide branching and those prohibiting branching (allowing unit banking); they are classified by population size. Numbers of banks rise and concentration declines as market size, measured by population, increases. Numbers of banks are generally higher and concentration lower in unit-banking than in statewide-branching states, though not too much should be made of this cross-section comparison.[25] Everywhere, however, there are relatively few banks and high concentration. In other words, the markets can, for the most part, be characterized as oligopolistic.

A recent comprehensive view of local-banking market concentration is provided in Table 31-3. Here concentration is measured by the Herfindahl Index and its numbers equivalent.[26] The average metropolitan area in 1973 had a Herfindahl Index of 0.21 or the equivalent of close to five banks of equal size. (Non-metropolitan-area markets, as

shown in Table 31-3, are considerably more concentrated.)

A number of banking studies in the past fifteen years have supported the hypothesis that concentration is a determinant of bank "prices." Typical findings have shown that higher concentration in local markets is associated with higher interest rates on business loans, consumer loans, and mortgages, with lower interest rates paid on time and savings deposits, and higher service charges on demand deposits. Most of the early studies found the magnitude of the concentration effect on "prices" to be small. For example, three prominent studies found that a 10 percent increase in local area deposit concentration was associated with a 4–8 percent increase in interest rates on business loans.[27] More recent studies, in attempting to remedy some of the deficiencies of the older studies, have found statistically significant relationships of greater magnitude.[28]

## The Effect of Regulation on Operational Efficiency

Operational efficiency concerns the ability of individual firms to produce at the lowest possible costs in the long run. The ability to do so normally requires a firm to achieve a size above some minimum level. The long-run average total cost curve for the industry reflects the minimum optimum size for firms in any industry and the rate at which costs change as such size is approached. A major factor determining the shape of the long-run cost curve is real economies of scale.

Economies of scale will, in part, determine the number of firms that can efficiently exist. At an extreme, substantial economies of scale may preclude sufficient numbers to provide competition.

[24]See Bernard Shull and Paul M. Horvitz, "The Bank Merger Act of 1960: A Decade After," *The Antitrust Bulletin* (Winter 1971), 859–889.

[25]For an analysis of the effects of branching laws on concentration, see Bernard Shull, "Multiple Office Banking and Competition: A Review of the Literature," *Compendium of Issues Relating to Branching by Financial Institutions,* Subcommittee of Financial Institutions, Committee on Banking, Housing and Urban Affairs, U.S. Senate, Washington, D.C., October 1976.

[26]The Herfindahl Index is defined as the sum of the squares of the market shares of each bank in the market, and approaches 0 at low concentrations and 1 at high concentrations. It will vary, not only with the proportion of deposits held by an arbitrary number of large banks in the market, but with the relative distribution of deposits among all banks in the market. The numbers equivalent is the number of banks of equal size yielding the calculated value of $H$.

[27]Franklin R. Edwards, "Concentration in Banking and Its Effects on Business Loan Rates," *The Review of Economics and Statistics* (1964), 294–300; Almarin Phillips, "Evidence on Concentration in Banking Markets and Interest Rates," *Federal Reserve Bulletin* (June 1967), 916–926; and Donald Jacobs, *Business Loan Costs and Bank Market Structure,* Occasional Paper 115, National Bureau of Economic Research, Columbia University Press, New York, 1971.

[28]See, for example, Arnold Heggestad and John J. Mingo, "Prices, Nonprices and Concentration in Commercial Banking," *The Journal of Money, Credit and Banking* (February 1976), 107–117.

**Table 31-2  Number of Banks and Concentration in SMSAs, Classified by Population, in Statewide-Branching and Unit-Banking States, June 1962 and June 1974**

| Population and Branch Law Classifications | June 1962 | | June 1974 | | Change June 1962–June 1974 | |
|---|---|---|---|---|---|---|
| | No. of Banks | Percentage of Deposits Held by Largest | No. of Banks | Percentage of Deposits Held by Largest | No. of Banks | Percentage of Deposits Held by Largest |
| Statewide branching | | | | | | |
| 50,000–99,999 | 4.8 | 53.0% | 6.7 | 41.9% | + 1.9 | −11.1% |
| 100,000–499,999 | 7.4 | 47.1 | 10.3 | 37.0 | + 2.9 | −10.1 |
| 500,000–999,999 | 12.4 | 44.7 | 19.8 | 37.5 | + 7.4 | − 7.2 |
| 1,000,000 and over | 27.6 | 37.3 | 36.6 | 33.8 | + 9.0 | − 3.5 |
| Unit banking | | | | | | |
| 50,000–99,999 | 6.2 | 42.1 | 7.4 | 38.7 | + 1.2 | − 3.4 |
| 100,000–499,999 | 15.0 | 34.5 | 19.6 | 25.5 | + 4.6 | − 9.0 |
| 500,000–999,999 | 38.8 | 27.5 | 56.0 | 20.3 | +17.2 | − 7.2 |
| 1,000,000 and over | 105.7 | 28.0 | 171.5 | 17.2 | +65.8 | −10.8 |

Source: Bernard Shull, "Multiple Office Banking and Competition: A Review of the Literature," *Compendium of Issues Relating to Branching by Financial Institutions,* Subcommittee on Institutions, Committee on Banking, Housing and Urban Affairs, U.S. Senate, Washington, D.C., October 1976, p. 134.

**Table 31-3  Cumulative Distribution of Concentration Levels in U.S. Banking Markets[a]**

| Percentage of Markets with Concentration Less Than Indicated Herfindahl Index | SMSAs | | Non-SMSA Counties | |
|---|---|---|---|---|
| | Herfindahl Index | Numbers Equivalent | Herfindahl Index | Numbers Equivalent |
| 10 | .1079 | 9.3 | .1017 | 5.0 |
| 20 | 1427 | 7.0 | .2536 | 3.9 |
| 30 | .1649 | 6.1 | .2969 | 3.4 |
| 40 | .1899 | 5.3 | .3472 | 2.9 |
| 50 | .2121 | 4.7 | .3858 | 2.6 |
| 60 | .2359 | 4.3 | .4492 | 2.2 |
| 70 | .2647 | 3.8 | .5130 | 1.9 |
| 90 | .3455 | 2.9 | 1.0000 | 1.0 |
| 100 | .5759 | 1.7 | 1.0000 | 1.0 |
| Mean | .2220 | 4.5 | .4587 | 2.2 |
| Median | .2121 | 4.7 | .3858 | 2.2 |
| Mode | not unique | | 1.0000 | 1.0 |

[a]Based on 1973 total deposits.

Source: Arnold Heggestad and John Mingo, "The Competitive Condition of U.S. Banking Markets and the Impact of Structural Form," *The Journal of Finance* (June 1977), 656.

New entry may be effectively foreclosed. With only a few producers, noncompetitive behavior is likely and, under such conditions, neither customers nor the economy would fully benefit from the efficiency achieved.

As has been noted, a number of legal and regulatory restrictions have impeded the growth of depository institutions. Laws that prevent branch banking, restrict mergers and acquisitions, and limit lending activity to narrow geographic areas all affect the ability of institutions to grow. In evaluating such restrictions, it is important to consider their impact on the ability of firms to achieve minimum optimum size, and the effect on costs at smaller sizes.

There have been a number of empirical studies of long-run costs for depository institutions.[29] The

[29] For reviews of the literature, see Gary Gilbert and William Longbrake, "The Effects of Branching by Fi-

most persuasive have utilized "direct costs" for separable functions: the functions of providing demand deposit services, time deposits, business loans, real estate loans, and so forth. They have used multiple regression techniques to relate functional costs to a "physical" measure of functional output—the number of accounts. Other characteristics of the accounts affecting costs are included as independent variables to provide for "output homogeneity," as are measures of factor prices and branching structure. Indirect costs associated with administration, business development, and occupancy are analyzed separately.[30]

The investigation of statistical cost curves along functional lines, however, prevents easy generalization. Economies of scale in commercial banks have been found for demand deposits, instalment loans, business loans, and real estate loans. For example, Bell and Murphy found that a 10 percent increase in the total number of demand deposits increased direct costs by only 9.1 percent. But economies were not found for some other functions, including time deposits, administration, and occupancy.

In the past savings and loan associations have been far more specialized in their functions than commercial banks, providing only two major services, savings accounts and real estate loans. Benston used the average number of loans serviced, the number of loans made, and the average number of savings accounts as alternative indices of output.[31] His results were close to identical with each

measure. He found that a 10 percent increase in output was associated, on average, with about 9.2 percent increase in expenses.

The finding of economies of scale for both commercial banks and S&Ls, and the existence of large numbers of small institutions, would seem to indicate extensive suboptimal operations. However, no such straightforward conclusion is warranted. Among the factors held constant by the statistical analyses is branching structure. Bell and Murphy found additional costs associated with the number of branch offices a bank had. For their sample of banks, the additional costs of branching fully offset the economies of larger numbers of accounts. Consequently, it could not be inferred that the combination of, say, ten independent unit banks into a single branch-banking organization with ten offices would reduce average costs, even though the resulting firm was considerably larger than any of the individual banks that composed it. Benston also found that branching involved diseconomies for savings and loan associations, but in Benston's sample these diseconomies did not offset economies associated with larger size.

Recently, additional light has been thrown on the branch–unit bank efficiency argument.[32] But no definitive statements on the advantages of branching versus unit banking have emerged or, indeed, seem likely to emerge. It has been noted that:

In general, production of financial services which are not easily centralized in the main office [for example, demand deposits] is less costly in unit banks. However, production of services centralized in the main office [for example, business loans] is less costly in branch banks.[33]

It seems reasonable to conclude that law and regulation, particularly those laws restricting branching, have impeded operational efficiency in varying degrees depending on what kinds of functions depository institutions undertake. Thus, there is no

nancial Institutions on Competition, Productive Efficiency and Stability: An Examination of the Evidence," Part II, *Journal of Bank Research* (Winter 1974), 298–307; George Benston, "Economies of Scale of Financial Institutions," *Journal of Money, Credit and Banking* (May 1972), 312–341; and Jack Guttentag, "Branch Banking: A Summary of the Issues and the Evidence," *Compendium of Issues Relating to Branching by Financial Institutions,* Subcommittee on Financial Institutions, Committee on Banking, Housing and Urban Affairs, U.S. Senate, Washington, D.C., October 1976.

[30]George Benston, "Economies of Scale and Marginal Costs in Banking Operations," *The National Banking Review* (June 1965), 507–549; F. W. Bell and N. B. Murphy, *Costs in Commercial Banking: A Quantitative Analysis of Bank Behavior and Its Relation to Bank Regulation,* Research Report No. 41, Federal Reserve Bank of Boston, 1968.

[31]George Benston, "Cost of Operations and Economies of Scale in Saving and Loan Associations," in *Study of*

*the Saving and Loan Industry,* Federal Home Loan Bank Board, Washington, D.C., 1970, pp. 971–1209.

[32]See Guttentag, "Branch Banking"; also Gilbert and Longbrake, "The Effects of Branching by Financial Institutions on Competition, Protective Efficiency and Stability," for discussion of recent contributions.

[33]Gilbert and Longbrake, "The Effects of Branching by Financial Institutions on Competition, Protective Efficiency, and Stability," 302.

simple way to determine *the extent* to which restrictions have prevented banks from growing to optimum size. Since, however, the mix of services offered by depository institutions is determined largely by customer demands and competition, there is a presumption against any restriction that prevents institutions from attaining whatever branching structure, office, and firm size they perceive as optimal.

## Summary

As indicated by the studies we have reviewed, regulation has had observable and quantifiable anticompetitive effects. The needs test has significantly reduced the numbers of competitors. Fewer numbers and higher concentration have resulted in higher "prices" for the services provided. It is also likely that branching restrictions have had adverse effects on operational efficiency. We now turn to recent developments that have tended to offset these effects.

## The Revival of Competition and Competitive Policies

Competition between and among depository institutions revived in the 1950s and 1960s before government policies began to promote it. It revived because relatively unregulated institutions and markets responded to profitable opportunities denied to the more regulated ones. Competition intensified, encouraged the circumvention of regulation, and placed pressure on regulators to liberalize restrictions.

From the point of view of commercial banks, competitive pressures developed in the late 1950s—from savings and loan associations whose rates on deposits were not then regulated and from rising rates on U.S. Treasury securities sold in open markets. In 1957, and over the next several years, increases in Regulation Q maximums were made necessary by the willingness of S&Ls to pay higher rates to savers and the growing sophistication of business in substituting higher-yielding Treasury bills for bank deposits. It is worth noting that these developments were forerunners of a series of institutional adaptations to regulation which, in turn, have tended to undermine regulation itself.

A number of procompetitive policy changes interacted with the revival of competition in the early 1960s and contributed to the changes taking place. These included the granting of more new commercial bank charters; new controls over horizontal mergers and acquisitions; new controls over market-extension acquisitions; and new policies to support geographic and product market diversification.

## More New Charters

Between 1950 and 1961 an average of roughly 90 commercial banks per year were granted new charters. Then, in 1962, the rate of new charters increased dramatically: to 179 in 1962, to 300 in 1963, and to 335 in 1964. The substantial increase reflected a more liberal policy on the part of a new Comptroller of the Currency, James Saxon. The 200 new national bank charters in 1964 alone were close to the number granted during the entire decade of the 1950s.

## Restrictions on Bank Acquisitions

The Bank Holding Company Act of 1956 required the Federal Reserve Board to evaluate the competitive effects of multiple-bank holding company formations and acquisitions before approving them. The Bank Merger Act of 1960 required the Federal Reserve, the Comptroller of the Currency, and the Federal Deposit Insurance Corporation to evaluate the competitive effects of bank mergers. In 1963, the Supreme Court held that bank mergers were subject to Section 7 of the Clayton Antitrust Act, so that even mergers approved by the banking agencies could be challenged by the Justice Department.[34] Mergers of other depository institutions became subject to antitrust considerations also. In 1966 Congress amended both the Bank Holding Company Act and the Bank Merger Act to clarify the relationship between them and the antitrust laws. Among other things, the 1966 amendments established an identical competitive standard to be applied by the three federal bank regulatory agencies in evaluating mergers and acquisitions by incorporating language from Section 7 of the Clayton Act.

[34]*United States* v. *Philadelphia National Bank,* 374 U.S. 321 (1963).

Under current law, a bank regulatory agency may not approve, under any circumstances, acquisitions that would violate Section 2 of the Sherman Antitrust Act (the "monopolizing" provision). It may not approve acquisitions that violate Section 1 of the Sherman Antitrust Act (that "would be in restraint of trade") or Section 7 of the Clayton Act (that "may be substantially to lessen competition or to tend to create a monopoly") unless "the anticompetitive effects . . . are clearly outweighed in the public interest by the probable effect of the transaction in meeting the convenience and needs of the community to be served."[35] Even if an acquisition is approved by the responsible bank regulatory agency, the Justice Department may bring suit under the Clayton and/or Sherman Acts.[36]

The enforcement of these laws contributed significantly to a decline in the number of horizontal mergers among large banks. It seems also to have contributed to reductions in local market concentration.[37]

## Potential Competition and Deconcentration

Restrictions on horizontal mergers can help prevent increases in concentration but cannot bring about reductions. Permitting established banks and bank holding companies to enter new local market areas could conceivably bring about reductions.

New entry by established banks, however, has been severely constrained by branch-banking and holding company laws. Even where laws are permissive, geographic expansion must hold promise of profit for banks to undertake it.

In the 1960s several states altered their banking laws so as to permit statewide operations by holding companies.[38] In other states, bank holding companies began to take advantage of permissive laws.

In several decisions regarding bank holding companies in the 1960s, the Federal Reserve Board, with sole authority under the Bank Holding Company Act, developed a policy aimed at reducing concentration in local areas in those states where holding companies embarked on statewide expansion.[39] The Board denied formations and acquisitions that involved combinations of large banks in separate markets. It argued that these large banks were potential competitors, and that their combination would substantially lessen *potential* competition. The express purpose was to require large, actual or potential, statewide banking organizations to enter new local areas *de novo* or by acquiring small, rather than large, local banks, by what has been called "foothold acquisitions." Such foothold acquisitions, it was hypothesized, would result in deconcentration, while entry by large acquisition could support existing levels of concentration. There is some empirical evidence that the Board's policy worked to reduce concentration in local market areas.[40]

The Justice Department undertook a similar policy with regard to potential competition. However, the department has repeatedly lost potential competition cases in the courts.[41] In 1977 the Federal Reserve expressly modified its own policy, indicating that it would no longer be as restrictive in permitting combinations of large banks in separate local market areas.[42] More recently, however, the

---

[35]This "justification" has been interpreted by the Supreme Court in a restrictive fashion in *United States* v. *Third National Bank of Nashville,* 300 U.S. 171 (1968). The Court held, in effect, that the banks must show that there is no less anticompetitive alternative that would yield the same benefits to the community. The Court stated: "This test does not demand the impossible or unreasonable. It merely insists that before a merger injurious to the public interest is approved, a showing be made that the gain expected from this merger cannot reasonably be expected through other means."

[36]If the department does not act within thirty days, it is thereafter barred from entering suit except under Section 2 of the Sherman Act. If the department does sue within thirty days, the banks may not consummate the merger until the suit is disposed of by the court.

[37]Shull and Horvitz, "The Bank Merger Act of 1960," 879.

[38]Notably New York and Virginia.

[39]See the following orders under the Bank Holding Company Act: *Morgan New York State Corporation to Become a Bank Holding Company,* 48 *Federal Reserve Bulletin* 567 (1962); *B T New York Corporation to Acquire Liberty National Bank,* 54 *Federal Reserve Bulletin* 225 (1968).

[40]Bernard Shull, "Multiple Office Banking and Competition: A Review of the Literature."

[41]See, for example, *U.S.* v. *Marine Bancorporation,* 418 U.S. 602 (1974); and *U.S.* v. *Connecticut National Bank,* 418 U.S. 656 (1974).

[42]Thus, see the Federal Reserve's decision in the merger of Texas Commerce Bancshares with the Ban-Capital Finance Corporation, 63 *Federal Reserve Bulletin* 504 (1977).

Federal Reserve has fluctuated. In 1980 the Justice Department lost two additional potential competition cases, one in New Jersey and one in Utah, at the District Court level.

### Product Diversification

Along with permitting more new charters in the early 1960s, the Comptroller of the Currency embarked on a liberal reinterpretation of the National Banking Act, permitting national banks to engage in activities previously thought to be prohibited. These included the leasing of equipment, certain insurance activities, the underwriting of municipal revenue bonds, the offering of data processing services, and the offering of travel agency services.[43]

Product diversification by large national banks placed pressure on state-chartered banks to obtain similar powers and on other regulatory agencies to reinterpret their own restrictions. The federal-state dualism that permeates the regulation of depository institutions makes it possible for banks to switch from state to national charters (and vice versa); a number of large state-chartered banks did become national banks in the 1960s to take advantage of the Comptroller's interpretations.[44]

The offering of new products by national banks brought them into competition with nonbanking firms. Leasing firms, insurance agencies, data processing companies, travel agencies, and others strenuously objected to the new competition; and a number of legal actions were undertaken to forestall bank expansion into new lines of activity.

Commercial banks ultimately found a less vulnerable avenue for product diversification in the bank holding company. The Bank Holding Company Act of 1956 required multiple-bank holding companies to register with the Board of Governors of the Federal Reserve System and imposed severe legal restrictions on noncommercial banking activities. However, one-bank holding companies had been exempted from regulation in 1956; Congress had found that they were typically (though not invariably) small concerns holding small banks, among other properties, and not important enough to require regulation.

In 1968 and in 1969, however, many of the largest banks in the nation organized one-bank holding companies to hold their banks' stock; by April 1970 there were over 1,100 such companies holding banks with close to $150 billion in deposits, about 35 percent of total deposits of all insured commercial banks in the United States. (There were, in 1977, close to 1,800.) Because of their unregulated status, these one-bank holding companies were, prior to 1971, free from regulation governing the acquisition of noncommercial banking firms. Through noncommercial bank affiliates, they could also enter towns and cities outside the branching areas dictated by state law and outside the states in which the banks were located.

An amendment to the Bank Holding Company Act adopted in December 1970 brought one-bank holding companies under Federal Reserve Board regulation. They were restricted to the same non-banking activities permitted multiple-bank holding companies, *but* the range of activities permitted all holding companies was liberalized. The Board was given authority to establish activities in which bank holding companies could engage and to permit specific entry into such permissible lines by acquisition or *de novo*.

Under the law, in order to be permissible an activity must be (a) "closely related to banking or managing or controlling banks," *and* (b) "a proper incident thereto." To qualify as "closely related to banking," the activity itself, or a similar one, must have been engaged in by banks, or be integrally related to services that banks do provide. To be "a proper incident thereto," the activity must pass a "net public benefits" test. The Board would have to conclude that likely public benefits deriving from bank holding company entry—benefits in the form of increased competition, gains in efficiency, or greater public convenience—more than offset the likely adverse effects stemming from increased concentration, less competition, or diminished bank soundness.

The Board has approved a substantial number of activities and denied a number of others. Table 31-4

---

[43]National banks are expressly permitted by law to receive deposits and lend money and to exercise "all such incidental powers as shall be necessary to carry on the business of banking." Permissible activities for national banks were expanded through a liberal interpretation of the "incidental powers" clause. See Howard Hackley, "Our Baffling Banking System," *Virginia Law Review,* Parts I and II, (May-June 1966), 565–632, 771–830.

[44]A notable example was the conversion of the Chase Manhattan Bank from a state to a national charter in 1965.

summarizes approved and denied activities as of March 1977.

It is of particular interest that the Board denied "saving and loan associations" as a permissible activity for bank holding companies. The Board stated that S&Ls were, in fact, "closely related to banking," but that they were not "a proper incident thereto." Bank holding company acquisitions of S&Ls did not pass the Board's public benefit test.

As indicated in the previous section, other depository institutions have also expanded their services, increasingly becoming more like one another. With the acquisition of demand-deposit-like "third party payment powers" and more liberalized lending powers under DMCA, they have become more like commercial banks.

## Summary

The past twenty years have seen the revival of public policy aimed at supporting and promoting competition, particularly among commercial banks. Freer entry by new and established banks, passage of the Bank Merger and Holding Company Acts, enforcement of the antitrust laws, and product diversification have combined to intensify competition among commercial banks and between banks and other depository institutions. In fact, bank holding company expansion has brought banks into competition with a host of financial (and some nonfinancial) institutions in distant geographic areas well beyond those to which state law has limited them.

## Current Issues

The revival of competition and the changing regulatory framework, along with the recent development of a new electronic payments technology, has raised a series of interrelated public-policy issues. This section considers a number of them.

### Interest Payments on Deposits

Interest restrictions on time deposits, initiated in 1933, have in recent years been modified in purpose, character, and effect; and, as noted previously, they are scheduled to be phased out by 1986. Nevertheless, it seems worthwhile to review the issue of ceilings on deposits, since it seems likely that the phase-out will continue to be controversial.

After 1957, when the Regulation Q maximums were raised for the first time in twenty years, maximums were changed frequently, extended to savings banks and S&Ls, eliminated on large denomination ($100,000 and over) CDs, and applied to negotiable orders of withdrawal (NOW accounts). In this period, the Federal Reserve also, on occasion, managed Regulation Q so as to restrict deposit flows to large banks during periods of inflation; that is, Regulation Q has served as a tool of monetary policy. The striking difference between the 1936–1956 regulation and the elaborated version in early 1980 before DMCA is shown in Table 31-5.

Unlike Regulation Q for time deposits, the prohibition of interest payments on demand deposits has not been modified since 1933, although, as we have seen, DMCA authorized a number of demand-deposit-like accounts (such as NOW accounts) nationwide beginning January 1, 1981. Nevertheless, commercial banks have used other means to compete for demand deposits. Deposit balances of businesses have been used as payment for lines of credit. Service charges on demand deposits have been reduced or eliminated. Branch offices have proliferated, where possible, substituting convenience of location for monetary return to depositors.

There was also a tendency to eradicate the distinction between time and demand deposits even before DMCA. Banks undertook, with the acquiescence of regulators, the rapid shifting of funds (either by telephone or automatically) from interest-bearing savings accounts to non-interest-bearing checking accounts. And NOW accounts, which function like demand deposits and pay interest like time deposits, were developed by thrift institutions in New England.[45]

[45]In June 1972, state-chartered mutual savings banks in Massachusetts, with state approval, began offering NOW accounts and, in September 1972, the practice spread to savings banks in New Hampshire. By 1974 all depository institutions in Massachusetts and New Hampshire (except credit unions) were authorized by Congress to offer NOW accounts. And, in February 1976, federal legislation authorizing NOW accounts in other New England states (Connecticut, Maine, Rhode Island, and Vermont) became effective. Authorization for NOW accounts was extended to New York State in 1978 and to New Jersey in 1979 before DMCA in 1980.

**Table 31-4   Status of Bank Holding Company Nonbanking Activities Under Section 4(c)(8) (as of March 11, 1977)**

*Activities Approved by the Board*

1. Dealer in bankers' acceptances[b]
2. Mortgage banking[b]
3. Finance companies[b]
   a. Consumer
   b. Sales
   c. Commercial
4. Credit card issuance[b]
5. Factoring company[b]
6. Industrial banking
7. Servicing loans
8. Trust company[b]
9. Investment advising[b]
10. General economic information[b]
11. Portfolio investment advice[b]
12. Full payment leasing[b]
    a. Personal property
    b. Real property
13. Community welfare investments[b]
14. Bookkeeping and data processing services[b]
15. Insurance agent or broker-credit extensions[b]
16. Underwriting credit life and credit accident and health insurance
17. Courier service[b]
18. Management consulting to nonaffiliate banks[b]
19. Issuance of traveler's checks[b]
20. Bullion broker[a]
21. Land escrow services[a,b]
22. Issuing money orders and variable denominated payment instruments[a,b,d]

*Activities Denied by the Board*

1. Equity funding (combined sale of mutual funds and insurance)
2. Underwriting general life insurance
3. Real estate brokerage[b]
4. Land development
5. Real estate syndication
6. General management consulting
7. Property management
8. Nonfull-payout leasing[a]
9. Commodity trading[a]
10. Issuance and sale of short-term debt obligations ("thrift notes")[a]
11. Travel agency[a,b]
12. Savings and loan associations[a]

*Activities Pending Before the Board*

1. Armored car services[b]
2. Underwriting mortgage guarantee insurance[c]
3. Underwriting and dealing in U.S. government and certain municipal securities[a,b]
4. Underwriting the deductible part of bankers' blanket bond insurance (withdrawn)[a]
5. Management consulting to nonaffiliated, depository type, financial institutions[a,b]

[a]Added to the list since January 1, 1975.
[b]Activities permissible to national banks.
[c]These were found to be "closely related to banking," but the proposed acquisitions were denied by the Board of Governors as part of its "go slow" policy.
[d]To be decided on a case-by-case basis.

Source: Dale S. Drum, *Economic Perspectives,* Federal Reserve Bank of Chicago (March-April 1977), 14.

**Table 31-5  Regulation Q Comparison, 1936–1980 (percentages per annum)**

*January 1, 1936 to December 31, 1956*

| Type and Maturity of Deposits | Commercial Banks and Mutual Savings Banks |
|---|---|
| Savings deposits | 2½ |
| Other time deposits payable | |
| 6 months or more | 2½ |
| 90 days to 6 months | 2 |
| Less than 90 days | 1 |

*January 1, 1980*

| Type and Maturity of Deposits | Commercial Banks | S&Ls and Mutual Savings Banks |
|---|---|---|
| Savings deposits | 5 | 5½ |
| NOW accounts[a] | 5 | 5 |
| Time deposits (fixed ceilings) | | |
| 8 years or more[b] | 7½ | 8 |
| 6–8 years[b] | 7½ | 7¾ |
| 4–6 years[b] | 7¼ | 7½ |
| 2½–4 years[b] | 6½ | 6¾ |
| 1–2½ years[b] | 6 | 6½ |
| 90 days–1 year | 5½ | 5¾ |
| 30–89 days | 5¼ | — |
| Governmental units (all maturities) | 7¾ | 7¾ |
| Denominations of $100,000 or more (all maturities) | Ceiling suspended in mid-1973 | |

[a]Permitted in New England States as of Feb. 27, 1976.
[b]Minimum amounts for deposits may be specified.

Source: *Federal Reserve Bulletin*, various issues.

The interest-payment restrictions did not meet their original purpose to prevent competition for deposits among commercial banks. Nor did they eliminate competition for deposits between commercial banks and thrift institutions, an apparent purpose of the Interest Rate Adjustment Act of 1966, which gave the FHLBB authority to establish Regulation Q-type maximums. Competition was suppressed and rechanneled, but not eliminated. Where close substitutes for deposits existed (as in the case of commercial paper and Treasury securities for time deposits), the restrictions had to be relaxed or abandoned. Even NOW accounts and other interest-bearing substitutes for demand deposits received increasing competition in 1979 and 1980 from the explosive growth of money-market mutual fund drafts made payable to third parties.

There is little evidence to support the contention that banks failed in the pre-1933 period because of ruinous competition for deposits that resulted in their reaching out for high-yield, excessively risky assets.[46] The adoption of these pricing restrictions might be viewed as an industry attempt at self-regulation.[47]

However the purpose of these restrictions is evaluated, their consequences were significant. While they diverted rather than eliminated competition, the diversion had unfortunate distributive and allocative impacts. The elimination of Regulation Q maximums on large, but not on small, CDs discriminated against small depositors, who were already adversely affected by the oligopolistic structures in many local market areas. The development of circuitous intermediaries, like the money-market mutual fund, to finesse these discriminatory restrictions by pooling the funds of small depositors for investment in non-price-regulated substitutes is difficult to justify in terms of effort and resources. The elimination of service charges on demand deposits in lieu of interest payments, moreover, eliminated the incentive for customers to economize in the writing of checks. As a result, checking services tend to be overutilized.[48] Undoubtedly, depository intermediaries will be faced with a variety of new kinds of competitive problems following nationwide introduction of NOW accounts in 1981 and the scheduled phase-out of all interest rate ceilings on deposits by 1986.

## Bank Failure

From the mid-1940s to the early 1970s, relatively few commercial banks failed—no more than ten in any one year. These few failures were entirely confined to small banks (with deposits under $100 million) whose difficulties typically stemmed from mismanagement and fraud. While the number of failures did not increase to unusual levels in the 1970s, the size of the banks that failed did.[49]

In 1972 the Bank of the Commonwealth of Detroit, with about $1 billion in deposits, was kept from failure only through the financial assistance of the FDIC. In 1973 the U.S. National Bank of San Diego, also with about $1 billion in deposits, was declared insolvent. In October 1974, the fast-shrinking Franklin National Bank, in New York, with about $3 billion in deposits, also failed. In 1975 the Security National Bank of New York, with over $1 billion in deposits, was merged to avert failure, and in 1980 the First Pennsylvania Bank, the largest in Philadelphia, received FDIC assistance to prevent failure. In addition, the "problem lists" of the federal banking agencies, which became known to the public in the late 1970s, revealed that a number of other important banks were in serious condition.

The course of events leading to these failures is reasonably clear. Between 1970 and 1973, commercial bank assets increased by a remarkable 15 percent, faster than real GNP and faster than that of any other financial institution. Expansion through holding companies into new and unfamiliar activities and into new geographic areas was also rapid.

[46] See George Benston, "Interest Payments on Demand Deposits and Bank Investment Behavior," *Journal of Political Economy* (October 1964), 431–439; see also, Albert Cox, Jr., "Regulation of Interest on Bank Deposits," *Michigan Business Studies* (1966).

[47] See Charles M. Linke, "The Evolution of Interest Rate Regulation on Commercial Bank Deposits in the United States," *The National Banking Review* (June 1966), 449–469.

[48] This economic efficiency argument is spelled out in "The Impact of the Payment of Interest on Demand Deposits," A Study of the Staff of the Board of Governors of the Federal Reserve System, Washington, D.C., January 31, 1977, pp. 34–38.

[49] For background discussion, see Paul M. Horvitz, "Bank Risks in the New International Financial Structures—Lessons from Bank Failures," in *The Emerging International Order and the Banking System,* ed. Yair Ahoroui, University Publishing Projects, Tel Aviv, 1975.

The issuance of holding company debt to finance subsidiaries also expanded. Commercial bank expansion far outpaced additions to capital.

In 1973, and thereafter, the economy suffered a number of shocks, including the unprecedented oil embargo by the OPEC cartel, the surge in oil prices, widely fluctuating exchange rates, a serious business recession, major business bankruptcies, the failure of many highly leveraged real estate investment trusts, and the near bankruptcy of New York City. Substantial loan losses were incurred by many commercial banks.

Bank problems revived pressures for more intensive supervision and regulation. In mid-1974, the Federal Reserve strongly urged banks to improve their capital positions and backed its views through a "go slow" policy for bank holding companies. It virtually ceased to expand permissible lines and turned down many applications for acquisitions because of dissatisfaction with the banks' financial or managerial capabilities. A notable case was its denial of the application of the giant BankAmerica Corporation to join with Allstate Insurance (a subsidiary of Sears Roebuck) in owning and operating a general insurance underwriting company in Europe (Allstate International S.A., Zurich, Switzerland).[50] Among the reasons given for the denial was that "the present capital position of the applicant is somewhat lower than what the Board would consider appropriate in light of its recent asset growth."[51]

In March 1977, the Chairman of the Board warned that

> companies whose asset composition, capital or liquidity raises doubts, ought now to know that the Board will be extremely skeptical of proposals that divert financial or managerial resources to new undertakings.[52]

Some economists accepted the failures of the post-1972 period as a more or less "normal" experience in a competitive system, a period in which the unwise and incompetent were shaken out. They observed that the failure rate was still quite low, and that runs on "sound" banks had not occurred even when large banks failed.[53] Other economists were more concerned. They argued that runs had been narrowly averted in the Franklin National failure by the extraordinary financial support provided by the Federal Reserve, thereby permitting large depositors to withdraw their funds prior to failure, and that such support provided de facto insurance to large depositors.[54]

Such a policy seemed to imply that the bank regulatory agencies would not permit the largest multibillion dollar banks to fail and would make large banks more immune to market and regulatory pressures for caution. Also, this policy would not be consistent with a *competitive* banking system because it gave the largest banks a significant advantage over all others.[55]

Regardless of the underlying economic causes, the proximate cause of bank failure can always be ascribed to mismanagement. A careful study by the Comptroller General of the United States (General Accounting Office) did find this cause to be important in the failures of the 1970s. It reported that most were caused by "bad management practices." Such practices included improper loans to officers, directors, or owners; poor quality loans made to others; and general managerial incompetence. A number of cases involved embezzlement or other crimes.[56] An extreme case was the failure of the U.S. National Bank of San Diego, which examiners of the Comptroller of the Currency characterized as the result of "massive fraud."

In addition to the renewed emphasis on capital adequacy, the regulatory agencies reappraised their examining procedures. If, in fact, mismanagement was the problem, it would seem that better supervision and examination might be the solution. Among other things, new "early warning systems"

[50]See *Federal Reserve Bulletin* (July 1974), 517–519.
[51]Ibid., 519.
[52]Statement of Arthur F. Burns, Committee on Banking, Housing and Urban Affairs, U.S. Senate, Washington, D.C., March 10, 1977.

[53]For the general principles underlying this view, see A. Dale Tussing, "The Case for Bank Failure," *Journal of Law and Economics* (1969), 129–147.
[54]Franklin National had deposit runoffs of about $1.8 billion between May and September 1974. These runoffs were made possible by Federal Reserve loans to Franklin prior to failure.
[55]See, for example, the statement of Hyman Minsky, Committee on Banking, Housing and Urban Affairs, U.S. Senate, March 11, 1977; and Thomas Mayer, "Should Large Banks Be Allowed to Fail?" *Journal of Financial and Quantitative Analysis* (November 1975), 603–610.
[56]*Federal Supervision of State and National Banks*, A Study by the Comptroller General of the United States, January 1977.

were developed in an attempt to detect problems before they became serious and to help focus the limited examining resources on the banks in real difficulty.[57] Dissatisfaction was also expressed with the coordination among the agencies in cases of failure; in many cases, all three banking agencies were involved in the process that led to declarations of insolvency.[58] Finally, the Senate Banking Committee undertook oversight responsibilities for the condition of the banking system, scheduling annual hearings on the subject.[59] As mentioned earlier, FIRA created the Federal Financial Institutions Examination Council to coordinate efforts toward improving examination procedures.

## Electronic Fund Transfer Systems (EFTS) and the Payments Mechanism

EFTS incorporate a number of electronic devices and systems serving different but potentially interrelated functions. These include customer-bank communication terminals (CBCTs), which may do no more than dispense cash when a card is inserted and the right buttons pushed, as well as more sophisticated machines, such as automated tellers (ATMs) that will receive deposits and make loans as well as provide cash. So-called "point-of-sales" (POS) machines can connect registers in retail establishments with computers and debit customer accounts on purchases. Automated clearing houses (ACHs) process information on computer tapes to clear and settle accounts and are of central importance to developing EFTS.

The CBCTs do not yet provide all the services offered by branch offices of depository institutions; for example, they do not open accounts, nor do they offer financial counseling or receive complaints. However, they have the potential to lower

unit and marginal costs for those services they do provide. In part, lower costs may result from the substitution of capital for labor and the associated centralization of administration; in part, from new economies of scale increasing the minimum efficient size of banks.[60] If EFT makes limited forms of branching less expensive than now, and if it introduces new economies of scale, it will encourage depository institutions to reach out for customers located in new geographic areas and to intensify their coverage in existing markets. From the customer's point of view, EFT reduces the inconvenience of dealing with a bank whose offices are at a distance by substantially reducing the number of times per year the offices need be visited.

As CBCTs come into use, depository institutions formerly isolated from one another by distance should tend to confront one another competitively. The fringes of existing local markets for retail banking services should tend to become more tightly integrated, and the markets themselves should expand in size. An immediate effect would be that the number of competitors in the expanded markets will be greater and concentration will fall. Geographic market expansion would further augment declines in concentration resulting from expanded powers for thrift institutions, particularly if thrifts are tied into ACHs.

The development of EFTS has raised a number of regulatory issues: (a) whether or not CBCTs legally constitute branch banks; (b) the participation of noncommercial banks in automated clearing houses; and (c) the role of the Federal Reserve as a developer and operator of ACHs. These issues will be considered in turn.

In December 1974, the Comptroller of the Currency ruled that EFT devices connecting national banks and their customers were not branches and, therefore, could be established in any desired location notwithstanding federal and state restrictions on branching. A number of national banks

---

[57]See, for example, Leon Korobow and David Stuhr, "Toward Early Warning of Changes in Banks' Financial Condition," *Monthly Review,* Federal Reserve Bank of New York (July 1975).

[58]For a discussion of some of the difficulties, and a suggestion for change, see Paul M. Horvitz, "Failures of Large Banks: Implications for Banking Supervision and Deposit Insurance," *Journal of Financial and Quantitative Analysis* (November 1975), 589–601.

[59]See *Problem Banks,* Hearings before the Committee on Banking, Housing and Urban Affairs, U.S. Senate, 94th Cong., 2d Sess., Washington, D.C., February 5, 1976.

[60]The ultimate impact of EFT devices on economies is not yet clear. For some early work on the subject, see David A. Walker, "An Analysis of EFTS Activity Levels, Costs and Structure in the United States," *Proceedings of a Conference on Bank Structure and Competition,* Federal Reserve Bank of Chicago, May 6 and 7, 1976; and David A. Walker, "An Analysis of Financial and Structural Characteristics of Banks with Retail EFT Machines," FDIC Working Paper 79-1, October 13, 1979.

thereafter set up CBCTs in locations in which they would not be permitted to have branch offices and, in some cases, across state lines. A series of law suits followed, with the result that CBCTs were found by several U.S. Courts of Appeal to be branches subject to state legal restrictions. The U.S. Supreme Court declined to review these decisions.[61]

After a two-year study commissioned by Congress, the National Commission on Electronic Fund Transfers recommended that the rules governing "the deployment of off-premise EFT terminals should be separate and distinct from and less restrictive than rules regarding the establishment of conventional brick and mortar branches."[62] In part, this finding was motivated by a legal advantage of thrift institutions over commercial banks. The FHLBB and NCUA can authorize federally chartered S&Ls and credit unions to deploy terminals without regard to state branching restrictions, which apply to branching by national banks; the McFadden Act applies only to nationally chartered commercial banks and not to the thrift institutions.[63]

An ACH association is a group of private depository institutions that have agreed to exchange payments recorded on computer tape. The information is sorted at the ACH and transmitted to the relevant depository institutions. Settlement may be accomplished by crediting and debiting reserve balances at Federal Reserve banks. The automated clearing house was initially conceived in the late 1960s, when it appeared that the growing volume of paper checks would overwhelm existing technical abilities to clear them. Such ACHs will, in all likelihood, eventually be "on line" to depository and other institutions, thus permitting the full electronic clearing and settling of accounts.

At the beginning of 1980, there were over thirty ACHs in the United States. All except two in New York and Chicago received operational support from the Federal Reserve on Reserve bank prem-

ises. The Federal Reserve has borne most of the cost of research and development.

The issue of institutional participation in ACHs is part of a large issue of cooperative sharing in various elements of EFT. "Joint ventures" may be desirable because they permit relatively small firms to invest on a cooperative basis where capital requirements are large and perhaps to achieve economies of scale. However, joint ventures can be objectionable in two respects: they can facilitate anticompetitive behavior among independent competitors, and they can preempt the project to the exclusion of entry by others.

Some ACH associations have excluded depository institutions other than commercial banks. The thrifts have found an ally in the Justice Department, which filed civil antitrust suits in Los Angeles and Denver to compel ACHs to grant membership status to other financial institutions.[64]

Concern has also been expressed about Federal Reserve involvement in EFT. The Justice Department has argued that Federal Reserve investment and operations are anticompetitive, potentially reducing the volume of private investment, forestalling the development of superior technology and systems, and distorting resource allocation. It has been suggested that the Federal Reserve withdraw from the operation of automated clearing houses in order to promote efficiency and innovation. Short of full withdrawal in favor of private financial institutions and clearing houses, it has been argued that the Federal Reserve adopt a fee schedule that covers the "full cost" of the services offered to avoid discouraging the development of private systems.[65] In 1980 DMCA required that the Federal Reserve implement a schedule of fees for ACH and other services by September 1, 1981.

Government agencies, perhaps the Federal Reserve more than others, are potentially unbeatable competitors. The threat alone of Federal Reserve subsidization could be sufficient to deter independent investment and could result in uneconomic uses of resources. Unfortunately, the withdrawal of the Federal Reserve from EFT operations could have

---

[61]*Independent Bankers Association of America* v. *Smith,* 402 F. Supp. 207 (1975); *State of Illinois* v. *Continental Illinois Bank and Trust Co.,* 409 F. Supp. 1167 (1975).

[62]*EFT and the Public Interest,* A Report of the National Commission on Electronic Fund Transfers, February 1977, Chap. 3, p. 35.

[63]Ibid., p. 33.

[64]*Wall Street Journal,* May 8, 1977. On the broader issue of sharing, see Stephen A. Rhoades, "Sharing Arrangements in an Electronic Funds Transfer System," *Journal of Bank Research* (Spring 1977), 8–15.

[65]"Justice Department Comments on the Federal Reserve's Proposed Regulation J," May 27, 1976.

equally unhappy results if, as seems likely, there are externalities (social benefits in this case) that are not taken into consideration by private investors. The approach of DMCA is to allow Federal Reserve participation in development of ACHs, but also to require that the Federal Reserve begin to charge for its services.

In part, at least, the discrepancy between the Board's view of a worthwhile investment expenditure and the view of private firms can be attributed to the existence of benefits that would not accrue to private investors, but which probably exist or at least seem apparent to the Federal Reserve. Among these are the prospects for a virtual elimination of Federal Reserve and other forms of float and a reduction in the costs associated with a rising volume of check usage.[66]

There are, however, a host of practical problems in setting prices for Federal Reserve services so as to minimize distortion in the allocation of resources. With substantial economies of scale likely to exist, and external benefits associated with the extent to which individuals and institutions participate in a compatible EFT system, it is not completely clear what kind of price schedule is economically desirable. "Subsidization," in theory, would certainly tend to discourage private firms. However, "full-cost" pricing requires careful definition that does not ignore long-run economies and benefits; otherwise, it will encourage an economically inefficient multiplicity of private cooperative arrangements.[67] In mid-1980, the system was forced

to grapple with these problems in earnest, as the September 1981 deadline for pricing began to draw near.

### Reorganization of the Regulatory Agencies

The current distribution of responsibilities and authority among agencies regulating depository institutions is not the result of a master plan. It developed on an ad hoc basis over a long period of time and reflects a good measure of political accommodation.

Most criticism has been directed at the overlapping powers of the three federal and fifty state agencies that regulate commercial banking.[68] The former chairman of the Federal Reserve Board has articulated some of the general objections:

> the most serious obstacle to improving the regulation and supervision of banking is the structure of the regulatory system . . . our system . . . is indeed a jurisdictional tangle that boggles the mind. . . . [It] fosters what has sometimes been called "competition in laxity" . . . is conducive to subtle competition among regulatory authorities, sometimes to relax constraints, sometimes to delay corrective measures . . . agencies are sometimes played off against one another. . . . banks should [not] continue to be free to choose their regulators. . . . we should not fail to face up to the difficulties created by the diffusion of authority and accountability that characterizes the present regulatory system.[69]

Nevertheless, commercial banks, and other depository institutions as well, have strongly supported the current arrangements and, in particular, those aspects of it referred to as the "dual banking system." In a limited sense, the dual banking system refers to the option depository institutions enjoy to have either a state or federal charter and to switch back and forth. More broadly, it encompas-

[66]It is reasonably clear that the suppression of non-par banking (the deduction of "exchange charges" in the payment of checks by banks on whom they were drawn) as a result of the Federal Reserve's entry into clearing and settlement after 1913 represents a case of public investment to attain social benefits that were not attainable through the operations of private banks. For a discussion of the inefficiencies created by non-par banking and the Federal Reserve's policy in this regard, see "Federal Reserve Operations in Payment Mechanisms: A Summary," *Federal Reserve Bulletin,* Board of Governors of the Federal Reserve System, Washington, D.C. (June 1976), 481–489.

[67]For an interesting proposal in this regard, and comments on it, see Robert Eisenmenger, Alicia Munnel, and Steven Weiss, "Pricing and the Role of the Federal Reserve in an Electronic Funds Transfer System"; and Almarin Phillips, "Discussion," in *The Economics of a National Electronic Funds Transfer System, Proceedings of a Conference,* Federal Reserve Bank of Boston, October 1974, pp. 97–114.

[68]Some observers maintain that the Federal Financial Institutions Examination Council and the Depository Institutions Deregulation Committees constitute fourth and fifth federal banking agencies.

[69]Arthur F. Burns, "Maintaining the Soundness of Our Banking System," address at the American Bankers Association Convention, Honolulu, Hawaii, October 21, 1974.

**Table 31-6  Major Reform Proposals for Regulation of Depository Institutions and Recent Legislation**

| | CMC (1961) | Hunt (1971) | FINE Discussion Principles (House, 1975) | FIA (Senate, 1975) | DMCA 1980 |
|---|---|---|---|---|---|
| **1. Activity prohibitions and balance-sheet constraints** | | | | | |
| a. Loans, investments, and other assets | Broader powers for depository institutions, on uniform basis, including some investment in equities | Broader powers for depository institutions, including some investment in equities, elimination of geographic lending restrictions on savings banks and S&Ls | Broader powers for thrifts, particularly in making consumer loans and issuance of credit cards, and trust powers. Underwriting municipal revenue bonds permitted commercial banks | Broader powers for thrifts, including consumer loans and trust powers; with some balance-sheet constraints. (Separate investigation of restrictions on commercial bank dealings in securities underway.) | Broader powers for federally chartered thrifts, including authority for S&Ls to invest up to 20 percent of assets in consumer loans, commercial paper, and corporate debt securities |
| b. Liabilities | Precise definition for time and savings deposits to prevent them from becoming more like demand deposits. | Provision of third-party-payment services for individuals at savings banks, S&Ls, and credit unions on same basis as commercial banks. | Permit demand deposits and other third-party-payment accounts at all thrifts institutions. | Permit third-party-payment accounts at all thrift institutions. | Permit NOW accounts and automatic transfer accounts for banks, S&Ls, and mutual savings banks; permit share drafts for credit unions. |
| c. Reserve requirements | Eliminate reserve requirements on time and savings deposits. | Mandatory membership in Federal Reserve for all state-chartered banks and all S&Ls and savings banks offering third-party payments. | F.R. reserve requirements for all depository institutions to be phased in over a period of 5 years. | F.R. reserve requirements for all institutions having substantial amounts of third-party-payment accounts. | F.R. reserve requirements for all institutions on transaction accounts and nonpersonal time deposits. |
| d. Capital, taxes | Tax incentives to increase capital ratios, bad debt reserves, and encourage risk taking. | Permit mutual savings banks and mutual S&Ls to convert to stock bases. Uniform tax formula for all depository institutions. | Equal tax treatment for all depository institutions. Tax credit and subsidized loan rates for lower- and moderate-income housing. | Tax credits when mortgages comprise 10 percent or more of assets. | |
| **2. Entry restrictions** | | | | | |
| a. Chartering | Federal charters for mutual savings banks. | Federal charters for stock S&Ls and savings banks. | Mutual savings banks and S&Ls permitted to convert to national bank charters. | | State-chartered stock S&Ls may convert to federal charters under certain conditions. (Federal chartering of mutual savings banks permitted by FIRA in 1978.) |

| | | | | | |
|---|---|---|---|---|---|
| b. Branching | Regional ("trading area") branching irrespective of state boundaries for commercial banks, savings, and S&Ls. | Statewide branching for all commercial banks, S&Ls, and mutual savings banks—both de novo and by merger. | Permit interstate branching for all federally insured depository institutions under certain rules. | (Separate investigation of in-state branching restrictions underway.) | (Separate investigation of McFadden Act branching restrictions underway in accordance with the International Banking Act of 1978.) |
| 3. Pricing restrictions | | | | | |
| a. Demand deposits | Continue interest-payment prohibition. | Continue interest-payment prohibition. | Permit interest payments on demand deposits and other third-party-payment accounts in no later than 5 years. | Permit interest payments on checking accounts Jan. 1, 1978, with possible delay to Jan. 1, 1980. | Continues interest payment prohibition on demand deposits but permits demand-deposit-like accounts such as NOW accounts. Eliminate maximum over 6 years after passage of bill. |
| b. Time and savings deposits | Extend Reg. Q to thrifts and place on "stand-by" basis; maximums to be imposed on determination by authorities that further interest rate competition not in public interest. | Eliminate maximums over 10-year period at all depository institutions. | Eliminate maximums in not later than 5 years. | Eliminate maximums 5½ years after passage of bill. | |
| 4. Agencies | | | | | |
| a. Coordination | Functions of FDIC and Comptroller transferred to Federal Reserve. Single federal agency to examine all federally insured S&Ls. | Consolidation of federal examining and supervisory functions over commercial and mutual savings banks into new agencies. Establish new federal insurance agency to oversee insurance for commercial banks and thrifts. | Establish a single Federal Depository Institutions Commission incorporating the regulatory and supervisory functions of the Comptroller of the Currency, Federal Reserve, FDIC System, and NCUA. | (Federal Bank Commission Act to consolidate powers of Comptroller of Currency, Federal Reserve, and FDIC introduced separately.) | Depository Institutions Deregulation Committee established. (Federal Financial Institutions Examination Council established under FIRA in 1978.) |
| b. Deposit insurance | | Uniform standards for meeting claims. Pay-out minimization should not be standard; rather public and community welfare. | Federal deposit insurance agency functions for all depository institutions combined under the aegis of Federal Depository Institutions Commission. | | |

Act and the standards applied under Section 7 of the Clayton Act.

8. Why did public concern about bank failure revive in the 1970s even though relatively few banks failed each year? What policy change developed to meet those concerns? Is such concern likely to continue? Why?

9. What is the economic rationale for eliminating the prohibition of interest payments on demand deposits? Is this prohibition likely to be eliminated? Why or why not? How about the Regulation Q maximums on time deposits?

10. What is the likely effect on allocational efficiency of permitting noncommercial bank thrift institutions to offer third-party-payment services? What will be the likely effect of permitting savings and loan associations to make consumer loans?

11. Are EFTS likely to increase or diminish competition in local financial markets? Explain your answer by indicating the specific conditions on which it is based. What is the economic rationale for permitting thrift institutions to become members of ACHs?

12. Develop the arguments for and against reorganization of the agencies regulating the depository institutions.

## Selected Bibliography

Benston, George. "Economies of Scale of Financial Institutions." *Journal of Money, Credit and Banking* (May 1972).

*Compendium of Issues Relating to Branching by Financial Institutions,* Subcommittee on Financial Institutions, Committee of Banking, Housing and Urban Affairs, U.S. Senate, 94th Cong., 2d Sess. Government Printing Office, Washington, D.C., October 1976.

*Compendium of Major Issues in Bank Regulation,* Committee Print No. 2, Committee on Banking, Housing and Urban Affairs, U.S. Senate 94th Cong., 1st Sess. Government Printing Office, Washington, D.C., August 1975.

*Despite Positive Effects, Further Foreign Acquisitions of U.S. Banks Should Be Limited Until Policy Conflicts Are Fully Addressed.* Report by the Comptroller General of the United States, U.S. General Accounting Office, Washington, D.C., August 26, 1980.

*Federal Supervision of State and National Banks.* A Study by the Comptroller General of the U.S., Washington, D.C., 1977.

*Financial Institutions and the Nation's Economy (FINE).* Compendium of Papers Prepared for the FINE Study, Books I & II, Committee on Banking, Currency and Housing, House of Representatives, 94th Cong., 2d Sess. Government Printing Office, Washington, D.C., June 1976.

Gilbert, Gary, and William Longbrake. "The Effects of Branching by Financial Institutions on Competition, Productive Efficiency and Stability: An Examination of the Evidence." *Journal of Bank Research.* Part I and Part II (Autumn 1973 and Winter 1974).

Lapidus, Leonard, et al. *State and Federal Regulation of Commercial Banks.* Vols. 1 and 2. Task Force on State and Federal Regulation, Federal Deposit Insurance Corporation, 1980.

McNeill, Charles R., and Denise M. Rechter. "The Depository Institutions Deregulation and Monetary Control Act of 1980." *Federal Reserve Bulletin* (June 1980).

*Report of the President's Commission on Financial Structure and Regulation* (Hunt Commission). Government Printing Office, Washington, D.C., December 1971.

Shull, Bernard. "Concentration, Prices, Profits and Public Policy." In *The Vital Majority: Essays Marking the Twentieth Anniversary of the U.S. Small Business Administration.* Ed. Deane Carson. Government Printing Office, Washington, D.C., 1973.

*Study of the Savings and Loan Industry.* Vols. 1–4. Directed by Irwin Friend, Federal Home Loan Bank Board. Government Printing Office, Washington, D.C., July 1969.

# 32

## Economic Efficiency and Financial Reform in the Securities Markets

An efficient process is one with a high ratio of useful outputs to costly inputs. In security markets, as pointed out initially in Chapter 19, there are at least three different kinds of efficiency: operational efficiency, informational efficiency, and allocational efficiency. We will now examine each of these in turn.

When a security is sold, the buyer ordinarily pays more than the seller receives. The difference represents payments to brokers, market makers, and others who help to facilitate the transaction. Transaction costs include this difference and the internal costs incurred by the buyers and sellers themselves for such things as telephone calls. In an *operationally efficient* securities market, transaction costs are as low as possible.

Informational efficiency refers to the speed and accuracy with which inputs of information are transformed into outputs of security values. Before a transaction takes place, both the buyer and the seller will ordinarily evaluate the security, taking into account what they know about the characteristics of the issuer and about the comparative value of this security and of other more or less similar securities. The prices at which transactions take place change as the information available changes. Investors have an incentive to buy undervalued securities and sell overvalued ones. A securities market is said to be *informationally efficient* if security prices promptly reflect all of the relevant information then available to society.

Securities represent claims on the income and wealth of their issuers. The price at which new securities can be issued, or at which previously issued securities are traded, can profoundly influence the behavior of the issuers. For example, an organization may not be able to undertake a new project unless it can sell enough securities to raise the funds required. Sale of the securities, in turn, depends on how the market prices the securities that the organization is prepared to issue. In addition, managers may be affected by the prices of securities even when no new issues are planned. Security prices may influence dividend policy, management rewards, acquisition strategies, and many other management decisions. *Allocational efficiency* deals with the extent to which securities' prices induce the issuers of securities (that is, resource users) to allocate resources to their most productive use.[1]

In summary then, there are three types of efficiency that are relevant to the securities market. They are *operational efficiency, informational efficiency,* and *allocational efficiency.* This chapter expands on the discussion of efficiency begun in Chapter 19. However, this chapter concentrates on the first two types of efficiency. Allocational efficiency is beyond the scope of this work.[2]

It is possible to make some judgments about the extent of economic efficiency by examining both market structures and market conduct.[3] For example, when the market for a good or service can be classified as having a competitive structure, there is a strong basis for believing that the good or service will be produced in an efficient manner. If some of the existing participants are inefficient, a competitive market structure should provide more efficient competitors an opportunity to displace them. However, although evidence on market structure is important, it is also desirable, whenever possible, to complement it with evidence

about actual market conduct. Do market participants actually behave in a competitive manner?

In securities markets, there is a great variety of services that facilitate transactions; it would be impossible to consider all of them. Happily, the most important of these services fall into three broad categories: brokers' services, the services of providing a marketplace, and dealers' services.

This chapter considers the structure and conduct for each of these for equities and then turns to the debt markets. In the debt markets, customers typically do business directly with dealers, and no formal marketplace organization exists. Our ultimate concern regarding both equity and debt markets will be the need for reform. Are markets reasonably efficient or is government action necessary to improve them? Or to look at it in another way, are there government regulations now in effect that prevent securities markets from being as efficient as they might be? We begin with a brief review of the characteristics and historical background of the equity securities markets.

## The Equities Market

### Characteristics of the Market

A few important features of equity markets should be noted at the outset. Common stock equity represents a residual, but unlimited, interest in the assets of the issuing corporation. Also, it has no predetermined retirement date. As a consequence, any information affecting the value of a corporation's assets or its future investment opportunities will affect the value of its common stock. Furthermore, since the term of the stock is indefinite, events in the distant future can be significant.[4]

Because the price of equity securities can be so profoundly affected by the firm's own fortunes, some people believe that each corporation's secu-

[1]Friend defines allocational efficiency in terms of the price of a security and the subsequent rate of return of the underlying asset. See Irwin Friend, ''The SEC and the Economic Performance of the Securities Industry,'' in *Economic Policy and the Regulation of Corporate Securities,* ed., Henry G. Manne, American Enterprise Institute, Washington, D.C., 1969, p. 190. In our terms, informational efficiency requires that, when adjusted for risk, all securities will have equal expected rates of return on their market prices; allocational efficiency requires that, when adjusted for risk, all real capital assets will have equal expected rates of return on their costs of reproduction.

[2]For an analysis of the links between the price of a stock and the earnings that will be generated by its underlying assets, see William J. Baumol, ''Performance of the Firm and Performance of Its Stocks,'' in Manne, *Economic Policy and the Regulation of Corporate Securities,* pp. 127–141.

[3]See Richard Caves, *American Industry: Structure, Performance, and Conduct,* Prentice-Hall, Englewood Cliffs, N.J., 1972. According to Caves, the main elements of market structure are seller concentration, product differentiation, and barriers to the entry of new firms. The main areas of market conduct are policies toward setting prices, policies toward setting the quality of product, and policies aimed at coercing rivals.

In this study, we will measure conduct of performance mainly in terms of efficiency. Caves lists other goals that are relevant, including full employment, technological improvement, and an equitable distribution of income.

[4]For example, consider a share of common stock whose market value is $100. The stock is currently paying a dividend of $8 per share and stockholders anticipate a growth in money dividends of approximately 9 percent per year. Of the $100 value of the stock, approximately one-third represents the present value of the dividends that will be received in the first five years and two-thirds represents the present value of the dividends that will be received after this five-year-period. It is apparent that stockholders will have a significant interest in events in the relatively distant future that could affect the company.

rities are unique and have a unique market. They point out that to appraise the value of a company's common stock requires a detailed study of its specific circumstances. Generalizations about the industry and the economy do not suffice. Others believe that the common stock of any one firm is a relatively good substitute for the common stock of many other firms. Those who take this approach claim that investors are primarily interested in the risks and expected returns associated with any stock ownership and that stocks are compared to one another on the basis of these characteristics. In this case, there is one stock market and the demand and supply curves facing investors are extremely price elastic. If, in contrast, the market for each issue is unique, the relevant market is smaller and much less price elastic. We will return to a fuller discussion of this very fundamental issue when we consider the informational efficiency of the equity markets.

It is important to distinguish between primary and secondary markets. In a primary market, the security is sold by the issuing corporation and, consequently, the assets of the corporation change as a result of the transaction: new securities are created. In a secondary market, both the buyer and the seller are financial investors; no cash is received by the issuer and no new securities are created. Most transactions in equities are secondary market transactions. Because equity securities have an indefinite life, issuers never need to raise new equity to re-fund expiring securities. Corporations that need additional equity capital can either retain earnings or sell more stock. In practice, most additions to equity capital are from retained earnings rather than from primary issues of stock (see Table 32-1).

### Historical Background

The basic structure of the American securities industry was determined in the last half of the nineteenth century and remained amazingly stable until the early 1970s despite a substantial increase in government regulation.[5] The nineteenth century

saw communications developments, such as the telephone and the stock-ticker system, which allowed the New York Stock Exchange to evolve into something like its modern form. Since its formation, the NYSE has dominated trading in the common stock of the largest companies in the United States. There was very little government interference with the operation of the exchange until, in response to the stock market collapse of 1929, the U.S. Congress passed the Securities Acts of 1933 and 1934. Even these significant laws did not cause fundamental structural changes in the securities industry. Major thrusts of these laws were to improve the flow of information from corporate issuers to investors and to strengthen the fraud provisions applicable in cases of deliberate dissemination of misleading information. These laws represented a sharp break from the past in that the federal government expressed its special concern for the securities industry as a vital and strategically important part of the economy.

Major changes have occurred in the ownership of common stocks. Before World War II, the owners of common stock were mainly individuals. Bank trust departments managing trusts and estates for the wealthy were the single important institutional investor. The post–World War II period has seen the rapid development of two other kinds of institutional portfolios: pension funds and mutual funds (see Table 32-2). The accumulation of stock in the hands of institutions has taken place gradually but has had important impacts on the securities industry. These changes have affected the structure of the securities industry in recent years. What brought institutions to public attention in a dramatic way was a rapid shift in their patterns of trading. In the pre-1960 era, institutions had lower rates of portfolio turnover than did individuals. During the 1960s, institutions, led by mutual funds, began trading more—with the result that turnover rates for the institutions rose substantially above those for individual investors. The growing importance of institutional trading undermined the tra-

---

[5]A good brief history of the NYSE is contained in Robert W. Doede, *The Monopoly Power of the New York Stock Exchange,* unpublished Ph.D. dissertation, Department of Economics, University of Chicago, 1967. An excellent source on relations between the NYSE and

other exchanges is Robert Sobel, *The Curbstone Brokers,* The Macmillan Company, New York, 1970. For more recent periods, see Robert Sobel, *NYSE: A History of the New York Stock Exchange, 1935–1975,* Weybright and Tulley, New York, 1975; also Chris Welles, *The Last Days of the Club,* E. P. Dutton & Co., New York, 1975.

**Table 32-1    Estimated Additions to Corporate Equity (in billions of dollars)**

| Common and Preferred Stock | 1973 | 1974 | 1975 | 1976 | 1977 |
|---|---|---|---|---|---|
| New issues | $12.1 | $ 8.0 | $12.8 | $14.1 | N.A. |
| Retirements | 3.0 | 3.7 | 2.4 | 3.1 | N.A. |
| Net change | 9.1 | 4.3 | 10.4 | 11.0 | N.A. |
| Undistributed profits | 39.3 | 44.4 | 33.2 | 56.4 | 58.4 |
| Net additions to corporation equity | $48.4 | $48.7 | $43.6 | $67.4 | N.A. |

Note: N.A. = Not Available. Series discontinued.

Source: *Federal Reserve Bulletins*, August 1976 and April 1978.

**Table 32-2    Market Values of Professionally Managed Common Stock, by Managment Type and by Portfolio Type, 1969 (in billions of dollars)**

| Management Type | Portfolio Type | | | | | |
|---|---|---|---|---|---|---|
| | Foundations & Educational Endowments | Pension Funds | Insurance | Investment Companies | Trusts, Estates, & Personal Advisory Accounts | Totals |
| Self-administered | $14.2 | $13.4 | | | | $ 27.6 |
| Insurance companies | | 4.4 | $17.4 | $ 0.5 | | 22.4 |
| Investment advisors | 4.7 | 9.9 | 1.3 | 51.6 | $ 28.0 | 95.5 |
| Banks | 4.1 | 50.4 | | | 110.6 | 165.1 |
| Totals | $23.0 | $78.1 | $18.7 | $52.1 | $138.6 | $310.6 |

Source: Securities and Exchange Commission, *Institutional Investor Study,* Summary Vol., p. 18.

ditional price structure of the securities industry during the late 1960s. Success in the competition for institutional business depended increasingly on the broker's ability to offer valuable services in addition to brokerage to institutional customers. A series of studies by the SEC and the Congress led to important policy changes in the early 1970s that were designed to facilitate price competition and the use of improved communications and data processing technology.[6] Since then the industry has been undergoing rapid change in structure and conduct. It is in the context of this rapidly changing scene that we will attempt to assess the state of efficiency of the stock market and the efforts at market reform now under way.

## Operational Efficiency and the Brokerage Function

The securities industry provides a variety of related services. The most important, from the point of view of revenues generated, are brokerage, market-making and related trading activities, and underwriting. Figure 32-1 shows the distribution of revenues and expenses during 1978 for those broker/dealers registered with the Securities and Exchange Commission whose total revenues exceeded

[6]Summaries of the main studies are contained in the following documents: Securities and Exchange Commission, *Institutional Investor Study Report, Summary Volume,* House Document 92-64, part 8, Government Printing Office, Washington, D.C., 1971; U.S. Congress, House of Representatives, Subcommittee on Commerce and Finance of the Committee on Interstate and Foreign Commerce, *Securities Industry Study Report,* House Report No. 92-1519, 92nd Cong., 2nd Sess., Government Printing Office, Washington, D.C., 1972; U.S. Congress,

Senate, Subcommittee on Securities of the Committee on Banking, Housing and Urban Affairs, *Securities Industry Study Report* (for the period ending February 4, 1972), 92nd Cong., 2nd Sess., Government Printing Office Washington, D.C., 1972; and U.S. Congress, Senate, Subcommittee on Securities of the Committee on Banking, Housing, and Urban Affairs, *Securities Industry Study Report,* 93rd Cong., 1st Sess., Government Printing Office, Washington, D.C., 1973.

**Figure 32-1    The Securities Industry Dollar: 1978**

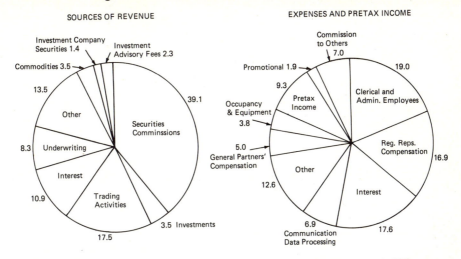

SOURCES OF REVENUE

EXPENSES AND PRETAX INCOME

Note: Includes information for firms with securities-related revenues of $500,000 or more in 1978.

Source: Securities and Exchange Commission, *1979 Annual Report*.

$500,000. Fewer than 20 percent of the firms registered with the SEC fall into this category, but they generate over 95 percent of the revenues and control over 99 percent of the assets of all firms in the industry.[7]

It should not be thought that all firms in the securities industry provide a similar mix of services to a similar mix of customers. There is considerable differentiation among the firms. An accurate classification of firms in the securities industries would need to take into account the mix of services offered, the securities covered, and the types of customers serviced. Some firms specialize in certain services: research, underwriting new issues, market making, or brokerage. Some firms will handle almost any kind of security. Such a firm could handle a customer's transactions in Treasury bills, government bonds, municipal bonds, Eurodollar securities, common and preferred stocks, government bonds, commodity futures, puts and calls, commercial paper, and more. Other firms may specialize in certain securities, such as over-the-counter common stocks. Some firms will deal with individuals, institutions, and other broker/dealers.

[7]Many of the firms excluded specialize in retail sales of mutual fund shares.

Other firms will deal primarily or exclusively with one of these categories. There are regional differences as well. Some firms operate on a national or international basis, while others restrict themselves to particular regions of the United States. This section focuses on the brokerage services of firms. This is the largest single revenue-producing activity of the securities industry, and it is, therefore, a logical place to start the discussion of efficiency. However, since most firms engaged in brokerage also offer one or more related services, these should also be considered.

*Restrictions on Entry and Market Structure*
Restrictions on entry are a key factor in evaluating the extent of competition in any industry. If entry is easy, it is unlikely that monopoly profits could continue for any long period of time, at least if their existence were known to others outside of the industry. In many respects, the brokerage industry is characterized by easy entry and exit. For example, the capital requirements are modest compared to those in heavy manufacturing. Certain skills and knowledge are required, but they are available to hundreds, perhaps thousands, of persons who are employed in the industry. Membership on an exchange is a necessity to conduct cer-

tain kinds of brokerage activities and purchasing a seat on the exchange creates a monetary barrier, but it also is not in itself a significant barrier to entry. There are, though, some economically significant restrictions on entry—restrictions that have the potential effect of limiting competition—to which we now turn our attention.

One type of entry restriction is restriction of individuals. Purchase of an exchange membership gives the member the right to conduct transactions on the floor of the exchange. Most stock exchange members use their seats to perform brokerage functions facilitating the securities transactions of non-members. A wealthy individual who does a lot of trading might join a stock exchange merely to save brokerage commissions on personal investment transactions. However, restrictions imposed by the SEC have practically eliminated this motivation for membership in the last few decades.[8]

There are also some regulations and restrictions that apply to a new firm wishing to enter the brokerage industry. For example, a firm must register with the Securities and Exchange Commission and satisfy the minimum capital requirements in effect at the time. In addition, most brokerage firms find it necessary to become member firms of the New York Stock Exchange. This requires that an officer purchase a seat on the NYSE—and the number of seats is limited. Seat prices have ranged from $17,000 (1942) to $515,000 (1968). A firm controlled by persons with a previous record of violations of the federal securities laws, or by a commercial bank, would not be eligible for membership. The principals of the firm would have to pass certain tests administered by the New York Stock Exchange. Thus, there is not, in any literal sense, complete freedom of entry.

A barrier to entry is significant, though, only if it permits firms in the industry to earn materially higher rates of return than firms outside of the industry that are exposed to comparable risks. At present, there is no basis for believing that the restrictions on entry of the type we have described have led to economically significant barriers to en-

try for brokerage firms that do business mainly with individual or institutional investors.[9]

The securities industry is actually characterized by a relatively rapid rate of entry and exit of new firms.[10] Also, existing firms adapt themselves quickly to changes in the characteristics of the available business. This flexibility is dramatically demonstrated, for example, by the experience of the 1960s in which the amount of highly profitable institutional business dramatically increased. As the Securities and Exchange Commission's *Institutional Investor Study* reported, "Because of the more profitable nature of institutional commission business during the 1960's, it was widely sought by broker/dealers. Firms attempted to gain additional business by tailoring their services and advertising to the institutional investor. Conferences and seminars, where broker/dealers and institutional investors could meet, became commonplace."[11] Of the firms that were in the industry in both 1962 and 1968, 43 percent had substantially increased the proportion of their brokerage revenues obtained from institutions in response to the increased amount of this highly profitable business available.

There are, however, some restrictions that prevent existing firms from expanding the products they offer. Certain members of the New York Stock Exchange are assigned special responsibilities in connection with the trading in certain listed securities and are designated by the exchange as *specialists* in these securities. Specialists are primarily dealers and, therefore, they will be discussed in detail under the dealership function. However, New York Stock Exchange Rule #113 prevents NYSE specialists from accepting brokerage business in their specialty stocks from institutions. This rule, which was first introduced in the early 1960s, was apparently intended, in part, to prevent specialists from competing with the regular brokerage firms who ordinarily handled institutional business.[12] It also makes it difficult for bro-

---

[8]There are categories of exchange members who are not mainly brokers. However, they are also not investors seeking to economize on brokerage costs; rather, they are in the business of being dealers. The dealership function is considered later in this chapter.

[9]These firms own only a small proportion of the seats on the NYSE. The prices of seats are believed to reflect mainly the expected excess profits of market makers (specialists) and floor brokers.

[10]For details, see Securities and Exchange Commission, *Institutional Investor Study,* vol. 4, pp. 2182–2183.

[11]Ibid., p. 2182.

[12]Apparently, the NYSE at first opposed the rule when it was proposed by the SEC. However, while the issue

kerage firms who do a substantial institutional business to become specialists.[13]

Restrictions also affect other institutions. The banking reform legislation in the mid-1930s has generally been interpreted as barring commercial banks from becoming brokers. Although the statutory language is somewhat unclear, no American commercial bank has ever applied for membership in an American stock exchange.

In the decade before fixed-minimum commission rates were abolished, there was considerable pressure from many other kinds of financial institutions to join stock exchanges. Most financial institutions, including many of the large insurance firms that joined or were seeking to join exchanges, did so primarily as a means of recapturing part of the commissions on their portfolio transactions and not with the intention of entering the general brokerage business. Connecticut was the first and only state to create a brokerage subsidiary for the purpose of joining a stock exchange to reduce the brokerage commissions paid by the state's pensions funds, although New York State threatened to follow a similar course.

Some observers voiced concern about possible conflicts of interest that could arise when the same firm had investment responsibility for a common stock portolio and did the brokerage for that portfolio as well.[14] For example, the institution in its role as investment adviser might undertake more stock purchases and sales than necessary, in order to generate profits from the resulting brokerage business. According to a Senate report on the subject: "While there is no evidence that the conflicts of interest described above have led to widespread breaches of fiduciary duty, the existence of these conflicts is troublesome."[15] The solution finally

imposed by the Congress was to allow institutions, except banks, to join stock exchanges, but to prohibit any broker/dealer from providing brokerage services to any institutional portfolio it managed.

In sum, there are no important natural obstacles, such as the need for large amounts of capital or specialized knowledge, that restrict entry into the brokerage industry. Regulations imposed by the Congress, the SEC, and some stock exchanges tend to make it difficult for brokers' customers to become brokers themselves. However, in the late 1960s, these restrictions were circumvented by growing numbers of financial institutions. The primary motive of financial institutions was to reduce their brokerage service costs. The introduction of competitive brokerage rates in the early 1970s eliminated this motive. The threat that institutions would enter the brokerage field in ever-increasing numbers was certainly one important force leading to the introduction of competitive rates. Today, there are no significant obstacles that prevent newly formed firms from entering the brokerage industry when it is sufficiently profitable. Nor are there significant obstacles that would prevent firms from leaving the industry when it is unprofitable. Market structure, then, seems consistent with the hypothesis of operational efficiency in the brokerage function. Now we can look at market conduct to see whether any evidence supports this hypothesis.

*Brokerage Commission Rates* From the early days of our country's history until the late 1960s, it seems that the custom in the securities industry was for nearly all firms to follow a common, publicly agreed, brokerage commission rate schedule. When Congress adopted the securities reform legislation in the 1930s, this practice was not even discussed.

On January 26, 1968, the SEC asked for public comment on a New York Stock Exchange proposal to change its commission rate schedule to allow a volume discount for large orders. In response, the Antitrust Division of the Department of Justice asked whether fixed-minimum commission rates were "necessary to make the Securities Exchange Act work." The Justice Department's view was that if fixed rates were not necessary, then they were illegal under the antitrust laws. In order to study the matter, the SEC began a series of public

---

was under consideration, one specialist firm invited large financial institutions to place their orders directly with the firm in its specialty stocks. At this point, the large wirehouses decided that they would support the SEC's proposal and the exchange reversed its position.

[13]If they became specialists, they would have to refuse orders from institutions in their specialty stocks.

[14]These concerns are summarized in the U.S. Senate, Subcommittee on Securities, Committee on Banking, Housing and Urban Affairs, *Security Industry Study Report,* 93rd Cong., 1st Sess., Government Printing Office, Washington, D.C., 1973, pp. 75 ff.

[15]Ibid., p. 77.

hearings on commission rate structure and related matters on July 1, 1968. Shortly afterward on December 5, 1968, a commission rate schedule incorporating volume discounts for large orders went into effect. On February 10, 1971, the SEC stated that "fixed minimum commissions on institutional-sized orders are neither necessary nor appropriate,"[16] and required the exchanges to introduce competitive rates on at least that portion of institutional transactions in excess of $500,000 beginning June 30, 1971. Following further studies by the Commission and by Congress and the filing of private antitrust suits, the SEC directed an end to fixed-minimum commission rates beginning on May 1, 1975.

The period from December 5, 1968 to May 1, 1975, can be considered a transition period for commission rates. Before the transition period, the commission rate was a function of the price per share for 100-share orders and multiples of the 100-share commission for larger orders. Consequently, an institution that purchased or sold 10,000 shares as a result of one order paid exactly 100 times as much as an individual who purchased or sold 100 shares of the same stock.

During the transition period, the rate structure was gradually changed so as to lower the rates on large orders and to allow competitively determined rates on the largest orders. Beginning on May 1, 1975, brokerage firms were free to use whatever rate schedule they preferred or to negotiate the commission on a transaction-by-transaction basis. In discussing the conduct of the brokerage industry, we will compare the period of fixed rates (before the transition period) and the period of competitive rates (after the transition period).

The basic mechanism that determined equilibrium in the brokerage industry under fixed-minimum commission rates was the adjustment of the cost of service to the existing rate schedule. If the average cost of serving a particular category of customer was less than the fixed-minimum commission rates charged, then serving that customer would be extremely attractive. A brokerage firm serving such customers would attempt to increase its market share by developing additional services to attract customers. Other brokerage firms that were not presently serving that market segment

would attempt to attract a share of the business and its excess profits. In the course of developing new services, the brokerage firms tended to raise their costs. Similarly, if the marginal cost of serving a particular group of customers exceeded the fixed-minimum commission rates, brokers would attempt to achieve a more profitable situation by cutting their costs or by ceasing altogether to serve that category of customers. In either case, an equilibrium would be reached when the rates charged equaled both marginal and average costs.

As a result of this pricing method, the level and structure of the chosen fixed-minimum commission rates would determine the pattern of auxiliary services offered to customers. For example, in the closing days of the fixed-minimum commission rates era, the cost of handling low-dollar, odd-lot transactions was greater than the amount that could be charged under the then prevailing fixed-minimum commission schedule. Not only did such customers not receive many extra services, but brokerage firms adopted internal policies that discouraged acceptance of such orders. Some firms refused to handle the orders if the total dollar amount of the order was below a certain minimum, or they refused to pay their registered representatives a commission on such orders.

In contrast to the small orders, large orders (500 shares or more) tended to be extremely profitable under the commission rate schedules in effect in the late 1960s. Furthermore, the number of such orders available was increasing, although the extent to which this increase may have resulted from aggressive efforts by brokerage firms to attract such orders cannot be determined with certainty. What is known is that in order to attract clients to this extremely profitable business, brokerage firms developed supplementary products and services which they *gave* to institutional investor customers, a practice known as "reciprocity." They also developed more efficient means of marketing and of delivering these supplementary services. Some of the services tended to be of interest to almost all institutions, while others were aimed at particular ones.

One service of interest to nearly all institutions is better trading. Before 1965, when an institution wished to buy or sell a large amount of stock, it would typically undertake a large number of small transactions spread out over days, weeks, or even

[16]Securities Exchange Act Release, No. 9079.

months. This behavior was intended to conceal the institution's portfolio changes and to avoid moving the price in an unfavorable direction, but it had a number of disadvantages. First, it created a great deal of paperwork for the institution since there were many different transactions involved. Second, the institution by concealing its intentions from its brokers, effectively prevented the broker from giving the institution advice as to the most effective way to carry out the transactions. Third, and most important, it took a long time. Large position changes are typically initiated because the institution feels that the stock is overpriced or underpriced. However, if the position change takes a long time to carry out, the market may adjust before it is completed.

To meet the needs of the institutions, some institutional brokerage firms developed a new trading technique called the *block trade* for transactions that are too large to arrange easily on the floor of a stock exchange. To arrange a block trade, the brokerage firm with an institutional customer wanting to sell a large quantity of stock would search among its other customers for someone willing to take the other side of the transaction. If both the seller and the buyer agreed on a price, the brokerage firm would then finalize the transaction on the floor of the stock exchange. In these trades, when a brokerage firm represented both the buyer and the seller, it collected brokerage commissions from both sides. Thus, block trading not only provided excellent service to the institution initiating the trade; it also could be extraordinarily profitable to brokerage firms since they collected commissions from both the seller and buyer.[17]

In order to acquire more of the block-trading business, block-trading firms developed elaborate communication procedures to contact potential buyers and sellers quickly—procedures that tended to raise costs. Frequently, a broker would find that it had a seller and some, but not all, of the necessary buyers. In such cases, some brokers were willing to buy the balance of the shares for their own account to complete the trade, a process known as *block positioning*. On the average, the price the broker/dealer paid for the shares bought this way was more than the price that could be obtained when the broker/dealer subsequently sold the shares. However, when the commissions earned on both sides of the transactions were taken into account, block trading could still be very profitable.[18]

Brokerage firms also developed other services for institutional investors, such as the establishment of costly research departments that provided statistical reports and other financial analysis to the institutional client.

Some brokerage firms would even deposit cash in a checking account at a bank even though the account was never used to conduct the firm's business, in effect giving the bank an interest-free loan. In return the bank would use the broker for part of its trust department business. The larger the broker's deposit, the more business it would receive from the bank. If the broker's profits on the extra business obtained in this way were large enough, they would offset the interest that might otherwise have been earned on the idle funds.

The brokerage industry also developed efficient means of distributing these supplementary services to institutions. A distribution system was necessary because the brokerage firm that was best able to handle a particular transaction was not necessarily the one with the best research or the best mutual fund sales record. Should an institution give its business to the firm that provided the best brokerage service or to the one that provided the best supplementary services? To minimize these problems, a practice known as the "customer directed give-up" was developed.[19] With customer directed give-ups, the broker that actually performed the brokerage service gave a part of the commission to another brokerage firm chosen by the customer. The second brokerage firm was one that the institution wanted to reward for some unrelated service, such as research. Eventually, a third level was introduced in which the institution would direct all of the give-ups it controlled to one brokerage firm, which, in turn, would distribute money to the ultimate beneficiaries.

---

[17]Prior to December 5, 1968, the commission for a 100-share order of a $40 stock was $39. A firm that represented both buyer and seller on a 10,000-share order of a $40 stock would receive commissions of $7,800 for the single transaction.

[18]The economics of block trading are discussed in Chapter 11 of SEC, *Institutional Investor Study.*

[19]Give-up practices are discussed in the SEC's Securities Exchange Act Release No. 8339, dated January 26, 1968.

The fact that brokerage firms were willing to provide costly services or give up a part of their commissions appears to indicate clearly that the fixed-minimum commissions charged to institutions prior to 1968 exceeded the cost of producing the brokerage service. However, another hypothesis takes issue with this approach by suggesting that fixed-minimum commissions charged institutions prior to 1968 plus a well-developed system of reciprocal services did provide the equivalent of competitive commission rates. That is, the institution and the broker, in negotiating for reciprocal services, were in effect negotiating a competitive commission rate. If this hypothesis were correct, the post-1968 elimination of fixed-minimum commissions would have had no real effects. It would have reduced brokerage commissions paid and increased by exactly the same amount the payments received by brokers for nontransaction services. The total payments by institutions to the securities industry and the total amount and variety of services provided by the securities industry to the institutions would remain the same.

An alternative hypothesis is that fixed-minimum commissions did make a difference: the mix of reciprocal services provided under a fixed-commission system was not the same as the mix of services that would have been purchased in separate, independent transactions in a competitive market. If fixed-minimum commissions plus reciprocal services did not provide the equivalent of a competitive solution, the shift to competitive commission rates would tend to reduce the dollar value of the services sold by the securities industry to the institutions.

During the interim period from December 1968 through May 1, 1975, the commission rate schedule was adjusted a number of times to make the rates charged conform more closely to execution costs. Nevertheless, when fixed-minimum commission rates were completely abolished on May 1, 1975, further substantial adjustments took place. These adjustments clearly support the hypothesis that fixed-minimum commission rates plus reciprocal services were not equivalent to competitive rates. The average commission rate paid by institutions declined from 0.84 percent of the principal value of the order in April 1975 to 0.47 percent in February 1977. This represents a rate decrease of approximately 44 percent. The percentage decrease was less on small orders and slightly more on larger orders. By February 1977, the average commission paid by institutions ranged from 1.04 percent of the principal value for orders of less than 200 shares to 0.32 percent for orders of more than 10,000 shares.[20]

During this same period, the average commission rate charged to individuals also declined but by a smaller amount from 1.73 percent (of the principal value) in April 1975 to 1.54 percent in February 1977, a decrease of 11 percent. For individuals, the trend by size of order was quite diverse. On orders of less than 200 shares, there was a decrease in the commission rate from 2.03 percent of the principal value in April 1975 to 1.99 percent in February 1977. For orders in the 200- to 1,000-share range, there was a 6 percent decline during this period to 1.75 percent. For orders in the 1,000- to 10,000-share range, there was a decrease of 15 percent to 1.16 percent of the principal value. For orders of 10,000 shares or more, however, there was a dramatic decline in the average commission rate from 0.76 percent in April 1975 to 0.4 percent in February 1977. However, since very little individual business is in this size range, the dramatic rate decrease in these very large orders had little effect on the overall average rate charged individuals.

Fortunately for the brokerage firms, the elimination of fixed-minimum commissions coincided with a substantial increase in trading volume. The SEC estimated that the elimination of fixed-minimum commissions saved customers of NYSE member firms an average of $34,000,000 per month during the first twenty months. However, because trading volume was high, the total revenue and the economic results for the firms were very favorable during 1975 and 1976; the average pre-tax return on equity was 32.6 percent during 1976.

Firms whose specialty was providing research to institutions appear to have been hardest hit by the demise of the fixed-minimum commission rates. Most of these firms went out of business or merged with other firms.

*Summary: Operational Efficiency of the Brokerage Industry*  Under fixed-minimum commission rates, brokerage firms tended to adjust the mix of

[20]U.S. Securities and Exchange Commission, *Fifth Report to Congress on the Effect of the Absence of Fixed Rates of Commission,* Washington, D.C., May 26, 1977.

brokerage and related services they offered so that the marginal cost of the services offered to each group of customers equaled the rates charged. The relative ease with which new firms could enter or exit from the industry, or with which existing firms could expand or contract, tended to insure that capital was invested in the industry when prospective returns were above the competitive level and withdrawn when they were below it.

The combination of fixed-minimum commission rates and restrictions on the ability of brokers' customers to integrate backward into the industry made it difficult for customers to force the industry to provide brokerage services by themselves at prices reflecting their cost. Fixed-minimum commission rates were associated with substantial operating inefficiencies but not with excessive rates of return to brokers.

In the 1960s the rapid growth of institutional trading created strains that eventually led to the complete elimination of fixed-minimum commission rates on May 1, 1975. Among the immediate consequences of competitive rates was a dramatic decline in the level of commission rates charged to institutions. Brokerage firms now face substantial competitive pressures to cut costs by increasing operating efficiency and eliminating unnecessary services. They also have greater freedom to adjust the types of services they offer to the needs of each category of customer, although dramatic changes in this area have not yet taken place.

On balance, the introduction of competitive commission rates is a good example of an important reform that appears to have led to a substantial increase in operating efficiency.

## Operational Efficiency and the Marketplace: Competition Between Marketplaces

This section begins by distinguishing between a market, a marketplace, and a market maker.[21] A *market* includes all of the potential buyers and sellers of a product or group of related products. Markets function through one or more *marketplaces,*

which are organizations specifically designed to facilitate transactions. The marketplace organization may be formal or informal. A stock exchange is an example of a formal marketplace. A *market maker* is a dealer who buys and sells securities for his or her own account in order to help customers complete their transactions. Market-making can be distinguished from other types of investing or dealer activity in that the market maker trades in a predominantly passive manner. The initiative for the trade comes from the customer who is anxious to buy or sell; the market maker responds by taking "the other side" of the transaction when necessary. This section deals with competition between marketplaces by examining both structure and conduct. The behavior of market makers is considered in the next section.[22]

In the securities market, most marketplaces can be readily classified as exchanges or over-the-counter markets, although there are also some hybrid types that do not neatly fall into one of these classifications. As a first step in analyzing competition among marketplaces, however, we will consider the conventional classifications.

*Over-the-Counter Markets*   The over-the-counter (OTC) market is an informal marketplace in which brokers and dealers buy and sell securities from each other and from their customers on the basis of telephone contacts. Individuals wanting to buy stock in a company traded in the OTC market will call their brokers, who will call other firms that might be interested in selling the stock. When a satisfactory offer has been located, the buyer's broker tells the other firm that its offer has been accepted. The actual stock delivery and transfer of money will take place later through some other mechanism, perhaps through the U.S. mails or a clearing corporation.

A number of characteristics of this market are worth mentioning. First, restrictions on the freedom of brokers and dealers to enter the market are minimal.[23] Second, it is necessary to search for the

---

[21]On the distinction between a market and a marketplace, see James L. Hamilton, "The Economic Role of the Stock Exchange in the Stock Market," Amos Tuck School Seminar on Regulation and Public Utilities, Dartmouth College, August 22, 1972.

[22]Dealer activities other than market-making, such as arbitrage, are not considered in this chapter. There is relatively little systematic knowledge of such activities. Block trading is considered to be a form of market-making. In the author's opinion, most dealer activity consists of market-making.

[23]There are some applicable government regulations, such as the requirement that a securities broker/dealer

"other side" of a transaction. Even when the search ends, there is ordinarily no assurance that the price accepted is the best one available, since it is not practical to check every possible source.[24] A third characteristic of the traditional OTC market is the relative privacy of the transactions. The transaction is essentially agreed to during a telephone conversation between two parties and is not directly known to any other party at that time. A fourth characteristic of such markets is that brokers are not necessary. Individuals ordinarily use brokers; financial institutions or large corporations may or may not, depending on their preferences.

There are thousands of different issues traded in the OTC market and hundreds of different firms that make markets in one or more issues. A private firm, the National Quotation Bureau, Inc., collects quotation information from dealers and publishes daily and monthly reports showing, for each security, the bids and offers of each firm. These quotation sheets provide a convenient guide to brokers as to which dealers have an interest in buying or selling a particular security.

In 1970 the National Association of Security Dealers Automatic Quotation System, known as NASDAQ, began operation. This system uses a random-access computer file containing bids and offers from market makers in about 3,500 of the most active stocks traded in the OTC stock market. A broker wishing to buy or sell a security can have displayed on his video screen the bids and offers from each market maker, greatly accelerating the search process. A broker must still call the market

maker to complete the transaction but, in the future, the system could be modified to provide for automatic execution.

*Exchanges* A major characteristic of present-day stock exchanges is the physical propinquity of their participants. In the early days of the country, merchants interested in buying or selling government bonds and other well-known securities met on the street or in coffee houses to do business. As recently as the 1920s, securities were bought and sold on the sidewalks of the Wall Street section of New York City. The open-air trading of securities disappeared in the United States when the predecessors of what is now the American Stock Exchange purchased a hall and moved indoors.

On both the New York and American Exchanges, many aspects of the outdoor trading were simply transferred indoors. Each security was assigned a floor location. A broker wanting to buy or sell the security would find at that location anyone else who was interested in buying or selling the same security. If the broker could not find a satisfactory trading partner to complete his customer's order, he might simply wait at the location, but this could be expensive since it prevented him from doing other business. A logical division of labor for some traders was to specialize as brokers' brokers. Such a broker, who later came to be called a specialist, would stay at the trading location in a particular stock and would accept limit orders from other brokers to be executed when a buyer (or seller) could be found.[25] Thus, the original broker could move from one location to another, and still be sure that his customer's order would be executed when an offsetting order arrived at the market.

On the New York Stock Exchange in the 1920s and 1930s, there was often enough business to support more than one specialist at one trading location and the specialists competed against one another to attract brokerage business. One way a specialist could attract additional business was to eliminate the need for waiting. If a broker arrived at the trading location with an order that was close to the current market but no offsetting order was imme-

---

register with the Securities and Exchange Commission or join a self-regulatory organization like the National Association of Securities Dealers. Stock exchanges have attempted to restrict the freedom of their members to trade in listed stocks in the OTC market.

[24]In active stocks, most dealers tend to quote the same bid or offer much of the time unless they purposely wish to discourage business on one side or the other. Those wishing to buy or sell frequently contact several dealers before making a transaction. A dealer whose bid or offer was different from the bids and offers of other dealers would quickly discover this fact. If his quotation was more favorable than those of the others, he would attract business very quickly; if it was less favorable than those of his competitors, he would find that the amount of business he was doing decreased rapidly. In such an active market, the customer needs only a few telephone calls to find out the prevailing prices. The expected value of additional calls is likely to be very low.

[25]A limit order is an order to buy or sell at a specified price. A market order, which instructs the broker to buy or sell at the best available price, would not require the broker to wait in order to complete the trade.

diately available, a specialist would sometimes be willing to accommodate the customer by taking the other side of the transaction. The specialist's main objective on these transactions was to earn the goodwill of the customer's broker and thus attract future brokerage business. In this way the specialist, in order to attract brokerage business, became a market maker. By the 1950s, the market-making function had become a more important activity for many specialists than the brokerage function. But competing specialists on one exchange have largely disappeared.[26] The official policy of the NYSE seems to be to encourage competition among specialists, but it has not yet succeeded to any substantial extent.

Other systems of organizing the trading activity on an exchange are possible. For example, the Toronto Stock Exchange discourages members from performing the market-making function except in a very limited way. On the Chicago Board of Options Exchange (CBOE), the market-making functions are performed by several market makers who compete with each other and who are not permitted to act as brokers. On most commodity futures exchanges, members have the right to trade on the floor as a principal or as a broker, and there are no restrictions as to the roles they can perform. The trading systems of the different exchanges have evolved independently to a considerable degree and there are few studies that attempt to compare the efficiency of the various systems.[27]

*Hybrid Systems* Some recent developments have tended to blur the distinction between an over-the-counter market and an exchange market. The use of automatic quotation systems and the potential of automatic systems for executing orders make the over-the-counter markets in stock seem more like an exchange. On the other hand, when the same security is traded on more than one exchange, one must search to find the best price just as in a conventional over-the-counter market. At this writing, brokers do not regularly check the quotations on several exchanges before sending their order to one of them, and there is no system to enable brokers automatically to ensure their customers of the best price on an order.[28] The SEC, as one of its major objectives, is attempting to develop a national market system that will provide better communication among stock exchanges. The proposed national market system is discussed later in this chapter.

Block trading is another example of a kind of hybrid system since block trades are arranged through telephone communications between customers and brokers. There is really no great difference between the processes of arranging a large block trade in listed stocks or in bonds or in some other security traded in the OTC market. There is a distinction only at the final step on a listed stock. An exchange member must (under rules in effect in June 1977) take the listed stock trade to the specialist's post on the floor of an exchange where the stock is traded and publicly bid and offer the stock before completing the transaction. This provides an opportunity for limit buy and sell orders held by the specialist and other brokers to be executed but, in other respects, the trade is processed as though it took place in an OTC market.

*Competition Between Marketplaces* One characteristic of the American capital markets is competition between marketplaces. Each marketplace acts as if one of its objectives is to increase the volume of trading taking place throughout its facilities. A reasonable question is why marketplaces compete since, with minor exceptions, they are not organized as businesses. Nevertheless, competition is a fact.

Marketplaces compete because, associated with each marketplace, are individuals whose careers or businesses are more or less tied to the fortunes of that marketplace and these individuals have an incentive to promote the marketplace. The individ-

---

[26]It is not entirely clear why competing specialists disappeared at this time. No study focusing on this issue is known to the author. Possible explanations include changes in the character of trading on the floor of the exchange (fewer limit orders and more market orders) and the encouragement of the NYSE and the SEC. These are not necessarily contradictory explanations. The philosophy of the SEC at the time was to assign more responsibility to specialists for maintaining fair and orderly markets, and it is hard to allocate responsibility among competing specialists.

[27]Among the few relevant studies are Seha Tinic and Richard R. West, "Marketability of Common Stocks in Canada and the USA: A Comparison of Agent versus Dealer Dominated Markets," *Journal of Finance* (June 1974), 729–746; and James L. Hamilton, "Marketplace Organization and Marketability: NASDAQ, The Stock Exchange and the National Market System," *Journal of Finance* (May 1978), 487–503.

[28]See *Wall Street Journal,* June 8, 1977.

uals may be officials of the marketplace or proprietors or employees of firms that have a comparative advantage in that marketplace. If a brokerage firm operates in many competing marketplaces, the firm's partners or managers in charge of its operations in a particular marketplace may tend to promote the interests of that marketplace as well as the interests of their employer.

There is often a geographic dimension to the competition. Cities and states work to attract more business for the financial marketplaces within their boundaries, just as they compete to attract new factories. A financial marketplace will tend to generate additional business for nearby banks and other finance-related firms, so some of these firms also take an active interest in promoting the interests of the marketplace.

*Competition for Securities* In Table 32-3, some major categories of securities are classified by the type of marketplace where they are traded and by type of investor. There appear to be no instances in which a security that is mainly owned by institutions is traded on an exchange. If individuals and institutions both own the same security, it may be traded on an exchange or in the OTC market, depending on the volume of trading. Small-volume issues are likely to be traded in an over-the-counter market even though they are held mainly by individuals. Large-volume issues whose owners include a substantial number of individuals are likely

to be traded on exchanges. There is no hard evidence as to why these generalizations occur, but it is worthwhile to speculate about some of the factors that may be important.

One important characteristic of a marketplace is the extent to which it provides an impersonal trading environment. In an impersonal trading environment the principals do not know each other and the characteristics of the principals do not affect the transaction. It is not necessary to know who is buying or selling when no one trader is large enough to have a noticeable impact on the market price for even a short period of time. However, in markets in which institutions are an important factor, trading by one institution may have at least a temporary impact on the market price that is large enough to be of concern to market makers and others.

Suppose an institution wishes to undertake a transaction large enough to have at least a temporary influence on price. A market maker would be reluctant to take the other side on such a transaction if the principal is anonymous because of the danger of a second transaction of similar magnitude from the same source. In such cases, the market maker's risk would be considerably less if he had the assurance of no similar transactions from the same source. This requires disclosing the identity of the principals involved in large transactions to the market maker, and it may be one reason why OTC markets predominate where transactions are undertaken mainly by institutions. When the char-

**Table 32-3  Capital Market Instruments Outstanding, by Type of Investor and Type of Secondary Marketplace**

| Predominant Marketplace Type | Type of Investor | | |
| --- | --- | --- | --- |
| | *Mainly Institutions* | *Mixed* | *Mainly Individuals* |
| OTC | 1. U.S. govt. bills and bonds<br>2. Corporate bonds[a]<br>3. Mortgages<br>4. Foreign exchange (spot & futures) | Municipal bonds | Stocks of small corporations & investment companies |
| Exchange | | 1. Stock of large corporations<br>2. Listed options<br>3. Commodity futures | Stocks of large investment companies |

[a]Small transactions in some corporate bonds still take place on exchanges. But even in those listed bonds, large transactions take place mainly in the OTC market.

acteristics of the investors in a security change, trading in the security may shift to a marketplace which is more appropriate to those investors.

*The Role of a Corporation in Selecting a Market-place* A common stock becomes listed on an exchange when the issuing corporation and the exchange sign a listing agreement. This contract specifies the obligations of both the exchange and the corporation. In general, the exchange agrees to provide a marketplace as long as the corporation meets certain conditions, the most important of which deal with disclosure of information to investors, stockholder rights, and the payment of listing fees to the exchange. A few large corporations have prevented their stocks from being listed on the major stock exchanges because they are not willing to enter into such listing agreements, but this situation is not too common. Some corporations have listing agreements with more than one exchange. Others may have a listing agreement with only one exchange, but their stock is traded on an unlisted basis on other exchanges.

Prior to 1975, federal securities laws prevented a stock exchange from providing a marketplace in a common stock unless the company had a listing agreement with at least one exchange but, in that year, the securities law was amended to permit an exchange, with SEC approval, to allow trading in the stock of a corporation that had not signed a listing agreement with any exchange. This unlisted trading rule has not yet been widely used.

An OTC market maker can make a market in a stock whether or not it is listed on an exchange and no company permission is needed. There is a special name for the over-the-counter market in stocks that are also listed on an exchange. This OTC market is known as the *Third Market*.

Under some conditions, a company may help to pay for the operation of a marketplace for its stock. Most listing agreements require the company to pay a fee to the exchange. When a company offers its stock to the public for the first time, the underwriter may agree to make a market in the stock after the offering. In a sense, the underwriting fee might be considered to include a payment for this later market-making operation. It is not known whether, or to what extent, companies may otherwise subsidize the operations of OTC market makers who make markets in their stock, but it is believed that this practice is not common.

*Restrictions on Competition Between Market-places* A brokerage firm can be a member of more than one stock exchange and most large brokerage firms are members of all of the important stock exchanges. If a stock is traded on more than one exchange, brokers take their customers' orders to any of these exchanges.[29]

Prior to 1976 the New York and American Stock Exchanges had an agreement under which companies were delisted from the American when they listed on the New York Stock Exchange. The effect was that a company could not be traded on more than one stock exchange within the City of New York. Under pressure from the SEC, these restrictions were eliminated in 1976.

For many years, a New York Stock Exchange rule (Rule 394) effectively prevented members of that exchange from executing a customer's order in the Third Market, but congressional action eliminated this restriction. Member firms are still restricted in their ability to buy stock from their customers, as principals, without first taking the transaction to the floor of the exchange. Because this restricts the ability of member firms to compete with specialists, the SEC is seriously considering eliminating this restriction as well.[30]

*Classification of Exchanges* Traditionally, stock exchanges are classified as national and regional. In the past, the regional stock exchanges provided an exchange marketplace for small companies whose stockholders mainly lived in the region in which the exchange operated. When the company and its stockholder base had grown to the point where stockholders were spread all over the country, the stock was often listed on the American Stock Exchange (ASE). If the company grew in size to the point where it met the criteria for listing on the NYSE, it would move to that exchange and the ASE would drop its listing.

The concept of the regional stock exchange as a marketplace for regional companies has long been out of date. Most transactions on the regional stock

---

[29]In the 1930s, the NYSE attempted to restrict the freedom of its members to undertake transactions on other exchanges in stocks that were listed on the NYSE. The SEC objected in the famous *Multiple Trading Case* and the NYSE never imposed this restriction.

[30]For an excellent discussion of this issue, see Carter T. Geyer, "The Abrogation of Rule 390," *Financial Analysts Journal* (January-February 1978), 22–30.

exchanges today are in the shares of companies that are listed on a national exchange. Thus, the regionals function as alternative marketplaces for well-known companies. Evidence of this is presented in Table 32-4. Over 90 percent of the issuers whose stocks are listed on any exchange are listed on either the New York or American Exchanges.

A large proportion of the transactions on regional stock exchanges are in stocks listed on the NYSE; only a small proportion consists of stocks listed on the ASE or stocks not listed on either of those exchanges. As Table 32-4 shows, typically more than 90 percent of the dollar volume of all common stock transactions on exchanges takes place on one of the two major exchanges in New York City.

Economies of scale are one possible explanation for this concentration of volume among exchanges. The data in Table 32-4 provide some crude support for this hypothesis.[31] For example, in recent years the NYSE accounted for 84 percent of the dollar volume of all stock transactions, but only 55 percent of the costs of all stock exchanges. Without exception, each of the other exchanges had a higher proportion of the industry cost than of the industry volume. This cannot be taken as more than a crude indication of economies of scale, but it is consistent with this interpretation. One cannot rely too strongly, however, on these cost comparisons to explain the concentration of trading in exchanges. First, not all the exchanges offer the same services. Second, the absolute magnitude of the costs of operating an exchange are small compared to either the dollar volume of the trading taking place on the exchange (0.1 percent) or of total transaction costs (about 10 percent). In deciding which marketplace is more efficient, the total transaction costs must be considered. It is quite possible that, by spending one dollar, an exchange (or other marketplace) could save more than a dollar that would otherwise be incurred by a broker or by the customer.

There appear to be substantial external economies in locating the paperwork-processing operations of one brokerage firm near similar operations of other firms and near similar operations of the

exchange on which the transactions being processed take place. The advantages are obvious when paper needs to be transferred from one office to another or when people need to confer about possible errors in recording transactions. When a firm does not have a processing operation in the vicinity of an exchange, it will often contract with another firm to provide the back-office processing.

In this situation, there is an incentive for a brokerage firm to have its main back-office processing center near the exchange on which it does the greatest volume. Thus, given the location of the back-office processing center, there may be a cost advantage, other things being equal, to doing business at that location rather than at some other location. Thus, a substantial countervailing advantage appears necessary to move a substantial business out of the vicinity of New York City. While this may become less important as electronic data processing replaces manual operations, it still appears to be a significant factor.

*Summary*   The function of a financial marketplace is to provide facilities and services that make trading more efficient. In principle, the several marketplaces can be thought of as competing with each other for trading volume by providing a more efficient trading environment. The development of NASDAQ is a notable example of how such competition might work. As an example, however, it is more the exception than the rule. In practice, the existing marketplaces have not been able to attract substantial volume from competitors by offering greater efficiency. Brokers do not routinely check alternative markets to obtain best execution for their customers, and most orders are routinely sent to whatever marketplace is most convenient from the point of view of the broker's processing system.

Thus, the major marketplace, the NYSE, has had a relatively stable market share over long periods of time. This predominant market share was eroded slightly in the late sixties and early seventies as other markets competed by offering means of avoiding fixed-minimum commission rates; it has been rebuilt as fixed-minimum commission rates were eliminated. As might be expected in these circumstances, important technological changes have been introduced at a modest rate. In the 1970s, government policy had been committed to increasing competition among (and within) market-

---

[31]See also Doede, *The Monopoly Power of the New York Stock Exchange*. The competitive position of regional exchanges is to be found in a symposium volume of the National Bureau of Economic Research, *Explorations in Economic Research*, ed. Donald E. Farnar, (Summer 1975).

**Table 32-4  Selected Statistics on Stock Exchanges**

|  | NYSE | ASE | MSE[b] | PSE[b] | PHLX[b] | BSE[b] | Others | Total |
|---|---|---|---|---|---|---|---|---|
| Number of stocks traded,[a] 1978 | | | | | | | | |
| Listed | 2,227 | 1,096 | 366 | 814 | 290 | 126 | —[c] | 3,676 |
| Unlisted | -0- | 39 | 303 | 167 | 792 | 740 | —[c] | 36 |
| Total | 2,227 | 1,135 | 669 | 981 | 1,082 | 866 | —[c] | 3,717 |
| Number of issuers | 1,926 | 1,088 | 596 | 816 | 914 | 819 | —[c] | 3,179 |
| Dollar volume of trading, 1978 (in billions of dollars) | $210.4 | $15.2 | $10.5 | $7.1 | $4.1 | $1.5 | $0.4 | $249.3 |
| Percentage distribution of dollar volume | | | | | | | | |
| 1977 | 83.96% | 4.60% | 4.79% | 3.53% | 1.62% | 0.74% | 0.76% | 100.0% |
| 1975 | 85.04 | 3.66 | 4.82 | 3.25 | 1.72 | 1.18 | 0.29 | 100.0 |
| 1970 | 78.44 | 11.11 | 3.76 | 3.81 | 1.99 | 0.67 | 0.18 | 100.0 |
| 1965 | 81.82 | 9.91 | 2.72 | 1.95 | 1.04 | 0.60 | 0.81 | 100.0 |
| 1955 | 86.31 | 6.98 | 2.44 | 1.90 | 1.03 | 0.78 | 0.55 | 100.0 |
| 1945 | 82.75 | 10.81 | 2.00 | 1.78 | 0.96 | 1.16 | 0.54 | 100.0 |
| 1935 | 86.64 | 7.83 | 1.32 | 1.39 | 0.88 | 1.34 | 0.60 | 100.0 |
| Expenses of exchanges,[d] 1977 | | | | | | | | |
| Millions of dollars | $108.2 | $35.6 | $28.7 | $16.1 | $4.8 | $4.0 | —[e] | $197.4 |
| Percentages | 54.8% | 18.0% | 14.5% | 8.2% | 2.4% | 2.0% | —[e] | 100.0% |

[a]Common and preferred.
[b]The names of the main regional stock exchanges are abbreviated as follows: Midwest Stock Exchange (MSE); Pacific Coast Stock Exchange (PSE); Philadelphia Stock Exchange (PHLX); and Boston Stock Exchange (BSE).
[c]Unduplicate counts not available.
[d]Revenues less pre-tax income. From SEC's *Second Report to Congress on the Effect of the Absence of Fixed Rates of Commission.*
[e]Not included in total.

Source: Securities and Exchange Commission, *Annual Report,* 1976, 1978.

places by developing a national market system. The effectiveness of this policy remains to be determined.

## Operational Efficiency and Market Makers

A market maker is a dealer who buys and sells for his or her own account in order to help others complete their transactions. If there were no market maker, an anxious buyer would have to wait for the arrival in the market of a seller with whom satisfactory terms could be negotiated. Even for listed stocks, it is not infrequent for several hours to elapse between transactions; this waiting time can be important to an anxious buyer or seller. The anxious buyer who is not prepared to wait may raise the bid price to meet that of the best available offer. (Similarly, an anxious seller could lower the offering price.) The market maker reduces the ex-

tent of the price concession an anxious buyer or seller has to make to complete the transaction quickly.

The market maker's role is largely passive—buying because others want to sell and selling because they want to buy. By comparison, other trading activity is presumably motivated by some external source, such as the desire to earn an investment return by holding a security over a sustained period of time or the desire to profit from a belief that the price level of a security is likely to change.

The existence of a modest volume of trading in any security seems sufficient to call forth professional market-making activity unless such behavior is in some way prohibited or prevented. Market-making is often combined with other activities. The particular form market-making takes varies substantially from market to market. On the NYSE, members who perform the market-making function on the floor of the exchange are known as specialists.

Rule 103 of the Exchange states that "no member shall act as a specialist on the floor in any security unless such member is registered as a specialist in such security with the Exchange and unless the Exchange has approved of his so acting. . . ." The NYSE specialists are responsible for handling limit orders in the stocks in which they specialize as well as providing for the market-making function.

The Exchange defines the function of market-making as "the maintenance, insofar as reasonably practicable, of a fair and orderly market." As a market maker, the specialist's transactions on the exchange "must constitute a course of dealing reasonably calculated to contribute to the maintenance of price continuity with reasonable depth, and to the minimizing of the effects of temporary disparity between supply and demand, immediate or reasonably to be anticipated. Transactions not a part of such a course of dealing are not to be affected."[32]

The members of the NYSE who are engaged in block trading also perform a market-making function. However, they are not considered to be specialists because they do not function on the exchange floor and they have no responsibility for any particular security. In the OTC market, any dealer can perform a market-making function by advertising bids and offers. There are no significant restrictions on entry and exit in this regard. On the Chicago Board of Options Exchange (CBOE), members are specifically appointed to perform market-making functions in a particular class of options, but they are not allowed to handle limit orders or to act as brokers in the option class in which they are performing a market-making function. On the CBOE, there is an average of six market makers for each stock listed for option trading.[33] By comparison, for the overwhelming majority of stocks listed on the NYSE, there is only one specialist.

*The Cost of Market-Making* The revenue of a market maker is realized in the form of trading profits. These trading profits represent the difference between the average price paid by other buyers and the average price received by other sellers. If the buyers and sellers conducted business directly with one another, this difference would be zero. If both deal with the market maker, the market maker's gross revenues will be equal to this difference.

Since the market maker responds to customers' initiatives, he is ordinarily willing to either buy or sell a particular security. The price at which the market maker is willing to buy a small quantity is called the bid price, and the price at which he is willing to sell a small quantity is called the offer or asking price. The difference per share between the bid and the offer is called the bid/ask spread. The spread is taken, by some writers, to indicate the cost of market-making services.[34] In a competitive market, average gross trading profit of a market maker will equal the spread plus the average inventory profits; but the spread by itself is not an accurate measure of the cost of market-making unless average inventory profits are zero.

Most market makers are willing to provide bid and offer prices on request as well as to indicate the number of shares they would be willing to buy or sell at those prices. Ordinarily, those quotations would be honored if accepted promptly and within the quantity limitations specified. However, market makers universally reserve the right to alter their bid and offer quotations after a transaction has taken place.

The willingness of market makers to buy more than the minimum quantities for which their bid and offer are quoted is one aspect of the provision of "depth." If market makers find it necessary to purchase and add to inventory a large quantity of stock to perform the market-making function, they will ordinarily pay a lower average price per share than they would require if they were purchasing only a small quantity. Similarly, if market makers were required to sell a large quantity short to satisfy their customers' needs, they would ordinarily require a higher price per share than would be necessary for a small transaction. In either case the inventory risk is greater. This quantity effect will be observed whether a market maker is presented with one large transaction or with a large number of small transactions of the same kind.[35]

---

[32] Rule 104 of the NYSE.

[33] Chicago Board of Options Exchange, *Annual Report,* 1973, p. 11.

[34] The initial work in this tradition is that of Harold Demsetz, "The Cost of Transacting," *Quarterly Journal of Economics* (February 1968), 33–35.

[35] For reasons explained earlier in connection with block trading, the quantity effect is likely to be less with one large negotiated transaction than with a large number

When there are a large number of small transactions, market makers are able to adjust the average price at which they purchase or sell by changing their quotations after each transaction. If there is a sequence of transactions that consist mostly of sales to an individual market maker, the market maker will tend to lower the price as inventory increases. Thus, the average price at which the market maker buys stock will be less than one would have estimated from the observed bid at the time of the first transaction. Evidence for the existence of this depth effect is contained in Table 32-5, which shows the relationship between the percentage price change in a stock and the change in the dollar value of the market maker's inventory in that stock. The price change is measured relative to the change in the Standard and Poor's Index in that stock on that day. It can be seen that market makers tend to increase their inventories on days when prices decline and decrease their inventories on days when prices rise. Furthermore, the amount of inventory change is related to the amount of price change. NYSE specialists are tightly regulated; NASDAQ market makers are not; yet the qualitative similarity of the response is striking.

An important consideration that influences a market marker's gross trading profits is the extent of that market maker's inventory profits. A market maker will tend to have inventory profits if he is better informed than those with whom he trades so that he is able to buy in advance of price increases and sell in advance of price decreases. On the other hand, if others are better informed, the market maker will tend to have inventory losses. The evidence in Table 32-6 shows that both NYSE specialists and over-the-counter market makers have an information disadvantage relative to the persons with whom they trade. Thus, they increase their inventories on days before a price decline and decrease their inventories on days before a price rise and, therefore, tend to have inventory losses on average.

Not all investors are better informed than the market makers with whom they trade. Since market makers lose money to those investors who are bet-

of small transactions because there will be less uncertainty on the part of the market maker as to the future flow of orders.

**Table 32-5   Average Net Inventory Change of a Group of Market Makers, on a Given Day, by Change in the Price of the Stock Relative to a Market Index on That Day (in thousands of dollars)**

| Percentage Change in Price of the Stock Relative to a Market Index | Dollar Value of the Inventory Change in the Corresponding Stocks of a Group of | |
|---|---|---|
| | NYSE Specialists | NASDAQ Market Makers |
| 5.0 or more | (90) | (88) |
| 3.0 to 4.99 | (87) | (68) |
| 1.0 to 2.99 | (51) | (13) |
| −.99 to .99 | 2 | (7) |
| −2.99 to −1.0 | 42 | 6 |
| −4.99 to −3.0 | 88 | 55 |
| −5.00 or less | 137 | 82 |

Source: Column 1, *Institutional Inventory Study*, vol. 4, p. 1876; Column 2, Hans Stoll, "Dealer Inventory Behavior; An Empirical Investigation of NASDAQ Stock," *Journal of Financial and Quantitative Analysis* (September 1976), 376.

ter informed, they must charge other investors enough to make up these losses and to cover their operating costs and profits.[36]

*The New York Stock Exchange Specialist System*   Since most common stock trades occur on the floor of the NYSE, any analysis of the market-making system for common stock requires one to focus substantial attention on the NYSE specialist system. Fortunately, there have been three major studies of this system in the last twenty years; the most recent of these was undertaken by the NYSE itself. The chairman of the committee conducting the study, William M. Batten, subsequently became chairman of the Exchange. Thus, the study deserves special attention.[37]

[36]Walter Bagehot, "The Only Game in Town," *Financial Analyst's Journal* (March-April 1971); also Armir Barnea and Dennis E. Logue, "The Effect of Risk on Market Makers Spread," *Financial Analysts Journal* (November-December 1975).

[37]*The Special Study of the Securities Industry*, 1963, and the *Insitutional Investors Study*, 1971, were both conducted by the SEC. Substantial parts of both studies dealt with specialist and other market-making activities. The third study is officially entitled *Report of the Committee to Study the Stock Allocation System*, January 1976, NYSE, but is commonly referred to as the Batten Committee Report after the study committee's chairman, William M. Batten.

**Table 32-6  Average Net Inventory Change of a Group of Market Makers on a Given Day, by Change in the Price of the Stock Relative to a Market Index on the Following Day (in thousands of dollars)**

| Percentage Change in the Price of the Stock Relative to a Market Index on the Following Day | Dollar Value of the Inventory Change in the Corresponding Stocks on the Given Day for a Group of | |
|---|---|---|
| | NYSE Specialists | NASDAQ Market Makers |
| 5.0 or more | (24) | (46) |
| 3.0 to 4.99 | (12) | (82) |
| 1.0 to 3.99 | (10) | (19) |
| −.99 to .99 | 1 | (11) |
| −2.99 to −1.0 | 8 | 16 |
| −4.99 to −3.0 | 10 | 67 |
| −5.0 or less | 22 | (22) |

Source: Same as Table 32-5.

With respect to entry, the Batten Committee Report contains the following comments:

> While there are no rules to prevent the entry of qualified outsiders into the Exchange specialist business, there are immense practical difficulties in achieving entry in any way other than by joining an existing specialist firm. The Exchange requires high qualifications for registration of an individual specialist and a very substantial minimum capital for this firm; it requires, further, that not less than three regular specialists be registered with each specialist unit. We believe that these requirements are in the public interest, but they mean that a new firm must be able to make markets in a sufficient number of stocks to cover the cost of a substantial business venture.
>
> The allocation of newly listed stocks is at present an unsatisfactory means to the establishment of a viable new unit. Even if the new firm were favored in allocation decisions, despite its lack of a record of past performance, it could be many years before a sufficient number of attractive stocks were thus acquired to permit a reasonable return on the required minimum capital. Such favoritism would be manifestly unfair to existing units applying for additional stocks.

> We believe that there should be no unreasonable barriers to entry into the specialist business by fully qualified outsiders. We have considered a variety of means through which entry could be achieved without unreasonable difficulty, and we conclude that the only practical means is to permit qualified and approved newly formed units to compete directly on the Exchange floor with whichever existing units they may choose.[38]

The report then goes on to describe the problems of creating competition on the floor of the Exchange.

Since this statement was released, very little progress has been made in achieving competition between specialist units on the floor of the Exchange. One specialist unit announced that it was going to do a public brokerage business at discount rates after May 1, 1975. Within a short period of time, a new specialist firm was formed to compete with the discount broker specialist. The new specialist firm is allegedly supported by some brokerage firms, which are concerned about competition from specialists in their brokerage business. The situation is under investigation by the Antitrust Division of the Justice Department. Another competitive episode lasted only six months, when the new entrant withdrew.

*Variations in Specialist Performance and Profits* Market makers normally behave in a stabilizing manner, buying stock in the face of selling pressure and selling stock in the face of buying pressure. This provision of depth tends to reduce the size of the price fluctuations that would otherwise occur and is consistent with the responsibilities of NYSE specialists. Since unregulated OTC market makers behave in a similar manner, however, it appears that this behavior is normal for market makers because it is profitable.

The *Institutional Investor Study* reported finding considerable variations among specialist firms in the extent to which they were willing to behave in a stabilizing manner. After controlling for the volume of trading and the proportion of institutional trading, the study found that stocks assigned to specialists who provided greater depth experienced

[38]Ibid., p. 56.

fewer temporary price fluctuations than did the stocks assigned to specialists providing less depth.

The study concludes its analysis of the profitability of NYSE specialists with the following statement:

The business of the NYSE specialist unit is a rewarding one. Indeed, in the one out of five stocks that fall in the high dollar volume category each month, the average annual gross incomes of NYSE specialist units range from $225,000 per stock per year to $312,000 depending on the inventory activity group of the specialist unit. In the case of the two categories of specialists that respond less to market demands for liquidity, the annual gross incomes per stock exceed the average overnight positions in the stock."[39]

These figures are on a before-tax basis and they include only those expenses other than interest that could be charged directly to a particular stock. Overhead expenses, such as office rents, are not included.

The Batten Committee Report contains information on specialist gross commission income and gross dealer profits but does not report much information on capital employed. The best available figure is the total net liquid assets committed to NYSE specialist activities as of June 30, 1975—just under $200 million. (This would be roughly equal to equity plus subordinated loans.) During the six months ending June 30, 1975, the total of commission income and dealer profits before taxes amounted to $90 million. The yearly average for the previous five years was $83,500,000. If net liquid assets employed were at the June 30, 1975 level, this would imply an average gross before-tax return on total capital of over 40 percent per year.

*Competition Facing Specialists* Even though there may be only one specialist for a particular stock on the floor of the NYSE, that specialist is not totally immune from competition. "The main types of competition emanate from (1) rivalry for the specialist's job; (2) competing markets; (3) outsiders who submit limit orders rather than market orders; (4) floor traders who may bypass the spe-

cialist by crossing buy and sell orders themselves; and (5) other specialists."[40] Rivalry for the specialist's job could take several forms. If a specialist were doing a poor job of maintaining markets in a particular stock, his or her registration in that stock could be revoked and the stock assigned to another specialist. This has not been a significant factor in the past although, on a few occasions, the NYSE has used informal pressure to merge specialist firms doing an unsatisfactory job into other firms believed to be performing better. Presumably, this carries some economic sanction, the magnitude of which is not clear. Alternatively, the NYSE could allow another specialist to compete in the same stocks. The Batten Committee recommended that this be done, but it had not occurred to any significant extent by July 1979. Specialists are also rivals for the right to specialize in newly listed stocks. Before 1971, a specialist's performance does not appear to have been a significant factor in allocating new stocks. However, the Batten Committee reports that statistical evidence on a specialist's performance (and particularly his or her ranking in opinion surveys of floor brokers) was a significant factor in allocating common stocks during 1973.[41]

Competition from other marketplaces can be a serious consideration. During 1972, 20 percent of the trading in securities listed on the NYSE took place on markets other than the NYSE. This percentage was higher in 1972 than in any preceding or subsequent year. Of the 20 percent of the trading that took place in other markets, approximately two-thirds took place on regional exchanges and one-third on the OTC market. Undoubtedly, the largest single factor accounting for this competition from other marketplaces was the fixed-minimum commission rates, which still applied to most transactions on the NYSE during that year. Since 1972, the introduction of volume discounts followed by competitive commission rates has tended to concentrate trading volume on the NYSE and, therefore, to further protect NYSE specialists from potential competition from other market makers. By early 1978, the Third Market had essentially disappeared.

[40]Demsetz, "The Cost of Transacting."

[41]*Report of the Committee to Study the Stock Allocation System*, The New York Stock Exchange, New York, January 27, 1976, pp. 157–158.

[39]*Institutional Investor Study*, vol. 4, p. 1929.

At present, there is no system that makes it practical for a broker to ensure that an individual investor's order is sent to the market at which it will be executed at the best price. Attempts to create such a system and, therefore, to increase the degree of competition among market makers in different marketplaces are major objectives of public policy. These attempts are discussed in the next section.

In a sense, the specialist and block trader are competitors. However, competition is heavily weighted in favor of the block trader because the block trader can earn a brokerage commission on some or all of the block trade while the specialist cannot (because of Rule 113). When the block trader is able to find customers for both sides of the transaction, the specialist does not even have the opportunity to participate by purchasing a part of the block.

Floor traders and investors who submit limit orders rather than market orders compete with specialists for the right to take the other side of the market orders that do arrive. Limit orders play an ambiguous role. On the one hand, limit orders provide competition for the specialist in the dealer function. On the other hand, the specialist as a broker profits by executing limit orders. During 1972, specialists earned an estimated $63 million in commission income as a result of handling limit orders on their books. This works out to an average of about $3.77 per hundred shares. The brokerage commission rates charged by specialists were subject to fixed-minimum commissions until May 1, 1975. In April 1976, the average brokerage income per 100 shares earned by specialists was $2.90. After the specialist brokerage commission rates became subject to competition, they declined by about 20 percent, so that the average brokerage commission rate per 100 shares was about $2.30.[42]

Table 32-7 presents data for a five-year period on the average gross profits per 100 shares that specialists earned from their dealer transactions. In 1972, this average gross profit was $6.84 but the five-year average was about $4.46. These gross profits are calculated before taxes but after deducting clearing charges. It appears that the average profit per 100 shares earned by NYSE specialists is greater when they act as dealers than when they act as brokers. If the average dealer profit from Table 32-7 still applies, and brokerage commission rates are $2.30 per 100 shares, the average advantage gained from being a dealer rather than a broker is about $2.00 per 100 shares ($4.46 − $2.30). In evaluating the advantage to the specialists of handling an order as a dealer rather than as a broker, one needs to take into account the fact that a dealer transaction involves a commitment of capital and substantially more risk.

The final form of competition is "other specialists," by which is meant transactions in other securities. Besides other common stocks, one should also include close substitutes for stocks, such as convertible bonds and puts and calls. In this sense, trading in listed options presents competition for specialists. However, the existence of active markets in listed puts and calls may also tend to increase the volume of trading in the underlying equity securities as a result of hedging and arbitrage activity.

*Summary*   Market makers perform an important function by allowing investors to buy and sell stocks quickly at better prices than would otherwise prevail, thus reducing price fluctuations. Contrary to popular belief, the evidence suggests that market makers are not able to anticipate the direction of price changes in common stocks and, thus, are not better informed than investors, on the average, about factors that would cause stock price changes.

NYSE specialists are the single most important group of market makers for common stocks. Institutional evidence indicates substantial barriers to entry into this phase of market-making, and this conclusion is confirmed by statistical evidence that NYSE specialists as a group earn rates that exceed competitive levels. There is substantial agreement among policymakers that more effective competition in this phase of market-making would be desirable.

## The National Market System

Two major related policy objectives of the Securities and Exchange Commission in the decade of the 1970s were the creation of a *national market*

---

[42]Securities and Exchange Commission, *Fifth Report to Congress on the Effect of the Absence of Fixed Rates of Commission*, p. 19.

**Table 32-7 Average Dealer Gross Profit per 100 Shares Earned by NYSE Specialists in Principal Transactions**

| Year | (1) Specialists' Purchases and Sales (millions of shares)[a] | (2) Specialists' Dealer Gross Profits (Losses) (millions of dollars)[a] | (3) Average Gross Profit (Loss) per 100 Share Round Trip[b] |
|------|------|------|------|
| 1970 | 867.6 | $ 26.822 | $6.183 |
| 1971 | 1,139.1 | 53.365 | 9.370 |
| 1972 | 1,232.7 | 42.179 | 6.843 |
| 1973 | 1,175.9 | (17.792) | (3.026) |
| 1974 | 957.1 | 15.322 | 3.202 |
| Total | 5,372.4 | $119.896 | $4.463[c] |

[a]Source: New York Stock Exchange, *Report of the Committee to Study the Stock Allocation System,* January 27, 1976, pp. 185, 190.
[b]Round trips computed by author, assuming purchases equal sales. The number of 100 share round trips is the amount in column (1) divided by 200 shares.
[c]Five-year average.

*system* and the strengthening of competitive forces within the securities industry. A central or national market system was first mentioned officially by the SEC on March 10, 1971, in transmitting the *Institutional Investor Study* to the Congress.[43] In discussing obstacles to the creation of a central market, the commission recognized that monopoly power, particularly among dealers, was an important obstacle and signaled its intention to rely more heavily in the future on competition rather than regulation. In discussing the guiding principles that it would use in creating a national market, the commission anticipated many of the problems with which it has subsequently dealt. In this connection, the commission wrote:

It may or may not be possible for the central market to be largely an auction market, although the values of the agency auction market must be preserved. Under present considerations, it appears that such a market will also require strong dealers. These may perform the traditional functions of offsetting temporary imbalances in supply or demand or they may have a more limited function such as block positioning. To provide for dealer functions, all responsible market makers should have access to the central market. In this connection it should be noted that, given present technology, it is neither necessary nor desirable that all such dealers be present in any

one geographical location, since any such requirement would among other things prevent the regional exchanges from having the meaningful role in a market system which they could have.

The participation of competing dealers in the central market will also reduce the element of monopoly power which has accompanied past efforts to establish a central market and will make it possible for potential abuses of such monopoly power to be controlled not only by regulation but to an increasing degree by competition. An essential characteristic of such a system would be the prompt reporting of all securities trades to the public on a comparable basis.[44]

In the Securities Act Amendments in 1975, Congress directed the SEC to appoint an advisory board to make recommendations on the appropriate steps to establish a national market system.

The precise form a national market system may take cannot now be foreseen. Many questions related to it are under active study. Some will undoubtedly require practical experience before satisfactory answers are reached. However, certain major components can be anticipated.

For nearly one hundred years, the NYSE operated a transaction reporting system commonly known as a "tape" that reported each trade taking place on its floor. The American Stock Exchange and some of the regional stock exchanges operated

[43]Securities and Exchange Commission, *Letter of Transmittal, Institutional Investor Study Report,* Summary Vol., p. xxiv.

[44]Ibid., pp. xxiv–xxv.

similar systems, although they were not as widely used. The smaller stock exchanges and the OTC market had no transaction-reporting systems. As a result, there was no way in which a person could be aware in a reasonable period of time of all the transactions that were taking place in any one security. Creation of a consolidated tape system was the first step taken by the SEC toward creating a national market system. An industry group began working on the project in the fall of 1971, shortly after the *Institutional Investors Study* was completed and, with repeated SEC prodding, a consolidated tape became fully operational with respect to all transactions on stocks listed on the NYSE in whatever markets they occurred on June 16, 1975. About a year later, a similar facility became operational with respect to stocks listed on the American Stock Exchange and selected issues on the other exchanges.[45]

A second necessary facility for a national market system is an efficient means of discovering the bids and offers available in various marketplaces for a particular stock. A rudimentary automated quotation system is now in operation, and the SEC is engaged in efforts to make it more useful and more widely used.

One problem with geographically dispersed markets is that a transaction may take place in one marketplace at a particular price even though a limit order or a dealer quote offering a better price exists in another marketplace. It is not yet clear how this difficulty will be overcome. Some people have proposed the creation of a composite limit order book, which would be maintained electronically at a central location. Presumably, transactions in all marketplaces would have access to this limit order book.

After a transaction has been agreed on through the trading mechanism, it is still necessary to complete the transaction by transferring ownership of the stock to the buyer and cash to the seller. The banking system has developed efficient methods for transferring ownership of cash through checks and electronic funds transfer systems. Traditionally,

the stock certificate has been the primary attribute of ownership of a share of common stock, and the transfer of ownership has required canceling one certificate and issuing a new one. This involves an extremely cumbersome paper-handling system. The extent of the problems involved may be appreciated when one considers that the buyer may be located in one part of the country, the broker in another, and the exchange on which the transaction takes place in a third. The SEC is in the process of approving the merger of the three largest clearing associations, which play a key role in completing security transactions.

Other steps under way to increase the operational efficiency of the stock market include efforts to eliminate or dramatically reduce the use of stock certificates and to reduce substantially the duplication of regulatory effort that now takes place when a broker/dealer belongs to more than one regulatory organization. As the national market system develops, studies will be needed to determine how it should be operated and by whom it should be regulated and controlled.

### Informational Efficiency

To understand the relationship between informational efficiency and stock price behavior, it is helpful to think of investors as competing with one another in an effort to discover stocks that are underpriced or overpriced. Competition takes the form of a search for new information that would enable the investor to classify some stocks as underpriced, and, therefore, more likely to increase in value compared to the average stock, and others as overpriced and, therefore, more likely to decrease in value compared to the average. If a stock is neither underpriced nor overpriced, it is just as likely to increase in value compared to the average as to decrease in value. In other words, if a stock is fairly priced, one would be equally surprised to see it increase or decrease in value. In this sense, the efficient market hypothesis implies that for fairly priced stocks the direction of future changes in their prices is unpredictable.

Tests of the efficient market hypothesis are all based on the idea that if relevant information about the value of a stock is *not* incorporated in the price, then an investor knowing the information should

[45]A brief history of the efforts required to create these consolidated tapes is contained in National Market Advisory Board, *Report to the Congress: The Possible Need for Modifications of the Scheme of Self-Regulation in the Securities Industry so as to Adapt It to a National Market System*, December 31, 1976, pp. 12–17.

be able to predict the direction of future changes in the price of the stock. On the other hand, if relevant information about the value of a stock is incorporated into its price, then an investor would find that knowledge of the information would not help in predicting the direction of future price changes.

Profits motivate the search for new information. New information that is easily available at the same time to all investors is not likely to be profitable, because prices are likely to respond to such new information almost immediately. On the other hand, new information is likely to be profitable to some of these investors only if they learn about the information and are able to complete transactions based on it before the price adjusts. Whether new information will be profitable depends, in part, also on the operational efficiency of the market since there is no profit potential if transaction costs exceed the expected price change from the new information.

Evidence presented earlier indicates that market makers tend to suffer inventory losses as a result of trading with better-informed investors. The expected inventory losses of market makers are a part of their costs and must be made up by charging higher transaction costs (for example, larger bid-asked spreads) to all traders. Therefore, a market in which new information is not made available to all investors at the same time will tend to have higher transaction costs.

Tests of the efficient market hypothesis have been classified into three broad categories. In so-called weak-form tests, an effort is made to predict the direction of a future price change by looking at past price changes. Suppose a stock tended to have a higher price in the morning than in the evening; or a higher price on Mondays than on Wednesdays. If such patterns existed, they would be violations of the weak form of the efficient market hypothesis, because it would be possible to make above average returns by knowing only these price patterns. Weak-form tests of the efficient market hypothesis have generally found no tendency for prices to follow predictable patterns. Where predictable patterns have been identified, the magnitudes of the movements have been too small to be profitable to a typical investor although they may be of significance to dealers and other security market professionals.

A second category of tests is referred to as the "semistrong category." Tests in this category make an effort to use specific kinds of information as a basis for predicting the direction of future price changes. For example, does the announcement of a stock dividend affect the price of a stock? (It should not and it does not.) Or, do stocks that are selling below book value or which have had a particularly poor past earnings record tend to be underpriced? (The answer is they do, but the magnitude of the underpricing is small relative to the transaction costs that would be incurred in attempting to eliminate it.)

A third category of tests is referred to as "strong-form tests." The objective of strong-form tests is to determine if groups of persons who might have access to nonpublic information are able to use that information to forecast stock prices. Most of the studies in this area have dealt with corporate insiders, and the evidence does indicate that they may be able to achieve somewhat higher rates of return in timing the purchases and sales of the stock of companies with which they are affiliated.

The evidence suggests that information about companies is very quickly reflected in the prices of stocks, at least for the larger, well-known companies, which have been the object of most of these studies. It is quite possible to exaggerate or misinterpret the significance of these findings, however. To avoid these pitfalls, it is helpful to remember that informational efficiency is a consequence of competition among investors to discover stocks that are undervalued or overvalued.

One common misinterpretation leads to the belief that security analysis is unnecessary—"that throwing darts at a stock list is just as effective a way of selecting securities as studying their characteristics." The fallacy here is that even in an informationally efficient market, different securities will be exposed to different degrees of risk. At the very least, security analysis is necessary in order to identify the risk characteristics of the different securities.

A more difficult question is whether security analysis devoted to discovering stocks that are undervalued or overvalued is worthwhile. The answer cannot be an unqualified yes or no. The market will be efficient only if some individuals and institutions seek out undervalued and overvalued stocks. In deciding whether this is a worthwhile objective for any particular investor, whether individual or institutional, one must evaluate both the comparative advantage of that investor and the extent of the competition. If there are too many searchers, then even the best analysts may have difficulty finding enough undervalued or overvalued securities to justify the costs of the search. On the other hand, if too many people withdraw from the effort, then even mediocre analysts may find that it is relatively easy to discover such situations. The intelligent investor will attempt to evaluate the costs and benefits of security research for investment portfolios.

## Summary and Conclusions: Equity Markets

A combination of factors has made the reform of the securities industry a high priority item on the agenda of the Securities and Exchange Commission. These factors include the development of dramatically improved communications and data processing technology, which make a reformed securities market technologically possible; the increasing importance of institutional investors as traders, which, in turn, generated competitive forces that broke down the previous commercial arrangements; and the back-office crunch of the late 1960s, which demonstrated the limitations of a manually operated back-office system and exposed to glaring publicity some dramatic managerial weaknesses among an important minority of firms in the securities industry. First the SEC and then the Congress studied the industry exhaustively, both reaching similar conclusions. The reform efforts presently under way are aimed at strengthening competition and increasing efficiency.

The elimination of fixed-minimum commissions has already substantially reduced transaction costs for institutions. This cost reduction took place as institutions were reducing their portfolio turnover rates from the excessively high levels of the late 1960s. If the reform efforts succeed, we can expect a further decline in transaction costs. The potential decline is perhaps relatively greater for individual investors, who have not yet benefited substantially, than it is for institutions, which have already reaped some of the benefits. If the overall cost of transacting declines substantially, it would not be surprising to find that at least some categories of individual investors substantially increase their volume of trading.

## The Market for Debt Securities

### Characteristics and Scope

The major issuers of marketable debt in the United States are the U.S. government and its agencies, state and local governments, and private corporations. Residential mortgages, which are an important form of long-term debt, are not yet sufficiently marketable to be classified as securities. However, debt instruments, backed by mortgages and issued by specialized financial intermediaries—such as the Government National Mortgage Association—are highly marketable and are becoming increasingly important.

Most marketable debt is owned by financial institutions or nonfinancial corporations and, as a result, most secondary market transactions in debt take place in the over-the-counter market. In the typical over-the-counter debt transaction, one side of the trade is taken by a dealer who makes a market in the issue. If a large corporation or financial institution is on the other side, it is likely to be represented by a skilled and experienced officer. Individuals and smaller corporations and institutions are likely to be represented by brokers. Occasionally, one dealer may use a broker to trade with other dealers. Some corporate bonds are listed and traded on stock exchanges, but the volume of trading is insignificant.

If corporate bonds are not registered with the SEC, there are serious legal obstacles that restrict subsequent trading. Thus, nonregistered corporate bonds should not be classified as marketable securities. These legal obstacles do not apply to U.S. government or to state and local government issues. The transaction costs on small issues of some state and local government issues are so high that they are usually purchased with the intention of holding them to maturity. In such cases, the securities are technically, but not practically, marketable.

### Operational Efficiency

The transaction costs incurred in the purchase and subsequent sale of a debt security may vary from as little as 0.10 percent to 10.0 percent or more of the dollar value of the security. The single most important determinant of unit transaction costs is the volume of transactions in the security: high volume is associated with low unit costs and vice versa. An industry in which higher volumes lead to lower average costs is characterized as having economies of scale. With economies of scale, marginal costs must be below average costs.[46]

Economies of scale are said to be internal if an individual firm can lower its average cost by increasing its volume of transactions in a particular security, even when the total volume of transactions among all firms is not increasing. Internal economies of scale can be expected to lead to monopoly, since the firm that has the highest share of the transactions in a security will have lower costs than its competitors and should eventually be able to dominate the market. Economies of scale are said to be external if the costs of each individual firm are decreased when the total volume of trading among all firms in a particular security increases. Scale economies of this kind do not, by themselves, give individual firms any particular competitive advantage.

Evidence on rates of profit indicates that market-making in high-volume debt securities is definitely not characterized by monopoly. Thus, we can conclude that at least for high-volume securities, internal economies of scale do not predominate. Less evidence is available regarding trading in low-volume securities. If there were a total absence of internal economies, there should be a large number of dealers interested in trading inactive securities. However, this does not appear to be the case, so we can conclude that some internal economies may be present. One plausible theory is that internal economies of scale are substantially or completely exhausted at rather low levels of trading volume, and that beyond that point the economies of scale are mainly external. Thus, only a few firms might be interested in inactive securities where total volume is low, but more firms might want to trade active securities.

Even with internal economies of scale for market makers, no monopoly profits would be expected if there were freedom of entry. There is only one important restriction on entry into the dealer activity. As a result of the financial reform legislation passed in the 1930s, commercial banks are prohibited from being underwriters or dealers in corporate bonds and in revenue bonds issued by state and local governments.[47] Restrictions on entry by other kinds of firms do not appear to be significant.

Direct studies of operational efficiency in debt markets are available only for the government securities market.[48] For other segments of the bond market, judgments about efficiency must be based on judgments about market structure.

One important direct indicator of the degree of competition among government securities dealers is their rate of profit. Profits for bank dealers are generated from three sources: the spread or trading income arising from differences in the price at which dealers buy and sell; inventory appreciation or depreciation as the values of securities held in inventory change; and "carry" income, the difference between interest earned on the securities in inventory and the financing charges associated with carrying that inventory. The rate of profit of government security dealers is available on an annual basis for the decade 1948–1957 and for two later years, 1964 and 1965. The average rate of profit during the earlier decade was 13.6 percent before taxes. This was roughly equal to the rate achieved by all insured commercial banks, but government security dealers experienced substantially greater earning variability than did the banks.[49] Government securities dealers also experienced lower average returns than most manufacturing industries.

---

[46]If the average costs per transaction were less than the marginal costs, increases in the number of transactions would increase the average cost per transaction since the additional transactions would cost more than the average.

[47]Commercial banks can and do participate as dealers and underwriters in U.S. government issues and in issues of states and localities that are backed by the municipality's full faith and credit. Both bank and nonbank dealers appear to be able to compete effectively with one another, at least in the huge U.S. government securities market.

[48]Allan H. Meltzer and Gert von der Linde, *A Study of the Dealer Market for Government Securities,* Joint Economic Committee, 86th Cong., 2nd Sess., Government Printing Office, Washington, D.C., 1960; also William G. Colby, Jr., "Dealer Profits and Availability in the U.S. Government Securities Industry, 1955–1965," U.S. Treasury Federal Reserve Study of the U.S. Government Security Market, May 1967 (mimeographed).

[49]Meltzer and Linde, *A Study of the Dealer Market of Government Securities,* Table VII-14.

15. What is the main determinant of transaction costs for bonds? Should the issuer of a bond be concerned about transactions costs in the secondary market for the bonds it has issued?
16. What explanations might account for the apparent differences in informational efficiency between utility bonds and industrial bonds? How could you determine whether your explanations were correct?

## Selected Bibliography

Barnes, Amir, and Dennis E. Logue. "The Effect of Risk on the Market Maker's Spread." *Financial Analysts Journal* (November-December 1975).

Baumol, William S. *The Stock Market and Economic Efficiency*. Fordham University Press, New York: 1965.

Demsetz, Harold. "The Cost of Transacting." *Quarterly Journal of Economics* (February 1968).

Manne, Henry G. "Economic Policy and the Regulation of Corporate Securities." American Enterprise Institute, Washington, D.C., 1969.

New York Stock Exchange. *Report of the Committee to Study the Stock Allocation Decision*. New York Stock Exchange, New York, January 1976.

———. *A History of the New York Stock Exchange, 1935–1975*. Weybright and Tulley, New York, 1975.

Securities and Exchange Commission. *Institutional Investor Study Report, Summary Volume*. House Document 92-64, Part 8. Government Printing Office, Washington, 1971.

Smidt, Seymour. "Which Road to an Efficient Stock Market: Free Competition or Regulated Monopoly?" *Financial Analysts Journal* (September-October 1971).

Sobel, Robert. *The Curbstone Brokers*. The Macmillan Company, New York, 1970.

U.S. House of Representatives, Subcommittee on Commerce and Finance of the Committee on Interstate and Foreign Commerce. *Securities Industry Study Report*. 92nd Cong., 2nd Sess. Government Printing Office, Washington, 1972.

U.S. Senate, Subcommittee on Securities of the Committee on Banking, Housing and Urban Affairs. *Securities Industry Study Report*. 93rd Cong., 1st Sess. Government Printing Office, Washington, D.C., 1973.

Welles, Chris. *The Last Days of the Club*. E. P. Dutton & Co., New York, 1975.

# INDEX